Opera on

Screen

About the author

Ken Wlaschin has worked for the American and British Film Institutes for the past 27 years directing the London and Los Angeles film festivals and the national film theaters of England and the U.S. He has published many books and articles about opera and cinema including a guide to Menotti's opera film *The Medium,* an encyclopedia of movie stars, a collection of poems about the cinema, a humorous guide to the movies and a book about Rome. He has also published several novels and worked as a film, music and theater critic in Italy, England and America. He was awarded an MBE in England for services to cinema and the equivalents in Italy and France.

Opera on Screen

A guide to 100 years of films and videos

featuring operas, opera singers and operettas

by

Ken Wlaschin

BEACHWOOD PRESS

LOS ANGELES

Designer: Scott Wlaschin
Producer: Mo Kennedy Martin

Library of Congress Cataloging-in-Publication Data
Wlaschin, Ken
Opera on Screen: A guide to 100 years
of films and videos featuring
 operas, opera singers and operettas
Includes bibliography
1. Opera - Film and video adaptations
I. Wlaschin, Ken

Library of Congress Catalog Card Number: 96-79577
ISBN: 1-888327-00-6

British Library Cataloguing in Publication Data is available.

First published in 1997.

Beachwood Press,
2597 Dearborn Drive,
Los Angeles, CA 90068

Printed in the United States of America

Contents

Introduction

This is a guide in book form and on CD-ROM to the thousands of films and videos featuring operas and opera singers made in the last one hundred years. There is no other guide like it so it should be a useful reference tool for those interested in opera and operetta on screen. Hopefully it can be read for enjoyment as well.

Opera on the screen goes back to the beginnings of cinema and its future was predicted at once by Thomas Edison. In 1893 he told *The New York Times* that "My intention is to have such a happy combination of photography and electricity that a man can sit in his own parlor, see depicted upon a curtain the forms of the players in opera upon a distant stage and hear the voices of the singers." In 1894 he told *Century Magazine* that "I believe that in coming years grand opera can be given at the Metropolitan Opera House in New York with artists and musicians long since dead."

We are the heirs of Edison's dream, the first generation to have access in our homes to a century of screen opera. A large majority of the films and television programs of operatic interest are now on video and laserdisc and it is quite easy to survey the riches of the opera legacy at home with high quality sound. Though audio has dominated the home experience of opera for the past 100 years, video is likely to dominate the next 100. As opera has always been as much theater as music, this change should make the art more popular.

This guide is intended to show what it is possible to view. It has been organized alphabetically as an encyclopedia with entries on operas, operettas, zarzuelas, singers, composers, writers, conductors and subjects of interest. The net is wide and inclusive and includes, for example, singers whose opera career was only on the movie screen and operas that have not been filmed but have cinema content. There are entries on operas composed as films and imaginary operas as well as television directors who have created TV operas and film directors who have worked on the opera stage.

Special subject entries include Animated Opera, Best Opera on Film, Best Operetta on Film, Castratos, Divas, Directors of Opera on Film, Directors of Opera on TV, Filmmakers On Stage, First Operas on Film, First Operas on TV, Imaginary Operas in Films, Operas and Operettas about the Movies, Operas as Movies, Operas Based on Movies, Operetta, Puppet Opera, Silent Films about Opera, Silent Films of Operas, Television Operas, Vitaphone Opera Films, Voice of Firestone, Worst Opera on Film, Worst Operetta on Film, Zarzuelas.

Major opera singers, of course, have their own entries with descriptions of their concert videos and a cross-referenced list of their screen operas. As most opera singers have also sung in operettas, European and traditional operettas that have been filmed or videotaped are discussed including some operettas composed only for the screen. The entries on composers include screen biographies and cross-referenced lists of their operas that have been filmed or taped. In the CD-ROM version these entries can be viewed with a click of the mouse. In book form you have to turn a few pages.

There are some noticeable gaps in the video market. *Faust*, for example, despite its popularity, is not available in a major modern production. There is no American video of Caruso's favorite opera *Martha* and very little of classical Viennese operetta. Modern American operas are also hard to find with nothing in complete form on commercial video by Adams, Barber, Beeson, Glass, Floyd, Moore or Thomson.

Opinions about the quality of the films and videos have been kept to a minimum. After reading thousands of reviews of opera films and videos and finding the same production praised by one critic and condemned by another, it is apparent that opera lovers rarely agree. As a rule of thumb, if you like a particular singer, you will probably enjoy seeing him/her in almost any production.

In addition to the chronological entries of the screen operas, there are entries on films of related interest using music from the opera or based on the same story. Early and silent versions of operas are listed after the more recent ones as being of a more specialized interest. Operas that were more fashionable in the early years of the century than now often have many silent versions.

The Carmen story is the major literary source and this book includes some 75 entries under *Carmen*, 22 of them screen versions of the opera. Nearly as popular are *La Traviata* with 53 entries, (18 of the opera) and *The Barber of Seville* with 47 entries (but only 13 of the opera). There are 17 screen versions of *Tosca*, 16 of *Pagliacci* and *Don Giovanni*, 14 of Aida and 13 of *The Magic Flute* and *La Bohème*. The most popular composers for screen biographies are Mozart with 25 entries including the famous *Amadeus* and Beethoven who has been the subject of 15 biopics. Verdi has the largest number of different operas on screen with 19 followed by Mozart with 13.

The most popular opera personalities, judging by the number of videos, are the three tenors (Domingo, Pavarotti, Carreras,) and the three sopranos (Sutherland, Ti Kanawa, Stratas). Placido Domingo is way ahead with films and videos of 49 operas and 93 entries. The major screen opera directors, who are both virtually unknown to the film world, are Kirk Browning and Brian Large; each has directed over 200 operas for TV and video. The most prolific opera-on-film directors are Carmine Gallone with 27 films, 14 of them based on operas, and Jean-Pierre Ponnelle with 20 opera movies, most based on his own stage productions.

Operas are listed in their original language except for the very popular operas which are usually titled in English on their videos, e.g., *The Barber of Seville*. Slavic operas are also listed in English. European operettas are listed in their original language unless they are best known in English (like *The Chocolate Soldier*) or in French (like *Trois Valses*). The accent marks used in most European languages are retained with the exception of some of the accents peculiar to Czech which do not exist in Word 6 and which tend to confuse the word processor and CD-ROM. My apologies to Dvorák, Janácek and Martinu.

The principal words in the titles of operas and films are capitalized as is normal in English even when they are not capitalized in texts in their own languages. This is the standard practice of publications like *The New York Times* and the *Metropolitan Opera Annuals* and is the usual practice on American films and videos.

When it is known, the video company that distributes, or once distributed, an opera is named. Distribution is always in flux and the companies handling videos often change. There are usually library or second-hand copies to be found if there is no current distributor. When a film or video is available at one of the television or film museums, this is noted. When a video is indicated as English, French, Italian or German, it is in the PAL or SECAM systems, not the American NTSC system. These must be played on a multi-standard or European video player.

The New Grove Dictionary of Opera has been used as the definitive source of information about operas though its Slavic spellings are not always followed. Kurt Gänzl's *Encyclopedia of Musical Theatre* is the most complete single source of data about operettas though in this book the word is used in a more restricted sense. The information about films and television programs comes from a variety of catalogs and journals but especially *Variety, The New York Times, The American Film Institute Feature Film Catalogs* and the film catalogs of Italy, France, Germany and England. Most of the information about the videos has been taken off the videos themselves. I have been able to view a vast number of the films and videos listed but certainly not all and there are sure to be errors and omissions. Corrections will be included in future editions.

I would like to thank the many people around the world who have helped with this book over the past four years from David Meeker in London to Sandro Massimini in Rome to Susan Dalton in Washington. There are hundreds of others including, notably, Howie Davidson and Torene Svitil who helped proof the text. I am above all grateful to Mo Kennedy Martin, who produced and edited the book, and Scott Wlaschin, who designed it and the CD-ROM. Without their help the book could not have been written .

Ken Wlaschin

Abbreviations of Film & Video Sources

AFI - American Film Institute, Los Angeles and Washington, D.C.
BFI - British Film Institute, London
IN - Inter Nationes, Goethe Institutes
LOC - Library of Congress, Washington, D.C.
MOMA - Museum of Modern Art Film Department, New York
MPRC - Music Performance Research Center, Barbicon, London
MTR - Museum of Television and Radio, New York and Los Angeles
NFTA - National Film and Television Archive, British Film Institute, London.
NYPL - New York Public Library for the Performing Arts, Lincoln Center, New York
UCLA - University of California, Los Angeles Film and Television Archive, Los Angeles

A

ABBADO, CLAUDIO

Italian conductor (1933-)

Claudio Abbado is part of a modern musical dynasty in Italy with his father, brother and nephew. The Milan-born conductor is thought of as a specialist in Italian opera but his range is wide. He has been conducting professionally since 1958 and was music director of the Vienna State Opera from 1986 to 1991. He is featured on a number of non-opera videos including *Abbado in Berlin*, and a book he wrote about La Scala was made into a film. See also THE BARBER OF SEVILLE (1972), LA CENERENTOLA (1982), ELEKTRA (1989), FIERRABRAS (1988), KHOVANSHCHINA (1989), LOHENGRIN (1989), THE MARRIAGE OF FIGARO (1991), LUCIANO PAVAROTTI (1996), SIMON BOCCANEGRA (1978), WOZZECK (1987).

1990 The House of Magical Sounds
Claudio Abbado's autobiographical book was made into a film by Daniele Abbado. It tells the story of a boy so impressed by what he hears at La Scala that he determines to make music the center of his life. The film includes music by Mozart, Beethoven, Debussy and Schubert performed by the Youth Orchestra of United Europe conducted by Abbado. Raul Julia narrates the story. Color. In English. 60 minutes. Sony video.

ABC TELEVISION ARCHIVE

ABC, the American Broadcasting Company, never developed its own opera productions like its rival networks NBC and CBS but it had the distinction of telecasting the first three live operas from the Metropolitan Opera. In November 1948, ABC telecast the opening night of *Otello*, in November 1949 it telecast the opening night of *Der Rosenkavalier* and in November 1950 it telecast the opening of *Don Carlo* to an estimated four million viewers. ABC then ended its prestigious but rather expensive collaboration with the Met. See OTELLO

ABDUCTION FROM THE SERAGLIO, THE

1782 opera by Mozart

Die Entführung aus dem Serial was Mozart's first opera in German and the first major opera in that language. Gottlieb Stephanie's libretto tells the story of nobleman Belmonte's attempt to rescue captive lover Konstanze from the palace of the Pasha Selim in 16th century Turkey. Belmonte's servant Pedrillo loves her servant Blonde and the unfriendly guard Osmin lusts after her. In the end, as in most Mozart operas, there is forgiveness and understanding. *Abduction* has been popular with filmmakers in recent years but was not filmed in the silent era. See also WOLFGANG A. MOZART.

1954 NBC Opera Theatre
Nadja Witkowska stars as Konstanze in this early color telecast of the opera in English by the adventurous NBC Opera Theatre. David Cunningham portrays Belmonte, Virginia Haskins is Blonde, David Lloyd is Pedrillo, Leon Lishner is Osmin and Norman Rose is the Pasha. Samuel Chotzinoff's production is traditional with sets by Rouben Ter-Arutunian. Herman Peter Adler conducted the Symphony of the Air Orchestra and Kirk Browning directed the telecast on Oct. 31, 1954. Color. In English. 90 minutes. Video at MTR.

1954 Vienna State Opera
The Austrian film *Unsterblicher Mozart* features a highlights version of *Abduction* performed on stage by the Mozart Ensemble of the Vienna State Opera. Wilma Lipp is Konstanze, Emmy Loose portrays Blonde, Rudolf Christ is Belmonte, Peter Klein is Pedrillo and Ludwig Weber is Osmin. Alfred Stöger directed the film and Rudolf Moralt conducted the Vienna Philharmonic. Color. In German. 95 minutes. Taurus (Germany) video.

1962 Heinz Liesendahl film
Heinz Liesendahl's German film of the opera features Anneliese Rothenberger as Konstanze, Peter Pasetti as Belmonte, Judith Blegen as Blonde, Werner Krenn as Pedrillo, Oscar Czerwenka as Osmin and Gerhard Stolze as the Pasha. The orchestra was conducted by Georg Solti, the choreography arranged by Heinz Schmiedel and

the sets designed by Jean-Pierre Ponnelle. Color. In German. 110 minutes. On video.

1970 NET Opera Theater
Kirk Browning directed and staged this experimental chroma-keyed production of the opera for NET Opera Theater. The abstract sets, designed by Robert Israel, consisted of patterned backdrops and solid color flat props giving the opera a two dimensional feeling. Peter Herman Adler was the artistic director who devised this unusual production. Color. In English. 90 minutes. Video at MTR.

1976 Dresden State Opera
Armin Ude sings the role of Belmonte in this Dresden State Opera production staged and filmed by Harry Kupfer for East German Television. Rolf Tomaszewaki is Osmin, Carolyn Smith-Myer is Konstanze, Barbara Sternberger is Blonde, Uwe Peper is Pedrillo and Werner Haseleu is the Pasha. Peter Gulke conducted the Dresden State Opera Orchestra and Chorus. Unitel. Color. In German. 129 minutes. VIEW video/Japanese laser.

1980 Glyndebourne Festival
This charming Glyndebourne Festival production by Peter Wood stars Ryland Davies as Belmonte , Valerie Masterson as Konstanze, Lillian Watson as Blonde, James Hoback as Pedrillo, Willard White as Osmin and Joachim Bissmeier as the Pasha. William Dudley designed the pastel sets and Gustav Kuhn conducted the London Philharmonic Orchestra and Glyndebourne Festival Chorus. Dave Heather directed the video. Color. In German with English subtitles. 145 minutes. VAI video.

1980 Bavarian State Opera
Francisco Araiza sings Belmonte with Edita Gruberova as Konstanze in this Bavarian State Opera production in Munich by August Everding. Reri Grist is Blonde, Norbert Orth is Pedrillo, Martti Talvela is Osmin and Thomas Holtzman is the Pasha. Max Bignens designed the sets and costumes and Karl Böhm conducted the Bavarian State Opera Chorus and Orchestra. Karl-Heinz Hundorf directed the video. Unitel. Color. In German with English subtitles. 146 minutes. DG Video.

1984 Paris Opera
Giorgio Strehler directed this notable production of the opera at the Paris Opera in 1984, utilizing the influential *commedia dell'arte* ideas he had developed

at the Salzburgh Festival. Kathleen Battle stars as Konstanze with Gerhard Unger as Belmonte and Catherine Malfitano as Blonde. The stage production was videotaped by INA. Color. In German. 140 minutes.

1986 Royal Opera
Elijah Moshinsky staged this lavish Royal Opera production with George Solti conducting the Royal Opera Orchestra and Chorus. Deon van der Walt is Belmonte, Inga Nielsen is Konstanze, Lillian Watson is Blonde, Kurt Moll is Osmin, Lars Magnusson is Pedrillo and Oliver Tobias is Pasha Selim. Timothy O'Brien and Sidney Nolan designed the sets and Humphrey Burton directed the video. Color. In German with English subtitles. 140 minutes. Home Vision video.

1989 Salzburg Festival
Deon van Der Walt is Belmonte with Inga Nielsen as Konstanze in this Salzburg Festival production by Johannes Schaaf. Kurt Rydl is Osmin, Lillian Watson is Blonde, Heinz Zednik is Pedrillo and Ulrich Wildgruber is the Pasha. Andreas Reinhardt designed the sets and Horst Stein conducted the Vienna State Opera Orchestra. The video was also directed by Schaaf and telecast in the *Great Performances* series on Jan. 5, 1990. Color. In German with English subtitles. 150 minutes.

1990 Drottningholm Court Theatre
This delightful Swedish production was filmed at the Drottningholm Court Theatre near Stockholm. Mozart specialist Arnold Östman conducts the Drottningholm Court Theatre Orchestra which performs in costume on period instruments. The singers are Richard Croft as Belmonte, Aga Winska as Konstanze, Elisabet Hellstrom as Blonde, Beng-Ola Morgny as Pedrillo, Tamäs Szüle as Osmin and Emmerich Shaeffer as Pasha Selim. Harald Clemen was stage director and Tomas Olofsson directed the video. Color. In German with English subtitles. 130 minutes. EMI video and laser.

1991 Théâtre du Châtelet, Paris
This lively authentic production was conducted by John Eliot Gardiner and staged by Lluis Pasqual at the Théâtre du Châtelet in Paris. Gardiner leads the English Baroque Soloists and the Monteverdi Choir with sets by Carlo Tommasi. The production stars Luba Orgonasova, Cyndia Sieden, Cornelius Hauptmann, Stanford Olsen, Uswe Paper and Hans Peter Minetti. Robin Lough directed for video.

Amaya distribution. Color. In German. 140 minutes. On video.

Related films

1958 Lotte Reiniger animated film
Animation pioneer Lotte Reiniger made an abbreviated animated silhouette version of the opera titled *A Night at the Harem*. Color. 14 minutes.

1971 Giorgio Strehler Rehearses *Abduction from the Seraglio*
Strehler is shown at work on his famous staging of The *Abduction from the Seraglio*, originally created for the Salzburg Festival in 1965. The highly influential production featured *commedia dell'arte* ideas and memorable shadow-type silhouettes of the singers. Norbert Beilharz directed this documentary film for SDR. Color. In German. 60 minutes.

1994 Guarding Tess
In the film Shirley MacLaine falls asleep during a scene from *The Abduction from the Seraglio* and is woken up by her bodyguard Nicolas Cage. The opera singers seen on stage are Julie Kursawa and Michael Consoli. The duet "Ich gehe, doch rate ich dir is sung" by Günther Missenhardt and Elzbieta Szmytka with the Vienna Symphony conducted by Bruno Weil. Hugh Wilson wrote and directed the film. Color. 98 minutes.

ABRAHAM, PAUL
Hungarian composer (1892-1960)

Paul Abraham (in Hungary it's Pál Ábrahám) has never become an American favorite but his operettas were often performed in Canada and England and continue to be popular in Europe. *Viktoria und ihr Husar* has been staged in Montreal, London and Paris and filmed twice. *Ball im Savoy* starred opera singer Gitta Alpar on stage and screen and was presented in London by Oscar Hammerstein II who wrote a new book for it. *Die Blume von Hawaii* is still in the central European repertory. Abraham also wrote memorable film musicals like *Die Privatsekretärin* (1931) which was filmed in four languages and in England became Victor Saville's *Sunshine Susie*. Abraham was Jewish so he had to flee from Berlin when the Nazis took over and then from Vienna, Budapest and Paris. He ended up in New York where he wrote no more operettas. See BALL IM SAVOY, DIE BLUME VON HAWAII, FRANZ SCHUBERT (1939), VIKTORIA UND IHR HUSAR.

ACCUSED, THE
1961 TV opera by Strauss

American soprano Patricia Neway stars in this one-character television opera composed by John Strauss to a libretto by Sheppard Kerman. It's a monologue by a woman accused of being a Salem witch. At a key moment in her defense she reveals that she is pregnant. The opera, with a set by Neil De Luca, was produced by John McGiffert for the adventurous *Camera Three* series. John Desmond directed the telecast on June 4, 1961. This was composer Strauss's only opera. Black and white. In English. 30 minutes.

ACIS AND GALATHEA
1718 opera by Handel

Acis and Galathea was George Friderich Handel's first dramatic work in English and was composed to a libretto by John Gay. It's based on Dryden's version of the 13th book of Ovid's *Metamorphoses* and concerns the love between the shepherd Acis and the semi-divine sea nymph Galathea. After he is killed by the monster Polyphemus, she turns him into a fountain. See also GEORGE F. HANDEL.

1985 RTSI Lugano
Barbara Schlick and Paul Ellit star in this television production of the opera staged by Helge Thomas in Lugano. The cast includes Guy de Mey, Michael Schopper, Sarah Leonhard and Michael Chance. Helmuth Müller-Bruhl conducted the orchestra and Klaus Lindemann directed the video. Color. In English. 65 minutes. Inter Nationes video.

ADAM, ADOLPHE
French composer (1803-1856)

Adolphe Adam, the opera-comique composer "of catchy little tunes that one can whistle," according to waspish Hector Berlioz, is best known today for his ballet *Giselle*. However, he also wrote many successful operas and five of them are available on CD. The most popular is *Le Postillon de Lonjumeau* which is especially liked in German-speaking countries when tenors like to show off their high notes in a tuneful fashion. There are no modern videos but there is a German film of the opera. See LE POSTILLON DE LONJUMEAU.

ADAM, THEO
German bass-baritone (1926-)

Theodor Adam has a big voice and a commanding presence even on the small screen, and has been a major figure in German opera since his 1949 debut in Dresden. He was a star performer at that opera house and especially noted for his Wagner, Handel and Beethoven. Two of his best roles are Handel's Julius Caesar and Beethoven's Pizarro and both are available on video. He can also be seen in concert with the Berlin Deutschen Staatsoper. See LUDWIG VAN BEETHOVEN (1989 film), BERLIN (1976), CAPRICCIO (1990), FIDELIO (1969/1977), DER FREISCHÜTZ (1985), GIULIO CESARE (1977), THE MAGIC FLUTE (1991), RICHARD WAGNER (1988).

ADAMS, DONALD
English bass (1929- 1996)

Bristol-born Donald Adams was principal bass with the D'Oyly Company from 1953 to 1969 and became a mainstay of their Gilbert and Sullivan productions. He is featured in twelve videos of Gilbert and Sullivan operas, including a D'Oyly Carte production of *The Mikado* in which he starred at least 2000 times. He also toured the world with a G. & S. Group he organized with tenor Thoomas Round. In 1983 Adams began a new career singing bass roles in grand operas at Covent Garden, the ENO and other major opera houses. He was starring in *Don Pasquale* at the Royal Opera when he died. See THE GONDOLIERS (1974), H.M.S. PINAFORE (1974), IOLANTHE (1974), THE MIKADO (1967/1974), PATIENCE (1974), THE PIRATES OF PENZANCE (1974), RUDDIGORE (1967, 1974, 1982), THE SORCERER (1982),THE YEOMAN OF THE GUARD (1974).

ADAMS, JOHN
American composer (1947-)

John Adams has become one of the most popular modern American composers with an attractive minimalist style that has a wide appeal. He has written two operas on modern political subjects that have won critical and audience favor. His 1987 *Nixon in China*, created with director Peter Sellers, has been one of the most publicized modern operas. It has been televised and is viewable on tape but there is not yet a commercial video. The 1991 *The*

Death of Klinghoffer, based on the hi-jacking of the cruise ship Achille Lauro, was less well received when it premiered but is winning acclaim on CD. See NIXON IN CHINA.

ADLER, PETER HERMAN
Czech-born American conductor(1899-?)

Peter Herman Adler was one of the triumvirate who created NBC Opera Theatre and made American television opera into a major cultural force. He was musical and artistic director of the series with Samuel Chotzinoff as producer and KirkBrowning as director from 1949 to 1959. Their productions included everything from *Amahl and the Night Visitors* to *War and Peace*. In 1969 he created the NET Opera Company in collaboration with Browning and they produced some of the most innovative TV operas seen up to that time. Original NET Opera production ended in 1973 when Henze's opera *Rachel the Cubana* exploded its small budget. See KIRK BROWNING, SAMUEL CHOTZINOFF, NBC OPERA THEATRE, NET OPERA, RACHEL THE CUBANA.

ADRIANA LECOUVREUR
1902 opera by Cilea

Francesco Cilea's theatrical melodrama focuses on an actress of the Comedie-Francaise in the 18th century. Her ill-fated love for Maurizio ends with her being poisoned by a jealous princess. The opera was written by Arturo Colautti and is based on a play by Scribe and Legouve about a real person. The opera has been a favorite of sopranos of a certain age since Angelica Pandolfini (and Enrico Caruso) launched it in 1902. It's also a favorite for set designers who like the chance to be theatrically monumental. The composer was especially fond of Magda Olivero in the role and brought her out of retirement in 1951 to sing it once more. She continued to do so for another 40 years and there is a video of her in the role. See FRANCESCO CILEA.

1976 Monserrat Caballé in Tokyo
Monserrat Caballé stars as Adriana Lecouvreur with José Carreras as her lover Maurizio and Fiorenza Cossotto as her deadly rival in this outstanding production of the opera in Tokyo. Attilio D'Orazi sings the role of the stage manager Michonnet. Gianfranco Masini leads the NHK Lirica Italiana Orchestra and Chorus. The opera was taped on Sept. 20, 1976, for Japanese television. In

Color. In Italian. 145 minutes. Lyric Legato Classics video.

1984 Australian Opera
Joan Sutherland is Adriana Lecouvreur in this Sydney Opera production by John Copley. Sutherland sings well but this is not a role suited for her acting talents. Anson Austin is her lover Maurizio, Heather Begg is the nasty Princess of Bouillon, John Wegner is her jealous husband and John Shaw is the stage manager Michonnet. Richard Bonynge conducts the Elizabethan Sydney Orchestra. Hugh Davison directed the video. Color. In Italian with English subtitles. 135 minutes. Sony Video.

1989 Teatro alla Scala
Mirella Freni is a dramatic and beautiful Adriana and Peter Dvorsky a handsome, imposing Maurizio in this monumental La Scala production by Lamberto Puggelli. Fiorenza Cossotto is Princess de Bouillon, Ivo Vinco plays Prince de Bouillon and Alessandro Cassis is Michonnet. Paolo Bregni designed the monumental sets and Gianandrea Gavazzeni conducted the La Scala Orchestra. Brian Large directed the video at a June 2, 1989 performance. Color. In Italian with English subtitles. 157 minutes. Home Vision video/ Japanese laser.

Related films

1910 Sarah Bernhardt film
Sarah Bernhardt stars as Adrienne Lecouvreur in this French film based on the play. It was directed by Alberto Capellani and Louis Mercanton for Pathé. Black and white. About 10 minutes.

1938 Magda Olivero video
Magda Olivero, the composer's favorite Adriana, can be seen in the role in two amazing excerpts on the compilation video Magda Olivero: the Last Verismo Soprano. She is first shown singing the role at the age of 26 in 1938 opposite Beniamino Gigli. Then she is shown in 1993 at the age of 81 (that's 55 years later) singing the same role. Black and white & color. 59 minutes. Bel Canto Society video.

1938 Adrienne Lecouvreur
Soprano Yvonne Printemps stars as Adrienne Lecouvreur in this French film based on Scribe and Legouve's play about the Comédie-Française actress. Pierre Fresnay is her Maurice. F.A. Wagner was the cinematographer for director Marcel l'Herbier. It's not the same as the opera but close enough for interesting comparisons. In Italy the film was screened with a score based on the opera music. Black and white. In French. 110 minutes

---

AFRICAINE, L'
1865 opera by Meyerbeer

The African Woman is the best of the spectacular "grand operas" in the French manner by Giacomo Meyerbeer. It invokes the age of Portuguese exploration with great passion and glorious music. Eugène Scribe's libretto revolves around the adventures of explorer Vasco Da Gama. He returns to Portugal after a long voyage bringing as captives Nelusko and Sélika, the "African woman" of the title. She loves Vasco, Vasco loves Ines and Nelusko loves Sélika. On the next voyage they are shipwrecked in Africa near where Sélika is a Queen and the power structure is reversed.

1988 San Francisco Opera
Shirley Verrett portrays Sélika and Placido Domingo is Vasca da Gama in this splendid and grandiose San Francisco Opera production by Lotfi Mansouri. Ruth Ann Swenson sings the role of Ines, Justino Diaz is Nelusko, Michael Devlin is Don Pedro and Philip Skinner is Don Diego Wolfram Skalaicki designed the sets and Maurizio Arena conducted the San Francisco Opera Orchestra and Chorus. Brian Large directed the video. Color. In French with English subtitles. 192 minutes. Home Vision video/Pioneer laserdisc.

Early films

1929 Titto Ruffo in *L'Africaine*
The great Italian baritone Tito Ruffo made three early opera films for MGM. On the first he performs, in costume and in Italian, Nelusko's invocation "Adamastor, re dell'onde profonde" from *L'Africaine*. Black and white. About 8 minutes.

1927 Charles Hackett in *L'Africana*
Chicago Opera tenor Charles Hackett sings the *L'Africaine* aria "O paradiso" in Italian on this early sound film made by the Vitaphone company. Black and white. 8 minutes.

AGNESE DI HOHENSTAUFEN
1829 grand opera by Spontini

Gaspare Spontini's grand historical opera *Agnese von Hohenstaufen* was composed to a German libretto by Ernest Rapuach but is usually performed now in an Italian version as *Agnese di Hohenstaufen*. It's a complex and rather emotional love story set amongst aristocratic intrigues in the 12th century. Agnes, a cousin of Emperor Henry VI, is in love with Heinrich, the son of the Emperor's Guelph enemy Henry the Lion. See also GASPARE SPONTINI.

1986 Montserrat Caballé video
Montserrat Caballé, who stars as Agnes in this Rome Opera production, first sang the role in a RAI broadcast in 1970. Caballé is supported here by tenor Veriano Luchetti as a very intense Heinrich, basso Silvano Pagliuca and soprano Glenys Linos. Maximiamo Valdes conducts the Rome Opera Orchestra. Color. 150 minutes. Bel Canto Society/Lyric/Opera Dubs videos.

AGRIPPINA
1709 opera by Handel

Handel composed this opera while he was living in Italy and his libretto writer was the powerful Cardinal Vincenzo Grimani. The Cardinal's contribution ensured its success and it made Handel famous. The opera is a fictional story about Emperor Claudius's conniving second wife Agrippina and her schemes to obtain the crown for her son Nero. She is willing to murder for it. See also GEORGE F. HANDEL.

1911 Enrico Guazzoni film
Enrico Guazzoni wrote and directed this early Italian film of the story with Adele Bianchi Azzarilli as the scheming Agrippina. The cast includes Cesare Moltini, Mrs. Sturla and Mr. Dolfini. Black and white. About 10 minutes.

1985 Schwetzingen Festival
Barbara Daniels stars as Agrippina and sings the difficult music brilliantly in this Schwetzingen Festival production by Michael Hampe, Tenor David Kuebler is Nero (a role written for a castrato), Claudia Nicolai is Ottone, Carlos Feller is Lesbo, Gunter von Kannen is Claudius and Janice Hall is Poppea. Maurice Pagano designed the striking sets and Arnold Östman conducts the London Baroque Players. Thomas Olofsson directed the video. Color. In Italian with English subtitles. 160 minutes. Home Vision video.

AIDA
1871 opera by Verdi

Aida is the most popular of the "grand operas" and its grandiose spectacle and stirring music have made it a favorite at outdoor arenas like Verona where elephants can join the triumphal march. Its spectacle has also made it a favorite of filmmakers. Librettist Antonio Ghislanzoni focuses the story on Aida, daughter of an Ethiopian king. She is a captive slave in Egypt in love with Ramades, the man chosen to lead the Egyptian army. The Pharaoh's jealous daughter Amneris also fancies Ramades so Aida's love eventually leads to death. The opera premiered in Cairo soon after the opening of the Suez Canal. See also GIUSEPPE VERDI.

1949 NBC Toscanini video
This is an historic concert version of the opera with Arturo Toscanini conducting on a 1949 NBC telecast. It's rather formal but wonderful all the same. The singers are Herva Nelli as Aida, Richard Tucker as Radames, Eva Gustavson as Amneris, Giuseppe Valdengo as Amonasro, Dennis Harbour as the King, Norman Scott as Ramfis and Teresa Stich-Randall as the Priestess. Toscanini conducts the NBC Symphony Orchestra and Robert Shaw Chorale. The telecast was produced by Don Gillis and directed by Doug Rodgers. Black and white. In Italian. 149 minutes. BMG video and laser.

1953 Sophia Loren film
This famous film was launched like a live spectacle by impresario Sol Hurok and was promoted as the first opera film in color. Sophia Loren stars as Aida with her singing dubbed by Renata Tebaldi. The film was a major production with top La Scala and Rome Opera singers and grandiose sets. Amneris is played by Lois Maxwell and sung by Ebe Stignani, Radames by Luciano della Marras sung by Giuseppe Campora, Amonasro by Afro Poli sung by Gino Bechi and Ramfis by Giulio Neri sung by Antonio Cassinelli. Flavio Mogherini designed the sets and Pietro Portalupi was the cinematographer. Renzo Rossellini conducted the Italian State Radio Orchestra and Clemente Fracassi directed the film. Oscar Film. Color. In Italian. 95 minutes. On video.

1958 Leontyne Price in Canada

Price sings the role of Aida and performs the third act of the opera for a Radio-Canada TV concert on Oct. 23, 1958. William McGrath portrays Ramades and Napoleon Bisson plays Amonasro. The music is played by the Radio-Canada Orchestra. François Bernier directed the film. Black and white. 30 minutes.

1961 Mario Del Monaco video

Mario del Monaco is a powerful Ramades with Gabriella Tucci as his Aida in this production taped in Tokyo for Japanese television. Giulietta Simionato portrays Amneris and Aldo Protti is Amonasro with Franco Capuana conducting the Lirica Italiana Orchestra. Black and white. In Italian with English and Japanese subtitles. VAI video/Japanese laser.

1963 Verona Arena

Tullio Serafin, then aged 85, conducts the Verona Arena Chorus and Orchestra in this vintage performance of the opera. Leyla Gencer portrays Aida opposite Giulietta Simionato as Amneris, Gastone Limarilli is Ramades, Giangiacomo Guelfi is Amonasro and Bonaldo Giaotti is Ramfis. Black and white. In Italian. 83 minutes. Video in INA Archives, Verona.

1966 Verona Arena

Leyla Gencer again stars as Aida with Carlo Bergonzi as her Ramades in this wonderful production at the open-air Verona Arena. Fiorenza Cossotto is Amneris, Anselmo Colzani is Amonasro and Bonaldo Giaiotti is Ramfis. Acting styles and production values have changed a lot at Verona in the past thirty years but these voices have never been superseded. Franco Capuana conducts the Verona Arena Chorus and Orchestra. Black and white. In Italian. 150 minutes. Bel Canto video.

1976 Orange Festival

Grace Bumbry sings the role of Amneris, Mexican soprano Gilda Cruz-Romo is Aida and Bulgarian tenor Peter Gougaloff is Ramades in this open-air production in the old Roman theater in Orange, France. Invar Wixell sings Amonasro and Thomas Schippers conducts the Turin Regio Theater Orchestra. The opera was filmed live by Pierre Jourdan. Color. In Italian with Japanese subtitles. 149 minutes. Lyric video/Japanese laser.

1981 Verona Arena

The Arena di Verona, an open air Roman amphitheater seating 25,000, is the perfect spectacular setting for *Aida*. This production by Giancarlo Sbragia is of real grandeur with sets by Vittorio Rossi of a size most designers can only dream about. Maria Chiara sings Aida, Nicola Martinucci is Radames, Fiorenza Cossotto is Amneris, Carlo Zardo is Ramfis, Alfredo Zanazzo is the King and Giuseppe Scandola is Amonasro. Anton Guadagno conducts the Verona Arena Orchestra and Chorus. Brian Large directed the video and provides a better view of the opera than the real audience gets. Color. In Italian with English subtitles. 150 minutes. HBO video.

1981 Opera Stories

A highlights laserdisc version of the Verona Arena production described above. Charlton Heston narrates the story from Egypt where he filmed his introductions to the opera scenes in 1989 under the direction of Keith Cheetham. Color. In English and Italian with subtitles. 52 minutes. Pioneer Artists laser.

1985 Metropolitan Opera

Leontyne Price stars as Aida, one of her great roles, with James McCracken as Radames in this Metropolitan Opera production by John Dexter. Fiorenza Cossotto is Amneris, Simon Estes is Amonasro, John Macurdy is Ramfis and Dimitri Kavrakos is the King. David Reppa designed the sets and James Levine conducted the Metropolitan Opera Orchestra and Chorus. Brian Large directed the Live from the Met telecast on Jan. 3, 1985. Color. In Italian with English subtitles. 150 minutes. Video at MTR.

1986 Teatro alla Scala

An impressive staging at the Teatro alla Scala in Milan with Maria Chiara as Aida partnered by Luciano Pavarotti as Ramades. Stage director Luca Ronconi wanted spectacular sets and designer Mauro Pagano certainly provided them. Ghena Dimitrova is a powerful Amneris, Juan Pons is Amonasro, Nicolai Ghiaurov is Ramfis and Paata Burchuladze is the King. The La Scala Orchestra and chorus are conducted by Lorin Maazel. Derek Bailey directed the video. Color. In Italian with English subtitles. 160 minutes. Home Vision video/Pioneer laser.

1988 Claes Fellbom film

Claes Fellbom's Swedish film is a fascinating attempt to create a genuine primitive setting for the opera with Egyptian society envisioned as a barbaric kingdom. It was filmed on the island of Lanzarote by cinematographer Jorgen Persson and is sung in Swedish by members of the Swedish Folk Opera. It was reviewed in America as the "topless" *Aida* because of the women's costumes. Aida is played by Margareta Ridderstedt, Ramades is played by Niklas Ek but sung by Robert Grundin, Amneris is Ingrid Tomasson and Jan Van Der Schaaf is Amonasro. The music is performed by the Swedish Folk Opera Orchestra and Chorus conducted by Kerstin Nerbe. The film premiered in the U.S. at the AFI Cinetex Festival in Las Vegas. Color. In Swedish with English subtitles. 116 minutes. On video.

1989 Metropolitan Opera

Aprile Millo is an intense Aida and Placido Domingo a powerful Ramades in this fine Metropolitan Opera production by Sonja Frisell. Dolora Zajick sings Amneris, Paata Burchuladze is Ramfis, Dimitri Kavrakis is the King and Sherrill Milnes is Amonasro. Gianni Quaranta designed the sets, Rodney Griffin created the impressive dance sequences and James Levine led the Metropolitan Opera Orchestra and Chorus. Brian Large directed the video. The telecast won an Emmy as the Outstanding Classical Program in the Performing Arts. Color. In Italian with English subtitles. 158 minutes. DG video/laser.

1994 Royal Opera

Cheryl Studer sings Aida with Dennis O'Neill as Radames in this excellent Royal Opera, Covent Garden, production by Elijah Moshinsky. Luciana D'Intino is Amneris, Robert Lloyd is Ramfis and Alexandru Agache sings Amonasro. Michael Yeargan designed the sets and Edward Downes conducted the Royal Opera House Orchestra and Chorus. Brian Large directed the video. Color. In Italian with English subtitles. 152 minutes. Home Vision video/ Pioneer laser.

1994 Verona Arena

Placido Domingo celebrated twenty five years of appearances at the Verona Arena with a special program of staged opera scenes that was televised in Italy. The program includes Act III of *Aida* with Domingo as Radames. Nello Santi conducts the Verona Arena Orchestra. SACIS. Color. 90 minutes. On video.

Early/related films

1911 Edison film

Mary Fuller portrays Aida in this Edison film based on the Verdi opera. Marc MacDermott is Ramades, Miriam Nesbitt is Amneris and Charles Ogle is the Pharaoh. The film premiered May 6, 1911 with live *Aida* music. Contemporary critics thought it a magnificent reproduction of the opera. Oscar Apfel and J. Searle Dawley wrote and directed. Black and white. About l2 minutes.

1911 Bianca Lorezoni film

Bianca Lorezoni stars as Aida in this early Italian film from the Film d'Arte Italiana company. The cast includes Virgilio Frigerio as Ramades and Rina Agozzino Alessio as Amneris. Black and white. About 10 minutes. Print in Dutch film archive.

1914 The Nightingale

Ethel Barrymore portrays a street singer who becomes an opera star in Paris and the Met singing the title role in *Aida*. The plot of this American film foreshadows what occurred at the Met four years later when Rosa Ponselle became an opera star with no prior experience. Black and white. About 30 minutes.

1927-1930 Giovanni Martinelli films

Giovanni Martinelli of the Metropolitan Opera made three Vitaphone sound films in 1927 and 1930 featuring excerpts from *Aida*. In two he sings "Celeste Aida," in the other he joins soprano Ina Bourskaya in the duet from the Temple Scene. Black and white. Each film about eight minutes.

1960 The Girl with a Suitcase

Valerio Zurlini's film *La Ragazza con la Valigia* has as its heroine a girl named Aida (Claudia Cardinale). As she walks down her boyfriend's staircase "Celeste Aida" is played on a phonograph as sung by Beniamino Gigli. Black and white. In Italian. 113 minutes.

1962 Leontyne Price on Voice of Firestone

Leontyne Price, one of the most famous interpreters of the role of Aida, is shown performing on the *Voice of Firestone* television show. She sings *O Patria mia* in costume with set. Howard Barlow conducts. The program was telecast Dec. 30, 1962. Black and white. In Italian with English introductions. About 7 minutes. VAI video *A Firestone Verdi Festival*

1987 The Aida File

An informative documentary about the opera tracing its origins with footage of past performances by great Aidas. It includes interviews with Eva Turner, Renata Tebaldi, Grace Bumbry, Carlo Bergonzi and Luciano Pavarotti. The Verdi material was shot in the La Scala Museum and in Parma and features George Barker as Verdi and Colin Jeavons as libretto writer Antonio Ghislanzoni. The film was made for the South Bank Show by producer Hilary Chadwick and director Derek Bailey. Color. 77 minutes. Home Vision Video.

AKHNATEN

1984 opera by Glass

Philip Glass's minimalist opera tells the story of Egyptian pharaoh Akhnaten, the first historical personage to set up worship of a single all-powerful god. His people, however, eventually rebel and restore the old gods. The opera was very popular when staged in London, Houston and Germany but remains controversial. There is no video of the complete opera but there is a documentary with excerpts from productions. See also PHILIP GLASS.

1985 A Composer's Notes

At the core of this excellent documentary about Glass, subtitled *Philip Glass and the Making of an Opera*, are simultaneous productions of *Akhnaten* in 1985 in Germany and. America. The production at the Wurttemberg State Theater in Stuttgart is directed by Achim Freyer with Paul Esswood as Akhnaten and Milagro Vargas as Nefertiti and the music conducted by Dennis Russell Davies. The Houston Grand Opera production is directed by David Freeman with Christopher Robson as Akhanaten and Marta Senn as Nefertiti with the music conducted by John DeMain. Michael Blackwood produced and directed the documentary photographed by Mead Hunt. Color. 87 minutes. VAI video.

ALAGNA, ROBERTO

French tenor (1966-)

Roberto Alagna was the talk of London in 1994 for his performance at Covent Garden in *Roméo et Juliette* with hopes that he could be the next great tenor or even Pavarotti. His American debut was nearly as successful. He made his debut at Glyndebourne in 1988 as Alfredo in *La Traviata* and has also sung Hoffmann in *The Tales of Hoffmann*,

Rodolfo in *La Bohème* and the Duke in *Rigoletto*. Born in Paris of Sicilian parents, he studied privately and is bilingual in French and Italian. He can be seen on two videos including his breakthrough *Roméo et Juliette* and a superb *La Traviata* at La Scala. See ROMÉO ET JULIETTE (1994), LA TRAVIATA (1994)

ALBANESE, LICIA

Italian-born American soprano (1913-)

Licia Albanese is noted for her Puccini and Verdi heroines and was Toscanini's choice to sing Violetta in *La Traviata* and Mimi in *La Bohème* in his NBC radio broadcasts. Albanese made her debut in Milan in 1934 and her first appearance at the Metropolitan Opera in 1940. She sang with the Met that year in the first American opera telecast. She was so popular that she decided to move to the U.S and become an American citizen. Albanese was praised for the intensity of her singing and her work is widely available on record. She starred as Desdemona in Verdi's *Otello* in the first complete opera telecast from the Metropolitan in 1948 and is featured in a documentary about *Tosca*. See METROPOLITAN OPERA (1940), OTELLO (1948), TOSCA (1983 film), ARTURO TOSCANINI (1985).

1951 Licia Albanese in Opera and Song

Albanese finished her career before extensive filming and televising of operas but left some television records. Before she retired from the Metropolitan Opera in 1966, she made an appearance on the *Voice of Firestone* television series. Her performance was taped on Feb. 19, 1951. Albanese sings arias from Leoncavallo's *Pagliacci* and Meyerbeer's *Le Prophète*. Black and white. 26 minutes. VAI Video.

1956 Serenade

Licia Albanese plays herself in this Hollywood film. She appears on a New York opera theater stage resembling the Met singing Desdemona opposite Mario Lanza as Otello. It's his Met debut in the film but he abandons Albanese on stage because Joan Fontaine doesn't turn up for the performance. Anthony Mann directed this adaptation of a James M. Cain novel. MGM. Color. 121 minutes. Warner Bros. video.

ALBERGHETTI, ANNA MARIA
Italian-born American soprano (1936-)

Italian-born Anna Maria Alberghetti began her career rather splendidly singing Monica in the 1951 film of Gian-Carlo Menotti's *The Medium.* Paramount thought she might be another Deanna Durbin and had her sing an aria in the Bing Crosby musical *Here Comes the Groom.* She was fine as a girl with a good opera voice in *The Stars are Singing* with the Metropolitan's Lauritz Melchior. After that her films were less musical and interesting. High points of her later career were a Tony for the Broadway music *Carnival* and a TV production of *Kismet* with José Ferrer. She also worked with the Long Beach Civic Light Opera Company. In addition to the films below she appeared in the westerns *The Last Command* (1955) and *Duel at Apache Wells* (1957). See also KISMET (1967), THE MEDIUM (1951).

1951 Here Comes The Groom
Blind war orphan Alberghetti gives a touching performance of Gilda's aria "Caro nome" at the beginning of this excellent musical. She is auditioning in Paris for an American conductor who decides to adopt her and arranges for her to sing at the Met. Most of the singing is by Bing Crosby who has to get married so he can adopt two orphans. The Oscar-winning song "In the Cool Cool Cool of the Evening" is sung by Crosby and Jane Wyman. Frank Capra directed. Black and white. 113 minutes. Paramount video.

1953 The Stars Are Singing
Anna Maria Alberghetti plays a 15-year-old Polish girl who jumps ship in New York and hides out from the police with family friend Lauritz Melchior, a former Metropolitan Opera star. She has a terrific voice and demonstrates it by singing "Una voce poco fa" from *The Barber of Seville* and "Sempre libera" from *La Traviata.* Alberghetti is also heard in duet with Melchior and is helped by singer Rosemary Clooney. Norman Taurog directed this enjoyable film. Paramount. Color. 99 minutes. Paramount video.

1957 Ten Thousand Bedrooms
Alberghetti is a gold digger in Rome in this old-fashioned musical and throws herself at millionaire Dean Martin. Richard Thorpe directed. Color. 114 minutes. Paramount video.

1960 Cinderfella
Alberghetti is a princess opposite Jerry Lewis in her last film. Frank Tashlin directed. Color. 90 minutes.

ALBERNI, LUIS
American character actor (1887-1962)

Luis Alberni is not from the world of opera but for moviegoers in the 1930s he was the personification of opera stereotypes. Whether portraying an opera singer, maestro, singing teacher or impresario. he always climbed to heights of frenzy and temperament. He acted opposite opera singers like Grace Moore, Marion Talley and Michael Bartlett and even sang the baritone part of the *Lucia* sextet to a haddock in *Follow Your Heart.* The New York Times hailed him as its favorite screen musician saying "Mr. Alberni may not know one note from another, but he has done so much of this sort of thing for the screen that he achieves a fervor comparable to that of an inspired conductor in the throes of *L'Africaine.*" Operatic Alberni films include *One Night of Love, Love Me Forever, Metropolitan* and *Follow Your Heart.*

ALBERT HERRING
1947 opera by Britten

Benjamin Britten's popular comic opera is based on a de Maupassant story transposed to England with a libretto by Eric Crozier. Albert Herring is picked to be the virgin May Day King in a small Suffolk village when no virginal May Queen can be found. After he is crowned, he has a little too much to drink and ends ups disqualifying himself from the crown.

1978 St. Louis Opera
A St. Louis Opera company video production of the Britten opera was shown in Minneapolis in 1978 during a national conference devoted to television opera.

1985 Glyndebourne Festival
Peter Hall directed this superb Glyndebourne Festival production of modern British opera at its best with good singers, direction and production values. Tenor John Graham-Hall stars as Albert Herring, Patricia Johnson is the unlikeable Lady Billows, Felicity Palmer is the maid Florence, Elizabeth Gale is the teacher Miss Wordsworth, Richard van Allen is police superintendent Budd,

Alan Opie is butcher's assistant Sid and Jean Rigby is baker's assistant Nancy. Bernard Haitink conducts the London Philharmonic Orchestra and Robin Lough directed the video. 145 minutes. Color. In English. Kultur or Home Vision video.

ALBERT, EUGEN D'
German composer (1864-1932)

Eugen d'Albert was truly international, a Euro composer ahead of his time. His family came from Italy, his name was French, his parents were Germans living in England, he was born in Scotland, he became Swiss and he died in Latvia. Although he wrote many operas, only one has remained in the repertoire and it is naturally the most international. *Tiefland* (1903) is a German opera based on a Catalan play composed in the Italian verismo style. Maria Callas helped build her early reputation starring in it. See TIEFLAND.

ALCESTE
1767 opera by Gluck

Gluck's opera was ahead of its time when it premiered in 1767, the second of his reform operas with librettist Ranieri de' Calzabigi. Alceste is a rather noble wife who promises to sacrifice herself to the gods if husband Admète will recover from an illness. He does and she does but all ends well with supernatural help from Apollo. See also CHRISTOPH WILLIBALD GLUCK.

1982 Janet Baker at Covent Garden
Dame Janet Baker is seen preparing for, rehearsing and performing in *Alceste* at Covent Garden in the documentary film *Full Circle*. She is pictured on stage singing the aria "Divinités du Styx" with Charles Mackerras conducting the Royal Opera House Orchestra. Bob Bentley's fine film follows Baker's final opera season. NVC. Color. 75 minutes. Kultur video.

ALDA, FRANCES
New Zealand/U.S. soprano (1883-1952)

New Zealand-born Frances Alda is noted for many things besides her splendid voice and her long, notable career at the Metropolitan Opera. She is the focal point of a great many opera anecdotes as she had a quick temper, was often involved in quarrels and lawsuits and was a "close friend" of conductor Arturo Toscanini and Met director Giulio Gatti-Casazzo, whom she later married. She was once hired to train Ganna Walska, the opera singer who became the prototype for the singer in *Citizen Kane*. Her entertaining 1937 autobiography is titled *Men, Women and Tenors*. See CITIZEN KANE.

1927-1930 Vitaphone films
"Madame Frances Alda" starred in three sound shorts made by the Vitaphone company in 1927, 1929 and 1930. She sings "The Star Spangled Banner" on the 1927 film, "The Last Rose of Summer" from *Martha* and the song "Birth of Morn" on the 1929 film and "Ave Maria" from *Otello* on the 1930 film. Black and white. Each film about 8 minutes. Bel Canto Society video.

ALEGRÍA DEL BATALLÓN, LA
1909 zarzuela by Serrano

Luis Buñuel wrote and produced and Jean Gremillon directed a famous film based on this zarzuela by José Serrano. It has a lightly anti-militaristic theme that shows the realities of military life and ridicules the comic self importance of soldiers. The libretto is by Carlos Arniches and F. Quintana. See also JOSÉ SERRANO.

1925 Maximiliano Thous film
The first film of the zarzuela stars Anita Giner, Leopoldo Pitarch and Julio Simón and was shot in Spain by Maximiliano Thous. It was a silent film but was screened with Serrano's music live. Black and white. In Spanish. 76 minutes.

1936 Luis Buñuel/Jean Gremillon film
This Spanish film, a collaboration between Spanish producer/writer Luis Buñuel and French director Jean Gremillon, became one of the most popular films in the zarzuela genre. It was widely seen and admired by critics as well as audiences but neither filmmaker took a credit. Angelillo, Ana Maria Custodio and Luis Heredia are the stars. Buñuel wrote the script with Eduardo Ugarte and even dubbed the voice of a peasant. José Maria Beltrán was the cinematographer. Black and white. In Spanish. 90 minutes.

ALEKO

1893 opera by Rachmaninoff

Aleko was composed as a graduation exercise by the nineteen-year-old Sergei Rachmaninoff and immediately staged at the Bolshoi Opera where it launched the young composer's career. It was an even bigger success four years later when Chaliapin sang the title role in a Kirov production and the opera entered the Russian repertory. The libretto, by Vladimir Nemirovich-Danchenko, is based on Pushkin's story *The Gypsies* and is a kind of one-act variation on *Carmen*. Young Aleko joins a group of gypsies because he is attracted by the gypsy Zemfira. When she decides to leave him for another man, he kills her. See also SERGEI RACHMANINOFF.

1954 Alexander Ognivtsev film
Soviet bass Alexander Ognivtsev stars as Aleko in this Soviet film based on a Kirov Opera production in Leningrad. The cast includes Mark Reizen, I. Soubkovaskaja, S. Kouznetsov and B. Elatogorova. This is a fairly direct film of the stage production but there are cinematic location scenes added to open it up including river and sea views. Grigory Roshal and Serge Sidelev produced and directed the film for Lenfilm. Black and white. In Russian. 61 minutes.

1986 Yevgeny Nesterenko film
Yevgeny Nesterenko stars as Aleko in this Soviet television film of the opera. The other roles are played by actors with singers dubbing their voices. Svetlana Volkova sings Zemfira acted by Nelli Volshaninova, Vladimir Matorin sings Zemfira's father acted by Vladimir Golovin, Raisa Kotowa sings the old Gypsy woman acted by Maria Papasjan and Michael Muntjan sings the Young Gypsy acted by Sphandor Semjonov. Vladimir Lebedov designed the sets and Pavel Sasjadko was cinematographer. Dimitri Kitaenko conducts the Moscow Philharmonic Symphony Orchestra and USSR TV and Radio Chorus. Victor Okunzov directed the film. Color. In Russian. 62 minutes. Lyric video/ Japanese laser.

ALLEN, THOMAS

English baritone (1944-)

Thomas Allen has sung at the Royal Opera for over twenty years. He began his career with the Welsh National Opera in 1969 in *La Traviata* and in 1971 sang Donald in *Billy Budd* at Covent Garden. By the age of 25 he was considered one of the best British baritones in half a century but he did not make his debut at the Metropolitan Opera until 1981. Allen has won wide praise as Don Giovanni and in 1987 became the first Englishman to sing the part at La Scala, a portrayal that is on video. He has been taped extensively and can be seen in many opera videos. See BILLY BUDD (1988), LA BOHÈME (1982), CARMINA BURANA (1989), COSÌ FAN TUTTE (1975), THE CUNNING LITTLE VIXEN (1995), DON GIOVANNI (1989/ 1993), MANON LESCAUT (1983), THE MARRIAGE OF FIGARO (1985), IL RITORNO D'ULISSE IN PATRIA (1985).

1992 Songs of Northumbria
Durham-born Thomas Allen returns home for a gala concert in Durham Cathedral to mark its 900th anniversary. Appearing with him are Sheila Armstrong and the Northumbrian Chamber Orchestra and Chorus. The regional songs, arranged by David Haslam, range from nursery rhymes to mining disaster ballads. Color. 70 minutes. Mawson and Wareham Music (England) video.

ALPAR, GITTA

Hungarian soprano (1903-)

Gitta Alpar (in Hungary it's spelled Alpár) began her career in Budapest in 1923 and became popular in coloratura roles in Munich and Vienna. She had great success in Berlin as Violetta, the Queen of the Night and the leads in operettas by Millöcker and Lehár. Her biggest hit was *Die Dubarry* which starred Grace Moore when it came to New York. Alpar had to leave Germany in 1933 when the Nazis came to power, first living in Austria and then moving to the U.S. in 1936. She married actor/ director Gustav Fröhlich and starred in many films in Germany, Austria, England and the U.S. See BALL IM SAVOY, DIE DUBARRY.

1932 Die - Oder Keine
Die - Oder Keine stars Alpar as a prima donna appearing in a production of *La Traviata*, an opera in which she had been very popular on the Berlin stage. She also wins the love of a young prince and helps him defeat his rivals for the throne. Gustav Fröhlich directed with music by Otto Stransky. *The New York Times* gave high praise to Alpar when the film opened in the U.S. as *She or Nobody* Black and white. In German. 92 minutes.

1932 Gitta Endeckt ihr Herz

Gitta Discovers Her Heart is a somewhat autobiographical film operetta featuring Alpar as a Hungarian singer named Gitta who becomes famous singing in Berlin. Husband Gustav Fröhlich directed and plays the young composer she loves and helps make a success. The music is by Nikolaus Brodszky and Hansom Milde-Meissner. Black and white. In German. 92 minutes.

1936 Guilty Melody

Alpar plays an opera singer in this odd British film which mixes espionage with music. She sings arias by Gounod and Verdi while her impresario husband Nils Asther sends code messages on her records. British intelligence officer John Loder suspects Alpar of being the spy. The film was based on Hans Rehfisch's novel *The Guilty Voice*. Richard Potter directed. Black and white. In English. 75 minutes

1936 Le Disque 413

The French version of *Guilty Melody* also stars Alpar but has a different supporting cast, cameraman and scriptwriter. The actors include Jules Barry, Jean Galland and Cecile Meunier. Richard Potter again directed. Black and white. In French. 82 minutes.

1941 The Flame of New Orleans

Gitta Alpar is seen on stage singing in *Lucia di Lammermoor* opposite Anthony Marlowe as Edgardo in this fine René Clair film. The Donizetti opera is being presented at the New Orleans Opera House in the opening scene. Clair uses Alpar's singing as an atmospheric backdrop for Marlene Dietrich who is seen baiting a honeyed trap for a rich man. Black and white. 78 minutes.

ALTMAN, ROBERT
American film director (1925-)

Robert Altman, acclaimed for such films as *Nashville* and *The Player*, has directed two operas on stage. First was *The Rake's Progress* produced in Lyons and in Ann Arbor for the University of Michigan. William Bolcom and Ardis Krainik of Lyric Opera of Chicago saw the Michigan production and invited Altman to collaborate on Bolcom's opera *McTeague*. Altman co-wrote the libretto and directed the opera on stage in October 1992. He also made a documentary about it. Altman's only opera film is based on Rameau's *Les Boreades* and is an episode in *Aria*. See ARIA, LES BOREADES, MCTEAGUE.

AMAHL AND THE NIGHT VISITORS
1951 TV opera by Menotti

This was the first opera created for television and marks the coming of age of TV. It was written, composed and staged by Gian Carlo Menotti for NBC Opera Theatre as a Christmas Eve special for Hallmark. It proved so popular that it was repeated annually for many years in the Hallmark Hall of Fame series. It was commissioned by Samuel Chotzinoff who had earlier commissioned Menotti's radio opera *The Old Maid and the Thief*. The story, inspired by Bosch's painting of *The Adoration of the Magi*, tells of a crippled boy whose family is visited on Christmas Eve by the Three Kings on their way to Bethlehem with gifts. When the boy offers his crutch as a gift, he is miraculously healed and joins the Kings on their visit to the Holy Child carrying his crutch. See also GIAN CARLO MENOTTI.

1951 NBC Opera Theatre

The opera premiered on Dec. 24, 1951, on NBC TV with Rosemary Kuhlmann singing the role of the Mother and Chet Allen as Amahl. The Three Kings were David Aiken as Melchior, Leon Lishner as Balthazar and Andrew McKinley as Kaspar. Menotti directed the staging, Samuel Chotzinoff produced, Thomas Schippers conducted the NBC Orchestra, Eugene Berman designed the costumes and sets and John Butler created the choreography. Kirk Browning directed the live telecast. Black and white. In English. 60 minutes. Videos at UCLA & MTR.

1952-1954 NBC Opera Theatre

Amahl and the Night Visitors was the first production in the Hallmark Hall of Fame series. It was so well received that it was presented seven more times in the following fourteen years, all but one as live productions. The same cast was featured in an Easter special telecast on April 13, 1952, but Bill McIver replaced Chet Allen in the third performance on Dec. 25 1952. The telecast on Dec. 20 1953 was the first in color and featured Sarah Churchill as narrator. The fifth telecast was on Dec. 19, 1954. Videos at UCLA.

1955 Swedish Television

The opera was produced in Swedish on Swedish television on Dec. 25 1955 with the title *Amahl och de Nattliga Besökarna*. Black and white. 60 minutes.

1963 NBC Opera Theater

The 1963 NBC Opera production of the opera was also issued on LP. It stars Martha King as the Mother, Kurt Yaghjian as Amahl and John McCollum, Richard Cross and Willis Patterson as the Three Kings. Herbert Grossman conducts the NBC Orchestra and Chorus. Kirk Browning directed the telecast which featured an introduction from Kookla, Fran and Olly. Black and white. 60 minutes. Video at MTR.

1979 Teresa Stratas film

Teresa Stratas stars as the Mother in this film of the opera shot in Israel and London with Arvin Brown as director and Menotti as music consultant. It is quite splendid visually with a formidable cast. Robert Sapolsky is the crippled Amahl, Giorgio Tozzi is Melchior, Willard White is Balthazar and Nico Castel is Kaspar. Ivy Baker Jones designed the costumes and Jesus Lopez-Cobos conducts the Ambrosian Opera Chorus and the Philharmonia Orchestra. Color. In English. 52 minutes. VAI video.

AMARA, LUCINE

Armenian-American soprano (1927-)

Lucine Amara made her debut at the Metropolitan Opera in 1950 in *Don Carlo* after starting in the chorus in San Francisco. She became a regular at Glyndebourne and was known for her performances in Italian operas. She was not, however, of Italian but of Armenian origin (her birth name was Armaganian) and she was born in Hartford. Her career ended before the advent of video but she can be seen in the opera montage scenes in the 1951 Caruso biography THE GREAT CARUSO.

AMATO, PASQUALE

Italian baritone (1878-1942)

Neapolitan baritone Pasquale Amato was a colleague of Caruso at the Metropolitan Opera and played Jack Rance opposite Caruso's Dick Johnson in the world premiere of *La Fanciulla del West* at the Met in 1910. Amato made his debut in his native Naples in 1900, was soon at La Scala and Covent Garden and first sang at the Metropolitan in 1908.

Amato became a member of the Met company and sang there until 1921. Afterwards he taught opera in New York and Louisiana. He appeared in only two films but left many recordings.

1928 A Neapolitan Romance

Amato is the star of this 1928 Vitaphone sound short titled *Pasquale Amato* in *A Neapolitan Romance*. It features him singing the Toreador aria from *Carmen* and the popular "Torna a Surriento." Black and white. About eight minutes.

1928 Glorious Betsy

Pasquale Amato portrays Napoleon in this patriotic part-talkie American film. He is seen but not heard though Met bass Andre De Segurola gets to sing "La Marseillaise." Dolores Costello, Conrad Nagel and Betty Blythe star in a tale about Napoleon's younger brother falling in love with an American girl, the Betsy of the title. Alan Crosland directed. Black and white. 80 minutes.

AMERICAN FILM INSTITUTE

The American Film Institute (AFI) is the major cultural film organization in the U.S. founded by President Lyndon Johnson in 1967. It has its main offices in Los Angeles and its film theater in Washington, DC. The AFI Catalogs of American Feature Films by decade are an invaluable source of information about opera and opera singers in American cinema since 1893. The AFI has also presented important opera-on-film series at its National Film Theater in the Kennedy Center in Washington, in collaboration with the Washington Opera, and in its Los Angeles International Film Festival (AFI Fest). In addition it is a leader in the film preservation movement.

AMFITHEATROF, DANIELE

Russian/American composer (1910-)

Daniele Amfitheatrof, who began his professional career as assistant conductor at La Scala, wrote an imaginary opera that is central to the plot of Max Ophuls great 1934 film *La Signora di Tutti*. He also wrote the original music for the 1953 Hollywood film *Salome*. See IMAGINARY OPERAS IN FILMS (1934), SALOME (1953 FILM).

AMORE DEI TRE RE, L'

1913 opera by Montemezzi

Italo Montemezzi's *The Love of Three Kings* was once a very popular opera and considered a masterpiece but it has nearly vanished from the repertory. Sem Benelli's libretto from his play is set in Italy in the tenth century and revolves around the loves of the Princess Fiora. She has been forced to marry blind King Archibaldo's son Prince Manfredo but really loves Prince Avito. When the king catches her with her lover, he strangles her and spreads poison on her lips. Lover and husband both kiss her lips and die. The king is left alone. See also ITALO MONTEMEZZI.

1962 NBC Opera Theatre

Phyllis Curtin is Princess Fiora with Giorgio Tozzi as the blind king in this NBC Opera Theatre production by Samuel Chotzinoff. Richard Torigi plays the husband and Frank Poretta is the lover. The opera was presented in English in a translation by Joseph Machlis. Alfred Wallenstein conducted the orchestra and Ed Wittstein designed the sets. Kirk Browning directed for television using eight cameras to show its elaborate four-level castle set. Black and white. In English. 93 minutes.

1983 Providence Opera Theater

Louise Cash stars as Princess Fiora in this Providence, Rhode Island, production. Michael Harrison plays Avito, Lawrence Cooper is Manfredo and John Seabury is Archibaldo. William Radka was the stage director, Preston McClanahan designed the sets and Alvaro Cassuto conducted the orchestra. A narrator explains the action before each act. Ray Fass directed for television. The video is an off-air copy of a telecast. Color. In Italian. 100 minutes. Lyric video.

AMRAM, DAVID

American composer (1930-)

Philadelphia-born David Amram composed for theater, cinema and the opera house. He began writing music for Ford's Theater in Washington in 1951 and later was music director of Joseph Papp's Shakespeare Festival in New York. His first opera, *The Final Ingredient* (1965), was written for television. His second, *Twelfth Night* (1968), was based on the Shakespeare play as revised by Papp. His notable film scores include *Splendor in the Grass* and *The Arrangement* for Elia Kazan and *The Manchurian Candidate* for John Frankenheimer.

1965 The Final Ingredient

The Final Ingredient was commissioned for Passover by the ABC television series *Directions '65*. It's based on a television play by Reginald Rose with a libretto by A. Weinstein and tells the story of a group of prisoners in a World War II concentration camp. They are short one ingredient for their forbidden Passover supper, an egg, and so they stage a breakout to get it. The opera was telecast on April 11, 1965, with the composer conducting. Color. In English.

ANDERSON, JUNE

American soprano (1952-)

Boston-born June Anderson made her debut at the New York City Opera in 1978 as the Queen of the Night in *The Magic Flute*. Since then her coloratura mastery has been heard everywhere from Covent Garden to the Met. She is known for her *bel canto* roles, has been compared to Joan Sutherland and has developed a strong stage presence to go with her powerful voice. She is very impressive in the video of *Candide* as Cunegonde and portraying Adelina Patti in a film about the 19th century diva. See CANDIDE (1989), LA DONNA DEL LAGO (1992), LUISA MILLER (1988), WOLFGANG A. MOZART (1984), OTELLO BY ROSSINI (1988), PARIS (1989), ADELINA PATTI (1993), LUCIANO PAVAROTTI (1991), RICCIARDO E ZORAIDE (1990), SEMIRAMIDE (1990).

1989 June Anderson, The Passion of Bel Canto

This French documentary film about the soprano shows her rehearsing, singing and talking about her *bel canto* roles in cities around Europe. Anderson says she enjoys roles as what she calls "crazy ladies." She is seen as Lucia in *Lucia di Lammermoor* with Alfred Kraus at Covent Garden, Desdemona in Rossini's *Otello* directed by Jean-Pierre Ponnelle and Elvira in Bellini's *I Puritani* directed by André Serban. At the Opéra Comique in Paris she appears in the title role of *The Daughter of the Regiment* and at La Scala she portrays Amina in Bellini's *La Sonnambula*. Color. 57 minutes. View video.

ANDERSON, MARIAN

American contralto (1899-1993)

Marian Anderson, one of the real-life heroines of opera, paved the way for the great African-

American divas of today. She never had the chance to become an opera star herself as her Metropolitan Opera debut did not take place until 1955 when she was long past her prime. She was still the first African-American to sing a solo role at the Met when she portrayed Ulrica in *Un Ballo in Maschera*. As much as for her voice ("A voice like yours is heard only once in a hundred years" said Toscanini), she is memorable for her integrity. A central moment in her career was singing outdoors at the Lincoln Memorial in Washington, DC in 1939 after the DAR had refused her permission to sing in the Constitution Hall. Anderson was then hired by 20th Century-Fox to sing at the premiere of the film *Young Mr. Lincoln* in Springfield, Illinois, where she was refused as a guest at the Lincoln Hotel. See also SOL HUROK (1956).

1953 Marian Anderson
Jules Dassin directed this film for the *Meet the Masters* film series. It features Anderson in a program of spirituals and Schubert lieders and includes a reconstruction of her famous 1935 introductory concert. There are also scenes of her home life and friends and her Connecticut farm. Produced by World Artists. Black and white. 27 minutes. Kultur video.

1957 The Lady from Philadelphia
Edward R. Murrow's film about Marian Anderson's goodwill tour of Southeast Asia for the State Department was first shown on Murrow's CBS television program *See It Now*. Anderson sings fifteen songs from "Ave Maria" to "Mon coeur s'ouvre a ta voix" as she visits seven countries from Korea to India. The film won warm praise when it was screened on Dec. 30, 1957 and the State Department arranged to show it in seventy countries. The soundtrack is also on record. Black and white. 60 minutes. Video at MTR.

1969 The Lady in the Lincoln Memorial
A short film tracing the career of Marian Anderson from her childhood through her early church and concert hall successes to her triumphs in Europe and America. The highlight of the film is Anderson's performance at the Lincoln Memorial in 1939. Color. 18 minutes.

1977 Peerce, Anderson & Segovia
One of the three segments of this 1977 video is a twenty-minute compilation history of the life and career of Marian Anderson, probably based on Jules Dassin's 1953 film. It contains interviews and historic film of her 1939 concert at the Lincoln Memorial in Washington, DC and other appearances. The video begins with a re-creation of her Town Hall concert of 1935 and shows her in recital singing "Deep River," "Ave Maria" and other spirituals. Black and white. 20 minutes. Kultur video.

1991 Marian Anderson
This superb film portrait, produced by Dante J. James for WETA, includes interviews and scenes of concerts from the 1930s to the 1960s with a section devoted to her appearance at the Metropolitan Opera. It examines her life and music in the context of the social and political life of the time. There are interviews with, among others, violinist Isaac Stern, Hurok associate Martin Feinstein, Jessye Norman and Mattiwilda Dobbs. Anderson, who was 88 when the film was made, reflects on her life and music throughout the film. Juan William wrote the script and Avery Brooks narrates the film. Color. 60 minutes. PBS video.

ANDREA CHÉNIER
1896 opera by Giordano

This romantic *verismo* opera by Italian composer Umberto Giordano, set at the time of the French Revolution, was written by the ubiquitous Luigi Illica. It is based on the life of poet Andrea Chénier and tells of his love for the aristocrat Maddalena. She is also loved by a former servant who becomes the revolutionary leader Gérard. Despite sacrifices all round, the lovers end up on the guillotine. *Andrea Chénier* offers a wonderful opportunity for a divo tenor to show off and Maddalena's aria "La mamma morta" has become widely popular because of the film *Philadelphia*. See also UMBERTO GIORDANO.

1955 Mario Del Monaco/ Antonietta Stella film
Mario Del Monaco, one of the great interpreters of *Andrea Chénier*, was at the peak of his powers when he made this film for Italian television. Antonietta Stella is an excellent partner singing Maddalena and Giuseppe Taddei is a nicely evil Gérard. Luisa Mandelli is Bersi and Maria Amadini is the Countess. Angelo Questa conducts the RAI Italian Television Orchestra and Chorus. Mario Landi directed the film. Black and white. In Italian. 115 minutes. Legato Classics/SRO/Bel Canto videos.

1961 Mario Del Monaco/Renata Tebaldi video

Mario Del Monaco is again superb as Chénier with Renata Tebaldi as an equally splendid Maddalena in this stage production filmed for Tokyo television. Aldo Protti is the trouble-making baritone Gérard. Franco Capuana conducts the Lirica Italiana orchestra in a performance recorded Oct. 1, 1961. Black and white. In Italian with English and Japanese subtitles. 118 minutes. VAI video/ Japanese laser.

1973 Franco Corelli film

Franco Corelli is the featured performer in this Italian television film as Andrea Chénier. He is supported by the vibrant Celestina Casapietra as Maddalena and the great Piero Cappuccilli as Gérard. Color. In Italian. 115 minutes. Lyric/Bel Canto Society videos.

1979 Vienna State Opera

Placido Domingo is featured as Chénier in this solidly professional Vienna Staatsoper production by Otto Schenk with Nello Santi conducting the Vienna State Opera Orchestra. Gabriele Benackova sings the role of Maddalena and Piero Cappuccilli is Gérard. Beta film. Color. In Italian. 162 minutes. On video.

1985 Teatro alla Scala

José Carreras stars as Chénier in this massive Teatro alla Scala production by Lamberto Puggelli. Eva Marton portrays Maddalena, Piero Cappuccilli is the malevolent Gérard and Nella Veri is the Countess. Paolo Bregni designed the impressive sets and Luisa Spinatelli the costumes based around the French tricolor. Riccardo Chailly conducts the La Scala Orchestra and Chorus. Brian Large directed the video. Color. In Italian with English subtitles. 123 minutes. Home Vision video/ Pioneer Artists laser.

1985 Royal Opera

Placido Domingo stars as Chénier in this Royal Opera, Covent Garden, production by Michael Hampe. Anna Tomowa-Sintow is Maddalena, Giorgio Zancanaro is Gérard, Cynthia Buchan is Bersi and Patricia Johnson is the Countess. William Orlandi designed the sets and Julius Rudel conducted the Royal Opera Orchestra. Humphrey Burton directed the video. Color. In Italian with English subtitles. 119 minutes. Kultur video.

1985 Opera Stories

Placido Domingo stars as Chénier in this Opera Stories highlights version of the production above. Charlton Heston provides introduction and narration from Paris. Color. In English and Italian with English subtitles. 52 minutes. Pioneer Artists video.

Early/related films

1909 Léonce Perret film

Léonce Perret directed this silent film of the opera titled *André Chénier*. It was accompanied in cinemas by Giordano's music. About 10 minutes.

1955 Clemente Fracassi film

Giordano's music is used as the score of this narrative adaptation of the opera. Antonella Lualdi stars as Maddalena (i.e., Madeleine), Michel Auclair is Andrea Chénier and Raf Vallone is Gérard. Clemente Fracassi directed this French/ Italian coproduction. Black and white. In Italian or French. 97 minutes.

1993 Philadelphia

Tom Hanks, a lawyer dying of AIDS, listens to Maria Callas sing the aria "La mamma morta" from *Andrea Chénier* in a crucial scene in this Oscar-winning film. It's his favorite aria and has an intense effect on him and his lawyer. What he hears is the 1955 recording Callas made with Mario Del Monaco and Renata Tebaldi. Jonathan Demme directed the film. Tri-star. Color. 119 minutes. On video.

ANDRIESSEN, LOUIS
Dutch composer (1939-)

Louis Andriessen has worked with English filmmaker Peter Greenaway on two operas, one for television, the other for the stage, both with cinematic techniques. Their opera *Rosa: A Horse Drama* attracted international attention in 1994. Andriessen's best known earlier operas are the collaborative *Reconstructie* (1969) and *De materie* (1989).

1993 M is for Man, Music and Mozart

Andriessen composed the music for this British television opera written and directed by Peter Greenaway. It was created for the *Not Mozart* series and shot in Amsterdam using a dazzling combination of song, dance, animation and computer wizardry. The film opens with singer Astrid Seriese running through the alphabet and concentrating on the letter M for man. Nude dancers Kate Gowar and Karen Potisk perform rituals before a medical theater audience and revive choreographer/ dancer Ben Croft who dances the rest of the film. Color. 30 minutes. Connoisseur Academy (England) video.

1994 Rosa: A Horse Drama

Andriessen and his librettist/director Peter Greenaway attracted international attention for this innovative opera when it was staged by Netherlands Opera in Amsterdam in 1994. It is dominated by cinematic techniques with three levels of screens on stage. *Rosa* is the story of the composer Juan Manuel de Rosa who lives in an abattoir in Uruguay and writes scores for Hollywood westerns, He loves his horse more than his girl Esmeralda so she tries to turn herself into a horse to get him to love her. Eventually he and his horse are killed by cowboys firing from the screen of a Western movie and all ends in fire. Critics praised Greenaway's stagecraft.

AND THE SHIP SAILS ON
1983 opera film by Fellini

E La Nave Va is an operatic fantasy by Federico Fellini featuring a shipful of opera personalities on a luxury liner sailing from Naples in 1914. They are headed for the island birthplace of diva Edmea Tetua (Janet Suzman) whose ashes are to be scattered there and whose life is remembered in flashback. The passengers include singers, musicians, journalists, aristocrats and an Austrian grand duke. Some of the singers even descend to the boiler room and serenade the stokers in an operatic competition. After a boatload of Serbian refugees is picked up, the liner is sunk by a battleship to music by Rossini and Verdi including the *Forza del Destino* overture. The opera singer characters include soprano Ildebranda Cuffari (Barbara Jefford, sung by Mara Zampieri), tenor Aureliano Fuciletto (Victor Poletti, sung by Giovanni Bavaglio), soprano Inez Ruffo Saltini (sung by Elizabeth Norberg Schulz), mezzo Teresa Valegnani (sung by Nucci Condo), tenor Sabatino Lepari (sung by Carlo Di Giacomo) , basso Ziloev (sung by Boris Carmeli), mezzo Maria Augusta Miceli and tenor Bruno Beccaria. Gianfranco Plenezio conducted the RAI Symphony Orchestra and Chorus and arranged the music. Fellini and

Tonino Guerra wrote the screenplay with texts for the opera passages by Andrea Zanzotto. Giuseppe Rotunno was the brilliant cinematographer. Color. In Italian with English subtitles. 138 minutes. On video. See also FEDERICO FELLINI.

ANIMATED OPERA

Some of the most enjoyable opera films have been animated cartoons using opera music by Rossini, Wagner, Mozart, etc. in unusually inventive ways. Rossini's overtures to *The Barber of Seville* and *William Tell* have been especially popular with animators. The best animated opera films would certainly include Chuck Jones's *What's Opera, Doc?* and *The Rabbit of Seville*, Walt Disney's *The Whale Who Wanted to Sing at the Met* and Walter Lantz's *The Barber of Seville*. Most of the films in this genre are listed under their operas or creators. See CARMEN, LA DAMNATION DE FAUST, DICK DEADEYE, WALT DISNEY, GIANINI & LUZZATI, CHUCK JONES, WALTER LANTZ, THE LEGEND OF THE INVISIBLE CITY OF KITEZH, THE MAGIC FLUTE, OPERA IMAGINAIRE, OPERAVOX ANIMATED OPERAS, GEORGE PAL, LOTTE REINIGER, DAS RHEINGOLD, RIGOLETTO, RUDDIGORE, TURANDOT, WARNER BROS. CARTOONS, WILLIAM TELL.

1935 Opera Night

Paul Terry and Frank Moser created this American animated opera film in 1935. Black and white. 6 minutes.

1952 Off to the Opera

American Connie Rasinki created this animated opera film. Color. 7 minutes.

1967 The Opera Caper

This Paramount cartoon from the series Go-Go Toons was started by Shamus Culhane and finished by Ralph Bakshi. Color. 7 minutes.

1969 The World in Opera

Polish animator Jerzy Kotowski created this lively animated opera film. Color. 8 minutes.

1972 Opera

An Italian cartoon about opera by the inventive animation genius Bruno Bozzetto. Animated comic lampoons of opera scenes form the background to commentary about modern madnesses. Color. 11 minutes.

ANNA BOLENA

1830 opera by Donizetti

Anna Bolena is the earliest of Donizetti's operas regularly performed. Felice Romani's libretto tells the story of the second wife of English King Henry VIII and her tribulations as the King attempts to get rid of her so he can marry lady-in-waiting Jane Seymour. It has one of Donizetti's great mad scenes when Anne reveals her love for Lord Percy and her hatred of Henry and Jane as she awaits execution in the Tower of London. Joan Sutherland's recording of the opera is much admired. See also GAETANO DONIZETTI.

1985 New York City Opera

Joan Sutherland stars in this New York City Opera concert version of the opera at Avery Fisher Hall. Singing with Sutherland are mezzos Cynthia Clarey and Judith Forst, tenor Jerry Hadley and bass-baritones Gregory Yurisich and Jan Opalach. Richard Bonynge conducts the New York City Opera Orchestra and New York Choral Artists. The opera was presented in the Live from Lincoln Center series and telecast Nov. 25, 1985. Color. In Italian. 120 minutes.

ANTHOLOGIES

There have been a number of opera anthologies, guides and compilations released on film and video with multiple opera scenes and excerpts. These are mostly excerpts from operas that already exist in more complete form on film or video but some of them are unique and most of them are helpful guides. Those with music by a single composer are listed under the composer's entry but the mixed anthologies are described below. See also LATE ADDITIONS, OPERA NORTH.

1948 First Opera Film Festival

This film consists of highlight versions of four operas staged at the Rome Opera House: *William Tell*, *The Marriage of Figaro*, *Don Pasquale* and *Carmen*. Most roles are portrayed by actors and dubbed by singers like Tito Gobbi, Cloe Elmo and Piero Brasini. Owen Downes introduces the operas and Angelo Questa conducts the orchestra. George Richfield produced the film released theatrically in the U.S. Classic Pictures. Black and white. In Italian. 90 minutes. On video. See individual operas for full details.

1962 Musikalisches Rendezvous

This is an anthology of DEFA opera films made in East Berlin. It includes highlights from the East German films of *The Beggar Student*, *The Merry Wives of Windsor*, *Zar and Zimmermann* and *The Marriage of Figaro*. Color. In German. 83 minutes. See individual operas for full details.

1964 Stars of Bel Canto

This is a compilation of excerpts from TV studio appearances by nine top singers in the early 1960s. The singers are Renata Tebaldi, Regina Resnick, Leonie Rysanek, Giulietta Simionato, Roberta Peters, Hilde Guden, George London, Lawrence Winters and Fernando Corena. They sings arias by Rossini, Offenbach, Verdi, Puccini, Mozart and Bizet. RTBF. Black and white. 60 minutes.

1987 The Music of Man

A Canadian series about the history of music in eight 60-minute programs on four videos with Yehudi Menuhin as narrator and guide. Among the opera composers discussed in the series with staged scenes are Monteverdi, Lully, Mozart, Beethoven and Verdi. Richard Bocking and John Thomason directed. Color. Home Vision videos.

1988 Opera Favorites

Placido Domingo and Kiri Te Kanawa star in scenes from six operas. Te Kanawa, Hildegarde Heichele and Hermann Prey are Rosalinde, Adele and Eisenstein in *Die Fledermaus* at the Royal Opera House. Domingo is Hoffmann in *The Tales of Hoffmann* at Covent Garden with Agnes Baltsa as Giulietta and Dick Johnson's in *La Fanciulla del West* at Covent Garden. At the Verona Arena, Te Kanawa is Desdemona and Vladimir Atlantov is Otello in *Otello*. At La Scala, Domingo is Ernani and Mirella Freni is Elvira in *Ernani*. The video ends at Covent Garden with Domingo as Des Grieux and Te Kanawa as Manon in *Manon Lescaut*. Color. In original languages with English subtitles. 59 minutes. HBO video.

1988 History of Italian Music

An Italian series on video by Elio Rumma tracing chronologically the history of opera and other forms of music in Italy. Each is about an hour long and is devoted to one aspect of music, e.g., *Opera Buffa in Naples*. Color. In Italian. About 60 minutes. Mastervideo (Italy) video.

1990 Essential Opera

An introduction-to-opera compilation video featuring twelve scenes from famous operas like *La Bohème* and *Carmen* with top stars. The singers include Placido Domingo, Maria Ewing, Raina Kabaivanska, Leo Nucci, Joan Sutherland, Mirella Freni and Luciano Pavarotti. The opera scenes are excerpts from existing videos. Color. In original language with English subtitles. 82 minutes. London video and laser.

1990 Essential Opera 2

A second introduction-to-opera compilation of scenes from twelve operas. The singers include Cecilia Bartoli as Rosina in *The Barber of Seville*, Placido Domingo as Cavaradossi in *Tosca*, Mirella Freni as Mimi in *La Bohème*, José Carreras, Kiri Te Kanawa and Luciano Pavarotti. Color. In original language with English subtitles. 83 minutes. London video and laser.

1992 My World Of Opera

Kiri Te Kanawa gives a tour of the Royal Opera House and introduces scenes from various operas. They include Te Kanawa singing the *Der Rosenkavalier* trio with Barbara Bonney and Anne Howells, Robert Lloyd in *Don Carlo*, José Carreras in *Andrea Chénier*, Placido Domingo in *The Tales of Hoffmann*, Janet Baker in *Orfeo ed Eurydice*, Domingo and Mirella Freni in *Ernani*, Vladimir Atlantov in *Otello* plus *Die Fledermaus*, *La Bohème* and *Nabucco*. Keith Cheetham directed and Robin Scott produced the video. Color. 59 minutes. Teldec video.

1994 Classics In Vision

A sampler of twelve scenes from the Decca video catalogue, most with operatic content. The opera excerpts are from *Rigoletto, Tosca, Lucrezia Borgia* and *The Marriage of Figaro*. The singers include José Carreras, Cecilia Bartoli, Kiri Te Kanawa, Luciano Pavarotti, Placido Domingo, Joan Sutherland and Sherrill Milnes. Color. In original language with English subtitles. 60 minutes. Decca video.

1995-1997 Music in the 20th Century

John Huszar and FilmAmerica's ten-part series on modern music contains a number of entries of operatic interest. *Fire and Ice*, the first program, has excerpts from and discussions of operas by Wagner and Debussy. *Musical Stages*, the eighth program, focuses on opera and musical theater. They are being televised and will be available on video from FilmAmerica.

ANTONY AND CLEOPATRA
1966 opera by Barber

Samuel Barber's operatic adaptation of Shakespeare's play was commissioned to open the new Metropolitan Opera House at Lincoln Center on September 16, 1966. The premiere was dominated by the extravagant staging of Franco Zeffirelli and badly received by critics. The libretto is mostly Shakespeare's words arranged by Zeffirelli, who condensed the play to seventeen scenes. The composer later revised the libretto and the opera and his version was a success when it was presented at the Lyric Opera of Chicago in 1991. See also SAMUEL BARBER.

1966 The New Met: Countdown to Curtain

A documentary about the final preparations for the opening of *Antony and Cleopatra* at the new Metropolitan Opera House at Lincoln Center in 1966. Soprano Leontyne Price is shown rehearsing the role of Cleopatra with conductor Thomas Schippers while director Franco Zeffirelli has problems with a giant turntable that won't work and general manager Rudolf Bing is threatened with a walkout by the orchestra. Robert Drew produced and directed the documentary telecast on the Bell Telephone Hour on NBC on Nov. 20, 1966. Black and white. 60 minutes. Kultur video.

1983 Spoleto Festival USA

Gian Carlo Menotti's production of *Antony and Cleopatra* at the 1983 Spoleto Festival in Charleston is featured in the video *Festival! Spoleto, USA*. Scenes from various parts of the opera are seen. The video was directed by Kirk Browning and telecast June 27. Color. 60 minutes.

1991 Chicago Lyric Opera

Catherine Malfitano stars as Cleopatra with Richard Cowan as Antony and Jacques Trussel as Octavius in this Chicago Lyric Opera production by Elijah Mojinsky. Erick Halfvarson is Enobarbus, Wendy White is Charmian, Nancy Maultsby is Iras, Michael Wadsworth is Agrippa, Paul Kreider is Dolabella, Philip Zawisza is Eros and William Walker is Alexas. Michael Yeargan designed the sets lit by Duane Schuler. Richard Buckley conducted the Chicago Lyric Opera Orchestra. Kirk Browning directed the video in October 1991 and it was later telecast in the Great Performances series. Color. In English. 120 minutes.

Related film

1972 Charlton Heston film

For comparison purposes the most interesting film of the original Shakespeare play is the 1972 version directed by Charlton Heston. It stars Heston as Antony and Hildegard Neil as Cleopatra. Color. In English. 160 minutes.

APOLLO AND HYACINTHUS

1767 opera by Mozart

Mozart's first stage work is in Latin, an intermezzo composed when he was only eleven years old. Rufinus Widl wrote the libretto loosely based on Ovid. Most of the parts are meant for boy sopranos and boy altos. Apollo wants to marry Melia but runs into a problem when his rival Zephyrus accuses him of killing Hyacinthus. See also WOLFGANG A. MOZART.

1983 José Montes-Bacquer video

Treble Cedric Rossdeutscher and tenor Michel Lecocq are among the featured singers in this German television production by José Montes-Bacquer. Helmut Muller-Bruhl conducts the orchestra. Color. In Latin with German and Japanese subtitles. 40 minutes. Japanese laserdisc.

ARABELLA

1933 opera by Richard Strauss

Richard Strauss' delightful opera is set in Vienna in 1860 at Carnival time. It concerns Arabella and her sister Zdenka and their suitors and how their love affairs get sorted out. The role of Arabella is a demanding one, calling for a silvery soprano voice that can soar over the high notes. It also helps if she is quite beautiful. This was the last of the operas written by Hugo von Hofmannsthal for Strauss. See also RICHARD STRAUSS.

1963 Bavarian State Opera

Lisa Della Casa stars as a highly believable Arabella in this historic Bavarian State Opera production in Munich. Dietrich Fischer-Dieskau is outstanding as her suitor Mandryka and Anneliese Rothenberg is superb as her sister Zdenka. Joseph Keilberth conducts the Bavarian State Opera Orchestra and Chorus. Black and white. In German. 175 minutes. Lyric video

1977 Vienna State Opera

Gundula Janowitz performs brilliantly in the title role in this studio film based on a Vienna State Opera production by Otto Schenk. Mandryka is nicely sung by Bernd Weikl, Zdenka is Sona Ghazarian and Matteo is René Kollo. Edita Gruberova sings the coloratura Fiakermilli while Martha Modl is the Fortuneteller. Jan Schulbach designed the sets, Bernd Müller designed the costumes and Jörg Neumann was the cinematographer. Georg Solti conducts the Vienna Philharmonic Orchestra. Unitel. Color. In German with English subtitles. 149 minutes. London video.

1984 Glyndebourne Festival

Ashley Putnam sings and acts beautifully as Arabella in this Glyndebourne Festival production by John Cox. John Brocheler is her suitor Mandryka, Gianna Rolandi is impulsive Zdenka and Keith Lewis plays Matteo. The coloratura soprano role of the Fiakermilli is sung by Gwendolyn Bradley. Bernard Haitink conducts the London Philharmonic Orchestra and Glyndebourne Chorus. Julia Trevelyan Oman designed the sets and costumes. John Vernon directed the video. Color. In German with English subtitles. 154 minutes. HBO Video.

1994 Metropolitan Opera

Kiri Te Kanawa is superb as Arabella in this Metropolitan Opera production by Otto Schenk. Wolfgang Brendel is Mandryka, Marie McLaughliln is Zdenka, David Kuebler is Matteo, Natalie Dessay is the Fiakermilli and Arabella's parents are sung by Helga Dernesch and Donald McIntyre. Gunther Schneider-Siemssen designed the sets, Milena Canonera designed the costumes and Christian Thielemann conducted the Metropolitan Orchestra and Chorus. The video was directed by Brian Large from a performance in November 1994 and telecast on PBS in 1995. Color. In German with English subtitles. 160 minutes.

ARAGALL, GIACOMO

Spanish tenor (1939-)

Giacomo Aragall is one of the top tenors in the world and a major force in Spanish singing. He was born in Barcelona, studied in Milan and made his debut at La Fenice in Venice in 1963. He sang at La Scala for three years and arrived in Covent Garden in 1966 as the Duke in *Rigoletto*. He was again the Duke in the Verdi opera at the Metropolitan in

1968 and in San Francisco in 1972. He is featured on both records and videos. See GALA LIRICA, TOSCA (1984), LA TRAVIATA (1984 film), VERONA (1988).

ARAIZA, FRANCISCO
Mexican tenor (1950-)

Francisco Araiza, one of the top Mozart tenors in the world, is also popular in Rossini and Verdi operas. He studied with Mexican soprano Irma Gonzalez, made his debut in Mexico City in 1970 and went to Europe in 1975. He sang in 1983 at Covent Garden (*Don Pasquale*) and in 1984 in San Francisco (*La Cenerentola)* and at the Metropolitan (*The Abduction from the Seraglio*). He is featured on many videos including several Mozart operas. See THE ABDUCTION FROM THE SERAGLIO (1980), LA CENERENTOLA (1981/1989), COSÌ FAN TUTTE (1983), DON GIOVANNI (1989), FALSTAFF (1982), THE MAGIC FLUTE (1983/1991), MANON (1983), WOLFGANG A. MOZART (1991), IL RITORNO D'ULISSE IN PATRIA (1980), DER ROSENKAVALIER (1979).

ARGENTINA, IMPERIO
Spanish soprano (1906-1996)

Imperio Argentina (born Magdalena Nilo del Rio in Buenos Aires) was the leading Spanish female film star of the 1930s, famous for singing, dancing and acting in musicals directed by husband Florian Rey and Benito Perojo. Her most popular Spanish movie was *Morena Clara* (1936) but her most notable films are the Italian *Tosca* (1940), on which Renoir and Visconti worked, and the Spanish film of Granados' opera *Goyescas* (1942). She also made films in Germany and Argentina. She made a comeback in 1986 at the age of 80 when director José Luis Borau featured her singing once again `in the Spanish film *Tata Mia*. See CARMEN (1938 film), GOYESCAS (1942), TOSCA (1941 film).

ARGENTO, DARIO
Italian film director (1943 -)

Italian director Dario Argento specializes in stylish horror films and often features opera music on his soundtracks. His horrific 1987 film *Opera* centers around a production of Verdi's bad-luck opera *Macbeth* in Parma. The supernatural 1979 *Inferno* features the appropriate chorus from *Nabucco* on its soundtrack. His 1973 *The Five Days*, about the Milan Revolution of 1848, features the La Scala Orchestra playing excerpts from *The Thieving Magpie*. See LA GAZZA LADRA (1973 film), MACBETH (1987 film), NABUCCO (1979 film).

ARGENTO, DOMINICK
American composer (1927-)

Dominick Argento, one of the most successful modern American opera composers, created the screen opera *The Dream of Valentino* which premiered at the Washington Opera in 1994. It is based on the life of silent film star Rudolph Valentino and uses movie techniques to enhance its Hollywood background. His operatic adaptation of *The Aspern Papers* (1988) was telecast from the Dallas Opera. Argento has written thirteen operas in all including *Postcard from Morocco* (1972), *The Voyage of Edgar Allen Poe* (1976) and *Miss Havisham's Fire* (1979). See THE ASPERN PAPERS, THE DREAM OF VALENTINO.

ARIA
1987 English opera film

English producer Don Boyd asked ten top directors to make a film around an opera aria of their choice. The result was the controversial *Aria* which closed the Cannes Film Festival in 1987 and opened AFI Fest in Los Angeles in 1988. Some episodes are better than others but all are innovative interpretations of opera music. Some of the filmmakers have also directed opera on stage. Critics have tended to dismiss this film because it falls in that uncertain area between cinema and opera but the episodes stand up well to repeated viewing. They are described under their operas: ARMIDE (Jean-Luc Godard), UN BALLO IN MASCHERA (Nicolas Roeg), LES BOREADES (Robert Altman), LA FORZA DEL DESTINO (Charles Sturridge), LOUISE (Derek Jarman), PAGLIACCI (Bill Bryden), RIGOLETTO (Julien Temple), TRISTAN UND ISOLDE (Franc Roddam), DIE TOTE STADT (Bruce Beresford), TURANDOT (Ken Russell). Color. 90 minutes. Lightyear Entertainment video and laser.

ARIADNE AUF NAXOS
1912 opera by Strauss

Richard Strauss and librettist Hugo von Hofmannsthal had problems working out the final form of this sophisticated opera-within-an-opera. It's a witty story about an *opera seria* company putting on a production for an 18th century patron and learning that a light comedy troupe will perform simultaneusly. The leading roles are all sopranos and there is great rivalry between the very serious Prima Donna, the effervescent comedy troupe leader Zerbinetta and the deeply concerned Composer. See also RICHARD STRAUSS.

1955 NBC Opera Theatre
This ambitious NBC Opera Theatre production attempts to re-create the original production by featuring short versions of the opera and the play first staged with it, Moliere's *The Would-Be Gentleman*. The performers are Wilma Spence, Virginia MacWattes, Robert Marshall and Joan Carroll. The comic arias are sung in English and the *seria* music is in German. Samuel Chotzinoff produced, John Schwartz directed and Reuben Ter-Arutunian designed the sets and costumes. Peter Herman Adler conducted the orchestra. Kirk Browning directed the telecast. Black and white. In English. 90 minutes. Video at MTR.

1978 Vienna State Opera
Gundula Janowitz stars as Ariadne with Edita Gruberova as Zerbinetta in this Vienna State Opera production by Filippo Sanjust. Trudeliese Schmidt is the Composer and René Kollo is Bacchus. The cast also includes Walter Berry, Heinz Zednik, Manfred Jungwirth, Hilda de Groote and Gaxelle Gall. The Prologue is staged in a realistic 18th century setting and the opera-within-the-opera in stylized sets. Karl Böhm conducted the Vienna Philharmonic Orchestra. John Vernon directed the film for television. Unitel/ Beta Film. Color. In German. 128 minutes. On video.

1988 Metropolitan Opera
A delightful Metropolitan Opera production by Bodo Igesz featuring a terrific trio of American star sopranos. Jessye Norman is the Prima Donna/ Ariadne, Kathleen Battle is Zerbinetta and Tatiana Troyanos is the Composer. James King sings the role of the Tenor/ Bacchus, Franz Ferdinand Netwig is the Music Master, Dawn Upshaw is Echo, Barbara Bonney is Naiade, Gweneth Bean is Dryade and Stephen Dickson is Harlequin. Oliver Messel designed the sets and Jane Greenwood the costumes. James Levine conducts the Metropolitan Opera Orchestras. Brian Large directed the video. A short documentary about the production is included. Color. In German with English subtitles. 148 minutes. DG video and laser.

ARIANE
1958 opera by Martinů

Czech composer Bohuslav Martinu wrote his last opera to a libretto based on Georges Neveux's play *Le Voyage of Thésée*. It was created for a bravura soprano and grew out of the composer's admiration for Maria Callas. The story concern the Greek myth about Ariadne and her relationship with Theseus during the time he was fighting the Minotaur. See also BOHUSLAV MARTINU.

1968 Celina Lindsay film
American soprano Celina Lindsay stars as Ariane in this Czechoslovakian television film directed by Tomás Simerada. The others in the cast are Norman Phillips, Vladmir Dolezal, Lubomir Mati, Richard Novak, Miroslav Kopp and Ludek Vele. Václav Neumann conducts the Czech Philharmonic Orchestra. Color. In Czech. 45 minutes.

ARIODANTE
1735 opera by Handel

George Frideric Handel's opera *Ariodante* tells the story of the tribulations of Princess Ginevra (Guinevere), daughter of the King of Scotland. She is in love with the vassal prince Ariodante, a mezzo-soprano role originally sung by a castrato. The opera, which has never really entered the Handel repertory, is set in Edinburgh though based on a work by Antonio Salvi derived from Ariosto's *Orlando Furioso*. See also GEORGE F. HANDEL.

1990 English & Welsh National Opera
American director David Alden produced this rare and vocally difficult opera as a co-production of the English National Opera and the Welsh National Opera. Mezzo Ann Murray stars as Ariodante with soprano Joan Rodgers as Princess Ginevra. The opera was telecast by the BBC from the ENO. RM Arts. Color. In Italian. 110 minutes. On video.

ARKHIPOVA, IRINA
Russian mezzo-soprano (1924-)

Irina Arkhipova began singing professionally in 1954 and made her debut at the Bolshoi in 1956 as Carmen. She quickly became one of the top stars of Bolshoi, originating roles in new operas and travelling with the company abroad. She was particularly admired for her Azucena in *Il Trovatore* at Orange in 1972, a performance that is on video. In 1988 she sang the role of Ulrica at Covent Garden. See BOLSHOI OPERA (1989), KHOVANSHCHINA (1979), MARIO DEL MONACO (1985), IL TROVATORE (1972).

1959 Irina Arkhipova Recital
Arkhipova was filmed in Moscow for television singing arias from some of her favorite operas. Included are *Carmen, Aida, Boris Godunov* and other Russian operas. Black and white. In Russian. 70 minutes.

ARMENIAN OPERA

Armenian opera and operetta began while the Armenian people were living in Turkey in the 19th century but is now centered in the Armenian capital of Erevan(formerl Yerevan). The first operetta composer was Chouhajian, best known for *The Chick-pea Seller,* and the first opera composer was Tigran Tchukhatjian whose 1868 *Arshak II* is considered the first Armenian grand opera. Armen Tigran Tigranyan's 1912 *Anush,* however, holds pride of place as the Armenian national opera. There have been a number of Armenian opera singers of note with Gohar Gasparian the most acclaimed. There are apparently no films of the Armenian operas but there are excerpts from them in a Gasparian film. She also stars in a movie based on the operetta *The Chick-pea Seller.* See LUCINE AMARA, GOHAR GASPARIAN.

ARMIDE
1686 opera by Lully

Jean-Baptiste Lully's opera, libretto by Philippe Quinault based on Tasso's *Jerusalem Delivered,* is the story of the enchantress Armide. She bewitches the Crusader knight Renaud who resisted her charms. He is eventually rescued by two friends. See also JEAN-BAPTISTE LULLY.

1987 Jean-Luc Godard film
French director Jean-Luc Godard uses arias from the opera to create an updated version of its story of an heroic knight held in a spell by a sorceress. His episode of the British opera film *Aria* is set in the Weider body building gym in Paris. Two young women wander around the gym in frustration trying to awaken response from the musclemen who seem to be frozen in enchantment. The arias on

the soundtrack are sung by Rachel Yakar, Zeger Vandersteene and Daniele Boorst. Philippe Herreweghe conducts the Ensemble Vocale et Instrumental de la Chappelle Royale. Color. In French. About 10 minutes. See also ARIA.

ARRIETA, EMILIO
Spanish composer (1823-1894)

Pascual Emilio Arrieta y Corera wrote many operas but is mostly remembered as a composer of zarzuelas. The most popular is the 1855 Italian-influenced *Marina* which is virtually a full-scale opera and has remained in the repertory of most Spanish-speaking countries. There have been recent productions in Spain, Mexico and Venezuela with top Spanish singers. See MARINA.

ASHLEY, ROBERT
American composer (1930-)

Robert Ashley's television operas have found many admirers in the avant-garde and mixed-media worlds. The Michigan-born composer has composed a dozen television operas since 1964 that mix his music with spoken and written texts and fascinating visual imagery. The longest is the 14-hour *Music with Roots in the Aether* which also involves six other composers. The best known is the 1980 *Perfect Lives* which has been telecast in seven 25-minute episodes. Both of these are on video. Ashley feels that television/video should be creating re-viewable works of art, which like musical compositions, need to be seen more than once. See MUSIC WITH ROOTS IN THE AETHER, PERFECT LIVES.

ATALANTA (ACTS OF GOD)
Ashley's 1982 opera *Atalanta (Acts of God)* premiered in 1985 in three 90-minute episodes at the Museum of Contemporary Art in Chicago. A 1984 highlights version titled *Atalanta Strategy* is available on video. It is based on "Willard," the second episode of the opera, and includes a flying saucer scene, a mule in a tree and an interview with Ashley. The performers include "Blue" Gene Tyranny, Ronald Vance and David van Tieghem. Lawrence Brickman directed the video. Color. In English. 28 minutes. Lovely Music video.

1983 Robert Ashley (4 American Composers)
Peter Greenaway's excellent film about Robert Ashley focuses on the origin, composition and

design of his opera *Perfect Lives* and segments of its episodes are shown. The film is based around performances of the opera in a London theater. It features Ashley as the storyteller, "Blue" Gene Tyranny on keyboards and Jill Kroesen and David Van Tieghem as the singers. Ashley uses a multitude of video monitors and multiple images in the opera. The film was made for Channel Four in England. Color. 60 minutes. Mystic Fire video.

ASPERN PAPERS, THE
1988 opera by Argento

Dominick Argento's adaptation of Henry James' novel shifts the location from Venice to Lake Como where Aspern becomes a Bellini-like composer rather than a poet. The action takes place in both 1835 and 1895. Aspern's lost opera *Medea* is the focus of the story. It was composed for his diva mistress Juliana but he drowned before finishing it. A modern scholar, called the Lodger, tries to obtain the suppressed manuscript from the aged Juliana through her niece Tina. The opera was premiered by Dallas Opera on November 19, 1988. See also DOMINICK ARGENTO.

1988 Dallas Opera
Elisabeth Soderstrom portrays Juliana both young and old in this Dallas Opera production by Mark Lamos. Frederica von Stade sings the role of her niece Tina, Richard Stillwell is the Lodger, Neil Rosenshein is Aspern, Katherine Ciesinski is Sonia and Eric Halfvarson is Barelli. John Conklin designed the sets and costumes. Dallas Opera artistic director Nicola Rescigno conducts the Dallas Symphony Orchestra. The opera was taped in November 1988 with its premiere cast and then telecast on PBS on June 9, 1989. Kirk Browning directed the video. Color. In English. 120 minutes. Video at MTR.

ASQUITH, ANTHONY
English film director (1901-1968)

Anthony Aquith's 36-year career in cinema includes two films with notable opera content. The 1952 *The Importance of Being Earnest* features ironic use of an aria from *Rigoletto*. The 1955 *On Such A Night* is a charming film about a young American attending a performance of *The Marriage of Figaro* at the Glyndebourne Festival. Sesto Bruscantini and Sena Jurinac are singing. Asquith also directed the opera *Carmen* on stage at Covent Garden and made Covent Garden ballet films. See THE MARRIAGE OF FIGARO (1955 film), RIGOLETTO (1952 film).

ATLANTOV, VLADIMIR
Russian tenor (1939-)

Vladimir Atlantov has become widely known singing in Western opera houses from La Scala to Covent Garden. He is the son of an opera singer, made his debut at the Kirov Opera in 1963, became a member of the Bolshoi Opera in 1967 and has toured widely with the company. He made his Covent Garden debut in 1987 in *Otello* and can be seen in this role in a Verona Arena video. He can also be seen in three Russian operas on video. See KHOVANSHCHINA (1989), OTELLO (1982), THE QUEEN OF SPADES (1983), THE STONE GUEST (1967), PYOTR TCHAIKOVSKY (1970).

ATTILA
1846 opera by Verdi

Italians who first experienced Giuseppe Verdi's opera in 1846 felt it was a portrait of their time as Italy was again overrun by barbarians. They loved its patriotism and it still stirs the blood today with its magnificent early Verdian rhythms. Temistocle Solera's libretto is the story of Attila the Hun who has conquered most of Italy and stopped to celebrate after sacking the town of Acquileia. The woman warrior Odabella swears revenge on him for killing her father and stabs him on the day she has promised to marry him. See also GIUSEPPE VERDI.

1985 Verona Arena
Russian bass Yevgeny Nesterenko stars as Attila the Hun in this magnificent Verona Arena production by filmmaker Giuliano Montaldo. He has a voice built to conquer the giant arena as well as the Romans and really dominates the production. Supporting him are Maria Chiara as the strong-minded Odabella, Silvano Carroli as Ezio and Veriano Luchetti as Foresto. The grandiose sets are by Luciano Ricceri and the costumes by Nana Cecchi. Nello Santi conducts the Orchestra and Chorus of the Arena di Verona. Brian Large directed the video. Color. In Italian with English subtitles. 120 minutes. Home Vision video.

1991 Teatro alla Scala
A major La Scala production with American basso Samuel Ramey in the role of Attila. He is well

supported by soprano Cheryl Studer as Odabella, Giorgio Zancanaro as Ezio, Kaludi Kaludov as Foresto, Ernesto Gavazzi as Uldino and Mario Luperi as Leoni. The production was directed by Jerome Savary with Michel Lebois in charge of design. Riccardo Muti conducted the orchestra and chorus of the Teatro Alla Scala. Christopher Swann directed the video. Color. In Italian with English subtitles. 115 minutes. Home Vision video/Japanese laser.

ATYS
1676 opera by Lully

Atys seems to be the only complete opera on video by Jean-Baptiste Lully, the founder of French opera. It is set in classical Greece and tells the tragic story of the high priest Atys and his confused relationships with the goddess Cybèle and the mortal Sangaride. In the end he kills Sangaride and is transformed into a tree by Cybèle. See also JEAN-BAPTISTE LULLY.

1987 Montpellier Opera
American conductor William Christie won warm praise for his performance and recording of *Atys* in 1987. His record was the first complete Lully opera to be issued on CD and some of the same cast can be seen in an off-air video of a telecast from Montpellier. Tenor Howard Crook sings the role of Atys, Agnès Mellon is Sangaride, Guillemette Laurens is Cybèle, Francoise Semmelez is Doris and Noemi Rime is Mélisse. Color. In French. 185 minutes. Opera Dubs video.

AUBER, DANIEL
French composer (1782-1871)

Daniel Auber wrote light operas that were immensely popular in their time and are usually thought of as the forerunners of operetta. He is as important historically as Rossini though none of his operas are currently available in modern professional videos. His most popular works were *Fra Diavolo*, a kind of French Robin Hood story, and *La Muette di Portici*, a revolutionary opera that once had a very wide appeal. See FRA DIAVOLO, LA MUETTE DE PORTICI.

AUDEN, W. H.
British poet/librettist (1907-1973)

W. H. Auden was the most prominent 20th century poet involved in writing opera and called himself an "opera addict." He began by collaborating with Benjamin Britten on *Paul Bunyan* in 1941 and then wrote *The Rake's Progress* for Stravinsky in 1948 in tandem with Chester Kallman. He worked on a number of other operas and created English language versions of Mozart's *The Magic Flute* and *Don Giovanni*. See THE MAGIC FLUTE (1956), THE RAKE'S PROGRESS.

AUDRAN, EDMOND
French composer (1840-1901)

Audran, a hugely popular composer in his time and an international rival of Lecocq, is not widely known today outside France. He had a fine gift for melody and many of his airs are still popular while his comic operas continue to be produced on the French stage. The best known and most enduring of his works is his 1880 opera-comique *La Mascotte* which was made into a French film in 1935. His *Le Grand Mogol* and *La Poupée* are on French CDs. See LA MASCOTTE.

AUFSTIEG UND FALL DER STADT MAHAGONNY
See RISE AND FALL OF THE CITY OF MAHAGONNY

B

BAA BAA BLACK SHEEP
1993 opera by Berkeley

British composer Michael Berkeley and librettist David Alouf based their opera on Rudyard Kipling's story *Baa Baa Black Sheep* which they superimposed on the *Jungle Book* tales. The boy Punch is in a bleak British seaside boarding house with his sister Judy and begins to create imaginary jungle characters based on the people he knows. He identifies himself with Mogli, the hero of the stories. The opera was premiered at the Cheltenham Festival by Opera North.

1993 Opera North
BBC Television taped and telecast the Opera North production by Jonathan Moore in Leeds with its original cast. Malcolm Lorimer is Punch, William Dazely is Mogli the man, Ann Taylor-Morley is Judy/Grey Wolf, Fiona Kimm is evil Auntirosi, Philip Sheffield is Harry and Eileen Hulse is Wolf-Messua. David Blight designed the sets and Paul Daniel conducted the English Northern Philharmonic Orchestra. Barrie Gavin directed for video. Color. 100 minutes. On video.

BABES IN TOYLAND
1903 operetta by Herbert

Victor Herbert's operetta is as much fun for adults as for children with an inventive libretto by Glen MacDonough, memorable tunes by the composer and a wonderful fairy tale setting. It tells the story of two children who escape from their wicked uncle to Mother Goose Land and become involved with nursery rhyme characters. There have been six screen adaptations of the operetta. See also VICTOR HERBERT.

1934 Laurel and Hardy film
Stan Laurel and Oliver Hardy star as Stannie Dum and Ollie Dee in this MGM film of the operetta produced by Hal Roach and directed by Charles Rogers and Gus Meins. Most of the Herbert score is retained and the film itself is a minor classic. Metropolitan Opera tenor Felix Knight is Tom-Tom, Charlotte Henry is Little Bo Peep, Johnny Downs is Little Boy Blue, Jean Darling is Curly Locks, Marie Wilson is Mary Quite Contrary, William Burress is the Toy Maker, Ferdinand Munier is Santa Claus and Virginia Karns is Mother Goose. The adaptation is by Nick Grinde and Frank Butler, the music director is Harry Jackson and the cinematography is by Art Lloyd and Francis Corby. Also known as *March of the Wooden Soldiers*. Black and white. In English. 78 minutes. Goodtimes video.

1950 NBC Musical Comedy Time
Dennis King is Dr. Electronic, Robert Weede is Santa Claus and Edith Fellowes is Bo Peep in this heavy-handed NBC TV version by Alexander Kirkland. Also in the cast are Dorothy Jarnac, Gil Lamb and Robert Dixon. Bill Corrigan directed and Harry Sosnick conducted the orchestra. It was telecast live on Dec. 25, 1950. Black and white. In English. 60 minutes.

1954 NBC Color Special
Barbara Cook is Jane Piper, Wally Cox is the Toymaker, Dennis King is Tom-Tom and Dave Garroway is Santa Claus in this lavish NBC TV color production by Max Liebman. Jack E. Leonard is Silas Barnaby, Ellen Barrie is Joan, Mary Mace is the Widow Piper, Jack Powell is the Clown and Jo Sullivan is Bo Peep. The operetta, adapted by Neil Simon, Will Glickman, William Freidberg and Fred Saidy, was telecast on Dec. 18, 1954. Color. In English. 90 minutes.

1960 Shirley Temple's Storybook
Shirley Temple stars opposite Jonathan Winters in a version of the Herbert operetta featured as an episode of the TV series *Shirley Temple's Storybook*. It was telecast on Dec. 25, 1960. Color. In English. 60 minutes.

1961 Walt Disney film
Ray Bolger is the villain Barnaby and Ed Wynn is the Toymaker in this elaborate Disney film by Jack Donohue. Annette Funicello is Mary Contrary, Tommy Sands is Tom Piper, Tommy Kirk is Grumio, Kevin Corcoran is Boy Blue, Mary McCarty is Mother Goose, Ann Jillian is Bo Peep, Henry Calvin is Gonzorgo and Gene Sheldon is Roderigo. Ward Kimball, Joe Rinaldi and Lowell S. Hawley wrote the adaptation. Critics disliked the

film but it got Oscar nominations. Color. In English. 126 minutes. Disney video.

1986 Clive Donner film
Clive Donner's television film of the operetta stars Drew Barrymore, Richard Mulligan, Eileen Brennan, Keanu Reeves, Jill Schoelen and Pat Morita. Critics didn't much like this one as little of Herbert's scores survives. "Toyland" and "March of the Wooden Soldiers" are heard but take second place to music by Leslie Bricusse. Paul Zindel wrote the adaptation. Color. 150 minutes. On video.

BACCALONI, SALVATORE
Italian bass (1900-1969)

Good-humored Salvatore Baccaloni, in addition to being a star at La Scala and the Metropolitan, acted in a number of American films, usually as the comic father. He began his American opera career in 1930 in Chicago and was a regular at the Met until 1962. He kept his opera and movie careers separate and made no opera films. His film career began in 1956 opposite Judy Holliday and Richard Conte in Richard Quine's *Full of Life*, the story of a New York Italian couple expecting a baby. In 1958 he was in Frank Tashlin's *Rock-a-Bye Baby* with Jerry Lewis and Marilyn Maxwell. Also in 1958 was Michael Kidd's *Merry Andrew* with Danny Kaye and Pier Angeli. In 1960 he appeared in Joshua Logan's *Fanny*, a Marcel Pagnol adaptation with Charles Boyer and Leslie Caron. In 1962 he was in Mel Shavelson's *The Pigeon That Took Rome* playing the father of Elsa Martinelli.

BACCHAE, THE
1991 Swedish opera by Börtz

Backanterna (The Bacchae), Swedish composer Daniel Börtz's opera written to a libretto by filmmaker Ingmar Bergman, is based on the Euripides play. It's meant to show the foolishness of fundamentalism as seen across the tragedy of the last great matriarchy. Bergman changed Euripides' unified chorus of Bacchantes into individual characters so that their murdering fury in the second act could appear more realistic. Börtz's music is full of insistent rhythms and percussive climaxes. The opera premiered at the Royal Opera Stockholm on November 2, 1991, under Bergman's direction. See also INGMAR BERGMAN.

1992 Ingmar Bergman video
Ingmar Bergman directed a video of his stage production at the Royal Opera, Stockholm for a television broadcast. Sylvia Lindenstrand stars as Dionysus with Peter Mattei as Pentheus, Laila Andersson-Palme as Tiresias, Sten Wahlund as Kadmos, Anita Soldh, Mariane Orland and Berit Lindholm. Lennart Mörk designed the sets and costumes and Kjell Ingerbretsen conducted the Royal Opera House Orchestra. Amaya Distribution. Color. In Swedish. 129 minutes. Video at MTR.

BACH, P.D.G.
Mythical German composer (1807-1742)

Musical jester, scholar and broadcaster Peter Schickle (1935-) invented this member of the Bach family and attributes parodistic pieces of baroque and classical music to him. P.D. Q. Bach supposedly composed operas and seven have been staged beginning with *The Stoned Guest* in Carnegie Hall in 1967. The most popular opera of this imaginary genius and the only one on video is a pastiche parody titled *The Abduction of Figaro* staged in Minneapolis in 1984. Other P. D. Q. Bach operas that have been staged include *Hansel & Gretel & Ted & Alice*, *The Magic Bassoon*, *Oedipus Tex* and *Prelude to Einstein on the Fritz*.

1984 The Abduction Of Figaro
This inventive pastiche is subtitled "A Simply Grand Opera" with such characters as Donna Donna, Donald Giovanni, Al Donfonso and Susanna Susannadonna. *Abduction* begins on the deathbed of Figaro and goes downhill from there in a series of operatic clichés. The cast includes LeRoy Lehr, Dana Krueger, Bruce Edwin Ford, Marilyn Brustadt, Lisbeth Lloyd, Michael Burt, Jack Walsh, Will Roy and John Ferrante. The video was taped at the premiere of the opera in April 1984 when it was performed by the Minnesota Opera with Schickle conducting. John Lee Beatty designed the sets, Michael Montel was stage director and Kaye S. Lavine directed the video. Color. In English. 144 minutes. VAI Video.

BACH, JOHANN SEBASTIAN
German composer (1685-1750)

Johann Sebastian Bach did not compose operas, mores the pity though his cantatas are nearly the equivalent, but some of his works have been produced on stage as operas or on film with opera singers.

1950 St. Matthew Passion
Major German opera singers are featured in this 1950 Austrian film of Bach's *St. Matthew Passion* commissioned for the 200th anniversary of the composer's death. Soprano Elisabeth Schwarzkopf heads the group that includes mezzo-soprano Elisabeth Höngen, tenor Walter Ludwig, baritone Karl Schmitt-Walter, Hans Braun and Raoul Aslan. Herbert von Karajan conducts the Vienna Philharmonic and Viennese choirs. Ernst Marischka wrote and directed the film which features paintings of the life and suffering of Christ as depicted by Michelangelo, Raphael, Leonardo da Vinci, Rubens and other major artists. Vaclav Vich was the cinematographer. The German title of the film is *Matthau-Passion.* Black and white. In German. 90 minutes.

1984 St. John's Passion
St. John's Passion was produced on stage in 1984 as an opera by director/designer Pier Luigi Pizzi and taped live. Zeger Vandersteen plays the Evangelist, Florian Prey is Jesus, Margarita Zimmermann is Mary, Brigitte Poschner is Magdalen, Thomas Thomaschke is Peter and Harry Nicoll is John. Alan Hacker conducts the Teatro La Fenice Orchestra, the Salzburg Kammerorchestrer, the Handel Collegium Kö In and the Toelzer Knabenchor of Munich. Color. In German with Japanese subtitles. 130 minutes. On Japanese laserdisc.

BACQUIER, GABRIEL
French baritone (1924-)

Gabriel Bacquier, who was born in Béziers, began his career in 1950 and has become one of the most popular opera singers on the circuit today. He has sung in most of the major opera houses and his admirers feel that his voice and his acting have grown in power and quality with the years. Falstaff is considered one of his great roles. See GIANNI SCHICCHI (1981), DON PASQUALE (1979), FALSTAFF (1979), THE LOVE OF THREE ORANGES (1989), THE TALES OF HOFFMANN (1993).

BADINGS, HENK
Dutch composer (1907-1987)

Henk Badings began to experiment with electronic music in 1952 and attracted acclaim with his 1954 electronic radio opera *Orestes.* His 1957 electronic screen opera *Salto Mortale* was the first to have its whole score recorded electronically. It was commissioned by Dutch television, Nederlandse Televisie Stichting, and is his only TV opera.

1957 Salto Mortale
Badings wrote music and words for *Salto Mortale* which premiered on Dutch television on June 19, 1957. The first opera composed for a fully electronic accompaniment, it was scored for five voices and electronic tape. The story, concerns a biochemistry professor who brings a poet back to life after his suicide. When the poet tries to seduce his laboratory assistant, the professor decides to kill him.

BAILEY, DEREK
English television director

Derek Bailey is one of the leading television opera directors today and his excellent work can been seen on a wide array of opera videos shot around the world from Glyndebourne, the ENO and Covent Garden to La Scala, La Fenice and the Bolshoi. He has also made superb documentaries on *Aida* and Joan Sutherland. See AIDA (1986/ 1987 film), BORIS GODUNOV (1987), GLORIANA (1984), JENUFA (1988), KATYA KABANOVA (1988), A LIFE FOR THE TSAR (1992), MADAMA BUTTERFLY (1986), MITRIDATE, RE DI PONTO (1991), ORPHÉE AUX ENFERS (1983), RUSALKA (1986), SALOME (1991), JOAN SUTHERLAND (1991), LA TRAVIATA (1987/ 1992).

BAJADERE, DIE
1921 operetta by Kálmán

Emmerich Kálmán's popular 1921 operetta *Die Bajadere*, libretto by Julius Brammer and Alfred Grünwald, features an operetta within an operetta. The heroine is the prima donna of an operetta called *La Bayadère* who is being pursued by an Eastern prince. It was a major hit in Vienna and staged in New York in 1922 as *The Yankee Princess* with Vivienne Segal as the star. See also EMMERICH KÁLMÁN.

1992 Sandro Massimini video
Highlights and a history of the operetta known in Italy as *Bajadera* were featured by operetta master Sandro Massimini and his associates on his Italian TV series *Operette, Che Passione!* The selections available on video include "Un piccol bar," "Oh Bajadera," "Quando in cielo ridino le stelle" and

"Ci si dié la man." Color. In Italian. About 17 minutes. Ricordi (Italy) video.

BAKER, JANET
English mezzo-soprano (1933-)

Dame Janet Baker began her career in 1956 and is especially admired for her performances of operas by Handel and Gluck. She created the role of Kate in the 1971 TV version of Benjamin Britten's *Owen Wingrave* and later sang the role at Covent Garden. She retired from opera in 1982 after singing the roles of Mary Stuart at the ENO and Orpheus at Glyndebourne. Some of her best opera roles are preserved on video and there is an excellent film biography. See GIULIO CESARE (1984), MARY STUART (1982), ORFEO ED EURIDICE (1982), IL RITORNO D'ULISSE IN PATRIA (1973).

1982 Full Circle: Her Last Year in Opera
Baker describes her final opera season and her career in this documentary film. Her stage career had begun 26 years earlier at Glyndebourne and she makes her farewell from that stage. She is seen preparing for Gluck's *Alceste* at Covent Garden, rehearsing *Mary Stuart* for television and performing at Carnegie Hall and Haddo Hall in Scotland. The film ends with Baker's performance in *Orfeo* at Glyndebourne. John Copley, Charles Mackerras, Janine Reiss, Martin Isepp, Peter Hall and Raymond Leppard also appear in Bob Bentley's film. NVC. Color. 75 minutes. Kultur video.

1987 Christmas at Ripon Cathedral
Baker is seen in fine voice in this video of a Christmas concert with Robert Hardy at Rippon Cathedral in Yorkshire. It includes a Baker's dozen of carols from "Mary Had a Baby" to "Come All Ye Faithful." Also performing are the Huddersfield Choral Society, the Black Dyke Mills Band and organists Simon Lindley and Robert Marsh. Terry Henebery directed for Yorkshire Television. Color. 55 minutes. Home Vision video.

BALADA, LEONARDO
Spanish-born U.S. composer (1933-)

Leonardo Balada, a Catalan from Barcelona, came to the U.S. in 1956 as a student and remained as a teacher and composer. His first opera, the 1982 *Hangman, Hangman!*, is based on a cowboy ballad and is a satire about the American West with a thief as hero. His major opera, the 1982 *Cristóbal Colón,*

tells the story of Columbus's voyage. It premiered in his native Barcelona with José Carreras and Montserrat Caballé in the main roles. See CRISTÓBAL COLÓN.

BALFE, MICHAEL
Irish composer (1808-1870)

Dublin-born Michael Balfe was one of the most popular light opera composers of the 19th century but fashions have changed and his operas are no longer performed. His best-known opera is *The Bohemian Girl* (1843) which contains the famous aria "I dreamt I dwelt in marble halls." It has been filmed several times. Balfe was one of the three "Irish" opera composers, Vincent Wallace and Julius Benedict are the others, who dominated British opera in the 19th century before Gilbert and Sullivan. See THE BOHEMIAN GIRL.

BALLAD OF BABY DOE, THE
1956 opera by Moore

Douglas Moore's frontier opera about the Colorado mining era and the romance of Baby Doe Tabor has a memorable libretto by John Latouche. It premiered at the Central City Opera House, scene of the first act of the opera, and arrived at the New York City Opera in 1958 with Beverly Sills as Baby Doe. The opera is based on events concerning the love triangle of mining magnate Horace Tabor, his wife Augusta and his lady love Baby Doe. For a time it was ranked as the Great American Opera and during the 1976 Bicentenary celebrations was given five professional productions. Surprisingly there are presently no commercial videos of this important opera. See also DOUGLAS MOORE.

1957 Omnibus
Virginia Copeland portrays Baby Doe in this production by Michael Myerberg created for the Omnibus TV series. William Johnson portrays Horace Tabor and Martha Lipton repeats the role of Augusta which she created in Central City. Sylvan Levin conducts the Symphony of the Air. Charles S. Dubin directed the telecast on ABC Television on Feb. 10, 1957. Black and white. In English. 60 minutes.

1976 New York City Opera
Ruth Welting stars as Baby Doe in this New York City Opera production by Patrick Bakman with Richard Fredricks portraying Horace Tabor and

Frances Bible as his wife Augusta. Judith Somogi conducts the New York City Opera Orchestra and Chorus. This was a pioneer *Live from Lincoln Center* telecast of the April 21, 1976, performance. It was produced by John Goberman and directed by Kirk Browning. Color. In English. 120 minutes.

1992 Lancaster Opera
New York City Opera baritone John Darrenkamp, a Lancaster native, stars as Horace Tabor in this production by the Lancaster Opera Company at the Fulton Theater in Lancaster, PA. Andrea Rose Folan sings the role of Baby Doe. This is the only available video of this major opera but it is a poor quality non-professional tape shot from a balcony. Color. In English. 131 minutes. Opera Dubs video.

BALL IM SAVOY
1932 operetta by Abraham

The Ball at the Savoy is an operetta by Hungarian Paul Abraham that was highly successful when it premiered in Germany with Hungarian opera diva Gitta Alpar as the star. It was turned into English by Oscar Hammerstein II for its London production where it had 148 performances, but it never came to New York. The story revolves around jealous behavior during a honeymoon that threatens to break up a marriage. Alfred Grünwald and Bela Löhner-Beda wrote the libretto. See also PAUL ABRAHAM.

1935 Gitta Alpar film
Gitta Alpar, the soprano who originated the role, stars as singer Anita Helling in *Bál a Savoyban*, a Hungarian film of the operetta. Hans Jaráy portrays Baron André von Wollheim, Rosi Barsony is Mary von Wollheim and Felix Bressart is Birowitsch. This was the first musical film made in Hungary. Istvan (Steve) Szekeley directed. Black and white. In Hungarian. 82 minutes.

1955 Nadja Tiller film
Nadja Tiller stars in this modern German film opposite Eva-Engeborg Scholz and Rudolf Prack. Paul Martin directed. Color. In German. 90 minutes.

1994 Ballo al Savoy
Italian singer Sandro Massimini describes the history of the operetta in Italian, outlines its plot and presents highlights on his television show *Operette, che Passione*. The TV series about operettas

is directed by Pierluigi Pagano. Color. In Italian. 52 minutes. Ricordi (Italy) video.

BALLO IN MASCHERA, UN
1859 opera by Verdi

A Masked Ball was a controversial opera in its time because it showed the assassination of a king, Sweden's Gustavus III, slain in 1792 at a masked ball. The censors objected so Verdi changed the venue to 17th century Boston and changed the king into colony governor Riccardo. The story concerns his love for Amelia, the wife of his best friend, her love for him, their honorable behavior and an assassination plot. Producers often change the setting back to Sweden or to another time or place and this is reflected in the videos. See also GIUSEPPE VERDI.

1967 Carlo Bergonzi film
Carlo Bergonzi stars as the love-stricken governor Riccardo with Antonietta Stella as his beloved Amelia in this production filmed in Tokyo for Japanese television. Adding support are Mario Zanasi, Margherita Guglielmi and Lucia Danieli. The original American setting of the opera is used. Oliviero de Fabritiis is the conductor. Color. In Italian with Japanese subtitles. 140 minutes. Lyric video.

1980 Metropolitan Opera
Luciano Pavarotti stars as Riccardo with Katia Ricciarelli as his Amelia in this fine Metropolitan Opera production by Eliljah Moshinsky. Judith Blegen is a delight as Oscar, Bianca Berini is Ulrica and Louis Quilco is Renato. The time of the opera has been moved forward to 18th century Boston on the eve of the American Revolution. Peter Wexler designed the modernistic sets and Peter J. Hall the costumes. Giuseppe Patanè conducts the Metropolitan Opera Orchestra and Chorus. Brian Large directed the video on Feb. 16, 1980. Color. In Italian with English subtitles. 150 minutes. Paramount video/Pioneer laser.

1991 Metropolitan Opera
This Metropolitan production by Piero Faggione moves the setting of the opera back to Sweden as originally planned by Verdi. Luciano Pavarotti repeats his role in the opera but this time as Gustavus III, King of Sweden. Aprile Millo is his Amelia, Leo Nucci is Renato, Florence Quivar is Ulrica and Harolyn Blackwell is his delightful

Oscar. The realistic sets, costumes and lighting are also by Faggioni. James Levine conducts the Metropolitan Orchestra and Chorus. Brian Large directed the video. Color. In Italian with English subtitles. 137 minutes. DG video.

Related film

1987 Nicolas Roeg film
Director Nicolas Roeg creates an ironic variation on the story of *Un Ballo in Maschera* in his episode of the film *Aria*. It is 1931 Vienna and King Zog of Albania (Teresa Russell) sneaks out of the opera house for an assignation with a baroness (Stephanie Lane). The opera being performed is *Un Ballo in Maschera* and Zog has to fight off an assassination attempt outside the theater. The singers are Leontyne Price, Carlo Bergonzi, Robert Merrill, Shirley Verrett and Reri Grist. Erich Leinsdorf conducts the RCA Italiana Opera Orchestra. Color. In Italian. About 10 minutes. See also ARIA.

BALTSA, AGNES
Greek mezzo-soprano (1944-)

Agnes Baltsa was born in Lefkas, Greece, and studied singing in Athens and Munich. She made her stage debut in Frankfurt in 1968 as Cherubino and her American debut in Houston as Carmen. Her performance as Carmen has been particularly admired for its dramatic quality and earthiness but her repertoire is quite wide ranging. See CARMEN (1987), JOSÉ CARRERAS (1991), DON CARLO (1986), DER ROSENKAVALIER (1984), THE TALES OF HOFFMANN (1981).

BARBE-BLEUE
1866 opéra bouffe by Offenbach

Jacques Offenbach's *Barbe-Bleue* is a satirical version of the Bluebeard legend composed to a libretto by Henry Meilhac and Ludovic Halévy. Bluebeard's wives are not killed but given sleeping potions and come back for a little vengeance at the end. The best known modern production was the creation of Germany's Walter Felsenstein and an adaptation exists on video. See also JACQUES OFFENBACH.

1902 Alber's Electro Talking Bioscope
An aria from the operetta was presented with sound and picture in Holland in September 1902. Alber's Electro Talking Bioscope was brought from France and used equipment bought from Clement Maurice at the 1900 Paris Exhibition.

1973 Berlin Komische Oper
Walter Felsenstein's most popular production was his 1963 *Ritter Blaubart* for the Komische Oper, repeated many times over the years. In 1973 he made a film version of it in a television studio. Hans Nocker portrays Bluebeard, Rudolf Asmus is the magician Popolani, Anny Schlemm is Boulotte and Werner Enders is Bobeche. Karl F. Voigtmann conducted the orchestra and Felsenstein made the film with help from Georg Mielke. Color. In German. 120 minutes. Classic Video Dreamlife (Japan) video and laser disc.

BARBER OF SEVILLE, THE
1816 opera by Rossini

Gioachino Rossini's opera *Il Barbiere di Seviglia* has been an audience favorite for nearly 200 years. Cesare Sterbini based his libretto on the famous Beaumarchais play and the story is continued in *The Marriage of Figaro*. Set in Seville, it tells how the match-making barber Figaro helps Count Almaviva marry the beautiful Rosina despite opposition from her guardian Bartolo. *Barber* has been filmed a great many times beginning with a French version in 1903. One of the best recordings features Maria Callas and Tito Gobbi but there is no film of them together in the opera. Gobbi was filmed in the complete opera with other Rosinas and Callas was filmed singing "Una voce poco fa" in concert. The videos of the opera with Cecilia Bartoli, Teresa Berganza, and Maria Ewing have been critical favorites. See also GIOACHINO ROSSINI.

1933 Le Barbier de Séville
This film combines Rossini's opera with Mozart's *The Marriage of Figaro*. It tells the story of both operas with music from both. There are also plot changes, e.g., Rosina and Almaviva get married during the music lesson. Hélène Robert portrays Rosine, André Baugé is Figaro, Jean Galland is Almaviva, Pierre Juvenet is Bartholo, Fernand Charpin is Basile, Josette Day is Suzanne, Monique Rolland is Cherubin and Yvonne Yma is Marceline. Pierre Maudru wrote the screenplay, Marcel Lucine was the cinematographer and L. Masson conducted the music. Hubert Bourlon and Jean Kemm directed the film. Black and white. In French. 93 minutes. Video Yesteryear video.

1946 Tagliavini/Gobbi film

Ferrucio Tagliavini portrays Almaviva and Tito Gobbi is Figaro in this Italian film. Tagliavini was hugely popular at the Metropolitan Opera at the time and his name rather than Gobbi's was on cinema marquees. Nelly Corradi is Rosina, Vito de Taranto is Bartolo and Italo Tajo is Basilio. The film is a record of a Rome Opera House production. Massimo Terzano was cinematographer and Giuseppe Morelli conducted the orchestra. Mario Costa directed the film. It premiered in the U.S. with narration by Deems Taylor. Black and white. In Italian. 110 minutes. Lyric video.

1947 Paris Opéra-Comique film

Roger Bourdin is impressive as Basile in this film of an Opéra-Comique production in Paris. It is sung in French with spoken dialogue and is well-made and well-acted, an excellent record of a French production of the time. Lucienne Jourfier stars as Rosine, Raymonde, Amade portrays Almaviva, Roger Bussonet is Figaro, Louis Musy is Bartholo and Renée Gilly is Marceline. René Colas was the cinematographer and André Cluytens conducts the Opéra-Comique Orchestra and Chorus. Jean Loubignac directed the opera production and Claude Dolbert made the film. Black and white. In French. 90 minutes. René Chateau (France) video.

1948 Tito Gobbi Film

Tito Gobbi stars as Figaro in this highlights version of the opera with Angelica Tuccari as Rosina (acted by Pina Malgharini), Cesare Valletti as Almaviva (acted by Mino Russo) and Giulio Tomei as Bartolo (acted by Gino Conti). It was shot on stage at the Rome Opera House and released as part of the First Opera Film Festival series with narration. Angelo Questo conducts the Rome Opera House Orchestra and Chorus. George Richfield produced and directed the film. Black and white. 23 minutes. In Italian and English.

1952 NBC Opera Theatre

Ralph Herbert sings the role of Figaro with Virginia Haskins as Rosina and Davis Cunningham as Almaviva in this NBC Opera Theatre production by Samuel Chotzinoff. Emile Renan is Bartolo and Carlton Gauld is Basilio. The opera was sung in English in a translation by Townsend Brewster. Charles Polacheck directed the stage action and Peter Herman Adler conducted the orchestra. Kirk Browning directed for television. Black and white. In English. 60 minutes. Video at MTR.

1955 Figaro il Barbiere di Siviglia

Tito Gobbi stars as Figaro in this cinematic adaptation by Camillo Mastrocinque. Giulietta Simionato sings the role of Rosina acted by Irene Gemma, Nicola Monti sings Almaviva acted by Armando Francioli, Vito De Taranto sings Bartolo acted by Cesco Baseggio and Guilio Neri sings and acts Basilio. Many of the opera's musical numbers have been cut and the film has spoken dialogue. Color. In Italian. 93 minutes. Lyric Bel Canto video.

1959 Bavarian State Opera

Hermann Prey sings Figaro, Erika Koth is Rosina, Fritz Wunderlich is Almaviva, Hans Hotter is Bartolo and Max Proebstl is Basilio in this Bavarian State Opera production in Munich. Ferdinand Leitner conducts the Bavarian State Opera Orchestra. The video is an off-air copy of a telecast. Black and white. In German. 155 minutes. Lyric video.

1972 Jean-Pierre Ponnelle film

One of the best films of the opera with terrific performances by Hermann Prey as Figaro and Teresa Berganza as Rosina. Director Jean-Pierre Ponnelle is highly inventive with a mobile camera that helps bring out the best of Rossini. This is a companion to Ponnelle's film of *The Marriage of Figaro* shot on the same sound stage. Luigi Alva is a suave Almaviva and Enzo Dara a fine Bartolo. Ernst Wild was the cinematographer and Claudio Abbado conducted the La Scala Orchestra and Chorus. Unitel. Color. In Italian with English subtitles. 142 minutes. DG video.

1975 Peter Seabourne film

Peter Seabourne filmed this English highlights version in Knebworth House in Hertfordshire. Margaret Eels stars as Rosina, Michael Wakeham is Figaro, Edmund Bohan is Almaviva, Malcolm Rivers is Bartolo and Philip Summerscales is Basilio. Peter Murray wrote the translation and John J. Davies conducted the Classical Orchestra. Color. In English. 54 minutes.

1976 New York City Opera

Beverly Sills stars as a sparkling Rosina in this New York City Opera production by Sarah Caldwell who also conducts. The cast is costumed like their roles with Figaro striped like a barber pole, Rosina wearing feathers like a bird in a cage and the others sporting the symbols of their occupations. The effect is odd and sometimes silly but certainly original.

Alan Titus portrays Figaro, Henry Price is Almaviva, Donald Gramm is Bartolo and Samuel Ramey is Basilio. Kirk Browning directed the video and telecast on Nov. 3, 1976. Color. In Italian with English subtitles. 156 minutes. Paramount video/Pioneer laser.

1982 Glyndebourne Festival
Maria Ewing is an alluring Rosina and John Rawnsley a zesty Figaro in this inventive production by John Cox. Max-René Cosotti is a dashing Count Almaviva, Claudio Desderi is Bartolo and Ferrucio Ferlanetto is Basilio. William Dudley's bright sets enliven the comedy as does the lively playing by the London Philharmonic Orchestra led by Sylvain Cambreling. Dave Heather directed the video. Color. In Italian with English subtitles. 156 minutes. Home Vision video/Pioneer Artists laser.

1988 Metropolitan Opera
Kathleen Battle stars as Rosina and steals the show with a sparkling performance in this big but unexciting production by John Cox. Leo Nucci is Figaro, Rockwell Blake is Almaviva, Enzo Dara is Bartolo and Ferruccio Furlanetto is Basilio. Robin Wagner designed the sets and Ralf Weikert conducted the Metropolitan Opera Orchestra. Brian Large directed the video with Peter Gelb as producer. Color. In Italian with English subtitles. 161 minutes. DG Video.

1988 Schwetzinger Festival
Mezzo soprano Cecilia Bartoli established her reputation singing the role of Rosina in this entertaining production by Michael Hampe at the Schwetzinger Festival. She is quite magnificent, radiant in personality and a sheer delight to watch and hear. Gino Quilico is Figaro, David Kuebler is Almaviva, Robert Lloyd is Basilio and Carlos Feller is Bartolo. Mauro Pagano designed the sets and costumes and Gabriele Ferro leads the Stuttgart Radio Symphony Orchestra and Cologne City Opera Chorus. Claus Viller directed the video. Color. In Italian with English subtitles. 159 minutes. RCA video and laser.

Early/related films

1903 Georges Méliès sound film
The first film of the opera was made in 1903 by French pioneer Georges Méliès. It was a long film for its time, 402 meters and seven scenes, and was publicized as a genuine "reproduction" of the opera with sound. Rossini's music was played on discs with the film in screenings. In Rome it was called the Cinematofonio and in Florence the Cinetofonio.

1908 Sigrid Arnoldsen sound film
Barbarenen i Sevilla is a Swedish sound film of the aria "Una voce poco fa" sung by Swedish soprano Sigrid Arnoldsen. N. H. Nylander directed the film made with the Biophon sound system and produced by Svenska Biografteatern. There is also a Danish version made for Kosmorama.

1910 Le Barbier de Séville
Le Barbier de Séville is a French silent film of scenes from the opera starring Jean Perier and Georges Beir. It was made for Pathé. Black and white. 10 minutes.

1913 Luigi Maggi film
Gigetta Morano stars as Rosina, Ubaldi Stefani is Figaro and Umberto Scapellin is the Count in this Italian film directed by Luigi Maggi. It was based on the opera and play and made for the Ambrosio studio of Turin. The same team made a version of *The Marriage of Figaro*.

1915 Oskar Messter sound film
This sound film of *The Barber of Seville* was copyrighted in the USA in 1915 by German sound film pioneer Oskar Messter. It may be the same as the Swedish film listed above.

1923 Pineschi Brothers sound film
The Italian brothers Azeglio and Lamberto Pineschi invented a camera that recorded sound on film and their highlights version of *Il Barbiere di Siviglia* was acclaimed by contemporary critics. It stars soprano Gabriella Di Veroli as Rosina and tenor Giovanni Manurita as Almaviva. Black and white. In Italian. 20 minutes.

1927 Giuseppe De Luca sound film
This Vitaphone sound film is titled *Giuseppe De Luca of the Metropolitan Opera Company as Figaro singing 'Largo al Factotum' from The Barber of Seville*. He is accompanied by the Vitaphone Symphony Orchestra. Black and white. In Italian. About 7 minutes.

1928 Apollo Granforte sound film
Italian baritone Apollo Granforte bounces on stage in Figaro costume with guitar and sings the "Largo al factotum" aria in an energetic style with full orchestra in this early Australian sound film. It was made by RCA with its Photophone system while he was on tour in Australia with Melba. Black and white. In Italian. About 6 minutes. Lyric video.

1929 Gaston Ravel film
Gaston Ravel's French film *Figaro* is based on the entire Beaumarchais trilogy. It follows the story from *The Barber of Seville* through *The Marriage of Figaro* to *The Guilty Mother*. Edmund Van Duren stars as Figaro, Tony D'Algy is the Count, Arlette Marchal is Rosine, Marie Bell is Suzanne and Jean Weber is Cherubin. Black and white. In French. 76 minutes.

1930 Tito Ruffo sings Largo al Factotum
The great Italian baritone Tito Ruffo made three opera films for MGM in 1929 and 1930 singing in costume. On the second he performs Figaro's "Largo al Factotum." The soundtracks of the aria has been issued on record. Black and white. About 8 minutes.

1931 Figaro e la sua Gran Giornata
Figaro's Great Day is an excellent Italian film about a touring opera company staging the Rossini opera in a provincial city. It was directed by the very able Mario Camerini and was a major hit in its time. Gianfranco Giachetti stars as an opera teacher who agrees to sing the role of Figaro with the company when the baritone quits. Rossini's music is played by an orchestra conducted by Felice Lattuada. Black and white. In Italian. 80 minutes.

1934 Apples To You
Billy Gilbert, son of two Metropolitan Opera singers, stars in *Apples to You*, a Hal Roach comedy based around *The Barber of Seville*. He portrays a burlesque theater impresario hired to revive the fortunes of a bankrupt opera company. He does this with an amazing version of *Barber* lacing the opera with burlesque routines and "20 Beautiful Barberettes." The opera audience loves it. Peter Sellars take note. Black and white. In English. 20 minutes.

1937 Broadway Melody Of 1938
An opera-loving racehorse wins its big race when Met baritone Igor Gorin sings Figaro's "Largo al Factotum" aria over the racetrack loudspeakers. This is a central plot point of this delightful Eleanor Powell musical. Roy Del Ruth directed. Black and white. 110 minutes. MGM-UA video.

1938 El Barbero de Sevilla
This Spanish film, made in Germany by Benito Perojo during the Spanish Civil War, is a zarzuela version of the story. Estrillita Castro, Robert Rey, Raquel Rodrigo and Miguel Ligero star. Black and white. In Spanish. 88 minutes.

1941 Citizen Kane
Dorothy Comingore makes a miserable attempt to sing "Una voce poco fa" and vocal coach Fortunio Bonanova tells her husband Charles Kane (Orson Welles) that she has no future as an opera singer. Kane pays no attention. Welles directed. Black and white. 119 minutes.

1941 Notes to You
An alley cat sets up a sheet music stand on a backyard fence and begins Figaro's Factotum aria to the annoyance of Porky Pig who is trying to sleep. Friz Freleng directed this Warner Bros. cartoon. Color. About 7 minutes.

1944 The Barber of Seville
The first Woody Woodpecker cartoon, one of the great screwball comedies, was inspired by the Rossini opera. Woody substitutes for barber Figaro and sings the "Largo al Factotum" while he gives shaves and haircuts. Walter Lantz produced and James Culhane directed. Color. 7 minutes.

1946 The Whale Who Wanted to Sing at the Met
Willie, the opera-singing whale with the voice of Nelson Eddy, imagines he is about to be discovered and auditions all over the ocean with Figaro's "Largo al Factotum" aria. Hamilton Luske directed this Disney cartoon as part of the feature *Make Mine Music*. Color. 12 minutes.

1948 For the Love of Mary
Deanna Durbin sings a comic rendition of "Largo al factotum" in this film in which she plays a telephone operator. Frederick De Cordova directed for Universal. Black and white. 90 minutes.

1948 Back Alley Oproar
Sylvester the Cat tries out his vocal style with the opening Figaro aria as Elmer Fudd tries to sleep in

this remake of the Warner Bros. Cartoon *Notes to You*. Friz Freleng directed. Color. 7 minutes.

1950 Figaro qua, Figaro la
Italian comic Toto stars in this Italian film based around the opera. It uses the music, plot and characters but is mostly farce. Toto portrays Figaro, Isa Barzizza is Rosina and Gianni Agus is Almaviva. Carlo Ludovico Bragaglia directed. Black and white. In Italian. 85 minutes.

1950 The Rabbit of Seville
Bugs Bunny has a grand time to music from *The Barber of Seville* in this brilliant cartoon. Elmer Fudd chases Bugs across the stage of the Hollywood Bowl. When the curtain goes up the rabbit is the barber and Elmer is his customer. Bugs sings as he shaves Elmer and ends up marrying him. Chuck Jones directed and Michael Maltese wrote the script and the new lyrics. Warner Bros. Color. 7 minutes.

1952 The Magical Maestro
Tex Avery's classic cartoon revolves around *The Barber of Seville*. A magician transforms a baritone in various strange ways as he tries to sing. Warner Bros. 7 minutes.

1955 Teatro Girolamo marionettes
This is a condensed version of the opera performed by marionettes of the Teatro Girolamo in Milan. The singing voices belong to Graziella Sciutti as Rosina, Antonio Pirino as Almaviva, Walter Monachesi and Bruno Scalchiero accompanied by the Rome Opera Orchestra. Filmeco. Color. Sung in Italian with English narration. 26 minutes.

1961 Un Aussi Longe Absence
Director Henry Colpi uses the romantic tenor aria " Ecco ridente in cielo" in a magical moment as the lovers reunite in this Cannes Grand Prize winner. The film is the story of a woman who finds her lost husband. Color. In French. 90 minutes.

1963 8 1/2
The Barber overture is used in a key moment in Federico Fellini's portrayal of a movie director in a creative crisis. Marcello Mastroianni escapes into fantasies and memories in a hotel washroom as the overture swells up on the soundtrack. Black and white. In Italian. 138 minutes.

1964 Bell Telephone Hour
Judith Raskin and William Walker of the Met are featured in a duet from *The Barber of Seville* on the Bell Telephone Hour television program on Jan 14, 1964. Sid Smith directed. Color. 60 minutes. Video at MTR.

1972 Lollipop Opera
Author-artist Don Freeman uses the music from *Barber of Seville* to tell an animated tale about a boy's visit to a barber. He draws both the shop and the customer and then mixes animation with live action. Color. 9 minutes.

1972 Joan Sutherland puppets
Joan Sutherland stars in this highlights version made for the *Who's Afraid of Opera?* series intended for children. Sutherland tells the story to puppets and performs the role of Rosina with Tom McDonnell as Figaro, Ramon Remedios as Almaviva, Spiro Milas as Bartolo and Clifford Grant as Basilio. The dialogue is in English but the arias are sung in Italian. George Djurkovic designed the sets and Richard Bonynge conducted the London Symphony Orchestra. Ted Kotcheff directed the film. Color. 30 minutes. Kultur video.

1984 Maestro's Company Puppets
This Australian Maestro's Company highlights version for children features puppets rehearsing the opera under an abandoned theater. The singers are Teresa Berganza as Rosina, Manuel Auseni as Figaro, Ugo Benelli as Almaviva, Fernando Corena as Bartolo and Nicolai Ghiaurov as Basilio. Silvio Varviso conducts the Naples Rossini Orchestra. William Fitzwater directed and Jim George produced; the series was created by Marcia Hatfield. Color. Dialogue in English, arias in Italian. 30 minutes. VAI video.

1985 Prizzi's Honor
The *Barber* overture is featured in this John Huston film about the Prizzi crime family and a love affair between killers Jack Nicholson and Kathleen Turner. Color. 130 minutes. Vestron video.

1987 Dark Eyes
Nikita Mikhalkov's film about turn-of-the-century Italian roué Marcello Mastroianni has an elegant use of "Une voce poco fa." At an aristocratic health resort Evelina Megnagi (with the voice of Magali Damonte) sings the aria at the start of his long affair

with a married Russian woman. He spends most of the movie remembering her. Color. 118 minutes.

1993 Mrs. Doubtfire
Star Robin Williams sings a parody of Figaro's "Factotum" aria as he records the voices of cat and canary animated cartoon characters during the opening scenes of this movie. Chris Columbus directed. Color. 125 minutes.

1995 Operavox Animated Opera
Christmas Films, a Moscow animation studio, created this model animation version of *The Barber of Seville* for the British Operavox series. The Welsh National Opera Orchestra plays a specially recorded score. Gareth Jones was music editor. Color. 27 minutes.

BARBER, SAMUEL
American composer (1910-1981)

Samuel Barber is best known to the wider public because of the film *Platoon* which uses his "Adagio for Strings" so effectively. Adagio is said to be the most popular American classical composition of the twentieth century and was also used in the film *Lorenzo's Oil* and the Swedish film *The Best Intentions*. Barber's operas have had mixed receptions but *Vanessa* seems likely to become a repertory staple and *Antony and Cleopatra* was popular in its revival. Both have been telecast and are on CD but are not on commercial video. See ANTONY AND CLEOPATRA, VANESSA.

1977 Happy Birthday, Samuel Barber
A CBS Camera Three television program celebrating the composer's birthday with Barber talking about his life and career to James Tocco. Esther Hinds performs one of the soprano arias from *Antony and Cleopatra*. Roger England produced and directed the telecast on March 6, 1977. Color. 30 minutes. Video at MTR.

BARBERILLO DE LAVAPIÉS, EL
1874 zarzuela by Barbieri

The Little Barber of Lavapiés is the most popular zarzuela by Spanish composer Francisco Asenjo Barbieri and its songs are a part of Spanish culture. Its hero Lamparilla is a Figaro-type barber in working-class Madrid in 1766 with a sweetheart called Paloma. They are caught up in a conspiracy to replace the hated prime minister and end up hiding the aristocrat Estrella and her fiancé. Luis Mariano de Larra wrote the libretto. See also FRANCISCO BARBIERI.

1968 Juan de Orduña film
Juan De Orduña directed this Spanish television film with Federico Moreno Torroba conducting the Spanish Lyric Orchestra and Madrid Chorus. The singers are Maria Carmen Ramirez, Luis-Sagi Vela, Dolores Prez, Francisco Sura, Ramon Alonso and Luis Frutos with actors portraying the characters on screen. The film was written by Manuel Tamayo and produced by TVE for its Teatro Lirico Español series. The soundtrack is on record. Color. In Spanish. 96 minutes.

BARBIERI, FRANCISCO
Spanish composer (1823-1894)

Francisco Asenjo Barbieri is one of the most popular Spanish composers of zarzuelas and is known for *El Barberillo de Lavapiés* and *Pan y Toros*. He wrote his first zarzuela in 1850 and completed over seventy that premiered in Madrid. He also made major contributions to Spanish music as writer, historian and teacher. See EL BARBERILLO DE LAVAPIÉS.

BARBIER VON BAGDAD, DER
1858 opera by Cornelius

Peter Cornelius's opera *The Barber of Baghdad* is based on tales from *The Arabian Nights*. Cornelius wrote the libretto which tells the story of Nureddin's love for Margiana and the unhelpful assistance he gets from an eager barber. Nureddin gets the girl but the barber gets the best music, including a fine buffo patter song. The opera, comparable to the work of Nicolai and Lortzing, is rarely performed outside German-speaking countries. See also PETER CORNELIUS.

1960 Bavarian Television
Der Barbier von Bagdad was made into a Bavarian television film in Munich in 1960 by Herbert Junkers with the music performed by the Bavarian Television Orchestra. The opera was adapted for the small screen by Heinrich Hollreiser. Color. In German. 88 minutes.

BARCLAY, JOHN
British baritone (1899-)

John Barclay was born in England but came to the U.S. in 1921 for a successful recital and recording career. He sang on two of the early Vitaphone sound films but his best known movie is the 1939 British *The Mikado*. See THE MIKADO (1939).

1927 Barclay Sings Pagliacci
The full title of this Vitaphone sound film is *John Barclay Offering Impersonations of Famous Characters Singing the Prologue from Pagliacci*. It features him singing the Prologue from *Pagliacci* plus Mephisto's Serenade from *Faust*, an aria from *Boris Godunov* and the Toreador Song from *Carmen*. Black and white. About 10 minutes.

1927 Barclay Sings Faust
The full title of this early Vitaphone sound film is *John Barclay Offering his Famous Character Interpretations of Mephisto's Calf of Gold*. He performs the aria "The Calf of Gold" from Gounod's *Faust* plus songs by Damrosch and Logan. Black and white. About 10 minutes.

BARITONE, THE
1985 Polish opera film

The story of *The Baritone* (Baryton in Polish) centers around a famous Polish opera singer who returns to Poland in 1933 as Hitler is coming to power. He has been abroad for 25 years and has returned to his home town with plans to build an opera house in Strasburg. Much of the film is concerned with plots against him by his secretary, wife, manager and mysterious others in the shadow of encroaching fascism. The film was written by Feliks Falk and directed by Janusz Zaorski. Color. In Polish. 95 minutes.

BARSTOW, JOSEPHINE
English soprano (1940-)

Josephine Barstow joined Sadler Wells in 1967 and made her debut at Covent Garden in 1969. Her first appearance at the Metropolitan was in 1977 as Musetta. Her repertoire ranges from classic Mozart to modern Tippet. She can be seen on video at Glyndebourne in *Idomeneo* as Electra and in *Macbeth* as Lady Macbeth. See IDOMENEO (1974), MACBETH (1972).

BARTERED BRIDE, THE
1866 opera by Smetana

Smetana's *Prodaná Nevesta* is the quintessential Czech opera and the standard against which other Czech operas are measured. It has charm galore with its roots in Bohemian folk music and has remained popular in central Europe and in Germany as *Der Verkaufte Braut*. The libretto by Karel Sabina tells the story of the lovers Marenka and Jenik. Each contrives an elaborate stratagem so they can marry after she has been betrothed to another. The opera's popularity is reflected in the many films based on it. See also BEDRICH SMETANA.

1932 Max Ophuls film
Die Verkaufte Braut, Max Ophuls' film of the opera in German, is one of the major opera films and a cinema classic. Jarmila Novotná sings Marenka and Willy Domgraf-Fassbaender is her Jenik. Comedians Max Nadler as the Mayor, Karl Valentin as Brummer and Paul Kemp as Wenzel are fun. Annemarie Sörensen is Esmeralda, Otto Wernicke is Kezal and Herman Kner is Micha. Theo Mackeben made the adaptation of this first German opera film. Black and white. In German. 75 minutes. Lyric, Bel Canto and Opera Dubs videos.

1933 Ota Horakova film
Prodaná Nevesta is a straightforward Czech film of the opera made in Prague as a kind of authentic answer to the German version. Ota Horakova sings Marenka with support from Jaroslav Gleich, Demil Pellert, V. Toms, J. Konstantin and D. Sudikova. Svatopluk Innemann, Jaroslav Kvapil and Emil Pollert co-directed with help from writer Jaroslav Kvapil who worked on the Ophuls film. Karel Degl, Vaclav Vich and Otto Heller were the cinematographers. Espofilm. Black and white. In Czech. 80 minutes.

1957 Elsie Morison video
Australian soprano Elsie Morison stars as Marenka in this *Bartered Bride*, a lively English version by Christopher Muir shot in the ABC Studios in Melbourne. Victor Franklin is Jenik, Muriel Luyk is Ludmila, Keith Nelson is Kezal, Raymond MacDonald is Vashek, June Barton is Esmeralda and Alan Eddy is Micha. John Peters designed the sets, Rex Reid arranged the choreography and Clive Douglas conducted the Victoria Symphony Orchestra and Melbourne Singers. Black and white. In English. 117 minutes. Opera Dubs video.

1975 Teresa Stratas film

Teresa Stratas stars as Marie with René Kollo as Hans and Walter Berry as Kecal in *Die Verkaufte Braut*, a German film of the opera made for Bavarian television. Janet Perry is Esmeralda, Margarethe Bence is Ludmila, Alexander Malta is Micha and Jörn W. Wilsing is Kruschina. Jaroslav Krombholc conducted the Munich RadioTelevision Orchestra and Chorus. Color. In German. 120 minutes.

1976 Benacková/Zedek film

Gabriela Benacková sings the role of Marenka acted by Vanda Svarcova in this Czechoslovakian film of the opera directed by Václav Kaslík. It features actors in the main roles with Czech opera singers dubbing their voices. Ivo Zedek sings the part of Jenik acted by Petr Skarke with Cesmir Randa as Kecal and Vaclav Sioup as Vasek. Barrandov Studios. Color. In Czech. 119 minutes.

1978 Metropolitan Opera

Teresa Stratas stars as Marenka with Nicolai Gedda as Jenik and Jon Vickers as Vasek in this Metropolitan Opera production by John Dexter. Martti Talvela is Kecal, Colette Boky is Esmeralda, Elizabeth Cross is Ludmila and Derek Hamond-Stroud is Krusina. Josef Svoboda designed the sets and James Levine conducts the Metropolitan Orchestra. Kirk Browning directed the telecast on Nov. 21, 1978. Color. 130 minutes. Video at New York Public Library and MTR.

1980 Vienna State Opera

Lucia Popp stars as Maria opposite Siegfried Jerusalem and Karl Ridderbusch in this German-language Vienna State Opera production by Otto Schenk. Hungarian conductor Adam Fischer leads the Vienna Staatsoper Orchestra The opera was filmed on stage and later telecast. Beta Film. Color. In German. 135 minutes. On video.

1981 Benacková/Dvorsky film

Gabriela Benacková stars as Marenka with Peter Dvorsky as Jenik in this colorful Czech film. Mirslav Kopp is Vasek, Richard Novak is Kecal, Jinrich Jindrak is Krusina, Marie Vesela is Ludmila and Jaroslav Horácek is Micha. Frantisek Filip directed for Prague TV stressing the folklorist elements. Zdenek Kosler conducts the Czechoslovakian Philharmonic Orchestra and Chorus. The opera is on CD with the same cast.

Supraphon Prag. Color. In Czech. 132 minutes. Topaz (Germany) video/ Japanese laser.

Early films

1908 Pathé sound film

A German sound film of a scene and aria from the opera was made in 1908. and screened with the music on a phonograph. About 4 minutes.

1913 Max Urban film

The first Czech film of the opera was made by Max Urban, one of the top Czech directors in the 1910s. Marie Slechtova stars as Marenka, Tadeus Dura is Jenik, Adolf Krossing is Vasek, Emil Pollert is Kecal and Emil Burian is Krusina. The screenplay was based on the libretto and the film was screened with live music. Black and white. About 45 minutes.

1922 Oldrich Kminek film

The second Czech film of the opera was made in 1922 by Oldrich Kminek. Laura Zelenska stars as Marenka, Frantisek Beransky is Vasek, Karel Noll is Kecal and Frantisek Kudlacet is Krusina. The film was screened with live music. Black and white. In Czech. About 70 minutes.

BARTLETT, MICHAEL
American tenor (1901-?)

Michael Bartlett was born in Massachusetts, studied in Milan and made his debut in Trieste in 1928 in *Lucia di Lammermoor*. In the U.S. he sang with the Franco-Italo Opera Company and on Broadway and made his film debut as himself in the 1935 film *Love Me Forever*. After a film musical in England, he returned to stage musicals. In 1939 he starred in Clarence Loomis's folk opera *Susanna, Don't You Cry* and joined the San Francisco Opera where he sang opposite Jarmila Novotná in *Madama Butterfly*. In 1944 he was Romeo to Jeanette MacDonald's Juliette in a Chicago Opera production of Massenet's *Roméo et Juliette*. He continued to sing on stage into his sixties.

1935 Love Me Forever

Bartlett made his film debut as himself in this Grace Moore film. He sings Rudolfo opposite Moore's Mimi in the climactic stage production of *La Bohème*. She portrays a soprano who gets to sing the Puccini opera at the Met with the help of gangster Leo Carrillo. The film features a mockup of the old Met and a caricature of Met general manager Giulio Gatti-Casazza as "Maurizzio" with Thurston Hall made up to look like him. The *Rigoletto* quartet was expanded to 40 voices in true Hollywood style. Victor Schertzinger wrote and directed. In England the film was called *On Wings of Song*. Columbia. Black and white. 90 minutes.

1935 She Married Her Boss
Bartlett portrays a rich playboy who fancies Claudette Colbert in this romantic comedy. Her boss is Melvyn Douglas. Gregory La Cava directed. Columbia. Black and white. 90 minutes.

1936 The Music Goes Round
Bartlett portrays himself and sings the title song as an operatic aria in this Columbia movie. It stars Harry Richman and Rochelle Hudson and tells the story of a showboat troupe and their problems. Victor Schertzinger directed. Columbia. Black and white. 85 minutes.

1936 Follow Your Heart
Bartlett stars opposite Met soprano Marion Talley in this Republic opera film made by a company better known for horse operas. He portrays a gifted tenor and she is a soprano from an eccentric family. This is a downhome opera film for the folks, written tongue-in-cheek by Nathaniel West, Lester Cole and Samuel Ornitz, e.g., the Sextet from *Lucia de Lammermoor* is a comic number with Bartlett singing the tenor part to a ham and baritone Luis Alberni singing to a fish. Black and white. 82 minutes.

1937 The Lilac Domino
Bartlett stars as a philandering gambling Hungarian count with June Knight as a baron's schoolgirl daughter who fascinates him in her disguise as the Lilac Domino. This British musical was an adaptation of a 1912 German operetta by Charles Cuvillier which had been staged in New York and London. Bartlett sings well but acts badly. Friedrich Zelnick directed. Black and white. 79 minutes.

BARTÓK, BÉLA
Hungarian composer (1881-1945)

Béla Bartók has the ability to strike universal chords with his music, possibly because of his use of folk music and legend. His only opera is about Bluebeard and invites interpretations on psychological and historical levels. His main connection with the movies was through his collaborator Béla Belazs, a noted screenwriter and film theorist. Bartók's ballet *The Miraculous Mandarin* has been turned into a quasi-operatic Hungarian film by Milos Szinetar. See BLUEBEARD'S CASTLE.

1964 Bartók
Ken Russell's television biography of the composer was one of his most successful. It intercuts shots of Bartok in a room with music and scenes from *Bluebeard's Castle* and *The Miraculous Mandarin*. Russell's extravagant style includes an acetylene torch, a steel mill furnace and a rocket launch in the Bluebeard section. Black and white. 60 minutes.

1989 After the Storm
Subtitled *The American Exile of Bela Bartok*, this biographical program about Bartok is a production of the BBC and Hungarian television. The composer spent the last five years of his life in the U.S. and died in New York in 1945. Donald Sturrocks directed. Color. 75 minutes. Home Vision video.

BARTOLI, CECILIA
Italian mezzo soprano (1966-)

Cecilia Bartoli made her stage debut in 1987 and attracted wide attention in 1988 singing Rosina in *The Barber of Seville* in Cologne, Schwetzingen and Zurich. In a short time she became one of the most talked-about singers in the world, noted especially for her interpretations of Rossini and Mozart. She made her debut at the Met as Despina in a fine production of *Così Fan Tutte* and her American TV debut as the star of Rossini's *La Cenerentola*. The hype does not seem to have harmed her and her delightful stage personality and superb voice promise an enduring career. See THE BARBER OF SEVILLE (1988), LA CENERENTOLA (1995), HERBERT VON KARAJAN (1987), MOZART REQUIEM (1991).

1992 Cecilia Bartoli: A Portrait
An excellent two-part documentary by David Thomas. Part One is biographical with Bartoli recording Rossini at La Fenice in Venice, practicing with her mother, talking about her life and discussing Rossini and Mozart. Part Two is a concert at the Savoy Hotel in London with Gyorgy Fischer at the piano. She sings arias by Rossini, Mozart, Vivaldi and Pergolesi and gives two encores. LWT/Decca. Color. 107 minutes. London video and laser.

BASTIANINI, ETTORE
Italian baritone (1922-1967)

Ettore Bastianini, whose remarkable voice was stilled at the early age of 45, began as a bass in Rome in 1945 and switched to baritone in 1951. He made his debut at the Met in 1953 as Germont and sang many other roles there and at La Scala. He was especially noted for his passionate singing of Verdi roles, two of which are preserved on video. See Don Carlo (1958), Il Trovatore (1957).

BATTLE, KATHLEEN
American soprano (1948-)

Kathleen Battle was brought up in a small town in Ohio and learned about opera from the small screen by watching television broadcasts. She became interested in singing at the University of Cincinnati and made her debut with the New York City Opera in 1976. She has now sung in most of the major opera houses, including the Metropolitan and Covent Garden, and her attractive stage presence is evident in her recital videos. She is also noted for her temperament which has led to professional clashes and a parting of the ways with the Met. See The Abduction from the Seraglio (1984), Ariadne auf Naxos (1988), The Barber of Seville (1989), Carmina Burana (1989), Carnegie Hall (1991), Don Giovanni (1987), L'Elisir d'Amore (1992), Herbert von Karajan (1987), The Magic Flute (1992).

1990 Spirituals in Concert
Kathleen Battle teams with Jessye Norman at Carnegie Hall for this program of spirituals. The divas, dressed in contrasting shades of blue, interact beautifully as they sing in a variety of styles. Battle is particularly fine singing "Swing Low, Sweet Chariot" and in duet with flautist Hubert Laws. James Levine leads the orchestra and a 70-member chorus. Brian Large directed the video. Color. 91 minutes. DG/Cami Video.

1991 Battle at the Metropolitan Museum
Battle in a formal recital with pianist Warren Jones in front of the Egyptian Temple of Dendur at the Metropolitan Museum in New York. Battle, wearing a striking formal red dress, performs seventeen arias and songs from Mozart and Puccini to Strauss and Gershwin. Her voice is stunning. Humphrey Burton directed the video. Color. 55 minutes. Cami/PolyGram video.

1992 Baroque Duet
Battle and jazz trumpeter Wynton Marsalis make a recording and are observed on film by Susan Froemke, Peter Gelb, Albert Maysles and Pat Jaffe. The film shows rehearsals, a recording session and a studio performance as well as Battle visiting her home town in Ohio and Marsalis playing with friends. John Nelson conducts the Orchestra of St. Luke's. The recording itself was filmed by Michael Chapman. Color. 85 minutes. Cami video.

1995 An Evening with Kathleen Battle and Thomas Hampson
Battle and Hampson join forces for this *Live from Lincoln Center* concert telecast on March 1, 1995. They perform arias and duets by Mozart, Rossini, Massenet, Verdi, Lehár and Korngold in the first half and American musical theater tunes in the second. During the interval baritone Sherrill Milnes hosts a backstage segment with Battle and Hampson TALKING about their work plus ideas from Stephen Sondheim. Color. 90 minutes.

BAYOU LEGEND, A
1941 opera by Still

William Grant Still's opera *A Bayou Legend* was composed in 1941 to a libretto by his wife Verna Arvey and first staged in 1974 by Opera/South in Jackson, Mississippi. They based the story on a Mississippi legend they found in a book in the Los Angeles Public Library. Clothilde (mezzo) rejects Leonce (baritone) as she wants to marry Bazile (tenor) who she says is the father of her unborn child. The spirit maiden Aurore (soprano), who loves Bazil, tells him this is not true so Clothilde accuses him of witchcraft to gain revenge. The villagers hang him and his spirit joins Aurore's. See also William Grant Still.

1981 Opera/South film
Still's opera was filmed on location on a Mississippi bayou in 1979 with an Opera/South cast. Raeschelle Potter sings Clothilde, Gary Burgess is Bazile, Peter Lightfoot is Leonce and Carmen Balthrop is Aurore. They were taped singing in the natural background of the opera and the music, performed by the Opera/South orchestra under the direction of Leonard de Paur, was added later. John Thompson directed the film produced by Curtis W. Davis. The opera was telecast on PBS on June 15, 1981. Color. In English. 120 minutes.

BAYREUTH

Not many composers have the ego to build an opera house to present only their own operas but Richard Wagner did. His Bayreuth Festspielhaus was completed in 1876 and remains a place of Wagnerian piligrimage. Its epic construction is often featured in the biographical films about Wagner, most notably in Tony Palmer's epic biopic. There are many videos of operas filmed on stage at Bayreuth, including two of the complete *Ring*. See also DER FLIEGENDE HOLLÄNDER (1985), GÖTTERDÄMMERUNG (1980 & 1992), LOHENGRIN (1982 & 1990), DIE MEISTERSINGER VON NÜRNBERG (1984), PARSIFAL (1981), DAS RHEINGOLD (1980/ 1991), DER RING DES NIBELUNGEN (1980 & 1991), SIEGFRIED (1980 & 1992), TANNHÄUSER (1978 & 1990), TRISTAN UND ISOLDE (1983), RICHARD WAGNER, DIE WALKÜRE (1980 & 1991) .

1960 Wagner in Modern Dress

Phänomen Bayreuth (distributed in English as *Wagner in Modern Dress*) is a German film about rehearsals at Bayreuth for the 1959 and 1960 festivals. It features Wieland and Wolfgang Wagner, Rudolf Kempe, Wolfgang Sawallisch, Anja Silja, Hans Knappertsbusch, Lorin Maazel and Jerome Hines. Werner Lütje directed for Nord-Sud Television. Black and white. In German or English. 33 minutes.

1976 100 Years of Bayreuth

A portrait of the Bayreuth Festival on its one hundredth anniversary made to celebrate Wagner's achievements. It includes scenes from the 1976 production of the *Ring* under Pierre Boulez. Color. 40 minutes. On video.

1980 Wagner and Bayreuth

Hans Jürgen Rojek wrote and directed this German film about Wagner's associations with the city of Bayreuth and the building of his opera house. Young musicians have gone there for the International Youth Festival since 1950. Color. In English or German. 27 minutes. Inter Nationes video.

1985 Wagner in Bayreuth

Wolfgang Wagner presents an introduction to Wagner followed by excerpts from ten operas staged at Bayreuth from 1978 to 1985. Colin Davis, Woldemar Nelsson, Pierre Boulez, Horst Stein and Daniel Barenboim conduct the Bayreuther Festspiel Orchestra and Chorus in performances by an array of singers. Brian Large directed the video. Unitel. Color. In German. Philips laserdisc.

1994 Die Verwandlung der Welt in Musik

The Transformation of the World in Music is a documentary about Bayreuth today by German filmmaker Werner Herzog who has directed Wagner operas on stage. There are interviews with Wolfgang Wagner, Daniel Barenboim and Placido Domingo plus scenes from stagings of *Parsifal, The Flying Dutchman* and *Tristan und Isolde*. Unitel/ZDF. Color. In German. 90 minutes.

BBC TELEVISION

BBC Television in England was the first in the world to present opera on TV when 25 minutes of highlights from Albert Coates' opera *Pickwick* were shown on Nov. 13, 1936. The following year a complete *La Serva Padrona* was telecast. From 1936 to September 1939 when BBC Television closed down for the war, thirty operas were presented. Lionel Salter gives a wonderful description of this amazing early venture into TV opera in two articles in *Opera*. Unfortunately it does not appear as if any of this pioneering material was preserved on film. The BBC began to telecast opera again on Nov. 26, 1946, with *The Beggar's Opera*. It began outside broadcasts of opera from the New London Opera Company in 1947. The first opera commissioned by the BBC was Arthur Benjamin's *Mañana* telecast in 1956. The first BBC live broadcast from Covent Garden was not made until 1968.

BEATRICE

1959 TV opera by Hoiby

Lee Hoiby's television opera *Beatrice* is based on a story by Maurice Maeterlinck called *Sister Beatrice*. M. Nardi's libretto tells the story of a medieval nun, her fall from grace and her redemption. The opera was commissioned by WAVE-TV in Louisville, Kentucky and was telecast on Oct. 23, 1959, in the Louisville Orchestra First Edition series. It was given a stage production a week later by the Kentucky Opera Association. Black and white. In English. See also LEE HOIBY.

BECCE, GIUSEPPE
Italian composer (1877-1973)

Giuseppe Becce occupies an important place in the history of early opera film. In 1913 he portrayed Wagner in Oskar Messter's biofilm *Richard Wagner* and also composed the score - the first specially composed for a German silent film. He quickly became the most important composer of scores for German silent films and edited the definitive collection of film themes. One of his later scores was for a 1954 version of *Hänsel and Gretel*.

BECHI, GINO
Italian baritone (1913-1993)

Gino Bechi was the leading Italian dramatic baritone of his time. He was born in Florence, made his debut in *Empoli* in 1936 and sang regularly at Rome and La Scala from 1938 to 1953. He also made guest appearances at Covent Garden and other opera houses until 1961. Bechi was featured in a dozen Italian films, usually in singing roles, sometimes just as a voice. Two of his films were cinema versions of operas. See AIDA (1953), MAD ABOUT OPERA, FRANZ SCHUBERT (1955), LA TRAVIATA (1967).

1943 Fuga a Due Voce
Fugue for Two Voices is a sentimental musical about a film company that can't get the right story for its baritone star. He tells them a story about missing a train, spending the night with a girl who also missed it and ending up in jail with her. It becomes the story of film. Carlo Ludovico Bragaglia directed. Black and white. In Italian. 66 minutes.

1945 Pronto, Chi Parla?
This lighthearted love story with music was released in the U.S. as *The Voice of Love*. Bechi portrays a famous singer who poses as his own butler to woo and win countess Annette Bach. He sings the Prologue to *Pagliacci* and other arias. Carlo Ludovico Bragaglia directed. Black and white. In Italian. 80 minutes.

1946 Torna a Sorrento
Bechi stars opposite Adriana Benetti in *Return to Sorrento*, a romantic Italian musical. She's a young woman who has lost her fiancee and he helps her look for him. After a few songs they fall in love. Carlo Ludovico Bragaglia directed. Black and white. In Italian. 88 minutes.

1947 Il Segreto di Don Giovanni
This cinematic opera buffa was released in the U.S. as *When Love Calls*. Bechi stars as a singer with an irresistible charm for women including Silvana Pampanini. When he loses his voice, he despairs and decides to end his life by hiring killers. When he changes his mind, he has problems. Mario Costa directed. Black and white. In Italian. 85 minutes.

1947 Amanti in Fuga
Lovers in Flight is an historical musical with Bechi portraying 17th century composer Alessandro Stradella. The film tells of his love affair in Venice with Ortensia Foscarini (Annette Bach), the daughter of the Inquisitor. Her father objects and orders Stradella's murder. Giacomo Gentilomo directed. Black and white. In Italian. 83 minutes.

1948 Arrivederci, Papá!
Bechi portrays a singer undergoing a mid-life career crisis. A philosopher tells him he is about to meet the woman of his life and have two children. And so he does. Camillo Mastrocinque directed. Black and white. In Italian. 86 minutes.

1949 Signorinella
The song "Signorinella mio" was the inspiration for this Bechi musical with Antonella Lualdi. The plot revolves around a confidence swindle. Mario Mattoli directed. Black and white. In Italian. 87 minutes. Opera Dubs/Lyric video.

1950 Una Voce nel tuo Cuore
The singing by Bechi and Beniamino Gigli is the best thing in *A Voice in Your Heart*. They play themselves in opera sequences. Vittorio Gassman stars as a war correspondent who loves a nightclub singer who wants to sing opera. Alberto D'Aversa directed. Black and white. In Italian. 98 minutes.

1954 Canzoni a Due Voci
Songs for Two Voices is an excuse to allow stars Gino Bechi and Tito Gobbi to sing. Gobbi is a famous baritone while Bechi plays his voice in this musical fantasy directed by Gianni Vernuccio. Black and white. In Italian. 84 minutes.

1957 La Chiamavan Capinera...
Bechi portrays a famous baritone in his last film. Singer Irene Galter comes to live with him and falls in love with his son. Piero Regnoli directed. Black and white. In Italian. 95 minutes.

BED AND SOFA
1996 screen opera by Pen

This is a "silent movie opera" based on a Soviet film of the 1920s. The original *Bed and Sofa*, a delightful 1926 satirical comedy by Abram Room, concerns a trio of working folk living in a one-room apartment. The married couple sleep on the bed and their friend sleeps on the sofa; when the husband goes away for a short time, the friend moves into the bed. The chamber opera with a libretto by Laurence Klavan and music by Polly Pen premiered in February 1996 at the off-Broadway Vineyard Theater in a production by Andre Ernotte. It starred Terri Klausner as the wife Ludmilla, Michael X Martin as the husband Nikolai and Jason Workman as the old friend Volodya. G. W. Mercier designed the sets and costumes, Phil Monat created the clever lighting and Alan Johnson conducted the four-piece orchestra. The critics were very impressed. 90 minutes.

BEECHAM, THOMAS
English conductor (1879-1971)

Sir Thomas Beecham is not well represented on film though he left a strong legacy on disc. The founder of the London and Royal Philharmonic orchestras was one of the major figures in opera in England and his recording of *La Bohème* is considered the best by many opera enthusiasts. Beecham appears in person conducting in the Powell-Pressburger film of *The Tales of Hoffmann*. See CONDUCTORS (1995), NELLIE MELBA (1918), WOLFGANG A. MOZART (1936), THE TALES OF HOFFMANN (1951).

BEESON, JACK
American composer (1921-)

Indiana-born Jack Beeson, who began composing tuneful accessible operas in 1950, tends to favor American subjects. He seems particularly fond of William Saroyan and both *Hello Out There* and *My Heart's in the Highlands* are based on plays by the Armenian-American writer. *Lizzie Borden* tells the story of the legendary Massachusetts murder trial protagonist while *Captain Jinks of the Horse Marines* derives from an early American play. Beeson's operas mix folk idioms with operatic lyricism and most of them are on record though not yet on commercial video. See LIZZIE BORDEN, MY HEART'S IN THE HIGHLANDS

1916 Captain Jinks of the Horse Marines
Beeson and librettist Sheldon Harnick based their 1975 light opera *Captain Jinks of the Horse Marines* on a 1916 play by Clyde Fitch. Captain Jonathan Jinks bets a friend he can seduce visiting opera singer Aurelia Trentoni. Naturally the two fall in love and the bet becomes a problem. There is apparently no video of the opera but the play was filmed in 1916 by Essanay. It stars Ann Murdock as Aurelia and Richard Travers as Jinks. Fred E. Wright directed. Black and white. In English. About 70 minutes.

BEETHOVEN, LUDWIG VAN
German composer (1770- 1827)

Beethoven was indebted to Mozart's *Magic Flute* collaborator Emanuel Schikaneder for getting started in the opera field. Schikaneder commissioned Beethoven to compose an opera to his libretto *Vestas Feuer*. Beethoven then abandoned it to work on an opera called *Leonore* which became *Fidelio*. The opera is widely available on video as are various film biographies. Beethoven's life has proven a great attraction to filmmakers, perhaps because his scowl, deafness and temperament are seen as cinematic. Most of the films romanticize him. See FIDELIO.

1918 Beethovens Lebensroman
Fritz Kortner portrays Beethoven in *Beethoven's Life Story*, an Austrian silent film about the composer. Emil Justitz directed for Sascha Film and Oskar Nedbal arranged the Beethoven music for the screenings. Also known as *Der Martyrer seines Herzens*. Black and white. About 75 minutes.

1927 The Life of Beethoven
Fritz Kortner portrays Beethoven again in this major Austrian film biography. Director Hans Otto Löwenstein shows the chief events and love affairs in the composer's life in a film made for the Beethoven centenary. Ernst Baumeister is Haydn, Lillian Gray is Countess Guiccardi, Heinz Altringen is Ries and Will Schmieder is Prince Liechnowsky. Allianz. Black and white. Silent. About 70 minutes.

1936 Un Grand Amour de Beethoven
Napoleon director Abel Gance's *The Life and Loves of Beethoven* stars Harry Baur as Beethoven. It's a big romantic movie with powerful scenes including one demonstrating the composer's deafness. Gance's bravura direction is as impressive as the music arranged by Louis Masson. Supporting actors

include Annie Ducaux, Jean-Louis Barrault, Jany Holt, Marcel Dalio, and Jean Debucourt. The cinematography is by Robert LeFebvre and Marc Fossard. The video is titled *Abel Gance's Beethoven*. Black and white. In French with English subtitles. 120 minutes. Connoisseur video.

1941 The Melody Master
Albert Basserman plays Beethoven and encourages Schubert (Alan Curtis) in this Hollywood version of Schubert's life. Reinhold Schunzel directed. The film was originally titled *New Wine* and is known in England as *The Great Awakening*. Black and white. In English. 89 minutes. Video Yesteryear video.

1949 Eroica
An Austrian film biography based around the creation of the Eroica Symphony. Ewald Balser gives a sensitive portrayal of Beethoven under the direction of Walter Kolm-Veltee and Karl Hartl. The cast includes Marianne Schonauer and Judith Maria Holzmester. Color. In German. 100 minutes.

1954 Napoleon
Filmmaker/actor Erich von Stroheim portrays Beethoven in this French biography of Napoleon. It contains a famous scene in which an angry Beethoven crosses out his dedication of his "Eroica" Symphony to Napoleon. Sacha Guitry directed. Color. In French. 182 minutes.

1962 The Magnificent Rebel
A Walt Disney film about the young Beethoven, portrayed by Karl Boehm, shot in Vienna with careful attention to period detail. Also in the cast are Ernst Nadhering, Ivan Desny and Gabriele Porks. It was directed by George Tressler, written by Joanne Court and photographed by Goran Strindberg. Technicolor. 94 minutes.

1969 Beethoven 1814
Herbert Vesely's German film portrait shows Beethoven's hard life in Vienna in 1814 and examines his work then as a composer. Orchestra rehearsals of the third *Leonore* overture with conductor Vjaceslaw Neumann are featured. Color. In English. 14 minutes. Inter Nationes film.

1970 Ludwig van Beethoven
Hans Conrad Fischer, a specialist in factual musical biography, made this fine film for the Beethoven bicentennial. It tells the story of Beethoven's life without actors using a narrator and a visual collage while visiting the places and events of the composer's life. The visuals include houses, concert halls, manuscripts, letters, photographs and memorabilia. Beethoven's music is played by various orchestras and chamber groups and there is an excerpt from a film of *Fidelio*. It was written by Erich Koch and photographed by Ivan Putora. Austria-West Germany. Color. In German. 100 minutes.

1970 Beethoven - Tage aus einem Leben
Russian actor Donatas Banionis, who bears a close resemblance to the composer, is the star of *Beethoven - Days from a Life*, an East German film. It presents reflective episodes from the life of Beethoven in Vienna from 1813 to 1819. Stefan Lisewiski is Johann Beehoven, Hans Tuscher is Karl Beethoven, Renate Richter is Josephine and Fred Delmare is Maelzel. Horst Seeman directed and collaborated on the screenplay with Gunter Kundert. DEFA. Color. In German. 110 minutes.

1971 Beethoven's Birthday
Leonard Bernstein narrates this documentary subtitled *A Celebration in Vienna*. It was made to show how Vienna marks the composer's 200th birthday and there are excerpts from a production of *Fidelio* with Gwyneth Jones, James King and Theo Adam. Humphrey Burton produced and directed. Color. In English. 60 minutes. Video at MTR.

1981 Bernstein/Beethoven
An eleven-part series devoted to the music of Beethoven as analyzed and performed by Leonard Bernstein with the Vienna Philharmonic. Program Four discusses *Fidelio*. The series was directed by Humphrey Burton and screened on CBS in 1981. Color. Videos at MTR.

1985 Beethoven's Nephew
Paul Morrissey's film revolves around the composer's supposed obsession with his nephew and one critic described it as "a high-minded subject with some genuine low-down fun." Wolfgang Reichmann stars as Beethoven, Dietmar Prince is his nephew and Natalie Baye is Leonore. It was written by Morrisey and Mathieu Carriere. Color. In English. 103 minutes. On video.

1989 Beethoven

Anthony Quayle and Balint Vaszonyi visit Beethoven's home in Bonn, talk about his life and music and actors re-create scenes from his turbulent life in Vienna. A film made for the Klassix 13 series. Color. 60 minutes. On video.

1992 Beethoven Lives Upstairs

Beethoven rents the upstairs room in his house and a young boy is annoyed and then impressed by the composer. This Canadian film, shot in Vienna with a good deal of music, is pleasant and innocuous and intended for young people. It stars Neil Munro, Ilya Woloshyn and Fiona Reid and won a TV Emmy. Heather Conkie wrote the screenplay and David Devine directed. Color. In English. 52 minutes. BMG video.

1994 Immortal Beloved

Gary Oldman stars as Beethoven in this big-budget romantic biography written and directed by Bernard Rose and shot on location in Europe and Prague. It focuses on the relationship between the composer and the supposed woman of his life, the "immortal beloved" of the title. Also featured are Jeroem Krabbe and Isabella Rossellini. The glory of the film is the music as performed by Sir Georg Solti and the London Symphony Orchestra. Columbia Pictures. Color. In English. 123 minutes.

BEGGAR'S OPERA, THE

1718 opera by Gay

The Beggar's Opera is the most famous ballad opera and the ancestor of operas by Gilbert & Sullivan and Brecht & Weill. It is the only opera considered to have been created by its writer, John Gay, rather than its composer/arranger, Johann Pepusch. It tells the cynical story of the highwayman Macheath, his involvement with a number of women, his betrayal and imprisonment and his purely arbitrary reprieve. Jonathan Swift suggested the story to Gay when the idea of a corrupt gang of crooks, whores, and informers as protagonists was a novelty. The opera still has bite; the corruption and hypocrisy which Gay satirized have not gone away. See also JOHN GAY.

1952 CBS Television Workshop

Stephen Douglass portrays Macheath with Doretta Morrow as Polly in this American television production on CBS. Also in the cast are Joseph Silver, Odette Myrtil, Bernard Kates, Jack Diamond,

Karen Lindgren and Wyatt Cooper. Norris Houghton produced and Dick Linroum directed. Black and white. 75 minutes. Video at MTR.

1953 Laurence Olivier film

Laurence Olivier stars as Macheath in this British film directed by Peter Brook. Stanley Holloway sings the role of Lockit but the others are dubbed. Dorothy Tutin is Polly Peachum, Athene Seyler is Mrs. Trapes, George Devine is Peachum, Yvonne Furneaux is Jenny Diver, Daphne Anderson is Lucy Lockit, Hugh Griffith is the Beggar, Mary Clare is Mrs. Peachum and Margot Grahame is the Actress. Dennis Cannan and Christopher Fry adapted the text and Arthur Bliss updated the score. The cinematography is by Guy Green and the art direction by Georges Wakhévitch and William C. Andrews. Color. 90 minutes. On video.

1973 Chelsea Theater Center

Timothy Jerome stars as Macheath with Leila Martin as Polly and June Gable as Lucy in this television adaptation of an Obie-winning stage production. The original was produced at the Chelsea Theater Center by George Cappannelli. The cast includes Gordon Connell, Howard Ross, John Long, Joe Palmieri and Jill Eikenberry. It was produced for cable television by Cappannelli and Edward F. Simon. Color. 120 minutes.

1983 Jonathan Miller film

Jonathan Miller produced and directed this production for BBC Television. Roger Daltrey is a stylish Macheath, Carol King a fine Polly, Stratford Johns a powerful Peachum, Patricia Routledge a delightful Mrs. Peachum and Rosemary Ashe a superb Lucy Lockit. The other singing actors are good and the music is authentic with John Eliot Gardiner and Jeremy Barlow arranging the ballads played by the English Baroque Soloists. The choreography by Sally Gilpin is fine and the filming is lively and intelligent. This should be an exciting video but it isn't and somehow never catches fire. Color. 135 minutes. Home Vision & Polygram videos/ Philips laser.

1986 Opera Do Malandro

This is a loose uncredited Brazilian film adaptation of *The Beggar's Opera* which also borrows material from the Brecht-Weill *Threepenny Opera*. The music is by Chico Buarque and the film is based on his stage production set in the 1940s. Smalltime crook Max seduces the daughter of the boss of the prostitution ring and gets himself in hot water. The film stars Edson Celulari and Claudia Ohana and was directed by Ruy Guerra. Color. In Portuguese. 105 minutes.

1991 Jerí Menzel film
Jerí Menzel based the Czech film *Zebrácká Opera* on a 1972 play by Václav Havel derived from the Gay opera. The characters and story are basically the same though Havel updates the story and gives it contemporary relevance. Josef Abraham stars as Macheath, Libuse Sifrankova is Jenny, Barbara Leichnerova is Polly, Veronika Freimanova is Lucy and Marian Labuda is Peachum. Jan Klusak composed the music. Barrandov Film. Color. In Czech. 102 minutes.

BELLA DORMENTE NEL BOSCO, LA
1922 opera by Respighi

The Sleeping Beauty in the Woods is an attractive musical fairy tale and Ottorino Respighi's best opera. It has never entered the repertory because Respighi composed it for Vittorio Podrecca's puppet theater, the Teatro dei Piccoli, but it had great success around the world. The singers sit with the orchestra and lend their voices to the puppets. The opera has unusual singing roles including the spindle that pricks the Princess asleep and the spiders who weave a protective web around her. Gian Bistolfi's libretto follows the Perrault fairy tale closely but Beauty's sleep lasts into the 20th century. See also OTTORINO RESPIGHI

1954 CBS Omnibus video
Jo Sullivan is the Princess with Jim Hawthorne as Prince Charming in this *Omnibus* TV production by Robert Banner. Nadia Witkowska is the Good Fairy, Rosemary Kuhlmann the Queen, Frank Rogier the King, Helen Scott the Nurse, Gloria Lane the Witch and Leon Lischener the Ambassador. Leslie Renfield designed the costumes, George Bassman conducted the orchestra and Julius Rudel supervised the chorus. The opera is sung in English with text by Arnold Schulman and lyrics by William Engvick. It was telecast by CBS on Jan. 31, 1954. Black and white. In English. 55 minutes. Video at MTR.

BELLE ET LA BÊTE, LA
1946 Cocteau film

Jean Cocteau's classic 1946 French film *La Belle et la Bête* retells the romantic fairy tale of Beauty and the Beast most beautifully and poetically. It has had a powerful effect on modern opera composers (as well as make-up artists and set designers) with at least three quasi-operas based on it. Beauty is portrayed in the film by Josette Day with the great Jean Marais superbly effective as the Beast. Cocteau wrote the screenplay as well as directing the film while Henri Alekan created the stunning imges. Georges Auric composed a wonderful score for the film and it has not really been bettered by the opera composers. Black and white. In French. 100 minutes.

1982 Stage work by Bill Nelson
Bill Nelson's score for a stage adaptation of the film by the Yorkshire Actor's Company is not strictly a screen opera though his music, as much as gesture and dialogue, helps to recreate the effect of the film. It was staged in 1982 following the success of a collaboration between the composer and the company on a stage version of the silent film *The Cabinet of Dr. Caligari.*

1994 Screen opera by Philip Glass
Philip Glass's 1994 screen opera *Beauty and the Beast* is an attempt to literally make the movie into an opera. It was composed to be presented with four soloists singing exactly the same words as the actors recite on screen while the film is projected without sound. Whether the Glass music improves the words or the images dominate his atmospheric score is debatable but it is certainly unusual. The opera premiered in New York on Dec. 8, 1994, at the Brooklyn Academy of Music with Glass leading the Philip Glass Ensemble. Alexandra Montano sang La Belle and Gregory Purnhagen was La Bête. The others singers were Hailie Neill and Zheng Zhou. 100 minutes. See also PHILIP GLASS.

1994 Screen opera by Mathias Ruegg
Swiss composer Mathias Ruegg created this version of the Cocteau film for his Vienna Art Orchestra. Ruegg's version is much different from the Glass opera as it does not show scenes from the movie. Instead there are slide projections of text and shapes from Cocteau's films, including *Orphée* and *The Blood of a Poet,* and a Cocteau-like statue that comes to life. When the opera was staged at the

Huddersfield Festival on Contemporary Music in November, 1994, Corin Curshellas sang Beauty and tuba player Jon Sass was the voice of the Beast. In French. 80 minutes.

BELLE HÉLÈNE, LA
1864 opéra-bouffe by Offenbach

The Beautiful Helen is a humorous operetta by Jacques Offenbach based around the saga of Helen of Troy, the most beautiful woman in the world. It features the usual cast of Greek heroes and delights in telling how Paris captured Helen. Henri Meilhac and Ludovic Halévy wrote the libretto for the operetta which has been a hit all over the world. Hortense Schneider starred in the Paris production and Lillian Russell starred in New York. It was revived at the New York City Opera in 1975 with Karan Armstrong. See also JACQUES OFFENBACH.

1951 Sköna Helena
A Swedish adaptation titled *Sköna Helena* was filmed by the Sandrews company in 1951 under the direction of Gustaf Edgren and R. Waldekranz. Black and white. In Swedish.

1957 Lotte Reiniger animated film
Animation pioneer Lotte Reiniger made an abbreviated animated silhouette version of the operetta in 1957. Color. 12 minutes.

1974 Die Schöne Helena
American soprano Anna Moffo stars as the beautiful Helen opposite René Kollo in this well-produced film of the operetta sung in German. The cast includes Josef Meinrad, Ivan Rebroff and Harald Serafin. Franz Allers conduct the Stuttgart Radio-television Orchestra. Axel von Ambesser shot the film in 35mm and stereo for German. television. Unitel. Color. In German. 110 minutes.

BELLINI, VINCENZO
Italian composer (1801-1835)

Vincenzo Bellini is one of the big three of early 19th century Italian opera though he had only ten years in which to compose his masterpieces. He was born in Catania, began his career in Naples in 1825 and became famous in 1826 when `Il Pirata` premiered in Milan. His mastery of the art of *bel canto* was amply demonstrated in *I Capuleti e i Montecchi, La Sonnambula* and *Norma*. He died after

his opera, *I Puritani*, was produced in Paris in 1835. There are surprisingly few videos of Bellini's operas but there are several biographical films with opera scenes. See I CAPULETI ED I MONTECCHI, CASA RICORDI, NORMA, I PURITANI, LA SONNAMBULA.

1935 The Divine Spark
This romantic film about Bellini and his love for singer Maddalena Fumaroli was made in English and Italian versions by opera film specialist Carmine Gallone. A lavish production for its period, the English version stars Phillips Holmes as Bellini, Martha Eggerth as Maddalena, Benita Hume as Giuditta Pasta and Edmond Breon as Rossini. The film tells us that Bellini was a dreamy romantic inspired to write the aria "Casta diva" because of his feelings for Maddalena. Black and white. In English or Italian. 81 minutes.

1935 Casta Diva
The Italian version of the film stars Sandro Palmieri as Bellini with Eggerth again in the role of Maddalena, Bruna Dragoni as Giuditta Pasta, Achille Majeroni as Rossini and Gualtiero Tumiata as Paganini. Walter Reisch wrote the screenplay. It was named Best Italian Film at the 1935 Venice Film Festival. Black and white. In Italian. 95 minutes.

1954 Casta Diva
Carmine Gallone directed this Technicolor remake of his 1935 Bellini biography. The new version stars Maurice Ronet as Bellini with Antonella Lualdi as Maddalena Fumaroli, Nadia Gray as Giuditta Pasta and Fausto Tozzi as Donizetti. The plot is more or less the same with Maddalena again inspiring Bellini to write "Casta diva" so *Norma* can be a success. France/Italy. Color. In Italian or French. 85 minutes.

BELL TELEPHONE HOUR
American television series (1959-1968)

The *Bell Telephone Hour* premiered on television in 1959 after nineteen years on radio and quickly became an important addition to TV opera. Joan Sutherland made her U.S. debut on the program in 1961 and singers like Birgit Nilsson were regular guests. The programs were produced with genuine quality and the specials are still enjoyable on video. Several were produced by Roger Englander and directed by Kirk Browning. See also ANTONY AND CLEOPATRA (1966), THE BARBER OF SEVILLE (1964),

Benjamin Britten (1967), Kirk Browning (1990), Faust (1963), Joan Sutherland (1964).

1947 Rehearsal
Ezio Pinza and Blanche Thebom star in this documentary about the *Bell Telephone Hour* radio show, the predecessor of the TV program. It shows the singers at a Monday afternoon rehearsal for the NBC program. Pinza sings Tosti's "L'Ultima Canzone," Thebom sings "Amour! viens aider mon faiblesse" from *Samson et Dalila* and they join on the duet "La ci darem la mano" from *Don Giovanni*. The film, a Peabody Award winner, ends with Pinza singing as the rehearsal fades into the formal evening performance. Donald Voorhees conducts the Bell Telephone Orchestra. Black and white. 24 minutes. Bel Canto/Video Yesteryear videos.

1967 First Ladies Of The Opera
Sopranos Birgit Nilsson, Leontyne Price, Joan Sutherland and Renata Tebaldi appear on this *Bell Telephone Hour* special on Jan. 1, 1967. Each sings and talks with Donald Vorhees who conducts the Telephone Hour Orchestra. Nilsson sings "Dich teure Halle" from *Tannhäuser* and "In questa reggia" from *Turandot*. Price sings "Io son l'umile ancella" from *Adriana Lecouvreur* and "Pace, pace, mio Dio" from *La Forza del Destino*. Joan Sutherland sings the Bell Song from *Lakme* and "Io no sono piu l'Annete" from the Ricci brothers comic opera *Crispino e la Comare*. Tebaldi finishes the program with "Voi lo sapete" from *Cavalleria Rusticana* and "Suicidio" from *La Gioconda*. Henry Jaffe produced and Charles R. Meeker directed. Color. 53 minutes. VAI video.

1968 Opera: Two To Six
A superb *Bell Telephone Hour* program of Great Operatic Ensembles. Joan Sutherland and Tito Gobbi sing the Duet from Act II of *Tosca*. Phyllis Curtin, Nicolai Gedda and Jerome Hines join for the Trio from *Faust*. Sutherland and Gobbi team with Gedda and Mildred Miller for the Quartet from *Rigoletto*. Curtin, Miller, Gedda and Hines are joined by Charles Anthony for the Quintet from *Die Meistersinger*. And finally the Sextet from *Lucia Di Lammermoor* is sung by Sutherland, Gobbi, Miller, Gedda, Anthony, and Hines. Donald Vorhees conducts the Bell Telephone Hour Orchestra and talks to the singers about their roles. Henry Jaffe produced and Charles R. Meeker directed. Color. 52 minutes. Kultur video.

BELSHAZZAR
1745 oratorio by Handel

Handel's oratorio *Belshazzar*, composed to an English libretto by Charles Jennes, is the story of King Belshazzar of Biblical and Babylonian fame. Handel was very taken with the story of the great king and composed a fine aria for Belshazzar's mother Nitocris describing the tragic fate of empires. The famous writing on the wall is interpreted by Daniel just before the Persians triumph. See also George F. Handel.

1985 Hamburg State Opera
Harry Kupfer staged this production of the oratorio for the Hamburg State Opera. The soloists are Helen Donath, Jeanne Piland, Jochen Kowalski, Walter Raffeiner, Harald Stamm and Karl Schulz. Gerd Albrecht conducts the Hamburg State Opera Choir and Philharmonic State Orchestra. Gunther Bock directed the film for German television. NDR. Color. In English. 139 minutes. Inter Nationes video.

BENATZKY, RALPH
Moravian composer (1884-1957)

Ralph Benatzky is remembered today for his spectacular operetta *White Horse Inn* (Im Weissen Rössl) and his Strauss pastiche operetta *Casanova* with its famous "Nun's Chorus." He was a popular songwriter in Vienna in the 1910s but his greatest success came later in Berlin with the lavish *White Horse Inn*. He also composed a famous Vienna stage musical about Hollywood called *Axel an der Himmelstür* with Zarah Leander as star. Benatzky contributed music to many films, mostly in Germany but also in England and the U.S. He is said to have created 5,000 songs, 250 film scores and 92 stage shows. See White Horse Inn.

BENEDICT, JULIUS
German/English composer (1804-1885)

Sir Julius Benedict, a student of Weber and a friend of Malibran, was an opera composer and conductor in Austria and Italy before coming to England for his greatest success. He was involved with all of the big three "Irish" operas popular in 19th century Britain. He produced Michael Balfe's *The Bohemian Girl* and Vincent Wallace's *Maritana* at Drury Lane and won wide popularity with his own opera *The Lily of Killarney*. He was also associated with Jenny

Lind as her conductor and accompanist. See THE LILY OF KILLARNEY.

BENJAMIN, ARTHUR
Australian composer (1893-1960)

Australian Arthur Benjamin has a place in screen opera history as one of the first composers commissioned to create an opera for BBC television. He was apparently chosen because he had already written an opera for BBC radio. Benjamin began writing operas in 1931 but completed only five. His most popular composition is *Jamaican Rumba*.

1956 Mañana
Mañana was one of the first operas commissioned by BBC Television. It was based on Caryl Brahms' *Under the Juniper Tree* and Brahms wrote the libretto with G. Foa. Benjamin was fond of Latin American rhythms hence the title of this light opera telecast on Feb. 1, 1956.

1958 A Tale Of Two Cities
Benjamin's operatic adaptation of the Dickens novel *A Tale of Two Cities* was composed to a libretto by J. C. Cliffe. It had its premiere on BBC Radio's Third Program in 1953, was staged at Sadler's Wells in 1957 and was then adapted for television and telecast by the BBC in 1958.

BERESFORD, BRUCE
Australian film director (1940-)

Australian director Bruce Beresford, known for such memorable movies as *The Getting of Wisdom* and *Tender Mercies*, has also become a stage director of opera. He has made two films with an operatic connection. His episode of the opera film *Aria* features a romantic homage to Korngold's *Die Tote Stadt*. His Oscar-winning *Driving Miss Daisy* features an aria from Dvořák's *Rusalka*. See ARIA, RUSALKA (1989 film), DIE TOTE STADT (1987).

BERG, ALBAN
Austrian composer (1885-1935)

Alban Berg is known for only two operas, *Wozzeck* and *Lulu*, both derived from works by major writers famous in their own right. Berg's operas have become staples of the international repertory and his reputation continues to grow. They are strangely popular despite their pessimism and their

musical difficulty, perhaps because of the strong emotions he explores and his unique style. He apparently composed slowly and painfully but he infused his operas with genius. See WOZZECK, LULU.

BERGANZA, TERESA
Spanish mezzo-soprano (1935-)

Teresa Berganza was born in Madrid and made her debut in France in 1957 in *Così Fan Tutte*. Her rich, warm voice helped her became one of the most admired singers of her generation, particularly liked in Rossini and Carmen. In the 1980s she appeared mostly in recitals. Berganza's great voice and personality are seen in two major opera films. In Losey's *Don Giovanni*, she plays Zerlina and in Ponnelle's *The Barber Of Seville*, she sings Rosina. See THE BARBER OF SEVILLE (1972/ 1984), CARMEN (1980), DON GIOVANNI (1970), GALA LIRICA, L'ITALIANA IN ALGERI (1957), PARIS (1989).

BERGER, ERNA
German soprano (1900-1990)

Erna Berger made her debut at the Dresden Staatsoper in 1925 in *The Magic Flute* as First Boy and later became one of the world's most famous interpreters of the Queen of the Night. She can be seen in the role in a 1942 film about Mozart and singing a duet from *La Traviata* with Beniamino Gigli in the 1936 film *Ave Maria*. Berger sang at Salzburg from the 1930s to the 1950s and can be seen there as Zerlina in a film made of *Don Giovanni*. She made her debut at the Metropolitan in 1949 as Sophie in *Der Rosenkavalier*. See BENIAMINO GIGLI (1936), DON GIOVANNI (1954), THE MARRIAGE OF FIGARO (1949), WOLFGANG A. MOZART (1942), OTTO NICOLAI (1940), DER ROSENKAVALIER (1949).

BERGMAN, INGMAR
Swedish film director (1918-)

Swedish filmmaker Ingmar Bergman has filmed two operas, used opera in other films, directed opera on stage and written an opera libretto. His *Magic Flute* is one of the great opera films and a fine introduction to the Drottningholm Opera House. Mozart is central to three of his other movies. In the 1952 *Face to Face*, the music is by Mozart. In the 1960 *The Devil's Eye*, Bergman tells his version of the Don Juan legend. In the 1968 *Hour Of The Wolf* a tiny Pamino performs an aria from *The Magic Flute* on a minute stage. Bergman directed for video the

Daniel Börtz opera *The Bacchae* which he staged and for which he wrote the libretto. See THE BACCHAE, THE MAGIC FLUTE.

Börtz, Bergman and the Bacchae
A Swedish documentary about the production of the Daniel Börtz opera *The Bacchae*. It shows director/librettist Ingmar Bergman in rehearsal and features interviews with those involved in the production at the Stockholm Royal Opera. The opera, based on Euripides, was written at the instigation of Bergman. Mans Reuterswärd directed the documentary. Color. In Swedish. 57 minutes. Video at MTR.

BERGONZI, CARLO
Italian tenor (1924-)

The golden-voiced Italian tenor Carlo Bergonzi made his debut in 1948. He sang at La Scala from 1953 to 1970 and was a regular at the Metropolitan Opera from 1956 to 1988. He recorded more than forty roles, most Verdi, and is sometimes considered the heir of Gigli in singing style and quality of voice. Bergonzi's voice is featured on the soundtrack of the films *Moonstruck* and in the *Un Ballo in Maschera* episode of *Aria*. See AIDA (1966), UN BALLO IN MASCHERA (1967), DON CARLO (1950), L'ELISIR D'AMORE (1989), VERONA (1990).

1985 Bergonzi Celebrates Gigli
In October 1985 Bergonzi gave a recital at Carnegie Hall celebrating the art of Beniamino Gigli with nineteen songs and arias made popular by Gigli. The recital was later videotaped in a studio before an invited audience. Bergonzi is accompanied on piano by Vincenzo Scalera while George Jellinek acts as host and commentator. The recital won warm praise from *The New York Times* which noted the continuing quality of Bergonzi's singing. The video includes a pictorial essay by Jellinek comparing the careers of Bergonzi and Gigli. Color. 87 minutes. V & E video.

1989 Carlo Bergonzi as Nemorino
Bergonzi as Nemorino sings two arias on stage in a dress rehearsal of *L'Elisir d'Amore* in a small New Jersey theater. He was 65 at the time and still sounds pretty good. The arias, " Quanta é bella" and "Un furtiva lagrima," are included on the video *Legends of Opera*. Color. In Italian. 8 minutes. Legato Classics video.

BERLIN

Berlin is home to three notable opera houses. Most famous is the Staatsoper Unter den Linden, formerly in East Berlin, which began as the Lindenoper in 1742. The present building dates from 1955. Near it is the Komische Oper which opened in 1966. The biggest is the Deutsche Opera which dates from 1961. All three are fine places to see quality opera in person or on video. See BARBE-BLEUE (1973), JOSÉ CARRERAS (1987), THE CUNNING LITTLE VIXEN (1965), FIDELIO (1970), GIULIO CESARE (1977), LES HUGUENOTS (1993), DER JUNGE LORD (1967), MACBETH (1987), OTELLO (1969), PARSIFAL (1993), SALOME (1990), DIE TOTE STADT (1986), TRISTAN UND ISOLDE (1993).

1976 Gala Unter den Linden
This East German film celebrating the Staatsoper Unter den Linden opera house is a record of a gala evening featuring major stars of the theater who perform arias identified with them. The singers are Theo Adam, Eberhard Buchner, Celestina Casapietra, Renate Hoff, Fritz Hubner, Isabella Nawe, Harald Neukirch, Ruggiero Orofino, Martin Ritzmann, Peter Schreier, Gisela Schroter, Ingeborg Springer, Reiner Suss, Anna Tomova-Sintow, Uta Trekel-Burkhardt and Siegfried Vogel. DEFA. Color. In German. 90 minutes.

1989 Berlin: Capitale de l'Opéra
Claire Newman directed *Berlin: Opera Capital*, a French television documentary about Berlin's high reputation for innovative opera production. It includes footage of noted director Harry Kupfer rehearsing a production of *The Tales of Hoffmann* in Berlin. FR 3. Color. In French. 60 minutes.

1990 The German Center: Kroll
This is a video about a famous now-vanished opera house, the Kroll Opera in Berlin which stood on the Platz der Republik, the "German Center." It opened in 1844 and Caruso was among the many stars who sang there over its century of existence. Johann Strauss was house conductor for two years and Otto Klemperer began to conduct there in 1927. The Kroll was closed in 1931 and torn down in 1951. Jörg Moser-Metius wrote and directed this history of the theater. Color. In English or German. 58 minutes. Inter Nationes video.

BERLIOZ, HECTOR

French composer (1803-1869)

Berlioz wrote five operas but did not have much luck with them in his lifetime. His first surviving opera, the 1838 *Benvenuto Cellini*, was a failure when it premiered and he had problems in getting later operas on stage in any form. His desperate life has inspired two screen biographies. The popular conception of Berlioz is reflected in Claude Chabrol's thriller *Un Double Tour* in which the murderer likes to conduct Berlioz. In recent years *Les Troyens* and *The Damnation of Faust* have been staged and are on commercial video. *Béatrice et Bénédict* and *Benvenuto Cellini* are available as off-air telecast videos from Lyric. See LA DAMNATION DE FAUST, LES TROYENS.

1941 La Symphonie Fantastique
Jean-Louis Barrault portrays Berlioz in this romantic French film about his life and love affairs. Renée Saint-Cyr is singer Marie Martin, who dies while singing one of his arias, and Lise Delamare is actress-wife Harriet Smithson. The music is played by the Conservatory Orchestra of Paris conducted by Marius-Paul Guillot. Christian-Jaque directed. Black and white. In French. 95 minutes.

1992 I, Berlioz
Tony Palmer created this powerful film biography which concentrates on the opera *Les Troyens* and the difficulties Berlioz had in creating and staging it. Corin Redgrave portrays the composer. There are large extracts from *Les Troyens* with soloists and choruses of the Zurich Opera House. Palmer made the film for London's South Bank Show. Color. In English. 90 min. On video.

BERNSTEIN, LEONARD

American composer (1918-1990)

Massachusetts-born composer-conductor Leonard Bernstein had a long association with the movies but not just for opera. He wrote the Oscar-nominated score for *On the Waterfront* and the stage musicals *On the Town* and *West Side Story* which were made into films. *Trouble in Tahiti* and its sequel *A Quite Place* are his only more-or-less traditional operas but the operatic operetta *Candide* and operatic musical *West Side Story* have been staged by opera companies and could enter the opera repertory. Bernstein himself considered them operatic enough to record with opera singers. *On*

the Town has also been filmed with opera singers while *Wonderful Town* was telecast but never filmed. Bernstein had a major television career, beginning in 1954 with *Omnibus*, and won a dozen Emmys. Around 250 Bernstein TV programs from 1954 to 1990 can be viewed at the Museum of Television and Radio which published a catalog of his TV work for a 1985 tribute. Many of his programs are also on commercial video. Selected programs only listed below. See also LUDWIG VAN BEETHOVEN (1981), CANDIDE, THE CREATION (1986), CONDUCTORS (1995), PAUL HINDEMITH (1964), ON THE TOWN, A QUIET PLACE, TROUBLE IN TAHITI, WEST SIDE STORY.

1949-1969 Hollywood Films
Bernstein's earliest connection with Hollywood movies was through the screen adaptation of *On The Town* in 1949. He was nominated for an Oscar for his score for *On the Waterfront* (1954) and composed the scores of *To Kill A Mockingbird* (1962), *Heaven's Gate* (1980) and *Terms of Endearment* (1983). He appears in person in *Satchmo the Great* (1957) and *A Journey to Jerusalem* (1969).

1954-1958 Omnibus TV series
Leonard Bernstein won his first Emmy in 1957 for his *Omnibus* TV programs which were telecast from 1954 to 1958. The March 23, 1958 program was "What Makes Opera Grand?" and on it Bernstein examined facets of opera with excerpts from *Carmen*, *Faust*, *Tristan und Isolde* and *La Bohème*. Black and white. Videos at MTR.

1958 Wonderful Town
Bernstein's 1953 musical, created with lyric writers Betty Comden and Adolph Green, was based on the 1940 play *My Sister Eileen*. It tells the romantic story of two sisters and their adventures in Greenwich Village and has entered the repertory of some opera houses. *Wonderful Town* was never filmed but a TV adaptation was made in November 1958 with Rosalind Russell, Sidney Chaplin, Jacquelyn McKeever and Joseph Buloff. Mel Ferber directed. Black and white. 120 minutes. Video at MTR.

1958-1973 Young People's Concerts
Bernstein telecast these programs on CBS from 1958 to 1973 with the New York Philharmonic. He was an enthusiastic teacher and on these award-winning programs he explains and demonstrates many forms of music including opera. There are also talks about individual composers from Beethoven and

Strauss to Charles Ives. Roger Englander produced and directed the telecasts. Bernstein Society and Sony videos.

1971/1981 Leonard Bernstein's Mass
There are two videos of productions of Bernstein's *Mass*, "A Theatre Piece for Singers, Players and Dancers," which was composed for the opening of the Kennedy Center in 1971. The first dates from 1974 when the work had its European premiere at the Vienna Konzerthaus with John Mauceri conducting the Yale Symphony Orchestra and Vienna choirs. James Schaffer was stage director and Brian Large directed the video. The second production was telecast from the Kennedy Center on Sept. 19, 1981, with Mauceri again conducting. Tom O'Horgan was stage director and Emile Ardolino directed the video. Videos at MTR.

1973 The Unanswered Question
A six-part musical lecture series in which Bernstein examines music using Noam Chomsky's ideas as springboard. The lectures include performances by Bernstein with the Boston Symphony and the Vienna Philharmonic and works by Beethoven, Debussy, Mahler and Stravinsky. The series originated as the Charles Eliot Norton Lectures at Harvard in 1973 and were telecast in 1976. Humphrey Burton was consulting producer. Color. 15 hours. Kultur video.

1974-1989 Great Performances
Bernstein conducted a great many concerts and recitals in America and Europe for the *Great Performances* TV series on PBS. They range from Tanglewood to Vienna and from Mahler to Brahms. Humphrey Burton directed most of these for video. Videos at MTR.

1988 Leonard Bernstein at 70
The Emmy Award-winning video record of Leonard Bernstein's birthday gala directed by Kirk Browning. The performers include Barbara Hendricks, Christa Ludwig, Kurt Ollmann, Beverly Sills, Michael Tilson Thomas, Dawn Upshaw, Frederica von Stade, John Williams and the Boston Symphony Orchestra. Color. 126 minutes.

1993 The Gift of Music
This ambitious documentary attempts to tell the story of Bernstein's musical life with commentary by Lauren Bacall. There are clips of the young Bernstein at the 1947 Prague Festival, on *Person to Person* in 1955 and in later appearances. There are performance extracts, scenes from operas and musicals and archival film footage plus comments from friends. Horant Hohlfeld directed for LWT. Color. 90 minutes. DG video.

1993 Leonard Bernstein's Place
A 75th birthday salute to Bernstein by his friends at Alice Tully Hall in Lincoln Center. Family members and friends remember him including Lauren Bacall, Isaac Stern, Wynton Marsalis and Phyllis Newman. Color. 87 minutes. On video.

1994 Bernstein on Broadway
This is a highlights video featuring excerpts from three of Bernstein's Broadway productions as recorded by opera singers. Featured are *On The Town* with Tyne Daly, Frederica von Stade, Thomas Hampson and Samuel Ramey; *Candide* with Jerry Hadley, June Anderson, Christa Ludwig, Kurt Ollmann and Adolph Green; and *West Side Story* with Kiri Te Kanawa, José Carreras and Tatiana Troyanos. Color. 90 minutes. On video.

BERTOLUCCI, BERNARDO
Italian film director (1940-)

Bernardo Bertolucci, the Oscar-winning director of *The Last Emperor* and *Last Tango in Paris*, has been described as having an "operatic sensibility." The Parma-born director admits to strong influences from Verdi and certainly three of his films have overt opera content. *La Luna* focuses on an American opera singer in Italy and her operatic tour. *The Spider's Stratagem* revolves around a plot to kill Mussolini during a performance of *Rigoletto*. See LA LUNA, RIGOLETTO (1970 film).

1976 Novecento (1900)
1900 is an epic film about modern Italy but it is also a homage to Giuseppe Verdi. The two boys who are the protagonists of the film are born on January 27, 1901, the day on which Verdi dies. Twentieth century Italian history is surveyed across their two families who live in Verdi's Emilia-Romagna region. There is Verdi music on the soundtrack and even a hunchback clown called Rigoletto. Robert De Niro and Gérard Depardieu star. Color. In Italian. 320 minutes. On video.

BEST OPERA ON FILM

The best operas on film are usually operas made by major filmmakers. The consensus best film and probably the most popular is Francesco Rosi's 1984 *Carmen* but Ingmar Bergman's 1974 *The Magic Flute* has a lot of admirers.There are also those who like Franco Zeffirelli's 1982 *La Traviata*, Joseph Losey's 1978 *Don Giovanni*, Max Ophuls' 1932 *The Bartered Bride* and Michael Powell and Emeric Pressburger's 1951 *The Tales of Hoffmann*. However, there is very strong support for a lesser known film described by the British film journal *Sight & Sound* as "an almost forgotten picture with some claim to being the most successful filmed opera." This is Gian Carlo Menotti's 1951 *The Medium*, the only major opera ever filmed by its composer, and it is still as effective today as it was when it was made. It may not be the best opera but *Opera News* once described it as "the most cinematic opera on film." See CARMEN (1984), THE MEDIUM (1951).

BEST OPERA ON VIDEO

The best operas shot on videotape rather than film are records of live performances at major opera houses. The quality of the work by the masters of video techniques like Brian Large and Kirk Browning is such that it often enhances the stage performances. " Best" in this context usually depends on the stage production itself and the quality of the singers involved. Nearly every production shot live at the Metropolitan, San Francisco, Covent Garden, Glyndebourne, La Scala, Salzburg, etc. is finely made and usually worth watching. Videos that have been strongly admired by critics include the Met's FRANCESCA DA RIMINI and THE GHOSTS OF VERSAILLES, Glyndebourne's ALBERT HERRING and DEATH IN VENICE, ENO's MARY STUART and PETER GRIMES, La Scala's LA FANCIULLA DEL WEST, Kirov's THE FIERY ANGEL, Bolshoi's THE QUEEN OF SPADES, Bayreuth's DIE WALKÜRE (1980), Bavarian Opera's THE MAGIC FLUTE and San Francisco's TURANDOT. One of the best recent opera videos is the 1993 Australian Opera production of LA BOHÈME staged by Baz Luhrmann and directed for video by Goeffrey Nottage.. The best series of opera videos are the eight Mozart operas taped at the DROTTNINGHOLM COURT THEATER by Thomas Olofsson for Swedish TV with Arnold Östman conducting relatively unknown singers. They are a pleasure to watch and listen to over and over and are available on laser as well as video for optimum sound.

BEST OPERETTA ON FILM

Operettas have not been well treated by the cinema, possibly because they have been out of fashion for seventy years. Most of the operetta films were made in the 1930s and often much of the original music was abandoned in the filming. The most popular operettas on film in America have been the MacDonald and Eddy pictures for MGM which treat the source material with little respect. The best French film is Straus's *Trois Valses* filmed by Ludwig Berger in 1938 with its stage star Yvonne Printemps. The best English film is the 1939 *The Mikado* directed by Victor Schertzinger with stars of the D'Oyly Carte Opera Company. The best German film operetta is probably Werner Heymann's *Congress Dances* as directed by Erik Charell but the most impressive German film of a stage operetta is a 1975 version of Strauss's *Die Zigeunerbaron* with a starry cast headed by Wagnerian tenor Siegfried Jerusalem. The best operetta film of them all, however, is the 1934 U.S. movie of *The Merry Widow*. It was directed by the masterful Ernst Lubitsch, stars Maurice Chevalier and Jeanette MacDonald with English lyrics by Lorenz Hart. It's a film liked even by those who dislike operettas. See THE MERRY WIDOW (1934).

BEST OPERETTA ON VIDEO

There is not a wide choice in the area as little operetta has been videotaped live in recent years but certainly one of the best is the 1955 American TV production of Herbert's NAUGHTY MARIETTA. It stars Patrice Munsel and Alfred Drake and was directed by Max Liebman who did a fine job of making the operetta into a fine screen experience. The most televised operetta is Strauss's DIE FLEDERMAUS and there are several good video versions featuring top opera singers. The most impressive is the 1983 Covent Garden production with Kiri Te Kanawa as Rosalinde and Herman Prey as Eisenstein in a video by Humphrey Burton.

BETTELSTUDENT, DER
1882 operetta by Millöcker

Karl Millöcker, once as popular as Strauss, had his greatest success with *The Beggar Student*, a combination of romance and revolutionary politics. It has been popular all over the world including Athens where young Maria Callas starred in it in 1945. It is set in Cracow in Poland in 1704. Saxon governor Ollendorf, spurned by Countess Nowalska's daughter Laura, revenges himself by getting her to marry a poor student disguised as a rich count. The two fall in love and the student ends up condemned to death. All ends happily with Polish rule re-established and the student transformed into a real count. The libretto is by F. Zell and Richard Genée. See also KARL MILLÖCKER.

1931 Jarmila Novotná film

The first sound film of the operetta was made simultaneously in two languages with German and English casts. The German film stars Czech soprano Jarmila Novotná as Laura and Hans Heinz Bollmann as the beggar student. The cast includes Fritz Schulz, Hans Juray and Truus van Aalten. Viktor Janson directed. AAFA. Black and white. In German. 64 minutes.

1931 Margaret Halstan film

Margaret Halstan stars as Countess Novalska in the English film of the operetta. Shirley Dale is Laura, Lance Fairfax is the beggar student, Frederick Lloyd is Ollendorff and Jerry Verno is Jan. John Harvel and Victor Hansbury directed. British Lion. Black and white. In English. 64 minutes.

1936 Marika Rökk film

This German film made a star of Marika Rökk who portrays Laura's sister Bronislawa. Carola Höhn is Laura, Johannes Heesters is the beggar student, Bernhold Ebbecke is his friend Jan, Ida Wüst is the Countess and Fritz Kampers is Ollendorf. Georg Jacoby directed for UFA. Black and white. In German. 85 minutes.

1956 Werner Jacobs film

Werner Jacobs directed this West German film of the operetta starring Gustav Knuth as Ollendorf, Waltraud Hass as Laura, Gerhard Riedmann as the beggar student and Elma Karlowa as the Countess. It was written by Fritz Boetiger. Carlton Film. Color. In German. 95 minutes.

1957 Hans Müller film

Hans Müller directed this East German version of the operetta shot in East Berlin with the title of *Mazurka der Liebe*. It stars Bert Fortell, Albert Garbe and Eberhard Krug with a screenplay by A. Arthur Kuhnert. DEFA. Color. In German. 87 minutes.

1977 Laszlo Seregi film

Koldusdiák is a Hungarian film of the operetta made for Budapest television and directed by Laszlo Seregi. The singing is reasonable, the costumes colorful, the acting adequate and the style only a bit kitschy. Harvath Tivadar portrays Ollendorf with Marika Németh as the countess, Zsuzsa Domonkos as daughter Laura, József Kovács as the beggar student, Maria Sempléni as Laura's sister and József Virágh as Jan. Herbert Magg conducts the Hungarian Television Orchestra and Chorus. Color. In Hungarian with English subtitles. 90 minutes. European Video Distributors video.

Early/related films

1908 Henny Porten film

Henny Porten, Germany's first film star, and her father Franz star in this Messter sound film directed by Franz. It features an aria by Ollendorf. About 4 minutes. A print survives in a German film archive.

1922 Hans Steinhoff film

A silent version of the operetta was made in Germany in 1922 directed by Hans Steinhoff. Black and white. About 70 minutes.

1927 Harry Liedtke film

Harry Liedtke and Hans Junkermann, popular German actors in the silent era, star in this film of the operetta. Pioneers Jacob and Luise Fleck produced and directed. Black and white. About 70 minutes.

1962 Musikalisches Rendezvous

This anthology of DEFA opera films made in East Berlin includes highlights from Hans Müller's 1957 film of *The Beggar Student*. Color. In German. 83 minutes.

BETTONI, VINCENZO
Italian bass (1881-1954)

Vincenzo Bettoni made his opera debut in 1902 and began his long Teatro alla Scala career in 1905. He was a popular partner for Conchita Supervia in Rossini operas in the 1920s and sang Don Alfonso in *Così Fan Tutte* in the first Glyndebourne season. He continued to sing until 1950 and can be seen in comic form in two films. See LA SERVA PADRONA (1932/1934).

BEZANSON, PHILIP
American composer (1916-1975)

Philip Bezanson taught music at Iowa University and Amherst and is known primarily as a composer of choral and chamber music but he also wrote two operas, *Western Child* and *Stranger in Eden*. *Western Child* was first performed at the State University of Iowa in 1959 and then revised and presented on NBC television as the television opera *Golden Child*. See GOLDEN CHILD.

BILLY BUDD
1951 opera by Britten

Benjamin Britten's all-male opera tells what happens when pure evil meets pure goodness. The libretto by E. M. Forster is based on a story by Herman Melville and is set on a British warship. Billy Budd is press-ganged into service on the ship and is persecuted by master-of-arms John Claggart. When Budd accidentally kills Claggart, Captain Vere is forced to hang him though he could have spoken in his defense. The opera is told as a memory by the haunted Vere. See also BENJAMIN BRITTEN.

1952 NBC Opera Theatre
American baritone Theodor Uppman, who created the role, stars as Billy Budd in this television production by Samuel Chotzinoff, the American premiere of the opera. Andrew McKinley is Captain Vere and Leon Lishner is Claggart with a cast that includes David Williams, Paul Ukena, Robert Holland, Kenneth Smith and Robert Gross. William Molyneaux designed the sets and Peter Herman Adler conducted the Symphony of the Air Orchestra. Kirk Browning directed the telecast on Oct. 19, 1952. Black and white. In English. 90 minutes. Video at MTR.

1966 BBC Television Opera
Peter Pears sings the role of Captain Vere and Britten conducts the orchestra in this BBC production by Cedric Messina. Peter Glossop as Billy Budd and Michael Langdon as Claggart head a starry cast that includes John Shirley-Quirk, Robert Tear, David Bowman, Bryan Drake, David Kelly and Kenneth MacDonald. Tony Abbott designed the sets and Basil Coleman directed. Black and white. In English. 160 minutes.

1988 English National Opera
Thomas Allen is Billy Budd and Philip Langridge is Vere in this fine English National Opera production by Tim Albery. The cast includes Richard van Allan as Claggart with Neil Howlett, Philip Guy-Bromley, Clive Bayley and Edward Byles. Tom Cairns and Antony McDonald designed the sets and David Atherton conducted the ENO orchestra and chorus. Barrie Gavin's video provides a brief history of the opera. Color. In English. 157 minutes. Home Vision video.

BIOPHON FILMS
Early German sound films (1903-1911)

Biophon films were one-reel movies with sound supplied from gramophone records and many were of opera and operetta arias. They were developed by Oskar Messter beginning in 1903 in Germany and were widespread in Sweden and Denmark within a year. Production of them seems to have finished about 1911. The films usually featured a famous aria in a scene from an opera. Perhaps 300 to 400 were made though not many survive. The difficulty in presenting them was not the film or the disc but the poor loudspeaker systems in the theaters. Biophon films are listed under operas when known.

BIRTWISTLE, HARRISON
English composer (1934-)

Harrison Birtwistle, considered by many as the leading opera composer in England today, is still best known for his first opera, the 1968 *Punch and Judy* created for the Aldeburgh Festival. He was musical director of the National Theatre for many years and learned a good deal about stage techniques. His 1986 opera *The Mask of Orpheus* includes electronic inserts and requires action at an accelerated pace like silent movies comedies of the Keystone Cops genre. His other 1986 opera *Yan Tan Tethera* could also be considered a screen opera as it was commissioned for television. His very cinematic 1995 opera *The Second Mrs Kong*, which was inspired by the RKO film *King Kong*, premiered at Glyndebourne and was filmed by the BBC. See PUNCH AND JUDY, THE SECOND MRS. KONG.

BITTER SWEET
1929 operetta by Coward

Bitter Sweet, Noël Coward's deliberately old-fashioned Viennese-style operetta, was inspired by Strauss's *Die Fledermaus*. It tells the story of Sarah, an English lady of high social position who elopes with her musical teacher Carl. They have a good life in Vienna until he dies in a duel with a count. She later becomes a famous singer. Like its Viennese model, the operetta has a big waltz, "I'll See You Again" and a rousing gypsy song "Ziguener." Coward wrote both music and libretto. See also NOEL COWARD.

1933 Anna Neagle film
Anna Neagle stars as Sarah in this well-crafted adaptation of the Coward operetta produced and directed by Herbert Wilcox. Fernand Gravey is her music teacher Carl with Miles Mander as the amorous count with whom he duels. British and Dominion film. Black and white. 93 minutes.

1940 MacDonald/Eddy film
Jeanette MacDonald and Nelson Eddy star as Sarah and Carl in this lavish film version of the Coward operetta directed by W.S. Van Dyke. George Sanders plays the baron who duels with Carl. The film includes most of Coward's songs and MacDonald is dressed in Adrian's plushest camp creations. Victor Saville produced and Lester Samuels made the screen adaptation. Color. 92 minutes. MGM-UA video.

BIZET, GEORGES
French composer (1838-1875)

Parisian George Bizet began his professional career when his *Le Docteur Miracle*, a comic operetta, won a competition organized by Offenbach and was staged in 1857. His career ended in 1875 with the seeming failure of the tragic opera *Carmen*. He was never to know that he had composed what was to become the most popular opera of all time. Bizet wrote other fine and popular operas like *The Pearl Fishers* and *The Fair Maid of Perth* but it is for *Carmen* that he is acclaimed and will continued to be remembered. It is because of Bizet that the Carmen story has entered the realm of myth. See CARMEN, LES PÊCHEURS DE PERLES.

1930 Georges Bizet
This "musical novelty" about the composer was made by James Fitzpatrick, the creator of the famous cineamtic *Travelogues*. Black and white. In English. 10 minutes.

1942 Hommage à Georges Bizet
A French film about the life of the composer including excerpts from *L'Arlésienne* and *Carmen*. The main singer is Yvonne Gouverné with Julien Bertheau as the poet. Louis Cuny wrote and directed. Black and white. In French. 36 minutes.

1952 Immortal Bizet
A short film telling the story of the composer's life using his homes in Paris and Italy as settings. The film includes selections from several of his operas. Black and white. 26 minutes.

1988 Bizet Concert in Soissons Cathedral
Monserrat Caballé stars in this Bizet concert filmed at the Soissons Cathedral in France. Highlight is a performance of the cantata *Clovis and Clotilda* with Caballé, tenor Gerard Garino, bass Boris Martinovic and the Lille National Orchestra conducted by Jean-Claude Casadesus. Color. 95 minutes. Kultur video.

1995 Bizet's Dream
Maurice Godin portrays Bizet in this HBO film intended for young people. His young piano student learns he is composing *Carmen*, an opera about a soldier and gypsy. As her soldier father is away in Spain, she begins to imagine he has been seduced by someone like Carmen. Brittany Madgett plays the girl and Micaela, Yseult Lendvai is Genevieve and Carmen, Vlastimil Harapes is her father and Don José and R. H. Thomson is Delaborde and Escamillo. The music is played by the Slovak Philharmonic Orchestra of Bratislava conducted by Ondrej Lenard with tenor Gurgen Ousepian but there is very little singing. A bit of *Carmen* is shown on stage at the end. The film was shot in the Czech Republic and directed by David Devine. Color. In English. 60 minutes. Sony video.

BJÖRLING, JUSSI
Swedish tenor (1911-1960)

Jussi Björling is the greatest tenor of the century after Enrico Caruso and some prefer his radiant voice to all others. He joined the Royal Swedish Opera in Stockholm in 1930. In the late 1930s he began to sing in England and America and was a favorite at the Metropolitan. His voice recorded exceptionally well and his records remain popular. His recording of *La Bohème* with Victoria De Los Angeles and Thomas Beecham is considered by many to be the best. Björling can be seen on stage in the video of the Met's pioneer 1950 telecast of *Don Carlo*, in three Swedish films and in videos of television shows. See DON CARLO (1950).

1938 Fram för Framgang
Jussi Björling portrays a young tenor in *Heading for Success*, a Swedish comedy about a singer who has trouble getting heard but eventually becomes an opera star. There are excerpts from *Un Ballo in Maschera* and other operas. The plot revolves around his relationships with a playwright and an actress. The film opened in the U.S. when Björling was appearing at the Met. Gunnar Skaggund directed. Black and white. In Swedish. 89 minutes. Lyric/Bel Canto Society video.

1948 En Svensk Tiger
Björling portrays an opera singer like himself in *A Swedish Tiger*, a Swedish film by Gustaf Edgren. It includes music from *Don Giovanni, The Tales of Hoffmann* and *L'Africaine*. The stars of the picture are Edvin Adolphson, who portrays the "tiger" of the title, with support from Margareta Fahlen, Sven Lindberg and Marianne Löfgren. Black and white. In Swedish. 87 minutes.

1950 Jussi Björling in Opera and Song 1
Björling appeared on the *Voice of Firestone* television series a number of times in the 1950s. Volume One includes scenes from telecasts on March 6, 1950 and Nov. 19, 1951. He is seen in arias and duets from *Faust, Gianni Schicchi, La Bohème, Princess Pat* and *Pagliacci* plus songs by Beach, Brahms and Richard Strauss. His singing partner is his wife Anna-Lisa. Black and white. 40 minutes. VAI video.

1950 Jussi Björling in Opera and Song 2
This second video of highlights from the *Voice of Firestone* TV programs features the tenor on a Nov. 20, 1950 telecast. Björling sings the Flower Song from *Carmen*, the "Neapolitan Love Song" from Herbert's *Princess Pat* and songs by Leoncavallo and Schubert. Black and white. 26 minutes. VAI video.

1953 Resan till Dej
Björling is a featured performer in the Swedish film *Journey to You* directed by Stig Olin. Appearing

with him are Alice Babs, Sven Lindberg and Karl-Arne Holmsten. Color. In Swedish. 88 minutes.

BLACK RIVER
1989 opera by Schultz

Black River is an Australian opera about race relations with music by Andrew Schultz and libretto by Julianne Schultz. A group of people have taken shelter from a storm in a jail where an aboriginal had been found hung. Discussion on how this could have happened leads to an examination of the realities of the relationship between aboriginals and whites. The opera is a collaboration between Australians of European and aboriginal descent.

1993 Kevin Lucas film
This Australian film of the opera stars mezzo-soprano Maroochy Barambah. It was the winner of the Grand Prix at the Opera Screen Festival in Paris in 1993 and toured England in an Australian film festival. It was produced and directed by Kevin Lucas for BBC Television. Color. In English. 90 minutes.

BLAKE, ROCKWELL
American tenor (1951-)

Rockwell Blake made his debut as Lindoro in Washington in *L'Italiana in Algeri* and at the Metropolitan in 1981 in the same role. He has become popular in Europe and sings regularly at the Rossini Festival in Pesaro and at the Aix-en-Provence Festival. He has been given special honors in France where he is considered by critics to be the finest Rossini tenor of our time. See THE BARBER OF SEVILLE (1988), LA CENERENTOLA (1980), DON GIOVANNI (1992), LA DONNA DEL LAGO (1990/1992), ERMIONE (1987), MITRIDATE (1983), OTELLO BY ROSSINI (1988), GIOACHINO ROSSINI (1992).

BLEGEN, JUDITH
American soprano (1941-)

Montana-born Judith Blegen, who began her career at the Santa Fe Festival, learned her craft in Italy and Germany starting in Spoleto in 1963. She sang a wide variety of roles in Nuremberg, Vienna and Salzburg and then made her debut at the Met in 1970 as Papagena. In 1975 she appeared at Covent Garden as Despina. Blegen is particularly admired for the purity and sweetness of her voice. See THE ABDUCTION FROM THE SERAGLIO (1967), UN BALLO IN MASCHERA (1980), THE CREATION (1986), L'ELISIR D'AMORE (1981), DIE FLEDERMAUS (1986), HANSEL AND GRETEL (1982) DER ROSENKAVALIER (1982).

BLISS, ARTHUR
British composer (1891- 1975)

Sir Arthur Bliss is a major figure in film music as well as opera and his score for the 1935 film *Things To Come* was both popular and influential. His other films include *Conquest of the Air, Christopher Columbus* and *Seven Waves Away*. He also prepared the music for the 1953 film of *The Beggar's Opera*. He composed only two operas but one was for the small screen. After the success of *The Olympians* in 1949, BBC television commissioned the opera *Tobias and the Angel* which was telecast in 1960. See THE BEGGAR'S OPERA (1953), TOBIAS AND THE ANGEL.

BLITZSTEIN, MARC
American composer (1906-1964)

Marc Blitzstein was one of the most overtly political of American opera/ music theater composers and wrote his best-known work with encouragement from Bertolt Brecht. The staging of *The Cradle Will Rock* in 1937 was a political event in itself; the cast was locked out of the theater and had to present it at another location. Blitzstein's major opera is his 1949 *Regina* based on Lillian Hellman's *The Little Foxes* but it is not on video. He is also much admired for his contribution to Weill-Brecht's *The Threepenny Opera*. His translation of the opera led to it becoming a popular success in the 1950s and spurred the revival of interest in Weill's European stage work. See THE CRADLE WILL ROCK.

BLOND ECKBERT
1994 opera by Weir

Judith Weir's opera, premiered by the English National Opera in 1994, is based on a mystifying but fascinating 1796 German story by Ludwig Tiech. Eckbert has his wife Berthe tell her life story to Walther. She was raised by an old woman with a dog and a bird that laid jewels and she later ran away with the jewels. Walther says he knows the name of the dog so Eckbert kills him and Berthe dies. Eckbert goes to the old woman's house where some explanations of the psychodrama are revealed. See also JUDITH WEIR.

1994 English National Opera
Nicholas Folwell stars as Eckbert in the English National Opera production by Tim Hopkins at the Coliseum. Anne-Marie Owens is Berthe, Nerys Jones is the Bird and Christopher Ventris is Walter, Hugo and the Old Woman. Sian Edwards conducted the ENO Orchestra. The opera was videotaped and telecast on England's Channel 4 on July 3, 1994 as part of a series on women composers. Color. In English. 70 minutes.

BLOSSOM TIME
See DAS DREIMÄDERLHAUS

BLUEBEARD'S CASTLE
1918 opera by Bártok

Béla Bártok composed only one opera but it is a highly original one with a brilliant libretto by Béla Balazs. *A Kekszakallu Herceg Vara*, also translated as *Duke Bluebeard's Castle*, can be seen in four visually exciting television films. The opera, based on the Bluebeard legend, is the symbolic story of an inquisitive woman who marries a reticent man. She insists in looking behind seven closed doors in his castle despite rumors she has heard. See also BÉLA BÁRTOK.

1964 Michael Powell film
English filmmaker Michael Powell created this version of the Bártok opera for South German Television. Norman Foster stars as Bluebeard and Anna Raquel Sartre plays Judith. Cinematographer Hannes Staudinger and production designer Hein Heckroth helped Powell create the feeling of Bluebeard's torment through decor and lighting. Milan Horvath conducts the orchestra. SDR. Color. In German. 60 minutes.

1981 Miklos Szinetar film
Miklos Szinetar's Hungarian television film is a visual and aural feast. It begins at night with the wife's arrival at Bluebeard's castle and each door she opens becomes a treat for the eyes and the imagination. Kolos Kováts stars as Bluebeard with Sylvia Sass as his new wife Judith. Gabor Bachmann designed the imaginative sets and the splendid costumes were created by Judith Schaffer. Sir Georg Solti conducts the London Philharmonic Orchestra. Unitel/Magyar Televizio. Color. In Hungarian with English subtitles. 58 minutes. London video.

1988 Leslie Megahey film

Director Leslie Megahey interprets the story as if it takes place in Bluebeard's mind. When his new wife visits a room and brings back a souvenir, Bluebeard weeps like the walls of his castle. Robert Lloyd portrays Bluebeard and Elizabeth Laurence is Judith. The opera was produced by Dennis Marks, designed by Bruce Macadie and costumed by Anna Buruma. Adam Fischer conducts the London Philharmonic Orchestra. The film won the 1989 Prix Italia Music Prize. Color. In Hungarian with English subtitles. 64 minutes. Teldec video.

1989 Metropolitan Opera

Samuel Ramey stars as Bluebeard with Jessye Norman as Judith in this Metropolitan Opera production by Göran Järvefelt. Chester Kallman wrote the English translation, F. Murray Abraham acted as host and Hans Schavernoch designed the sets. James Levine conducted the Metropolitan Opera Orchestra. Brian Large directed the telecast in the *Metropolitan Opera Presents* series on March 31, 1989. Color. In English. 70 minutes.

BLUME VON HAWAII, DIE
1931 operetta by Abraham

The Flower of Hawaii is a rather exotic operetta by Hungarian Paul Abraham about an Hawaiian princess working as a French waitress in Paris who falls in love with an American officer. She is taken back to Hawaii to marry the king but true romance wins out in the end. The libretto is by Alfred Grünwald and Bela Löhner-Beda. The operetta was popular in Montreal and is still in the Berlin repertory. See also PAUL ABRAHAM.

1933 Marta Eggerth film

Marta Eggerth stars as the Hawaiian princess in this German film of the operetta directed by Richard Oswald. She is supported by Hans Fidesser, Ivan Petrovitch and Hans Junkermann. Black and white. In German. 85 minutes.

1953 Geza von Cziffra film

Geza von Cziffra directed this German film of the operetta with a greatly changed plot. The story now is about actresses who finally get the roles they want and the men to go with them. It stars Mario Litto, Ursula Justin, William Stelling and Rudolf Platte. Color. In German. 95 minutes.

1992 Sandro Massimini video

Highlights from *Fiore d'Haway* are sung by Italian operetta master Sandro Massimini and his associates on a video from the Italian TV series *Operette, Che Passione!* Featured are "Un paradiso in riva al mare," "Un bambolino piccolino," "My golden baby" and "Bimbe floride." Color. In Italian. About 16 minutes. Ricordi (Italy) video.

BOCCACCIO
1879 operetta by Suppé

This is the most popular of Franz von Suppé's operettas with music worthy of a comic opera and a libretto by Zell and Genée. It tells the story of Italian writer Boccaccio and his life in 14th century Florence when his tales scandalized his fellow citizens. Using intrigues he wins the love of the beautiful Fiametta, the daughter of the Duke. Maria Callas made her stage debut in this operetta in 1940 in Athens at the Royal Opera. See also FRANZ VON SUPPÉ

1920 Michael Curtiz film

Michael Curtiz, the director of *Casablanca*, made a film based on the operetta in Austria after he moved from Budapest to Vienna. Black and white. In German. About 65 minutes.

1936 Willy Fritsch film

German singing star Willy Fritsch portrays Boccaccio in this German film of the operetta directed by Herbert Maisch. Supporting him are Heli Finkzeller as Fiametta, Albrecht Schoenhals, Fita Benkoff, Paul Kemp and Gina Falkenberg. Black and white. In German. 86 minutes.

1940 Clara Calamai film

This Italian film is based on the libretto by Zell and Genée and uses Suppé's music and songs but has a revised plot by Luigi Bonelli. Clara Calamai, best known as the sensual star of Visconti's film *Ossessione*, stars as Giannina, the writer's niece. She disguises herself as Boccaccio but this causes problems for her cousin who is also pretending to be Boccaccio. Osvaldo Valenti is Berto, Silvana Jachino is Fiametta and Luigi Amirante is Scalza. Black and white. In Italian. 80 minutes.

BOHÈME, LA
1896 opera by Puccini

Giacomo Puccini's *La Bohème*, one of the most melodius of all operas with unforgettable arias and great romantic ensembles, has done more to create romantic ideas about Bohemian life than any other work. Early films of the opera are based more on Henri Murger's source novel *Scènes de la Vie de Bohème* than on the poetic libretto by Giuseppe Giacoso and Luigi Illica. At least that's what the film producers claimed when the opera was still in copyright. *La Bohème* is the story of four Bohemians who share an apartment in Paris in the 1830s. Poet Rodolfo has a wistful love affair with seamstress neighbor Mimi while painter Marcello has a tempestuous relationship with flirtatious Musetta. Philosopher Colline and musician Schaunard complete the quartet. Mimi dies of consumption after four acts of the most romantic music ever written. See also GIACOMO PUCCINI.

1949 NBC Opera Theatre
Evelyn Case is Mimi, Glen Burris is Rodolfo, Norman Young is Marcello, Virginia Cards is Musetta and Edwin Stoffe is Colline in this pioneer but still enjoyable English-language NBC Opera Theatre production. Only the last act was presented. Peter Herman Adler conducts the Symphony of the Air orchestra and Kirk Browning directed the telecast. Black and white. In English. 30 minutes. Video at MTR.

1953 Metropolitan Opera
Nadine Conner stars as Mimi in this Metropolitan Opera production telecast in English on the *Omnibus* TV series. Brian Sullivan is Rodolfo, Brenda Lewis is Musetta, Frank Guarrera is Marcello, Norman Scott is Colline and Clifford Harvuot is Schaunard. Rolf Gerard designed the sets and costumes, Howard Dietz wrote the translation and Alistair Cooke made the introductions. Alberto Erede conducted the Metropolitan Orchestra and Chorus and Bob Banner directed the CBS telecast on Feb. 23, 1953. Black and white. In English. 81 minutes. Video Yesteryear video.

1956 NBC Opera Theatre
Dorothy Coulter sings the role of Mimi with John Alexander as Rodolfo in the NBC Opera Theatre production by Samuel Chotzinoff. Jan McArt is Musetta, Richard Torigi is Marcello, Thomas Tipton is Colline and Chester Watson is Schaunard. Peter Herman Adler conducts the Symphony of the Air orchestra. The opera is sung in a translation by Joseph Machlis. Kirk Browning directed the live telecast. Color. In English. 120 minutes. Video at MTR.

1965 Franco Zeffirelli film
Mirella Freni stars as Mimi with Gianni Raimondi as Rodolfo in this film based on a Franco Zeffirelli production at La Scala. Adriana Martino is Musetta, Rolando Panerai is Marcello, Ivo Vinco is Colline and Gianni Maffeo is Schaunard. Herbert von Karajan conducts the La Scala Theater Orchestra and Chorus. Werner Krien photographed and Wilhelm Semmelroth directed the film in a Milan studio but the music was recorded in the Munich Opera House. Historic note: this was the first opera film produced by Unitel and the first music film conducted by Karajan. Color. In Italian with English subtitles. 105 minutes. DG video.
(Highlights version available in Great Moments video series as Volume 11).

1977 Metropolitan Opera
Renata Scotto stars as Mimi opposite Luciano Pavarotti as Rodolfo in this historic Metropolitan Opera production by Fabrizio Melano. It was the first opera to be televised from the new Met at Lincoln Center. Maralin Niska is Musetta, Ingvar Wixell is Marcello, Paul Plishka is Colline, Allan Monk is Schaunard and Italo Tajo is Benoit. Pier Luigi Pizzi designed the sets and James Levine conducted the Metropolitan Opera Orchestra. Kirk Browning directed the telecast on March 15, 1977. Color. In Italian with English subtitles. 120 minutes. Video at MTR.

1982 Metropolitan Opera
Franco Zeffirelli directs Teresa Stratas as Mimi and José Carreras as Rudolfo in this famous Metropolitan Opera production. Renata Scotto is Musetta, Richard Stilwell is Marcello, James Morris is Colline, Allan Monk is Schaunard and Italo Tajo is Alcindoro. Zeffirelli also designed the impressive sets which are applauded. James Levine conducts the Metropolitan Opera Orchestra and Chorus and Kirk Browning directed the video taped Jan. 16 and telecast Jan. 20, 1982. It includes a 20-minute film *Zeffirelli on Bohème*. Color. In Italian with English subtitles. 141 minutes. Paramount video/ Pioneer laser.

1982 Royal Opera House

Ileana Cotrubas stars as Mimi with Neil Schicoff as Rodolfo in this fine Royal Opera House production by John Copley at Covent Garden. Marilyn Zschau is Musetta, Thomas Allen is Marcello, Gwynne Howell is Colline and John Rawnsley is Schaunard. Julia Trevelyan Oman designed the sets and Lamberto Gardelli conducted the Royal Opera House Orchestra. Brian Large directed the video. Color. In Italian with English subtitles. 115 minutes. HBO video and Pioneer laser.

1982 Opera Stories

Charlton Heston narrates a highlights laser version of the above Royal Opera House production. His introductions were filmed in the Latin Quarter in Paris by Keith Cheetham in 1989. Color. In Italian with English subtitles. 50 minutes. Pioneer Artists laserdisc.

1983 Pavarotti in Philadelphia

Pavarotti stars as Rodolfo with the winners of a competition in this Philadelphia production of *La Bohème*. Nine million people, the largest audience for an opera in public TV history, watched the telecast. Brazilian Leila Guimaraes is Mimi, Texan Mary Jane Johnson is Musetta, Italian Franco Sioli is Marcello, Hungarian Laszlo Plgar is Colline, Bulgarian Ivan Konsulov is Schaunard, Brazilian Carmo Barbosa is Benoit and Californian John del Carlo is Alcindoro. Gian Carlo Menotti staged the opera, Franco Colavecchia designed the sets and Olivero de Fabritiis conducted the Philadelphia Opera Orchestra. Kirk Browning directed the video. Color. In Italian. 120 minutes.

1986 Pavarotti in China

Luciano Pavarotti stars as Rodolfo in this production filmed in Beijing's Tianquiao Theater during his China tour. Fiamma Izzo D'Amica is Mimi, Madelyn Renee is Musetta, Roberto Servile is Marcello, Jeffrey Mattsey is Schaunard and Francesco Ellero D'Artegna is Colline. Granco Colavecchia designed the Latin Quarter sets and Gian Carlo Menotti staged the opera. Leone Magiera conducted the Genoa Opera Orchestra and Chorus. Color. In Italian with English subtitles. 120 minutes. Kultur Video.

1988 Luigi Comencini film

Barbara Hendricks stars as Mimi in this film by Luigi Comencini. He films the opera straight but adds ideas of his own, e.g., Mimi knows that Rodolfo is alone in the garret and initiates their meeting by pretending her candle has gone out. José Carreras sings the role of Rodolfo which is acted by Luca Canonici, Angela Maria Blasi is Musetta, Gino Quilico is Marcello, Richard Cowan is Schaunard and Francesco Ellero D'Artegna is Colline. Armando Nannuzzi was cinematographer, Daniel Toscan du Plantier produced and James Conlon conducted the National Orchestra of France and the Radio France Choir. Eastmancolor. In Italian with English subtitles. 107 minutes. Erato video.

1989 San Francisco Opera

Mirella Freni and Luciano Pavarotti star as Mimi and Rodolfo in this acclaimed San Francisco Opera production by Francesca Zambello. Sandra Pacetti is Musetta, Gino Quilico is Marcello, Nicolai Ghiaurov is Colline, Stephen Dickson is Schaunard and Italo Tajo is Benoit and Alcindoro. David Mitchell designed the sets and Tiziano Severini conducted the San Francisco Opera Orchestra and Chorus. Brian Large directed the video. Color. In Italian with English subtitles. 111 minutes. Home Vision video.

1993 Baz Luhrmann film

Australian filmmaker Baz Luhrmann, known for the movie *Strictly Ballroom*, directs the opera as a Paris love story of the late 1950s with a superb young cast. The Bohemians live behind a neon sign that proclaims "L'Amour" and the subtitles make reference to Sartre and Mary Poppins. This is a production that really surprises and delights. David Hobson is outstanding as Rodolfo, Cheryl Barker is fine as Mimi, Roger Lemke is Marcello, Christine Douglas is Musetta, Gary Rowley is Colline and David Lemke is Schaunard. Catherine Martin designed the revolving set and Julian Smith conducted the Sydney Opera House Orchestra. The opera was produced by Australia Opera at the Sydney Opera House in 1990, taped in 1993 and televised in the U.S. in 1994. Color. In Italian with English subtitles. 110 minutes. On video.

1994 Verona Arena

Placido Domingo celebrated twenty five years of appearances at the Verona Arena with a special program of staged opera scenes that was televised in Italy. The program includes Act III of *La Bohème* with Domingo as Rodolfo and Cecilia Gasdia as Mimi. Nello Santi conducts the Verona Arena Orchestra. SACIS. Color. 90 minutes. On video.

Early/related films

1910 Edison film
Enrico Berriel directed this film of scenes from the opera for the Edison Studio. It stars Vittoria Lois and Maria Moscieka and was presented in theaters with live music. Black and white. In English. About 12 minutes. A print has been preserved.

1910 Albert Capellani film
Alberto Capellani directed this French film based on the Murger play for Pathé. Paul Capellani, Suzanne Révonne and Juliette Clarens are the stars. About 15 minutes.

1916 Alice Brady film
Alice Brady, who stars as Mimi, sang Mimi's introductory aria from the theater stage when this American film premiered. Titled *La Vie de Bohème,* it was based on the Murger novel but used Puccini's music as its live orchestral accompaniment. Paul Capellani plays Rodolfo, Zena Keefe is Musetta, Chester Barnett is Marcello and D. J. Flanagan is Schaunard. Albert Capellani directed for Paragon-World. Black and white. In English. About 70 minutes.

1917 Leda Gys film
Leda Gys stars as Mimi in this Italian film by Amleto Palermi. Luigi Serventi is Rodolfo, Alberto Nepoti is Marcello, Biana Lorenzoni is Musetta, Vittorio Pierri is Colline and Camillo Di Riso is Schaunard. The film was based on both opera and novel and was meant to be accompanied by Puccini's music but the composer refused permission. Black and white. In Italian. About 70 minutes.

1923 Wilhelm Dieterle film
Wilhelm Dieterle stars as Rudolfo with Maria Jacobini as his Mimi in this German film directed by Gennaro Righelli. Hans Krähly and Rigelli adapted the Murger-Puccini story. Black and white. In German. About 80 minutes.

1926 Lillian Gish film
Lillian Gish stars as Mimi with John Gilbert as Rudolphe in this *La Bohème,* the most famous silent version of the story. Renée Adorée portrays Musette, George Hassell is Schaunard, Edward Everett Horton is Colline and Gino Carrado is Marcel. The film follows the plot of the opera but

the publisher refused to allow the studio to use Puccini's music. MGM commissioned a new score by William Axt which was then played with the film. King Vidor directed. Black and white. In English. About 96 minutes.

1926 Mi Chiamano Mimi
This Italian children's film takes its title from Mimi's introductory aria and tells the story of *La Bohème* with child actors under the age of ten. This Italian answer to the American *Our Gang* films was written and directed by Washington Borg. Black and white. In Italian. About 60 minutes.

1935 Mimi
Gertrude Lawrence stars as Mimi in this British film with Douglas Fairbanks, Jr. as Rudolphe. It's an adaption of the Murger novel but it uses some music from the Puccini opera. Carol Goodner portrays Musette, Harold Warrender is Marcel, Richard Bird is Colline and Martin Walker is Schaunard. Paul Stein directed. Black and white. In English. 94 minutes. Video Yesteryear.

1937 The Charm of La Bohème
Zauber de Bohème is a "parallel" story of *La Bohème* in that what happens to the opera characters is reflected in the lives of the "real" characters. Hungarian soprano Marta Eggerth stars as Denise with Polish tenor Jan Kiepura as the man she loves. They are opera singers who want to sing together and perform Puccini arias and Robert Stolz songs. When Eggerth learns she will die of an incurable illness, she goes nobly away so he can have a career without worrying about her. They both become famous and finally appear on stage together in *La Bohème.* At the end of the opera she dies on cue just like Mimi. This Austrian film was written by Ernst Marischka, photographed by Franz Planer and directed by Geza von Bolvary. Black and white. In German. 95 minutes. Lyric video.

1939 La Vida Bohemia
An American Spanish-language film based on the story of the opera but without the music. The film has titles informing the audience that the poet and flowermaker got married and so were not immoral lovers. Rosita Diaz is sweet as Mimi while Gilbert Roland is fine as Rodolfo. Joseph Berne directed. Columbia Pictures. Black and white. In Spanish. 88 minutes.

1940 It's a Date
Deanna Durbin sings "Musetta's Waltz" in this Universal film. She portrays the daughter of a Broadway star who wins the role her mother wants. William Seiter directed. Black and white. 100 minutes.

1942 La Vie de Bohème
Maria Dennis portrays Mimi and Louis Jourdan is Rodolfo in this film by Marcel L'Herbier based on the Murger novel. It uses the opera music as its score. Gisele Pascal is Musette, André Roussiin is Marcel, Louis Salou is Colline and Alfred Adam is Schaunard. France-Italy. Black and white. In French or Italian. 92 minutes.

1947 Her Wonderful Lie
The 1937 film *The Charm of La Bohème* was such a success that it was remade ten years later with the same stars, Jan Kiepura and Marta Eggerth. Shot in English in Italy, it again parallels the "real" life of two opera singers with the story of Mimi and Rodolfo. The couple sing Puccini and a bit of *Martha*. The American cast includes Janis Carter, Sterling Holloway, Gil Lamb, Franklin Pangborn and Douglass Dumbrille. The "wonderful lie" is the heroine's denial of her love for the hero so he can be a success. Angelo Questa conducted the Rome Opera House Orchestra, Carmine Gallone directed and Ernst Marischka, Hamilton Benz and Rowland Leigh wrote the screenplay. The Italian title is *Addio, Mimi*. Columbia Pictures. Black and white. 89 minutes. On video.

1953 So This is Love
Kathyrn Grayson portrays Metropolitan Opera soprano Grace Moore in this biopic and finishes on stage at the Met singing "Mi chiamano Mimi." Gordon Douglas directed for Warner Bros. Color. 101 minutes.

1979 Thriller
Sally Potter's provocative film examines the victim role Mimi plays in the opera and reconstructs her death as a possible murder. Colette Laffont portrays Mimi with Rose English as Musetta though much of the film is told through still photographs of performances at the Royal Opera House plus the opera music. The voices on the soundtrack are Licia Albanese as Mimi, Tatiana Menotti as Musetta and Beniamino Gigli as Rodolfo. Color. In English. 33 minutes.

1987 Moonstruck
This film is virtually an homage to *La Bohème*. It begins in front of the Metropolitan Opera as *La Bohème* billboards are put up and focuses on romantic love. Nicolas Cage takes his brother's fiancée Cher to see the opera at the Met after their instant attraction has already disrupted their lives. Act Three is shown with Renata Tebaldi and Carlo Bergonzi singing and Martha Collins and John Fanning acting though the stage scenes were actually shot in Toronto. Musetta's Waltz and the duet "Donde lieta uscì" are also on the soundtrack. *Moonstruck* was directed by Norman Jewison and written by John Patrick Shanley. Color. 103 minutes. MGM video.

1990 Once Upon a Time an Opera
Ugo Gregoretti's under-valued Italian film *Maggio Musicale* revolves around a production of *La Bohème* at the Florence Maggio Musicale. It's a gentle satire on Italian opera people and productions. Malcolm McDowell stars as a producer who battles with singers Shirley Verrett and Chris Merritt who appear as themselves. Pierluigi Santi photographs Florence most beautifully and Ivan Stefanutti's set designs are entertaining. Color. In Italian. 107 minutes.

1990 Awakenings
Nicolai Gedda and Mirella Freni are heard on the soundtrack singing "O soave fanciulla" in this fascinating film based on the experiences of Dr. Oliver Sacks. The music is performed by the Rome Opera House Orchestra led by Thomas Schippers. Robin Williams and Robert De Niro star as doctor and patient under the direction of Penny Marshall. Color. 121 minutes.

1992 La Vie de Bohème
Finnish director Aki Kaurismäki's bittersweet adaptation of the Murger novel is set in a timeless though modern Paris. The plot revolves around painter Rodolfo, poet Marcelle and composer Schaunard and their loves affairs with Mimi and Musette. Color. In French. 100 minutes.

1994 Heavenly Creatures
Kate Winslet is heard singing Mimi's final aria "Sono andati" in this New Zealand film set in the early 1950s. The story is about two strange teenage girls. Peter Jackson directed. Color. 95 minutes. On video.

BOHEMIAN GIRL, THE
1838 opera by Balfe

Fame is fleeting for some famous operas and their composers. Despite his 19th century fame, Irish composer Michael Balfe is known today mostly because of one aria from this opera, "I dreamt I dwelt in marble halls." It is sung by the heroine of the opera, Arline, the daughter of a count who was kidnapped as a child from her father's castle by gypsies as she dreams of her original home. The libretto is by Alfred Bunn. There are some early films and a complete CD but no modern videos of the opera. See also MICHAEL BALFE.

1909 Pathé Frères color film
The earliest film of the opera was made by Pathé Frères in France and released in the U.S. in a tinted version. Color. About 7 minutes.

1922 Ivor Novello film
This is the opera libretto without the music starring England's leading stage musical star of the period, Ivor Novello. Harley Knoles directed this British film with Novello as Thaddeus, Gladys Cooper as Arline and C. Aubrey Smith as Devilshoff. Constance Collier is the Queen of the Gypsies and Ellen Terry is the nurse Buda. The high point of the film is an elaborate visualization of the aria, "I dreamt I dwelt in marble halls," which was accompanied by live music when the film was screened. It was a big success. Black and white. Alliance Film. About 85 minutes.

1927 Johnson and Langley film
Pauline Johnson stars as Arline opposite Herbert Langley as Thaddeus in this silent British Song Films highlights version. Live singers and orchestra performed the arias in synchronization with the screen. H. B Parkinson directed for the *Cameo Opera* series. Black and white. About l5 minutes.

1936 Laurel and Hardy film
Stan Laurel and Oliver Hardy star in this comedy version of the opera. The plot is basically the same with Laurel and Hardy as gypsy pickpockets who raise the stolen girl. The aria "I dreamt I dwelt in marble halls" is beautifully sung by Arline (Jacqueline Wells) over breakfast in their gypsy caravan. Met tenor Felix Knight appears as a gypsy singer. Also featured are Mae Busch, Antonio Moreno and Thelma Todd. James Horne directed and Hal Roach produced. Black and white. 74 minutes. MGM video.

1986 Jessye Norman video
Jessye Norman sings "I dreamt I dwelt in marble halls" on stage at the Royal Opera House in London on April 21, 1986. This scene from the opera was produced for *Fanfare for Elizabeth*, an all-star gala telecast in honor of the Queen. Color. 90 minutes. Video at MPRC.

1993 The Age of Innocence
Martin Scorsese's adaptation of Edith Wharton's novel features the aria "I dream I dwelt in marble halls." Michelle Pfeiffer and Daniel Day-Lewis are the stars. Columbia. Color. 132 minutes.

BOHEMIOS
1904 zarzuela by Vives

Spanish composer Amadeo Vives' famous zarzuela *Bohemians*, like the opera *La Bohème* that preceded it, takes place in the Paris Latin Quarter around 1830. It was also inspired by the Murger novel and probably by the Puccini opera. The Bohemians here are the penniless composer Roberto, who is writing an opera called *Luzbel*, and his poet/librettist friend Victor. Aspiring opera singer Cossette lives next door and falls in love with Roberto through listening to his music. She ends up singing a love duet from his opera with him at an audition. *Bohemios* was written by Guillermo Perrin and Miguel de Palacios and has been very successful in Spain. See also AMADEO VIVES.

1934 Rafael Portas film
The first film of *Bohemios* was directed by Rafael E. Portas and produced in Mexico for Cinematográfica Mexicana. Black and white. In Spanish. 80 minutes.

1937 Francisco Elias film
Spanish cinema pioneer Francisco Elias wrote, directed and edited this film of *Bohemios*. Most of the roles are played by singers and include Emilia Aliaga as Cossette, Amparo Bosch as Roberto, Roma Taeni, Antonio Gaton, Fernando Vallejo and Antonio Palacios. Black and white. In Spanish. 90 minutes.

1968 Juan de Orduña film
Josefina Cubeiro sings Cossette acted by Dianik Zurakowska while Carlo del Monte sings Roberto

acted by Julián Mateos in this fine Spanish film directed by Juan de Orduña. Enrique del Portal sings Victor and Ramon Sola is the impresario Girard. Federico Moreno Torroba conducts the Spanish Lyric Orchestra for this film made for Spanish television and also released on record. Color. In Spanish. 100 minutes.

BÖHM, KARL
Austrian conductor (1894-1981)

Karl Böhm, considered one of the great opera conductors of the century, was particularly admired for his Mozart operas, two of which are on film. He was also a good friend of Richard Strauss, who dedicated an opera to him, and fortunately there are videos of Strauss operas which he conducted. See THE ABDUCTION FROM THE SERAGLIO (1980), ARIADNE AUF NAXOS (1978), ELEKTRA (1981/1981 film), FIDELIO (1970), DIE FLEDERMAUS (1971), THE MARRIAGE OF FIGARO (1976), SALOME (1974).

1994 I Remember...Dr. Karl Böhm
Subtitled *His Life - His Music*, this documentary portrait of the conductor was created to celebrate the 100th anniversary of the conductor's birth on August 28, 1894. The video was conceived and directed by Horant H. Hohlfeld. Color. In German. 60 minutes.

BOHNEN, MICHAEL
German bass-baritone (1887-1965)

German Bass-baritone Michael Bohnen sang at the Metropolitan Opera regularly from 1923 to 1932 and at the Deutsche Opernhaus in Berlin from 1933 to 1945. He was Intendant of the Berlin Städtische Oper from 1945 to 1947 and continued to sing on stage until 1951. Bohnen is featured in a number of German opera and operetta films made in the 1920s and 1930s, including one with Richard Strauss and an attempt to make a "film opera." He was also a featured actor in many non-musical movies. See BENIAMINO GIGLI (1937), OPERAS AS MOVIES (1930), JOHANN STRAUSS (1932), DER ROSENKAVALIER (1926), TIEFLAND (1922), VIKTORIA UND IHR HUSSAR (1931), DER ZIGEUNERBARON (1927).

1929 Sajenko, the Soviet
Bohnen was billed as the bass-baritone from the Metropolitan Opera in this film, a story about Russian refugees in Berlin. Bohnen stars as Sajenko, the Soviet spy, opposite Suzy Vernen as a princess.

Friedl Behn-Grund directed. Black and white. About 80 minutes.

1934 Gold
Bohnen plays a mining scientist with a method of creating gold, Brigitte Helm is his daughter and Hans Albers is the German engineer who opposes him. Karl Hartl directed. Black and white. In German. 120 minutes.

1935 Der Gefangene des Königs
Bohnen plays brawny King Augustus the Strong in this German historical film. Augustus was a Saxon Elector who was King of Poland from 1697 to 1733. Franz Koch directed. Black and white. In German. 105 minutes

1935 Liselotte von der Pfalz
Bohnen plays King Louis XIV of France in this historical drama shown in the U.S. as *The Private Life of Louis XIV*. Renate Müller is the Princess Liselotte. Carl Froelich directed. Black and white. In German. 91 minutes.

1936 August Der Starke
Bohnen is the powerful king Augustus the Strong for a second time on screen. The king has a weakness for wine and women, especially Lil Dagover. Paul Wegener directed. Black and white. In German. 105 minutes.

1939 Das Unsterbliche Herz
Bohnen has a minor role in *The Immortal Heart*, a film about Peter Henlein, the man who invented the pocket watch in 1510. Veit Harlan directed. Black and white. In German. 104 minutes.

1940 Achtung Feind Hört Mit!
Bohnen has a small role in this spy movie starring Kirsten Heiberg. Arthur Maria Rabenalt directed. Black and white. In German. 100 minutes.

1940 Der Liebe Augustin
Bohnen gets to sing again in this Austrian musical about a famous Viennese beer cellar singer of the 18th century. E. W. Emo directed. Black and white. In German. 94 minutes.

1940 Die Rothschilds
Bohnen has a small role in this film about the Rothschild banking family. It was banned after the

war. Erich Waschneck directed. Black and white. In German. 94 minutes.

1943 Münchhausen
This famous color fantasy extravaganza features Bohnen as Count Karl von Braunschweig. Hans Albers plays Baron Munchausen. Josef von Backy directed. Color. In German. 130 minutes.

1945 Meine Herren Söhne
Bohnen has a small role in this family-style movie starring Monika Burg. Robert A. Stemmle directed. Black and white. In German. 85 minutes.

BOITO, ARRIGO
Italian composer/librettist (1842-1918)

Arrigo Boito is famous both as a composer (*Mefistofele*) and a librettist for Verdi and Ponchielli. His texts for *Falstaff* and *Otello* are among the finest and much credit is given him for persuading Verdi to write his last two operas. Boito studied at the Milan Conservatory and wrote the text for Verdi's *Inno delle Nazione* a year after graduation. His other noted librettos are *La Gioconda* for Ponchielli, and the revision of *Simon Boccanegra*. His other opera, *Nerone*, is not widely performed though the publication of its libretto was a literary event. Arrigo's brother Camillo was also a writer and his story provided the basis for Visconti's operatic film *Senso*. See MEFISTOFELE , NERONE.

BOLCOM, WILLIAM
American composer (1938-)

William Bolcom, who moves between ragtime, cabaret and classical music with his wife Joan Morris, began his opera career in 1960 with *Dynamite Tonight*. He has tried to avoid European styles in his operas and has made recordings of many different kinds of music. His 1990 opera *Casino Paradise* is on CD. His opera career was spotlighted when his opera *McTeague* premiered at the Chicago Lyric Theater in 1992. Based on the novel that inspired the film *Greed* and directed by Robert Altman, it attracted attention for connecting cinema and opera. See MCTEAGUE.

BOLES, JOHN
American baritone (1895-1969)

Texas baritone John Boles was a mainstay of the Hollywood operetta in its heyday in the 1930s after creating a reputation on Broadway. He was the Red Shadow in the first film version of *The Desert Song* in 1929 and the singing hero of the even more successful *Rio Rita* the same year. In 1934 he co-starred with Gloria Swanson in the film of Jerome Kern's operetta *Music in the Air*. He sang with Met soprano Gladys Swarthout in two movies, first in the 1935 *Rose of the Rancho* and then in the 1938 *Romance in the Dark*. In the last he fihad the chance to try his voice out on a genuine opera duet, joing her in "La ci darem la mano" from *Don Giovanni*. See THE DESERT SONG (1929), MUSIC IN THE AIR (1934), RIO RITA (1929), GLADYS SWARTHOUT (1935, 1938).

BOLSHOI OPERA
Moscow opera house (1856-)

The Bolshoi (the word means "Grand") Opera is the principal opera house in Russia and one of the most famous in the world. The original theater was built in 1825 and the present building dates from 1856. The opera house can be seen in all its glory in a number of films and videos. See BORIS GODUNOV (1978/ 1987), MONTSERRAT CABALLÉ (1989), EUGENE ONEGIN (1993), KHOVANSHCHINA (1979), A LIFE FOR THE TSAR (1992), MLADA (1992), THE QUEEN OF SPADES (1983).

1951 The Grand Concert
Bolshoi Koncert, released in the U.S. as *The Grand Concert*, is a first-class opera/dance recital film directed by Vera Stroyeva who also made two major Soviet films of operas. The first 45 minutes is devoted to excerpts from *Prince Igor* with Alexander Pirogov as Igor, Yevgeniya Smolenskay as his wife and Maxim Mikhailov as Khan Konchak. Olga Lepeshinskaya is the main dancer in the Polovetsian Dances sequence. Other highlights include Mark Reizen singing an aria from *Ivan Susanin* and Ivan Kozlovsky singing Lensky's aria from *Eugene Onegin*. Black and white. In Russian. 105 minutes. On Japanese laser.

1989 Great Gala for Armenia
This is an all-star gala concert at the Bolshoi Opera in 1989 held to raise money for the victims of the earthquake in Armenia. The singers include

Yevgeny Nesterenko, Alfredo Krauss, Hermann Prey, Carlo Bergonzi and Irina Arkhipova. Color. 120 minutes. Kultur video.

BONANOVA, FORTUNIO
Spanish baritone (1896-1969)

Fortunio Bonanova is better known as a film actor than as an opera singer but he sang widely in Europe in the 1920s. He began his opera career in Madrid, appeared as Escamillo in *Carmen* in Paris and then toured Europe and Latin America. He reached Broadway in 1930 and then moved on to Hollywood. His first film was made in 1922 in Spain, a version of the classic *Don Juan Tenorio*, and he was featured in Spanish-language shorts at the beginning of the sound era. His real Hollywood career began in 1932 with *A Successful Calamity* in which he played a musician sponsored by Mary Astor. His greatest role came in the Orson Welles film *Citizen Kane* in which he plays the despairing vocal coach of would-be opera singer Susan Alexander Kane. When she attempts to sing "Una voce poco fa," he knows she can't make the grade and so does she. His other films include *Tropic Holiday, The Black Swan, Five Graves to Cairo, Blood and Sand, An Affair to Remember, Double Indemnity, For Whom the Bell Tolls, The Moon Is Blue* and *September Affair*. He also appeared in a few Mexican films and in television series. See also CITIZEN KANE.

BONELLI, RICHARD
American baritone (1887-1980)

Richard Bonelli studied under Jean de Reszke in Paris and made his debut at the Brooklyn Academy in 1915 as Valentin in *Faust*. He established his reputation in Europe with the San Carlo Opera and other companies and then returned to the U.S. for performances in Chicago and San Francisco. He made his debut at the Metropolitan in 1932 as Germont opposite Rosa Ponselle's Violetta. He was usually cast in Verdi operas but he also featured as Valentin and as Tonio in *Pagliacci*.

1928 Fox Movietone Numbers
Bonelli starred in two sound films for Fox in 1928 in a series titled *Movietone Numbers*. They were intended to compete with the Vitaphone opera shorts. In the films he performs Tonio's Prologue from *Pagliacci* and Figaro's "Largo al Factotum" from *The Barber of Seville*. Black and white. About eight minutes each.

1933 Enter Madame
Richard Bonelli and Nina Koschetz are the featured singers in this romantic comedy set partially in the world of opera. There are selections from *Cavalleria rusticana, Tosca* and *Il Trovatore*. The film is the story of millionaire Cary Grant and his marriage to opera singer Elissa Landi. Elliott Nugent directed. Paramount. Black and white. 81 minutes.

1941 The Hard-boiled Canary
Richard Bonelli is featured opposite soprano Susanna Foster just getting started in movies. She plays a hard-boiled burlesque singer named Toodles who becomes an opera diva at a music camp. Andrew L. Stone directed. Also known as *There's Magic in Music*. Paramount. Black and white. 80 minutes.

BOORMAN, JOHN
English film director (1933-)

John Boorman, known for such powerful films as *Point Blank* and *Deliverance*, has featured Wagnerian opera music in several of his films. In *Excalibur* (1981) there are extracts from *Die Götterdämmerung, Tristan und Isolde* and *Parsifal*. In *Hope and Glory* (1987) it is the appropriate music from *Die Meistersinger* that helps a World War II blimp to soar. See DIE MEISTERSINGER VON NÜRNBERG (1987 film).

BOREADES, LES
1763 opera by Rameau

French composer Jean-Philippe Rameau's opera Les Boreades, composed to a libretto by Louis De Cahusac, has been recorded by John Eliot Gardiner but is rarely staged. The Boreads of the title are descendents of the wind god Boreas. Their Queen wants to marry a non-Boread and decides to abdicate for love but the Gods work out a better solution. The opera was considered subversive when abdication was considered a very bad idea. Folklore holds that the Paris Opera house burned down during its rehearsals.

1987 Robert Altman film
Robert Altman's episode of the opera film *Aria* is based around Rameau's opera and derives from the legend that inmates of French insane asylums in the 18th century were invited to the opera once a year. In the film they attend a performance of *Les Boreades* at the Ranelagh Theater in Paris. Altman made the

film after staging *The Rake's Progress* in Lyons, the final scene of which is set in a Hogarthian lunatic asylum. The stage performance of the opera is never shown in the film, we see only the audience. The actors include Genevieve Page as a brothel keeper, Julie Hagerty, Bertrand Bonvoisin, Cris Campion and Delphine Rich. The singers are Jennifer Smith, Anne-Marie Rodde and Philip Langridge with John Eliot Gardiner conducting the Monteverdi Choir and English Baroque Soloists. See also ROBERT ALTMAN, ARIA.

BORIS GODUNOV
1869 opera by Mussorgsky

Mussorgsky's *Boris Godunov* was completed in 1869, first performed in 1874 and then promoted to success by Rimsky-Korsakov with a revised orchestration (of which purists now disapprove). It became popular in the West when Chaliapin began singing the role of Boris in the great opera houses. Mussorgsky based his libretto on a Pushkin tragedy. Tsar Boris Godunov murders Dimitri, the young heir, so he can assume the throne. When another young man, Grigory, pretends to be Dimitri, many people believe him and Boris himself is full of doubts. The opera has been very popular with filmmakers. See also NICOLAI GHIAUROV (1986), KIROV OPERA HOUSE (1992), MODEST MUSSORGSKY.

1954 Alexander Pirogov film
Alexander Pirogov stars as Boris in this excellent Soviet film directed by Vera Stroyeva. There are massive sets, huge crowds, elaborate costumes and location scenes at the Kremlin, Moscow squares and monasteries. Georgy Nellep sings Dimitri, Maksim Mikhailov is Pimen, Aleksei Krivchenya is Varlaam, Ivan Kozlovsky is the Fool and Larissa Avdeyeva is Marina. Vasily Nebolsin conducts the Bolshoi Theater Orchestra and Chorus. N. Golovanov and Stroyeva wrote the screenplay and V. Nikolayev was cinematographer. Mosfilm. Color. In Russian with English subtitles. 105 minutes. Corinth video and laser.

1961 Giorgio Tozzi video
Giorgio Tozzi stars as Boris in this NBC Opera Theatre production by Samuel Chotzinoff. Frank Poretta is Dimitri, Gloria Lane is Marina, Richard Cross is Pimen, Andrew McKinley is Prince Shuisky, Joan Caplan is the Nurse and Lee Cass is Rangoni. Peter Herman Adler conducts the Symphony of the Air Orchestra. The English translation is by John Gutman. Kirk Browning directed for TV. Black and white. In English. 120 minutes. Lyric Video.

1962 Jerome Hines video
Jerome Hines sings the role of Boris in an extended scene from the opera on the *Voice of Firestone* television program on Nov. 18, 1962. The excerpt begins with the introduction to the Coronation Scene and presents the Farewell and Death of Boris. The scenes are staged with sets and extras and Howard Mitchell conducts the orchestra. The excerpt is on the video *Jerome Hines in Opera and Song*. Black and white. In Russian with English introduction. 12 minutes. VAI video.

1978 Yevgeny Nesterenko at the Bolshoi
Yevgeny Nesterenko stars as Boris Godunov in this powerful Bolshoi Opera stage production with Boris Khaikin conducting the Bolshoi Theater Orchestra and Chorus. Vladislav Piavko is Dimitri the Pretender, Artur Eisen is Varlaam, Irina Arkipova is Marina, Valery Yaroslavtsev is Pimen, Galina Kalinina is Xenia and Aleksei Maslennikov is the Fool. This is the Rimsky-Korsakov version. Color. In Russian with English subtitles. 181 minutes. Kultur video.

1980 Ruggero Raimondi in Paris
Ruggero Raimondi stars as Boris in this production at the Paris Opéra House. He is supported by contralto Zehava Gal, soprano Christine Barbaux and tenor Kenneth Riegel. Ruslan Raichev conducts the Paris Opéra Orchestra and Chorus. Color. In Russian. 180 minutes. Lyric video/Japanese laserdisc.

1987 Yevgeny Nesterenko at the Bolshoi
Yevgeny Nesterenko stars as Boris for the second time in this Bolshoi Opera production by Irina Morozova with Alexander Lazarev conducting the Bolshoi Opera Orchestra and Chorus. Vladislav Piavko is Dimitri, Tamara Sinyavskaya is Marina, Alexander Vedernikov is Pimen, Artur Eizen is Varlaam, Alexander Fedis is the Fool, Nelya Lebedeva is Xenia, Tatiana Yerastova is Fyodor, Raisa Kotova is the Nurse and Vladimir Kudryashov is Prince Shuisky. Leonid Baratov staged the original production of the Rimsky-Korsakov version. Derek Bailey directed the video. Color. In Russian with English subtitles. 171 minutes. Home Vision video.

1989 Ruggero Raimondi film

Ruggero Raimondi stars as Boris in this film by Polish director Andrzej Zulawski. Kenneth Riegel is Prince Shuisky, Galina Vishnevskaya sings Marina acted by Delphine Forest, Romuald Tesarowicz is Varlaam, Paul Pliska sings Pimen acted by Bernard Lefort, Vyaceslav Pokosov sings Dimitri acted by Pavel Slaby and Nicolai Gedda sings the Simpleton also acted by Pavel Slaby. The cinematography is by Andrzej Jaroszewic and Pierre-Laurent Chenieux and the set designs are by Nicolas Dvigoubsky. Mstislav Rostropovitch conducted the National Symphony Orchestra of Washington. Color. In Russian. 115 minutes.

1990 Andrei Tarkovsky video

Soviet film director Andrei Tarkovsky first staged this powerful production at Covent Garden in 1983. It was restaged at the Kirov Theater in St. Petersburg by Stephen Lawless with a mostly Russian cast. Robert Lloyd stars as Boris, Alexei Steblianko is Grigory, Olga Borodina is Marina, Alexander Morozov is Pimen, Vladimr Ognovenko is Varlaam, Sergei Leiferkus is Rangoni, Larissa Dyatkova is Fyodor and Yevgeny Boitsov is Shuisky. Nicholas Dvigoubsky designed the sets and costumes and Valery Gergiev conducts the Kirov Theater Orchestra and Chorus. Humphrey Burton directed the video. In Color. In Russian with English subtitles. 221 minutes. London video and laser.

1991 Vladimir Matorin film

Russian basso Vladimir Matorin stars as Boris in this Russian film of the opera shot in Moscow by Olga Ivanova. The other singers include Sasha Belyaev, T. Yas'ko, V. Kirnos, L. Kurdiumova, V. Voinarovsky and A. Kicighin. V. Kolobov conducts the orchestra. Color. In Russian. 292 minutes. Italian video/ Japanese laserdisc.

Early/related films

1907 Boris Godunov

This historic silent Russian film of scenes from the Pushkin play on which the opera is based was the first fiction film ever made in Russia. Director I. Shuvalov filmed the scenes at the Eden summer theater in St. Petersburg. About 11 minutes.

1927 John Barclay on Vitaphone

English baritone John Barclay sings an aria from Boris Godunov in imitation of Chaliapin in this Vitaphone sound film. Black and white. About 10 minutes.

1953 Boris Gmirya film

Ukrainian basso Boris Gmirya (or Borys Hmyrya in Ukrainian) is the main star of the 1953 Soviet concert film *Ukrainian Concert Hall* and his aria from *Boris Godunov* is the highlight of the concert. Boris Barnett directed the film. Color. In Russian with English subtitles. 52 minutes.

1963 Panorama of Russia

The Soviet documentary *Pesni Rossii* (Panorama of Russia) is basically a musical tour of the USSR with opera singers Irina Arkipova and Boris Shtokolov. The selections include an excerpt from *Boris Godunov*. Yefil Uchitel directed the film. Black and white. In Russian. 65 minutes.

1966 The Opera Makers

Bulgarian basso Nicolai Ghiaurov stars as Boris in this documentary about preparations for a production of *Boris Godunov* at the Chicago Lyric Opera. The filmmakers follow the production from casting through first night. Bruno Bartoletti leads the Chicago Lyric Opera Orchestra and Chorus. The film was written by Hal Wallace, photographed by Morry Bleckman and directed by Al Schwartz for WBKB-TV in Chicago. Color. In English. 60 minutes.

1986 Boris Godunov

This is an epic non-operatic Soviet film of the story of Tsar Boris based on the original Pushkin poem. It was directed by Sergei Bondarchuk who made the seven-hour Soviet film of *War and Peace*. Bondarchuk portrays Boris with support from Alexander Soloviev, Adriana Bierdjinskay and Antatoli Romanchine. Color. In Russian. 164 minutes.

BORKH, INGE
Swiss soprano (1921-)

The great Swiss lyric/dramatic soprano Inge Borkh was most famous for her performances as Salome and Elektra. They are widely available on record but there appears to be only one video of her in performance. She sings the role of Jocasta in Stravinsky's *Oedipus Rex* on a Leonard Bernstein television program. See LEONARD BERNSTEIN (1961).

BORODIN, ALEXANDER
Russian composer (1833-1887)

Borodin attempted to be both a chemist and a composer and not surprisingly did not have time to finish most of his operas. He labored over *Prince Igor*, for example, for eighteen years and never did complete it. What we see on stage is the completion made by colleagues Rimsky-Korsakov and Glazunov even though the magnificent melodies are all Borodin's. To the non-opera public Borodin is known as the man who wrote the original music for the pastiche operetta *Kismet*, a success on stage and screen and now a classic of music theater. See KISMET, PRINCE IGOR.

BOSE, HANS-JÜRGEN VON
German composer (1953-)

Hans-Jürgen von Bose is not yet well known in the U.S. but he has completed a number of operas and two have been filmed for German television. They are the 1981 *Die Nacht aus Blei* (A Night of Lead) and the 1984 *Die Leiden des Jungen Werthers* (The Sorrows of Young Werther). See DIE LEIDEN DES JUNGEN WERTHERS.

1987 Hans-Jürgen von Bose
A German documentary about Bose made for the *Young German Composers* series. It includes scenes from *A Night of Lead* and *The Sorrows of Young Werther* and extracts from his *Three Songs*. Detlef-Michael Behrens wrote and directed the film. Color. In English or German. 17 minutes. Inter Nationes video.

BOULEZ, PIERRE
French conductor/composer (1925-)

Pierre Boulez was not attracted to opera when he was a composer and once suggested that opera houses should be blown up. He changed his mind after he became an opera conductor. His *Ring Cycle* at Bayreuth was the first complete *Ring* to be televised and made available on video. See BAYREUTH (1985), GÖTTERDÄMMERUNG (1980), PELLÉAS ET MÉLISANDE (1992), DAS RHEINGOLD (1980), DER RING DES NIBELUNGEN (1980/1980 film), ARNOLD SCHOENBERG (1989), SIEGFRIED (1980), IGOR STRAVINSKY (1968), TRISTAN UND ISOLDE (1967), RICHARD WAGNER (1987), DIE WALKÜRE (1980).

1989 Pierre Boulez - The Birth of Gesture
Oliver Mille's documentary centers around classes given by Boulez at Villeneuve-les-Avignon in July 1988. He is shown advising young conductors as they direct the InterContemporain Ensemble. There is also footage of Boulez in rehearsal in 1988 with the BBC Symphony Orchestra and Jessye Norman. Included are extracts from compositions by Boulez sung by Phyllis Bryn-Julson. Amaya. Color. In French. 55 minutes. On video.

BOWMAN, JAMES
English countertenor (1941-)

James Bowman is one of the singers who has helped make the countertenor voice popular today. He made his debut as Oberon at Aldeburgh in Britten's *A Midsummer Night's Dream* in 1967 and became famous singing the role around the world. He can be seen on video in the role at Glyndebourne. Bowman is well suited to both modern and baroque operas but is particularly associated with Handel. He is the villainous Ptolemy in the ENO English production of Handel's `Giulio Cesare` and portrays the castrato who originated the role of Rinaldo in the film *Honour, Profit and Pleasure*. See DEATH IN VENICE (1981), GIULIO CESARE (1984), A MIDSUMMER NIGHT'S DREAM (1981), RINALDO.

BRECHT, BERTOLT
German librettist/dramatist (1898 - 1956)

German poet-playwright Bertolt Brecht is important in the operatic world for his collaborations with composer Kurt Weill from 1927 to 1933 in Germany. Together they revolutionized ideas about the relevance of the musical stage, especially with their hugely successful *The Threepenny Opera*. Nearly as notable are *Happy End, Rise and Fall of the City of Mahagonny* and *The Seven Deadly Sins*. Although both men fled the Nazi regime and ended up in the U.S. they never worked together again. See also MARC BLITZSTEIN, HAPPY END, DER LINDBERGHFLUG, RISE AND FALL OF THE CITY OF MAHAGONNY, THE SEVEN DEADLY SINS, THE THREEPENNY OPERA, KURT WEILL.

BREEN, BOBBY
Canadian/American boy soprano (1927-)

Bobby Breen, who began his vocal career on the Eddie Cantor radio show and became the singing equivalent of Shirley Temple for RKO, sometimes featured opera arias in his films of the late 1930s. He became an instant star with his opera-oriented first film, the 1936 *Let's Sing Again*, and made eight films in all. Also successful were *Rainbow on the River*, *Make a Wish* and *Hawaii Calls*. After his movie career ended in 1942, Breen became a nightclub singer.

1936 Let's Sing Again

Breen plays a boy living in an orphanage, the son of a opera singer, who joins an old Italian singer called Pasquale (Henry Armetta) in a travelling theater. Pasquale is a once-famous tenor who has lost his voice but kept the opera records he made in his early years. He teaches Breen to sing opera arias beginning with "La donna é mobile" and the boy is a hit in the show. Eventually Breen's opera singing father, who has been searching for him, finds him for a happy ending. Black and white. 65 minutes. Video Yesteryear video.

BRETÓN, TOMAS

Spanish composer (1850-1923)

Tomas Bretón y Hernandez is one of the best known composers of zarzuelas. He devoted much of his life to trying to create truly Spanish operas but could never arouse great interest in his own except for *La Dolores*. He is primarily remembered for his enjoyable 1894 zarzuela *La Verbena de la Paloma*. It is especially liked for its portrayal of working class Madrid street life and has been filmed three times. See LA VERBENA DE LA PALOMA.

BRIGANDS, LES

1869 opéra-bouffe by Offenbach

Jacques Offenbach's satirical operetta is the story of an Italian bandit band as imagined by creative librettists Ludovic Halévy and Henry Meilhac. Business is bad for the bandits as there are bigger thieves in banks and government. The bandit chief's daughter and a chocolate shop owner have a flirtation but the Duke of Mantua wins her heart. The Carabinieri police threaten but always arrive too late. *Les Brigands* is the French counterpart of a Gilbert and Sullivan satire, a pleasant diversion with infectious melodies and double-dyed deception. It was very popular in the 19th century and has had many recent revivals. See also JACQUES OFFENBACH.

1989 Lyons Opera

This lively Opéra de Lyon production transposes the high jinks of the Italian bandits to gangland Chicago. Michel Trempont is gang leader Falsacappa with Valerie Chevalier as his fickle daughter Fiorella and Colette Alliot-Lugas as Fragoletto, the chocolate shop owner who loves her. Stage directors Louis Erlo and Alain Maratrat use a gigantic but well-utilized three-level set designed by Gian Maurizio Fercioni. The updated libretto is by Maratrat. Claire Gibault conducts the Opéra de Lyon Orchestra and Chorus. Jean-Marie Bergis photographed and Yves André Hubert directed the film. Color. In French with English subtitles. 122 minutes. Pioneer laser and video.

BRIGNONE, GUIDO

Italian film director (1887-1959)

Guido Brignone began working in the cinema in 1913 and directed movies from 1930 to 1958. He was a specialist in musical films which often featured opera singers. Brignone helped create Tito Schipa's cinema career with the hit movie *Vivere*, directed Beniamino Gigli in *Mamma* and made three of Giuseppe Lugo's films. One of his best movies is the 1943 *Maria Malibran* with Maria Cebotari as the great diva. See BENIAMINO GIGLI (1941), GIUSEPPE LUGO (1939/1940/ 1942), MARIA MALIBRAN (1943), TITO SCHIPA (1936/1938), LA WALLY (1932).

BRITTEN, BENJAMIN

English composer (1913-1976)

Benjamin Britten almost single-handedly revived the reputation of British opera. His 1945 *Peter Grimes* created a sensation and nearly every work afterwards was accepted as a classic. His sympathy for innocence badly treated is seen in many of his operas including *Peter Grimes* and *Billy Budd*. Some critics see in this a reflection of his problems in being gay in a less tolerant era. The potency of his last opera, *Death in Venice* based on the Thomas Mann novel, is another aspect of this. Britten's lifetime companion Peter Pears had roles in almost all of Britten's operas. Britten was given a peerage in 1976. The first operas by Britten to be televised were *Let's Make an Opera* on BBC in 1950 and *Billy Budd* on NBC TV in 1952. Britten also composed music for films including memorable scores for documentaries like *Night Mail*. He founded the famous Aldeburgh Festival in Suffolk in 1948. See ALBERT HERRING, BILLY BUDD, DEATH IN VENICE,

GLORIANA, A MIDSUMMER NIGHT'S DREAM, PETER GRIMES, THE TURN OF THE SCREW, WAR REQUIEM.

1936-1938 British documentary films
Britten wrote music for British documentary films from 1936 to 1938. The most famous is *Night Mail*, a film poem about a mail train on which he collaborated with poet W. H. Auden. Auden later wrote the libretto for Britten's opera *Paul Bunyan*. The other documentary films include *Coal Face, The Savings of Bill Blewit, Line to Tschierva, The Calendar of the Year, The Tocher, Advance Democracy* and *The Way to the Sea*. They were made for the GPO and government film units.

1937 Love From a Stranger
Britten wrote the score for only one fiction feature film, this suspense thriller about a woman who thinks she may have married a maniac. It stars Ann Harding and Basil Rathbone and was based on an Agatha Christie story. Rowland V. Lee directed. Black and white. 90 minutes.

1950 Let's Make an Opera
Britten's "entertainment for young people" is about a group preparing and presenting the opera *The Little Sweep*. It premiered at Aldeburgh in June 1949, and was telecast by the BBC from the Theatre Royal in Stratford on February 5, 1950. It features Shirley Eaton, Michael Nicholls, Alan Woolston and Jean Galton with commentary by Douglas Smith. The music was played by Norman Del Marr and his orchestra. Black and white. In English. 60 minutes.

1959 Benjamin Britten
British filmmaker John Schlesinger was at the beginning of his career when he directed this first-class documentary about the composer for the BBC Television *Monitor* series. Black and white. 60 minutes.

1963 Britten at 50
Humphrey Burton produced this BBC Television tribute to Britten for the composer's 50th birthday. Britten and Peter Pears make appearances, W.H. Auden talks about their collaboration, Michael Tippett talks about the music, there are clips from films like *Night Mail* and excerpts from operas like *Peter Grimes*. Gennadi Rozhdestvensky conducts the London Symphony Orchestra. Huw Wheldon is the moderator. Black and white. In English. 65 minutes.

1967 Britten and His Aldeburgh Festival
This *Bell Telephone Hour/BBC* program celebrates the 20th anniversary of the founding of the Aldeburgh Festival. There are extracts from *A Midsummer Night's Dream* and *The Burning Fiery Furnace* plus interviews with Peter Pears and other Britten associates. Humphrey Burton produced and Tony Palmer directed. Black and white. 55 minutes. Video at MTR.

1980 A Time There Was...A Profile of Benjamin Britten
Peter Pears supplies the narrative framework for this documentary by Tony Palmer which focuses on the operas. Britten's colleagues talk about their understanding of the musician. They include E. M. Forster, Leonard Bernstein, Julian Bream, Frank Bridge, Paul Rotha, Rudolf Bing and Mstislav Rostropovich. Palmer's film also includes archival material and home movies It won the Italia Prize for 1980. LWT. Color. 102 minutes. Kultur video.

1992 The British Documentary Movement: Volume 3, Benjamin Britten
The British Documentary Movement is a six-part series examining the growth and development of the British documentary film movement. Volume Three is devoted to Benjamin Britten. His contribution was considered especially important because of the films *Night Mail* and *Coal Face*. Color and black and white. 60 minutes. On video.

BROOK, PETER
English director (1925-)

Peter Brook was director of productions at the Royal Opera House from 1947 to 1950 but then left to concentrate on theater and film. He made his first opera film in 1953, *The Beggar's Opera* with Laurence Olivier, but won more praise 30 years later with his three films of his minimalist production of Bizet's *Carmen*. Brook's film career began in 1943 but stage rather than screen has always been his main love. See THE BEGGAR'S OPERA (1953), CARMEN (1983/1978 film)

BROSCHI, RICCARDO
Italian composer (1698-1756)

Riccardo Broschi was the brother of the famous castrato male soprano Farinelli and wrote several operas for him. Farinelli's most famous aria "Son qual nave ch'agitata" was composed by Broschi for the pasticcio opera *Artaserse* which premiered in

London in 1734. It can be seen and heard in the 1994 film *Farinelli*. See FARINELLI.

BROWNING, KIRK
Television opera director (1921-)

Kirk Browning is the D.W. Griffith of television opera, one of the great pioneers of the operatic screen. Browning essentially invented the vocabulary of filming opera for television in America and directed most of the early TV opera productions. He began at NBC-TV in 1948 and became director of NBC Opera Theatre in 1949 under NBC music director Samuel Chotzinoff. He collaborated with conductor Peter Herman Adler on NBC and NET Opera and also worked on the Bell Telephone Hour. He directed the first *Live from Lincoln Center* and *Live from the Met* telecasts, worked with opera companies in Washington, Chicago, Philadelphia and Dallas on their telecasts and won numerous awards including an Emmy for *La Gioconda* in 1980. Browning helped create many TV operas including Menotti's *Amahl and the Night Visitors*, Stravinsky's *The Flood*, Pasinetti's *The Trial of Mary Lincoln* and Foss's *Griffelkin*. His influence on style and technique can be seen in every opera televised. He has directed well over a hundred different operas for television listed in this book as well as such specials as the Metropolitan Opera Centennial telecast. He is noted for his restless camera and for his emphasis on the close-up. There are 168 videos directed by Browning at the Museum of Television and Radio. See most opera entries plus NBC OPERA THEATRE, NET OPERA.

1986 Metropolitan Opera Seminar
A panel discussion featuring Kirk Browning talking about the Metropolitan Opera telecasts held at the Museum of Broadcasting (now the MTR) on Oct. 1, 1986. The moderator is Robert M. Batscha. Also participating are Bruce Crawford, John Charles and Martin Meyer. Color. 58 minutes. Video at MTR.

1990 Bell Telephone Hour Seminar
A second panel discussion featuring Kirk Browning, this time talking about the Bell Telephone Hour telecasts. It was held at the Museum of Broadcasting on Oct. 1, 1986, with Robert Sherman as moderator. Color. 22 minutes. Video at MTR.

BRUNDIBAR
1938 Czechoslovakian opera by Krása

Hans Krása created the children's opera *Brundibar* (The Bumble Bee) for a Prague orphanage using a libretto by Adolf Hoffmeister. It's based on a Czech fairy tale and tells how two children get the better of evil organ grinder Brundibar with the help of friendly animals. Krasna's opera became known when the Nazis allowed a showcase production in the Terezin (Theresienstadt) prison camp for the International Red Cross. Krása later died in Auschwitz. The opera has been revived in recent years because of interest in music suppressed by the Nazis. It is on CD and has been filmed and telecast. See also HANS KRÁSA, TEREZIN OPERAS.

1995 BBC Television film
Brundibar, first staged by Mecklenburg Opera in 1993, was filmed at the Harrow School Theatre in England in 1995. John Abulafia's production, directed for BBC TV by Simon Broughton, uses set designs based on Frantisek Zelenka's originals. Anne Manson conducts the orchestra with the singing done by children from the New London Children's Choir. Color. 30 minutes.

BRUSCANTI, SESTO
Italian bass-baritone (1919-)

Sesto Bruscanti, who began his career in Rome in 1946, was popular at the Glyndebourne Festival in the 1950s for his performances in Mozart and Rossini. He made his first apperance there as Don Alfonso in *Così Fan Tutte* in 1951 and also sang Guglielmo, Figaro and Dandini. He was the archetypal Glyndebourne Mozart Figaro and made a famous recording of *The Marriage of Figaro* in 1955 with Sena Jurinac as the Countess. They can be seen in scenes from this production in the film *On Such a Night*. See THE MARRIAGE OF FIGARO (1955 film).

BRUSON, RENATO
Italian baritone (1936-)

Renato Bruson is a noted *bel canto* baritone and has sung in seventeen Donizetti operas but he is also popular in Verdi operas. He made his debut in Spoleto in 1961 as Count di Luna, came to the Metropolitan as Enrico in *Lucia di Lammermoor* in 1969 and made his debut at La Scala as Antonio in Donizetti's *Linda di Chamounix*. He now sings around the world in a wide variety of roles ranging from Falstaff to Don Giovanni and has made many videos. See CAVALLERIA RUSTICANA (1982), I DUE FOSCARI (1988), ERNANI (1982), FALSTAFF (1982), GIOVANNA D'ARCO (1989), LUCIA DI LAMMERMOOR (1992), LUISA MILLER (1980), MACBETH (1987), METROPOLITAN OPERA (1983), NABUCCO (1981/1986).

1992 Renato Bruson
A video portrait of the great baritone made for the Italian opera television series *I Grandi della Lirica*. Color. In Italian. 60 minutes. Center (Italy) video.

BRYDEN, BILL
English director (1942-)

Bill Bryden, who directed the *Pagliacci* segment of the film *Aria*, is primarily a theater director with a continuing association with opera on stage. He wrote the libretto for the 1975 opera *Hermiston* and in 1988 staged a famous production of *Parsifal* set in a bomb-damaged cathedral like Coventry. His films include the excellent *Ill Fares the Land* (1982). See ARIA, PAGLIACCI (1987 film).

BUMBRY, GRACE
American mezzo/soprano (1937-)

Grace Bumbry won a Metropolitan Opera audition in 1958 but didn't make her Met debut until 1965. Her career began in Paris in 1960 and in 1961 she became the first African-American to sing at Bayreuth when she was cast as Venus. She sings in a wide range of but is noted for her Carmen, Tosca and Amneris. See AIDA (1976/ 1987 film), CARMEN (1966), DON CARLO (1983), METROPOLITAN OPERA (1983), TOSCA (1983).

BUÑUEL, LUIS
Spanish film director (1900-1983)

Luis Buñuel, one of the masters of cinema, was obsessed by Richard Wagner's operas, especially *Tristan und Isolde,* and featured Wagner music in a number of his films. His first, *Un Chien Andalou* (1928), has music from *Tristan und Isolde* as does *L'Age d'Or* (1930) which also has *Siegfried* music. His 1954 film of *Wuthering Heights* uses themes from *Tristan und Isolde* as its entire music track. His last film, *That Obscure Object of Desire* (1977), highlights a duet from *Die Walküre*. Buñuel was also involved in Spanish opera and zarzuela films. His first job in

Paris was as set designer for a production of Manuel de Falla's *El Retablo de Maese Pedro*. In 1935 he began to produce, write and direct zarzuela films but did not want his name on the credits. His adaptation of Guerrero's *Don Quintin el Amargao* (1935) was so successful that he remade it in Mexico sixteen years later. His production of Serrano's *La Alegría del Batallón* was also popular. *Lucia di Lammermoor* has an intriguing if unexplained connection to his film *The Exterminating Angel*. See LA ALEGRÍA DEL BATALLÓN (1936), DON QUINTIN EL AMARGAO (1935), LUCIA DI LAMMERMOOR (1960 film), SIEGFRIED (1930 film), TRISTAN UND ISOLDE (1930 film/1950 film), DIE WALKÜRE (1977 film).

BURCHULADZE, PAATA
Georgian bass (1951-)

Georgian basso Paata Burchuladze made his debut in his native Tbilisi in 1976, came to Covent Garden in 1984 as Ramfis and then sang Don Basilio at the Metropolitan Opera in 1989. He has now become internationally popular in a wide variety of roles but especially in his portrayals of Russian opera roles like Boris Godunov. See AIDA (1986/1989), DON GIOVANNI (1987), KHOVANSHCHINA (1989), MEFISTOFELE (1989), NABUCCO (1986), PRINCE IGOR (1990), PYOTR TCHAIKOVSKY (1993).

BURTON, HUMPHREY
English producer/director (1931-)

Humphrey Burton is one of the most important and creative producer/directors of opera for television and video. He has worked for BBC, LWT and Channel 4 and in 1965 made a famous film about the first complete recording of the Ring. He has produced or directed the videos of many of the stage productions at Glyndebourne and Covent Garden and has also made several fine films about performers and composers. See THE ABDUCTION FROM THE SERAGLIO (1986), ANDREA CHÉNIER (1985), KATHLEEN BATTLE (1991), LUDWIG VAN BEETHOVEN (1971/1981), LEONARD BERNSTEIN (1973/1974), BORIS GODUNOV (1990), BENJAMIN BRITTEN (1963/1976), CANDIDE (1989), THE CREATION (1986), DIE FLEDERMAUS (1983/ 1990), THOMAS HAMPSON (1991), MACBETH (1972), THE MARRIAGE OF FIGARO (1973), MOZART REQUIEM (1988/1991), PRINCE IGOR (1990), DER RING DES NIBELUNGEN (1965 FILM), GEORG SOLTI (1990), IGOR STRAVINSKY (1982), JOAN SUTHERLAND (1991), WAR AND PEACE (1991), KURT WEILL (1964), WEST SIDE STORY (1985).

C

CABALLÉ, MONTSERRAT
Spanish soprano (1933-)

One of the great voices of the 20th century, Montserrat Caballé made her debut in Basle in 1956 singing Mimi and won acclaim in New York in 1965 as Lucrezia Borgia. Caballé, a proud and supportive Catalan, helped launch countryman José Carreras on his career. They have starred together in films and stage productions which are on video. She has devoted more time in recent years to recitals and concerts than operas but remains one of the great interpreters of Italian opera. See AGNESE DI HOHENSTAUFEN (1986), GEORGES BIZET (1988), CRISTÓBAL COLÓN (1989), ERMIONE (1987), LA FORZA DEL DESTINO (1978), GALA LIRICA, JULIÁN GAYARRE (1986), GLYNDEBOURNE (1992), METROPOLITAN OPERA (1972/ 1983), NORMA (1974/1977), TOSCA (1983 film), VERONA (1988), IL VIAGGIO A REIMS (1988).

1983 Montserrat Caballé: The Woman, the Diva
Antonio Chic's documentary examines the person as well as the singer. Caballé talks about her husband and family but, more importantly, sings with consummate brilliance. There are arias from her favorite operas including *Giulio Cesare, Adriana Lecouvreur, La Bohème, La Forza de Destino* and *Mefistofele* plus songs and zarzuela arias. She comes over as a warm human being as well as a splendid singer. Color. 67 minutes. Kultur video.

1983 Caballé Subjugates La Scala
Caballé's recital at La Scala on March 26, 1983, followed her problems and withdrawal from *Anna Bolena* the year before. This time she triumphed with a program that includes arias by Spontini, Cherubini, Bellini, Vives and Rossini. Color. In Italian. 118 minutes. Bel Canto Society video.

1989 Caballé and Carreras in Moscow
The two Catalan stars appear in concert together at the Bolshoi Opera. The program includes nineteen solos and four duets with compositions by Bellini, Verdi, Vivaldi, Tosti, Granados, Scarlatti and others. They are accompanied on piano by Miguel Zanetti. Color. 60 minutes. Kultur video.

1990 Evviva Bel Canto/Le Grande Primadonne
These two videos are from one concert with Caballé appearing with Marilyn Horne at the Philharmonie Hall in Munich. They sing arias and duets from Vivaldi, Meyerbeer, Rossini, Handel, Puccini, Offenbach and Mercadente. They work well together and seem to give each other inspiration, notably on a magnificent duet from *Semiramide*. Nicola Rescigno leads the Munich Rundfunk Orchestra in support. Evelyn Paulman and Helmut Rost directed the videos. Color. 47/41 minutes. MCA video.

1993 Montserrat Caballé
Chris Hunt's fine documentary film about the diva's life and career traces her life from the early years. She is shown in performance and rehearsal and relates fascinating anecdotes. There are also interviews with Joan Sutherland, Placido Domingo, José Carreras and Cheryl Studer. Made for the South Bank Show. Color. 60 minutes.

1993 Christmas Concert from the Vatican
Montserrat Caballé is the operatic star of this Vatican Christmas concert arranged by RAI TV. Renato Serio conducts the St. Cecilia National Academy Symphony Orchestra. Color. 97 minutes. On video.

CABALLERO, MANUEL FERNÁNDEZ
Spanish composer (1835-1906)

Manuel Fernández Caballero is one of the major zarzuela composers, best known for his 1898 *Gigantes y Cabezudos*. He began as a violinist and conductor, started to compose zarzuelas in 1854 and became successful after spending some time in Cuba absorbing new musical ideas. Caballero wrote over one hundred zarzuelas and his works are especially popular in South America. See GIGANTES Y CABEZUDOS, LOS SOBRINOS DEL CAPITÁN GRANT.

CABINET OF DR. CALIGARI, THE
1981 musical stage work by Nelson

Robert Wiene's expressionist 1919 German film *The Cabinet of Dr. Caligari*, one of the first great horror movies, was widely influential for its stylist acting and powerful set design. Conrad Veidt, Werner Krauss and Lil Dagover star in a paranoiac story about a hypnotist who uses a somnambulist to commit murders. Carl Mayer and Hans Janowitz wrote the screenplay. It was turned into a quasi-opera by 1981 by composer Bill Nelson who created an electronic music score based on the film for an English stage production. The Yorkshire Actors' Company used the music in their theatrical adaptation of the film to complement storytelling through gesture, mime and dance.

CACOYANNIS, MICHAEL
Greek film director (1922-)

Michael Cacoyannis, who began his moviemaking career in 1953, is known for classic films like *Zorba the Greek* (1964) and *Electra* (1961). He has not made any opera films but he has directed opera on stage. One of his most notable productions was an American opera derived from *Electra* staged at the Metropolitan in 1967. Marvin David Levy's *Mourning Becomes Electra*, based on the Eugene O'Neill play, starred Evelyn Lear and Sherrill Milnes.

CALDWELL, SARAH
American conductor/director (1924 -)

Sarah Caldwell founded the Boston Opera Company in 1958 and served as both administrative and musical director. She won much praise for her innovative productions including modern and little known operas. Caldwell was the first woman to conduct opera at the Metropolitan and has been influential in a number of different ways. See THE BARBER OF SEVILLE (1976), ZAIDE.

1973 What Time is the Next Swan?
A short film of a behind-the scenes visit to the Boston Opera Company while Caldwell rehearses with performers and works with her staff. The film shows the preparation and planning for a Boston production. Color. 8 minutes.

CALLAS, MARIA
American/Greek soprano (1923-1977)

Maria Callas is by consensus the greatest female opera singer of the 20th century and the reason that many people become attracted to opera. Callas was born Mary Kalogeropoulou in New York City in

1923, made her debut in Athens in 1941 and became famous in Italy in the late 1940s with the help of conductor Tullio Serafin. Film directors Luchino Visconti and Franco Zeffirelli influenced her and directed her in operas on stage but not in films. She ended her public career in 1965, returned for a concert tour in 1973-1974 and died in 1977 at the age of 53. Callas's career ended before televising operas became common and there is no video of her in a complete opera. Even her concerts and recitals are sparsely covered. What survives gives a powerful indication of how she could immerse herself in a role and effectively become the character she portrayed. See also TOSCA (1964).

1956 Ed Sullivan Show Tosca
Maria Callas made her American TV debut on the *Ed Sullivan Show* on CBS on Nov. 25, 1956. Rudolf Bing, general manager of the Metropolitan Opera, introduces her in a scene from *Tosca* staged by John Gutman. George London sings Scarpia with Dimitri Mitropoulos conducting the Metropolitan Opera Orchestra. Black and white. 18 minutes. Video at MTR.

1958 Ed Sullivan Show Interview
Maria Callas made her second television appearance on the Ed Sullivan Show on CBS on Jan. 24, 1958. In this program Sullivan talks to her about her life and career. Black and white. 60 minutes. Video at MTR.

1958 Lisbon La Traviata
Callas is interviewed at the Lisbon Airport and shown briefly on stage in *La Traviata* with Alfredo Kraus in the Act III party. The material is included on the video *Legends of Opera*. Black and white. In Italian and French. 7 minutes. Legato Classics video.

1958 Maria Callas Debuts in Paris
The most important Callas video, a gala concert presented as it was televised live from the Palais Garnier on Dec. 19, 1958. The first half features arias from *Norma*, *The Barber of Seville* and *Il Trovatore*. The second half is a staging of Act II of *Tosca* with Callas partnered by Tito Gobbi as Scarpia and Albert Lance as Cavaradossi. Georges Sebastian conducts the Paris Opéra Orchestra and Chorus. Roger Benamou staged the production. Black and white. French narration. 107 minutes. EMI Classics video/ Pioneer Artists laser.

1959 Hamburg Concert

The first of two live concerts of Callas taped performing in Hamburg. She sings wonderfully and truly embodies her roles. The arias are from *Macbeth, The Barber of Seville, Don Carlo, Il Pirata* and *La Vestale*, all operas she had sung at La Scala. Nicola Resigno, who conducted her American debut in 1954 in Chicago, conducts the NDR Symphony Orchestra of Hamburg. The concert was taped on May 15, 1959. Black and white. 68 minutes, Kultur video and on laser.

1962 Hamburg Concert

Callas is in terrific form in the second of the two concerts taped in Hamburg, this one on March 16, 1962. She sings arias from *Carmen, Ernani, Le Cid* and *La Cenerentola*, operas which she had never performed on stage, plus *Don Carlo*. Georges Prêtre, who conducted for her *Norma* and *Tosca* in Paris, leads the NDR Symphony Orchestra. Black and white. 67 minutes. Kultur video and on laser.

1962 Covent Garden Gala Concert

Maria Callas was featured singer in this November 1962 concert with Giuseppe Di Stefano at the Royal Opera House in Covent Garden. She sings "Tu che la vanita" from *Don Carlo* and the Habanera and Seguidilla arias from *Carmen*. George Prêtre conducts the Royal Opera House Orchestra. Sir David Webster introduces the video produced by Bill Ward for ATV television. Black and white. 60 minutes. EMI Classics video.

1968 The Callas Conversations

Maria Callas looks relaxed and elegant in her Paris apartment talking with Lord Harewood. The conversation concerns her career, her early life, her means of preparing for a performance and her ideas of interpretation. She discusses particularly her conception of her roles in *Norma, Tosca* and *La Traviata*. The *Conversations* were produced by John Culshaw, directed by Barrie Gavin and first shown in fifty-minute segments on BBC TV in December 1968. Color. 100 minutes. On video.

1968 Werner Schroeter films

German filmmaker Werner Schroeter, who was obsessed with Callas at the start of his career, made three 8mm films about her in 1968. They are *Callas Walking Lucia* (3 minutes), *Maria Callas Portrait* (17 minutes) and *Maria Callas singt 1957 Rezitativ und Arie der Elvira aus Ernani 1844 von Giuseppe Verdi* (15 minutes).

1970 Medea

This Italian film is the only genuine movie Callas made. She and the film are superb though it is not an opera and Callas does not sing. She portrays the Medea of the Euripides' tragedy, not the Cherubini opera, under the direction of Italian filmmaker Pier Paolo Pasolini. These two great artists create a memorable film with Callas at her most emotional and charismatic and Pasolini at his most powerful and lucid. The film tells the story of Medea's horrific revenge on Jason after he betrays her. Color. In Italian with English subtitles. 118 minutes. VAI video.

1978 Callas in Japan

This is a video made of a concert given by Maria Callas in Japan wjen she was on her last tour. Color. 56 minutes. Video at NFTA in London.

1978 Vissi d'Arte

Alain Ferrari created this French television documentary on Callas to explore what was unique about her work vocally and artistically. Through interviews with collaborators, directors and conductors, he examines the high demands Callas made on those she worked with and how it influenced her artisty. INA. Color. In French. 75 minutes. On video.

1978 Maria Callas

A documentary about the singer and her career written and directed by John Ardoin. Color. 90 minutes. Video at New York Public Library.

1983 Callas

A major international television tribute to Maria Callas introduced by Leonard Bernstein. The program includes live performances by singers from La Scala in Milan, Covent Garden in London, the Opéra in Paris and the Lyric in Chicago through linkage by satellite. There are also many interviews and film clips. Color. 150 minutes.

1987 Maria Callas: the Life and Legend

Tony Palmer's documentary traces Callas's life and career from birth to death using archival footage interspersed with interviews. Franco Zeffirelli is especially interesting as he attempts to explain her magic as a singer and her relationship with Onassis. The film opens and closes with scenes from her 1958 Paris debut but also includes much rare newsreel and interview material. There are excerpts of her singing arias from *The Barber of Seville, Il*

Pirata, La Gioconda, Don Carlo, Norma, Carmen, Tosca, Il Trovatore and *La Sonnambula*. Color & black and white. 90 minutes. On video/Pioneer Artists laser.

1988 Maria Callas: Life and Art

This informative documentary about Callas by Alan Lewens and Alistair Mitchell follows her career intelligently in a chronological format. There are excerpts from most of her films and videos, excellent interviews with those who knew her well and many insights into her life and singing. She is seen performing arias from *Tosca, The Barber of Seville, Carmen, Cavalleria Rusticana* and *L'Elisir d'Amore*. Black and white. 80 minutes. Kultur video/ Pioneer laser.

1988 Onassis: The Richest Man in the World

Jane Seymour gives a fiery performance as Maria Callas in this highly fictional American TV movie directed by Waris Hussein. Raul Julia portrays Aristotle Onassis, Anthony Quinn is his father and Francesca Annis is Jackie Kennedy in an adaptation of a book by Peter Evans. Color. 200 minutes. On video.

1992 Casta Diva: Tribute to Maria Callas

Maria Callas is honored at a concert in the open-air Herodion Theater on the Athens Acropolis with introductions from Irene Pappas. The concert includes "Casta Diva" and other arias associated with Callas sung by sopranos Mariella Devia, Raina Kabaivanska, Daniela Dessi and Francesca Pedaci. Giuseppe Sabbatini, Giacomo Prestia and Paolo Coni lend support. Gianluigi Gelmetti conducts the Stuttgart Radio Symphony Orchestra. Color. 111 minutes. Lyric video.

1993 Philadelphia

This film about a gay lawyer with AIDS (Tom Hanks) helped acquaint the wide American public with the voice of Maria Callas. The crucial central scene of the film is built around Hanks and his lawyer listening to Callas sing the aria "La mamma morta" from *Andrea Chénier*. She is also heard in the film singing "Ebben? ne andrò lontano" from *La Wally*. Tristar. Color. 119 minutes.

CAMBIALE DI MATRIMONIO, LA
1810 opera by Rossini

The Bill of Marriage is Rossini's first professional opera, a one-act comedy written when he was only

eighteen. It revolves around a marriage bill that is the center of romantic confusion. When Sir Tobias tries to marry off his daughter Fanny to the rich Canadian Slook who has the bill, her lover Edoardo has to find a quick solution. Gaetano Rossi wrote the libretto. See also GIOACHINO ROSSINI.

1989 Schwetzingen Festival

Michael Hampe's charming Cologne Opera production in a rococo theater in the town of Schwetzingen was staged with other early Rossini operas in a celebratory cycle. Janice Hall stars as daughter Fanny, David Kuebler is her lover, John Del Carlo is her father, Alberto Rinaldi is the Canadian Slook and Amelia Felle is the servant. Gianluigi Gemetti conducts the Stuttgart Radio Symphony Orchestra. Carlo Tommasi designed the sets and Carlo Diappi the costumes. Color. In Italian with English subtitles. 85 minutes. Teldec video/Pioneer laser.

CAMEO OPERAS
1927 British film series

Cameo Operas, a 1927 British film series devoted to opera, condensed well-known operas to about 20 minutes and presented them with live vocalists and cinema orchestras. They were produced by John E. Blakeley and directed by H. B. Parkinson for Song Films. Parkinson also produced the earlier *Tense Moments in Opera* series. The operas selected for the series are a reflection of what interested the British public at the time. See THE BOHEMIAN GIRL, CARMEN, THE DAUGHTER OF THE REGIMENT, FAUST, THE LILY OF KILLARNEY, MARITANA, MARTHA, RIGOLETTO, DER RING DES NIBELUNGEN, SAMSON ET DALILA, LA TRAVIATA, IL TROVATORE.

CAMERA
1994 TV opera by Moore

Anthony Moore's television opera stars John Harris as a tax collector who is sent to a derelict house to collect arrears from a woman called Melusina (Dagmar Krause). She says her house is a country called Camera and only the laws of imagination are in effect. He returns to his office without the taxes and is fired. A more ruthless tax collector (Quentin Hayes) is sent to complete the job. The opera was commissioned by Channel Four. Jane Thorburn directed the telecast on Feb. 6, 1994. Color. In English. 60 minutes.

CAMERA THREE
CBS television series (1953-1978)

The adventurous CBS art and culture series *Camera Three* presented opera in a bare-bones recital format. Its extreme low budget and early Sunday morning time slot meant that it could present almost anything that didn't cost much money. There were programs devoted to composers Thomas Pasatieri and Kurt Weill, singers Marilyn Horne, Dorothy Kirstein, Richard Tucker and Judith Blegan, historic operas like Galuppi's *Il Filosofo di Compagne* and modern chamber operas like *The Accused*. The series was dropped by CBS in 1978 but revived on PBS in 1979 with new and repeat programs. Roger Englander was a producer/director on the series for three years. See THE ACCUSED, SAMUEL BARBER (1977), THE CRADLE WILL ROCK (1967), BALDASSARE GALUPPI, TOM JOHNSON, DOROTHY KIRSTEN (1978), THOMAS PASATIERI (1977), DER SCHAUSPIELDIREKTOR (1961), MICHAEL TIPPETT (1975).

CAMPANARI, GIUSEPPE
Italian baritone (1855-1927)

Giuseppe Campanari made his debut at the Metropolitan in 1984 and had a major success as Ford in the U.S. premiere of *Falstaff* the following year. He was much liked as Figaro in both the Mozart and Rossini operas and sang over 200 performances at the Met before retiring in 1912. He made a number of recordings and was featured in one early sound film. See CARMEN (1917).

CAMPORA, GIUSEPPE
Italian tenor (1927-)

Tenor Giuseppe Campora made his debut in 1949 as Rodolfo in Bari and soon was performing around the world from New York to Buenos Aires. He made many recordings, mostly of Verdi and Puccini operas. Opera film enthusiasts know him as the voice declaring love for Sophia Loren in the Italian movie of *Aida*. Campora is the voice of Radames. See AIDA (1953).

1958 Lisa Della Casa in Opera and Song
Giuseppe Campora is featured with soprano Lisa Della Casa on this *Voice of Firestone* telecast on Sept. 22, 1958. He sings "Recondita armonia" from *Tosca* and joins the soprano on the opening and closing songs by Idabelle Firestone. Black and white. 30 minutes.

CANDIDE
1965 operetta by Bernstein

Candide veers from opera to high-octane operetta but seems likely to enter the opera house repertory. Based on Voltaire's sharply funny and still relevant satire, it tells the story of the naive couple Candide and Cunegonde. They start off believing the optimistic teachings of the philosopher Pangloss who says this is the best of all possible worlds. After a series of disasters, they find that such a philosophy is of little relevance in the real world. The libretto for the original Broadway production was by Lillian Hellman with lyrics by so many writers it became a joke. The overture is a marvel and Cunegonde's aria "Glitter and Be Gay" has become a favorite of coloratura sopranos. See also LEONARD BERNSTEIN.

1986 New York City Opera
David Eisler is Candide, Erie Mills is Cunegonde and John Langston is Pangloss in this New York City Opera production by Harold Prince . The cast includes James Billings, Deborah Darr, Jack Harrold, John Lankston and Muriel Costa-Greenspon. Scott Bergeson conducts the New York City Opera Orchestra. Beverly Sills was host for the telecast in the Live from Lincoln Center series on Nov. 12, 1986. Color. In English. 150 minutes.

1989 Barbican Center, London
It looks like an oratorio but it sounds like an opera. Jerry Hadley sings the role of Candide with June Anderson as Cunegonde in this revised concert version of the operetta presented at the Barbican Center in London. Adolph Green is Pangloss, Christa Ludwig is the Old Lady and Kurt Ollmann is Maximillian. Anderson is particularly fine in the difficult "Glitter and be Gay" aria. Bernstein himself conducts the London Symphony Orchestra and Chorus. Humphrey Burton directed the video. Color. In English. 147 minutes. Polygram Video and laser.

Related film

1960 Candide
This is a non-musical French film based on the Voltaire satire which makes an interesting comparison to the operetta. Writer-director Norbert Carbonneaux keeps the basic story but updates the time to the World War II period. It stars Jean-Pierre Cassel as Candide, Dahlia Lavi as Cunegonde and

Pierre Brasseur as Pangloss with support from Michel Simon, Louis De Funès and Jean Richard. Black and white. In French. 88 minutes.

CANIGLIA, MARIA
Italian soprano (1905-1979)

Maria Caniglia was born in Rome, studied in Naples and made her debut in Turin. She became a regular at La Scala and sang at Covent Garden and the Met in the late 30s. She brought a warm humanity to her specialty Verdi roles but was also a much admired Tosca. She made a few Italian films including one about La Scala. See TEATRO ALLA SCALA (1943), MAD ABOUT OPERA, MANON LESCAUT (1940 film), TOSCA (1956).

1947 Il Vento mi ha Cantato una Canzone
Maria Caniglia plays a singer in *The Wind Sang Me A Song*, an Italian musical starring Laura Solari and Alberto Sordi. It's the story of a musician who finally succeeds in his ambitions with the help of an amateur. Camillo Mastrocinque directed. Black and white. In Italian. 95 minutes.

CAPPUCCILLI, PIERO
Italian baritone (1929-)

Piero Cappuccilli was born in Trieste and made his debut in Milan in 1957 in *Pagliacci*. His international career began in 1960 when he sang *La Traviata* at the Metropolitan and recorded *Lucia di Lammermoor* with Maria Callas. By 1964 he was rated as one of the leading baritones in the world and sang regularly at La Scala and other major opera houses. He is featured in a number of opera videos and tributes. See ANDREA CHÉNIER (1979), DON CARLO (1986), NICOLAI GHIAUROV (1986), OTELLO (1982), LUCIANO PAVAROTTI (1991), SIMON BOCCANEGRA (1978), IL TRITTICO (1983).

CAPRICCIO
1942 opera by Strauss

The question of the relative importance of words and music in opera is the self-referential focus of this philosophical opera by Richard Strauss. The libretto, by the composer and conductor Clemens Krauss, is set in a castle in Paris in 1775 and tells the story of Countess Madeleine and her two suitors. One is a poet and the other is a composer. A heated debate is held on the value of words and music in opera. The suitors are asked to write an opera using the people present as the characters. The countess is still unable to choose. The opera premiered in Munich in the middle of World War II. See also RICHARD STRAUSS.

1975 Glyndebourne Festival
Elisabeth Söderström stars as the Countess torn between words and music in this remarkable Glyndebourne Festival production by John Cox. Cox updates the opera to the 1920s with superb art deco sets. Andrew Davis conducts the orchestra. The opera was telecast by the BBC but, as the Strauss estate no longer approves of modern dress productions, it has never been released on video. Color. In German with English subtitles. 145 minutes. Video in BBC TV archives.

1990 Salzburg Festival
Anna Tomowa-Sintow is outstanding as the Countess with the esthetic problem in this Salzburg Festival production by Johannes Schaaf. It is his conceit to begin the opera in the 1920s and then regress to the 18th century. Eberhard Buchner is the composer Flamand, Andreas Schmidt is the poet Oliver, Wolfgang Schone is the Count, Iris Vermillion is the actress Clairon, Theo Adam is stage director La Roche and Heinz Zednik is the Prompter. Andreas Reinhardt designed the sets and costumes and Horst Stein conducts the Vienna Philharmonic Orchestra. Schaaf also directed the video. Color. In German with English subtitles. 150 minutes. On video.

1992 San Francisco Opera
Kiri Te Kanawa sings brilliantly as the Countess Madeleine in this San Francisco Opera production by Stephen Lawless. Tatiana Troyanos portrays the actress Clairon in what was to be her final stage role. Simon Keenlyside is the poet Olivier, David Kuebler is the composer Flamand, Håkan Hagegård is the Count, Victor Braun is the stage director La Roche and Michel Senechal is the Prompter. Mauro Pagano was the set designer, Donald Runnicles conducted the San Francisco Opera Orchestra and Peter Maniura directed the video. Color. In German with English subtitles. 144 minutes. London video and laser.

CAPULETI ED I MONTECCHI, I
1830 opera by Bellini

The Capulets and the Montagues is Vincenzo Bellini's version of the Romeo and Juliet story. Felice Romani's libretto is based on the original Italian stories rather than Shakespeare's play but the story is essentially the same. The leading roles are for women singers with Juliet cast as a soprano and Romeo a mezzo. The role of Romeo was composed for the diva Giuditta Grisi who starred when the opera premiered at La Fenice in 1830. The final duet between the two lovers is much admired .See also VINCENZO BELLINI.

1991 La Fenice, Venice
Italian soprano Katia Ricciarelli stars as Juliet in this highlights version of the opera produced at La Fenice Theater in Venice and filmed for the *My Favorite Opera* series. Rehearsals and staged performances of scenes are shown in the order they appear in the opera. Romeo is sung by Diane Montague, Dano Raffanti is Tebaldo, Marcello Lippi is Capellio and Antonio Salvador is Lorenzo. Ugo Tesitore is the stage director and Pier Luigi Pizzi designed the sets and costumes. Bruno Campanella leads the La Fenice Orchestra and Chorus and Allan Miller directed the film. Color. 60 minutes. Kultur video.

CARDILLAC
1926/1952 opera by Hindemith

Paul Hindemith's first full-length opera, originally created in 1926, is based on a novella by E. T. Hoffmann. It is the bizarre story of the psychotic goldsmith René Cardillac and his strange behavior at the Paris court of King Louis XIV. Unable to give up his creations, he murders his clients to recover them. His story is counterpointed by his daughter's love affair. Hindemith revised the opera in 1952 and enlarged it with a new libretto. See also PAUL HINDEMITH.

1986 Bavarian State Opera
Donald McIntyre stars as the mad artist Cardillac in this Bavarian State Opera production by Jean-Pierre Ponnelle. Maria de Francesca-Cavazza portrays his daughter with a supporting cast that includes Robert Schunk, Hans Gunter Nocker and Josef Hopferweiser. Wolfgang Sawallisch conducted the Bavarian State Opera Orchestra and Brian Large directed the video. Unitel. Color. In German. 89 minutes.

CARMEN
1875 opéra comique by Bizet

The story of Carmen has transmuted into a genuine myth and is now the most popular literary source for movies. It is also the largest single entry in this book with sixty-nine films and videos. The idea of a strong sensual woman killed by an ordinary man she has seduced and abandoned seems to have universal resonance ; it has inspired a large number of movies with opera singers. Early films often claim to be based on the Prosper Mérimée source story rather than the libretto by Henri Meilhac and Ludovic Halévy for Georges Bizet's opera but this was usually for copyright reasons. Non-operatic movies often feature arias or other references to the opera and a selection of these is included below. The best version of the complete opera on video is undoubtedly the 1984 Francesco Rosi film with Julia Migenes. See also GEORGES BIZET.

1931 Gypsy Blood
This British movie of the opera stars American soprano Marguerite Namara as Carmen and is sung and spoken in English. Namara had just finished touring Europe in a stage production of the opera. Thomas Burke portrays Don José with Lance Fairfax as Escamillo. Malcolm Sargent conducts the New Symphony Orchestra and Cecil Lewis directed the film. The film was retitled *Carmen* when it was shown in the U.S. BIP. Black and white. In English. 79 minutes.

1932 Operalogue highlights film
This English-language highlights version of *Carmen* was produced in the U.S. in 1932 for the Operalogue series. Lew Seller directed it for Educational Films. Black and white. In English. 28 minutes.

1948 Tito Gobbi film
Tito Gobbi stars as Escamillo in this highlights version filmed at the Rome Opera House. Cloe Elmo is the voice of Carmen acted by Fernanda Candoni. Giancinto Prandelli plays Don José and Pina Malgharini is Micaela. George Richfield produced it for the anthology *First Opera Film Festival*. Angelo Questa conducted the Orchestra and Chorus of the Rome Opera House, E. Fulchignoni was stage director and E. Cancelleri

directed the film. The English narration is by Olin Downes. Black and white. In Italian. 25 minutes.

1950 CBS Opera Television Theater
Gladys Swarthout is Carmen, Robert Rounseville is Don José and Robert Merrill is Escamillo in this acclaimed CBS Opera Television Theatre production. It was the first in a CBS opera series and was narrated by Lawrence Tibbett. Henry Souvaine produced, Byron Paul directed and Boris Goldovsky conducted the orchestra. The opera was telecast on Jan. 1, 1950. Black and white. In French. 75 minutes.

1950 NBC Opera Theatre
Vera Bryner is Carmen, David Poleri is Don José and Andrew Gainey is Escamillo in this NBC Opera Theatre production with the story told in flashback by Don José in prison. It was produced by Samuel Chotzinoff, directed by Charles Polacheck and designed by George Jenkins with the orchestra conducted by Peter Herman Adler. Kirk Browning directed the telecast on Dec. 17, 1950. Black and white. In English. 60 minutes.

1951 Cloe Elmo highlights film
La Scala mezzo-soprano Cloe Elmo stars in this highlights version of *Carmen* which includes an Englsh narrative explaining the story of the opera. Black and white. In Italian and English. 18 minutes.

1952 Risë Stevens at the Metropolitan
Risë Stevens portrays a sexy Carmen in this dynamic Metropolitan Opera production by Tyrone Guthrie, hugely famous at the time. It was captured for posterity when it was telecast on closed circuit television to 31 theaters in 27 cities on Dec. 11, 1952. The audience was about 70,000. The *Variety* reviewer pretended to be shocked by its sexuality and the cleavage displayed by Stevens. Richard Tucker is Don José, Robert Merrill is Escamillo and Nadine Conner is Micaela. Unfortunately only Act Four of the telecast has survived on video. Black and white. About 40 minutes. At MTR.

1953 First Color Telecast Opera
The first color telecast of any opera anywhere was this NBC Opera Theatre production of *Carmen*. It could be seen in color only by an invited audience but was judged a brilliant success. Vera Bryner is the colorful Carmen, Robert Rounseville is Don José and Warren Galjour is Escamillo. It was produced by Samuel Chotzinoff, directed by Charles

Polacheck and designed by William Monyneux with the orchestra conducted by Peter Herman Adler. Kirk Browning directed the telecast on Oct. 31, 1953. Color. In English. 60 minutes.

1954 Carmen Jones
Oscar Hammerstein's Americanized, modernized stage adaptation of the opera was revised for the film. Dorothy Dandridge stars as Carmen Jones, a worker in a World War II parachute factory, with her singing voice dubbed by a very young Marilyn Horne. Harry Belafonte portrays Joe, the American soldier who falls for Carmen, with his singing by LaVern Hutcherson. Husky Miller (Escamillo) is a boxer acted by Joe Adams and sung by Marvin Hayes with a notable "Stand Up and Fight." Pearl Bailey is Carmen's friend Frankie and does her own singing on the splendid "Beat Out dat Rhythm with a Drum." Now that modernized versions of classic operas are common, it is time to look again at this undervalued film produced by Samuel Goldwyn and directed by Otto Preminger. 20th Century-Fox. Color. CinemaScope. In English. 94 minutes. Fox video/Pioneer laser.

1959 Robert Merrill video
Robert Merrill sings Escamillo in scenes from *Carmen* staged for the *Voice of Firestone* television show. Rosalind Elias is his Carmen and Nicolai Gedda is Don José with Alfred Wallenstein conducting the Firestone orchestra. The scenes, with sets and extras, were telecast on April 27, 1959 and are on the video *Firestone French Opera Gala*. Black and white. In French with English introductions. 20 minutes. VAI video.

1961 Luigi Vanzi film
Italian director Luigi Vanzi made a television film of the opera for the Vides company. It stars Marta Rose as Carmen, Nino Carta as Don José and Antonio Annaloro as Escamillo. Color. In Italian. 100 minutes.

1963 Rudolph Cartier telecast
Rudolph Cartier's lavish BBC Television production stars Rosalind Elias as Carmen with Raymond Nilsson as Don José and John Shirley-Quirk as Escamillo. Cartier eliminated spoken dialogue and the role of Micaela for his version and added film of Seville as background. Charles Mackerras conducts the Philharmonia Orchestra, Glyndebourne Festival Chorus and Ealing Boys' Grammar School Choir.

The opera was telecast on Jan. 11, 1963. Black and white. In Italian. 100 minutes.

1967 Salzburg Festival
Grace Bumbry stars as Carmen with Mirella Freni as Micaela and Jon Vickers as Don José in this film of a Salzburg Festival production staged and filmed by Herbert von Karajan. Justino Diaz is Escamillo and Olivera Miljakovic is Fraquita with Karajan conducting the Vienna Philharmonic Orchestra and Vienna State Opera Chorus. The sets are by Theo Otto and the art direction by Georges Wakhévitch. The cast is terrific and Bumbry is a magnficent Carmen but Karajan does not really succeed in making the opera come alive. The film was shown theatrically in the U.S. Unitel. Color. In French with English subtitles. 163 minutes. Philips video and laser.

1978 Vienna State Opera
Franco Zeffirelli's influential production of *Carmen* at the Vienna Statsoper won him wide acclaim. Elena Obraztsova stars as Carmen with Placido Domingo as her Don José in an opulent and dramatic production. The cast includes Juri Mazurok, Isobel Buchanan and Cheryl Kanfoush. Carlos Kleiber conducts the Vienna Staatsoper Orchestra. Unitel/Beta Film. Color. In French. 176 minutes. On video.

1980 Paris Opéra
Teresa Berganza sings Carmen with Placido Domingo as her Don José in this live production by Piero Faggioni at the Théâtre National L'Opéra de Paris. Ruggero Raimondi portrays Escamillo with Katia Ricciarelli as Micaela. Pierre Dervaux conducts the Paris Opéra Orchestra and Chorus. Color. In French. 157 minutes. Lyric video/Japanese laser.

1983 Peter Brook film
La Tragédie de Carmen is Peter Brook's film of his minimalist Paris stage production. There are actually three films with different casts, each using four singers, two actors and fifteen musicians. This is a slimmed-down neo-realistic version of the opera with Micaela, for example, portrayed as a tough-minded country girl who has a knife fight with Carmen over Don José. The adaptation is by screenwriter Jean Claude Carrière in collaboration with Brook, music director Marius Constant and producer Micheline Rozan. The casts are Hélène

Delavault, Eva Saurova and Zehava Gal as Carmen, Howard Hensel and Laurence Dale as Don José, Agnes Host and Veronique Dietschy as Micaela, and Jake Gardner and John Rath as Escamillo. The three films with different Carmens were shot by Ingmar Bergman's cinematographer Sven Nykvist. Color. In French with English subtitles. 82 minutes. Home Vision video (Delavault version).

1984 Francesco Rosi film
Italian director Francesco Rosi's *Carmen* is a model for what a great opera film can be and works nearly as well on the small screen as in the cinema. He uses the spoken dialogue of the original stage production to create effective cinema as well as fine opera. Julia Migenes as Carmen acts as well as she sings and her sensual personality is at the center of the drama. José is Placido Domingo at his best, a country boy in the army with a potential for violence brought to the surface by Carmen. Ruggero Raimondi is a grand full-of-himself Escamillo while Faith Esham is touching as the girl-from-back-home Micaela. Lorin Maazel conducts the National Orchestra of France and the Radio France Chorus and Children's Choir with real sizzle while Pasqualino De Santis's cinematography is as glorious as the music. Daniel Toscan du Plantier produced. Color. In French with English subtitles. 151 minutes. RCA/Columbia video.

1984 New York City Opera
Frank Corsaro's controversial production stars Chilean mezzo-soprano Victoria Vergara as Carmen, Jacques Trussel as Don José and Robert Hale as Escamillo. Corsaro updates the opera to the 1930s during the Spanish Civil War. Carmen is portrayed as an anti-Franco loyalist while Don José is a fascist soldier. The New York City Opera Orchestra is conducted by Christopher Keene. The opera was telecast in the Live from Lincoln Center series on Sept. 26, 1984. Color. In French. 210 minutes.

1985 Glyndebourne Festival
Maria Ewing gives an electrifying performance as Carmen opposite Barry McCauley as Don José in this starkly realistic Glyndebourne Festival production by Peter Hall. David Holloway sings the role of Escamillo with Marie McLaughlin as Micaela. John Bury designed the sets and costumes and Bernard Haitink conducted the London Philharmonic Orchestra and Glyndebourne Festival Choir. Hall himself directed the sizzling video.

Color. In French with English subtitles. 175 minutes. Home Vision video.

1986 Vancouver Opera
Romanian film and stage director Lucian Pintile created this controversial updated English-language version of *Carmen* for Vancouver Opera. It's presented as a fantasy play-within-a-play in a carnival in a Latin American country. Escamillo is now a rock singer and Micaela is blind. Canadian mezzo Jean Stillwell stars as Carmen with Jacques Trussel as Don José, Tom Fox as Escamillo and Martha Collins as Micaela. Tony Gilbert directed the telecast on June 17, 1986. Color. In English. 180 minutes. Lyric video.

1987 Metropolitan Opera
Agnes Baltsa is an earthy Carmen opposite José Carreras as Don José in this lavish Metropolitan Opera production by Paul Mills. Leona Mitchell is Micaela, Samuel Ramey is Escamillo, Myra Merritt is Frasquita and Diane Kesling is Mercedes. John Bury designed the sets and the costumes and James Levine conducted the Metropolitan Opera Orchestra and Chorus. Brian Large directed the telecast and video. Color. In French with English subtitles. 172 minutes. DG video/on laser.

1989 Earl's Court, London
Maria Ewing is a fine Carmen in this mammoth production by Steven Pimlott at Earl's Court in London. It cost some $10 million to stage with a cast of 500 singers, dancers, horse riders, fire eaters and even musicians. Stefanos Lazaridis designed the giant set in the round. Jacques Trussel is Don José, Alain Fondary is Escamillo and Miriam Gauci is Micaela. There is no dialogue but Paco Pena and his flamenco troupe do fine dancing. Gavin Taylor did a excellent job of directing the video. Color. 150 minutes. Arena Home Entertainment (England) video.

1991 Royal Opera
Maria Ewing, already acclaimed in the role at Glyndebourne and Earl's Court, stars as Carmen in this Royal Opera House production. Luis Lima is her Don José, Gino Quilico is Escamillo, Leontina Vaduva is Micaela, Judith Howarth is Fraquita and Jean Rigby is Mercedes. The stage director is Spanish actress Nuria Espert. Zubin Mehta leads the Royal Opera House orchestra and chorus. The sets were designed by Gerardo Vera and the video director was Barry Gavin. Color. In French with

English subtitles. 164 minutes. Home Vision video/Pioneer laser.

Early/related films

1894 Carmencita
This Thomas Edison film, made in his Black Maria studio in March 1894, features a Spanish dancer named Carmencita. In the Bizet opera, it will be recalled, the heroine tells us her name is "Carmencita." It was not recorded at the time whether Carmencita danced to Bizet's music for the film but it is probable. About 30 seconds

1902 Bioscope sound film
An aria from *Carmen* was featured in this sound film shown in September 1902 by Alber's Electro Talking Bioscope in the Netherlands. About 3 minutes.

1906 G. W. Bitzer film
D. W. Griffith's great cameraman G. W. Bitzer shot this early American version of *Carmen* in a New York studio for the American Mutoscope and Biograph company. About 7 minutes.

1907 Chronophone sound film
This British sound film features several arias and scenes from the opera. It was directed by Arthur Gilbert for Gaumont using the Chronophone sound-on-disc system. About 12 minutes.

1908 Antonio Cataldi sound film
Antonio Cataldi is featured singing the "Toreador Song" from *Carmen* in this sound film made in Brazil using a synchronized record. About four minutes.

1909 Vittoria Lepanto film
Vittoria Lepanto, one of the top Italian stars of the period, portrays Carmen in this film directed by Gerolamo Lo Savio. Alberto Nepoti portrays Don José and Annibale Ninchi is Escamillo. Film d'Arte Italiana. About 10 minutes.

1909 Torero Song "Carmen"
The American Lubin company made this sound film for its Bizet series and titled it both *Carmen* and *Torero Song "Carmen."* Escamillo's aria was synchronized with the film using the Lubin sound

system with a disc. About 4 minutes. NFTA in London has sound disc.

1910 Régine Badet film
André Calmettes directed this French film of the story with Régine Badet as Carmen and Max Dearly as Don José. A Films d'Art Pathé production. About 10 minutes.

1913 Marion Leonard film
Marion Leonard stars as Carmen in this American film of the story made for the Monopol company. This was one of two rival films of *Carmen* made in 1913 and was the first released. About 45 minutes.

1913 Marguerite Snow film
Thanhouser star Marguerite Snow portrays Carmen in this rival American version of the story released one month later. Her co-stars are William Garwood and William Russell. Theodore Marston directed. About 45 minutes.

1915 Toreador Song
German sound film pioneer Oskar Messter made a film of the "Toreador Song" with his synchronized sound-on-disc system for his Berlin Biophon Theater. It was copyrighted in the USA in 1915 but probably made earlier. About five minutes.

1915 Geraldine Farrar film
Geraldine Farrar, who had sung *Carmen* on stage at the Metropolitan Opera, made her cinema debut as Carmen in this famous Cecil B. DeMille film. Wallace Reid is her Don José and Pedro De Cordoba is Escamillo. The film was liked by both audiences and critics and launched Farrar on a very successful film career. De Mille claimed that the opera copyright owners wanted too much money so only the Mérimée story was used but nobody believed him; a 50-piece symphony orchestra played the opera music on opening night. Lasky-Paramount. Black and white. About 75 minutes.

1915 Theda Bara film
Theda Bara stars as Carmen in this rival film made for Fox and directed by Raoul Walsh. It was released on the same day as the Geraldine Farrar film and won reasonable acceptance though critics felt that vamp Bara was not well cast as a tempestuous gypsy. Don José is Einar Linden and Escamillo is Carl Harbaugh. Black and white. About 75 minutes.

1916 Charlie Chaplin film
Charlie Chaplin's Burlesque on Carmen is the best known of the silent Carmen movies. Chaplin wrote and directed and plays a soldier with the punning name of Darn Hosiery. Edna Purvience is his enticing Carmen. This is a very funny movie with many Chaplinesque delights including satirical jabs at opera acting and the rival movies by Geraldine Farrar and Theda Bara. There is also a happy ending; the knife Chaplin uses to kill Carmen is a palpable fake. Essanay. Black and white. About 60 minutes.

1916 Marguerite Sylva film
Belgian-born American opera star Marguerite Sylva, who sang the role of Carmen on stage 600 times around the world, stars in this Italian film of the opera and won praise from critics for her intense performance. Her co-stars are André Habay, Susanna Arduini and C. Servant. Giovanni Doria and August Turchi directed for Cines. Black and white. About 75 minutes.

1917 Giuseppe Campanari sound film
Metropolitan Opera baritone Giuseppe Campanari stars as Escamillo in this sound film of highlights of the opera. He is seen performing the Toreador Song with soprano Marie Conesa, Salvatore Giordano and bass Léon Rothier. The film was made for Webb Singing Pictures and premiered at the Cohan & Harris Theater in New York in the presence of Enrico Caruso and other colleagues from the Met. George Webb was an early sound film entrepreneur. About 10 minutes.

1918 Pola Negri/Ernst Lubitsch film
Ernst Lubitsch's famous film stars Pola Negri as Carmen and Harry Liedtke as Don José. It was made in Germany and was based more on the novel than the opera but the video includes Bizet's music as its score. Lubitsch and Negri won high praise from U.S. critics and later had notable Hollywood careers. The film was titled *Carmen* in Germany but was released in the U.S. in 1921 as *Gypsy Blood*. Black and white. About 75 minutes. On video.

1919 Annie Bos film
Dutch actress Annie Bos stars as Carmen in a film of the opera story shot in the Netherlands in 1919. About 70 minutes.

1920 Ernest Vollrath film
A Mexican film of the Carmen story was produced in Mexico in 1920 by Germán Camus. It was directed by Ernest Vollrath. About 65 minutes.

1922 Tense Moments from Operas film
Patricia Fitzgerald stars as Carmen in this British highlights film made for the *Tense Moments from Operas* series. Ward MacAllister is Don José and Maresco Maresini is Escamillo. George Wynn directed and H. B. Parkinson produced for Master/Gaumont. Black and white. About 10 minutes.

1926 Raquel Meller/ Jacques Feyder film
Raquel Meller stars as Carmen in this famous French film directed by Jacques Feyder. Meller is superb as the gypsy temptress and has a fine partner in Louis Lerch as Don José. *The New York Times* called it "vastly superior" to earlier screen versions of the story. Feyder based his realistic film on the Mérimée source novel but there are overtones from the opera. Albatros Film. Black and white. About 75 minutes.

1927 Giovanni Martinelli film
Metropolitan Opera tenor Giovanni Martinelli portrays Don José and sings selections from Act II of *Carmen* in this Vitaphone sound film. He is joined by contralto Jeanne Gordon as Carmen on three of the excerpts accompanied by the Vitaphone Symphony Orchestra. Black and white. About 10 minutes.

1927 John Barclay on Vitaphone
English baritone John Barclay sings the Toreador Song in "imitation of a famous character" in this Vitaphone sound film. Black and white. About 10 minutes.

1927 The Loves of Carmen
Dolores Del Rio is a memorable Carmen in this version of the Carmen story, the second directed by Raoul Walsh. Don Alvarado plays Don José but it is Victor McLaglen as Escamillo that Carmen really pursues. Bizet's influence was fully acknowledged with a live prologue of music from the opera performed at the New York premiere and selections played during the film. Critics praised Del Rio's fiery performance. Black and white. About 93 minutes.

1927 Cameo Opera film
Zeda Pascha stars as Carmen opposite Herbert Langley as Don José in this British Song Films highlights version. Live singers and orchestra performed in synchronization with the scenes on screen. H. B. Parkinson directed for the *Cameo Opera* series. Black and white. About 20 minutes.

1928 Pasquale Amato film
Baritone Pasquale Amato sings the Toreador aria from *Carmen* in this 1928 Vitaphone sound short titled *Pasquale Amato in A Neapolitan Romance*. Black and white. 8 minutes.

1928 Julius Pinschewer film
Julius Pinschewer's German animated film of *Carmen* was screened with music from the Bizet opera. Black and white. 7 minutes.

1929 Eleanor Painter film
"Eleanor Painter, The Lyric Soprano" sings, in costume, the "Habanera" from *Carmen* in this early sound short made for Vitaphone. Black and white. About 9 minutes.

1933 Lotte Reiniger film
German silhouette artist Lotte Reiniger's animated film of the opera is still widely admired. It is one of the most famous early "artistic" cartoons. Black and white. 10 minutes.

1936 Anson Dyer film
England animator Anson Dyer made a charming burlesque version of *Carmen*. It's based around the Stanley Holloway character Sam who becomes a matador. Color. 9 minutes

1937 Broadway Melody of 1938
The first shot of the movie shows crowds in front of the old Metropolitan Opera and posters of *Carmen*. An orchestra plays Escamillo's music and a voice is heard beginning the 'Toreador Song.' The camera pans right to a barber shop where a barber (played by Met baritone Igor Gorin) is singing the aria while shaving Buddy Ebsen. Roy Del Ruth directed. MGM. Black and white. 110 minutes.

1938 Carmen la de Triana
Imperio Argentina stars as Carmen in this Spanish version of the story directed by Florian Rey and shot in Berlin during the Spanish Civil War. The basic music is Bizet but there are many new songs.

In the cast are Rafael Rivelles, Manuel Luna and Alberto Romea. Black and white. In Spanish. 102 minutes.

1938 Andalusische Nachte
The German version of the above *Carmen* features Imperio Argentina singing in German under the direction of Herbert Maisch. The cast includes Friedrich Benfer, Erwin Biegel and Karl Kousner. Black and white. In German. 102 minutes.

1939 Balalaika
The Toreador Song and the Gypsy Song from *Carmen* are featured in this Nelson Eddy/Ilona Massey musical about the Russian revolution. He plays a prince, she's a cabaret singer. Reinhold Schunzel directed. Black and white. 102 minutes.

1941 Ridin' the Cherokee Trail
This Tex Ritter B western contains what is surely the most bizarre version of the Toreador Song in the cinema. See RIDIN' THE CHEROKEE TRAIL

1942 I Married an Angel
The last of the Jeanette MacDonald-Nelson Eddy films was an adaptation of a Rodgers and Hart musical about a man who dreams he marries an angel. The duo also sing the "Chanson Bohème" from *Carmen*. W.S. Van Dyke directed. Black and white. 84 minutes.

1943 Viviane Romance film
Viviane Romance stars as Carmen opposite Jean Marais as Don José in this French film based on the opera libretto and using Bizet's music as score. This is an elaborate and colorful film, splendidly made and well directed by period film specialist Christian-Jaque. Black and white. In French. 105 minutes.

1943 Nini Marshall film
Singer Nini Marshall stars in this Argentine comedy based around the opera. She plays a dressmaker who gets hit on the head at the opera house and dreams she is part of the on-stage *Carmen*. It turns into an updated burlesque with the smugglers dealing in black market tires. Luis Cesar Amadori directed. Sono Film. Black and white. In Spanish. 96 minutes.

1944 Going My Way
Metropolitan Opera star Risë Stevens portrays Carmen in this film before she ever performed the role on stage and it helped identify her with the part. Bing Crosby plays a priest who needs to raise money for his church. He goes backstage at the Met and watches with admiration as his friend Stevens sings the Habanera. Leo McCarey directed. Black and white. 126 minutes. Paramount video.

1948 The Loves of Carmen
Rita Hayworth is Carmen in this Hollywood version of the story set in 1820 Seville. Glenn Ford portrays the soldier captivated by her. Hayworth is beautiful but the music is by Mario Castelnuova-Tedesca, not Bizet. Charles Vidor directed for Columbia Color. 99 minutes. On video.

1952 Forbidden Carmen
Aña Esmerald stars as a Spanish dancer called Carmen in *Carmen Proibita*, an Italian film based on a modern version of the story directed by Giuseppe Maria Scotese. Fausto Tozzi is the José who is seduced and corrupted by her. A Spanish version was made at the same time as *Siempre Carmen* and directed by Alejandro Perla. Black and white. 93 minutes.

1956 Serenade
The Carmen myth is central to James Cain's novel *Serenade* and the Mario Lanza film based on it. The hero is an opera singer, his favorite opera is *Carmen*, his real-life Carmen is a rich American and his Escamillo is a Mexican woman who fights figurative bulls and nearly kills Carmen to save him. The book is more resonant than the film but director Anthony Mann keeps its interesting. Warner Bros. Color. 121 minutes. On video.

1959 The Devil Made A Woman
Sara Montiel's Carmen is a Spanish cabaret singer in *Carmen, la de Ronda*, a revised Spanish version of the story set in Spain during the Napoleonic wars. She falls in love with a French soldier named José and attempts to save his life. Tulio Demicheli directed and Benito Perojo produced. Color. In Spanish. 98 minutes.

1962 The Drama of Carmen
Leonard Bernstein examines the opera using Metropolitan Opera singers and Broadway actors in this television show with the New York Philharmonic. Jane Rhodes and William Ovis sing

the roles of Carmen and Don José while Zohra Lampert and James Congdon portray them in the spoken version. Bernstein contrasts the original opera with its spoken dialogue and the later sung version. William A. Graham directed the telecast. Black and white. 60 minutes.

1962 Black Tights
Zizi Jeanmaire is Carmen, Roland Petit is Don José and Henning Kronstam is the toreador in a thirty-minute ballet version of *Carmen* in this French film. Petit devised the choreography and Terence Young directed the film. The French title is *Les Collants Noirs.* Color. 120 minutes.

1962 Carmen of Trastevere
Giovanna Ralli is Carmen in *Carmen di Trastevere*, an Italian attempt to transfer the story to the working class district of Trastevere in Rome. Don José is a policeman and his rival is now a motorcyclist. Opera film specialist Carmine Gallone directed. Black and white. In Italian. 90 minutes.

1970 The Clowns
Italian director Federico Fellini features the Toreador music in his brilliant semi-documentary about the world of clowns. Color. In Italian. 93 minutes.

1972 Carmen: The Dream and the Destiny
Huguette Tourangeau is Carmen, Placido Domingo is Don José and Tom Krause is Escamillo in this documentary about a Hamburg production of the opera by Regina Resnik. The film shows both preparation and performance and explores the history of the opera. Alain Lombard conducts the Hamburg Opera Orchestra. Swansway Productions. 90 minutes. Print at NFTA.

1976 The Bad News Bears
Themes from *Carmen* are featured rather ironically as the score of this excellent satirical comedy. Michael Ritchie's fable about a Little League baseball team stars Walter Matthau and Tatum O'Neal. Color. 103 minutes.

1978 Peter Brook & the Tragedy of Carmen
A documentary film by Tony Cash about Peter Brook and his production of a bare-bones *Carmen* at the Théâtre des Bouffes du Nord in Paris. After revising the libretto with screenwriter Jean Claude Carrière and music director Marius Constant, the result is a highly theatrical production with four singers, two actors and 15 musicians. Brook used three casts on the production for 150 performances. LWT. Color. 52 minutes. On video.

1978 Carmen, Who Was Only 16
Mayra Alejandra stars as Carmen in *Carmen, la que Contaba 16 Años*, a Venezuelan version of the story set in the harbor of La Guaira. Director Roman Chalbaud follows the story fairly closely in its new setting and ends the film with Don José killing Carmen at the bull ring. Color. In Spanish. 102 minutes.

1978 To Forget Venice
Franco Brusati's *Dimenticare Venezia*, which takes place at the home of a dying opera star, received an Oscar nomination for Best Foreign Language film. The story of some complicated relationships, it features the Habanera from *Carmen*. Color. In Italian. 107 minutes.

1983 Carlos Saura film
Laura Del Sol dances the role of Carmen in this superb film by Carlos Saura. The screenplay of this flamenco-centered story is based on the opera and the novella. Choreographer Antonio Gades discovers Carmen as an untrained dancer and hires her for a production of *Carmen*. He falls in loves with her, finds her fickle and kills her when she betrays him. Arias from *Carmen* are sung in the film by Regina Resnik as Carmen, Mario del Monaco as Don José and Tom Krause as Escamillo. Color. In Spanish with English subtitles. 101 minutes.

1983 First Name Carmen
Jean-Luc Godard's updated version of the story, *Prénom Carmen*, is more Godard than Bizet but includes snatches of music from the opera. Maruschka Detmers is Carmen, a terrorist rather than a smuggler, but still a femme-fatale. She seduces a policeman called Joseph and leads him to a life of crime. She's also an aspiring filmmaker with a film director uncle played by Godard. Color. In French. 85 minutes. On video and laser.

1988 Jessye Norman Sings Carmen
A behind-the-scenes film of Jessye Norman making a recording of *Carmen* in Paris. She is observed at various stages of the process singing arias, giving a press conference, having problems and talking about her interpretation. Neil Shicoff sings Don José and Simon Estes is Escamillo in this Philips

recording with Seiji Ozawa conducting the National Orchestra of France and the Radio France Chorus. The film was made by Susan Froemke, Peter Gelb, Albert Maysles and Charlotte Zwerin. Color. In English and French with subtitles. 59 minutes. Cami video.

1994 The Hudsucker Proxy
Grace Bumbry sings the Habanera on the soundtrack as Tim Robbins dances with a Carmen figure in a dream. Rafrael Frübeck de Burgos leads the Paris Opera Orchestra and Chorus. The film is an odd Capra-eque fantasy about an innocent running a big business. Joel Coen directed. Color. 111 minutes.

1995 Operavox Animated Opera
The British Pizzazz animation studio created this computer-enhanced live action animated version of *Carmen* for the British Operavox series. The Welsh National Opera Orchestra plays the music. Julian Smith was music editor. Color. 27 minutes.

1995 Babe
A trio of mice briefly sing the Toreador Song in this Australian children's fantasy about a piglet that wants to herd sheep. Chris Noonan directed. Color. 91 minutes.

1996 Natasa Barbara Gracner film
Natasa Barbara Gracner stars as a hooker Carmen in the Slovenian film *Carmen*, a retelling of the mythic tale set in the urban underworld of Slovenia. Sebastijan Cavazza plays the Don José equivalent. Metod Pevec directed. Color. 94 minutes.

CARMINA BURANA
1937 scenic cantata by Orff

Carl Orff's *Carmina Burana* (Songs of Beuren), which he called a "scenic cantata," is not an opera or oratorio in the traditional sense but it was meant to be staged and danced with orchestra and choir in the pit and it has influenced modern ideas about opera. Orff used as "libretto" a collection of poems by 13th century monks rediscovered 600 years later. The thread of narrative that runs through the cantata concerns the workings of fate/fortune with sections devoted to spring, the tavern and seduction. There are solos for soprano, tenor and baritone. See also CARL ORFF.

1976 Jean-Pierre Ponnelle film
Jean-Pierre Ponnelle and Jean Louis Martinot directed this film of a staged version of *Carmina Burana* for Bavarian and Czech television. The soloists are Lucia Popp, John Van Kesteren and Hermann Prey with Kurt Eichhorn conducting the orchestra and chorus. Color. In Latin. 65 minutes. BMG video.

1981 Cardiff Festival of Choirs
Thomas Allen, Kenneth Bowen and Norma Burrows are the soloists at this superb subtitled concert performance of the cantata at the Cardiff Festival of Choirs in Wales. Walter Weller conducts the Royal Philharmonic Orchestra with the Cardiff Polyphonic Choir, the Dyfed Choir and the Llandaff Cathedral Choristers. Terry de Lacey produced and directed the video for Welsh television. Color. In Latin with English subtitles. 60 minutes. Kultur video.

1989 Berlin Philharmonic Hall
Kathleen Battle, Frank Lopardo and Thomas Allen are the soloists at this splendid performance of *Carmina Burana* filmed at the Berlin Philharmonic Hall. Seiji Ozawa leads the Shin-Yu Kai Chorus, the Boys' choir of the Staats-und-Domchor of Berlin and the Berlin Philharmonic Orchestra. Barrie Gavin directed the video for ZDF. Color. In Latin. 62 minutes. Philips video.
(A highlights version is available in the *Great Moments* video series as Volume 5).

1995 Horant Hohlfeld video
Horant H. Hohlfeld directed this video of a staged version of *Carmina Burana* for German television. The soloists are Anna Korondi, Thomas Mohr and Donald George-Smith with Daniel Nazareth conducting the Middeldeutschen Rundfunk Orchestra and Chorus. The ballet is performed by the MDR Deutsches Fernsehballett. Unitel. Color. In Latin. 62 minutes.

CARNEGIE HALL
American concert hall (1891-)

Carnegie Hall is the most famous concert hall in America and has crowned the reputation of opera singers from Caruso to Callas. Despite an attempt to replace this repository of musical memory with an orange skyscraper, Carnegie Hall looks set to celebrate another century of music. It has been the subject of two films and appears as a character in movies like *On The Town*, *Unfaithfully Yours* and *Home Alone 2*. It is also the subject of America's most famous classical music joke. Question: "How do you get to Carnegie Hall?" Answer: "Practice!"

1947 Carnegie Hall
This pleasant film is a fiction framework for a series of numbers by classical stars of the period. Ezio Pinza performs arias from *Don Giovanni* and *Simon Boccanegra*, Risë Stevens sings arias from *Carmen* and *Samson et Dalila*, Lily Pons sings the Bell Song from *Lakmé* and Jan Peerce sings "O Sole Mio." The other performers include Bruno Walter, Leopold Stokowski, Artur Rubenstein and Jascha Heifitz. Karl Lamb's script is about a lady who works at the Hall and dreams her pianist son will one day play there. William Miller photographed it and Edgar G. Ulmer directed. Federal Films. Black and white. 134 minutes. Allegro/Bel Canto Society videos.

1991 Carnegie Hall at 100
This splendid documentary, subtitled *A Place of Dreams*, celebrates the centennial of the hall and includes archival footage of opera personalities who appeared there. Marilyn Horne is interviewed, Leonard Bernstein talks about his first appearance and Lily Pons performs her party piece Bell Song. The hero of the film is Isaac Stern who organized the group that saved the building from being torn down in 1961. The documentary was directed by Peter Rosen and written by Sara Lukinson. BMG. Color. 57 minutes. RCA Victor video and laser.

1991 Carnegie Hall Live at 100
A gala at Carnegie Hall celebrating its birthday. The performers include Placido Domingo, Marilyn Horne, Leontyne Price and Samuel Ramey with Zubin Mehta conducting the orchestra. The concert was telecast on PBS in May 1991. Color. 57 minutes.

1991 A Carnegie Hall Christmas
Kathleen Battle and Frederica von Stade perform seasonal favorites in this concert at Carnegie Hall on Dec., 8, 1991. They join voices on the "Evening Prayer" from Humperdinck's *Hansel and Gretel*, "Mariä Wiegenlied" and "Gesu Bambino" and ensembles. Also featured are trumpeter Wynton Marsalis, harpist Nancy Allen, the American Boys Choir, the Christmas Concert Chorus and the Orchestra of St. Luke's led by André Previn. Brian Large directed the video. Color. 88 minutes. Sony video.

CAROUSEL
1945 musical by Rodgers & Hammerstein

Carousel is one of the most powerful of the great musicals produced by Richard Rodgers and Oscar Hammerstein II. It is based on Ferenc Molnar's 1921 play *Liliom* with the setting transferred to a 19th century New England fishing village. Carnival barker Billy Bigelow marries factory worker Julie Jordan but as they have no money they move into Cousin Nettie's home. He is killed during a robbery attempt but is allowed to return to earth for a good deed and sing "You'll never walk alone" to his daughter. Counterpointing their story is the plain but satisfying marriage of Carrie to Mr. Snow. See also OSCAR HAMMERSTEIN II, RICHARD RODGERS.

1956 Claramae Turner/Robert Rounseville film
Metropolitan Opera contralto Claramae Turner portrays Cousin Nettie in this classic film version of *Carousel* and New York City Opera tenor Robert Rounseville is seen in the role of Enoch Snow. Gordon MacRae stars as the swaggering carousel barker who marries simple factory girl Shirley Jones. Turner and Rounseville's songs include "June is bustin' out all over," "When the children are asleep" and "A real nice clambake." The musical, mainly shot on location by Charles G. Clarke, was directed by Henry King for Twentieth Century-Fox. Color. 128 minutes. On video and laserdisc.

1967 Patrica Neway video
New York City Opera soprano Patricia Neway portrays Nettie in this ABC television production by Norman Rosemont. Roubert Goulet stars as Billy Bigelow with Mary Grover as Julie Jordan, Marlyn Mason as Carrie and Jack De Lon as Mr. Snow. Jack Ellcott was the musical director and Paul Bogart directed. Color. 120 minutes.

CARRERAS, JOSÉ
Spanish tenor (1946-)

José Carreras has become one of the most popular tenors of our time as evidenced by his participation in the Three Tenors concerts and his many recordings, films and videos. He made his debut in his home town of Barcelona in 1970, was aided in the early part of his career by fellow Catalan Montserrat Caballé and soon won acclaim in the major opera houses. He can be seen portraying Julián Gayarré in a famous Catalan film. Carreras had to fight against leukemia but he made a courageous comeback. Carreras's warm personality comes across strongly in his videos and films. See also ANDREA CHÉNIER (1985), ADRIANA LECOUVREUR (1976), LA BOHÈME (1982/1988), MONTSERRAT CABALLÉ (1989/1993), CARMEN (1987), ENRICO CARUSO (1994), CRISTÓBAL COLÓN (1989), DON CARLO (1986), LA FORZA DEL DESTINO (1978), GALA LIRICA, JULIÁN GAYARRE (1986), NICOLAI GHIAUROV (1986), I LOMBARDI ALLA PRIMA CROCIATA (1984), METROPOLITAN OPERA (1983), MOZART REQUIEM (1994), SOUTH PACIFIC (1986), STIFFELIO (1993), THE THREE TENORS, TURANDOT (1983),VERDI REQUIEM (1982), VERONA (1988), VIENNA (1991/1992), WEST SIDE STORY (1985), ZURICH (1984).

1985 Silent Night with José Carreras
A Christmas journey to Austria with Carreras filmed in and around Salzburg. The tenor talks about Christmas, visits the place where "Silent Night" was composed and sings it with style. He also performs such favorites as "White Christmas" and "Come All Ye Faithful." Color. 40 minutes. On video.

1987 José Carreras in Concert
Carreras is shown performing in concert at the Komische Oper in East Berlin on Jan. 9, 1987, to enormous applause. He sings arias and songs by Puccini, Tosti, Bellini, Leoncavallo, Cilea, Respighi, Ginastera, Sorozabal and others. Vincenzo Scalera accompanies him on piano. Color. 90 minutes. Kultur video.

1988 José Carreras Comeback Recital
Carreras's comeback recital at Peralada Castle in Spain in the summer of 1988 carries an emotional charge. It was his first appearance after being hospitalized with leukemia and two operations. He sings a variety of songs by Tosti, Hahn, Duparc, Massenet, Catala, Monpou, Turina, Puccini, Grieg and Lara. The closing number is a strong "Granada." Carreras is accompanied on piano by Vincenzo Scalera. Color. 82 minutes. Kultur video.

1990 Music Festival in Granada
Carreras gives performances of songs by Scarlatti, Bononcini, Tosti, Puccini, de Falla, Turina, Ginastera and Nacho in this concert filmed in Granada during a 1990 summer music festival. Color. 93 minutes. Kultur video.

1990 Carreras: Four Days on the Road
A documentary about the tenor during the four days on which he was working on the film *Misa Criolla*. He follows in the footsteps of his ancestors from Barcelona to Mallorca and prepares for his journey to the Mission Dolores in California. Once there he performs Ariel Ramirez's *Misa Criolla*. A camera team follows Carreras in rehearsal, talking with fans, meeting his son and returning home. Andrea Thomas directed. Color. 31 minutes. Kultur video.

1990 Misa Criolla
Carreras sings Ariel Ramirez's *Misa Criolla* (La Palabra y la Voz) in a performance shot in the Mission Dolores in San Francisco. Carlos Caballé conducts the orchestra. Color. 60 minutes. Kultur video.

1991 Tribute to Mario Lanza
José Carreras salutes his youthful idol Mario Lanza in a recital from the Royal Albert Hall in London. He sings Lanza favorites like "Be My Love," "Serenade" and "Because You're Mine" plus the Donizetti aria "Una furtiva lagrima" which Lanza sang in *That Midnight Kiss*. The video, subtitled *With a Song in My Heart*, includes film of Lanza singing "Ave Maria." Enrique Ricci conducts the BBC Concert Orchestra and English Concert Chorus. Declan Lowney directed. Color. 83 minutes. Teldec video.

1991 Carreras Sings Andrew Lloyd Weber
Carreras sings the songs of Andrew Lloyd Webber in concert joined by Marti Webb, Jane Harrison and Stephanie Lawrence. They are supported by St. Paul's Cathedral Choir. Richard Harroway produced the video. Color. 55 minutes. Teldec video.

1991 José Carreras and Friends
An evening of arias, duets and songs with Carreras joined by singing friends Katia Ricciarelli, Agnes Baltsa and Ruggero Raimondi. They are accompanied by the London Arts Orchestra led by Jacques Delacote. Color. 60 minutes. On video.

1992 José Carreras: A Life Story
Chris Hunt's documentary is an excellent biography of the singer and includes a version of "La donna è mobile" recorded by the tenor when he was seven years old. The film shows Carreras's rise to success, his fight against leukemia, his

triumphant return and his first Three Tenors concert. There are comments from Caballé, Domingo and Pavarotti plus interviews with the singer and his father. Color. 60 minutes. London video.

CARUSO, ENRICO
Italian tenor (1873-1921)

Caruso was the first opera singer to become famous on record. He had a phonogenic voice, the acoustical equivalent of the cinema's photogenic face, and the primitive recording apparatus loved him. Caruso was born in Italy and became a star there but his main career was at the Metropolitan Opera from 1903 to 1920, when he was the center of the Met's Golden Age. Caruso was signed up by the movie moguls, of course, and there was talk of a silent version of *Pagliacci* but the camera apparently didn't love him in the way the recording machine did. His films were not successful and his movie career was brief. His voice, however, is often used in films and there are several entertaining film biographies. His biopic, *The Great Caruso*, is by far the most popular opera film ever made and a German film centering around him, *Fitzcarraldo*, is one of the best. See FITZCARRALDO, THE GREAT CARUSO.

1908 Caruso on Synchronoscope
Jules Greenbaum's Synchronoscope was an early attempt at synchronizing a record with a film image. Universal Pictures founder Carl Laemmle exhibited one at the Majestic Theater in Evansville, Indiana in the summer of 1908 that reportedly included a "sound film" with the voice of Caruso singing an aria.

1912 Caruso on Cinephonograph
Caruso is reported to have sung the Sextet from *Lucia di Lammermoor* with basso Pol Plançon in this legendary early Edison Studio attempt to synchronize sound and image. Caruso did make records of the Sextet during this period but no film has ever been found.

1917 Caruso on Webb's Singing Pictures
Caruso turned up in person at the Cohen & Harris Theater in New York on Jan, 14, 1917, for the premiere of an early attempt at sound cinema from George Webb's Singing Pictures. As an actor appeared on screen in costume in a scene from *Pagliacci*, Caruso's voice was heard singing the aria

"Vesti la giubba" over loudspeakers. The singing came from a Caruso record. A second film featured actors on screen in *Rigoletto* while Caruso sang "La donna è mobile."

1918 My Cousin
This was Caruso's first film as an actor and he is pretty good in the double role of a great opera singer and his poor but likable cousin. The film includes scenes at the Metropolitan Opera House, shows Caruso's dressing room and features him singing in *Pagliacci* but was mostly filmed at the Artcraft studio on 56th Street in New York. His co-star was a young American opera singer named Carolina White. Caruso's film career never took off but it is not true that this was simply a bad film and Caruso a bad actor. He is quite watchable and his personality shines through. Reviews were favorable: *The New York Times* praised the film and said Caruso's acting was "thoroughly enjoyable," *Variety* called him a "master" and *Photoplay World* said the film was "unqualifiedly a success." Edward José directed. The film was inspired by a popular song of 1908 titled "My Cousin Caruso" which was based on a theme from *Pagliacci*. Famous Players/Lasky/ Artcraft. Black and white. About 60 minutes (4,710 feet).

1919 The Splendid Romance
Caruso's second film features him as Prince Cosimo, an aristocrat sought out in Rome by young American Ormi Hawley who wants to become an opera singer. They have a romance. The film was again made by Artcraft in its New York studio for Famous Players-Lasky and directed by Edward José. Margaret Turnbull wrote the screenplay for both Caruso films. *This Splendid Romance* was released in June 1919 but apparently not in the U.S. Black and white. About 74 minutes (five reels).

1935 El Cantante de Napoles
Enrico Caruso Jr. plays opera star Enrico Daspurro in *The Singer from Naples*, an American Spanish-language film based on Caruso Sr.'s life. As a young man in Naples he dreams of singing at La Scala and eventually succeeds with help from Mona Maris. Caruso sings arias from *Il Trovatore, The Barber of Seville* and *L'Africaine* as well as Neapolitan songs. Emilia Leovalli plays his mother with Carmen Rio as his sweetheart. Betty Reinhardt wrote the script based on a novel by Arman Chelieu. Howard Bretherton directed. Black and white. In Spanish. 77 minutes.

1951 The Young Caruso

Ermanno Randi stars as Caruso with his singing dubbed by Mario Del Monaco in the Italian film *Enrico Caruso, Leggenda di una voce*. Gina Lollobrigida is his co-star. Like the American film it is romanticized biography, but this one focuses on the singer's early years and ends when he signs his first professional contract. It was based on a novel by Frank Thies titled *Leggenda Napoletana*. There are arias by Giordano, Flotow, Donizetti and Leoncavallo. Giacomo Gentilomo directed. Color & black and white. In Italian. 91 minutes. Video Yesteryear/Opera Dubs videos.

1956 The Day I Met Caruso

Frank Borzage's charming film about Caruso's meeting with a little Quaker girl was made for the Screen Directors Playhouse. Lotfi Mansouri, who later became an important opera director, portrays Caruso with his singing provided by Caruso recordings. Sandy Descher is the little girl who meets Caruso on a Boston train to New York and is won over by his voice. Zoe Atkins' screenplay is based on a story by Elizabeth Bacon Rodewald. The film was made at the Hal Roach studios. Black and white. 30 minutes.

1960 Pay or Die

Caruso received blackmail threats from the Mafia-like Black Hand when he was singing at the Met in 1909. This real event is incorporated into this period American crime thriller set in New York City's Italian neighborhood. Howard Caine portrays Caruso and is seen on stage at the Met performing an aria from *Lucia de Lammermoor* with the singing done by David Poleri. The plot to kill Caruso is thwarted by heroic Italian police detective Ernest Borgnine. Richard Wilson directed. Black and white. 109 minutes. Allied Artists video.

1978 Metropolitan Opera

An intermission feature on Caruso was featured with the telecast of Pagliacci in April 1978. Color. 17 minutes. Video at New York Public Library.

1985 The Grey Fox

Richard Farnsworth, an aging train robber in the early years of the century, is attracted to a woman by her outdoor phonograph playing Caruso's recording of "M'appari" from *Martha*. Their joint love of Caruso leads to a permanent relationship. Philip Borsos directed this fine Canadian film. Color. 92 minutes. Media video.

1987 John Hurt sings Caruso

The final episode of the British opera film *Aria* features John Hurt singing with Caruso's voice. After wandering around between episodes of the film, he enters an opera house where he makes up as a clown. On stage he has a vision of a girl he once loved, mimes to Caruso singing "Vesti la giubba" from *Pagliacci* and dies. Bill Bryden directed. See ARIA.

1994 A Tribute to Caruso

Omaggio a Caruso is a gala evening in honor of Caruso at the San Carlo Opera House in his native Naples. The singers include José Carreras, Shirley Verrett and Lucio Dalla. There are memories and anecdotes as well as music. Walter Licastro directed the program. Color. 147 minutes. On video.

CASA RICORDI

1954 Italian opera film

This is a grand Hollywood-on-the Tiber opera film, the romanticized story of the Milan opera publishing house Ricordi with an all-star cast of Italian singers re-creating and inventing operatic history under the direction of Carmine Gallone. The film traces the history of Italian opera through tales about great composers. First there is Rossini having a tempestuous love affair while writing *The Barber of Seville*, after which Tito Gobbi and Giulio Neri sing scenes from the opera. Then we see Donizetti (Marcello Mastroianni) taming a temperamental diva during rehearsals of *L'Elisir d'Amore*. Bellini (Maurice Ronet) dies as *I Puritani* is being premiered. Verdi makes a comeback with *Otello* and Mario Del Monaco sings the final scene as Francesco Tamagno, the tenor who created the role. Puccini is inspired to write *La Bohème* by a girl he meets in a shop, but she dies of TB before the premiere at which Renata Tebaldi sings Mimi's last aria. Other featured singers include Giulietta Simionato, Gianni Poggi, Giulio Neri and Italo Tajo. The actors include Paolo Stoppa as the founder of the Ricordi firm, Marta Toren, Nadia Gray and Micheline Presle. *The New York Times* critic loved this movie. Color. In Italian. 120 minutes. Opera Dubs/ Lyric videos. See also CARMINE GALLONE.

CASA VERDI

Milan retirement home (1902 -)

The Casa Verdi in Milan is a retirement home for opera singers founded and funded by composer

Giuseppe Verdi in 1902. Many of its residents were major stars of the opera world in their youth. Casa Verdi has always been a place of fascination to opera enthusiasts and has been the focus of two documentary films.

1943 Casa Verdi
Italian director Giovanni Paolucci made a number of acclaimed documentaries in the 1940s about aspects of Italian life including a notable one about music and the St. Cecilia Academy. His wartime film *Casa Verdi* is an informative documentary about the Milan retirement home and its opera singers. Black and white. In Italian. 30 minutes.

1985 Tosca's Kiss
Il Bacio di Tosca is a feature-length Swiss film by Daniel Schmid about the Casa Verdi that focuses on retired singers Sara Scuderi, Giovanni Puligheddu, Leonida Bellon, Salvatore Locapo and Giuseppe Manacchini. They still consider themselves resting between jobs and, at the age of 85, keep suitcases packed in case they might be suddenly called to sing at the Met. They are also more than willing to demonstrate a scene from *Tosca* in a phone booth. Schmid's film is filled with opera music as well as warmth, humor, conflict and delight. Color. In Italian with English subtitles. 87 minutes. VAI video. See also DANIEL SCHMID.

CASE, ANNA
American soprano (1889-1984)

Anna Case made her debut at the Metropolitan Opera in 1909 and sang Sophie in the first Met performance of *Der Rosenkavalier* in 1913. She stopped performing in operas in 1920 but continued to give concerts until 1931. She also made nearly a hundred Edison recordings as her voice was highly phonogenic and recorded well in the early systems. She starred in one silent film and was featured in one of the first Vitaphone sound opera films where her Met connection was highly publicized.

1918 The Hidden Truth
Anna Case stars as a mining town singer in her only feature film, a romantic Western directed by Julius Steger. The plot revolves around her taking on another woman's identity because of love. Select Pictures. Black and white. About 68 minutes (5,050 feet).

1926-27 Vitaphone sound films
Case's cinematic moment of glory arrived with the premiere of the John Barrymore film *Don Juan* on August 6, 1926. She was a featured performer in this famous prelude to the sound era starring in the Vitaphone short *La Fiesta* with the Metropolitan Opera House Chorus. The sheet music for *Don Juan* carries a banner announcement: "Sung by Anna Case of the Metropolitan Opera." *La Fiesta* is available with the other Vitaphone shorts featured that historic evening on a laserdisc with *Don Juan*. A second Anna Case Vitaphone short was made in 1927 and featured her singing Stephen Foster's "Old Folks at Home." Black and white. Each about 7 minutes. On video.

CASERIO, EL
1916 zarzuela by Guridi

Basque composer Jesus Guridi's zarzuela *El Caserio* (The Homestead) is set in the Basque countryside and uses Basque rhythms and musical instruments. The libretto by Guillermo Fernández Shaw and Federico Romero is a country love story. Middle-aged Santi has a nice estate and will leave it to young relatives Ana Mari and José Miguel if they will marry. When José doesn't want to settle down, Santi says he will marry the girl himself. See also JESUS GURIDI.

1968 Juan de Orduña film
Federico Moreno Torroba conducts the Spanish Lyric Orchestra and Madrid Chorus in this colorful film. The principal roles are sung by Dolores Pérez, Rosa Sarmiento, Luis-Sagi Vela, Carlo del Monte and Enrique del Portal with actors portraying the characters on screen. The film was directed by Juan De Orduña, written by Manuel Tamayo and produced by TVE for its Teatro Lirico Español series. The film soundtrack is on record. Color. In Spanish. 92 minutes.

CASTELNUOVO-TEDESCA, MARIO
Italian composer (1895-1968)

Italian-born American opera composer Mario Castelnuovo-Tedesca, who wrote two imaginary screen operas, is known in Italy for stage operas like *The Importance of Being Earnest* and *The Merchant of Venice*. He was forced to flee Italy in 1939 because of anti-Semitism and settled in Los Angeles where he wrote music for films as well as the stage. He created effective imaginary operas for the movies *Everybody Does It* in 1949 and *Strictly Dishonorable* in 1951. He also wrote the score for the Rita Hayworth film of *Carmen*. See CARMEN (1948), IMAGINARY OPERAS IN FILMS (1949, 1951).

CASTRATOS

Castratos were male sopranos or contraltos castrated when young to preserve high voices with masculine power. Many early operas were written for them and, for a period, the castrati were the highest paid singers. Handel wrote many operas for castratos and the famous castrato Farinelli had many admirers. No one today knows what they really sounded like but Farinelli had a range of three and one-half octaves, could sing 250 notes in a row and could hold a single note for a minute. It must have been impressive. The last opera written for a castrato was Meyerbeer's 1824 *Il Crociato in Egitto*. Most roles composed for castratos are now sung by contraltos and countertenors. The era of the castrati in opera has been explored in several films. See also FARINELLI.

1964 White Voices
Le Voce Bianche is an Italian film set in 18th century Italy. Paolo Ferrari tries to sell his brother as a castrato but ends up having to take his place. He bribes the surgeon not to perform the operation and enjoys a special position with women until fate catches up with him. There are several elegant operatic scenes. Pasquale Festa Campanile and Massimo Franciosa wrote and directed the film. Color. In Italian. 103 minutes.

1989 Les Voix du Serail
The Voices of the Seraglio is a video of a televised concert of music written for castratos presented at the 1989 Marrakesh Festival in Morocco. The singers include Charles Brett, Elizabeth Vidal, Aris Christofellis and Paulo Abel Donascimento. Color. In French. 60 minutes. Lyric video.

1992 The Reluctant Angels
Michael Bartlett's documentary, subtitled "The World of the Castrati," explores the why and how of the era of the castratos. The practice seems to have grown up when women were not allowed in the Vatican choir and on stage in Italy. Most castrati came from poor families who learned that successful singers became wealthy. The film journeys from Venice to Dresden with arias sung by countertenor Jochen Kowalski. Color. English narration. 56 minutes. Opera Dubs video.

CATALANI, ALFREDO
Italian composer (1854-1893)

Alfredo Catalani, a romantic composer who died young and is sometimes compared to Puccini, is remembered primarily for his opera *La Wally*. It has a heated plot about a mountain woman and her ill-fated love affair. The libretto is by Luigi Illica who wrote *La Bohème* and other Puccini operas. Catalani suffered from a persecution complex in the latter part of his life intensified by a continuing illness and died a year after the premiere of *La Wally*. The cinematic public became aware of the glories of Catalani's opera in 1981 when the French film *Diva* used an aria as a plot point. See LA WALLY.

CAT AND THE FIDDLE, THE
1931 operetta by Kern & Harbach

Jerome Kern's 1931 *The Cat and the Fiddle* is called a "musical romance" but is usually considered a rather successful attempt to put the traditional operetta into a contemporary form. Otto Harbach wrote the lyrics and book about the love affair between two operetta composers, a serious Romanian and a jazz-oriented American. Their music finally harmonizes in the operetta they create together. See OTTO HARBACH, JEROME KERN.

1934 Jeanette MacDonald film
Jeanette MacDonald stars opposite Ramon Novarro in the film version of the operetta directed by William K. Howard. Writers Sam and Bella Spewack changed most of the plot but kept the music and the couple are still composers. Novarro is not very successful so they break up but he needs her help to premiere his stage operetta. She finally gives in and true love takes over as the film changes into color at the end. The songs include "The Night Was Made for Love." MGM. Color and black and white. 90 minutes.

CAVALIERI, LINA
Italian soprano (1874 - 1944)

Lina Cavalieri was as famous for her extravagant life style and beauty as for her voice but she was a notable singer in her time. She was also publicized as the "most beautiful woman in the world." Born in poverty in Viterbo, she had a career as a cafe singer before making her opera debut in 1900 in *La Bohème* in Naples and going on to sing in Paris, Covent Garden and other major opera houses. She made her American debut at the Metropolitan in 1906 opposite Caruso in Giordano's *Fedora*, and then sang at the Manhattan and Chicago Opera Houses. After marrying tenor Lucien Muratore, her fourth husband, she starred in silent films with reasonable success. Cavalieri had a preference for opera roles like Manon which allowed display of costume and jewels, so it was not surprising that she began her film career in *Manon Lescaut*. She died in a freak accident during an air raid on Florence in 1944. Gina Lollobrigida portrayed her in a film biography.

1914 Manon Lescaut
Lina Cavalieri made her film debut in America portraying Manon, the beautiful convent girl who becomes a courtesan. Her husband Lucien Muratore plays her lover, the Chevalier des Grieux. The film was supposedly based on the Abbé Prévost source novel rather than the Puccini opera which was in copyright. It was directed by Herbert Hall. Playgoers Film Co. Black and white. About 80 minutes.

1915 La Sposa della Morte
Cavalieri's second film, *The Bride of Death*, was made back in Italy for Tiber Film under the direction of Emilio Ghione. Her tenor husband Lucien Muratore was again featured along with Alberto Collo, Ida Carloni Talli and Luigi Scotto. Black and white. About 75 minutes.

1916 La Rosa di Granata
Cavalieri's third film was made in Italy with Emilio Ghione directing. Appearing with her in the film are husband Lucien Muratore, Diomira Jacobini and Kally Sambucini. Black and white. About 75 minutes.

1917 The Eternal Temptress
Cavalieri's second American film features her as a princess of extraordinary beauty living in Venice and loved madly by every man she meets. It has a melodramatic plot about secret papers and her sacrifice for the man she finally loves. Emile Chautard directed for Famous Players. Black and white. About 72 minutes.

1918 Love's Conquest
Cavalieri stars as Gismonda, the beautiful Duchess of Athens, in this film based on Sardou's play *Gismonda*. She has many suitors but loves only her son. Eventually she falls for the huntsman who rescues her boy from kidnappers. Edward José directed for Famous Players. Black and white. About 70 minutes.

1918 A Woman of Impulse
Cavalieri portrays an opera singer in this film, the Parisian prima donna Leonora "La Vecci." The film has faint autobiographical elements as the singer, like Cavalieri, comes from a poor Italian family and cannot afford voice lessons until a rich admirer buys them. Lucien Muratore has only a small role in this film directed by Edward José for Famous Players. Black and white. About 60 minutes.

1919 The Two Brides
Cavalieri plays Diana di Marchesi, the beautiful daughter of a sculptor. The film tells the story of her love for two men and revolves around a lifelike statue of her created by her father. Edward José directed for Famous Players. Black and white. About 72 minutes.

1921 Amore che Ritorna
Cavalieri's last film, an Italian melodrama called *Love that Returns*, is listed in her credits but does not appear to have been reviewed and may not have been completed.

1955 Beautiful but Dangerous
Gina Lollobrigida portrays Lina Cavalieri in *La Donna Piu Bella del Mondo* (The Most Beautiful Woman in the World), an Italian film biography of the diva released in America as *Beautiful but Dangerous*. It pictures her rise from the cheapest of cafes to the best of opera houses. Lollobrigida, who had once trained to be an opera singer, sings Tosca's aria "Vissi d'arte" in the film. Mario Del Monaco is the singing voice of Gino Sinimberghi who portrays the tenor who loves her. Vittorio Gassman is the ardent Russian Prince Sergio and Robert Alda is the nasty conductor Doria. Robert Z. Leonard directed. Color. In Italian. 104 minutes. On video.

CAVALLERIA RUSTICANA
1890 opera by Mascagni

Pietro Mascagni's instantly famous opera, based on a story by Giovanni Verga, is his only opera in the repertory. It has long been a favorite for Italian-American filmmakers both as story and as musical mood setter. Francis Ford Coppola's *The Godfather Part III* has its final sequence set at a production of the opera and Martin Scorsese's *Raging Bull* also uses music from the opera to good effect. Giovanni Targioni-Tozzetti and Guido Menasci's libretto tells a story of infidelity and revenge in a Sicilian village. Turiddu has seduced Santuzza and is now having an affair with Alfio's wife Lola. The jealous Santuzza tells Alfio of the affair and he challenges Turiddu to a duel. Turiddu asks his mother Lucia to look after Santuzza, who is pregnant, as he knows he will be killed in the duel. See also PIETRO MASCAGNI.

1952 Mario del Monaco film
Mario del Monaco stars as Turiddu opposite Rina Telli as Santuzza and Richard Torigi as Alfio in this film made for the *Opera Cameos* series. The staging is by Anthony Stivanello while the film was produced and directed by Carlo Vinti and Marion Rhodes. The orchestra is conducted by Giuseppe Bamboschek with the Opera Cameos chorus. It was released in the U.S. in a double bill with *La Traviata* with an introduction by John Ericson. Color. In Italian. 53 minutes. Lyric/Bel Canto videos.

1960 NBC Opera Company
Virginia Copeland stars as Santuzza in this NBC Opera Company production by Samuel Chotzinoff. David Poleri is Turiddu, Jan McArt is Lola, Chester Ludgin is Alfio and Anna Carnevale is Mamma Lucia. Peter Herman Adler conducts the Symphony of the Air Orchestra. The opera is sung in English in a translation by Joseph Machlin. Kirk Browning directed the telecast on Jan. 31, 1960. Color. In English. 75 minutes.

1961 Giulietta Simionato video
Giulietta Simionato stars as Santuzza with Angelo Loforese as Turiddu in this production in Tokyo filmed for Japanese television. Attilio D'Orazi sings the role of Alfio while Giuseppe Morelli conducts the Lirica Italiana orchestra. Black and white. With English and Japanese subtitles. 72 minutes. VAI video.

1968 Teatro alla Scala
Fiorenza Cossotto is Santuzza and Gianfranco Cecchele is Turiddu in Åke Falck's film of a famous La Scala production by Giorgio Strehler. It was shot in a studio usually in close-ups but opened up by location shots of Sicilian landscapes. Giangiacomo Guelfi is Alfio, Adriana Martino is Lola and Anna di Stasio is Mamma Lucia. Herbert von Karajan conducts the La Scala Chorus and Orchestra and Ernst Wild was the cinematographer. The film was released theatrically in the U.S. Unitel. Color. In Italian. 73 minutes. London video.

1975 Covent Garden
Placido Domingo stars as Turiddu in this Royal Opera House, Covent Garden, production. It was telecast by the BBC in 1975 but not released on video until 1995. Color. In Italian. 70 minutes. Pioneer video and laser.

1978 Metropolitan Opera
Tatiana Troyanos stars as Santuzza with Placido Domingo as Turiddu in this Metropolitan Opera production. Cornell MacNeil is Alfio, Jean Kraft is Mamma Lucia and Isola Jones is Lola. The production was designed by Franco Zeffirelli but staged by Fabrizio Melano. James Levine conducts the Metropolitan Opera Orchestra and Chorus and Kirk Browning directed the video telecast on April 5, 1978. Color. In Italian. 70 minutes. Video at MTR.

1982 Franco Zeffirelli film
Franco Zeffirelli shot this realistic film on location in a Sicilian village and on stage in Milan basing it on his La Scala production. Placido Domingo stars as Turiddu with Elena Obraztsova as Santuzza, Renato Bruson as Alfio, Fedora Barbieri as Mamma Lucia and Axelle Gall as Lola. The art direction is by Gianni Quaranta, the costumes by Anna Anni and the cinematography by Armando Nannuzzi. Georges Prêtre conducts the Teatro alla Scala Orchestra and Chorus. Color. In Italian. 70 minutes. Philips video and laser.

1990 Shirley Verrett in Siena
Shirley Verrett stars as Santuzza in this production filmed in the Teatro Comunale dei Rinnovati in Siena. Kristjan Johannsson is Turiddu, Ettore Nova is Alfio, Rosy Orani is Lola and Ambra Vespasiani is Mamma Lucia. Baldo Podic leads the Philharmonia Orchestra of Russe. Italian filmmaker Mario Monicelli directed the stage production while Peter Goldfarb directed the video. RAI TV. Color.

In Italian with English subtitles. 80 minutes. VAI video/ Japanese laserdisc.

1992 New York City Opera
Jonathan Eaton, who staged this New York City Opera production, moves the setting to an Italian neighborhood in New York in the late 19th century. Sharon Graham is Santuzza, Craig Sirianni is Turiddu, Melanie Sonnenberg is Lola, Max Wittges is Alfio and Dulce Reyes is Mamma Lucia. The sets are by Paul Short and the costumes by Eduardo V. Sicangco. John Goberman produced the opera for television and Kirk Browning directed the telecast on Sept. 20, 1992, in the *Live from Lincoln Center* series. Color. In Italian. 75 minutes.

Early/related films

1908 Mario Gallo film
An early Italian film version of the Verga/Mascagni story was directed by Mario Gallo. About 10 minutes.

1909 Victorin Jasset film
A French film of the opera and Verga play was directed by Victorin Jasset for the Éclair company. It stars Charles Krauss, Dupont Morgan, Eugénie Nau and Mme. Barry. About 10 minutes.

1910 Giovanni Grasso film
Sicilian actor Giovanni Grasso, who often portrayed Alfio on the stage, stars as Alfio in this Italian film of the Verga/ Mascagni story. About 15 minutes.

1916 Sanzogno film
Two Italian films of *Cavalleria Rusticana* were made in 1916, this one by the Italian Flegrea film company with authorization from the Sanzogno publishing house. Mascagni objected to both films, sued to stop them and lost. The film was directed by Ubaldo Maria Del Colle who appears as Turiddu with Tilde Pini as Santuzza, Bianca Lorenzoni as Lola and Ugo Gracci as Alfio. About 50 minutes.

1916 Giovanni Verga film
The second of the two Italian films of *Cavalleria Rusticana* made in 1916 was produced by the Tespi film company and authorized by writer Giovanni Verga. Mascagni objected and sued to stop it but lost. The film was co-directed by Ugo Falena and Mario Gargiulo and stars Gemma Belincioni, Luigi Serventi, Bianca V. Camagni, Signora Campioni and Gioacchini Griss. About 50 minutes.

1924 Mario Gargiulo film
Mario Gargiulo directed a second version of *Cavalleria Rusticana* in 1924 with Sicilian actor Giovanni Grasso in his famous portrayal of Alfio. Tina Xeo is Santuzza, Livio Pavanelli is Turiddu, Lia Di Marzio is Lola and Mary-Cleo Tarlarini is Nunzia. The film was based on the Verga story. Black and white. In Italian. About 70 minutes.

1927 Beniamino Gigli film
Beniamino Gigli sings three selections from *Cavalleria Rusticana* on this Vitaphone sound film and is joined by baritone Millo Picco and contralto Minnie Egener. Black and white. In Italian. About 10 minutes.

1932 Vendetta
This highlights version of *Cavalleria Rusticana* was produced in the U.S. and released as *Vendetta*. It is an abridgment created for the Operalogue series and directed by Lew Seller for Educational Films. Black and white. In English. 28 minutes.

1939 Isa Pola film
Isa Pola stars as Santuzza in this *Cavalleria Rusticana* which was intended to be an adaptation of the Mascagni opera. When the composer refused to cooperate, the Verga novel became the basis for the story and new music was written by Alessandro Cicognini. Leonardo Cortese is Turiddu, Carlo Ninchi is Alfio, Doris Duranti is Lola and Bella Starace Sainati is Nunzia. Amleto Palermi directed for Scalera film. The film was released in the U.S. in 1947. Black and white. In Italian. 75 minutes.

1953 Fatal Desire
Opera film specialist Carmine Gallone directed this Italian narrative version of *Cavalleria Rusticana* basing it on the opera and the Verga novel. It features Tito Gobbi as an off-screen singing voice but the on-screen actors are Anthony Quinn as Alfio, May Britt as Santuzza, Kerima as Lola, Ettore Manni as Turiddu and Virginia Balistieri as Mamma Lucia. Oliviero De Fabritiis conducted the music and Carlo Ponti produced the film. It was shown in the U.S. as *Fatal Desire*. Color. In Italian. 106 minutes.

1963 La Scala Rehearsal with Corelli

Franco Corelli as Turiddu and Giulietta Simionato as Santuzza join in duet at a piano rehearsal of the opera at La Scala in 1963. Film of the scene is included in the video *Legends of Opera*. Black and white. 4 minutes. Legato Classics video.

1990 The Godfather Part III

A production of *Cavalleria Rusticana* at the Palermo Opera house in Sicily is the focus of the final scene of this Francis Ford Coppola film. Michael Corleone (Al Pacino) is there to see his son Anthony make his operatic debut as Turiddu. Plot and revenge threads converge in counterpoint to the unfolding opera, culminating in an assassination attempt on the steps of the opera house. The opera performers are Franc D'Ambrosio as Anthony and Turiddu (sung by Gianni Lazzari), Elena Lo Forte as Santuzza (sung by Madelyn Renée Monti), Corinna Vozza as Lucia, Angelo Romero as Alfio (sung by Paolo Gavanelli) and Madelyn Renée Monti as Lola. Anton Coppola conducts the Orchestra and Chorus of the Academia Musicale Italiana. Color. In English with opera scenes in Italian. 162 minutes. Paramount video.

CAVANI, LILIANA

Italian film director (1936-)

Liliana Cavani is best known in the U.S for her controversial 1974 film *The Night Porter*. She began directing in 1966 and won her critical reputation with strong historical films on St. Francis, Galileo and Nietzsche. She has also become a notable director of opera on stage including highly praised La Scala productions of *La Traviata* in 1992 and *La Vestale* in 1994. She also filmed the 50th anniversary concert of the rebuilt La Scala. See LA TRAVIATA (1992), TEATRO ALLA SCALA (1996).

CAVE, THE

1993 screen opera by Reich

American composer Steve Reich describes his visually complex opera *The Cave* as "documentary music video theater." It's a collaboration with video artist Beryl Korot and uses five video screens to tell its story about the underpinnings of the Middle East conflict. The focus is the Cave of the Patriarchs in Hebron where Abraham is supposed to be buried and long a center of conflict. The music is based around filmed interviews with Jews, Muslims and Americans talking about Abraham, Sarah, Isaac and Hagar. The screens provide text, imagery and documentary information. The opera is not yet on video but is available on CD performed by the Steve Reich Ensemble. The singers on the CD are sopranos Cheryl Bensman Rowe and Marion Beckenstein, tenor James Bassi and baritone Hugo Munday. See also STEVE REICH.

CBC TELEVISION OPERA

CBC, the Canadian Broadcasting Company, regularly produces operas and operettas, many of which are seen on U.S. television. The most popular and the widely seen are the Gilbert and Sullivan productions, some of which have been released on video. Canadian opera singers who later acquired world reputations, like Jon Vickers and Teresa Stratas, often made their screen opera debut on CBC and some of their work is also available on video. See EUGENE ONEGIN (1986 film), THE GONDOLIERS (1962), HANSEL AND GRETEL (1970), H.M.S. PINAFORE (1960), IOLANTHE (1984), THE MAGIC FLUTE (1987), THE MERRY WIDOW (1988 film), THE MIKADO (1959/1982), PAGLIACCI (1955), PETER GRIMES (1970), THE PIRATES OF PENZANCE (1961/1985), LA RONDINE (1970), TERESA STRATAS (1983), JON VICKERS (1954/1984).

CBS TELEVISION OPERA

CBS, the Columbia Broadcasting System, began its television opera programming in 1949 with a concert presentation of *Aida* conducted by Arturo Toscanini. It was followed by a similar Toscanini *Falstaff* in 1950. CBS's *Opera Television Theater*, which staged productions in the studio, began in 1950 under the direction of singer Lawrence Tibbett and producer Henry Souvanine. The first presentation was a New Year's Day telecast of *Carmen* in French starring Gladys Swarthout as Carmen. It was followed the same year with *La Traviata* in English starring Elaine Malbin. The series ended when CBS could not find sponsors. However, as the list below indicates, CBS presented many operas and operettas in other formats. See AIDA (1949), MARIAN ANDERSON (1957), SAMUEL BARBER (1977), LUDWIG VAN BEETHOVEN (1981), THE BEGGAR'S OPERA (1952), LA BELLA DORMENTE NEL BOSCO (1954), LEONARD BERNSTEIN (1958), LA BOHÈME (1953), MARIA CALLAS (1956/1958), CAMERA THREE, CARMEN (1950), AARON COPLAND (1961), ED SULLIVAN SHOW, FALSTAFF (1950), DIE FLEDERMAUS (1953), THE FLOOD (1962), GALLANTRY (1962), BALDASSARE GALUPPI, GEORGE

GERSHWIN (1953), BERNARD HERRMANN (1954/1955), THE IMPRESARIO (1961), TOM JOHNSON (1972), JENNY LIND (1951), EZRA LADERMAN (1973), MADAMA BUTTERFLY (1957), MARTIN'S LIE, THE MEDIUM (1948), THE MERRY WIDOW (1954), METROPOLITAN OPERA (1953/1957/ 1975), THE MIGHTY CASEY (1955), OEDIPUS REX (1951), OMNIBUS, THOMAS PASATIERI (1977), THE PIRATES OF PENZANCE (1955), THE RED MILL (1958), THE SECOND HURRICANE (1960), IGOR STRAVINSKY (1966), THE TELEPHONE (1953), TOSCA (1956), LA TRAVIATA (1950), TRIAL BY JURY (1950/1953), THE TRIALS OF GALILEO (1967), ALEC WILDER (1953).

CEBOTARI, MARIA
Bessarabian soprano (1910-1949)

Maria Cebotari (born Cebutaru) was the leading coloratura soprano in Germany during the Nazi era. She made her debut as Mimi in Dresden in 1931 and created Aminta in Strauss's *Die Schweigsame Frau*. She also sang in Vienna, Salzburg and Covent Garden. Her attractive voice and personality translate well to records and to the opera films she made in which she portrays divas like Malibran and Stolz and sings opposite Gigli. Her films based around *Madama Butterfly* and *La Traviata* were very popular. Cebotari's death at 40 and career in Nazi Germany meant that she never had the chance to become as well-known internationally as she could have been. See BENIAMINO GIGLI (1937), MADAMA BUTTERFLY (1939 film), MARIA MALIBRAN (1943), LA TRAVIATA (1940 film), GIUSEPPE VERDI (1938).

1936 Madchen in Weiss
Cebotari's voice is the chief attraction of her debut film *The Girl in White*. It's a Cinderella-type musical set in pre-revolutionary St. Petersburg. Her aristocratic fiancé (Ivan Petrovich) doesn't want her to sing but she goes ahead anyway like her mother before her. Her tenor partner is Norberto Ardelli. Viktor Janson directed the film shown in the U.S. in 1939 as *Alles die Treue*. Black and white. In German. 83 minutes.

1937 Stark Herzen
This is an important lost film about a production of *Tosca* during a Communist uprising in Hungary in 1918. Cebotari portrays the actress who sings the role of Tosca with a cast that includes Gustav Diesl and René Deltgen. Herbert Maisch directed the film which was banned and probably no longer exists. UFA. Black and white. In German. 79 minutes.

1942 Odessa in Flames
Cebotari portrays a Romanian opera singer seeking her young son in war-torn Europe in *Odessa in Fiamme*, an Italian-Romanian film directed by Carmine Gallone. When the boy is taken to Odessa, she follows. Her hero husband eventually rescues them. The film was shown at the Venice Film Festival in 1942. Black and white. In Italian or Romanian. 83 minutes.

CENDRILLON
1899 opera by Massenet

Jules Massenet's version of the Cinderella story is no longer a fashionable opera but is quite charming all the same. The story follows the traditional Perrault fairy tale more closely than the Rossini version. Cinderella has a wicked stepmother and two vile sisters but goes glamorously to the ball anyway, meets Prince Charming and leaves her glass slipper behind. The opera is on CD with Frederica von Stade as Cinderella and Nicolai Gedda as the Prince. See JULES MASSENET.

1979 National Arts Center
Frederica Von Stade stars as Cendrillon in this Canadian telecast of a Centre National des Arts production by Brian Macdonald. Delia Wallis sings Prince Charming, Ruth Welting is the Fairy Godmother, Maureen Forrester is Madame de la Haltiere, Michele Boucher is Noemie and Louis Quilico is Pandolfe. Mario Bernardi conducts the Centre National des Arts Orchestra and Jean-Yves Landry directed the telecast. Color. In French. 110 minutes. Lyric video.

Early/related films

1899 Georges Méliès film
This seven-minute film by French film pioneer Georges Méliès was inspired by the premiere of Massenet's opera in Paris in 1899. It was an epic production for its time with twenty scenes, a cast of thirty-five and delightful special effects. With such a popular theme and the opera to publicize it, Méliès had a surefire hit. The film is like the opera but the screen version has many more attractive young women. Tinted. In French. About 7 minutes (410 feet).

1902 Dutch sound film

An early sound film featuring an aria from *Cendrillon* was shown at the September 1902 screenings of Alber's Electro Talking Bioscope in the Netherlands. About 3 minutes.

1994 Celestial Clockwork

Mécaniques Célestes is a magical film about the Cinderella story in which a Venezuelan opera singer goes to Paris to attempt to be the diva who stars in the film version. At one point a poster of Maria Callas even sings and winks. Ariadna Gil stars as the singer under the direction of Fina Torres. Color. In Spanish. 86 minutes.

CENERENTOLA, LA

1817 opera by Rossini

Rossini's charming *Cinderella* is not quite the story of the fairy tale as we know it as there is no magic and no fairy godmother. The Prince's elderly tutor Alidoro takes the godfather role and a silver bracelet replaces the glass slipper but the sisters are as mean as always. Cinderella's father Don Magnifico is a major comic character counterpointed by the Prince's valet Dandini, who impersonates the Prince for plot reasons. The libretto by Jacobo Ferretti is based it on another libretto, not the Perrault tale. This is a delightful *opera buffa* with grand comedy, memorable music, amazing ensembles, touching arias and a very happy ending. See also GIOACHINO ROSSINI.

1948 Fedora Barbieri film

This was a famous film in its day, the first screen version of a then little-known Rossini opera, shot in palaces near Milan with a sizable budget. Cinderella's voice is Fedora Barbieri but the woman seen on screen is Lori Randi. The mean sisters are sung by Fiorella Carmen Forti and Fernanda Cadoni (acted by Franca Tamantini) while the scene stealer is their father Don Magnifico, a blustering Vito de Taranto. The Prince is Gino del Signore, Dandini is Afro Poli and Alidoro is Enrico Formichi. Oliviero de Fabritiis conducts the Rome Opera House Orchestra and Chorus. Fernando Cerchio directed the film and his cameraman was Mario Albertelli. Black and white. In Italian with English narration. 94 minutes. VIEW video.

1980 New York City Opera

Rockwell Blake stars in this New York City Opera production of the Rossini opera sung in English with Brian Salesky conducting the NYCO Orchestra and Chorus. Leading the cast are Susanne Marsee as Cinderella, Gianna Rolandi, Alan Titus, Ralph Bassett and James Billings. Gimi Beni wrote the translation and Beverly Sills hosted. Kirk Browning directed the telecast on Nov. 6, 1980. Color. In English. 180 minutes.

1981 Jean-Pierre Ponnelle film

Director-designer-producer Jean Pierre Ponnelle's film of *La Cenerentola* is one of the best with a superb cast headed by Frederica von Stade as Cinderella. It's based on Ponnelle's stage production at La Scala for which he designed sets and costumes and was shot there without an audience. Francisco Araiza is a princely Prince, Paolo Montarsolo is a magnificent Don Magnifico, Claudio Desderi is Dandini, Laura Zannini is sister Tisbe, Margherita Guglielmi is sister Clorinda and Paul Pliska is Alidoro. Claudio Abbado leads the La Scala Orchestra and Chorus. Unitel. Color. In Italian with English subtitles. 152 minutes. DG video/ laser.

1983 Glyndebourne Festival

Kathleen Kuhlmann stars as Cinderella in this Glyndebourne production by John Cox staged in a fairy book manner, a genial if not a memorable production. The Prince is Laurence Dale, his valet Dandini is Alberto Rinaldi and the pompous Don Magnifico is Claudio Desderi in excellent form. Cinderella's sisters are Marta Taddei and Laura Zannini while Roderick Kennedy portrays Alidoro. Donato Renzetti conducts the London Philharmonic and John Vernon directed the video. Color. In Italian with English subtitles. 145 minutes. HBO video.

1989 Salzburg Festival

Irish mezzo soprano Ann Murray shines as Cinderella in this Salzburg Festival production by Michael Hampe. Francisco Araiza is a commanding Prince and Gino Quilico an amusing Dandini. Angela Denning and Daphne Evangelatos are the mean sisters, Walter Berry is Don Magnifico and Wolfgang Schone is Alidoro. Mauro Pagano designed the sets and Riccardo Chailly conducted the Vienna Philharmonic. Claus Viller directed the video. Color. In Italian with English subtitles. 147 minutes. Home Vision and HBO videos/Pioneer Artists laser.

1994 Houston Grand Opera

Cecilia Bartoli is superb vocally and dramatically as Cinderella in this splendid Houston Grand Opera production by Robert De Simone. Enza Dara is very funny as Don Magnifico, Raul Gimenez is fine as the Prince, Laura Knoope is Clorinda, Jill Grove is Tisbe, Alessandro Corbelli is Dandini and Michele Pertuse is Alidoro. Bruno Campanella conducts the Houston Grand Opera Orchestra. Brian Large directed for video at a November 1995 performance telecast on PBS on April 3, 1996. Color. In Italian with English subtitles. 150 minutes. London video.

Related film

1996 Celestial Clockwork

This romantic fantasy film is based around *La Cenerentola* and is basically a version of the Cinderella story. A young Venezuelan bride abandons her bridegroom at the altar and heads for Paris to become an opera singer like her role model Maria Callas. She ends up starring in a new production of *La Cenerentola*. Spanish actress Ariadna Gil plays the Cinderella role and French-based Venezuelan director Fina Torres wrote and directed. The excerpts from the opera in the film are performed by mezzo sopranos Lucia Valentini Terrani and Elsa Maurus, tenor Francisco Araiza, bass Domenico Trimarchi and the West German Radio-Television Chorus. Color. In French. 85 minutes.

CHABRIER, EMMANUEL

French composer (1841-1894)

The eclectic French composer Emmanuel Chabrier was influenced by both Offenbach and Wagner but managed to create his own delightful style out of the amalgam. His best known works are the comic operas *L'Étoile* (1877) and *Le Roi Malgré Lui* (1887) and the somewhat Wagnerian *Gwendoline* (1886). Only one of his operas is on video. See L'ÉTOILE.

CHALIAPIN, FEODOR

Russian bass (1873-1938)

Feodor Chaliapin (or Fyodor Shalyapin) is the most famous bass of the early 20th century with an unforgettable voice heard on over 200 records. He was influential in restoring acting to the opera stage and popularizing Russian opera. His career began in Tibilsi in 1892, he reached La Scala in 1901 and he sang at the Metropolitan in 1907. He was noted for his Russian roles but also his Mefistofele, Don Basilio and Don Quichotte. His acting style can be seen in Pabst's film of *Don Quixote* and in a Russian film about Ivan the Terrible. Ezio Pinza portrays him in the Sol Hurok biopic *Tonight We Sing*. Hollywood actor Feodor Chaliapin Jr. is his son. See DON QUICHOTTE (1935), IVAN THE TERRIBLE (1915), TONIGHT WE SING.

1940 Yakov Sverdlov

Sergei Yutkevich's official Soviet film biography of the first president of the Soviet Republic. One of the people portrayed in the film is Chaliapin in a much admired performance by Nicolai Okhlopkov. Black and white. In Russian. 100 minutes.

1969-1972 Chaliapin

This Soviet film directed by Mark Doskoi appears in many filmographies and was certainly a long planned project of the director. However, it does not appear to have been made.

CHANCE, MICHAEL

English countertenor (1955-)

Michael Chance made his opera debut in 1983 at the Buxton Festival in Cavalli's *Giasone* and was soon popular in both baroque and modern operas. He has recorded Monteverdi and Gluck operas and is much liked in oratorio as well as in opera. See ACIS AND GALATHEA (1985), MESSIAH (1992), CLAUDIO MONTEVERDI (1989).

CHAPÍ, RUPERTO

Spanish composer (1851-1909)

Ruperto Chapí y Lorente created many kinds of music drama, including operas, but is best known for his zarzuelas. Chapí became famous in the genre in 1882 with *La Tempestad* which was followed by *La Bruja* and *El Rey que Rabió*. Most popular with the movie industry has been *La Revoltosa* which has been filmed four times. *La Chavala* was filmed in 1914 and 1925 and *La Bruja* was made into a silent film in 1923. Juan de Orduña, who made a series of zarzuela films for Spanish television in 1968, starred in the silent versions of *La Revoltosa*, *El Rey que Rabió* and *La Chavala*. See LA REVOLTOSA , EL REY QUE RABIÓ, LA TEMPESTAD.

CHARLIE CHAN AT THE OPERA

1936 operatic murder mystery movie

Boris Karloff plays an opera baritone (singing dubbed by Rico Ricardi) suffering from amnesia and a desire for revenge. He is suspected of a murdering a woman onstage but detective Charlie Chan (Werner Oland) has his doubts. This was one of the best of the low-budget Chan films based around the Honolulu detective created by Earl Derr Biggers. Oscar Levant composed an imaginary opera called *Carnival* for this film including overture and arias. The libretto by William Kernell was created around a Mephistopheles costume used by Lawrence Tibbett in *Metropolitan*. It was given to the Chan picture to be worn on-stage by Chaney in the stabbing scene. Levant discusses this opera in his autobiography *A Smattering of Ignorance* and there is an analysis of it by Irene Hahn Atkins in *Source Music in Motion Pictures*. H. Bruce Humberstone directed for 20th Century Fox. Black and white. 66 minutes. Key video. See also IMAGINARY OPERAS IN FILMS (1936), OSCAR LEVANT.

CHARPENTIER, GUSTAVE

French composer (1860-1956)

Gustave Charpentier was the very model of a Parisian Montmartre Bohemian and affected its life style. He eventually created a great opera out of that atmosphere. *Louise* is the story of a girl who chooses Bohemian life in sin with an artist over obedience to her parents. It was considered scandalous when it premiered but today is viewed as a romantic tribute to Paris and its aria "Depuis le jour" has become a soprano standard. Charpentier was strongly involved in the making of a film of this opera with Grace Moore as Louise. He also wrote a sequel called *Julien* but it was not successful. See LOUISE.

CHICAGO

Chicago has been a major site for opera since the middle of the 19th century. It was especially famous when Mary Garden was its prima donna from 1910 to 1933 and vast sums were spent on premieres like *The Love of Three Oranges*. The major company today, the Lyric Opera of Chicago, dates from 1954 and first became famous for importing top stars like Maria Callas, Tito Gobbi and Renata Tebaldi. It has mounted many important and adventurous productions and is now one of the five or six top opera companies in the U.S. The smaller Chicago Opera Theater, founded in 1974, has been even more adventurous with an emphasis on modern American operas like Floyd's *Susannah* and Hoiby's *Summer and Smoke*. See ANTONY AND CLEOPATRA (1991), BORIS GODUNOV (1966 film), MARIA CALLAS (1983), EUGENE ONEGIN (1985), FAUST (1988), THE LOVE OF THREE ORANGES, MCTEAGUE (1991), THE MERRY WIDOW (1983 film), SUMMER AND SMOKE (1980), SUSANNAH (1986).

CHOCOLATE SOLDIER, THE

1908 operetta by Straus

Oscar Straus's *Der Tapfere Soldat* is based on the 1894 play *Arms and the Man* by George Bernard Shaw. Its central character is a soldier who keeps chocolates in his cartridge box rather than bullets and wins the heart of a woman for his non-heroics. Shaw let Straus use the play for an operetta on condition that he receive no royalties, a condition he regretted when the operetta became a world success. The German title translates as *The Valiant Soldier* and the German libretto is by Rudolf Bernauer and Leopold Jacobson; however, the operetta was more successful and truer to Shaw in its English translation by Stanislaus Stange. It opened in New York in 1909 and in London in 1910 as *The Chocolate Soldier* and has been popular ever since. See also OSCAR STRAUS.

1914 Stanislaus Stange Film

The first film of the operetta was made in 1914 by the people who introduced it to the New York stage in 1909. Stanislaus Stange, who wrote the English libretto and lyrics and directed the operetta on Broadway, directed the film with Walter Morton. The Broadway cast is featured in the film. Alice Yorke stars as Nadina Popoff, Tom Richards is Lieutenant Bumberli, Lucille Saunder is Aurelia Popoff and Francis J. Boyle is Massakroff. Fred C. Whitney, who brought the operetta to America, produced the film under the auspices of the Daisy Feature Film Company. It was screened with live music from the operetta score. Black and white. In English. About 75 minutes.

1941 Risë Stevens MGM film

Metropolitan Opera diva Risë Stevens and Nelson Eddy star in this version of the operetta which uses the Straus music without the Shaw story. Shaw wanted more money than MGM wanted to pay so *Arms and the Man* was replaced as plot by Molnar's

The Guardsman. The music was loosely adapted to the new book. Stevens and Eddy play husband and wife opera stars. He is suspicious of her fidelity so he disguises himself as a Cossack and tries to seduce her. She knows what he is doing and just strings him along. Roy Del Ruth directed and Herbert Stothart was music director. Black and white. 102 minutes. MGM-UA video.

1955 Risë Stevens NBC film

Risë Stevens stars for the second time in the Straus operetta *The Chocolate Soldier* but this time she is able to sing and speak the original libretto based on the George Bernard Shaw play *Arms and the Man*. The NBC television production by Max Liebman also features Eddie Albert and Akim Tamiroff. Black and white. In English. 90 minutes.

CHOTZINOFF, SAMUEL
Russian-born U.S. producer (1889-1964)

Samuel Chotzinoff is one of the great pioneers of screen opera. As NBC music director he was the first to commission an opera for television, Menotti's 1951 NBC *Amahl and the Night Visitors*. He founded and ran NBC Opera Theatre from 1949 to 1964 in association with conductor Peter Herman Adler and director Kirk Browning and during that time commissioned an impressive number of operas by major composers. In many ways he helped create television opera and the NBC series ended with his death. Chotzinoff began his musical career as a pianist and a music critic. In 1937 he convinced Toscanini to return to America to lead the NBC Symphony Orchestra. In 1939 he commissioned Menotti's 1939 radio opera *The Old Man and the Thief*. Chotzinoff was one of those most responsible for bringing opera to the wider American public. In 1953 he told *Time* magazine that "television is the only hope of opera in America." See PETER HERMAN ADLER, KIRK BROWNING, NBC OPERA THEATRE.

CHRISTINÉ, HENRI
French composer (1867-1941)

Henri Christiné was born in Switzerland but his career as an operetta composer took place in Paris. He first achieved fame as a song writer and then had a big success with his 1918 operetta *Phi-Phi* about the Greek sculptor Phidias. Equally successful was the 1921 *Dédé* which starred Maurice Chevalier. Both were made into French films. The song "Valentine," which virtually became Chevalier's theme song, was composed by Christiné for a 1925 revue. See DÉDÉ, PHI-PHI.

CRISTÓBAL COLÓN
1989 opera by Balada

Leonardo Balada's opera tells the story of the voyage of Christopher Columbus in flashbacks using a libretto by A. Gala. The opera, composed to mark the 500th anniversary of Columbus's journey, includes diverse types of music from Catalan and Andalusian themes to Native American elements. It was well received by critics at its Barcelona premiere. See also LEONARDO BALADA.

1989 Montserrat Caballé/ José Carreras video

José Carreras and Montserrat Caballé star in the world premiere of Balada's opera produced at the Gran Teatre de Liceu in Barcelona Sept. 24, 1989. They are supported by mezzo soprano Victoria Vergara and bass-baritone Carlos Chausson. M. Alcantara conducts the Liceu Opera Orchestra. The video is a copy of a Spanish telecast. Color. In Spanish. 118 minutes. Lyric/Opera Dubs videos.

CHRISTOFF, BORIS
Bulgarian bass (1914-1993)

Boris Christoff was the most famous Bulgarian opera singer of his time and one of the world's great basses. He won recognition after his debut at Covent Garden in 1949 as Boris Godunov and was equally admired for his Phillip II in *Don Carlo*. Christoff was born in Plovdiv and studied in Rome and Salzburg. His career was slowed by the war but he finally made his opera debut in 1946 at the Teatro Argentina singing Colline in *La Bohème*. After his successes in the roles of Boris Godonuv and Philip II, they became virtually his property for many years and his recordings of them are famous. He can be seen in one complete opera on video and in excerpts on others. See LA FORZA DEL DESTINO (1958).

1956 NBC Festival of Music

Christoff is featured in the Death of Boris scene from *Boris Godunov* in this NBC telecast for the *Producer Showcase* series. He is supported by Nicola Moscona, Michael Pollock and Kirk Jordan with Alfred Wallenstein conducting the NBC Symphony of the Air Orchestra. It was shown on Dec. 10, 1956. Black and white. In English. 30 minutes. On video.

1962 Profile in Music: Boris Christoff

Christoff is interviewed and seen in staged performances of scenes from two operas in this historic British television program. The BBC interviewer is John Freeman who narrates the program. Christoff sings the aria "Ella giammai m'amo" from *Don Carlo* and the death scene from *Boris Godunov*. He is accompanied by the Philharmonia Orchestra conducted by Marcus Dods. Patricia Foy produced the program. Black and white. In English. 30 minutes. Video at MPRC.

1972 Christoff as Philip II

Christoff, on stage as King Philip II in *Don Carlo*, sings his great aria "Ella giammai m'amo" in an excerpt from a 1972 production. The excerpt is featured on the video *Legends of Opera*. Color. In Russian. 7 minutes. Legato Classics video.

1976 Profilo di una Voce

The 62-year-old basso is interviewed by Italian critic Giorgio Gualerzi for television and performs some of his most famous arias. Featured are Osmin's aria from *The Abduction from the Seraglio*, the Calumny aria from *The Barber of Seville* and Boris's Death Scene from *Boris Godunov*. B. Amaducci conducts the RTSI Orchestra. Color. In Italian. 65 minutes. On video.

CIBOULETTE

1923 operetta by Hahn

French composer Reynaldo Hahn's best known operetta is set in Les Halles in 1867 and is almost an homage to the light operas of Messager and Lecocq. *Ciboulette* is also of interest to admirers of *La Bohème* because one of its main characters is the poet Rodolfo, now thirty years older and calling himself Duparquet. In one scene he sings of his sad love affair with Mimi. Ciboulette herself is a Parisian market girl who is having a bad time with her fickle suitor Antonin. After she becomes an operetta singer, her lover returns. See also REYNALDO HAHN.

1935 Claude Autant-Lara film

Reynaldo Hahn supervised this controversial film of his operetta directed by Claude Autant-Lara with dialogue by Jacques Prévert. Simone Berriau stars as Ciboulette, André Urban is Duparquet, Robert Burnier is Antonin, Thérèse Dorny is Zenobie, Madeleine Guitty is Mother Pingret and Armand Dranem is Father Grenu. Black and white. In French. 100 minutes.

1985 Monte Carlo Opera

Pierre Jourdan created this post-modern production of the operetta for French television. It begins with Hahn telling the story of the operetta he is composing to his maid Françoise and fades into Act I on stage at the Salle Garnier at the Monte Carlo Opera House. The story cuts back and forth between the narrators and the operetta characters. Agnes Host plays Ciboulette, Jacques Jansen is Duparquet, Antonine Norman is Antonin, Mariel Berger is Zenobie and Nicolas Riven is Roger with appearances by Madeleine Robinson and François Perrot. Cyril Diederich conducts the Monte Carlo Opera Philharmonic Orchestra and Chorus and André Brasilier designed the sets and costumes. Color. In French. 123 minutes. Opera Dubs video.

CILEA, FRANCESCO
Italian composer (1866-1950)

The early careers of Francesco Cilea and promising new singer Enrico Caruso were richly intertwined at the turn of the century. Caruso starred in the premieres of Cilea's two major operas at the Teatro Lirico in Milan and they helped make him and the operas famous. *L'Arlesiana* in 1897 was Caruso's first major world premiere and was a big success. An even greater triumph, however, came with *Adriana Lecouvreur* which premiered on Nov. 6, 1902. Six days later Caruso recorded an aria from the opera, "No, piu nobile," one of his earliest and best records. *Adriana Lecouvreur* is still the most popular of Cilea's operas and the only one on commercial video. See ADRIANA LECOUVREUR.

CIMAROSA, DOMENICO
Italian composer (1749-1801)

Domenico Cimarosa composed wonderful tunes, witty ensembles and enjoyable comic operas and was justly popular in the 18th and 19th centuries. He was born in Naples, rose to fame in 1772 with his opera *Le Stravaganze del Conte* and was soon popular all over Europe. He was court composer in St. Petersburg, Naples and Vienna (where he replaced Salieri) and he wrote over 60 operas. Today he is really remembered for only one, the delightful 1792 *Il Matrimonio Segreto*. *Il Maestro di Capella* is also available on video. See IL MATRIMONIO SEGRETO, IL MAESTRO DI CAPELLA.

CINESI, LE
1754 opera by Gluck

The Chinese Women was originally a palace entertainment for future Empress Maria Theresa. Metastasio's libretto is a kind of light-hearted *opera seria* about three young ladies suffering from boredom. The fashion of the time was *chinoiserie* so the ladies are supposedly Chinese. Lisinga and her friends are showing off their dramatic abilities to each other when her brother Silango interrupts. They play scenes and sing arias. He plays Sivene's lover with too much feeling for the jealous Tangia who imitates and mocks him. Lisinga sings a tragic aria. They end up dancing. See also WILHELM CHRISTOPH GLUCK.

1987 Schwetzingen Festival
Kurt Streit stars as Silango with Sophie Boulin as Sivene, Christina Hogman as Lisinga and Eva Maria Tersson as Tangia in this elegant, entertaining production from the Schwetzingen Festival in Germany. Herbert Wernicke staged the opera and designed sets and costumes while René Jacobs conducted the Concerto Cologne Orchestra. Claud Viler directed the video. Color. In Italian with English subtitles. 69 minutes. Home Vision video.

CINOPERA
1985 French opera documentary

Cinopera is an informative French television documentary which examines the art of opera on film through a series of interviews and excerpts. It ranges over a wide range of opera movies with discussion of them by the program's creators Eric Lipman, Levon Sayan (who set up the first opera film festival in 1976) and Daniel Toscan du Plantier (who produced many major opera films). Among the subjects discussed are Gina Lollobrigida's fine acting in *Pagliacci*, Franco Zeffirelli's direction of *La Traviata* and *Otello*, Julia Migenes-Johnson's qualities in *Carmen*, Ruggero Raimondi's work in *Don Giovanni*, Placido Domingo's style as a film actor and Sophia Loren's appearance in *La Favorita*. The program was directed by Yvon Gerault. Color. In French. 90 minutes. Lyric video.

CITIZEN KANE
1941 opera film by Welles

Kiri Te Kanawa has recorded an opera aria composed for this movie by Bernard Herrmann and that is only one of the reasons why *Citizen Kane* is among the more interesting opera films. Herrmann wrote the imaginary opera *Salammbô* for the film because diector Orson Welles wanted an opera in which the soprano heroine is on stage when the curtain goes up and has to sing over a powerful orchestra. This is a disaster for Kane's singer wife Susan Alexander whom he has forced into an opera career. The actress is Dorothy Comingore but the singing is by soprano Jean Forward, a professional who forced herself to sound amateurish and could barely be heard over the booming orchestra. It's a great scene with many ramifications, including the sacking of Kane's critic friend Joseph Cotten. The *Salammbô* aria sounds quite splendid in Te Kanawa's recording. In an another memorable scene, Comingore attempts to sing Rosina's "Una voce poco fa" to the despair of opera coach Fortunio Bonanova, a former Met baritone. Bonanova knows that she can't make the grade but Kane won't allow her to quit. William Randolph Hearst, one of the prototypes for Kane, did have an opera singer girlfriend called Sibyl Sanderson but she was a success. She went to Paris and seduced composer Jules Massenet who wrote operas for her. A better prototype is Chicago newspaper magnate Harold McCormick who tried to promote a somewhat untalented Polish soprano called Ganna Walska. He hired Met diva Frances Alda to develop her voice and arranged for her to star in Leoncavallo's opera *Zaza* at the Chicago Opera Company of which he was chief funder. Like Susan Alexander, Walska had a disastrous experience and fled the city before the premiere. Welles kept notes on the Walska affair. RKO. Black and white. 119 minutes. On video. See also BERNARD HERRMANN, IMAGINARY OPERAS IN FILMS (1941), GANNA WALSKA, ORSON WELLES.

CLAIR, RENÉ
French film director (1898-1981)

René Clair became famous in France in the silent era for comedies like *The Italian Straw Hat* and even more famous in the sound era for musicals like *Sous les Toits de Paris*. He also made fine movies in England and America. Opera is used with great skill in his films. The delightful 1931 French opéra-bouffe film *Le Million* was probably the model for the Marx Brothers *A Night at the Opera* and features one of the great opera house comedy scenes. The 1941 American film *The Flame of New Orleans* opens with *Lucia di Lammermoor* on stage sung by the great Hungarian diva Gitta Alpar. See LUCIA DI LAMMERMOOR (1941 film), LE MILLION.

CLASSIC VIEWS
Video music magazine

Classic Views is a magazine on video devoted to opera and classical music. Published quarterly, it includes interviews with opera singers and extracts of performances of operas as well as reviews of new videos and CDs. Color. In English. Each 80 minutes.

CLEMENZA DI TITO, LA
1791 opera by Mozart

The Clemency of Titus, Mozart's last *opera seria,* is set in Rome in 80 AD, and is the story of an unsuccessful assassination plot against the Emperor Titus. In the end he pardons the plotters. The opera was not an original text for Mozart (it was adapted by Caterina Mazzolá from a Metastasio libretto) but it fits well with the composer's usual themes of betrayal and forgiveness. There are three excellent videos, one filmed on location in Rome and two taped from stage performances in Sweden and England. See also WOLFGANG A. MOZART.

1980 Jean-Pierre Ponnelle film
Jean-Pierre Ponnelle directed this film at various sites in Rome including the Arch of Titus in the Roman Forum, the Baths of Caracalla and the Villa Adriana in the Tivoli Gardens. He opens up the opera with interesting images and camera work and creates surrealistic effects through the use of dummy figures. Eric Tappy portrays Tito, Tatiana Troyanos is the would-be assassin Sesto, Carol Neblett is the plotting Vitellia, Anne Howells is Annio, Catherine Malfitano is Servilia and Kurt Rydl is Publio. Giovanni Agostiniucci and Pet Lalmen were the designers and James Levine conducts the Vienna Philharmonic Orchestra and Vienna State Opera Chorus. Color. In Italian with English subtitles. 135 minutes. DG video and laser.

1987 Drottningholm Court Theater
One of a series of intimate Mozart operas filmed at the Drottningholm Court Theater outside Stockholm. Conductor Arnold Östman wears a period costume like his orchestra players who perform on period instruments. Stefan Dahlberg sings Tito, Anita Soldh is Vitellia, Lani Poulson is Sesto, Maria Hoeglind is Annio, Pia-Marie Nilsson is Servilia and Jerker Arvidson is Publio. The set designs are 18th century and the stage direction is by Göran Järvefelt. Thomas Olofsson directed the video. Color. In Italian with English subtitles. 145 minutes. Philips video and laser.

1991 Glyndebourne Festival
Philip Langridge stars as Tito in this modernist Glyndebourne Festival production by Nicholas Hytner. Ashley Putnam sings Vitellia, Diana Montague is Sesto, Martine Mahé is Annio, Elzbieta Symytka is Servilia and Peter Rose is Publio. David Fielding's sets are tilted and eye-catching but go well with the Roman costumes. Drew Davis leads the London Philharmonic Orchestra and Glyndebourne Festival Choir. Robin Lough directed the video. Color. In Italian with English subtitles. 150 minutes. Home Vision video/ Pioneer laser.

CLO-CLO
1924 operetta by Lehár

This light-hearted Franz Lehár operetta centers around a musical comedy star whose manager causes her constant trouble by planting imaginative stories about her in the gossip press. Eventually one of the stories affects her love life and causes her real problems. Béla Jenbach wrote the libretto. See also FRANZ LEHÁR.

1935 Marta Eggerth film
Marta Eggerth portrays the musical comedy star in *Die Ganze Welt Dreht sich um Liebe,* an Austrian film of the operetta released in the U.S. as *The World's in Love.* Eggerth is in fine form and lights up the film. Leo Slezak plays the old farmer whose son Rolf Wanka wins Eggerth after mother Ida Wüst sorts out a stumbling block to romance. Hans Moser provides the comedy as the manager Anton. Viktor Tourjansky directed. Black and white. In German. 87 minutes.

CLOUZOT, HENRI-GEORGES
French director (1907-1977)

Henri-Georges Clouzot, the Hitchcock of France, directed two of the great French thrillers, *The Wages of Fear* and *Diabolique.* In 1949 he filmed a modernized non-operatic version of *Manon.* He also made two splendid films of musical interest. In *Karajan: Early Images* he places his cameras in unusual places and conveys the intensity of the music and Karajan's conducting through camera movements, odd angles and jump cuts. In his film of Verdi's *Requiem* shot at La Scala, his powers as a filmmaker are wonderfully evident. See HERBERT VON KARAJAN (1966), MANON LESCAUT (1949 film), VERDI REQUIEM (1967).

COMENCINI, LUIGI
Italian film director (1916-)

Italian film director Luigi Comencini, who began his movie career just after World War II, is best known in the U.S. for his 1954 film *Bread, Love and Dreams* with Gina Lollobrigida. His 1988 film of *La Bohème* stars American soprano Barbara Hendricks as Mimi. He films the opera straight but adds his own ideas about the story like having Mimi initiate her meeting with Rodolfo by pretending her candle has gone out. See LA BOHÈME (1988)

CONDUCTORS

The great opera conductors have been recorded for posterity on film like the great singers and there is film of some going back to the silent era. Most videos of stage opera performances include scenes of the conductors at work. A major series of videos about conductors was held at the Museum of Television and Radio in New York in 1994 with fifty hours of taped performances and can be viewed there. Videos about individual conductors are described under their names, the others are listed below.

1993 Great Conductors, Vol I.
A compilation showing nine conductors at work. They are Bruno Walter, Leo Blech, Fritz Busch, Joseph Keilberth, Ferenc Fricsay, Karl Elmendorff (an excerpt from *Gotterdämmeriing* at Bayreuth), Hans Knappertsbusch (with Erna Berger and Torsten Ralf), Carl Schuricht and Erich Kleiber. 60 minutes. Bel Canto Society video.

1994 Great Conductors, Vol. 2
A second Bel Canto Society compilation of conductors at work. They are Arthur Nikisch, Pietro Mascagni, Fritz, Fritz Busch, Richard Strauss, Arturo Toscanini, Sergiu Celibidache, Bruno Walter, Igor Stravinsky, Wilhelm Furtwängler, Hans Knappertsbusch, Charles Munch, Herman

Scherchen, Karl Böhm, Josef Krips, Herbert von Karajan, George Solti, Rafael Kubelik and Lorin Maazel. 80 minutes. Bel Canto Society video.

1995 The Art of Conducting: Great Conductors of the Past
This superb video, based on a BBC series, features sixteen giants of the conductor world, and includes a 1913 film of Arthur Nikisch demonstrating his technique with the baton. They are John Barbirolli, Thomas Beecham, Leonard Bernstein, Wilhelm Furtwangler, Herbert von Karajan, Otto Klemperer, Sergei Koussevitsky, Fritz Reiner, Leopold Stokowski, Richard Strauss, George Szell, Bruno Walter, Fritz Busch with a 1932 Dresden *Tannhäuser*, Arturo Toscanini with a 1944 *La Forza del Destino* and Felix Weingartner with a 1932 *Der Freischütz*. Sue Knussen directed the video. Color and black and white. 117 minutes. Teldec video.

1995 Great Conductors of the Third Reich
A survey of conductors working in Germany during the Nazi era. There is performance footage plus newsreel material with Hitler and Goebbels. The conductors include Leo Blech, Wilhelm Furtwangler, Herbert von Karajan, Hans Knappertsbusch, Clemens Krauss and Max von Schillings. Black and white. 70 minutes. Bel Canto Society video.

CONGRESS DANCES
1931 German operetta film

Congress Dances, the English version of the best known and most popular of German operetta films, stars England's Lillian Harvey in a frothy tale about aristocratic dalliance at the 1815 Congress of Vienna. The Russian Tzar has a fling to splendid music by Werner Heymann. Henri Garat is Harvey's love in English and in the French version titled *Le Congrès S'amuse* while the German *Der Kongress Tanzt* co-stars Willy Fritsch. Karl Hoffmann was the fine cinematographer, Norbert Falk and Robert Liefmann wrote the script, Erich Pommer produced for UFA and Erik Charell directed. Black and white. 92 minutes

CONNER, NADINE
American soprano (1913-)

Nadine Conner was born in Los Angeles and began her career in the film capital in 1941 singing Marguerite in *Faust*. She made her debut at the Metropolitan Opera soon after as Pamina in *The*

Magic Flute and became known for her Mozart roles. She remained a regular at the Met until 1958 and also sang in Europe in the 1950s. Conner made records of *Carmen* and *Fidelio*, is seen in telecasts as Mimi in *La Bohème* and Micaela in *Carmen*, starred in a classical music film and is featured in *Voice of Firestone* videos. See LA BOHÈME (1953), CARMEN (1952), GEORGE LONDON (1953), OF MEN AND MUSIC.

1952 Nadine Conner in Opera and Song

Nadine Conner is seen as she appeared on the *Voice of Firestone* NBC television program that featured opera stars in recital and scenes from operas. She is shown in performance on April 16, 1952 when she sang the "Jewel Song" from *Faust* and other songs. Black and white. 30 minutes. VAI video.

CONSUL, THE

1950 opera by Menotti

Gian Carlo Menotti's political opera *The Consul* won the Pulitzer Prize and has been presented in more than twenty countries. It can be interpreted as a sinister modern variation on *Tosca* as it also revolves around getting a visa to leave a police state. Menotti's story is set somewhere in Europe in the late 1940s and tells the story of freedom fighter John Sorel and his wife Magda. He has to flee the country because the secret police want to arrest him, but he wants his wife to get a visa from a foreign consulate and follow him. She tries but is blocked by a Kafka-esque bureaucracy. After her baby dies, she kills herself in a vain attempt to stop him from returning. The leading roles were created on stage by Cornell MacNeil as Sorell, Patricia Neway as Magda and Marie Powers as the Mother. See also GIAN CARLO MENOTTI, MARIE POWERS.

1952 Cleveland Play House

Mary Simmons stars as Magda Sorel with Salvatore Colluras as John Sorel in this television adaptation of a Cleveland Play House production. Zelma George is the Mother, Shirley Abrams is the Secretary, Jack Lee is the Magician, Michael Sandry is Mr. Korner and Edgar Power is the Secret Agent. Frederick McConnell and George Dembo designed the sets and Harold Fink was music director. Earl Keyes directed the telecast in February 1952 on WEWS. Black and white. In English. 60 minutes.

1978 Spoleto Festival, USA

A production of the opera at Menotti's Spoleto Festival USA in Charleston, SC, telecast by PBS in the In Performance series. The performers are Mavalee Cariaga, David Clatworthy, Fredda Rakusin, Vern Shinall and Jerold Siena. Christopher Keene conducted the Spoleto Festival Orchestra and Kirk Browning directed the telecast before an invited audience. Critics felt the opera was particular suitable for TV. Color. In English. 115 minutes. Video at New York Public Library.

COPLAND, AARON

American composer (1900-1990)

Aaron Copland, one of the most popular modern American composers, is also noted for his film scores and won an Academy Award for one. He wrote two operas but neither was a real success. *The Second Hurricane* deals with students helping out during a natural disaster and was given its premiere in 1937 by Orson Welles before he went to Hollywood. Leonard Bernstein revived it for television. *The Tender Land* tells the story of a young woman's coming of age in the Midwest. It was originally created for television but NBC rejected it so Copland revised it for the stage. It premiered at the New York City Opera in 1954. A CD version was released in 1989 but there is no video. See THE SECOND HURRICANE.

1939-1988 Hollywood films

Copland began writing scores for Hollywood films in 1939 beginning with *The City*. He was nominated for Oscars for his scores for *Of Mice and Men*, *Our Town* and *North Star* and won an Academy Award for *The Heiress* in 1949. He also gained acclaim for *The Red Pony* and *Love and Money*. His last score was for the 1988 film *Miles From Home*. Copland adapted some of his film scores into orchestral suites, notably *The Red Pony*.

1961 Aaron Copland's Birthday Party

Leonard Bernstein and the New York Philharmonic celebrate Copland's birthday on CBS television. The program includes William Warfield singing Copland songs, Bernstein conducting Copland works and Copland himself conducting *El Salon Mexico*. Roger Englander directed the telecast on Feb. 12, 1961, in the *Young People's Concert*s series. Black and white. 60 minutes.

1972 Copland on Copland

Music commentator Karl Haas filmed Copland at his mountain retreat in New York for this program. Copland is seen in his garden, at his piano thinking about a composition and orchestrating at his desk. He discusses his work and career with Haas and there is an excerpt from the film *The City*. Black and white. 30 minutes. Video at MTR.

1976 The Copland Portrait

A film made by the U.S. Information Service as a portrait of the composer's life, work and music. He is shown with friends discussing his career and some of the significant moments in his life. Color. 29 minutes.

1980 An American Birthday: Copland at 80

Copland conducts the American Symphony as it plays *Fanfare for the Common Man* and *Short Symphony*. He narrates *A Lincoln Portrait* as Leonard Bernstein conducts in this birthday concert at Carnegie Hall filmed and telecast by Bravo. Color. 40 minutes.

1985 Aaron Copland: A Self-Portrait

Allan Miller's film is in the form of an autobiography tracing the life and career of the composer. Copland's music is prominently featured and there are interviews with Leonard Bernstein, Ned Rorem, Michael Tilson Thomas and Agnes de Mille. Vivian Perlis was the writer and Ruth Leon the producer of the film telecast in October 1985. Color. 60 minutes.

COPLEY, JOHN
English director (1933-)

John Copley became a top London stage director in the 1970s with notable productions at Covent Garden and the English National Opera. He began to work internationally in the 1980s, moving from Europe to Sydney to New York producing operas with such major stars as Joan Sutherland. He has been much admired for his ability to work with singers. See ADRIANA LECOUVREUR (1984), JANET BAKER (1982), LA BOHÈME (1982), L'ELISIR D'AMORE(1991), LA FORZA DEL DESTINO (1988 film), GIULIO CESARE (1984), LUCIA DI LAMMERMOOR (1986), THE MARRIAGE OF FIGARO (1991), MARY STUART (1982), SEMIRAMIDE (1986/ 1990), TOSCA (1986).

COPPOLA, FRANCIS FORD
American film director (1939-)

Francis Ford Coppola, after filming *The Godfather* in 1972, directed the stage production of Gottfried von Einem's opera *The Visit of the Old Lady* for the San Francisco Opera. His success resulted in invitations from Vienna and the Met to direct productions for them and he even had plans to stage *La Bohème* for Joseph Papp. None of these happened but opera is featured in several Coppola movies. In *The Godfather III* the end of the film revolves around a production of *Cavalleria Rusticana* at the Palermo Opera House. Coppola himself has stressed the operatic qualities of *Apocalypse Now*; he says that the smoke at the beginning signals that it is an opera and that he used *Turandot* as his model for the bodies in the compound. The use of the "Ride of the Valkyries" music during the helicopter attack helped make this scene one of the most memorable in cinema. The Coppola name actually has an operatic history in Italy for Giuseppe and Pietro Coppola composed operas in Naples in the 18th and 19th centuries. See CAVALLERIA RUSTICANA (1990 film), DIE WALKÜRE (1979 film).

COQ D'OR, LE
See THE GOLDEN COCKEREL

CORBIAU, GÉRARD
Belgian film director (1945-)

Gérard Corbiau wrote and directed two of the most interesting opera-oriented films of recent years after a long period making music programs for television. His 1987 *The Music Teacher* (Le Maître de Musique) stars José Van Dam as a retired opera singer who becomes a teacher. His 1994 *Farinelli* tells the story of the famous 18th century castrato. Both films utilize large amounts of opera music. See FARINELLI (1994), JOSÉ VAN DAM (1987).

CORELLI, FRANCO
Italian tenor (1921-)

A major cult has emerged around this Italian tenor in recent years and there was real excitement when his 1958 San Carlo performance of *La Forza del Destino* with Tebaldi was released from the Italian TV archives. The Modena-born tenor made his debut in 1951 in Spoleto in *Carmen* and sang widely around the world in the 1950s and 1960s. There are several videos of Corelli in concert compiled by the Bel Canto Society, mostly off-air television tapings. See also ANDREA CHÉNIER (1973), CAVALLERIA RUSTICANA (1963 film), LA FORZA DEL DESTINO (1958), TOSCA (1956).

1959 Renata Tebaldi and Franco Corelli

The first half of this video is devoted to an appearance by Franco Corelli on the *Voice of Firestone* television series on June 2, 1963. He sings three opera arias and two songs. The arias are the "Brindisi" and "Addio alla madre" from *Cavalleria Rusticana* and "Non piangere, Liù" from *Turandot*. The orchestra is conducted by Wilfrid Pelletier. Black and white. 35 minutes. VAI video.

CORIGLIANO, JOHN
American composer (1938-)

John Corigliano had real success with his first major opera, *The Ghosts of Versailles*. It premiered at the Metropolitan Opera in 1991 to critical praise, was a hit when telecast, is a consistent seller on video and laser disc and has already been revived by the Met. Corigliano had some success with earlier dramatic works. His 1970 *Naked Carmen* is based on the Bizet opera but uses unusual instruments and singers and is available on record only. He also wrote the Oscar-nominated score for Ken Russell's film *Altered States* (1980) and a less popular score for Hugh Hudson's *Revolution* (1985). See THE GHOSTS OF VERSAILLES.

CORNELIUS, PETER
German composer (1824-1874)

Peter Cornelius is not as well known in the U.S. as in Germany but holds an important position in the development of modern German opera. He was urged by Liszt to write his most famous opera, *Der Barbier von Bagdad*. Liszt conducted the premiere in 1858 but it was a fiasco. Cornelius had to leave town and the opera was not performed again until after his death. Cornelius became a close friend of Wagner, who also encouraged him, and his second opera *Der Cid* had a successful premiere in 1865. His opera *Gunlöd* was not complete when he died in 1874. See DER BARBIER VON BAGDAD.

CORTE DE FARAÓN, LA
1910 zarzuela by Lleó

Vincente Lleó's famous zarzuela *La Corte de Faraón* (The Court of the Pharaoh) is set in ancient Egypt in the time of the Pharaohs. Its Biblical tone is somewhat reminiscent of Cecil B. De Mille and it had censorship problems because it was considered risqué in its dialogue and in its scanty feminine costumes. It has been filmed twice in very different

ways and was even banned for a time in Spain. See also VINCENTE LLEÓ.

1943 Mexican film

The first film of the zarzuela was a black-and-white version made in a traditional manner in Mexico City in 1943. It was directed by Julio Bracho for Films Mundiales. Black and white. In Spanish. 85 minutes.

1985 José Luis García Sánchez film

Spanish director José Luis García Sánchez made this film to get even with the censors who had banned the zarzuela. In the movie an amateur company is performing the zarzuela in Madrid in the late 1940s when its members are arrested and hauled off to the police station in their Egyptian costumes. A priest has objected to the production of the forbidden zarzuela. While the police investigate, there are flashbacks of the musical numbers in the zarzuela and the relationships in the company are explored. The film stars Ana Belén, Fernando Fernán Gómez and Antonio Banderas. Color. In Spanish. 96 minutes.

CORTI, AXEL
Austrian film director (1933-)

Axel Corti, who was born in Paris but made his reputation directing film and theater in Austria, is known for movies like *Welcome to Vienna* and *The Refusal*. He has included opera music in his many films about Vienna and directed opera on film and stage. See ZAR UND ZIMMERMANN.

COSÌ FAN TUTTE
1790 opera by Mozart

Così Fan Tutte looks slight at first sight but it may well be Mozart's and librettist Lorenzo Da Ponte's most complex opera. Unlike their other two collaborations, it is an original story. It has only six characters and everything is balanced and orderly (or so it seems) as it tells the tale of two men testing the love of their fiancées with the connivance of an old cynic and a chameleon-like servant. The opera went out of fashion during the 19th century and was not popular with filmmakers until the present day. There seem to be no early films of the opera when it was unfashionable but there are a great many modern ones. See also WOLFGANG A. MOZART.

1958 NBC Opera Company

Phyllis Curtin portrays Fiordiligi with Frances Bible as Dorabella in this lively NBC Opera Company production by Samuel Chotzinoff. Mac Morgan is Guglielmo, John Alexander is Ferrando, James Pease is Don Alfonso and Helen George is Despina. The opera is sung in English in a translation by Ruth and Thomas Martin. Ed Wittenstein designed the sets and costumes and artistic director Peter Herman Adler conducted the NBC Symphony of the Air Orchestra. Kirk Browning directed the telecast on April 6, 1958. Black and white. In English. 59 minutes.

1970 Vaclav Kaslik film

The earliest version of *Così Fan Tutte* on film is by Czech composer/conductor Vaclav Kaslik. It was filmed in eight scenes in baroque settings introduced by *comedia dell'arte* figures bearing captions or icons. Gundula Janowitz is Fiordiligi, Christa Ludwig is Dorabella, Olivera Miljakovic is Despina, Luigi Alva is Ferrando, Hermann Prey is Guglielmo and Walter Berry is Don Alfonso. The cinematographer was Jan Stallich and Karl Böhm conducted the Vienna Philharmonic Orchestra. The film was released theatrically in the U.S. Unitel. Color. In Italian. 159 minutes.

1975 Glyndebourne Festival

This is a traditional but nicely acted and sung Glyndebourne Festival production by Adrian Slack. Helena Döse sings Fiordiligi, Sylvia Lindenstrand is Dorabella, Daniele Perriers is Despina, Thomas Allen is Guglielmo, Anson Austin is Ferrando and Franz Petri plays Don Alfonso. Emanuel Luzzati designed the sets, John Pritchard conducted the London Philharmonic Orchestra and Glyndebourne Festival Chorus and Dave Heather directed the video. Color. In Italian with English subtitles. 150 minutes. VAI video.

1977 Curtis Institute of Music

This is a video of the opera *Così Fan Tutte* as it was produced and performed by students of the Curtis Institute of Music. It was taped at the Walnut Street Theater in Philadelphia on April 24, 1977. Color. In Italian. 155 minutes. Video at New York Public Library for the Performing Arts.

1983 Dresden State Opera

German tenor Armin Ude sings Ferrando with Ana Pusar as Fiordiligi in this Dresden State Opera production by Joachim Herz. Elisabeth Wike is Dorabella, Andreas Scheibner is Guglielmo, Cornelia Wosnitza is Despina and Werner Haseleu is Don Alfonso. Hans F. Vonk conducts the Dresden Staatsoper Orchestra. Color. In German with Japanese subtitles. 148 minutes. Japanese laserdisc.

1984 Drottningholm Court Theater

This is sheer delight, an effervescent but complex version of this multi-faceted opera videotaped at the Drottningholm Court Theater. There is nothing apparently dark about this production with its young cast but appearances are deceptive and there is actually a good deal of Bergmanesque concern about the frailty of human beings hidden under the charm. Thomas Olofsson, who directed the video, sets the mood by showing the cast arriving by bus, bike and foot during the overture and then segueing into the opening stage scene. Arnold Östman, noted for bringing authenticity back to Mozart, is superb conducting the Drottningholm Orchestra in period costume playing period instruments. The stage direction by Willy Decker combines a dark center and a light surface. Anne Christine Biel is Fiordiligi, Maria Hoeglind is Dorabella, Magnus Linden is Guglielmo, Lars Tibell is Ferrando, Ulla Severin is Despina and Enzo Florimo is Don Alfonso. Color. In Italian with English subtitles. 141 minutes. Color. Philips video and laser.

1988 Jean-Pierre Ponnelle film

Jean-Pierre Ponnelle directed this fine cinematic version of *Così fan tutte* in June 1988, the last film he made before his fatal accident. Edita Gruberova is Fiordiligi, Delores Ziegler is Dorabella, Teresa Stratas is Despina, Luis Lima is Ferrando, Ferruccio Furlanetto is Guglielmo and Paolo Monarsolo is Don Alfonso. Wolfgang Treue was the cinematographer and does a fine job of enhancing Ponnelle's interpretation of the opera. Nikolaus Harnoncourt conducts the Vienna Philharmonic Orchestra and Chorus. Unitel/Beta Film. Color. In Italian with English subtitles. 178 minutes. London video and laser.

1989 Teatro alla Scala

Michael Hampe's lavish, large-scale production at La Scala is good but the opera seems lost in such a large theater. Daniela Dessi is Fiordiligi, Delores Ziegler is Dorabella, Josef Kundiak is Ferrando, Alessandro Corbelli is Guglielmo, Adelina Scarabelli is Despina and Claudio Desderi is Don Alfonso. Mauro Pagano designed the opulent sets and costumes and Riccardo Muti conducted a relatively small Teatro alla Scala Orchestra and Chorus. Ilio Catani directed the video on April 15, 1989. In Italian with English subtitles. 186 minutes. Home Vision video/on laser.

1989 Peter Sellars film
This is director Peter Sellars' attempt to give *Così Fan Tutte* contemporary relevance. His updated setting is a small-town diner called Despina's and the opera characters are modern in dress and attitudes. The interpretation is bleak and the subtitles slangish but this *Così* is intelligent, well thought out and justifies its modernity. Susan Larson portrays Fiordiligi, Janice Felty is Dorabella, Frank Kelley is Ferrando, James Maddalena is Guglielmo, Sanford Sylvan is Don Alfonso and Sue Ellen Kuzma is Despina. Sellars filmed the opera in a Vienna television studio in 1989 but the concept originated with his Pepsico Summerfare Festival staging in New York. Adrianne Lobel designed the striking sets and Craig Smith conducted the Vienna Symphonic Orchestra and Arnold Schoenberg Choir. Color. In Italian with American subtitles. 184 minutes. London video/on laser.

1992 Théâtre du Chatelet, Paris
John Eliot Gardiner's admirable production is performed on period instruments at the Théâtre du Chatelet in Paris. Amanda Roocroft is Fiordiligi, Rosa Monnion is Dorabella, Rodney Gilfry as Guglielmo, Rainer Trost is Ferrando, Eirian James is Despina and Claudio Nicolai is Don Alfonso. Carlo Tommasi designed the sets and costumes and Gardiner conducted the English Baroque Soloists and Monteverdi Choir. Peter Mumford directed the video. Color. In Italian with English subtitles. 193 minutes. Archiv video and laser.

Related films

1971 Sunday Bloody Sunday
There is a fine use of the trio "Soave sia il vento" in the British film *Sunday Bloody Sunday*. A love triangle ends when Murray Head decides to leave both Peter Finch and Glenda Jackson and go to America. Finch reacts by putting on a record of the trio sung by Pilar Lorengar, Yvonne Minto and Barry McDaniel. This is true Mozartian reconciliation for it allows him to express his emotional best wishes for the trip without even speaking. Joseph Losey, who filmed *Don Giovanni*, directed. Color. In English. 110 minutes. On video.

1978 Portrait of Solti
The same trio, "Soave sia il vento," is used with a different kind of irony in the TV documentary *Portrait of Solti*. It is played over grim newsreel scenes of German tanks rolling into Hungary at the beginning of World War II. It's not where you travel but how. Color and black and white. 60 minutes. On video.

1989 My Left Foot
Director Jim Sheridan features the tenor aria "Un aura amorosa" on the soundtrack of this film about Irish artist and cerebral palsy victim Christy Brown. Daniel Day-Lewis won an Oscar for his portrayal of Brown. Color. 103 minutes.

1995 Così
This is a superb and fascinating Australian comedy about a production of *Così Fan Tutte* in a mental hospital. The inmates can't speak Italian but they try it anyway. Louis Nowra wrote the screenplay basing it on his stage play and Mark Joffe directed the film. Color. 100 minutes.

COSSIRA, EMILE
French tenor (1854-1923)

Emile Cossira was one of the first opera singers to be both seen and heard on the movie screen. One of his most famous roles was as Romeo in the Gounod opera *Roméo et Juliette* and he was featured singing an aria from it in a pioneering sound film shown at the Paris Exhibition of 1900. Cossira was at the Paris Opéra from 1888 to 1891, sang the role of Romeo at Covent Garden in 1891 and was the first French Tristan in 1896. He was noted for the stylishness of his singing. See ROMÉO ET JULIETTE (1900).

COSSOTTO, FIORENZA
Italian mezzo-soprano (1935-)

Fiorenza Cossotto, who was born in Vercelli, made her debut at La Scala in 1957. After that she sang there regularly and was also welcomed at most of the other great opera houses from Covent Garden to the Metropolitan. She made her debut at the Met in 1968 as Amneris and found American audiences admired her fine singing. See ADRIANA LECOUVREUR (1976/1989), AIDA (1966/1981/1985), CAVALLERIA RUSTICANA (1968), WOLFGANG A. MOZART (1967), IL TROVATORE (1985), VERDI REQUIEM (1967).

COSTA, MARIO
Italian composer (1858-1933)

Taranto-born composer Mario Costa began as a Neapolitan songwriter and first found success on stage with his 1909 light opera *Il Capitan Fracassa*. He created five operettas but his greatest success and one of the classics of the genre in Italy is the *La Scugnizza* first performed in 1922. It is still popular after 70 years.

LA SCUGNIZZA
La Scugnizza is a lighthearted romantic operetta about a millionaire named Toby, his daughter Gaby and his secretary Chic. He visits a small Italian town and falls for a local girl called Salomè. A 1992 highlights version of the operetta was featured by operetta master Sandro Massimini and his associates on the Italian TV series *Operette, Che Passione!* It includes the songs "Napoletana," "Bada Salomè," "Salomè, un rondine non fa primavera" and "Vedo un cielo tutto azzurro." Color. In Italian. About 20 minutes. Ricordi (Italy) video.

COSTA, MARIO
Italian film director (1908-)

Director Mario Costa, who is credited with discovering Gina Lollobrigida, began his movie career in 1938 with a documentary based on Respighi's *The Fountains of Rome*. He made a number of opera films including a 1946 *Barber of Seville* that spearheaded the postwar Italian opera film boom. They usually featured the top Italian opera singers of the period, notably the all-star *Mad About Opera*, and are valuable records of an era. See THE BARBER OF SEVILLE (1946), GINO BECHI (1947), L'ELISIR D'AMORE (1947), MAD ABOUT OPERA, MANON LESCAUT (1955 film), PAGLIACCI (1948).

COSTA, MARY
American soprano (1934-)

Mary Costa began her film career with *Marry Me Again* in 1953 before she went into opera. She also married its director, Frank Tashlin. She had, however, been singing and studying voice since high school in Knoxville and had sung at the Hollywood Bowl. She sang in *The Bartered Bride* in Los Angeles in 1958, joined the San Francisco Opera company and was invited to London in 1962 to sing Violetta at Covent Garden. She made her debut at the Metropolitan Opera in 1964 in the same role.

Costa made four films and appeared on the *Voice of Firestone* television opera series. See FAUST (1963), VICTOR HERBERT (1973), JOHANN STRAUSS (1972).

1953 Marry Me Again
Costa's first Hollywood film was a comedy directed by Frank Tashlin. It stars Robert Cummings as an aviator romancing beauty contest winner Marie Wilson. Costa portrays Wilson's best friend. Black and white. 73 minutes.

1957 The Big Caper
Costa's second film was a crime drama directed by Rory Calhoun. Costa and co-star Calhoun pose as a married couple in a town to set up a robbery. Life in the town reforms them and they undo the planned crime. Black and white. 84 minutes.

1959 Sleeping Beauty
Costa won praise for giving voice to the Princess in this Disney animated feature. "Mary Costa's rich and expressive voice for the title character gives substance and strength to it" commented *Variety*. "It is a stronger voice than Disney ordinarily uses and its choice was wise." The music was adapted by George Bruns from Tchaikovsky's *Sleeping Beauty* ballet and Costa was particularly admired singing "Once Upon a Dream." The film is based on the Perrault version of the fairy tale. Clyde Geronimi directed. Color. 75 minutes. On video and laser.

COTRUBAS, ILEANA
Romanian soprano (1939-)

Ileana Cotrubas made her debut in Bucharest in 1964 and soon won recognition in the great opera houses. She sang Mimi at La Scala in 1975 and at the Met in 1977. Her voice has a truly touching quality in roles like Mimi and Violetta and this is evident in her video of *La Bohème* made at Covent Garden in 1982. Cotrubas retired from the opera stage in 1989 but came back for the *Three Sopranos* recital in 1991. See LA BOHÈME (1982), DIVAS (1991), DON CARLO (1987), IDOMENEO (1982), THE MARRIAGE OF FIGARO (1973), A MIDSUMMER NIGHT'S DREAM(1981), GIACOMO PUCCINI (1990), THE TALES OF HOFFMANN (1981), VERONA (1988).

COUNTERTENORS

The renaissance and popularity of countertenors, which began with England's Alfred Deller, continues apace with a widening number of roles and singers to fill them. Not only are countertenors prominent on video in the operas of Handel and other baroque composers, they can also been seen and heard in many modern operas written for them including works by Britten and Glass. Countertenors with entries in this encyclopedia are JAMES BOWMAN, MICHAEL CHANCE, PAUL ESSWOOD, JOCHEN KOWALSKI, CHRISTOPHER ROBSON,

COWARD, NOËL
English composer (1899-1973)

Noël Coward is best known as a wit, playwright, song writer and musical comedy composer but he also wrote a deliberately old-fashioned Viennese operetta. *Bitter Sweet* was inspired by Strauss's *Die Fledermaus* and Coward wrote both the music and libretto. Like its Viennese predecessor, it has a gypsy song, "Ziguener," and a big waltz, "I'll See You Again." See BITTER SWEET.

COX AND BOX
1866 operetta by Sullivan

Sir Arthur Sullivan's operetta, *Cox and Box, or the Long Lost Brothers*, was composed prior to his collaboration with William S. Gilbert and was meant as a private entertainment. The libretto by Francis C. Burnard tells the farcical story of two men who share a rented room without knowing it. Cox works by day and Box works by night and landlord Bouncer gets double rent for their room. They also share the same unwanted widow and are long lost brothers. See also GILBERT AND SULLIVAN.

1948 New York University Players
William Whalen is Cox, Stanley Weiler is Box and Earle Woodberry is Bouncer in this early telecast of the operetta by students at New York University. Albert M. Greenfield, their professor, directed them and the music was played by the University Orchestra. It was telecast on Dec. 1, 1948, from WPIX in New York. Black and white. In English. 60 minutes.

1982 George Walker Film
John Fryatt stars as Box and Russell Smythe is Cox in this film produced by Judith De Paul for George Walker. Tom Lawlor is Bouncer and there are a large number of atmospheric non-singing roles. Alexander Faris conducts the London Symphony Orchestra and the Ambrosian Opera Chorus. David

Alden was stage director and Dave Heather directed the film. Color. In English. 55 minutes. Braveworld (England) video.

THE CRADLE WILL ROCK
1937 "play in music" by Blitzstein

The Cradle Will Rock was Marc Blitzstein's first major "play in music" and was probably influenced by the Weill/Brecht political operas. It was composed after encouragement from Brecht who was enthusiastic about the song "Nickel Under the Foot" sung in the play by the prostitute Moll. The story takes places in Steeltown, U.S.A., where the workers are struggling to organize. It's told in flashback from a night court; the hero is a labor organizer and the villain is the town strongman. The premiere was directed by Orson Welles and was presented despite heavy-handed attempts to block it. It has been staged a number of times since. See also MARC BLITZSTEIN.

1967 Blitzstein's Cradle
Scenes from the opera are available in recital form in the television program *Blitzstein's Cradle* which originated on the New York Camera Three television series. Color. In English. 30 minutes. New York State Education Department video.

1986 American Place Theater
Patti LuPone stars in this production by the Acting Company at the American Place Theatre in New York. The cast includes Casey Biggs, James Harper, Tom Robbins, Mary Lou Rosato, David Schramm and Charles Shaw-Robinson. Bruce Minnix was the director and Glen Litton and John Lollos were the producers. The show was telecast on Jan. 26, 1986. Color. 90 minutes.

CREATION, THE
1878 oratorio by Haydn

Josef Haydn was a major opera composer whose work is now being re-evaluated but his operas are not yet on video. His writing for voice is finely demonstrated in his vocal masterpiece, the popular oratorio *Die Schöpfung* (The Creation). It is based on Milton's epic narrative poem *Paradise Lost* with a libretto by Gottfried van Swieten. It tells the story of the creation and of Adam and Eve. See also JOSEF HAYDN.

1986 Leonard Bernstein in Munich

Judith Blegen sings the role of Gabriel, Thomas Moser is Uriel, Kurt Moll is Raphael, Lucia Popp is Eve and Kurt Ollmann is Adam in this impressive performance in Munich Cathedral. Leonard Bernstein leads the Bavarian Radio Chorus and Symphony Orchestra. Humphrey Burton directed the video for Unitel. Color. In German. 120 minutes. DG video.

1990 Christopher Hogwood in Gloucester

Christopher Hogwood conducts the Choir of New College, Oxford, and the Academy of Ancient Music in this excellent performance at Gloucester Cathedral. Emma Kirkby, Anthony Rolfe Johnson and Michael George are the soloists. Chris Hunt, who directed the video, intercuts the performance with creation images from art and the natural world. Color. In German. 105 minutes. Decca video.

CRESPIN, RÉGINE

French soprano (1927-)

Régine Crespin was born in Marseilles, made her debut in 1960 and began to sing at the Paris Opéra in 1951. She rose to international fame singing both French and German operas and was particularly noted as the Marschallin and Sieglinde. She made her first appearance at the Metropolitan in 1962. After 1975 she turned to mezzo roles like Carmen. Crespin retired from the stage in 1991 and became an important singing teacher. See LES DIALOGUES DES CARMÉLITES (1987), LA GRANDE-DUCHESSE DE GÉROLSTEIN (1981), TOSCA (1983 film).

1974 Régine Crespin Recital

Crespin gives a recital on French television with the Orchestre National de France conducted by Jean Doussard. The program includes works by Massenet, Wagner and Berlioz. Yvonne Courson directed the program for INA. Color. 25 minutes.

1985 Tribute to Régine Crespin

This French television documentary includes an interview with the singer and performance excerpts from *Ariadne auf Naxos*, *Tosca* and *La Grand-Duchesse de Gérolstein*. She is also seen in rehearsals of *Die Walküre* with Herbert von Karajan. Color. In French. 88 minutes. Opera Dubs video.

CRISPINO E LA COMARE

1850 opera by Luigi and Federico Ricci

Luigi and Federico Ricci's *Crispino and the Fairy* was one of the most successful comic operas in Italy in the 19th century. It's a fantasy about a poor cobbler who is saved from suicide by a fairy godmother. The fairy helps him realize his desire to become a doctor but success goes to his head. In the end she changes him back into a cobbler. Francesco Maria Piave's libretto sews medical satire and buffo fun onto infectious melodies. See also LUIGI AND FEDERICO RICCI.

1989 Savona Festival

Roberto Coviello stars as Crispino in this Savona Festival production with Daniel Lojarro as his wife Annetta, Simone Alaimo as Fabrizio, Antonio Marani as Mirabolano and Serena Lazzarini as the Fairy. Paolo Carignani conducts the San Remo Symphony Orchestra. This is the only modern video of this rare opera but it is a non-professional version shot from the audience. A CD of the opera is available with the same cast. Color. In Italian. 100 minutes. Lyric video.

Early/related films

1916 Camillo De Riso film

Camillo De Riso directs and stars as Crispino in this Italian film made for the Ambrosio Studio. Emma Saredo plays Annetta. Black and white. About 50 minutes.

1938 Vincenzo Sorelli film

Ugo Céresi stars as Crispino in this Italian film based on the opera and using its music as soundtrack. Silvana Jachino is the Marchesina, Mario Pisu is the young painter and Guglielmo Sinaz is the doctor. The cinematographer was Piero Pupilli and Vincenzo Sorelli directed for Caesar Film. Black and white. In Italian. 72 minutes.

CSÁRDÁSFÜRSTIN, DIE

1915 operetta by Kálmán

Die Csárdásfürstin (The Gypsy Princess) is Emmerich Kálmán's most successful and enduring operetta. A Budapest cabaret singer named Sylva is in love with a German prince called Edwin. They face a lot of problems and there is much confusion but love finally wins out. In the course of the story she becomes known as the Gypsy Princess. The operetta was very popular in Europe in its time; it arrived in America in 1917 as *The Riviera Girl* in an adaptation by P.G. Wodehouse and Guy Bolton with new songs by Jerome Kern and was staged in London in 1921 as *The Gipsy Princess*. It has been filmed many times in German, Hungarian and Russian. The Hungarian title is *Csárdáskirályno*. See also EMMERICH KÁLMÁN.

1934 Martha Eggerth film

Hungarian soprano Martha Eggerth is the Gypsy Princess in this delightful German film of the tuneful operetta. Hans Söhnker portrays her handsome prince and Paul Kemp and Inge List are memorable singing the "Swallow Song" in an elevator. Georg Jacoby directed with Carl Hoffmann as cameraman. UFA. Black and white. In German. 97 minutes. Lyric/ Opera Dubs video.

1934 Meg Lemonnier film

The French version of the above production titled *Princesse Czardas* was shot in Germany at the same time with a cast headed by Meg Lemonnier. The cast includes Marcel Vibert, Lucine Dayle, Lyne Clevers, Marfa Dhervilly and Pierre Pierade. André Beucler directed with help from Georg Jacoby. UFA. Black and white. In French. 85 minutes.

1951 Marika Rökk film

German musical star Marika Rökk is the Gypsy Princess in this colorful film version of the Kálmán operetta directed by George Jacoby. Johannes Heesters is Prince Edwin, Franz Schafheitlin is Leopold and Hubert Marsischka is Feri. Color. In German. 94 minutes.

1971 Anna Moffo film

American opera soprano Anna Moffo sings Sylva and René Kollo is her Prince Edwin in this lively Hungarian-German film of the operetta directed by Miklós Szinetár. Dagmar Koller plays Countess Stasi and the cast includes Sandor Németh, Laszlo Mensaros, Elisabeth Ried, Irén Psota, Karl Schönböck, and Zoltan Latinovits as Miska the headwaiter. Bert Grund conducts the Graunke Symphony and Zigeuner Orchestras and two choruses. The film was released in the U.S. as *The Czardas Queen*. Mafilm/Unitel. Color. In Hungarian or German. 97 minutes.

1992 Sandro Massimini video

Italian singer/director Sandro Massimini produced this Italian stage version of the operetta titled *La Principessa della Czarda*. He stars as the dapper Count Boni with Sonia Dorigo as Sylva, Edoardo Guarnera as Prince Edvino, Gabriele Villa as Mirko and Vincenzo De Angelis as Feri. Don Lurio arranged the choreography, Umberto Di Nino designed the sets and Roberto Negri conducted the orchestra. G. F. Principe and Pierluigi Pagano directed the video for television. Color. In Italian. 121 minutes. Ricordi (Italy) video.

Early films

1919 Ida Russka film

Ida Russka stars as the Gypsy Princess in this Austrian silent film of the operetta written and directed by Emil Leyde. The cast includes Max Brod, Karl Bachmann and Susanne Bachrich. Black and white. In German. About 70 minutes.

1927 Liane Haid film

Liane Haid is the Csardas Princess in this elaborate silent film of the operetta made as a German/Hungarian collaboration. The operetta music was played live with the film in theaters. Ladislaus Vajda and Wilhelm Thiele wrote the film and Hans Schwarz produced it. Black and white. In German. 85 minutes.

CUNNING LITTLE VIXEN, THE
1924 opera by Janácek

Leo Janácek's Czechoslovakian opera *The Cunning Little Vixen* (Príhody Li ky Bystrou ky) takes place in a netherworld between reality and fantasy with its principal characters both animals and people. Janácek based the libretto on a tale by Rudolf Tesnohlídek. It tells the story of the vixen Sharp Ears and the Forester who captures her. After she escapes, mates with the Fox and has cubs, she is killed by a poacher. See also LEO JANÁCEK.

1965 Komische Oper, Berlin

Walter Felsenstein's Komische Opera production in Berlin features a famous performance by Rudolf Asmus as the Forester with Imgart Arnold as the Vixen. Manfred Hopp is the Fox, Ruth Schob-Lipka is the Forester's Wife and Owl and Werner Enders is the Schoolmaster. Rudolf Heinrich designed the sets and Vaclav Neumann conducted the Komische

Oper Orchestra. Felsenstein, who emphasized acting as much as singing, taped the opera in a studio for East German television. The German title is *Schlaue Füchslein*. Black and white. In German. 104 minutes. Japanese Classic Video/ Dreamlife laser.

1983 New York City Opera
Gianna Rolandi stars as Vixen Sharp Ears with Richard Cross as the Forester in this New York City Opera production by Frank Corsaro. The fairy tale sets and costumes created from designs by Maurice Sendak enchanted the critics. John Lankston and Nadia Pelle are also in this English-language version. Scott Bergeson conducted the New York City Opera Orchestra and Kirk Browning directed the telecast in the Live from Lincoln Center series on Nov. 9, 1983. Color. In English. 100 minutes. Video at NYPL.

1988 Czechoslovakian TV film
Rudolf Asmus plays the Forester in this Czechoslovakian television film made in Prague. Soprano Libuse Domanidska is the Fox with M. Ledererova as the Vixen. N. Bakala conducts the orchestra. Color. In Czech with Japanese subtitles. 102 minutes. Japanese laser.

1995 Nicholas Hytner film
Thomas Allen is the Forester with Eva Jenis as the Vixen in this film of the opera by Nicholas Hytner. Sir Charles Mackerras conducts the orchestra. RM Arts. Color. 100 minutes. On video.

CURTIZ, MICHAEL
American film director (1888-1962)

Michael Curtiz, whose *Casablanca* has become an icon of the American cinema, began his career in his native Hungary in 1912. In his early years he made several opera-related movies in Hungary and Austria. They include films of Flotow's *Martha*, Wedekind's *Lulu*, Lehar's *The Merry Widow* and Suppé's *Boccaccio*. In Hollywood he filmed Friml's *The Vagabond King*. See BOCCACCIO (1920), LULU (1918), MARTHA (1913), THE MERRY WIDOW (1918), THE VAGABOND KING (1956).

CYRANO DE BERGERAC
1913 opera by Damrosch

American composer Walter Damrosch was one of the most influential figures in American music in the first half of the century as both conductor and composer. His opera *Cyrano de Bergerac* uses Edmund Rostand's complete play as its libretto and was premiered at the Metropolitan Opera on Feb. 27, 1913. It was well received but was considered overly long and is no longer in the repertory. See also WALTER DAMROSCH.

1922 Augusto Genina film
Italian director Augusto Genina based his 1922 silent film *Cirano di Bergerac* on the Rostand play and followed the original as exactly as Damrosch. When the film came to America in 1925, the Damrosch score was considered the perfect accompaniment as they had the same text. The film opened at the Colony Theater accompanied by musical numbers from the Damrosch opera and won warm praise from the critics. Pierre Magnier stars as Cyrano de Bergerac with Linda Moglia as Roxanne and Angelo Ferrari as Christian. Black and white. In Italian. About 95 minutes.

CZINNER, PAUL
Hungarian opera film director (1890-1972)

Paul Czinner was one of the great opera film pioneers. He was a Hungarian who began making movies in Austria in 1919 and carried on his cinema career in England and the U.S. after the Nazis came to power. He was married to actress Elisabeth Berger who starred in many of his films including *Catherine the Great* and *As You Like It*. He turned to ballet and opera films in the 1950s. His 1954 Salzburg Festival *Don Giovanni* is one of the earliest complete operas filmed in performance on stage and was a harbinger of the multi-camera live TV operas of the future. In 1960 he filmed *Der Rosenkavalier* at Salzburg preserving a classic performance by Elizabeth Schwarzkopf. He also made a short film about Salzburg. See DON GIOVANNI (1954), DER ROSENKAVALIER (1960), SALZBURG (1956).

D

DAISI
1923 opera by Paliashvili

Daisi (Twilight), the second opera of Georgian composer Zakhary Paliashvili, was the first opera ever staged in Georgia, then part of the Soviet Union. V. Guniya's libretto is based on Georgian poems and is a romantic and highly patriotic folk legend set in 18th century Georgia.Two men are rivals for a woman at a time when the country is being attacked by a foreign power. Love and patriotism are entertwined. The opera premiered at the Georgia National Opera House in Tbilsi. See also ZAKHARY PALIASHVILI.

1966 Georgian film
Nikolai Sanishvili directed this film of the opera with Georgian actors dubbed by Georgian opera singers. The actors are Nana Kipiani, Dahli Tushishvili, Otar Koberidze and Kartolso Miradishvili while the singers include Medea Amiramashvili, Tamara Gurgenidze and Zurab Andjaparidze. The film emphasizes the necessity of struggling against foreign invaders even in the midst of love. Director Sanishvili collaborated on the film with Djansug Charkviani and Valeriano Tunia while Dudar Margiev was the cameraman. Gruzia film. Color. In Georgian. 73 minutes.

DAL MONTE, TOTI
Italian soprano (1899-1975)

Toti Dal Monte, once proclaimed by Melba to be her successor, remains a major cult figure for opera enthusiasts in Italy and her records are still popular. Dal Monte made her debut in 1916 at La Scala and in 1924 sang Lucia and Gilda at the Metropolitan Opera. She starred in four Italian films, at least one of which is available on video.

1940 Il Carnevale di Venezia
Critics thought the best thing about *The Venice Carnival* was Dal Monte's singing of arias from *Lucia di Lammermoor* and *La Sonnambula*. She plays a retired opera singer whose daughter is supposed to sing for the Carnival. When daughter panics, mother sings instead. Giacomo Gentilomo and Giuseppe Adami directed. Black and white. In Italian. 68 minutes.

1944 Fiori d'Arancio
Orange Blossoms, Dal Monte's second movie, was made in Venice in the chaos of war at the end of 1944 and was seen by almost no one. It was based on a play by André Birabeau and directed by the journalist Dino Hobbes Checchini. Black and white. In Italian. 70 minutes.

1949 Il Vedovo Allegro
The Merry Widower was written and directed by Mario Mattoli and features Dal Monte in a supporting role in a slight story about a revue performer. Black and white. In Italian. 90 minutes

1954 Cuore di Mamma
Dal Monte plays a retired opera singer in her last film, *Heart of a Mother*, and gets her final chance to sing on screen. The simple plot revolves around love complications after false accusations about a jewel theft. Luigi Capuano directed. Black and white. In Italian. 87 minutes. Bel Canto Society video.

DALIBOR
1868 opera by Smetana

Bedrich Smetana's opera *Dalibor* occupies a place in Czechoslovakia comparable to that of *Fidelio* in Germany and expresses similar patriotic ideas about national freedom. Josef Wenzig's libretto has a story reminiscent of the Beethoven opera. Dalibor is in prison for attacking a castle and killing a high official. Milada, the sister of that official, has fallen in love with Dalibor. She disguises herself as a boy musician to get into the prison and eventually dies in an attempt to rescue him. So does he. See also BEDRICH SMETANA.

1956 Vaclav Krska film
Vaclav Krska's patriotic Czech film of the opera uses actors to portray the characters with their voices dubbed by top opera singers. Karel Fiala portrays Dalibor as sung by Beno Blachut, Vera Heroldava is Milada with the voice of Milada Surtova, Jana Ryabarova is Jitka sung by Libuse Domaninska and Karel Bednar is the King. Krska

also made a film about Smetana's life. Black and white. In Czech. 92 minutes.

DAMNATION DE FAUST, LA
1846 opera by Berlioz

Hector Berlioz did not intend this concert opera for the stage in its present form but had plans to adapt it. He died before he could do so. There have been many attempts to stage it all the same. Berlioz wrote the libretto based on Goethe's *Faust*. Aging scholar Faust sells his soul to Mephistopheles for youth, love and glory and ends up betraying the lovely Marguerite. He goes to Hell and she goes to Heaven. See also HECTOR BERLIOZ.

1989 Royal Albert Hall
Anne-Sofie von Otter sings the role of Marguerite with Keith Lewis as Faust, José van Dam as Mephistopheles and Peter Rose as Brander in this concert version of the opera. It was presented at the Royal Albert Hall in London as a dramatic cantata in the form Berlioz conceived it. Sir Georg Solti leads the Chicago Symphony Chorus and Orchestra. Rodney Greenberg directed the video on August 28, 1989. Color. In French. 133 mins. London video.

Early/related films

1898 George Méliès film
Damnation de Faust is an early George Méliès film of the opera, the predecessor of the more ambitious film he made in 1903. About 1 minute.

1903 George Méliès epic
French film genius George Méliès created a tinted epic adaptation of the Berlioz opera released in France as *Faust aux Enfers* and in the U.S.A as *The Damnation of Faust*. Méliès stars as Méphistophélès and much of the film is devoted to Faust being taken to Hell after the death of Marguerite. This film was considered epic in its time because of its fifteen magnificent scenes and its extreme length. Tinted. In French. About 9 minutes (493 feet).

1992 The Ride to the Abyss
Swiss animator Georges Schwitzgebel's made an expressionistic animated version of scenes from the opera using the Berlioz music. Color. 10 minutes.

1992 L'Affaire Faust
French animator Jacques Houdin created this updated version of the Faust story using Berlioz music for its soundtrack. Color. 5 minutes.

DAMROSCH, WALTER
American composer (1862-1950)

Walter Damrosch, who was born in Germany but spent most of his life in the U.S., was an influential figure in American music as composer and conductor. He wrote four operas and two were produced at the Metropolitan opera house, *Cyrano de Bergerac* (1913) and *The Man Without a Country* (1937). See CYRANO DE BERGERAC.

DANGEROUS LIAISONS, THE
1994 opera by Susa

Conrad Susa's fourth opera *The Dangerous Liaisons* was successfully premiered at the San Francisco Opera on Sept. 10, 1994. Philip Littell's libretto, based on the 1782 epistolary novel *Les Liaisons Dangereuses* by Pierre Choderlos de Laclos, was probably influenced by the three films of the novel. *The Dangerous Liaisons* is an exploration of decadent sexuality and power games in the 18th century. It revolves around the aristocratic rake Valmont and the Marquise de Merteuil, his colleague in erotic intrigues. His seductions of Cecile de Volanges and Madame de Tourvel lead to love and tragedy. The opera maintains the wit and style of the novel. See CONRAD SUSA.

1994 San Francisco Opera
Thomas Hampson stars as Valmont with Frederica von Stade as Merteuil in this superb San Francisco production by Colin Graham. Renée Fleming sings the role of Mme. de Tourvel, Judith Forst is Madame de Volanges, Mary Mills is Cecile de Volanges, David Hobson is the Chevalier de Danceny and Johanna Meier is Madame de Rosemond. Gerard Howland designed the period sets and costumes and Donald Runnicles conducted the San Francisco Opera Orchestra. Gary Halvorson directed the video telecast on Oct. 17, 1994. Color. In English. 150 minutes.

Related films

1959 Roger Vadim film

Roger Vadim's *Les Liaisons Dangereuses* 1960 is an updated French version of the story. Gérard Philippe plays Valmont with Jeanne Moreau as his intrigue-spinning partner, Annette Stroyberg as Tourvel, Jeanne Valérie as Cecile and Jean-Louis Trintignant as Danceny. Black and white. In French. 105 minutes.

1988 Stephen Frears film

Stephen Frears' *Dangerous Liaisons* is a film of Christopher Hampton's stage adaptation of the novel. John Malkovich portrays Valmont with Glenn Close as Merteuil, Michelle Pfeiffer as Tourvel, Uma Thurman as Cecile and Keanu Reeves as Danceny. Color. In English. 120 minutes.

1989 Milos Forman film

Milos Forman's *Valmont* was scripted by Jean-Claude Carriere. Colin Firth plays Valmont with Annette Bening as Merteuil, Meg Tilly as Tourvel, Fairuza Balk as Cecile and Jeffrey Jones in the Danceny role. Color. In English. 137 minutes.

DANZA DELLE LIBELLULE, LA

1916/1922 operetta by Lehár

Franz Lehár's operetta was first staged in Vienna in German in 1916 as *Der Sterngucker* and concerned a young astronomer involved with three women. It was a failure. It was an even bigger failure in English in New York in 1917 where it was staged as *The Star Gazer*. The operetta was saved from extinction when it was translated into Italian and revised by Italian entrepreneur Carlo Lombardo. He worked with Lehár to transform it into *La Danza delle Libellule* (The Dance of the Dragonflies) for its Milan premiere in 1922. In the new plot the protagonist is a Duke in search of a wife and there are many elaborate dances. This version was a hit, especially for the song "Gigolette," and it returned to Vienna in its new form as *Libellentanz*. It was staged in England in 1924 as *The Three Graces* and then revived in Milan in 1926 as *Gigolette*. See also FRANZ LEHÁR.

1990 Sandro Massimini production

La Danza delle Libellule was staged in Milan in 1990 by Italian operetta maestro Sandro Massimini and taped for video. He directs and also appears as Bouquet Blum. Edoardo Guarnera stars as the Duke of Nancy with Simona Bertini as the Widow Cliquot, the woman who will become his Duchess. Annalena Lombardi is Tutù Gratin, Donatella Zapelloni is Carlotta Pommery, Gabriele Villa is Piper and Giorgio Valente is Gratin. Robert Negri conducted the orchestra, Umberto Di Nino designed the sets and Don Lurio arranged the choreography. Color. In Italian. 112 minutes. Ricordi (Italy) video.

DA PONTE, LORENZO
Italian librettist (1749-1838)

Lorenzo Da Ponte, who wrote some of the most beautiful words in opera for Mozart, is probably the best known of all opera librettists. The Da Ponte-Mozart operas stand on an operatic peak all their own. Surprisingly Da Ponte has been almost ignored in the many Mozart film biographies including *Amadeus*. His highly enjoyable *Memoirs* make his life seem fictional even if it actually happened. After he left Vienna, he moved on to London and then ended his life in New York where he assisted in importing opera. He wrote librettos for Salieri and many others besides Mozart but these operas have not remained in the repertory. There is, however, a video of a Salieri opera. See also COSÌ FAN TUTTE, DON GIOVANNI, THE MARRIAGE OF FIGARO, WOLFGANG A. MOZART, ANTONIO SALIERI, TARARE.

DARGOMIZHSKY, ALEXANDER
Russian opera composer (1813-1869)

Alexander Dargomizhsky, the first important Russian opera composer after Glinka, is known for three operas. The first was *Esmeralda* based on a novel by Victor Hugo. *Rusalka*, based on a poem by Pushkin, became a favorite of Russian singers like Chaliapin. Dargomizhsky's last opera, *The Stone Guest*, a variation on the Don Giovanni story based on a Pushkin poem, is his masterpiece and is still in the Russian repertory. A Soviet film of *The Stone Guest* was distributed internationally. See THE STONE GUEST.

DAUGHTER OF THE REGIMENT, THE

1840 opera by Donizetti

Gaetano Donizetti's *La Fille du Régiment* was composed to a French libretto but is usually staged in Anglo countries in English as *The Daughter of the Regiment*. In any language it's a romp, the colorful story of Marie who was found on a battlefield as a child and raised by a French regiment as its mascot. She wants to marry Tonio but a Marquise intervenes saying Marie is her long-lost niece and must marry a nobleman. After some rollicking fun and lots of bugle and drum playing, everything works out for the best. The French libretto is by J. H. Vernoy de Saint-Georges and Jean-François Bayard. Donizetti also made an Italian version. See GAETANO DONIZETTI.

1933 Pierre Billon film

Pierre Billon's French film modernizes the opera, moves the setting to Scotland, turns the French regiment into Scottish Highlanders and Anglicizes the names. Anny Ondra stars as Mary with a cast that includes Claude Dauphin as Lt. Williams, Marfa Dhervilly as Lady Diana and Paul Asselin as Sergeant Bully. The adaptation was written by Hans Zerlett and Hans Hannes. Vandor Film. Black and white. In French. 90 minutes.

1933 Karel Lamac film

This German-language version of the opera titled *Die Tochter des Regiment* was shot in Austria at the same time as the French film with the same changes in plot and names. It also stars Anny Ondra as Mary but with a supporting Austrian cast that includes Werner Fuetterer, Adele Sandrock and Otto Wallburg. Karel Lamac directed. Vandor Film. Black and white. In German. 90 minutes.

1972 Who's Afraid of Opera? series

Joan Sutherland stars in this highlights version intended for children and directed by Ted Kotcheff. Sutherland tells the story of the opera to puppets and performs the role of Marie with Ramon Remedios as Tonio, Spiro Milas as Sergean Sulpice and Monica Sinclair as the Marchioness. George Djurkovic designed the sets and Richard Bonynge conducted the London Symphony Orchestra. Color. Dialogue in English, arias sung in French. 30 minutes. Kultur video.

1974 Wolf Trap Park

Beverly Sills is delightfully exuberant and really enjoys herself as Marie in this English-language production of the opera staged by Lotfi Mansouri at Wolf Trap Park in Virginia. William McDonald is Tonio, Spiro Malas is Sergeant Sulpice and Muriel Costa-Greenspon plays the Marquise. Charles Wendelken-Wilson conducts the Filene Center Orchestra and the Wolf Trap Company Chorus. Ruth and Thomas Martin wrote the translation and Kirk Browning directed the video. Color. In English. 118 minutes. VAI video.

1986 Australian Opera

Joan Sutherland is in terrific voice as Marie in this enjoyable French-language Sydney Opera House production by Sandro Sequi. Anson Austin is Tonio, Gregory Yurisich is Sergeant Sulpice and Heather Begg is the Marquise. Henry Bardon designed the sets and Michael Stennett the costumes. Richard Bonynge conducted the Elizabethan Sydney Orchestra and Australian Opera Chorus. Peter Butler directed the video. Color. In French with English subtitles. 122 minutes. Kultur video.

Early/related Films

1898 American Mutoscope Film

A very early film of a scene from this opera was made in July 1898 in the New York City studio of the American Mutoscope Co. It was distributed with the title *The Daughter of the Regiment*. Black and white. About 2 minutes (155 feet).

1900 Phono-Cinéma-Théâtre

This was one of the first sound films. It features La Scala opera singer Polin performing an aria from *La Fille du Régiment*. The film was first shown at the Phono-Cinéma-Théâtre at the Paris Exhibition of 1900. Black and white. About 3 minutes.

1909 Deutsches Mutoscop und Biograph

A German sound film featuring the aria "Weiss nich die Welt" from the German version of *Die Regimentstochter*. It was made by the Deutsches Mutoscop und Biograph company. Black and white. In German. About 4 minutes.

1913 Cines film

The Italian film company Cines made a silent version of the Donizetti opera in 1913 with the

Italian title *La Figlia del Reggimento*. About 20 minutes.

1915 Pittaluga film
Another Italian silent film of the opera was made two years later and also titled *La Figlia del Reggimento*. It was distributed by Pittaluga. About 40 minutes.

1920 Vidali film
The popularity of the opera was so strong in Italy at this time that a third and somewhat longer version of the opera was produced and again titled *La Figlia del Reggimento*. Liliane de Rosny stars as Mary (not Marie) opposite Umberto Mozzato as Toni. The film was directed by Enrico Vidali for Subalpina Films of Turin. Black and white. About 50 minutes (1000 meters).

1927 Cameo Operas series
Kitty Barling stars as Marie in this British Song Films highlights version with Oscar Sosander as Tonio and Algernon Hicks as Baron Bertrand. It was screened with live singers and an orchestra in synchronization with the screen. H. B Parkinson directed as part of the *Cameo Opera* series. About 20 minutes.

1929 Betty Balfour film
English movie star Betty Balfour was brought to Berlin to star as Marie in this silent version of the opera adapted by Hans Zerlett. Alexander D'Arcy plays the man she loves and Kurt Gerron is the Sergeant. Hans Behrendt directed this German-British co-production. Black and white. About 80 minutes.

1944 Mapy Cortes film
Mapy Cortes stars as Maria in this Spanish-language film based on the Donizetti opera and made in Mexico under the direction of Jamie Salvador. It was released by Aguila Films with the Spanish title *La Hija del Regimiento*. Black and white. In Spanish. 86 minutes.

1953 Geza von Bolvary film
Antonella Lualdi stars as the daughter in this narrative film of the opera made in three languages with Isa Barzizzi, Hannelore Schroth, Michel Auclair and Theo Lingen. The Italian version is called *La Figlia del Reggimento*, the German version *Die Tochter der Kompanie* and the French version *La Fille du Régiment*. All three were directed by Geza von Bolvary with help from Tullio Covazi in Italy. Black and white. In Italian, German or French. 90 minutes.

THE DEAD
1987 opera film by Huston

John Huston's wonderful last film *The Dead* is not ostensibly about opera but opera is central to its story. Based on a story by one-time opera singer James Joyce, it revolves around a 1904 New Year's Eve party in Dublin where one of the guests is a professional opera tenor. The conversation is often about opera including *La Bohème* which has just premiered in Dublin. The discussion ranges from Verdi to *bel canto* and ends with talk about Caruso and memories of another great tenor. There is a touching scene in which the elderly woman giving the party sings Elvira's aria "Son vergin vezzosa" from *I Puritani*. It is sung in English as "Arrayed for the Bridal" by Cathleen Delany who sings badly but charmingly over a montage of mementos. The final scene of the film, the memory of a long-dead love, is triggered by the tenor singing "The Lass of Aughrim." Color. 82 minutes. Vestron video. See also JOHN HUSTON.

DEATH IN VENICE
1973 opera by Britten

Benjamin Britten's *Death in Venice* is based on the novella by Thomas Mann which was also made into a major film by Luchino Visconti. The libretto by Myfanwy Piper consists of vocal scenes connected by dance interludes. It tells the story of a famous German writer who goes to Venice and falls in love with a young boy. Cholera strikes the city but he is unable to leave and dies. The roles of the characters who lead the writer to his destiny are sung by the same baritone. The boy does not sing but dances. This was Britten's last opera. See also BENJAMIN BRITTEN.

1981 Tony Palmer film
Robert Gard stars as Aschenbach in this fascinating film of the opera directed by Tony Palmer and actually shot on location in Venice. James Bowman is the Voice of Apollo and John Shirley-Quirk sings all the baritone roles from Elderly Fop to Hotel Barber. Charles Knode designed the costumes and Nick Knowland was cinematographer. Steuart

Bedford conducts the English Chamber Orchestra. Color. 132 minutes. London Trust (England) video.

1990 Glyndebourne Festival

Robert Tear is poignant as the writer Aschenbach and Alan Opie is strong in the baritone roles in this Glyndebourne production by Stephen Lawless. The boy Tadzio and his Polish family are portrayed by dancers choreographed by Martha Clarke. Graeme Jenkins conducted the London Sinfonietta and the Glyndebourne Chorus while Robin Lough directed the video. Color. In English. 140 minutes. Home Vision video/Pioneer laser.

Related film

1971 Luchino Visconti film

This superb adaptation of the Thomas Mann source novel makes a good companion to the Britten adaptation and possibly influenced it. Director Luchino Visconti and co-scripter Nicola Badalucco, like Britten, emphasize that this is a story of homosexual love. Dirk Bogarde as Aschenback is made up to look like German composer Gustav Mahler and Mahler's music is used as the score. Bjorn Andresen is Tadzio, Silvana Mangano is the Mother and Romolo Valli is the hotel manager. Color. In English or Italian. 130 minutes.

DEBUSSY, CLAUDE
French composer (1862-1918)

Claude Debussy, one of the real revolutionaries of modern music, had plans for many operas but completed only one, *Pelléas et Mélisande*, based on a play by Maurice Maeterlinck. His version of the story of El Cid, *Rodrigue et Chimène*, was nearly finished when he died and it has been staged. Debussy also had projects to make operas out of Edgar Allen Poe stories and one of them, *La Chute de la Maison Usher*, has been completed by others and staged. See PELLÉAS ET MÉLISANDE, RODRIGUE ET CHIMÈNE.

1965 The Debussy Film

Oliver Reed portrays Debussy in Ken Russell's television film which centers around a group of people making a film about Debussy. The lives of the actors and the characters they portray begin to interact. Vladek Sheyball, for example, plays both the film director and the character who takes photographs of Debussy in the film-within-the film.

The film is an ingenious study in reflexive self-referential biography and was very adventurous for its time. Melvyn Bragg co-scripted. BBC. Black and white. 60 minutes.

DE CORDOBA, PEDRO
American bass (1881-1950)

Pedro De Cordoba, a New Yorker of Cuban and French parents, began his career as a bass. His first film was the 1915 Cecil B. De Mille version of *Carmen* in which he portrays the bullfighter Escamillo opposite Geraldine Farrar. He also appeared with Farrar in De Mille's 1915 *Temptation*. He was tall, good looking and gaunt and became a popular Hollywood character actor usually playing aristocratic Latinos. He made a large number of films but few with operatic connections and he was never a screen singer. His memorable movies include *Captain Blood*, *The Mark of Zorro*, *Blood and Sand*, *Saboteur* and *The Song of Bernadette*. See CARMEN (1915), GERALDINE FARRAR (1915).

DÉDÉ
1921 operetta by Christiné

Maurice Chevalier made Henri Christiné's tuneful French operetta *Dédé* into a major success on the Paris stage. He portrayed a shoe salesman in a shop with the comic André Urban as his manager. The *Dédé* of the title is a rich man who has bought the shop in order to meet a married woman without compromising her. Albert Willemetz wrote the libretto. See also HENRI CHRISTINE.

1934 Albert Prejean/Danielle Darrieux film

Christiné's operetta was made into a 1934 French film starring Danielle Darrieux as the saleswoman Denise and Albert Prejean as the shoe salesman Robert. The cast also includes Mireille Perrey, Viviane Romance, Ginette Leclerc and Claude Dauphin. René Guissart directed. Black and white. In French. 75 minutes. René Chateau (France) video.

DEHN, PAUL
English librettist (1912-1976)

Paul Dehn was a notable screenwriter, who also found time to write opera librettos. He wrote *The Bear* for William Walton and *A Dinner Engagement* and *Castaway* for Lennox Berkeley. He had great success writing for the movies, winning an Oscar for his story for *Seven Days to Noon* in 1950 and a British Academy Award for his screenplay for *Orders to Kill* in 1958.

DE KOVEN, REGINALD
American composer (1859-1920)

Reginald De Koven was one of the most popular American composers of light operas and operettas at the end of the 19th century. His 1891 *Robin Hood* was a major success in its time and the source of the still popular wedding song "Oh, promise me." There was even a sequel called *Maid Marian.*

1937 The Adventures of Robin Hood
This great Hollywood adventure film is partially based on Harry B. Smith's libretto for De Koven's *Robin Hood*. The De Koven/Smith version of the story is the only one in which Robin and Sir Guy duel over Maid Marian and the movie certainly would not be the same without that marvelous sword fight. Errol Flynn stars as Robin, Basil Rathbone is Guy and Olivia De Havilland is Marian. Erich Wolfgang Korngold wrote the score which apparently does not use any of De Koven's music. Michael Curtiz and William Keighley directed. Color. 102 minutes.

1981 S.O.B.
Director Blake Edwards features the hit song from De Koven's opera at the end of this Hollywood satire. Star Julie Andrews sings "O Promise Me" rather well. Color. 121 minutes.

DELIBES, LEO
French composer (1836-1891)

Leo Delibes used to be better known as the composer of the ballet *Coppelia* than for his operas. Since British Airways began to use music from his *Lakmé* in their commercials, however, he is once again a popular operatic favorite. Tchaikovsky was a great admirer of Delibes' operas which include *Le Roi l'a dit, Jean de Nivelle* and *Kassya*. Only the famous *Lakmé* is available on video. See LAKMÉ .

DELIUS, FREDERICK
English composer (1862-1934)

Frederick Delius is not usually thought of as an opera composer but he wrote a fair number of them in the early part of his career. The most successful

and the only one on video is the bucolic love story *A Village Romeo and Juliet*. See A VILLAGE ROMEO AND JULIET.

1968 Song of Summer
Ken Russell's elegiac film about Delius stars Max Adrian as the composer at the end of his life and Christopher Gable as his devoted helper Eric Fenby. Color. 50 minutes.

DELLA CASA, LISA
Swiss soprano (1919-)

Lisa Della Casa, who won wide praise for her performances in Mozart, Strauss and Wagner operas, is probably best-known for her Arabella. She made her debut in Solothurn in 1941, was soon a regular at the Zurich Stadttheater and sang at the Metropolitan Opera from 1953 to 1968. She retired from the stage in 1974 but can be seen as Donna Elvira in the 1954 Salzburg *Don Giovanni*, in a 1963 *Arabella* and in her *Voice of Firestone* TV shows. See ARABELLA (1963), DON GIOVANNI (1954), FAUST (1963 Bell Telephone Hour).

1958-1962 Lisa Della Casa in Opera & Song
A selection of highlights from Lisa Della Casa's appearances on the *Voice of Firestone* television shows in 1958 and 1962. In one she performs arias and scenes from *La Bohème* in collaboration with tenor Nicolai Gedda; he joins her in duet on "O soave fanciullla" and sings "Che gelida manina." On the other program she joins her voice in *Tosca* with Giuseppe Campora and Richard Tucker and in *La Bohème* with Tucker. She also sings the opening and closing songs by Idabelle Firestone. Black and white. 30 minutes.

1969 Four Last Songs by Strauss
Lisa Della Casa sings the *Four Last Songs* by Richard Strauss in a television studio, apparently using her 1953 recording of the songs with Karl Böhm as the playback soundtrack. Kurt Grigoleti directed the film. Color. In German. 45 minutes.

1970 Portrait of Lisa Della Casa
Heinz Liesendahl directed this documentary portrait of Lisa Della Casa for WDR television in Germany. She talks about her career and sings arias by Mozart, Strauss and Puccini. Color. In German. 32 minutes.

DELLO JOIO, NORMAN
American composer (1913-)

Pulitzer Prize-winning composer Norman Dello Joio, who has written operas for stage and television, thinks his 1961 *Blood Moon* is his major achievement. He has also written three operas about St. Joan including *The Trial at Rouen* (1956) created for the NBC Opera Theatre. His other TV operas are *All is Still* (1971), a monologue based on a letter from Mozart to his father, and *The Louvre* (1965) which won an Emmy. Dello Joio has also written scores for films and television shows including the 1956 *Air Power* TV series. See THE TRIAL AT ROUEN.

1958 Dello Joio on *The Seven Lively Arts*
Dello Joio is the narrator of this program created for *The Seven Lively Arts* series which attempts to show the sources of his ideas and techniques. He discusses the influence of his organist father and uses a piano to explain patterns in his music. He talks about writing for film and television and his score for the *Air Power* TV series. Lending support are conductor Alfredo Antonini, a symphony orchestra, a ballet company and a Japanese pianist. The program was telecast on Feb. l6, 1958. Black and white. 60 minutes.

DEL MONACO, MARIO
Italian tenor (1915-1982)

Mario Del Monaco is in the tradition of those Italian tenors who felt that their powerful voices were meant to thrill audiences; his did from his debut in Milan in 1941 until his retirement in the 1960s. He began his international career at Covent Garden in 1946 with the San Carlo Company and made his first appearance at the Metropolitan in 1950. He was admired for his Otello, which he sang around the world, but his range of roles included even Wagner. He began making movies in 1949 and had a small but successful cinema career. He has singing roles in films about Cavalieri, Caruso, Mascagni and Verdi. Many of his operas were televised in Italy and are on video including his *Otello*. See AIDA (1961), LINA CAVALIERI (1955), ANDREA CHÉNIER (1958/1961), ENRICO CARUSO (1951), CASA RICORDI, MADAMA BUTTERFLY (1957), PIETRO MASCAGNI (1952), OTELLO (1958), PAGLIACCI (1961), RIGOLETTO (1954), IL TROVATORE (1957), GIUSEPPE VERDI (1953), LJUBA WELITSCH (1960).

1948 The Man with the Grey Glove
Mario Del Monaco portrays a tenor fresh from the country in Camillo Mastrocinque's Italian thriller *L'Uomo dal Guanto Grigio*. He's a bit naive but he sings some arias, wins Annette Bach and solves the crime. The film was released in the U.S. on the strength of Del Monaco's popularity. Black and white. In Italian. 85 minutes.

1955 Guai ai Vinti!
Mario Del Monaco has a small role in *Getting in Trouble!*, a rather didactic Italian film about abortion. Two women are raped during World War I and become pregnant but only one has an abortion. Lea Padovani and Anna Maria Ferrero are the stars while Raffaello Matarazzo directed. Black and white. In Italian. 100 minutes.

1959 Mario Del Monaco in *Carmen*
Mario Del Monaco sings the "Flower Song" from *Carmen* on stage in Tokyo. The aria is included on the video *Legends of Opera*. Black and white. In Italian. 4 minutes. Legato Classics video.

1966 Ein Sängerporträt
Portrait of a Singer is a German documentary film about Del Monaco which includes excerpts from *Tosca, Turandot, Rigoletto, La Bohème, Il Trovatore* and *Otello*. It was shot on 35mm for WDR television in Germany. Color. 29 minutes.

1978 Primo Amore
Mario Del Monaco is the director of a retirement home for show business personalities in the Italian film *First Love*. Ugo Tognazzi portrays a retired star who begins a love affair with Ornella Muti. Dino Risi directed. Color. In Italian. 112 minutes. Opera Dubs video.

1985 Mario del Monaco in Moscow
De Monaco sings in recital with Russian soprano Irina Arkhipova in this video made for Soviet television. The program includes works by Verdi, Bizet and Leoncavallo. Color. 61 minutes.

1992 Mario Del Monaco
This is a video portrait of the great tenor made for the Italian opera singer series *I Grandi della Lirica*. Color. In Italian. 60 minutes. Center (Italy) video.

DE LOS ANGELES, VICTORIA
See LOS ANGELES, VICTORIA DE

DE LUCA, GIUSEPPE
Italian baritone (1876-1950)

Giuseppe De Luca's impressive Italian career, which began in 1897, includes the world premieres of Cilea's *Adriana Lecouvreur* and Puccini's *Madama Butterfly* as Sharpless. He sang at La Scala for eight years and at the Metropolitan Opera for 25 years from 1915 to 1940. In New York he created another famous role, that of Puccini's Gianni Schicchi in *Il Trittico*. De Luca made many recordings and starred in three Vitaphone films.

1927-1928 Vitaphone opera films
Giuseppe De Luca, billed as "of the Metropolitan Opera Company," appeared in three sound films for the Vitaphone company. In the first he sings one of his specialties, Figaro's "Largo al Factotum" from *The Barber of Seville*. In the second he sings the Quartet from *Rigoletto* with Beniamino Gigli as the Duke, Marion Talley as Gilda and Jeanne Gordon as Maddalena. In the third he joins Gigli in one of the great performances of the Friendship Duet from Act I of Bizet's *The Pearl Fishers*, sung in Italian. Black and white. Each film about 7 minutes. Bel Canto Society video.

DELVAUX, ANDRÉ
Belgian film director (1926-)

André Delvaux, one of Belgium and the world's great modern filmmakers, has had wide recognition for films like *The Man Who Had His Hair Cut Short* (1968) *and Rendezvous in Bray* (1971). His 1985 film *Babel Opera* revolves around a stage production of *Don Giovanni*. See DON GIOVANNI (1985 film).

DEMME, JONATHAN
American film director (1944-)

Jonathan Demme, who won an Oscar for *The Silence of the Lambs*, began his Hollywood career in the 1970s with B-pictures for Roger Corman. He has created some of the more thought-provoking Hollywood films and his AIDS-oriented film *Philadelphia* has a notable use of opera, especially the Maria Callas version of "La Mamma Morta" from *Andrea Chénier*. See ANDREA CHÉNIER (1993 film), MARIA CALLAS (1993), IDOMENEO (1993 film).

DE PALMA, BRIAN
American film director (1940-)

Brian De Palma, whose films have some stylistic similarities to those of Alfred Hitchcock, is known for such shocking thrillers as *Carrie, Body Double* and *Wise Guys*. Like other Italian-American directors, he occasionally uses opera in his films. See PAGLIACCI (1987 film).

DE PAOLIS, ALESSIO
Italian tenor (1893-1964)

Alessio De Paolis made his debut at Bologna in 1919 and sang Fenton in *Falstaff* at La Scala in 1923. He was a top tenor in Italy for fifteen years before going to the Metropolitan Opera in 1938 where, incredibly, he sang for 26 more years. He seems to have appeared in only one film.

1932 La Cantante dell'Opera
Alessio De Paolis and soprano Laura Pasini, both singing at La Scala at this time, are featured in the opera scenes in this colorful Italian film. The plot revolves around a young opera singer in Venice and her involvement with an American who is not what he seems. Nunzio Malasomma directed. Black and white. In Italian. 90 minutes.

DE SEGUROLA, ANDRÉS
See SEGUROLA, ANDRÉS DE

DESERET
1961 TV opera by Kastle

American composer Leonard Kastle was working for the NBC Opera Theatre when it produced his opera about Mormon leader Brigham Young and his last romance. "Deseret" was the Mormon's name for their country before it was forced to become the American state of Utah. Librettist Anne Howard Bailey sets the opera in Young's mansion at the time of Civil War. It tells how he loses his proposed 25th wife to a Union Army captain. Kenneth Smith sings the role of Brigham Young, Judith Raskin is the woman and John Alexander is the army captain. Samuel Chotzinoff produced, Jan Scott designed the sets and Peter Herman Adler conducted the orchestra. Kirk Browning directed the telecast on Jan. 8, 1961. Color. In English. 120 minutes. See also LEONARD KASTLE.

DESERT SONG, THE
1926 operetta by Romberg

Sigmund Romberg's *The Desert Song* may not be grand opera but it's certainly grand operetta as the many films and stagings of this classic piece of melodic hokum demonstrate. It was the first operetta to be filmed in the sound era. Otto Harbach, Oscar Hammerstein II and Frank Mandel's libretto tells the story of a mysterious cloaked figure called the Red Shadow who leads the Moroccan Riffs against the French. He is actually Pierre Birbeau, the supposedly wimpy son of the French Governor. He secretly loves and eventually wins Margot, the fiancée of his bitter rival, the French commander. The operetta's famous songs include "The Riff Song" and "One Alone." See also SIGMUND ROMBERG.

1929 First operetta film
This 1929 movie was the first operetta to be filmed and was advertised as the "first all-singing and talking operetta." It was made by by Warner Brothers soon after the operetta premiered on stage and was promoted as having a chorus of 132 voices backed by 109 musicians. Baritone John Boles stars as the Red Shadow opposite Carlotta King as Margot and Louise Fazenda as Susan. Harvey Gates wrote the adaptation, Bernard McDilled filmed it and Roy del Ruth directed it. Black and white. 106 minutes.

1932 Alexander Gray film
Warner Brothers also made a two-reel version of the operetta titled *The Red Shadow* and starring Alexander Gray as the Shadow with Bernice Claire as his Margot. They had sung the roles opposite each other on the stage. Warners made many short films based on their own musicals as the costs were minimal. Black and white. 20 minutes.

1943 Dennis Morgan Film
This Hollywood feature version of the operetta stars Dennis Morgan as the rebel Red Shadow who leads a double life. His lady love is played by Irene Manning. As this version of the story was made during World War II, the Germans turn out to be the real villains. Robert Florey directed. Warner Bros. Color. 96 minutes.

1953 Gordon McRae film
Gordon McRae portrays the mysterious rebel leader with a double life in this film of the Romberg operetta. Kathryn Grayson is the woman he loves. This is the best of the film versions and much helped by the musical arrangements of Max Steiner. Bruce Humberstone directed for Warner Brothers. Color. 110 minutes.

1955 Nelson Eddy TV Film
Nelson Eddy stars as the Red Shadow rebel with a voice in this NBC Television production by Max Liebman. Margot is sung by soprano Gale Sherwood with whom he was appearing in a nightclub act at the time. The supporting cast includes Salvatore Baccaloni, Otto Kruger, Rod Alexander and Bambi Lynn. Black and white. 90 minutes.

DESTINN, EMMA
Czech soprano (1878-1930)

Emma Destinn, the great soprano from Prague who became a heroine in her homeland, made her debut in 1898 in Berlin as Santuzza and sang there for ten years. She made her first appearance at the Metropolitan Opera in New York in 1908 as Aida and in 1910 created the role of Minnie in the world premiere of Puccini's *La Fanciulla de West*. She was an important part of the Met's golden age and a recording artist of great merit but also a important Czech patriot. She did not appear in any movies but there is a Czech film about her.

1979 Divine Emma
Bozidara Turzonovova stars as Emma Destinn (Ema Destinová in Czech) in *Bozská Ema*, a Czechoslovakian film biography. The film is as much about her love for her country as it is about her opera career. It begins with a triumphal tour of America by Destinn while World War I rages in Europe and the U.S. remains neutral. When she returns home, she is at first put in prison as a spy by the Austro-Hungarian authorities. Eventually she is allowed to tour the country singing patriotic songs. The film was directed by Jiri Krejcik, written by Krejcik and Zdenek Mahler and photographed by the famous Miroslav Ondricek. Color. In Czech. 110 minutes.

DEVIL AND KATE, THE
1899 opera by Dvořák

Antonín Dvořák's Czech opera *The Devil and Kate* (Cert a Káca) is a comic tale centering around a strong-minded woman named Kate. She dances with a Devil called Marbuel at a village fair and goes off to his home at his invitation. Home turns out to be Hell but Kate proves to be too much for this Devil. With the help of Jirka, the shepherd, she saves and reforms the local princess and makes everything right. The libretto by Adolph Wenig is based on a Czech folk tale. See also ANTONÍN DVORÁK.

1988 Wexford Festival
Peter Lightfoot stars as the Devil Marbuel with Anne Marie Owens as Kate in this lively English-language production by Francesca Zambello at the Theatre Royal at the Wexford Festival in Ireland. Kristine Ciesinksi portrays the Princess, Joan Davies is Kate's Mother, Marko Putkonen is Lucifer, Alan Fairs is the Marshall, Kathleen Tynan is the Chambermaid, Joseph Evans is Jirka and Philip Guy Bromley is Hell's Gatekeeper. Neil Peter Jampolis designed the sets and Albert Rosen conducts the RadioTelefisEireann Symphony Orchestra. The overture is played over scenes of Wexford in the telecast and video. Color. In English. 115 minutes. Lyric video.

DEVILS OF LOUDUN, THE
1969 opera by Penderecki

Krzysztof Penderecki's remarkable *Die Teufel Von Loudun*, an operatic version of what happened to a priest and a group of nuns in 17th century Loudun, has been widely produced. Erotic fantasies in a religious setting with blasphemy for spice apparently can count on popularity even if the music is difficult. Penderecki's German libretto is based on a play by John Whiting derived from a book by Aldous Huxley. The opera begins by saying the devil cannot be trusted even when he tells the truth. Father Grandier is accused of corrupting the nuns in a convent and especially its prioress Mother Jeanne. The truth is much more complicated. See also KRZYSZTOF PENDERECKI.

1969 Hamburg State Opera
After the premiere at the Hamburg State Opera House, the opera was presented on Hamburg television with the same cast. Tatiana Troyanos portrays Mother Jeanne, Andrzej Hiolski is Father Grandier, Bernard Ladysz is Father Barré, Horst Wilhelm is Father Mignon, Heinz Blankenburg is Mannoury, Kurt Marschner is Adam and Ingeborg Krüger is Philippe. Marek Janowski conducts the Hamburg State Opera Orchestra and Chorus and

Joachim Hess directed. Color. In German. 120 minutes.

Related film

1970 The Devils
Ken Russell's film, like Penderecki's opera, is based on the play by Whiting and the book by Huxley. This may be Russell's most bizarre film but it's hysterically fascinating. Vanessa Redgrave stars as Mother Jeanne and Oliver Reed is Father Granier. The music in the film is by Peter Maxwell Davies. Color. 111 minutes. On video.

DEW, JOHN
English director (1944-)

English director John Dew, who studied with Walter Felsenstein and Wieland Wagner, began directing operas in Germany in 1971. He began to stage modern operas at Bielefeld in 1981 and later worked at the Deutsche Oper, Berlin. He is particularly well known for updating classic operas including *Les Huguenots* which is on video. See LES HUGUENOTS (1993).

1993 Portrait of John Dew, Opera Producer
Hubert Orthkemper made this video documentary about the English producer for German television. It pictures Dew at work on opera and explains the extent of his career. Color. In German. 44 minutes.

DEXTER, JOHN
English director (1925-1990)

John Dexter began his career as a director producing plays for the English Stage Company and the National Theater. His first opera was *Bevenuto Cellini* staged at Covent Garden in 1966. Dexter became director of productions for the Metropolitan Opera in 1974 and many of his productions there are on video. See AIDA (1985), THE BARTERED BRIDE (1978), DON CARLO (1980/1983), DON PASQUALE (1979), LA FORZA DEL DESTINO (1984), LULU (1980), RIGOLETTO (1981), RISE AND FALL OF THE CITY OF MAHAGONNY (1979).

DIALOGUES DES CARMÉLITES, LES

1957 opera by Poulenc

Dialogues of the Carmélites is an opera based on a movie screenplay. The story originated in the memoirs of a nun who survived the French Revolution. Her story was turned into a novel by German writer Gertrude von Le Fort. Austrian priest Raymond-Leopold Bruckberger wrote a film script based on the novel and asked French novelist Georges Bernanos to write the dialogue. The screenplay was at first judged uncinematic by producers, even though Bruckberger later made a film from it, so Bernano turned his script into a stage play in 1948. Composer Francis Poulenc saw the play and wrote his libretto based it. The opera, composed in 1953, was not staged until 1957. It tells the story of a group of nuns during the French Revolution who are forced to become martyrs. Blanche is the fragile new nun who decides to join her sister nuns when they are led to the guillotine by Prioress Madame Lidoine. See also FRANCIS POULENC.

1957 NBC Opera Theatre
Leontyne Price portrays Prioress Madame Lidoine with Elaine Malbin as Blanche in this much-praised NBC Opera Theatre production by Samuel Chotzinoff. The cast includes Rosemary Kuhlman as Mother Marie, Patricia Neway as the old Mother Superior, Judith Raskin as the prophetic Sister Constance, David Lloyd as the priest and Robert Rounseville as the Chevalier de la Force. Trew Hocker designed the sets, Peter Herman Adler conducted the Symphony of the Air Orchestra and Kirk Browning directed the telecast. Color. In English. 120 minutes.

1985 Australian Opera
Joan Sutherland stars as Prioress Madame Lidoine in this Australian Opera English language production by Elijah Moskinsky at the Sydney Opera House. Isobel Buchanan is the fearful Blanche, Heather Begg is Mother Marie, Ann-Marie MacDonald is Constance, Patricia Price is Mother Jeanne, Geoffrey Chard is the Marquis de la Force, Paul Ferris is the Chevalier de la Force and Lone Kopple is the old Prioress. John Bury designed the sets and Richard Bonynge conducted the Elizabethan Sydney Orchestra and Australian Opera Chorus. Brian Adams produced and Henry

Prokop directed the video for ABC TV. Color. In English. 155 minutes. Sony video.

1987 Canadian Opera
Irena Welhasch portrays Blanche in this Canadian Opera Company production originally staged by Lotfi Mansouri at the O'Keefe Center. The cast includes Maureen Forrester as the old Prioress, Janet Stubbs as Mother Marie, Harolyn Blackwell as Constance, Carol Vaness, Gaetan Laperriere and Mark DuBois as the Chevalier de la Force. Jean Fournet conducts the Canadian Opera Orchestra. Norman Campbell directed the telecast on Jan, 25, 1987. Color. In English. 180 minutes.

1987 Metropolitan Opera
Maria Ewing stars as Blanche opposite Jessye Norman as Prioress Madame Lidoine, Régine Crespin and Florence Quivar in this all-star Metropolitan Opera production by John Dexter. David Kuebler lends male support as del la Force. Manuel Rosenthal, a friend of Poulenc, conducts the Metropolitan Opera Orchestra and Chorus. Brian Large directed the video taped April 4 and telecast on May 6, 1987. Color. In French with English subtitles. 180 minutes.

Related film

1959 Bruckberger film
This French film, *Les Dialogues des Carmélites*, is based on the original screenplay of the story and makes a fascinating comparison with the opera. It was directed by Raymond-Leopold Bruckberger, the priest who wrote the screenplay that inspired the opera, in collaboration with Philippe Agostini. The script now is credited to George Bernanos, Bruckberger and Agostini. The story is basically the same: a young nun learns the spirit of sacrifice during the Terror of the French Revolution. The film stars Alida Valli as Blanche, Jeanne Moreau as the Prioress and Madeleine Renaud. Black and white. In French. 112 minutes.

DICK DEADEYE
1975 pastiche by Gilbert & Sullivan

This is a pastiche operetta in the form of a British animated film based on the characters of William S. Gilbert, the music of Arthur Sullivan and the drawings of Ronald Searle. It was created by animator Bill Melendez and the graphics are its chief delight. The main character is Dick Deadeye, the villain of H.M.S. Pinafore, transformed here into a hero commissioned by the Queen to undertake a dangerous mission. He is joined in his adventure by Little Buttercup, Yum-Yum, the twins Nanki and Poo, a Modern Major General and other G & S characters. Some of the songs have recognizable lyrics while others have new words by Robin Miller. The voices belong to John Baldry, Barry Cryer, George A. Cooper, Miriam Karlin, Victor Spinetti, Linda Lewis, Peter Reeves and others. Jimmy Horowitz arranged and conducted the music to a libretto by Leo Rost and Robin Miller. Color. In English. 80 minutes. Proscenium Entertainment video. See also GILBERT AND SULLIVAN.

DIDO AND AENEAS
1689 opera by Purcell

Henry Purcell's opera is usually considered the first great English opera and often ranked as the best before the 20th century. Nahum Tate's libretto is based on the *Aeneid.* Queen Dido of Carthage loves Prince Aeneas who has fled Troy and is now a guest at her court. An envious sorceress sends a false messenger from the gods to tell Aeneas he must abandon Dido and leave the island. Dido is so heartbroken when he goes that she dies. Janet Baker is often associated with the role and she was featured in a Glyndebourne Festival production telecast by the BBC in the mid Sixties. See also HENRY PURCELL.

1951 Kirsten Flagstad film
Kirsten Flagstad stars as Dido with Maggie Teyte as her lady-in-waiting Belinda in scenes from a production by the Elizabethan Theatre Opera at the old Mermaid Theatre in St. John's Wood, London. Bernard Miles produced this famous inaugural production of the theater with Geraint Jones conducting. BBC Television shot the film at a stage rehearsal on Sept. 14, 1951, with both singers in costume. Black and white. In English. 10 minutes. Video at MPRC.

1989 Reggio Emilia Opera
Argentine mezzo Margarita Zimmermann stars as Dido in this production at the Valli Municipal Theater in Reggio Emilia designed and directed by Pier Luigi Pizzi. It also features Nicolas Rivenq, Fiorella Pediconi, Nathalie Stutzmann, Susanna Anselmi and Alessandra Ruffini with M.

Francombe conducting. Color. In English. 60 minutes. Lyric video.

1995 Maria Ewing film
Maria Ewing stars as Dido in this BBC film with Karl Daymond as Aeneas. Peter Maniura filmed this opulent version of the opera on location at an old mansion, Hampton Court House, keeping the camera constantly on the move. Rebecca Evans sings the role of Belinda, Sally Burgess is the Sorceress and James Bowman is Mercury. Richard Hickox conducts the Collegium Musicum 90 on period instruments. The film premiered on BBC TV in November 1995. Color. In English. 60 minutes. Warner Music Vision (England) video.

DIDUR, ADAM
Polish bass (1874-1946)

Adam Didur was born in Poland in 1874, made his debut in Rio de Janeiro in 1894 and then sang with the Warsaw Opera, La Scala and Covent Garden. The most important segment of his career was at the Metropolitan Opera. He made his debut there in 1908 and remained a stalwart of the company for the next 25 years. He was a notable Figaro, a fine Almaviva and an outstanding Boris. He left a film record of his opera style before returning to Poland.

1927 Vitaphone opera film
Adam Didur joins tenor Giovanni Martinelli and an unseen soprano in excerpts from *Aida* in this 1927 Vitaphone opera film. It was shot at the Manhattan Opera House and seems to have been Didur's only film. Black and white. About nine minutes.

DIETZ, HOWARD
American librettist (1896-1983)

Howard Dietz wrote English adaptations of *La Bohème* and *Die Fledermaus* for the Metropolitan Opera that aroused so much interest they were sold as books. Small wonder. Dietz was one of the great Hollywood publicists and more or less created the public image of MGM. He is credited with the company's trademark Leo the Lion, Latin motto *Ars Gratia Artis* and Greta Garbo campaigns. At the same time, he was a successful opera and musical comedy lyricist and librettist. His shows included *The Little Show* (1929) and *The Band Wagon* (1931). His autobiography *Dancing in the Dark* (1975) tells all. See LA BOHÈME (1953), DIE FLEDERMAUS (1953), METROPOLITAN OPERA (1953).

DIMITROVA, GHENA
Bulgarian soprano (1941-)

Ghena Dimitrova made her debut in Sofia in 1966 in one of her most famous roles, Abigaille in Nabucco. She began to sing in western Europe in 1975 and her powerful voice was first heard in America in Dallas in 1982 in *Ernani*. She made her Metropolitan debut in 1988 as *Turandot*, another of her great roles. See AIDA (1986), I LOMBARDI ALLA PRIMA CROCIATA (1984), NABUCCO (1981/1986), TURANDOT (1983), VERONA (1988).

DIRECTORS OF OPERA ON FILM

A thousand film directors have made opera films, too many to list here, but there are a number of important filmmakers who deserve to be highlighted. First are the directors whose work is not well known in cinema circles as their films were made primarily for TV presentation. They include Jean-Pierre Ponnelle who made sixteen important opera films, influential East German producer Walter Felsenstein, Pierre Jourdan who filmed at the Orange Festival, Joachim Hess who directed Hamburg operas for Rolf Liebermann and Spain's Juan de Orduña who made a fine series of zarzuelas. Second are the filmmakers who, although they have made a number of excellent opera films, are not as widely recognized as they deserve including the Italians Carmine Gallone and Mario Costa and the Russians Vladimir Gorikker, Vera Stroyeva and Roman Tikhomirov. Third are the major filmmakers whose opera films are among the glories of the genre from Ophuls, Powell, Bergman and Losey to Rosi and Comencini. Finally there are the composers who have directed films of their own operas led by Gian Carlo Menotti. See INGMAR BERGMAN, LUIS BUÑUEL, LUIGI COMENCINI, MARIO COSTA, JUAN DE ORDUÑA, WALTER FELSENSTEIN, CARMINE GALLONE, ABEL GANCE, VLADIMIR GORIKKER, JOACHIM HESS, PIERRE JOURDAN, JOSEPH LOSEY, GIAN CARLO MENOTTI, MAX OPHULS, JEAN-PIERRE PONNELLE, MICHAEL POWELL, FRANCESCO ROSI, VERA STROYEVA, ROMAN TIKHOMIROV.

DIRECTORS OF OPERA ON TV

The pioneer television and video opera directors have not received the recognition they deserve and are often not even listed in reference books. Kirk Browning and Brian Large, for example, who directed most of the Metropolitan Opera telecasts and videos, do not have entries in the *Metropolitan Opera Encyclopedia*. Opera on video and the small screen could not have developed so well without their craft and genius in creating effective images of live opera. Most of the pioneers who helped create the genre are still working. Kirk Browning, the first great director in the field, developed television opera on American television along with Roger Englander who collaborated with Menotti and Bernstein. The dominant director in the field today is England's ubiquitous Brian Large. Other British TV opera directors of note are Derek Bailey, Humphrey Burton, Barrie Gavin, Dave Heather and John Vernon. Also important are Thomas Olofsson who made the Drottningholm Mozart videos and Claus Viller who made many of the Schwetzingen Festival videos. Filmmakers who have directed the videos of their stage productions include Ingmar Bergman, Peter Brook, Peter Hall, Peter Sellars and Franco Zeffirelli. See INGMAR BERGMAN, DEREK BAILEY, PETER BROOK, KIRK BROWNING, HUMPHREY BURTON, ROGER ENGLANDER, BARRIE GAVIN, PETER HALL, DAVE HEATHER, BRIAN LARGE, THOMAS OLOFSSON, PETER SELLARS, JOHN VERNON, CLAUS VILLER.

DISNEY, WALT
American film producer (1901-1966)

Walt Disney was the genius behind the greatest animation studio in the history of movies and created such cinematic icons as Mickey Mouse and Donald Duck. He also created many impressive films using opera and operetta music including the remarkable *The Whale Who Wanted to Sing at the Met*. Most Disney animated films are also musicals and most of the Disney feature films from *Snow White and the Seven Dwarfs* to *Beauty and the Beast* are really film operettas. Listed below are the films with music from operas. See also THE WHALE WHO WANTED TO SING AT THE MET.

1935 The Band Concert
Mickey Mouse conducts a band playing opera tunes in the park in his first color film. After the audience cheers the selections from the opera *Zampa*, the band plays the *William Tell* Overture until it is interrupted by Donald Duck. Wilfred Jackson directed. Color. 7 minutes.

1936 Mickey's Grand Opera
Mickey Mouse, the first star of the studio, is featured in his earlier and funnier years in this Disney operatic cartoon. Wilfred Jackson directed. Color. 7 minutes.

1940 Fantasia
This Disney classical musical extravaganza features a famous melody from Ponchielli's grand opera *La Gioconda* in one of its more memorable scenes. The "Dance of the Hours" is performed in the film by a pink hippopotamus with an alligator as her partner and a ballet corps made up of ostriches and elephants. Color. 120 minutes.

DI STEFANO, GIUSEPPE
Italian tenor (1921-)

Italian tenor Giuseppe Di Stefano accompanied Maria Callas on her last tour in 1973 and was still in reasonable voice. He had made his debut in 1946 in Reggio Emilio as Des Grieux in *Manon* and first sang at La Scala from 1947. He arrived at the Metropolitan in 1948 and sang there regularly until 1965. His great period of recording with Callas and Tito Gobbi in the 1950s resulted in a legacy of disc masterpieces. In recent years Di Stefano has been teaching his techniques in masterclasses. He can be seen and heard in performance on film and video and appears in some of the videos about Maria Callas. He is a featured singer on the soundtrack of Martin Scorsese's 1990 film *Goodfellas*. See MARIA CALLAS (1962, 1988), THE IMPRESARIO.

1953 Canto per Te
De Stefano stars in *I Sing For You* as a tenor who has trouble with a detective who covets his girl Hélène Remy. De Stefano is given ample opportunity to sing but not enough to save the film from being ordinary. Marino Girolami directed. Black and white. In Italian. 90 minutes. Bel Canto Society video.

1987 Maria Callas Life and Art
De Stefano is seen in performance with Maria Callas on the final night in Japan of their 1973-74 recital tour and they're both splendid. He is also interviewed about their relationship and talks of her with warmth and admiration. Alan Lewens and Alistair Mitchell produced. Black and white. 80 minutes . Kultur video.

DIVAS

There have been a number of excellent films and videos about the great female singers of today and yesterday. In addition to those listed below, there are documentaries about the divas who have sung *Tosca* (*I Live for Art*) and *Aida* (*The Aida File*) and a remarkable gathering of great divas on the *Bell Telephone Hour* (*First Ladies of the Opera*). See AIDA (1987 film), BELL TELEPHONE HOUR (1967), TOSCA (1983 film).

1987 Le Cinéma des Divas
A compilation documentary created from scenes in opera films featuring the great divas. It was put together by and premiered at the Cannes Film Festival in 1987 when the festival mounted a series devoted to Cinéma & Opéra. Color & black and white. 90 minutes.

1990 Donne e Dive
Women and Divas is an Italian video featuring three top women singers performing in Bologna in 1990. They are Marilyn Horne, Katicia Ricciarelli and Daniela Dessi. Valery Gerghiev conducts the orchestra. Color. In Italian. 60 minutes. Lyric video.

1991 The Three Sopranos
Not to be bested by mere tenors, three top sopranos got together for their own concert at the Roman Amphitheater in Syracuse in Sicily in 1991. The three were Renata Scotto, Ileana Cotrubas and Elena Obraztsova. They sing arias and ensembles from *Pagliacci*, *Le Villi*, *Samson et Dalila*, *La Bohème*, *Un Ballo in Maschera*, *The Tales of Hoffmann*, *Gianni Schicchi*, *Carmen*, *Der Fledermaus* and *Aida*. Armando Krieger conducts the Czech Symphony Orchestra. Color. 67 minutes. Kultur video/Pioneer laser.

1991 Primadonna Belcanto Italiano
Eight top Italian sopranos perform in the open air in St. Mark's Square in Venice on June 24, 1991. The setting is marvelous and the singing just as enjoyable. Regina Resnik introduces the divas. Renata Scotto sings "Bondi cara Venezia" from Wolf-Ferrari's *Il Campiello*, Raina Kabaivanska sings "Io son l'umile ancella" from *Adriana Lecouvreur*, Daniela Dessi sings "Tue che le vanitá" from *Don Carlo*, Mariella Devia sings "Ardon gli incensi" from *Lucia di Lammermoor*, Cecilia Gasdia sings "Al dolce guidami castel natio" from *Anna Bolena*, Katia Ricciarelli sings "Ebben n'andro lontana" from *La Wally*, Luciana Serra sings "Der Holle Rache" from

The Magic Flute, Lucia Valentini Terrani sings "Les trigles des sistres tintailent" from *Carmen* and all eight join voices *The Tales of Hoffmann* Barcarolle. Massimo Manni directed. Color. In Italian. 80 minutes. Ricordi (Italy)/Lyric video.

1991 Queens from Caracalla

A gala concert of women opera singers arranged to mark the 50th anniversary of the opening of the 6000-seat theater at the Baths of Caracalla. They include Marilyn Horne, Eva Marton, Cecilia Gasdia, Aprile Millo, Lucia Alibert, Giusi Devinu and Mariella Devia. Carlo Franci conducts the Rome Opera House Orchestra. Luigi Bonori directed the video. Color. 112 minutes. Lyric video.

1994 Restless In Thought, Disturbed In Mind

Mary Jane Walsh's documentary traces the history of women in opera. Female singers were not allowed by the church so it was not until opera became a valued art that they achieved status by singing. The film begins with Hildegard of Bingen and traces operatic women to the present time. It examines the Mad Song, the lament, virtuosity, the idea of the diva and why opera composers are fascinated by fallen and abandoned women. There are interviews with composer Judith Weir, director Francesca Zambello and John Rosselli. Emma Kirkby and Jane Manning perform staged sequences. The film was telecast on Channel 4 in England. Color. 60 minutes.

1995 Divas

Elijah Moshinsky investigates the phenomenon of the diva for this British *Omnibus* television program shown in England in 1995 as *Where Have All the Divas Gone?* and in the U.S. in 1996 as *Divas*. He believes that the days of the great divas are over because the toll on the personal lives of female singers is becoming too great. Appearing in the film are Birgit Nilsson, Kiri Te Kanawa, Jessye Norman, Elisabeth Schwarzkopf, Dennis Marks, Jeremy Isaacs and Kathleen Battle's chauffeur. Color. 60 minutes.

DOLLARPRINZESSIN, DIE

1907 operetta by Fall

The "princess" of Leo Fall's charming Viennese operetta *The Dollar Princess* is the daughter of a New York millionaire. The rich father and sought-after daughter and their loves and problems provide the plot. It is set in New York and Canada rather than Vienna. But the musical hasn't changed much The principal waltz of the operetta was so popular that it helped the New York stage production to run for 200 performances. See also LEO FALL.

1971 Tatjana Iwanow film

Tatjana Iwanow is the sexy cabaret star of this modern German film of the operetta with Horst Niendorf as her co-star. Bert Grund conducted the Kurt Graunke Symphonic Orchestra. Klaus Überall directed in 35mm and stereo for German television. Color. In German. 87 minutes.

Early films

1908 Alfred Duskes sound film

Alfred Duskes' German sound film of the duet "Wir tanzen Ringelreih'n" was screened with synchronized music from a record. The singers are Arnold Riech and Hélène Winter. Black and white. About 3 minutes.

1910 Charles Magnusson film

Charles Magnusson directed this Swedish sound film made with the Biophon system. It features the aria "Entresangen" from *Dollarprinzessan* sung by Carl Barcklind. Black and white. About 3 minutes.

1927 Liane Haid film

Liane Haid, Hans Albers and George Alexander star in this silent feature-length version of the operetta made in Germany by Felix Basch. The film was titled *Die Dollarprinzessin un ihre Sechs Freier.* Black and white. In German. About 80 minutes.

DOMGRAF-FASSBÄNDER, WILLI

German baritone (1897-1978)

Willi Domgraf-Fassbänder, the father of mezzo-soprano Brigitte Fassbaender was the lyric baritone at the Berlin Staatsoper from 1930 to 1946. He sang Figaro at Glyndebourne on the opening night in 1934 and later returned as Guglielmo and Papageno. He also appeared in several opera films, including Max Ophul's famous version of *The Bartered Bride* and a notable *Marriage of Figaro.* See THE BARTERED BRIDE (1932), THE MARRIAGE OF FIGARO (1949), CARL MARIA VON WEBER (1934).

DOMINGO, PLACIDO
Spanish tenor (1941-)

Placido (or Plácido) Domingo may be the best tenor of our time with a remarkable voice that has allowed him a wide repertory. He can be seen in an enormous number of operas on film and video, far more than Pavarotti or any other opera singer and over a much wider range of roles. Born in Madrid but raised in Mexico, he began his career in 1957. He sang zarzuelas with his parents before making his American debut in Dallas in 1961 as Arturo in *Lucia di Lammermoor*. He began to build an international reputation in Israel from 1962 to 1965 and was soon established as one of the best tenors in the world. His *Three Tenors* concerts confirmed that position and he published his autobiography in 1984. Domingo is featured in two of the best opera films, Rosi's *Carmen* and Zeffirelli's *La Traviata*, and a large number of videos. See L'AFRICAINE (1988), AIDA (1989), ANDREA CHÉNIER (1979/1985), MONTSERRAT CABALLÉ (1993), CARMEN (1978/1980/ 1984/1972 film), CARNEGIE HALL (1991), JOSÉ CARRERAS (1992), CAVALLERIA RUSTICANA (1975/ 1982), DON CARLO (1983), ERNANI (1982), LA FANCIULLA DEL WEST (1983/1991/1992), FEDORA (1993), DIE FLEDERMAUS (1983), FRANCESCA DA RIMINI (1984), GALA LIRICA, EL GATO MONTÉS (1994), ANGELA GHEORGHIU (1994), LA GIOCONDA (1986), GOYA (1986), DER GRAF VON LUXEMBURG (1963), IL GUARANY (1994), MARIO LANZA (1983), LOHENGRIN (1990), LUISA FERNANDA (1963), LUISA MILLER (1979/1980), MADAMA BUTTERFLY (1979), MANON LESCAUT (1980/1983), MARINA (1963), THE MERRY WIDOW (1963), METROPOLITAN OPERA (1972/1983/1986/ 1991), SHERRILL MILNES (1985), JESSYE NORMAN (1991), OTELLO (1979/1984/1993), PAGLIACCI (1975/ 1978/1982), PARIS (1989), EL POETA (1980), RIGOLETTO (1977), SAMSON ET DALILA (1980), BEVERLY SILLS (1981), SIMON BOCCANEGRA (1995), STIFFELIO (1993), IL TABARRO (1994), THE TALES OF HOFFMANN (1981), PYOTR TCHAIKOVSKY (1993), KIRI TE KANAWA (1988), THE THREE TENORS, TOSCA (1976/1985/1992), LA TRAVIATA (1981/1982), LES TROYENS (1983), TURANDOT (1988), VERONA (1988/1994), SHIRLEY VERRETT (1985), VIENNA (1992/1993/1994), ZARZUELA (1991).

1982 Hommage a Sevilla
Domingo sings arias in their Seville setting in Jean-Pierre Ponnelle's film about the city and its place in opera history. Don Giovanni boasts of his conquests from the Giralda tower, Domingo duets with himself as Figaro and Almaviva in the Barrio Santa Cruz and Florestan's aria is heard in the Roman ruins in Italica. There are two duets in the Maestranza Bullring, one from *Carmen* with Victoria Vergara, the other from Penella's *El Gato Montés* with Virginia Alonzo. James Levine leads the Vienna Symphony Orchestra. Color. In English. 60 minutes. DG video.

1984 A Year in the Life of Placido Domingo
Revel Guest follows Domingo around the world with a camera for a year. He rehearses with Kiri Te Kanawa for *Manon Lescaut*, Katia Ricciarelli for *Otello* and Marilyn Zschau for *La Fanciulla del West*. He makes his debut as a conductor at Covent Garden with *Die Fledermaus* and is seen in performance in *Tosca, Tales of Hoffmann, Ernani, Otello, La Fanciulla del West, Manon Lescaut* and Zeffirelli's film of *La Traviata*. Color. 105 minutes. Kultur video.

1987 An Evening with Placido
This is a video of Domingo in concert at Wembley Arena in London on June 21, 1987. He sings arias and duets from Giordano, Puccini, Verdi, Lehár and Spanish composers and is joined on duets by Columbia mezzo soprano Marta Seen and Romanian baritone Eduard Tomagian. Eugene Kohn conducts the English Chamber Orchestra and Madeleine French directed the film. 55 minutes. Kultur video.

1989 Great Arias with Domingo and Friends
Domingo is shown in concert with four singers in Paris. He sings "Quando le sere al placido" from *Luisa Miller*, Shirley Verrett sings "Vissi d'arte" and they join in duet on "Non sono tuo figlio" from *Il Trovatore*. Barbara Hendricks sings "Senza mamma, o bimbo" from *Suor Angelica*, Simon Estes performs Iago's "Credo" and Wang Yan Yan sings an aria from *Don Carlos*. Lorin Maazel conducts the National Orchestra of France. André Frederick directed the video. Color. 46 minutes. View video.

1990 Placido Grandisimo
A film of Domingo and friends in a Seville Stadium concert.   Julia Migenes joins him for some outstanding scenes from *Carmen* and then solos with an aria from *La Rondine* and Gershwin's "Summertime." Domingo sings "E lucevan le stelle," joins Spanish soprano Guadalupe Sanchez on an aria from Penella's *El Gato Montés* and teams with guitarist Ernesto Bitetti on songs by Manuel Alejandro. Eugene Kohn and Alejandro conduct

the National Symphonic Orchestra of Spain. Juan Villaescusa filmed the concert. Color. 60 minutes. On video.

1990 Songs of Mexico Volumes 1 & 2
Two travelogue-type videos of Domingo performing songs on location in Mexico with Mexican folk singers, mariachi bands and folk dancers. Color. Each 60 minutes. On video.

1991 Concert for Planet Earth
Domingo filmed in concert in Rio de Janeiro. He sings arias from *L'Africaine, Tosca, Candide* and some zarzuelas and duets with American mezzo Denyce Graves in a scene from *Carmen*. He is joined by the Wynton Marsalis septet, Antonio Carlos Jobin and violinist Sarah Chang. John De Main of the Houston Opera leads the Rio De Janeiro Municipal Theater Orchestra. Color. 60 minutes. Sony video.

1991 Domingo and Rostropovich Concert
Domingo at an open air concert at the ancient Roman Theater in Merida, Spain. He is joined by Olga Borodina for a duet from *Carmen* and sings Lensky's aria from *Eugene Onegin*. Rostropovich performs the Haydn Cello Concerto in C and joins Domingo on Massenet's "Elegie" with the tenor singing and playing the piano. Eugene Kohn and the two stars conduct the St. Petersburg Kirov Theater Orchestra. Juan Vallaescusa directed. Color. 60 minutes. Kultur video.

1991 Domingo Live From Miami
Domingo filmed in concert in the Miami Arena. He sings arias from *L'Africaine, Lucia di Lammermoor, Tosca, La del Manoja de Rosas* and *Luisa Fernanda* and joins soprano Ana Panagulias in duets from Donizetti's *L'Elisir d'Amore* and Penella's *El Gato Montés*. She also sings arias from *Don Pasquale* and *Gianni Schicchi*. Eugene Kohn leads the Symphonic Orchestra of Miami and Francisco Suarez filmed the concert. Color. 60 minutes. Kultur video.

1994 Placido in Prague
Domingo in concert at the Royal Hall in Prague with Romanian soprano Angela Gheorghiu on April 24, 1994. Eugen Kohn conducts the Czech Symphony Orchestra in a recital that includes Domingo in arias and duets by Mozart, Donizetti, Meyerbeer, Puccini, Verdi and Penella. The concert was taped by Czech Television, telecast and later released on video. The video was later released in England under Gheorghiu's name because of her success in *La Traviata*. Thomas Simerda directed the video. Color. 60 minutes. Kultur video.

1994 Tales at the Opera
Four films about Domingo made as a series by BBC television. The first, shot in Vienna, features his debut in *Die Walküre*. The second was made in Los Angeles with Domingo conducting *La Bohème*. The third features him at the Met in *Otello* and the fourth is built around a production of Gomes's *La Guarany* in Bonn. Daniel Snowman and Martin Rosenbaum produced. Color. Each 55 minutes.

1994 Domingo at Verona Arena
This gala was arranged in honor of Domingo's 25th anniversary as a performer at the Verona Arena and was staged on August 9, 1994. It consists of scenes from operas with sets and costumes including Domingo singing Rudolfo in *La Bohème* and Ramades in *Aida*. The production was by Mario Dradi. Claudio Colupi was cinematographer and Drazen Siriscevic directed the video. A SACIS production telecast on A & E. Color. In Italian. 60 minutes. On video.

1995 Placido Domingo: A Musical Life
An excellent documentary about the life and career of the tenor. It follows him from early days in Mexico and Israel to triumphs around the world. He is seen in scenes from *Otello, Tales of Hoffmann, Rigoletto* and *L'Africaine*, recording a zarzuela and relaxing with his family. His wife Marta makes some interesting contributions. Mike Csaky directed the video. Color. 90 minutes. Kultur video.

1997 Placido Domingo on CD-ROM
Domingo is the first opera star to be featured on an operatic CD-ROM. It includes original audio and video material as well as excerpts from previous performances, behind-the-scenes material and background information. The CD-ROM is by by Calliope Media and EMI Classics.

DOMINO NOIR, LE
1837 opéra-comique by Auber

The Black Domino was one of the most popular of Daniel Auber's operas and was performed a thousand times at the Opéra-Comique in Paris. It's the story of a man who falls in love with a woman wearing a "black domino" at a masked ball in Spain. The woman, Lady Angela, continues to re-emerge in various garbs and always fascinates him. Finally the mystery is unraveled and they get married. There does not appear to be a modern video of the opera. See also DANIEL AUBER.

1929 Victor Janson film
This silent film was based on the libretto of the Auber opera and was presented with the opera music. It was directed by Victor Janson with Harry Lidetke as Orazio de Massarena, Vera Schmiterlow as his beloved Angela, Hans Junkermann as the Conte de St. Lucar, Lotte Lorring and Herman Picha. Aafa Film. Black and white. About 80 minutes.

DOÑA FRANCISQUITA
1923 zarzuela by Vives

Amadeo Vives's *Doña Francisquita*, one of the major Spanish zarzuelas, is based on Lope de Vega's play *La Discreta Enamorada* updated to the mid-19th century. It is Carnival time in Madrid. Francisquita loves the student Fernando but he fancies the actress Aurora. Fernando's widowed father Don Matías courts Francisquita and she encourages him to make Fernando jealous. Fernando woos Francisquita to make Aurora jealous and so it gets very complicated. The libretto is by Federico Romero and Guillermo Fernández Shaw. See also AMADEO VIVES.

1934 Raquel Rodrigo film
Raquel Rodrigo stars as Francesquita in this Spanish film. Puerto Rican singer Fernando Cortes portrays Fernando, Matilde Vazquez is the seductive Aurora and Antonio Palacios is Fernando's eccentric friend Cardona. All won praise for their singing. Hans Behrendt directed the film and Enrique Guerner was the cinematographer. Black and white. In Spanish. 88 minutes.

1952 Marimi del Pozo film
Marimi del Pozo sings the role of Francisquita but the role is portrayed on screen by Mirtha Legrand in this Spanish film. Luly Bergman sings Aurora as acted by Emma Penella. Armando Calvo, Antonio Casal and Manola Moran are also featured. This is a more lavish production than the 1938 film with spectacular Carnival scenes. Benito Perojo produced, Ladislas Vajda directed and Antonio Ballesteros was cinematographer. Black and white. In Spanish. 90 minutes.

1988 Gran Teatre del Liceu, Barcelona
Enedina Lloris stars as Francisquita with Alfredo Kraus as Fernando in this stage production at the Gran Teatre del Liceu in Barcelona. Rosalina Mestre is Aurora, Josep Ruiz is Cardona, Maria Rus is Doña Francisca and Tomas Alvarez is Don Matias. José Luis Alonso staged the production for the Teatro Lirico Nacional de la Zarzuela while Valdes conducted the Liceu Orchestra and Chorus. Francisco Montolo directed the telecast. The video is an off-air recording of the telecast. Color. In Spanish. 135 minutes. Opera Dubs video.

DON CARLO
1867 opera by Verdi

A young man (Don Carlo) and a young woman (Elizabetta) fall in love but she is forced to marry his father. As the father is Phillip II of Spain, they have a major problem. Throw in a Grand Inquisitor of doubtful morality, a noble friend (Rodrigo), a scheming rival (Eboli) and a heap of political intrigue and you have grand soap opera. It's an overheated story but Giuseppe Verdi's music turns it into a great opera and it only requires half a dozen magnificent singers to make it sound right. The original French libretto by Joseph Mery and Camille du Locle is based on Schiller's verse play *Don Carlos*. In French as *Don Carlos* the opera was not a success but when it was translated into Italian and sung as *Don Carlo*, it became a major hit. All available videos are in Italian and titled *Don Carlo*. See also GIUSEPPE VERDI.

1950 Metropolitan Opera
Don Carlo is sung by Jussi Björling, Rodrigo by Robert Merrill and the Grand Inquisitor by Jerome Hines in this pioneer American television effort on ABC with an estimated four million viewers. The occasion was the opening night of the 1950-1951 season at the Metropolitan on November 6. The opera was directed by Margaret Webster, the first woman to stage a Met production. Fritz Stiedry conducted the Metropolitan Opera Orchestra and Milton Cross introduced each scene. Black and white. In Italian. 225 minutes.

1980 Metropolitan Opera
Renata Scotto stars as Elizabetta, Sherrill Milnes is Rodrigo and Tatiana Troyanos is Eboli in this Metropolitan Opera production by John Dexter. Vasile Moldoveanu portrays Don Carlo, Paul Pliska is Filippo (Philip II) and Jerome Hines is the

Grand Inquisitor. The sets were designed by David Reppa and the costumes by Ray Diffin. James Levine conducted the Metropolitan Orchestra and Chorus. Kirk Browning directed the video taped on Feb. 21 and telecast on April 12, 1980. Color. In Italian with English subtitles. 205 minutes. Video at MTR.

1983 Metropolitan Opera
John Dexter's outstanding Metropolitan production stars singers perfectly fitted for their roles. Placido Domingo is Don Carlo, Mirella Freni is Elizabetta, Nicolai Ghiaurov is Philip II, Grace Bumbry is Eboli, Ferruccio Furlanetto is the Grand Inquisitor and Louis Quilico is Rodrigo. David Reppa designed the sets and Ray Diffin the costumes. James Levine conducts the Metropolitan Opera Orchestra and Chorus. Brian Large directed the video taped March 20, 1983, and telecast Feb. 1, 1984. Color. In Italian with English subtitles. 214 minutes. Paramount video/Pioneer laser.

1985 Royal Opera
Ileana Cotrubas and Robert Lloyd star in this Royal Opera House, Covent Garden, production designed by Luchino Visconti in 1958 and re-staged by Christopher Renshaw. Cotrubas is a strong Elizabeth, Lloyd a powerful Philip II and Joseph Rouleau a frightening Grand Inquisitor. Luis Lima sings well as Don Carlo, Giorgio Zancanaro is a joy as Rodrigo and Bruna Baglioni is a stylish Eboli. Bernard Haitink conducted the Royal Opera House Orchestra and Chorus and Brian Large directed the video. Color. In Italian with English subtitles. 207 minutes. Home Vision video.

1986 Salzburg Festival
José Carreras is in fine fettle in a commanding performance as Don Carlo, Fiamma Izzo d'Amico is impressive as Elizabeth and Agnes Baltsa is at her best as Eboli. Piero Cappuccilli is Rodrigo, Ferruccio Furlanetto is Philip II and Matti Salminen is the Grand Inquisitor. This is one of the operas filmed by Herbert von Karajan in his "legacy for home video" series. He leads the Berlin Philharmonic Orchestra, Bulgarian National Opera Chorus, Vienna State Opera Chorus and Salzburg Chamber Choir. Ernst Wild directed the film. Color. 180 minutes. In Italian. Sony Classical video/laser.

1992 Teatro alla Scala
Franco Zeffirelli's superb production of the opera at La Scala stars Luciano Pavarotti as Don Carlo and Samuel Ramey as Philip II, both in great form. Daniella Dessi is Elizabeth, Luciana d'Intino is Eboli, Paolo Coni is Rodrigo and Alexander Anisimov is the Grand Inquisitor. Anna Anni designed the costumes while Zeffirelli designed the sets and directed the video. Riccardo Muti conducted the Teatro alla Scala Orchestra and Chorus. Color. In Italian with Italian subtitles. 182 minutes. EMI Classics video and Pioneer laser.

Early films

1909 Cines film
An early Italian silent film of scenes from the opera made by Cines. It was released in the USA in September 1909 as *Don Carlos* and screened with music from the opera. About 10 minutes (742 feet).

1909 André Calmettes film
A French film of scenes from the opera directed by André Calmettes for the Société du Film d'Art and featuring Paul Mounet, Dehelly and Bartet. It was released in the USA in May 1910 as *Don Carlos* and screened with the Verdi music. About 14 minutes (975 feet).

1921 Antamoro film
A second silent Italian film based on the opera and the Schiller play was directed by Giulio Antamoro, a moviemaker known primarily for religious films. Alfredo Bertone, Elena Lunda and Enrico Roma star. About 70 minutes (1637 meters).

DON CÉSAR DE BAZAN
1872 opera by Massenet

Jules Massenet's fading reputation has meant that this opera has dropped almost out of sight but it was very popular with filmmakers in the early part of the century. It's based on the play by Adolphe d'Ennery and Philippe Dumanoir which also inspired Vincent Wallace's English opera *Maritana*. Don César is a nobleman who becomes the surrogate husband for the gypsy Maritana after she attracts the interest of the Spanish king. See also JULES MASSENET.

1909 Victorin Jasset film
Victorin Jasset directed this French film of the opera for the Eclair company. It stars Charles Krauss, Harry Bauer, Marie de l'Isle and Suzanne Goldstein. About 10 minutes.

1912 Irving Cummings film

Irving Cummings directed this American silent film of the opera for the Reliance company. About 15 minutes.

1915 Kalem film

This American film is called *Don Caesar de Bazan* but the screenplay was actually based on Wallace's opera *Maritana*. The plots, however, are virtually the same. Robert G. Vignola directed it for the Kalem studio. About 70 minutes.

DON GIL DE ALCALÁ

1932 opera by Penella

Spanish composer Manuel Penella's *Don Gil de Alcalá* is one of his most popular operas. It's set in 18th century Mexico and focuses on the adventures of Captain Don Gil de Alcalá and his rescue of a convent girl from a wicked Spanish nobleman. Penella, who alsowrote the libretto, went to Mexico in 1938 to supervise the making of a film based on the opera and died while there. See also MANUEL PENELLA.

1938 José Mojica film

Mexican tenor José Mojica stars as Don Gil de Alcalá in this tuneful Mexican film based on Penella's opera but retitled *El Capitan Aventurero*. Mojica saves beautiful Manolita Saval from villainous nobleman Alberto Marti with support from comic sergeant Carlos Orellana. Margarita Mora portrays a happy-go-lucky countess. The film allows Mojica ample time to sing Penella's melodies. Arcady Boytler directed the film which was also released in the U.S. Black and white. In Spanish. 91 minutes. Bel Canto Society/Lyric videos.

DON GIOVANNI

1787 opera by Mozart

Don Giovanni reached the cinema as early as 1900 when a sound film of a scene from the opera was shown at the Paris Exposition. A silent version was made in 1922 and arias have been featured regularly in films since the coming of sound. *Don Giovanni* is one of the three Mozart operas written in Italian by Lorenzo Da Ponte and he tells the great libertine's story brilliantly. Many consider this the greatest opera ever written. George Bernard Shaw wrote an ironic sequel play called *Don Juan in Hell* which describes what happens to the main characters in the opera when they meet up in Hell. There are also many films from Spanish-speaking countries titled *Don Juan Tenorio* but they are based on a Spanish play and not the opera. See also LORENZO DA PONTE, WOLFGANG A. MOZART.

1954 Salzburg Festival

This British film is one of the earliest complete operas filmed in performance on stage. Paul Czinner shot it at the 1954 Salzburg Festival with S. D. Onions as his cinematographer. Cesare Siepi stars as Don Giovanni with Otto Edelmann as Leporello, Elisabeth Grummer as Donna Anna, Lisa della Casa as Donna Elvira, Erna Berger as Zerlina, Walter Berry as Masetto and Deszö Ernster as the Commendatore. Herbert Graf was the stage director and Wilhelm Furtwängler conducted the Vienna Philharmonic Orchestra and the Vienna State Opera Chorus. Color. In Italian. 169 minutes. VAI video/Japanese laserdisc.

1954 H. W. Kolm-Veltee film

This cinematic version of the opera in German by H.W. Kolm-Veltee was released in the U.S.A. as *Don Juan*. It eliminates many of the arias and turns the opera into a swashbuckler film with duels, dancing and music. The music is by the Vienna Symphony Orchestra, the dances are by the Vienna State Opera Ballet and the duels are of the Errol Flynn type. Cesare Danova stars as Don Giovanni but the role is sung by Alfred Poell, Josef Meinrad is Leporello sung by Harald Progelhof, Evelyn Cormand is Zerlina sung by Annie Felbermeyer, Hans von Vorsody is Masetto sung by Walter Berry, Lotte Tobisch is Donna Elvira sung by Hanna Loeser, Jean Vinci is Don Ottavio sung by Hugo Meyer-Welfing, Marianne Schoenauer is Donna Anna sung by Annie Felbermeyer and Fred Hennings is the Commendatore sung by Gottlob Frick. Willy Sohm-Hannes Fuchs was cinematographer. Color. In German. 85 minutes.

1954 Vienna State Opera

The Austrian film *Unsterblicher Mozart* (Immortal Mozart) features a highlights version of *Don Giovanni* sung in German and performed on stage by the Mozart Ensemble of the Vienna State Opera. Paul Schöffler is Don Giovanni, Hilde Gueden is Zerlina, Erich Kunz is Leperello, Carlo Martiris is Donna Anna, Hilde Zadek is Donna Elvira, and Ludwig Weber is the Commendatore. Alfred Stöger directed the film and Rudolf Moralt conducted the

Vienna Philharmonic. Color. In German. 95 minutes. Taurus (Germany) video.

1960 NBC Opera Theatre

Cesare Siepi stars as Don Giovanni with Leontyne Price as Donna Anna in this lively NBC Opera Theatre production by Samuel Chotzinoff. James Pease portrays Leporello, Helen George is Donna Elvira, Judith Raskin is Zerlina , Charles K. L. Davis is Don Ottavio, John Reardon is Masetto and John Macurdy is the Commendatore. The opera is sung in an English translation by W. H. Auden and Chester Kallman. Don Shirley designed the sets and Peter Herman Adler conducted the Symphony of the Air. Kirk Browning directed the telecast on April 10, 1960. Black and white. In English. 160 minutes.

1961 Berlin Deutsche Oper

Dietrich Fischer-Dieskau stars as Don Giovanni in this historic video of a telecast of a famous Deutsche Oper Berlin production with a multi-national cast. They include Elisabeth Grümmer, Donald Grobe, Pilar Lorengar and Walter Berry. Ferenc Fricsay conducts the Deutsche Oper Berlin orchestra. Black and white. In German with Japanese subtitles. 166 minutes. On Japanese laserdisc.

1966 Berlin Komische Oper

Director Walter Felsenstein created this famous production of *Don Giovanni* at the Berlin Komische Oper at the height of his fame. Zdenek Kosler directs the Berlin Komische Oper Orchestra. The stage production was filmed by East German television. There is also a 1967 documentary film showing Felsenstein rehearsing the opera. Color. In German. 164 minutes.

1977 Glyndebourne Festival

Peter Hall staged this controversial Glyndebourne Festival production set in the Victorian period. Benjamin Luxon makes a strong Don Giovanni with solid support from Stafford Dean as Leporello, Rachel Yakar as Donna Elvira, Horiana Branisteanu as Donna Anna, Leo Goeke as Don Ottavio, Elizabeth Gale as Zerlina, John Rawnsley as Masetto and Pierre Thau as the Commendatore. John Bury designed the sets and Bernard Haitink conducted the London Philharmonic Orchestra and Glyndebourne Festival Chorus. Dave Heather directed the video. Color. In Italian with English subtitles. 173 minutes. VAI video.

1978 Joseph Losey film

One of the major opera films. Joseph Losey shot it on location in Vicenza near Venice with unusual visual ideas. The film opens at a glass factory with Don Giovanni on a visit accompanied by Donna Anna. Leporello's "Catalogue" aria is a visual joke with the catalogue shown as a scroll that unrolls down the stairs. A mysterious non-singing valet in black is always with the Don and seemingly influencing him. Ruggero Raimondi is a cynical, charming Don Giovanni matched in duplicity by José Van Dam as Leporello. Kiri Te Kanawa plays Donna Elvira and is most convincing as a wronged woman determined on vengeance. Edda Moser is equally vengeful as Donna Anna while Teresa Berganza is an earthy and sensual Zerlina. John Macurdy is a gruff Commendatore, Kenneth Riegel a wimpy Don Ottavio and Malcolm King a put-upon Masetto. The music is wonderfully played by the Orchestra and Chorus of the Paris Opera conducted by Lorin Maazel. Gerry Fisher and Carlo Poletti were the cinematographers and Losey wrote the screenplay with Franz Salieri and Patricia Losey. Daniel Toscan du Plantier produced. Technicolor. In Italian with English subtitles. 177 minutes. Kultur video/Pioneer laser.

1978 Metropolitan Opera

Joan Sutherland stars as Donna Anna with James Morris as Don Giovanni in this Metropolitan Opera production by Herbert Graf. Julia Varady is Donna Elvira, John Brecknock is Don Ottavio and John Macurdy portrays the Commendatore. Richard Bonynge conducts the Metropolitan Opera and Chorus. Kirk Browning directed the telecast on March 16, 1978. Color. In Italian with English subtitles. 190 minutes. Video at MTR.

1987 Drottningholm Court Theater

Håkan Hagegård stars as Don Giovanni in this charming production by Göran Järvefelt at the Drottningholm Court Theater in Sweden. Erik Saedén is Leporello, Helena Döse is Donna Anna, Birgit Nordin is Donna Elvira, Tord Wallström is Masetto, Anita Soldh is Zerlina, Gösta Winbergh is Don Ottavio and Bengt Rundgren is the Commendatore. Arnold Östman conducts the Drottningholm Court Theater Orchestra whose members wear period costume and play period instruments. Thomas Olofsson directed the video for Swedish Television SVT-1. Color. In Italian with English subtitles. 155 minutes. Philips video and laser.

1987 Salzburg Festival

Samuel Ramey stars as Don Giovanni with Kathleen Battle as Zerlina in this Salzburg Festival production by Michael Hampe. Ferruccio Furlanetto plays Leporello, Anna Tomowa-Sintow is Donna Anna, Julia Varady is Donna Elvira, Gösta Windbergh is Don Ottavio, Alexander Malta is Masetto and Paata Burchuladze is the Commendatore. Herbert von Karajan conducts the Vienna Philharmonic Orchestra and Vienna State Opera Chorus. Claude Vilar directed the video. Color. In Italian. 193 minutes. Sony video and laser.

1989 Teatro alla Scala

Thomas Allen sings Don Giovanni in this sumptuous La Scala production by Giorgio Strehler of Piccolo Teatro fame. Edita Gruberova is Donna Anna with Ann Murray as Donna Elvira, Suzanne Mentzer as Zerlina, Claudio Desderi as Leporello, Natale de Carolis as Masetto, Francisco Araiza as Don Ottavio and Sergei Koptchak as the Commendatore. Ezio Frigiero designed the sets and Riccardo Muti conducted the La Scala Opera Orchestra and Chorus. Color. Carlo Battistoni directed the video. In Italian with English subtitles. 176 minutes. Home Vision video/on laserdisc.

1990 Peter Sellars film

Peter Sellars sets his bleak modern *Don Giovanni* in the back streets of Brooklyn where the Don is a vicious drug addict. Leporello is his doppelganger in this version with the roles played by twin brothers. Sellars' vision is striking but so dark we lose sympathy for the Don and the other characters. Eugene Perry is Giovanni, Herbert Perry is Leporello, Dominique Labelle is Donna Anna, Lorraine Hunt is Donna Elvira, Ai Lan Zhu is Zerlina, Carroll Freeman is Don Ottavio, Elmore James is Masetto and James Patterson is the Commendatore. Sellars filmed the opera in a Vienna TV studio with Craig Smith conducting the Vienna Symphony and the Arnold Schoenberg Choir. Color. In Italian with English subtitles. 190 minutes. London video and laser.

1990 Metropolitan Opera

Samuel Ramey stars as Don Giovanni in this Metropolitan Opera production by Franco Zeffirelli. Carol Vaness is Donna Anna, Dawn Upshaw is Zerlina, Ferruccio Furlanetto is Leporello, Karita Mattila is Donna Elvira, Jerry Hadley is Don Ottavio, Philip Cokorinos is Masetto and Kurt Moll is the Commendatore. Zeffirelli designed the sets and Anna Anni the costumes. James Levine conducted the Metropolitan Opera and Chorus and Brian Large directed the video of an April 1990 performance. Color. In Italian with English subtitles. 190 minutes.

1991 Stavovské Theatre, Prague

This Czech film of the Prague version of the opera was shot in the Stavovské Theatre in Prague. Featured are Emilia Markova, Lude Vele, Eva Randova, M. Bestchastney and L Petrenko. Charles Mackerras conducts the orchestra. Color. In Italian with Japanese subtitles. 180 minutes. On Japanese laserdisc.

1992 Ruggero Raimondi: My Favorite Opera

Ruggero Raimondi stars as Don Giovanni in this film from the *My Favorite Opera* series. It shows him preparing and performing scenes from the opera in a production by Luca Ronconi at the Teatro Communale in Bologna. Alessandro Corbelli is Leporello, Jane Eaglen is Donna Anna, Daniel Dessi is Donna Elvira, Adelina Scarbelli is Zerlina, Rockwell Blake is Don Ottavio, Giovanni Fulanetto is Masetto and Andrea Silvestrelli is the Commendatore. Margherita Pali designed the sets and Vera Marzot the costumes. Riccardo Chailly conducted the Teatro Communale Orchestra and Paul Smaczny and Clara Fabry directed the film for EuroArts. Color. In Italian with English narration and English subtitles. 60 minutes. Kultur video.

1993 Cologne Opera

Thomas Allen stars as Don Giovanni in this Cologne Opera production by Michael Hampe. The cast includes Carol Vaness, Kjell-Magnus Sandvé, Matthias Holle, Karita Mattila, Ferrucio Furlanetto, Reinhard Dorn and Andrea Rost. James Conlon conducted the Cologne Gurzenich Orchestra and Cologne Opera Chorus. José Montes-Baquer directed the video. WDR/ EuroArts. Color. In Italian. 173 minutes. On video.

1995 Glyndebourne Festival

Gilles Cachemaille stars as Don Giovanni in this exciting if controversial updated Glyndebourne Festival production by Deborah Warner. This is a not a very glamorous portrait of the Don who is portrayed like a street hood womanchaser. Hillevi Martinpelto sings Donna Anna, Steven Page is Leporello, Juliane Banse is Zerlina, Adrianne Pieczonka is Donna Elvira, John Mark Ainsley is Don Ottavio, Roberto Scaltriti is Masetto and Gudjon Oskarsson is the Commendatore.

Hildegarde Bechtler designed the costumes (with Nicky Gillibrand) and the nowhereland sets that complement the lighting effects by Jean Kalman. Yakov Kreizberg conducts the Orchestra of the Age of Enlightenment and Derek Bailey directed the superb video, much of it shot in close-up. Color. In Italian with English subtitles. 176 minutes. Warner Vision (England) video.

Early/related films

1900 First sound opera film

Victor Maurel, the French baritone who created the roles of Iago, Falstaff and Canio, is heard singing an aria from *Don Giovanni* in the first sound opera film. It was shown in Paris on June 8, 1900 at Clément Maurice's Phono-Cinéma-Théâtre at the Paris Exhibition and used a synchronized phonographic cylinder for its sound. Also on the program and sharing first honors were films of Maurel in *Falstaff* and Emile Cossira in *Romeo et Juliette*. Black and white. About 3 minutes.

1905 Albert Capellani film

Albert Capellani directed this French Pathé film titled *Don Juan* starring Paul Capellani and Henry Desfontaines. It was re-released in Germany in 1908 with an aria from the opera played on a phonograph. Black and white. About 7 minutes.

1911 La Fin de Don Juan

Victorin Jasset directed this early film of scenes from the opera for the French Éclair company. A contemporary critic noted how pleasant it was to see films based on operas because one could imagine the music that accompanied the scenes. About 10 minutes.

1922 Tense Moments from Operas series

J. R. Tozer stars as Don Giovanni in this British highlights version of the opera made for the *Tense Moments from Opera* series. Pauline Peters portrays Zerlina, Lillian Douglas is Donna Anna and Kathleen Vaughan is Donna Elvira. Edwin J. Collins directed. Black and white. In English. About 10 minutes.

1922 Don Juan et Faust

Marcel L'Herbier directed this French feature based on a novel which combines the two legends into one story. Jaque Catelain is a sympathetic Don Juan, Vanni Marcoux is an evil Faust and Marcelle Pradot

is the Donna Anna they both desire. Gaumont. About 80 minutes.

1929 Charles Hackett film

Chicago Opera tenor Charles Hackett sings the aria "Il mio tesoro" from *Don Giovanni* in this early sound film made by the Vitaphone company. Black and white. 8 minutes.

1932 The Great Lover

Adolphe Menjou portrays a Don Juan-esque opera star/philander who seduces women with the help of the duet "La ci darem il mano." He is pictured on stage at the Met in *Don Giovanni* with Irene Dunne. Harry Beaumont directed. MGM. Black and white. 79 minutes.

1940 Her First Romance

Shy Edith Fellows sings the duet "La ci darem il mano" with Chicago opera star Wilbur Evans at a dance soon after they meet in this Monogram film. Naturally he asks her to marry him. Black and white. 77 minutes.

1942 Dino Falconi film

Dino Falconi directed this Italian film titled *Don Giovanni* that tells more or less the same story as the opera and uses Mozart's music as its score. Adriano Rimoldi stars as Giovanni with Dina Sassoli as Donna Anna and Elena Zasreschi as Donna Elvira. Black and white. In Italian. 85 minutes.

1945 The Picture of Dorian Gray

The Oscar Wilde-like Lord Harry Wotton (George Sanders) invites Dorian Gray (Hurd Hatfield) to the opera to hear de Reszke sing after Gray has seduced and caused the suicide of pub entertainer Angela Lansbury. He then leaves singing the aria "La ci darem la mano." Albert Lewin directed. Black and white. 110 minutes.

1949 Kind Heart and Coronets

Dennis Price sits in the death cell in an English prison writing his memoirs and remembering how his opera singer father sang Don Ottavio's aria "Il mio tesoro" and eloped with his mother. She was cut off by her aristocratic family and Price has bumped them all off in revenge. Robert Hamer directed this fine black comedy. Black and white. 104 minutes.

1967 Felsenstein Inszeniert

American filmmaker Michael Blackwood shot the German TV documentary *Felsenstein Director* while Walter Felsenstein was rehearsing the second act of *Don Giovanni* at the Berlin Komische Oper in 1966. It shows him staging and commenting on the opera. NDR. Color. In German. 67 minutes.

1967 Mozart in Prague: Don Giovanni 67

Dietrich Fischer-Diescau as Don Giovanni, Birgit Nilsson as Donna Anna and Peter Schreier as Don Ottavio are filmed during rehearsals for and recording of *Don Giovanni* in Prague. They also talk about their approach to singing Mozart. Karl Böhm conducts the Prague National Theater Chorus and Orchestra. Wolfgang Esterer directed the film. The recording is still available on DG. Radio Bremen. Color. 60 minutes.

1970 Carmelo Bene film

Carmelo Bene's conscientiously outrageous and experimental Italian film *Don Giovanni* is loosely based on the opera. Bene's music might be called mock-Mozart. Bene plays Don Giovanni, Lydia Mancinelli is the woman, Gea Marotta is her daughter and Salvatore Vendittelli is the Commendatore. Color. In Italian. 80 minutes.

1980 Don Juan, Karl-Liebknect-Strasse 78

Siegfried Kuhn's film revolves around the problems a Berlin opera producer confronts in a provincial theater in East Germany when he tries to stage *Don Giovanni*. His personal problems parallel the opera, especially his relations with the women portraying Donna Anna and Donna Evira. The stars are Hilmar Thate, Beata Tyszkiewicz, Ewa Szykulska and Helmut Strassburger. DEFA. Color. In German. 99 minutes.

1984 Amadeus

Milos Forman's Mozart biography features a memorable scene of the Commendatore's statue bursting on to the stage at the end of the opera. It was shot in the theater where *Don Giovanni* had its world premiere, the Tyl Theater in Prague, and was staged by Twyla Tharpe with the orchestra conducted by Neville Marriner. Karel Fiala portrays Don Giovanni (but the role is sung by Richard Stilwell), Zdenek Jelen is Leporello (sung by Willard White) and Jan Blazek is the Commendatore's statue (sung by John Tomlinson). The statue is presented as if it were Mozart's father

coming back from the grave to chastise his errant son. Color. 160 minutes. HBO/ Cannon video.

1985 Babel Opera

Babel Opéra, ou La Répétition de Don Juan is a Belgian film by master director André Delvaux. It's built around preparations for a production of *Don Giovanni*. The "real" characters in the film are involved in situations similar to those in the opera. The opera features José van Dam as Don Giovanni, Ashley Putnam as Donna Anna, Stuart Burrows as Don Ottavio, Christiane Eda-Pierre as Donna Elvira and Pierre Thau as the Commendatore. Color. In French. 94 minutes.

1986 The Mozart Brothers

Broderna Mozart is a Swedish film by Suzanne Osten about the problems of staging *Don Giovanni* with a hint of homage to the Marx Brothers in *A Night at the Opera*. A stage director wants to stand the "old war-horse opera" on its head and create a vital new production. The singers lose hair and clothes, the musicians get angry and the union becomes outraged. Only the ghost of Mozart seems happy with what is going on. Many of the actors in the film are from the Stockholm Opera. Etienne Glaser portrays the stage director, Loa Falkman is Eskil who plays Don Giovanni on stage, Agneta Ekmannder is Marian who plays Donna Elvira, Lena T. Hansson is Ia and Donna Anna, Helge Skoog is Olof and Don Ottavio, Grith Fjelmose is Therese and Zerlina, Rune Zetterstrom is Lennart and Leporello, Krister Sit Hill is Philip and Masetto and Zander is the rehearsal conductor and Mozart's ghost. Swedish Film Institute production. Color. In Swedish. 98 minutes.

1987 Harry Kupfer Rehearses *Don Giovanni*

Rainer Milzkott directed this TV documentary showing German director Harry Kupfer at work staging a production of *Don Giovanni*. SFB. Color. In German. 44 minutes.

1987 Babette's Feast

This Academy Award-winning Danish film features notable scenes from *Don Giovanni*. The suitor of one of the protagonists is a French opera singer first seen on stage in *Don Giovanni*. He takes a holiday in a Jutland village where he is attracted to the daughter of the local pastor and offers to give her singing lessons. After a seductive session singing "Ci darem il mano," she gives up singing. Years later the singer sends the French chef Babette to the woman and sets in motion the banquet that is the climax of the film. Gabriel Axel directed. Color. In Danish with English subtitles. 102 minutes. Orion video.

1989 Karajan in Salzburg
A documentary film about Herbert von Karajan at the 1987 Salzburg Festival with extensive scenes of the rehearsals and opening of *Don Giovanni* with Samuel Ramey as Don Giovanni. Susan Froemke, Peter Gelb and Deborah Dickson directed the film. Color. In English and German. 84 minutes. On video.

1992 Don Gio
Czech filmmakers who worked with Milos Forman on *Amadeus* created this experimental version of the Don Giovanni story. Don Giovanni is sung by Andrej Bescasny and Zdenek Klumpar, Leporello by Ludek Vele, Zerlina by Bara Basikova and Donna Elvira by Jirina Markova. Mozart's music is played by the National Theatre Orchestra conducted by Jose Kuchinka. Directors Simon and Michal Caban intercut the opera and rehearsals with modern music and contemporary events. Color. In Czech with English subtitles. 88 minutes.

1995 Guarding Tess
Shirley MacLaine and Nicolas Cage star in this Hollywood comedy drama about a bodyguard and a wayward lady which features Leporello's aria "Madamina, il catalogo é questo." It is sung by Giuseppe Taddei with the Philharmonia Orchestra conducted by Carlo-Maria Guilini and derives from a classic EMI recording. Hugh Wilson wrote and directed the film. Color. 98 minutes.

DONIZETTI, GAETANO
Italian composer (1797-1848)

Gaetano Donizetti was born in Bergamo in 1797 and composed his first opera in 1818. During his lifetime he wrote 66 more, many still in the international opera repertory. His first great opera was *Anna Bolena* in 1930 followed by *L'Elisir d'Amore* in 1932 and *Lucia di Lammermoor* in 1935. Also still popular are *La Fille du Régiment, Don Pasquale* and *La Favorita*. His last opera was the 1844 *Caterina Cornaro*. Donizetti has been much better served on film and video than his *bel canto* colleague Bellini. At least six of his operas are on commercial video and others have been telecast. *La Fille du Régiment* (The Daughter of the Regiment)

and *Maria Stuarda* (Mary Stuart) are on video in English. See ANNA BOLENA, THE DAUGHTER OF THE REGIMENT, DON PASQUALE, L'ELISIR D'AMORE, LA FAVORITA, LINDA DI CHAMOUNIX, LUCIA DI LAMMERMOOR, LUCREZIA BORGIA, MARY STUART, ROBERTO DEVEREUX.

1946 The Life of Donizetti
Il Cavaliere del Sogno is an Italian film about the life of the composer starring Amedeo Nazzari as Donizetti. His life is told in flashback from his deathbed with many scenes shot in his native Bergamo. The plot is mostly concerned with his love affair with Luisa di Cerchiara but there are ample opera excerpts. Tito Schipa appears as the French tenor Gilbert Duprez who created the role of Edgardo in *Lucia di Lammermoor* and also sings excerpts from *L'Elisir d'Amore* and *Don Pasquale*. Camillo Mastrocinque directed the film which was released in the U.S. in 1952. Black and white. Film is in Italian but video is dubbed English. 92 minutes. View video.

DONNA DEL LAGO, LA
1819 opera by Rossini

Gioachino Rossini's opera is based on Sir Walter Scott's poem *The Lady of the Lake* as adapted by libretto writer Andrea Leone Tottola. It is set in 16th century Scotland in the time of James V and revolves around that king's unrequited love for the lady of the lake. He is traveling in disguise and is staying in an enemy household. The lady is the daughter of his chief enemy and she doesn't like him at all. The score is one of Rossini's best. See also GIOACHINO ROSSINI.

1990 Teatro Regio, Parma
Conductor Arnold Östman, whose Drottningholm Mozart opera videos are highly regarded, does an equally impressive job in Parma leading the Teatro Regio Orchestra and Chorus. Cecilia Gasdia is superb as Elena, the Lady of the Lake. She is ably partnered by Kathleen Kuhlmann as Malcolm, Rockwell Blake as King James, Luca Canonici as Rodrigo and Boris Martinovic as Douglas. Gae Aulenti staged the production with sets designed by Lorenza Codignola. The video is an off-air taping of an Italian telecast. Color. In Italian. 153 minutes. Lyric video.

1992 Teatro alla Scala

German film director Werner Herzog staged this impressive Milan production of the opera which stars June Anderson as Elena, the Lady of the Lake. Rockwell Blake is King James, Chris Merritt is Rodrigo, Martine Dupuy is Malcolm, Giorgio Surjan is Douglas and Marilena Laurenza is Albina. Maurizio Balo designed the sets and Franz Blumauer the costumes. Riccardo Muti conducted the La Scala Orchestra and Choir and Ilio Catani directed the video. Color. In Italian. Home Vision video/Japanese laser.

DON PASQUALE
1843 opera by Donizetti

Gaetano Donizetti's very popular comic opera has a highly entertaining libretto by Giovanni Ruffini and the composer. A foolish old miser named Don Pasquale opposes his nephew Ernesto's marriage to a young woman named Norina. When he seeks a wife for himself through Dr. Malatesta, an elaborate trick is set in motion. Norina poses as his wife and makes his life a misery. Afterwards Pasquale is happy for her to marry his nephew. There are excellent patter songs, delightful comic scenes and wonderful arias and duets. See also GAETANO DONIZETTI.

1948 Rome Opera

Tito Gobbi stars as Malatesta in this highlights version of the opera shot on stage at the Rome Opera House. The cast features Luciano Neroni as Don Pasquale (acted by Giulio Tomei), Angelica Tuccari as Norina (acted by Pina Malagarina) and Cesare Valletti as Ernesto (acted by Mino Rosso). The music is played by the Rome Opera House Orchestra conducted by Angelo Questa. George Richfield produced the film for the First Opera Film Festival. English commentary explains the plot. Black and white. In Italian. 25 minutes.

1955 Italo Tajo & Sesto Bruscantini on RAI

Italo Tajo stars as Don Pasquale with Sesto Bruscantini as Malatesta in this RAI production for Italian television. Alda Noni sings the role of Norina and Cesare Valletti is Ernesto. Alberto Erede conducts the RAI Orchestra and Chorus. Black and white. In Italian. 110 minutes. Hardy Classic (France) video.

1979 Welsh National Opera

Geraint Evans stars as Don Pasquale in this TV film based on a production by the Welsh National Opera and directed by Basil Coleman. Lillian Watson is Norina, Russell Smythe is Malatesta, Ryland Davies is Ernesto and John Dobson is the Notary. Richard Armstrong conducts the Welsh National Opera Chorale and Welsh Philharmonia. Color. In Italian with English subtitles. 112 minutes. On video.

1979 Metropolitan Opera

Gabriel Bacquier stars as Don Pasquale with Beverly Sills as Norina in this Metropolitan Opera production by John Dexter. Alfredo Kraus sings the role of Ernesto and Håkan Hagegård is Dr. Malatesta. Desmond Heeley designed the sets and Nicola Rescigno conducted the Metropolitan Opera orchestra. Kirk Browning directed the video on Jan. 11, 1979 and it was telecast on May 17, 1980. 115 minutes. Color. In Italian. On video.

1990 Alfredo Mariotti film

Italian bass Alfredo Mariotti stars as Don Pasquale in this Italian television film with Susanna Rigacci as his Norina. Tenor William Matteuzzi sings the role of Ernesto and Bruno Pola is Dr. Malatesta. Color. In Italian. 110 minutes. Lyric video/Japanese laser.

1991 Barbara Hendricks: My Favorite Opera

American soprano Barbara Hendricks is the focus of this film in the *My Favorite Opera* series which features an Aix-en-Provence production of *Don Pasquale*. Hendricks stars as Norina and is shown with the cast in rehearsal and on stage. Gabriel Bacquier portrays Don Pasquale, Gino Quilico is Malatesta and Luca Canonici is Ernesto. Patricia Gracis is the stage producer, Lauro Crisman designed the sets and Gabriele Ferro conducts the orchestra. The film was superbly directed by Hungarian Márta Mészaros. Color. In English. 60 minutes. Kultur video.

Early/related films

1927 Meine Tante, Deine Tante

Henny Porten stars as Norina in this loose adaptation of the Donizetti opera by Walter Supper. W. R. Heymann wrote new music for the film which was directed by Carl Froelich. The cast includes Ralph Arthur Roberts, Angelo Ferrari and Harry Grunwald. Black and white. In German. About 75 minutes.

1940 Don Pasquale

This Italian film is a narrative version of the story using the libretto of the opera as its script and Donizetti's music as its score. It stars Armando Falconi as Don Pasquale, Laura Solari as Norina, Franco Coop as Malatesta and Maurizio D'Ancora as Ernesto. Camillo Mastrocinque directed. Black and white. In Italian. 98 minutes.

DON QUICHOTTE
1910 opera by Massenet

Jules Massenet's opera is based on Cervantes great novel about the aged, idealistic and somewhat mad Spanish knight Don Quixote, known in France as Don Quichotte. Henri Cain's libretto concentrates on the Don's relationship with his ideal woman Dulcinea (Dulcinée in French) and on his death. Ironically it also reflects Massenet's own life in its mocking story about an elderly man infatuated with a young girl. The girl in his case was singer Lucy Arbell for whom he wrote the role of Dulcinée. The role of Quichotte was written for Feodor Chaliapin, who recorded it. When G. W. Pabst decided to make a film of the novel many years later, he persuaded Chaliapin to reprise the role of Quixote. See also JULES MASSENET.

1933 Don Quixote/Don Quichotte

Feodor Chaliapin stars as the chivalrous but somewhat crazy Knight of La Mancha in G. W. Pabst's excellent film of episodes from the Cervantes novel. There is music and singing in the film but the music is by Jacques Ibert, not Massenet. The film was made in English and French versions. In the English version George Robey is Sancho Panza, Sidney Fox is Dulcinea and Miles Mander is the Police Captain. In the French version Dorville is Sancho Panza, Renée Valliers is Dulcineé and Charles Martinelli is the Police Chief. At the end of the film, after the sadly sane knight returns home, all his romantic books about chivalrous adventures are burned. One book burns in reverse and is revealed to be the history of the knight Don Quixote. Ibert's music is played by an orchestra conducted by Alexander Drajomisjky. Black and white. In English or French. 82 minutes. Lyric/Opera Dubs video.

1986 Nicolai Ghiaurov video

Bulgarian bass Nicolai Ghiaurov appears in an extended scene from *Don Quichotte* in the video *Nicolai Ghiaurov: Tribute to a Great Basso*. The sequence begins with filmed scenes of the sheep episode and concludes with Ghiaurov on stage singing in Quichotte's death scene. Color. 79 minutes. VIEW video.

DON QUINTIN EL AMARGAO
1924 zarzuela by Guerrero

Jacinto Guerrero's tuneful zarzuela *Don Quintin el Amargao* has been filmed three times, twice by master filmmaker Luis Buñuel. The libretto by Carlos Arniches and José Estremera is pure melodrama. Don Quintin had abandoned his little girl when his unfaithful wife claimed he was not the father. Many years later the dying wife admits she lied out of spite and the father sets out to find his long lost daughter. The young woman had run away from her adopted parents and married but he eventually finds her. See also JACINTO GUERRERO.

1925 Manuel Noriega film

The first version of this zarzuela was a Spanish silent film scripted by Carlo Primelles and directed by Manuel Noriega. It stars Juan Nada as Don Quintin, Lina Moreno and Consuelo Reyes. Cartago Films, Madrid. Black and white. In Spanish. 75 minutes.

1935 Luis Buñuel Spanish film

Luis Buñuel's zarzuela film was a big commercial success even though he kept his name off the credits. Buñuel not only directed the film (Luis Marquin gets the screen credit), he also produced, wrote and edited it with José Maria Beltrán as his cinematographer. The street sets by José Maria Torres were widely praised. Alfonso Muñoz stars as Don Quintin, Ana Maria Custodio is Teresa, Luisita Esteso is Felisa, Fernando Granada is Paco and Isabel Noguera is Margot. Black and white. In Spanish. 85 minutes.

1951 Luis Buñuel Mexican film

Bunuel's Spanish version of the zarzuela was so successful that his Mexican producer persuaded him to remake it using the title *La Hija del Engaño*. It follows the original closely though some of the characters names are changed. Fernado Soler stars as Don Quintin, Rubén Rojo is Paco, Alicia Caro is Marta and Nacho Contla is Jonrón. Ultramar Films. Black and white. In Spanish. 80 minutes.

DOWN IN THE VALLEY
1948 opera by Weill

Kurt Weill's American folk opera has become one of his most popular works, partially because of its strong libretto by Arnold Sundgaard but mostly for its wonderful use of folksong. It begins with the Leader's song "Down in the Valley" which tells the story of the opera. Brack Weaver is in jail for killing Thomas Bouché in a fight over Jennie Parsons and has been sentenced to die. On the eve of his execution he escapes to spend the night with Jennie but returns to his death cell at dawn. Weill originally wrote the opera for radio. See also KURT WEILL.

1950 NBC Opera Theatre
Marion Bell, who created the role, stars as Jennie in this NBC Opera Theatre production by Samuel Chotzinoff. William McGraw is Brack, Ray Jacquemont is Thomas, Richard Barrows is Jennie's father, Roy Johnston is the Prison Guard and Kenneth Smith is the Leader/Preacher. The telecast included filmed inserts of a valley and a train at the beginning and fields and clouds at the end. Charles Polacheck staged the opera, Peter Herman Adler conducted the Symphony of the Air Orchestra and Kirk Browning directed the live telecast on January 14, 1950. This opera was the NBC Opera Theatre's premiere after four experimental telecasts. The television cast made a recording of the opera under Weill's supervision which is on an LP. Black and white. In English. 50 minutes.

1961 BBC Television
Stephanie Voss portrays Jennie opposite Joseph Ward as Brack in this BBC Television production by Douglas Craig. Richard Golding is Thomas, Bernard Turgeon is the Leader, John Hauxvell is the Preacher, Mark Baker is Jennie's father and Edumund Donleavy is the Prison Guard. Desmond Chinn designed the sets and Sheila Glassford the costumes. Charles Mackerras conducted the Pro Arte Orchestra and Charles R. Rogers directed the telecast and video. Black and white. In English. 30 minutes.

1988 Frank Cvitanovich film
Linda Lou Allen stars as Jennie with Hutton Cobb as Brack in this British film of the Weill folk opera. The cast also includes Phil Brown, Bob Sessions and Kenny Andrews. Carl Davis conducted the orchestra while Frank Cvitanovich directed the film

in 35mm and stereo for television. Unitel. Color. In English. 51 minutes.

DREAM OF VALENTINO, THE
1994 screen opera by Argento

Dominick Argento's Hollywood-style opera *The Dream of Valentino*, libretto by Charles Nolte, tells the story of film star Rudolph Valentino from his quick rise to mythical fame to his sudden death. It includes screen projections of films and other Hollywood images. The opera premiered at the Washington Opera on Jan. 15, 1994, with Robert Brubaker portraying Valentino, Suzanne Murphy in the role of screenwriter June Mathis who promoted him, Julia Ann Wolf as Natacha Rambova who shaped his career, Joyce Castle as movie star Alla Nazimova, Edrie Means as Valentino's first wife Jean Acker, Julian Patrick as the Mogul and Dan Dressen as Marvin Heeno, the Mogul's nephew. Ann-Margret Pettersson was the stage director, Valentino designed the costumes, John Conklin designed the sets and Christopher Keene conducted the Washington Opera Orchestra and Chorus. See also DOMINICK ARGENTO.

DREIGROSCHENOPER, DIE
See THREEPENNY OPERA, THE

DREI WALZER
See LES TROIS VALSES

DREIMÄDERLHAUS, DAS
1916 operetta by Schubert/Berté

It is ironic that Franz Schubert, one of the great composers for the voice, wrote fourteen operas without success and then became a success as an operetta composer a century after his death. *Das Dreimäderlhaus* (The House of the Three Girls) is a pastiche operetta cobbled together by Heinrich Berté from Schubert melodies. It tells the (fictional) story of Schubert's love for Hannerl who has sisters called Hederl and Haiderl. He is too shy to woo her and loses her to his poet friend Schober. The libretto by A. M. Willner and Heinz Reichert is based on a novel. The operetta was a hit in twenty languages with Richard Tauber playing the lead role in Germany and England. In England the operetta was first called *Lilac Time* and then *Blossom Time*, in Paris it was *Chanson d'Amour* and in the USA *Blossom Time*. The American version was arranged by

Sigmund Romberg who recomposed the score to a new libretto. See also FRANZ SCHUBERT.

1917 Richard Oswald film
Richard Oswald directed an early silent German film version of the operetta. It was screened in theaters with the music. Black and white. About 70 minutes.

1934 Blossom Time
Richard Tauber starred as Schubert on stage in London in 1933 in the English version of the operetta titled *Blossom Time*. In 1934 he played the role in an English film directed by Paul Stein. June Baxter portrays the woman Schubert loves and Carl Esmond is his friend Rudi. BIP. Black and white. In English. 90 minutes.

1936 Drei Mäderl um Schubert
Paul Hörbiger stars as Schubert in this German film of the operetta now titled *Three Girls and Schubert*. Else Elster is Hannerl, Maria Andergast is Heiderl and Gretl Theimer is Hederl Gustav with Waldau as Tschoell and Julia Serda as his wife. E. W. Emo directed. Black and white. In German. 88 minutes.

1958 Ernst Marischka film
Karl-Heinz Böhm stars as Schubert in this film of the operetta directed by Ernst Marischka. The cast includes Johanna Matz, Magda Schneider, Gustav Knuth, Rudolf Schock and Ewald Balser. Black and white. In German. 90 minutes.

DROTTNINGHOLM COURT THEATER
Swedish opera house (1766-)

The baroque Drottningholm Court Theater (Drottningholm Slottsteater) near Stockholm was built for the Swedish royal family and is one of the most beautiful old opera houses in the world. Operas are presented with their original machinery and 18th century sets and the orchestra dresses in period costume and plays period instruments. The theater was first seen on film in a reconstruction in Ingmar Bergman's *The Magic Flute* (1974) but has become better known through a series of superb videos of Mozart operas filmed by Thomas Olofsson for Swedish TV with conductor Arnold Östman. As a group these are among the finest screen operas and are all on laser disc. See THE ABDUCTION FROM THE SERAGLIO (1991), LA CLEMENZA DI TITO (1987), COSÌ FAN TUTTE (1984), DON GIOVANNI (1987), LA FINTA GIARDINIERA (1988), IDOMENEO (1991), THE MAGIC FLUTE (1974/1989), THE MARRIAGE OF FIGARO (1981).

1967 Drottningholm Court Theatre
A Swedish film demonstratings the glories of the Drottningholm Court Theater and showing how its decor is unchanged after two centuries. The ancient groove and shutter machinery is pictured in action during a performance of Gluck's *Iphigenia in Aulis*. Color. In English or Swedish. 28 minutes.

DUBARRY, DIE
1931 operetta by Millöcker/Mackeben

Karl Millöcker and Theo Mackeben's operetta *The Dubarry* was very popular in the 1930s and was staged in English in London and New York in 1932. Metropolitan opera diva Grace Moore starred in the New York production and her success led to her being invited back to Hollywood to become a movie star. Originally an 1879 Millöcker operetta called *Gräfin Dubarry*, it was revised by Theo Mackenben in 1931 with a new libretto by Paul Knepler and J.M. Welleminsky. The new version, which premiered in Berlin with diva Gitta Alpar, tells the story of a milliner's assistant in Paris who marries a count and becomes the mistress of Louis XV. It does not follow history too closely. There are many non-musical versions of the story starring everyone from Theda Bara to Martine Carol. See also THEO MACKEBEN, KARL MILLÖCKER.

1935 I Give My Heart
Hungarian opera diva Gitta Alpar, who originated the role, stars as Madame Dubarry in this British film of the operetta. Owen Nares is Louis XV, Arthur Margetson is Count Dubarry and Patrick Waddington is Dubarry's first love René. "I Give My Heart" is the hit song from the operetta. Marcel Varnay directed the film released in the U.S. as *The Loves of Madame Dubarry*. Black and white. In English. 91 minutes.

1951 Theo Mackeben film
Composer/arranger Theo Mackeben supervised a German television adaptation of the operetta which was filmed in 1951. Black and white. In German. 90 minutes.

DUCHESSA DEL BAL TABARIN, LA

1917 operetta by Lombardo

Italian composer Carlo Lombardo's 1917 operetta *La Duchessa del Bal Tabarin* is an adaptation of Bruno Granichstädten's 1911 Austrian operetta *Majestät Mimi* with a new libretto by A. Franci and C. Vizzotto. It was a big success in its reincarnation and became popular in Spain as well as Italy. The story focuses on the love affair of a Ruritanian prince and a Paris cabaret performer, Mimi in the original but Frou-Frou of the Bal Tabarin in the Italian version. See also CARLO LOMBARDO.

1963 Placido Domingo film
Placido Domingo stars in this Mexican TV film of the operetta called *Frou-Frou del Tabarin*. Domingo plays the prince with his wife Marta Ornelas as Frou-Frou and support from Ernestina Garfias and Franco Inglesias. The operetta, sung in Spanish, was filmed for Max Factor. Black and white. In Spanish. 90 minutes.

1975 Gianni Grimaldi film
Gianni Grimaldi wrote and directed this Italian feature film version of the operetta titled *Frou-Frou del Tabarin*. The somewhat revised storyline features Martine Brochard, Fabrizio Moroni, Carmen Scarpitta and Jacques Berthier. Color. In Italian. 88 minutes.

1992 Sandro Massimini video
Italian operetta master Sandro Massimini featured the Lombardo operetta on his TV series *Operette, Che Passione!* He talks about the history of the operetta and presents highlights from it in this video. The featured songs are "Frou Frou del Tabarin" and "Ombre siamo nella notte." Color. In Italian. About l5 minutes. Ricordi (Italy) video.

DUE FOSCARI, I

1844 opera by Verdi

Giuseppe Verdi's tragic opera *I Due Foscari* is based on a play by Lord Byron called *The Two Foscaris*. The libretto is by Francesco Maria Piave and it is one of the few operas in which evil wins out. *I Due Foscari* is set in the great days of power in Venice. The elderly Doge Foscari is unable to stop his son Jacopo from being exiled after a false accusation of murder. The son dies and the Doge is forced to resign and then dies as well. His enemy Loredano is jubilant. See also GIUSEPPE VERDI.

1988 Teatro alla Scala
Renato Bruson stars as the Doge Foscari in this Teatro alla Scala production designed and directed by Pier Luigi Pizzi. The cast includes Alberto Cupido as Jacopo, Linda Roark-Strummer as Linda, Luigi Roni, Renato Cazzaniga, Monica Tagliasacchi, Aldo Bottion and Aldo Bramante. Gianadrea Gavazzeni conducts the La Scala Orchestra and Chorus. SACIS. Color. In Italian with Japanese subtitles. 100 minutes. Castle video/ Fonit Cetra (Italy) /Japanese laserdisc.

Related films

1923 Amleto Novelli film
Amleto Novelli, the most famous Italian actor of the silent era, stars as Jacobo Foscari in this Italian adaptation of the Byron play titled *I Foscari*. The cast also includes Alberto Collo, Nini Dinelli, Vittorio Pieri and Lia Miari. Mario Almirante directed. Verdi's music was played with the film. Black and white. Italian titles. About 72 minutes.

1942 Rossano Brazzi film
Rossano Brazzi stars as Jacobo Foscari in this adaptation of the Byron play. It uses Verdi's music from the opera as it soundtrack as arranged by Fernando Previtali. Carlo Ninchi plays the Doge Foscari with a cast that includes Memo Benassi and Elli Parvo. Enrico Fulchignoni directed for Scalera Film. Black and white. In Italian. 85 minutes.

DUKE BLUEBEARD'S CASTLE
See BLUEBEARD'S CASTLE

DURBIN, DEANNA
Canadian soprano (1921-)

Deanna Durbin was not a stage singer but she introduced a lot of moviegoers to opera. She was signed by MGM to portray Ernestine Schumann-Heink in a biography but the contralto became ill and the film was cancelled. Durbin moved to Universal where her singing coach was Spanish bass Andres de Segurola, formerly of the Met. Her first feature, the 1936 *Three Smart Girls*, was a huge success and Durbin was soon a major star. Her producers usually found room for opera arias in her films and in one she duets with Met tenor Jan

Peerce. There was even a souvenir songbook of arias from her movies. Two of her films were based on operettas. Durbin's active film career ended in 1948 but she still has many fans today. Her films with operatic content are listed below. See also FRÜHJAHRSPARADE (1940), JAN PEERCE (1947), UP IN CENTRAL PARK (1948).

1937 100 Men and a Girl
Durbin sings the "Libiamo" aria from *La Traviata* in this picture about the spunky talented daughter of a musician. Her co-star is conductor Leopold Stokowski. Henry Koster directed. Universal. Black and white. 83 minutes.

1938 That Certain Age
Durbin gets a crush on Melvyn Douglas and sings "Daydreams" ("Ah! Je veux vivre") from Gounod's *Roméo et Juliette*. Edward Ludwig directed. Universal. Black and white. 95 minutes.

1939 Three Smart Girls Grow Up
Durbin sings "The Last Rose of Summer" from *Martha* and Weber's "Invitation to the Dance" in this film about three sisters and their romantic attachments. Henry Koster directed. Universal. Black and white. 87 minutes.

1939 First Love
Durbin sings an English version of "Un bel di" from *Madama Butterfly*. The aria ends with her Prince Charming rescuing her. She also does well with a song based on a Strauss waltz. Henry Koster directed. Universal. Black and white. 84 minutes.

1940 It's a Date
Durbin sings "Musetta's Waltz" from *La Bohème* and Schubert's "Ave Maria." She plays the daughter of a Broadway star who wins the role her mother wanted. William Seiter directed for Universal. Black and white. 100 minutes.

1943 The Amazing Mrs. Holliday
Durbin sings "Vissi d'Arte" from *Tosca* in this story about a missionary and Chinese orphans. Jean Renoir directed most of the film but Bruce Manning finished it for Universal. Black and white. 96 minutes.

1943 His Butler's Sister
Durbin sings the tenor aria "Nessun dorma" from *Turandot* at a butler's ball in this charming film about a girl and a composer. She also sings Victor Herbert and Russian songs. Frank Borzage directed with flair. Universal. Black and white. 94 minutes.

1948 For the Love of Mary
Deanna Durbin is a White House telephone operator in her last film and performs a comic version of Figaro's "Largo al factotum" from *The Barber of Seville*. Frederick De Cordova directed. Universal. Black and white. 90 minutes.

DVORÁK, ANTONÍN
Czech composer (1841-1904)

Antonín Dvorák is known to most Americans as the composer of the *New World Symphony* as his operas have never really entered the international repertory. He wrote ten of them, however, and they are quite popular in the Czech Republic. By far the most performed and admired is *Rusalka*, a version of the Undine legend that contains a much-performed soprano aria called "Song of the Moon." There are two videos of it. The other fairly popular Dvorák opera is the fun and folksy *The Devil and Kate*. See THE DEVIL AND KATE, RUSALKA.

á

This is a record of an American tribute to Dvorák shot at Smetana Hall in Prague with the Boston Symphony Orchestra conducted by Seiji Osawa. Mezzo-soprano Frederica von Stade sings the famous "Song of the Moon" aria. Brian Large directed the video. Color. 90 minutes. Sony video.

DVORSKY, PETER
Czech tenor (1951-)

Peter Dvorsky, a favorite of opera film specialist Petr Weigl, made his debut in Bratislava in 1972 and has sung widely around the world from La Scala and Covent Garden to the Metropolitan. Although he sings many Slavic operas, he is equally well known for his performances in Puccini and Verdi. Dvorsky is featured in many of Weigl's opera films and stars in his pastiche *The Love of Destiny*. He has also starred in Czech and Slovakian TV productions of operas including *La Bohème* and *Tosca*. See ADRIANA LECOUVREUR (1989), THE BARTERED BRIDE (1981), L'ELISIR D'AMORE (1984), EUGENE ONEGIN (1985), MADAMA BUTTERFLY (1986), VERONA (1988/1990), WERTHER (1985), PETR WEIGL (1983).

E

EATON, JOHN
American composer (1935-)

John Eaton began composing operas at Princeton beginning with the 1957 chamber opera *Ma Barker* which tells the story of the famous gangster mother. *Heracles*, based on Sophocles and Seneca, was composed in 1964 but not staged until 1972 in Bloomington. The 1973 *Myshkin* was commissioned and composed for television. His other operas include *The Cry of Clytemnestra* (1980), *The Tempest* (1985) and *The Reverend Jim Jones* (1989). See MYSHKIN.

ECHO ET NARCISSE
1779 opera by Gluck

Gluck wrote this little opera at the end of his career to a libretto by Ludwig Von Tschoudi based on Ovid's *Metamorphoses*. Echo loves Narcissus but he loves only his own image. In despair she dwindles into a voice and causes Narcissus to suffer. The god Amor won't allow him to die of despair as well so he restores Echo to life. The opera was successfully revived at the Schwetzingen Festival in 1987 and is on video. See also CHRISTOPH WILLIBALD GLUCK.

1987 Schwetzingen Festival
Kurt Streit is Narcisse, Sophie Boulin is Echo and Deborah Massell is Amor in this charming Schwetzingen Festival production, the first in the 20th century. Herbert Wernicke staged the opera and designed the sets and costumes while René Jacobs conducted the Concerto Cologne Orchestra. The cast includes Peter Galliard as Cynire, Gertrude Hoffstedt as Egle, Hanne Krogen as Thanais and Eva Marie Tersson as Sylphie. Claud Viler directed the video. Color. In French with English subtitles. 99 minutes. Home Vision video.

EDDY, NELSON
American tenor (1901-1967)

Tenor Nelson Eddy began his career on stage as a baritone singing Gilbert and Sullivan roles with the Savoy Opera Company in Philadelphia. He made his opera debut as Amonasro in *Aida* with the Philadelphia Civic Opera in 1924 and sang with them for six years. He even sang on the stage of the Met in *Pagliacci* and *Wozzeck* though not with the Met company. Eddy began his MGM film career in 1933 and teamed up with Jeanette MacDonald in 1935 for *Naughty Marietta*. They stayed a popular team for eight years. Eddy had a strong career on his own and gave voice to one of the best animated opera films, *The Whale Who Wanted to Sing at the Met*. He continued in films until 1947, then switched to television. He began touring with Gale Sherwood in the 1950s and sang with her in nightclub acts until the end of his life. Only films with a musical element are listed below. See also BITTER SWEET (1940), THE CHOCOLATE SOLDIER (1941), THE DESERT SONG (1955), LA FANCIULLA DEL WEST (1938 film), JEANETTE MACDONALD (1942/1993), MAYTIME (1937), NAUGHTY MARIETTA (1935), THE NEW MOON (1940), THE PHANTOM OF THE OPERA (1943), ROSE-MARIE (1936), SWEETHEARTS (1938), KURT WEILL (1944), THE WHALE WHO WANTED TO SING AT THE MET.

1937 Rosalie
Eddy sings Cole Porter in this MGM musical about a romance between West Point cadet Eddy and princess-in-disguise Eleanor Powell. His songs include "In the Still of the Night" and "Rosalie." W.S. Van Dyke directed. Black and white. 122 minutes. On video.

1939 Let Freedom Ring!
Eddy portrays the masked hero The Hornet who fights for the ranchers against railroad villain Edward Arnold and wins the heart of Virginia Bruce. He also sings songs like "America" and "Dusty Road." Ben Hecht wrote the screenplay and Jack Conway directed. Filmed in Sepia. 100 minutes.

1939 Balalaika
Nelson Eddy stars opposite Ilona Massey in this MGM operetta about the Russian revolution based on an Eric Maschwitz stage show. He's a prince, she's a cabaret singer. The film includes

excerpts from *Carmen* and an imaginary Rimsky-Korsakov opera at the Imperial Opera House. Reinhold Schunzel directed. Black and white. 102 minutes.

1947 Northwest Outpost
Nelson Eddy's last film for Republic was a musical western with a score by operetta composer Rudolf Friml. Ilona Massey co-stars in a story set in a Russian trading post in 19th century California. Allan Dwan directed. Black and white. 91 minutes. On video.

1992 Nelson and Jeanette: America's Singing Sweethearts
Michael Lorentz' documentary film about the careers and lives of Jeanette MacDonald and Nelson Eddy includes clips from their many films. It is hosted by Jane Powell and was written by Elayne Goldstein. Jeanette's husband Gene Raymond is one of the guests. The film was produced by WTTW Chicago and Turner Entertainment and was shown on PBS in 1993. Color. 57 minutes. Video for sale and at MTR.

EDISON, THOMAS ALVA
Opera film visionary (1847-1931)

The inventor of the phonograph and the cinema was an opera film visionary who dreamt of "Kinetoscope operas with phono." In *The New York Times* in 1893 he said his intention was "to have such a happy combination of photography and electricity that a man can sit in his own parlor, see depicted upon a curtain the forms of the players in opera upon a distant stage and hear the voices of the singers." In 1894 he made a prophecy for *Century Magazine*: "I believe that in coming years grand opera can be given at the Metropolitan Opera House in New York with artists and musicians long since dead." Edison's company made a number of opera films including a remarkable 1900 *Martha* and a famous 1904 *Parsifal*. See AIDA (1911), LA BOHÈME (1910), CARMEN (1894), ENRICO CARUSO (1912), FAUST (1909), MARTHA (1900), THE MERRY WIDOW (1908 film), PARSIFAL (1904).

1940 Young Tom Edison
A Hollywood biography with Mickey Rooney as Edison trying out his first experiments under the direction of Norman Taurog. MGM. Black and white. 82 minutes.

1940 Edison, the Man
Edison grows up and becomes Spencer Tracy and invents almost everything in this film directed by Clarence Brown. MGM. Black and white. 107 minutes.

ED SULLIVAN SHOW
CBS television series (1948-1971)

The Ed Sullivan Show, the most important television variety show in the 1950s, often featured opera singers and scenes from operas. One of the first was Roberta Peters who appeared in 1950 after her walk-on debut at the Met as Zerlina in *Don Giovanni*. Anna Moffo and Joan Sutherland each appeared six times. In November 1953 the TV show was broadcast live from the Met stage with an excerpt from *Carmen* with Risë Stevens and Richard Tucker. In 1956 Sullivan and the Met agreed to do five programs together. The first on Nov. 26, 1956, featured Maria Callas in a scene from *Tosca*, the second featured Dorothy Kirsten and Mario Del Monaco in *Madama Butterfly*. Audience response was so poor that the agreement was ended. The Met's final appearance on the show was on March 10, 1957 when Renata Tebaldi and Richard Tucker sang a duet from *La Bohème*.

1996 Great Moments in Opera
This compilation video includes 95 minutes of operatic highlights from the *Ed Sullivan Show* with many top opera stars of the fifties, sixties and early seventies. The singers presenting arias and ensembles include Maria Callas, Robert Merrill, Leontyne Price, Anna Moffo, Richard Tucker, Eileen Farrell, Beverly Sills, Franco Corelli, Lily Pons, Birgit Nilsson, Renata Tebaldi, Joan Sutherland, Marilyn Horne, Roberta Peters, Lillian Sukis and Jan Peerce. Color & black and white. 95 minutes. Consumer Video.

EGGERTH, MARTA
Hungarian soprano (1912-)

Hungarian soprano Marta Eggerth and her Polish tenor husband Jan Kiepura were the MacDonald and Eddy of German cinema. She began her career in opera and usually sang opera in her films, two were even based around *La Bohème*, but most of her movies were operettas. Eggerth came to the U.S. with Kiepura in 1936 when he was engaged to sing at the Met and they sang in *La Bohème* in Chicago. She appeared in two Hollywood films with Judy Garland. In 1944, she and Kiepura starred in *The Merry Widow* on Broadway and then toured it around the world. Kiepura died in 1966 but Eggerth was still singing in her 80s, including Sondheim's *Follies*. Most of her important theatrical films are listed but she also made European television shows. See VINCENZO BELLINI (1935), DIE BLUME VON HAWAII (1933), LA BOHÈME (1937/1947 films), CLO-CLO (1935), DIE CSÁRDÁSFÜRSTIN (1934), JAN KIEPURA (1934), DAS LAND DES LÄCHELNS (1952), ROBERT STOLZ (1990), WO DIE LERCHE SINGT (1936), DER ZAREWITSCH (1933).

1932 Where Is This Lady?
Eggerth starred in English and German versions of this film operetta written by Billy Wilder with music by Franz Lehár. Eggerth is Steffi, a Viennese charmer who helps a bankrupt banker turn his bank into a nightclub. Her English co-stars are Owen Nares, George Arthur and Wendy Barrie. Lazlo Vajda and Victor Hanbury directed. Black and white. In English. 77 minutes.

1932 Es War Einmal ein Walzer
Once There Was a Waltz is the German version of the Billy Wilder/Franz Lehár movie described above. Eggerth's co-stars in it are Paul Hörbiger, Rolf von Goth and Lizzie Natzler. Viktor Janson directed. Black and white. In German. 77 minutes.

1932 Kaiserwalzer
Eggerth stars in this musical by composer Nico Dostal based around themes by his operetta colleagues Strauss, Millöcker and Suppé. The cast includes Willi Eicheberger, Paul Hörbiger and Hansi Niese. Black and white. In German. 89 minutes.

1932 Der Frauendiplomat
Former Metropolitan Opera tenor Leo Slezak appears opposite Eggerth in this musical comedy set in the world of diplomats. Max Hansen, Theo Lingen and Anton Poinner lend support. Hans May wrote the music and E. W. Emo directed. Black and white. In German. 70 minutes.

1934 The Unfinished Symphony
Schuberts Unvollendete Symphonie is the German title of this romantic British-Austrian film about composer Franz Schubert and his impossible love for Count Esterhazy's daughter Caroline, portrayed by Eggerth. Eggerth sings Schubert's "Ave Maria." Willi Forst directed both English and German versions. Black and white. 90 minutes.

1935 Die Blonde Carmen
The Blonde Carmen is a German film operetta with Eggerth singing up a storm opposite Wolfgang Liebeneiner. He's a librettist who thinks theater women are no good so Eggerth set out to prove him wrong. Leo Slezak and Ida Wüst lend support. Viktor Janson directed and Franz Grothe wrote the music. Black and white. In German. 98 minutes.

1942 For Me and My Gal
Eggerth plays a glamorous singing star who almost teams up with Gene Kelly at the urging of Judy Garland in this MGM musical about a vaudeville team aiming for the big time. Eggerth sings "Do I Love You?" very nicely. Busby Berkeley directed. Color. 104 minutes. On video.

1943 Presenting Lily Mars
Eggerth has a large role as the star rival of Judy Garland in this MGM musical about a girl with theatrical dreams. She demonstrates her high notes singing three songs including "Is it Really Love" and "When I Look at You." Judy parodies her accent and singing style in a funny but rather unkind scene. Norman Taurog directed. Color. 104 minutes. MGM/UA video.

1949 La Valse Brillante
Eggerth and Kiepura's first film after the war is a French musical starring Eggerth as a singer receiving threatening letters. Jan Kiepura plays a tenor hired to be her bodyguard. He solves her problems and ends up as her singing partner and husband. The music is mostly by Mozart and Verdi. Jean Boyer directed. Vox film. Black and white. In French. 95 minutes.

EINSTEIN ON THE BEACH
1976 opera by Glass

Einstein on the Beach, the influential opera created by composer Philip Glass and playwright Robert

Wilson, is one of the most famous minimalist operatic collaborations. It was staged with great success in opera houses in Europe and then at the Metropolitan after its premiere in Avignon. The opera takes an offbeat aural and visual look at Einstein as scientist, musician, humanist and theorist of the atomic bomb. The music is scored for four soloists and a chorus of twelve with chamber orchestra. The opera is available on CD. See also PHILIP GLASS.

1976 Avignon Festival
There is no commercial video of the opera but Wilson's original production at the Avignon Theatre Festival in France was videotaped. It runs for four hours and forty minutes without intervals with its four acts connected by "knee plays." The character Einstein appears as a violinist positioned between the stage and the orchestra pit. Color. 280 minutes. Video source unknown.

1986 Einstein on the Beach: The Changing Image of Opera
Mark Obenhaus's film is a behind-the-scenes documentary about the revival of the opera at the Brooklyn Academy of Music in 1984. Glass and Wilson are shown at work on the production and discussing its creation, and there are scenes of the opera in rehearsal and performance. The film was telecast on Jan 31, 1986. Color. 60 minutes. Direct Cinema film or video.

1985 A Composer's Notes
The "Spaceship" episode from *Einstein on the Beach* is performed in this documentary by the Philip Glass Ensemble, though most of the film is devoted to productions of *Akhnaten*. Michael Blackwood directed the film. Color. 87 minutes. VAI video.

EISENSTEIN, SERGEI
Soviet film director (1898-1948)

Film director Sergei Eisenstein was also an opera director and enthusiast and opera affected much of his life. As a young man he queued all night to see Chaliapin in *Boris Godunov* though when Chaliapin asked him to direct a film of *Don Quichotte*, Eisenstein was not interested. Chaliapin played Ivan the Terrible in Rimsky-Korsakov's opera *The Maid of Pskov* and reprised the role in a 1915 Russian film which Eisenstein studied when preparing his own Ivan film. In

1940 Eisenstein staged Wagner's *Die Walküre* at the Bolshoi Opera during the period of the non-aggression pact with Germany. Eisenstein's production was controversial and his hopes for a complete *Ring* became impossible. He also wanted to stage Prokofiev's opera *War and Peace* but that wasn't possible either. It is hardly surprising then that he conceived *Ivan the Terrible* as virtually a film-opera with Prokofiev music. It has been described as the most operatic film ever made. Eisenstein's earlier *Alexander Nevsky* also has operatic overtones and music by Prokofiev. See IVAN THE TERRIBLE.

1937 Battleship Potemkin
Eisenstein's 1925 Soviet film *Battleship Potemkin* (Bronenosets Potemkin) inspired a Soviet opera with the same name in 1937. Both film and opera tell the story of a famous 1905 mutiny in Odessa by sailors on the Battleship Potemkin. Ukrainian composer Oles Semenovich Chishko wrote his Potemkin opera to a libretto by S. D. Spassky. It was produced at the Kirov and Bolshoi Operas and became one of the popular revolutionary operas of its time. German composer Edmund Meisel wrote an influential score to accompany the silent Eisenstein film, but the sound version issued by the USSR in 1950 used a score by Soviet composer E. Kriouskov.

EISINGER, IRENE
German soprano (1903-1994)

Irene Eisinger, German-born but a favorite at Glyndebourne after she left Germany in the mid-30s, sang the role of Despina in the first complete recording of *Così Fan Tutte* made at Glyndebourne in 1935. She made her debut in Basle in 1926 and sang in Berlin, Vienna, Prague and Salzburg before moving to England. She was noted for her performances in Mozart operas but also sang in operettas. Eisinger starred in a number of German films in the 1930s including *Two Hearts in 3/4 Time* and *The Merry Wives of Vienna*, both with music by operetta composer Robert Stolz. See DIE FÖRSTERCHRISTL (1931), ROBERT STOLZ (1930/1931).

ELDER, MARK
English conductor (1947-)

Mark Elder began as a chorister and bassoon player but turned to conducting at Cambridge.

He worked at both Glyndebourne and Sydney, but his major period came after he joined the English National Opera in 1974. He conducted more than thirty operas for the ENO, including Jonathan Miller's famous *Rigoletto*, and he helped established the company's world reputation through tours. See GLORIANA (1984), RIGOLETTO (1982), RUSALKA (1986).

ELEKTRA
1909 opera by Strauss

Richard Strauss asked Hugo von Hofmannsthal if he could use the playwright's German version of Sophocles' tragedy as the libretto for an opera. Hofmannsthal agreed and their long and fruitful collaboration began. The opera describes how Electra (Elektra in German) seeks revenge for the death of her father King Agamemnon. While he was at the Trojan Wars, Queen Clytemnestra took a new lover called Aegisthus and they killed Agamemnon when he returned. Electra's brother Orestes has been sent into exile and her younger sister Chrysothemis is ineffectual. Electra dreams of revenge when Orestes finally returns. See also HUGO VON HOFMANNSTHAL, RICHARD STRAUSS.

1969 Rolf Liebermann film
American soprano Gladys Kuchta stars as Elektra with Regina Resnik as Klytemnestra in this German film of the opera produced by Rolf Liebermann. It was shot in a Hamburg TV studio but based on a production by the Hamburg State Opera. The cast includes Ingrid Bjoner, Hans Sotin and Helmut Melchert. Leopold Ludwig conducts the Hamburg State Opera Chorus and Philharmonic Orchestra. The film was released theatrically in the U.S. Color. In German. 107 minutes.

1980 Metropolitan Opera
Birgit Nilsson is 61 but still in good form as Elektra in this Metropolitan Opera production by Herbert Graf. Leonie Rysanek portrays Chrysothemis, Mignon Dunn is Klytemnestra, Donald McIntyre is Orest and Robert Nagy is Aegisth. The opera was directed by Paul Mills and designed by Rudolf Heinrich. James Levine conducted the Metropolitan Opera and Chorus. Brian Large directed the video on Feb. l6, 1980 but it was not telecast until Jan. 28, 1981. Color.

In German with English subtitles. 112 minutes. Paramount video/ Pioneer laser.

1981 Götz Friedrich film
Leonie Rysanek stars as Elektra in this Austrian film by Götz Friedrich shot in a somewhat expressionist in Vienna. Dietrich Fischer-Dieskau is Orest, Astrid Varnay is Klytemnestra, Catarina Ligendza is Chrysothemis and Hans Beirer is Aegisth. Josef Svoboda was the set designer, Rudolf Blahacek was the cinematographer and Karl Böhm conducted the Vienna Philharmonic Orchestra and Vienna State Chorus Concert Ensemble. Color. In German with English subtitles. 117 minutes. London video and laser.

1989 Vienna State Opera
Eva Marton stars as Elektra with Cheryl Studer as Chrysothemis and Brigitte Fassbaender as Klytemnestra in this strong Vienna State Opera production by Harry Kupfer. James King Is Aegisth and Franz Grundheber is Orest. Hans Scavernock designed the sets and Reinhard Heinrich the costumes. Claudio Abbado conducted the Vienna State Opera Orchestra and Chorus. Brian Large directed the video. Color. In German with English subtitles. 108 minutes. Home Vision video/Pioneer laser.

1993 South Australian Opera
Marilyn Zschau stars as Elektra in this South Australian Opera production by Australian film director Bruce Beresford. Others in the cast are Yvonne Minton, Claire Primrose and Florian Cemy. Richard Armstrong conducted the South Australian Orchestra. The production was taped and telecast by the Australian Broadcasting Corporation. Color. In German with English subtitles. 1l0 minutes.

1994 Metropolitan Opera
Hildegard Behrens stars as Elektra with Deborah Voigt as Chrysothemis and Brigitte Fassbaender as Klytemnestra in this Metropolitan Opera production by Otto Schenk. James King is Aegisth and Donald McIntyre is Orest. Jurgen Rose designed the sets and costumes and Paul Mills was the stage director. James Levine conducted the Metropolitan Opera Orchestra and Chorus. Brian Large directed the video in January 1994 but it was not telecast until Sept. 12, 1994. Color. In German with English subtitles. 110 minutes.

Early/related films

1910 Vitagraph film
Mary Fuller stars as Elektra in this Vitagraph film inspired by the success of the Strauss opera. Maurice Costello is her co-star. The film, released in April 1910, was screened with music but not always by Strauss. Black and white. About 12 minutes (942 feet).

1961 Electra (Sophocles)
Anna Synodinou stars as Electra in this film of the play by Sophocles which provided the basis for the libretto for the Strauss opera. Director Ted Zarpas filmed Sophocles' tragedy on stage at the ancient outdoor Epidaurus Theater with G. Eptamenitis as his cinematographer. Black and white. In Greek. 115 minutes.

1961 Electra (Euripides)
Irene Pappas stars as Electra in this famous film version of the story based on the rival play by Euripides and directed by Michael Cacoyannis. Walter Lassally was the cinematographer and Mikis Theodorakis wrote the music. Black and white. In Greek. 110 minutes. On video.

1981 The Filming of Elektra
"Do I hear the music? It pours out of me." Norbert Beilharz shot this documentary film about the making of the famous Götz Friedrich film of the opera with Leonie Rysanek and Dietrich Fischer-Dieskau. Conductor Karl Böhm is shown in rehearsal with the singers and the Vienna Philharmonic Orchestra. The actors are Mechthild Grossman and Siemen Rühaak. Color. In German. 90 minutes.

ELIAS, ROSALIND
American mezzo-soprano (1929-)

Rosalind Elias began her opera career with the New England Opera in 1948, built her reputation at La Scala and San Carlo and joined the Metropolitan in 1954. She appeared in over 400 performances at the Met and was a featured singer in the premieres of *Vanessa* and *Antony and Cleopatra*. See CARMEN (1959/1963), HANSEL AND GRETEL (1982), METROPOLITAN OPERA (1975), THE RAKE'S PROGRESS (1977), VANESSA.

ELISIR D'AMORE, L'
1832 opera by Donizetti

The Elixir of Love has always been one of Gaetano Donizetti's most popular comic operas, helped by an entertaining libretto by Felice Romani. Shy peasant Nemorino loves beautiful Adina but she lives in a fantasy world and ignores him. He buys an alcoholic love potion from the quack medicine man Dr. Dulcamara which makes him drunk and drives annoyed Adina into the arms of his rival, Sergeant Belcore. A second bottle of elixir and Nemorino is in the Army as well but Adina now finds she loves him and buys his enlistment paper back. The famous tenor aria "Una furtiva lagrima" is sung by Nemorino. See also GAETANO DONIZETTI.

1947 Tito Gobbi film
Tito Gobbi is Sergeant Belcore with Nelly Corradi as Adina and Gino Sinimberghi as Nemorino in this Italian film. Italo Tajo is the quack doctor Dulcamara and Loretta di Lelio is Giannetta. Gina Lollobrigida, in her second film, plays a friend of Adina's. Giuseppe Morelli conducted the music and Mario Costa directed the film which was shown in the US as *The Wine of Love*. Black and white. In Italian. 85 minutes. Applause (USA)/ Mastervideo (Italy) videos.

1959 Ferruccio Tagliavini video
Ferruccio Tagliavini, noted for his portrayal of Nemorino, stars in this Italian stage production in Tokyo filmed live on Feb. 9, 1959, for Japanese TV. Alda Noni is Adina, Paolo Montarsolo is Dulcamara, Arturo La Porta is Belcore and Santa Chissari is Giannetta. Alberto Erede conducts the Lirica Italiana Orchestra and Chorus. Black and white. In Italian with Japanese subtitles. 96 minutes. Lyric Legato Classics video.

1981 Metropolitan Opera
Judith Blegen is the heartless Adina with Luciano Pavarotti as the lovesick Nemorino in this Metropolitan Opera production by Nathaniel Merrill. Brent Ellis is Belcore, Sesto Bruscantini is Dulcamara and Louis Wohlafka is Giannetta. Nicola Rescigno leads the orchestra and choir of the Metropolitan Opera. Kirk Browning directed the video on March 2, 1981. Color. In Italian with English subtitles. 132 minutes. Paramount video/Pioneer laser.

1984 Melanie Holliday film

American soprano Melanie Holliday stars as vivacious school teacher Adina in this picturesque Czech film of the opera shot on location in the country. Miroslav Dvorsky is the lovesick housepainter Nemorino, Alfredo Mariotti is Belcore, Armando Ariostini is Dulcamara and Bozena Plonyova is Giannetta. The music is played by the Bratislava Radio Symphony conducted by Piero Bellugi. Frank DeQuell directed. Color. In Italian. 80 minutes. European video / Japanese video and laserdisc.

1989 Carlo Bergonzi as Nemorino

Carlo Bergonzi stars as Nemorino in a filmed dress rehearsal of *L'Elisir d'Amore* in a small New Jersey theater. He was 65 at the time and still sounds pretty good. Roberta Peters sings the role of Adina and Alfredo Silipigni conducts the orchestra. The arias, "Quanta é bella" and "Un furtiva lagrima," are also on the video *Legends of Opera*. Color. In Italian. 125 minutes. Lyric video.

1991 Metropolitan Opera

Kathleen Battle stars as Adina with Luciano Pavarotti again portraying Nemorino in this Metropolitan Opera production by John Copley. Juan Pons is Belcore, Enzo Dara is Dulcamara and Korliss Uecker is Giannetta. The sets are by Beni Montresor. James Levine conducts the Metropolitan Opera Orchestra and Chorus. Brian Large directed the video. Color. In Italian with English subtitles. 129 minutes. DG video and laser.

1996 Lyons Opera

Robert Alagna stars as Nemorino in this Opéra de Lyon production directed by Frank Dunlop. The time of the action has been modernized to the 1930s. Brian Large directed the video for RM Arts. Color. In Italian. 130 minutes.

Early/related films

1914 Imp film

An early American film made by the Imp company was based on the libretto of the opera. About 20 minutes.

1930 Call of the Flesh

Ramon Novarro sings the "Cavatina" from the opera in this early MGM sound film about a café singer who becomes an opera star. Charles Brabin directed. Black and white. 110 minutes.

1941 Tagliavini/Bettoni film

This Italian film, with singing by Ferruccio Tagliavini and Vicenzo Bettoni, has an interesting conceit: the opera story is told in flashback. Love potion salesman Dr. Dulcamara makes a return visit to the village where his elixir solved Nemorino's love problem twenty years before and finds Nemorino and Adina's son facing the same problem. Armando Falconi is Dulcamara with Margherita Carosio as Adina, Roberto Villa as Nemorino, Giuseppe Rinaldi as their son, Carlo Romano as Belcore and Jone Salinas as Giannetta. Amleto Palermi directed the film released in the U.S. as *Elixir of Love*. Black and white. 85 minutes. In Italian. Bel Canto Society video.

1955 Bellissima

Luchino Visconti's film makes important use of themes from *L'Elisir d'Amore*. It opens with the opera being performed in a Rome broadcast studio and one gradually realizes that the magic elixirs of today are the movies. A film company announces it is looking for a child actress and Anna Magnani sets out to get her girl the role. The film director is played by the veteran film director Alessandro Blasetti whose every appearance is accompanied by the "Charlatan" music from the opera. Visconti also uses the aria "Quanto è bella" (How beautiful she is) as the ironic theme music for Magnani's plain child. The music was arranged by Franco Mannino. Black and white. In Italian. 112 minutes.

1985 Prizzi's Honor

A tenor is singing "Una furtiva lagrima" on stage during a Prizzi mob family celebration towards the climax of the film when the event is fire bombed by rival gangsters. John Huston directed. Color. 130 minutes. Vestron video.

1992 Lorenzo's Oil

Australian director George Miller features "Un furtiva lagrima" as sung by Tito Schipa in this harrowing film about a boy dying of a seemingly incurable disease. Parents Susan Sarandon and Nick Nolte refuse to accept his fate and set out to find a cure. Color. 135 minutes.

ELLIS, MARY
American soprano (1900-)

New York-born Mary Ellis made her debut at the Metropolitan Opera in 1918 as the Novice in the world premiere of *Suor Angelica*. She was just 18. She sang opposite both Caruso and Chaliapin in major operas but then four years later switched from opera to operetta and musical comedy. In 1924 she created the title role in Friml's *Rose Marie* and in 1932 moved to England. Her London stage shows include Ivor Novello's *Glamorous Night* in 1935 and *The Dancing Years* in 1939 and she played the role inspired by diva Mary Garden in Novello's 1943 *Arc de Triomphe*. Her film career began in England with *Bella Donna* in 1934 and ended with *The Three Worlds of Gulliver* in 1960. At the age of 95 she was still working in television. See IVOR NOVELLO (1937).

1934 Bella Donna
Ellis made her film debut in this British film about a woman who tries to poison her husband because of her love for an Egyptian. It was based on a Robert Hichens play and directed by Robert Milton. Black and white. 91 minutes.

1935 All the King's Horses
Ellis made her American screen debut in this Ruritanian operetta based on a stage musical by Edward Horan. It's a kind of musical *Prisoner of Zenda* with Carl Brisson playing both a king and an actor who looks like him. Ellis is his somewhat confused queen. Frank Tuttle directed. Paramount. Black and white. 85 minutes.

1936 Fatal Lady
The New York Times called this "a prima donna's vehicle, duly affording Miss Ellis opportunities of singing choice bravura passages in nearly every world capital." Ellis plays an opera diva who runs away after accusations of murder and sings under a false name. Back-stage intrigue and murder follow her to the new opera house but Walter Pidgeon finally solves the mystery. The film includes excerpts from *William Tell* and two imaginary operas, *Isabelle* with music by Gerard Carbonara and *Bal Masque* with music by Carbonara and Victor Young. Edward Ludwig directed. Paramount. Black and white. 72 minutes.

1936 Paris in Spring
Ellis plays a Paris nightclub singer opposite Tullio Carminati. He's a count who loves her but she ignores him until he makes her jealous by wooing young Ida Lupino. The songs are by Harry Revel and Mack Gordon and Lewis Milestone directed. Paramount. Black and white. 82 minutes.

1960 The Three Worlds of Gulliver
Ellis's last theatrical film was a British fantasy based on *Gulliver's Travels* with Kerwin Matthews as Gulliver. Ellis portrays Queen Brobdingnag, the forty-foot-tall ruler of the giants. Jack Sher directed. Color. 98 minutes.

ELMO, CLOE
Italian mezzo-soprano (1910-1962)

Elmo Close, the leading mezzo-soprano at La Scala from 1936 to 1945, began her career in Cagliari in 1934. She came to the Metropolitan Opera in 1947, sang Mistress Quickly in a Toscanini telecast of *Falstaff* and made American recordings. She returned to La Scala in 1951. She can also be seen on film as Carmen and Cherubino. See CARMEN (1948, 1951), FALSTAFF (1950), THE MARRIAGE OF FIGARO (1948).

ELVERHØJ
1828 stage work by Kuhlau

The Elf Hill is not strictly an opera but became the patriotic equivalent in Danish stage music history. Friedrich Kuhlau (1786-1832), a major Danish composer, wrote five singspiels but his major stage work is *Elverhøj*, a play by Johan Ludwig Heiberg for which he wrote songs and music. Created for a royal wedding, it tells the story of a girl raised by elves. Kuhlau based the music on Danish folk tunes arranged to fit the incidents in the play. One song, "Kong Christian stod ved højen mast" (King Christian stood by the high mast) became the Danish national anthem.

1902 Royal Danish Ballet film
The "Children's Dance" from *The Elf Hill* is performed by the Royal Danish Ballet in this film. The soloists are Gudrun Christen and Helga Smith. About 3 minutes. Print in the Danish Film Archive.

1909 Solborg Fjeldsøe sound film

The first film of the musical was a sound short made for Talende. It pictures singer Solborg Fjeldsøe performing an aria from *The Elf Hill* called "Der vanker en Ridder." About 4 minutes.

1910 Jørgen Lund film

Jørgen Lund portrays King Christian IV and also directed this film for Biorama. Carl Petersen is Erik Walkendorff, Agnes Lorentzen is Elisabeth Munk, Franz Skondrup is Albert Ebbesen and Victoria Petersen is Elisabeth. About 20 minutes.

1910 Gunnar Helsengreen film

Gunnar Helsengreen directed this film for Fotorama Film. Philip Bech stars as King Christian IV, Johannes Rich is Erik Walkendorf, Marie Nidermann is Elisabeth Munk, Pater Malberg is Albert Ebbesen, Martha Helsengreen is Martha and Jenny Roelsgaard is Agente. About 13 minutes.

1939 Svend Methling film

Svend Methling's film for Palladium gives prominence to the music of Kuhlau and was based on an adaptation by Gunnar Robert Hansen. The stars are Nicolai Neilendam, Carlo Wieth, Eva Heramb and Peter Poulson. Black and white. In Danish. 80 minutes.

1965 Bent Barfod animated film

Bent Barfod, one of the leading animation artists of Denmark, made an animated cartoon version of the story in 1965. Color. About 10 minutes.

EMMELINE

1996 opera by Picker

Santa Fe Opera commissioned composer Tobias Picker and librettist J.D. McClatchy to create the opera Emmeline. Based on a novel by Judith Rossner, it is a reworking of the Oedipus myth transposed to 19th century New England. The 13-year-old mill worker Emmeline is seduced, has a baby and gives it up for adoption. Twenty years later she marries a young man who she later discovers is her own son. This was the first opera by Picker and is composed in the conservative style now associated with modern American operas but incorporating some jazz syncopation and even the hymn "Rock of Ages." It premiered at Santa Fe on July 27, 1996.

1996 Santa Fe Opera

Patricia Racette stars as Emmeline in this world premiere production staged for Santa Fe Opera by Francesca Zambello. Curt Peterson plays her son-husband Curt, Victor Ledbetter is her seducer Mr. Maguire, Anne-Marie Owen is Aunt Hannah, Kevin Langan is Henry Mosher, Melanie Sarakatsannis is Sophie, Joseph Gayer is Mrs Bass and Herbert Perry is Pastor Avery. Robert Israel designed the effective set, Amy Appleyard did the lighting and Dunya Ramicova made the costumes. George Manahan conducted the Santa Fe Opera Orchestra. The opera was videotaped and telecast in the PBS *Great Performances* series. Color. In English. 115 minutes.

EMPRESS, THE

1993 TV opera by Gough

Composer Orlando Gough, librettist David Gale, director Jane Thorburn and producer Mark Lucas were asked to create a TV opera by Avril MacRory of England's Channel 4. They adapted a wordless play by Frank Wedekind called *The Empress of Newfoundland*. A doctor prescribes marriage as a cure for the Empress of Newfoundland who is ill. She rejects suitors who represent mind, money and power and chooses the strongest man in the world. When he leaves her, she kills herself. Amanda Dean sings the role of the Empress, Valerie Morgan is the Prime Minister, Richard Stuart is the Doctor and Mike Ahearne is the strong man with the voice of Jeremy Birchal. The opera was filmed in comic strip style and telecast on Channel 4 on Sept. 26, 1993. Color. In English.

ENESCU, GEORGE

Romanian composer (1881-1955)

Romania's greatest composer George Enescu wrote only one opera, the 1936 *Oedipe*, but it is considered a masterpiece. However, it has never been popular outside Romania and is rarely staged elsewhere. The libretto by Edmund Flegg is partially based on the Sophocles plays but tells the whole story of the tragic life of Oedipus from birth to death in an expressionist manner. The opera is on CD with José Van Dam as Oedipus but the only video comes from Romania.

1980 David Ohanesian video
Romanian baritone David Ohanesian, who became famous for his portrayal of Oedipus in the opera, stars in this Romanian stage production. The video is an off-air recording of a Romanian telecast. Color. In Romanian. 155 minutes. Opera Dubs video.

ENFANT ET LES SORTILÈGES, L'
1925 opera by Ravel

French novelist Colette wrote the libretto for this delightful Maurice Ravel opera about a naughty child sent to his room for misbehavior. In a tantrum he destroys toys, furniture and books and assaults the family cat. The maltreated objects comes to life and the scene moves outdoors where the child finally redeems himself with an act of kindness. See also MAURICE RAVEL.

1986 Netherlands Dance Theatre
This is a dance video with an opera soundtrack. Netherlands Dance Theatre dancers perform on the stage but the soundtrack comes from a 1961 opera recording. Francoise Ogéas sings the role of the child danced by Marly Knoben, Janine Collars sings the Mother danced by Roslyn Anderson and Camille Maurane sings the cat danced by Nacho Duato. Hans Hulscher produced and directed with choreography by Jirí Kylián and sets and costumes by John Macfarlane. Lorin Maazel conducts the Paris Orchestre National and RTF Chorus. Color. In French without subtitles. 50 minutes. Home Vision video.

1987 Glyndebourne Festival
Maurice Sendak designed the eye-catching sets for this Glyndebourne Festival production by Frank Corsaro. Cynthia Buchan stars as the Child with Fiona Kimm as both Mother and Cat, Malcolm Walker as Tomcat and Clock, François Loup as Armchair and Tree, Hyacinth Nicholls as Louis XV Chair and Bat and Thierry Dran as Teapot and Frog. Ronald Chase designed the slides and animation and Jenny Weston arranged the choreography. Simon Rattle conducts the London Philharmonic Orchestra, Glyndebourne Festival Chorus and Trinity Boys Choir. Tom Gutteridge directed the video. Color. In French with English subtitles. 46 minutes Home Vision video.

1993 Lyons Opera
This chamber version of the opera was re-orchestrated by Didier Punto for nine soloists and four intrumentalists and staged by the Opéra de Lyon Workshop. Isabelle Eschenbrenner stars as the Child with Marie Boyer as Mother, Chinese Cup and Dragonfly, Nathalie Dessay as Fire, Sylvaine Davene as Nightingale, Catherine Dubosc as the Princess, Jean-Louis Meunier, Christophe Lacassagne, Christopher Goldsack and Doris Lamprecht. Didier Punto conducts for the Atelier Lyrique de l'Opéra de Lyon. Moshe Leiser and Patrice Caurier created the production and filmed it. Color. In French with English subtitles. 52 minutes. On video.

ENGLANDER, ROGER
American TV director/producer (1935-)

Roger Englander, one of the real pioneers of television opera, was involved with producing Menotti operas for NBC television as early as 1948. He later produced *The Old Maid and the Thief*, Bell Telephone Hours, Leonard Bernstein programs (including *The Second Hurricane)* and *Omnibus* programs. Much of his later TV work was in filming non-operatic classical music. He has also produced stage productions and written an excellent beginner's guide to opera with stills of some of his early TV productions. See BELL TELEPHONE HOUR, LEONARD BERNSTEIN (1958), CAMERA THREE, AARON COPLAND (1961), THE MEDIUM (1948), THE OLD MAID AND THE THIEF (1953), THE SECOND HURRICANE (1960), THE TELEPHONE (1948).

ENGLISH NATIONAL OPERA

The English National Opera, which presents operas in English in the Coliseum in London, began at the Old Vic, then became the Sadler's Wells Opera and was renamed the ENO in 1973. It has been innovative and adventurous in its productions with new English operas, lesser known French works and radical stagings of classics. Its most famous productions on video are Jonathan Miller's Mafia *Rigoletto* and the award-winning *Xerxes*. See BILLY BUDD (1988), GIULIO CESARE (1984), GLORIANA (1984), MARY STUART (1982), THE MIKADO (1987), RIGOLETTO (1982), XERXES (1988).

ERKEL, FERENC
Hungarian composer (1810-1893)

Ferenc Erkel, the most important 19th century Hungarian opera composer, wrote a large number of operas but they are mostly unknown outside Hungary. The most famous and important is the 1861 *Bánk Bán*. Recordings of many Erkel operas are available on Hungarian labels including the popular *Hunyádi László*.

1914 Bánk Bán
Erkel's 1861 opera tells of a 13th century rebellion against a hated queen who is killed by a hero named Bánk bán. A film of the opera was made in 1914 by Hungarian director Mihály Kertéz who later became famous in Hollywood as Michael Curtiz. It stars actors from Jenö Janovic's theater at Kolozsvar. Palatine Bánk bán is portrayed by László Bakó, his wife Melinda by Erzsi Paulay, Queen Gertrud by Mari Jászai, and the peasant Tiborc by István Szentgyörgyi. The film was screened with the opera music. Black and white. About 60 minutes.

ERMIONE
1819 opera by Rossini

Gioachino Rossini's once-forgotten opera has been hailed in recent years as a masterpiece and is now on video and CD. Andrea Leone Tottolo's libretto, based on Racine's play *Andromaque*, tells the story of some ill-fated liaisons in the period following the Homeric war. The jealous, sex-obsessed and rather mad Ermione persuades Oreste (Orestes) to kill Pirro (Pyrrhus) who plans to marry Hector's widow Andromache instead of her. She then denies she gave the order. See also GIOACHINO ROSSINI.

1987 Pesaro Festival
Montserrat Caballé is Ermione in this Pesaro Festival production by Roberto De Simone which led to the opera being re-evaluated. Marilyn Horne is Andromaca, Chris Merritt is Pirro, Rockwell Blake is Oreste, Giuseppe Morino is Pilade and Giorgio Surjan is Fenicio. Enrico Job designed the sets and Gustav Kuhn conducted the Italian Youth Orchestra and the Budapest Radio Chorus. Ilio Catani directed the video. Color. In Italian. 154 minutes. Lyric video.

1995 Glyndebourne Festival
Anna Caterina Antonacci stars as Ermione in this powerful Glyndebourne Festival production by Graham Vick. Diana Montague sings the role of Andromaca, Jorge Lopez-Yanez is Pirro, Bruce Ford is Oreste, Paul Austin Kelly is Pilade, Paul Nilon is Attalo, Junile Unwin is Cleone, Lorna Windson ir Cefisa, Oliver Bridge is Astianatte, and Gwynne Howell is Fenicio. Richard Hudson designed the sets. Andrew Davis conducts the Glyndebourne Chorus and London Philharmonic Orchestra. Humphrey Burton directed the video for a May 30, 1995, Channel 4 telecast. Color. In Italian with English subtitles. 152 minutes. Warner Vision (England) video.

ERNANI
1844 opera by Verdi

Giuseppe Verdi's fifth opera, a rather full-blooded melodrama, made him famous. Francesco Maria Piave's libretto is based on Victor Hugo's play *Hernani* and tells the story of three men who desire the same woman in 16th century Spain. Elvira is the fiancée of Silva but loves the nobleman-turned-bandit Ernani. Don Carlo, the King of Spain, takes her hostage so the other two plot against him. In the end Ernani wins Elvira but has to kill himself because of a pledge of honor. See also GIUSEPPE VERDI.

1982 Teatro alla Scala
Four great Verdi singers star in this fine production by Luca Ronconi at Milan's Teatro alla Scala. Placido Domingo is the heroic bandit Ernani, Mirella Freni is the gentle heroine Elvira, Renato Bruson is the scheming Don Carlo and Nicolai Ghiaurov is the grandee Silva. Ezio Frigerio designed the sets and Riccardo Muti conducted the La Scala Orchestra and Chorus. Preben Montell directed the video. Color. In Italian with English subtitles. 135 minutes. HBO video.

1982 Opera Stories
This is a laserdisc highlights version of the opera based on the above La Scala production. Charlton Heston narrates the story of the opera and the history behind it from a castle in Spain and from the plains of Aragon. Keith Cheetham directed the framework material filmed in 1989. Color. In English and Italian with English subtitles. 52 minutes. Pioneer Artists laser •

1983 Metropolitan Opera

Luciano Pavarotti joins Sherrill Milnes and Ruggero Raimondi to create a beautifully sung Metropolitan Opera production by Pier Luigi Samaritani. Pavarotti dominates as the bandit Ernani with Milnes as Don Carlo, Raimondi as Silva and Leona Mitchell as Elvira. Samaritani designed the sets, Peter J. Hall designed the costumes and James Levine conducted the Metropolitan Opera Orchestra and Chorus. Kirk Browning directed the video taped on Dec. 17 and telecast on Dec. 21, 1983. Color. In Italian with English subtitles. 142 minutes. Paramount video.

Early/related films

1909 Albert Capellani film

Alberto Capellani directed this French film of the story for Pathé. It stars Henry Krauss, Jeanne Delvair and Paul Capellani. About 10 minutes.

1910 Francesca Bertini film

Italy's first film diva Francesca Bertini stars as Elvira in scenes from the Verdi opera. Geralamo Lo Savio directed. About 10 minutes.

1911 Spanish film

A Spanish film of the opera was made by the Barcelona Film company. It consists of highlight scenes from the opera. About 10 minutes.

1972 Il Caso Pisciotta

Eriprando Visconti's Italian film, which features excerpts of music from *Ernani*, is also concerned with bandits. A magistrate investigates the killing of *Salvatore Giuliano's* chief lieutenant by the Mafia. Color. In Italian. 98 minutes.

1982 Fitzcarraldo

This film contains a fine historical though fictional presentation of the opera. The protagonist Fitzcarraldo (Klaus Kinski) travels thousands of miles to see the last few moments of a Teatro Amazonas production of *Ernani* starring Enrico Caruso and Sarah Bernhardt. The short scene, staged by Werner Schroeter, is sung by Mietta Sighele, Veriano Luchetti and Dimiter Petkov with actors on stage. A singer in the pit provides the vocals for the non-operatic Bernhardt. The music is performed by the Venice Philharmonic. Color. In German. 157 minutes. Warner video.

ERWARTUNG

1909 opera by Schoenberg

Erwartung (Expectation) is a one-act one-person opera about a woman looking for her lover in a forest in the moonlight and worrying out loud about his infidelity with another woman. She eventually comes upon his bloody corpse but we suspect that she may have been the one who killed him. Arnold Schoenberg's opera, with a libretto by Marie Pappenheim, was composed in 1909 but not premiered until 1924. See also ARNOLD SCHOENBERG.

1989 Metropolitan Opera

Jessye Norman stars as the Woman in this Metropolitan Opera production by Göran Järvefelt with set designs by Hans Schavernoch. James Levine conducts the Metropolitan Opera Orchestra in the *Metropolitan Opera Presents* series. Brian Large directed the telecast on PBS on March 31 1989. The performance is on CD. Color. In German with English subtitles. 30 minutes.

ESSWOOD, PAUL

English countertenor (1942-)

Paul Esswood, one of the best-known countertenors in the world, made his debut in 1968 and has now sung around the world in both modern and baroque operas. He was featured in the famous Ponnelle-Harnoncourt Monteverdi opera cycle at Zurich in the late 1970s and created the title role of Akhnaten in the Philip Glass opera. See AKHNATEN (1985), L'INCORONAZIONE DI POPPEA (1979), IL RITORNO D'ULISSE IN PATRIA (1980).

ESTES, SIMON

American bass-baritone (1939-)

Simon Estes was born in Iowa but began his career with the Deutsche Oper in Berlin singing Ramfis in *Aida*. He won praise for Wagnerian roles and in 1978 became the first African-American man to sing at Bayreuth when he starred in *Der Fliegende Holländer*. In 1982 he made a triumphal entry to the Metropolitan as the Landgrave in *Tannhäuser*. He also sings in Italian and Russian operas and was the first Porgy at the Metropolitan in 1985. His *Dutchman* at Bayreuth is on video. See AIDA (1985), CARMEN (1988 film), DER FLIEGENDE HOLLÄNDER (1985), PLACIDO DOMINGO (1989), JESSYE NORMAN (1988), IL RITORNO D'ULISSE IN PATRIA (1980), SALOME (1990).

1990 Concert For Peace

Simon Estes sings with Frederica Von Stade in this concert filmed in Oslo, Norway. The music includes arias by Mozart and Handel, spirituals and the fourth movement of Mahler's Symphony No. 4. Audrey Hepburn and Gregory Peck hosted the program telecast on PBS in 1991. Color. 55 minutes.

ÉTOILE, L'
1877 opéra bouffe by Chabrier

Emmanuel Chabrier's charming comic opera *The Star* is about a mythical king caught in a Catch 22 quandary. King Ouf I likes to hold a public execution once a year and his choice for victim this year is a peddler called Lazuli. However, his astrologer says their stars are tied together and advises the king that he will die 24 hours after Lazuli. The peddler is immediately recognized as a person of real importance by the king and even wins the hand of Princess Laoula. Lazuli is a mezzo-soprano trouser role. See also EMMANUEL CHABRIER.

1986 Lyons Opera

Colette Alliot-Lugaz stars as Lazuli in the production by Louis Erlo at the Opéra de Lyon. George Gautier plays the King, Ghyslaine Raphanel in the Princess, François Le Roux is the pompous Hérisson de Porc Epic and Antoine David is his secretary Tapioca. John Eliot Gardiner conducts the Lyons Opera Orchestra and Chorus. Bernard Maigrot directed the video. Color. In French. 105 minutes. RM Arts. Polygram (France) video/Japanese laserdisc.

EUGENE ONEGIN
1879 opera by Tchaikovsky

A deceptively simple but resonant bitter-sweet love story provides the basis for *Yevgeny Onegin*, Tchaikovsky's best loved opera. The libretto by Konstantin Shikovsky and the composer is based on a famous Pushkin verse novel. It tells of the love of the innocent Tatyana for the world-weary aristocrat Eugene Onegin. She writes him a passionate love letter but he rejects her and flirts with her sister, the fiancée of his friend Lensky. They duel and Lensky is killed. Years later Onegin discovers that he loves Tatyana but she is married to another and it is too late. Tatyana's "Letter Aria" is one of the most famous arias in Russian opera. See also PYOTR TCHAIKOVSKY.

1958 Roman Tikhomirov film

Roman Tikhomirov, who specialized in movies of Russian operas, made this film of *Eugene Onegin* with actors dubbed by top singers. Tatyana is sung by the great soprano Galina Vishnevskaya and acted by Ariadna Shengelaya, wife of Georgian filmmaker Eldar Shengelaya. Eugene Onegin is sung by Yevgeny Kibkalo acted by Vadim Medvedev, Anton Gregoriev sings Lensky acted by Igor Ozerov, Ivan Petrov both sings and acts Gremin and Olga is sung by Larissa Adveyeva and acted by Svetlana Nemolyneva. Alexander Ivanovsky wrote the adaptation and Yegeny Shapiro photographed it. Boris Haikin conducts the Kirov Opera Orchestra and Chorus. Lenfilm. Color. In Russian with English subtitles. 104 minutes. Corinth Video.

1962 Munich State Opera

Fritz Wunderlich sings the role of Lensky with Herman Prey as Eugene Onegin in this telecast of a Bavarian State Opera production in Munich. Brigitte Fassbaender is Olga and Ingeborg Bremert is Tatyana. Joseph Keilberth conducts the Bavarian State Opera Orchestra. Black and white. In German. 105 minutes. Lyric Legato Classics Archives video.

1968 Teresa Stratas film

Teresa Stratas stars as Tatyana with Herman Prey as Eugene Onegin in this German-language film of the opera made in Stuttgart for television. Vaclav Neumann conducts the Stuttgart Opera Orchestra. Color. In German. 110 minutes. Lyric video.

1984 Kirov Opera

Sergei Leiferkus stars as Eugene Onegin with Tatyana Novikova as Tatyana in this Kirov Opera production from Leningrad. Yuri Marusin portrays Lensky, Larissa Dyadkova is Olga, Nikolai Okhotnikov is Prince Gremin and

Evgenya Gorskovskaya is Madame Larina. Yuri Temirkanov conducts the Kirov Opera Orchestra and Chorus. Color. In Russian with English subtitles. 155 minutes. Kultur video.

1985 Chicago Lyric Opera
Mirella Freni is superb as Tatyana in this Lyric Opera of Chicago production by Pier Luigi Samaritani who also designed the sets and costumes. Wolfgang Brendel is Eugene, Peter Dvorsky is Lensky, Nicolai Ghiaurov is Gremin and Sandra Walker is Olga. Bruno Bartoletti conducts the Lyric Opera Orchestra and Chorus and Chicago City Ballet. Kirk Browning directed the video. Color. In Russian with English subtitles. 157 minutes. Home Vision video.

1988 Petr Weigl film
Petr Weigl's beautiful film was shot on location with Czech actors dubbed by opera singers. Teresa Kubiak sings the role of Tatyana acted by Magdalena Vasaryova, Bernd Weikl portrays Eugene Onegin acted by Michal Docolomansky, Stuart Burrows sings Lensky acted by Emil Horvath, Nicolai Ghiaurov sings Gremin acted by Premysl Koci, Julia Hamari sings Olga acted by Kamila Magalova and Anna Reynolds sings Madame Larina acted by Antonie Hegerlikova. George Solti conducts the Royal Opera House Orchestra and John Aldiss Choir. Color. In Russian with English subtitles. 116 minutes London video.

1993 Bolshoi Opera
Galina Gorchakova sings the role of Tatyana in this Bolshoi Opera production by Boris Pokrovsky with sets designed by Alexander Levental. Alexander Lazarev conducts the Bolshoi Opera Orchestra and Choir. Brian Large directed the video. NVC Arts. Color. In Russian. 117 minutes. On video.

1994 Glyndebourne Festival
Graham Vick's magical Glyndebourne Festival production stars Russian soprano Elena Prokina as Tatyana and Polish baritone Wojciech Drabowicz as Eugene Onegin. Both are superb singers and actors and they get excellent support from Martin Thompson as Lensky, Louise Winter as Olga, Frode Osen as Gremin, Yvonne Minton as Larina and Ludmilla Filatova as Filipyevna. Richard Hudson designed the sets and Glyndebourne music director Andrew Davis

conducted the London Philharmonic Orchestra and Glyndebourne Chorus. Humphrey Burton directed this outstanding video in June 1994 and it was telecast on July 24, 1994. Color. In Russian. 156 minutes. Warner Vision (England) video.

Early/related films

1911 Vasilij Goncharov film
This Russian silent film by Vasilij Goncharov was the first based on the Tchaikovsky opera. A. Goncharova stars as Tatyana, Andrei Gromov is Lensky and P. Biryukov is Onegin. Black and white. About 14 minutes. Print in Russian Film Archive.

1935 Anna Karenina
Anna Karenina (Greta Garbo) and her lover Count Vronsky (Fredric March) attend a production of *Eugene Onegin* at the Moscow Opera after she has left her husband. Their presence is considered a scandal. The opera was chosen by music director Herbert Stothart for its ironic effect as it is about a woman who refuses to leave her husband for a lover. What is actually seen on stage is the Act I "Dance of the Peasants." Clarence Brown directed. Black and white. 95 minutes.

1986 Onegin
Onegin is a film of John Cranko's ballet adaptation of the Tchaikovsky opera and Pushkin poem directed by Norman Campbell. It stars Sahina Sallemann as Tatyana, Frank Augustyn as Eugene Onegin, Jeremy Ranson as Lensky and Cynthia Lucas as Olga. Kurt-Heinz Stolze arranged Tchaikovsky's music for the ballet. The film was first shown on CBC-TV in Canada on Nov. 9, 1986. Color. 120 minutes.

EVA
1911 operetta by Lehár

Eva has never been one of Franz Lehár's most popular operettas but is still much liked in Spain and Italy. It is subtitled *The Factory Girl* and the plot revolves around the love life of factory worker Eva and her efforts to stave off attention from factory owner Octave Flaubert. By the end of the operetta, however, she has agreed to marry him. *Eva* was staged in London and New York and its big waltz was popular. The libretto is by

A. M. Willner and Robert Bodanzky. See also FRANZ LEHÁR.

1918 Alfred Deesy film
A silent film of the Lehár operetta was made in Hungary during the period of the Councils' Republic. Alfred Deesy directed. About 60 minutes.

1936 Magda Schneider film
Magda Schneider stars as Eva in this German film of the operetta directed by Johannes Riemann. Hans Ruhmann is Octave with a cast that includes Hans Sohnker, Adele Sandrock and Hans Moser. The adaptation was made by Ernst Marischka. Black and white. In German. 94 minutes.

1992 Sandro Massimini video
Highlights from *Eva* are sung by Italian operetta master Sandro Massimini and his associates on the Italian TV series *Operette, Che Passione!* Featured are "Sia pur chimera, felicità," "Oh Parigina bella ed legante" and "Perchè tremate così." Color. In Italian. About 15 minutes. Ricordi (Italy) video.

EVANS, GERAINT
Welsh baritone (1922-1992)

Sir Geraint Evans, one of the great figures in Welsh opera, was much admired in comic roles like Don Pasquale and Falstaff. He joined Covent Garden in 1948 and while there created roles in two operas by Benjamin Britten. He became a regular at Glyndebourne in Mozart roles and sang Falstaff at the Metropolitan in 1964. There is a film of him as Falstaff at Glyndebourne in 1960, a video of his 1979 *Don Pasquale* with the Welsh National Opera and a video of his performance as Coppelius in *The Tales of Hoffmann* at Covent Garden in 1981. See DON PASQUALE (1979), FALSTAFF (1960), THE TALES OF HOFFMANN (1981).

EWING, MARIA
American mezzo-soprano (1950-)

Maria Ewing can be watched on video changing from a delightful Cherubino to an alluring Carmen to a depraved Salome and she is wonderful as all three. Ewing, who began her career in 1973 under the guidance of James Levine, broke into the big time in 1976 singing Cherubino at Salzburg and the Met. Her other Met roles include Rosina, Carmen, Zerlina and Dorabella and she was also popular at Glyndebourne under the direction of then husband Peter Hall. Her *Carmen* and *Salome* videos are particularly fine. See THE BARBER OF SEVILLE (1982), CARMEN (1985/1991), LES DIALOGUES DES CARMÉLITES (1987), L'INCORONAZIONE DI POPPEA (1984), THE MARRIAGE OF FIGARO (1976), MOZART REQUIEM (1988), SALOME (1991).

F

FALENA, UGO
Italian film director (1875-1931)

Italian pioneer filmmaker Ugo Faleno directed many early cinema versions of operas and opera subjects, often starring diva Francesca Bertini. He usually worked for the Film d'Arte Italiana and Bernini Film companies. See ADRIANA LECOUVREUR (1918), CARMEN (1909), CAVALLERIA RUSTICANA (1916), FRANCESCA DA RIMINI (1911), OTELLO (1909), RIGOLETTO (1910), LA TRAVIATA (1909), IL TROVATORE (1909).

FALL, LEO
Austrian composer (1873-1925)

Leo Fall was not very successful as an opera composer but when he turned to operettas he became a rival for Lehár and Straus. He had a genuine gift for melody and is sometimes considered the Viennese equivalent of Offenbach. He first won fame with *Der Fidele Bauer* (1907), *Die Dollarprinzessin* (1907) and *Die Geschiedene Frau* (1908). The most popular of his later operettas are *Die Rose von Stambul* (1916) and *Madame Pompadour* (1922), considered his masterpiece. Many of his operettas were staged in New York and London and some are still popular on stage in Germany. Joan Sutherland included six of his tunes in her influential record album *The Golden Age of Operetta*. See also DIE DOLLARPRINZESSIN, DER FIDELE BAUER, DIE GESCHIEDENE FRAU, MADAME POMPADOUR, DIE ROSE VON STAMBOUL.

FALLA, MANUEL DE
Spanish composer (1876-1946)

Manuel De Falla is the most important Spanish composer of the 20th century but his impact on opera has been relatively small. He created two popular one-act operas, *La Vida Breve* (1904) and *El Retablo de Maese Pedro* (1923). The cantata called *Atlántida* was unfinished at his death but is highly ranked. Falla also composed six zarzuelas but they have not found popularity. See EL RETABLO DE MAESE PEDRO

1990 When the Fire Burns...
A documentary film on the life and music of Manuel De Falla. It includes an extract from his opera *La Vida Breve* with Gabriel Moreno as the Cantaor (singer) and Carmen Casarrubios as the solo dancer. There are extracts from his other major musical works as well as interviews and places associated with his music. Edward Atienza is the narrator and Larry Weinstein directed the video. Color. In English and Spanish with English subtitles. 84 minutes. London video (with *El Retablo de Maese Pedro*).

FALSTAFF
1893 opera by Verdi

Falstaff was Verdi's last opera and many consider it his masterpiece. Librettist Arrigo Boito made a brilliant adaptation of Shakespeare's *The Merry Wives of Windsor* with additions from the Henry IV plays. The opera premiered at La Scala with Victor Maurel as Falstaff and seven years later Maurel was filmed in the role in the first sound opera film. The vain, fat knight Sir John Falstaff is caught sending the same love letter to both Alice and Meg. Alice's husband Ford is suspicious and Falstaff ends up in the Thames in a laundry basket. He is humiliated a second time when he agrees to meet Alice in the forest. See also GIUSEPPE VERDI.

1950 NBC Toscanini telecast
An historic concert version of the opera with Arturo Toscanini conducting a NBC telecast. Many consider this one of the greatest operatic performances. The singers are Giuseppe Valdengo as Falstaff, Herva Nelli as Alice, Nan Merriman as Mistress Page, Cloe Elmo as Mistress Quickly, Teresa Stich-Randall as Nanetta and Frank Guarrera as Ford. Toscanini conducts the NBC Symphony Orchestra and the Robert Shaw Chorale. The telecast was produced by Don Gillis and directed by Doug Rodgers. Black and white. In Italian. 141 minutes.

1960 Glyndebourne Festival
Geraint Evans stars as Falstaff in this famous Glyndebourne Festival production televised by the BBC on Sept. 15, 1960. The cast includes Ilva Ligabue, Oralia Dominguez, Hugues Cuenod, Mariella Adani, Juan Oncina and Sesto Bruscantini.

Osbert Lancaster designed the sets and costumes and Vittorio Gui led the Royal Philharmonic Orchestra and Glyndebourne Festival Chorus. The film was produced for BBC television by Peter Ebert and Noble Wilson. Black and white. In Italian. 145 minutes. Film in National Film Archive, London.

1976 Glyndebourne Festival

Jean-Pierre Ponnelle was in peak form when he staged this exuberant production emphasizing the comedy of the opera. Donald Gramm is delightful in the role of Falstaff, but then everyone is good. Benjamin Luxon is Ford, Nucci Condo is Mistress Quickly, Kay Griffel is Alice, Reni Penkova is Meg, Max-René Cosotti is Fenton and Elizabeth Gale is Nanetta. John Pritchard conducted the London Philharmonic Orchestra and Glyndebourne Choir while Dave Heather directed the video. Color. In Italian with English subtitles. 123 minutes. VAI video.

1979 Götz Friedrich film

Götz Friedrich shot this version of the Verdi opera on a sound stage with Gabriel Bacquier as the Shakespearean knight. The sound is post-synchronized so the singers have the opportunity for some strenuous acting. Karan Armstrong is Alice Ford, Marta Szirmay is Mistress Quickly, Jutta-Renate Iholoff is Nannetta, Max-René Cosotti is Fenton and Richard Stillwell is Ford. Jörg Neumann and Thomas Riccabona designed the sets. Sir Georg Solti conducted the Vienna Philharmonic Orchestra, the Vienna State Opera Chorus, the Berlin Deutsch Opera Chorus and the Schönberg Boys Choir. Color. In Italian with English subtitles. 126 minutes. London video and laser.

1982 Salzburg Festival

Giuseppe Taddei is a most believable Falstaff in this Salzburg Festival production staged by Herbert von Karajan. This is a solid but conventional production with good live sound and first class singing. Raina Kabaivanska is Alice, Christa Ludwig is Mistress Quickly, Janet Perry is Nanetta, Francisco Araiza is Fenton and Rolando Panerai is Ford. Karajan leads the Vienna Philharmonic Orchestra and Vienna State Opera Chorus. Karajan and Ernst Wild made the video. Color. In Italian. 135 minutes. Sony Classical video/laser.

1982 Royal Opera, Covent Garden

Renato Bruson stars as Falstaff in this lively Covent Garden production by Ronald Eyre. Katia Ricciarelli is Mistress Ford, Brenda Boozer is Meg, Lucia Valentini Terrani is Mistress Quickly, Barbara Hendricks is Nanetta, Dalmacio Gonzalez is Fenton and Leo Nucci is Ford. Hyden Griffin Carlo designed the sets. Carlo Maria Giulini conducted the Royal Opera House Orchestra and Chorus and Brian Large directed the video. Color. In Italian with English subtitles. 141 minutes. HBO video/Pioneer laser.

1982 Opera Stories

A highlights version of the above Royal Opera production with Charlton Heston telling the story of the opera and setting the scenes. Keith Cheetham directed the framework material shot in 1989. Color. In English and Italian with subtitles. 52 minutes. Pioneer Artists laser.

1992 Metropolitan Opera

Paul Plishka stars as Falstaff with Mirella Freni as Alice and Marilyn Horne as Mistress Quickly in this Metropolitan Opera production. Franco Zeffirelli designed and staged the original 1964 production restaged by Paul Mills with emphasis on the humor. Barbara Bonney is Nannetta, Frank Lopardo is Fenton and Bruno Pola is Ford. James Levine conducts the Metropolitan Orchestra and Chorus. Brian Large directed the video taped on Oct. 10, 1992 and telecast Sept. 13, 1993. Color. In Italian with English subtitles. 126 minutes. DG video.

Early/related films

1900 First sound opera film

Victor Maurel, the French baritone who created the role of Falstaff at La Scala, was seen and heard as Falstaff in the first sound opera film. It was shown in Paris on June 8, 1900, at the Phono-Cinéma-Théâtre at the Paris Exhibition using a synchronized phonographic cylinder. The film was made by Clément Maurice. Also on the program and sharing first honors were films of Maurel in *Don Giovanni* and Emile Cossira in *Romeo et Juliette*. Black and white. About 3 minutes.

SILENT OPERA FILMS

There are many early *Falstaff* films based on the Shakespeare play they do not appear to have a connection to the opera. A 1911 French film by

Henri Desfontaines, however, may have been based on the opera libretto. French film critic Jean Mitry says it was but Shakespeare expert Robert Hamilton Ball disagrees in his definitive book *Shakespeare on Silent Film*.

SHAKESPEARE FILMS

The most interesting modern film based on the Shakespeare character is Orson Welles' 1966 *Falstaff*, also known as *Chimes at Midnight*. Like the Verdi opera it is a combination of all the plays in which Falstaff appears, and Welles is superb in the role. Black and white. In English. 115 minutes.

FALSTAFF BY SALIERI

1799 opera

Antonio Salieri's likeable comic opera *Falstaff*, which preceed Verdi's, is one of the earliest operas based on a Shakespeare play. Librettist Carlo Prospero Defranceschi adapted *The Merry Wives of Windsor* with such skill that it inspired Mozart's rival to compose one of his most enjoyable scores. The story concentrates on Falstaff and his relationship with the Fords and the Pages and omits the young lovers. It has been successfully revived. See also ANTONIO SALIERI.

1995 Schwetzingen Festival

John Del Carlo stars as Falstaff in this Schwetzingen Festival revival production of the opera staged by Michael Hampe and taped for telecast. Teresa Ringholz is Alice Ford and Richard Croft is Ford. Arnold Östman conducts the Stuttgart Radio Symphony Orchestra. Color. In Italian. 140 minutes.

FANCIULLA DEL WEST, LA

1910 opera by Puccini

The Girl of the Golden West was the name of the American play by David Belasco on which Puccini based this opera. The libretto by Carlo Zangarini and Guelfo Civinini follows the play fairly closely. Minnie, the "girl" of the title, runs a saloon in a gold mining town and falls in love with stranger Dick Johnson. He turns out to be a bandit wanted by the miners but she saves his life anyway. There were many non-operatic films based on the play in the silent era. There are presently three videos of the opera and Placido Domingo stars as Johnson in all three. See also GIACOMO PUCCINI.

1983 Royal Opera House

Carol Neblett sings the role of Minnie in this atmospheric Covent Garden production with sets by Ken Adams, the designer of the James Bond films. She is ably supported by Placido Domingo as Dick Johnson with Silvano Carroli as Sheriff Jack Rance, his nemesis. Francis Egerton is Nick, Robert Lloyd is Ashby and Gwynne Howell is Jake Wallace. Piero Faggoni directed the production and designed the costumes and lighting while Nello Santi conducted the Royal Opera House Orchestra and Chorus. John Vernon directed the video. Color. In Italian with English subtitles. 139 minutes. HBO video.

1991 Teatro alla Scala

Placido Domingo steals the limelight as Dick Johnson in this massive La Scala production by Jonathan Miller. Minnie is Mara Zampieri with Juan Pons as an almost sympathetic Sheriff Rance. Sergio Bertocchi is Nick, Luigi Roni is Ashby and Antonio Salvador is Sonora. The realistic set designs are by Stephanos Lazaridis. Lorin Maazel conducted the La Scala Orchestra and Chorus while John Michael Phillips directed the video. Color. In Italian with subtitles. 142 minutes. Home Vision video & on laser.

1992 Metropolitan Opera

Barbara Daniels is a warm-hearted Minnie in this much praised realistic production by Giancarlo Del Monaco. Placido Domingo is very strong as Dick Johnson and Sherrill Milnes is in excellent form as his implacable enemy Rance. Michael Scott designed the sets and costumes and Leonard Slatkin conducted the Metropolitan Opera Orchestra and Chorus. Brian Large directed the video and telecast. Color. In Italian with English subtitles. 140 minutes. DG Video/ Japanese laser.

Early/related Films

1915 Cecil B. De Mille film

Cecil B. De Mille directed the first film of the David Belasco play with Mabel Van Buren as Minnie and Theodore Roberts as Dick Johnson. Jesse Lasky had acquired the movie rights to Belasco's theatrical productions and Belasco said this famous film achieved a realism he could not match on stage. Black and white. About 70 minutes.

1923 Sylvia Breamer film

Sylvia Breamer stars as Minnie with J. Warren Kerrigan as Dick Johnson in this silent film of the play directed by Edwin Carewe. First National. Black and white. About 65 minutes.

1930 Ann Harding film

Ann Harding is Minnie and James Rennie is Dick Johnson in this film based on the Belasco play and directed by John Francis Dillon. First National. Black and white. 78 minutes.

1938 MacDonald/Eddy film

MGM did not want to use the Puccini music for their Jeanette MacDonald/ Nelson Eddy film of the story so the studio commissioned a new score from Sigmund Romberg. It was not his best. In this version Jeanette becomes Mary Robbins but she's still a saloon lady with a heart of gold that melts for bandit Eddy and she still plays poker with Rance (Walter Pidgeon) for his life. Robert Z. Leonard directed. Black and white. 120 minutes. MGM/UA video.

1993 The Man Without a Face

Loner Mel Gibson plays a 78 rpm record of Jussi Björling singing "Ch'ella mi creda libero" as he sits alone in his house reciting the opening lines of the *Aeneid*. Gibson also directed this film about a teacher with a scarred face who mentors a 12-year-old with problems. Color. 114 minutes.

FARINELLI
Italian male soprano (1705-1782)

Farinelli was a famous castrato singer and a major cultural figure in 18th century Europe. He was born Carlo Broschi, made his debut in Naples in 1720 and was trained by Nicola Porpora. It was said he had a three and one-half octave range, could sing 250 notes in a row and sustain a single note for a minute. Farinelli lived in London for three years singing with Handel's competitors and then quit the stage. He spent the next two decades in Spain singing for and advising Philip V and Ferdinand VI about opera, music and horses. After he retired to Bologna he was visited by the great musicians of the time including Mozart and Gluck.

1994 Farinelli

Gérard Corbiau's film is a visually opulent biography which focuses on Farinelli's relationship with his composer brother Riccardo Broschi, with his teacher Nicola Porpora and with Handel. There are elaborate re-creations of opera productions of the period. Among the featured castrato arias are Porpora's "Alto Giove" from *Polifemo* , Broschi's "Son qual nave" from *Artaserse* and "Ombra fedele anch'io" from *Idaspe*. They are staged with the supposed sound of a male soprano created by fusing the voices of soprano Ewa Mallas-Godlewska and countertenor Derek Lee Ragin. The sound is extraordinary. Also featured are arias from Handel's *Rinaldo* and Hasse's *Cleofide*. Farinelli is played by Stéfano Dionisi with Jeroen Krabbe as Handel and Enrico Lo Verso as Broschi. The superb production design is by Gianni Quaranta and the music is played by Christophe Rousset with Les Talens Lyriques. Color. In Italian, French and English. 100 minutes.

FARRAR, GERALDINE
American soprano (1882-1967)

Geraldine Farrar, a Massachusetts-born soprano who made her early career in Germany, joined the Metropolitan Opera in New York in 1906. She made her debut as Juliet in Gounod's *Roméo and Juliette* and became one of the glories of the Met's Golden Age. She sang at the Met until 1922 in a variety of roles but was most popular as Butterfly and Carmen. Her success in *Carmen* led producer Jesse Lasky to invite her to make films. Even without her voice she had great appeal and a winning personality and became a real movie star. She was helped by having a major filmmaker, Cecil B. De Mille, as the director of her first six films. She was so popular that her numerous female fans became known as Gerryflappers. She made fourteen films before giving up the movies in 1920. See CARMEN (1915).

1915 Maria Rosa

Farrar made this Cecil B. De Mille film before *Carmen*, supposedly as a cinematic warm-up, but it was not released until afterwards. She portrays a Catalan woman who is the center of a bitter rivalry between two men, Wallace Reid and Pedro de Cordoba. Paramount. Black and white. About 70 minutes.

1915 Temptation

Farrar portrays an opera singer, the villain is an opera impresario (dressed like the Met's Giulio Gatti-Casazza) and the hero is an opera composer. Farrar almost has to make the ultimate sacrifice to help the composer but is saved at the last minute. Cecil B. De Mille directed with an eye on the Metropolitan Opera. Paramount. Black and white. About 70 minutes.

1916 Joan the Woman

Geraldine Farrar is outstanding as Joan of Arc in this superb film about the French heroine written by Jeanie Macpherson. This was the first of director Cecil B. De Mille's film epics. The story is framed within a soldier's dream during World War I in France. Wallace Reid portrays the English lover who eventually betrays her. Some of the film was made in color in the Wyckoff Process. About 120 minutes.

1917 The Woman God Forgot

Farrar portrays a daughter of Montezuma who falls in love with a Spanish captain during the Cortez invasion of Mexico. She betrays her people but finds consolation in Christianity under the direction of one of that religion's great promoters, Cecil B. De Mille. Artcraft. Black and white. About 70 minutes.

1917 The Devil Stone

The last Farrar film directed by Cecil B. De Mille and produced by Jesse Lasky. She portrays a Breton fisherwoman in a story about a priceless emerald with a curse on it. She later gets rich so she has a chance to wear the fine clothes her fans expected. Artcraft. Black and white. About 70 minutes.

1918 The Hell Cat

In Farrar's first film for Goldwyn Pictures, she portrays Pancho O'Brien, the high-spirited but beautiful daughter of an Irish ranch owner. She is loved by the sheriff but prefers the outlaw in this melodramatic love story. Reginald Barker directed. Black and white. About 80 minutes.

1918 The Turn of the Wheel

Farrar is a beautiful American woman on vacation in Monte Carlo who falls in love with a gambler and helps him win a fortune. When he's arrested for wife murder, she sets out to find who really did it. Reginald Barker directed for Goldwyn. Black and white. About 70 minutes.

1919 Flame of the Desert

Farrar plays Isabelle Channing, a lady who falls in love with a charming sheik (Lou Tellegen) in Egypt. A few reels later he rescues her and turns out to be a noble Englishman in disguise. Reginald Barker directed for Goldwyn. Black and white. About 70 minutes.

1919 Shadows

Farrar is a devoted wife and mother but she was once a dance hall girl in Alaska. A friend of her husband finds out and attempts blackmail. Milton Sills is her co-star. Reginald Barker directed for Goldwyn. Black and white. About 70 minutes.

1919 The Stronger Vow

This is a kind of Spanish grand opera variation on *Romeo and Juliet* with Farrar in love with the man (Milton Sills) she believes killed her brother in a family feud. Reginald Barker directed for Goldwyn. Black and white. About 80 minutes.

1919 The World and Its Women

Farrar portrays a famous opera singer and is seen on stage in a scene from Massenet's *Thais*. Off stage she is in love with a Russian prince (Lou Tellegen) who rescues her from the Bolshevists during the Revolution. They escape to America together. Frank Lloyd directed. Goldwyn. Black and white. About 80 minutes.

1920 The Woman and the Puppet

Pierre Louys wrote the novel and play on which the film is based but the shadow of *Carmen* is evident. Farrar is a Spanish cigarette maker who dances wonderfully and is loved by a nobleman. She scorns him because she believes he has tried to buy her. Reginald Barker directed for Goldwyn. Black and white. About 80 minutes.

1920 The Riddle: Woman

Farrar's last film was directed by Edward José, the man who directed Caruso's and Cavalieri's unsuccessful movies. He was apparently not a good director for opera singers; Farrar hated him and the film so much that she gave up moviemaking. The story derives from a Danish play about a woman blackmailed by a former lover. Pathé. Black and white. About 80 minutes.

FARRELL, EILEEN
American soprano (1920-)

Eileen Farrell began her singing career in concerts and didn't make her stage debut until after singing opera on screen. She was the voice of opera singer

Marjorie Lawrence in a 1955 film biography and made her own debut in 1956 as Santuzza in Tampa. She made her first appearance at the Metropolitan in 1960 as Gluck's Alcestis and sang at the Met for five seasons. She was also noted for her Wagnerian heroines on concert stage. Farrell made no more films but she did sing on television and left a splendid legacy of records. See also SPOLETO (1959).

1955 Interrupted Melody
Eileen Farrell is outstanding as the voice of Australian soprano Marjorie Lawrence in this well-crafted film biography. It contains excellent opera sequences from Lawrence's debut in Monte Carlo through her successes in Paris to her triumphs at the Metropolitan. Farrell recorded nine arias for Eleanor Parker who portrays Lawrence on screen. There are stage scenes from *La Bohème*, *Il Trovatore*, *Madama Butterfly*, *Carmen*, *Samson et Dalila*, *Die Walküre* and *Tristan und Isolde*. Curtis Bernhardt directed. Color. 106 minutes. MGM-UA video.

1960 The Creative Performer
Leonard Bernstein featured Farrell on his 1960 CBS television program *The Creative Performer*. She sings the "Suicidio" aria from Ponchielli's *La Gioconda* with accompaniment by the New York Philharmonic. William A. Graham directed the Jan 31 telecast. Black and white. 60 minutes. Video at MTR.

FAUST
1859 opera by Gounod

Charles Gounod's opera was by far the most popular opera in the world at the beginning of the century and its arias among the best known. The Faust legend itself is one of the favorite subjects of filmmakers with at least fifty movies, most based to a certain extent on the opera. Gounod's music was played with the silent film versions even when they were not based on the opera. The opera is based on Goethe's great play but the focus of Jules Barbier and Michel Carré's libretto is on Faust's love affair with Marguerite. Faust promises his soul to Mephistopheles if he can become young again and have Marguerite. After she has been seduced, her brother Valentin challenges Faust to a duel and is killed. Marguerite goes mad, kills her baby, is sentenced to death and is forgiven by heaven. The opera is also a central plot concept in *Phantom of the Opera* movies. See also CHARLES GOUNOD, THE PHANTOM OF THE OPERA.

1936 Anne Ziegler color film
Anne Ziegler stars as Marguerite, Webster Booth is Faust and Dennis Hoey is Mephistopheles in this British highlights version of the opera. It is sung in English, was directed by Albert Hopkins and was shot in an early color system. Critics consider this one of the worst opera films ever made. Color. In English. 63 minutes.

1949 Faust and the Devil
Italo Tajo stars as Mephistopheles in *La Leggenda di Faust*, an Italian-American film of the opera. Gino Mattera plays Faust, Nelly Corradi portrays Marguerite on screen with her singing done by Ornella Fineschi, Gilles Quéant is Valentin and Thérèse Dorny is Martha. Carmine Gallone directed for producer Gregor Rabinovitch and Columbia Pictures. Black and white. In Italian. 90 minutes.

1963 Richard Tucker on Firestone
Richard Tucker sings Faust in this highlights version of the opera telecast on June 16, 1963 on the *Voice of Firestone* television show. Mary Costa is Marguerite and Jerome Hines is Mephistopheles. The scenes are staged with sets and extras. Harry John Brown conducts the orchestra. The opera is on the video *A Firestone French Opera Gala*. Black and white. In French with English introductions. 16 minutes. VAI video.

1973 Scotto/Ghiaurov in Japan
Renata Scotto is a splendid Marguerite and Alfredo Kraus a superb Faust in this classic production of the opera in Tokyo taped live on Sept. 9, 1973. Nicolai Ghiaurov is exceptionally strong as Mephistopheles and Lorenzo Saccomani is fine as Valentin. Milena Dal Piva is Siebel, Anna Di Stasio is Marthe and Guido Mazzini is Wagner. Paul Ethuin conducts the Lyrica Italiana Orchestra and Chorus. Color. In French with Japanese subtitles. 159 minutes. Lyric Legato Classics video.

1973 Who's Afraid of Opera? series
Joan Sutherland stars in this highlights version of the opera directed by Canadian filmmaker Ted Kotcheff. Sutherland tells the story to three puppets and performs the role of Marguerite with Ian Caley as Faust, Pieter Van Der Stolk as Mephistopheles and Margreta Elkins as Siébel. The dialogue is in English but the arias are sung in French. The music is played by the London Symphony Orchestra conducted by Richard Bonynge with sets designed

by George Djurkovic. Color. In English and French. 30 minutes. Kultur video.

1975 Paris Opéra
Nicolai Gedda sings Faust with Mirella Freni as Marguerite and Roger Soyer as Mephistopheles in this production by Jorge Lavelli at the Théâtre National L'Opéra de Paris. Tom Krause sings the role of Valentin and Charles Mackerras conducts the Paris Opéra Orchestra and Chorus. Color. In French. 159 minutes. Lyric video/ Japanese video and laser.

1985 Philadelphia Opera
James Morris sings the role of Mephistopheles, Valerie Masterson is Marguerite and Alain Vanzo is Faust in this Opera Company of Philadelphia production by Grethe Holly. Gino Quilico is Valentin and Marta Senn is Siébel. Serge Baudo conducts the Philadelphia Opera Orchestra. Brian Large directed the video telecast on PBS April 7, 1985. Color. In French. 141 minutes.

1988 Chicago Lyric Opera
Nicolai Ghiaurov is Mephistopheles, Mirella Freni is Marguerite and Alfredo Kraus is Faust in this Chicago Lyric Opera production by Alberto Fassini. Georges Prêtre conducts the Chicago Lyric Opera Orchestra. Color. In French. 139 minutes. On video.

Early/related films

1898 Faust et Marguerite
French filmmaker George Méliès' first film of the Faust legend is merely a transformation trick. Mephistopheles draws a sword across Marguerite's throat causing her to disappear and Faust to appear in her place. It was distributed in the U.S. in 1900 by Edison. About 1 minute (60 feet).

1898 Faust and Mephistopheles
British film pioneer G. A Smith, who invented Kinemacolor, made a magical Faust film in the same year as Méliès. Mephistopheles conjures up a vision of Marguerite to persuade Faust to sign a pact for his soul. Faust is transformed into a young man. About 1 minute (75 feet).

1900 Faust and Marguerite
Edwin S. Porter , later famous for *The Great Train Robbery*, directed this version of the story for the Edison company. About 3 minutes.

1902 Faust et Méphisto
Alice Guy, the first woman director, filmed this adaptation of the opera for Gaumont. About 3 minutes (150 feet).

1902 Faust Opera (Colored Views)
Faust Opera (Colored Views) was the announcement made for the September 1902 screenings of Alber's Electro Talking Bioscope in the Netherlands. The film used sound and film equipment purchased at the Paris Exhibition of 1900. About 3 minutes.

1904 La Damnation du Docteur Faust
The Damnation of Dr. Faust, George Méliès' second version of the Faust legend, is a colorful epic adaptation of the Gounod opera. It tells the story of the opera in twenty scenes in thirteen minutes. Méliès himself portrays Mephistopheles. Also known as *Faust et Marguerite*. Tinted. About 14 minutes (853 feet).

1907 First complete opera film
Arthur Gilbert's 1907 English film of *Faust* is the first complete opera to be filmed according to the *Guinness Book of Records*. It was made in the Gaumont Chronophone sound-on-disc system and advertised as the "complete opera with 22 arias" on disc. About 66 minutes.

1908 Henny Porten sound films
Two early German sound films were made of *Faust* for Oskar Messter's Berlin Biophon-Theater. Henny Porten stars as Marguerite and is directed by her father Franz. The "Jewel Song" is sung by Sigrid Arnold and the duet by Arnold and Joh. Lembach. Each about 3 minutes.

1909 Soldiers' Chorus sound film
The "Soldiers' Chorus" from *Faust* is featured on this early German sound film made by Deutsche Bioscop. About 3 minutes.

1909 Edison opera film
This adaptation of the opera was written and directed by J. Searle Dawley under the supervision of Edwin S. Porter. It was intended to be the first of an Edison series of films of operas. William J. Sorelle stars as Mephistopheles. The critics called it a classic. About 12 minutes.

1910 Ferdinand Zecca film
Ferdinand Zecca stars in this hand-colored French film directed by Henri Andreani and Georges Fagot for Pathé. It was distributed with a score based on the Gounod opera. About 18 minutes.

1910 British Animatophone film
A British sound film of scenes from the opera was made in the Animatophone system by David Barnet. The arias sung on screen were synchronized with phonograph records. About 10 minutes.

1910 Enrico Guazzoni film
Enrico Guazzoni directed this Italian film for the Cines company. It was based on the Gounod opera and stars Amleto Novelli, Gustavo Serena, Lea Orlandini and Gianna Terribili Gonzales. About 14 minutes. Print in British film archive.

1910 Éclair sound film
The French Éclair company made this sound film of an aria from the opera with a Paris Opera basso. His recording of the aria was played on a synchronized phonograph. About 4 minutes.

1911 Hepworth sound film
This British Hepworth sound film of scenes from *Faust* uses the Vivaphone system with the images synchronized to records. Hay Plumb is Faust, Claire Pridelle is Marguerite, Jack Hulcup is Mephistopheles and Frank Wilson is Valentine. Cecil Hepworth directed. Black and white. About l5 minutes

1913 Stanislav Hlavsa film
Czech director/singer Stanislav Hlavsa was influenced by Méliès when he made this Czechoslovakian film based on the Gounod opera. He starred himself as Mephistopheles and toured the country with the film singing the role from behind the screen. Antonin Pech produced the film which occupies an important niche in early Czech cinema. Black and white. About 30 minutes.

1915 Edward Sloman film
Edward Sloman directed and featured himself as Mephistopheles in this two-reel British film of the story. About 30 minutes.

1915 Biophone sound film
This British sound film of arias from the opera was made by the Commercial Biophone company. About 10 minutes.

1916 The Woman Who Dared
Beatriz Michelena portrays an opera singer in this American film and is seen on stage in her most famous role as Marguerite in *Faust*. These scenes were staged by her father Fernando Michelena, who had been an opera tenor. California Motion Picture Company. Black and white. About 80 minutes.

1918 Find the Woman
Alice Joyce portrays a soprano with the French Opera Company in New Orleans in this film and is seen as Marguerite in the Gounod opera. Tom Terriss directed for Vitagraph. About 70 minutes.

1918 Mefistofele e la Leggenda di Faust
Mario Gargiulo directed this Italian film version of the Faust story for Flegrea Film in 1918. Black and white. About 65 minutes.

1922 Sylvia Caine film
Sylvia Caine stars as Marguerite with Dick Webb as Faust and Lawford Davidson as Mephistopheles in this *Faust*, a British highlights version made for the *Tense Moments from Operas* series. Gordon Hopkin is Valentine and Minnie Rayner is Martha. Challis Sanderson directed for Gaumont. Black and white. About 15 minutes.

1922 Gerard Bourgeois film
Jeanne Leduc stars as Marguerite with Georges Wague as Méphistophélès and Maurice Varyy as Faust in this French film based on the opera and warmly praised by critics. Gerard Bourgeois directed. Black and white. In French. About 72 minutes.

1922 Don Juan et Faust
Marcel L'Herbier directed this French feature based on a novel which combines the two legends into one story. Jaque Catelain is a sympathetic Don Juan, Vanni Marcoux is an evil Faust and Marcelle Pradot is the Donna Anna they both desire. Gaumont. About 80 minutes.

1926 F. W. Murnau film
F. W. Murnau made this German *Faust* with Emil Jannings as Mephistopheles, Gosta Ekmann as

Faust and Camilla Horn as Marguerite. It was based on Goethe, Marlowe and German folk tales but not the opera. About 80 minutes.

1927 Cameo Operas series
Margo Lees is Marguerite, Herbert Langley is Faust and A. B. Imeson is Mephistopheles in this British highlights version made for the silent *Cameo Operas* series. Live singers and orchestra performed in synchronization with the screen. H. B. Parkinson directed. Black and white. About 18 minutes.

1927 John Barclay Vitaphone films
English baritone sings arias from *Faust* in English versions on two Vitaphone sound films made in 1927. On one he performs "The Calf of Gold," on the other "Mephisto's Serenade." Black and white. Each about 8 minutes.

1929 Charles Hackett sound film
Tenor Charles Hackett of the Chicago Opera portrays Faust in this two-reel Vitaphone sound film of Act One of the opera. Basso Chase Baromeo is his tempter Mephistopheles and the music is played by the Vitaphone Symphony Orchestra. About 20 minutes.

1930 Martinelli in The Prison Scene
Giovanni Martinelli stars as Faust in this Vitaphone sound film of the Prison Scene. Yvonne Benson sings Marguerite and Louis d'Angelo is Mephistopheles in the famous trio with the music played by the Vitaphone Symphony Orchestra. About 10 minutes.

1936 San Francisco
Jeanette MacDonald impresses Clark Gable by singing Marguerite's prayer aria "Anges purs." MacDonald is appearing in *Faust* at the Tivoli Opera House and Gable goes on opening night to stop the show. He changes his mind when he hears her sing. W. S. Van Dyke directed and Herbert Stothart was music director. MGM. Black and white. 115 minutes.

1937 La Grand Illusion
Jean Renoir's magnificent World War I prison film uses the "Anges purs" aria in a rather different way. It's sung by the French prisoners with extra words to warn new arrivals to hide their gold and watches from their German captors. Black and white. In French. 117 minutes.

1942 I Married an Angel
The last of the MacDonald-Eddy films was this adaptation of a Rodgers and Hart musical about a man who dreams he marries an angel. MacDonald naturally has to sing Marguerite's prayer "Anges purs." W.S. Van Dyke directed. Black and white. 84 minutes.

1949? Alexander Pirogov as Mephistopheles
This excerpt from a Soviet feature film of the 1940s features the great Russian bass Alexander Pirogov as Mephistopheles singing the "Serenade." Black and white. In Russian. 10 minutes.

1963 Bell Telephone Hour
The NBC television program included the prison scene from *Faust* on Nov. 22, 1963. Lisa della Casa sings the role of Marguerite, Nicolai Gedda is Faust and Cesare Siepi is Mephistopheles. Sid Smith directed. Black and white. 60 minutes. Video at MTR.

1965 Jean-Louis Barrault at the Met
This is a French news film showing Jean-Louis Barrault preparing a production of *Faust* at the Metropolitan Opera in September 1965. Seen in rehearsal and performance are Nicolai Gedda as Faust, Gabrielle Tucci as Marguerite and Cesare Siepi as Mephistopheles along with designer Jacques Dupont, choreographer Flemming Flindt and conductor George Pretre. The Oct. 2 opening night is also shown. This Pathé-Cinéma news film is titled *Chroniques des France No. 14.* Black and white. 7 minutes. Print in NFTA, London.

1983 Faust in Film
A German documentary about silent film versions of the Faust story which are shown in counterpoint to a production of the Goethe play by Gustav Gründgens. Gerd Albrecht, Hauke Lange-Fuchs and Steffen Wolf wrote and directed it. Color & black and white. In English. 36 minutes. Inter Nationes video.

1993 The Age of Innocence
Martin Scorsese's adaptation of Edith Wharton's novel begins, like the book, with the principal characters at a production of *Faust* in the 1870s. The plot begins to unfold as we observe Faust and Marguerite on stage in Act III. A similar ill-fated love affair becomes the central concern of the film and the opera is later featured in ironic counterpoint when the affair is forced to end. Linda

Faye Farkas portrays Marguerite on stage with Michael Rees Davis as Faust. Columbia. Color. 132 minutes.

1994 Jan Svankmajer film

Czech animator Jan Svankmajer's Kafka-esque film takes an ordinary man in Prague and turns him into Faust in a puppet production of the Gounod opera. A strange but powerful movie. Color. 60 minutes.

FAVORITA, LA
1840 opera by Donizetti

Italian Gaetano Donizetti originally created this as a French opera called *La Favorite* but outside France most productions are now in Italian. The fourteenth century Spanish monk Fernando falls in love with Leonora, not realizing she is the king's mistress. With her as inspiration he becomes a soldier and a hero, returns in glory and marries her. When he discovers her past, he renounces the marriage and returns to monastic life. She pleads for forgiveness and dies. The libretto is by Alphonse Royer and Gustav Vaez. See also GAETANO DONIZETTI.

1952 Sophia Loren film

Sophia Loren stars as a very beautiful Leonora with her singing done by Palmira Vitali Marini. Gino Sinimberghi is Fernando (sung by Piero Sardelli), Franca Tamantini is Ines (sung by Miriam Di Giove), Paolo Silver is Alfonso and Alfredo Colella is Baldassare. Nicola Rucci leads the Rome Opera orchestra and Cesare Barlacchi directed the film. Black and white. In Italian (English narration on video). 80 minutes. VIEW/Video Yesteryear videos.

Early films

1902 Dutch sound film

This Dutch sound film picturing the singing of an aria from *La Favorite* in French was one of the opera films featured at Alber's Electro Talking Bioscope screening in Holland in September 1902. About 3 minutes.

1910 Georges Denola film

This French film of *La Favorite* was directed by Georges Denola and made for Pathé. It was distributed in New York where American reviewers felt it was a good adaptation of the opera. About 12 minutes.

FEDORA
1898 opera by Giordano

Fedora is no longer fashionable on the stage though its tenor aria "Amor ti vieta" remains popular. Umberto Giordano's opera has some similarities to *Tosca*, perhaps both are based on plays written by Sardou for Sarah Bernhardt. Arturo Colautti created the melodramatic libretto. Russian princess Fedora goes to Paris to avenge the murder of her fiancé and falls in love with Loris, whom she believes is his murderer. Her plans for revenge cause multiple deaths and she kills herself when she discovers too late that her fiancé's killing was justified. See also UMBERTO GIORDANO.

1942 Luisa Ferida film

Camillo Mastrocinque's film is based on the opera libretto and uses Giordano's music as its score but it is a narrative film, not the opera. Luisa Ferida stars as Fedora with Amedeo Nazzari as Loris, the object of her vengeance and love. Also in the cast are Osvaldo Valenti, Rina Morelli and Sandro Ruffini. Ferida and Valenti were fanatical fascists and were shot by partisans at the end of the war. Black and white. In Italian. 90 minutes.

1993 Teatro alla Scala

Mirella Freni sings the role of Fedora with Placido Domingo as her enemy/ lover Loris in this Teatro alla Scala production. Gianandrea Gavazzeni conducted the La Scala Orchestra and Chorus. The video is an off-air recording of an Italian telecast. Color. In Italian. 120 minutes. Lyric video.

FELLINI, FEDERICO
Italian film director (1920-1994)

Federico Fellini said he did not understood opera so he never directed opera on stage. However opera music does feature in many of his films and is the central focus of *And the Ship Sails On*. Fellini became famous in 1954 with his Oscar-winning circus film *La Strada*, which was turned into a stage opera in 1982 by Czech composer Václav Kaslík. Fellini attracted even greater attention in 1960 with his scandalous *La Dolce Vita*. In a recent *Sight and Sound* poll of filmmakers, Fellini was voted the greatest film director of all time. See AND THE SHIP SAILS ON, THE BARBER OF SEVILLE (1963 film), CARMEN (1970), LA STRADA, THE THREEPENNY OPERA (1979), DIE WALKÜRE (1970).

FELSENSTEIN, WALTER
Austrian director (1901-1975)

Walter Felsenstein was one of the most influential modern opera producers. Although much of his work was done in East Berlin at Komische Oper, his ideas permeated opera ideas around the world. He believed that opera was as much theater as it was music and that acting was as important as singing, a radical concept at the time. His ideas have been so assimilated that what was once revolutionary now seems less surprising. Nevertheless his fine qualities as a director can still be experienced on a number of films. His 1955 *Fidelio* was for a long time the only film of that opera and was shown widely around the world. See also BARBE-BLEUE, (1973), THE CUNNING LITTLE VIXEN (1965), DON GIOVANNI (1966), FIDELIO (1955), THE MARRIAGE OF FIGARO (1976), OTTO KLEMPERER (1985), OTELLO (1969), THE TALES OF HOFFMANN (1970).

1967 Felsenstein Inszeniert
Felsenstein Director was filmed by noted American documentary filmmaker Michael Blackwood while Walter Felsenstein was rehearsing the second act of *Don Giovanni* in Berlin in 1966. It shows him at work on the staging and commenting on his ideas about the opera. The film was made for the German television company NDR. Color. In German. 67 minutes.

1972 Walter Felsenstein, a Portrait
This is a German television documentary film about the career of the director, showing aspects of his numerous productions and discussing his ideas about putting opera on the stage. It was made for Hessischer Rundfund. Color. In German. 62 minutes.

FERNANDEZ, WILHELMENIA
American soprano (1955-)

Wilhelmenia Wiggins Fernandez was the African-American soprano who became famous singing an aria from *La Wally* in the 1981 film *Diva*. She made her debut in 1982 singing Musetta in *La Bohème* with the New York City Opera. She later appeared as Carmen Jones in the first London Old Vic production of Oscar Hammerstein's adaptation of the Bizet opera. She has made a number of records and has been a guest on Sesame Street. See RISE AND FALL OF THE CITY OF MAHAGONNY (1976).

1981 Diva
Fernandez portrays African-American opera singer Cynthia Hawkins in this stylish French thriller by Jean-Jacques Beineix. She is wonderfully mysterious because she refuses to allow her voice to be recorded. A young admirer secretly tapes her singing "Ebben...ne andro lontana," an aria from Catalani's opera *La Wally*, at the Théâtre de les Bouffes du Nord in Paris. The tape gets confused with a tape about a drug king and is central to the plot. The film, which made Fernandez famous and aroused fresh interest in Catalani's opera, is based on a French crime novel by Delacorta. Color. In French with English subtitles. 117 minutes. MGM/UA Video.

1991 La Grouchiata (La Traviata)
Wilhelmenia Fernandez is a delight in this episode of *Sesame Street* which attempts to show young viewers the joys of opera. Puppet opera star Grundgetta prefers screaming to singing so she quits the show and Wilhelmenia has to step in and save the day singing in *La Traviata*. Color. 30 minutes.

FERRER, JOSÉ
American actor-singer (1912-1992)

Puerto Rico-born José Ferrer was an actor, director and singer whose primary career was in the movies but who also sang in operas, operettas and musicals. In 1960 he was featured at Santa Fe Opera in the title role of the Puccini one-act opera *Gianni Schicchi*. In 1964 he won acclaim on Broadway singing the Prince in Noel Coward's musical *The Girl Who Came to Supper*. He won a Tony and an Oscar playing Cyrano De Bergerac on stage and on film, and is a delight as Sigmund Romberg in the film *Deep in My Heart* singing opposite Helen Traubel. Even when he isn't singing, his voice is a sonorous marvel. See also KISMET (1967), SIGMUND ROMBERG (1954).

FIDELIO
1814 opera by Beethoven

Beethoven's opera had its premiere in the form we know it in Vienna in 1814. Leonore disguises herself as the boy Fidelio so she can work in the Seville jail and attempt to rescue her husband Florestan. The evil Pizarro, meanwhile, has plans to kill him. The opera is filled with Beethoven's ideas about liberty, heroism and the triumph of hope. The libretto in its final form is by George Friedrich Treitschke and Josef Sonnleithner. See also LUDWIG VAN BEETHOVEN.

1955 Walter Felsenstein film

The earliest *Fidelio* is an Austrian film by influential director Walter Felsenstein which features actors on screen but opera singers on the soundtrack. Leonore is sung by Magda Laszlo and acted by Claude Nollier, Florestan is Richard Holm, Pizaro is sung by Heinz Rehfuss and acted by Hannes Schiel and Fernando is sung by Alfredo Poli and acted by Erwin Gross. Felsenstein internalizes the music and uses a lot of visual symbolism including waterfalls, falling rocks and flowery meadows. Niklaus Hayer was cinematographer and Fritz Lehmann conducted the Vienna Philharmonic Orchestra and Vienna Opera Chorus. Black and white. In German with English subtitles. 90 minutes.

1959 NBC Opera Theatre

Irene Jordan sings the role of Leonore in this highly-praised NBC Opera Theatre production by Samuel Chotzinoff. John Alexander is Florestan, Lee Cass is Pizarro, Judith Raskin is Marzelline, Chester Watson is Rocco and Fred Cushman is Jaquino. The opera is sung in English in a translation by Joseph Nachlis. Peter Herman Adler conducted the orchestra and Kirk Browning directed the telecast on Nov. 8, 1959. Color. In English. 120 minutes. Video at MTR.

1963 Deutsche Oper, Berlin

Christa Ludwig is Leonore with James King as Florestan and Josef Greindl as Pizarro in this historic telecast of a Deutsche Oper Berlin production. Artur Rother conducts the Deutsche Oper Berlin Orchestra. Black and white. In German with Japanese subtitles. 123 minutes. Japanese laser.

1969 Rolf Liebermann film

Anja Silja is Leonore, Richard Cassilly is Florestan and Theo Adam is Pizarro in this West German film produced by Rolf Liebermann and based on a Hamburg State Opera production. Lucia Popp is Marzelline, Hans Sotin is Fernando and Ernest Wiemann is Rocco. Leopold Ludwig conducts the Hamburg State Opera Chorus and Philharmonic Orchestra. Guenther Rennert directed the stage production and Joachim Hess directed the film which was shown theatrically in the U. S. Polyphon Film. Color. In German. 128 minutes.

1970 Deutsch Oper, Berlin

Welsh soprano Gwyneth Jones is Leonore in this film of a Berlin Deutsche Oper stage production by Gustav Rudolf Sellner. James King is Florestan, Gustav Neidinger is Pizarro, Olivia Miljakovic is Marzelline, Josef Greindl is Rocco, Martti Talve is Fernando and Donald Grobe is Jaquino. Karl Böhm conducted the Deutsch Oper Orchestra. West Germany-Austria. Unitel. Color. In German. 115 minutes.

1977 Orange Festival

Jon Vickers is Florestan, Gundula Janowitz is Leonore and Theo Adam is Pizarro in this French film of the opera. Pierre Jourdan shot it on stage at the Orange Festival without an audience. Stella Richmond is Marzelline, William Wildermann is Rocco and Misha Raitzin is Jaquino. Zubin Mehta directs the Israel Philharmonic Orchestra and London New Philharmonia Chorus. The production is by Alfred Wopmann and the sets are by Marco Arturo Marelli. Jourdan's film was not released until 1979. Color. In German. 120 minutes. Japanese video and laser.

1978 Vienna State Opera

Gundula Janowitz is Leonore and René Kollo is Florestan in this Vienna State Opera stage production staged and directed for video by Otto Schenk. Lucia Popp is Marzelline, Manfred Jungwirth is Rocco, Hans Sotin is Pizzaro, Hans Helm is Fernando and Adolf Dallapozzo is seen as Jaquino. Leonard Bernstein conducts the Vienna Philharmonic Orchestra. There is also an audio version on CD. ORF. Color. In German. 145 minutes. On video.

1979 Glyndebourne Festival

Elisabeth Soderstrom is particularly fine as Leonore in this Glyndebourne production by Peter Hall. Anton de Ridder is Florestan, Robert Allman is Pizarro, Elizabeth Gale is Marzelline, Michael Langdon is Fernando, Ian Caley is Jaquino and Curt Appelgren is Rocco. John Bury designed the sets and Bernard Haitink led the London Philharmonic Orchestra and Glyndebourne Festival Chorus. Dave Heather directed the video. Color. In German with English subtitles. 130 minutes. VAI video.

1987 Bad Hersfeld Festival

A production of the opera by Erhard Fischer for the Bad Hersfeld Festival with members of the Hersfeld Festival Choir and the Frankfurt and Marburg

Concert choirs. Siegfried Heinrich conducts the Prague Radio Symphony Orchestra. Akos Ravasz directed the video which includes scenes of the town. Color. In German. 134 minutes. Inter Nationes video.

1990 Royal Opera House
Gabriela Benacková is Leonore in this thoughtful and very effective Royal Opera House production by Adolf Dresen. Josef Protschka plays Florestan, Monte Pederson is Pizarro, Marie McLaughlin is Marzelline, Robert Lloyd is Rocco and Neill Archer is Jaquino. Christoph von Dohnanyi conducts the Royal Opera House Orchestra and Chorus. Color. 129 minutes. In German with English subtitles. Home Vision video/Pioneer Artists laser.

1995 Bregenz Festival
Stig Andersen and Jane Thorner-Mengedoht star in this impressive Bregenz Festival production by David Pountney on the giant floating stage. Stefano Lazardis designed the mammoth sets. Also in the performance taped for television are Mark Holland and Pavlo Hunka. Ulf Schirmer conducts. Color. In German. 130 minutes.

Related films

1937 Yoshiwara
Max Ophuls' splendid film about a Japanese woman (Michiko Tanaka) who sells herself to a brothel to provide for her little brother features an homage to *Fidelio*. Her Russian protector (Pierre Richard Willm) takes her on an imaginary train ride to the opera and teaches her how to applaud. The opera, appropriately, is about another self-sacrificing woman. Black and white. In French. 88 minutes.

1970 Fidelio: A Celebration of Life
Leonard Bernstein takes a look at Beethoven's "flawed masterpiece" and discusses its story and problems. Four selections from Act II are presented preceded by analysis and plot summary. This film derives from Bernstein's *Young People's Concert* series on television. Black and white. 54 minutes. Video at MTR.

FIDELE BAUER, DER
1907 operetta by Fall

Austrian composer Leo Fall's 1907 operetta The *Merry Peasant* was his first success and one of the most popular of its time. Victor Léon's libretto tells the story of German peasant Matthäus who idolizes his son and makes sacrifices in order to give him an education. When the son marries a woman from the city, he is embarrassed to have his very countrfied family attend the wedding. In the end both families meet and all goes well. See also LEO FALL.

1927 Franz Seitz film
This silent German film of the operetta stars Hungarian actor S. Z. Sakall, English actress Ivy Close, German actor Werner Krauss, Mathias Wieman and Leo Peukert. It was screened with Fall's music played lived in the theater. Franz Seitz directed. Black and white. German titles. About 75 minutes.

1951 Hubert Marischka film
Paul Horbiger stars as the merry peasant in this Austrian film of the operetta with a somewhat altered story written and directed by Hubert Marischka. Erich Auer plays the son and Amarianne Wicschmann is the woman he loves (now an American). Black and white. In German. 90 minutes.

FIERRABRAS
1823 opera by Schubert

Franz Schubert's best-known opera was composed in 1823 but didn't get staged until 1897. It was then ignored until 1988 when it was revived at the Vienna State Opera. Josef Kupelwieser's libretto deals with the legend of Charlemagne and his heroic knight Roland. Moorish prince Fierrabras loves Charlemagne's daughter Emma while Roland loves Fierrabras's sister, Florinda. All ends more or less well after many complications. See also FRANZ SCHUBERT.

1988 Vienna State Opera
Thomas Hampson is Roland and Josef Protschka is Fierrabras in this Vienna Staatsoper production by Ruth Berghaus arranged in collaboration with conductor Claudio Abbado. Karita Mattila is Emma, Ellen Shade is Florinda, Peter Hofmann is Ogier, Robert Holl is Charlemagne and Robert Gambill is Eginhard. Berghaus sets the action in a timeless era

with abstract modernist sets by Hans-Dieter Schaal. Marie Luise Strandt designed the costumes and Abbado conducts the Europe Chamber Orchestra and Arnold Schoenberg Choir. P. W. R. Lauscher directed the video. Color. In German. 120 minutes. Lyric video.

FIERY ANGEL, THE
1927 opera by Prokofiev

Sergei Prokofiev's opera *Ognennyi Angel* premiered in Paris in 1954 after the composer's death but has since been recongized as one of his finest works. Based on a novel by Valery Bryussov with a libretto by the composer, it is the sexually-charged story of a 16th century mystic called Renata who has visions of a fiery angel. Ruprecht tries to help her and fights a duel on her behalf but she ends up being tried as a witch. See also SERGEI PROKOFIEV.

1993 Kirov Opera
Galina Gorchakova stars as a potent Renata with Sergei Lieferkus as a fine Ruprecht in this superb Kirov Opera production by David Freeman. Larissa Diadkova plays the Fortuneteller, Konstantin Pluzhnikov portrays Mephistopheles, Vladimir Ognovenko is the Inquisitor and members of the St. Petersburg Maryinsky Acrobatic Troupe portray Renata's evil demons. Valery Gergiev conducts the Kirov Orchestra and Chorus. Brian Large directed the video. Color. In Russian. 120 minutes. Philips Classics video and laserdisc.

FILLE DE MADAME ANGOT, LA
1872 operetta by Lecoq

French composer Charles Lecoq's tuneful operetta *Madame Angot's Daughter* is set in Paris during the French Revolution. Clairette, the daughter of Madame Angot, is in love with the poet Ange Pitou but her fishwife mother has arranged for her to marry Pomponnet. Her rival is Mlle. Lange, an actress who was once a schoolmate. The libretto is by Clairbille, Siraudin and Koning. See also CHARLES LECOQ.

1935 André Bauge film
This French film version of the operetta stars André Bauge as Ange Pitou, Moniquella as Clairette, Danièle Brégis as Mlle Lange, Robert Arnoux as Pomponnet and Arletty as Ducoudray. Jean Bernard-Derosne directed. Black and white. In French. 85 minutes.

FILLE DU RÉGIMENT, LA
See THE DAUGHTER OF THE REGIMENT

FILMMAKERS ON STAGE

A number of major filmmakers, in addition to making opera films, have turned to actually producing operas on stage. This has become more common in recent years and appears to be a growing trend. The first and most influential were probably Visconti and Zeffirelli, whose stage work is as important as their filmmaking. Some of the better known film directors working on stage who have entries in this encyclopedia are ROBERT ALTMAN, ANTHONY ASQUITH, BRUCE BERESFORD, INGMAR BERGMAN, LILIANA CAVANI, AXEL CORTI, SERGEI EISENSTEIN, PETER GREENAWAY, PETER HALL, WERNER HERZOG, JOHN HUSTON, HERBERT ROSS, KEN RUSSELL, JOHN SCHLESINGER, DANIEL SCHMID, ISTVÁN SZABÓ, ANDREI TARKOVSKY, LUCHINO VISCONTI, FRANCO ZEFFIRELLI.

FINTA GIARDINIERA, LA
1775 opera by Mozart

Mozart was eighteen when he composed this entertaining opera to a libretto attributed to Ranieri de Cazabigi. *The False Woman Gardener* is the story of a marchioness who pretends to be the gardener Sandrina so she can look for her fiancé Count Belfiore who believes her dead after he stabbed her in a quarrel. She is hired by foolish old Don Achise who falls in love with her. Meanwhile the maid Serpetta wants to marry the old man and rejects the advances of the countess's servant, also in disguise. Sandrina finally reveals her identity to save her fiancé from the charge of murdering her after numerous amorous and identity complications. See also WOLFGANG A. MOZART.

1988 Drottningholm Court Theatre
This Drottningholm Court Theater production by Göran Järvefelt is quite charming. Britt-Marie Aruhn stars as the aristocratic gardener Sandrina, Richard Croft is her fiancé Belfiore, Stuart Kale is the foolish Don Achise, Eva Pilat is Arminda, Ann Christine Biel is Serpetta, Annika Skoglund is Ramiro and Petteri Salomaa is Nardo. Arnold Östman conducts the Drottningholm Court Theater Orchestra and Chorus and Thomas Olofsson directed the video. Color. In Italian with English subtitles. 149 minutes. Philips video and laser.

1989 George F. Mielke video

This German-language production of the opera as *Gärtnerin aus Liebe* was produced by George F. Mielke for East German and Austrian television. Brigitte Eisenfeld sings the role of Sandrina with James O'Neal as Belfiore, Heinz Zednik as Don Anchise, Ute Selbig as Arminda, Elvira Dreen as Ramiro, Ulrike Steinsky as Serpetts and Juergen Harfield as Nardo. Max Pommer conducts the Berlin Radio-Television Orchestra. Color. In German with Japanese subtitles. 145 minutes. On Japanese video and laser.

1990 Théâtre Royal de la Monnaie

This Belgian production at La Monnaie opera house in Brussels was telecast in Europe and is available on both CD and laser. It stars soprano Joanna Kozlowska as Sandrina with support from tenor Ugo Benelli, tenor Marek Torzewski and soprano Malvina Major. Silvain Cambreling conducts the La Monnaie Orchestra. Color. In French. 148 minutes. On Japanese laserdisc.

FIREFLY, THE
1912 operetta by Friml

Rudolf Friml was invited to take over from Victor Herbert as the composer of this operetta. Herbert had quarreled with prima donna Emma Trentini and refused to work with her anymore so the producers decided to take a risk on Friml. Otto Harbach's libretto tells the story of an Italian street singer who travels to Bermuda as a cabin boy and ends up as an opera star. Friml wrote a fine score and composed three hit songs, "Giannina Mia," "Love is Like a Firefly" and "Sympathy." The operetta's famous "Donkey Song" was also written by Friml but was created for the 1937 film. See also RUDOLF FRIML.

1937 Jeanette MacDonald film

MGM abandoned the stage libretto in favor of a new screenplay by Frances Goodrich, Albert Hackett and Ogden Nash. Jeanette MacDonald stars as a singer called "The Firefly," a Spanish spy during the Napoleonic War with France. Co-star Allan Jones introduced "The Donkey Serenade" and became famous for it. The film retains most of the songs from the stage show including "Giannina Mia," "Love is Like a Firefly" and "Sympathy." The cast includes Henry Daniell, Warren William, George Zucco and Billy Gilbert. Robert Z. Leonard directed the film and Herbert Stothart conducted the music. Black and white. 131 minutes. MGM-UA video.

FIRST OPERAS ON FILM

The first opera film appears to have been an American movie shot in July 1898 by the American Mutoscope Company. It was a two-minute version of Donizetti's *The Daughter of the Regiment* filmed at a New York City studio.

French director Georges Méliès made two films in 1898 inspired by operas, *Faust et Marguerite* and *Damnation de Faust*. In 1899 he made *Cendrillon*, a film inspired by the Massenet opera.

The first films about opera composers were made in 1898 by Italy's first filmmaker, Leopoldo Fregoli. He shot films satirizing Verdi, Rossini, Mascagni and Wagner conducting.

The first film of an actual opera is American. In March 1900 the Edison Company released *Opera of Martha* with four genuine opera singers performing Act Two of the Flotow opera.

The first opera films with sound were presented at the Phono-Cinéma-Théâtre at the Paris Exhibition. on June 8, 1900. Victor Maurel sang arias from *Don Giovanni* and *Falstaff* and Emile Cossira sang an aria from *Roméo et Juliette*. In a later sound film the same year Polin performed an aria from *La Fille du Régiment*.

The first epic opera film was Edison's 1904 *Parsifal* shot in eight episodes with elaborate sets. It ran for twenty whole minutes and created a minor scandal as Edison made the film without permission. He was emulating the Metropolitan Opera which had staged the Wagner opera in 1903 without permission. Edwin S. Porter directed.

The first complete opera to be filmed was a sound version of Gounod's *Faust* according to the *Guinness Book of Records*. Arthur Gilbert's 1907 English film was advertised for sale as the "complete opera with 22 arias." The music was played on records synchronized through the Chronophone sound-on-disc system. It was about 60 to 70 minutes long.

The first complete opera to be filmed in America was *Pagliacci* according to the Guinness Book of Records. It was in three reels and was made in 1913 by the Vi-T-Ascope Co. using the Vi-T-Phone sound system. It was about 30 to 40 minutes long.

The first full-length opera adapted for the screen with sound and photographed as a movie rather than a stage production was a 1930 version of Auber's *Fra Diavolo*. Mario Bonnard made this 90-minute film in French, Italian and German versions with Croatian tenor Tino Pattiera.

The first sound era film of a full opera was a 1931 *Pagliacci* filmed as a stage production on Long Island by Italian-Americans of the San Carlo Grand Opera Company. The 80-minute movie was directed by Joe W. Coffman with Leoncavallo's music played by the San Carlo Symphony Orchestra

FIRST OPERAS ON TELEVISION

The first opera shown on TV was Albert Coates' little known English opera *Pickwick*. Twenty-five minutes of scenes from the opera were telecast by BBC Television on Nov. 13, 1936 just before the opera's Covent Garden premiere.

The first opera televised in its entirety was Pergolesi's relatively short *La Serva Padrona* which was shown in September 1937 on BBC.

BBC Television transmitted about 30 operas before closing down for the war in September 1939 and was far ahead of its rivals in the field. It restarted telecasts of opera on Nov. 26, 1946, beginning with *The Beggar's Opera*.

The first opera on German television was a film of Mozart's relatively short *Der Schauspieldirektor* (The Impresario) telecast over the Paul Kipnow Sender station in Berlin in 1938.

The first opera on U.S. television was an amateur version of *Carmen* shown on NBC's experimental W2XBS in November 1939. The Miniature Opera Company staged scenes from the opera with child singers.

The first opera presented on American television with professional singers was *Pagliacci*. The Metropolitan Opera staged the first act at NBC's Radio City television studio in March 1941.

The first telecast of a complete opera in the U.S. was *Hansel and Gretel*. It was sung in English by Hartford music students from Schenectady's WRGB studio in December 1942.

The first full-length opera telecast from a stage was Verdi's *Otello* from the Metropolitan Opera on Nov. 29, 1948.

The first color telecast of an opera was NBC Opera Theatre's *Carmen* on Oct. 31, 1953 starrring Vera Bryner in the role of Carmen.

The first French opera telecasts did not occur until the early 1950s with a series directed by Henri Spade that included *Mireille, Don Quichotte* and *Manon Lescaut*.

The first live telecast from the Paris Opéra was the Maria Callas gala evening on Dec. 19, 1958.

The first international opera telecast was on June 3, 1961 when Renata Tebaldi's *Tosca* from the Stuttgart State Opera inaugurated a consortium of European stations.

FIRST OPERETTAS ON FILM

The first film of an operetta seems to have been made by German pioneer Max Skladanowsky at the end of 1896. Operetta stars Fritzi Massary and Josef Gianpietro appeared in a scene from either *Der Vogelhander* or *Der Bettelstudent*.

The first operetta film made in America was a 1902 Lubin movie featuring a scene from *The Mikado*.

The first film of a French operetta was a 1902 excerpt from Offenbach's *Barbe-Bleue*. An aria from the operetta was presented with sound and picture in Holland in September 1902.

The first operetta to be filmed complete in the sound era was Sigmund Romberg's *The Desert Song*, advertised in June 1929 as the "first all-singing and talking operetta." Baritone John Boles starred as the Red Shadow in this Warner Bros. Film.

The first European operetta to be filmed in the sound era was an adaptation of Oscar Straus's *Hochzeit in Hollywood*. It premiered on stage in Vienna in December 1928 and by September 1929 was showing in American movie houses as *Married in Hollywood*. It was advertised by Fox as "the first Viennese operetta."

FISCHER-DIESKAU, DIETRICH
German baritone (1925-)

Dietrich Fischer-Dieskau, who is as famous for lieder as for opera, retired in 1993 but his recordings maintain his reputation as one of the major singers of our time. He made his debut in 1948 in *Don Carlo* in Berlin and became known for his studied, intellectual style. He said he did not want to be a screen opera singer so he did not make films and rarely appeared on TV. Luckily there is a small legacy of his work on video that includes *Don Giovanni* and *The Marriage of Figaro*. See DON GIOVANNI (1961), ELEKTRA (1982), THE MARRIAGE OF FIGARO (1976), THE MAGIC FLUTE (1971), WAR REQUIEM (1988).

1960 Concert for the United Nations

Fischer-Dieskau was filmed in Paris in 1960 at the Salle Player when he took part in a concert in honor of the birth of the United Nations. He sings Mahler's *Lieder eines fahrenden Gessellen* with the NHK Tokyo Symphonic Orchestra conducted by Paul Kletzki. The film was directed by Denise Billon for the INA. Color. In German. 20 minutes.

1987 Fischer-Dieskau Sings Mahler

Fischer-Dieskau was taped in 1987 giving a performance of the songs from Mahler's *Der Knaben Wunderhorn*. He is accompanied on piano by Hartmut Höll. Klaud Lindeman directed the video for SWF. Color. In German. 71 minutes.

1988 Die Schöne Magelone

Fischer-Dieskau sings and recites romances from Brahms' *Die Schöne Magelone* which he had made famous on earlier recordings. He is accompanied by Hartmut Höll on piano. Klaus Lindemann directed the video for SWF. Color. In German. 95 minutes.

1990 Winterreise

The great baritone was 66 when he was filmed on stage in Berlin in this performance of Schubert's *Winter Voyage* song cycle. He first performed the songs in 1948 and nearly half a century later his voice is still impressive. He is accompanied on piano by Murray Perahia. Rodney Greenberg directed the video. Color. In German. 70 minutes. Sony video and laser.

1992 Master Class with Fischer-Dieskau

Fischer-Dieskau at 68 gives a master class to young singers in Berlin. He talks about opera and lieder with the emphasis on Mozart, Schubert and Schumann. Bruno Monsaingeon directed the video for Idéale Audience. Color. In German. 90 minutes.

FITZCARRALDO
1982 opera film by Herzog

Fitzcarraldo is one of the great opera films, the story of a man so obsessed with Enrico Caruso and opera that he decides to build an opera house for him in the Amazon jungle. Klaus Kinski stars as the opera-mad Fitzcarraldo whose ideas about opera dominate the film. It begins with Kinski and his mistress Molly (Claudia Cardinale) rowing 1200 miles to Manaus to hear the last few moments of Caruso on stage with Sarah Bernhardt in *Ernani* in the Teatro Amazonas. He decides to open a shipping route on the Amazon and raise the money to bring opera to the jungle even if he has to haul a ship over a mountain to do it. The ship is called the "Molly Aida" and the film is filled with opera talk and music by Verdi, Bellini, Leoncavallo, Meyerbeer and Massenet. Caruso's voice is heard on a phonograph at various times singing *Pagliacci*, *L'Africana* and *La Bohème*. When a missionary says he can't cure Indians of their "notion that normal life is an illusion behind which lies the reality of dreams," Fitzcarraldo comments that he is also "a man of the opera." At the end of the film there are *I Puritani* scenes on the boat with Isabel Jimenz de Cisneros as Elvira, Liborio Simonella as Arturo and the Lima Repertory Symphony Orchestra. The opening *Ernani* scene, staged by Werner Schroeter, is sung by Mietta Sighele, Veriano Luchetti and Dimiter Petkov with actors on stage and music by the Venice Philharmonic. Color. In German. 157 minutes. Warner video. See also WERNER HERZOG.

FLAGSTAD, KIRSTEN
Norwegian soprano (1895-1962)

Kirsten Flagstad had an extraordinary career. She was about to retire in 1933 after a modestly successful career in Scandinavia when she was engaged to sing at Bayreuth in small roles. By the following year she was being acclaimed as one of the best Wagnerian singers of the century. She made her debut at the Metropolitan Opera in 1935 at the age of 40 as Sieglinde in *Die Walküre* and was such a powerful singer that she did not, in fact, retire for another 20 years. She made only one film, in which she sings Brunhilde's "Ho-jo-to-ho!" from *Die Walküre*, but she can be seen in a BBC television program as Dido in scenes from Purcell's *Dido and Aeneas*. See DIDO AND AENEAS (1951), DIE WALKÜRE (1935 film).

FLEDERMAUS, DIE

1874 operetta by Strauss

The Bat is Johann Strauss's most popular operetta and has honorary opera status in most opera houses. The libretto by Carl Haffner and Richard Genée is based on *Le Réveillon* by Henri Meilhac and Ludovic Halévy. The philandering Eisenstein has been sentenced to jail for a minor infraction but goes first to a masked ball given by Prince Orlofsky. His wife Rosalinde disguises herself and goes to the ball to catch her husband flirting. Their maid Adele goes with her sister Ida pretending to be an actress. Rosalinde's old flame Alfred goes to jail pretending to be Eisenstein. Falke set all this up in revenge for a trick played on him once when he was wearing a bat costume. The ball scene usually includes guest stars. See also JOHANN STRAUSS II

1931 Anny Ondra film

Czech actress Anny Ondra stars in the first sound film of the operetta which was made in Paris in French and German versions. In the French *La Chauve-Souris*, Ondra portrays Arlette, Marcelle Denya is Caroline Gaillardin, Mauricet is Isodore Gaillardin, George Bury is Alfred and Ivan Petrovich is Orlofsky. In the German *Die Fledermaus*, Ondra has support from Georg Alexander, Oskar Sima Karel, Betty Werner and Petrovich. Karel Lamac directed both films at the Pathé Studios in Joinville. Black and white. 80 minutes.

1933 Evelyn Laye film

Evelyn Laye stars as Rosalinde in this free adaptation of the operetta titled *Waltz Time*. Philanderer Eisenstein is a writer researching a book at a masked ball outwitted by his wife in disguise. German singer Fritz Schultz portrays Eisenstein, Gina Malo is Adele, Parry Jones is Alfred, Ivor Barnard is Falke and George Baker is Orlofsky. A. P. Herbert wrote the screenplay and William Thiele directed. Gaumont-British. Black and white. 82 minutes.

1937 Paul Verhoeven film

Paul Verhoeven directed this self referential version of *Die Fledermaus*. Hans Sohnker portrays a tenor who has starred in the operetta for 300 shows and has become bat-obsessed. He falls asleep and dreams the operetta with his wife and friends in the various roles. Lida Baarova plays his wife and Frieda Czepa is the maid. Black and white. In German. 105 minutes.

1946 Marte Harell film

This Agfa color film of the operetta was made at the end of World War II in the Barrandov Studios in Prague. The negative was then seized by the Soviets who premiered the film in East Berlin in 1946. Marte Harell stars as Rosalinde, Johannes Heesters is Eisenstein, Dorit Kreysler is Adele, Siegfried Breuer is Orlofsky, Willi Dohm is Falke and Willy Fritsch is Frank. Geza von Bolvary directed. The film was released in the U.S. in 1958. Color. In German. 100 minutes.

1950 NBC Opera Theatre

This NBC Opera Theatre production by Samuel Chotzinoff was televised in English as *The Bat*. It was directed by Charles Polacheck and designed by Carl Kent while the orchestra was conducted by Peter Herman Adler. Kirk Browning directed the telecast. Black and white. 60 minutes.

1953 Metropolitan Opera on Omnibus

Jarmila Novotná stars as Prince Orlovsky in this Omnibus TV version of a famous Metropolitan Opera production. The opera, with English libretto by Garson Kanin and lyrics by Howard Dietz, was the centerpiece of Rudolph Bing's first season as general manager. Brenda Lewis is Rosalinde, Lois Hunt is Adele, Charles Kullman is Eisenstein and Thomas Hayward is Alfred. Herbert Graf staged the operetta for the Met and William Spier produced it. Eugene Ormandy conducted the Metropolitan Opera orchestra. Bob Banner directed for CBS television on Jan. 2, 1953. Black and white. In English. 65 minutes. Video at MTR.

1955 Oh Rosalinda!!

Oh Rosalinda!! is a British modernization written and directed by Michael Powell and Emeric Pressburger and set in post-World War II occupied Vienna. The songs have new lyrics, the sets are deliberately artificial and the direction is deft. The film opens with Anton Walbrook (Falke) explaining his practical joke. Adele is splendidly portrayed by Anneliese Rothenberger. Rosalinda (acted by Ludmilla Techerina, sung by Sari Barabas) is married to French colonel Eisenstein (Michael Redgrave) and pursued by American captain Alfred (Mel Ferrer). The masked ball is given by Russian general Orlofsky (Anthony Quayle) and attended by British major Frank (Dennis Price). Color. In English. 101 minutes.

1955 Jarmila Ksirowa film
Jarmila Ksirowa, Sonja Schoner and Eric Arnold star in this East German version of *Die Fledermaus* written and directed by E. W. Fiedler and shot in East Berlin. It was released with the title *Rauschende Melodien* (Sumptuous Melodies). DEFA production. Color. In German. 86 minutes.

1962 Marianne Koch film
Marianne Koch sings Rosalinde with Marika Rökk as Adele in this Austrian film directed by Geza von Cziffra. Peter Alexander is Eisenstein, Boy Gobert is Prince Orlofsky, Rolf Kutschera is Alfred and Willy Millowitsch is Frank. The libretto has been somewhat changed and the time moved to the turn of the century. Kurt Edelhagen conducted the Vienna State Opera Orchestra. Color. In German. 107 minutes.

1966 Flagermusen
Lily Broberg stars as Rosalinde in this Danish film of the operetta directed by Annelise Meineche. Poul Reichhardt plays Eisenstein, Ghita Norby is Adele, Holger Juul-Hansen is Falke, Grethe Morgensen is Orlofsky, Karl Steggera is Frank and Dario Campeotto is Alfred. The Royal Danish Ballet is featured in the ball scene. Color. In Danish. 99 minutes.

1970 Vienna Volksoper
Peter Minich, Mirjana Irosch and Dagmar Koller star in this Vienna Volksoper production directed by Karl Dönch. Franz Bauer-Theussl conducted the Volksoper Orchestra. Color. In German. 156 minutes. On video.

1972 Gundula Janowitz film
Gundula Janowitz sings the role of Rosalinde, Eberhard Wächter is her husband Eisenstein and Renate Holm is the maid Adele in this lavish Austrian film. Wolfgang Windgassen portrays Prince Orlofsky and Eric Kunz is Frank. Karl Böhm conducts the Vienna Philharmonic Orchestra and State Opera Choir. Otto Schenk directed in 35mm for television. Unitel. Color. In German. 137 minutes. Taurus (Germany) video.

1982 Australian Opera
Joan Sutherland stars as Rosalinde in this Sydney Opera House production by Anthony Besch. Robert Gard portrays Eisenstein, Monique Brynnel is Adele, Anson Austin is Alfred, Heather Begg is Orlofsky and Michael Lewis is Falke. The English translation is by David Pountnoy and Leonard Hanock. John Stoddart designed the colorful sets and costumes and Richard Bonynge conducts the Elizabethan Sydney Orchestra. Hugh Davison directed the video for the Australian Broadcasting Corp. Color. In English. 142 minutes. Sony video.

1983 Royal Opera
Kiri Te Kanawa sings Rosalinde in this splendid Covent Garden production by Leopold Lindtberg and Richard Gregson. Herman Prey portrays Eisenstein, Hildegarde Heichele is Adele, Doris Soffel is Orlofsky, Benjamin Luxon is Falke and Dennis O'Neill is Alfred. Julia Trevelyan Oman designed the sets and costumes and Placido Domingo conducts the Royal Opera House Orchestra and Chorus. Humphrey Burton directed the video. Color. In English and German with English subtitles. 175 minutes. HBO video.

1983 Opera Stories
This is a laserdisc highlights version of the above Royal Opera House production. Charlton Heston tells the story of the operetta from Vienna in framing material shot in 1989. Color. 52 minutes. In English and German with English subtitles. Pioneer Artists laser.

1986 Metropolitan Opera
Kiri Te Kanawa stars as Rosalinde in this Metropolitan Opera production by Otto Schenk. The strong cast assembled for a live New Year's Eve telecast includes Judith Blegen, Tatiana Troyanos, David Rendall, Hakan Hagegard and Michael Devlin. Joanne Woodward hosted the evening and Jeffrey Tate conducted the Metropolitan Opera Orchestra and Chorus. Kirk Browning directed the telecast on Dec. 31, 1986. Color. 210 minutes. Video at MTR.

1986 Bavarian State Opera
Pamela Coburn stars as Rosalinde with Eberhard Wachter as Eisenstein in this high-powered Bavarian State Opera production by Otto Schenk. Janet Perry is Adele, Brigitte Fassbaender is Orlofsky, Wolfgang Brendel is Falke and Josef Hopferwieser is Alfred. Gunther Schneider-Sienssen designed the sets and Carlos Kleiber conducted the Bavarian State Opera Orchestra and Chorus. Brian Large directed the video. Unitel. Color. In German with English subtitles. 154 minutes. DG video.

1990 Royal Opera

Joan Sutherland bids farewell to Covent Garden as a party guest in this spirited production by John Cox. Nancy Gustafson sings Rosalinde with Judith Howarth as Adele, Louis Otey as Eisenstein, countertenor Jochen Kowalski as Orlofsky, Anthony Michaels-Moore as Falke and Bonaventura Bottone as Alfredo. Sutherland's farewell includes duets with Luciano Pavarotti and Marilyn Horne and a nostalgic "Home Sweet Home" emulating her Australian predecessor Nellie Melba. Richard Bonynge conducted the Royal Opera Orchestra and Chorus. John Mortimer wrote the English translation and Humphrey Burton directed the video. Color. In English. 197 minutes. Home Vision video and laser.

1992 Sandro Massimini video

Highlights from *Il Pipistrello* are sung by Italian operetta master Sandro Massimini and his associates on this videotape from the Italian TV series *Operette, Che Passione!* Featured are "Delioziose che maniere," "Aria di Adele" and "Inno allo champagne." Color. In Italian. About 15 minutes. Ricordi (Italy) video.

Early films

1908 Alfred Duskes film

A trio from *Die Fledermaus* is pictured and sung by Edmund Binder and Hermine Hoffman in this early German sound film directed by Alfred Duskes. Film is in a German archive. About 3 minutes.

1923 Lya de Putti film

This German silent version of the operetta was directed by Max Mack and stars Lya de Putti as Rosalinde, Harry Liedtke, Paul Heidemann, Eva May, Ernst Hoffman and Wilhelm Bendow. It was screened with live music.

FLIEGENDE HOLLÄNDER, DER

1843 opera by Wagner

The Flying Dutchman, the earliest Wagner opera in the repertory, is based on a tale by Heinrich Heine but was probably already a folk legend. It tells of a Dutch ship captain condemned to sail around the world until he is redeemed by the love of a faithful woman. He is allowed to land every seven years to search for her. When he docks in Norway, he meets Senta who is obsessed with his legend and falls in love with him. When he sails away because he thinks she has been unfaithful, she throws herself off a cliff and provides his redemption. See also RICHARD WAGNER.

1964 Joachim Herz film

Fred Dueren portrays the Flying Dutchman with the singing done by Rainer Lüdeke in this East German film of the opera directed by Joachim Herz. Anna Prucnal portrays Senta sung by Gerda Hannemann, Gerd Ehlers is Daland sung by Hans Krämer, Mathilde Danegger is Mary sung by Katrin Wölzl, Herbert Graedke is Eric sung by Rolf Apreck and Hans-Peter Reineck is the Steersman sung by Friedrich Hölze. Rolf Leuter conducts the Leipzig Gewandhaus Orchestra and the Leipzig Opera Chorus. DEFA. Black and white. In German. 98 minutes. On Japanese video and laser.

1980 Grand Théâtre de Genève

Danish baritone Leif Roar stars as the Dutchman in this Geneva Grand Théâtre production by Jean-Claude Riber which was taped live. Romanian soprano Maria Slatinaru is Senta, German bass Hans Ridderbusch is Daland and Ro bert Shunk is Erik. Pier-Luigi Pizzi designed the sets and costumes and Horst Stein conducted the Orchestre de la Suisse Romande. Color. In German with Japanese subtitles. 130 minutes. Japanese video and laserdisc.

1985 Bayreuth Festival

Lisbeth Balslev stars as Senta with the story seen from her point of view in this famous Bayreuth Festival production by Harry Kupfer. Simon Estes portrays the Dutchman with Matti Salminen as Daland, Anny Schlemm as Mary, Robert Schunk as Erik and Graham Clark as Daland's Steersman. Peter Sykora designed the sets, Reinhard Heinrich designed the costumes and Woldemar Nelsson conducted the Bayreuth Festival Orchestra and Chorus. Brian Large directed the video. Color. In German with English subtitles. 136 minutes. Phillips video and laser.

1987 Bavarian State Opera

New Zealand bass-baritone Donald McIntyre portrays the Dutchman with Catarina Ligendza as Senta in this television film of a Bavarian State Opera production by Vaclav Kaslik. The cast includes Bengt Rundgren, Hermann Winkler and Ruth Hesse. Wolfgang Sawallisch conducts the

Bavarian State Opera Orchestra and Chorus. Unitel Film. Color. In German. 117 minutes. On video.

1989 Savonlinna Opera Festival
Franz Grundheber sings the role of the Dutchman with Hildegarde Behrens as Senta in this Savonlinna Opera Festival production by Ilkka Bäckman in the courtyard of the Olavinlinna Castle in Finland. Matti Salminen is Daland with Anita Välkki as Mary, Raimo Sirkiä as Erik and Jorma Silvasti as the Steersman. Juhani Pirskanen designed the sets and Leif Segerstam conducted the Savonlinna Opera Festival Orchestra and Chorus. Juhani Pirskanen was stage director and Aarno Cronvall directed the video. Color. In German with English subtitles. 139 minutes. Teldec video and laser.

1991 Bavarian State Opera
Robert Hale portrays the Dutchman with Julia Varady as Senta in this Bavarian State Opera production in Munich by Henning von Gierke Schmidt. Jaako Ryhänen sings the role of Daland, Anny Schlemm is Mary, Peter Seiffert is Erik, and Ulrich Ress is the Steersman. Wolfgang Sawallisch conducts the Bavarian State Opera Orchestra and Chorus. Eckhard Schmidt directed the video. Color. 135 minutes. In German. EMI Classics video and laser.

Early films

1918 Leo Schützendorf film
Leo Schützendorf stars as the Dutchman with Olga Desmond as Senta in this German silent film. It was directed by Hans Neumann for Harmonie Film. About 70 minutes.

1919 Delog touring film
The German Delog company, which made this silent version of *Der Fliegende Höllander*, had an original answer to the silence of screen opera. They sent the films on tour with the company's own soloists, chorus and orchestra. About 70 minutes.

1923 Lloyd Carleton film
This American silent film was based on the Wagner opera but writer-director Lloyd B. Carleton departed considerably from the libretto. Philip Vanderdecker falls asleep while reading *The Flying Dutchman* and imagines he is the accursed sailor. He becomes involved with Melissa, who is unable to be faithful, and then Zoe who redeems him. Lawson Butt stars as Philip, Nola Luxford is Melissa and Ella Hall is Zoe. R. C. Pictures/FBO. Black and white. About 70 minutes.

FLOOD, THE
1962 TV opera by Stravinsky

Igor Stravinsky was asked by CBS in 1960 to compose a new work for television and decided on a Biblical dance/ drama about Noah. He said he was drawn to the story after visiting Venice and seeing its flooded streets. Robert Craft's libretto is based on the *Bible* and the English Miracle plays. Stravinsky worked with George Balanchine to create the visual effects he wanted on television and especially the masks and use of ritual. The opera was put on stage later the same year. See also IGOR STRAVINSKY.

1962 CBS Television premiere
Stravinsky worked on the production of his television "musical play" with choreographer George Balanchine, designer Rouben Ter-Arutunian and TV director Kirk Browning. Laurence Harvey is the Narrator, Jacques D'Amboise is Adam, Suzanne Farrell is Eve, Sebastian Cabot is Noah, Elsa Lancaster is Noah's wife, Paul Tripp is The Caller, Richard Robinson is Lucifer and John Reardon and Robert Oliver are God. Robert Craft conducted the Columbia Symphony Orchestra and Chorus. The opera, preceded by a documentary about its production, was telecast on June 14, 1962. Black and white. In English. 60 minutes. Video at MTR.

1985 Jaap Drupsteen video
This inventive production uses the original CBS soundtrack of the opera as the basis for a new video production. Jaap Drupsteen designed and directed it with new actors and some electronic wizardry. As in the original, the opera is narrated by Laurence Harvey with the same singing cast and orchestra conducted by Robert Craft. However, the visuals are completely different with the nudity of Adam and Eve an indication of changing times. Color. In English. 30 minutes. Home Vision video.

FLOTOW, FRIEDRICH VON
German composer (1812-1883)

Friedrich von Flotow composed a large number of operas in the 19th century but is known today for only one, the 1847 *Martha*. At the turn of the century *Martha* was an opera house regular and a great favorite of Caruso. It is currently out of fashion in the English-speaking world and there are no commercial videos of it but its tenor aria "Ach so fromm" remains popular, especially when sung in Italian as "M'appari." There is also still interest in Flotow's 1844 "serious" opera *Alessandro Stradella* but it has not been widely recorded. See MARTHA.

FLOYD, CARLISLE
American composer (1926-)

Carlisle Floyd is one of the most popular American opera composers and his works are continually being staged though mostly in regional venues. He is best known for *Susannah* (1956), a modern version of the Biblical story of Susannah and the Elders. Its combination of folk idiom and classical opera has helped it become what the most often performed American opera. Other Floyd operas of note are *Wuthering Heights* (1958), *Of Mice and Men* (1970) and *Willie Stark* (1981). His opera *The Sojourner and Mollie Sinclair* was created for television but first produced on stage. Despite their popularity, Floyd's operas are badly served on video. See SUSANNAH, WILLIE STARK.

1963 The Sojourner and Mollie Sinclair
A comic opera about Scottish settlers in the Carolinas. The "Sojourner" of the title is a clan chieftain trying to maintain highland traditions with opposition from young Mollie who thinks its time for new ideas. The opera was commissioned for television by the Carolina Charter Tercentenary Commission but premiered on stage at East Carolina College in Raleigh, NC, on Dec. 2, 1963. The production was videotaped for presentation on Carolina television stations.

FLYING DUTCHMAN, THE
See DER FLIEGENDE HOLLÄNDER

FOCILE, NUCCIA
Italian soprano (1959-)

Nuccia Focile is one of the rising stars of the international opera world with an agile voice and fine acting ability. She first won attention for her comic roles with particular success as Nanneta in *Falstaff* in Cardiff in 1988. She has also been acclaimed for her portrayals of Violetta and Tatyana

and for her Ascanio in the rarity *Lo Frate 'Nnamorato*. To top it off she has sung in concert with Pavarotti. See L'ITALIANA IN ALGERI (1987), LUCIANO PAVAROTTI (1993), LO FRATE 'NNAMORATO (1990).

FORFAITURE
1921 screen opera by Erlanger

Camille Erlanger's opera *Forfaiture*, the first to be based on a motion picture scenario, used as its source the 1915 Paramount movie *The Cheat*. The film, directed by Cecil B. De Mille, tells of the relationship between a rich Japanese man (Sessue Hayakawa) and a woman who is in desperate need of money (Fannie Ward). Hector Turnbull and Jeanie McPherson wrote the screenplay. Erlanger (1863-1919) is best known for a 1906 opera called *Aphrodite* which was introduced by Mary Garden. He saw the De Mille picture in Paris in 1916 and was so impressed he obtained permission to make it into an opera. The libretto by P. Milliet and A. De Lorde uses the screenplay of the film as its basis. The opera was first staged at the Opéra-Comique in Paris in 1921, two years after Erlanger's death. The movie has been itself has been remade three times: in 1923 with Pola Negri, in 1931 with Tallulah Bankhead and in 1937 in French as *La Forfaiture* with Sessue Hayakawa reprising his original role under the direction of Marcel L'Herbier. The original 1915 movie is considered by French critics to be as important in the development of film as *Citizen Kane*.

FORMAN, MILOS
Czech-born U.S. film director (1932-)

The first movie that Milos Forman saw was a silent version of Smetana's opera *The Bartered Bride*. That was in 1937 in Czechoslovakia and it made a lasting impression. Forman won acclaim in the late 1960s for the Czech new wave films *Loves of a Blonde* and *The Fireman's Ball* but moved to the U. S. in 1969 after the USSR invaded Czechoslovakia. His American movies included the Oscar-winning *One Flew Over the Cuckoo's Nest*. In 1984 he returned to Czechoslovakia to make *Amadeus*, a brilliant biographical tribute to Mozart who had premiered two of his operas in Prague. See THE DANGEROUS LIAISONS (1989 film), WOLFGANG A. MOZART (1984).

FORRESTER, MAUREEN
Canadian contralto (1930 -)

Maureen Forrester sang mainly in Canada in concert in the early part of her career but turned towards opera in 1962. Her success was rapid and she has now sung on the stages of most of the major opera houses of the world including the Met and La Scala. Forrester is noted for her witty characterizations as well as her splendid voice and has been featured in a number of screen operas including Madame Flora in *The Medium*. See CENDRILLON (1979), LES DIALOGUES DES CARMÉLITES (1987), HANSEL AND GRETEL (1970), IOLANTHE (1984), THE MEDIUM (1975).

1982 Portrait of Maureen Forrester
Auréle Lecoste directed this musical portrait of Forrester for a Canadian telecast in January 1982. She talks about her life and career and sings arias by Offenbach, Dvořák, Ponchielli and Gershwin. John Newmark accompanies her on piano. Color. In English. 60 minutes.

FÖRSTERCHRISTL, DIE
1907 operetta by Jarno

The Forester's Daughter is Hungarian composer Georg Jarno's most popular operetta and has been filmed four times. It tells the tuneful if somewhat bucolic story of a romance between the Austrian Emperor Franz Joseph and Christl, the beautiful daughter of a forester. The libretto is by Gerhard Buchbinder. See also GEORG JARNO.

1925 Friedrich Zelnick film
Friedrich Zelnick directed this silent film of the operetta which was screened with live music. It stars William Dieterle, who later became a notable American film director, with Harry Liedtke and Eduard von Winterstein. Black and white. In German. About 75 minutes.

1931 Irene Eisinger film
German opera soprano Irene Eisinger stars as Christl, the forester's daughter, in the first sound film of the operetta. Paul Richter plays the Emperor, Oskar Karlweiss is Mozart and Adele Sandrock, André Pilot and Paul Hörbiger lend support. Some of the songs in this version are based on music by Mozart. Friedrich Zelnick directed. Black and white. In German. 90 minutes.

1952 Johanna Matz film
Johanna Matz stars as the forester's daughter Christl in this 1952 German film of the operetta directed by Arthur Maria Rabenalt. Karl Schönbock portrays the Emperor, Angelika Hauff is Ilona, Will Quadflieg is Joseph, Ivan Petrovich is the Count, Jochen Hauer is the forester and Oskar Sims plays Leisinger. Black and white. In German. 104 minutes.

1962 Franz-Josef Gottlieb film
Franz-Josef Gottlieb directed this German film of the operetta. It stars Sabine Sinjen as Christl, Peter Weck and Sieghardt Rupp. Franz Grothe arranged the music, Dieter Wedekind was cinematographer and Janne Furch and Fritz Böttger wrote the adaptation. Black and white. In German. 104 minutes.

FORTUNE TELLER, THE
1898 operetta by Herbert

Victor Herbert's operetta *The Fortune Teller* is full of tuneful Hungarian gypsy music. Harry B. Smith's libretto tells the story of a rich heiress called Irma and a gypsy fortune teller who looks just like her. Both roles were created on stage by Alice Nielsen in a production that also featured opera singer Marguerita Sylva. The operetta is still being staged; there was a recent off-Broadway production by the Light Opera of Manhattan. See also VICTOR HERBERT.

1934 La Buenaventura
Enrico Caruso Jr. stars as Enrico Baroni in this Spanish-language adaptation of the Herbert operetta made by the Warner Brothers studio in Los Angeles. The film includes most of Herbert's songs with new lyrics plus some arias from the operas *Don Pasquale*, *L'Elisir d'Amore* and *L'Africaine*. Anita Campillo plays the double role of Irma and Elvira with Luis Alberni as Fresco and Alfonso Pedroza as Sandor. Black and white. In Spanish. 77 minutes.

FORZA DEL DESTINO, LA
1862 opera by Verdi

Giuseppe Verdi's melodramatic opera *The Force of Destiny* has a libretto by Francesco Maria Piave based on a Spanish play and is set in 18th century Spain. Don Alvaro accidentally shoots Donna Leonora's father who has caught them trying to elope. Her brother Don Carlo swears revenge and the lovers have to separate. Leonora becomes a hermit with the help of Father Guardiano and Alvaro becomes a monk in a nearby monastery. Carlo finds him and is killed in the resultant duel but manages to stab his sister before dying. Alvaro retreats into prayer. See also GIUSEPPE VERDI.

1949 Tito Gobbi film
Tito Gobbi was 37 when he starred in this film of the opera directed by Carmine Gallone. It was shot in natural settings near Rome with most of the actors dubbed by opera singers. Gobbi sings and acts the role of Don Carlo, Catherina Mancini sings Leonora acted by Nelly Corradi, Galliano Masini sings Don Alvaro acted by Gino Sinimberghi and Vito de Taranto is Fra Melitone. Gabriele Santini leads the Rome Opera House Orchestra and Chorus. Black and white. In Italian without subtitles. 110 minutes. Bel Canto Society/ Pickwick (England) videos.

1951 Opera Cameos series
This highlights version of the third act of the opera was produced for the *Opera Cameos* TV series. Soprano Rina Telli sings the role of Leonora, bass-baritone Nicola Moscona is Don Carlo and basso Lloyd Harris is Father Guardiano. Hugh LaRue introduces the arias and explains the plot while Giuseppe Bamboschek conducts the orchestra. Joseph Vinti wrote the script and Carlo Vinti directed the film. Black and white. 30 minutes.

1958 Teatro di San Carlo, Naples
An historic live performance of the opera at the San Carlo Opera in Naples with an all-star cast. Renata Tebaldi is Donna Leonora, Franco Corelli is Don Alvaro, Ettore Bastianini is Don Carlo, Boris Christoff is Padre Guardiano, Oralia Dominguez is Preziosilla and Renato Capecchi is Fra Melitone. The opera was televised by RAI in March 1958. The picture quality of this archival copy is poor but the sound is wonderful and the singers are magnificent. Francesco Molinari-Pradelli conducts the San Carlo Theatre orchestra and chorus. Black and white. In Italian. 156 minutes. Legato Classics/Bel Canto Society videos.

1978 Teatro alla Scala
Montserrat Caballé portrays Leonora in this La Scala production telecast in the U.S. in 1980. José Carreras is Don Alvaro, Piero Cappuccilli is Don Carlos, Nicolai Ghiaurov is Padre Guardiano and Sesto Bruscanti is Melitone. Giuseppe Patanè

conducts the La Scala Opera Orchestra and Chorus. Color. In Italian with English subtitles. 155 minutes. Lyric video.

1984 Metropolitan Opera
Leontyne Price stars as Leonora in this Metropolitan Opera production by John Dexter. Giuseppe Giacomini is Don Alvaro, Leo Nucci is Don Carlo, Isola Jones is Preziosilla, Bonaldo Giaiotti is Padre Guardiano and Enrico Fissore is Fra Melitone. Eugene Berman designed the sets and Peter J. Hall the costumes. James Levine conducts the Metropolitan Opera Orchestra and Chorus. Kirk Browning directed the video on March 24, 1984, which was telecast Oct. 31. Color. In Italian with English subtitles. 179 minutes. Paramount video/Pioneer laser.

1996 Metropolitan Opera
Sharon Sweet sings the role of Leonora opposite Placido Domingo as Don Alvaro in this Metropolitan Opera production by Giancarlo Del Monaco. Vladimir Chernov is Don Carlo, Gloria Scalchi is Preziosilla, Robert Scandiuzzi is Padre Guardiano and Bruno Pola is Fra Melitone. Michael Scott designed the sets and costumes and Gil Wechsler arranged the lighting. James Levine conducts the Metropolitan Opera Orchestra and Chorus. Brian Large directed the video of a performance in March 1996 telecast on Sept. 11, 1996. Color. In Italian with English subtitles. 180 minutes.

Early/related films

1911 La Force du Destin
This 1911 French Pathé film was praised by critics for being a good screen adaptation of the opera. About 14 minutes.

1986 Jean de Florette/Manon of the Spring
The overture of *La Forza del Destino* is used very effectively in these French films which tell a harsh story about the force of destiny. They were directed by Claude Berri and based on a novel by Marcel Pagnol. Color. In French. 122/113 minutes.

1976 Hans Glanzmann animated film
This short animated film titled *La Forza del Destino* was created by Hans Glanzmann at the London International Film School. It tells the tragic destiny of a man seduced by a woman. Color. 3 minutes.

1987 Charles Sturridge film
British director Charles Sturridge directed the lyrical black-and-white *Forza del Destino* episode of *Aria*. It shows the children Nicola Swain, Jack Kyle and Marianne McLoughlin in church, stealing a car and learning about violence. They seem to need the protection asked for in "La vergine degli Angeli" sung by Leontyne Price as Leonora with Giorgio Tozzi and Ezio Flagello. Thomas Schippers conducts the RCA Italiana Orchestra. Color. 10 minutes.

1988 Making Opera
Subtitled "The Creation of Verdi's *La Forza del Destino*," this informative Canadian film revolves around a production of the opera by the Canadian Opera Company. The filmmakers observe the preparations of some 500 people involved with the opera and show how it looked when it was finally staged. The opera director is John Copley and his cast includes Stefka Evstatieva as Leonora, Allan Monk, Judith Forst and Ernesto Veronelli. Maurizio Arena conducts the orchestra. Anthony Azzopardi directed the film with Ron Stannett as cinematographer. Color. In English. 88 minutes. VIEW video.

1994 Desperate Remedies
The music of *La Forza del Destino* is central to this New Zealand film about a 19th century woman and her odd relationships. The film opens with her cracking her whip to the overture and includes a moment of understanding set to the aria "Pace, pace, mio dio." Jennifer Ward-Lealand is the woman, Peter Scholes arranged the music and Peter Wells and Stewart Main directed the film. Color. 101 minutes.

FOSS, LUKAS
German-born U.S. composer (1922-)

Pianist-conductor-composer Lukas Foss has written three operas. *The Jumping Frog of Calaveras County* (1949) is based on the Mark Twain story and the whimsical *Introductions and Good-byes* (1960) was created for the Spoleto Festival. His best-known opera, however, is the devilish folk tale *Griffelkin* which he composed for NBC Opera Theatre. It premiered on television in 1955 but has been staged three times since, the last a popular 1993 New York City Opera production. See GRIFFELKIN.

FOSTER, SUSANNA
American soprano (1924-)

Susanna Foster had an extraordinary voice and though she never appeared on the opera stage except in movies, she did eventually become a star on the operetta stage. Foster was born in Chicago and was signed for a film by MGM at the age of eleven as she was a child prodigy singer who could sing F above high C. She and her family moved to Hollywood in 1935 but the film that was to have been called *B Above High C* was never made and she returned to voice lessons. She was then signed by Paramount who featured her in four films beginning with *The Great Victor Herbert* in 1939. After that she went to Universal for eight more including her best movie *The Phantom of the Opera*. In 1948 she quit filmmaking and starred in a West Coast production of the operetta *Naughty Marietta*. She later joined the Cleveland Light Opera Company and toured in *The Merry Widow*. In 1955 she sang in *Brigadoon* and *Show Boat*. See THE PHANTOM OF THE OPERA (1943), VICTOR HERBERT (1939).

1941 There's Magic in Music
Foster had good reviews for her singing and her acting in this semi-musical. She plays a hard-boiled burlesque singer named Toodles LaVerne taken by Allan Jones to a children's summer music camp where she becomes an opera diva. Andrew L. Stone directed. Aka *The Hard-Boiled Canary*. Paramount. Black and white. 80 minutes.

1941 Glamour Boy
Foster is the girl loved by Jackie Cooper in this story about a grown up child star hired to coach a kid in a remake of his old success *Skippy*. She sings "Sempre Libera" from *La Traviata* and two songs. Ralph Murphy directed. Paramount. Black and white. 79 minutes.

1942 Star Spangled Rhythm
Foster is one of the many guest stars in this all-star Paramount extravaganza featuring every star on the lot in a show for the Navy. It was her last film for the studio. George Marshall directed. Black and white. 99 minutes.

1943 Top Man
Foster stars opposite Donald O'Connor in this putting-on-a-show musical with silent movie star Lillian Gish playing her mother. Foster's hit song in

the film is "Wrap Your Troubles in Dreams." Charles Lamont directed for Universal. Black and white. 74 minutes.

1944 The Climax
Foster once again portrays an opera singer in this thriller follow up to *Phantom of the Opera*. Boris Karloff plays a killer who years before had killed a singer who looked like Foster. There are a number of opera sequences with Foster. George Waggner directed. Color. 86 minutes.

1944 Bowery to Broadway
Jack Oakie and Donald Cook have rival beer gardens in old New York. Foster is one of the Universal stars who sing for them when they join forces to produce musicals. Charles Lamont directed. Black and white. 94 minutes.

1944 Follow The Boys
Foster has a cameo role as herself in this all-star Universal musical with Orson Welles, Jeanette MacDonald, et al. Edward Sutherland directed. Black and white. 122 minutes.

1944 This Is the Life
Foster is a singer, the fickle girlfriend of Donald O'Connor, but she really fancies an older man, Patrick Knowles. She sings some popular songs including "With a Song in My Heart." Felix Feist directed. Universal. Black and white. 87 minutes.

1945 Frisco Sal
This is a Western mystery but Foster still gets to sing. She portrays a woman who goes west to find the man who killed her brother. Universal. George Waggner directed. Black and white. 94 minutes.

1945 That Night With You
Foster's last film was a kind of musical screwball comedy that featured her singing a feminine version of *The Barber of Seville* and not liking either the idea or the make-up. She portrays a singer who becomes a Broadway success. William A. Seiter directed. Universal. Black and white. 84 minutes.

FRA DIAVOLO
1830 opera by Auber

Daniel Auber's most famous comic opera is based on legends about a Robin Hood-type bandit in southern Italy who was hanged by Napoleon. In Eugène Scribe's libretto he is not very altruistic and seems mostly just interested in robbing. He disguises himself as a Marquis and goes to a tavern where he plans to rob an English lord and lady. Lorenzo dreams of capturing the bandit and claiming a reward so he can marry Zerlina, the innkeeper's daughter. Fra Diavolo was one of the most popular operas of the 19th century and has been filmed in various ways. There is no modern commercial video but Lyric offers copies of telecasts in French and German. See ALSO DANIEL AUBER.

1930 Tino Pattiera film
This 1930 film is important historically as the first full-length opera adapted for the screen with sound and photographed as a movie rather than a stage production. Mario Bonnard made French, Italian and German versions with opera star Tino Pattiera portraying Diavolo in all three. Pattiera, a Croatian tenor who sang in Chicago in the early 1920s, is the only opera singer in the film except outside the chorus. The Zerlina role, here called Anita, is played by Madeleine Breville in the French version and Brigitte Horney in the German. Auber's music was arranged by Giuseppe Becce and the opera was cinematized with spoken dialogue and swashbuckling action. Black and white. In French, German or Italian. 90 minutes.

1933 Laurel and Hardy film
Bonnard's film was the model for the best known cinematic adaptation of the opera, the 1933 Laurel and Hardy film directed by Hal Roach for MGM and known as *Fra Diavolo* or *The Devil's Brother*. Dennis King portrays the bandit Diavolo and, as in the Bonnard film, is the only singer except for the chorus. There is not a lot of the opera left but it is one of the most amusing Laurel and Hardy sound films. Stan Laurel plays Stanlio Laurelo and Oliver Hardy is Olivero Hardio. Black and white. In English. 88 minutes. On video and laserdisc.

1948 La Scala in Rome
A highlights version of the opera with La Scala singers performing on stage at the Rome Opera House. The film features Nemo Adami as Fra Diavolo, Palmira Vitali Marina as Lady Pamela, Luciano Neorni and Gino Conti. Angelo Questa conducted the Rome Opera House Orchestra and Chorus and George Richfield produced and directed the film. There is an English narration. Black and white. In Italian and English. 20 minutes.

Early/related films

1906 Hedwig Francillo sound film
A film of an aria from *Fra Diavolo* was made with soprano Hedwig Francillo for Oskar Messter and his Biophon-Theater in Berlin. The scene was shown on screen while the aria played on a phonograph. About 3 minutes.

1909 Albert Capellani film
This French film of the story was directed by Albert Capellani for Pathé and stars Jean Angelo and Germaine Rouer. About 10 minutes.

1912 Alice Guy-Blaché film
This adaptation of the opera was made by the first woman film director, Alice Guy-Blaché, for her Solax company. It stars Billy Quirk as Fra Diavolo, George Paxton as Lord Allcash, Fanny Simpson as Lady Allcash, Darwin Karr as Lorenzo and Blanche Cornwall as Zerlina. It was warmly received by contemporary critics who felt it augured well for the future of opera on the screen. Black and white. In English. About 45 minutes.

1913 Ambrosio film
A silent Italian film was made for the Ambrosio company based on the story of Fra Diavolo. About 20 minutes.

1915 Éclair film
A silent French film was made for the Éclair company based on the story of Fra Diavolo. About 30 minutes.

1922 Tense Moments from Opera series
Gordon Hopkirk stars as Fra Diavolo in this British highlights version of the opera made for the *Tense Moments from Opera* series. Vivian Gibson plays Zerlina, Lionel Howard is Lorenzo and Amy Willard is Lady Allcash. Challis Sanderson directed for Master film. Black and white. About 12 minutes.

1924 Emilio Zeppieri film
Emilio Zeppieri directed this sound version of the opera using real opera singers. Their voices were recorded and the film was screened with synchronized music using the Zeppieri Fotocinema system. Apparently it didn't work very well as it was pulled from circulation after the first few screenings. Bosia film. About 70 minutes.

1925 Gustavo Serena film
This *Fra Diavolo* tells the story of the bandit Michel Pezza on whom the Fra Diavolo legend is based but is not the opera. It stars Gustavo Serena as Diavolo and was directed by Roberto Roberti and Mario Gargiulo. About 75 minutes.

1942 Luigi Zampa film
Enzo Fiermonte portrays Diavolo in this *Fra Diavolo* which tells a similar story about the Italian bandit. However, it is based on a play and not the opera. Luigi Zampa directed. 90 minutes.

1952 Donne e Briganti
Amedeo Nazzari stars as Diavolo in this Italian film of the story directed by Mario Soldati. Black and white. 88 minutes.

1962 I Tromboni di Fra Diavolo
Francisco Rabal stars as Fra Diavolo in the Italian film directed by Giorgio C. Simonelli. It uses music from the opera as its soundtrack. Color. 90 minutes.

1962 La Leggenda di Fra Diavolo
Tony Russell stars as Fra Diavolo in this Italian film about the legendary bandit directed by Leopold Savona. Color. 90 minutes.

FRANCESCA DA RIMINI
1914 opera by Zandonai

The tragic story of the 13th century Italian lovers Paolo and Francesca has similarities to the Tristan and Isolde legend. It originated in Dante's *Inferno* and has inspired over 30 operas. The best known is Riccardo Zandonai's 1914 version composed to a libretto by Tito Ricordi. It's based on a play written by Gabriele D'Annunzio for Eleanora Duse. Paolo is sent by his brother Giociotti to bring back bride-to-be Francesca. They fall in love, are eventually found out by the brother and killed. The opera was produced at the Metropolitan Opera in 1916 soon after its premiere in Milan and was revived in 1984. The story inspired many early films which have no direct connection with the opera but at least two were based on the D'Annunzio play. See also RICCARDO ZANDONAI.

1984 Metropolitan Opera
Renata Scotto is in fine form as Francesca with Placido Domingo as Paolo in this colorful Metropolitan Opera production by Piero Faggioni.

Cornell MacNeil is a properly villainous Gianciotto, William Lewis is the nasty Malatestino, Isola Jones is Francesca's handmaiden Smadragdi and Richard Fredericks is Francesca's brother. Ezio Frigerio designed the lavish sets and Franca Squarciapino the costumes while James Levine conducted the Metropolitan Opera Orchestra and Chorus. Brian Large directed the video. Color. In Italian with English subtitles. 148 minutes. Paramount video/ Pioneer laser.

Related film

1910 Jeanne Delvair film
This French film was made before the opera but was based on the D'Annunzio play. It was directed by Alberto Capellani for Pathé and stars Jeanne Delvair as Francesca, Jacques Gretillat and Paul Capellani. About 10 minutes.

1912 Florence Turner film
Florence Turner stars at Francesca in this American film of the story made for Vitagraph and apparently inspired by the play. Playing opposite her are William Raymond and Hector Dean. About 15 minutes.

FRASER-SIMSON, HAROLD
British composer (1872-1944)

Harold Fraser-Simson composed the hugely popular light opera *The Maid of the Mountains* which opened in London in 1916 and ran for 1352 performances. It was a must-see operetta for World War I soldiers on leave and was revived in 1972. Its most popular song, a waltz called "Love will find a way," begins with the first four notes of Lehar's *Merry Widow* waltz twice repeated. Joan Sutherland recorded this aria on her influential album *The Golden Age of Operetta*. The story concerns a mountain brigand, his involvement with the Governor's daughter and the true love he inspires in Teresa, the maid of the mountains.

1932 The Maid of the Mountains
Harry Welchman, England's answer to Laurence Tibbett, stars as the bandit who robs the rich and helps the poor in this rather stodgy film of the operetta directed by Lupino Lane. Betty Stockfeld plays the Governor's daughter with Nancy Brown as the maid of the mountains. Black and white. 80 minutes.

FRASQUITA
1922 operetta by Lehár

Richard Tauber starred as Armand when this Franz Lehár operetta premiered in Vienna in 1922. It came to London in 1925 but didn't make it to New York until 1953. *Frasquita* is the story of a gypsy woman and her protracted love-hate relationship with Armand. He starts off intending to marry Dolly but gives her up to his friend Hippolyt when he finds he prefers Frasquita. Several notable opera sopranos have found the role of Frasquita to their liking including Conchita Supervia, Jarmila Novotná and Ilona Massey. See also FRANZ LEHÁR.

1934 Jarmila Novotná film
Czech soprano Jarmila Novotná, who later became a Metropolitan Opera star, portrays Frasquita in this Austrian film of the operetta. Her singing was hailed by critics as the highlight of the movie. Baritone Hans Heinz Bollmann sings the Armand role with Heinz Ruhmann as Hippolyt and Charlotte Dauder as Dolly. Hans Moser provides comic relief as the servant Jaromir. Carl Lamac directed for Atlantis Film. Black and white. In German. 82 minutes.

FRATE 'NNAMORATO, LO
1731 comic opera by Pergolesi

Giovanni Pergolesi is best known for his intermezzo *La Serva Padrone* but this full-scale comic opera, *The Beloved Brother*, was his first success. The dialogue is in Neapolitan dialect and this prevented the opera from being widely known in other Italian cities. The complicated libretto by Gennaro Antonio Federico (who wrote *La Serva Padrone*) tells the story of the Neapolitan twin sisters Nina and Nena. They think they love Ascanio but then he turns out to be their long-lost brother. He is the ward of rich Marcaniello, who has designs on the sisters, while his daughter Lucrezia fancies Ascanio. The La Scala production of the opera is on CD and video.See also GIOVANNI PERGOLESI.

1990 Teatro alla Scala
This colorful La Scala production was a important revival arranged by conductor Riccardo Muti and director Robert De Simone. Amelia Felle portrays Nena, Bernadette Manca Di Nissa is Nina, Nuccia Focile is Ascanio, Alessandro Corbelli is Marcaniello, Luciana D'Intino is Lucrezia, Ezio Di Cesare is Carlo, Elizabeth Norberg-Schulz is

Vanella, Nicoletta Curiel is Cardella, Bruno De Simone is Don Pietro and Luca Bonini is the swordsman. The sets are by Mauro Carosi and the costumes by Odette Nicoletti. John Phillip directed the video. Color. In Italian with English subtitles. 132 minutes. Home Vision video/ Japanese laser.

FRAU, DIE WEISS, WAS SIE WILL, EINE

See A WOMAN WHO KNOWS WHAT SHE WANTS

FRAU IM HERMELIN, DIE

1919 operetta by Gilbert

German composer Jean Gilbert's *The Lady in Ermine* is a tuneful multi-generation operetta about beautiful barefooted women aristocrats who use ermine coats as weapons. The "lady" is supposedly a ghost who defends a castle from invaders in times of peril. This was Gilbert's most Lehár-like operetta and was staged in London in 1921 as *The Lady of the Rose* with Phyllis Dare as its star. It reached New York in 1922 as *The Lady in Ermine* with splendid English lyrics by Lorenz Hart. Rudolf Schanzer and Ernest Welisch wrote the original German libretto. Athough the story has been filmed three times, Gilbert's music has hardly been used. See also JEAN GILBERT.

1927 Corinne Griffith film
Silent diva Corinne Griffith stars as the resourceful woman with an ermine weapon in *The Lady in Ermine*, a silent version of the operetta directed by James Flood for First National Pictures. Francis X. Bushman is the invading general and Eoinar Hasen is her husband. The film was shown in cinemas with Gilbert's music played live. Black and white. In English. About 70 minutes.

1930 Vivienne Segal film
Vivienne Segal stars in this adaptation of the operetta titled *Bride of the Regiment* with Gilbert's music replaced by songs by Al Dubin, Al Bryan and Eddie Ward. The plot is the same with Segal playing the countess defending the castle, Walter Pidgeon as the invading colonel and Alan Prior as the husband. In Australia the film was called *The Lady of the Rose* after the stage production. John Francis Dillon directed for First National. Black and white. In English. About 80 minutes.

1949 Betty Grable film
Gilbert's operetta provided the basis for Ernst Lubitsch's last movie, *That Lady in Ermine*. He died during the filming and the movie was completed by Otto Preminger. Betty Grable has a double role as noblewomen from two generations who know how good a weapon an ermine coat can be. Douglas Fairbanks Jr. is the army chief who has to be overcome in both generations and Cesar Romero is the cowardly husband. Gilbert's music has again been shunted aside, this time replaced by songs by Leo Robin and Frederick Hollander. Twentieth Century-Fox. Color. In English. 89 minutes.

FRAU LUNA

1899 operetta by Lincke

Frau Luna is Paul Lincke's most popular operetta and has become symbolic of Berlin, especially since his Berlin theme tune "Berliner Luft" was incorporated into a revised version. The operetta originated as an 1899 fantasy about a group of Berliners visiting the moon via balloon where they meet Frau Luna, the lady-in-the-moon. It's an Offenbach-type burlesque and many of Lincke's better songs have been added to it over the years. The songs remain popular and the operetta is still being staged in Berlin today. See also PAUL LINCKE.

1941 Lizzi Waldmuller film
The operetta was filmed in Berlin in 1941 with Lizzi Waldmuller as its top star. The story was changed considerably and was now a backstage romance set at the time of the opening of *Frau Luna* on stage but the most popular songs were retained. The cast includes Fita Benkhoff, Irene von Meyendorff, Georg Alexander and Theo Lingen. Theo Lingen also directed. Black and white. In German. 96 minutes.

FRAU OHNE SCHATTEN, DIE

1919 opera by Strauss

Richard Strauss's *The Woman without a Shadow* is a "magic fairy tale," a highly symbolic opera with an original libretto by Hugo von Hofmannsthal. The Empress, daughter of the King of the Spirits, is without a shadow, a sign of her childlessness. She must find one to keep the Emperor from being turned to stone and so makes a bargain to buy the shadow of the wife of the dyer Barak. In the end she decides not to take the other woman's shadow when she realizes the harm this action will cause.

Her humanity results in happiness all round. See also HUGO VON HOFMANNSTHAL, RICHARD STRAUSS.

1992 Salzburg Festival
Cheryl Studer portrays the Empress and Eva Marton is the Dyer's Wife in this record of a performance staged by Götz Friedrich at the Salzburg Festival in 1992. Studer is in terrific form with Thomas Moser as her Emperor, Robert Hale as the dyer Barak, Marjana Lipovsek as the Nurse and Bryn Terfel as the Spirit-Messenger. Rolfe and Marianne Glittenberg designed the atmospheric sets and Sir Georg Solti conducted the Vienna Philharmonic and Vienna Stage Opera Chorus. Brian Large directed the video and his mastery helps clarify the action. Color. In German with English subtitles. 204 minutes. London video and laser.

FREGOLI, LEOPOLDO
Italian filmmaker (1867-1936)

Italian stage performer Leopold Fregoli, known as the "Protean Artiste" in England, is considered the first Italian film director. He was a quick-change illusionist who transformed himself into famous people including composers Rossini and Verdi conducting their operas. Fregoli saw the first Lumière films in 1896, constructed what he called a "Fregoligraphe" shortly afterward and made about 25 short films in 1897. These were screened at his stage performances when he would stand behind the screen and sing or talk in synchronization with the moving pictures.

1898 Maestri di Musica
Fregoli's famous film of great opera composers, *Maestros of Music*, is one of the first opera films and survives in an Italian film archive. In it illusionist Fregoli is seen as Rossini, Verdi, Mascagni and Wagner as they conduct their own operas. It was presented with the appropriate music of each composer. In England the film was titled *Fregoli the Protean Artiste* and was distributed by film pioneer R. W. Paul. About 6 minutes.

FREISCHÜTZ, DER
1821 opera by Weber

The Freeshooter is Carl Maria von Weber's best known opera. Max has to win a shooting contest if he is to marry Agathe. At midnight in the Wolf Glen he obtains seven magic bullets from the evil spirit Samiel. In the competition the seventh bullet is controlled by Samiel and is intended for Agathe. However, a holy hermit intervenes and the bullet kills the villainous huntsman Kaspar instead. Friedrich Kind's libretto is based on a tale from the *Gespensterbuch* by Johann Apel and Friedrich Laun. The Wolf Glen scene became one of the central images of 19th century German romanticism. See also CARL MARIA VON WEBER.

1968 Rolf Liebermann film
Ernst Kozub sings the role of Max with Arlene Saunders as Agathe in this Rolf Liebermann film based on a Hamburg State Opera production. Tom Krause is Ottokar, Edith Mathis is Aennchen, Bernard Minetti is Samiel, Gottlieb Frick is Kaspar and Hans Sotin is the Hermit. Leopold Ludwig conducts the Hamburg State Opera Orchestra and Chorus. Hannes Schindler was cinematographer and Joachim Hess directed. It was released theatrically in the U.S. Polyphon Films. Color. In German. 127 minutes.

1981 Wurttemberg State Opera
Director/designer Achim Freyer created this mysterious but intriguing production of the opera for the Wurttemberg State Opera in Stuttgart. The sets are striking, the singing good and the production engrossing. Toni Krämer is Max, Catarina Ligendza is Agathe, Raili Viljakainen is Aennchen, Wolfram Raub is Samiel, Wolfgang Schone is Ottokar and Wolfgang Probst is Caspar. Hans Joachim-Haas's lighting enhances the nightmarish quality of the production. Dennis Russell Davies leads the Wurttemberg State Opera Orchestra and Chorus. Hartmut Schottler directed the video. Color. In German with English subtitles. 150 minutes. Home Vision video.

1985 Dresden Semper Opera
Der Freischütz was the signature opera of the Semper Opera House in Dresden and was chosen to re-open the rebuilt theater on Feb. 13, 1985. Dresden star tenor Rainer Goldberg sings Max, Jana Smitkova is Agathe, Andrea Ihle is Aennchen, Hans-Joachim Ketelsen is Ottokar, Ekkehard Wlaschiha is Kaspar and Theo Adam is the Hermit. Joachim Herz directed the production and Wolf-Dieter Hauschild conducted the Dresden State Opera Chorus and Orchestra. The opera was telecast in Germany. Color. In German. 148 minutes. On Japanese laserdisc.

Early/related films

1908 Henny Porten sound film

Henny Porten, Germany's first important silent film star, is featured as Agathe in this Messter Biophone sound film based on a recording of an aria from the opera. Porten's father Franz, a former opera singer, directed the film in a Berlin studio using Oskar Messter's synchronization process. About 3 minutes.

1917 German silent film

A silent feature-length German film was apparently made of the opera in 1917. About 70 minutes.

1954 Melody Beyond Love

Excerpts from *Der Freischütz* are featured in the German film *Konsul Strotthoff* (released in the U.S. as *Melody Beyond Love)* which is set in Salzburg and Hamburg. They are a counterpoint to a love triangle story revolving around a singer studying at the Salzburg Mozarteum. Inge Egger and Willy Birgel are the stars and Erich Engel directed. Black and white. In German. 103 minutes.

1967 Five Girls to Deal With

Evald Schorm's Czech film *Pet Holek na Krku* revolves around performances of *Der Freischütz* staged by a repertory company in the provincial city of Liberec. The five girls of the title attend every night as they are infatuated with the tenor; the romanticism of the opera is counterpointed with the girls' romantic behavior. Black and white. In Czech. 100 minutes.

1994 Ildiko Enyedi film

Hungarian filmmaker Ildiko Enyedi, who won an Oscar nomination for *My 20th Century*, based her narrative film *Der Freischütz* on the Weber opera but updated it to Budapest in the 1990s. Max is a policeman married to Eva. He makes a pact with the Devil who gives him six bullets which never miss. Gary Kemp is Max, Sadie Frost is Eva and Alexander Kajdanovski plays the Devil. Alliance Communications. Color and black and white. In Hungarian and German. 110 minutes.

FRENI, MIRELLA

Italian soprano (1935-)

Mirelli Freni has been singing at the Metropolitan Opera for over thirty years and has won many admirers for her voice and personality. She began her career in Italy but has now sung in most major opera houses. Freni is noted for her Butterfly and her recording of the opera is used effectively in the films *Fatal Attraction* and *M. Butterfly*. Freni is married to Bulgarian basso Nicolai Ghiaurov and appears with him in his video biography. See ADRIANA LECOUVREUR (1989), LA BOHÈME (1965/ 1989), CARMEN (1966), DON CARLO (1983), ERNANI (1982), EUGENE ONEGIN (1985), FALSTAFF (1992), FAUST (1988), FEDORA (1993), NICOLAI GHIAUROV (1986), MADAMA BUTTERFLY (1974), THE MARRIAGE OF FIGARO (1976), METROPOLITAN OPERA (1983/ 1986/1991), OTELLO (1974), SHERRILL MILNES (1985), SIMON BOCCANEGRA (1978), LA TRAVIATA (1975).

FRICK, GOTTLOB

German bass (1906-)

Gottlob Frick, one of the great basses of the century, has recorded a wide range of operas but is generally thought of as one of the masters of Wagner. He began to sing professionally in Germany in 1927 and was a regular at Covent Garden from 1957 to 1967. Unfortunately he has left only a small legacy of film performances. He can been seen as Hagen in the film about the recording of the *Ring* in 1965 and as Kaspar in *Der Freischütz*. In his other two films he simply a memorable voice on the soundtrack. See DON GIOVANNI (1954), DER FREISCHÜTZ (1968), WOLFGANG A. MOZART (1955), DER RING DES NIBELUNGEN (1965 film).

FRIEDERIKE

1928 operetta by Lehár

Richard Tauber starred as Goethe in the Berlin premiere of this bittersweet Franz Lehár operetta. Friederike is his first love, a young woman who loves him as much as he loves her. She realizes, however, that unless she gives him up, he will never leave the village and become what he is destined to become. She makes him believe that she no longer cares and he leaves for Weimar. When he returns years later, he discovers the truth but it is too late. One of the most famous arias is Friederike's question, "Warum hast du mich wachgeküsst?" The operetta was staged in New York in 1937 as *Frederika*. See also FRANZ LEHÁR.

1932 Mady Christians film

Mady Christians is extremely beautiful as Friederike in this German film version of the Lehár operetta. Hans Heinz Bollmann portrays Goethe and sings the Lehár melodies exceptionally well. Viet Harlan is the Duke of Weinmar and Ida Wust is Magdalena. The film was directed by Fritz Friedman-Frederich. Black and white. In German. 90 minutes.

FRIML, RUDOLF

Czech-born U.S. composer (1879-1972)

Rudolf Friml was one of the last major American composers of European-style operettas. Friml began his career in his native Prague but moved to New York in 1904. In 1912 Victor Herbert quarreled with Emma Trentini and Friml was asked to take over and create a new operetta for her. Friml composed *The Firefly* and it launched him on a popular music theater career. Friml had major successes with European-style operettas like *Rose-Marie* (1924) and *The Vagabond King* (1925) but was less successful with American-style musicals like *Cinders*. His 1927 operetta *The White Eagle* is based on the same play as Cecil B. De Mille's 1913 debut film *The Squaw Man*. As European operettas became outmoded, Friml switched to Hollywood and composed music for films ranging from Jeanette MacDonald's 1930 operetta *The Lottery Bride* to Nelson Eddy's 1947 western *Northwest Outpost*. Friml created a style of music so uniquely recognizable as his own that musical satirist Tom Lehrer wrote a lyric describing a tune as "quite Rudolph Friml-y." See NELSON EDDY (1947), THE FIREFLY, THE LOTTERY BRIDE, ROSE-MARIE, THE VAGABOND KING.

FROM THE HOUSE OF THE DEAD

1930 opera by Janáček

Leo Janáček's powerful opera *From the House of the Dead* (Z Mrtvého Domu) is an adaptation of Dostoevsky's autobiographical 1862 novel *The House of the Dead*. It is set in a prison camp in Siberia and begins with a prisoner being flogged. Despite the grimness of the story, the opera is considered both exhilarating and uplifting. For many in Czechoslovakia it was a prophetic opera about the Communist future. See also LEO JANÁČEK.

1969 NET Opera
Producer Peter Herman Adler added flashbacks to this expressionistic English version of the opera presented by National Educational Television Opera. Adler conducted the NET Opera Orchestra

and Kirk Browning, who had worked with Adler on the NBC Opera Theatre, directed. Black and white. In English. 55 minutes.

1992 Salzburg Festival
Nicolai Ghiaurov stars as Goryanchikov with Philip Langridge as Skuratov in this Salzburg Festival production by Klaus Michael Gruber. Monte Pederson sings Shishkov, Barry McCauley is Luka, Heinz Zednik is Shapkin, and Elzbieta Szymtka is Alyeya. Claudio Abbado conducts the Vienna Philharmonic Orchestra and Vienna State Opera Chorus. Brian Large directed the video. Color. In Czech with English subtitles. 93 minutes. DG video/Japanese laserdisc.

FRÜHJAHRSPARADE

1934/1954 operetta by Stolz

Robert Stolz's operetta *Frühjahrsparade* (Spring Parade), originally a 1934 Hungarian film operetta, became a stage operetta in 1954. Ernst Marischka wrote the original screenplay, Geza von Bolvary was the film director and Joseph Pasternak the producer. The film was remade twice before it was staged at the Vienna Volksoper on March 25, 1964. The operetta story focuses on a young Hungarian woman who travels from a country town to Emperor Franz Josef's Vienna where, of course, she finds true love. See also ROBERT STOLZ.

1934 Franziska Gaal film
Hungarian soprano Franziska Gaal stars as the Hungarian country girl who goes to Vienna in the film that begat the operetta and won the Best Musical award at the 1934 Venice Film Festival. The cast includes Paul Hörbiger, Theo Lingen and Annie Rosar. Geza von Bolvary directed the film shot in Vienna. Black and white. In Hungarian or German. 97 minutes.

1940 Deanna Durbin film
Deanna Durbin stars as Ilonka Tolnay in *Spring Parade*, an American film of the operetta produced by Joe Pasternak, who made the original film. Robert Stolz, who was working in Hollywood, provided new songs including the Oscar nominee "Waltzing in the Clouds." Durbin's co-stars are Robert Cummings, Mischa Auer and Henry Stephenson. Henry Koster directed. Universal. Black and white. In English. 89 minutes.

1955 Romy Schneider film

Romy Schneider is the star of *Ein Deutschmeister*, an Austrian film of the operetta written and directed by Ernst Marischka. The cast includes Paul Hörbiger (who was also in the original film), Hans Moser and Magda Schneider. Color. In German. 92 minutes.

FULL CIRCLE
1968 opera by Orr

Scottish composer Robin Orr (1909-) wrote the one-act opera *Full Circle* for Scottish Opera. It premiered on April 10, 1968, as a companion to Stravinsky's *Histoire du Soldat* and was scored for the same instruments. The libretto by Sydney Goodsir Smith in Clydeside dialect tells the story of an unemployed man during the 1930s Depression. He is driven to steal and is arrested for killing a policeman.

1968 Scottish TV

Robin Orr's one-act opera was produced by Scottish Opera for Scottish TV and telecast on Oct. 8, 1968. Alexander Gibson conducted the Scottish Opera Chamber Orchestra. Bryan Izzard directed. Color. 32 minutes. Film of telecast at NFTA in London.

FURTWÄNGLER, WILHELM
German conductor (1886-1954)

Wilhelm Furtwängler is admired for his ability as a conductor but remains controversial for his political attitudes as he stayed in Germany during the Nazi era. The only film of him conducting a complete opera is the Paul Czinner *Don Giovanni* shot in Salzburg. See CONDUCTORS (1994/1995), DON GIOVANNI (1954).

G

GALA LIRICA
1991 Seville concert video

Eight major Spanish opera singers team up for a concert in 1991 to inaugurate the Gran Teatro de la Maestranza in Seville: Giacomo Aragall, Teresa Berganza, Montserrat Caballé, José Carreras, Placido Domingo, Alfredo Kraus, Pilar Lorengar, Pedro Lavirgen and Juan Pons. They end with "Libiamo" toasting the new theater. Aragall sings "E lucevan le stelle," Berganza sings "Tu che accendi" from *Tancredi* and two arias from *Carmen*, Caballé sings "Pleurez, pleurez mes yeux" from *Le Cid*, Carreras sings "No puede ser" from Sorozabal's *La Tabernera del Puerto*, Domingo performs an aria from *Macbeth* and a duet from *La Forza del Destino* with Pons, Kraus sings arias from *Daughter of the Regiment* and *Rigoletto*, Lorengar sings arias from *La Wally* and *El Barberillo de Lavapies*, Lavirgen sings an aria from *Alma de Dios* and Pons sings an aria from *Rigoletto*, Color. In Spanish and Italian. 72 minutes. RCA Victor video.

GALLANTRY
1958 opera by Moore

American composer Douglas Moore described *Gallantry* as a "soap opera" when it premiered at Columbia University in March 1958. It is intended to be a parody of the traditional radio/ television soap opera and includes satiric commercials within a tale about a romantic triangle. See also DOUGLAS MOORE.

1962 CBS telecast
Martha Wright sings the operatic commercials in this television production by Pamela Hott directed by Martin Carr. The three involved in the love triangle are Ronald Holgate, Laurel Hurley and Charles Anthony. Alfredo Antonini conducted the CBS Symphony Orchestra and Jan Peerce introduced the opera presented in a program titled *Arias and Arabesques*. Black and white. In English. 30 minutes.

GALLONE, CARMINE
Italian film director (1886-1973)

Carmine Gallone specialized in opera films and probably made more films in the genre than any other theatrical filmmaker. He started making movies in 1913 and was an active filmmaker until the 1960s. His films were usually liked by the public and often by the Italian critics but he does not have an international reputation. His films are not to everyone's taste but they are made with understanding of both cinema and opera. Most are superior to their Hollywood operatic equivalents and as a group they provide a wide-ranging portrait of Italian opera and its singers. Gallone was one of the inventors of the "parallel" opera film in which a modern story parallels the plot of the opera. *Casa Ricordi*, a history of Italian opera through the story of the Ricordi publishing firm, is his epic achievement. See VINCENZO BELLINI (1935/1954), LA BOHÈME (1947 film), CARMEN (1962 film), CASA RICORDI, CAVALLERIA RUSTICANA (1953), MARIA CEBOTARI (1942), FAUST (1949), LA FORZA DEL DESTINO (1949), BENIAMINO GIGLI (1937/1938/1950), JAN KIEPURA (1930/1934/ 1936), MADAMA BUTTERFLY (1939 film/1955), MANON LESCAUT (1940 film), WOLFGANG A. MOZART (1940), GIACOMO PUCCINI (1952), RIGOLETTO (1947), TOSCA (1946 film/1956), LA TRAVIATA (1940 film/1947), IL TROVATORE (1949), GIUSEPPE VERDI (1938).

GALUPPI, BALDASSARE
Italian composer (1706-1785)

Baldassare Galuppi was an important figure in 18th century Italian opera composing over a hundred operas. He was one of the creators of the comic opera as well as being a major *opera seria* composer. His collaboration with Venetian playwright Carlo Goldoni marked a major advancement in the development of *opera buffa*. The most successful of their operas was *Il Filosofo di Campagna* (The Country Philosopher), first staged in 1756.

1960 Il Filosofo de Campagna
Galuppi and Goldoni's 1756 comic opera centers around the philosophical country farmer Nardo and the connivances of his maid Lesbina as a series of marital arrangements develop. It is rarely staged today but the adventurous CBS television program *Camera Three* devoted a program to it in 1960. It was structured as a highlights recital with excerpts

and scenes from the opera sung in a semi-staged manner. Black and white. In Italian. 30 minutes.

GANCE, ABEL
French film director (1889-1981)

French film genius Abel Gance, known to the wider public for his epic 1927 film *Napoleon*, was involved with a number of films of operatic interest during his long career. The most important is *Louise*, a 1938 film based on the opera by Gustave Charpentier and starring Grace Moore. Also of note are his 1934 *La Dame aux Camélias*, with music by Reynaldo Hahn and starring Yvonne Printemps, and his 1936 biography *Un Grand Amour de Beethoven* starring Harry Baur as Beethoven. See LUDWIG VAN BEETHOVEN (1936), LOUISE (1938), YVONNE PRINTEMPS (1934).

GANNE, LOUIS
French composer (1862-1923)

Louis Ganne began writing operettas in 1893 and had his first real success with the 1899 opéra-comique *Les Saltimbanques* which has a colorful circus setting. It is still his best known stage work and has remained a favorite in France. Ganne was also a noted conductor and was popular for his concerts at the Monte Carlo Opera. His operettas *Hans, le Joueur de Flûte* (1906) and *Rhodope* (1910) were both produced at Monte Carlo before being staged in Paris. See LES SALTIMBANQUES.

GARDEN, MARY
Scottish-born U.S. soprano (1874-1967)

Mary Garden, who came to live in the U.S. as a child, made her opera debut back in Europe singing the title role of *Louise* in Paris in 1900. Her success in French operas led to Massenet writing *Chérubin* for her in 1905. She made her American debut in 1907 in *Thais* at the Manhattan Opera House and was then hailed as the greatest singing actress in the world. In 1910, she began a twenty-year association with the Chicago Grand Opera. Her great rival was Geraldine Farrar, so it was not surprising that she followed her into movies. Garden was hired by the Goldwyn Studio at $10,000 a week for two pictures, beginning with her great New York operatic success. Her personality and acting style did not translate to the screen as had Farrar's and she did not have an expert director like Cecil B. De Mille to help her. Her film career ended as quickly as it began.

1917 Thais
Mary Garden's first film was intended to be a "picturization" of her great opera success so it was obviously not conceived cinematically. Most of the film showed Garden posing in a statuesque opera manner. Audiences, not surprisingly, didn't care for it. The plot is more or less the same as the opera and revolves around the loves of the courtesan Thais and the monk who saves her soul (played by Hamilton Revelle). It was shot at the Goldwyn Studios in Fort Lee, NJ, with location scenes in Florida. Frank H. Crane and Hugo Ballin directed. This is said to be the first film ever shown at the Vatican. Black and white. About 60 minutes.

1918 The Splendid Singer
Garden's second and last film was a modern story set during World War I. She plays a woman who had once loved a wealthy German but is now married to an American doctor. She ends up on the war front shot as a spy by her German lover. Audiences didn't like this film either. It was directed by Edwin Carewe. Black and white. About 80 minutes.

1953 So This is Love
Mabel Albertson portrays Mary Garden in this glossy film biography of Grace Moore (played by Kathryn Grayson). Garden is seen as the role model idol who persuades Moore to go to Europe and become an opera singer. Moore returns in glory two years later for her 1928 Met debut. AKA *The Grace Moore Story*. Gordon Douglas directed. Warner Bros. Color. 101 minutes.

GARDINER, JOHN ELIOT
English conductor (1943-)

John Eliot Gardiner is particularly known for his promotion of early music and for his period performance of operas, especially Mozart. He began his career conducting Monteverdi while still at university and he talks about his interest in conducting on a video of Monteverdi's *Vespro della Beata Vergine*. He is filming an excellent series of Mozart operas at the Chatelet Theater in Paris. See THE ABDUCTION FROM THE SERAGLIO (1991), THE BEGGAR'S OPERA (1983), LES BORÉADES (1987 film), COSÌ FAN TUTTE (1992), L'ÉTOILE (1986), THE MARRIAGE OF FIGARO (1993), CLAUDIO MONTEVERDI

(1989), MOZART REQUIEM (1991), PELLÉAS ET MÉLISANDE (1987), HENRY PURCELL (1995), WAR REQUIEM (1988).

GARGIULO, MARIO
Italian film director (1895-1927?)

Mario Gargle was a workhorse director of the early Italian cinema and filmed a number of opera story adaptations from 1916 to 1926, mostly for Flegrea Film. They included two versions of *Cavalleria Rusticana, Faust, Manon Lescaut, Mignon* and *Fra Diavolo.* Sicilian diva Tina Xeo starred in four of them. See also CAVALLERIA RUSTICANA (1916, 1926), FAUST (1918), FRA DIAVOLO (1925), MANON LESCAUT (1918), MIGNON (1921).

GARLAND, JUDY
American musical entertainer (1922-1969)

Judy Garland is one of the great American singers but she didn't do much to further the cause of opera in her films. As she tells us in *Babes in Arms,* "If I sang a duet from an opera, Mr. Verdi would turn over in his grave." In fact, she represented the jazzy opposite end of the musical spectrum in three films. She sang "hot" against classical opponents and seemed to enjoy poking fun at the operatic manner. See also IGOR GORIN (1937), JEROME KERN (1946), RICHARD RODGERS (1948).

1936 Every Sunday
Judy Garland is matched again the operatic Deanna Durbin in this MGM short, her first film. She and Durbin both sing to help save their town's park concerts. Judy is hot and jazzy while Deanna sings the classical "Il Bacio." Black and white. 20 minutes.

1939 Babes In Arms
Garland partners with Betty Jaynes in the "Opera Vs. Jazz" section of this memorable musical. Roger Edens created the words and most of the music for a five-part number about twin sisters with different musical tastes. Judy swings a jazzy *Barber of Seville* number while Betty has to sing the sextet from *Lucia di Lammermoor* all by herself. It's very clever but opera comes out a poor second. Black and white. 96 minutes.

1943 Presenting Lily Mars
Hungarian opera soprano Marta Eggerth is Garland's rival in this MGM musical about a girl

with theatrical ambitions. Eggerth sings well in her European manner but Garland parodies her accent and singing in a funny if rather unkind scene. Norman Taurog directed. Color. 104 minutes.

GASDIA, CECILIA
Italian soprano (1960-)

Verona-born Cecilia Gasdia, who began her career singing Giulietta in *I Capuleti e I Montecchi* in Florence in 1981, has become known for her *bel canto* roles and coloratura technique. She sang in most major European opera houses before coming to the Metropolitan in 1986 as Juliet in Gounod's *Roméo et Juliette.* She has also recorded a wide range of Italian operas by Rossini, Verdi, Donizetti and Puccini. See DIVAS (1991/1993), PLACIDO DOMINGO (1994), LA DONNA DEL LAGO (1990), GIANNI SCHICCHI (1983), TURANDOT (1983), IL VIAGGIO A REIMS (1988).

GASPARIAN, GOHAR
Armenian soprano (1924-)

Coloratura soprano Gohar Gasparian, one of Armenia's most famous opera singers, was born in the Armenian colony in Cairo where she made her debut. She moved to Soviet Armenia in 1948 and became the principal soprano of the Spendiarian Opera and Ballet Company in 1949. She later sang around the world touring both England and the U.S. Gasparian has portrayed the heroines of most of the Armenian operas as well as singing in the major Russian, Italian and French operas. She has also been an instructor at the Komitas Conservatory in Yerevan.

1971 Gohar Gasparian
Grigory Melik-Avakyan produced this Soviet Armenian film as a showcase for the great soprano. It consists of eleven episodes, in each of which she sings a different aria. Two are from famous Armenian operas: Anush's final aria from Armen Tigran Tigranyan's 1912 *Anush,* the Armenian national opera, and an aria from Tigran Tchukhatjian's 1868 *Arshak II,* the first Armenian grand opera. The film also includes the Mad Scene from *Lucia di Lammermoor,* Oxana's aria from Mussorgsky's *Christmas Eve,* the Queen of the Night's first aria from *The Magic Flute,* Auber's "A Burst of Laughter," Ter-Tatevosyan's "Song of Armenia," Grieg's "Solvejg's Song," Schubert's "Barcarolle" and the Bach-Gounod "Ave Maria."

Armenfilm Studio. Color. In Armenian and Russian. 70 minutes.

1979 Gariné

Gasparion stars as Gariné, the heroine of this film of an operetta by Armenian composer Chouhajian, known in English as *The Chick-pea Seller*. It's a love story set in 19th century Istanbul. Chouhajian lived in Istanbul and was the creator of the first Turkish operettas. Color. In Armenian. 93 minutes.

GASPARONE

1884 operetta by Millöcker

Carl Millöcker's last major operetta, a bandit-type romance written by F. Zell and Richard Genee, is still occasionally performed. Gasparone is the name of a bandit evoked by almost every character in the operetta and blamed for almost everything that happens but he is never actually seen. Carlotta falls in love with Erminio after he rescues her from a danger he himself devised. However, she has promised to marry the mayor's son if he will help her on an important matter. True love, of course, wins out. See also CARL MILLÖCKER.

1937 Marika Rökk film

Metropolitan Opera tenor Leo Slezak is in the cast of this German film version of the Millöcker opera but glamorous Marika Rökk is the featured star. Johann Heesters portrays Erminio, Edith Schollwer is the countess and Oskar Sima is the smuggler. Rökk's husband Georg Jacoby directed. The film was released in the U.S. Black and white. In German. 92 minutes.

1963 Haas/Riedmann telecast

Waltraud Haas and Gerhard Riedmann, who were also featured in the 1956 German TV version of *Der Bettelstudent*, are the stars of this German ARD television production. It was directed by Hans Hollmann. Black and white. In German. 90 minutes.

GATO MONTÉS, EL

1916 opera by Penella

Manuel Penella's *El Gato Montés* (The Wildcat) has the best known melody in Spanish music, a pasodoble that has become the theme music of the Spanish bullfight. The opera was first staged in the U.S. in New York in 1922 in English as *The Wildcat*. More recently Placido Domingo has been promoting it in Spanish producing it in Los Angeles, recording it in Spain and featuring it in a film about Seville. *El Gato Montés* is roughly the Spanish equivalent of the French *Carmen* with a love triangle involving a bandit known as the "Cat," a bullfighter called Rafael and a Gypsy woman named Soleá. There is a major scene at the Seville Bullring and all three end up dead because of love. Penella wrote both words and music. See also MANUEL PENELLA.

1924 Howard Hawks film

The first film of the opera was made in America after the New York stage success of *The Wildcat* and was adapted for the screen by Howard Hawks before he became a director. Paramount retitled it *Tiger Love* and Hawks changed the plot considerably. Antonio Moreno stars as the Wildcat, an aristocratic Robin Hood of the Spanish mountains, who loves Estelle Taylor. He kidnaps her before she can be forced to marry Raymond Nye. The film was screened with Penella's music played by a live orchestra. Black and white. In English. About 70 minutes.

1935 Rosario Pi film

This film of the opera was the first Spanish feature film to be directed by a woman. Rosario Pi made two other films including a screen adaptation of Pablo Luna's zarzuela *Molinos de Viento*. Penella himself adapted the opera for the screen. It stars Pablo Hertogs, Maria del Pilar Lebron, Mary Cortes and Consuelo Company. Agustin Macasoloi was the cinematographer. Black and white. In Spanish. 88 minutes.

1994 Los Angeles Music Center

Placido Domingo stars as the bullfighter Rafael in this Los Angeles Music Center Opera production of the opera. It was staged by Emilio Sagi and based on a production by the Teatro Lirico National de la Zarzuela in Madrid. Verónica Villaroel plays the gypsy Soleá and Justino Diaz portrays the Wildcat. Julian Gahan designed the sets and Miguel Roa conducted the Music Center Opera Orchestra. Gary Halvorsen directed the video taped in January 1994 and first telecast on Oct. 5, 1994. Color. In Spanish with English subtitles. 115 minutes.

GAVIN, BARRIE
English TV opera director

Barrie Gavin has directed a number of excellent operas for television that are now available on video. Some are unique copies of operas. They include BAA BAA BLACK SHEEP (1993), BILLY BUDD (1988), CARMEN (1991), CARMINA BURANA (1989), MLADA (1992), PETER GRIMES (1994), RUDDIGORE (1982), WAR REQUIEM (1992), KURT WEILL (1994).

GAY, JOHN
English librettist (1685-1732)

The only opera usually credited to its libretto writer rather than its composer is John Gay's *The Beggar's Opera*. His partner on the first ballad opera was Johann Pepusch (1667-1752) who compiled rather than wrote the popular songs for the opera. Gay's work changed the face of English theater though his other ballad operas like *Polly* and *Achilles* have not remained in the repertory. However, Gay did become wealthy through his first beggarly production. His influence has continued into the 20th century inspiring the Weill-Brecht *The Threepenny Opera* and even a Brazilian variation. See THE BEGGAR'S OPERA.

GAYARRE, JULIÁN
Spanish tenor (1844-1890)

Julián Gayarre was the most famous Spanish opera performer of the 19th century. He was born near Pamplona, studied in Madrid and Milan, made his debut in Varese in 1867 and was then recognized as one of the great tenors of his age. He was eventually invited to sing in most of the major opera houses and created the role of Enzo in *La Gioconda* in 1876. Gayarre collapsed on stage in Madrid in 1889 singing in *The Pearl Fishers* and died aged 45. He has become a symbol of Spanish opera and is the subject of two biographical films.

1959 Gayarre
Spanish tenor Alfredo Kraus portrays Gayarre in this Spanish film, one of two biographies of the singer. Kraus sings many of the arias associated with Gayarre's career as the film shows his rise to fame. Among the operas featured are *Don Pasquale*, *La Favorita, Rigoletto, I Puritani, Lucia di Lammermoor* and *Les Pecheurs de Perles*. Luz Marquez portrays his love Luisa while Lina Huarte appears as the diva Adelina Patti. Domingo Viladomat directed. Color.

In Spanish. 100 minutes. Bel Canto/Lyric/Opera Dubs videos.

1986 Final Romance
Jose Carreras portrays Gayarre in *Romanca Final*, a romantic Catalan biopic. It tells of the tenor's rise to fame and his love for his childhood sweetheart. The film has fascinating re-creations of the 19th century opera milieu as well as first-class singing. There are excerpts from many operas including Gomes's *Il Guarany, Les Pecheurs de Perles, La Favorita, L'Elisir d'Amore, Martha, Un Ballo in Maschera* and *Lohengrin*. Monserrat Caballé makes an appearance singing with Carreras in a production of *Il Guarany*. Romano Gandolfi leads the Orchestra and Chorus of the Theatre del Liceu. José M. Forque directed. Color. In Spanish with English subtitles. 120 minutes. Kultur video.

GAZZA LADRA, LA
1817 opera by Rossini

The Thieving Magpie is a mixture of drama and comedy, what was once called an *opera semiseria*, and has one of Rossini's more famous overtures. Giovanni Gherardini based the libretto on a French comedy. The magpie thief of the opera causes real trouble when it steals a silver spoon. The maid Ninetta is accused of the theft and because of circumstantial evidence is sentenced to be hanged by the mayor who is angry because she has rejected him as a suitor. Her father ends up in jail trying to save her and her lover Giannetto seems unable to help. She is saved at the end by the discovery of the real thief. See also GIOACHINO ROSSINI.

1984 Cologne Opera
Ileana Cotrubas stars as Ninetta in this much-praised production from the Cologne Opera in Germany. David Kuebler is Gianetto, Brent Ellis is Ninetta's father Fernando, Alberto Rinaldi is the pompous mayor and Carlo Feller is Gianetto's father Fabrizio. Maurice Pagano designed the sets and costumes while Bruno Bartoletti conducted the Cologne Gurzenich Orchestra and the Cologne Opera Chorus. José Montes-Baquer directed the video. Color. In Italian with English subtitles. 176 minutes. Home Vision video/Pioneer Classics laser.

Related films

1954 Johnny Green film
Bandleader Johnny Green conducts the MGM Symphony Orchestra in the overture to *La Gazza Ladra* in this CinemaScope short titled *The Thieving Magpie*. Color. 9 minutes.

1964 Luzzati/Gianini cartoon
Emanuele Luzzati and Giulio Gianini's animated film *La Gazza Ladra*, based on the overture to the opera, is one of the masterpieces of animation and has become one of the world's best known cartoons. The story of the film has no direct relation to the opera. A king and his noblemen ride out to hunt birds so a magpie steals the king's crown and the birds attack the hunters. The patterns and colors of the film create the effect of a medieval painting. Color. 10 minutes.

1971 A Clockwork Orange
Music from *The Thieving Magpie* is featured on the soundtrack of this Stanley Kubrick film. It's a dystopian vision of England in the not-too-distant future as imagined by Anthony Burgess. Color. 136 minutes.

1973 The Five Days
Dario Argento's Italian film *Le Cinque Giornate* tells of the five days of the Milan Revolution against the Austrians in 1848. It features music from *La Gazza Ladra* as performed by the Teatro alla Scala Orchestra. Color. In Italian 126 minutes.

GEDDA, NICOLAI
Swedish tenor (1925-)

Nicolai Gedda made his debut in Stockholm in 1951, sang at La Scala in 1953 as Don Ottavio in *Don Giovanni* and arrived at Covent Garden in 1955. The focus of his career, however, was the Metropolitan Opera. He sang there for 22 seasons beginning in 1957 and was featured in a wide variety of roles including Anatol in the world premiere of Samuel Barber's *Vanessa*. See THE BARTERED BRIDE (1978), BELL TELEPHONE HOUR (1968), BORIS GODUNOV (1989), CARMEN (1959), CENDRILLON, FAUST (1963/ 1965/ 1975), LISA DELLA CASA (1958), THE MAGIC FLUTE (1971), METROPOLITAN OPERA (1983), OPERA IMAGINAIRE, ROMÉO AND JULIETTE (1963), ROBERT STOLZ (1990), VANESSA, VOICE OF FIRESTONE (1950-63).

1985 Nicolai Gedda in Concert Vols. 1 & 2
Two compilation videos of excerpts from Gedda concerts have been put together by the Bel Canto Society. Volume One features Russian songs and arias from *Fedora* and *L'Arlesiana*. Volume Two includes arias from *L'Elisir d'Amore*, *Paganini*, *The Merry Widow*, *The Land of Smiles*, *Giuditta* and *Eugene Onegin*. Color. Each 60 minutes.

GENÉE, RICHARD
German librettist/composer (1823-1895)

Richard Genée was one of the great operetta librettists, mainly in partnership with Camillo Walzel who wrote under the penname F. Zell. His major achievement was the 1874 *Die Fledermaus* for Johann Strauss on which he worked out melodic as well as plot ideas. He wrote other librettos for Strauss, Suppé (*Boccaccio*), Millöcker (*Der Bettelstudent*), etc. He also wrote music and conducted. His biggest success as a composer was the operetta *Nanon* (1877) which was filmed in Germany with coloratura Erna Sack as its star. See DER BETTELSTUDENT, BOCCACCIO, DIE FLEDERMAUS, NANON.

GENCER, LEYLA
Turkish soprano (1924-)

Leyla Gencer studied in Istanbul, made her debut in Ankara in 1953 and began to sing in Italy in 1953. She was Madame Lidone in the premiere of *Dialogues des Carmélites* at La Scala in 1957, and soon after began to sing around the world in a variety of roles. Her voice is unique and her style absorbing. It can be experienced on video in two of her great Verdi roles, as Aida and Leonora. See AIDA (1963/ 1966), IL TROVATORE (1957).

GENTLE, ALICE
American mezzo soprano (1889-1958)

Mezzo soprano Alice Gentle, who began her opera career in San Francisco in 1915, made her debut at La Scala the following year. After the war she sang with the Metropolitan Opera and then travelled around the world giving concerts. She was brought to Hollywood in 1930 during the first musical boom and starred in two Techncolor operettas, Gershwin's *Song of the Flame* and Kálmán's *Golden Dawn*. She made her final movie appearance in a small role in *Flying Down to Rio*. See GOLDEN DAWN, SONG OF THE FLAME

1934 Flying Down to Rio

Gentle has a tiny role as a featured singer in this famous RKO musical. It launched the screen collaboration of Fred Astaire and Ginger Rogers and made the Carioca into a national dance craze. The music is by Vincent Youmans with lyrics by Edward Eliscu and Gus Kahn. Black and white. 80 minutes.

GEORGIAN OPERA

Georgian opera history began in the capital Tbilisi in 1851 when the first opera house opened in what was then a part of Russia. All of the operas performed in the 19th century were Italian or Russian but Georgian operas began to be staged in 1919. Zakhary Paliashvili is considered the father of Georgian opera and the opera theater in Tbilisi is named after him. His opera Daisi has been filmed. The famous bass Paata Burchuladze is one of the best-known of the many Georgian opera singers. See PAATA BURCHULADZE, ZAKHARY PALIASHVILI.

GERSHWIN, GEORGE
American composer (1898-1937)

George Gershwin is now recognized as a major opera composer though he wrote only three "operas". The first was the twenty-minute *Blue Monday/135th Street* staged in 1922, which is like a sketch for an opera. The second was the 1925 "romantic opera" *Song of the Flame* which is really an operetta. The third, of course, was *Porgy and Bess* which premiered in 1935 and is now accorded full operatic status even though it was first staged on Broadway. It has been filmed twice and is on video. In addition there was a "Jewish opera" tentatively titled *The Dybbuk* which was commissioned by the Metropolitan Opera in 1929 but never completed. Gershwin's success in importing jazz and blues idioms into other forms of music has been widely copied and his stage and film scores are among the best of their kind. The major movies based around Gershwin music are the Oscar-winning *An American in Paris* and the Fred Astaire films *Damsel in Distress, Shall We Dance* and *Funny Face*. Gershwin died while working on the 1938 film *The Goldwyn Follies* which has operatic content. There is also a romantic Hollywood biography called *Rhapsody in Blue*. George's brother Ira (1896-1983), the lyricist of most of his songs and an important contributor to *Porgy and Bess*, also wrote lyrics for Kurt Weill and

Aaron Copland. See also HELEN JEPSON (1938), PORGY AND BESS, SONG OF THE FLAME.

1953 135th Street

Gershwin's first opera "a la Afro-American" was called *Blue Monday* when it was first presented as a part of the *George White Scandals of 1922*. It was composed by Gershwin to a text by B.G. De Sylva which focuses for twenty minutes on love problems in Harlem. Ferde Grofé re-orchestrated it in 1925 for presentation at Carnegie Hall under the new title of *135th Street*. The Grofé version was produced on television on the CBS *Omnibus* program in 1953 with choreography by Valerie Bettis. Black and white. In English. 20 minutes.

1945 Rhapsody in Blue

This is a romantic Hollywood film version of Gershwin's career with Robert Alda portraying the composer and Ray Turner dubbing his piano playing. His lyricist brother Ira Gershwin is played by Herbert Rudley. The film contains an extract from Gershwin's mini-opera *Blue Monday*, arias from *Porgy and Bess* and a performance of *Rhapsody in Blue*. Irving Rapper directed. Black and white. 139 minutes. On video.

GESCHIEDENE FRAU, DIE
1908 operetta by Fall

Leo Fall's 1908 operetta *Die Geschiedene Frau* (The Divorcée) traveled to London and New York in 1910 as *The Girl in the Train*. Viktor Leon's libretto was considered slightly scandalous as most of the first act is set in a Dutch divorce court. Joan Sutherland has recorded a medley of tunes from it in her influential album *The Golden Age of Operetta*. See also LEO FALL.

1926 Mady Christians film

Mady Christians stars as the divorced woman in this 1926 German silent film of the operetta directed by Victor Janson. Carl Drews was the cinematographer. The film was shown in cinemas with Fall's music played live. Black and white. In German. About 75 minutes.

1953 Marika Rökk film

Marika Rökk stars as the scandalous divorcée opposite Johannes Heesters in this modern German film version of the operetta. The cast includes Trude Hesterberg and Hans Nielsen with Konstantin

Tschet as cinematographer. Georg Jacoby directed. Black and white. In German. 100 minutes.

GHEORGHIU, ANGELA
Romanian soprano (1965-)

Angela Gheorghiu, born in Ajud and trained in Bucharest, began to sing internationally from 1990 in Vienna, London, Zurich and New York. She became one of the most talked-about sopranos in the world after being acclaimed in 1994 as Violetta in *La Traviata* at Covent Garden with Sir Georg Solti conducting. She is not yet well represented on video but can be seen in her breakthrough performance as Violetta in London with Solti and in concert with Placido Domingo in Prague. See LA TRAVIATA (1994).

1994 Angela Gheorghiu
The soprano is featured live in concert in Prague on April 24, 1994, with tenor Placido Domingo. Domingo was the star at the time and the original telecast was under his name but after the success of her London Violetta, the video was released in England under her name. She sings duets with Domingo from *La Traviata*, *Otello* and *L'Elisir d'Amore* plus a number of arias including "Porgi amor" from *The Marriage of Figaro*, "Ebben, ne andrò lontana" from *La Wally*, and the Romanian aria "Muzika" by Grigoriu. The music is performed by the Czech Symphony Orchestra under the direction of Eugen Kohn. Thomas Simerda directed the video. Color. 80 minutes. Bechmann (England) video.

GHIAUROV, NICOLAI
Bulgarian bass (1929-)

Nicolai Ghiaurov, the most famous Bulgarian opera singer of our time and one of the most impressive bassos of any country, made his debut in Sofia in 1955 as Don Basilio in *The Barber of Seville* and began his international career in Bologna in 1958 as Méphistophélès in *Faust*. He first sang at Covent Garden in 1962 and at the Metropolitan in 1965. His popular roles include Boris Godunov, Philip II and Don Quichotte. See also AIDA (1986), LA BOHÈME (1989), BORIS GODUNOV (1966 film), DON CARLO (1983), ERNANI (1982), FAUST (1988), LA FORZA DEL DESTINO (1978), FROM THE HOUSE OF THE DEAD (1992), EUGENE ONEGIN (1985/ 1988), KHOVANSHCHINA (1989), METROPOLITAN OPERA (1983), SIMON BOCCANEGRA (1978), VERDI REQUIEM (1967).

1986 Nicolai Ghiaurov: Tribute to a Great Bass
This is a video of a Bulgarian television program in honor of the great basso and featuring Ghiaurov, his wife Mirella Freni and friends. He is shown in performance alone and with José Carreras and Piero Cappuccilli and in rehearsal with Herbert von Karajan. The video begins with a stage performance of the Golden Calf aria from *Faust* and includes excerpts from *Don Quichotte*, *La Bohème*, *Simon Boccanegra*, *The Barber of Seville* and *Boris Godunov*. Mirella Freni is seen with him in *Faust* at La Scala and in *La Bohème*. Color. 79 minutes. VIEW video.

GHOSTS OF VERSAILLES, THE
1991 opera by Corigliano

American composer John Corigliano's opera, a commission from the Metropolitan Opera, premiered with great success in 1991. It was then telecast and revived on stage in 1995. William M. Hoffman's libretto borrows characters from *La Mére Coupable*, the third play in Beaumarchais' Figaro trilogy, and the musical influence is mostly Mozart and Rossini who composed operas to the first two plays. *Ghosts* takes place on three levels and is set beyond time in the lands of history, theater and ghosts. Beaumarchais is a character in the opera and falls in love with Marie Antoinette. She feels her trial and execution were unfair so he tries to change history by rewriting his plays but his characters will no longer take his orders. In the end Marie Antoinette accepts her fate. The music is a splendid pudding of Mozart, Rossini, Turkish dances and spectacle. See also JOHN CORIGLIANO.

1992 Metropolitan Opera
Teresa Stratas stars as Marie Antoinette in the premiere production at the Metropolitan Opera. Håkan Hagegård is excellent as Beaumarchais, Gino Quilico is splendid as Figaro, Marilyn Horne is grand as Samira and Graham Clark is most villainous as Bégears. The large cast also includes Judith Christin as Susanna, Renée Fleming as Rosina, Peter Kazaras as Almaviva and Stella Zambalis as Cherubino. It is brilliantly staged by Colin Graham with sets and costumes by John Conklin. James Levine conducts the Metropolitan Opera Orchestra. Video director Brian Large not only captures the spectacle but enhances it. Color. In English. 180 minutes. DG video and laserdisc.

Related film

1938 Marie Antoinette

Norma Shearer stars as Marie Antoinette in this lavish big-budget film that has the same major problem as the opera: how to make a frivolous queen into a sympathetic character. Scripters Donald Ogden Stewart, Claudine West and Earnest Vajda do a fine job and art director Cedric Gibbons creates a bigger-than-life Versailles for this opulent MGM epic. W. S. Van Dyke directed. Black and white. 149 minutes.

GIANINI & LUZZATI
Italian film animators/designers

Italian animation masters Giulio Gianini and Emanuele Luzzati became famous in 1964 for one of the most popular opera-inspired animated films. *The Thieving Magpie* (La Gazza Ladra) is based on the Overture to the Rossini comic opera and tells of three kings who make war on birds but get outwitted by a magpie. In 1968 they followed it with *L'Italiana in Algeri* (The Italian Girl in Algiers), also inspired by a Rossini comic opera. In 1974 they created an animated version of Puccini's *Turandot* and in 1977 a longer version of Mozart's *The Magic Flute* with a live Papageno. Luzzati has also designed sets for a number of stage operas. See Così Fan Tutte (1975), La Gazza Ladra (1964), L'Italiana in Algeri (1968), Macbeth (1972), The Magic Flute (1977).

GIANNINI, VITTORIO
American composer (1903-1966)

Vittorio Giannini came from a family of opera singers. His sister Dusolina helped him get his first opera *Lucedia* staged in Munich in 1934 and created the role of Hester Prynne when his *The Scarlet Letter* was produced in Hamburg in 1938. He also wrote three radio operas for CBS in the 1930s including a version of the Beauty and the Beast legend. His most popular opera, however, is *The Taming of the Shrew* based on the Shakespeare play. It captured national attention as an NBC Opera Theatre production in 1954. Giannini's *The Servant of Two Masters* (1967), based on the Goldoni play, has also been well received. See THE TAMING OF THE SHREW.

GIANNI SCHICCHI
1918 opera by Puccini

Giacomo Puccini's one-act opera *Gianni Schicchi* is best known for its soprano aria "O mio babbino caro" sung by Gianni Schicchi's daughter Lauretta. The libretto by Gioachino Forzano tells the story of a crafty medieval Florentine who devises a way to get a man's will changed after he has died. This is modern *opera buffa* and very clever both in plot and music. It is the third opera in Puccini's triptych *Il Trittico* and is usually performed with *Il Tabarro* and *Suor Angelica*. It had its world premiere at the Metropolitan Opera. See also Giacomo Puccini.

1951 NBC Opera Theatre

Ralph Herbert stars as Gianni Schicchi with Virginia Haskins as his daughter Lauretta in this NBC Opera Theatre production by Samuel Chotzinoff. Robert Marshall is Rinuccio with a cast that includes Jean Handzlick, Kenneth Smith and Paul Ukena. Charles Polacheck directed, H. M. Crayon designed the sets and Peter Herman Adler conducted the orchestra. The opera is sung in English in a translation by Townsend Brewster. Kirk Browning directed for television. The production was repeated live in the 1952 NBC Opera series. Black and white. In English. 60 minutes.

1981 Metropolitan Opera

Gabriele Bacquier portrays Schicchi with Renata Scotto as Lauretta and Philip Creech as Rinuccio in this Metropolitan Opera production by Fabrizio Melano. David Reppa designed the sets and James Levine conducts the Metropolitan Opera Orchestra. Kirk Browning directed the telecast on Nov. 14, 1981, as a part of *Il Trittico*. Color. In Italian with English subtitles. 50 minutes.

1983 Teatro alla Scala

Juan Pons stars as Schicchi with Cecilia Gasdia as his daughter Lauretta and Yuri Marusin as Rinuccio. All are splendid but Gasdia's "O mio Babbino caro" is especially memorable. The opera was staged by Silvano Bussoti with Gianandrea Gavazzeni conducting the Teatro alla Scala Orchestra and Chorus. Brian Large directed the video. Color. In Italian with English subtitles. 50 minutes. Home Vision video.

Related film

1970 Pennsylvania State documentary
This film is titled *Gianni Schicchi* but it is not the opera but a documentary about the preparations for and rehearsals of a production by the music department of Pennsylvania State University. The film was made by students of the university's Theatre Arts Department. Black and white. In English. 23 minutes.

1985 A Room with a View
Director James Ivory features the aria "O mio babbino caro" at a key moment in this superb E. M. Forster adaptation. Helena Bonham Carter portrays a confused young woman discovering herself in the Florence of yesteryear. Color. 115 minutes. On video.

GIGANTES Y CABEZUDOS
1898 zarzuela by Caballero

Manuel Fernández Caballero's patriotic zarzuela *Gigantes y Cabezudos* gets its odd title from Carnival figures called "giants and bigheads." The story is set in Carnival time in Zaragoza in Spain and tells of the ordinary people of that town and of the love between the orphan Pilar and the soldier Jesus. The other main characters are the town policeman Timoteo, his wife Antonia, Pilar's uncle Isidoro and the Sergeant who fancies Pilar and tells lies about Jesus. Miguel Echegaray wrote the libretto. See also MANUEL FERNÁNDEZ CABALLERO.

1925 Florián Rey film
Carmen Viance stars as Pilar in this popular silent film version of the zarzuela directed by Florián Rey. The cast includes José Nieto, Marina Torres, Guillermo Munoz, Francisco Marti and the noted comic José Gimeno, the Ben Turpin of the Spanish cinema. Alberto Arroyo was the cinematographer. Black and white. In Spanish. 80 minutes.

1968 Juan De Orduña film
Isabel Rivas sings the role of Pilar with an actress portraying her on screen in this excellent film of the opera. It was directed by Juan De Orduña and made by Spanish Television for its *Teatro Lirico Español* series. The other principal roles are sung by Carlo del Monte, Rosa Sarmiento, Jesus Aguirre and Ramon Alonso. Manuel Tamayo wrote the script and Federico Moreno Torroba conducted the Spanish Lyric Orchestra and Madrid Chorus. The soundtrack is also on record. TVE. Color. In Spanish. 100 minutes.

GIGLI, BENIAMINO
Italian tenor (1890-1957)

Beniamino Gigli possessed one of the great voices of the century and his recordings are likely to keep him popular for a long time. He made his debut in Italy in 1914 and was one of the stalwarts of the Metropolitan Opera in the 1920s as the successor to Caruso. He returned to Italy in 1932 after declining to accept a cut in salary during the Depression. He was, sadly, a favorite of Mussolini and a supporter of Fascism but the Italian public loves him all the same. He began making fiction movies in English, Italian and German in 1935 and can be seen in eighteen features and six earlier Vitaphone shorts. He is by no means one of the great film actors but his screen personality is attractive and his incredible voice carries all else before. Most of his films are available on video though it is sometimes difficult to distinguish between them as they have different titles and casts in three different languages. His first feature, for example, is known under four different names. See also CARLO BERGONZI (1985), MAD ABOUT OPERA, PAGLIACCI (1943 film), GIUSEPPE VERDI (1938), VERONA (1990).

1927-1928 Vitaphone opera films
Gigli began his movie career in America where he starred in six Vitaphone sound films shot at the old Manhattan Opera Theater in 1927 and 1928. He can be seen and heard singing selections from *La Gioconda*, *The Pearl Fishers* (a great duet in Italian with baritone Giuseppe De Luca), *Lucia di Lammermoor* (a duet with soprano Marion Talley), *Rigoletto* (the famous Quartet with De Luca, Talley and contralto Jeanne Gordon) and *Cavalleria Rusticana* (with baritone Millo Picco and contralto Minnie Egener). There is also "A program of concert favorites." Black and white. Each about 8 minutes.

1935 Forget Me Not/ Non Ti Scordar di Me
Gigli's first feature, made in English, Italian and German, takes its title from its theme song "Non ti scordar di me" by Ernesto De Curtis. Gigli sings it a number of times and it has remained so popular that Pavarotti featured it in the Los Angeles *Three Tenors* concert. Gigli portrays an opera singer who marries a younger woman (Joan Gardner in the

English version) who is rebounding from a failed love affair. She almost leaves Gigli when she meets her old love a few years later. Gigli is pictured on an operatic world tour which allows him to sing arias from *Rigoletto, Martha, L'Africaine* and *L'Elisir d'Amore*. Augusto Genina directed the Italian and German versions (*Non Ti Scordar di Me* and *Vergiss Mein Nicht*) which premiered in November 1935. Zoltan Korda directed the English version which premiered in March 1936. It opened in the U.S. in 1937 as *Forever Yours*. Black and white. 72 minutes in English. HBO video and laser.

1936 Ave Maria
Gigli portrays an opera singer with a lost love who falls for torch singer Käthe Von Nagy. She's a night club performer in Paris who sets out to trap him but ends up falling in love with him. The arias include "Un di felice" from *La Traviata* with Erna Berger singing Violetta opposite Gigli's Alfredo and "Di quella pira" from *Il Trovatore*. The music is played by the Berlin State Opera Orchestra. Johannes Riemann directed Italian and German versions. Released in August 1936. Black and white. 85 minutes. Bel Canto/SRO Lyric/Opera Dubs videos.

1936 Du Bist Mein Gluck/Thou Art My Luck
Italian actress Isa Miranda is featured opposite Gigli in a double role as mother and daughter in this melodramatic musical. As the mother she is a music teacher's wife in love with Gigli who collapses while he is on stage in *Aida*. As the daughter she also loves him. The singing is terrific and Miranda is a fine screen actress. Gigli sings arias from *Aida, Tosca* and *Manon Lescaut* with backing from the Bavarian State Opera Orchestra and Chorus. Karl Heinz Martin directed it. The U.S. title is *Thou Art My Luck*. The Italian title is *Sinfonia di Cuori*. Released in November 1936. Black and white. 95 minutes. In German. Bel Canto/Lyric/Opera Dubs videos.

1937 Die Stimme des Herzens
Gigli stars opposite Geraldine Katt in this musical which translates as "Voice of the Heart" and is also known as *Der Sanger Ihrer Hoheit*. He's an opera singer, she's a princess who plays piano for him as a favor and they become involved in a sentimental mistaken identity mix-up. Gigli has the opportunity to sing arias from *Martha* and *Lohengrin* plus songs by Giuseppe Becce and Ernesto de Curtis. Karl Heinz Martin directed for Bavaria Film. Released

March 1937. Black and white. In German. 91 minutes. Lyric video.

1937 Solo Per Te/Mutterlied
Bessarabian soprano Maria Cebotari, who makes a wonderful singing and acting partner, stars opposite Gigli in this pleasant Carmine Gallone film. He's an opera singer married to a woman with a secret (Cebotari) while German bass-baritone Michael Bohnen is the man from her past who reappears in their opera company. The film begins with Gigli on stage in Boito's *Mefistofele*, spotlights a scene from *Andrea Chénier*, includes a sequence where Gigli sings a duet with himself as Don Giovanni and Zerlina on "La, ci darem la mano" and features a back stage murder during *Un Ballo in Maschera*. The Italian title is Solo Per te, the German version is *Mutterlied*. Black and white. 84 minutes. In Italian or German. Lyric/Opera Dubs videos.

1937 When You're in Love
Gigli is heard singing "M'appari" on a phonograph record in this Hollywood film about an opera singer. It stars Grace Moore as the singer. Robert Riskin directed for Columbia. Black and white. 104 minutes.

1938 Marionette/Dir Gehört Mein Herz
Carla Rust plays a journalist who hears aristocrat opera singer Gigli working in a vineyard on his estate and thinks she has discovered a great peasant tenor. He allows her to promote him but she soon finds she's been deceived. Gigli sings arias from *Rigoletto, Martha* and *Nina* plus Italian popular songs. Carmine Gallone shot the film on location in Rome and Naples in German and Italian. The Italian version is *Marionette*, the German one is *Dir Gehört Mein Herz*. U.S. title is *My Heart Belongs to Thee*. Black and white. In Italian. 102 minutes. Lyric/ Opera Dubs videos.

1939 Casa Lontana/Der Singende Tor
Gigli portrays an opera singer whose ballerina wife leaves him for another man. He meets his wife again in South America and kills an evil impresario in self defense. Gigli sings arias from *L'Arlesiana, Lucia di Lammermoor, Giulietta et Roméo, Fedora* and *Pagliacci*. Liva Caloni is his soprano partner. Johannes Meyer shot the film in Rome in Italian and German. Italian version is called Casa Lontana, the German version is *Der Singende Tor*. U.S. title: *Legittima Difesa/Self Defense*. Black and white. In Italian. 84 minutes. Lyric/Opera Dubs videos.

1940 Traummusik/Ritorno

Gigli plays himself in this musical starring Marte Harell. She's been cast in a new opera called *Penelope* created by her Italian boyfriend (Rossano Brazzi) and based on the Greek legend of the most faithful wife in history. She asks Gigli to be her Ulysses. The scenes from the imaginary opera were actually composed by Riccardo Zandonai. The film also includes a scene from *La Bohème* and the singer who provides the voice for Harell in the opera sequences is Mafalda Favero. Geza Von Bolvary directed in German and Italian. The German film is called *Traummusik* and the Italian one is *Ritorno*. Black and white. 80 minutes. In German or Italian. Bel Canto/ Lyric/Opera Dubs videos.

1941 Mamma/Mutter

A three-handkerchief movie. Opera star Gigli's aging mother (the legendary Emma Gramatica) prevents her daughter-in-law from leaving her son for another man. To do this she has to run through the rain while Gigli is on stage tearfully singing *Otello* with backing from the Rome Opera Orchestra. Mamma dies of the strain but she dies happy. Gigli also sings an aria from *Rigoletto*. Guido Brignone shot the film in Rome in Italian and German. The Italian version is called *Mamma*, the German version is *Mutter*. Black and white. In Italian. 83 minutes. Bel Canto/ Lyric/ Opera Dubs videos.

1942 Vertigine/Tragödie einer Liebe

Gigli sings Rodolfo opposite Tito Gobbi as Marcello in the *La Bohème* sequence of this film with Liva Caloni as Mimi, Tatiana Menotti as Musetta and Gino Conti as Colline. Gigli plays an opera singer who breaks up with his girl and suffers gambling losses because of another woman. His true love eventually rescues him. The film features scenic views of Venice, Rome and San Remo with music by Puccini, Wagner, Giordano and Cilea including an excerpt from *Adriana Lecouvreur*. Guido Brigone directed. The Italian version is called Vertigine, the German *Tragödie einer Liebe*. Black and white. In Italian or German. 88 minutes. Lyric/ Opera Dubs videos.

1944 Silenzio: Si Gira!/Achtung Aufnahme

Gigli portrays a famous opera singer who gets a girl that he fancies a role in a film he is making. He becomes jealous when she prefers a younger actor and stops the filming out of spite. He also sings arias from *Rigoletto* and *Lohengrin*. Rossano Brazzi and Mariella Lotti are the other stars in this film made in Rome by Carlo Campogalliani. The chief screenwriter was Cesare Zavattini, one of the creators of Italian neorealism. The Italian version is *Silenzio: Si Gira!*, the German *Achtung Aufnahme*. Black and white. In Italian or German. 86 minutes. Bel Canto Society/Lyric videos.

1946 Voglio Bene Soltanto a Te

Gigli's first movie after the war has a plot almost the same as the above film which had limited distribution. He stars as a tenor making a movie in Rome who fancies a female co-star who prefers another younger man. The film includes arias from *La Favorita, Tannhäuser, Martha, Die Walküre, Lohengrin, L'Africana* and *L'Elisir d'Amore* as well as clips from Gigli's film *Mamma*. Giuseppe Fatigati directed. Black and white. In Italian. 80 minutes. Lyric/ Opera Dubs videos.

1950 Taxi di Notte/Singing Taxi Driver

Gigli is at his best in this charming film about a taxi driver who sings opera for his customers for extra tips. The story takes place within a 48-hour period in Rome during which time Gigli has the chance to sing Donizetti and Leoncavallo arias as well as Italian folk songs. He also gets an offer to sing opera in America but it doesn't work out. Carmine Gallone directed. US title: *Singing Taxi Driver*. Black and white. In Italian. 100 minutes. Lyric/Opera Dubs/ Bel Canto Society videos.

1950 Una Voce nel Tuo Cuore/A Voice in Your Heart

The singing of Gigli and baritone Gino Bechi enliven this lightweight musical. They play themselves as opera singers and their operatic sequences are the best thing in the film. Vittorio Gassman stars as a war correspondent who loves a nightclub performer who wants to be an opera singer. Alberto D'Aversa directed. US title: *A Voice in Your Heart*. Black and white. In Italian. 98 minutes.

1953 Carosello Napoletano/Neapolitan Carousel

Gigli's last feature film, *Carosello Napoletano*, was based on a famous stage musical and tells the story of Naples in music and dance from the 16th century to the present day. Gigli's voice is used in the movie along with the voices of Carlo Tagliabue, Mario Cioffi and Marinelli Meli. Ettore Giannini directed the film which stars Sophia Loren. It was released in the U.S. in 1963 as *Neapolitan Carousel*. Color. In Italian. 116 minutes. Bel Canto Society/Lyric videos.

211

1960 Beniamino Gigli, Una Voce nel Mondo

Beniamino Gigli, A Voice in the World is an Italian television film about the singer written by Enrico Roda and directed by Giorgio Ferroni. It traces the life and singing career of the singer. The film was also made in a German version narrated by Hans Petsch and in an English version. Black and white. In Italian. 40 minutes.

1994 Portrait of Beniamino Gigli

An Italian television documentary portrait of the singer was broadcast in 1994. Color. In Italian. 60 minutes.

GILBERT and SULLIVAN
Operetta librettist and composer

The poet and the composer, different as they were, are almost never separated on film and video so they are considered here together. William S. Gilbert (1836-1911) wrote the words, Arthur Sullivan (1842-1900) wrote the music and Richard D'Oyly Carte forged their collaboration. Together they created the Savoy Operas, a species of comic opera or operetta unique to the English-speaking world. Sullivan was first in the field and wrote the music for *Cox and Box* before teaming up with Gilbert. Their first effort together went over the heads of audiences and it wasn't until the 1875 *Trial By Jury* that the collaboration took off. The team wrote 14 operettas, most of which remain popular; *The Mikado, The Pirates of Penzance* and *H.M.S. Pinafore* are the most often filmed and telecast. There have been two comprehensive series of the operettas: Eight were made as *World of Gilbert and Sullivan* productions and filmed in 1974 with a company formed by bass DonaldAdams and tenor Thomas Round. Eleven were made as George Walker productions and filmed in 1982. The D'Oyly Carte Opera Company, which controlled copyrights until 1961, has also been captured on film at different periods. There do not appear to be any videos of their last operettas, *Utopia Limited* and *The Grand Duke*, but there is one of a pastiche called *Dick Deadeye*. See COX AND BOX, DICK DEADEYE, THE GONDOLIERS, IOLANTHE, H.M.S. PINAFORE, THE MIKADO, PATIENCE, PRINCESS IDA, THE PIRATES OF PENZANCE, RUDDIGORE, THE SORCERER, THESPIS, TRIAL BY JURY, THE YEOMAN OF THE GUARD.

1937 The Girl Said No

This little-known American film contains scenes of Gilbert and Sullivan operettas performed in a traditional manner by members of the "Gilbert and Sullivan Opera Company of New York." William Danforth, who sings the role of the Mikado, is said to have performed it for 25 years on stage. The other Savoyards are Frank Moulan, Vivian Hart and Vera Ross. They play old-style troupers down on their luck but running a restaurant where they can still sing G & S. Robert Armstrong (the hero of *King Kong*) seeks revenge on Irene Hervey by arranging a fake staging of *The Mikado* in which she can star. The G & S troupe sells its restaurant believing the swindle real. The film was also released as *With Words and Music*. Grand National Films. Black and white. In English. 63 minutes. Video Yesteryear.

1940 Lillian Russell

Nigel Bruce portrays Gilbert and Claude Allister impersonates Sullivan in this American film biography of singer Lillian Russell. She starred in many of their operettas but they are only minor characters in this film. Black and white. 127 minutes.

1953 The Story of Gilbert and Sullivan

Maurice Evans is Sullivan and Robert Morley is Gilbert in this lavish British film biography by Frank Launder and Sidney Gilliat. It tells the story of their career intertwined with that of theater manager D'Oyly Carte (Peter Finch). The singers include Martyn Green, Owen Brannigan, Webster Booth, Elsie Morison and Marjorie Thomas. The screenplay is based on a book by Leslie Baily. The film was released in the U.S. as *The Great Gilbert and Sullivan*. Color. In English. 109 minutes.

1974 Gilbert and Sullivan

This documentary about the two Savoy Opera masters was made for the Music Shop television series. It is hosted by Jerry H. Bilik and focuses on the growth of the team and the nature of their genius. Color. In English. 27 minutes. Michigan Media video.

1982 Gilbert & Sullivan Present Their Greatest Hits

This is a concert at the Royal Albert Hall presented as if Gilbert and Sullivan were present in Victorian costume to celebrate the centenary of the first presentation of *Iolanthe*. They discuss their operettas and career as they listen to their most famous compositions. The featured soloists of the D'Oyly Carte Singers appear in costume to perform favorite songs backed by a choir of 1,000 voices. Michael Heyland directed the concert. The video was produced by John Urling Clark and directed by Alan Birkinshaw. Color. 54 minutes. Vestron video.

GILBERT, JEAN
German composer (1879-1942)

Jean Gilbert, whose operetta career was primarily in Berlin, is little remembered in the English-speaking world today but in the early part of the century his operettas were quite popular in London and New York. The most successful was the 1910 *Die Keusche Susanne* (Modest Susanne) which was staged in most major cities and filmed in five countries; it remains popular in Latin America. Gilbert's 1913 *Die Kinokönigen* (The Cinema Queen) was one of the first operettas about the movies. It was staged in London in 1914 as *The Cinema Star* with Jack Hulpert, Cicely Courtneidge and Fay Compton and in New York as *The Queen of the Movies*. Unfortunately it was not filmed. The operetta *Die Frau im Hermelin* (The Lady in Ermine), staged in New York in 1922, was filmed three times, once by Ernst Lubitsch. See DIE FRAU IM HERMELIN, DIE KEUSCHE SUSANNE, OPERAS & OPERETTAS ABOUT THE MOVIES.

GIOCONDA, LA
1876 opera by Ponchielli

Even those who have never seen *La Gioconda* on stage recognize music from it. The famous "Dance of the Hours" ballet is performed by pink hippopotami in Disney's *Fantasia* and the aria "Cielo e mar" is a favorite recital piece for tenors. *La Gioconda* is Amilcare Ponchielli's most famous opera and the only one still in the repertory. It has a strong if somewhat melodramatic libretto by Arrigo Boito based on a play by Victor Hugo. Set in Venice, it tells the story of the street singer La Gioconda, Prince Enzo whom she loves, her blind mother La Cieca, Laura whom Enzo loves and the villain Barnaba who loves Gioconda and causes a lot of trouble. See also AMILCARE PONCHIELLI.

1980 San Francisco Opera
Luciano Pavarotti stars as Enzo with Renata Scotto as La Gioconda in this San Francisco Opera production by Lotfi Mansouri. It is memorable both for its fine singing and for its famous feud between Scotto and Pavarotti. After he took a disputed solo bow, she refused to take her final bow and sat in her dressing room. Kurt Herbert Adler conducted the San Francisco Opera Orchestra and Chorus. The

opera was telecast like a mini-series in April, 1980, one act each night following a documentary about its production. Color. In Italian with English subtitles. 170 minutes.

1986 Vienna State Opera
Eva Marton stars as La Gioconda with Placido Domingo as Enzo in this Vienna State Opera production staged and designed by Filippo Sanjust. Margarita Lilova sings La Cieca, Matteo Manuguerra is Barnaba, Kurt Rydl is Alvise and Ludmilla Semtschuk is Laura. Adam Fischer conducted the Vienna State Opera Orchestra and Chorus. Hugo Käch directed the video for ORF. Color. In Italian with English subtitles. 169 minutes. Home Vision video.

Early/related films

1927 Gigli Sings La Gioconda
Tenor Beniamino Gigli sings extracts from the second act of *La Gioconda* in this early sound film made by the Vitaphone company at the old Manhattan Opera House in New York. The selections begin with "Sia gloria ai canti dei naviganti" and end with the famous aria "Cielo e mar!" Gigli is accompanied by the Vitaphone Symphony Orchestra. Black and white. In Italian. About 9 minutes.

1953 Alba Arnova film
Boito's libretto was used as the screenplay for this Italian film and Ponchielli's music was used as the score but it's a narrative not an opera film. Alba Arnova stars as La Gioconda, Paolo Carlini is Enzo, Elena Kleus is Laura and Peter Trent is the Grand Inquisitor Alvise. Giacinto Solito directed. Black and white. In Italian. 88 minutes.

1970 Richard Tucker sings "Cielo e mar"
Tenor RichardTucker sings the aria "Cielo e mar" from *La Gioconda* on stage in a 1970 concert. The aria is included on the video *Legends of Opera*. Black and white. In Italian. 5 minutes. Legato Classics video.

1980 Opening Night-The Making of an Opera
This famous documentary about the production of *La Gioconda* at the San Francisco Opera in 1980 is mostly remembered because it shows Renata Scotto's feud with Luciano Pavarotti. However, the film is also very informative about what goes on backstage when an opera is staged, from the

troubles at rehearsals to the instructions to ushers. Conductor Kurt Herbert Adler, 75, is seen as the company director and Lotfi Mansouri as the producer. The documentary was telecast on April 13, 1980, preceding the screening of the opera. Color. In English. 60 minutes.

GIORDANO, UMBERTO

Italian composer (1867-1948)

Umberto Giordano's *Fedora* has more or less remained in the repertory and he had other popular successes during his life but it is really the love of tenors for *Andrea Chénier* which has kept his reputation alive. The opera has become a regular part of the international repertory because it offers wonderful opportunities for a divo tenor to show off his abilities. In modern times it has been a speciality of Franco Corelli, Placido Domingo, Mario Del Monaco and José Carreras, all of whom can be seen in the opera on video. See ANDREA CHÉNIER, FEDORA.

GIOVANNA D'ARCO

1845 opera by Verdi

Joan of Arc is Verdi's version of the story of the Maid of Orleans to a libretto by Temistocle Solera based on a Shiller play. Joan (Giovanna in the opera) urges French King Charles VII and his troops on to victory after hearing celestial voices. Joan and Charles fall in love but she knows it is impossible. Her father Giacomo denounces her as a witch, saying she is in league with the Devil. When the French begin to lose the next battle, however, she rushes to help them and inspires victory. During the fighting she is killed. *Giovanna d'Arco* was seen as a patriotic opera about the Austrian occupiers when it was first staged. See also GIUSEPPE VERDI.

1989 Bologna Opera
German film director Werner Herzog staged this production at the Teatro Comunale in Bologna. Susan Dunn is impressive as Joan, Renato Bruson quite convincing as her father Giacomo and Vincenzo La Scola sings well as Charles VII. This is a straightforward production which highlights the strengths of the opera. Richard Chailly conducts the Bologna Teatro Comunale Orchestra and Chorus. Herzog and Keith Cheetham directed the video. Color. In Italian with English subtitles. 128 minutes. Teldec video and laser.

GIUDITTA

1934 operetta by Lehár

Jarmila Novotná starred as Giuditta and Richard Tauber as Octavio when Franz Lehár's operetta *Giuditta* premiered at the Vienna State Opera in 1934. It's the story of a working class wife who runs off with an Italian Army officer. She eventually becomes a night club dancer and he becomes a cabaret pianist. Its biggest hit was Novotná's aria "Meine Lippen, sie Küssen so heiss." *Giuditta* has never been among Lehár's most popular works but it has fine roles for opera singers. The libretto is by Paul Knepler and Fritz Löhner. See also FRANZ LEHÁR.

1970 Teresa Stratas film
The young Teresa Stratas stars as the lovely Giuditta in this lavish German film of the Lehár operetta. Rudolf Schock, sometimes considered the successor to Richard Tauber, is featured opposite her as the obsessed Army officer Octavio while Maria Tiboldi portrays Anita. Wolfgang Ebert conducted the Berlin Symphony Orchestra. Günther Hassert directed the film in 35mm for German television. Unitel. Color. In German. 97 minutes.

GIULIO CESARE

1724 opera by Handel

Handel's opera *Julius Caesar* is not based on the Shakespeare play. It is set in Egypt and focuses on the relationships between Caesar and Cleopatra and her brother Ptolemy. Ptolemy kills Pompey and is himself killed by Sestus when he tries to rape Cornelia. The libretto by Nicola Haym, based on an earlier libretto by Bussani, is in Italian though the opera was written for English audiences in London. This is currently the most popular of Handel's operas and there are three very different videos in German, English and Italian. See also GEORGE F. HANDEL.

1977 Berlin State Opera
Theo Adam stars as a powerful and dominating Caesar in this Berlin State Opera production sung in German and staged by Ehard Fischer. Celestina Casapietra is Cleopatra, Siegfried Vogel is Ptolemy, Annelies Burmeister is Cornelia, Eberhard Büchner is Sextus and Günther Leib is Achillas. Gustaf Hoffman designed the sets and Peter Schreier conducted the Berlin State Opera Orchestra and Chorus. George F. Mielke directed the video. Color.

In German. 124 minutes. VIEW video/ Japanese laser.

1984 English National Opera
Janet Baker is superb as Caesar in this English National Opera production by John Copley. The production originated in 1979 but the film was made in 1984 in a studio. Counter tenor James Bowman is superb as the villainous Ptolemy and Valerie Masterson is alluring as Cleopatra with an impressive collection of dresses. Costume designer Michael Stennett enjoyed himself with this opera. Sarah Walker is Cornelia, Della Jones is Sextus and John Tomlinson is Achillas. John Pascoe designed the sets and Sir Charles Mackerras conducted the ENO Orchestra. Brian Trowell wrote the English translation and John Michael Phillips directed the video. 180 minutes. Color. In English. HBO video/Pioneer laser.

1990 Peter Sellars film
Peter Sellars updates the opera to the near future with Caesar now an American President staying at the Nile Hilton and Cleopatra something like an Egyptian Valley girl. Jeffrey Gall portrays Caesar, Susan Larson is Cleopatra, Drew Minter is Ptolemy, Mary Westbrook-Geha is Cornelia, Lorraine Hunt is Sextus and James Maddalena is Achillas. Craig Smith conducts the Dresden Sachsische Staatskapelle Orchestra. Sellers based the film on his production of the opera at the Monnaie Théâtre in Brussels. Color. In Italian with English subtitles. 151 minutes. London video/laser.

GIUSTINO
1737 opera by Handel

Handel's Giustino is a ploughboy who becomes involved in heroic deeds in ancient Greece. He rescues Leoncasta, the emperor's sister, from a bear and Arianna, the widow of the old emperor, from a sea monster. In the end he is discovered to be the long lost brother of Vitaliano, a noble tyrant. The new emperor Anastasio rewards him with a share of the throne and a royal bride. The role was originally sung by an alto castrato. See also GEORGE F. HANDEL.

1985 Komische Oper, Berlin
German countertenor Joachen Kowalski stars as Giustino in this Komische Opera production by Harry Kupfer. Michael Rabsilber is Anastasio, Dogner Schellenberger is Arianna and Violetta

Madjarowa is Leocasta. Hans Haenchen conducts the Komische Oper Orchestra. Color. In German with Japanese subtitles. 120 minutes. On Japanese video and laserdisc.

GLASS, PHILIP
American composer (1937-)

Philip Glass is the best-known avant-garde composer in America today. The Baltimore-born minimalist has had popular acceptance of the operas *Einstein on the Beach* (1976) and *The Voyage* (1992), both staged at the Metropolitan Opera, and *Akhnaten* (1984), staged in Houston. His film scores are an integral part of Godfrey Reggio's visual new age films *Koyaanisqatsi* (1983) and *Powaqqatsi* (1988) and add greatly to the power of films like *Mishima* (1985), *The Thin Blue Line* (1988) and *A Brief History of Time* (1992). He has also composed for Hollywood movies including *Breathless* (1983), *Hamburger Hill* (1987) and *Candyman* (1992). Glass has recently begun to transmute films by Jean Cocteau into operas. His operas, however, are not in complete form on video. See AKHNATEN, LA BELLE ET LA BÊTE, EINSTEIN ON THE BEACH, ORPHÉE.

1976 Music with Roots in the Aether
Glass is interviewed and performs a scene from *Einstein on the Beach* in a two-hour video produced by fellow composer Robert Ashley. He also performs *Music in 12 Parts: Part 2* with his ensemble including Jon Gibson, Dickie Landry, Richard Peck, Kurt Munkacsi, Joan La Barbara and Michael Rieman. Ashley produced and directed seven videos about new composers under this title and they were edited into one-hour television programs in 1985. Color. 60 or 120 minutes.

1979 Skyline: Philip Glass
A television portrait of Philip Glass with excerpts from various compositions. It features the opera *Einstein on the Beach*, parts of which are played. The program was produced by Peggy Daniel and directed by John Merl. Color. 19 minutes.

1983 4 American Composers: Philip Glass
British filmmaker Peter Greenaway based this excellent film portrait of Glass around performances at the Sadler Wells Theatre in London. It includes interviews with and about Glass and shows the Philip Glass Ensemble performing passages from *Einstein on the Beach* and

Glassworks. Transatlantic Films. Color. 60 minutes. Mystic Fire video.

GLINKA, MIKHAIL
Russian composer (1804-1857)

Mikhail Glinka is considered the father of Russian opera and was the first Russian composer to become known abroad. He wrote two operas, the Italianate 1836 *A Life for The Tsar* and the genuinely Russian 1842 *Ruslan and Ludmilla,* both of which are still popular in Russia. Glinka pioneered many types of Russian national music and has been the subject of two major Soviet screen biographies. See also A LIFE FOR THE TSAR, RUSLAN AND LYUDMILA.

1946 The Great Glinka
Boris Chirkov portrays Glinka in this Soviet film biography of the composer by Lev Arnshtam. Valentina Serova plays Glinka's wife, Peter Aleynikov is Pushkin, Vasili Merkuriev Is Ulynanich and Boris Livanov is Tsar Nicholas I. The film traces Glinka's search for a Russian musical idiom and includes highlights from *Ivan Susanin* sung by members of the Bolshoi Opera. The cinematography was by Alexander Shelenkov and Chen Yu-lan, the set designs by Vladimir Kaplunovsky and the music supervision by Vissarion Shebalin. The film was released in the U.S. in 1947. Mosfilm. Black and white. In Russian. 98 minutes.

1952 Man of Music
Boris Smirnov portrays Glinka in this Soviet film biography of the composer directed by Grigori Alexandrov. It focuses on Glinka's music as much as on his life and contains stagings of scenes from *Ivan Susanin* and *Ruslan and Lyudmilla.* Critics were impressed with the musical sequences and especially Sviatoslav Richter as Liszt. The cast also includes Lyubov Orlova as Ludmilla Glinka, I. Durasov as Pushkin and B. Vinogradova as the singer Giuditta Pasta. The film was released in the U.S. in 1953 as *Man of Music.* Color. In Russian. 100 minutes.

GLORIANA
1953 opera by Britten

Benjamin Britten wrote *Gloriana* on commission from the Royal Opera House to celebrate the coronation of Queen Elizabeth II. It was not well received at its premiere but has since been re-evaluated and restored to a position of importance. The opera concentrates on the later years of Elizabeth's reign and focuses on the tragic relationship between the Queen and the Earl of Essex. This was also the subject of Rossini's opera *Roberto Devereux.* Librettist William Plomer says that Lytton Strachey's *Elizabeth and Essex* was his starting point. Joan Cross starred as the Queen in the premiere with Peter Pears as Essex. See also Benjamin Britten.

1984 English National Opera
This intense English National Opera production was an important step in the re-evaluation of the opera. Sarah Walker stars as a dominating Queen Elizabeth I, Essex is sung by Anthony Rolfe Johnson, Richard van Allan is Sir Walter Raleigh, Elizabeth Vaughan is Lady Rich and Alan Opie is Cecil. It was designed and directed for the stage by Colin Graham with assistance from designer Alix Stone. Mark Elder conducted the ENO Orchestra and Derek Bailey directed the video. Color. In English. 146 minutes. HBO video.

Related film

1939 The Private Lives of Elizabeth and Essex
This colorful film version of the story stars Bette Davis as Elizabeth and Errol Flynn as Essex. It was based on Maxwell Anderson's play *Elizabeth the Queen* and makes an interesting comparison to the opera. One opera critic felt Sarah Walker modelled herself on Davis. Michael Curtiz directed. Warner Bros. Color. 106 minutes.

GLUCK, CHRISTOPH WILLIBALD
Austrian composer (1714-1787)

Christoph Gluck was influential in reforming ideas about opera. He worked with librettist Ranier de' Calzabigi to make operas musical dramas rather than showcases for singers. Gluck composed his early operas in Italy and Vienna but spent the later part of his career in Paris writing operas in French. His most famous opera is *Orfeo ed Euridice* though many critics consider *Iphigénie en Tauride* his masterpiece. At least ten of his operas are available on CD. See LE CINESI, DROTTNINGHOLM COURT THEATER, ECHO ET NARCISSE, ORFEO ED EURIDICE.

1979 Dimenticare Venezia

One of Gluck's most famous arias is "Oh del mio dolce ardor" from the 1770 opera *Paride ed Elena*, the story of Paris and Helen. It is featured in Franco Brusati's 1979 Italian film *Dimenticare Venezia* (Forget Venice) where it is sung by Adriana Martino. Much of the film takes place at the estate of a retired opera soprano. Color. In Italian. 107 minutes.

1988 Christoph Willibald Gluck, Portrait

Christine Eichel's German film is a film portrait of the composer made for the 200th anniversary of his death. It centers around scenes from two of his most important operas, *Orfeo ed Euridice* and *Iphigénie en Tauride*, and an exhibition of Gluck opera sets and costume designs. The production of *Orfeo* in Kassel was directed by Herbert Wernicke. Color. In Engosh. 44 minutes. Inter Nationes video.

GLYNDEBOURNE
English opera festival (1934 -)

The Glyndebourne Festival Opera, which opened in 1934 with *The Marriage of Figaro*, is noted for its fine Mozart productions and innovative stagings. Many of its more recent successes were directed by Peter Hall. Glyndebourne was one of the first opera houses to telecast operas starting with the BBC in the 1950s and continuing to the present day with Southern, TVS, and Channel 4. There are a large number of Glyndebourne productions on video, many with Dave Heather as director and Humphrey Burton as producer, including a notable 1973 *Marriage of Figaro*. There are also videos showing the history of the old and the new theaters. See THE ABDUCTION FROM THE SERAGLIO (1980), ALBERT HERRING (1985), ARABELLA (1984), THE BARBER OF SEVILLE (1982), CARMEN (1985), LA CENERENTOLA (1983), LA CLEMENZA DI TITO (1991), COSÌ FAN TUTTE (1975), DEATH IN VENICE (1990), DON GIOVANNI (1977), L'ENFANT ET LES SORTILÈGES (1987), EUGENE ONEGIN (1994), FALSTAFF (1960/1976), FIDELIO (1979), L'HEURE ESPAGNOLE (1987), HIGGLETY PIGGLETY POP! (1985), IDOMENEO (1974/1983), L'INCORONAZIONE DI POPPEA (1984), INTERMEZZO (1983), JENUFA (1988), KATYA KABANOVA (1988), THE LOVE OF THREE ORANGES (1982), MACBETH (1972), THE MAGIC FLUTE (1978), THE MARRIAGE OF FIGARO (1973/1994), A MIDSUMMER NIGHT'S DREAM (1981), ORFEO ED EURIDICE (1982), PORGY AND BESS (1989), THE QUEEN OF SPADES (1992), THE RAKE'S PROGRESS (1977), IL RITORNO D'ULISSE IN PATRIA (1973), LA TRAVIATA (1987), WHERE THE WILD THINGS ARE (1985).

1955 On Such A Night

Anthony Asquith's famous film promotes the experience of seeing opera at the Glyndebourne Festival. Sesto Bruscantini as Figaro and Sena Jurinac as the Countess are seen performing on stage. David Knight stars as an American who goes to see *The Marriage of Figaro* at the Glyndebourne Festival. Oliver Messel designed the sets. Frank North was cinematographer and Paul Dehn wrote the script. Color. 37 minutes.

1992 The Glyndebourne Gala

The final gala evening at the old Glyndebourne in 1992 was filmed with an all-star recital. Frederica von Stade is a joy singing "Voi che sapete" and Montserrat Caballé is extraordinary singing Desdemona's "Willow Song." Other performers include Kim Begley, Ruggero Raimondi, Benjamin Luxon, Felicity Lott and Cynthia Haymon with Andrew Davis and Bernard Haitink conducting the London Philharmonic Orchestra. Also making appearances are Geraint Evans, Elisabeth Söderström and Janet Baker. Christopher Swann directed the film telecast in America by Bravo in 1994. Color. 110 minutes. Kultur video.

1994 Glyndebourne: The House that George Built

A documentary about the history of Glyndebourne and the building of its new opera house filmed by Christopher Swann over a three-year- period. It begins with the meeting at which Sir George Christie's group decides to knock down and rebuild the opera house then continues through design, demolition and re-opening. The film was first screened on British television when Glyndebourne re-opened on May 28, 1994, with *The Marriage of Figaro*. Color. 90 minutes. Praxis (England) video.

GOBBI, TITO
Italian baritone (1913-1984)

Tito Gobbi, one of the great singers of the 20th century, starred in many opera and operatic films. His stage debut was in 1936 and his film debut followed in 1937 when he was featured as a singer in the medieval epic *I Condottieri*. He appears in films as both singer and actor and while his acting is good, his singing is better. He was featured in a number of postwar Italian films of complete operas, all of which are available on video. Gobbi was a notable partner for Maria Callas in her golden years and can be seen with her on video in Act II of *Tosca*. See also THE BARBER OF SEVILLE (1946/ 1955), CASA RICORDI, L'ELISIR D'AMORE (1947), LA FORZA DEL DESTINO (1950), LUCIA DI LAMMERMOOR (1948), MAD ABOUT OPERA, PAGLIACCI (1949), RIGOLETTO (1947), TOSCA (1946 film/ 1964), LA TRAVIATA (1948), GIUSEPPE VERDI (1938/1953), WILLIAM TELL (1947).

1937 I Condottieri

Gobbi made his debut as Nino the Singer in this epic heroic film, one of a number made in the Mussolini era with history twisted to justify the Fascists. It's the story of a Medici and his "black shirts" in the 16th century. There's lots of spectacle but not much truth. It was directed by Luis Trenker, who starred himself as Giovanni, and was released in the U.S. as *Giovanni De Medici, the Leader*. Black and white. In Italian. 88 minutes.

1943 Musica Proibita

Gobbi has an operatic double role in this film as a famous baritone and his son. The son wants to marry the niece of a woman the father had been involved with years before. She opposes the marriage after she hears Gobbi sing the "Forbidden Music" of the title and learns his name. The film is spiced with opera tunes and was directed by Carlo Campogalliani. Black and white. In Italian with English subtitles. 93 minutes. Video Yesteryear.

1946 O Sole Mio

Gobbi is an Italian-American army officer and singer who is parachuted into Naples during the famous "four days, " the subject of a popular film by Nanni Loy. Gigli broadcasts coded messages to the Allies through his radio songs until he is betrayed by a girl. Giacomo Gentiluomo directed. Black and white. In Italian. 90 minutes.

1946 Les Beaux Jours du Roi Murat

Gobbi is a singing revolutionary in the old Kingdom of Naples who charms his way into the palace and nearly gets himself executed. This French-Italian film co-stars Claude Génia and Junie Astor and has the Italian title of *L'Eco della Gloria*. It was directed by Théophile Pathé. Black and white. In French or Italian. 85 minutes.

1950 The Glass Mountain

Tito Gobbi portrays an opera singer partisan called Tito who sings in an opera composed for the film by Nino Rota. The opera is called *The Glass Mountain* and is the focus of the story. Michael Denison plays the composer of the opera who falls in love with Valentina Cortese after his plane crashes in the Italian Alps. Elena Rizzieri sings with Gobbi in the opera scenes with the music played by the La Fenice Opera Orchestra of Venice led by Franco Ferrara. The film was directed by Henry Cass. The Italian version is called *La Montana di Cristallo*. Black and white. In English or Italian. 91 minutes. Lyric/Opera Dubs videos.

1952 The Firebird

Gobbi plays an opera singer who falls in love with ballet dancer Ellen Rasch in this odd Swedish-Italian film made in English. Gobbi's singing is the highlight of the film which includes excerpts from *Don Giovanni*. Rasch is seen in excerpts from ballets and there is also singing by Sweden's Leon Bjorker. The film was originally made as two Gevacolor ballet shorts and the Gobbi material was added to create a feature. Sweden's Hasse Ekman directed. The Swedish title is *Edlfageln*, the Italian *L'Uccello di Fuoco*. Color. In English. 100 minutes.

1954 Songs for Two Voices

Canzoni a Due Voci is more or less an excuse to allow Tito Gobbi and Gino Bechi a chance to sing. Gobbi is a famous baritone who hides out when he finds out someone wants to kill him and Bechi plays his voice, which seems to have a mind of its own. This operatic fantasy was directed by Gianni Vernuccio. Black and white. In Italian. 84 minutes.

GODARD, JEAN-LUC
French film director (1930-)

Jean-Luc Godard, arguably the most influential European director of the modern era, became instantly famous with his 1959 *Breathless* (A Bout de Souffle). His versions of classic stories are as individualistic as his contemporary stories and two have an operatic connection. His episode of the opera film *Aria* is based around Lully's *Armide*. His updating of the Carmen story, *First Name Carmen*, turns her into a modern day terrorist and a filmmaker. See ARMIDE, CARMEN (1983 film).

GOLDEN CHILD
1960 opera by Bezanson

Philip Bezanson's opera *Golden Child*, libretto by Paul Engle, was called *Western Child* when it was first performed on July 28, 1959 at Iowa State

University. It is an adaptation of the Nativity story set in Sutter's Fort during the 19th century California Gold Rush. It was heavily revised for television presentation as *Golden Child*. See also PHILIP BEZANSON.

1960 Hallmark Hall of Fame
Golden Child was staged on the *Hallmark Hall of Fame* series on NBC television on Dec. 16, 1960. Jerome Hines sings the role of Captain Sutter, Patricia Neway is Martha, Brenda Lewis is Sara, Stephen Douglass is Martin and Patrica Brooks is Annabelle. Herman Grossman was the conductor and Robert Hartung directed. Black and white. In English. 60 minutes. Video at MTR.

GOLDEN COCKEREL, THE
1909 opera by Rimsky-Korsakov

Nicolai Rimsky-Korsakov's last and greatest opera, *Zolotoi Petushok*, was first produced in the West as the Diaghilev ballet *Le Coq d'Or* so the singers had to perform from theater boxes. It has now been restored to its authentic operatic form and is performed in English as *The Golden Cockerel*. It's an anti-war satire based on a Pushkin poem with a libretto by Vladimir Bielsky. A cockerel with a gift of prophecy is given to King Dodon by the Astrologer to warn him of danger. When the King falls in love with the Queen of Shemakha, the Astrologer wants her as his payment. The most famous aria is the Queen's "Hymn to the Sun." See also NICOLAI RIMSKY-KORSAKOV.

1971 New York City Opera
Beverly Sills stars as Queen Shemakha with Norman Treigle as King Dodon in this New York City Opera production. Syble Young portrays the Golden Cockerel and Enrico Di Giuseppe is the Astrologer. Elena Denda staged and choreographed the opera and Jules Rudel conducted the NYCO Orchestra and Chorus. Kirk Browning directed the closed circuit cable telecast. Color. 120 minutes.

Related film

1953 Mood Contrasts
Pioneer film artist Mary Ellen Bute created this abstract film as a visual interpretation of Rimsky-Korsakov opera music. The mood of the "Hymn to the Sun" from *The Golden Cockerel* is contrasted to that of "The Dance of the Tumblers" from *The Snow Maiden*. Color. 7 minutes.

GOLDEN DAWN
1927 operetta by Kálmán

Hungarian composer Emmerich Kálmán created this American operetta during a visit to New York when his *Gypsy Princess* was a Broadway hit. *Golden Dawn*, composed with Herbert Stothart to a libretto by Oscar Hammerstein and Otto Harbach, is an odd and somewhat dubious achievement. The setting is East Africa during World War I but the music is Viennese and the songs better suited for Mayfair. White actors in blackface plays the Africans and the plot is ludicrous. Dawn, a blonde African princess who doesn't know she is white, falls in love with a British officer being held prisoner by the Germans. The black overseer Shep is the baddie and his hit song is about his whip. The score was liked, however, so the operetta ran for half a year and was filmed. The film has become a cult classic. See also EMMERICH KÁLMÁN.

1930 Alice Gentle film
Metropolitan Opera mezzo soprano Alice Gentle portrays Mooda, the African woman who reared Dawn (Vivienne Segal) in this bizarre Warner Bros. film of this strange operetta. She has two major songs and performs them rather well with her dark powerful voice. Segal is a excellent Broadway singer in an embarrassing sarong role. Noah Beery in blackface is the villainous African overseer; his acting is hammy but he sings his whip song splendidly. Broadway baritone Walter Woolf has the hero role of the British officer. Some critics rate this as the worst operetta ever filmed. Ray Enright directed in early two-color Technicolor and the *New York Times* reviewer felt even the color was weird. The version available on laser is in black and white. 75 minutes. On laserdisc.

GOLONDRINAS, LAS
1914 lyric drama by Usandizaga

José Maria Usandizaga is one of the most famous Basque composers and his opera *Las Golondrinas* (The Swallows) is a permanent fixture in the Spanish repertory. It's a tragic love story about a group of traveling players led by Puck who loves Cecilia and is loved by Lina. Cecilia pretends to love Puck to spite Lina but when she scorns him, Puck kills her. *Las Golondrinas* was written as a zarzuela but converted into an opera by the composer's brother. Gregorio Martinez Sierra wrote the libretto. See also JOSÉ MARIA USANDIZAGA.

1969 Juan De Orduña film
Vincente Sardinero sings the role of Puck acted by José Moreno, Isabel Rivas sings Cecilia acted by Maria Silva and Josefina Cuberio sings Lina acted by Dianik Zurakowska in this excellent Spanish film directed by Juan De Orduña. Federico Moreno Torroba conducts the Spanish Lyric Orchestra and Madrid Chorus. The film, written by Manuel Tamayo, was produced by Spanish TVE for its *Teatro Lirico Español* series. The soundtrack is on record. Color. In Spanish. 90 minutes.

GOMES, CARLOS
Brazilian composer (1836-1896)

Carlos Gomes is the best known Brazilian opera composer, mostly because of the success of *Il Guarany* in Europe. He was born in Campinas, studied in Rio de Janeiro at the Imperial Conservatory with an Italian teacher and had his first opera, *A Noite do Castelo,* produced in 1861. He spent most of the later part of his life in Italy where *Il Guarany* won him renown in 1870 after its premiere at La Scala. It was produced in Rio the same year. Gomes' later successes include *Salvator Rosa* (1874) and *Lo schiavo* (1889). *Il Guarany* was in the international opera repertory for many years and remains popular in Brazil. See IL GUARANY.

1948 Guarany
An Italian film biography of the composer starring Antonio Vilar as Carlos Gomes. It tells the story of his life from his childhood in Brazil, where some of the scenes were shot, to his opera achievements in Italy. The film uses Gomes' music as its score. The cast includes Mariella Lott as Lindita, Anita Vargas as the composer's mother and Luigi Pavese as his father. Riccardo Freda wrote and directed the film. Black and white. In Italian. 85 minutes.

GONDOLIERS, THE
1889 comic opera by Gilbert & Sullivan

The Gondoliers or *The King of Barataria* is the last of the Gilbert and Sullivan operettas still regularly performed. It's set in Venice and has a complicated story about gondolier twin brothers, Marco and Giuseppe. One of them is really a prince who was married as a child to Casilda, the daughter of the Duke and Duchess of Plaza-Toro. This is a problem as no one knows which one is the prince, and they are already married to Gianetta and Tessa. The Grand Inquisitor orders them to rule the kingdom of Barataria jointly until things get sorted out. The music is among the best in the Savoy operas. See also GILBERT AND SULLIVAN.

1962 Stratford Festival
A Canadian television adaptation of a Stratford Festival stage production by Norman Campbell. John Arab and Victor Braun are the gondolier brothers and head a cast that includes Douglas Campbell, Ilona Kombrink, Ann Casson, Jack Creley and Alexander Gray. Alan Lund was the choreographer and Louis Applebaum conducted the CBC Orchestra. CBC. Black and white. In English. 90 minutes.

1974 World of Gilbert & Sullivan film
Donald Adams stars as the Grand Inquisitor in this highlights version produced by John Seabourne for the *World of Gilbert and Sullivan* series. Helen Landis is the Duchess of Plaza-Toro, John Cartier is the Duke, Thomas Round is Marco Palmieri, Michael Wakeham is Giuseppe Palmieri, Gillian Humphreys is Gianetta, Ann Hood is Tessa and Joy Roberts is Casilda. They are supported by the Gilbert and Sullivan Festival Orchestra and Chorus. Trevor Evans directed the film. Color. In English. 50 minutes.

1982 George Walker film
Keith Michell is the Grand Inquisitor and Eric Shilling is the Duke of Plaza-Toro in this film produced by Judith De Paul for the George Walker series. Sandra Dugdale is Casilda, Francis Egerton is Marco, Tom McDonnell is Giuseppe, Nan Christie is Gianetta, Fiona Kimm is Tessa and Anne Collins is The Duchess. Alexander Faris conducted the London Symphony Orchestra and the Ambrosian Opera Chorus. Peter Wood was stage director and Dave Heather directed the film. Color. In English. 111 minutes. CBS Fox video.

1983 Stratford Festival
Brian Macdonald was stage director of this entertaining Stratford Festival production directed for Canadian television by Norman Campbell. Douglas Chamberlain stars as the Duchess of Plaza Toro, Eric Donkin is the Duke, Richard MacMillan is the Grand Inquisitor, Deborah Milson is Casilda, Marie Baron is Gianetta, John Keane is Marco, Paul

Massel is Giuseppe and Karen Skidmore is Tessa. Douglas McLean and Susan Benson designed the sets and costumes. Berthold Carriere conducts the Stratford Festival Orchestra and Chorus. Color. In English. 154 minutes. Connaisseur/Home Vision video.

1995 Australian Opera
Brian Macdonald was also stage director of this fine updated version of the operetta at the Australian Opera in Sydney. Graeme Ewer plays the Duchess of Plaza Toro, Robert Gard plays the Duke, the Gondoliers are sung by David Hobson and Roger Lemke while Susanne Johnston and Christine Douglas are seen as their lady loves. Frank Dobbs conducted the orchestra and chorus and Martin Dobbs directed the video. Color. In English. 150 minutes. Polygram (England) video.

GOOD FRIDAY 1663
1995 English TV opera by Westbrook

Good Friday 1663 is an English television opera composed by Mike and Kate Westbrook to a libretto by Helen Simpson and is based on her story. A pregnant woman trapped in a loveless marriage sits in church in 1663 listening to a gloomy Good Friday sermon while remembering events in her life. Kate Westbrook plays the woman and sings all the roles except for the preacher. Peter Jaques produced and Frank Cvitanovich directed the opera filmed on location in Suffolk. It was commissioned by Channel Four and telecast on March 12, 1995. Color. In English. 51 minutes.

GORCHAKOVA, GALINA
Russian soprano (1960-)

Rising star Galina Gorchakova emerged from Siberia to become the prima donna of the Kirov Opera in St. Petersburg. She attracted international attention singing Tatyana in *Eugene Onegin* in Sverdlovsk in 1988 and was much admired in Prokofiev's *The Fiery Angel* in London. She can be seen on video as Tatyana with the Bolshoi Opera. See EUGENE ONEGIN (1993).

GORETTA, CLAUDE
Swiss film director (1929-)

Claude Goretta is known for such internationally successful films as *The Lacemaker* (1977) and *The Girl*

From Lorraine (1980), both made with notable sensitivity. His controversial film version of the Monteverdi opera *Orfeo* premiered at the Venice Film Festival in 1985. See ORFEO.

GORIKKER, VLADIMIR
Russian opera film director

Soviet filmmaker Vladimir Gorikker specialized in creating films of classic Russian operas. They were made as genuine shot-on-location movies with actors portraying the opera personages and the singing dubbed by top opera stars. His 1965 version of Rimsky-Korsakov's The Tsar's Bride has been particularly admired for its visual and vocal qualities but all of his films have real quality. See Iolanta (1963), Mozart and Salieri (1962), The Stone Guest (1967), The Tsar's Bride (1965).

GORIN, IGOR
Ukrainian/American baritone (1908-1982)

Metropolitan Opera baritone Igor Gorin was born in the Ukraine in 1908 but his family moved to Vienna after the Soviet Revolution. He made his debut at the Vienna Volksoper in 1930, emigrated to the U.S. in 1933 and worked for many years in American radio. He first appeared on screen in the 1937 MGM movie *Broadway Melody of 1938* singing arias from *Carmen* and *The Barber of Seville*. Gorin was a regular guest on the *Voice of Firestone* opera TV series in the 1950s and also starred in the NBC Opera Theatre productions of *Rigoletto* and *La Traviata* (both on video). He finally made his debut at the Met in 1964 singing the role of Germont in *La Traviata* but it was late in his career. Two years later he sang the role of Ford opposite Norman Foster's *Falstaff* in a film of *The Merry Wives of Windsor*. After he retired from the stage, he taught voice at the University of Arizona. See also THE MERRY WIVES OF WINDSOR (1966), RIGOLETTO (1958), LA TRAVIATA (1957).

1937 Broadway Melody Of 1938
Charles Igor Gorin portrays the operatic barber Nicki Papaloopas in this entertaining musical about an opera-loving racehorse. The first shot of the movie shows crowds in front of the old Metropolitan Opera and posters of *Carmen*. An orchestra plays Escamillo's music and a voice is heard singing the "Toreador Song." The camera pans right to a barber shop where barber Gorin is singing the aria while shaving customer Buddy

Ebsen. Later racehorse owner Eleanor Powell finds that when Gorin sings Figaro's "Largo al Factotum" from *The Barber of Seville*, her horse can win steeplechase races. The horse has to win so that Robert Taylor can finance a Broadway show starring Powell. With Gorin and Rossini's help it does and the show goes on. The film also features Judy Garland and Sophie Tucker. Jack McGowan and Sid Silvers wrote the screenplay, William Daniels was cinematographer and Roy Del Ruth directed for MGM. Black and white. 113 minutes. MGM-UA video.

1951-1952 Igor Gorin in Opera & Song

Baritone Igor Gorin is seen in performances on *Voice of Firestone* television programs in 1951 and 1952 in this video of highlights from the series. He sings arias from *La Traviata, Pagliacci, The Barber of Seville* and *Herodiade* as well as a selection of popular songs including "The Way You Look Tonight" and "For You Alone." Howard Barlow conducts the orchestra. Black and white. 55 minutes. VAI video.

GÖTTERDÄMMERUNG
1876 opera by Wagner

The Twilight of the Gods is the fourth and final opera in Richard Wagner's epic *Ring* tetralogy. Hagen, son of Alberich, plots to get back the Ring. The hero Siegfried is given a drug at the castle of Gunther and Gutrune which obliterates his love for Brünnhilde. He agrees to marry Gutrune, abducts Brünnhilde as a bride for Gunther and takes the Ring from her. When Siegfried's memory returns, Hagen kills him. The distraught Brünnhilde joins Siegfried on his funeral pyre thereby setting fire to the castle and destroying Vahalla. The Rhine floods and the Ring is finally restored to the Rhinemaidens. The era of the Gods is over. See also RICHARD WAGNER.

1980 Bayreuth Festival

Gwyneth Jones (Brünnhilde) and Manfred Jung (Siegfried) star in Patrick Chereau's famous 1977 Bayreuth Festival Centenary production set in the 19th century. Jeannine Altmeyer is Gutrune, Franz Manura is Gunther, Fritz Hubner is Hagen, Gwendolyn Killebrew is Waltraute and Hermann Becht is Alberich. Richard Peduzzi designed the sets and Jacques Schmidt the costumes. Pierre Boulez conducts the Bayreuth Festival Orchestra and Chorus. Brian Large directed the video. Color.

In German with English subtitles. 266 minutes. Philips video and laserdisc.

1989 Bavarian State Opera

René Kollo sings Siegfried with Hildegard Behrens as Brünnhilde in this modernist Bavarian State Opera production by Nikolas Lehnhoff with Wolfgang Sawallisch conducting. Lisabeth Balslev is Gutrune, Hans Gunter Nocker is Gunther, Matti Salminen is Hagen, Waltraud Meier is Waltraute and Ekkerhard Wlaschiha is Alberich. Erich Wonder designed the symbolic high-tech sets and Shokichi Amano directed the video. Color. In German with English subtitles. 230 minutes. EMI video and Japanese laser.

1990 Metropolitan Opera

Siegfried Jerusalem sings Siegfried with Hildegarde Behrens as Brünnhilde in this solidly traditional Metropolitan Opera production by Otto Schenk with James Levine conducting. Christa Ludwig is Waltraute, Matti Salminen is Hagen, Anthony Raffell is Gunther, Hanna Lisowska is Gutrune and Ekkehard Wlaschiha is Alberich. Gunther Schneider-Siemssen designed the naturalistic sets and Rolf Langenfass the costumes. Brian Large directed the video which was telecast on PBS. Color. In German with English subtitles. 252 minutes. DG video and laserdisc.

1992 Bayreuth Festival

Siegfried Jerusalem portrays Siegfried with Anne Evans as Brünnhilde in this modernist Bayreuth Festival production by Harry Kupfer with Daniel Barenboim conducting. Gunter von Kannen sings the role of Alberich and the cast includes Waltraud Meier and Philip Kang. The minimalist SF-style sets are by Hans Schavernoch and Horant H. Hohlfeld directed the video. Color. In German with English subtitles. 230 minutes. Teldec video and laser.

Related films

1932 Rehearsal at Bayreuth

Frida Lieder as Brünnhilde and Max Lorenz as Siegfried are seen on stage at Bayreuth rehearsing Siegfried's farewell scene. Karl Elmendorff conducts. Winifred Wagner is shown watching in this film included on the video Legends of Opera. Black and white. In German. 2 minutes. Legato Classics video.

1990 Highlander II - The Quickening

Christopher Lambert as the Highlander hero of this fantasy set in a rather dismal the-world-is-about-to-end future goes to the opera for a little relaxation. The opera, appropriately, is *Götterdämmerung*. Birgit Nilsson is heard on the soundtrack singing with the Vienna Philharmonic Orchestra conducted by Georg Solti. The Seattle Symphony and Symphony Chorale under Gerard Schwarz are also featured. Color. 100 minutes.

GOUNOD, CHARLES
French composer (1818-1893)

Charles Gounod was ranked as one of the major opera composers at the end of the 19th century when *Faust* was the favorite opera of Queen Victoria but his reputation has been in decline for the last hundred years. Only *Faust* has remained in the standard repertory and even it is accused of sentimentality. The decline in Gounod's reputation can be measured by the films made of his operas; there were a great many at the beginning of the century and virtually none in recent years. Gounod's other major operas are *Mereille* (1864) and *Roméo et Juliette* (1867). Gounod's "Ave Maria" based on Bach is very popular with opera singers on record and in recitals. See FAUST, MIREILLE, ROMÉO ET JULIETTE.

1904 Cinéma-Gramo-Théatre

Mme. Landouzy of the Paris Opéra-Comique sings Gounod's "Ave Maria," accompanied by her husband on cello, in this early French sound film using a system called Cinéma-Gramo-Théatre. It was produced by Henri Joly and George Mendel. Black and white. 3 minutes.

1960 I Survive My Death

A Czech opera singer in a World War II Nazi concentration camp sings Gounod's "Ave Maria" instead of the more usual "Internationale" in a crucial scene in this Czechoslovakian film. Vojtech Jasny directed. Czech title: *Prezil Jsem Sviu Smrt*. Black and white. In Czech. 92 minutes.

GOYA
1986 opera by Menotti

Gian Carlo Menotti's opera *Goya* was created for Placido Domingo for presentation at the Kennedy Center by the Washington Opera. The libretto by Menotti tells the story of the Spanish painter Goya and his relationships with the Duchess of Alba and the Queen of Spain. See also GIAN CARLO MENOTTI.

1986 Washington Opera

Placido Domingo stars as the painter Goya caught between the Queen of Spain, portrayed by Karen Huffstodt, and the Duchess of Alba, sung by Victoria Vergara. Raphael Fruhbeck de Burgos conducts the Washington Opera Orchestra. The Washington production was telecast on PBS from the Kennedy Center on Nov. 28, 1986, under the direction of Menotti himself. Kirk Browning directed the telecast and video. Color. In English. 120 minutes.

GOYESCAS
1916 opera by Granados

Spanish composer Enrique Granados premiered his most famous opera at the Metropolitan Opera on Jan. 28, 1916, the first opera in the Spanish language presented in a major American opera house. It is set in Madrid around 1800 and is based on a piano suite by the composer. Fernando Periquet's libretto was based around paintings by Goya. The bullfighter Paquiro is engaged to the singer Pepa but flirts with the aristocratic Rosario and arouses the animosity of her lover, Captain Fernando. The two end up dueling and Fernando is killed. The opera has a famous intermezzo and a noted aria, "La maja y el ruiseñor." See also ENRIQUE GRANADOS.

1942 Imperio Argentina film

Spanish singer Imperio Argentina stars in a double role in *Goyescas*, a Spanish film based on the opera. She portrays both of the women who love Captain Fernando but the plot is considerably altered. Granados' music is played by the Madrid Symphonic Orchestra as arranged by Jose Munoz Molleda. Argentina sings and acts well and director/adapter Benito Perojo is expert at this genre of film. The cast also includes Rafael Rivelles as Captain Fernando, Armando Calvo and Marina Torres. The film was released in the U.S. in 1944. Black and white. In Spanish. 97 minutes.

GRAF VON LUXEMBURG, DER
1909 operetta by Lehár

Franz Lehár's *The Count of Luxemburg* is the story of René, the penniless Count of Luxembourg, who agrees for payment to marry an opera singer named

Angèle. This has been arranged so she will have a title and be able to marry Prince Basil. The marriage takes place without either seeing the other. Naturally they later fall in love but don't know they are already married to each other. After various problems are solved, they become a happy couple. The libretto is by A.M. Willner & Robert Bodansky. The operetta was staged in English in London in 1911 and in New York in 1912. See also FRANZ LEHÁR.

1926 George Walsh film

George Walsh stars as René, the penniless Count, in this American silent film version of the operetta directed by Arthur Gregor. It was screened with live music by Lehár. Helen Lee Worthing portrays the actress Angèle with Michael Dark as the Duke. Chadwick Films. Black and white. In English. About 70 minutes.

1957 Renate Holm film

Renate Holm stars as Angèle in this German movie version of the Lehár operetta with Gerhard Riedmann as René. It was directed by Werner Jacobs for the CCC company. Color. In German. 90 minutes.

1963 Placido Domingo film

Placido Domingo stars as the Count of Luxembourg in this Spanish-language film of the operetta made for Mexican television by Max Factor. His co-stars are his wife Marta Ornela as Angèle, his mother Pepita Embil and his father Placido. Black and white. In Spanish. 80 minutes.

1972 Eberhard Wächter film

Wagner baritone Eberhard Wächter portrays the Count in this colorful German film of the operetta. Lilian Sukis plays the opera singer Angèle Didier, Erich Kunz is Prince Basil, Peter Frölich is the painter Armand Brissard and Helga Papouschek is his mistress Juliette Vermont. The music is played by the Kurt Graunke Symphony Orchestra. Wolfgang Glück directed the film in 35mm for television. Unitel. Color. In German. 95 minutes. Taurus (Germany) video.

1992 Sandro Massimini video

Highlights from *Il Conte de Lussemburgo* are sung by Italian operetta master Sandro Massimini and his associates on the Italian TV series *Operette, Che Passione!* Featured are "Lei di qui lui di là" and "Cuoricin, tesorin." Color. In Italian. About 16 minutes. Ricordi (Italy) video.

GRÄFIN MARIZA
1924 operetta by Kálmán

Countess Mariza is Emmerich Kálmán's most popular operetta after *Die Csárdásfürstin*. It includes one of his best known melodies, sung in English as "Play Gypsies, Dance Gypsies" when it was presented on Broadway in 1926. Beautiful Hungarian Countess Mariza hires disguised Count Tassilo to work on her estate and then falls in love with him though she is pursued by the boorish Baron Zsupán. The libretto is by Julius Brammer and Alfred Gruenwald. See also EMMERICH KÁLMÁN.

1925 Hans Steinhoff film

Vivian Gibson stars as the Countess with support from Harry Liedtke as Tassilo in this silent German film of the operetta. It was directed by Hans Steinhoff who also made silent versions of *Die Fledermaus* and *Der Bettelstudent*. Black and white. In German. About 70 minutes.

1932 Hubert Marischka film

Hubert Marischka, who originated the role of Count Tassilo in the Vienna premiere of the operetta, repeats his performance in this German film with Dorothea Wieck as the Countess. The cast includes Charlotte Ander, Ferdinand von Alten and Anton Pointner. Richard Oswald directed. Black and white. In German. 110 minutes.

1958 Rudolf Schock film

Rudolf Schock, often described as the successor to Richard Tauber, stars as Count Tassilio in this German film of the operetta. Christine Gorner portrays the Countess with Renate Ewert in support. Rudolf Schündler directed. Color. In German. 110 minutes.

1973 René Kollo film

Wagnerian tenor René Kollo stars as Count Tassilo in this colorful German film with Erzsebet Hazy as Countess Mariza, Dagmar Koller as Lisa and the great Ljuba Welitsch as Princess Bozeno. It was shot on location in the country with plenty of colorful dancing and inventive Busby Berkeley-like camera work. Wolfgang Ebert conducts the Vienna Symphony Orchestra and the Vienna Operetta

Choir. Rolf and Alexandra Becker designed the sets and Eugen York directed the film. Unitel. Color. In German. 102 minutes. Taurus (Germany) video.

1992 Sandro Massimini video

Highlights from *La Contessa Maritza* are sung by Italian operetta master Sandro Massimini and his associates on the Italian TV series *Operette, Che Passione!* Featured are "Se vieni a Varasdin," "Vien Tzigon" and "Il trillare delle viole." Color. In Italian. About 18 minutes. Ricordi (Italy) video.

GRANADOS, ENRIQUE
Catalan composer (1867-1916)

Enrique Granados is one of the best known Catalan composers especially for his opera *Goyescas* and his piano compositions. His Catalan operas, known only in Barcelona in his lifetime, include *Petrarca*, *Follet* and *Picarel* written to librettos by Catalan poet Apeles Mestres. His most famous opera, *Goyescas*, premiered at the Metropolitan Opera in 1916. The composer was returning home from the premiere when his ship was torpedoed in the English Channel. See GOYESCAS.

GRANDE BRETÈCHE, LA
1957 TV opera by Hollingsworth

Stanley Hollingsworth's opera *La Grande Bretèche* was commissioned by the adventurous NBC Opera Theatre. Harry Duncan's libretto is based on a Balzac story that has been made into an opera by five composers. It's a grim tale about a woman's lover being walled up in a closet by a jealous husband. Gloria Lane stars as Countess Marie with Hugh Thompson as her husband, David Cunningham as her lover, Adelaide Bishop as the maid and Kimi Beni as the handyman. Samuel Chotzinoff produced, John Schwartz directed and Gerald Ritholz designed the sets. Peter Herman Adler conducted the Symphony of the Air Orchestra and Kirk Browning directed the telecast on Feb. 10, 1957. Color. In English. 45 minutes. See also STANLEY HOLLINGSWORTH.

GRANDE-DUCHESSE DE GÉROLSTEIN, LA
1867 opera-bouffe by Offenbach

Jacques Offenbach's *The Grand Duchess of Gérolstein*, a satire about war and petty German principalities,

was one of his greatest successes. Its popularity continued to the time of Lillian Russell who sang its famous "Saber Song" to President Cleveland in one of the first long-distance phone calls. It was written for Offenbach's good friend Hortense Schneider to a libretto by Henri Meilhac and Ludovic. The Duchess fancies private Fritz whom she promotes to commander-in-chief to the dismay of bombastic General Boum. But as Fritz prefers Wanda he loses his promotion. See also JACQUES OFFENBACH.

1981 Paris Opéra

Régine Crespin has an affection for Offenbach and has recorded many of his operettas. She stars as the Grand Duchess in this Paris Opéra production, a role she then reprised in San Francisco in 1983. Supporting her in this production are tenor Remy Corazza, baritone Michel Roux, tenor Charles Burles and tenor Trempont. Michel Plasson conducts the orchestra. The video is an off-air copy of a telecast. Color. 110 minutes. Lyric/Opera Dubs video.

1992 Sandro Massimini video

Highlights from *La Granduchessa di Gérolstein* are sung by Italian operetta master Sandro Massimini and his associates on this video from the Italian TV series *Operette, Che Passione!* Featured are "Ah, que j'aime les militaires" sung by Sonia Dorigo and "Il generale Bum-Bum" sung by Massimini. Color. In Italian. About 16 minutes. Ricordi (Italy) video.

GRANFORTE, APOLLO
Italian baritone (1886-1975)

Apollo Granforte began his career in Argentina where he made his debut in 1913. He sang with Melba on Williamson tours in Australia in 1924 and 1928 and became a regular at La Scala in the 1930s. He sang a wide variety of operas from Mascagni's *Nerone* to *Parsifal* but was especially admired in Rossini and Verdi. He can be seen as Rossini's Figaro in a film made in Australia in 1928 while he was on tour and in a biopic about Verdi. See also GIUSEPPE VERDI (1938).

1928 Granforte sings *The Barber of Seville*

Granforte bounces on stage in Figaro costume with guitar and sings the "Largo al factotum" aria in an energetic manner backed by a full orchestra. He made this sound film in Australia while he was on tour with Melba. The title on the screen is "Efftee Presents Signor Apollo Granfort of La Scala, Milan, and the Williamson-Imperial Grand Opera Company. Selections from 'The Barber of Seville' (Rossini)." The film was made by RCA with its Photophone Recording system. Black and white. In Italian. About 6 minutes. Lyric video.

GRAN SCENA OPERA, LA

1981 satirical opera group

La Gran Scena Opera Company of New York is an extraordinary satirical male theatrical opera troupe which has been successful in poking gentle fun at opera around the world. It was founded in 1981 by Ira Siff who, in addition to being artistic director, stars as Madame Vera Galupe-Borszkh, a "traumatic" soprano known as La Dementia. His singing, like that of his colleagues, is unusual and quite funny.

1985 La Gran Scena in Munich
This La Gran Scena show was staged for the Munich Theater Festival and taped by Bavarian Television. It features the company in scenes from *Die Walküre, Semele, La Bohème, Lucia di Lammermoor, Carmen* and *La Traviata*. The performers are Siff, Keith Jurosko, Philip Koch, Bruce Hopkins, Luis Russinyol, Charles Walker, Dennis Raley and Dan Brack. Ross Barentyne is music director, Kenneth M. Young designed the costumes and Christopher Banner the wigs and make-up. The stage directors are Siff, Peter Schloser and Jane Whitehill. Christina Haberlik directed the video. Color. In English with arias in original language. 112 minutes. VAI video.

GRAYSON, KATHRYN

American soprano (1922-)

Kathryn Grayson became an opera singer on stage after her Hollywood career. She was the successor to Jeanette McDonald at MGM in the 1940s and 1950s singing the difficult soprano roles in films based on operettas and films featuring opera arias. Grayson was born Zelma Kathryn Hedrick in North Carolina and grew up wanting to be an opera diva. She had a florid coloratura soprano voice, photographed well and was a fine star for MGM in its musical heyday. She made an adequate operatic partner for Mario Lanza and Lauritz Melchior and was able to sing enough opera to star as Grace Moore in a biopic. She was featured in the second version of the operetta *Rio Rita* but her greatest successes were her partnerships with Howard Keel in versions of *Show Boat* and *Kiss Me Kate*. The

Vagabond King in 1956 was her last film. In 1960 she went on stage in productions of the operas *Madama Butterfly, La Bohème* and *La Traviata*. In 1961 she turned to operettas and was on stage in *The Merry Widow, Naughty Marietta* and *Der Fledermaus*. Her films with operatic content are listed below. See also THE DESERT SONG (1953), RIO RITA (1941), SHOW BOAT (1951), THE VAGABOND KING (1956).

1941 Andy Hardy's Private Secretary
Grayson, in her first film, portrays a high school student hired by fellow student Mickey Rooney to sort out his mixed-up affairs. She sings the "Mad Scene" from *Lucia di Lammermoor* at the school graduation. George Seitz directed. MGM. Black and white. 101 minutes.

1943 Thousands Cheer
Grayson sings the aria "Sempre libera" from *La Traviata* in this all-star film in which she is the love interest of Army private Gene Kelly. George Sidney directed. Black and white. 126 minutes.

1946 Two Sisters from Boston
Kathryn Grayson sings opposite Metropolitan Opera tenor Lauritz Melchior in this turn-of-the-century musical directed by Henry Koster. Grayson sings in Jimmy Durante's Bowery saloon to earn money but really wants to get into opera. Sister June Allyson and family think she's already an opera star so she has to pretend to be one and sneak on stage with Melchior. They team up first in an imaginary opera based on Mendelssohn and later join voices an imaginary opera called *Marie Antoinette*. Black and white. 112 minutes. MGM video.

1947 It Happened in Brooklyn
Grayson stars opposite Frank Sinatra in a story about Brooklynites trying to break into musical show business. She sings an aria from *Lakme*. Richard Whorf directed. Black and white. 105 minutes.

1949 That Midnight Kiss
Grayson stars opposite Mario Lanza in his first film. She's an heiress who wants to be an opera singer, he's a truck driver with a great voice and there is music from *Aida, Cavalleria Rusticana* and *L'Elisir d'Amore*. Norman Taurog directed. MGM. Color. 96 minutes.

1950 The Toast of New Orleans

Grayson plays the prima donna of the French opera house in turn-of-the-century New Orleans and Mario Lanza is a Louisiana fisherman who becomes an opera star with her tutoring. She is seen on stage in scenes from *Mignon*, *The Marriage of Figaro*, *Carmen* and *Madame Butterfly*. Cio-Cio was Grayson's favorite opera role. Norman Taurog directed. MGM. Color. 97 minutes.

1950 Grounds for Marriage

Grayson is an opera star again in this comedy but there's not much singing. The film is mainly concerned with her relationship with ex-husband Van Johnson. Robert Z. Leonard directed. MGM. Black and white. 91 minutes.

1953 So This is Love

Grayson finishes this film on stage at the Metropolitan Opera as Mimi in *La Bohème* singing "Mi chiamano Mimi." She portrays diva Grace Moore in her struggle to become a opera star. After success on Broadway and at the Met, Moore went to Hollywood and also became a film star. Gordon Douglas directed. AKA *The Grace Moore Story*. Warner Bros. Color. 101 minutes.

GREAT CARUSO, THE
1951 opera film

Mario Lanza portrays Enrico Caruso in *The Great Caruso*, one of the most popular opera films ever made. Ann Blythe plays his wife, Jarmila Novotná is seen as a temperamental prima donna and Dorothy Kirsten plays Met soprano Louise Heggar, his regular stage partner. Other singers seen in staged opera sequences include Blanche Thebom, Teresa Celli, Nicola Moscone, Giuseppe Valdengo, Lucine Amara and Marina Koshetz. The film is a romantic biography partially based on a book by Caruso's American wife with all the legends as facts, but it is still good entertainment. It did a great deal to make the wider public interested in opera and many major singers like José Carreras and Placido Domingo have acknowledged its influence on them. Richard Thorpe directed. MGM. Color. 109 minutes. MGM video.

GREAT LOVER, THE
American opera film series

The Great Lover originated as a 1915 Broadway play set in the world of opera. It was filmed in 1920 and 1932. A third film to star Enzio Pinza, Jan Peerce, Robert Peters and Robert Merrill was announced in 1952 but never made. The play by Leo Ditrichstein and Frederick and Fanny Hatton revolves around a love affair between a famous opera baritone and a rising young soprano.

1920 John Sainpolis film

John Sainpolis stars as world famous baritone Jean Paurel who becomes engaged to American soprano Claire Adams. She has just returned from study in Europe and joined his opera company. Prima donna Rose Dion becomes jealous as does young singer John Davidson. Paurel loses his voice and eventually gives up the girl to the young man who turns out to be his son. Several scenes take place on the opera house stage. Frank Lloyd directed for Goldwyn Pictures. Black and white. About 70 minutes.

1932 Adolphe Menjou film

Adolphe Menjou stars as the famous opera baritone and philanderer Jean Paurel who seduces women by singing Don Giovanni's "La ci darem il mano." He is attracted to American singer Irene Dunne and arranges for her to come to the Metropolitan. There is much back stage strife as he wins her, loses his voice and finally gives her up to her true love. The film features *Don Giovanni* on stage at the Met plus arias from *Die Walküre*, *The Barber of Seville* and *Roméo and Juliette*. Ironically in real life Dunne had wanted to be an opera singer but was rejected by the Met. Harry Beaumont directed for MGM. Black and white. 79 minutes.

GREAT PERFORMANCES
PBS opera series (1975-)

This PBS television series is a kind of cultural umbrella brand name rather than a particular program but includes many operas. It has presented many European productions as they were telecast in Europe.

GREEK
1988 opera by Turnage

Mark-Anthony Turnage's first opera *Greek* was commissioned for the Munich Biennale by Hans Werner Henze. It premiered in Munich and was then staged at the Edinburgh Festival and at the ENO in London. The libretto by the composer and Jonathan Moore is based on Stephen Berkoff's play of the same title. It's a modern variation on the Oedipus legend set in London's East End with the plague seen as unstoppable unemployment and racism. The protagonist Eddy discovers he has killed his father and married his mother. The opera was well received and interpreted as an political anti-Thatcher statement. See also MARK-ANTHONY TURNAGE.

1990 BBC Television
Turnage's opera was adapted for BBC television in London after its stage success. Quentin Hayes stars as Eddy, Fiona Kimm plays sister/wife/Sphinx, Richard Stuart is father/cafe manager/police chief and Helen Charnock is mother/waitress/Sphinx. Richard Bernas conducts the Almeida Ensemble, David Blight and Raymond Langhorn designed the sets and Keith Alexander produced. Peter Maniura and Jonathan Moore directed the video. Color. In English. 81 minutes. RM Arts (England) video.

GREEK PASSION, THE
1961 opera by Martinu

Bohuslav Martinu's opera *The Greek Passion* is based on Nikos Kazantzakis' novel *Christ Recrucified*. The story is set in a Greek village where a young man Manolios becomes identified with Christ after he is chosen for the role for a Passion play. There are also counterparts of Mary Magdalene and Judas. The Judas figure kills the Christ figure at the end of the opera. See also BOHUSLAV MARTINU.

1981 Indiana Opera Theater
This Indiana Opera Theater production, telecast in 1981, stars Tim Nobel, Rebecca Field, Rudolf Neufeld and Joannes Kosters. Bryan Balkwith conducts the Indiana Opera Theater Orchestra and Chorus. Color. In English. 145 minutes. Video at New York Public Library.

GREENAWAY, PETER
English film director (1942-)

Peter Greenaway writes and directs operas as well as films and makes documentaries about opera composers. He began as painter, turned to films in 1965 and became internationally known in 1982 for his first feature *The Draughtsman's Contract* with a Purcell-esque score by Michael Nyman. There were operatic qualities in subsequent films including *The Cook, the Thief, His Wife and Her Lover* and *Prospero's Books*. In 1993 he created a television opera with

Dutch composer Louis Andriessen. In 1994 he wrote the libretto and directed Andriessen's stage opera *Rosa: A Horse Drama* using cinematic techniques. He has also made films about Robert Ashley, Philip Glass and Meredith Monk for the British *4 American Composers* series. See LOUIS ANDRIESSEN, ROBERT ASHLEY, PHILIP GLASS, MEREDITH MONK.

GRÉMILLON, JEAN
French film director (1902-1959)

French filmmaker Jean Grémillon, known for films like *Remorques* and *Le Ciel est à Vous*, began with the intention of being a professional musician. He was strongly influenced by Debussy's *Pelléas et Mélisande* which he saw fifteen times. He turned to cinema in 1923. In 1934 he made a film based on a famous Spanish opera, Jose Serrano's *La Dolorosa*. In 1935 he shot the musical *La Valse Royale*, the French version of the German operetta *Königswalzer*. In 1936 he collaborated with Luis Buñuel and directed a popular zarzuela film based on Serrano's *La Alegría del Batallón*. See LA ALEGRÍA DEL BATALLÓN, JOSÉ SERRANO.

GRIFFELKIN
1955 TV opera by Foss

Lukas Foss's opera, commissioned by NBC Opera Theatre, has a libretto by Alastair Reid. It is based on the fairy tale "The Little Devil's Birthday" told to Foss when he was a boy and is intended to be opera with appeal for children and adults. Griffelkin is a little devil whose birthday present is a day in our world to create mischief. The experience changes him as he finds he likes things in this world and especially one little girl. He is so corrupted that he commits a good deed and is expelled from hell and forced to become a human. The opera was staged in Tanglewood in 1956 and at New York City Opera in 1993. See also LUKAS FOSS.

1955 NBC Opera Theater
Adelaide Bishop stars as Griffelkin in this NBC Opera Theatre production by Samuel Chotzinoff. Mary Kreste plays his Grandmother, Alice Richmond is the Mother whose life he saves, Rose Geringer is the Little Girl he loves and Lee Cass is the bewildered Policeman. Robert Jouffrey choreographed and staged the production, Rouben Ter-Arutunian designed the sets and Peter Herman Adler conducted the Symphony of the Air orchestra. Kirk Browning directed the telecast on

November 6, 1955. Black and white. In English. 60 minutes. Video at MTR.

GROSS TENOR, DER
1930 German opera film

Emil Jannings stars as a world-famous opera tenor named Alberto Winkelmann in *The Great Tenor*, a German film made at the height of the actor's stardom. There are opera house scenes in Germany, Brazil and Austria and scenes of Jennings on stage in *Otello* and *Lohengrin* with his singing dubbed. The film shows his pampered philandering life, his jealousy about a rising singer, his loss of voice and his eventual redemption. Renate Muller plays his faithful wife and Evaristo Signorini is the rival. Hans Schwartz directed. Also known as *Liebling der Gotter*. Black and white. In German. 103 minutes.

GUARANY, IL
1870 opera by Gomes

This opera, which made Brazilian composer Carlos Gomes famous when it premiered at La Scala in 1970, is the best known Brazilian opera and the only opera by a 19th century Latin American composer to enter the repertory. Set in 1560 near Rio de Janeiro, it tells the story of the Guarani Indian Peri and his love for the Portuguese noblewoman Cecilia. A Spanish adventurer named Gonzales is the villain. The libretto is by Antonio Scalvini and Carlo D'Ormeville. *Il Guarany* is modeled on Italian opera but uses Brazilian Indian melodies and rhythms. It was presented in most major opera houses in the 19th century but is now rarely staged outside Brazil. In its time it was admired by Verdi and its arias were recorded by Caruso, Gigli and Destinn. There have been recent productions by Werner Herzog in Vienna and Washington, DC. See also CARLOS GOMES.

1986 Campinas video
Ivo Lessa stars as Peri with Niza de Castro Tank as Cecilia in the only video of the complete opera, a tape of a telecast from Campinas in the state of Sao Paulo in Brazil. Eduardo Janho-Abumrad is Don Antonio and Nelson N. Di Marzio is Gonzales. The music is played by the Campinas Municipal Symphony Orchestra led by Benito Juarez. Video by RTC, Sao Paulo. Color. In Italian with Portuguese titles. 148 minutes. Opera Dubs video.

Early/related films

1916 Brazilian "singing" film
O Guarani, the first film of the opera, was made in Brazil in the silent era as what was known as a "singing" film. Singers stood behind the screen and sang arias from the opera at the appropriate moments. The movie starred Georgina Marchiani as Cecilia and was a considerable success. Black and white. Sung in Portuguese. About 40 minutes.

1923 Salvatore Aversano film
The second screen production was a silent version made in Italy by Salvatore Aversano. It was a big production for its time and praised for its advanced special effects. Gino Soldarelli stars as Peri with Elisenda Annovazzi as Cecilia and Camillo de Rossi as Gonzales. Black and white. In Italian. About 70 minutes.

1986 Carreras/Caballé scenes
José Carreras and Monserrat Caballé sing the roles of Peri and Cecilia in the fictional premiere of *Il Guarany* in the Spanish film *Romanca Final*. The movie is the biography of 19th century Navarese tenor Julián Gayarré. The music is performed by the Orchestra and Choir of the Theatre del Liceu conducted by Romano Gandolfi. Jose M. Forque directed the film. Color. In Spanish with English subtitles. 120 minutes. Kultur video.

1994 Placido Domingo in Bonn
Placido Domingo stars as Peri in a production of *Il Guarany* in Bonn in Part Four of the BBC TV film series *Placido Domingo's Tales at the Opera*. The German stage production, directed by filmmaker Werner Herzog, was the first in Europe in modern times. Domingo introduces the opera and explains that it had long been his ambition to sing in it. The series was produced by Daniel Snowman and Martin Rosenbaum. Color. In Italian. 55 minutes.

GUEDEN, HILDE
Austrian soprano (1917-1988)

Hilde Gueden made her debut at the Volksoper in Vienna in an operetta by Robert Stolz. After singing in Zurich, Munich and Salzburg, she became a member of the Vienna State Opera. She appeared at the Metropolitan for nine seasons and was much admired for her vocal technique. She can been seen as Zerlina and Cherubino in Vienna State Opera

videos and at a rehearsal at the Met. See DON
GIOVANNI (1954), THE MARRIAGE OF FIGARO (1954),
METROPOLITAN OPERA (1953), WOLFGANG A.
MOZART (1956).

GUERRERO, JACINTO
Spanish composer (1895-1951)

Jacinto Guerrero y Torres, one of the most popular
Spanish composers of zarzuelas, first became
known through the song "Hymn to Toledo." He
created over 200 musical stage works in addition to
composing for films and revues and was a major
promoter of the zarzuela genre. His best-known
zarzuelas are *Los Gavilanos* (1923), *Don Quintin el
Amargao* (1924) which has been filmed by Luis
Buñuel and *El Huésped del Sevillano* (1926). See DON
QUINTIN EL AMARGAO, EL HUÉSPED DEL SEVILLANO.

GUILLAUME TELL
See WILLIAM TELL

GURIDI, JESUS
Basque composer (1886-1961)

Jesus Guridi, one of the most popular Basque
musicians, composed several zarzuelas and operas
in the Basque language. The libretto of the opera
Mirentxu (1910) is in Basque and includes quotes
from Basque folk music. His opera Amaya (1920) is
based on a famous Navarrese novel. His most
famous work, however, is the Basque zarzuela El
Caserio (1916) which has been acclaimed as one of
the masterpieces of the genre. See EL CASERIO.

H

HACKETT, CHARLES
American tenor (1889-1942)

Massachusetts tenor Charles Hackett began his opera career in Italy and France and made his debut at the Metropolitan Opera in New York in 1919. He sang with the Chicago Opera from 1922 to 1935. He was able to sing at Covent Garden with Melba and continued singing professionally until 1939. His records include duets with Rosa Ponselle and he can be heard in fine form on a 1935 Met broadcast of Gounod's *Roméo et Juliette*.

1927-1929 Vitaphone opera films
Hackett made seven Vitaphone sound opera films in the 1927 to 1929 period and was described on them as the "Leading tenor of the Chicago Civic Opera Co." The films include a duet from *Roméo et Juliette* with Rosa Low and arias from *Rigoletto, Don Giovanni, L'Africana, Faust* and *Sadko* as well as various art songs. Black and white. Each about 8 minutes.

HADLEY, JERRY
American tenor (1952-)

Jerry Hadley made his debut as Lyonel in *Martha* in Sarasota in 1978 and then sang with the New York City Opera for several seasons in a wide range of roles. His European career began in Vienna in 1982 as Nemorino in *L'Elisir d'Amore* and afterwards he sang in most of the major European opera houses. He made his debut at the Metropolitan Opera in 1987 as Des Grieux in *Manon Lescaut*. Hadley is featured in a large number of videos and was chosen by Leonard Bernstein to be his final Candide. See ANNA BOLENA (1985), LEONARD BERNSTEIN (1994), CANDIDE (1989), DON GIOVANNI (1990), IDOMENEO (1983), MADAMA BUTTERFLY (1982), MESSIAH (1992), MOZART REQUIEM (1988), WOLFGANG A. MOZART (1991), THE RAKE'S PROGRESS (1992), IL RE PASTORE (1989), FREDERICA VON STADE (1990).

HÅGEGARD, HÅKAN
Swedish baritone (1945-)

Håkan Hagegård delighted audiences in 1974 as the superb Papageno in Ingmar Bergman's film of *The Magic Flute*, even though he was then an unknown baritone singing in Swedish. The part was his debut role at Sweden's Royal Opera in 1968. Hagegård has since become one of the most popular baritones in the world. He made his first appearance at the Metropolitan as Malatesta in *Don Pasquale* and in 1991 created the role of Beaumarchais in Corigliano's *The Ghosts of Versailles*. He can been on video in all these roles as well as Don Giovanni at Drottningholm and as the *Capriccio* Count at San Francisco. See CAPRICCIO (1993), DIE FLEDERMAUS (1986), DON GIOVANNI (1987), DON PASQUALE (1979), THE GHOSTS OF VERSAILLES (1992), THE MAGIC FLUTE (1974), THE RAKE'S PROGRESS (1995).

HAHN, REYNALDO
French composer (1875-1947)

Reynaldo Hahn, one of the leading modern composers of French operettas, was also a specialist in conducting Mozart and an intimate friend of Proust. His biggest success was *Ciboulette* (1923) which is set in Les Halles in 1867 and is virtually an homage to the operettas of Messager and Lecocq. He also wrote a popular operetta with Mozartian themes called *Mozart* which premiered with Yvonne Printemps portraying the composer. His last operetta was *Malvina* (1935). Hahn also composed movie music including *La Dame aux Camélias* with Printemps. See CIBOULETTE, YVONNE PRINTEMPS.

HAITINK, BERNARD
Dutch conductor (1929-)

Bernard Haitink is one of the major opera conductors of the world and is well represented on video. He can be seen leading the London Philharmonic Orchestra at the Glyndebourne Festival, often for Peter Hall productions, and at Covent Garden where he was music director. See ALBERT HERRING (1985), ARABELLA (1984), CARMEN (1985), DON CARLO (1985), DON GIOVANNI (1977), FIDELIO (1979), IDOMENEO (1983), THE LOVE OF THREE ORANGES (1983), THE MAGIC FLUTE (1978), THE MARRIAGE OF FIGARO (1994), A MIDSUMMER NIGHT'S DREAM (1981), PRINCE IGOR (1990), THE RAKE'S PROGRESS (1977), PYOTR TCHAIKOVSKY (1993), LA TRAVIATA (1987).

HALÉVY, FROMENTAL
French composer (1799-1862)

Fromental Halévy wrote around 40 operas, many of them grand in the manner of Meyerbeer, but only *La Juive* (The Jewess) is available on CD. Halévy, who was Jewish, was also much appreciated for the comic opera *L'Éclair* and the grand opera *La Reine de Chypre*. His operas are not currently fashionable and are not on video but there are two Vitaphone films of Giovanni Martinelli in scenes from *La Juive*. See LA JUIVE.

HALKA
1848 opera by Moniuszko

Stanislaw Moniuszko's *Halka* was the first Polish "grand opera" and is still the most famous. It has become a national symbol and its arias are a part of Polish popular culture. Although it has not entered the international repertory, it is available on CD and has been filmed twice. The story has similarities to that of *Madama Butterfly*. Halka is the heroine, a village girl seduced and abandoned by the rich nobleman Janusz who is marrying another. Jontek, who loves Halka, tries to help but she kills herself on Janusz's wedding day. Wlodzimierz Wolski's libretto is based on a story by Kazimierz Wojcicki. See also STANISLAW MONIUSZKO.

1913 Edward Pulchalski film
The first screen adaptation of Moniuszko's opera was a 1913 film, one of the earliest Polish movies. Edward Pulchalski adapted the opera for the screen and directed the film which was presented in cinemas accompanied by the opera music. Black and white. In Polish. About 15 minutes.

1937 Wladislaw Ladis-Kiepura film
Polish tenor Wladislaw Ladis-Kiepura, brother of Jan Kiepura and the leading tenor of the Hamburg Opera at this time, stars as Jontek in this Polish film of the opera. Polish soprano Ewa Brandrowska-Turska portrays the doomed Halka. Film director Jules Gardan collaborated with stage director Leon Schiller in producing the film which was a huge success in Poland. It was produced by Rex Films and was originally intended to be a Polish-British production. Black and white. In Polish. 90 minutes.

HALL, PETER
English director (1930-)

Sir Peter Hall is known primarily for his theater and opera direction but he has also had a lively cinema career. His films include *The Homecoming, Perfect Friday* and *Three in Two Won't Go*. He directed a film of Shakespeare's *A Midsummer's Night's Dream* and his stage production of Britten's opera based on the play is on video. Hall began directing opera in 1957 at Sadler's Wells and has been a regular at Covent Garden and Glyndebourne. Many of his opera stage productions are now on video. See ALBERT HERRING (1985), CARMEN (1985), DON GIOVANNI (1977), FIDELIO (1979), L'INCORONAZIONE DI POPPEA (1984), THE MARRIAGE OF FIGARO (1973), A MIDSUMMER NIGHT'S DREAM (1981), ORFEO ED EURIDICE (1982), IL RITORNO D'ULISSE IN PATRIA (1973), SALOME (1991), LA TRAVIATA (1987).

HALLMARK HALL OF FAME
American television series (1951-)

The Hallmark Hall of Fame television series began on NBC on Dec. 24, 1951, with the premiere of Menotti's TV opera *Amahl and the Night Visitors*. It was a major success and was repeated in the following years. The Hallmark series, which continues to the present day, has featured other operas and operettas including Bezanson's Nativity opera *Golden Child* and Gilbert and Sullivan's *The Yeoman of the Guard*. The Hallmark programs are preserved at the UCLA Film and Television Archive which mounted a major tribute in 1991.

HAMMERSTEIN, OSCAR II
American lyricist/librettist (1895-1960)

Oscar Hammerstein II is the major bridge between the worlds of European-style operetta and American musical comedy. His collaborations with composers Sigmund Romberg and Rudolph Friml on one side and Jerome Kern and Richard Rodgers on the other are especially notable. His European-style operettas, like *The Desert Song* and *The New Moon*, are deservedly popular but it was his ground-breaking American-style "operettas" like *Show Boat* (with Jerome Kern) and *Oklahoma* (with Richard Rodgers) that created the modern musical as we know it. Hammerstein also transformed Bizet's *Carmen* into the American opera *Carmen Jones*. Oscar Hammerstein II's impresario grandfather Oscar I created the old Manhattan

Opera House. See BALL IM SAVOY, CARMEN (1954), CAROUSEL, THE DESERT SONG, JEROME KERN, JEANETTE MACDONALD (1934) THE NEW MOON, RICHARD RODGERS, SIGMUND ROMBERG, ROSE-MARIE, SOUTH PACIFIC.

1946 Till the Clouds Roll By
Paul Langton portrays Oscar Hammerstein II in this all-star film biography of composer Jerome Kern and (to a limited degree) Hammerstein. It ends with their triumph with *Show Boat*. Richard Whorf directed. MGM. Color. 137 minutes. On video.

HAMPSON, THOMAS
American baritone (1955-)

Indiana-born Thomas Hampson studied in Los Angeles but made his debut in Dusseldorf in 1981. He sang a variety of roles in small European and American opera houses and had great success in Zurich singing in *Don Giovanni* and *The Barber of Seville*. He made his debut at the Metropolitan as Almaviva in *The Marriage of Figaro* in 1986 and now sings in major theaters in most countries. He is particularly noted for his fine singing and stage presence in Mozart operas. See THE DANGEROUS LIAISONS (1994), DON GIOVANNI (1991), FIERRABRAS (1988), METROPOLITAN OPERA (1991), ON THE TOWN (1992), GIOACHINO ROSSINI (1992), A VILLAGE ROMEO AND JULIET (1989), ZURICH (1984).

1991 Mahler Concerts in Vienna
Hampson sings Mahler songs at concerts in 1989 and 1991 at the Great Hall of the Vienna Musikverein. "Five Ruckert Songs" and "Songs of a Wayfarer" were taped in 1991 with Leonard Bernstein conducting the Vienna Philharmonic. A selection of Mahler's "Kindertotenlieder" was taped in 1989. Humphrey Burton directed the video. Color. In German. 70 minutes. DG video.

1995 An Evening with Kathleen Battle and Thomas Hampson
Battle and Hampson join forces for this *Live from Lincoln Center* concert telecast on March 1, 1995. They perform arias and duets by Mozart, Rossini, Massenet, Verdi, Lehár and Korngold in the first half and American musical theater tunes in the second. During the interval baritone Sherrill Milnes hosts a segment with Battle and Hampson talking about their work and Stephen Sondheim talking about his. Color. 90 minutes.

HAMPTON, HOPE
American soprano (1899-1982)

Hope Hampton was a movie star who decided to become an opera star. The Texas-born singer-actress, née Kennedy, arrived in Hollywood as a beauty contest winner and immediately found a sugar daddy. Wealthy Jules E. Brulatour set up a film company for her and during the 1920s she starred in 13 films from *The Bait* and *A Modern Salome* in 1920 to *The Unfair Sex* in 1926. In *Star Dust* (1921) she portrays an opera singer and she also appeared in the first *Gold Diggers* film in 1923. In 1927 she began to study singing and in 1928 made her opera debut in Philadelphia as Manon in the Massenet opera. In 1929 Warner Brothers made a Vitaphone film of her in the role. She made her debut with the San Francisco Opera in 1930 as Marguerite in *Faust* opposite Ezio Pinza. In the 1930s she sang leading roles in the operas *Thaïs* and *La Bohème* with regional opera companies. In 1938 she was featured in a Hollywood film singing Musetta's Waltz from *La Bohème*. She made her last film in 1961. Only her films with some opera relevance are listed.

1920 A Modern Salome
This film was suggested by the Oscar Wilde poem that provided the basis for the Strauss opera. Hampton portrays a woman who causes a lot of problems before she dreams she is the Biblical Salome and reforms. About 80 minutes.

1921 Star Dust
Hampton plays a singer who goes to New York, has the usual problems, is discovered by a voice teacher and becomes an opera star. She makes her debut in Massenet's *Thaïs*. The film is based on a Fannie Hurst novel. Hobart Henley directed. First National. About 75 minutes.

1929 Hope Hampton in Fourth Act of Manon
Hampton's stage debut in Philadelphia in Massenet's *Manon* in 1928 led to her being asked to appear in a sound film of excerpts from the opera. This one-reel Vitaphone film features scenes from Act IV of the opera with accompaniment by the Vitaphone Symphony Orchestra and Chorus. About 10 minutes

1938 The Road to Reno
Hampton is on stage singing Musetta's Waltz from *La Bohème* in the opening scenes of this film. She

portrays a New York opera singer trying to divorce her ranch owner husband Randolph Scott. S. Sylvan Simon directed for Universal. 68 minutes.

HANDEL, GEORGE FRIDERIC
German/English composer (1685-1759)

George Frideric Handel was for long remembered as the creator of the oratorio *Messiah* rather than as a opera composer. This has changed dramatically in recent years and he is now equally famous as the German composer who wrote Italian operas for the English. Most of his operas have been given modern productions and are available on CD and video. Handel's life has been the subject of three films and his music is often used in non-operatic movies like Bunuel's *Viridiana* and the Japanese *The Makioki Sisters*. See also ACIS AND GALATHEA, AGRIPPINA, ARIODANTE, BELSHAZZAR, FARINELLI, GIULIO CESARE, GIUSTINO, ISRAEL IN EGYPT, MESSIAH, RINALDO, THE SORCERESS, XERXES.

1942 The Great Mr. Handel
Wilfred Lawson stars as the composer in this British film about Handel's fall from Royal favor and his rise again after composing *Messiah*. The plot concerns Handel's feud with the Prince of Wales (Max Kirby). In addition to *Messiah*, the film includes arias from *Xerxes*, the overture to *Alcides* and some *Water Music*. Elizabeth Allen portrays prima donna Mrs. Cibber with her singing dubbed by Gladys Ripley. Malcolm Keen is Lord Chesterfield and Hay Petrie is the valet Phineas. Norman Walker directed from a screenplay by Gerald Elliott and Victor MacClure. Black and white. 103 minutes.

1985 Honor, Profit and Pleasure
Simon Callow portrays Handel in this fine British film biography written and directed by Anna Ambrose. It begins with a performance of *Rinaldo*, Handel's first opera for London, beautifully reconstructed with a feeling for period and performance style. There is a delightful scene when Handel goes to Italy in search of sopranos and is serenaded in a coach by two of them. Alan Devlin plays Handel's friend James Quin who narrates the film, Jean Rigby is Susannah Cibber, Christopher Benjamin is Heidegger, T. P. McKenna is Jonathan Swift, John Moffatt is Richard Steel and James Villiers is Richard Addison. Anne Skinner was producer, Peter MacDonald was the cinematographer and Peter Luke was co-scripter.

Nicholas Kraemer was musical director and the music is performed by the Raglan Baroque Players. Color. 70 minutes. Films for the Humanities video.

1985 Georg Frideric Handel (1685-1759)
Musical biography specialist Tony Palmer directed this documentary film to mark the 300th anniversary of the composer's birth in 1685. It was created for British television. Color. In English. 90 minutes.

1990 Handel's Resurrection
This is a German music film by Klaus Lindemann based on Stefan Zweig's novel *Händels Augerstehung*. The soloists are soprano Gundula Janowitz, mezzo Marga Hoeffgen and trumpeter Maurice André with Karl Richter conducting the Munich Bach Orchestra and Choir. The actors seen in the film are Heinrich Schweiger, Enrico Dondi and Mike Gwilym. Color. In German. 100 minutes.

1995 The Madness of King George
Handel's music is used as the soundtrack music for this superb English film and is performed by a baroque orchestra led by Nicholas Kraemer. Nicholas Hytner directed from a screenplay by Alan Bennett based on his own play. Color. 105 minutes.

1996 My Night With Handel
Arias and duets by Handel are performed in modern London settings during a 24-hour period as imagined by Jonathan Keates. Sarah Connolly sings "Scherza infida" while watching a couple in a London square, Alastair Miles sings a Zoroaster's aria in a psychiatrist's chair, Rosa Mannion and John Mark Ainsley join in a duet from *Il Moderato* as commuters hurry to work and Claron McFadden and Christopher Robson are lovers singing a duet from *Sosarme* in an Italian café. Harry Bicket leads the Orchestra of the Age of Enlightenment and Nicolas McGegan and David Field set the context. Alex Maregno directed the film for Channel 4 television in England. Color. 60 minutes.

HANSEL AND GRETEL
1893 opera by Humperdinck

Hansel and Gretel (*Hänsel und Gretel* in German) is the only opera by German composer Engelbert Humperdinck that has remained popular. As it is a major musical achievement as well as a children's favorite, it is likely to survive a few more centuries. It is usually performed in English in the U.S. and Great Britain. The original German libretto by Adelheid Wette is based on a Grimm Brothers story about two children who wander off one day and end up at the gingerbread cottage of a witch. She tries to bake them in an oven but ends up there herself and all the children she had captured before reappear magically. The best of the many videos is the 1982 Met production in English but there is also a fine 1981 version in German. The first telecast of a complete opera in the U.S. was a production of *Hansel and Gretel* in English in December 1942. See CARNEGIE HALL (1991), ENGELBERT HUMPERDINCK.

1942 WRGB telecast

This December 1942 studio production of *Hansel and Gretel* was the first telecast of a complete opera in the U.S. It originated from WRGB-TV, General Electric's pioneer station in Schenectady, New York. The opera was sung in English by students from a Hartford music school. Black and white. 80 minutes.

1950 NBC Opera Theatre

Metropolitan Opera soprano Claramae Turner sings the role of the Witch in this NBC Opera Theatre production. Virginia Haskins and David Lloyd are featured as Hansel and Gretel while Frances Lehnerts and Paul Ukena portray their parents. The opera was produced by Samuel Chotzinoff and directed by Charles Polacheck from an English translation by Townsend Brewster. Kirk Browning directed the telecast on Dec. 25, 1950. Black and white. In English. 60 minutes. Video at MTR.

1954 Anna Russell puppet film

Electronic puppets called Kimemins are the stars of this charming film of the opera in English. The voices of the puppets are Anna Russell as the Witch, Constance Brigham as both Hansel and Gretel, Mildred Dunnock as Mother, Frank Rogier as Father, Delbert Anderson as the Sandman, Helen Boatwright as the Dew Fairy and the Apollo Boys Choir as angels and children. The music was scored by Giuseppe Becce, the orchestra was conducted by Franz Allers, the sets were designed by Evalds Dajevskis and the puppets were created by James Summers. The film was produced by Michael Myerberg, adapted for the screen by Padraic Colum and directed by John Paul. Color. In English. 75 minutes. On video.

1970 Maureen Forrester on CBC

Canadian contralto Maureen Forrester stars as the Witch in this CBC-TV production of the opera by Norman Campbell. Judith Forst sings the role of Hansel, Christine Anton is Gretel and Bob Lawson designed the sets. The critics loved the special effects. NET and BBC co-produced the opera with the Canadian Broadcasting Corporation. Color. In English. 90 minutes.

1981 Brigitte Fassbaender/Edita Gruberova film

Brigitte Fassbaender and Edita Gruberova are outstanding as Hansel and Gretel in this Austrian film. Director August Everding filmed the opera in 35mm as if it were being performed for an audience of children at a small theater. Sena Jurinac sings the Witch, Helga Dernesch is Mother, Hermann Prey is Father, Norma Burrowes is the Sandman and Elfriede Hobarth is the Dew Fairy. Gerhard Janda designed the sets while Friedrich Hechelmann designed the costumes and paintings. Georg Solti conducted the Vienna Phiharmonic Orchestra and Boys Choir. Color. In German with English subtitles. 109 minutes. London video.

1982 Metropolitan Opera

Frederica von Stade and Judith Blegen are the stars of this Metropolitan Opera production in English which is as good as one can hope for. Von Stade and Blegen are superb as Hansel and Gretel, Rosalind Elias is a terrific witch, Robert O'Hearn's sets and costumes are a delight and Nathaniel Merrill's direction is just right. Jean Kraft and Michael Devlin are the parents, Betsy Norden is the Dew Fairy and Diane Kesling is the Sandman. Thomas Fulton conducted the Metropolitan Orchestra and Chorus and Kirk Browning directed the video on Dec. 25, 1982. Color. In English. 104 minutes. Paramount video/Pioneer laser.

1984 Maestro's Company puppets

The Australian Maestro's Company presents scenes from the opera with puppets and the singing voices of opera singers. The story involves children who discover the puppets rehearsing operas under an old theater. The *Hansel and Gretel* singing voices belong to Brigitte Fassbaender, Lucia Popp, Walter Berry, Anny Schlemm and Julia Hamari. The music is by the Vienna Philharmonic Orchestra conducted by Georg Solti. William Fitzwater directed the video. Color. Dialogue in English, arias in German. 30 minutes. VAI video.

Related films

1954 Lotte Reiniger animated film
Animation pioneer Lotte Reiniger made an abbreviated animated silhouette version of the opera in 1954. Color. 10 minutes.

1958 Risë Stevens on NBC
Risë Stevens stars as the Mother in this NBC-TV production and won wide praise for singing Humperdinck's "Lullaby." The rest of the composer's music, however, was not used as Alec Wilder wrote new songs. The cast includes Barbara Cook, Hans Conried, Rudy Vallee, Stubby Kaye and Red Buttons. Paul Bogart directed. Black and white. In English. 60 minutes.

1987 Cloris Leachman film
Cloris Leachman stars as the Witch in this Cannon film of the Hansel and Gretel story. It uses Humperdinck's music only as background score. David Warner is the Father, Emily Richard is the Mother, Hugh Pollard is Hansel and Nicola Stapleton is Gretel. Len Talen directed. Color. In English. 84 minutes. Cannon video.

HANSON, HOWARD
American composer (1896-1981)

Howard Hanson, who was born in the same tiny Nebraska town as Hollywood movie mogul Daryl Zanuck, wrote a good deal of music but only one opera. *Merry Mount* was first staged at the Metropolitan Opera in 1934 with Lawrence Tibbett in the leading role of Wrestling Bradford and Tullio Serafin as the conductor. It was a huge success with fifty curtain calls but is no longer in the repertory. The libretto by Richard L. Stokes is based on Nathaniel Hawthorne's story *The Maypole of Merry Mount* and is a tale of witchcraft and sexual obsession among the Puritans.

1957 Merry Mount
Howard Hanson, who was director of the Eastman School of Music when this film was made, explains how a composer conveys the ideas and emotions of the characters in an opera. Hanson uses his opera *Merry Mount* as a demonstration work. The film was made for the *Music as a Language* series. Black and white. In English. 29 minutes. On l6mm film.

HAPPY END
1929 stage musical by Weill & Brecht

Happy End is Kurt Weill and Bertolt Brecht's successor to their hit *The Threepenny Opera* though it has never had the same popularity. Some of its songs, however, are among their best known including "Surabaya Johnny" and "Bilbao Song." It tells the story of a Salvation Army woman named Lilian Holliday who reforms a gang of criminals in Chicago after falling for the charms of dance hall boss Bill Cracker. The libretto is by Elisabeth Hauptmann writing as Dorothy Lane. See also BERTOLT BRECHT, KURT WEILL.

1986 Arena Stage, Washington
Garland Wright staged this production of the Weill musical at the Arena Stage in Washington, DC The cast includes Judith Anna Roberts, Marilyn Caskey, Casey Biggs, Kevin McClaron, Richard Bauer, Joe Palmiere, Lisabeth Pritchett and Henry Strozier. Martha Schlamme hosted the program and Greg Harney directed the telecast on Jan 19, 1986. Color. 120 minutes.

HARBACH, OTTO
American librettist (1873-1963)

Otto Harbach, although not as influential as Oscar Hammerstein II, was one of the principal creators of the words for the major American operettas in their great period. He was both librettist and lyricist and worked most famously on operettas with Rudolf Friml (*The Firefly* and *Rose-Marie*), Sigmund Romberg (*The Desert Song*), George Gershwin (*Song of the Flame*), Emmerich Kálmán (*Golden Dawn*)) and Jerome Kern (*The Cat and the Fiddle*). His musicals include *No No Nanette* with Vincent Youmans and *Roberta* with Kern. See THE CAT AND THE FIDDLE, THE DESERT SONG, THE FIREFLY, GOLDEN DAWN, ROSE-MARIE, SONG OF THE FLAME.

HARNONCOURT, NIKOLAUS
Austrian conductor (1929-)

Nikolaus Harnoncourt, one of the leading exponents of the period instrument opera, formed the Vienna Concentus Musicus in 1953 to perform early music. In 1971 he conducted his first Monteverdi opera and subsequently made a number of films of Monteverdi and Mozart operas, usually in collaboration with director Jean-Pierre Ponnelle. See COSÌ FAN TUTTE (1988), IDOMENEO

(1988), L'INCORONAZIONE DI POPPEA (1979), MITRIDATE (1986), ORFEO (1978), IL RITORNO D'ULISSE IN PATRIA (1980).

HART, LORENZ
American lyricist (1895-1943)

The greatest song lyricist of the 20th century never collaborated on an opera but he did write English words for two operettas, Jean Gilbert's *The Lady in Ermine* and Franz Lehar's *The Merry Widow*. *Lady* was presented on the New York stage while the *Widow* lyrics were used in Ernst Lubitsch's film of the operetta with Jeanette MacDonald and Maurice Chevalier. Hart also wrote the lyrics of a wartime patriotic song for Metropolitan Opera tenor Jan Peerce. His lengthy collaboration with composer Richard Rodgers culminated in one of the greatest of all American musicals, *Pal Joey*. In the 1948 Rodgers and Hart film biography *Words and Music*, he is portrayed by Mickey Rooney. See DIE FRAU IM HERMELIN, JEANETTE MACDONALD (1932, 1942), THE MERRY WIDOW (1934), JAN PEERCE (1943), RICHARD RODGERS.

HÁRY JÁNOS
1926 opera by Kodály

This Hungarian opera by Zoltán Kodály celebrates the imagination and virtues of a bragging old veteran whose fantastic adventures reflect the qualities and folk music of his country. He tells how he rescued a French princess, won a battle against Napoleon and gained the love of the Emperor's wife. However, he preferred to return to his native village and his first love. The libretto by Bela Paulini and Zsolt Harsany is based on an epic comic poem by Janos Garay. The opera music is widely known through an orchestral suite. See also ZOLTÁN KODÁLY.

1965 Miklos Szinetar film
Miklos Szinetar directed this Hungarian film of the opera with actors on screen and opera singers dubbing their voices. Adam Szirtes (sung by Gyorgy Melis) stars as the veteran tall tale teller Háry János with Maria Medgyesi (sung by Maria Matyas) as his sweetheart Orzse. Teri Torday (sung by Judith Sandor) is the French princess Marie-Louise, Laszlo Markus (sung by Jozsef Refi) is Ebelastin, Gyula Bodrogi is Napoleon and Manyi Kiss (sung by Eva Gombos) is the Empress. The Budapest Philharmonic Orchestra is conducted by János Ferencsik. Mafilm. Color. In Hungarian. 109 minutes.

HAUNTED MANOR, THE
1865 opera by Moniuszko

Polish composer Stanislaw Moniuszko's opera *Straszny Dwór* is not as well known as *Halka*, possibly because it was banned after its premiere because of a too patriotic aria. It's a comic opera about two soldier brothers and the women they decide to wed after a night in the haunted house of the title. The libretto by Jan Checinski is based on a story by Kazimierz Wojcicki. It is available on CD in a 1978 Cracow production. See also STANISLAW MONIUSZKO.

1986 Marek Grzesinski film
Marek Grzesinski's film of the opera stars Isabella Klosinska as Hanna and Stanislaw Kowalski as Stefan, the soldier she loves. Elzbieta Panko plays Jadwiga who is loved by Zbigniew, played by Leonard Mroz. Andrzej Hiolski is their friend Miecznik who owns the haunted manor, Krzysztof Szmyt is Damazy and Krystyna Szostek-Radkowa is Czesnikowa. Irena Bieganska designed the sets and costumes and Robert Satanowski conducts the Warsaw Grand Theater Orchestra and Chorus. Color. In Polish. 134 minutes. On video.

HAYDN, FRANZ JOSEF
Austrian composer (1732-1809)

Franz Josef Haydn wrote many operas and some contemporaries ranked his dramatic works above Mozart's. They have been neglected until recently but are now beginning to be re-evaluated. Haydn himself considered his operas among his most important works. At least ten are available on CD but there are still none on video. However, his great dramatic oratorio *The Creation*, based on Milton's *Paradise Lost*, has been filmed twice. Haydn often appears as a character in films about Beethoven and Mozart. See LUDWIG VAN BEETHOVEN (1927 film), THE CREATION, WOLFGANG A. MOZART (1948 film).

1984 Haydn and Mozart
Haydn's life, times and musical career are explored and illustrated by André Previn on this video. It's Volume One in the series *The Story of the Symphony* written and directed by Herbert Chappell. There is also a performance of Haydn's Symphony No. 87

by Previn and the Royal Philharmonic Orchestra. Color. In English. 90 minutes. Home Vision video.

1990 Haydn at Esterháza
A film about the composer's life and work at Prince Esterhazy's Palace where he conducted hundreds of operas. There are explanatory comments from H.C. Robbins Landon, Christopher Hogwood and Melvyn Bragg. At the end of the narrative Hogwood leads the Academy of Ancient Music in performances of three Haydn symphonies. Chris Hunt directed. Color. In English. 100 minutes.

HEATHER, DAVE
English TV opera director

Dave Heather is one of the pioneers of directing television opera and there are many videos of his work available from as early as 1972. He directed most of the Glyndebourne Festival telecasts for Southern Television and most are on commercial video. In 1982 he directed Gilbert and Sullivan operas for George Walker. See THE ABDUCTION FROM THE SERAGLIO (1980), THE BARBER OF SEVILLE (1982), COSÌ FAN TUTTE (1975), DON GIOVANNI (1977), FALSTAFF (1976), FIDELIO (1979), THE GONDOLIERS (1982), IDOMENEO (1974), IOLANTHE (1982), MACBETH (1972), THE MAGIC FLUTE (1978), A MIDSUMMER NIGHT'S DREAM (1981), PATIENCE (1982), PRINCESS IDA (1982), THE RAKE'S PROGRESS (1977), IL RITORNO D'ULISSE IN PATRIA (1973), THE SORCERER (1982), KIRI TE KANAWA (1978), THE YEOMAN OF THE GUARD (1982).

HENDRICKS, BARBARA
American soprano (1948-)

Barbara Hendricks was born in Arkansas, studied science at the University of Nebraska and didn't consider music as a career until she was twenty. In 1969 she went to Juilliard to study with Jennie Tourel and her musical life began. She made her debut in San Francisco in 1974 in Cavalli's *Ormindo* and soon began to sing in opera houses around the world. In 1982 she made her debut in Paris as Gounod's Juliette. She did not reach the Metropolitan Opera until 1986 when she sang Sophie in *Der Rosenkavalier*. Luigi Comencini chose her to play Mimi in his film of *La Bohème* and Márta Mészaros made a film about her performing on stage in *Don Pasquale*. See LA BOHÈME (1988), DON PASQUALE (1991), PLACIDO DOMINGO (1989/1991),

FALSTAFF (1982), PARIS (1989), ROMÉO ET JULIETTE (1982), THE TALES OF HOFFMANN (1993).

1988 Fauré/Poulenc Concert
Barbara Hendricks is featured in a live concert at the Saint Denis Basilica in France. The program consists of Fauré's *Requiem* and Poulenc's *Gloria*. Hendricks is partnered by baritone Carl-John Falkam while Jean-Claude Casadesus conducts the Lille National Orchestra. Mate Rabinovsky directed the video for French television. Color. 70 minutes. Kultur video.

1990 Barbara Hendricks
Jean-Luc Leon directed this French documentary about the soprano. She is shown on the set of Comencini's film of *La Bohème*, at the Met with Brigitte Fassbaender for *Der Rosenkavalier*, at La Scala for *The Marriage of Figaro* with conductor Riccardo Muti and in Berlin for *Rigoletto* with conductor Silvio Varsivo. She is also shown at home studying a role and working for the United Nations. Made for France's La Sept. Color. 47 minutes. On video.

HENRY VIII
1883 opera by Saint-Saens

Camille Saint-Saens French opera Henry VIII about the English king was popular in the late 19th century but has never really entered the international repertory like his *Samson et Dalila*. The libretto by Léonce Détroyat and Armand Silvestre tells of Henry's split with the Catholic Church when he divorces Catherine of Aragon in order to marry Anne Boleyn, formerly the lover of the Spanish ambassador Don Gomez. See also CAMILLE SAINT-SAENS.

1991 Théâtre Impérial, Compiègne
Philippe Rouillon stars as Henry VIII in this famous production of the opera at the Théâtre Impérial in Compiègne north of Paris. Michèle Command portrays Catherine of Aragon, Lucile Vignon is Anne Boleyn and Alain Gabriel is Don Gomez de Feria. Alain Guingal conducts the French Lyric Orchestra and Rouen Theatre Chorus. The restored 19th century theater reopened in September 1991 with this production which is on CD with the same cast. Color. In French. 180 minutes. Lyric video.

HENZE, HANS WERNER
German composer (1926-)

Hans Werner Henze, one of the leading modern German composers, had had a strong interest in stage works. His first full-length opera was the 1952 *Boulevard Solitude*, a variation on the *Manon Lescaut* story. His best-known operas are *Elegy for Young Lovers, Der Junge Lord* and *The Bassarids*. His American TV opera *Rachel la Cubana* was well received but its production cost overruns led to the demise of original opera on NET. Henze had a strong influence on Mark-Anthony Turnage's career and commissioned his opera *Greek*. See DER JUNGE LORD, RACHEL LA CUBANA, IL RITORNO D'ULISSE IN PATRIA (1985), MARK-ANTHONY TURNAGE.

1990 El Cimarrón
El Cimarrón is a musical theater piece for four musicians composed by Henze in 1970. The libretto by Hans Magnus Enzensberger is based on Miguel Barnet's *Biography of the Runaway Slave Estaban Montejo* and consists of 15 episodes from the book. It was videotaped in performance for German television in 1990 with baritone/narrator William Pearson, flutist Karlheinz Zöller, guitarist Wilhelm Bruck and percussionist Stomu Ymash'ta. Color. In German. 79 minutes.

HERBERT, VICTOR
Irish-born U.S. composer (1859-1924)

Victor Herbert is the most important of the American Viennese-style operetta composers. He composed over thirty of them and dominated the Broadway scene at the turn of the century. His major operettas can be as vocally demanding as operas for they were often written for opera sopranos like Alice Nielsen, Fritzi Scheff and Emma Trentina. Herbert was born in Dublin and brought up in Germany, coming to the U.S. as a cellist when his wife was engaged to sing at the Metropolitan Opera. He composed his first operetta in 1894 and is probably best known for *Naughty Marietta, Babes in Toyland* and *The Red Mill*. Seven of his operettas have been filmed and there is a Hollywood film about his musical career. *Rosalie*, which he co-composed with George Gershwin, was also filmed but without the Herbert-Gershwin music. Herbert also wrote two operas, *Natoma* and *Madeleine*, which are more or less forgotten today. See also BABES IN TOYLAND, THE FORTUNE TELLER, MLLE. MODISTE, NAUGHTY MARIETTA, THE RED MILL, SWEETHEARTS.

1915 Old Dutch
Victor Herbert's 1909 operetta *Old Dutch* was written for comedian Lew Fields and tells the story of an inventor who develops a video-phone far ahead of its time. The Shubert Film company turned it into a silent film in 1915 with Fields reprising his stage role. Frank Crane directed. Black and white. About 75 minutes.

1939 The Great Victor Herbert
Walter Connolly portrays Herbert in this romantic film which masquerades as a biography but is really the story of a couple who sing his music. Mary Martin and Allan Jones star in Herbert's operettas until Jones' career starts to decline and hers starts to rise. In the end their daughter Susanna Foster becomes a star in a revival of *The Fortune Teller* singing "Kiss Me Again" with a remarkable B above high C. The film features performances of many Herbert songs from "Ah, Sweet Mystery of Life" to the "March of the Toys." Andrew L. Stone directed for Paramount. Black and white. 84 minutes. On video.

1946 Till the Clouds Roll By
Paul Maxey portrays Victor Herbert who appears as a minor character in this all-star film biography of Jerome Kern. Richard Whorf directed. MGM. Color. 137 minutes. On video.

1973 The Music of Victor Herbert
This is a Canadian television tribute to Victor Herbert featuring performances of his songs by various singers. They include Mary Costa, Anna Shuttleworth, Judith Forst and Robert Jeffrey with Richard Bonynge accompanying on piano. Color. In English. 60 minutes. Opera Dubs video.

HÉRODIADE
1890 opera by Massenet

Jules Massenet's French opera is a rather different version of the Biblical Salome story as filtered through a story by Flaubert and librettist Paul Milliet. Salome, who is a much nicer person than in the Strauss opera, fancies John the Baptist (here called Jean) while Herod desires Salome. She refuses Herod's attentions but wins Jean's love. Both end up in jail waiting to be beheaded. Neither Herod nor wife Hérodiade know that Salome is her daughter. See also JULES MASSENET.

1994 San Francisco Opera

Placido Domingo stars as Jean opposite Renée Fleming as Salome in this San Francisco Opera production by Lotfi Mansouri. Dolora Zanick portrays Hérodiade, Juan Pons is Hérode and Kenneth Cox is Phanuel. Gerard Howland designed the sets and Valery Gergiev conducted the San Francisco Opera Orchestra. Color. In French. 175 minutes. Sony Classics video.

HERRMANN, BERNARD
American composer (1911-1975)

Bernard Herrmann, one of the great movie composers, also wrote operas. His *Wuthering Heights* is on CD and two of his short operas have been presented on television. Herrmann was brought to Hollywood by Orson Welles and later worked with Alfred Hitchcock and Martin Scorsese. His film scores include Welles' *Citizen Kane* for which he wrote part of an imaginary opera called *Salambó*, Hitchcock's *Psycho* whose music has become a cinema icon and Scorsese's influential *Taxi Driver*. In his Hitchcock scores, he paid homage to Wagner: the music for the love scene on the train in *Rear Window* is a variation of the love theme from *Tristan und Isolde* while *Vertigo* contains a variation of the Magic Fire music from *Die Walküre* as well as echoes of *Tristan und Isolde*. See also ALFRED HITCHCOCK, CITIZEN KANE.

1954 A Christmas Carol

Herrmann composed this enjoyable lightweight "television opera," really a musical, as a CBS Christmas special and also conducted the 40-piece orchestra and Roger Wagner Chorale. Maxwell Anderson wrote the libretto based on the Dickens story and the lyrics for the songs/arias. Fredric March is Scrooge, Basil Rathbone is Marley, Rob Sweeney as Crachit and Ray Middleton as Scrooge's nephew. It was produced and directed on film by Ralph Levy and telecast on Dec. 23, 1954. Black and white. In English. 60 minutes.

1955 A Child is Born

Herrmann's first Christmas television opera for CBS was a success so they commissioned a second. This one is based on a short story by Stephen Vincent Benet and was telecast on Dec. 25, 1955. Black and white. In English. 60 minutes.

HÉROLD, FERDINAND
French composer (1791-1833)

Ferdinand Hérold was one of the most popular composers of the 19th century and his 1831 opera *Zampa* was almost constantly on stage. He was a mainstay of the Paris Opéra-Comique in the early 19th century and his other major opera, *Le Pré aux Clercs* (1832), was almost as much of a hit as *Zampa*. His operas are not currently fashionable, though the *Zampa* overture is still popular at open-air band concerts. *Le Pré aux Clercs* and *Le Muletier* are available on French CDs and his ballet *La Fille Mal Gardée* is on video. See ZAMPA.

HERVÉ
French composer (1825-1892)

Hervé (real name Louis August Joseph Florimond Ronger) is the father of French operetta, the precursor of Offenbach and a major composer in his own right. He began creating operettas in 1842 but his most important light opera and the only one on film is the 1883 *Mam'zelle Nitouche*. It's the autobiographical story of a convent organist who writes operettas and a convent girl who wants to go on stage. Like the protagonist, Hervé led a double life in his early years working simultaneously as a church organist and an operetta composer. His other popular operettas include *Chilpéric* (1868) and *Le Petit Faust* (1869). See MAM'ZELLE NITOUCHE.

HERZOG, WERNER
German film director (1942-)

Werner Herzog, one of the best modern directors and creator of one of the great opera films, has also become a major director of opera on stage and this work can be seen on video. His film *Fitzcarraldo* revolves around an obsession with Caruso, examines the meaning of opera and features a good deal of operatic music. Herzog features music from *Das Rheingold* in his vampire film *Nosferatu* and music by Wagner in his aboriginal film *Where the Green Ants Dream*. His *Woyzeck* makes an interesting contrast with the Berg opera. After directing Wagner operas on stage, he made a documentary about the world of Richard Wagner operas. See BAYREUTH (1994), FITZCARRALDO, LA DONNA DEL LAGO (1992), GIOVANNA D'ARCO (1989), IL GUARANY (1994), LOHENGRIN (1990), DAS RHEINGOLD (1979 film), WOYZECK (1979 film).

HESS, JOACHIM

German opera film director

Joachim Hess directed a number of opera films in collaboration with producer Rolf Liebermann when Liebermann was in charge of the Hamburg State Opera. An impressive group of them were screened in New York in 1970 at an opera film festival. See THE DEVILS OF LOUDUN (1969), FIDELIO (1969), DER FREISCHÜTZ (1968), THE MAGIC FLUTE (1971), THE MARRIAGE OF FIGARO (1967), ORPHÉE AUX ENFERS (1968), WOZZECK (1967), ZAR UND ZIMMERMANN (1968).

HESTON, CHARLTON

American actor (1924-)

Charlton Heston, one of the monuments of the American cinema, is best-known for epic roles like Moses and Ben Hur. He is also quite good at commenting on opera. He is featured on a series of laser discs called *Opera Stories* in which he introduces highlights from major operas and describes the stories behind them from their supposed actual locations. The discs include about fifty minutes of scenes from productions at Covent Garden, La Scala and Verona. The framing material with Heston was shot by Keith Cheetham in 1989 and was written by Gerald Sinstadt. See AIDA (1981), ANDREA CHÉNIER (1985), ANTONY AND CLEOPATRA (1972 film), LA BOHÈME (1982), ERNANI (1982), FALSTAFF (1983), DIE FLEDERMAUS (1983), MANON LESCAUT (1983), JESSYE NORMAN (1991), OTELLO (1982), TOSCA (1984), IL TROVATORE (1985).

HEUBERGER, RICHARD

Austrian composer (1850-1914)

Richard Heuberger was an Austrian music critic and teacher who composed four operas and a number of operettas. He is remembered today for the 1898 operetta *Der Opernball* (The Opera Ball) which has similarities to *Die Fledermaus* and continues to be staged in Vienna. It has been filmed three times. Heuberger was the first person to compose music for *The Merry Widow* libretto but his attempt was rejected by the producers and Lehár took over. See DER OPERNBALL.

HEURE ESPAGNOLE, L'

1911 opera by Ravel

Maurice Ravel composed this clockwatcher's delight to a risqué vaudeville by Franc-Nohain set in Toledo. *The Spanish Hour* is the time every Thursday when the clockmaker Torquemada leaves his wife alone and goes off to wind the town clocks. The wife plans to meet her lover during this hour but it gets complicated when there are too many suitors. The first two end up stuck in grandfather clocks while she dallies with the mule driver Ramiro. See also MAURICE RAVEL.

1985 French television video

This production of *L'Heure Espagnole* was created for French television by François Porcile who used a number of video techniques to create its illusions. Armin Jordan conducts the orchestra. INA. Color. In French. 52 minutes.

1987 Glyndebourne Festival

Maurice Sendak designed the sets and costumes for this colorful Glyndebourne Festival production by Frank Corsaro. Anna Steiger stars as the amorous wife Concepcion, François Le Roux is the new man in her life Ramiro, Rémy Corazza is the clockmaker Torquemada, Thierry Dran is Galzalve and François Loup is Don Ingo Gomez. Ronald Chase designed the slides and animated films and Sian Edwards conducted the London Philharmonic Orchestra and Glyndebourne Festival Chorus. Color. In French with English subtitles. 50 minutes. Home Vision video/laser.

HIGGLETY PIGGLETY POP!

1985 opera by Knussen & Sendak

American artist and author Maurice Sendak, whose colorful children's books are both controversial and delightful, was inspired to create this fairy tale by his Sealyham terrier Jennie. The pampered dog sets out to explore the world and meets lions, pigs, cats and babies. She eventually becomes the star of a Mother Goose theater. English composer Oliver Knussen set the witty story to impressionistic music. The opera premiered at Glyndebourne in 1985 and a definitive version was staged in Los Angeles in 1990. See also OLIVER KNUSSEN, MAURICE SENDAK.

1985 Glyndebourne Festival

Cynthia Buchan stars as the dog Jennie in search of "something more than everything" in this bright and cheerful Glyndebourne production. It was staged and choreographed by Frank Corsaro with wondrous costumes and set designs by Sendak. The splendid cast includes Andrew Gallacher, Rosemary Hardy, Neil Jenkins, Deborah Rees and Stephen Richardson. Knussen conducted the London Sinfonietta and Christopher Swann directed the video. Color. In English. 60 minutes. Home Vision video and laser.

HINDEMITH, PAUL

German composer (1895-1963)

Paul Hindemith, one of the most influential composers of the century, came to the U.S. after his work was banned by the Nazis for being degenerate. He created a number of operas of which the best known are *Cardillac, Mathis der Maler* and *The Long Christmas Dinner*. Little of his work is presently available on video. See also CARDILLAC.

1964 The Genius of Paul Hindemith

Leonard Bernstein pays tribute to Hindemith on a 1964 CBS Television Young People's Concert soon after the composer's death. He talks about the importance of his compositions and leads the orchestra in excerpts including a section of *Mathis der Maler*. Roger Englander directed the telecast on Feb. 23, 1964. Black and white. 60 minutes. Video at MTR.

HINES, JEROME

American bass and composer (1921-)

Jerome Hines is a six-foot six-inch basso who sang for forty consecutive years with the Metropolitan Opera. He was noted for his portrayals of Boris Godunov and Philip II. He also composed a religious opera called *I Am the Way* in which he portrayed Christus and an excerpt is available on a *Voice of Firestone* video. Hines was born in Hollywood and made his debut in San Francisco in 1941 as Nerone. He joined the Met in 1946 and sang most of the great bass roles with the company. He sang also in Europe including La Scala, Bayreuth and the Bolshoi. In 1989 he returned to sing in New Orleans 45 years after his first appearance there. See DON CARLO (1950), FAUST (1963).

1951-1963 Jerome Hines in Opera & Song

A highlights video featuring Jerome Hines in performance on six *Voice of Firestone* television programs broadcast over twelve years. He sings arias from *Faust, The Magic Flute, Porgy and Bess* and Thomas's *Le Caïd* plus songs by Tosti, Speaks and Rodgers. His portrayal of *Boris Godunov* is featured in an eleven-minute excerpt in the program of Nov. 18, 1962. His sacred opera *I Am the Way* is featured in a ten-minute excerpt in the program of March 31, 1963, with Hines as Christus, Mildred Miller as Mother Mary, William Walker as St. Peter and David Starkey as St. John. Black and white. 58 minutes. VAI video.

HITCHCOCK, ALFRED

English film director (1899-1980)

Music is an essential element in Alfred Hitchcock's films and eight of his main characters are musicians though opera and operetta are rarely central. His 1934 musical *Waltzes From Vienna* is the exception as it is one of the many films about the Strauss father/son rivalry. In *Shadow of a Doubt* the villainous uncle (Joseph Cotten) is associated with Lehar's *Merry Widow* waltz and is known as the Merry Widow murderer. Hitchcock's musical collaborator Bernard Herrmann liked to pay homage to Wagner in his scores. The music for the love scene on the train in *Rear Window* is a tongue-in-cheek variation of the love theme from *Tristan und Isolde* and the score for *Vertigo* contains a variation on the Magic Fire music from *Die Walküre*. See THE MERRY WIDOW (1943 film), JOHANN STRAUSS (1934).

H.M.S. PINAFORE

1878 comic opera by Gilbert & Sullivan

H.M.S. Pinafore or The Lass That Loved a Sailor is one of the most filmed of the Savoy operas and was a hit from its first appearance. The target of Gilbert's satire is the British Navy and class distinctions. First Lord of the Admiralty Sir Joseph Porter, who tells us he started as an office boy, asks for the hand of Captain Corcoran's daughter Josephine. She, however, loves the common sailor Ralph Rackstraw. Their relationship is impossible until Little Buttercup reveals that she mixed up two babies many years ago and so Ralph is really the Captain and vice versa. See also GILBERT AND SULLIVAN.

1960 Stratford Festival

Tyrone Guthrie's film of the operetta is based on a Stratford Festival production by Norman Campbell. It stars Eric House as Sir Joseph Porter, Marion Studholme as Josephine, Howard Mosson as Dick Deadeye, Andrew Downie as Ralph Rackstraw, Harry Mossfield as Captain Corcoran, Irene Byatt as Buttercup and Douglas Campbell. Louis Applebaum conducted the CBC Orchestra. This Canadian production was telecast on NBC and released as a film. Black and white. In English. 90 minutes.

1973 D'Oyly Carte Opera Company

John Reed stars as Sir Joseph Porter in this version of the operetta created for television by the London D'Oyly Carte Opera Company. Pamela Field portrays Josephine, Malcolm Williams is Ralph Rackstraw, Lyndsie Holland is Little Buttercup, John Ayldon is Dick Deadeye and Michael Rayner is Captain Corcoran. Roystan Nash was the music director, Michael Heyland was the stage director and John Sichel produced and directed for television. Color. In English. 78 minutes. Magnetic/ITC (England) video.

1974 World of Gilbert & Sullivan film

John Cartier stars as Sir Joseph Porter in this highlights version of the operetta produced by John Seabourne for the *World of Gilbert and Sullivan* series. Valerie Masterson is Josephine, Thomas Round is Ralph Rackstraw, Helen Landis is Little Buttercup, Michael Wakeham is Captain Corcoran and Donald Adams is Dick Deadeye. The music is played by the Gilbert and Sullivan Festival Orchestra and Chorus. Trevor Evans directed the film. Color. In English. 50 minutes.

1982 George Walker film

Frankie Howerd is a delight as Sir Joseph Porter in this outstanding film produced by Judith De Paul for George Walker. Peter Marshall is Captain Corcoran, Meryl Drower is Josephine, Michael Bulman is Ralph Rackstraw, Della Jones is Little Buttercup and Alan Watts is Dick Deadeye. Alexander Faris conducts the London Symphony Orchestra and the Ambrosian Opera Chorus. Michael Geliot staged the production and Rodney Greenberg directed the film. Color. In English. 90 minutes. CBS Fox/ Braveworld (England) video.

Early films

1906 Iago Lewis sound film

An early British sound film with Iago Lewis singing "I am the Captain of the Pinafore." Arthur Gilbert directed it for Gaumont using the Chronophone sound system. About three minutes.

1944 Provincetown Players

Irwin Shayne and Tony Ferreira produced the operetta for an historic live telecast with the Light Opera Theatre of the Provincetown Players. Critics weren't overwhelmed but thought it was better than other TV musicals. The cast includes Ione Di Caron, Joseph De Stefano, James Gales, Robert Feytl, Josephine Lombardo and Charles Kingsley. The music is performed by the Light Opera Theatre Orchestra. Black and white. In English. 50 minutes.

1956 Paul Ashley puppet film

Barry Shear produced this adventurous puppet film version of the operetta with Paul Ashley puppets made to look like the Pinafore characters. They include Sir Joseph Porter, Josephine, Ralph Rackstraw, and Dick Deadeye. The voices are provided by D'Oyly Carte Company performers headed by Martyn Green. Black and white. In English. 90 minutes.

HOCHZEIT IN HOLLYWOOD
1928 operetta by Straus

Oscar Straus's operetta *Hochzeit in Hollywood* (Married in Hollywood) premiered in Vienna on Dec. 21, 1928, and then crossed the Atlantic with surprising speed. It became the first European operetta to be made into a sound film in Hollywood and was premiered in New York on Sept. 23, 1929. The libretto is by Leopold Jacobson and Bruno Hardt-Warden. The story revolves around a Ruritanian prince who falls in love with an American singer. He has to give her up for reasons of state but is reunited with her in Hollywood when she becomes a movie star. See also OSCAR STRAUS.

1929 Married in Hollywood

Fox produced the first European operetta in the Hollywood sound era with this adaptation of the Straus work. J. Harold Murray stars as Prince Nicholai with Norma Terris as his beloved Mary Lou Hopkins. After his family forces them to break up, she becomes a movie star. When he is forced to flee to America after a revolution, he gets a job playing a prince in one of her films. *The New York Times* loved the movie and its songs. Marcel Silver directed. Black and white and color. In English. 106 minutes.

HOCKNEY, DAVID
English painter (1937-)

David Hockney has become one of the best known painters in the world in recent years and has made important contributions to opera set design. His seemingly simple but extraordinarily effective use of color and design have enlivened many productions. He began in 1975 with a remarkable design for *The Rake's Progress* at Glyndebourne and an equally impressive *Magic Flute*. He has now designed ten operas including *Tristan und Isolde* for the Los Angeles Opera and *Turandot* for San Francisco. His work looks nearly as impressive on video as it does on stage. See THE MAGIC FLUTE (1978), THE RAKE'S PROGRESS (1977), TURANDOT (1993).

HODDINOTT, ALUN
Welsh composer (1929-)

Composer Alun Hoddinott, who founded the Cardiff Music Festival in 1967, began composing operas in 1974. He turned to screen opera in 1976 when he created *Murder the Magician* for Harlech Television. Myfanwy Piper, who wrote librettos for Benjamin Britten operas, also wrote librettos for Hoddinott. Her *What the Old Man Does is Always Right* is Hoddinott's most successful opera, possibly because of its many parts for children. *The Rajah's Diamond (1979)* was also composed for the small screen.

1976 Murder the Magician
Hoddinott's first television opera, *Murder the Magician*, has a libretto by J. Morgan. It was given its world premiere on Harlech Television in Wales on Feb. 11, 1976. Color. In English.

1979 The Rajah's Diamond
The Rajah's Diamond, Hoddinott's second TV opera and his second to a libretto by Myfanwy Piper, is based on a story by Robert Louis Stevenson. It was telecast on BBC Television on Nov. 24, 1979. Color. In English.

HOFMANNSTHAL, HUGO VON
Austrian poet and librettist (1874-1929)

Hugo von Hofmannsthal is considered the greatest modern opera librettist and his 23-year collaboration with Richard Strauss is said to have helped restore the word to equality with the music. Ironically Strauss composed an opera on the relative importance of word and music, *Capriccio*, many years after his collaborator's death. Hofmannsthal's collaboration with Strauss began when the composer asked to use his adaptation of Sophocles' *Electra* as a the basis of an opera. Their *Elektra* was a success as were most of their other operas with *Der Rosenkavalier* as the greatest achievement. See also ARABELLA, ARIADNE AUF NAXOS, ELEKTRA, DIE FRAU OHNE SCHATTEN, DER ROSENKAVALIER, RICHARD STRAUSS.

HOIBY, LEE
American composer (1926-)

Lee Hoiby is one of the most successful modern American opera composers. He won instant acclaim with his first opera, the Chekhovian *The Scarf*, presented at Spoleto in 1958 and then at the New York City Opera. His 1959 *Beatrice* was written for television but was later performed on stage. His other major successes include *A Month in the Country* based on the Turgenev novel, *Summer and Smoke*, based on the Tennessee Williams play, and *The Tempest* based on Shakespeare. Hoiby's operas are melodic and tonal and have a kinship with operas by his contemporaries Gian Carlo Menotti and Samuel Barber. See BEATRICE, SUMMER AND SMOKE.

HOLLINGSWORTH, STANLEY
American composer (1924 -)

Stanley Hollingsworth studied with Milhaud and Menotti. His first opera *The Mother*, based on a Hans Christian Andersen fairy tale, premiered in Philadelphia in 1954. In 1957 NBC Opera Theatre commissioned him to create the TV opera, *La Grande Bretèche*, based on a story by Balzac. He has also had success with his children's operas *The Selfish Giant* and *Harrison Loved his Umbrella*, both produced at Spoleto Festival USA in 1981. See LA GRANDE BRETÈCHE.

HOLLYWOOD BOWL

The Hollywood Bowl, one of the largest and most atmospheric outdoor opera venues in the world with 17,6019 seats, has a small place in screen opera history. The first opera presented there was William Parker's *Fairyland*. Regular seasons began in 1922 with Marguerite Sylva in *Carmen*. The Bowl has also been the site of the debut of a number of opera singers including Lawrence Tibbett in *Aida* in 1923, Felix Knight in *La Traviata* in 1935 and George London in *La Traviata* in 1941. The cinematic opera *Voices of Light* had its Los Angeles premiere there in 1984. Opera at the Bowl is featured in Hollywood movies but there is no film of an actual opera performance there. See ZUBIN MEHTA (1967), VOICES OF LIGHT.

1936 Moonlight Murder
Hollywood Bowl itself got the star reviews when this low-budget murder mystery opened ("the best part of the film is the setting," said *Variety*). A tenor is killed at the Hollywood Bowl during a performance of *Il Trovatore* and detective Chester Morris has to find the person whodunit. A mad composer is suspected but it turns out that poison gas was used in a misguided mercy killing. Leo Carrillo plays the tenor but the lengthy selections from the opera are actually sung by voice double Alfonso Pedroza. The onstage opera sequences were arranged by Wilhelm von Wymetal. Florence Ryerson and Edgar Allan Woolf wrote the screenplay, Charles Clarke was cinematographer and Edward R. Marin directed for MGM. Black and white. 80 minutes.

1937 Music For Madame
Italian tenor Nino Martini wins fame singing at the Hollywood Bowl at the climax of this enjoyable musical. He plays a naive immigrant hired to sing the *Pagliacci* aria "Vesti la giubba" in clown costume at a Hollywood wedding. His singing is actually a diversion for a robbery and if he sings again a famous conductor will recognize his voice and send him to jail. Instead the conductor (Alan Mowbray in a caricature of Leopold Stokowski) thinks he is so good that he hires him to sing at the Hollywood Bowl. Gertrude Purcell and Robert Harari wrote the screenplay, Joseph August was cinematographer and John Blystone directed for RKO. Black and white. 77 minutes. Lyric video.

HONEGGER, ARTHUR
French composer (1892-1955)

Arthur Honegger wrote seven dramatic works that can be loosely called operas and around 40 film scores including famous ones for Abel Gance. He was very interested in the new mediums of film and radio. Honegger's best known operatic works are *Antigone* (1927), *Jeanne d'Arc au Bûcher* (1938) and *L'Aiglon* (1937). The only one filmed was his Joan of Arc story which he described as a "dramatic oratorio." Honegger's scores for silent films include *Napoleon* and *Les Miserables*. His score for the Abel Gance film about a locomotive, *La Roue*, was later adapted into the concert piece *Pacific 231*. In 1949 Jean Mitry made a film about the music which was also titled *Pacific 231*. See JEANNE D'ARC AU BÛCHER.

HOPKINS, ANTONY
English composer (1921-)

Antony Hopkins has had nine of his operas staged. He is best known for the 1948 *Lady Rohesia* which some critics have compared in eccentricity to the American film *Hellzapoppin*. Hopkins was also a radio broadcaster and wrote an opera for radio called *Scena*. His comic opera *Hands Across the Sky* was premiered by the Intimate Opera Company at Cheltenham Town Hall in July, 1959.

1960 Hands Across The Sky
Hopkin's 1959 comic opera, composed to a libretto by G. Snell, was presented on BBC Television a year after its stage premiere. The TV production stars Eric Shilling, Julia Shelley and Stephen Manton and was directed by Charles Lefeaux. It was telecast on July 2, 1960. Black and white. 45 minutes. A film of the telecast is at the National Film Archive in London.

HORNE, MARILYN
American mezzo-soprano (1934-)

Mezzo-soprano Marilyn Horne studied singing in Los Angeles with Lotte Lehmann. She made her screen debut at the beginning of her career dubbing Dorothy Dandridge's voice in the 1954 film *Carmen Jones*. She made her stage debut the same year singing Hata in *The Bartered Bride* in Los Angeles. After she went to Europe, her career blossomed in association with Joan Sutherland. Her performances in Rossini operas have been particularly notable. She has also made TV appearances. On *The Odd*

Couple sitcom series she portrayed a Carmen who wouldn't sing unless Jack Klugman was her Don José. See MONTSERRAT CABALLÉ (1990), CARMEN (1954), CARNEGIE HALL (1991), DIVAS (1990/1993), DIE FLEDERMAUS (1990), ERMIONE (1987), FALSTAFF (1993), THE GHOSTS OF VERSAILLES (1992), L'ITALIANA IN ALGERI (1986), METROPOLITAN OPERA (1983), ORLANDO FURIOSO (1990), GIOACHINO ROSSINI (1992), SEMIRAMIDE (1986/1990).

1981 Sutherland Horne Pavarotti Concert
Marilyn Horne, Luciano Pavarotti and Joan Sutherland compete for honors in *a Live from Lincoln Center* concert telecast on March 23, 1981. Each sings an aria and joins the others in duets and trios. Horne's aria is "Mura felici" from *La Donna del Lago*, Pavarotti's is "Che gelida manina" and Sutherland's is "Tu del mio Carlo" from Verdi's I *Masnadieri*. Pavarotti sings a duet from *La Gioconda* with Horne and a duet from *Otello* with Sutherland. All three join in music from *Norma, Beatrice Di Tenda* and *Il Trovatore*. Richard Bonynge conducts the New York City Opera Orchestra. The concert has also been released as a recording. Color. 150 minutes.

1983 Marilyn Horne's American Songbook
Horne sings from the stage of Avery Fisher Hall in celebration of her 50th birthday and the 30th anniversary of her opera debut. The program includes songs by Stephen Foster, Jerome Kern and Aaron Copland plus spirituals and folk songs. Leonard Slatkin leads the American Symphony Orchestra in this Live from Lincoln Center telecast on Dec. 28, 1983, Color. 60 minutes.

1985 A Gala Concert
Horne and Joan Sutherland get together for a bel canto evening at the Sydney Opera House in 1985 singing some of their finest collaborations. The program includes arias and duets ranging from Handel, Bellini and Rossini to Auber and Meyerbeer. The operas are *Norma, Lakmé, The Tales of Hoffmann, Don Pasquale, Samson et Dalila, Fra Diavolo, Semele, Alcina, La Donna del Lago, La Cambiale di Matrimonio, Semiramide* and *Les Huguenots*. Richard Bonynge conducts. Color. 142 minutes. Kultur video.

1994 Marilyn Horne at 60
A portrait of the singer filmed to celebrate her 60th birthday. She and her husband talk about her career and her ideas about singing and she is seen in performance in operas by Rossini, Vivaldi and others. There are also excerpts from her birthday gala at Carnegie Hall and assessments of her work by colleagues. Nigel Wattis directed the film for London Weekend Television and Bravo with Melvyn Bragg as presenter. Color. 60 minutes.

HORSE OPERA
1994 TV opera by Copeland

Horse Opera is a television opera by Stewart Copeland of the rock group The Police. Jonathan Moore's libretto, based on Anne Caulfield's play *Cowboys*, tells the story of a clerk (Philip Guy-Bromley) who likes to pretend to be a cowboy. After a blow on the head he thinks he wakes up in the Old West and meets Wyatt Earp, Jesse James and Billy the Kid. Bob Baldwin directed the opera telecast on Feb. 13, 1994, on Channel Four in England. Color. In English.

HOTTER, HANS
Austrian bass-baritone (1909-)

Hans Hotter was an authentic Wagnerian in all aspects of style, power and grandeur. He began singing Wagner in the 1930s, quickly became the world's leading Wagnerian bass-baritone and remained so until his retirement from major roles in 1972. He also directed the *Ring Cycle* at Covent Garden. Hotter made a number of films in Germany and Austria between 1939 and 1950, mostly sentimental stories or musicals, but also a version of *Pagliacci* in which he sang the Prologue. See also THE BARBER OF SEVILLE (1959), PAGLIACCI (1943), TRISTAN UND ISOLDE (1967).

1939 Mutterliebe
Hans Hotter plays a country boy in *Mother Love*, a family-style Austrian film directed by Gustav Ucicky. Käthe Dorsch and Paul Hörbiger are his co-stars. Black and white. In German. 102 minutes.

1942 Bruderlein Fein
Hotter's second film is an Austrian biography of the Viennese poet Ferdinand Raimund. Marte Harell, Hans Holt and Winnie Markus are also featured. Hans Thimig directed. Black and white. In German. 100 minutes.

1943 Seine Beste Rolle
Hotter is the star of *His Best Role*, a Czech-German musical shot in Prague in the worst days of World

War II. The cast includes Marina von Ditmar, Paul Dahlke and Camilla Horn. Otto Pittermann directed. Black and white. In German. 90 minutes.

1950 Grosstadtnacht
Night in the Big City is an Austrian musical featuring opera arias sung by Hans Hotter. Hans Wolff directed. Black and white. In German. 82 minutes.

1950 Sehnsucht des Herzens
Yearnings of the Heart is a German film about a singer who falls in love with a married woman. Hotter stars opposite Linda Caroll and Rainer Penkert. Paul Martin directed. Black and white. Black and white. In German. 78 minutes.

HOUSTON, GEORGE
American baritone (1900-1944)

New Jersey baritone George Houston studied at Juilliard and then taught at Eastman where he joined the American Opera Company. He also sang operettas like *New Moon* and *Casanova* in New York. He made his first film in 1935, *The Melody Lingers On,* and played opera singers in his early films including *The Great Waltz.* Most of his films, however, were not musical. He was George Washington with Cary Grant in *The Howards of Virginia,* Marshall Duroc with Greta Carbo in *Conquest* and the cowboy hero the Lone Rider for PRC in low-budget pictures. Films of operatic interest are listed below. See also JOHANN STRAUSS (1938).

1935 The Melody Lingers On
Houston is featured in scenes from *Carmen* in this romantic love story. He portrays Carlo Salvini, an opera singer Army captain who returns home in 1917 for a benefit performance of *Carmen.* He meets and marries pianist Josephine Hutchinson and years later their son also becomes an opera star. UA. Black and white. 85 minutes.

1935 Let's Sing Again
Houston portrays Leon Alba, the opera singer father of Bobby Breen. Breen inherits his father's voice and also becomes a singer even though they are separated. Father and son are reunited at the end of this movie directed by Kurt Neumann. Black and white. 70 minutes.

HOUSTON GRAND OPERA

The adventurous and innovative Houston Grand Opera, housed in the Wortham Center since 1978, is noted for championing modern American opera. It has held the premieres of new operas by Bernstein, Tippett, Glass and Adams and arranged major revivals of operas by Joplin, Gershwin and Floyd. See PHILIP GLASS (1985), NIXON IN CHINA (1988), WILLIE STARK (1981), TREEMONISHA (1982).

HOWARD, KATHLEEN
Canadian mezzo-soprano (1880-1956)

Kathleen Howard had three careers in her long life as opera singer, movie actress and fashion editor. Her opera career began in Metz in 1907 and she sang with the Metropolitan Opera from 1916 to 1928. She was welcomed by other opera companies and made records for Edison and Pathé. Howard was also a costume expert and after she left the Met in 1928 she became fashion editor of *Harper's Bazaar.* After that she tried Hollywood and worked in movies from 1934 to 1950. Her films don't have opera content but many are cinema classics. Her first was the stylish 1934 *Death Takes a Holiday,* her last the classy 1950 *The Petty Girl.* She is best known to movie fans for her memorable performances as W. C. Fields' nagging wife in *It's a Gift* (1934), *You're Telling Me* (1934) and *The Man on the Flying Trapeze* (1935). Her later films included *Ball of Fire* (1941), *Laura* (1944) and the Jerome Kern musical *Centennial Summer* (1946).

HUÉSPED DEL SEVILLANO, EL
1926 zarzuela by Guerrero

Spanish composer Jacinto Guerrero's zarzuela *El Huésped del Sevillano* focuses on an imaginary incident in the life of *Don Quixote* creator Miguel Cervantes. It supposes that this event inspired him to write a famous story titled *La Ilustre Fregona.* Cervantes is not mentioned by name in the zarzuela but is called "the huésped" (guest) at an inn. He is, however, quite recognizable. The libretto was written by Enrique Reoyo and Juan Ignacio Luca de Tena. See also JACINTO GUERRERO.

1939 Antonio de Obregon film
Antonio de Obregon's film stars the famous zarzuela singer Luis Sagi-Vela at the peak of his career. He is supported by Charito Leonis, Marta Ruel and Julio Castro with Manuel Kayser in the

role of the Huésped Cervantes. Black and white. In Spanish. 88 minutes.

1969 Juan De Orduña film

Juan De Orduña's colorful film was produced by Spanish television for its *Teatro Lirico Español* series. Dolores Pérez sings the role of Raquel acted by Maria Silva, Carlo del Monte sings Juan Luis acted by Manuel Gil, Rosa Sarmiento sings Constancia acted by Maria Jose Alfonso and Angel Picazo portrays the Huésped Cervantes. Federico Moreno Torroba conducted the Spanish Lyric Orchestra. The soundtrack was released on record. Color. In Spanish. 92 minutes.

HUGUENOTS, LES

1836 opera by Meyerbeer

Giacomo Meyerbeer's *The Huguenots*, the second of the composer's spectacular collaborations with librettist Eugène Scribe, is grand opera in all senses. It requires seven major singers, gigantic sets and elaborate production to describe events leading up to the horrific St. Bartholomew's Day massacre of Protestant Huguenots by French Catholics. The plot revolves around Queen Marguerite de Valois and the love between Protestant aristocrat Raoul and Catholic noblewoman Valentine who both die in the massacre. The other main roles in the opera are Count de Nevers, Count de St. Bris, Urbain and Marcel. The opera is usually performed in Italy as *Gli Ugonotti* and in Germany as *Die Hugenotten*. See also GIACOMO MEYERBEER.

1990 Australian Opera

Joan Sutherland stars as Marguerite de Valois in this Sydney Opera House production by Lotfi Mansour. Amanda Thane is Valentine, Anson Austin is Raoul, John Pringle is Count de Nevers, John Wegner is Count de St. Gris, Clifford Grant is Marcel and Suzanne is Urbain. John Stoddart designed the sets, Michael Stennet the costumes and Lois Strike the choreography. Richard Bonynge conducted the Australian Opera and Ballet Orchestra and Chorus and Virginia Lumsden directed the video. Color. In French with English subtitles. 200 minutes. Home Vision video.

1993 Deutsche Oper, Berlin

American tenor Richard Leech stars as Raoul in *Die Hugenotten*, a famous modernized Deutsche Oper Berlin production by John Dew. Dew transplanted the setting of the opera to a divided Berlin. The others in the cast are Angela Denning, Lucy Peacock, Camille Capasso, Marcia Bellamy and Martin Blasius. Stefan Soltesz conducts the Deutsche Opera Berlin Orchestra and Chorus. Brian Large directed the video in HDTV. Color. In German. 156 minutes. On video and Japanese laserdisc.

Early/related films

1902 Dutch sound film

An aria from the opera was seen and heard in Holland in September 1902 in a sound film featured in screenings by Alber's Electro Talking Bioscope. About 3 minutes.

1909 Louis Feuillade film

French director Louis Feuillade shot a version of the story for Gaumont in 1909. About 12 minutes.

1933 La Canzone Del Sole

This Italian film ends with a live production of *Gli Ugonotti* in the giant open-air Verona Arena. Giacomo Lauri-Volpi stars as Raoul on stage in what was effectively the Italian premiere of the opera. In the film he portrays himself opposite Vittorio De Sica who acts as his lawyer. Max Neufeld directed. The movie was called *Das Lied Der Sonne* in Germany and was released in the USA as *Song of the Sun*. Black and white. In Italian or German. 80 minutes.

1937 Maytime

Jeanette MacDonald portrays an opera diva in 19th century Paris seen on stage at the Imperial Opera in a production of *Les Huguenots*. She sings "Noble seigneurs, salut" and "Une dame noble et sage" while admirer Nelson Eddy watches from the audience. Robert Z. Leonard directed. Black and white. 132 minutes. MGM-UA video and laserdisc.

1951 Madame de...

Max Ophuls' stylish study of relationships, known in the U.S. as *The Earrings of Madame de...*, features ironic theme music from *Les Huguenots*. The plot revolves around earrings that countess Danielle Darrieux pawns, husband Charles Boyer retrieves and baron lover Vittorio De Sica returns with unfortunate consequences. Black and white. In French. 100 minutes.

HUMPERDINCK, ENGELBERT
German composer (1854-1921)

Engelbert Humperdinck used to be known only as the composer of the hugely successful opera, *Hansel and Gretel*, a favorite of children and adults around the world after its premiere in 1893. He is now also known as the composer whose name was appropriated by a British rock singer. Fortunately Humperdinck's musical brilliance in *Hansel and Gretel* is likely to keep him in the limelight long after the pop star is forgotten. Humperdinck's other major opera, which is only occasionally performed, is the 1897 *Königskinder*. He also composed one of the earliest important film scores at the request of Max Reinhardt's for the 1912 spectacular *Das Mirakel*. See HANSEL AND GRETEL.

HUROK, SOL
American impresario (1889-1947)

Russian-born American impresario Sol Hurok helped popularize opera in America by touring top singers like Feodor Chaliapin. Among the singers whose reputations were enhanced by Hurok were Marian Anderson, Jan Peerce and Roberta Peters. Hurok also launched one opera film as if it were a major live spectacle, the 1953 Italian *Aida* with Sophia Loren. Hurok has been the subject of several biographies and a famous all-star film. See TONIGHT WE SING.

1956 Producers' Showcase
Sol Hurok produced this all-star television festival of opera singers. Leonard Warren sings the Prologue from *Pagliacci*, Zinka Milankov sings "Vissi d'arte" from *Tosca*, Roberta Peters sings Olympia's aria "Les oiseaux" from *The Tales of Hoffmann*, Jan Peerce sings "Vesti la giubba" from *Pagliacci*, Marian Anderson sings spirituals, Blanche Thebom and Mildred Miller join on the Barcarolle duet from *Tales of Hoffmann* and Risë Steven sings the Card Aria from *Carmen*. Max Rudolf conducted the orchestra, Herbert Graf directed the staging and Kirk Browning directed the telecast on Jan. 30. Black and white. 60 minutes. Video at MTR.

HUSTON, JOHN
American film director (1906-1987)

John Huston, whose splendid directing career began with *The Maltese Falcon* in 1941, featured opera in both *The Dead* and *Prizzi's Honor*. He also directed opera on stage. The Metropolitan approached him first to direct *La Fanciulla del West* but he turned them down saying their approach was shabby. La Scala then gave him the chance to direct Richard Rodney Bennett's *The Mines of Sulphur*. The production premiered in Milan on March 1, 1966. Critics called it a success but Huston never directed opera on stage again. His love of opera, however, is evident in his wonderful last film *The Dead*. See THE DEAD.

1966 The Life and Times of John Huston
A film portrait of John Huston that shows him directing Richard Rodney Bennett's *The Mines of Sulphur* at La Scala. The film includes interviews with Huston and colleagues and footage of him working on a film. Huston talks about his past, his philosophy of life, his successes and his failures. Black and white. 60 minutes.

1985 Prizzi's Honor
A tenor is singing "Una furtiva lagrima" on stage at a Prizzi family celebration when the event is fire bombed by rival gangsters. The film is the story of a love affair between killers Jack Nicholson and Kathleen Turner and their relationship with the Prizzi crime family. The parodistic use of Rossini, Verdi, Puccini and Donizetti contributes to the texture of many scenes. Tomasina Baratta is the opera singer and Alexandra Ivanoff is the soprano in the wedding scene. *The Barber of Seville* overture is also featured. Color. 130 minutes. Vestron video.

HYTNER, NICHOLAS
English director (1956-)

Nicholas Hytner, one of the most original of the new theater and opera directors, is becoming equally well known as a film director following the success of *The Madness of King George* and *The Crucible*. His first opera production was *The Turn of the Screw* for Kent Opera for whom he also directed *King Priam* and *The Marriage of Figaro*. His controversial *La Clemenza di Tito* at Glyndebourne is on video. Hytner has worked with the Royal Shakespeare Company and the National Theatre of Great Britain and is known for his staging of *Miss Saigon*. See LA CLEMENZA DI TITO (1991), GEORGE FRIDERIC HANDEL (1995), KING PRIAM (1985), XERXES (1988).

I

IDOMENEO
1781 opera by Mozart

Idomeneo, Re di Creta (Idomeneus, King of Crete) is the official name of Mozart's first major opera but the videos are titled simply *Idomeneo* as was its original poster. It's an impressive *opera seria*, considered by many critics the best ever written. Greek general Idomeneo has been shipwrecked and promises the god Neptune that he will sacrifice the first person he sees if allowed to return home to Crete. That person turns out to be his son Idamante who is in love with the Trojan princess Ilia. Elettra (ie, Electra) has also taken refuge on the island and is in love with Idamante and madly jealous. Neptune wants his pledge honored. The libretto by Giambattista Varesco is based on a French libretto by Antoine Danchet but has been given a happy ending. See WOLFGANG A. MOZART.

1966 Peter Pears on BBC
Peter Pears stars as Idomeneo in this BBC television production with the orchestra conducted by Benjamin Britten. The cast includes Heather Harper as Ilia, Robert Tear as Arbace, Rae Woodland as Elettra and Anne Pashley as Idamante. Black and white. In Italian. NFTA in London has 66 minute video of Act II.

1974 Glyndebourne Festival
Richard Lewis stars as Idomeneo with Josephine Barstow as Elettra in this Glyndebourne Festival production by John Cox. Bozena Betley is Ilia, Leo Goeke is Idamante, Alexander Oliver is Arbace, John Fryatt is the High Priest and Dennis Wicks is the Voice of Neptune. Roger Butlin designed the sets and John Pritchard conducted the London Philharmonic Orchestra and Glyndebourne Festival Chorus. Dave Heather directed the video. Color. In Italian with English subtitles. 127 minutes. VAI video.

1982 Metropolitan Opera
Luciano Pavarotti stars as Idomeneo opposite a powerful trio of women in this Metropolitan Opera production by Jean-Pierre Ponnelle. Ileana Cotrubas is Ilia, Hildegarde Behrens is Elettra and Frederica Von Stade is Idamante with John Alexander as Arbace, Timothy Jenkins as the High Priest and Richard J. Clark as the Voice of Neptune. Ponnelle also designed the sets and costumes while James Levine conducted the Metropolitan Opera Orchestra and Chorus. Brian Large directed the video taped Nov. 6, 1982 and telecast in the Live from the Met series on Jan. 26, 1983. Color. In Italian with English subtitles. 185 minutes. Paramount video/Pioneer laser.

1983 Glyndebourne Festival
Philip Langridge stars as Idomeneo in this Glyndebourne Festival production by Trevor Nunn. Yvonne Kenny sings the role of Ilia, Carol Vaness is Elettra, Jerry Hadley is Idamante, Thomas Hemsley is Arbace, Anthony Roden is the High Priest and Roderick Kennedy is the Voice of Neptune. Bernard Haitink conducted the London Philharmonic Orchestra and Glyndebourne Festival Chorus. Christopher Swann directed the video. Color. In Italian with English subtitles. 180 minutes. HBO video.

1988 Michael Kreihsl film
Michael Kreihsl wrote and directed this Austrian film of the opera. Pepi Griesser portrays Idomeneo, Joachim Bauer is Idamante, Elke Heinbücher is Ilia, Marisa Fernandino is Elettra, Hjalmar Este is Arbace and Uli Hoffmann is the High Priest. Nikolaus Harnoncourt conducted the Mozart Orchestra and the Zurich Opera Chorus. The film was produced by the Vienna Music School and presented at the Ghent and Göthenborg film festivals. Color. In German. 102 minutes.

1991 Drottningholm Court Theatre
An outstanding production from the ornate Drottningholm Court Theater in Sweden with Arnold Östman conducting the period instrument orchestra of the theater. Stuart Kale stars as Idomeneo, David Kuebler is Idamante, Ann-Christin Biel is Ilia, Anita Soldh is Elettra, John-Eric Jacobsson is Arbace, Lars Tibel is the High Priest and Olle Skold is the Voice of Neptune. The production was staged by Michael Hampe and designed by Martin Rupprecht. Thomas Olofsson directed the video. RM Arts. Color. In Italian with

English subtitles. 142 minutes. Philips video and laser.

Related films

1993 Philadelphia
This film about a gay lawyer with AIDS (Tom Hanks) features Lucia Popp on the soundtrack singing Ilia's aria from *Idomeneo* "Non temer amato bene". She's accompanied by the Vienna State Opera Orchestra led by John Pritchard. Tristar. Color. 119 minutes.

IMAGINARY OPERAS IN FILMS

There have been a number of imaginary operas created for the movies as a part of the plot, usually to allow the stars to behave or sing in ways that a traditional opera might not encompass. They are, of course, only parts of operas so they have never been transferred to the stage. An aria created by Bernard Herrman for an imaginary opera in *Citizen Kane*, however, has been recorded by Kiri Te Kanawa and appears to have a life of its own. The composers of these fascinating imaginary operas include Erich Wolfgang Korngold, Riccardo Zandonai, Kurt Weill, Herbert Stothart, Nino Rota, Oscar Levant, and Mario Castelnuovo-Tedesco. Irene Kahn Atkins discusses some of them in depth in her fine study *Source Music in Motion Pictures*.

1931 Les Bohèmiens
The imaginary opera *Les Bohèmiens* is seen in the climactic scenes of the René Clair film *Le Million* and is only vaguely related to Murger. There are two scenes on stage at the Opéra-Lyrique Théâtre in Paris. In the first a duet titled "Alone in the forest" is sung by tenor Sopranelli (Constantin Stroesco) and soprano Mme. Ravellina (Odette Talazac) with the romantic leads (Annabella and René Lefèvre) hidden behind the scenery. In the second scene, set in a gypsy camp, the Bohemians sing about happiness, the tenor wins a duel for his soprano's honor and his dying rival sings to his mother. The film centers around the hunt for a lottery ticket hidden in the coat the tenor is wearing. After a number of rival groups charge on stage in an attempt to seize it, the opera ends in chaos. *Les Bohèmiens* was composed by Georges van Parys, who also wrote stage operettas, with Philippe Parès and Armand Bernard. Black and white. In French. 91 minutes. Video Yesteryear/Bel Canto Society videos.

1934 La Signora di Tutti
An unnamed imaginary opera is at the center of this film and its plot is described in detail. The opera is the story of a young officer who is magically healed by a woman after he is shot. She becomes his lover and goes on a military campaign with him but the Emperor takes the woman away from him. The officer ends up in prison totally mad. In the film Isa Miranda is taken to the opera by a married man and they fall in love during the time he describes the plot to his wife. The music for the opera was written by Daniel Amfitheatrof who began his music career at La Scala. Black and white. In Italian. 89 minutes. Connoisseur video.

1936 Romeo and Juliet
Eric Wolfgang Korngold composed parts of an imaginary *Romeo and Juliet* opera for the 1936 Hollywood film *Give Us This Night*. Korngold, who had already had success on stage with his operas in Europe, was a friend of the movie's star Jan Kiepura. Kiepura and Gladys Swarthout star in Korngold's opera as part of the plot of the film. Alexander Hall directed the film. Paramount. Black and white. 70 minutes.

1936 Carnival
Oscar Levant created an imaginary opera called *Carnival* for the 1936 film *Charlie Chan at the Opera* with overture, prelude, marches and arias. The libretto by William Kernell was created around a Mephistopheles costume worn by Lawrence Tibbett in *Metropolitan*. The outfit was given to the low-budget Chan picture to be worn on-stage by a baritone in a stabbing scene. Boris Karloff plays the singer (singing dubbed by Rico Ricardi) suffering from amnesia and a desire for revenge. Levant discusses this neglected opera in his autobiography *A Smattering of Ignorance* and there is an analysis by Irene Hahn Atkins in her book. H. Bruce Humberstone directed for 20th Century Fox. Black and white. 66 minutes. Key video.

1936 Isabelle
The 1936 Mary Ellis movie *Fatal Lady* features two imaginary operas. The first to be seen is *Isabelle* with music by Gerard Carbonara and libretto by David Ormont. Ellis plays an opera diva who runs away after being accused of a murder and has to sing under a false name. Paramount. Black and white. 72 minutes.

1936 Bal Masque

Bal Masque is the second imaginary opera in the 1936 Mary Ellis opera movie *Fatal Lady*. It has music by Gerard Carbonara and Victor Young with a libretto by Sam Coslow. Ellis plays an opera diva accused of murder. Paramount. Black and white. 72 minutes.

1937 Czaritza

Composer Herbert Stothart created *Czaritza*, a 19th century French opera set in Russia, for the 1937 film *Maytime*. It is supposedly written by a Rossini-like Paris composer for American prima donna Jeanette MacDonald. Stothart based the opera on themes from Tchaikovsky's *Fifth Symphony* and ten minutes of it are fully staged at the climax of the film. MacDonald and Nelson Eddy sing the lead roles. MGM. Black and white. In English. 132 minutes. On video and laserdisc.

1939 Balalaika

An imaginary Rimsky-Korsakov opera based on *Scheherezade* is staged at the Imperial Opera House in the MGM operetta film *Balalaika*. It was devised by Herbert Stothart with help from pastiche masters Bob Wright and Chet Forest, the team that transmuted Borodin's music into the operetta *Kismet*. Nelson Eddy and Ilona Massey are the stars of this film set at the time of the Russian revolution and based on a British stage operetta by Eric Maschwitz. Reinhold Schunzel directed. Black and white. 102 minutes.

1939 Arlesiana

An imaginary opera called *Arlesiana* was composed by Sam Pokrass to a libretto by Armando Hauser for the film *Wife, Husband and Friend*. Opera soprano Nina Koshetz provides the singing voice for Binnie Barnes who portrays an opera diva while Warner Baxter and Loretta Young play would-be singers. The film was based on James Cain's story *Career in C. Major* which was filmed again in 1949 as *Everybody Does It* with yet another imaginary opera. Black and white. 75 minutes.

1940 Penelope

Italian opera composer Riccardo Zandonai created the imaginary opera *Penelope* for the 1940 Beniamino Gigli film called *Traummusik* in German and *Ritorno* in Italian. It's a retelling of the *Odyssey* story about Ulysses' wife Penelope who waited twenty years for his return. In the film the composer hero (Rossano Brazzi) has composed the opera for his beautiful soprano friend Marte Harell and she asks Gigli to be her Ulysses. A scene from the opera is shown with Mafalda Favero supplying the singing voice for the beautiful Harell. Geza von Bolvary directed. Black and white. 80 minutes

1941 Salammbô

Kiri Te Kanawa has recorded an aria from this imaginary opera created by Bernard Herrmann for *Citizen Kane*. Herrmann wrote *Salammbô* because director Orson Welles wanted a peculiar kind of opera, one in which the soprano is on stage as the curtain goes up and has to sing over a powerful orchestra. In the film this is planned as a disaster for Kane's singer wife Susan Alexander whom he has forced into an opera career. The actress is Dorothy Comingore but the singing was done by soprano Jean Forward, a professional who forced herself to sound amateurish. The *Salammbô* aria as sung professionally by Te Kanawa and other modern sopranos actually sounds pretty good. RKO. Black and white. 119 minutes. On video.

1943 Amour et Gloire

The 1943 version of *The Phantom of the Opera* includes scenes and arias from two imaginary operas created by composer Edward Ward and librettist George Waggner. The first, a charming, melodious French opera called *Amour et Gloire*, is based on music by Chopin. Nelson Eddy stars opposite soprano Susanna Foster in the opera and Foster hits some fine high notes. Arthur Lubin directed for Universal. Color. 92 minutes.

1943 Le Prince Masque de la Caucasie

The second opera created by composer Edward Ward and librettist George Waggner for the 1943 Universal film *The Phantom of the Opera* is a fiery Russian drama. It's called *Le Prince Masque de la Caucasie* and is based on themes from Tchaikovsky's Fourth Symphony. Nelson Eddy and soprano Susanna Foster sing the imaginary opera music. Arthur Lubin directed. Color. 92 minutes.

1945 Where Do We Go From Here?

Kurt Weill wrote a 12-minute mini-operetta about Christopher Columbus to a libretto by Ira Gershwin for this film musical. Fred MacMurray has a genie which allows him to travel backwards into American history. Gregory Ratoff directed. Color. 77 minutes.

1946 Marie Antoinette

Marie Antoinette is an imaginary opera based on music by Liszt and featured at the Met at the end of the 1946 film *Two Sisters from Boston.* Lauritz Melchior portrays a Metropolitan Opera tenor who sings some the opera on stage opposite Kathryn Grayson. He sings the role of the French king while she plays Marie and both are dressed in period costumes with dozens of extras and an elaborate set. MGM built a 500-foot-wide reproduction of the Old Met interior for the film. The film also features Melchior and Grayson in an imaginary unnamed opera with music by Mendelssohn. Charles Previn arranged the music, Joseph Pasterak produced and Henry Koster directed. Black and white. 112 minutes. MGM/UA video.

1949 The Loves of Fatima

Mario Castelnuovo-Tedesco created an opera called The Loves of Fatima for the 1949 film Everybody Does It with arias for soprano and baritone. Paul Douglas sings the baritone role in the opera with Arlene Dahl as the soprano in its "premiere" by the American Scala Opera Company. His singing is done by New York City Opera baritone Stephen Kemalyan while Dahl's singing is by San Francisco Opera soprano Helen Spann. The premiere turns into a comic disaster. Douglas plays a man whose wife wants to be an opera singer though he has the real voice. The film was based on James Cain's story `Career in C Major`. Edmund Goulding directed. Black and white. 98 minutes. On video.

1949 The Princess

Mario Lanza and Kathryn Grayson make their opera debut in an imaginary opera called *The Princess* in the 1949 film *The Midnight Kiss.* Arranger Charles Previn based it on themes from Tchaikovsky's Fifth Symphony. Lanza is a truck driver with a great voice while Grayson is an heiress who wants to be an opera singer,. There is also music from *Aida, Cavalleria Rusticana* and *L'Elisir d'Amore.* Norman Taurog directed for MGM. Color. 96 minutes.

1950 The Glass Mountain

Tito Gobbi stars in the opera *The Glass Mountain* created by Nino Rota for the 1950 film *The Glass Mountain.* Michael Denison, composer of the opera in the film, falls in love with Valentina Cortese after his plane crashes in the Italian Alps. Elena Rizzieri sings with Gobbi in the opera scenes. The theme from the opera became quite popular in England in the 1950s. Franco Ferrara conducts the La Fenice Opera Orchestra. Henry Cass directed the film. Black and white. 91 minutes. Lyric/Opera Dubs video.

1951 Il Ritorno de Cesare

Mario Castelnuovo-Tedesco created this opera for the film *Strictly Dishonorable.* The opera singer is Ezio Pinza who belts out the baritone aria "Il Ritorno de Cesare" with Janet Leigh as his sword bearer. He plays an operatic Don Juan and she an innocent who falls in love with him. He has to marry her to save her reputation. The film, based on a play by Preston Sturges, was directed by Melvin Frank and Norman Panama. MGM. Black and white. 94 minutes.

1962 Saint Joan

The imaginary opera *Saint Joan* written by the Phantom is the centerpiece of the 1962 British film *The Phantom of the Opera.* The music was actually composed and conducted by Edwin Astley. Herbert Lom portrays the Phantom with Heather Sears as the young soprano Christine. The Phantom teaches Christine how to sing his opera and saves her life when a chandelier falls. Terence Fisher directed. Color. 84 minutes.

1989 Don Juan Triumphant

Music director Misha Segal wrote an aria of the Phantom's lost opera *Don Juan Triumphant* for a 1989 version of *The Phantom of the Opera.* The opera is described in Leroux' source novel and is sung in the film by the Christine character Jill Schoelen. Robert Englund portrays the Phantom in this American film set in 19th century Covent Garden. Dwight H. Little directed. Color. 90 minutes.

IMPRESARIO, THE
1786 opera by Mozart

Der Schauspieldirektor is a delightful one-act comic *singspiel* (ie, the dialogue is spoken) in German about the rivalry of prima donnas. Mozart wrote it for an Imperial social event to a libretto by Gottlieb Stephanie Jr. An impresario is hiring performers for an engagement in Salzburg. Sopranos Herz and Silberklang audition with very different styles of arias and are both hired. They argue over who will be the prima donna and a tenor called Vogelsang tries to keep the peace. The roles were written for Aloysia Weber, who specialized in singing German opera with sentiment, and Catarina Cavalieri, who specialized in singing Italian opera with brilliance.

It is usually performed in English in the U.S. and England as *The Impresario* and often modernized. See also WOLFGANG A. MOZART.

1938 First opera on German television
A German film of *Der Schauspieldirektor* was the first opera shown on television in Germany. It was telecast by the small Paul Nipkow Sender station nine times between 1938 and 1940.

1961 Steber/Moody video
Eleanor Steber and Jacquelyne Moody star as the rival sopranos in this highly praised CBS Camera Three English-language production by John Desmond. Titled *The Impresario*, it is updated to the present time with a simple set of piano and desk. The sopranos arrive at the same time for their auditions with impresario John Kuhn. After a series of jealous arguments, he resolves the problem. Arnold Gamson conducts the CBS orchestra. Black and white. In English. 60 minutes. Videos at MTR and NYPL.

1980 Christie/Wise video
Patricia Wise portrays soprano Beverly Silvertone and Nan Christie is rival soprano Elisabeth Herzkoph in this excellent updated English version of *The Impresario*. The Nemesis Opera Company is presenting a Mozart opera with two star sopranos and it is to be filmed for TV. Giuseppe Di Stefano plays tenor Luciano Buffarotti and Patrick Cargill is impresario Rudolph Bang. After many problems they stage an opera called *Der Schauspieldirektor*. Vilem Tausky conducts the English Chamber Orchestra. Kenneth Corden wrote the adaptation with Francis Coleman and directed the telecast for BBC TV. Color. In English with some arias in German. 60 minutes. Lyric/ Opera Dubs video.

1989 Schönbrunn Schlosstheater, Vienna
Polish soprano Zdislawa Donat stars in this Austrian production of *Der Schauspieldirektor* filmed in German at the Schönbrunn Palace Schlosstheater in Vienna, a popular theater for chamber operas. The video is from a telecast on Austrian television. Color. 60 minutes. In German. Lyric video.

1991 Buckingham Palace
Yvonne Kenny and Ann Howard are the rival sopranos in this version of *The Impresario* staged at Buckingham Palace. Barry Banks is the tenor, Mathew Best is the impresario and Peter Shaffer is the narrator. Sir Colin Davis conducts the orchestra.

Color. In English with Japanese subtitles. 60 minutes. EMI video/Japanese laserdisc as *Mozart at Buckingham Palace.*

IM WEISSEN RÖSSL
See WHITE HORSE INN

INCORONAZIONE DI POPPEA, L'
1642 opera by Monteverdi

Claudio Monteverdi's last surviving opera *The Coronation of Poppea* has become quite popular in recent years, perhaps because the villains triumph in the end for a change. The story, loosely out of Roman history, tells of the love of the Emperor Nero for the beautiful Poppea and her desire to become empress in place of Octavia. The philosopher Seneca's opposition to a change of wife results in an order for his execution. An attempt to murder Poppea by Drusilla backfires. Octavia is divorced and exiled and the adulterous couple reign in full triumph. Of morality there is very little. See also CLAUDIO MONTEVERDI.

1979 Jean-Pierre Ponnelle film
Director Jean-Pierre Ponnelle and conductor Nicholaus Harnoncourt team on an adaptation of a Monteverdi production. Like their collaborations on *Orfeo* and *Il Ritorno d'Ulisse in Patria*, the film grew out of their acclaimed Monteverdi cycle at the Zurich Opera House in the early 1970s. The film has basically the same cast as the stage production. It stars Rachael Yakar as Poppea, Eric Tappy as Nerone, Trudeliese Schmidt as Octavia, Paul Esswood as Ottone and Matti Salminen as Seneca. Harnoncourt conducts the Monteverdi Ensemble of the Zurich Opera House. Unitel Film. Color. In Italian with English subtitles. 161 minutes. London video/laser.

1984 Glyndebourne Festival
Peter Hall's lively production of the opera stars Maria Ewing as Poppea, Dennis Bailey as Nero, Cynthia Clarey as Octavia, Robert Lloyd as Seneca, Elizabeth Gale as Drusilla and Dale Duesing as Ottone. The characters are dressed in Renaissance clothes in accordance with Hall's idea that the opera reflected the ideas of the time of its composition rather than the ideas of ancient Rome. Raymond Leppard conducts the London Philharmonic Orchestra and Glyndebourne Chorus. The video,

directed by Robin Lough, is introduced by Peter Hall. Color. In Italian. 148 minutes. HBO Video.

1993 Schwetzingen Festival
Michael Hampe staged a new production of the opera at the Schwetzingen Festival for a Monteverdi anniversary. It stars Patricia Schuman, Marianne Rotholm, Kathleen Kuhlmann, Jeffrey Gall, Harry Peters, Curtis Rayam and Richard Croft. Baroque music specialist René Jacobs conducted the Cologne Concerto Orchestra and José Montes-Baquer directed the video. EuroArts. Color. In Italian. 151 minutes. On video.

Related film

1969 Laughter in the Dark
Tony Richardson's film version of the Nabokov novel uses seduction music from Monteverdi's opera to underline a similar seduction situation. Nicol Williamson portrays the married man whose obsession with young Anna ruins his life. Color. 101 minutes.

INNOCENZA ED IL PIACER, L'
Operas by Gluck

The video set titled *L'Innocenza ed il Piacer* is comprised of two short operas by Christoph Willibald Gluck staged together at the Schwetzingen Palace in 1988. See LE CINESI, ECHO ET NARCISSE.

INTERMEZZO
1924 opera by Strauss

Richard Strauss wrote his own libretto for this autobiographical opera based on an incident in his marriage. The chief characters are based on his wife Pauline, a temperamental former opera singer, and himself. In the opera Christine, the annoying wife of the conductor Robert Storch, has a flirtation with young Baron Lummer but soon drops him. She then becomes incensed when she discovers a love letter apparently meant for her husband and threatens to divorce him. It is a misunderstanding and all ends well. See also RICHARD STRAUSS.

1983 Glyndebourne Festival
Felicity Lott is superb as Christine in this excellent English-language production of the opera by John Cox. She is ably supported by John Pringle as her husband Robert, Ian Caley as the Baron and Elizabeth Gale as the maid. Martin Battersby created the set designs and Andrew Porter made the English translation. Gustav Kuhn conducted the London Philharmonic and David Buckton directed the video. Color. In English. 155 minutes. Home Vision video.

IOLANTA
1892 opera by Tchaikovsky

Tchaikovsky's opera *Iolanta* was presented on film in the U.S. as *Yolanta* while the Sovexport publicity brochure calls it *Yolande* in both English and French. Whatever her proper name, Iolanta is the blind daughter of King René and has been kept away from the very idea of sight. However, it appears she can be cured if she wants to see light. After she falls in love with Vaudemont, she has to be cured to save his life. The libretto by Modest Tchaikovsky is based on a Danish play by Henrik Hertz. See also PYOTYR TCHAIKOVSKY.

1963 Vladimir Gorikker film
In this delightful Soviet film of the opera the charming Natalya Rudnaya portrays Iolanta on screen with her singing dubbed by Galina Oleynichenko. Opera film specialist Vladimir Gorikker wrote and directed the film using film actors dubbed by singers from the Bolshoi Opera. King René plays Fyodor Nikitin sung by Ivan Petrov, Vaudemont is Yuri Perov sung by Surab Andzhaparidze, Duke Robert is Alexander Belyavsky sung by Pavel Lisitsian, Eon-Hakkia is Pyotr Glebov sung by V. Valaitis, Martha is Valentina Ushakova sung by Y. Verbitskaya and Bertand is Valdis Sandberg sung by V. Yaroslavtev. The cinematography is by Vadim Mass and the costumes by U. Pauzer. Boris Khaikin conducts the Bolshoi Opera Orchestra. A Riga, Latvia, production. Color. In Russian. 82 minutes.

IOLANTHE
1882 comic opera by Gilbert & Sullivan

Iolanthe or The Peer and the Peri is an enjoyable combination of fantasy and satire with the House of Lords involved in a fairyland frolic. Iolanthe is a fairy who was banished years before for marrying a mortal and has had a son called Strephon. The other fairies entreat their Queen to forgive her. Strephon's fiancée becomes jealous of his beautiful mother, the Lord Chancellor and Peers of the Realm get involved, Strephon becomes a Peer to try to solve his problems and everything gets turned topsy-turvy. Arthur Sullivan's music is outstanding and William S. Gilbert's lyrics are among his best. See also GILBERT AND SULLIVAN.

1974 World of Gilbert & Sullivan film
A highlights film of the operetta produced by John Seabourne for the *World of Gilbert and Sullivan* series. It features singers from the D'Oyly Carte Opera Company and Sadler Wells including Thomas Round, Helen Landis, Michael Wakeham and Donald Adams. The music is played by the Gilbert and Sullivan Festival Orchestra and Chorus. Trevor Evans directed the film. Color. In English. 54 minutes.

1982 George Walker film
Derek Hammond-Stroud stars as the Lord Chancellor with Richard Van Allen as Private Willis in this enjoyable film produced by Judith De Paul for George Walker. Alexander Oliver is Strephon, Kate Flowers is Phyllis, Beverly Mills is Iolanthe, Anne Collins is the Fairy Queen, David Hillman is Earl Tolloller and Thomas Hemsley is the Earl of Mountararat. Alexander Faris conducts the London Symphony Orchestra and the Ambrosian Opera Chorus. David Poultney was stage director and Dave Heather directed the film. Color. In English. 116 minutes. Braveworld (England) video.

1984 Stratford Festival
An entertaining Stratford Festival production by Brian MacDonald with the libretto updated by Jim Betts and John Banks. The operetta is presented as if staged by a second-rate touring company in a provincial city. Maureen Forrester is a delight as the grande dame diva of the company who portrays the Queen of the Fairies. She gets strong support from Eric Donkin as the Lord Chancellor, Marie Baron as Phyllis, Paul Massel as Strephon, Katherina Megli as Iolanthe and Stephen Beamish and Douglas Chamberlain as the Earls. The sets and costumes are by Susan Benson and Berthold Carriere conducted the Stratford Festival Orchestra and Chorus. James Guthro directed the video. CBC. Color. In English. 138 minutes. Home Vision video and laser.

IRIS
1898 opera by Mascagni

Pietro Mascagni's influential opera *Iris* reflected his interest in the Japanese subjects fashionable at the time. It has a libretto by Luigi Illica, one of the authors of Puccini's similarly-themed *Madama Butterfly*, though *Iris* was written earlier and probably had an influence on the Puccini opera. Iris is the name of the heroine of the opera, an innocent Japanese girl who is kidnapped by her rich admirer Osaka and placed in a brothel run by Kyoto. She kills herself when she is discovered by her father and cursed. *Iris* helped spark a vogue for Oriental and Eastern settings for operas. See also PIETRO MASCAGNI.

1918 Giuseppe De Liguoro film
Giuseppe De Liguoro directed this silent Italian film adaptation of the Mascagni opera. It was screened in cinemas accompanied by music from the opera. Black and white. About 70 minutes.

1985 Masimo Tomiwako video
The only modern video of the opera is a recording of a telecast of a stylish Tokyo stage production with a Japanese cast. The opera is introduced in Japanese and has Japanese subtitles but is sung in Italian. Iris is portrayed by Masimo Tomiwako, Osaka is Yamadi Yosishisa and Kyoto is Kimara Tosimitu. Color. In Japanese and Italian. 100 minutes. Lyric video.

ISRAEL IN EGYPT
1738 oratorio by Handel

George Frideric Handel's dramatic *Israel in Egypt* has become one of his most popular oratorios. It opens with the Israelites lamenting the death of Joseph and telling the story of the plagues in Egypt that led eventually to their being allowed to depart and of their escape across the Red Sea. The miracle of their liberation is celebrated with exciting choruses and exhilarating solos. See also GEORGE F. HANDEL.

1991 Rodney Greenberg film
The oratorio was filmed live by Rodney Greenberg on the shore of the Red Sea in Israel. There is magnificent use of the actual location of the drama and the text of the oratorio appears as subtitles. John Currie conducts the John Currie Singers, the Edinburgh Festival Chorus, the Scottish National

Orchestra Chorus and the Jerusalem Symphony Orchestra. The soloists are sopranos Irene Drummond and Llyndall Trotman, basses John Hearne and Stephen Roberts, contralto Christine Cairns and tenor Stuart Patterson. Color. In English. 90 minutes. SISU video.

ITALIANA IN ALGERI, L'

1813 opera by Rossini

The Italian Woman in Algiers was Gioachino Rossini's first full-length comic opera and remains one of his most enjoyable. The libretto by Angelo Anelli is high-spirited fun, a comic counterpoint to Mozart's *The Abduction from the Seraglio*. Set in Algiers in the early 1800s, it tells the story of the Italian woman captive Isabella who bewitches and outwits her blustering captor, the Bey Mustafa. After causing him to behave in a most foolish manner, she escapes with her lover Lindoro and restores the Bey to his wife Elvira. See also GIOACHINO ROSSINI.

1957 Teresa Berganza video
Teresa Berganza stars as Isabella in this entertaining Italian television version of the opera. Director Mario Lanfranchi keeps the action in a kind of Arabian Nights fairytale land with help from designer Luca Crippa. Alvinio Misciano is Lindoro, Mario Petrias is Mustafa, Sesto Bruscantini is Taddeo, Rena Gary Falachi is Elvira, Vittoria Palombini is Zulma and Valerio Meucci is Haly. Nino Sanzogno conducted the Milan RAI Orchestra and Chorus. Black and white. In Italian. 118 minutes. Lyric/Bel Canto videos.

1986 Metropolitan Opera
Marilyn Horne is superb as Isabella in this outstanding Metropolitan Opera production by Jean-Pierre Ponnelle. Paolo Montsarsolo is Mustafa, Myra Merritt is Elvira, Douglas Ahlstedt is Lindoro, Allan Monk is Taddeo and Spiro Malas is Haly. Ponnelle also designed the sets while James Levine conducted the Metropolitan Opera Orchestra. Brian Large directed the Live from the Met telecast on Jan. 11, 1986. Color. In Italian with English subtitles. 150 minutes. Video at MTR.

1987 Schwetzingen Festival
Doris Soffel portrays Isabella in this excellent Schwetzingen Festival production by Michael Hampe. Robert Gambill is Lindoro, Gunther von Kannen is Mustafa, Nuccia Focile is Elvira, Enrico Serra is Taddeo, Rudolf A. Hartmann is Haly and

Susan McLean is Zulma. Mauro Pagano designed the sets and Ralf Weikert conducted the Stuttgart Radio Symphony Orchestra and Bulgarian Male Chorus of Sofia. Claus Viller directed the video. Color. In Italian with English subtitles. 149 minutes. RCA Victor video and laser.

Related film

1968 Gianini and Luzzati cartoon
Italian animation masters Giulio Gianini and Emanuele Luzzati, who became famous in 1964 for the Rossini-inspired *The Thieving Magpie*, followed it with another Rossini opera. Their cartoon version of *L'Italiana in Algeri* was also popular. Color. 8 minutes.

IVAN THE TERRIBLE

Russian tsar (1530-1584)

Tsar Ivan IV Vasilyevich, the 16th century Grand Duke who became the first Russian Tsar and a symbol of absolutist rule, has been the central character of operas, films and ballets. The first two films were based on operas, Rimsky-Korsakov's noted *The Maid of Pskov* and Raoul Gunsbourg's forgotten *Ivan le Terrible*. Paul Leni's 1924 film *Das Wachsfigurenkabinett* features Ivan as a principal character and Yuri Tarich's 1926 Soviet film *Wings of the Serf* (released in Paris as *Ivan the Terrible*) revolves around him but they have no apparent operatic connections. Eisenstein's magnificent two-part *Ivan the Terrible*, however, is highly operatic with music by Prokofiev. A Soviet ballet was later created around Prokofiev's music for the Eisenstein film and the ballet itself has been filmed.

1915 Ivan the Terrible
Feodor Chaliapin's most popular opera role in Russia was as Ivan the Terrible in Nicolai Rimsky-Korsakov's 1873 opera *Pskovityanka (The Maid of Pskov* or *Ivan the Terrible)*. The opera tells how Ivan spared the city of Pskov after the intercession of his daughter Olga. Chaliapin reprised the role in a 1915 Russian film of the opera called *Tsar Ivan Vasilyevich Grozny*. A. Ivanov-Gai produced and directed. Chaliapin was paid a generous 25,000 roubles as the film was to celebrate his 25th year on the stage but it did not become popular. Chaliapin hated it but Eisenstein studied it when he made his own Ivan film. Sharez Film. Black and white. In Russian. About 80 minutes.

1915 Ivan il Terrible

Raoul Gunsbourg aka Ginsberg (1859-1955), a Bucharest-born French impresario who managed opera houses in Moscow and St. Petersburg in the 1880s, became director of the Monte Carlo Opera in 1893. He wrote six operas, the second of which was the 1910 *Ivan le Terrible*. Chaliapin sang the lead role in its premiere production but said harsh things about it in his memoirs. In 1915 Enrico Guazzoni made an Italian film version called *Ivan il Terrible*. Amleto Novelli portrays Ivan, Matilde Di Marzio is the Romanov, Leda Gys is Elena and André Habay is Vladimir. Cines Film. Black and white. In Italian. About 60 minutes.

1946 Ivan the Terrible

Sergei Eisenstein's epic film *Ivan Groznyi* is not based on either of the above operas but they probably helped inspire the Soviet filmmaker to create an operatic film around the Tsar. James Agee has described Eisenstein's film as "a visual opera, with all of opera's proper disregard of prose-level reality." Eisenstein was working at the Bolshoi Opera staging Wagner's *Die Walküre* just before making the film so opera was very much on his mind. He was also hoping to stage composer's Sergei Prokofiev's opera *War and Peace* but that was not possible. Instead Prokofiev wrote the music for Eisenstein's film. Nikolai Cherkassov portrays Ivan in one of the great Soviet film performances. The film was made in two parts: the first finished in 1944 tells of Ivan's early life and struggles, the second completed in 1946 with color sequences focuses on the boyars' plot. Black and white and color. In Russian with English subtitles. 188 minutes. On video.

1977 Ivan the Terrible ballet film

Prokofiev's music for Eisenstein's film was then trasmuted into a ballet choreographed andd staged by Yuri Grigorovich in 1975. It was so popular that the ballet was then filmed by Grigorovich and Vadim Derbenev with the original stage cast. Yuri Vladimirov stars as the dancing Ivan with Natalya Bessmertnaya as his wife Anastasia and Boris Akimov as Prince Kurbsky. Color. 92 minutes.

IVORY, JAMES
American film director (1928-)

James Ivory teamed up with Indian producer Ismail Merchant in 1963 and since then the team has made an astonishing number of beautiful movies, many based on literary classics. Although Ivory has not made any films of opera per se, his movies often use opera to great effect. These include *Jefferson in Paris* (1995) with an elaborate staging of Antonio Sacchini's opera *Dardanus* and *A Room with a View* (1985) with its fine use of Puccini arias on the soundtrack. See GIANNI SCHICCHI (1985 film), LA RONDINE (1985 film), ANTONIO SACCHINI (1995).

J

JACOBS, WERNER
German film director (1909-)

Werner Jacobs, who began as an editor and assistant in the 1930s, started directing features in 1952. He has never been a critical favorite though his films have been popular with audiences. Jacobs adapted a number of operettas for the screen in French and German versions. See DER BETTELSTUDENT (1956), DER GRAF VON LUXEMBURG (1957), THE MERRY WIDOW (1962), WHITE HORSE INN (1960).

JANÁCEK, LEO
Czech composer (1854-1928)

Leo Janácek's operas have shown an amazing growth in popularity and critical esteem during the past seventy years. He didn't have an opera staged in a major opera house until 1916 when he was 62 years old but a burst of creativity during the last years of his life resulted in one of the major operatic legacies. He created a unique sound partially through his decision to set words to their sound as spoken rather than sung. His popularity today is shown by the large number of videos of his operas, His music has been used on the soundtrack of films as different as *Don's Party* (1976) and *The Unbearable Lightness of Being* (1988). See also THE CUNNING LITTLE VIXEN, FROM THE HOUSE OF THE DEAD, JENUFA, KATYA KABANOVA, THE MAKROPOULOS CASE.

1983 Leoš Janácek: Intimate Excursions
This is an extraordinary British puppet film about Janácek's operas created by the Brothers Quay and Keith Griffiths. The puppet Janácek reminisces about his life and introduces excerpts from his operas in which he also acts. Featured are *Diary of One Who Vanished, The Cunning Little Vixen, The Makropoulos Case, From the House of the Dead, The Excursion of Mr. Broucek* and *The Glagolitic Mass.* The singers include Pacel Kuhn, Bohumir Vich and Libuse Pylova and the music is played by the Czech Philharmonic Orchestra and Prague National Theatre Orchestra. Color. In English and Czech. 27 minutes.

JANOWITZ, GUNDULA
German soprano (1937-)

Gundula Janowitz was born in Berlin but began her professional opera career at the Vienna Staatsoper where she sang for thirty years. She came to the Met in 1967 as Sieglinde and also sang regularly at Salzburg and Bayreuth. She can be seen on video in a range of roles from Ariadne to Fiordiligi to Leonore. See ARIADNE AUF NAXOS (1978), COSÌ FAN TUTTE (1970), FIDELIO (1977), DIE FLEDERMAUS (1972), GEORGE F. HANDEL (1992), THE MARRIAGE OF FIGARO (1980).

JARMAN, DEREK
English film director (1942-1994)

Derek Jarman trained as an artist and worked as a designer for Ken Russell on several films. He created the sets for John Gielgud's controversial *Don Giovanni* at the Coliseum in 1968 and designed sets and costumes for Russell's innovative *The Rake's Progress* in Florence in 1982. His film of Benjamin Britten's *War Requiem* is of operatic interest as he virtually turned it into an opera. He also directed one of the most effective episodes of the opera film *Aria* around Charpentier's *Louise.* See ARIA, LOUISE (1987), THE RAKE'S PROGRESS (1982), WAR REQUIEM (1988).

JARNO, GEORG
Hungarian composer (1868-1920)

Hungarian composer Georg Jarno wrote tuneful Viennese-style operettas but his work is not well known in America. One of his operettas, *Die Försterchristl* (1907), has remained in the German stage repertory and has been filmed at least four times. His last operetta *Die Csikós-Baroness* was also turned into a film. Another of his operettas, *Das Musikantenmädel,* also has admirers. See DIE FÖRSTERCHRISTL.

1930 Die Csikós-Baroness
The Czardas Baroness is a Hungarian-style operetta based on a story by Sándor Petöfi with a libretto by Fritz Grünbaum. It was finished in 1920, the year Jarno died, and was an immdiate success. It was made into a German film ten years later with Gretl

Theimer, Ernst Verebes, Julius Falkenstein and Ida Wüst. Jakob and Luise Fleck directed the film for Hegewald film. Black and white. In German. 93 minutes.

JEANNE D'ARC AU BÛCHER
1938 dramatic oratorio by Honneger

Arthur Honneger described *Joan of Arc at the Stake* as a "dramatic oratorio" and it is certainly full of drama. It may not be a full-fledged opera but as staged by Roberto Rossellini in the major opera houses of Europe in 1953, it was assuredly a first cousin. The role of St. Joan is a spoken one and was performed on stage and film by Ingrid Bergman in Rossellini's revival. Paul Claudel's libretto tells the story of Joan's triumph and martyrdom. See also ARTHUR HONNEGER.

1954 Giovanna d'Arco al Rogo
Italian film director Roberto Rossellini produced this film version after directing the oratorio on stage in 1953 at San Carlo, La Scala, the Paris Opéra and the Stoll Theatre in London. Ingrid Bergman stars as Giovanna (St. Joan), Tullio Carminati is Fra Domenico, Giacinto Prandelli is Procus, Augusto Romani is the giant Heurtebise and Agnese Dubbini is Mrs. Botti. The singing voices belong to Myriam Pirazzini as Saint Catherine, Marcella Pobbe as the Virgin Mary, Florence Quartararo as St. Margaret, Pina Esca and Giovanni Avolant. The music was performed by the San Carlo Opera House Orchestra and Chorus. Color. In Italian. 80 minutes.

1986 August Everding Directs
A German film about a production of the oratorio by August Everding at the Bavarian State Opera in Munich. Joan is portrayed by Andrea Jonasson and Dominic by Christian Quadflieg. Director Werner Lütje follows the rehearsals and shows the production developing its form under Everding's direction. Color. In English. 26 minutes. Inter Nationes video.

1993 Saito Kinen Festival
Marthe Keller portrays Joan in this production at the Saito Kinen Festival in Japan. It is based on an earlier recorded production by conductor Seiji Ozawa in France. The soloists are Georges Wilson, Christine Barbaux and John Aler. Color. In French. 90 minutes. On Japanese laser.

JENSEITS DES STROMES
1922 opera written for the screen

Jenseits des Stromes (The Other Side of the River), said to be the first opera written expressly for the movies, is the work of Berlin opera composer Ferdinand Hummel (1855-1928). He wrote seven operas for the stage, the most famous being the 1893 *Mara*, but they are all but forgotten today. His film opera shares their fate. It was composed for singers and orchestra in the silent cinema era and provided its score literally on the screen. A strip of musical notation runs from left to right at the bottom of the image on screen as the picture progresses and provides guidance to singers and orchestra in theaters showing the film. Not many did.

JENUFA
1904 opera by Janácek

Leo Janácek's opera *Její Pastorkyna* (Her Stepdaughter) is based on a dialect play by Gabriela Preissová which is a realistic portrayal of peasant life. The opera made Janácek famous when it was staged in Prague in 1916. The grim story revolves around a young peasant named Jenufa who becomes pregnant by the miller Steva. The baby is murdered by her foster mother, the Kostelnicka, when it becomes an obstacle to Jenufa's marriage to Laca. See also LEO JANÁCEK.

1987 Janácek Theatre, Brno
Gabriela Benackova stars as Jenufa in this Janácek Theatre production in Brno. Vilem Pribyl portrays Lac, Nadezda Kniplova is the Kostelnicka, Anna Barova is the Grandmother and Vladimir Krejcik is Steva. Frantisek Jilek conducts the Janácek Opera Chorus and Orchestra. Color. In Czech with Japanese subtitles. 120 minutes. On Japanese laserdisc.

1989 Glyndebourne Festival
Roberta Alexander stars as Jenufa with Anja Silja as the Kostelnicka and Philip Langridge as Laca in this Glyndebourne Festival production by John Miller. Mark Baker sings the role of Steva, Alison Hagley is Karolka and Sarah Pring is Barena. The opera was originally staged by Nikolaus Lehnhoff with set designs by Tobias Hoheisel. Andrew Davis conducts the London Philharmonic Orchestra and Glyndebourne Festival Orchestra. Derek Bailey directed the video. Color. In Czech with English

subtitles. 119 minutes. Home Vision video/Japanese laserdisc.

JEPSON, HELEN
American soprano (1904-)

Helen Jepson made her opera debut in Philadelphia in 1928 in *The Marriage of Figaro* and her Metropolitan Opera debut seven years later in the premiere of John Seymour's *In the Pasha's Garden*. She sang in San Francisco as Flotow's *Martha* and in Chicago as Massenet's *Thais* with coaching from Mary Garden. Paramount put Jepson under contract in 1935 during the opera film boom but never used her. She was supposed to star in Grand National's *Something to Sing About* with James Cagney but it didn't happen. She finally appeared in a Samuel Goldwyn movie when he wanted a photogenic prima donna but it turned out to be her only film. Jepson continued to sing opera on stage until 1942.

1938 The Goldwyn Follies
Helen Jepson and Metropolitan opera tenor Charles Kullmann appear in a key scene in this famous George Gershwin film. Jepson portrays an opera singer called Leona Jerome who is first observed on stage in *La Traviata* with Kullman. Film producer Adolphe Menjou is looking for a class singer for a film he wants to make. Jepson as Violetta and Kullman as Alfredo perform "Libiamo" and "Sempre libera." Menjou hires her for the film he is making and she has a small role in the rest of the film. *Follies* is a musical kaleidoscope with songs by George Gershwin (who died while it was being made). They include "Love walked in" and "Love is here to stay." Ben Hecht's tongue-in-cheek screenplay revolves around an ordinary girl (Andra Leeds) hired by producer Menjou as an expert on ordinary people. George Marshall directed. Color. 115 minutes. On video.

JERITZA, MARIA
Czech soprano (1887-1982)

Maria Jeritza combined glamour with a remarkable voice and fine acting ability and still has many admirers today. She also had four husbands, one of whom was American film producer Winfield Sheehan. He was head of production at Fox in the 1930s and built her a showcase house in Beverly Hills where guests dined on gold plates. The novel *Bagage* is based on her life and she also starred in a film. She was a favorite in Vienna for two decades in the Puccini roles of Tosca, Minnie and Turandot and was equally popular at the Met. She created roles in Strauss's *Ariadne auf Naxos* and *Die Frau ohne Schatten* and Korngold's *Die Tote Stadt* and was much admired singing in operettas by Strauss and Suppé.

1933 Grand Duchess Alexandra
Grossfürstin Alexandra is an Austrian film starring Jeritza as a Russian Grand Duchess who flees to Vienna after the Revolution and becomes an opera singer. Franz Lehár wrote the original music for this musical set in Czarist Russia and postwar Vienna. Jeritza looks beautiful and sounds splendid in scenes from *Aida* and *La Forza del Destino*. Paul Hartmann plays Grand Duke Michael and Leo Slezak is Duke Nikolai. Wilhelm Thiele directed. Black and white. In German. 85 minutes.

1983 I Live for Art - Tosca
Jeritza is talked about quite a lot in this Tosca documentary, especially by Ljuba Welitsch who considers her the best Tosca ever. Jeritza is pictured singing on stage in *Aida* in her Austrian film but tells her teacher that she wants to sing the role of Tosca. She is told she will have to wait until she is ready. Muriel Balash directed the documentary. Color. In English. 91 minutes. Kultur video.

JERUSALEM, SIEGFRIED
German tenor (1940-)

Siegfried Jerusalem is noted primarily for his performances in Wagner but he can be seen in a lighter vein on video in Strauss's operetta *The Gypsy Baron*. It was his first professional singing appearance and afterwards he decided to stop being a bassoon player and become a singer. He made his opera debut with the Stuttgart Opera in 1975 in *Fidelio* and rose to fame at Bayreuth as Lohengrin, Siegmund and Siegfried. He became a member of the Deutsche Oper in 1978 and made his first appearance at the Metropolitan in 1980 as Lohengrin. A number of his Met performances are on video. See GÖTTERDÄMMERUNG (1990), MEISTERSINGER VON NÜRNBERG, DIE (1984), PARSIFAL (1981/1993), SIEGFRIED (1990), DER ZIGEUNERBARON (1975).

JESSEL, LÉON
German composer (1871-1942)

Léon Jessel, a talented German-Jewish composer killed by the Nazis in 1942, wrote sixteen operettas and some clever piano pieces like "The Parade of the Tin Soldier." He is best remembered for the charming, tuneful operetta *Das Schwarzwaldmädel* (The Black Forest Girl). It premiered at the Berlin Comiche Opera in 1917 with a rustic libretto by August Niehart and has become a favorite of film and TV directors. See DAS SCHWARZWALDMÄDEL.

JOHNSON, TOM
American composer (1939-)

Tom Johnson first became known as a music critic for the *Village Voice* when he helped promote new opera composers like Robert Ashley and Philip Glass. His 1972 *The Four Note Opera* became popular for its intriguing use of only four notes and was telecast and then reprised at universities after its New York premiere. His next opera was *Masque Of Clouds*, a collaboration with Robert Kushner staged at The Kitchen in 1976. Johnson moved to Paris in 1982 and began to write operas with French and German librettos. The most famous is the 1986 *Riemannoper* based on definitions from the German musical dictionary *Riemann Musik Lexikon*.

1972 The Four Note Opera
Johnson says his minimalist opera was strongly influenced by Pirandello's *Six Characters in Search of an Author*. It uses only the four notes A, B, D and E. The libretto by Johnson and Robert Kushner allows the singers to describe the music they sing. Like Pirandello's characters they are aware that they are only performers and that their destiny is to be obedient to the score. A version of the opera was telecast on the Camera Three program on CBS Television in 1972. Color. In English. 30 minutes.

JONES, CHUCK
American animation director (1920-)

Chuck Jones, one of the great masters of film animation, worked at Warner Brothers from 1938 to 1963 and created many of the studio's most inventive cartoons. His Bugs Bunny, Daffy Duck and Road Runner cartoons are amazing in their vitality and humor. His greatest achievement, however, are the opera cartoons *What's Opera, Doc?*

and *The Rabbit of Seville*. Jones was greatly assisted by his screenwriter Michael Maltese.

1949 Long-Haired Hare
This was Jones' first attempt to wed Bugs Bunny to the music of Rossini's *The Barber of Seville*. It features the tough-talking rabbit and the aria "Largo al factotum." Color. 7 minutes.

1950 The Rabbit of Seville
One of the great opera cartoons. Bugs Bunny has a grand time to *Barber of Seville* music including the Overture and "Largo al factotum." The film begins with hunter Elmer Fudd chasing Bugs across the stage of the Hollywood Bowl as the curtain goes up showing the rabbit as the barber and Elmer as his customer. Bugs sings to Elmer as he shaves him and ends up marrying him. Jones directed and Michael Maltese wrote the script and the new words. Warner Bros. Color. 7 minutes.

1957 What's Opera, Doc?
This Chuck Jones cartoon, one of the great animated opera films, was admired by Picasso for its awe-inspiring art. It's a brilliant pastiche of Wagner written by Michael Maltese. Elmer Fudd hunts Bugs Bunny singing "Kill da wabbit, kill da wabbit" to the "Ride of the Valkyries" music. When Bugs disguises himself as Brünnhilde, they sing a love duet. When Bugs loses his disguise, Elmer throws a lightning bolt at him. Jones says this was the most difficult film he ever made. It's also the best. Warner Brothers. Color. 8 minutes.

JONES, GWYNETH
Welsh soprano (1936-)

Dame Gwyneth Jones began her remarkable career as a mezzo-soprano in Zurich in 1962 but made her reputation as Lady Macbeth with the Welsh National Opera and the Royal Opera. She was soon a regular at Covent Garden, Bayreuth, Vienna and other opera houses and made her debut at the Metropolitan in 1972 as Sieglind. Her powerful voice and strong stage presence can be experienced on a number of videos including the 1980 Bayreuth *Ring* where she sings Brünnhilde. See FIDELIO (1970), GÖTTERDÄMMERUNG (1980), DER RING DES NIBELUNGEN (1980), DER ROSENKAVALIER (1979), SIEGFRIED (1980), TRISTAN UND ISOLDE (1993), IL TROVATORE (1964), LA VOIX HUMAINE (1990), DIE WALKÜRE (1980), ZURICH (1984).

JOPLIN, SCOTT

American composer (1868-1917)

Scott Joplin is the Chopin of ragtime, the composer who perfected the form of this style of music and created masterpieces in it like "The Maple Leaf Rag." He was much admired in the early years of the century but was almost forgotten when Joshua Rifkin and the film *The Sting* made him famous all over again. His recognition as an opera composer was late arriving. His great opera *Treemonisha* was performed only once in his life time. He produced it himself in Harlem in 1915 with only a piano and it was such a failure that it led to insanity and early death. The opera was virtually forgotten for fifty years but won warm admiration in 1972 when it was finally staged professionally. Joplin was awarded a posthumous Pulitzer Prize in 1974. See also TREEMONISHA.

1977 Scott Joplin
Billy Dee Williams portrays Joplin in this film biography in which his rise to success and his ambition to write the opera *Treemonisha* are central. The cast includes Art Carney as publisher John Stark, Margaret Avery, Eubie Blake, Godfrey Cambridge and Sam Fuller. It was written by Christopher Knopf and directed by Jeremy Paul Kagan. Color. 96 minutes.

JOURDAN, PIERRE

French film director

Pierre Jourdan has directed several films of operas on stage at the Orange Festival in France, most of them shot live and intended for television. Best known are his *Fidelio* with Gundula Janowitz shot on stage without an audience and a live *Norma* with Montserrat Caballé. His post-modern *Ciboulette* is highly entertaining and he had international distribution for his 1970 film with Rudolph Nureyev titled *I Am a Dancer*. Some of his Orange Festival films are on video and some on Japanese laserdiscs. See AIDA (1976), CIBOULETTE (1985), FIDELIO (1977), NORMA (1974), TRISTAN UND ISOLE (1973), IL TROVATORE (1973).

JUIVE, LA

1835 opera by Halévy

Fromental Halévy's grand opera *The Jewess* is not in fashion today and is not complete on video but it was hugely popular in the 19th century. The jewess

of the title is Rachel who loves Prince Leopold. When she refuses to convert to Christianity, Cardinal de Brogni has her thrown into a boiling cauldron. It is then revealed that she was actually de Brogni's daughter. Eugène Scribe wrote the libretto. The opera is on CD with José Carreras and June Anderson. See also FROMENTAL HALÉVY.

1927 Giovanni Martinelli films
Giovanni Martinelli made two one-reel sound films of arias from the opera for the Vitaphone company in 1927. In one he sings the aria "Va pronouncer la mort" from Act IV. In the other he sings the role of Lazarus opposite bass Louis d'Angelo who plays Cardinal de Brogni. They sing the duet from Act IV in costume in a staged scene. Black and white. About 6 minutes each. Bel Canto Society video.

JULIETTA

1938 opera by Martinu

Bohuslav Martinu's Czech opera is based on Georges Neveux's enigmatic play *Juliette ou la Clé des Songes* (Juliette or the Key of Dreams). It's a rather mysterious opera set somewhere out of time and concerning a man seeking an illusion of the past. Michael is the man who is looking for the dream that is Juliette. See also BOHUSLAV MARTINU.

1969 Václav Kaslík film
Czech director/conductor/composer Václav Kaslík created a film version of Martinů's opera for Czechoslovakian television. It was first screened in 1969. Color. In Czech. 100 minutes.

Related film

1951 Marcel Carné film
French director Marcel Carné made a famous film version of the Georges Neveux play that provided the libretto for the opera. Gérard Philipe stars as the dreamer Michel with Suzanne Cloutier as the mysterious Juliette. Black and white. In French. 90 minutes.

JUNGE LORD, DER

1965 opera by Henze

Hans Werner Henze's opera *The Young Lord* was commissioned by Berlin's Deutsche Oper and premiered there in 1965. A tribute to Italian *opera buffa*, it is based on a story by Wilhelm Hauff with a libretto by Ingeborg Bachmann. A young English lord arrives in a small German town in 1830 and upsets the local gentry with his odd behavior. The main characters are Luise and Wilhelm who fall in love. The lord himself is finally discovered to be a performing ape. See also HANS WERNER HENZE.

1968 Deutsche Oper, Berlin

Edith Mathis plays Luise with Donald Grobe as Wilhelm in this German film of the opera made with the original stage cast, director and orchestra. Gustav Rudolf Sellner, who staged the Deutsche Oper production, directed the film. The cast includes Barry McDaniel as the Secretary, Loren Driscoll as Barrat, Charles Williams, Lisa Otto, Margarete Anst and Vera Little. Christoph von Dohnanyi conducts the Berlin Deutsche Oper Chorus and Orchestra. The film was shown theatrically in the U. S. Unitel Color. In German. 136 minutes.

JURINAC, SENA
Yugoslav soprano (1921-)

Sena Jurinac, who made her debut in 1942 in Zagreb, was particularly admired in her early career for her performances in Mozart and was a favorite at the Glyndebourne Festival. She sang Dorabella in *Così Fan Tutte* with the Glyndebourne company at Edinburgh in 1948 and later appeared as the Countess and both Donnas in *Don Giovanni*. She made a famous recording of *The Marriage of Figaro* in 1955 at Glyndebourne with Sesto Bruscanti as Figaro and they can be seen on stage in it in Anthony Asquith's film *On Such a Night*. Her repertory also included Strauss, Verdi, Berg and Humperdinck. She can be seen as Octavian in Paul Czinner's Salzburg film of *Der Rosenkavalier*, as Marie in a German *Wozzeck* and as the Witch in *Hansel and Gretel*. See HANSEL AND GRETEL (1981), THE MARRIAGE OF FIGARO (1955 film), DER ROSENKAVALIER (1960), WOZZECK (1967).

K

KABAIVANSKA, RAINA
Bulgarian soprano (1934-)

Soprano Raina Kabaivanska is particularly liked as Madama Butterfly and Tosca but has a wide range of roles. She made her debut in Sofia in 1967, sang regularly at La Scala and the Metropolitan from the beginning of the 1960s and became popular all over the world for her warm voice and agreeable stage personality. There are excellent videos of her as Tosca and Butterfly. See MARIA CALLAS (1993), DIVAS (1991), FALSTAFF (1982), MADAMA BUTTERFLY (1983), PAGLIACCI (1968), LUCIANO PAVAROTTI (1991/1992), TOSCA (1976/1983/1993).

KACSÓH, PONGRAC
Hungarian composer (1873-1923)

Pongrac Kacsóh is little known in America but he is a national hero in Hungary. His 1904 operetta *János Vitéz* (John the Hero), adapted from a patriotic epic poem by Sándor Petöfi, is the most popular "Hungarian" operetta in contrast to the "Viennese" operettas of Emmerich Kálmán. Kacsóh wrote other music but is known primarily for this stirring work.

JOHN THE HERO
The 1904 operetta *János Vitéz* tells of the fantastic adventures of a peasant soldier named John and incorporates Hungarian songs in its telling. It has been filmed three times in Hungary. In 1917 a silent version was made by Jenö Illés and was screened with live music. In 1938 a 91-minute sound version was made by Béla Gaál and had great success including a U.S. release. In 1973 Marcell Jankovic made an animated feature film of the story.

KAISER VON ATLANTIS, DER
1943 opera by Ullman

The Emperor of Atlantis centers around an Emperor who forces people to make all-out war. Death is so dismayed by the senseless killing that he abdicates and refuses to allow people to die. The Emperor has to capitulate by offering himself as Death's first new subject. The other characters are the Soldier, the Girl, the Loudspeaker and the Drummer. Jewish composer Viktor Ullmann and librettist Peter Kien created the opera in the Terezin (Theresienstadt) concentration camp on the back of SS deportation forms but were sent to Auschwitz before they could stage it. The opera, with its echoes of Weill and Hindemith, has been revived in recent years because of new interest in music suppressed by the Nazis. See also TEREZIN OPERAS, VIKTOR ULLMANN.

1978 John Goldschmidt video
John Goldschmidt staged the opera dramatically in a set designed like a concentration camp with barbed wire and prison spotlights. Siegmund Nimsgern portrays the Emperor and Alexander Malta sings the role of Death while Kerry Woodward conducts the London Sinfonietta. The video production for ARD television in Germany won the Prix Italia. Color. In German. 57 minutes.

KALICH, BERTHA
Romanian soprano (1874-1939)

Bertha Kalich began her opera career in Bucharest singing *Carmen* and *Il Trovatore*. She emigrated to the U.S. in 1895, sang in New York productions of Offenbach's *La Belle Hélène* and Strauss's *The Gypsy Baron* and then moved into non-musical theater. She toured in the play *Marta of the Lowlands*, the basis of the opera *Tiefland*, and starred in a film version of it in 1914. She made three other films in 1916 for Fox but her film career did not take off.

1914 Marta of the Lowlands
Kalich repeats her stage success portraying a woman of the mountains who is kept by a rich man but married off by him to another. J. Searle Dawley directed the film for Famous Players. The play has the same literary source as Eugen D'Albert's opera *Tiefland*. Paramount. Black and white. About 70 minutes.

1916 Slander
Kalich has a happy marriage so a seducer sets out to destroy it so she will wed him. She discovers his duplicity and returns to her husband. Will S. Davis directed for Fox. Black and white. About 70 minutes.

1916 Ambition

Kalich plays the wife of an ambitious attorney. She leaves him when she finds he is willing to give her to another to advance his career. James Vincent directed the film for Fox. Black and white. About 70 minutes.

1916 Love and Hate

A man tells lies about Kalich so her husband will divorce her. In the end the truth comes out. James Vincent directed. Fox. Black and white. About 80 minutes.

KÁLMÁN, EMMERICH
Hungarian composer (1882-1953)

Emmerich Kálmán is out of fashion in America as are most other traditional operetta composers but he retains a strong following in central Europe. As he wrote lovely melodies, it is likely his star will rise again. In the meantime his major operettas can still be enjoyed on German videos. Kálmán was Hungarian but he modeled his operettas on the Viennese style created by Strauss and Lehár and he premiered most of his operettas in Vienna. His greatest success came with *Die Csárdásfürstin* in 1915 but *Gräfin Mariza* and *Die Zirkusprinzessin* were also popular. He also wrote one operetta for Broadway. Like many other composers, Kálmán had to flee when the Nazis took over Austria. He eventually settled in the U.S. where he continued to compose until his death. See DIE BAJADERE, DIE CSÁRDÁSFÜRSTIN, GOLDEN DAWN, GRÄFIN MARIZA, DIE ZIRKUSPRINZESSIN.

1931 Ronny

Kálmán wrote this German film operetta for Käthe von Nagy with Willy Fritsch as her romantic partner. It has the surefire operetta plot of the prince and the poor girl who wins his heart. In this variation the prince writes an operetta which stars the girl. Reinhold Schunzel directed for UFA. Black and white. In German. 87 minutes.

1958 Die Csárdaskönig

The Czardas King, subtitled *The Emmerich Kálmán Story*, is a German film biography of the composer. Gerhard Riedmann stars as Kálmán in what is essentially a potpourri of scenes and songs from his best-known operettas. Camilla Spira plays Mrs. Kálmán, Rudolf Schock is the tenor János and Marina Orschel is Vera. Harald Philipp directed for CCC. Color. In German. 96 minutes.

KANAWA, KIRI TE
See TE KANAWA, KIRI

KARAJAN, HERBERT VON
Austrian conductor (1908-1989)

Herbert von Karajan, the leading conductor of his time, was deeply involved with opera and film during much of his career and made sure he left a video legacy of his work. After he became director of the Salzburg Festival, he filmed virtually every opera he produced. His early telecasts were produced by the German firm Unitel and have been released on DG videos. He later formed the Telemondial company and filmed his operas himself aided by cinematographer Ernst Wild and audio producer Michel Glotz. Karajan also oversaw the editing of the videos. Most of his operas are available commercially and there are many others of him conducting non-operatic music. See LA BOHÈME (1965), CARMEN (1966), CAVALLERIA RUSTICANA (1968), DON CARLO (1986), DON GIOVANNI (1987), FALSTAFF (1982), LUDWIG II (1955), MADAMA BUTTERFLY (1974), OTELLO (1974), PAGLIACCI (1968), DAS RHEINGOLD (1978), DER ROSENKAVALIER (1960/1984), ST. MATTHEW PASSION, VERDI REQUIEM (1967).

1966 Karajan: Early Images

French master Henri-Georges Clouzot filmed these extraordinary early images of Karajan at work. He conveys the intensity of the music and conducting through fluid camera movement, unusual angles and jump cuts. Featured are Beethoven's Symphony No. 5, Dvorák's New World Symphony and Schumann's Symphony No. 4. Black and white. 95 minutes. DG video and laser.

1978 Impressions of Herbert von Karajan

Czech director Vojtech Jasny created this informative bi-lingual documentary produced for British and German television. It was made to mark the 70th birthday celebrations of the conductor. Color. In English at 50 minutes, in German at 60 minutes.

1975/1978 Karajan Conducts

Karajan leads the Berlin Philharmonic at New Year's Eve programs in 1975 and 1978. The programs include a number of opera overtures and intermezzi from *L'Amico Fritz*, *La Forza del Destino* and *Tannhäuser*. Karajan himself directed the videos. Color. DG video and laser.

1987 Karajan in Salzburg
Karajan, aged 80, is seen at work and at home during the 1987 Salzburg Festival. He talks about the 43 films he has made as his legacy and shows off his video editing room. *Don Giovanni*, *Tannhäuser* and *Tristan und Isolde* are seen in rehearsal and performance with Jessye Norman (*Tristan und Isolde*), Kathleen Battle and Samuel Ramey (*Don Giovanni*), Julia Varady and others. He also talks with two rising young singers, Sumi Jo and Cecilia Bartoli, both virtually unknown at the time. Susan Froemke, Peter Gelb and Deborah Dickson made this excellent documentary. Color. In English and German. 84 minutes. Sony video.

KASLÍK, VÁCLAV
Czech composer/conductor (1917-1989)

Václav Kaslík, who directed a number of operas and operettas for film and television, composed two screen operas. He composed the 1961 TV opera *Krakatit* based on a story by Karel Capek and he used Federico Fellini's film *La Strada* as the basis for a 1980 opera. Kaslík was a noted conductor and the founder of a grand opera house in Prague. See also JULIETTA (1969), RUSALKA (1962), LA STRADA, THE TALES OF HOFFMANN (1970), ZIGEUNERLIEBE (1974).

1961 Krakatit
Kaslík's television opera *Krakatit*, telecast on Czech TV in March 1961, is based on a 1925 novel by Karel Capek, the Czech writer who gave us the word "robot." The novel, published in English as *An Atomic Fantasy*, is the prophetic story of an inventor who discovers atomic power and finds that people want to make bombs out of it. In the opera the tenor inventor struggles to keep his explosive away from the deep-voiced militants. Black and white. In Czech. 90 minutes.

KASTLE, LEONARD
American composer (1929 -)

New Yorker Leonard Kastle helped stage Menotti operas on Broadway and was a music director on the ambitious NBC Opera Theatre. His first two operas were commissions for the NBC company, *The Swing* (1956) and *Deseret* (1961). Many of his operas are set in 19th century America. *Deseret* deals with Mormon leader Brigham Young, *The Pariahs* is

about American whalers and *The Calling of Mother Ann* and *The Journey of Mother Ann* are concerned with the Shakers. See also DESERET.

1956 The Swing
Kastle's opera *The Swing* was written on commission for the NBC Opera Theatre. It was telecast on June 11, 1956. Black and white. In English. 60 minutes.

KATERINA ISMAILOVA
1962 opera by Shostakovich

Dimitri Shostakovich's opera premiered in Leningrad in 1934 as *Lady Macbeth of the Mtsensk District* and was a success until Stalin went to see it in December 1935. He didn't like it. *Pravda* published a vicious attack on the opera in January 1936 and the opera was withdrawn. It did not surface again until after Stalin's death in 1962 when Shostakovich presented a revised version as *Katerina Ismailova*. This was filmed starring Galina Vishnevskaya; she talks about it and the different versions of the opera in her autobiography. The libretto by the composer and Alexander Preis is based on a famous story by Nikolai Leskov. Katerina is a bored housewife who has an affair with her servant Sergei. When her father-in-law Boris discovers this, she poisons him and then they murder her husband Zinovy. They are exiled to Siberia where Sergei seduces another woman and Katerina drowns her rival and herself. The original version of the opera has now been revived. See DIMITRI SHOSTAKOVICH.

1966 Galina Vishnevskaya film
Russian soprano Galina Vishnevskaya is outstanding as Katerina Ismailova in this superb Soviet film by Mikhail Shapiro shot on location in natural settings. The fine cinematography is by Rostislav Davydov. Most of the roles are played by actors with their singing dubbed. Sergei is played by V. Trepyak and sung by Artem Inozemtsev, Boris Ismailov is A. Verdernikov sung by Alexandrovich Sokolov and Zinovy is V. Reka sung by T. Gavirolova. Konstantin Simeonov conducts the Shevchenko Opera and Ballet Theater Orchestra of Kiev. Color. In Russian. 116 minutes. On Japanese laserdisc.

Related films

1962 Siberian Lady Macbeth
Polish director Andrezj Wajda's film is based on the same Leskov story and uses the Shostakovich music as its score. It stars Olivera Markovic as Katerina and Lujba Tadic as Sergei. It was made in Yugoslavia. Black and white. 94 minutes.

1994 Katia Ismailova
Valeri Todorovski's Russian film is based on a modernized version of the Leskov story and stars Ingeborga Dapkounaite as Katerina. The Shostakovich music is not used. Color. In Russian. 88 minutes.

KATYA KABANOVA
1921 opera by Janácek

Leo Janácek's powerful *Katya Kabanova* (Kát'a Kabanová) is based on Russian writer Alexander Ostrovsky's 1859 play *The Thunderstorm* and deals with adultery, guilt and suicide. Katya is the frustrated wife of the timid Tichon and is dominated by her shrewish mother-in-law Kabanicha but she is able to share spiritual ideas with her friend Varvara. She becomes infatuated with Boris and has a secret affair while her husband is away. When he returns during a thunderstorm, Katya makes a guilt-stricken public confession of her adultery. After a reunion with Boris, she drowns herself in the Volga. See also LEO JANÁCEK.

1977 Drahomíra Tikalova video
Czech soprano Drahomíra Tikalova stars as Katya Kabanova in this Czechoslovakian television production of the opera. Tenor Beno Blachut is her co-star while Jaroslav Krombholc conducts the Prague National Theater Chorus and Orchestra. This version is also available on CD. Color. In Czech. 105 minutes. On Japanese laserdisc.

1988 Glyndebourne Festival
Nancy Gustafson stars as Katya Kabanova in this outstanding Glyndebourne Festival production by Nicholaus Lehnhoff. Felicity Palmer is the domineering Kabanicha, Louise Winter is Varvara, Ryland Davies is Tichon and Barry McCauley is Boris. Andrew Davis conducts the London Philharmonic Orchestra and Glyndebourne Festival Chorus. Tobias Hoheisel designed the sets and

Derek Bailey directed the video. Color. In Czech with English subtitles. 100 minutes. Home Vision video.

KEENLYSIDE, SIMON
English baritone (1959-)

Simon Keenlyside is one of the new generation of baritones and a fine actor as well as singer. He had great success in *Billy Budd* in Glasgow in 1992 and his career is now widening from Glasgow and Hamburg to Geneva, Paris and Milan. He can be seen on video as the poet Olivier opposite Kiri Te Kanawa in a San Francisco production of *Capriccio*. See CAPRICCIO (1992).

KENNY, YVONNE
Australian soprano (1950 -)

Yvonne Kenny was born in Sydney but she made her professional debut in London in 1975 and then became a regular at Covent Garden. She has since returned to Australia for performances with the Australian Opera although her fine coloratura technique has made her in demand all over the world. She is featured as the voice of Melba in an Australian film. See also IDOMENEO (1983), THE IMPRESARIO (1991), THE MAGIC FLUTE (1986), MITRIDATE (1983, 1986), NELLIE MELBA (1988), ROYAL OPERA HOUSE (1986), WILLIAM WALTON (1987).

KERN, JEROME
American composer (1885 - 1945)

Most of the musicals of Jerome Kern, one of the finest composers of the century, are outside the boundaries of this reference book. *Show Boat*, which developed out of the operetta format and virtually created the new genre of the American musical, was the first musical to enter the opera house repertory and has been recorded by opera singers. Kern also dabbled on the edges of European-style operetta. He was involved in the American adaptation of Emmerich Kálmán's operetta *Die Csárdásfürstin* staged in 1917 as *The Riviera Girl*. His 1931 *The Cat and the Fiddle*, a kind of modernized operetta, was filmed in 1934 with Jeanette MacDonald. His 1932 *Music in the Air* is set in the Central European operetta milieu and features an operetta singer as one of its stars. Kern wrote as brilliantly for the cinema as for the stage including such classic movies as *Swing Time* and *Cover Girl*. There is also a film biography with an an all-star cast. See THE CAT AND THE FIDDLE, MUSIC IN THE AIR, SHOW BOAT.

1946 Till the Clouds Roll By
This all-star MGM film biography of Jerome Kern contains highlights from his musical career and a potted version of *Show Boat*. Robert Walker portrays Kern and the singers include Judy Garland, Frank Sinata, Kathryn Grayson, Dinah Shore, Tony Martin, Angela Lansbury, Caleb Peterson and Lena Horne. Richard Whorf directed. Color. 137 minutes

KEUSCHE SUSANNE, DIE
1910 operetta by Gilbert

Modest Susanne is an ironic operetta about people pretending to be more virtuous than they really are and centers around a baron caught at the Moulin Rouge in Paris. German composer Jean Gilbert is not much remembered in the English-speaking world today but his operetta was once very popular all over the world. It was staged in London as *The Girl in the Taxi* with Yvonne Arnaud and has been filmed in five countries. It remains popular on stage in Latin America where it has become part of the zarzuela repertory; it was last presented in the U.S. in Miami in 1978 in Spanish as a zarzuela. See also JEAN GILBERT.

1926 Lillian Harvey film
The first film of the operetta made British singer-dancer Lillian Harvey famous though it was shot before the coming of sound to the movies. *Die Keusche Susanne* was made in Germany starring Harvey as Susanne opposite Willy Fritsch. Richard Eichberg and Hans Sturm directed. Black and white. About 78 minutes.

1937 The Girl in the Taxi
The Girl in the Taxi is an English film of the operetta using the title it was given on stage in London. Frances Day stars as Suzanne, Henri Garat portrays René Boisiurette, Lawrence Grossmith is the Baron and Jean Gillie is Jacqueline. The film was directed by André Berthomieu, photographed by Roy Clark and produced by British Unity Pictures. Black and white. In English. 72 minutes.

1937 La Chaste Suzanne
The French version of the above production, shot in England at the same time with director André Berthomieu, has a different cast and is titled *La Chaste Suzanne*. Meg Lemonnier stars as Suzanne Pomarel, Henri Garat is René Boisiurette and Raimu is the Baron. Black and white. In French. 90 minutes.

1944 La Casta Susanna
The German operetta was made into a Spanish-language Argentine film in 1944 under the title *La Casta Susanna*. It was directed by zarzuela film specialist Benito Peroja during his period of exile from Spain. Black and white. In Spanish. 89 minutes.

1952 El Casto Susano
Joaquin Pardavé directed this Spanish-language variation of the operetta in Mexico with the masculine title *El Casto Susano*. It was produced by Filmex. Black and white. In Spanish. 87 minutes.

KHOVANSHCHINA
1886 opera by Mussorgsky

The Khovansky Affair, an epic historic opera, was left unfinished by Modest Mussorgsky when he died in 1881; it was completed by Rimsky-Korsakov in 1886. The opera was inspired by the bicentenary of Tsar Peter the Great and describes a plot at the beginning of Peter's reign. The complicated libretto by Mussorgsky and Vladimir Stassov concerns the struggle of a group of radicals led by Prince Ivan Khovansky and their collaboration with the Old Believers led by dissenter Dosifei. Khovansky's son Andrei and Old Believer prophetess Marfa have a hopeless love affair and all ends badly. There are, rather surprisingly, four screen versions of the opera. See also MODEST MUSSORGSKY

1959 Vera Stroyeva film
Vera Stroyeva directed this wide screen version of the opera with Mark Reisen as Dosifei. Alexei Krivchenya is Prince Ivan Khovansky, Anton Grigoriev is Andrei Khovansky, Vladimir Petrov is Prince Golitsyn, Kira Leonova is Marfa, Yevgeny Kibkalo is the boyar Shaklovity, and the Persian dancer is played by Maya Plistetskaya. The Bolshoi Opera Ballet and Orchestra provide support. The opera was adapted for the screen by Dimitri Shostakovich, Anna Abramova and Stroyeva. Color. In Russian with English subtitles. 131 minutes. Corinth video.

1979 Bolshoi Opera
Yevgeny Nesterenko stars as Dosifei in this Bolshoi Opera stage production. Irina Arkhipova is Marfa, Alexander Vedernikov is Ivan Khovansky, Georgi Andruschenko is André Khovansky, Evgeny Raikov is Prince Galitsyn, Vladislav Romanovsky is Shaklovity and Vitaly Vlasov is Scribe. Yuri Simonov conducts the Bolshoi Theater Orchestra and Chorus with the Rimsky-Korsakov orchestration. Color. In Russian with English subtitles. 172 minutes. Kultur video.

1989 Vienna State Opera
Nicolai Ghiaurov portrays Prince Ivan Khovansky in this fine Vienna State Opera production by Alfred Kirchner. Vladimir Atlantov is Prince Andrei Khovansky, Paata Burchuladze is Dosifei, Ludmila Semtschuk is Marfa, Yuri Marusin is Prince Vassily Golitsin, Brigitte Poschner-Klebel is Susanna and Anatoly Kocherga is the Boyar Shaklovity. Erich Wonder designed the sets and Joachim Herzog the costumes. Claudio Abbado conducted the Vienna State Opera Orchestra and Chorus, Slovak Chorus of Bratislava and Vienna Boys' Choir. The orchestration is by Dmitri Shostakovich with the final scene by Igor Stravinsky. Brian Large directed the video. Color. In Russian with English subtitles. 182 minutes. Home Vision video.

1992 Kirov Opera
Bulat Minzhilkiev portrays Prince Ivan Khovansky and Olga Borodina is Marfa in this strong Kirov Theater production originated by Fyodor Lopukhov and staged by L. Baratov. Yuri Marusin is Andrei Khovansky, Konstantin Pluzhnikov is Goltisin and the Scribe, Nikolai Okhotnikov is Dosifei and Tatiana Kratsova is Emma. The set design is by F. Fedorovsky. Valery Gergiev conducts the Kirov Orchestra, Chorus and Ballet and Brian Large directed the video. Color. In Russian. 210 minutes. Philips Classics video and laser.

KIENZL, WILHELM
Austrian composer (1857-1941)

Wilhelm Kienzl was heavily influenced by Richard Wagner but eventually found his own style and success with the 1895 religious opera *Der Evangelimann* (The Evangelist). It was a popular opera in the early years of the century, especially in German-speaking countries, but is now almost unknown outside Germany. It tells the story of a evangelist and how he comes to forgive his dying evil brother.

1924 Elisabeth Bergner film
Elisabeth Bergner is the star of *Der Evangelimann*, a 1924 German silent film based on the opera and directed by Forrest Holger-Madsen. The cast includes Paul Hartmann, Hanni Weisse, Henrich Peer and Jacob Feldhammer. Union Film. Black and white. In German. About 75 minutes.

KIEPURA, JAN
Polish tenor (1902-1966)

Jan Kiepura was a star of the Vienna State Opera from 1926 to 1937 and well like at La Scala and the Paris Opéra. He also starred in 19 films in Germany, England, France and America, most of which feature opera. His Hungarian soprano wife Marta Eggerth often appeared with him and they became a popular team on film and stage. He made his American debut in Chicago in 1937 in *Tosca*, an opera with which he was often identified. He sang *La Bohème* at the Met in 1938 and continued to sing in opera in America until 1942. That year he and wife began their long starring partnership in *The Merry Widow* on Broadway. His friendship with Erich Korngold resulted in his Hollywood film *Give Us This Night*. See also LA BOHÈME (1937/1947 films), DAS LAND DES LÄCHELNS (1952), MARTA EGGERTH (1949).

1930 City of Song
Jan Kiepura stars as a Neapolitan singer brought to London in this bi-lingual musical directed by Carmine Gallone. Claire Winter is his partner in the British version and Brigitte Helm teams with him in the German version titled *Die Singende Stadt*. In the U.S. it was called *Farewell to Love*. UFA. Black and white. In English or German. 101 minutes. Bel Canto video.

1932 Tell Me Tonight
Kiepura plays an Italian tenor who changes places with a fugitive and falls in love with the mayor's daughter. He sings arias from *La Bohème*, *Rigoletto*, *La Traviata* and *Martha* plus songs by Mischa Spoliansky. Anatole Litvak directed both English and German versions of the film. It was titled *Das Lied einer Nacht* in Germany and *Be Mine Tonight* in the U.S. Black and white. In English or German. 91 minutes. On video.

1934 My Song For You

Kiepura plays a famous tenor brought to Vienna to star in *Aida*. A young woman tries to use his influence to get her boyfriend a job in the opera. The English version was directed by Maurice Elvey with a cast that includes Sonnie Hale, Gina Malo and Emlyn Williams. The German version, titled *Ein Lied fur Dich*, was directed by Joe May and featured Jenny Jugo and Ida Wust. Black and white. In English or German. 87 minutes.

1934 My Heart Is Calling

This is the story of a opera company stranded in France with Kiepura as the company tenor and Marta Eggerth as the woman he loves. Their efforts to get an engagement at the Monte Carlo Opera form the basis of the film. The high point is a performance of *Tosca* on the steps of the opera house while the resident company performs inside. The outsiders win and the audience comes outside to hear the better singers. Carmine Gallone directed versions in English, Italian and German (as *Mein Herz ruft nach Dir*). Black and white. 90 minutes. Opera Dubs video.

1935 Ich Liebe alle Frauen

I Love All Women is a German musical with new music composed by operetta king Robert Stolz. Kiepura plays a singer with help from Lien Deyers and Theo Lingen. Carl Lamac directed. Black and white. In German. 94 minutes. Lyric/ Opera Dubs videos.

1936 Opernring

Kiepura portrays a singing taxi driver who becomes a successful opera tenor and sings in *Turandot* at the Vienna State Opera. Kiepura's co-stars are Friedl Czepa and Theo Lingen. Carmine Gallone directed this Austrian film which won a prize at the Venice Biennnale in 1936. The English title is *Thank You Madame*. Black and white. In German. 91 minutes

1936 Give Us This Night

Kiepura and soprano Gladys Swarthout are the stars of this American film about opera singers. When a tenor singing in *Il Trovatore* is booed, fisherman Kiepura demonstrates his own fine voice and causes a riot. Opera diva Swarthout refuses to sing with the lousy tenor when a new opera is premiered and Kiepura replaces him. The new opera is titled *Romeo and Juliet* and was created for the film by Erich Wolfgang Korngold. Kiepura and Swarthout also sing a duet from *Tosca*. Alexander

Hall directed for Paramount. Black and white. 70 minutes.

KING, JAMES
American tenor (1925-)

James King, who was born in the historic cowtown Dodge City made famous in western movies, began his opera career singing in Florence and moved on to San Francisco in 1961. He reached the Metropolitan in 1966 as Florestan in *Fidelio*. King is particularly popular in Wagner and Strauss operas in Germany. See ARIADNE AUF NAXOS (1988), ELEKTRA (1994), FIDELIO (1970), IL RITORNO D'ULISSE IN PATRIA (1985), DIE TOTE STADT (1986).

KING OF HEARTS
1995 television opera by Torke

King of Hearts is an English TV opera composed by American Michael Torke to a libretto by English writer/director Christopher Rawlence. It's a love triangle story set in contemporary London and involving two teachers, played by Hilton McRae and Lynne Davies, and a therapist, sung by Omar Ebrahim. There are evocations of *Madame Bovary* and the opera she attends in the novel, *Lucia di Lammermoor*. *King of Hearts* was commissioned by Channel Four and first telecast on Feb. 26, 1995. It was staged at Aspen in the summer of 1996. Color. In English. 51 minutes.

KING PRIAM
1962 opera by Tippett

King Priam was Michael Tippett's second major opera and he based his libretto on Homer's *Iliad*. It focuses on King Priam of Troy and through him on the meaning of love, violence, war and death. The opera begins with the birth of Paris, focuses on the Trojan War caused by the love match of Paris and Helen and ends compassionately with Priam's death. The deaths of Patroclus, Hector, Achilles and Paris precede his and are seen as linked. Tippett described the opera as about "the mysterious nature of human choice." See also MICHAEL TIPPETT.

1985 Kent Opera

Nicolas Hytner's outstanding production of the opera for Kent Opera also makes an impressive video. Rodney Macann is a powerful King Priam matched by Sarah Walker as Andromache. Janet

Price is Priam's wife Hecuba, Howard Haskin is Paris, Omar Ebrahim is Hector, Neil Jenkins is Achilles, John Hancorn is Patroclus, Christopher Gillet is Hermes and Anne Mason is Helen of Troy. David Fielding's set is timeless modern with sandbags and barbed wire as basic ingredients. Roger Norrington conducts the Kent Opera Orchestra and Chorus. Robin Lough directed the video. Color. In English. 135 minutes Home Vision video.

KIRKOP, ORESTE
Maltese tenor (1926-)

Oreste Kirkop is from the tiny island country of Malta which also has a tiny operatic tradition. Kirkop studied in Malta for a year, made his debut in Valletta in *Cavalleria Rusticana* and then went to sing in Italy. His career took off in England where he sang with the Carl Rosa Opera Company, Sadler Wells and Covent Garden. After his 1956 film of *The Vagabond King* for MGM with Kathryn Grayson, he sang a 1957 *La Bohème* in Las Vegas and worked with the NBC Opera Theatre. He was featured as the Duke in a 1958 color telecast of *Rigoletto* and afterwards returned to England and Covent Garden. See RIGOLETTO (1958), THE VAGABOND KING (1956).

1956 Bing Presents Oreste
Paramount promotes its new singer Oreste with some help from Bing Crosby in this VistaVision film special. Oreste sings "Vesti la giubba" from *Pagliacci* and joins Bing on some pop songs. Color. 10 minutes.

KIROV OPERA HOUSE
St. Petersburg opera theater

The Kirov Opera House in St. Petersburg (formerly Leningrad), once the Russian Imperial Court Theater, has gone back to its original name of Maryinsky Theater. The Kirov was the site of the premiere of Verdi's *La Forza del Destino* and of many Russian operas including Tchaikovsky's *The Queen of Spades*. It is featured in a number of Soviet opera videos. See BORIS GODUNOV (1990), EUGENE ONEGIN (1984), KHOVANSHCHINA (1992), PRINCE IGOR (1962), THE QUEEN OF SPADES (1960/ 1992), NIKOLAI RIMSKY-KORSAKOV (1952), SADKO (1994), WAR AND PEACE (1991).

1992 Welcome Back, St. Petersburg
A gala evening at the Royal Opera House, Covent Garden, with the Kirov Opera and Ballet and the Kirov Opera Orchestra. There are selections from works by Borodin, Drigo, Minkus, Mussorgsky, Prokofiev, Rimsky-Korsakov and Tchaikovsky. Highlights include arias from Tchaikovsky's *The Enchantress* and Mussorgsky's *Salammbo* and the Kromy Forest scene from *Boris Godunov*. Valery Gergiev conducts the opera sequences and Viktor Fedotov the ballets. Color. In Russian with English subtitles. 90 minutes. Philips video.

KIRSTEN, DOROTHY
American soprano (1915-1992)

Dorothy Kirsten was a protégé of Grace Moore so it was natural for her to appear in the movies. When she sang *Louise* at the Metropolitan Opera in 1947, she dedicated the performance to Moore. Kirsten made her debut in 1940 with the Chicago Grand Opera Company in *Manon*. After performing with the New York City Opera and the San Francisco Opera, she came to the Met in 1945 as Mimi in *La Bohème*. She sang at the Met regularly until her retirement in 1975. She was also featured on radio and TV and recorded popular songs. She can be enjoyed in two films and in Firestone television appearances. See THE GREAT CARUSO, MADAMA BUTTERFLY (1957).

1950 Mr. Music
Kirsten plays herself as Bing Crosby's guest star in this enjoyable musical. She sings a wonderful stage duet with Crosby on "Accidents Will Happen" written by James Van Heusen and Johnny Burke. She's on the Opera side of the stage, he's on the Vaudeville side but their voices intertwine. Crosby's problems as a Broadway composer provide the plot. Richard Haydn directed. Black and white. 113 minutes. Paramount video.

1955 Colgate Comedy Hour
Kirsten sings one aria on this NBC television program. Mannin Ostroff directed. Black and white. 60 minutes. Video at MTR.

1959/62 Dorothy Kirsten in Opera & Song
Kirsten is featured in opera scenes from 1959 and 1962 *Voice of Firestone* telecasts in this video. She portrays Minnie in an extended scene of the poker game in *La Fanciulla del West* with Mario Sereni as Jack Rance and also sings "Vissi d'arte" from *Tosca*.

In other excerpts she duets with Thomas L. Thomas on "And This is My Beloved" from *Kismet* and with Sereni on the song "Romance." Black and white. 23 minutes. VAI video.

1978 An Occasion with Dorothy Kirsten
The Camera Three television program devoted a program to the singer and titled it An *Occasion with Dorothy Kirsten*. In it she both sings and talks about her life and career. The program was telecast on April 18, 1978. Color. 30 minutes. Video at MTR.

KISMET
1953 Borodin pastiche operetta

The pastiche operetta *Kismet* by Robert Wright and George Forrest is based on themes by Russian composer Alexander Borodin, mostly from the opera *Prince Igor*. It tells the story of the witty Arabian poet-beggar Hajj and his success as a sorcerer deceiving a wicked Wazir in Baghdad. The role was created on Broadway by Alfred Drake in 1953. The book is by Charles Lederer and Luther Davis and was based on a 1911 play by Edward Knoblock. Memorable songs include "A Stranger in Paradise" and "Baubles, Bangles and Beads." See also ALEXANDER BORODIN.

1955 Howard Keel film
Howard Keel stars as the singing poet Hajj in this entertaining MGM film directed by Hollywood musical master Vincente Minnelli. Ann Blyth is the poet's daughter loved by young Caliph Vic Damone while Dolores Gray is the flirtatious wife of wicked Wazir Sebastian Cabot. André Previn and Jeff Alexander conducted the music. Color. In English. 113 minutes. MGM/UA video.

1967 José Ferrer film
José Ferrer is featured as the tongue-in-cheek poet who deceives all Baghdad in this ABC television production of the Borodin operetta. Anna Maria Alberghetti sings the role of his daughter Marsinah and George Chakiris portrays the Caliph. The operetta was telecast on Oct. 24, 1967. Color. In English. 90 minutes.

KLEIBER, CARLOS
German conductor (1930-)

Carlos Kleiber, whose father Erich was also a famous conductor, is one of the best-known conductors working today. He has led orchestras at Covent Garden and Edinburgh as well as most of the other major European opera houses. A few of his opera productions are available on video. See CARMEN (1978), DIE FLEDERMAUS (1978), DER ROSENKAVALIER (1979/1994), VIENNA (1991).

KLEMPERER, OTTO
German conductor (1885-1973)

Otto Klemperer, one of the great visionary conductors of the century, began his career in 1906 in Berlin with the Offenbach operetta *Orphée aux Enfers*. He was in demand all over Germany and became the director of the Kroll Theater at its height at the end of the 1920s when he premiered such modern classics as Stravinsky's *Oedipus Rex*. His German career ended when the Nazis took over and he left for America. He returned to conducting in Budapest in 1947 and helped to raise the opera company there to a high level. He made his debut at Covent Garden in 1961 with *Fidelio*. See also CONDUCTORS (1995).

1985 Otto Klemperers Lang Reise Durch Sein Zeit
Phil Bregstein's German documentary film *Otto Klemperer's Long Journey through His Time* places the conductor's life in the context of history. Klemperer talks about his career and about opera and there is commentary from colleagues like Pierre Boulez, Walter Felsenstein, Ernst Block, Paul Dessau, Gottfried Reinhardt and H. H. Stuckenschmidt. His promotion of modern composers caused him problems in both Nazi Germany and Communist Hungary but he also had problems in America where his passport was withdrawn during the anti-Communist witch hunt era. The film is an update of another made in 1974. RM/WDR/ ORF. Black and white. In German. 90 minutes.

KNIGHT, FELIX
American tenor (1913-)

Felix Knight's opera career began after he finished his film career. He worked first for Hal Roach in the Laurel and Hardy versions of two light operas. He is Tom-Tom in Herbert's *Babes in Toyland* and a gypsy singer in Balfe's *The Bohemian Girl*. The Georgian tenor made his opera debut in *La Traviata* at the Hollywood Bowl in 1935 and won a Metropolitan Opera competition in 1938. He did not actually make his Met debut until 1946 but then stayed with the company until the arrival of

Rudolph Bing. He spent the rest of his singing career in recitals and nightclubs. See BABES IN TOYLAND (1934), THE BOHEMIAN GIRL (1936).

KNUSSEN, OLIVER
English composer (1952-)

Glasgow-born Oliver Knussen spent his early musical years experimenting with concert work. He became known as an opera composer through collaborations with American author/illustrator Maurice Sendak. Together they created two of the most popular modern children's operas, *Higglety Pigglety Pop!* and *Where the Wild Things Are*. Knussen has also become one of the leading conductors of modern music and an advisor to musical festivals. See HIGGLETY PIGGLETY POP!, WHERE THE WILD THINGS ARE.

KODÁLY, ZOLTÁN
Hungarian composer (1882-1967)

Zoltán Kodály ranks with Bartók as one of the major modern Hungarian composers and his influence on other Hungarian composers has been notable. He is known to most of the rest of the world primarily for the folksy opera *Háry János* and the orchestral suite based on it. See HÁRY JÁNOS.

KOLLO, RENÉ
German tenor (1937-)

René Kollo is the grandson of Walter Kollo, the composer who wrote the first operetta about the movies. He was born in Berlin, began his career in operetta and made his opera debut in 1965 in *Oedipus Rex* singing at Dusseldorf from 1967 to 1971. He began in light lyric roles and was featured in television films of classic operettas but then shifted to heavier roles, especially the Wagnerian tenor parts. He became a regular at Bayreuth and made his first appearance at the Metropolitan Opera in 1976 as Lohengrin. He also much admired as *Otello* and for his Russian opera roles. See also ARABELLA (1977), ARIADNE AUF NAXOS (1978), LA BELLE HÉLÈNE (1975), DIE CSÁRDÁSFÜRSTIN (1971), FIDELIO (1978), GÖTTERDÄMMERUNG (1989), GRÄFIN MARITZA (1973), DAS LAND DES LÄCHELNS (1973), THE MAGIC FLUTE (1975 film), OBERON (1968), OEDIPUS REX (1973), RUDOLF SCHOCK (1983), SIEGFRIED (1989), TANNHÄUSER (1994), TRISTAN UND ISOLDE (1983/1993), VERONA (1988), WIENER BLUT (1974).

KOLLO, WALTER
German composer (1878-1940)

Walter Kollo was one of Germany's top musical theater composers in the early years of the century and wrote the first operetta about the movies. It was titled *Filmzauber* when it was first staged in Berlin in 1912 and *The Girl on the Film* when it came to London and New York in 1913. The story revolves around a film company's efforts to make a movie about Napoleon. Kollo's romantic 1913 operetta *Wie Einst im Mai*, which provided the basis for Sigmund Romberg's operetta *Maytime*, is still popular in Germany where it continues to be staged in its original form. It has also been filmed. Tenor René Kollo is Walter's grandson and appeared in a Berlin stage production of *Wie einst im Mai* in 1966. See OPERAS & OPERETTAS ABOUT THE MOVIES (1912), WIE EINST IM MAI.

KORJUS, MILIZA
Polish soprano (1902-1980)

Coloratura soprano Miliza Korjus, who starred in two operetta films and was nominated for an Oscar, was born in Warsaw of Swedish and Estonian parents. She sang for many years in Berlin opera houses and then in Vienna, Brussels and Stockholm. She is remembered today mostly for her starring role in *The Great Waltz* for which she received considerable acclaim and an Academy Best Supporting Actress nomination. MGM publicists promoted her with the slogan "Miliza Korjus rhymes with gorgeous." She had a automobile accident soon afterwards and moved to Mexico where she made one further operatic film. Korjus returned to the U.S. for a Carnegie Hall concert in 1944 and later lived in Los Angeles. Her fine coloratura voice can also be enjoyed on record.

1938 The Great Waltz
Korjus portrays Carla Donner, a singer with the Imperial Opera who falls in love with Johann Strauss in this Julien Duvivier film. Strauss (Fernand Gravet) loves Donner but marries sweetheart Poldi (Luise Rainer). Korjus sings his waltzes, get him a publisher and inspires him to write the operetta *Die Fledermaus*. Most of the singing in the film is by Korjus and critics felt it was done well. The film was a big success. Black and white. 100 minutes. On video.

1942 Caballería del Imperio

Chivalry of the Empire is a Mexican film musical that begins with Korjus on stage in Vienna in 1864 singing while Johann Strauss conducts. She goes to Mexico in the era of the Empress Carlotta and the Emperor Maximilian. When bandits invade a restaurant where she is dining, she tells them she is the ambassador from Strauss to Mexico. They believe her after she sings even though it's Bellini's "Casta Diva" rather than Strauss. The film also features Mexican tenor Pedro Vargas. Miguel Contreras Torres directed. Black and white. In Spanish. 139 minutes. Opera Dubs video.

KORNGOLD, ERICH
American composer (1897-1957)

Moravian-born Erich Wolfgang Korngold was a major opera composer in Europe before he came to Hollywood to compose what he called "operas without singing." There are certainly few opera scores more memorable than his music for *The Adventures of Robin Hood* or *The Sea Hawk*. He also wrote an imaginary opera called *Romeo and Juliet* for the film *Give Us This Night* and worked on the Wagner biopic *Magic Fire*. His most successful opera on stage was the symbolist *Die Tote Stadt* (1920) which is beginning to come back into fashion. See IMAGINARY OPERAS IN FILMS (1936), DIE TOTE STADT, RICHARD WAGNER (1956).

KOSHETZ, NINA
Ukrainian soprano (1894-1965)

Nina Koshetz, the Kiev-born daughter of a Bolshoi tenor, made her debut in 1913 with the Zimin Opera Company. She performed in Russia until 1920 when she went to Chicago to sing in the premiere of Prokofiev's *The Love of Three Oranges*. She continued to sing around the world until 1940 when she retired and opened a Hollywood restaurant. She also worked occasionally in Hollywood movies after starting with the French film *Casanova* in 1926. Her daughter Marina was also an opera singer and can be seen in *The Great Caruso*.

1926 Casanova

Nina Kochitz (so spelled on the film credits) portrays the Countess Vorontzvo in this epic French film version of the story of the great lover. Casanova is played by Ivan Mojoukine and there are many Russian expatriates in the cast. Alexandre Volkoff directed. Black and white. In French. 110 minutes.

1935 Enter Madame

Koshetz sings arias from *Tosca* and *Cavalleria Rusticana* for Elissa Landi in this charming film about a glamorous opera singer who marries millionaire Cary Grant. He follows her around the world from opera house to opera house. Elliott Nugent directed. Paramount. Black and white. 83 minutes.

1938 Algiers

Koshetz portrays Tania in this American remake of the French film *Pépé le Moko*. Charles Boyer and Hedy Lamar are the stars and John Cromwell directed. Black and white. 95 minutes.

1939 Wife, Husband and Friend

Koshetz provides the voice for Binnie Barnes who portrays an opera diva in this film of James Cain's story *Career in C. Major*. Warner Baxter and Loretta Young play would-be opera singers. Black and white. 75 minutes.

1944 Our Hearts Were Young and Gay

Koshetz plays a old-style grand opera diva in this fine comedy directed by Lewis Allen. The film is based on a book by two women who enjoyed 1920s Paris and wrote about the life that late they had led there. Paramount. Black and white. 81 minutes.

1944 Summer Storm

Kotshetz portrays a singer in 1912 provincial Russia in a Chekhov story about a judge who falls for a loose lady. George Sanders and Linda Darnell are the stars and Douglas Sirk directed. Black and white. 106 minutes.

1947 The Chase

Koshetz has a supporting role to stars Michèle Morgan and Robert Cummings in this *film noir* set in Cuba and based on a Cornell Woolrich novel. Arthur Ripley directed. Black and white. 86 minutes.

1950 It's a Small World

Koshetz has a small role in one of the odder Hollywood genre films. Midget Paul Dale has a bad time until he gets adjusted to his size. William Castle directed. Black and white. 68 minutes.

1952 Captain Pirate

Koshetz has only a supporting role in this pirate movie starring Louis Hayward and Patrica Medina. Ralph Murphy directed for Columbia. Black and white. 85 minutes.

1955 Hot Blood

Koshetz's last film was directed by Nicholas Ray. It stars Jane Russell and Cornel Wilde and tells a story about gypsies. Columbia. Black and white. 85 minutes.

KOWALSKI, JOCHEN

German countertenor (1954-)

Jochen Kowalski, who made his debut with the Komische Oper while still a student, has become one of the most popular countertenors in the world. He sings both modern and baroque but is especially noted for his Gluck Orpheus and his Handel operas. Some of his most enjoyable operas are on video. See BELSHAZZAR (1985), CASTRATOS (1992), DIE FLEDERMAUS (1990), GIUSTINO (1985), ORFEO ED EURIDICE (1991), MITRIDATE (1991).

KRÁSA, HANS

German composer (1899-1944)

Hans Krása was born in Prague, worked all over Europe and died in Auschwitz. His first opera, based on a story by Dostoyevsky, was composed in 1933. He is remembembered today mostly for his simple but highly effective children's opera *Brundibar*. It was created for children at a Prague orphanage in 1938 and the Jewish children took it with them when they were deported to the concentration camp at Terezin. It was staged there in 1943for the International Red Cross as a show piece. See BRUNDIBAR.

KRAUS, ALFREDO

Spanish tenor (1927-)

Lyric tenor Alfredo Kraus, who is known in Spain for his performances in both operas and zarzuelas, made his debut in Cairo in 1956. He rose to prominence in Italy and Spain singing in 1958 with Maria Callas in *La Traviata* and in 1959 with Joan Sutherland in *Lucia di Lammermoor*. Kraus can be seen in many operatic films and videos. He portrays the 19th century Navarese tenor Julián Gayarre in the film *Gayarre* and can be seen opposite Sutherland in a 1982 video of *Lucia*. See also JUNE

ANDERSON (1989), DON PASQUALE (1979), DOÑA FRANCISQUITA (1988), FAUST (1973/1988), GALA LIRICA, JULIÁN GAYARRE (1959), LUCIA DI LAMMERMOOR (1982), MARINA (1980/1987), METROPOLITAN OPERA (1983), PARIS (1989), OPERA STARS IN CONCERT, WERTHER (1991).

1958 The Vagabond and the Star

Kraus portrays an opera singer opposite dancer Ana Esmeralda in the Spanish musical *El Vagabundo y la Estrella*. He sings arias from *Lucia di Lammermoor, I Puritani, La Bohème, Il Trovatore* and *Xerxes*. Mateo Cano and Jose Luis Merino directed. Color. In Spanish. 80 minutes. Bel Canto/Opera Dubs/Lyric video.

KRAUSE, TOM

Finnish baritone (1934-)

Finland's Tom Kraus began his opera career in Berlin as Escamillo in *Carmen* and has been popular in the role ever since. He made his first appearance at the Metropolitan Opera in 1967 as Almaviva in *The Marriage of Figaro*. Krause now sings in a wide range of modern and traditional operas in German and Italian in opera houses around the world. See CARMEN (1972/1983 films), DER FREISCHÜTZ (1968), OEDIPUS REX (1973), THE MARRIAGE OF FIGARO (1968).

KRENEK, ERNST

Austrian composer (1900-1991)

Ernst Krenek, who emigrated to the U.S. because of his difficulties in Nazi Germany, is best known for his 1927 opera *Jonny Spielt Auf*. It was the biggest operatic hit of pre-Nazi Germany and hugely influential in its time because of its jazz characteristics. Krenek, who wrote his own librettos, began creating operas in 1922 starting with *Die Swingburg*. His other major operas include *Karl V* and *Orpheus und Eurydike*. He composed two operas for television.

1962 Ausgerechnet und Verspielt

Krenek's television opera, *Calculate and Gamble*, concerns a mathematician who believes he understands gambling. He works out a formula which he thinks will guarantee that he wins when he plays. It doesn't work, of course. The opera was telecast on July 25, 1962, on Austrian TV.

1968 Der Zauberspiegel
Krenek wrote a libretto with fourteen scenes for his television opera *The Magic Mirror*. It was telecast on Bavarian Television on Dec. 23, 1968.

KRUSCENISKI, SALOMEA
Ukrainian soprano (1872-1952)

Salomea Krusceniski (or Krushelnytska) was one of the great singing actresses of the operatic stage and an important interpreter of the roles of Butterfly, Salome and Aida. She made her debut in Lvov in 1893 and sang primarily in Russia until 1902. After 1903 she became one of the most popular stars of the Italian lyric stage. One of her most famous performances was as Butterfly in the revised production that made the opera a success following its initial failure. She was an exciting Salome and Electra, sang splendidly opposite Caruso and remained a major star until her retirement in 1925.

1987 The Return of Butterfly
Elena Safonova stars as Salomea Krushelnytska in *Vozrastchenié Batterflai*, a Soviet Ukrainian biography of the soprano. The film begins with the singer aged 80 telling the audience about her early life and remembering scenes from it, especially her triumph in *Madama Butterfly*. Her life from childhood to fame is presented with arias by Puccini, Mascagni, Strauss and Wagner as well as Ukrainian folk songs. The supporting cast includes Ivan Mikolaichuk, Ivan Gavriliuk and Galina Zolotareva. Valerie Vrublevskaya wrote the film and Oleg Fialko directed it. Dovzhenko Studios. Color. In Ukrainian. 90 minutes.

KUBRICK, STANLEY
American film director (1928-)

Stanley Kubrick began making movies in 1951 and won international acclaim in 1957 for the anti-war film *The Paths of Glory*. Three of his films have musical interest: *Barry Lyndon* (1975) uses instrumental operatic music in keeping with the period of the film including the Cavatina from Paisiello's *The Barber of Seville* and the March from Mozart's *Idomeneo*. There is also music by Bach, Handel, Schubert and Vivaldi. *2001: A Space Odyssey* (1968) uses music by Johann and Richard Strauss and Gyorgy Ligeti. *A Clockwork Orange* (1971) makes Beethoven's music an integral part of the story.

KULLMAN, CHARLES
American tenor (1903-1993)

Tenor Charles Kullman sang with the Metropolitan Opera for 25 seasons in a wide variety of roles and was noted for his pleasing stage personality. He studied at Yale and Juilliard and made his debut as Pinkerton in 1929 with the American Opera Company. He then went to Europe and built his career in Berlin, Vienna, Salzburg and Covent Garden. He returned to America and began his long Metropolitan career in 1935 singing in *Faust*. He appeared in only one film, *The Goldwyn Follies*, singing on stage in *La Traviata* opposite Met soprano Helen Jepson. See DIE FLEDERMAUS (1953), HELEN JEPSON (1938).

KÜNNEKE, EDWARD
German composer (1885-1953)

Edward Künneke was one of the German operetta composers whose work was so popular in London and New York in the 1920s. The most successful was the 1921 *Der Vetter aus Dingsda* staged in both London and New York and filmed twice. Also popular were *Marriage in Crisis* (1921) and *Casino Girls* (1923). He wrote the Offenbach-esque *The Love Song* (1926) for the Shuberts in New York and had a hit in London with *The Song of the Sea* (1928). Künneke composed twenty-five operettas and the best stand up to comparison with Lehár. See DER VETTER AUS DINGSDA

1960 Eduard Künneke Tribute
Hans Homeberg produced this German television tribute to the composer on what would have been his 75th birthday. The program features highlights from his career and interviews with composer Hans Carste, conductor Willy Stech and producer Heinz Hentsche. There are also reminiscences from his singer-daughter Evelyn Künneke. The program was made in Stuttgart. Black and white. In German. 40 minutes.

KUPFER, HARRY
German opera director (1935-)

The innovative German stage director Harry Kupfer made his debut with the opera *Rusalka* in 1958 and became chief director for the Dresden State Opera in 1972. His highly original interpretation of *Der Fliegende Holländer* at Bayreuth in 1978 made him world famous and his high tech production of *Der*

Ring there also aroused great interest. His *Elektra* for the Welsh National Opera in 1978 was considered a revelation by British critics. He is considered the spiritual heir of Walter Felsenstein for his radical productions. See also THE ABDUCTION FROM THE SERAGLIO (1976), BELSHAZZAR (1985), BERLIN (1989), DER FLIEGENDE HOLLÄNDER (1985), ELEKTRA (1989), GÖTTERDÄMMERUNG (1992), GIUSTINO (1985), PARSIFAL (1993), DAS RHEINGOLD (1991), DER RING DES NIBELUNGEN (1991), SIEGFRIED (1992), DIE SOLDATEN (1988), THE TALE OF TSAR SALTAN (1978), DIE WALKÜRE (1991).

1987 Harry Kupfer Rehearses *Don Giovanni*
Rainer Milzkott directed this TV documentary showing Harry Kupfer at work staging a production of *Don Giovanni*. SFB. Color. In German. 44 minutes.

1989 Der Musik Theater Macher Harry Kupfer
Music Theater Creator Harry Kupfer is a German documentary about the ideas and achievements of opera director Harry Kupfer. It was filmed by Lothar Spree for German and Austrian television. ZDF/ORF. Color. In German. 80 minutes.

L

LABYRINTH
1963 TV opera by Menotti

Gian Carlo Menotti's enigmatic television opera premiered on NBC Opera Theater as *Labyrinth: An Operatic Riddle.* A honeymoon couple looking for the key to their room in a grand hotel meet characters who perhaps represent their life and future. Judith Raskin portrays the Bride, John Reardon is the Groom, Elaine Bonazzi is the Spy, Robert White is the Old Chess Player, Beverly Wolff is the Executive Director and Leon Lishner is the Desk Clerk/Death. When the couple open doors, they see strange things with the help of special effects photography. A traditional opera is staged behind one door, an astronaut floats through space behind another, etc. The opera was staged by Menotti who introduces it. Samuel Chotzinoff produced, Warren Clyner designed the sets, Noel Taylor designed the costumes and Herbert Grossman conducted the Symphony of the Air Orchestra. Kirk Browning directed the telecast on March 3, 1963. Black and white. In English. 45 minutes. See GIAN CARLO MENOTTI.

LADERMAN, EZRA
American composer (1924-)

Ezra Laderman has written four screen operas, three for television and one about a movie star. The most famous is *The Trials of Galileo*, an examination of the life and ideas of the Italian astronomer, televised in 1967 and staged as *Galileo Galilei*. The 1971 *And David Wept* is the story of David and Bathsheba. Third was the 1973 *The Questions of Abraham* about the Jewish leader. His opera *Marilyn* about the life of Marilyn Monroe was staged in 1984 at the New York City Opera. See MARILYN MONROE, THE TRIALS OF GALILEO.

1971 And David Wept
Laderman wrote the television opera *And David Wept* on a commission from CBS News. Joseph Darion's libretto tells the story of the Biblical love affair of David and Bathsheba and its effect on her husband, Uriah the Hittite. The story is told in flashbacks as the protagonists describe how the affair began and how it ended with the death of Uriah. The opera was telecast by CBS on April 8, 1971. It was revised and staged in 1980. Color. In English. 50 minutes.

1973 The Questions Of Abraham
Laderman wrote the television opera *The Questions of Abraham* on commission from CBS. The libretto by Joseph Darion is based on the Biblical story of Abraham, the founder of the Hebrew people. According to the opera, his long life led him to have many questions and unresolved doubts. The opera was telecast by CBS Television on Sept. 30, 1973. Color. In English. 50 minutes.

LADY MACBETH OF THE MTSENSK DISTRICT
See KATERINA ISMAILOVA

LAKMÉ
1883 opera by Delibes

British Airways used the Flower Duet from Léo Delibes' opera in commercials and helped make *Lakmé* once again a popular favorite. It has always been Delibes' best-known work, one of the Far East themed operas favored in France at the end of the 19th century. The libretto by Edmond Gondinet and Philippe Gille is based on Pierre Loti's novel *Rarahu*. Lakmé is the daughter of a Brahmin priest in 19th century India who becomes doomed by her love for a British army officer. Coloratura sopranos love the opera for its showy "Bell Song" which Lily Pons and others often perform in films. See also LÉO DELIBES.

1976 Australian Opera
Joan Sutherland has a great voice and is eminently suited to singing the role of Lakmé. She is not so convincing acting the role of a demure Indian temple priestess but as she sings so superbly in this Sydney Opera House production it really doesn't matter. A highlight is the famous Flower Duet with Huguette Tourangeau as her servant Mallika. Clifford Grant plays the priest Nilakantha, Henri Wilden is Gerald and John Pringle is Frederick. Desmond Digby designed the sets and Richard Bonynge conducted the

Elizabethan Sydney Orchestra. Norman Ayrton was the stage director and John Charles directed the video on August 18, 1976. Color. In French. 153 minutes. Home Vision video/Japanese laserdisc.

Early/related films

1906 Lakmé: Les Stances
An early British sound film was made of a scene from the opera. The music was synchronized on a phonograph when the film was shown. About 3 minutes.

1906 Chronophone film
An excerpt from *Lakmé* was featured on this French sound film made by Leon Gaumont with the Chronophone system. It may be identical with the English film decribed above. About 3 minutes

1933 A Brahmin's Daughter
This American film highlights version of the opera was directed by Howard Highness and made for Kindle-De Valley. Black and white. In English. 22 minutes.

1935 I Dream Too Much
Lily Pons made her film debut opposite Henry Fonda in this RKO picture. She portrays a rising opera singer and sings her signature aria, the Bell Song. John Crumble directed. Black and white. 85 minutes. On video.

1937 Love and Hisses
French actress Simian Simon, who stars in this film as a French singer, apparently asked if she could perform the Bell Song. She does so under the direction of Sidney Lanfield. Black and white. 84 minutes.

1947 It Happened in Brooklyn
Kathryn Grayson sings the Bell Song in this story about Frank Sinatra and other Brooklynites trying to break into musical show business. Richard Whorf directed. Black and white. 105 minutes.

1947 Carnegie Hall
Lily Pons once again sings the Bell Song but this time on stage at Carnegie Hall. The film is a fictional framework for a series of concert numbers by classical music stars. Edgar G. Ulmer

directed. Black and white. 134 minutes. Bel Canto Society video.

1976 Joan Sutherland Making *Lakmé*
A behind-the-scenes documentary about the Australian Opera production of *Lakmé* with Joan Sutherland. It follows the production from concept through design, casting, costuming and rehearsal to opening night. Sutherland is shown rehearsing the Bell Song and Flower Duet with Huguette Tourangeau while conductor Richard Bonynge supervises the production. Color. In English. 60 minutes. Mastervision.

1987 Someone to Watch Over Me
Ridley Scott's film about a cop (Tom Berenger) who becomes involved with the woman he is guarding (Lorraine Bracco) features music from *Lakmé* on the soundtrack. Mady Mesplé sings the Flower Duet with Danielle Millet and the Paris Opéra-Comique Orchestra conducted by Alain Lombard. Color. 106 minutes.

1987 I've Heard the Mermaid Singing
The Flower Duet is featured in this sexually ambiguous Canadian film by Patricia Rozema. A young innocent recounts her life at a trendy art gallery. Color. 83 minutes

1987 Five Corners
Joan Sutherland sings an aria from *Lakmé* on the soundtrack of this Tony Bill film about Jodie Foster and her problem boyfriend. Richard Bonynge conducts the Monte Carlo Opera Orchestra. Color. 94 minutes.

1993 The Hunger
The highlight of Tony Scott's modern vampire movie features the glorious vampire Catherine Deneuve and Susan Sarandon in bed. The music on the soundtrack is, of course, the Flower Duet. Color. 97 minutes.

1993 True Romance
The Flower Duet is again featured in this Tony Scott film which has a screenplay by Quentin Tarantino. The odd couple at the center of the film do somehow live happily ever after. Color. 119 minutes.

1993 Carlito's Way
Brian DePalma's film about a criminal trying to go straight features Al Pacino and Sean Penn. It again features Joan Sutherland in an excerpt from *Lakmé*. Color. 144 minutes.

1995 The American President
The Flower Duet is sung by Mady Mesplé and Danielle Millet on the soundtrack of this film about a love affair between a widowed president (Michael Douglas) and a journalist (Annette Benning). They are accompanied by the Orchestre du Théâter National de l'Opéra-Comique conducted by Alain Lombard. Color. 98 minutes.

LAMAC, KAREL
Czechoslovak film director (1897-1952)

Prague-born Karel (aka Karl) Lamac directed or acted in some 265 films in five languages in Czechoslovakia, Austria, Hungary, Germany, France and England. He began directing in 1919 and a number of his movies were based on operas and operettas with singers like Jan Kiepura and Martha Eggerth. He was married to *Blackmail* star Anny Ondra and she became famous through his films. The pair were major figures in the early Czech cinema. Though never highly ranked by cineastes and mostly ignored in the film histories, Lamac's movies are well-made, entertaining and important in the history of opera and operetta on film. See THE DAUGHTER OF THE REGIMENT (1933), DIE FLEDERMAUS (1931), FRASQUITA (1934), JAN KIEPURA (1935), DIE LANDSTREICHER (1937), MAM'ZELLE NITOUCHE (1931), POLENBLUT (1934), LE POSTILLON DE LONJUMEAU (1936), WHITE HORSE INN 1935), WO DIE LERCHE SINGT (1936).

LAND DES LÄCHELNS, DAS
1923 operetta by Lehár

Franz Lehár's *The Land of Smiles* is about a Viennese woman who marries a Chinese prince and goes to live with him in Peking. She finds life there not as she had imagined and tries to return home but is prevented until the intervention of an old friend. The operetta was made famous by Richard Tauber who starred as Prince Sou-Chong in productions in Vienna, London and New York. In London the operetta was titled *The Land of Smiles*, in New York it was called *Yours Is My Heart* after its hit song "Dein ist mein ganzes herz." The libretto by Ludwig Herzer and Fritz Lohner is based on an earlier Lehár operetta. See also FRANZ LEHÁR.

1930 Richard Tauber film
Richard Tauber stars in this German film of the Lehár operetta made a year after its stage premiere in Berlin in 1929. It was produced by Tauber's own company and directed by Max Reichmann. Mary Losseff is Lisa and the cast includes Hans Mierendorff, Bruno Kastner, Karl Platen and Max Schreck. Black and white. In German. 89 minutes. Opera Dubs/Lyric video.

1952 Jan Kiepura film
Jan Kiepura sings the role associated with Tauber in this 1952 German film. His wife Marta Eggerth gets equal billing in a somewhat altered plot. Prince Sou is now a Siamese prince who meets a Viennese operetta soprano and marries her. They return to Bangkok where some of the film was actually shot. The rest is a comparable Easterner-married-to-Westerner problem. Hans Deppe directed. Black and white. In German. 107 minutes. Opera Dubs/Lyric video.

1973 René Kollo film
René Kollo stars as the Chinese prince with Birgit Pitsch-Sarata as the woman he loves in this lavish colorful German film of the operetta. The cast also includes Dagmar Koller, Heinz Zednik and Fred Liewehr while the South Korean State Ballet play the dancers. Wolfgang Ebert conducted the Stuttgart Radio-Television Orchestra. Arthur Maria Rabenalt directed the film in 35mm for German TV. Unitel/ZDF. Color. In German. 98 minutes.

1992 Sandro Massimini video
Highlights from *Il Paese del Sorriso* are sung by Italian operetta master Sandro Massimini and his associates on the Italian TV series *Operette, Che Passione!* Featured are "Chi nella nostra vita accese amor," "Duetto del the" and "Tu che mi hasi preso il cuor." Color. In Italian. About 15 minutes. Ricordi (Italy) video.

LANDSTREICHER, DIE
1899 operetta by Ziehrer

Die Landstreicher (The Hoboes) is Austrian composer Karl Michael Ziehrer's most popular operetta. It premiered in 1899 and tells the story of a resourceful vagabond husband and wife who find a diamond necklace and a large bank note. Being clever scam artists they find many ways to take advantage of their unexpected fortune. The operetta came to Broadway in 1901 as *The Strollers*. The libretto is by Leopold Krenn and Carl Lindau. See also KARL MICHAEL ZIEHRER.

1937 Karel Lamac film

The operetta was filmed in Germany in 1937 by Hungarian Karel Lamac with a strong cast headed by Paul Hörbiger, Lucie Englisch and Erika Drusovich. Black and white. In German. 89 minutes.

LANG, FRITZ
German film director (1890-1976)

Fritz Lang, who made notable films in Germany, France and America, created his own version of *Die Niebelungen* with a wonderful Siegfried and the Dragon sequence though he did not utilize Wagner's music. He did, however, feature Wagner in his American film *The Blue Gardenia* where Isolde's death music signals a crime of passion. See DER RING DES NIBELUNGEN (1924 film), TRISTAN UND ISOLDE (1953 film).

LANGRIDGE, PHILIP
English tenor (1939 -)

Philip Langridge made his debut at Glyndebourne in 1964 in a minor role but has since sung there as Florestan, Don Ottavio, Tito and Idomeneo. He has also become a regular at both the ENO and Covent Garden and sings at many top European opera houses. He has been most acclaimed for his performances in operas by Britten, Stravinsky and Janáček, many of which are on video. See BILLY BUDD(1988), LES BOREADES (1987), LA CLEMENZA DI TITO (1991), FROM THE HOUSE OF THE DEAD (1992), IDOMENEO (1983), JENUFA (1989), THE MIDSUMMER MARRIAGE (1984), OBERON (1986), OEDIPUS REX (1992), PETER GRIMES (1994), THE SECOND MRS. KONG (1995), THE TURN OF THE SCREW (1982), WOZZECK (1987).

LANTZ, WALTER
Animated film producer (1900-1994)

Walter Lantz created several popular cartoon characters, including Woody Woodpecker and Andy Panda, and received an Academy Award in 1979 in recognition of his contributions. Several of his films use classical music from Rossini to Chopin to Suppé.

1944 The Barber of Seville

The first Woody Woodpecker cartoon is one of the great screwball comedies of the genre and was inspired by music from Rossini's opera *The Barber of Seville*. Woody substitutes for the barber Figaro and sings the "Largo al Factotum" while he gives shaves and haircuts to a Native American and a construction worker. Walter Lantz produced and James Culhane directed. Color. 7 minutes.

1947 Overture to William Tell

This Walter Lantz's Musical Miniature is based around the overture of the Rossini opera *William Tell*. The cartoon features the character Wally Walrus and was directed by Dick Lundy. Color. 7 minutes.

LANZA, MARIO
American tenor (1921 - 1959)

Mario Lanza does not rate an entry in standard opera reference books like the *New Grove Dictionary* but he should. His influence is important and continuing and many of today's top opera singers, including Three Tenors Luciano Pavarotti, José Carreras and Placido Domingo, have noted the effect he had on their careers. Lanza did a real service in popularizing opera with a public which might otherwise not have learned about it. *The Great Caruso* may not be historically accurate or remarkable cinematically but it had great value in making opera accessible and is one of the all-time most popular opera films. Lanza, born in Philadelphia as Alfred Arnold Coccozza, auditioned for Serge Koussevitzky in 1942. This led to a scholarship and an appearance at Tanglewood in *The Merry Wives of Windsor*. In 1949 he joined George London in a performance of scenes from *La Bohème* for David Sarnoff which helped initiate opera on NBC. His film career also began in 1949 at MGM where he starred in a series of films with opera content. He enjoyed great popularity because of the power of the emotion in his voice. His best film is the 1951 *The Great Caruso* in which he appeared with known opera singers in a romantic biography of his role model. Personality, alcohol, barbiturate problems, obesity and perhaps even the Mafia helped end his brief career. For the record, Lanza did sing opera on stage; he performed the role of Pinkerton in *Madame Butterfly* with the New Orleans Opera and gave a concert that included opera arias at the Royal Albert Hall. His popularity on video remains strong and it is estimated that 50 million copies of his records have been sold. Philadelphia named a park in his honor and José Carreras taped a tribute to him, See also JOSÉ CARRERAS (1991) THE GREAT CARUSO, THE STUDENT PRINCE (1954).

1949 That Midnight Kiss
Lanza stars opposite Kathryn Grayson in his film debut and sings arias from *Aida*, *L'Elisir d'Amore* and *Cavalleria Rusticana*. He's a truck driver, she's an heiress who wants to become an opera singer, they fall in love. The film was very popular and launched his career into high gear. Norman Taurog directed. MGM. Color. 96 minutes. MGM-UA video.

1950 The Toast of New Orleans
Lanza is a Louisiana fisherman who becomes an opera star with tutoring from Kathryn Grayson in this enjoyable film set in turn-of-the-century New Orleans. She's the prima donna of the French opera house and naturally they fall in love. The film features scenes from *Mignon*, *The Marriage of Figaro*, *Carmen* and *Madame Butterfly* in which Lanza chases Grayson around the stage to win her love. Lanza also sings "Be My Love" which became his biggest hit. Norman Taurog directed, Joe Pasternak produced. MGM. Color. 97 minutes.

1952 Because You're Mine
Lanza portrays an opera star who is drafted into the Army and falls in love with Doretta Morrow, the sister of his sergeant, James Whitmore. This is one of Lanza's least interesting films and his last for MGM as an actor but the title song became popular. Alexander Hall directed. Color. 103 minutes. MGM-UA video.

1956 Serenade
Mario Lanza portrays a singer with emotional problems in this adaptation of James M. Cain's novel. He's the protégé of rich Joan Fontaine and abandons the Met stage during his debut as *Otello* with Licia Albanese when Fontaine doesn't come to see him. An attempt to sing Don Ottavio's aria "Il mio tesoro" at the Mexico City Opera leads to his losing his voice completely. Sarita Montiel helps him out and restores his "manhood." The film includes excerpts from *Il Trovatore*, *Turandot*, *La Bohème* and *La Traviata*. Anthony Mann directed. Warner Bros. Color. 121 minutes. Warner Bros. video.

1958 The Seven Hills of Rome
Lanza is a TV singer who goes to Rome to look for his runaway girlfriend and ends up finding true love with an Italian girl. The plot is mostly about his rise to success as a singer in a nightclub after he wows them belting "Questa o quella" from *Rigoletto*. There is a good deal of beautiful Roman tourist scenery and a bizarre scene in which he imitates various American pop singers. Roy Rowland directed. Color. 104 minutes. MGM/UA video.

1959 For the First Time
In Lanza's last film he is typecast as a temperamental opera singer who is always missing performances and behaving badly. He falls in love with a deaf girl in Capri (Johanna von Koszian) who reforms him. There is plenty of opera music and a tour of the opera houses of Europe. Lanza is seen in the rain outside the Rome opera house singing arias from *Rigoletto* and on stage in costume in *Pagliacci*, *Otello* and *Aida*. Lanza's screen career closes ironically with the Triumphal March from *Aida*. Rudolph Maté directed. Color. 97 minutes. MGM-UA video.

1983 Mario Lanza, the American Caruso
An informative documentary about Lanza's life and career hosted by Placido Domingo. The film traces his rise and fall, includes high praise for his singing ability from various opera singers who worked with him and features clips of scenes from his films. Domingo says that seeing Lanza in the film *The Great Caruso* inspired him to become an opera singer. Among those interviewed are Anna Moffo, Kathryn Grayson and Joe Pasternak. The film, which suggests his death may have been caused by the Mafia, was written by Jo Ann G. Young and directed by John Musilli. VPI. Color.

68 minutes. Kultur video and New York Public Library.

1994 Heavenly Creatures
Mario Lanza is literally worshipped by two strange teenage girls in this New Zealand film set in the early 1950s. There is an altar for their operatic god and Lanza's records and songs are recurrent symbols. The girls attend his films as often as they can and consider him without doubt as the greatest tenor in the world. Peter Jackson directed. Color. 95 minutes. On video.

LARGE, BRIAN
English TV opera director (1939-)

Brian Large is one of the major figures in the field of directing opera for television and video. He became the chief director of opera for BBC television in 1974 and is England's counterpart to American TV opera pioneer Kirk Browning. Their styles are rather different but equally effective. Large uses fewer close-ups and has a less restless camera than Browning, tending to favor medium shots and more painterly compositions. Large now directs the Metropolitan Opera telecasts originally handled by Browning. He directed Britten's TV opera *Owen Wingrave* and was TV director for the *Ring* at Bayreuth in 1980. A large number of the videos made in opera houses around the world today are the work of Large and well over a hundred are listed in this book. He wrote the informative entry on "Filming, videotaping" in *The New Grove Dictionary of Opera* and has written books on Smetana and Martinu.

1980 The Making of the Ring
Brian Large makes a rare personal appearance talking about his work in this documentary. Director Peter Wienberg focuses on the filming of the 1980 Bayreuth *Ring* for television and includes interviews with the creative personnel. The documentary is included with the video of *Die Walküre*. Color. In English and German with English subtitles. About 40 minutes. Philips video and laserdisc.

LAURI-VOLPI, GIACOMO
Italian tenor (1892-1979)

Giacomo Lauri-Volpi could sing with ease a high D above high C and made his last public appearance at the age of 85 hitting a high C

singing "La donna è mobile." He had a remarkable voice that endured into old age and was a role model for others tenors. Lauri-Volpi was born in Rome, made his debut in 1919 and was a star attraction at La Scala and Verona from 1922 through the 1940s. He sang at the Metropolitan from 1923 to 1933 and continued to perform in public until 1959 when he retired to Spain. He also wrote studies of singers and singing. His reputation today is based on his recordings but he also left a few films in which he can be seen singing during his best years.

1933 La Canzone Del Sole
Lauri-Volpi stars as himself in *Song of the Sun*, a musical with an original score by Pietro Mascagni. The film ends with a full-scale production at the Verona Arena where Lauri-Volpi sings Raoul in Meyerbeer's *Gli Ugonotti (Les Huguenots)*. His role in the film is primarily as a singer including arias from *I Puritani* and the title song composed by Mascagni. Vittorio De Sica plays his lawyer and gets mistaken by a German woman for the singer. Much of the film is picture postcard views of Italy. Max Neufeld directed and also made a German version as *Das Lied Der Sonne*. Black and white. In Italian. 80 minutes.

1950 Il Caimano del Piave
Lauri-Volpi makes a brief and apparently autobiographical appearance in this film about a musical incident during World War I in Piave. It is Christmas and the Italian troops ask their captain to sing. Lauri-Volpi does so and his voice floats beautifully over the trenches causing both Italian and German troops to stop fighting and listen. Black and white. In Italian. 100 minutes.

1983 Memories of Giacomo Lauri-Volpi
Ricordi di Giacomo Lauri-Volpi begins with the famous concert in Spain where the 85-year-old tenor sang "La donna è mobile" to warm applause. It features lengthy extracts from the film *La Canzone del Sole* showing Lauri-Volpi at his recital of *I Puritani* arias and at the Verona Arena in his production of *Les Huguenots*. Italian mezzo Gianna Pederzina, who sang in the Verona production, recalls working with him. The film also features other high points in his career including a "Nessuna dorma" sung when he was 80. Franco Corelli and Carlo Bergonzi are among those interviewed. Rodolfo Celetti and Tonino del Colle directed the documentary for Italian

television with commentary by Silvio Berbandini. Color & black and white. In Italian. 90 minutes. Opera Dubs video.

LAWRENCE, MARJORIE
Australian soprano (1909-1979)

Marjorie Lawrence was known in America for her portrayals of Wagner heroines at the Metropolitan but she actually sang a wide range of roles. She was born in Australia, studied in Paris and made her debut in Monte Carlo in 1932. She sang at the Paris Opéra for three years and then made her Metropolitan debut as Brünnhilde in *Die Walküre*. She sang at the Met until 1941 when she was stricken with polio. She refused to quit singing and resumed her career in 1943 in staged performances in which she was always seated. In 1946 she returned to the Paris Opéra to sing Amneris. Lawrence published her autobiography *Interrupted Melody* in 1949 and it became the basis of a film.

1955 Interrupted Melody
This film biography contains excellent opera sequences from Lawrence's debut in Monte Carlo through her success in Paris to her triumph at the Metropolitan in *Die Walküre*. Lawrence recorded nine arias for actress Eleanor Parker, who portrays her, but they were not used; the voice heard on screen belongs to Eileen Farrell. The film tells the story of Lawrence's early successes, her polio attack and her triumphant come back at the Met in *Tristan und Isolde*. It features stage scenes from *La Bohème, Il Trovatore, Madama Butterfly, Carmen, Samson et Dalila* and *Die Walküre*. The film was nominated for four Oscars and won two. Glenn Ford and Roger Moore lend support and Curtis Bernhardt directed. Color. 106 minutes. MGM-UA video.

LECOCQ, CHARLES
French composer (1832-1918)

Charles Lecocq replaced Offenbach as the king of French operetta with his brilliant and tuneful 1872 masterpiece *La Fille de Madame Angot*. He was seriously crippled and perhaps this inspired him to favor romance over reality. His operettas were the triumph of escapism over satire and mockery. Lecocq, who once shared first prize with Bizet in an Offenbach operetta competion, had continuing success with *Giroflé-Girofla, La Petite Mariée* and *Le*

Petit Duc. These operettas are on French CDs but only *Fille de Madame Angot* has been filmed. See LA FILLE DE MADAME ANGOT.

LEGEND OF THE INVISIBLE CITY OF KITEZH, THE
1907 opera by Rimsky-Korsakov

The full name of Nikolai Rimsky-Korsakov's opera is *Skazaniye o nevidomom grade Kitezhe I deve Fevronii* (The Legend of the Invisible City of Kitezh and the Maiden Fevroniya). It's a heroic, patriotic, religious opera set in medieval times telling of a miracle that made a city invisible and saved it from invading Tartars. The maiden is the one who prays for the miracle that saves the city. The libretto is by Vladimir Belsky. See also NIKOLAI RIMSKY-KORSAKOV.

1971 The Battle of Kerzhenets
This is one of the major animation films, an extraordinary portrayal of the battle at the center of the opera. The images are based on medieval frescoes and the filmmakers use the powerful Rimsky-Korsakov music to great effect. *Battle* was produced by two of the best Soviet animation directors, Ivan Ivanov-Vano and Yuri Norstein. It won the Grand Prize at the Zagreb animation festival in 1972. Color. 20 minutes.

LEGEND OF TSAR SALTAN
See THE TALE OF TSAR SALTAN

LEHÁR, FRANZ
Austro-Hungarian composer (1870-1948)

Franz Lehár, the leading operetta composer of the 20th century, is likely to remain popular for a few more centuries on the strength of *The Merry Widow* alone as it has now entered the opera repertory. Lehár, who was born in Hungary but spent most of his life in Austria and Germany, wrote so many infectious melodies that he is often called the Puccini of the operetta. He was an avid cinemagoer, enjoyed the films of his operettas and acted in some of the films made about him. His music was featured with early silent films like *Mit Herz und Hand furs Vaterland* (1915) and in the 1930s he composed music for films starring Richard Tauber (*Die Grosse Attraktion/* 1931), Marta Eggerth *(Where is This Lady?/*1932), Maria Jeritza (*Grossfürstin Alexandra /*1933) and Jarmila

Novotná (*Der Kosak und die Nachtigall*/ 1935). See also CLO-CLO, LA DANZA DELLE LIBELLULE, MARTA EGGERTH (1932), EVA, FRASQUITA, FRIEDERIKE, GIUDITTA, DER GRAF VON LUXEMBURG, MARIA JERITZA (1933), DAS LAND DES LÄCHELNS, THE MERRY WIDOW, JARMILA NOVOTNÁ (1935), PAGANINI, SCHÖN IST DIE WELT, RICHARD TAUBER (1931), WO DIE LERCHE SINGT, DER ZAREWITSCH, ZIGEUNERLIEBE.

1914 Die Ideal Gattin

Lehár's Spanish-themed 1913 operetta *Die Ideal Gattin* (The Ideal Wife) was made into a silent film in Austria in 1914. The actors included director-to-be Ernst Lubitsch and Lyda Salmonova. Hans Heins Ewers directed. Black and white. In German. About 50 minutes.

1923 Franz Lehár

This Austrian silent film about the composer was made with Lehár's cooperation in Vienna by Thalia Film. He also wrote the score to be played live with the film, utilizing his own operetta melodies. Wilhelm Thiele and Hans Torre directed. Black and white. In German. About 70 minutes.

1925 Franz Lehár, der Operettenkönig

Franz Lehár, the Operetta King is another tribute to the composer made in Vienna, this one by Allianz Film. Lehár appears in the film and is seen playing the piano and conducting a rehearsal. Music from his operettas was played with the film in theaters. Alfred Deutsch-German directed. Black and white. In German. About 80 minutes.

1927 Das Fürstenkind

Lehár's operetta *Das Fürstenkind* (The Prince's Child), first staged in 1909, was made into a 1927 silent film in Austria. It tells the story of a brigand, his beautiful daughter and the American naval officer she loves. The film stars Harry Liedtke. Jacob and Luise Fleck directed. Black and white. In German. About 90 minutes.

1927 Der Rastelbinder

Lehár's 1910 operetta *Der Rastelbinder* (The Tinker) was the basis of a silent Austrian film in 1927. Viktor Léon's libretto tells the story of a ill-matched engaged couple and is set in Slovakia, Vienna and an army barracks. The film features Ellen Davis as Mitzi, Franz Glawatsch as her father, Louis Treumann, Hanna Andrée and Mary Hadar. Maurice Armand Mondet, Heinz Hanus

and Arthur Göttlein directed. Black and white. In German. About 86 minutes.

1929 Franz Lehár

This film features Lehár himself with many friends and associates including Liesl Goldarbeiter (Miss Austria that year), Viktor Léon, Ida Ruska, Victor Fleming, Ossi Fuhrer, Hans Otto Löwenstein, Karl Juiles and Fritz Heller. Lehár wrote the orchestral score and Hans Otto Lowenstein directed for Norbert Film. Black and white. In German. 90 minutes.

1930 Amours Viennoise

Wiener Liebschafter (Viennese Loves) is a French-German film operetta with music by Lehár. The French version stars Janie Marèse, Lyne Clèvers, Roland Toutain and Michel Duran under the direction of Jean Choux. The German version stars George Alexander, Betty Bird, Max Schipper and Lotte Lorring. Black and white. 72 minutes.

LEHMANN, LOTTE

German-born U.S. soprano (1888-1976)

Lotte Lehmann, who originated roles in two of Richard Strauss's opera before being driven out of Austria by the politics of 1938, began her career in Berlin and Hamburg. She moved to Vienna in 1916, where she established her international reputation, and made her debut at the Met in 1934. Lehmann continued to give recitals until 1951. Her voice is well served on her many recordings and she can be seen singing in her only film made when she was sixty. See METROPOLITAN OPERA (1966).

1948 Big City

Lehmann sings four songs in her sole film appearance including Brahms' Lullaby, "The Kerry Dance," "Traumerci" and "God Bless America." She portrays the mother of Danny Thomas in this story about racial tolerance involving Jews, Catholics and Protestants. Margaret O'Brien plays an orphan adopted by a minister, a cantor and an Irish cop. Norman Taurog directed for MGM. Black and white. 103 minutes.

LEIDEN DES JUNGEN WERTHER, DIE

1986 German opera by Bose

German composer Hans-Jürgen von Bose's opera *The Sorrows of Young Werther* is based on the same Goethe novel as Massenet's *Werther*. Bose and Filippo Sanjust's libretto, however, is surrealistic rather than romantic and combines scenes from the novel with visions, dreams and poems by Goethe, Lenz and Hölderlin. The basic story is the same. Werther falls in love with Lotte but when he goes away, she marries Albert. When Werther returns and finds she cannot return his love, he shoots himself. The opera premiered at the Schwetzingen Festival. See also HANS-JÜRGEN VON BOSE.

1986 Marco Arthur Marelli video

Marco Arthur Marelli produced, designed and costumed this production of the opera for Suddeutscher Rundfunk in Stuttgart. Hans Zender conducts the Stuttgart Suddeutscher Rundfunk Orchestra and the Madrigal Quintet of the Stuttgart Schola Cantorum. Jose Monte-Baczuer directed the video. Color. In German. 117 minutes. Inter Nationes video.

LEIFERKUS, SERGEI

Russian baritone (1946-)

Sergei Leiferkus was born in Leningrad and spent his early years at the Kirov Opera where he made his debut as Prince André in *War and Peace*. In 1978 he toured Britain with the Kirov and was so well received that he made London his base. He sings regularly at both Covent Garden and the Metropolitan and is popular in Italian as well as Russian operas. His Russian roles remain his strongest suit and he is particularly liked as Tomsky in *The Queen of Spades*. See BORIS GODUNOV (1990), EUGENE ONEGIN (1994), OTELLO (1993), THE QUEEN OF SPADES (1992/1992), PRINCE IGOR (1990), PYOTR TCHAIKOVSKY (1993).

LEMESHEV, SERGEI

Russian tenor (1902-1977)

Sergei Lemeshev joined the Bolshoi Opera in 1931 and a combination of personal charm, acting ability and fine voice made him an instant star. It also helped that he studied with Stanislavsky at the Bolshoi Opera Studio. He made his debut in 1926 at Sverdlovsk and was a leading tenor with the Bolshoi into the 1950s singing the Russian repertoire as well as many Italian operas. In the early 1940s he was featured in a couple of Soviet classical music films. He began to direct in 1951 and published his memoirs in 1968.

1940 A Musical Story

Sergey Lemeshev made his film debut as the star of *Muzikalnaya Istoriya*, the first Soviet sound film to have an operatic theme. It is based around music by Bizet, Flotow, Borodin, Rimsky-Korsakov and Tchaikovsky. Lemeshev portrays the hero-chauffeur sent to the State Music Conservatory by his fellow workers. He falls in love with dispatcher Zoya Fyodorova and wins her over rival Erast Garin. Lemeshev won particular praise for singing arias from *Eugene Onegin*. The film was released in the U.S. in 1941. Black and white. In Russian. 80 minutes.

1941 Russian Salad

Lemeshev sings arias from Rigoletto and Martha in *Kino-Concert 1941*, a Soviet concert musical released in the West with the title *Russian Salad*. The six directors were Adolf Minkin, Herbert Rappoport, Sergei Timoshenko, I. Menaker, M. Tsekhanovsky and M. Shapiro. Black and white. In Russian. 86 minutes.

1948? Sergei Lemeshev Recital

A documentary film showing Lemeshev singing a recital that was filmed by Ostankino. Black and white. In Russian. 60 minutes.

LEMNITZ, TIANA

German soprano (1897-)

Tiana Lemnitz was a brilliant lyric soprano who made her debut at Heilbronn in 1920. She joined the Berlin Staatsoper in 1934 and remained with that company until she retired in 1957. She sang at Covent Garden in a number of roles in the mid-1930s. She sings the role of the Countess in a 1949 film of *The Marriage of Figaro* and appeared in an opera recital scene in a German narrative film. Her relationship with the Nazi Party during World War II is controversial. See THE MARRIAGE OF FIGARO (1948).

1939 Altes Herz wird wieder Jung

Tiana Lemnitz is featured in the opera scene in this German narrative film along with Berlin State Opera tenor Max Lorenz. Emil Jannings and Maria Landrock star in *An Old Heart Becomes Young*, family-type comedy directed by Erich Engel. Black and white. In German. 81 minutes.

LEONCAVALLO, RUGGERO
Italian composer (1857-1919)

Struggling composer Ruggero (or Ruggiero) Leoncavallo became famous in 1892 for creating *Pagliacci* after fifteen years of trying to get his operas produced. He was born in Naples and was 35 when his one-act opera about a group of traveling players made him world famous. He was never again to find such success. His earlier operas did not become popular and his excellent *La Bohème* was overshadowed by Puccini's rival version. The only other Leoncavallo opera currently on CD is *Zaza* and the rest are more or less forgotten outside Italy. Leoncavallo also wrote operettas in an attempt to make money, the best known being *La Reginetta delle Rose*. *Pagliacci*, however, is his masterpiece and remains among the most popular of all operas on stage, film, television and video. There are at least fifteen films and videos of it complete and many other movies that feature its music. See PAGLIACCI, LA REGINETTA DELLE ROSE.

LETZTE WALZER, DER
1920 operetta by Straus

The Last Waltz is one of Oscar Straus's most popular operettas and has been filmed in three languages. It tells the story of Count Dimitri's last night and last waltz at a masked ball in Poland in 1910. He is to be executed the next day for having struck a member of the Russian Royal family when he went to the rescue of Countess Vera. Vera, however, has other plans and succeeds in saving his life and marrying him. The operetta premiered in Berlin in 1920 and was a success in New York and London.See also OSCAR STRAUS.

1934 Camille Horn film

Camille Horn stars as Countess Vera in the first German film of the operetta. Ivan Petrovich sings the role of Count Dimitri, Ernst Dumcke is Grand Duke Paul and Adele Sandrock is Vera's mother.

George Jacoby directed. Black and white. In German. 90 minutes.

1936 Jarmila Novotná English film

Czech opera diva Jarmila Novotná portrayed Countess Vera in two films of the operetta shot simultaneously with different casts. In the English film titled *The Last Waltz*, Harry Welchman portrays Count Dimitri, Gerald Barry plays Prince Paul and Josephine Huntley Wright is Babushka. Gerald Barry directed. Black and white. 74 minutes.

1936 Jarmila Novotná French film

Novotná stars again as Countess Vera in this French film of the above production made with a different director and a slightly different cast. In *La Dernière Valse* Jean Martinelli portrays Count Dimitri under the direction of Leo Mittler. Black and white. 90 minutes.

1953 Eva Bartok film

Eva Bartok stars as Countess Vera in this modern German film of the operetta directed by Arthur Maria Rabenalt. The plot has been changed and updated. Curt Jurgens is Count Dimitri and O. E. Hasse the Grand Duke. Black and white. In German. 93 minutes.

LEVANT, OSCAR
American composer (1906-1972)

Oscar Levant was a fine composer as well as being an actor, writer, wit, pianist and notable interpreter of George Gershwin's music. His most famous film performance is in the Gershwin film *An American in Paris* where he acts up a neurotic storm and plays superb piano. In the Gershwin biography *Rhapsody in Blue* he portrays himself as a friend of Gershwin and performs the title tune. Other major films include *The Band Wagon*, *The Barkleys of Broadway* and *Romance on the High Seas*. His only opera is the imaginary screen opera *Carnival* which he composed for the 1936 film *Charlie Chan at the Opera*. See IMAGINARY OPERAS IN FILMS (1936).

LEVINE, JAMES
American conductor (1943-)

The indefatigable James Levine has become America's most famous opera conductor through his Metropolitan Opera telecasts. He made his Met debut in 1971, became the chief conductor in 1974, was named artistic director in 1986 and celebrated 25 years at the Met in 1996. He has helped the Met maintain its position as one of the great opera houses of the world and has also conducted extensively abroad. Levine is featured in too many operas videos to list, including most of the Met operas, but an A to C sampling includes AIDA (1985/1989), ARIADNE AUF NAXOS (1988), UN BALLO IN MASCHERA (1991), THE BARTERED BRIDE (1978), KATHLEEN BATTLE (1990), BLUEBEARD'S CASTLE (1989), LA BOHÈME (1977/1982), CARMEN (1987), CAVALLERIA RUSTICANA (1978), LA CLEMENZA DI TITO (1980).

1986 James Levine: The Life in Music

Peter Weinberg's documentary video follows the energetic conductor around the world. It shows Levine rehearsing, conducting and accompanying singers on piano from New York to Bayreuth. Among those interviewed are Placido Domingo, Jean-Pierre Ponnelle, Leonie Rysanek and Lynn Harrell. Joanne Woodward is the narrator. Unitel. The documentary was telecast Aug. 11, 1986. Color. 55 minutes.

1996 James Levine's 25th Anniversary Gala

James Levine's 25th anniversary at the Met was marked by a all-star seven-hour gala telecast live. While the singers appeared for only a few moments, the inexhaustible Levine conducted the entire marathon. Among the dozens of singers participating were Roberto Alagna, June Anderson, Gabriela Benackova, Carlo Benackova, Grace Bumbry, Placido Domingo, Maria Ewing, Gwyneth Jones, James King, Alfredo Kraus, Catherine Malfitano, Aprile Millo, Sherrill Milnes, James Morris, Birgit Nilsson, Jessye Norman, Samuel Ramey, Sharon Sweet, Ruth Ann Swenson, Kiri Te Kanawa, Bryan Terfel, Dawn Upshaw, Anne Sofie von Otter and Frederica Von Stade. Peter Allen was the narrator and Brian Large directed the video and telecast. Color. 420 minutes.

LEWIS, MARY

American soprano (1897-1941)

The beautiful Arkansas soprano Mary Lewis rose from extreme poverty to became one of the most notable Ziegfeld Follies girls. She then turned to opera and made her debut in Vienna in 1923 as Marguerite in *Faust*. In 1924 she sang the role of Mary in the premiere of Vaughan William's *Hugh the Drover* at Covent Garden and in 1925 starred in *The Merry Widow* in Paris. She returned to the U.S. with a Met contract and sang in *La Bohème*, *Pagliacci* and *The Tales of Hoffmann*. Her Met career ended after a drunken *Carmen* in 1930. Her film career was messy. She seems to have worked with Christie Comedies in 1919 and possibly appeared in the 1920 film *The Ugly Duckling*. After her Met career ended in 1930 she signed with Pathé to star in a film about her life. When that didn't work out, she started on a French Revolution film that was abandoned probably because of her drinking. After marrying a rich man, she resumed her singing career but mostly on radio. She died somewhat mysteriously at the age of 43 in 1941.

1927 Vitaphone sound films

Mary Lewis made two Vitaphone sound films but only one was released. The first was titled *Mary Lewis in Way Down South* and in it she sings songs by James Bland and Dan Emmett with backing from a male chorus. Her second Vitaphone film, started a month later, was to feature excerpts from *The Tales of Hoffmann* but it was never completed. Vitaphone sued her and claimed she was drinking on the set. Black and white. About 8 minutes.

LIBRARY OF CONGRESS

The Library of Congress (LOC) in Washington, D.C., has a large collection of films and television programs, many of which have operatic content. They are preserved by the Motion Picture, Broadcasting and Recorded Sound Division and can be viewed by interested researchers. Some of its holdings are relatively unique and it is probably the only place where one can view the withdrawn Samuel Goldwyn film of *Porgy and Bess*. A partial catalog of its TV holdings is available. It's titled *Three Decades of Television, A Catalog of Television Programs Acquired by the Library of Congress 1949-1979* and was compiled by Sarah Rouse and Katharine Loughney. In 1986 the Library's collection increased enormously with the acquisition of over 20,000 NBC television programs.

LIEBERMANN, ROLF

Swiss opera film producer (1910-)

Composer/administrator Rolf Liebermann, who has been in charge of the Hamburg State Opera and the Paris Opera at various times, is also a notable producer of opera films. Most of them were made in the late 1960s when he was director of the Hamburg Staatsoper and he brought an impressive selection of them to New York for an opera film festival in 1970. Although he did not direct the films (it was usually Joachim Hess), he was the driving force behind their creation. He talks about opera films in the documentary Cinopera. See CINOPERA, ELEKTRA (1969), FIDELIO (1969), DER FREISCHÜTZ (1968), THE MAGIC FLUTE (1971), THE MARRIAGE OF FIGARO (1967), DIE MEISTERSINGER VON NÜRNBERG (1969), IGOR STRAVINSKY (1968), THE TALES OF HOFFMANN (1970), WOZZECK (1967), ZAR UND ZIMMERMANN (1968).

LIFE FOR THE TSAR, A

1836 opera by Glinka

Mikhail Glinka's *A Life for the Tsar* (Zhizn' za Tsarya) is the first important Russian opera and its patriotism has ensured its continuing popularity. Yegor Rozen's libretto tells the story of the peasant Ivan Susanin who sacrifices his life to save the Tsar from invading Poles. It is also the story of his daughter Atonida, her fiancé Sobinin and his ward Vanya. The opera was banned in 1917 but revived in 1938 with a new libretto and the title Ivan Susanin. The hero in this version saves Moscow rather than the Tsar. The opera was revived in its original form after the collapse of the Soviet Union and is now available in Russian on video as written. See also MIKHAIL GLINKA.

1911 Goncharov film

This is a Russian silent film featuring highlights of the opera. It was directed by Valili M. Goncharov. Black and white. About 10 minutes.

1992 Bolshoi Opera

Evgeny Nesterenko stars as the patriotic Ivan Susanin in this traditional Bolshoi Opera production by Nicolai Kuznetsov. Marina Mescheriakova sings the role of Susanin's daughter Antonida, Alexander Lomonosov is her fiancé Sobinin, Elena Zaremba is his ward Vanya and Boris Bezhko is the Polish Commander.

Valery Levental designed the sets and Alexander Lazarev conducted the Bolshoi Symphony Orchestra and Chorus. Derek Bailey directed for video at the Bolshoi Theater in June 1992. Color. In Russian. 175 minutes. Teldec (England) video.

LILY OF KILLARNEY, THE

1862 opera by Benedict

Julius Benedict's light opera is one of the big three of 19th century Anglo-Irish light opera along with *The Bohemian Girl* and *Maritana*. It's based on Dion Boucicault's play *The Colleen Bawn* using a libretto by Boucicault and John Oxenford. In 19th century Ireland the peasant girl known as the Colleen Bawn (i.e., the blonde maiden) is secretly married to an aristocrat. He is being pushed to marry an heiress to solve his financial problems and an attempt is made by one of his associates to drown the Colleen. The opera's best-known airs include "Colleen Bawn" and "Eily Mavourneen." Its huge popularity in England led to it being filmed four times in the pre-World War II period. A 1934 version was released in the U.S. See also JULIUS BENEDICT.

1922 Betty Farquhar film

Betty Farquhar stars as the Colleen Bawn in this silent highlights version of the opera made for the English *Tense Moments from Operas* series. Bertram Burleigh is her aristocrat husband and Booth Conway is Myles na Coppaleen. Challis Sanderson directed and H. B. Parkinson produced. Black and white. About 15 minutes.

1927 Kathlyn Hillard film

Kathlyn Hillard is the Colleen Bawn Elly in this British highlights film made for the English *Cameo Operas* series. Herbert Langley portrays Hardress Cregan. The film was screened with singers standing by the stage performing the arias. John E. Blakeley produced and H. B. Parkinson directed for Song Films. Black and white. About 18 minutes.

1929 Pamela Parr film

Pamela Parr plays the Colleen Eily O'Connor in this feature film of the opera made at the end of the silent era. Cecil Landreau is Hardress Cregan, Dennis Wyndham is Myles-na-Coppaleen and Edward O'Neill is Corrigan. George Ridgwell directed. British International Pictures. Black and white. About 70 minutes.

1934 Gina Malo film

Gina Malo sings the role of Eileen O'Connor, the Colleen Bawn, in this tuneful adaptation of the opera released in the U.S. as *Bride of the Lake*. It's more musical than opera with extra Irish songs but it contains the opera's most famous airs. John Garrick is Sir Patrick Creegan, Leslie Perrins is his enemy Sir James Corrigan and Stanley Holloway is Father O'Flynn, a priest fond of singing and drinking. Maurice Elvey directed for Twickenham Films. Black and white. In English. 88 minutes. Video Yesteryear.

LINCKE, PAUL

German composer (1866-1946)

Paul Lincke's music is as symbolic of Berlin as Offenbach's is of Paris and Strauss's of Vienna. The march song "Berliner Luft" (Berlin Air), which originated in his 1904 operetta *Berliner Luft*, is practically the theme song of the city. Lincke was the first of the famous Berlin operetta composers and created his first stage show there in 1896. He is known to most Americans as the composer of the hit song "The Glow-Worm" which originated in his 1901 operetta *Lysistrata*. In Germany today his best-known operetta is *Frau Luna*, an 1899 fantasy about a group of Berliners visiting the moon via balloon. The operetta is still being staged in Berlin today. See FRAU LUNA.

LINDA DI CHAMOUNIX

1842 opera by Donizetti

Gaetano Donizetti's opera *Linda of Chamounix* is less well known but is considered by critics to be one of his finest . The heroine Linda is in love with the young painter Carlo, the Viscount Sirval in disguise. When she thinks he has left her, she goes mad. The libretto by Gaetano Rossi is based on a French play. There is currently no video of the complete opera though it is available on CD. See also GAETANO DONIZETTI.

1913 Matilde Granillo film

Matilde Granillo stars as Linda in this early Italian film of the opera featuring Arnaldo Arnaldi as the Viscount Sirval. It was produced for Centauro Films in Turin under the supervision of Giuseppe De Witten. Black and white. About 30 minutes.

1921 Nella Serravezza film

Nella Serravezza stars as Linda in this narrative film based on the libretto of the opera and directed by Luigi Ferrario. Antonio Solinas portrays the Viscount Sirval, Dillo Lombardi is Linda's father Antonio and Decio Jacobacci is the lecherous Marquis Boisfleury. The public approved of the film though the critics were not enthusiastic. The alternative title is *La Perla della Savoia*. Eden-Ferrario film. Black and white. In Italian. About 75 minutes.

LINDBERGHFLUG, DER

1929 opera by Weill

The Lindbergh Flight is a lesser known Bertolt Brecht/Kurt Weill collaboration that was originally intended to be a radio opera. It celebrates the flight of American aviator Charles Lindbergh. The opera is in fifteen tableaux separated by a radio commentator who reads the title of each new scene. See also KURT WEILL.

1994 Jean-François Jung video

Jean-François Jung created a German television video of the opera using newspaper clippings, photographs, images from films, models of airplanes and other montage effects. Richard Erin Samuel portrays Lindbergh and Peter Wallasch is the speaker. The singers are Wolfgang Schmidt, Herbert Feckler, Lorenz Minth, Christoph Scheeben and the Cologne Pro Musica Chorus. Jan Latham-König conducted the Cologne Radio-Television Orchestra. Color. In German. 60 minutes. On video.

LIND, JENNY

Swedish soprano (1829-1887)

American showman P. T. Barnum made Jenny Lind into one of the most famous singers of the 19th century with a truly amazing publicity campaign. The "Swedish Nightingale" made her debut at the Royal Opera in Stockholm in 1830 and was soon the most popular singer in Sweden. Voice problems in 1841 while singing *Norma* forced her to retrain with Manuel Garcia but she then became famous again singing that Bellini opera and *La Sonnambula*, *La Fille du Régiment* and *Robert le Diable*. Lind toured Europe in opera until 1849 and gave recitals in the U.S. from 1850 to 1852 when Barnum boosted her to new heights of celebrity. She has been portrayed on film by

Grace Moore, Hanna Schygulla, Françoise Rosay, Virginia Bruce and Priscilla Gillette among others.

1930 A Lady's Morals

Metropolitan Opera diva Grace Moore portrays Jenny Lind in this film, the first of the Hollywood show business film biographies after the coming of sound. After a successful career in Sweden, Lind loses her voice on stage in *Norma* in Italy. A composer who loves her (Reginald Denny) is blinded defending her though later he is able to help her recover her voice. Showman P.T. Barnum (Wallace Beery) brings Lind to America and makes her into a superstar. Moore sings arias from *La Fille du Régiment* and *Norma* and songs by Oscar Straus. Sidney Franklin directed and Adrian designed Moore's clothes. English title: *Jenny Lind*. Black and white. In English. 75 minutes.

1930 French Jenny Lind

A French version of *A Lady's Morals* was made with Grace Moore repeating her role as Jenny Lind but with a different supporting cast and director. In the French film André Berley portrays P.T. Barnum, André Luguet plays Lind's friend Paul, Georges Mauloy is Garcia and Françoise Rosay has a major role. Arthur Robison directed. Black and white. In French. 92 minutes.

1934 The Mighty Barnum

Virginia Bruce portrays Jenny Lind in this American film focusing on the great promoter. Bruce is shown singing "Casta Diva" and other arias by Bellini and Donizetti but the actual singing is by Frances White of the Los Angeles Civic Light Opera company. Wallace Beery impersonates P. T. Barnum with gusto. 20th Century Pictures. Black and white. 98 minutes.

1951 The Legend of Jenny Lind

Soprano Priscilla Gillette plays Jenny Lind in the Westinghouse Studio One television production with Thomas Mitchell as P. T. Barnum. The story concentrates on the relationship between the singer and the showman. Gillette, who starred on stage in Blitzstein's *Regina* and Moross's *The Golden Apple*, sings a number of arias associated with Lind. Paul Nickell directed the production telecast on CBS on Dec. 10, 1951. Black and white. 50 minutes. Video Yesteryear video.

1986 Barnum

German actress Hanna Schygulla, the notable star of many Fassbinder films, is superb as Jenny Lind opposite Burt Lancaster's Barnum in this Canadian film. He goes to Europe and mortgages his future to bring the soprano to the U.S. without ever hearing her sing. At her American debut Schygulla sings Lind's trademark Bellini aria "Come per me sereno" from *La Sonnambula* but the voice belongs to soprano Jeanine Thames. Michael Norell wrote the script, Reginald Morris was cinematographer and Lee Philips directed. Color. 94 minutes. Academy video.

1986 Barnum

Christina Collier portrays a *femme fatale* Jenny Lind in this London stage musical of the P.T. Barnum story. She sings, first in Swedish and then in English, but it is not quite opera. Michael Crawford stars as Barnum in a circus-like production with book by Mark Bramble, music by Cy Coleman and lyrics by Michael Stewart. Joe Layton directed the original stage production and Terry Hughes directed the video. Color. 110 minutes. Waterbearer video.

LIPP, WILMA
Austrian soprano (1925-)

Wilma Lipp made her debut in Vienna in 1943 as Rosina and joined the Vienna State Opera in 1945. She was popular in coloratura roles, especially as the Queen of the Night, and sang many Mozart heroines. She appeared as Konstanze at Glyndebourne in 1957 and can be seen in this role in a 1954 Vienna film. Lipp appeared in only one other film, singing Mozart in an Otto Preminger movie. Her recordings remain popular. See THE ABDUCTION FROM THE SERAGLIO (1954).

1963 The Cardinal

Wilma Lipp is featured soloist with the Wiener Jugendchor in Otto Preminger's film about the life of an American Roman Catholic priest (played by Tom Tryon). The priest spends two periods of his life in Vienna which is where he (and the film audience) hear Lipp sing the Alleluia from the "Exultate Jubilate" motet by Mozart. Columbia Pictures. Color. 175 minutes.

LIVE FROM LINCOLN CENTER
PBS television series (1976-)

Technical improvements led to live telecasts of opera from Lincoln Center in 1976 under the direction of the pioneer opera director Kirk Browning. The first broadcast in May 1976 was Douglas Moore's *The Ballad of Baby Doe*. It was telecast from the stage of the New York City Opera. Live opera from Lincoln Center continues to the present time.

LIVE FROM THE MET
PBS television series (1977-)

The Metropolitan Opera returned to live telecasting of its operas in March 1977 thirty years after its first experimental efforts. The first presentation was *La Bohème* starring Luciano Pavarotti with Kirk Browning as the genius behind the cameras. Live programs from the Met are now a staple of television and include not only operatic standards but Met premieres of new operas like *The Ghosts of Versailles*. Brian Large has now taken over directing duties from Browning. These two directors are the most influential in the history of television opera. See METROPOLITAN OPERA.

LIZZIE BORDEN
1965 opera by Beeson

Kenward Elm based his libretto for Jack Beeson's "family portrait" opera on a famous trial held in Fall River, MA, in 1892. Lizzie Borden, daughter of a banker, was accused of killing her father and stepmother with an axe but was acquitted. The story has become a part of American folklore and has inspired a number of songs. Beeson's opera tells the story of what may have happened. It was premiered by the New York City Opera in March 1965 and is on CD.

1967 NET Opera Theater
The New York City Opera cast that created the opera was also featured in an NET Opera Theater TV production by James Perrin. Brenda Lewis stars as Lizzie supported by Herbert Beattie, Ellen Faull and Ann Elgar. Anton Coppola conducted the Cambridge Festival orchestra and Kirk Browning directed the telecast in January 1967. Color. In English. 115 minutes. Video at MTR.

Related film

1975 The Legend of Lizzie Borden
Elizabeth Montgomery stars as Lizzie in this realistic TV film of the story written by William Bast and directed by Paul Wendkos. The cast includes Ed Glanders, Fionnuala Flanagan, Fritz Weaver and Katherine Helmond. Color. 100 minutes. Video at Library of Congress.

LLEÓ, VICENTE
Spanish composer (1870-1922)

Vincente Lleó y Balbastre is one of the best known Spanish zarzuela composers. He began composing in 1885 and wrote over one hundred musical works for the stage including operas. His greatest success and best-known zarzuela is *La Corte de Faraón* (The Court of the Pharaoh) first staged in 1910. It is the only popular zarzuela with a Biblical story and has been filmed twice. See LA CORTE DE FARAÓN.

LLOYD, ROBERT
English bass (1940-)

British basso Robert Lloyd has become so popular as Boris Godunov that he was invited to sing the role with the Russians in St. Petersburg following his success at Covent Garden. Lloyd made his debut in 1969, joined the Royal Opera in 1972 and has sung in most of the great opera houses of the world in various roles. He has in some ways assumed the mantle of Chaliapin as actor and singer. He has also worked with some of the world's top filmmakers including Hans-Jurgen Syberberg for the film of *Parsifal* and André Tarkovsky for the Covent Garden production of *Boris Godunov*. Many of his performances are on video including his Tarkovsky *Boris*. See THE BARBER OF SEVILLE (1988), BLUEBEARD'S CASTLE (1988), BORIS GODUNOV (1990), DON CARLO (1985), LA FANCIULLA DEL WEST (1983), FIDELIO (1991), L'INCORONAZIONE DI POPPEA (1984), PARSIFAL (1982), IL RITORNO D'ULISSE IN PATRIA (1973), THE TALES OF HOFFMANN (1981), TRISTAN UND ISOLDE (1993).

1990 Six Foot Cinderella
A BBC television film about various aspects of Lloyd's career showing the breadth and depth and especially height of his work as an actor and

a singer. One of its memorable moments is his singing simultaneously the roles of Don Giovanni, Leporello and the Statue in the closing scene of *Don Giovanni*. This was done through multiple takes to demonstrate the dramatic possibilities of the bass voice. Color. 60 minutes.

LOHENGRIN
1850 opera by Wagner

Lohengrin has been a favorite of filmmakers since 1902. There are many screen versions of Richard Wagner's opera, even one in Italian, but the most praised is the one staged by filmmaker Werner Herzog. All four available videos were directed by Brian Large. *Lohengrin* is set in Antwerp in the tenth century. The Swan Knight Lohengrin appears to defend the honor of Elsa who has been accused of murdering her brother by Telramund and his wife Ortrud. Elsa is saved and marries the knight but breaks her promise not to ask his name and origin. See also RICHARD WAGNER.

1947 Renata Tebaldi film
Renata Tebaldi sings the role of Elsa portrayed on screen by Jacqueline Plessis in this Italian film of the opera. Antonio Cassinelli is seen as Lohengrin with the voice of Giacinto Prandelli, Inga Borg is Ortrud sung by Elena Nicolai, Attilio Ortolani is Telramund sung by Giuseppe Modesti and Giulio Oppi is King Henry. Gian Maria Cominetti and Piero Ballerini wrote the script, Giuseppe Caraccio photographed the film and Max Calandri directed. Black and white. In Italian. 100 minutes.

1982 Bayreuth Festival
Peter Hofmann stars as Lohengrin in this Bayreuth Festival stage production by Götz Friedrich. Karan Armstrong is Elsa, Elizabeth Connell is Ortrud, Siegfried Vogel is King Henry the Fowler, Leif Roar is Telramund and Bernd Weikl is the Herald. Gunther Uecker designed the sets and Frieda Parmeggiani designed the costumes. Woldemar Nelsson conducted the Bayreuth Festival Orchestra and Chorus and Brian Large directed the video. Color. In German with English subtitles. 200 minutes. Philips video and laser.

1986 Metropolitan Opera
Peter Hofmann is Lohengrin, Eva Marton is Elsa and Leonie Rysanek is Ortrud in this strong Metropolitan Opera production staged by August Everding. John Macurdy is King Henry, Leif Roar is Telramund and Anthony Raffell is the Herald. Ming Cho Lee designed the sets and Peter J. Hall the costumes. James Levine conducted the Metropolitan Orchestra and Chorus and Brian Large directed the video on Jan. 10 and it was telecast on March 26. Color. In German with English subtitles. 220 minutes. Paramount video/Pioneer laser.

1990 Vienna State Opera
Placido Domingo stars as Lohengrin with Cheryl Studer as Elsa in this excellent Vienna State Opera production by Joachim Herz staged by Wolfgang Weber. Dunja Vejzovic is Ortrud, Robert Lloyd is King Henry, Hartmut Welker is Telramund and Georg Tichy is the Herald. Rudolf and Reinhard Heinrich designed the sets and costumes and Claudio Abbado conducted the Vienna State Opera Orchestra and Chorus. Brian Large directed the video. Color. In German with English subtitles. 218 minutes. Home Vision video.

1990 Bayreuth Festival
Film director Werner Herzog staged and designed this much acclaimed Bayreuth Festival production featuring Paul Frey as Lohengrin and Cheryl Studer as Elsa. Gabriel Schnaut sings the role of Ortrud, Ekkehard Wlaschiha is Telramund, Manfred Schenk is King Henry and Eike Wilm Schulte is the Herald. Peter Schneider conducted the Bayreuth Festival Orchestra and Chorus and Brian Large once again directed the video. Color. In German with English subtitles. 215 minutes. Philips video and laserdisc.

Early/related films

1902 Lubin film
The Lubin film company in Philadelphia distributed a film of a scene from the opera in the U.S. in January 1902. Black and white. About 3 minutes.

1907 Henny Porten sound film
This Oskar Messter Biophon Tonbilder sound film of an aria from the opera was made in Germany with the Porten family. Friedrich Porten directed and Henny and Franz Porten were the actors. The film was screened with the aria played on a phonograph. About 3 minutes.

1916 Felix Dahn film

Felix Dahn stars as Lohengrin in this silent German film adaptation of the opera with Elizabeth von Endert as Elsa and Frieda Langendorff as Ortrud. The film was produced by Opern Gesellschat and the screenings were accompanied by music and singing. Black and white. About 50 minutes.

1937 100 Men and a Girl

Deanna Durbin sneaks into a rehearsal at the Manhattan Concert Hall and watches Leopold Stokowski conduct the Prelude to Act One of *Lohengrin*. Henry Koster directed. Black and white. 84 minutes.

1940 The Great Dictator

The Prelude to Act One of *Lohengrin* is used as the musical background when Hitler clone Charlie Chaplin lifts a giant balloon of the world and sends it soaring in a mock ballet sequence. This was Chaplin's first talkie as director and actor. Black and white. 98 minutes.

LOLLOBRIGIDA, GINA

Italian actress (1927-)

Gina Lollobrigida is often considered simply an Italian cinema sex symbol, but the reality is more interesting. She was studied opera for a time, considered it as a profession and began her career in the opera movies *L'Elisir d'Amore* and *Lucia di Lammermoor*. In the Italian film about opera singer Lina Cavalieri, *The Most Beautiful Women in the World*, she plays Cavalieri and sings Tosca's aria "Vissi d'arte" which was released on record. In the excellent 1948 film of *Pagliacci* she is very good as Nedda though her singing is dubbed. In the Enrico Caruso biopic *The Young Caruso* she is the woman Caruso loves. In Mario Costa's *Mad About Opera* she brings the top Italian opera stars to London. She gets high praise in the opera film documentary *Cinopera*. See also ENRICO CARUSO (1951), LINA CAVALIERI (1955), CINOPERA, L'ELISIR D'AMORE (1946), LUCIA DI LAMMERMOOR (1946), MAD ABOUT OPERA, PAGLIACCI (1948).

LOMBARDI ALLA PRIMA CROCIATA, I

1843 opera by Verdi

The Lombards on the First Crusade has a complex story about family intrigues in the twelfth century ending with the Crusaders conquering the Holy Land. The libretto for Verdi was written by Temistocle Solera and is based on an epic poem by Tommaso Grossi. Pagano attempts to kill his brother Arvino but kills his father instead. As a result he becomes a hermit. Arvino's daughter Giselda falls in love with the Moslem Oronte. He is killed by the Crusaders but not before he is baptized by Pagano who is also mortally wounded. The highly regarded chorus "O Signore, dal tetto natio" has patriotic similarities to *Nabucco's* "Va pensiero." See also GIUSEPPE VERDI.

1984 Teatro alla Scala

José Carreras stars as Oronte, Ghena Dimitrova is Giselda and Silvano Carroli sings the bass role of Pagano in this La Scala production staged by Gabriele Lavia. Carlo Bini is Arvino and Luisa Vannini is Viclinda. Andrea Viotti designed the colorful costumes and Giovanni Agostinucci designed the much plainer sets. Gianandrea Gavazzoni leads the La Scala Orchestra and Chorus in a stirring production and Brian Large directed the video. Color. In Italian with English subtitles. 126 minutes. HBO video/ Pioneer laser.

1993 Metropolitan Opera

Luciano Pavarotti is Oronte, Samuel Ramey is Pagano and Lauren Flanigan is Giselda in this Metropolitan Opera production by Mark Lamos. Bruno Beccaria sings the role of Arvino and Imma Egida is Viclinda. John Conklin designed the sets and Dunya Ramicova the costumes. James Levine conducts the Metropolitan Opera and Chorus. Brian Large directed the video at a December 1993 production which was telecast on March 30, 1994. Color. In Italian with English subtitles. 139 minutes. On video.

LOMBARDO, CARLO

Italian composer/librettist (1869-1959)

Carlo Lombardo was involved in many aspects of Italian operetta production during the early years of the century as producer, composer and librettist. Most of his success came from adapting and revising foreign stage works. His Italian version of Franz Lehár's Viennese operetta *Der Sterngucker* (The Star Gazer) was a hit as *La Danza delle Libellule* after the German-language version had failed. He wrote librettos for Pietro Mascagni's operetta *Sì* and for Maria Costa's popular *La Scugnizza*. Lombardo's other operetta adaptations include *La Duchessa del Bal Tabarin* and *Madame di Tebe* which have both retained some popularity in Italy; *Duchessa* is also performed in Spain and Mexico in the zarzuela repertory as *Frou Frou del Tabarin*. Lombardo created one of the first operettas about the movies with his *La Signorina del Cinematografo* (1914) based on Carlo Weinberger's *Der Schmetterling* (1896). See LA DUCHESSA DEL BAL TABARIN , MARIO COSTA, LA DANZA DELLE LIBELLULE, OPERAS & OPERETTAS ABOUT THE MOVIES, PIETRO MASCAGNI.

1992 Madame di Tebe
Carlo Lombardo's lighthearted 1918 Italian operetta set in a Paris nightclub is based on Joseph Szulc's musical *Flup...!* with additional tunes from Cuvillier, Offenbach, Lehár and Lleó. A 1992 highlights version and history was featured by operetta master Sandro Massimini and his associates on the Italian TV series *Operette, Che Passione!* It includes the songs "Spesso a cori e picche," "Tango," "Montmartre" and "Occhio di ciel, core di gel." Color. In Italian. About 20 minutes. Ricordi (Italy) video.

LONDON, GEORGE
American bass-baritone (1920-1985)

George London made his debut at the Hollywood Bowl in 1941 in *La Traviata* but his career did not take off until 1949 when he sang at Vienna, La Scala and Glyndebourne. He came to the Met in 1951 as Amonasro in *Aida* and in 1960 became the first non-Russian to sing *Boris Godunov* at the Bolshoi. He was much admired for his acting abilty, especially in Mozart and Wagner. London went into opera management in Washington in 1968 and produced a complete *Ring* in Seattle in 1975. He made no films but there are videos of telecasts. His only complete opera on video is a superb *Tosca* in Germany with Renata Tebaldi. He can also be seen as Scarpia opposite Maria Callas in an American television show. See MARIA CALLAS (1956), METROPOLITAN OPERA (1953), TOSCA (1961).

1953-55 George London in Opera & Song
George London is shown in performance on four *Voice of Firestone* TV programs. He sings arias from *Boris Godunov* (Varlaam's Aria) and *The Marriage of Figaro* ("Non piu andrai"), duets with Dorothy Warenskjold and Nadine Conner in music from *Don Giovanni, Maytime* and *Show Boat* and sings songs by Kern, Romberg and Rodgers & Hammerstein. Black and white. 46 minutes. VAI video.

1962 George London Festival
George London performs operatic arias, songs and lieder for a filmed television concert created for the Festival of Performing Arts series. Included are Leporello's Catalog aria from *Don Giovanni* and the Death Scene from *Boris Godunov*. The concert was telecast on April 24, 1962,. Black and white. 30 minutes. Video at Library of Congress.

LOOSE, EMMY
Czech soprano (1914-1987)

Emmy Loose made her debut as Blonde in *The Abduction from the Seraglio* in Hanover in 1939 and can be seen in that role in a Vienna State Opera video. She sang with the Vienna opera house for 25 years from 1941 but also found time to visit Covent Garden and Salzburg. Loose, who was especially liked in Mozart, can also be seen as Susanna in a Vienna video of *The Marriage of Figaro*. See THE ABDUCTION FROM THE SERAGLIO (1954), THE MARRIAGE OF FIGARO (1954).

LOPEZ, FRANCIS
French composer (1916-1995)

Francis Lopez, the modern king of the French "opérette, was by far the most popular operetta composer in France when he died in 1995 and this is reflected in the many French videos of his stage works. Despite his Gallic popularity he remains virtually unknown in America and England. The Basque-born Lopez, who created forty stage musicals and a thousand songs, first became popular in 1945 with *La Belle de Cadix* starring Luis Mariano. It was followed by *Andalousie* and *Le Chanteur de Mexico*, both also starring Mariano. They were top box office hits as films. *La Belle de Cadix* was revived on stage in Paris in 1995 with José Todaro. Lopez created traditional, tuneful operettas with exotic settings and much Spanish style music which the French public greatly enjoyed. He also wrote music for over thirty French films including Clouzot's *Quai des Orfèvres* and Bernard's *La Dame aux Camélias*. Many of his operettas were filmed or taped live. A partial selection is listed below.

1950 Andalousie

Luis Mariano stars as the bullfighter Juanito in this film of Lopez's 1947 operetta. After a disagreement with his girl Dolores, he goes to Mexico and become a famous matador while she dedicates herself to dance and becomes the star Estrellita. Robert Vernay directed. Black and white. In French. 94 minutes. René Chateau (France) video.

1953 La Belle de Cadix

Luis Mariano re-creates his stage role as the movie star singer Carlos in this film of Lopez's 1945 operetta. It is reset in Spain in 1953 where a film company is shooting *La Belle de Cadix* and a singing partner is sought for Carlos. The gypsy Maria-Luisa (Carmen Sevilla) finally takes on the role. Raymond Bernard directed. Color. In French. 105 minutes. René Chateau (France) video.

Les Plus Belles Operettes De Francis Lopez

Six of the Lopez operettas were filmed on stage for television in the early 1980s under the supervision of Lopez and are available on video. They are *À la Jamaique* with José Villamor, *Aventure à Monte Carlo* with Georges Guetary, *La Belle de Cadix* with José Todaro, *La Perle des Antilles* with José Villamor, *Le Vagabond Tzigane* with Youri, *La Route Fleurie* and *Frenesie Tzigane*. Color. In French. About 120 minutes each. EMI (France) videos.

LOREN, SOPHIA

Italian opera film star (1934 -)

Sophia Loren doesn't sing opera but she did star in two major Italian opera films in her early movie career. In 1952 she portrayed Leonora most beautifully in Cesare Barlacchi's film of Donizetti's *La Favorita* using the singing voice of Palmira Vitali Marini. In 1953 she had the glorious singing voice of Renata Tebaldi when she played Aida in a famous screen version of Verdi's *Aida*. The film was directed by Clemente Fracassi and promoted in the U.S. by Sol Hurok like a theatrical event. It helped make Loren world

famous. In 1961 she won a Best Actress Oscar for her performance in *Two Women*. See AIDA (1953), LA FAVORITA (1952).

LORENGAR, PILAR

Spanish soprano (1928-1996)

Pilar Lorengar, who made her U.S. debut at the San Francisco Opera as Desdemona in 1964, was hugely popular in that city and sang there regularly for 25 years. She began her career in Spain as a zarzuela singer and moved into opera in 1955. She made her first appearance at the Met in 1966 but the main center of her activity was the Deutsche Oper in Berlin. She is only sparsely represented on film and video. See COSÌ FAN TUTTE (1971 film), DON GIOVANNI (1961), GALA LIRICA, LA TRAVIATA (1984 film).

LORTZING, ALBERT

German composer (1801-1851)

Albert Lortzing was the leading comic opera composer of German in the 19th century. He began creating operas in 1828 with *Ali Pascha von Janina* and finished his last in 1851 just before he died. His most famous comic operas in Germany are *Zar und Zimmermann* and *Der Wildschütz* although the romantic tragedy *Undine* is probably the best known internationally. *Zar und Zimmermann* is a favorite of German filmmakers. See UNDINE, ZAR UND ZIMMERMANN.

1919 Der Waffenschmied

Lortzing's 1846 opera *Der Waffenschmied* (The Armourer) is set in the city of Worms in the 16th century. Count Liebenau loves Marie, the daughter of Stadinger who disapproves of aristocrats. The count disguises himself as a commoner and goes to work for him as an armourer. The German Delog company filmed the opera in 1919 and sent it on tour with soloists, chorus and small orchestra. Presumably this was a way of bringing opera to small towns at low cost. Black and white. About 70 minutes.

LOS ANGELES, VICTORIA DE

Spanish soprano (1923-)

Victoria de los Angeles was born in Barcelona where she made her debut in 1941 as Mimi in *La Bohème*. She sang on the BBC in 1948, came to

Covent Garden in 1950 and to the Met in 1951. She is especially admired for her singing of lyrical roles like Mimi and her recording of *La Bohème* with Bjoerling and Beecham is considered by many to be unsurpassed. Los Angeles has now given up opera for the concert stage but she continues to charm audiences 50 years after she began her career. See MADAMA BUTTERFLY (1960), MAURICE RAVEL (1988).

1962 Victoria de los Angeles

John Freeman talks to Victoria de los Angeles about her life and her career in this BBC television film. She sings excerpts from *The Barber of Seville, Madame Butterfly* and *La Vida Breve.* The program was produced by Patricia Foy and transmitted on May 31, 1962. Black and white. 40 minutes. Print at National Film Archive, London.

1967 The Glory of Spain

Victoria de los Angeles is the featured singer in this tribute to the music and art of Spain filmed at Madrid's El Prado museum. She sings songs and arias by Palomin, Blas de la Cerna, Granados and Cabeson. The program also includes pianist Alicia de Larrocha and guitarist Andrés Segovia and the featured artists are El Greco, Goya and Velasquez. The video is introduced by Segovia, narrated by Donald Voorhes, written by John Somerset and directed by Nathan Kroll. Color. 54 minutes. VAI video.

1968 Magnificent Victoria de los Angeles

Los Angeles is shown in a recital taped for the BBC on Dec. 17, 1968. Pianist Gerald Moore acts as host and introduces the selections. She sings eighteen songs including "Zapateado" from Gimenez's *La Tempranica*, four songs by Ravel, three by Fauré, three by Nin and two by Toldra. She ends the program with Montsalvatge's "Canción de cuna par domir a un negrito." Color. 48 minutes. VAI video.

1989 The Jubilee Recital

Los Angeles made her recital debut at the Palacido de la Musica in Barcelona on May 19. 1944 at the beginning of her career. On May 19, 1989 she returned to the same stage for a Spanish song celebration of her 45 years as a singer. She performs songs by Falla, Del Vado, Mison, Pia, Esteve, Granados, Albeniz, Vives, Montsalvatge, Mompou and concludes with an aria from

Carmen. Manuel Garcia Morante is her pianist. Color. 90 minutes. VAI video.

LOSEY, JOSEPH
American film director (1909-1984)

Joseph Losey began his film career in America in 1941 but worked primarily in England after he was blacklisted in 1951. He is the cinema's equivalent of Henry James with artistic roots in both countries and one of his greatest movies was appropriately titled *The Go-Between.* His *Don Giovanni* is one of the truly great opera films and unlike any other in its visual and intellectual sensibility. See DON GIOVANNI (1979).

LOTT, FELICITY
English soprano (1947-)

Felicity Lott made her debut in 1973, began to sing with the English National Opera in 1975 and made her first appearances at Covent Garden and Glyndebourne in 1976. She sings in a wide variety of classic and modern operas but is especially noted for her Mozart and Strauss. She made her debut at the Met in 1990 as the Marshallin in *Der Rosenkavalier* and can be seen in this role on video. See GLYNDEBOURNE (1992), INTERMEZZO (1983), THE MAGIC FLUTE (1978), THE MARRIAGE OF FIGARO (1984 film), A MIDSUMMER NIGHT'S DREAM (1981), THE RAKE'S PROGRESS (1977), DER ROSENKAVALIER (1994).

LOTTERY BRIDE, THE
1930 film operetta by Friml

Rudolf Friml wrote an original score for this rather bizarre Hollywood film operetta produced by Arthur Hammerstein (Oscar II's uncle). Jeanette MacDonald portrays a woman whose love affair goes wrong so she allows herself to be the prize in an Alaskan marriage lottery. She ends up as the bride-to-be of her true love's brother and, horrors, he is there in the same cabin. He jumps on a passing German Zeppelin to get away but it gets lost on the ice. Jeanette sets out to rescue him and all ends impossibly well. The cast also includes Joe. E Brown and Zasu Pitts. Herbert Stothart originated the story, Horace Jackson wrote the screenplay, J. Kerin Brennan wrote the lyrics for the forgotten songs and Paul Stein directed. United Artists. Two color Technicolor 80 minutes. See also RUDOLF FRIML.

LOUISE

1900 opera by Charpentier

Louise is Gustav Charpentier's greatest opera and the only one for which he is remembered. It is virtually a love song to the Bohemian Paris of his time and tells the story of Louise who loves the artist Julien. Her parents refuse to allow them to marry so they set up house together in Montmartre. When her father becomes ill, she returns home to nurse him. After he recovers she rejoins Julien. The opera was a scandal when it premiered but today it is seen as merely romantic. It is best known for its famous soprano aria "Depuis le jour." Charpentier was involved in the making of a 1939 film of the opera but there are no modern videos. See also GUSTAV CHARPENTIER.

1939 Grace Moore film

Metropolitan Opera diva Grace Moore stars as Louise in this French film produced under the supervision of the 78-year-old composer. It is one of the classic opera films and was directed by cinematic master Abel Gance. The film's greatest asset, however, is Moore who filmed it after her Hollywood career when she was in peak form as singer and actress. The other singers include Georges Thill as Julien and André Pernet as Louise's father; they made a famous recording of the opera in 1935 with Ninon Vallin as Louise. Suzanne Desprès portrays Louise's mother, Ginette Leclerc is Lucienne and Robert Le Vigan is Gaston. Eugene Bigot conducted the orchestra. The dialogue in the film is spoken. Black and white. In French. 85 minutes.

1987 Derek Jarman film

Derek Jarman's segment of the British opera film *Aria* is based around "Depuis le jour" as sung by Leontyne Price. It features an aged opera singer taking her final curtain call and remembering the great love of her youth. Amy Johnson portrays the old lady, Tilda Swinton plays the lady as a girl and Spencer Leigh is the young man. The music is played by the RCA Italiana Orchestra conducted by Francesco Molinari-Pradelli. Color. In French. About 10 minutes. See also ARIA.

LOVE OF THREE ORANGES, THE

1921 opera by Prokoviev

Sergei Prokoviev's surrealistic opera *The Love of Three Oranges* (Lyubov' k tryom apel'sinam)

premiered in Chicago in 1921 in its French translation as *L'Amour des Trois Oranges*. Prokoviev based his libretto on a fantasy fable by Venetian playwright Carlo Gozzi. The story revolves around the Prince of Clubs who is dying because he is unable to laugh until Fata Morgana takes a pratfall. Under her spell he seeks out three oranges which contain three princesses, one of whom will be his love. See also SERGEI PROKOVIEV.

1980 BBC Television

Robin Leggate stars as the Prince in this Brian Large production for BBC TV. The opera is sung in French with Joseph Rouleau as the King of Clubs, Pauline Tinsley as Fata Morgana, Alexander Oliver as Truffaldino, Dennis Wicks as Celio, Tom McConnell as Leandro and Katharine Pring as Clarissa. Robin Stapleton conducts the London Philharmonic Orchestra and the Ambrosian Opera Chorus. Color. In French with English subtitles. 130 minutes. Video at MTR.

1982 Glyndebourne Festival

The star of this extravagant production is set designer Maurice Sendak whose zany designs, colors and puppets keep the eye constantly amused. Director Frank Corsaro features the *commedia dell'arte* story as a play within a play being staged in the middle of the French Revolution. It's outlandish fun with its acrobats, jugglers, oranges that grow princesses, animated sequences and giant baker. Ryland Davies is the Prince who can't be amused, Willard White is the upright King, Nelly Morpurgo is the bewitching Fata Morgana, Richard Van Allan is the Magician Celio, Ugo Benelli is Truffaldino, Derek Hammond-Stroud is Farfarello, Colette Alliot-Lugaz is Princess Ninetta, Nuccio Condo is Clarissa and John Pringle is Leandro. Bernard Haitink conducts the London Philharmonic. Rodney Greenberg directed for video. Color. In French with English subtitles. 120 minutes. Home Vision video.

1989 Opéra de Lyon

Gabriel Bacquier stars as the King of Clubs in Louis Erlo's zestful Lyons Opera production. Jean-Luc Viala is the Prince, Hélène Penaguin is Princess Clarissa, Catherine Dubosc is Ninetta, Consuelo Caroli is Linetta, Michèle Lagrange is Fata Morgana, Georges Gautier is Truffaldino, Didier Henry is Pantaloon and Farfarello, Jules Bastin is the Cook and Gregory Reinhart is the magician Celio. Jacques Rapp designed the sets and Ferdinando Bruni created the costumes. Kent Nagano conducted the Opéra de Lyon Orchestra and Jean-François Jung directed the video. Color. In French. 90 minutes. Polygram (England) video/ Japanese laserdisc.

LUBITSCH, ERNST
German/U.S. film director (1892-1947)

Ernst Lubitsch made film adaptations of operas and operettas in Germany and America. His famous "touch" extended to notable silent films of *Carmen* and *The Student Prince*. He filmed *Ein Walzertraum* in 1931 as *The Smiling Lieutenant*. He directed Jeanette MacDonald in musicals and made a superb version of *The Merry Widow* in 1934. Other plans didn't work out including an ambitious *Der Rosenkavalier* and a film of Kálmán's *Kaiserin Josephine* with Grace Moore. It was cancelled when she was killed in a plane crash. His last film was an adaptation of Jean Gilbert's operetta *That Lady in Ermine*; he died while shooting it. See CARMEN (1918), DIE FRAU IM HERMELIN (1949), JEANETTE MACDONALD (1929/1930/1932), THE MERRY WIDOW (1934), THE STUDENT PRINCE (1927), EIN WALZERTRAUM (1931).

LUCIA DI LAMMERMOOR
1835 opera by Donizetti

Lucy of Lammermoor is Donizetti's finest opera and has become a fixture in the modern repertory. Its extraordinary sextet and mad scene are among the most memorable in all opera. The melodramatic libretto by Salvadore Cammorano is based on Sir Walter Scott's novel *The Bride of Lammermoor*. Lucia's brother Enrico has usurped Edgardo's estate but Lucia and Edgardo are in love and meet secretly. Her brother persuades to marry Arturo by forging a letter but Edgardo returns on the day of the marriage to join in the famous sextet. Lucia goes mad, kills her husband and demonstrates her singing skills with the help of a flute. The blood and thunder plot has been popular with filmmakers and the opera has been used for dramatic effect in novels, most notably in Flaubert's *Madame Bovary*. See also GAETANO DONIZETTI.

1948 Nelly Corradi film
This was the first film of the complete opera and shows its age but it stays close to the original in text and music. Nelly Corradi stars as Lucia with Mario Filippeschi as Edgardo, Afro Poli as Ashton, Aldo Ferracuti as Arturo, Italo Tajo as Raimondo and Loretta Di Lelio as Alisa. Gina Lollobrigida has a small role. Oliviero De Fabritiis conducts the Rome Opera House Orchestra and Chorus. Piero Ballerini directed. Black and white. In Italian. 95 minutes. Lyric/Opera Dubs/Mastervideo (Italy) videos.

1948 Tito Gobbi film
Tito Gobbi stars as Lord Ashton in this highlights version of the opera filmed on stage at the Rome Opera House. Liliana Rossi sings Lucia (acted by Anne Lollobrigida), Giancinto Prandelli sings Edgardo (acted by Zwonko Gluk), Luciano Neroni sings Raimondo (acted by Giulio Tomei), Anna Marcangeli sings and acts Alisa and Cesare Valletti sings Arturo (acted by Gino Conti). Angelo Questa conducted the Rome Opera House Orchestra and Chorus. E. Fulchignoni staged the opera and George Richfield produced the film for the *First Opera Film Festival*. Black and white. In Italian. 23 minutes.

1964 NBC Opera Theatre
This notable NBC Opera Theatre production by Samuel Chotzinoff was presented in an English-language version. Peter Herman Adler conducted the Symphony of the Air Orchestra and Kirk Browning directed the live telecast. Black and white. In English. 100 minutes.

1967 Renata Scotto video
Renata Scotto was in peak form when she sang the role of Lucia in this Tokyo production. Carlo Bergonzi is her melancholic Edgardo, Mario Zanasi is a villainous Enrico, Plinio Clabassi is Raimondo, Mirella Fiorentini is Alisa, Giuseppe Baratti is Normanno and Angelo Marchiandi is Arturo. The opera was taped for Japanese television on Sept. 27, 1967, with rather old-fashioned cardboard sets. Bruno Bartoletti conducted the NHK Lirica Italiana Orchestra and Chorus. Color. In Italian with Japanese subtitles. 127 minutes. Legato Classics video.

1971 Anna Moffo film
Anna Moffo is marvelous as Lucia in this Italian film shot on location in a 17th century castle. Edgardo is portrayed by Lajos Kozma, Enrico is Giulio Fioravanti, Pietro di Vietri is the ill-fated Arturo, Paulo Washington is Raimondo and Anna

Maria Segatori is Alisa. The music is performed by the Rome Symphony Orchestra and the RAI Chorus led by Carlo Felice Cillario. Mario Lanfranchi directed. Color. In Italian with English subtitles. 108 minutes. VAI video.

1973 Joan Sutherland video
Joan Sutherland stars in this highlights *Who's Afraid of Opera* version of the opera intended for children. Sutherland tells the story of the opera to puppets and performs the role of Lucia with John Brecknock as Edgardo, Pieter Van Der Stolk as Enrico, Francis Egerton as Arturo, Clifford Grant as Raimondo and Alicia Gamley as Alisa. The dialogue is in English but the arias are sung in Italian. Richard Bonynge conducted the London Symphony Orchestra and Piers Haggard directed. Color. In English and Italian. 30 minutes. Kultur video.

1981 Bregenz Festival
Katia Ricciarelli portrays Lucia with José Carreras as Edgardo in this Bregenz Festival production in Austria. Leo Nucci sings the role of Enrico and Lamberto Gardelli conducts. Color. In Italian. 125 minutes. Legato video.

1982 Metropolitan Opera
Joan Sutherland, one of the great Lucias, was captured on tape in this superb Metropolitan Opera production by Bruce Donnell. This was the role that made Sutherland famous in 1959 and 23 years later she is still a vocal wonder. The Sextet and the Mad Scene set standards for the opera. Sutherland is ably partnered by Alfredo Kraus as Edgardo, Pablo Elvira as Enrico, Paul Plishka as Raimondo and Ariel Bybee as Alisa. Attilio Colonnello created the sets and costumes and Richard Bonynge conducts the Metropolitan Opera Orchestra and Chorus. Kirk Browning directed the video on Nov. 13, 1982, and it was telecast on Sept. 28, 1983. Color. In Italian with English subtitles. 128 minutes. Paramount video/Pioneer laser.

1982 New York City Opera
Gianna Rolandi stars as Lucia in this New York City Opera production heading a cast that includes Brent Ellis, Robert Hale and Barry McCauley. Judith Somogi conducts the New York City Opera and Chorus. Beverly Sills hosted the telecast on April 10, 1982. Color. In Italian with English subtitles. 180 minutes.

1983 Grand Théâtre de Genève
June Anderson stars as Lucia with Peter Dvorsky as her Edgardo in this Geneva Grand Théâtre production by Pier-Luigi Pizzi. Lajos Miller is Enrico and Agostino Ferrin sings the role of Raimondo. Nello Santi conducts the Suisse Romande Orchestra and the Grand Théâtre de Genève choirs. Color. In Italian with Japanese subtitles. 149 minutes. Lyric video/Japanese laser.

1986 Australian Opera
Joan Sutherland stars again as Lucia in this Sydney Opera House production by John Copley but it is not up to the 1982 Metropolitan Opera version. Sutherland is supported by Richard Greager as Edgardo, Malcolm Donnelly as Ashton, Clifford Grant as Raimondo, Patricia Price as Alisa and Sergei Baigildin as Arturo. Richard Bonynge conducts the Elizabethan Sydney Orchestra. Color. In Italian with English subtitles. 145 minutes. Kultur video.

1992 Teatro alla Scala
Baritone Renato Bruson stars as Enrico in this La Scala production with Mariella Devia as Lucia and Vincenzo La Scola as Edgardo. Pier'Alli staged the opera, designed the sets and costumes and directed the video. The cast includes Marco Berti, Carlo Colombara, Floriana Sovilla and Ernest Cravazzi. Stefano Ranzani conducts the Teatro alla Scala Orchestra and Chorus. SACIS. Color. In Italian. 140 minutes. On video and Japanese laser.

Early/related films

1907 Messter sound film
Otto Messter's Biophon German film of a scene from the opera was screened with an aria played on a synchronized phonograph. About 3 minutes.

1908 Rossi sound film
This early Italian sound film of scenes from the opera was made by the Rossi company with the sound-on-disc system. Black and white. About 9 minutes.

1908 Ernesto Maria Pasquali film
Italian director Ernesto Maria Pasquali made this version of the story for the Ambrosio company in 1908. About 10 minutes.

1909 Vitagraph film
The American Vitagraph company made this version of *The Bride of Lammermoor* in 1909. It was based on both the Scott novel and the opera. About 10 minutes.

1911 Mario Caserini film
Mario Caserini directed this version of the story for the Cinés studio of Turin, based on the opera and the Scott novel. Like Caserini's other opera films, it stars Alberto Capozzi and Maria Cleo Tarlarini and was written by Arrigo Frusta. About 10 minutes.

1912 Edison Cinephonograph
Caruso is rumored to have sung the Sextet from *Lucia* with basso Pol Plançon in a legendary early Edison attempt to synchronize sound and image. Caruso did make records of the Sextet during this period but the film, if it ever existed, has never been found.

1922 Tense Moments from Opera series
Vivian Gibson stars as Lucia in this English highlights version of the opera titled *The Bride of Lammermoor*. Gordon Hopkird portrays Edgardo and Olaf Hytten is Arturo. Challis Anderson directed for the *Tense Moments from Opera* series. The music was played live when the film was screened. Gaumont. Black and white. About 10 minutes.

1934 One Night of Love
Grace Moore's hit opera film contains a delightful *Lucia di Lammermoor* Sextet scene. It is cleverly arranged by Spanish bass Andrés De Segurola to divert the attention of a rent-collecting landlady. Victor Schertzinger directed. Black and white. 80 minutes.

1934 Madame Bovary
Flaubert set an important scene of his novel at a performance of *Lucia di Lammermoor* in Rouen. Director Jean Renoir includes the opera scene in his fine film adaptation. Black and white. In French. 101 minutes.

1935 Captain January
The Sextet is performed in this Shirley Temple movie as a trio by Temple, Guy Kibbee and Slim Summerville. The film tells the story of an orphan taken in by a lighthouse keeper. Black and white. 78 minutes.

1937 Swing It Professor
The Sextet is sung by a group of hoboes sitting around an outdoor campfire in this musical comedy about swing music. Pinky Tomlin plays the music professor who stumbles on the operatic bums. Black and white. 66 minutes.

1941 The Flame of New Orleans
René Clair's wonderful film begins with *Lucia di Lammermoor* on stage at the New Orleans opera house as Marlene Dietrich baits her trap for a rich man. Hungarian diva Gitta Alpar and Anthony Marlowe are shown singing Lucia and Edgardo's first act duet "Verrano a te sull'aure." Black and white. 78 minutes.

1941 Andy Hardy's Private Secretary
Kathryn Grayson portrays a singer hired by Mickey Rooney to sort out his mixed-up affairs. She sings the Mad Scene from *Lucia* at their high school graduation. George Seitz directed. MGM. Black and white. 101 minutes.

1941 Notes to You
An alley cat sets up a sheet music stand on a backyard fence and annoys Porky Pig who is trying to sleep. After the cat is shot, ghost cats return singing the Sextet from *Lucia di Lammermoor*. Friz Freleng directed. Warner Bros. Color. About 7 minutes.

1946 The Whale Who Wanted to Sing at the Met
Willie, the opera-singing whale with the voice of Nelson Eddy, imagines he is about to be discovered and auditions by singing three parts of the Sextet. He then fantasizes performing it on stage at the Met. Hamilton Luske directed this Disney cartoon as part of the feature *Make Mine Music*. Color. 12 minutes.

1948 Back Alley Oproar
Sylvester the Cat and heavenly friends sing the Sextet to the utter disgust of a Elmer Fudd in this delightful Warner Bros. cartoon. Friz Freleng directed. Color. 7 minutes.

1960 The Exterminating Angel
Lucia de Lammermoor is the unseen prelude to Luis Buñuel's extraordinary Mexican film *El Angel*

Exterminador. The high society folk in the film have just attended a performance of the opera when they turn up for a dinner party at the Nobile mansion. The diva Silvia (Rosa Elena Durgal) who sang Lucia and her conductor Mr. Roc (Enrique Garcia Alvarez) are among the guests. They find themselves unable to leave the room where the dinner is held. Black and white. In Spanish. 95 minutes.

1991 Where Angels Fear To Tread

Where Angels Fear To Tread is a 1905 novel by E. M. Forster with an opera scene built around *Lucia di Lammermoor* as performed in a provincial Italian opera house. Charles Sturridge filmed this sequence brilliantly and it becomes the occasion for a display of the different attitudes Italians and English have towards opera. An English family led by Harriet Herriton (Judy Davis) is in the town of Manteriano as she has hopes of taking back her late sister's child from his Italian father. The family go to the theater to see *Lucia* and find the Italian audience really enjoying itself. Harriet walks out saying she finds this gusto disgusting and the production "not even respectable." Her brother Philip thinks it's wonderful. Color. 112 minutes. New Line video.

1991 Madame Bovary

Claude Chabrol's film of the Flaubert novel stars Isabelle Huppert as Madame Bovary and includes the scene where she attends *Lucia di Lammermoor* in Rouen. The opera itself is not shown. Color. In French. 130 minutes.

LUCREZIA BORGIA
1833 opera by Donizetti

Lucrezia Borgia was Donizetti's most popular opera during the 19th century and has been a star vehicle in recent times for Montserrat Caballé and Joan Sutherland. The melodramatic libretto by Felice Romani is based on a Victor Hugo play about the most famous woman in the Borgia clan. Lucrezia is married to Alfonso but she has already poisoned three husbands and he is afraid he may be next. When Lucrezia poisons young Orsini and his companions out of spite, she discovers that her son Gennaro is one of her victims. She tries to save him but he rejects her and chooses to die.

1977 Australian Opera

Joan Sutherland was at her vocal peak when she sang Lucrezia in this Sydney Opera House production. Ronald Stevens is Gennaro, Margreta Elkins is Orsini and Robert Allman is Don Alfonso. The production was directed by George Ogilvie with Richard Bonynge conducting the Australian Opera Orchestra and Chorus. It was taped for Australian television in July 1977. Color. In Italian. 138 minutes. Home Vision video/Japanese laser.

LUDWIG II
King of Bavaria (1845-1886)

Richard Wagner's royal patron admired the composer so much that he provided him with financial aid from the moment he became King Ludwig II in 1864. This generous support allowed Wagner to create his most ambitious operas. The Wagner connection and the King's eccentric behavior have combined to inspire a number of film biographies. All use Wagner's music on the soundtrack and most have scenes from the operas.

1922 Ludwig II

Olaf Fjord stars as Ludwig II with Eugen Freiss as Richard Wagner in this silent Austrian film biography of the monarch. It was screened with live Wagner music. Otto Kreisler directed. Black and white. In German. About 70 minutes.

1929 Ludwig the Second, King of Bavaria

William Dieterle stars as Ludwig in *Ludwig der Zweite, König von Bayern* which he also directed just before the sound era in Germany. It was shot on location in Ludwig's castles. The cast includes Max Schreck, Theodor Loos and Hans Heinrich Von Twardowski. Black and white. German intertitles. About 90 minutes.

1955 Ludwig II

Helmut Kautner's romantic film about the King concentrates on his love for Elizabeth, Empress of Austria. O. W. Fischer portrays Ludwig with Ruth Leuwerik as the Empress, Paul Bildt as Richard Wagner and Erica Balque as Cosima. Wagner's music is performed by the Vienna Symphony Orchestra conducted by Herbert von Karajan. Color. In German. 115 minutes.

1972 Ludwig, Requiem for a Virgin King

Hans Jurgen Syberberg's eccentric approach to the story focuses on the King as a mad virgin homosexual visionary. Harry Baer portrays the King with Gerhard März as Richard Wagner I and Annette Tirier as Richard Wagner II. Ingrid Caven portrays Lola Montez and Hanna Kohler is Sissi. Dietrich Lohmann was the cinematographer. The German title is *Ludwig - Requiem für einem jungfräulichen König*. Color. In German. 140 minutes.

1972 Ludwig

Luchino Visconti's elaborate version of the story centers on the Bavarian king's fears, fantasies and neuroses. It was shot on location in Bavaria with authentic costumes and settings. Helmut Berger stars as Ludwig with Trevor Howard as Richard Wagner. There is strong support from Romy Schneider, Silvana Mangano and Gert Fröbe. Excerpts from *Lohengrin, Tannhäuser, Tristan und Isolde* and *Siegfried* are played by the Hollywood Bowl Symphony Orchestra conducted by Carmen Dragon. Armando Nannuzzi was the superb cinematographer. Color. In Italian.185 minutes.

1985 In the Ocean of Longing

Im Ozean der Sehnsucht is an impressionistic video about the life and death of King Ludwig directed by Christian Rischert. Color. In German. 103 minutes.

LUDWIG, CHRISTA
German mezzo-soprano (1928-)

Berlin-born Christa Ludwig made her debut as Orlovsky in *Die Fledermaus* in Frankfurt, established her reputation in Vienna which became her operatic home and then went on to sing at most of the great opera houses. She made her American debut in 1959 in Chicago and sang at the Metropolitan the same year. She was a Met regular until 1990 and sang Dido in the first U.S. production of *Les Troyens*. Ludwig gave her farewell performance in October 1993. See CANDIDE (1989), COSÌ FAN TUTTE (1970), FALSTAFF (1982), FIDELIO (1963), GÖTTERDÄMMERUNG (1990), MADAMA BUTTERFLY (1974), DAS RHEINGOLD (1990), DIE WALKÜRE (1990).

1972 Brahms Recital by Christa Ludwig

Christa Ludwig sings and Leonard Bernstein accompanies her on piano at this 1972 recital. The program consists of songs by Brahms. Roger Englander directed this 35mm film for television. Color. 59 minutes.

1992 Vienna Philharmonic 150th Anniversary

Christa Ludwig is in eloquent form singing five Mahler songs in this concert with the Vienna Philharmonic conducted by Riccardo Muti. It was taped at a performance in the Grosser Musikvereinsaal in Vienna on March 22, 1992. Hugo Kach directed. Color. 114 minutes. Sony video.

1994 Tribute to Vienna

Ludwig pays tribute to the city that provided some of her greatest musical moments in this recital taped at the Grosser Musikvereinssaal on April 24th, 1994. The concert includes selections from Beethoven, Mahler, Schubert, Bernstein, Strauss and Wolf. Charles Spencer accompanies her on piano and Elisabeth Birke-Malzer directed the video. Color. 77 minutes. RCA video.

LUGO, GIUSEPPE
Italian tenor (1898-1980)

Giuseppe Lugo starred in five Italian films in the late 1930s and early 1940s, usually portraying an Italian tenor like himself. He began his career at the Opéra Comique in Paris in 1931 singing Cavaradossi in *Tosca*. He returned to Italy in 1936 and had great success in Bologna in the same role. He then became popular at La Scala, Rome and other Italian opera houses and was much liked for his *Rigoletto* Duke as well as his Cavaradossi. Logo is not listed in the *New Grove* but has sizable entries in Italian and German reference books. His recordings are available in the U.S. and some films are on video.

1939 La Mia Canzone al Vento

Lugo portrays a famous tenor in *My Song in the Wind* and sings a number of opera arias. He becomes the prize in a charity lottery and agrees to visit the winner for a day. When the daughter of a small town official wins, Lugo arrives incognito to check out the situation. Guido Brignone directed. Black and white. In Italian. 82 minutes

1940 Cantante Con Me

Sing With Me features Lugo as the same famous tenor. A small town housewife has become infatuated with him and follows him to Rome to see him in *Tosca*. Lugo sends her back to her anxious husband. Director Guido Brignone allows Lugo the opportunity to sing Verdi, Leoncavallo and Puccini arias. Black and white. In Italian. 83 minutes.

1942 Miliardi, che follia!

Guido Brignone again directs Lugo, this time as a millionaire with a fine voice. After a kidnap attempt he hides out with a touring theater company. His singing makes them rich and he falls in love with a young woman in the troupe. Critics noted that Lugo hardly ever stopped singing in his films. Black and white. In Italian. 85 minutes.

1943 Senza una donna

Lugo had a new director, Alfredo Guarini, for *Without a Woman* but once again he is rich and very vocal. He portrays a woman-hating duke who hides away in his castle with two other tenors. Women are not allowed but a group of stranded ballerinas gain entry and change his life. Black and white. In Italian. 82 minutes.

1956 Il Tiranno del Garda

Lugo made only one film after the war and was featured in a supporting role as the opera singer Raniero. The film is a patriotic historical tale about an uprising in the Lake Garda area. Ignazio Ferronetti directed. Black and white. In Italian. 85 minutes.

LUHRMANN, BAZ

Australian film director (1962-)

Filmmaker Baz Luhrmann, best known for the 1992 hit movie *Strictly Ballroom,* has also become a successful producer of operas on stage in Australia. In 1986 he wrote and directed an opera called *Lake Lost* for Australian Opera. In 1990 he staged *La Bohème* and turned it into a highly effective 1950s Paris love story, with a lively young cast. The Bohemians live behind a neon sign that proclaims "L'Amour" and the subtitles on the video refer to Sartre and Mary Poppins. It was taped in 1993. See LA BOHÈME (1993).

LUISA FERNANDA

1932 zarzuela by Moreno Torroba

Spanish composer Federico Moreno Torroba's most popular zarzuela is set in Spain in the middle of the 19th century. Royalist and Republicans are at each other's throats, not unlike the time when the opera premiered. Luisa Fernanda loves Royal Hussar colonel Javiar but is courted by rich landowner Vidal. When Javiar turns his attentions to Duchess Carolina, Luisa Fernanda decides to marry republican Vidal. When the republicans win, Javiar admits his love for her. She decides to go into exile with him. See also FEDERICO MORENO TORROBA.

1963 Placido Domingo film

Placido Domingo stars in a film of the zarzuela made for Mexican television at the beginning of his career. It is part of a series of six sponsored by Max Factor. The production features Ernestina Garfias, Franco Inglesias and Domingo's father. Black and white. In Spanish. 90 minutes.

1968 Juan de Orduña film

Dolores Perez sings the role of Luisa Fernanda with Federico Moreno Torroba conducting the Spanish Lyric Orchestra and Madrid Chorus. Other roles are taken by Luis-Sagi Vela, Carlo del Monte, Josefina Cubeiro, Manuel Gonzalez, Ramon Alonso and Jesus Aguirre. The film was directed by Juan De Orduña, written by Manuel Tamayo and produced by Spanish Television for its *Teatro Lirico Español* series. The film soundtrack is on record. Color. In Spanish. 96 minutes.

1982 Teatro de Colón, Bogotá

Zorayda Salazar stars as Luisa Fernanda in this Teatro de Colón production designed and staged by Jaime Manzur and telecast from Bogotá, Colombia. Antonio Blancas is Vidal Hernando, Manuel Contreras is Xaviar Moreno and Beatriz Parra is Duchess Carolina. Jaime Leon conducts the Colombia Symphony Orchestra and Chorus. Color. In Spanish. 115 minutes. Opera Dubs video.

LUISA MILLER

1844 opera by Verdi

Giuseppe Verdi's popular early opera is set in 17th century Tyrol. Luisa Miller is in love with Rodolfo but his father plots to separate them as he wants his son to marry Federica. When Luisa's father is arrested, Luisa is forced to write a letter denying her love. The angry Rodolfo poisons Luisa and himself and defies his father by dying. The opera's famous tenor aria "Quando le sere al placido" is sung by Rodolfo. Salvadore Cammarano based his libretto on Schiller's play *Kabale und Liebe*. See also GIUSEPPE VERDI.

1979 Metropolitan Opera
Renata Scotto sings Luisa and Placido Domingo is Rodolfo in this Metropolitan Opera production by Nathaniel Merrill. Sherrill Milnes is Miller, Jean Kraft is Federica, Bonaldo Giaiotti is Count Walter and James Morris is Wurm. The sets were designed by Attilio Colonnello and the costumes by Charles Caine. Kirk Browning directed the video which was telecast on Jan. 10, 1979. Color. In Italian with English subtitles 150 minutes. Video at MTR.

1980 Covent Garden
Katia Ricciarelli portrays Luisa in this Royal Opera House, Covent Garden, production that was telecast in the U.S. Placido Domingo is Rodolfo, Renato Bruson is Miller, Gwynne Howell is Walter and Richard van Allen is Wurm. Lorin Maazel conducts the Royal Opera House Orchestra and Chorus. Color. In Italian with English subtitles. 149 minutes. Lyric video.

1988 Lyons Opera
June Anderson stars as Luisa in this Opéra de Lyon production by Jacques Lassale. Taro Ichihara is Rodolfo, Eduard Tumagian is Miller, Paul Plishka is Count Walter, Romuald Tesarowicz is Wurm and Susanna Anselmi is Federica. Maurizio Balo designed the sets and costumes. Maurizio Arena leads the Lyons Opera Orchestra and Chorus and Montpellier Opera Chorus. Claud Viller directed the video. Color. In Italian. 150 minutes. Home Vision video/Japanese laserdisc.

Early film

1910 Itala film
A early silent film of scenes from the opera was made in Italy by the Itala film company of Turin. It was released in the USA in August 1910. Black and white. About l4 minutes.

LULLY, JEAN-BAPTISTE
French composer (1632-1687)

Jean-Baptiste Lully, the founder of French opera, was born in Italy but came to Paris at the age of thirteen. His collaborations with the playwright Molière were highly influential, especially the comedy-ballet *Le Bourgeois Gentilhomme*. His *Cadmus et Hormione* is seen as the cornerstone of French opera. Lully wrote fifteen popular operas but they are hardly known today outside France. See also ARMIDE, ATYS.

1958 Le Bourgeois Gentilhomme
Lully wrote the music for *Le Bourgeois Gentilhomme* (The Would-Be Gentleman) to a libretto by Molière in 1670. It's really a play with songs and dances but definitely a close relative of opera. Jean Meyer directed the Comédie Francais in a good 1958 film adaptation. Louis Seigner plays the rich bourgeois Jourdain with a cast that includes Andrée de Chauveron, Jean Piat and Michèle Grellier. André Jolivet conducts the music. Black and white. In French. 96 minutes. Video Yesteryear video.

1959 Pickpocket
Robert Bresson's great existential film about a Paris pickpocket uses music by Lully as its soundtrack. Black and white. In French. 75 minutes.

LULU
1937 opera by Berg

Alban Berg based the libretto of *Lulu* on Frank Wedekind's plays *Erdgeist* and *Die Büchse der Pandora*. The opera, set in the 19th century, tells the story of the *femme fatale* Lulu who destroys the men in her life. Her first husband dies after she is seduced by a painter and she kills the newspaper editor Schön whom she has married. She is emprisoned but escapes with the help of her lesbian lover Countess Geschwitz and ends up as a prostitute in London where she is killed by Jack the Ripper. Film director Roman Polanski based a Spoleto stage production on the Pabst film of the story. See also ALBAN BERG.

1980 Metropolitan Opera
Julia Migenes-Johnson stars as Lulu in this Metropolitan Opera production by John Dexter. Franz Mazura is Schön and Jack the Ripper,

Kenneth Reigel is Alwa, Evelyn Lear is the Countess, Frank Little is the Painter and the Negro and Andrew Foldi is Schigolch. Jocelyn Herbert designed the sets and James Levine conducted the Metropolitan Orchestra. Brian Large directed the video telecast on Dec. 20, 1980. Color. In German with English subtitles. 175 minutes. Video at MTR.

1995 Salzburg Festival
Christine Schäfer portrays Lulu in this Salzburg Festival production by Peter Mussbach. The cast includes Marjana Lipovsek, Laurence Dale, John Bröcheler, David Rendall, Tom Fox, Theo Adam and Graham Clark. Michael Gielen conducted the orchestra and Brian Large directed the video. ZDF/ARTE/RM Arts. Color. In German. 150 minutes. On video.

1996 Glyndebourne Festival
Christine Schäfer takes the role of Lulu in this modern dress Glyndebourne Festival Opera production by Graham Vick. Supporting her are David Kuebler as Alwa, Norman Bailey as Schigolch, Wolfgang Schöne as both Dr. Schöne and Jack the Ripper and Kathryn Harries as Countess Geschwitz. Pal Brown designed the plain, basic set and Thomas Webster designed the lighting. Andrew David conducted the London Philharmonic orchestra to exceptional effect. Humphrey Burton directed the video for Channel Four Television. Color. In German with English subtitles. 182 minutes. NVC Arts (England) video.

Related films

1917 Erna Morena film
Erna Morena stars as Lulu in this silent German film loosely based on the stories and featuring Emil Jannings and Harry Liedtke. It was directed by Alexander von Antalfy. Black and white. About 70 minutes.

1918 Michael Curtiz film
Casablanca director Michael Curtiz filmed this *Lulu*, his version of the Wedekind stories, in Budapest in 1918. It features Claire Lotto as Lulu with Bela Lugosi and Sandor Goth in supporting roles. Black and white. In Hungarian. About 70 minutes.

1919 Asta Nielsen film
Danish star Asta Nielsen portrays Lulu in this German silent film titled *Die Büchse der Pandora* adapted from the Wedekind story. Arzan von Csersepy directed. Black and white. In German. About 70 minutes.

1922 Asta Nielsen film
Asta Nielsen portrays Lulu for the second time in the German silent film titled *Loulou* (or *Erdegeist*) adapted from Wedekind's story *Erdegeist*. Albert Basserman plays Schön and Leopold Jessner directed. Black and white. In German. About 75 minutes.

1929 Louise Brooks film
Louise Brooks stars as Lulu in G.W. Pabst's *Die Büchse der Pandora* (Pandora's Box), the classic German silent film adaptation of the Wedekind plays. In its own way the film is as powerful and memorable as the Berg opera and can withstand comparison. Brooks, an American actress, gives one of the great screen performances, unsurpassed even by operatic Lulus. Fritz Kortner portrays Schön, Alice Roberts is the Countess and Gustav Diessl is Jack the Ripper. Ladislaus Vajda wrote the screenplay and Gunther Krampf was the superb cinematographer. Roman Polanski based his production of the opera in Spoleto on this film. Black and white. In German. 97 minutes. On video.

1962 Nadja Tiller film
This Austrian film titled *Lulu* stars Nadja Tiller as Lulu in an adaptation of the Wedekind plays strongly influenced by the Pabst film. It was written and directed by Rolf Thiele and uses music by Carl de Groof rather than Berg. The film was released in the U.S. as *No Orchids for Lulu*. Black and white. In German. 88 minutes.

1979 Walerian Borowczyk film
Polish director Walerian Borowczyk wrote and directed this *Lulu*, a German-French-Italian adaptation of the Wedekind plays. It stars Anne Bennent as Lulu with support from Michèle Placido and Jean-Jacques Delbo. The music is by Gianfranco Chiaranello. Color. In German or French. 86 minutes.

1978 Ronald Chase film
Ronald Chase based his film *Lulu* on G. W. Pabst's film *Pandora's Box* but added music from the Berg

opera to the soundtrack. Color. In German. 94 minutes.

LUNA, LA
1978 opera film by Bertolucci

Jill Clayburgh portrays a famous American soprano on tour in Italy with her adolescent son in this remarkable opera film by Bernardo Bertolucci. It includes a visit to Verdi's villa and an affectionate parody of a production of *Un Ballo in Maschera* at the Baths of Caracalla at its climax as well as scenes from *Il Trovatore, La Traviata* and *Rigoletto*. The soundtrack singers include Maria Callas, Franco Corelli, Gabriella Tucci and Robert Merrill. Carlo Verdone plays the director of the Caracalla opera with Ronaldo Bonacchi as his assistant and Alessio Vlad as the orchestra conductor. Nicola Nicoloso portrays Manrico in the production of *Il Trovatore* with Mario Tocci seen as the Count di Luna. Vittorio Storaro was the fine cinematographer. Twentieth Century-Fox. Color. In English. 140 minutes. See also BERNARDO BERTOLUCCI.

LUNA, PABLO
Spanish composer (1879-1914)

Spanish composer Pablo Luna y Carné is best known for his 1910 zarzuela *Molinos de Vientos* (Windmills) set in the flat landscapes of Holland. It became famous not only for its fine music but because it was one of the first Spanish zarzuelas to shift away from traditional settings in Spain. Luna wrote over 170 works for the stage but only *Windmills* appears to have been filmed. The libretto is by Luis Pascual Frutos.

1937 Molinos de Viento
Rosario Pi, the first Spanish woman director, filmed Luna's famous zarzuela in Spain in 1937. It was made for Star Films of Barcelona and stars singer Pedro Teroi with support from Maria Mercader, Maria Gómez and Roberto Font. Agustin Macasoli was the cinematographer. Black and white. In Spanish. 88 minutes.

LUSTIGE WITWE, DIE
See THE MERRY WIDOW

LUSTIGEN WEIBER VON WINDSOR, DIE
See THE MERRY WIVES OF WINDSOR

LYONS

Lyons (or Lyon as the French call it) has been a center of operatic activity in France since 1687 and in recent years has been one of the most adventurous. The Opéra de Lyon under the direction of Louis Erlo with American Kent Nagano as chief conductor has created a number of impressive productions of operas new and old, many of which are on video. They are certainly not all to everyone's taste but they are genuinely stimulating. See LES BRIGANDS (1989), L'ELISIR D'AMORE (1996), L'ENFANT ET LES SORTILÈGES (1993), L'ÉTOILE (1986), THE LOVE OF THREE ORANGES (1989), LUISA MILLER(1988), MADAMA BUTTERFLY (1993 film), THE MAGIC FLUTE (1992), MITRIDATE (1983), PELLÉAS ET MÉLISANDE (1983), RODRIGUE ET CHIMÈNE (1993), THE TALES OF HOFFMANN (1993), LES TROIS SOUHAITS (1991).

M

MAAZEL, LORIN
American conductor (1930-)

Lorin Maazel conducts the music on some of the great opera films including Joseph Losey's *Don Giovanni*, Francesco Rosi's *Carmen* and Franco Zeffirelli's *Otello*. He has led orchestras in New York, London, Vienna, Rome and Berlin and conducted opera at Covent Garden, Bayreuth, La Scala and other major opera houses. See AIDA (1986), BAYREUTH (1960), CARMEN (1984), PLACIDO DOMINGO (1989), DON GIOVANNI (1978), L'ENFANT ET LES SORTILÈGES (1986), LA FANCIULLA DEL WEST (1981), LUISA MILLER (1980), MADAMA BUTTERFLY (1986), OTELLO (1986), TURANDOT (1983).

MACBETH
1847 opera by Verdi

Giuseppe Verdi's opera has a libretto by Francesco Mario Piave and Andrea Maffei that follows the Shakespeare play fairly closely. Lady Macbeth persuades Macbeth to kill Duncan so he can become king of Scotland but their consciences give them no peace. Lady Macbeth walks in her sleep and dies of anguish. Rebels led by Macduff kill Macbeth and Malcolm becomes king. There are many films of the play from the earliest days of cinema but only recently has the opera itself been put on film and video. See also GIUSEPPE VERDI.

1953 NBC Opera Theatre
Patricia Neway stars as Lady Macbeth with Warren Galjour as Macbeth in this NBC Opera Theater English-language production by Samuel Chotzinoff. Lee Cass is Banquo and the cast includes William Böhm, Robert Holland and William Ryan. John Bloch directed the singers, Peter Herman Adler conducted the orchestra and Giovanni Cardelli wrote the translation. Kirk Browning directed the telecast. Black and white. 90 minutes. Video at MTR.

1972 Glyndebourne Festival
Kosta Paskalis and Josephine Barstow give intense performances as Macbeth and Lady Macbeth in this acclaimed Glyndebourne Festival production by Michael Hadjimischer. James Morris is Banquo, Keith Erwen is Macduff and Ian Caley is Malcolm. Emanuele Luzzati designed the sets and Robert Bryan the lighting. John Pritchard led the London Philharmonic and Glyndebourne Chorus. The video, directed by Dave Heather and produced by Humphrey Burton, was revived at London's National Film Theatre on Dec. 27, 1994. Color. In Italian with English subtitles. 148 minutes. VAI video.

1987 Deutsche Oper, Berlin
Renato Bruson and Mara Zampieri star as Macbeth and his Lady in this German production but it was producer Luca Ronconi and conductor Giuseppe Sinopoli that attracted the critical attention. James Morris is Banquo, Dennis O'Neill is Macduff and David Griffith is Malcolm. The set designs and costumes by Luciano Damiani are lit by Kurt Oscar Herting. Ronconi's minimalist production is enhanced by Brian Large's video direction as is Sinopoli's conducting of the Deutsche Oper Berlin Orchestra. Color. In Italian with English subtitles. 150 minutes. Home Vision video.

1987 Claude D'Anna film
Leo Nucci and Shirley Verrett are the murderous Macbeths in this French film of the opera. Director Claude D'Anna shot it on location in Belgium at the castle of the Crusader Godefroy de Bouillon in the Ardennes in an attempt to make it as realistic as possible. Samuel Ramey sings the role of Banquo which is acted by John Leysen, Veriano Luchetti sings Macduff acted by Philippe Volter and Antonio Barasorda is Malcolm. Riccardo Chailly conducts the Bologna Teatro Comunale Orchestra and Chorus. Color. In Italian with English subtitles. 134 minutes. London video and laser.

1993 Savonlinna Festival
Jorma Hynninen and Cynthia Makris portray the ambitious Macbeths in this production staged by Ralf Langbacka at the Savonlinna Festival in Finland. It's set in the 16th century Olavinlinna castle. The supporting cast includes Jaakko Ryhanen, Peter Lindroos and Riso Saarman. Lief Segerstam conducts the Savonlinna Festival Orchestra. Aarno Cronvall directed the video.

Amaya distribution. Color. In Italian. 140 minutes. On video.

Related films

SHAKESPEARE FILMS
Shakespeare's 1606 play *Macbeth* has been popular with filmmakers since the early days of silent cinema and was even transposed to Japan in Akira Kurosawa's 1957 *Throne of Blood*. The most notable modern versions are the 1948 *Macbeth* directed by and starring Orson Welles and the 1971 Roman Polanski film with Jon Finch as Macbeth.

1987 The Secret of Macbeth
Anna Raphael shot this 16mm documentary film during the production of Claude d'Anna's film of Verdi's *Macbeth* with singers Leo Nucci and Shirley Verrett. It shows how the film was made and includes interviews with the principals. Color. 43 minutes.

1987 Opera
Dario Argento's Italian film *Opera* is built around a Parma production of *Macbeth*. There are a number of scenes of the opera on stage at the Teatro Regio with Cristina Marsillach portraying Lady Macbeth. The singers are Elisabetta Norberg Schulz, Paola Leolini, Andrea Piccini and Michele Pertusi accompanied by the Arturo Toscanini Symphony Orchestra of Emilia and Romagna. Maria Callas and Mirella Freni are also heard on the soundtrack. The film plot is similar to that of *The Phantom of the Opera* with a mysterious figure prowling the secret corridors of the opera house, furthering the career of a young soprano and killing those involved with her. The film was released in the U. S. as *Terror at the Opera*. Color. In Italian. 90 minutes. South Gate video.

McCORMACK, JOHN
Irish tenor (1884-1945)

John McCormack considered himself a poor actor, one of the reasons he gave for quitting the opera stage, but his films belie this and show a natural performer. The great Irish tenor was born in Athlone but studied in Italy where he made his debut in 1906 with a false Italian name. He first appeared at Covent Garden in 1907 as Turiddu in *Cavalleria Rusticana* and sang there until 1914. He made his Metropolitan Opera debut in 1910 as

Alfredo in *La Traviata* and sang in opera in America until 1918. After that he devoted himself to recital tours and records. Like Caruso, he had a voice that recorded beautifully and he is still a pleasure to hear. He starred in one rather enjoyable film and was featured in others.

1930 Song O' My Heart
McCormack is a delight in this charming musical directed by Frank Borzage. The story is mostly an excuse for the tenor to sing twelve songs, everything from "Then You'll Remember Me" from *The Bohemian Girl* to "Plaisir d'Amour" and "Kitty My Love." He portrays an opera singer living in an Irish village who quit singing years before when he lost the woman he loved to another man. When he returns to singing and goes on an America recital tour, she asks him to look after her children if she should die as she fears. Spanish bass Andres De Segurola appears in the film as a friend from La Scala days. McCormack seems at ease as a film actor and his singing is superb. Fox. Black and white. 91 minutes. VAI video.

1933 The Shepherd of the Seven Hills
John McCormack sings the "Paius Angelicus" in this documentary about the Pope. It depicts the history of Rome, Vatican City and the Papacy. The Medievalists sing the choral music and Lew White plays the organ. The film was sponsored by the Catholic Writers Guild of New York and the Vatican. Black and white. 60 minutes.

1937 Wings of the Morning
McCormack portrays himself in the first British Technicolor feature and sings Moore's "Believe Me If All Those Endearing Young Charms," Balfe's "Killarney" and the traditional "At the Dawning of the Day." Henry Fonda and Annabella star in a slight story about a racehorse called Wings of the Morning. Harold Schuster directed. Twentieth Century-Fox. Technicolor. 87 minutes.

1953 So This is Love
Ray Kellogg portrays McCormack in this glossy Hollywood film biography of soprano Grace Moore, played by Kathryn Grayson. In the film he introduces the future Met diva at a recital she gives early in her career. The movie finishes on stage at the Metropolitan Opera with Moore in *La Bohème*. Gordon Douglas directed. Also known as *The Grace Moore Story*. Warner Bros. Color. 101 minutes.

McCRACKEN, JAMES
American tenor (1926-1988)

James McCracken, who won world acclaim in the role of Otello, made his debut in 1952 in Central City as Rodolfo. He began at the Metropolitan in 1953 in minor roles but left for Europe in 1957 when his career seemed stymied. He sang in German in Bonn until he had built a reputation and was invited to sing Otello in Washington, D.C. in 1960. It was this engagement that made him famous in the role and he then sang it around the world, including the Met. He often sang in Europe with his wife Sandra Warfield. McCracken can be seen performing as Otello in two videos. See AIDA (1985), METROPOLITAN OPERA (1983), OTELLO (1961/1963).

MacDONALD, JEANETTE
American soprano (1903-1965)

Jeanette MacDonald studied with Lotte Lehmann and made her opera debut as Juliette in Gounod's *Roméo et Juliette* in Montreal in 1942. She also sang the role of Marguerite in *Faust* with the Chicago Civic Opera Company. MacDonald's stage opera performances, of course, are less important than her film career. The Pennsylvania soprano began her career on Broadway in 1921 and made her first Paramount film, *The Love Parade*, in 1929. She joined MGM in 1933 and increased her popularity by teaming up with Nelson Eddy in the most successful singing partnership in the movies. She made many films with opera content and even sang excerpts from *Madama Butterfly* in her last movie. Her operetta films with Eddy are out of fashion but they still have fans and are unlikely to be forgotten. Listed below are her films with musical content. See also BITTER SWEET (1940), LA FANCIULLA DEL WEST (1938 film), THE FIREFLY (1937), THE LOTTERY BRIDE, THE MERRY WIDOW (1934), MAYTIME (1937), NAUGHTY MARIETTA (1935), THE NEW MOON (1940), ROSE-MARIE (1936), ROMÉO ET JULIETTE (1936 film), SWEETHEARTS (1938), TOSCA (1936 film), THE VAGABOND KING (1930).

1929 The Love Parade
MacDonald's first film was made for Ernst Lubitsch and starred her opposite Maurice Chevalier. It's a sophisticated musical romance about a Ruritanian queen who marries a prince with a past. The song "Dream Lover" by Victor Schertzinger and Clifford Grey was a hit. Paramount. Black and white. 110 minutes

1930 Monte Carlo
Ernst Lubitsch again directs MacDonald, this time opposite England's Jack Buchanan. She plays an impoverished countess wooed by royal Buchanan in disguise. The memorable song was "Beyond the Blue Horizon." Paramount. Black and white. 90 minutes.

1930 Oh, For A Man
MacDonald plays an opera singer who marries the man who burglarizes her apartment. This little known film originally had strong operatic content but most of the arias were cut when the public turned against musicals. She does get to perform an aria from *Tristan und Isolde*. Fox. Black and white. 78 minutes

1932 One Hour with You
MacDonald was reteamed with Maurice Chevalier in this musical romance about a married couple whose life is disturbed by a flirtatious woman. She made the title song a hit. George Cukor and Ernst Lubitsch directed. Black and white. 80 minutes.

1932 Love Me Tonight
One of the great film musicals and one of MacDonald's finest films with innovative direction by Rouben Mamoulian and outstanding songs by Rodgers and Hart. Maurice Chevalier plays a tailor who falls in love with princess MacDonald and they sing such standards as "Lover" and "Isn't It Romantic?" Paramount. Black and white. 96 minutes.

1936 San Francisco
One of the better Hollywood epics with charismatic stars, a memorable earthquake and pretty good opera. MacDonald, Clark Gable and Spencer Tracy star in a story about a San Francisco opera singer who is loved by a saloon keeper at the time of the 1906 quake. She sings arias from *Faust* and "Sempre libera" from *La Traviata*. W.S. Van Dyke directed. MGM. Black and white. 115 minutes.

1939 Broadway Serenade
The highlight of this film is MacDonald singing Butterfly's aria "Un bel di" in a fine sequence staged by Seymour Felix. The film revolves around

the marital troubles of songwriter Lew Ayres and wife MacDonald. Robert Z. Leonard directed. MGM. Black and white. 114 minutes.

1941 Smilin' Through
This is the third film version of a sentimental story about romance and rivalry over two generations based on a 1919 play. MacDonald stars opposite real-life husband Gene Raymond under the genial direction of Frank Borzage. MGM. Color. 100 minutes.

1942 I Married an Angel
The last of the MacDonald-Eddy films was this Rodgers and Hart musical about a man who dreams he marries an angel. The songs are wonderful but the film is a disappointment. Opera extras include MacDonald singing "Anges Purs" from *Faust* and duetting on a bit of *Carmen*. W.S. Van Dyke directed. Black and white. 84 minutes.

1942 Cairo
MacDonald sings a duet from *The Marriage of Figaro* with Ethel Waters in this spy mystery. She portrays a movie star in Cairo whose high C eventually solves the secret. Robert Young co-stars and W.S. Van Dyke directs. MGM. Black and white. 101 minutes.

1949 The Sun Comes Up
MacDonald's last film. In an appropriate farewell she sings her favorite aria from her favorite opera, "One Fine Day" from *Madama Butterfly*. MacDonald plays a widowed singer who's lost her son but finds happiness with orphan Claude Jarman Jr. and his dog Lassie. Richard Thorpe directed. MGM. Color. 93 minutes.

1950 Jeanette MacDonald in Performance
MacDonald performs on the *Voice of Firestone* television show on Nov. 13, 1950. The program usually hosted major opera stars so she wisely does not attempt to compete. She sings "Will You Remember?" from *Maytime*, "Italian Street Song" from *Naughty Marietta*, "March of the Grenadiers" from *Love Parade* and the traditional "Charlie Is My Darling." Black and white. 23 minutes. VAI video.

1992 Nelson and Jeanette: America's Singing Sweethearts
Michael Lorentz' documentary film about the careers and lives of Jeanette MacDonald and Nelson Eddy includes clips from their many films.

It is hosted by Jane Powell and was written by Elayne Goldstein. Jeanette's husband Gene Raymond is one of the guests. The film was produced by WTTW Chicago and Turner Entertainment and was shown on PBS in 1993. Color. 57 minutes. Video for sale and at MTR.

McINTYRE, DONALD
New Zealand baritone (1934-)

Donald McIntyre, one of the leading Wagnerian singers of our time, has been particularly admired for his Wotan in the *Ring* at Bayreuth. He made his debut with the Welsh National Opera in 1959 in Nabucco and sang regularly at Sadler's Wells. He began to appear at Covent Garden in 1967 and came to the Metropolitan in 1975 as Wotan. He has a compelling stage presence as well as a quite formidable voice. See CARDILLAC (1986), ELEKTRA (1980/1994), DER FLIEGENDE HOLLÄNDER (1987), MARTIN'S LIE (1964), DIE MEISTERSINGER VON NÜRNBERG (1988), DAS RHEINGOLD (1980), DER RING DES NIBELUNGEN (1980/1980 film), SIEGFRIED (1980), DIE WALKÜRE (1980).

MACKEBEN, THEO
German composer (1879-1953)

Berliner Theo Mackeben is mostly remembered for his adaptations of other people's work. He brilliantly revised Karl Millöcker's unsuccessful 1879 operetta *Gräfin Dubarry* and made it an international success in 1931. The stage versions starred opera divas Gitta Alpar in Berlin and Grace Moore in New York. Mackeben was also the conductor of the original production of *The Three Penny Opera* in Berlin and collaborated with Kurt Weill in adapting it for the screen. He worked with Max Ophuls adapting Smetana's *The Bartered Bride* for the cinema and writing original music for Ophul's film *Liebelei*. Willi Forst and Zarah Leander were among the stars who appeared in his film musicals. See THE BARTERED BRIDE (1932), DIE DUBARRY (1931/1951), THE THREEPENNY OPERA (1931).

MacNEIL, CORNELL
American baritone (1922-)

Cornell MacNeil made his debut in 1950 in Philadelphia creating the role of John Sorel in Menotti's *The Consul*. He sang with the New York City Opera from 1953 to 1955 and went on to San

Francisco, Chicago and La Scala. He made his first appearance at the Metropolitan in 1959 as Rigoletto and continued to sing there in a variety of roles until 1987. He is an excellent Germont in Zeffirelli's film of *La Traviata* and is known especially for his fine singing in Verdi operas. See CAVALLERIA RUSTICANA (1978), FRANCESCA DA RIMINI (1984), OTELLO (1978), RISE AND FALL OF THE CITY OF MAHAGONNY (1979), IL TABARRO (1981), TOSCA (1978/1985), LA TRAVIATA (1982).

McTEAGUE
1992 opera by Bolcom

William Bolcom's opera was publicized as a kind of marriage between opera and cinema because it was partially based on a famous film and was co-written and staged by film director Robert Altman. The original source was Frank Norris's realistic 1899 novel *McTeague*. It tells the story of the brutal dentist McTeague, his stingy wife Trina who wins the lottery and the lust for gold that causes him to murder her and his best friend. The novel was the basis for Erich von Stroheim's famous though rather grim 1924 film *Greed*. The opera was created by Bolcom working with librettists Arnold Weinsten and Altman and premiered to good reviews at the Chicago Lyric Opera.

1993 The Real McTeague
This documentary includes a number of scenes from the opera's stage production at the Lyric Opera of Chicago in 1992. Ben Heppner sings the role of McTeague, Catherine Malfitano is his wife Trina, Timothy Nolen is Marcus and Emily Golden is Maria. Dennis Russell Davies conducts the Chicago Lyric Orchestra. The film compares the opera, the movie which inspired it and the novel on which it was based. There are clips from the film *Greed* and readings by Studs Terkel from the novel. Robert Altman, who staged the opera and wrote the libretto with Arnold Weinstein, directed this documentary which has been shown on television. In the film Bolcom explains his ideas about the opera while Altman admits that opera is not really what he does. Color. In English. 60 minutes. On video.

MAD ABOUT OPERA
1948 Italian opera film

Follie per L'Opera is a romantic opera film about the Italian community in London. They organize a concert with opera stars to raise funds to rebuild a Soho church. Gina Lollobrigida and Carlo Campanini are the concert organizers. The singers who appear in concert are Tito Gobbi, Beniamino Gigli, Gino Bechi, Tito Schipa and Maria Caniglia. Mario Costa directed, Mario Monicelli and Steno wrote the screenplay and Mario Bava was cinematographer. Black and white. In Italian. 95 minutes.

1950 Soho Conspiracy
The English film *Soho Conspiracy* is a cut-price remake of *Mad About Opera* with a different cast but the same plot and the same opera singers as guest stars; their scenes are simply lifted from the earlier film. Jacques Lebreque and Zena Marshall are the concert organizers here with Cecil H. Williamson as director. Black and white. In English 85 minutes.

MADAMA BUTTERFLY
1904 opera by Puccini

Madama Butterfly, libretto by Luigi Illica and Giuseppe Giacosa, was the first of the two Puccini operas based on plays by American David Belasco and derives from a short story by John Luther Long. Cio-Cio-San, known as Madame Butterfly, marries American naval lieutenant B. F. Pinkerton. He does not take the marriage very seriously and eventually returns to America. Butterfly has a child and waits three years for his return. When he does, she finds he is married to another and so she kills herself. The opera was a fiasco when it premiered at La Scala but became a success in a revised version. Early films based on the opera often claimed to be derived from the play or story for copyright reasons. See also GIACOMO PUCCINI.

1950 NBC Opera Theatre
Tomiko Kanazawa stars as Madame Butterfly with Davis Cunningham as Pinkerton in this NBC Opera Theatre production by Samuel Chotzinoff. The cast includes Conchita Gaston as Suzuki, Roger Sorenson, Johnny Silver and Paul Dennis. It was directed by Charles Polacheck and designed by Carl Kent while the orchestra was conducted by Peter Herman Adler. Kirk Browning directed the telecast. Black and white. In English. 60 minutes. Video at the MTR.

1955 Carmine Gallone film

This is an attempt to create a realistic *Madama Butterfly* by using Japanese designers and Japanese actors combined with the voices of singers from the Rome Opera House. It was filmed in Rome by Carmine Gallone with sets by Ryotaro Mitsubayashi. Kaoru Yachigusa of the Takarazuka Girls Opera Company portrays Cio-Cio-San most convincingly with Orietta Moscucci singing her arias. Suzuki is Michiko Tanaka sung by Anna Maria Canali while Pinkerton is Nicola Filacuridi sung by Giuseppe Camparo. Ferdinando Lidonni is the American Consul Sharpless. Oliviero De Fabritiis conducted the Rome Opera Orchestra and Claude Renoir was director of photography. Color. In Italian. 100 minutes.

1955 NBC Opera Theatre

Elaine Malbin portrays Butterfly in the NBC Opera Theatre production by Samuel Chotzinoff. Davis Cunningham is Pinkerton, Conchita Gaston is Suzuki and Warren Galjour is Sharpless. Herbert Grossman conducted the Symphony of the Air orchestra with Peter Herman Adler as music director. The opera is sung in an English translation by Ruth and Thomas Martin and the set design is by Trew Hocker. Kirk Browning directed the telecast. Color. In English. 135 minutes. Video at MTR.

1957 Dorothy Kirsten video

American soprano Dorothy Kirsten is featured in two scenes from *Madama Butterfly* opposite Italian tenor Mario Del Monaco as Pinkerton in this video. These are excerpts from a Metropolitan Opera production that were specially staged for a 1957 *Ed Sullivan Show* on CBS television. Black and white. About 15 minutes. Video at MTR.

1960 Victoria de los Angeles video

Victoria de los Angeles portrays Cio-Cio-San with Brian Sullivan as Pinkerton in scenes from *Madama Butterfly* on the *Bell Telephone Hour* television program. They appeared in the *Portraits in Music* series. Kirk Browning directed. Black and white. About 10 minutes. Video at the MTR.

1964 Grace Trester Jones video

Grace Trester Jones stars as Butterfly with Ronald Naldi as Pinkerton in this English-language version of *Madama Butterfly*. It was written by John Gutman and directed by Allen Ross and Herbert Seitz for Indiana University Television Theater.

Wolfgang Vacaro conducted the orchestra. Black and white. In English. 75 minutes. Video at MTR.

1974 Jean-Pierre Ponnelle film

Mirella Freni is Butterfly and Placido Domingo is Pinkerton in this popular film staged, designed and directed by Jean-Pierre Ponnelle who shot it in a Berlin studio. Christa Ludwig is Suzuki with Robert Kerns as Sharpless and Michel Senechal as Goro. Herbert von Karajan conducts the Vienna Philharmonic and Wolfgang Treu was the cinematographer. Unitel. Color. In Italian with English subtitles. 144 minutes. London video/London laser. (Highlights version available in the *Great Moments* video series as Volume 6).

1982 New York City Opera

Judith Haddon stars as Butterfly with Jerry Hadley as Pinkerton in this New York City Opera production by Frank Corsaro. Judith Christin sings the role of Suzuki and Alan Titus is Sharpless. Lloyd Evans designed the sets and costumes and Christopher Keene led the New York City Opera Orchestra and Chorus. Kirk Browning directed the video telecast on PBS on Oct. 20, 1982. Color. In Italian with English subtitles. 145 minutes.

1983 Verona Arena

An open-air arena like Verona isn't the ideal setting for an intimate love story like *Madama Butterfly* but it works reasonably well on video. Home viewers have close-ups and camera intimacies that the live audience doesn't. Bulgarian soprano Raina Kabaivanska plays Cio-Cio-San with Nazzareno Antinori as her Pinkerton, Eleonora Jankovic as Suzuki, Lorenzo Saccomani as Sharpless and Mario Ferrara as Goro. Giulio Chazalettes staged the opera with huge sets and colorful costumes by Ulisse Santicchi. Maurizio Arena conducted the Verona Arena Orchestra and Chorus and Brian Large directed the video. Color. In Italian with English subtitles. 150 mins. HBO Video.

1986 Teatro alla Scala

This is an attempt at an authentic production featuring a Japanese soprano, stage director, set designer and costume. Designer Keita Sari creates a Kabuki-like atmosphere with support from the clever sets of Ichiro Takada and effective costuming of Hanae Mori. Butterfly's house is built as the audience watches at the beginning of the opera. Yasuko Hayashi portrays Cio-Cio-San with

Czech Peter Dvorsky as her Pinkerton. They sing well but it's pretty hard to believe in them. Korean Hak-Nam Kim portrays Suzuki while Italians Giorgio Zancanaro and Enesto Gavazzi are Sharpless and Goro. American Lorin Maazel conducts the La Scala Orchestra and Derek Bailey directed the video. Color. In Italian with English subtitles. 150 minutes. Home Vision.

1994 Metropolitan Opera
Catherine Malfitano stars as Butterfly with Richard Leech as Pinkerton in Giancarlo del Monaco's production for the Metropolitan Opera. Wendy White is Suzuki, Dwayne Croft is Sharpless and Pierre Lefebvre is Goro. Gil Wechsler designed the lighting, Michael Scott designed the sets and costumes and Daniel Gatti conducted the Metropolitan Opera Orchestra and Chorus. Brian Large directed the video on Dec. 1, 1994, which was telecast on Dec, 27, 1995. Color. In Italian with English subtitles. 150 minutes.

1995 Frederic Mitterrand film
Chinese soprano Ying Huang stars as Butterfly in Frederic Mitterand's fine film of the opera with Richard Traxell as Pinkerton. The film was shot on location in Tunisia where a 1904 Nagasaki was reconstructed on a hilltop. The opera is filmed in a fairly straightforward manner with the addition of documentary footage of old Japanese inserted between Acts One and Two. Ning Liang is Suzuki, Richard Cowan is Sharpless and Jing Ma Fan is Goro. Philippe Welt was the cinematographer, Christian Gasc designed the costumes and Michele Abbe-Vannier was the production designer. James Conlon was the musical director and Daniel Toscan du Plantier produced. Color. In French. 135 minutes.

Early/related films

1915 Mary Pickford film
Mary Pickford stars as Cho-Cho-San in this silent film supposedly based on the 1898 source story by John Luther Long. Marshall Neilan portrays Pinkerton with Olive West as Suzuki. Sidney Olcott directed for Famous Players. Black and white. About 70 minutes.

1919 Fritz Lang film
Fritz Lang was just beginning his career when he made this silent German film version of Madama Butterfly. It was titled Harakiri, was written by Max

Jungk and was supposedly based on the Long story and Belasco play. The names of the characters are different but Lil Dagover portrays a young Japanese woman who falls in love with a naval officer (Niels Prien). When he deserts her, she commits suicide. Black and white. About 87 minutes.

1932 Cary Grant film
Cary Grant portrays Pinkerton with Sylvia Sidney as his Cho-Cho-San in this Hollywood version of the story based on the novel, the play and the opera. It uses Puccini's music as the background score. Grant does sing a bit but it's not Puccini. Marion Goring directed for Paramount. Black and white. 85 minutes.

1934 One Night of Love
Grace Moore ends this film appearing on stage at the Metropolitan Opera as Cio-Cio-San in Madama Butterfly and singing most beautifully. Victor Schertzinger directed. Black and white. 80 minutes.

1939 The Butterfly Dream
Maria Cebotari, a coloratura soprano who had sung the opera on stage, stars as a singer whose life parallels her role in Madama Butterfly. She falls in love with an American musician (Fosco Giachetti) who leaves her pregnant. When he returns four years later and visits her as she is about to go on stage, he is with his new wife. The singers include Tito Gobbi, Palmira Vidali Marini and Alfredo De Lidda. Carmine Gallone directed two versions, one in Italian titled Il Sogno di Butterfly, one in German called Premiere der Butterfly. Black and white. 95 minutes. On video.

1939 First Love
Deanna Durbin sings an English version of the Madama Butterfly aria "Un bel dì." The aria ends with her Prince Charming rescuing her in a modern version of the Cinderella story. Henry Koster directed for Universal. Black and white. 84 minutes.

1939 Broadway Serenade
The highlight of this film is Jeanette MacDonald singing "Un bel dì" in a splendid sequence staged by Seymour Felix. Robert Z. Leonard directed. MGM. Black and white. 114 minutes.

1949 The Sun Comes Up
This was Jeanette MacDonald's last film and in an appropriate farewell she sings her favorite aria from her favorite opera, "Un bel dì" from *Madama Butterfly*. Richard Thorpe directed. MGM. Color. 93 minutes

1950 The Toast of New Orleans
Mario Lanza is seen on stage as Pinkerton singing with Kathryn Grayson as Butterfly in the final scene of this MGM romp. It's the culmination of their relationship and she succumbs after he chases her around the opera house stage. Norman Taurog directed. Color. 97 minutes. On video.

1961 My Geisha
This Shirley MacLaine film is based around *Madama Butterfly*. She plays a movie star whose director husband Yves Montand goes to Japan to make a film of the opera with an unknown geisha. He wants to prove that he can be successful without her. She disguises herself as a geisha and gets the starring role. The selections from the opera are sung by Michiko Sunahara as Butterfly and Barry Morell as Pinkerton. Franz Waxman arranged the music, Norman Krasna wrote the script and Jack Cardiff directed. Paramount. Color. 100 minutes. Paramount video.

1971 Death in Venice
Though most of the music in the film is by Mahler, *Butterly*'s plaintive aria "Vogliateme bene" is appropriately featured in Luchino Visconti's epic film *Death in Venice*. Color. 130 minutes

1987 The Return of Butterfly
This is a Soviet film about Salomea Krushelnytska, the singer who helped make *Madama Butterfly* a success. She starred in the Brescia production that followed the Milan premiere fiasco. Elena Safonova portrays as the Ukrainian soprano who became famous in the role. Oleg Fialko directed this colorful biography. Color. 90 minutes.

1987 Fatal Attraction
In this movie about a woman who refuses to take rejection as gently as Cio-Cio-San, a fondness for *Madama Butterfly* is an indication of cultural closeness. Glenn Close turns up the volume on a recording so she and Michael Douglas can tell each other it's their favorite opera. He should have noticed it was the death scene. Heard singing on the soundtrack are Mirella Freni, Luciano Pavarotti

and Christa Ludwig. Adrian Lyne directed. Color. 119 minutes. On video.

1990 Soldiers of Music
Soviet diva Galina Vishnevskaya, famous for her performances as Madama Butterfly before she left the USSR with cellist husband Mstislav Rostropovich, returns with him after 16 years for a concert. She sings an aria from *Madama Butterfly*. Color. 89 minutes. Sony Video.

1991 Butterfly: the European Myth of the Oriental Woman
This British documentary examines the way Oriental women have been portrayed on the Western stage. It includes scenes from an English National Opera production of *Madama Butterfly* starring Janice Cairns. There is also commentary by David Henry Hwang, author of *M. Butterfly*, and Claude-Michel Schönberg, composer of *Miss Saigon*. Color. 60 minutes. On video.

1991 Jennifer 8
Bruce Robinson's taut thriller uses the Humming Chorus from *Madama Butterfly* on the soundtrack at a key moment. Andy Garcia stars as a cop trying to keep Uma Thurman from getting bumped off by a serial murderer. Color. 127 minutes.

1993 Kiju Yoshida Meets Madama Butterfly
Oliver Horn made this documentary about Kiju Yoshida's work as the director of a production of *Madama Butterfly* at the Opéra de Lyon in 1993. Michie Nakamaru sings the role of Butterfly, Vyacheslav M. Polosov is Pinkerton, Hak-Nam Kim is Suzuki and Richard Stillwell is Sharpless. Kent Nagano conducts the Lyons Opera Orchestra. Color. In French. 50 minutes. On video.

1993 M. Butterfly
David Cronenberg's film of Henry David Hwang's play tells the story of a French diplomat (Jeremy Irons) in China who falls in love with a female impersonator (John Lone) apparently because of the power of Puccini's music. He first sees her/him singing "Un bel dì" at a diplomatic reception and begins to live a story parallel to the opera. The voice belongs to soprano Michelle Couture singing with the Royal Philharmonic Orchestra conducted by Howard Shore. Later in the film Irons attends the Paris Opéra and we see Maria Teresa Uribe as Butterfly and hear the Hungarian State Opera Orchestra conducted by Adam Medveczky. At the end he himself becomes Butterfly and kills himself

miming to a record of Mirella Freni singing Butterfly's suicide aria with the Vienna Philharmonic. Color. 101 minutes.

1993 Household Saints
Madame Butterfly is virtually a running theme through this offbeat story of the odd love lives of two Italian women in New York including visions of Butterfly and Pinkerton. One character is so obsessed by the opera (and Asian women) that he commits hara-kiri to Butterfly's suicide music. The singers we hear are Toti Dal Monte and Beniamino Gigli with "Vogliatemi bene" and Toti solo with "Un bel dì." Oliviero de Fabritiis conducts the Teatro alla Scala Orchestra. Nancy Savoca directed the film based on a novel by Francine Prose. Color. 124 minutes.

1994 Heavenly Creatures
The Hungarian State Opera Chorus is heard on the soundtrack singing the Humming Chorus as two teenage girls prepare for murder. It is oddly effective. Peter Jackson directed this offbeat New Zealand film. Color. 95 minutes.

MADAME POMPADOUR
1922 operetta by Fall

Operetta diva Fritzi Massary had her greatest success in Leo Fall's operetta about the love triangle of Madame Pompadour, King Louis XV and Count René. She starred in the Berlin and Vienna productions in what was considered her greatest stage performance. Evelyn Laye played the part in London, Wilda Bennett sang it in New York and Paris Opéra soprano Raymonde Vécart was the Madame in Paris. This is Fall's finest operetta, comparable in its quality to Offenbach's best work. See also LEO FALL.

1927 Lillian Gish film
The success of the operetta on stage in London persuaded producer E. A. Dupont and director Herbert Wilcox to turn it into a British film in 1927. Lillian Gish is surprisingly sexy as Madame Pompadour with Antonio Moreno as Count René and Henri Bosc as the King. Frances Marion and E. A. Dupont wrote the screenplay. Black and white. About 80 minutes.

MADDALENA
1913 opera by Prokofiev

Sergei Prokofiev's opera *Maddalena* was composed in 1913 when he was twenty but he didn't finish it and it wasn't staged until 1981. It was completed by Edward Downes who conducted its premiere at Graz. The action is set in 15th century Venice. Faithless Maddalena is bored waiting for her husband Genaro to return. When he arrives, she swears she has been faithful but insists on hiding when her lover Stenio arrives. Both men want to kill her but she persuades them to kill each other instead. See also SERGEI PROKOFIEV.

1981 Graz Festival
Nancy Shade stars as Maddalena with Ryszard Karczykowski as Genaro in this Austrian film of the opera shot at the Graz Festival. This was the first stage performance of the opera and it was conducted by Edward Downes leading the Graz Philharmonic Orchestra. Jorge Lavelli directed the film. Beta Film. Color. In French. 59 minutes. On video.

MAESTRO DI CAPELLA
1792 opera by Cimarosa

Domenico Cimarosa's one-man comic opera *The Music Director* is a tour-de-force for a bass or baritone. The music master is conducting a large orchestra which pays little attention to his directions. In the end he has to imitate each instrument to get the musicians to play correctly and in harmony. There are two CDs of the opera and a non-professional video. See also DOMENICO CIMAROSA.

1958 Luigi Borgonovo video
Italian baritone Luigi Borgonova portrays the frustrated music director in this TV production of the opera directed by Vladi Orengo. It was filmed for Italy's RAI television. Color. In Italian. 86 minutes. Onda (Italy) video.

1987 Giuseppe Taddei video
Italian baritone Giuseppe Taddei, best known for his performances of comic roles in Mozart operas, portrays the music director in this recent production for Italy's RAI television. Color. In Italian. 86 minutes. Opera Dubs video.

MAGIC FLUTE, THE
1791 opera by Mozart

Die Zauberflöte is the most magical of Mozart's operas combining Masonic rituals and populist entertainment in an educational fairy tale. A prince is asked by a queen to rescue a princess from an evil wizard. She provides him with a magic flute and a birdman servant with magic bells. But things are not what they seem and he has many adventures before winning the princess. This singspiel (it has spoken dialogue) was commissioned by Emanuel Schikaneder who wrote the libretto and created the role of Papageno. It contains some of Mozart's greatest music. *The Magic Flute* was rarely filmed in the silent era but is quite popular with modern filmmakers and there is a choice of excellent videos. See also WOLFGANG A. MOZART.

1956 NBC Opera Theatre
Leontyne Price stars as Pamina with William Lewis as Tamino in this famous NBC Opera Theatre production. W.H. Auden and Chester Kallman created a controversial new English-language adaptation for the telecast, George Balanchine devised the choreography and Rouben Ter-Arutunian created the fanciful sets and costumes. John Reardon portrays Papageno, Laurel Hurley is the Queen of the Night, Yi Kwe Sze is Sarastro, Adelaide Bishop is Papagena and Andrew McKinley is Monostatos. Samuel Chotzinof produced the opera and artistic director Peter Herman Adler conducted the Symphony of the Air Orchestra. Kirk Browning directed the telecast on Jan. 15, 1956. Black and white. In English. 120 minutes. Video at MTR.

1971 Rolf Liebermann film
Rolf Liebermann produced this film of the opera based on a Hamburg State Opera production shot in a Hamburg TV studio. Nicolai Gedda is Tamino, Edith Mathis is Pamina, William Workman is Papageno, Cristina Deutekom is the Queen of the Night, Hans Sotin is Sarastro and Carol Malone is Papagena. Horst Stein conducts the Hamburg State Opera Orchestra. Peter Ustinov adapted the opera to the screen and Joachim Hess directed. Color. In German. 154 minutes.

1974 Ingmar Bergman film
Ingmar Bergman's *Trollflojten* is one of the great opera films and one of the most enjoyable. It is sung in Swedish by relatively unknown singers but this hardly seems to matter. Bergman and Oscar-winning cinematographer Sven Nykvist shot it as an opera in performance in a mock-up of the 18th century Drottningholm Court Theatre. Bergman first shows the audience, then focuses on a girl's wonder at seeing the opera and finally presents the opera itself beautifully staged and filmed. At intermission the camera observes the singers back stage. During the opera, lines of the libretto occasionally descend from the heavens and the two trios sing them in a charming manner. Indeed almost everyone in the opera is charming in Bergman's film which includes the idea that Pamina is the daughter of Sarastro and the Queen of the Night. Håkan Hagegård (who became known internationally after this film), is Papageno, Joseph Köstlinger is Tamino, Irma Urrila is Pamina, Elisabeth Erikson is Papagena, Birgit Nordin is the Queen of the Night, Ulrik Cold is Sarastro and Ragnar Ulfung is Monostatos. Britt-Marie Aruhn, Birgitta Smiding and Kirsten Vaupel are the Three Ladies and Urban Malberg, Erland von Haijne and Ansgar Krook are the Three Boys. Eric Ericson conducts the Swedish State Broadcasting Network Symphony. Color. In Swedish with English subtitles. 135 minutes. Home Vision/Paramount video.

1976 Leipzig Opera
Horst Gebhardt portrays Tamino in this Leipzig Opera production by Joachim Herz. Magadalena Falewicz is Pamina, Dieter Scholz is Papageno, Inge Uibel is Queen of the Night, Herman Christian Polster is Sarastro, Heidrun Halx is Papagena, Gutfried Speck is Monostatos and Jitka Kovarikova, Anne-Kristin Paul and Gertrud Lahusen-Oertel are the Three Ladies. Marion Schurath arranged the choreography and Gert Bahner conducts the Gewandhaus Orchestra. Georg F. Mielke directed the video for DDR television. Color. In German. 156 minutes. VIEW video/Japanese laser.

1978 Glyndebourne Festival
David Hockney's superb set designs are a central feature of this Glynebourne Festival production by John Cox. Leo Goeke is Tamino, Felicity Lott is Pamina, Benjamin Luxon is Papageno, May Sandoz is the Queen of the Night, Thomas Thomaschke is Sarastro, Elizabeth Conquet is Papagena, John Fryatt is Monostatos, Willard White is the Speaker and Teresa Cahill, Patricia Parker and Fiona Kimm are the Three Ladies.

Bernard Haitink conducted the London Philharmonic Orchestra and Glyndebourne Festival Chorus. Dave Heather directed the video. Color. In German with English subtitles. 164 minutes. VAI video.

1982 Salzburg Festival
Jean-Pierre Ponnelle directed this outstanding production from the Salzburg Festival and one critic rated it the best of all video operas. Peter Schreier is Tamino, Ileana Cotrubas is Pamino, Christian Boesch is Papageno, Edita Gruberova is Queen of the Night, Marti Talvela is Sarastro, Gundrun Seiber is Papagena, Walter Berry is the Speaker and Edda Moser, Ann Murray and Ingrid Mayr are the Three Ladies. James Levine conducted the Vienna Philharmonic. Color. In German. 190 minutes.

1983 Bavarian State Opera
Francisco Araiza is Tamino and Lucia Popp is Pamina in this Bavarian State Opera production by August Everding in Munich. Wolfgang Brendel portrays Papageno, Edita Gruberova is Queen of the Night, Kurt Moll is Sarastro, Gudrun Sieber is Papagena, Norbert Orth is Monostatos, Jan-Hendrik Rootering is Speaker and Pamela Coburn, Daphne Evangelatos and Cornelia Wulkopf are the Three Ladies. Wolfgang Sawallisch conducts the Bavarian State Opera Orchestra and Chorus. Peter Windgassen directed the video. Unitel. Color. In German with English subtitles. 160 minutes. Philips video and laser.
(Highlights version available in *Great Moments* video series as Volume 4).

1986 Australian Opera
Swedish director Göran Järvefelt's production for the Australian Opera features Gran Wilson as Tamino, Yvonne Kenny as Pamina, John Fulford as Papageno and Christa Leahmann as Queen of the Night. Donald Shanks portrays Sarastro, Peta Blyth is Papagena, Graeme Ewer is Monostatos, John Pringle is the Speaker and Nicola Ferner-White, Patricia Price and Rosemary Gunn are the Three Ladies. Richard Bonynge conducted the Elizabethan Sydney Orchestra and the Australian Opera Chorus. Color. In English 160 minutes. Kultur video.

1987 National Arts Centre
John Thomson staged this production for the National Arts Centre of Canada in Ottawa. It features David Rendall as Tamino, Patricia Wells, as Pamina, David Holloway as Papageno, Rita Shane as the Queen of the Night, Don Garrard as Sarastro, Nancy Hermiston as Papagena, Alan Crofoot as Monostatos and Barbara Collier, Diane Loeb and Janet Stubbs as the Three Ladies. Mario Bernardi conducted the National Arts Center of Canada Orchestra. Thomson also directed the video. Color. In English. 160 minutes. CBC video.

1987 New York City Opera
Faith Esham and Stephen Dickson star in this New York City Opera production of the opera by Lotfi Mansouri. The cast includes Jon Garrison, Rachel Rosales and Gregory Stapp. Sergiu Comissiona conducts the New York City Opera Orchestra. Beverly Sills was host on the telecast on Oct. 14, 1987. Color. In German. 195 minutes.

1989 Drottningholm Court Theater
A most enjoyable Drottningholm Court Theater production by Göran Järvefelt with Arnold Östman leading the Drottningholm Orchestra in period costume with authentic instruments. Ann Christine Biel is Pamina, Stefan Dahlberg is Pamino, Mikael Samuelson is Papageno, Birgitta Larsson is Papagena, Birgit Louise Frandsen is the Queen of the Night, Laszlo Polgar is Sarastro and Magnus Khyle is Monostatos. Anita Soldh, Linnea Sallay and Inger Blom are the Three Ladies and Elisabeth Berg, Ann-Christine Larsson and Anna Tomson are the Three Boys. Thomas Olofsson directed the video. Color. In German with English subtitles. 165 minutes. Philips video and laser.

1991 Metropolitan Opera
David Hockney designed the striking sets and costumes for this Metropolitan Opera production by John Cox restaged by Gus Mostart. Francisco Araiza portrays Tamino, Kathleen Battle is Pamina, Manfred Hemm is Papageno, Luciana Serra is Queen of the Night, Kurt Moll is Sarastro, Barbara Kilduff is Papagena, Andreas Schmidt is the Speaker, Heinz Zednik is Monostatos and Juliana Gondek, Mimi Lerner and Judith Christin are the Three Ladies. James Levine conducted the Metropolitan Opera Orchestra and Chorus and Brian Large directed the video. Color. In German with English subtitles. 169 minutes. DG video.

1991 Rens Groot film
An animated film version of the opera using chalk pictures on a blackboard with Colin Davis's

Dresden recording as soundtrack. It is quite clever and has some moments of magic. The singers are Peter Schreier as Pamino, Margaret Price as Pamina, Mikael Melbye as Papageno, Luciana Serra as the Queen of the Night, Kurt Moll as Sarastro, Maria Venuti as Papagena, Theo Adam as the Speaker, Robert Tear as Monostatos and Marie McLaughlin, Ann Murray and Hanna Schwarz as the Three Ladies. Colin Davis conducts the Dresden State Orchestra and Leipzig Chorus. Color. In Italian. 160 minutes.

1992 Une Petite Flûte Enchantée

A Little Magic Flute is an experimental production of the opera in French devised for the Atelier Lyrique of the Opéra de Lyon by Louis Urlo, Claire Gibault and Myriam Tanant. It is simplified, shortened and modernized (the three ladies shoot the dragon with pistols) and sung by relative unknowns. Jean Delescluse plays Tamino, Virginie Pochon is Pamina, Christophe Lacassagene is Papagena, Cyrille Gerstenhaber is Papagena, Isabelle Sabrié is the Queen of the Night, Frederic Caton is Sarastro and the three ladies are Caroline Pelon, Pomone Epoméo and Francine André. Montserrat Casanova designed the sets and costumes, Urlo directed the production and Gibault conducted the Lyons Opera Orchestra. Pierre Cavassilas directed the video for French television. Color. In French. 117 minutes. Imalyre (France) video.

Early/related films

1906 Pathé French film

A French film titled *La Flûte Enchantée* by Pathé was released in the U.S. in December 1906. About 5 minutes.

1908 American film

An American film titled *The Magic Flute* was distributed in the U.S. in November 1908. About 7 minutes.

1919 Max Mack German film

German director Max Mack produced a film of *The Magic Flute* in 1919. About 70 minutes.

1935 Pagageno

This is one of the best of German animation pioneer Lotte Reiniger's charming silhouette opera films. It features the birdcatcher from *The Magic Flute*. Black and white. 8 minutes.

1946 La Flute Magique

Music from *The Magic Flute* is used in a clever manner in this animated film by French master Paul Grimault. Roger Leenhardt wrote the script. Color. 11 minutes.

1948 Letter from an Unknown Woman

This fine film reaches its climax at a performance of *The Magic Flute* (sung in Italian) at the Vienna Opera House. Joan Fontaine sees her lover Louis Jourdan for the first time in ten years while her husband watches. Max Ophuls directed. Black and white. 86 minutes.

1967 Hour Of The Wolf

Ingmar Bergman's film *Vargtimmen* has several references to *The Magic Flute*. A moody artist (Max von Sydow) and his wife (Liv Ullman) live on a lonely island where he is beginning to encounter strange demons, perhaps of the mind. One is a bird man whom he thinks is related to Pagageno. A rich man invites him to dinner in his castle and displays a toy theater in which a tiny but seemingly real Tamino (Folke Sundquist) performs the aria "O ew'ge Nacht!" They talk about the meaning of the words "O eternal night! When will it end?" Color. In Swedish. 80 minutes. On video.

1974 Night Porter

There is a memorable use of the aria "Bei Manner" in the opera scene in this strange Liliana Cavani film. It is the story of an opera conductor's wife (Charlotte Rampling) who meets up with the SS Officer (Dirk Bogarde) who sexually abused her in a concentration camp. Color. 115 minutes.

1975 Gute Nacht, du Fasche Welt

This German documentary film shows rehearsals for a 1975 production of *The Magic Flute* at the Salzburg Festival directed by Giorgio Strehler. The title refers to Papageno's suicidal line "Goodbye, cruel world" near the end of the opera when he thinks he has lost his Papagena. The production stars Eidith Mathis, René Kollo, Hermann Prey and Reri Grist. Norbert Beilharz directed the film for SDR television. Color. In German. 43 minutes.

1977 Mozart by Ingmar Bergman

This is a German television documentary about the creation of Ingmar Bergman's 1975 film of *The Magic Flute*. WDR televison. Color. In German. 60 minutes.

1977 Gianini/Luzzati cartoon

An inventive cartoon version of the Mozart opera by the Italian masters of opera animation Giulio Gianini and Emmanuele Luzzati. Color. 25 minutes.

1984 Amadeus

Milos Forman's Mozart biography features the genesis of *The Magic Flute* and shows Mozart's (Tom Hulce) relationship with showman/librettist Emanuel Schikaneder (Simon Callow). Callow is seen on stage creating the role of Papageno (sung by Brian Kay) with Lisabeth Bartless as Papagena (sung by Gillian Fisher). There is a striking scene showing Milada Cechalova as the Queen of the Night with the singing done by June Anderson. Twyla Thorpe staged it and Neville Marriner conducted the Academy of St. Martin-in-the-Fields orchestra. Color. 160 minutes. On video.

1991 Papageno

British animator Sarah Roper's tribute to the birdman of *The Magic Flute*. Color. 7 minutes.

1994 Mark Hamill animated film

Mark Hamill is the voice of Tamino in this animated film for children based on the opera. Michael York is Sarastro, Samantha Eggar is the Queen of the Night, Joely Fisher is Pamina and Jerry Houser is Pagageno. Very little of the opera music is used. Rony Myrick and Marlene Robinson directed. Color. In English. 60 minutes

1995 Operavox Animated Opera

The Russian animation studio Christmas Films created this animated version of the Magic Flute for the British Operavox series. The Welsh National Opera Orchestra plays a specially recorded score. David Seaman was the music editor. Color. 27 minutes.

MAHLER, GUSTAV
Austrian composer (1860-1911)

Gustav Mahler wrote a number of stage works and completed Weber's *Die Drei Pintos* but there are no surviving operas by him. His operatic importance is on the performance side as he derived his primary income from conducting opera and had a major influence on opera presentation. Mahler headed the Vienna Hofoper (Staatsoper) from 1897 to 1907, directed opera orchestras in Budapest and Hamburg and was guest conductor at the Metropolitan Opera for two years.

1974 Mahler

Ken Russell's British film biography is structured as a flashback with Mahler recalling the events of his life during a train trip with his wife Alma. Most of the high and low points of his career and music are featured. Robert Powell, who looks like the composer, plays Mahler while Georgina Hale is Alma. Wagner's opera music is prominent including *Die Walküre* and *Tristan und Isolde*. In one dream sequence Mahler and Cosima Wagner sing new lyrics to the Ride of the Valkyries while he converts from Judaism. This scene is so bizarre that it has to be seen to be believed. Color. In English. 115 minutes.

MAID OF ORLEANS, THE
1881 opera by Tchaikovsky

Tchaikovsky's operatic version of the story of Joan of Arc, *Orleanskaya Deva*, is based on a play by Schiller. It is his most ambitious opera and a big success in its time though it has almost been forgotten outside Russia. The story is basically historic with Joan once again the savior of France even if there is an additional not so historic love story. Joan falls in love with a Burgundian knight called Lionel fighting on the English side and it becomes a central plot point. He is killed at the time she is taken prisoner by English. See also PYOTR TCHAIKOVSKY.

1993 Bolshoi Opera

Nina Rautio is superb as Joan of Arc in this June 1993 Bolshoi production by Boris Pokrovksy first staged in 1990 and seen at the Metropolitan Opera in 1993 with different singers. Vladimir Redkin plays Lionel, Oleg Kulko is King Charles, Maria Gavrilova is Agnès Sorel, Gleb Nikolsky is the Archbishop and Mikhail Krutikov is Dunois. Valery Levental designed the multi-level sets and Alexander Lazarev conducts the Bolshoi Opera Orchestra and Chorus. The video was shot on stage at the Bolshoi by Brian Large without an audience. Color. In Russian. 150 minutes. Teldec video.

MAKROPOULOS CASE, THE

1926 opera by Janácek

Leo Janácek's opera *Vec Makropoulos* is based on a play by Czech playwright Karel Capek. It's the story of opera singer Emilia Marty nèe Makropoulos who has lived for 342 years because of a drug developed by her father three centuries before. As she now needs more of the drug and must get the formula to make it, she visits a law office where a relevant lawsuit is in progress. She helps settle it and eventually gives herself to a man in return for the formula. However, she is now so disillusioned by life that she chooses to let herself to die. See also LEO JANÁCEK.

1989 Canadian Opera

Stephanie Sundine stars as the eternally young Emilia Marty in this Canadian Opera Company production by Lofti Mansouri at the O'Keefe Center in Toronto. Kathleen Brett is Kristina, Graham Clark is Albert Gregor, Cornelis Opthof is Jaroslav Prus, Robert Orth is Dr. Kolenaty, Richard Margison is Vitek and Benoit Butet is Janek. The opera was staged with help from Janácek specialist Elisabeth Soderstrom. Leni Bauer-Ecsy designed the sets and Berislav Klobucar conducted the Canadian Opera Company Orchestra. Norman Campbell directed the video. Color. In Czech with English subtitles. 123 minutes. VAI video.

1995 Glyndebourne Festival

The great German soprano Anja Silja stars as the ageless Emilia Marty in this much-admired Glyndebourne Festival production by Nicholas Lehnhoff. Tobias Hoheisel designed the highly effective mobile sets. Kim Begley portrays Gregor, Anthony Roden is Vitek, Manuela Krisak is Kristina, Victor Braun is Prus, Christopher Ventris is Janek, Andrew Shore is Kolenaty and Robert Tear is Hauk-Sendorf. Andrew Davis conducted the London Philharmonic Orchestra and Glyndebourne Festival Chorus and Brian Large directed the video under studio conditions. Color. In Czech with English subtitles. 95 minutes. Warner Vision (England) video.

MALFITANO, CATHERINE

American soprano (1948-)

Catherine Malfitano made her debut in 1972 with the Central City Opera and was a regular with the New York City Opera from 1973 to 1979. She began to sing at the Metropolitan in 1979 and was soon also a featured singer at European opera houses. She was Servilia in Ponnelle's 1980 film of *La Clemenza di Tito* and Tosca in a famous Live from Rome film in 1992. She has been especially praised for her Berlin *Salome* and much liked for her Chicago performances in *Antony and Cleopatra* and *McTeague*. See The ABDUCTION FROM THE SERAGLIO (1984), ANTONY AND CLEOPATRA (1991), LA CLEMENZA DI TITO (1980), MCTEAGUE (1993), THOMAS PASATIERI (1977), THE SAINT OF BLEEKER STREET (1978), SALOME (1990), STIFFELIO (1993), STREET SCENE (1979), TOSCA (1992).

MALIBRAN, MARIA

Spanish mezzo-soprano (1808-1836)

Maria Malibran is still one of the great myth figures of opera a century and a half after her death and is still a continuing subject for movies and emulation. Obviously the myth is about more than just her superb voice and notable acting ability. Malibran, who died at 28, has become the embodiment of the age of Romanticism. She was the friend of many major composers including Rossini, Donizetti, Bellini and Verdi. Her sister Pauline Viardot was also a famous singer and her father was the influential teacher Manuel Garcia.

1943 Maria Malibran

Soprano Maria Cebotari stars as Malibran in this romantic Italian film biography directed by Guido Brignone. It tells the story of the singer's life from her early years through her many love affairs to her death. Cebotari is well suited for the role, and sings several arias by Malibran's composer friends Rossini and Bellini. The cast includes Rossano Brazzi as Malibran's violinist lover de Beriot, Renato Cialente as husband Ernest Malibran, Loris Gizzi as Rossini and Roberto Bruni as Bellini. Black and white. In Italian. 92 minutes.

1943 La Malibran

Geori Boué stars as Maria Malibran in this French film of the singer's life written and directed by Sacha Guitry. Guitry portrays her husband Eugene Malibran, Jean Cocteau is Alfred de Musset and Mario Podesta is Manuel Garcia. Guitry says that Malibran "was born, lived and died on tour. Spanish, born in Paris, made her debut in Italy, continued her career in London, married a Frenchman in New York, married a Belgian and died in Manchester." Black and white. In French. 95 minutes. Montparnasse (France) video.

1971 The Death of Maria Malibran
Werner Schroeter's experimental film *Der Tod der Maria Malibran* features Magdalena Montezuma as Malibran and is a visual film to the point of wild extravagance. It consists of tableaux depicting the life and death of the soprano. High fashion and decadent art meet with lurid results. The opera selections include *Mignon, The Marriage of Figaro, Gianni Schicchi* and *Semiramide*. The cast includes Christine Kaufmann, Candy Darling, Ingrid Caven and Manuela Riva. Color. In German and Italian. 104 minutes.

MAM'ZELLE NITOUCHE
1883 operetta by Hervé

This light opera, the only Hervé work on film, has an inventive libretto by Henri Meilhac and Albert Millaud. It's the charming story of a convent organist (Célestin in the convent, Floridor in the theater world) who secretly writes operettas and of a convent girl named Denise who wants to go on the stage. Denise is turned into the mysterious "Mam'selle Nitouche" who saves the day by singing at the premiere of his operetta. An army lieutenant provides the love interest. The plot derives loosely from incidents in Hervé's own early years when he led a double life as a church organist and operetta composer and performer. See also HERVÉ.

1912 Gigetta Morano film
This early Italian film of the story, also known as *Santarellina*, stars two major Italian actors of the period and was a big hit in 1912. Gigetta Morano is Denise who becomes Mam'zelle Nitouche and Ercole Vaser portrays Célestin/Floridor. Mario Bonnard is the lieutenant and Mario Caserini directed for Ambrosio film. Black and white. In Italian. About 15 minutes.

1931 Raimu film
The first sound version of the operetta stars the great Raimu as Célestin/Floridor under the deft direction of Marc Allegret. Jeanie Marèse portrays Denise/Nitouche with Jean Rousseliere as the lieutenant, André Alerme as the major and Edith Mera as Corinne. In small roles are stars-to-be Simone Simon and Edwige Feuillère. Paramount.

Black and white. In French. 106 minutes. Montparnasse (France) video

1931 Anny Ondra film
Anny Ondra portrays Denise/Nitouche in this German-language version of the above production. It was shot in Paris at the same time with a different cast and director and was titled *Mamsell Nitouche*. Ondra's co-stars are Oskar Karlweis, Georg Alexander and Hans Junkermann. Karel Lamac directed. Black and white. In German. 105 minutes.

1953 Fernandel film
Fernandel, the top French comic actor of the period, stars as Célestin/Floridor with Pier Angeli as Denise/Nitouche in this colorful French film of the operetta. Jean Dubucourt is the Commandant, François Guerin is the lieutenant, Michèle Cordoue is Corine and Louis de Funès is the major. Yves Allegret directed. Color. 90 minutes. In French. Montparnasse (France) video.

MANON
1884 opera by Massenet

Jules Massenet's version of the Abbé Prévost novel, which had already provided the basis for an opera by Auber and would later become Puccini's first success, is one of the principal repertory works in French opera houses to this day. Massenet's opera, with a libretto by Henri Meilhac and Philippe Gille, follows the novel closer than Puccini's but the story is the same. Convent-bound Manon runs off with young Des Grieux whom she meets at an inn but later abandons him for a rich man. After a series of complications she dies in the arms of Des Grieux. See also JULES MASSENET and for films based on the Prévost novel, see MANON LESCAUT.

1977 New York City Opera
Beverly Sills stars as Manon in this New York City Opera production by Tito Capobianco. Henry Price is Des Grieux, Richard Fredricks is Lescaut, Samuel Ramey is the Count and Robert Hale is De Bretigny. Gigi Denda was the stage director and Marsha Louis Eck designed the sets. Julius Rudel conducts the New York City Opera Orchestra and Chorus. Kirk Browning directed the video. Color. In French with English subtitles. 152 minutes. Paramount video.

Edita Gruberova stars as Manon in this Vienna State Opera production by Jean-Pierre Ponnelle. Francisco Araiza supports her in the role of Des Grieux. Adam Fischer conducted the Vienna Staatsoper Orchestra and Chorus. Color. In French. 167 minutes. On video.

Early/related films

1910 Mlle. Regnier film
This early Pathé Frères film was based on the Massenet opera. It stars Mlle. Regnier as Manon, M. Dehelly and J. Perier. It was released in the U.S. in July 1910. Black and white. About 10 minutes.

1926 Lya de Putti film
The German film *Manon Lescaut* starring Lya de Putti as Manon was based on the Massenet opera and the Prévost novel. Vladimir Gaidarow is Des Grieux, Eduard Rothauser is his father and Marlene Dietrich appears in the small role of Micheline. Paul Leni designed the sets and Arthur Robison directed. UFA. Black and white. In German. About 88 minutes.

1929 Hope Hampton in the Fourth Act of *Manon*
Silent film actress Hope Hampton had just become a professional opera singer when she sang in this Vitaphone sound film. It features excerpts from Act IV of the Massenet opera with accompaniment by the Vitaphone Symphony Orchestra and chorus. Hampton made her opera debut in *Manon* with the Philadelphia Grand Opera on Dec. 21, 1928. Black and white. About 10 minutes.

1930 Call of the Flesh
Ramon Novarro's version of the "Ah fuyez, douce image" from Manon was featured in this early Technicolor musical. The film is the story of a dancer turned opera singer. Charles Brabin directed. Color. 89 minutes.

MANON LESCAUT
1893 opera by Puccini

Puccini's first major success was based on a novel by the Abbé Prévost which had already inspired operas by Auber and Massenet. His wonderful melodies and an excellent libretto by Illica, Giacosa and others have made it the most popular of the three versions. Manon Lescaut is a young woman about to be put in a convent by her brother. She meets the Chevalier des Grieux at an inn and runs away with him. She later leaves him for the wealthy Geronte, gets arrested as a prostitute and is deported to Louisiana. Des Grieux goes with her and she dies in his arms. Manon's aria "In quelle trine morbide" is popular with sopranos. See also GIACOMO PUCCINI.

1980 Metropolitan Opera
Renato Scotto is in peak form as Manon in this opulent Metropolitan Opera production by Gian Carlo Menotti. Equally fine are Placido Domingo as Des Grieux, Pablo Elvira as Lescaut and Renato Capecchi as Geronte. Desmond Heeley designed the sets and James Levine conducted. Kirk Browning directed the video at a March 29, 1980, performance telecast on Sept. 27. Color. In Italian with subtitles. 135 minutes. Paramount video.

1983 Covent Garden
Placido Domingo returns as Des Grieux with Kiri Te Kanawa as Manon in this production by Götz Friedrich at the Royal Opera House. They are well supported by Thomas Allen as Lescaut and Forbes Robinson as Geronte. Gunther Schneider-Siemssen designed the sets and Giuseppe Sinopoli conducted the Royal Opera House Orchestra and Chorus. Color. In Italian with English subtitles. 130 minutes. HBO video.

1983 Opera Stories
This is a laserdisc highlights version of the above. Covent Garden production. The excerpts are introduced and narrated by Charlton Heston from the authentic settings of the opera. The framing material was shot in 1989 and directed by Keith Cheetham. 52 minutes. In English and Italian with subtitles. Pioneer Artists laser.

Early/related films

1908 Carlo Rossi film
An Italian silent film of a scene from the opera made by the Carlo Rossi Studio and screened with music synchronized on a phonograph. It was distributed in the U.S. by Kleine. About 3 minutes.

1910 Marie Regnier film
Marie Regnier stars as Manon Lescaut in this French silent film of the story made by the Pathé Studio. About 10 minutes.

1911 Francesca Bertini film
Italian film diva Francesca Bertini stars as Manon in this Italian film directed by Giovanni Pastrone, later known for his epic *Cabiria*. About 12 minutes.

1911 Stacia Napierkowska film
Stacia Napierkowska stars as Manon in this French film based on the Prévost story. Léon Bernard and Romuald Joubé lend support. Alberto Capellani directed for Pathé. About 12 minutes.

1912 Bérangère film
The noted stage actress Bérangère stars as Manon in this French film based on the opera and the novel. M. Barry portrays Des Grieux and M. Barnier is Lescaut. Made for Pathé. About 12 minutes.

1914 Lina Cavalieri film
Italian soprano Lina Cavalieri, publicized as "the most beautiful woman in the world," had starred on stage as Manon in both the Puccini and Massenet operas. In this American silent film she plays the role opposite her husband, French tenor Lucien Muratore, who portrays Des Grieux. The film was supposedly based on the Prévost novel rather than the operas or so they claimed for copyright reasons. Herbert Hall Winslow directed. About 50 minutes.

1918 Tina Xeo film
Tina Xeo stars as Manon in this silent Italian film based on the novel/opera story and directed by Mario Gargiulo. About 60 minutes.

1919 Lya Mara film
Lya Mara stars as Manon Lescaut in this silent German film based on the opera/ novel story and directed by Fred Zelnik. About 70 minutes.

1926 Lya de Putti film
This major German silent film of the Prèvost novel stars Lya de Putti as Manon. Vladimir Gaidarow portrays Des Grieux. Arthur Robison directed. Black and white. About 90 minutes.

1927 When a Man Loves
Dolores Costello plays Manon with John Barrymore as Des Grieux in this silent Warner Bros. feature. It was based on the Prévost novel but the studio gave it a happy ending. Black and white. About 110 minutes.

1940 Alida Valli film
Alida Valli stars as Manon with Vittorio De Sica as Des Grieux in this opulent Italian film. Opera film specialist Carmine Gallone based it on the opera libretto and Puccini's music provides the background score. Italian soprano Maria Caniglia sings the Puccini arias heard on the soundtrack. Black and white. In Italian. 92 minutes.

1949 Cecile Aubrey film
Cecile Aubrey portrays Manon in Henri-Georges Clouzot's harsh updated version of the story set in post-World War II France. Michel Auclair appears as Des Grieux. Black and white. In French. 105 minutes.

1954 The Loves of Manon Lescaut
Gli Amori di Manon Lescaut is an Italian film based on the novel but using the Puccini opera music as its score. Miriam Bru stars as Manon with Francesco Interlenghi as Des Grieux. Mario Costa directed. Black and white. In Italian. 95 minutes.

1986 Mayra Alejandra film
Venezuelan television star Mayra Alejandra portrays a modern Manon who runs off with her lover to the Hilton Hotel. This updated adaptation of the story was filmed in Venezuela by Roman Chalbaud. Color. In Spanish. 112 minutes.

1986 Hannah and Her Sisters
Woody Allen's fine film about three sisters in New York and their complicated love lives features a Metropolitan Opera performance of *Manon Lescaut*. Sam Peterson takes Diane Wiest to the opera where the camera observes them ironically while the aria "Sola, perduta, abbandonata" is sung. Color. In English. 106 minutes.

MAN WHO MISTOOK HIS WIFE FOR A HAT, THE
1986 opera by Nyman

Michael Nyman's chamber opera is based on one of the cases described by Dr. Oliver Sachs in a book about his patients. Christopher Rawlence's libretto follows the original closely as it tells the story of a man with a memory defect; he is unable to recognize familiar objects and cannot distinguish his wife from his hat. The man is a professional opera singer suffering from what Sachs calls "visual agnosia" and he cannot make sense of what he sees until he restores order through music. Nyman's opera relates the diagnostic journey of the neurologist who helps him. The music combines popular and classical idioms and was first staged at London's Institute of Contemporary Arts (ICA). See also MICHAEL NYMAN.

1987 ICA film
Nyman worked with the ICA for a year after the stage premiere to produce a film of his opera which evolved through a collaboration with librettist/filmmaker Rawlence, stage director Michael Morris and Dr. Oliver Sachs who appears in the film. The featured singers are Emile Belcourt, Patricia Hooper and Frederick Westcott. Sacks says that the real hero of the opera is music, "the power of music to organize, knit and re-knit a shattered world into sense." The film premiered in the U.S. at an American Film Institute film festival in Los Angeles. Color. In English. 75 minutes.

MARIA GOLOVIN
1958 TV opera by Menotti

Gian Carlo Menotti created Maria Golovin for television, specifically the NBC Opera Theatre, but it actually premiered at the U.S. Pavilion at the Brussels World Fair on August 20, 1985. The production was by NBC's Samuel Chotzinoff who took the opera to New York for a run at the Martin Beck Theater before its television premiere. The opera is the story of Donato, a blind war veteran who falls in love with the married Maria Golovin, a tenant in his mother's house. When her prisoner of war husband returns, he is madly jealous and tries to kill her. See also GIAN CARLO MENOTTI.

1959 NBC Opera Theater
Maria Golovin was presented on NBC Opera Theatre in the Samuel Chotzinoff production devised for Brussels and New York. The cast was essentially the same as that seen on stage with Franca Duval as Maria Golovin, Richard Cross as Donato, Ruth Kobart as Agata, Maria Neway as Donato's Mother and Lorenzo Muti as Trottolo. Rouben Ter-Arutunian designed the sets and Peter Herman Adler conducted the Symphony of the Air Orchestra. Kirk Browning directed the telecast on March 8, 1959. Color. In English. 120 minutes. Video at the MTR.

MARIANO, LUIS
Spanish/French tenor (1914-1970)

Luis Mariano is the equivalent of Mario Lanza for the French cinema, an operatic tenor who became a popular movie star but inspired little critical respect. His 1950s operetta films were top box office, videos of them are still best-sellers, books about him continue to be written and his records remain popular. Mariano was born in Spain but fled to France in 1936 because of the Civil War. He studied opera in Bordeaux and began his opera career as Ernesto in *Don Pasquale* in Paris in 1943. His stardom began with the operettas of Francis Lopez. He starred on stage in Lopez's *La Belle de Cadix* in 1946 and *Andalousie* in 1947 and starred again in their successful film versions. Also top box-office films were *Le Chanteur de Mexique* and *Violettes Imperials*. Mariano's only foreign film is a German-made adaptation of *Der Zarewitsch*. Mariano is not well known in the U.S. but he appeared on the Ed Sullivan Show in 1951 and in 1953 as the guest of Frank Sinatra. See also FRANCIS LOPEZ (1950/1953), DER ZAREWITSCH (1954).

1946 Historie de Chanter
Mariano plays a popular opera singer in his first major film. He is seen on stage as the Duke in Act One of *Rigoletto* and as Alfredo in the second act of *La Traviata*. Gilles Grangier directed the film. Black and white. In French. 88 minutes.

MARIA STUARDA
See MARY STUART

MARINA
1855 zarzuela by Arietta

Spanish composer Emilio Arietta's most popular zarzuela was modeled on Italian operas and most probably *Lucia di Lammermoor*. Francisco Camprodan's libretto tells the story of Marina (soprano), a young woman in a Catalan fishing village, and her love for the ship captain Jorge (tenor). There are many problems and misunderstandings but love wins out in the end. The zarzuela has been filmed and telecast at least three times and remains popular. See also EMILIO ARIETTA.

1963 Placido Domingo film

Placido Domingo stars as Jorge with Ernestina Garfias as Marina in this Mexican television film. It was shot in 1963 in Mexico City for a Max Factor series. Black and white. In Spanish. 90 minutes.

1980 Alfredo Kraus video

Alfredo Kraus stars as Jorge with C. Albanese as Marina in this video of a Caracas, Venezuela, production. The cast includes F. Kraus, Aponte and Noguera. Carlo Piantini conducts the orchestra. The video is an off-air copy of a Venezuelan telecast. Color. In Spanish. 115 minutes. Lyric/Opera Dubs videos.

1987 Teatro Campoanor, Oviedo

Ana Gonzalez stars as Marina with Alfredo Kraus as Jorge in this fine Asturias Opera production in the Campoanor Theater in Oviedo, Spain. Juan Pons is Roque, Alfonso Echeverria is Pascual, Stefano Palatchi is the old Capitan and Lourdes Diaz is Teresa. Jorquin Vion is the stage director and Enrique Ricci conducts the Asturias Symphonic Orchestra. Color. In Spanish. 118 minutes. Lyric video.

MARITANA

1845 opera by Wallace

Maritana was one of the big three "Irish" operas of 19th century England with Balfe's *Bohemian Girl* and Benedict's *Lily of Killarney.* Composer Vincent Wallace was Irish but the libretto by Edward Fitzball was based on the French play *Don César de Bazan* set in 17th century Madrid. The plot is close to Offenbach's *La Perichole.* King Charles II is attracted to the gypsy Maritana so his prime minister Don José arranges for her to marry Don Caesar in prison so she can obtain a title. *Maritana* was popular in London, New York and Vienna and was staged at Sadler's Wells as late as 1931. Though it was filmed three times and remained in the English repertory until World War II, it is no longer in fashion. There is no modern video and only a highlights record. See also VINCENT WALLACE.

1915 Alice Hollister film

Alice Hollister stars as Maritana in this American film of the opera shot by the Kalem company on location at a Spanish fort in Florida. Lawson Butt plays Don Caesar, Robert D. Walker is King Charles, Helen Lindroth is Queen Mary Louise and

Harry Millarde is Don Jose. Robert G. Vignola directed. The film is titled *Don Caesar de Bazan.* Black and white. About 50 minutes.

1922 Vivian Gibson film

Vivian Gibson portrays Maritana in this English highlights film of the opera made for the series *Tense Moments from Opera.* Gordon Hopkirk is Don Caesar de Bazan and Wallace Bosco plays King Charles. George Wynn directed the film and H. B. Parkinson produced it. Black and white. About 15 minutes.

1927 Kathlyn Hillard film

Kathlyn Hillard stars as Maritana in this British highlights film of the opera made for the *Cameo Operas* series. Herbert Langley plays Don Caesar. John E. Blakeley produced and H. B. Parkinson directed for Song Films. The movie was shown with live singers performing the arias. Black and white. About 18 minutes.

MARRIAGE, THE

1953 TV opera by Martinu

The Marriage, Bohuslav Martinu's comic opera based on a play by Gogol, premiered on NBC Television Opera Theatre. A young man thinks he should get married so a friend finds him the perfect woman. A marriage broker brings the woman other suitors but she agrees to marry the young man. He then changes his mind. Donald Gramm plays the young man, Sonia Stollin is the woman and Michael Pollock is the friend. Samuel Chotzinoff produced, Otis Riggs designed the sets and Peter Herman Adler conducted the orchestra. John Block directed the telecast on Feb. 7, 1953. Black and white. In English. 60 minutes. See also BOHUSLAV MARTINU.

MARRIAGE OF FIGARO, THE

1786 opera by Mozart

Le Nozze di Figaro is nearly the perfect opera with memorable music, wonderful characterizations, an entertaining plot and amazing ensembles. Lorenzo Da Ponte's delightful libretto is based on an excellent play by Beaumarchais. Figaro and Susanna make plans to marry but have to counter the Count's designs on her. They get help from the Countess and the page Cherubino and eventually succeed after many close calls. The opera has been popular with filmmakers. See also WOLFGANG A. MOZART.

1933 Le Barbier de Seville
This French film, though titled *Le Barbier de Seville*, is actually a combination of the Rossini and Mozart Beaumarchais operas and uses the story and music of both. The second half of the film is based around the Mozart opera. Josette Day is Susanna, André Baugé is Figaro, Jean Galland is the Count, Hélène Robert is the Countess, Monique Rolland is Cherubino and Yvonne Yma is Marceline and Pierre Juvenet is Bartholo. Marcel Lucine was the cinematographer and L. Masson conducted the music. Pierre Maudru wrote the screenplay and Hubert Bourlon and Jean Kemm directed. Vega Production. Black and white. In French. 93 minutes. Video Yesteryear (52-minute version).

1948 Rome Opera film
Piero Brasini stars as Figaro in this highlights film shot on stage at the Rome Opera House by George Richfield. Gianna Perea Zabia sings Susanna acted by Pina Malgharini, Gabriella Gatti sings the Countess acted by Lidia Melasei, Luciano Neroni sings the Count acted by Giulio Tomei who sings Bartolo acted by Gino Conti and Cleo Elmo is Cherubino. Angelo Questa leads the Rome Opera House Orchestra and Chorus and Olin Downes explains the story in English. This film was originally part of a feature called the *First Opera Film Festival*. Black and white. In Italian. 23 minutes. Video Yesteryear.

1949 Georg Wildhagen film
Georg Wildhagen directed *Figaros Hochzeit*, a film of the opera sung in German with spoken dialogue. Willi Domgraf-Fassbaender portrays Figaro, Mathieu Ahlersmeyer plays the Count, Erna Berger sings the role of Susanna acted by Angelika Hauff, Tiana Lemnitz sings the Countess acted by Sabine Peters, Anneliese Muller sings Cherubino acted by Willi Puhlmann, Eugen Fuchs sings Bartolo acted by Victor Jansen, Paul Schmidtmann sings Basilio acted by Alfred Dalthoff and Margarete Klose sings Marcellina acted by Elsa Wagner. Arthur Rother conducted the Berlin State Chamber Orchestra. DEFA. Black and white. In German. 105 minutes. Lyric video/Japanese laser.

1954 NBC Opera Theatre
Ralph Herbert portrays Figaro with Virginia Haskins as Susanna in this NBC Opera Theatre production by Samuel Chotzinoff. Laurel Hurley plays the Countess, William Shriner is the Count, Ann Crowley is Cherubino, Emile Renan is Bartolo, Ruth Kobart is Marcellina, John McCollum is Basilio and Paul Ukena is Antonio. The opera was directed by Charles Polacheck and designed by William Monyneux with the English translation made by Edward Eager. Peter Herman Adler conducted the Symphony of the Air orchestra. Kirk Browning directed two 90-minute live telecasts in February 1954 on successive Saturdays. Black and white. In English. 180 minutes. Video at MTR.

1954 Vienna State Opera film
Unsterblicher Mozart (Immortal Mozart) is an Austrian film featuring a highlights version of *The Marriage of Figaro* performed in German on stage by the Mozart Ensemble of the Vienna State Opera. Emmy Loose portrays Susanna, Erich Kunz is Figaro, Paul Schöffler is the Count, Hilde Gueden is Cherubino, Hilde Zadek is the Countess and Peter Klein is Basilio. There are also scenes from *The Abduction from the Seraglio* and *Don Giovanni*. Alfred Stöger directed the film and Rudolf Moralt conducted the Vienna Philharmonic. Color. In German. 95 minutes. Taurus (Germany) video.

1967 Rolf Liebermann film
Rolf Liebermann produced this *Die Hochzeit des Figaro*, a German-language film based on a Hamburg State Opera production. Heinz Blankenburg sings Figaro, Edith Mathis is Susanna, Tom Krause is the Count, Arlene Saunders is the Countess, Elisabeth Steiner is Cherubino, Noël Mangin is Bartolo, Maria von Hosvay is Marcellina, Natalie Usselmann is Barbarina and Kurt Marschner is Basilio. Hans Schmidt-Isserstedt conducts the Hamburg State Opera Orchestra and Chorus. Hannes Schindler was the cinematographer and Joachim Hess directed. The film was shown theatrically in the U.S. Color. In German. 189 minutes.

1973 Glyndebourne Festival
Peter Hall assembled a starry cast for this excellent Glyndebourne Festival production. Kiri Te Kanawa portrays the Countess, Ileana Cotrubas is Susanna, Frederica von Stade is Cherubino, Benjamin Luxon is the Count, Knut Skram is Figaro, Marius Rintzler is Bartolo, John Fryatt is Basilio, Elizabeth Gale is Barbarina and Nucci

Condo is Marcellina. John Bury designed the sets and John Pritchard conducted the London Philharmonic Orchestra and Glyndebourne Chorus. Humphrey Burton produced and Dave Heather directed the video for Southern Television. Color. In Italian with English subtitles. 169 minutes. VAI video.

1976 Jean-Pierre Ponnelle film
Jean-Pierre Ponnelle designed and directed a strong cast in this superb film of the opera, a virtual continuation of his earlier *Barber of Seville* shot on a sound stage. Hermann Prey again portrays Figaro and Paolo Montarsolo is again Bartolo. Mirella Freni is Susanna, Kiri te Kanawa is the Countess, Dietrich Fischer-Dieskau is the Count, Maria Ewing is Cherubino, Heather Begg is Marcellina, John van Kesteren is Basilio and Janet Perry is Barbarina. Ernst Wild was the cinematographer and Karl Böhm conducted the Vienna Philharmonic Orchestra. Color. In Italian with English subtitles. 181 minutes. DG video.

1976 Komische Opera Berlin
Walter Felsenstein created this production of *Figaros Hochzeit* for the Komische Opera in Berlin and wrote the German translation as well. Jozsef Dene sings the role of Figaro, Ursual Reinhardt-Kiss is Susanna, Magdalena Falewicz is the Countess, Uwe Kreyssig is the Count and Ute Trekel-Burckhardt is Cherubino. Geza Oberfran conducted the Komische Oper Orchestra and Chorus. Color. In German. 163 minutes. Japanese laser disc.

1980 Paris Opéra
José Van Dam portrays Figaro in this all-star Paris Opéra production directed by Giorgio Strehler. Gundula Janowitz is the Countess, Lucia Popp is Susanna, Frederica von Stade is Cherubino, Gabriel Bacquier is the Count and Kurt Moll is Bartolo. Sir George Solti conducts the Paris Opera Orchestra and Chorus. Taped live for French television by INA. Color. In Italian. 177 minutes. Lyric video/ Japanese laser.

1981 Drottningholm Court Theater
Göran Järvefelt staged this delightful authentic Drottningholm Court Theater production in collaboration with Mozart specialist Arnold Östman who conducts the period orchestra and chorus. Mikael Samuelsson is Figaro, Georgine Resick is Susanna, Sylvia Lindenstrand is the Countess, Per-Arne Wahlgren is the Count, Ann Christine Biel is Cherubino, Karin Mang-Habashi is Marcellina, Erik Saedén is Bartolo, Torbjörn Lilliequist is Basilio, Bo Leinmark is Curzio, Birgitta Larsson is Barbarina and Karl-Robert Lindgren is Antonio. Thomas Olofsson directed the video. Color. In Italian with English subtitles. 179 minutes. Philips video and laser.

1985 Metropolitan Opera
Kathleen Battle stars as Susanna with Ruggero Raimondi as Figaro in this Metropolitan Opera production designed and directed by Jean-Pierre Ponnelle. Carol Vaness is the Countess, Thomas Allen is the Count and Frederica Von Stade is Cherubino. James Levine conducts the Metropolitan Opera Orchestra and Chorus. Brian Large directed the video on Dec. 14, 1985, telecast on April 23, 1986. Color. In Italian with English subtitles. 180 minutes. Video at MTR.

1990 Peter Sellars film
Peter Sellers set his innovative updated version of the opera in the Trump Tower with the Count a Trump-like rich man and Cherubino macho in an American football uniform. It works well most of the time and there are many enjoyable references to vintage film comedy. Sanford Sylvan is Figaro, Jeanne Ommerle is Susanna, Jayne West is the Countess, James Maddalena is the Count, Susan Larson is Cherubino, Sue Ellen Kuzma is Marcellina, Frank Kelley is Basilio, William Cotton is Don Curzio, Lyn Torgove is Barbarina and Herman Hildebrand is Antonio. The film was shot in a Vienna TV studio with sets by Adrianne Lobel and costumes by Dunya Ramicova. Craig Smith conducted the Vienna Symphony Orchestra and Arnold Schoenberg Chorus. Color. In Italian with English subtitles. 193 minutes. London video and laser.

1991 New York City Opera
Dean Peterson portrays Figaro and Maureen O'Flynn is Susanna in this New York City Opera production by John Copley. Elizabeth Hynes is the Countess, William Stone is the Count, Kathryn Gamberoni is Cherubino, Joseph McKee is Bartolo, Susanne Marsee is Marcellina, Jonathan Green is Basilio, Michele McBride is Barbarina, Don Yule is Antonio and Peter Blanchet is Curzio. Carl Toms designed the sets and costumes and Scott Bergeson conducted the New York City Opera Orchestra and Chorus. Kirk Browning directed the video

telecast on Sept. 25, 1991 in the *Live from Lincoln Center* series. Color. In Italian with English subtitles. 195 minutes.

1992 Vienna State Opera
Jonathan Miller's larger-than-life production of the opera at the Theater an der Wien in Vienna stars Marie McLaughlin as Susanna, Lucio Gallo as Figaro and Cheryl Studer as the Countess. Ruggero Raimondi is the Count, Gabriella Sima is Cherubino, Heinz Zednik is Basilio, Rudolph Mazzola is Bartolo, Margherita Lilowa is Marcellina, Yvetta Tannebergerova is Barbarina and Istvan Gati is Antonio. Peter J. Davison designed the huge revolving sets and Claudio Abbado conducted the Vienna State Opera Orchestra and Chorus. Shot in HDTV. Color. In Italian. 181 minutes. Sony video and laser.

1993 Théâter du Châtelet, Paris
Welsh baritone Bryn Terfel stars as Figaro with Alison Hagely as Susanna in this excellent John Eliot Gardiner production at the Châtelet theater in Paris. Rodney Gilfray is the Count, Hillevi Martinpelto is the Countess, Pamela Helen Stephen is Cherubino, Susan McCullock is Marcellina, Carlos Feller is Bartolo and Francis Egerton is Basilio. Conductor Gardiner collaborated with stage director Jean Louis Thamin and set designer Rudy Saboughi. Olivier Mille directed the video. Color. In Italian. 170 minutes. DG video and laser.

1994 Glyndebourne Festival
The first production of the rebuilt Glyndebourne Festival Theatre was appropriately *The Marriage of Figaro* which began the Glyndebourne legend. Gerald Finley is Figaro, Alison Hagley is Susanna. Renée Fleming is the Countess, Andreas Schmidt is the Count, Marie-Ange Todorovitch is Cherubino and Robert Tear is Bartolo. Stephen Metacalf produced the opera and Bernard Haitink conducted the London Philharmonic Orchestra and Glyndebourne Chorus. The opera was televised live in England on May 28, 1994, and directed for
TV and video by Derek Bailey. Color. In Italian. 190 minutes. Warner Vision (England) video.

1995 Music Theatre London
This excellent BBC adaptation of Music Theater London's updated version of the opera is in modern English with spoken recitatives. The new setting is a National Trust house in the Home Counties. The Count is a Tory Euro plutocrat, Susanna is a spunky Essex girl who kicks him in the groin when he gets fresh and the Countess is an exercise fanatic. Harry Burton is Figaro, Mary Lincoln is Susanna, Jan Hartley is the Countess, Andrew Wadsworth is the Count, Jacinta Mulcahy is Cherubino, Denis Quilley is Bartolo, Tricia George is Marcellina, Nigel Planer is Antonio and Simon Butteriss is Basilio. Nick Broadhurst staged the opera for Music Theatre London and wrote the translation with Tony Britten who conducted the nine-player orchestra. Geoff Posner produced the video adaptation for BBC Television. Color. In English. 180 minutes. Sony Classical (England) video.

Early/related films

1911 Cines Film
This is an early Italian adaptation of the play and the opera and was screened in theaters with music from the opera. Black and white. About 10 minutes.

1913 Luigi Maggi film
Luigi Maggi directed this Italian film based on the opera and play for the Ambrosio studio of Turin. It stars Gigetta Morano as Rosina, Ubaldi Stefani as Figaro, Umberto Scapellin as the Count, Eleuterio Rodolfi, Ernesto Vaser and Ada Mantero. It was partially shot on location in Seville. The same team made an earlier version of *The Barber of Seville*. Black and white. About 15 minutes.

1920 Figaros Hochzeit
This German silent film of the opera was written and directed by Max Mack who made several German opera films. Critics praised its painterly images. Black and white. About 60 minutes.

1929 Figaro
Gaston Ravel wrote and directed this French film based on the Beaumarchais trilogy of Figaro plays. It follows the story from *The Barber of Seville* through *The Marriage of Figaro* to *The Guilty Mother* in which the Countess has a child by Cherubino. E. H. Van Duren stars as Figaro, Tony D'Algy is the Count, Arlette Marchal is Rosine (Rosina/the Countess), Marie Bell is Suzanne (Susanna) and Jean Weber is Cherubin (Cherubino). Black and white. In French. 76 minutes.

1932 Educational Film
This is a film of a rehearsal of *The Marriage of Figaro*. It shows the singers on stage in scenes from the opera with the orchestra. Black and white. In English. 14 minutes.

1942 Cairo
Jeanette MacDonald sings a duet from *The Marriage of Figaro* with Ethel Waters in this spy mystery. She portrays a movie star in Cairo. W.S. Van Dyke directed. MGM. Black and white. 101 minutes.

1952 So Little Time
This story of a doomed romance in wartime Belgium between music student Maria Schell and German officer Marius Goring includes excerpts from *The Marriage of Figaro*. Compton Bennett directed. Black and white. 88 minutes.

1955 On Such A Night
Sesto Bruscantini (Figaro) and Sena Jurinac (the Countess) are seen rehearsing and performing at Glyndebourne in this famous film by Anthony Asquith. David Knight plays an American who goes to see *The Marriage of Figaro* at the Glyndebourne Festival. Oliver Messel designed the sets, Benjamin Frankel selected the opera excerpts and Glyndebourne musical director Carl Ebert assisted. Frank North was the cinematographer and Paul Dehn wrote the script. Color. 37 minutes.

1959 Le Mariage de Figaro
A French film of the Beaumarchais play using the Mozart opera music as its score. Jean Piat is Figaro, Micheline Boudet is Suzanne, Georges Descrières is the Count, Yvonne Gaudeau is the Countess, Denise Gence is Marceline, Jean Meyer is Basilio and Michele Grellier is Cherubin. Erna Berger's voice is heard on the soundtrack. Jean Meyer directed the film based on a Comédie-Française production. Color. In French. 105 minutes.

1959 The Nun's Story
Audrey Hepburn plays Cherubino's "Voi che sapete" on the piano with her father in a touching scene before leaving for the convent. Fred Zinnemann directed. Color. 149 minutes.

1965 The Ipcress File
British intelligence agent Michael Caine (Len Deighton's Harry Palmer) meets his Albanian counterpart by a bandstand in a park to ransom a kidnapped scientist. The band plays the overture to *Marriage* and the Albanian comments upon its delicacy. Sidney Furie directed. Color. 108 minutes.

1984 Kaos
Writer Luigi Pirandello sees the ghost of his mother and hears Barbarina's aria "L'ho perduto" (I've lost it) in this Italian film by the brothers Paolo and Vittorio Taviani. She appears at his window and tells him the story of her lost innocence to this appropriate aria. Color. In Italian. 188 minutes.

1984 Amadeus
Milos Forman's film features scenes from *Marriage* staged by Twyla Tharpe in Prague's Tyl Theater. Miro Grisa portrays Figaro (sung by Samuel Ramey), Zuzana Kadlecova is Susanna (sung by Isabel Buchanan), Helena Cihelnikova is the Countess (sung by Felicity Lott), Karel Gult is the Count (sung by Richard Stillwell), Magda Celakovska is Cherubino (sung by Anne Howells), Slavena Drasilova is Barbarina (sung by Deborah Rees, Eva Senkova is Marcellina (sung by Patricia Payne, Ladislav Kretschmer is Antonio (sung by Willard White), Leos Kratochvil is Basilio (sung by Alexander Oliver), Bino Zeman is Curzio (sung by Robin Leggate and Jaroslav Mikulin is Bartolo (sung by John Tomlinson). Color. In English. 160 minutes. On video and laser.

1988 The Moderns
Alan Rudolph's film about the American writers and artists in Paris in the 1920s features Cherubino's arias "Voi che sapete." Color. 128 minutes.

1989 Le Mariage de Figaro
This modern big-budget French film of the Beaumarchais play was shot in a chateau near Paris. It was directed by Roger Coggio and follows the original closely. Color. In French. 171 minutes.

1993 The Last Action Hero
The acceptance of opera music in even the most commercial Hollywood films is reflected by the inclusion of a bit of *Marriage* in *The Last Action Hero*. Arnold Schwarzenegger plays a fictional movie hero chasing criminals in the "real" world. He hears the opera overture on the radio and asks what it is. A woman tells him it is Mozart and asks

if he likes classical music. I will, he promises. John McTiernan directed. Color. 100 minutes.

1993 L'Accompagnatrice
Barbarina's aria is heard twice in this French film about life in Paris in 1942. Beautiful soprano Irene (Elena Safonova, sung by Laurence Monteyrol) sings it for her husband at his request accompanied by plain Sophie (Romane Bohringer, piano by Angeline Pondepeyre). It's repeated at an appropriate moment later in the film. Claude Miller directed. Color. In French with English subtitles. 100 minutes. On video.

1993 Trading Places
The Overture from the opera is nicely used on the soundtrack of this satirical comedy by John Landis. Eddie Murphy stars as the conman who is turned into a commodities broker. Color. 116 minutes.

1994 The Shawshank Redemption
Prisoner Tim Robbins uses the intercom system to let the inmates listen to some opera over the loudspeakers. Two women sing a duet and though the prisoners don't know what the women are singing, it's a liberating experience for Morgan Freeman and his fellow inmates. What they hear is the duet "Che soave zeffiretto" from Act III of *The Marriage of Figaro*. The recording is by Edith Mathis as Susanna and Gundula Janowitz as the Countess with the Deutsche Oper Berlin Orchestra conducted by Karl Böhm. Frank Darabont directed the film. Color. 142 minutes. On video.

MARSCHNER, HEINRICH
German composer (1795-1861)

Heinrich Marschner is considered the major opera composer in Germany between Weber and Wagner. He has mostly been forgotten by the modern opera public but some of his stage works still have admirers. He is best known for the Grand Guignol-like *Der Vampyr*. As the vogue for vampires never seems to abate, it is likely to stay in the repertory. It was recently updated in a stylish way for British television. See DER VAMPYR.

MARSHALL, EVERETT
American baritone (1901-)

Massachusetts-born baritone Marshall Everett studied in New York, London and Milan but made

his debut in Palermo in 1926 in *Il Trovatore*. He began his career at the Metropolitan Opera in 1927 in *Lohengrin* and remained with the Met for five seasons. His film career began in 1930 with the operetta *Dixiana* after which he shifted to Broadway for *George White's Scandals* in 1931 and the *Ziegfeld Follies* in 1934. He was back in Hollywood in 1935 for one more film but then turned to stage operetta and toured in standards like *The Student Prince*.

1930 Dixiana
Marshall stars opposite Bebe Daniels in this RKO operetta film set in 1840 New Orleans. It was made by the same team that made the very successful *Rio Rita* but it didn't quite jell this time. Daniels playscircus singer Dixiana and Marshall is from a wealthy Southern family. They want to marry but his family is snobbish. The film was made with two-color Technicolor sequences and songs by Harry Tierney and Anne Caldwell. Luther Reed directed. Black and white and color. 98 minutes.

1935 I Live For Love
Busby Berkeley directed this minor musical with Marshall as a singer who has a rivalous relationship with Delores Del Rio. After a series of theatrical and radio mix-ups, they get married. The songs are by Mort Dixon and Allie Wrubel. Warner Bros. Black and white. 64 minutes.

MARTHA
1847 opera by Flotow

Friedrich von Flotow's *Martha, oder Der Markt zur Richmond* used to be a very popular opera at the Met and was a particular favorite of Caruso's. Edison was certainly aware of this popularity because he made *Martha* the first opera to be filmed in America. Its tenor aria "Ach so fromm," its adaptation of "The Last Rose of Summer" and its fine quintet "Mag der Himmel" are still sung but the opera is rarely staged now in the U.S. Perhaps it's because librettist W. Friedrich has such an odd Germanic view of England in 1710. Lady Harriet and her maid Nancy attend the Richmond Market for a lark in disguise as Martha and Julia. They are hired by Lyonel and Plumkett (so spelled) who take them back to Plumkett's farm. The women escape but not before both men fall in love. Lyonel sees Lady Harriet at a Royal event but she pretends not to know him. They get together in the end. *Martha* has been filmed many times and remains popular in Germany. See also FRIEDRICH VON FLOTOW.

1932 Milady's Escapade
This is a highlights version in English of *Martha* filmed in the U.S. and distributed with the title *Milady's Escapade*. Howard Higgins directed it for the Operalogue series produced by Educational Films. Black and white. In English. 30 minutes.

1936 Helge Roswaenge film
Dane Helge Roswaenge, who was the leading tenor at the Berlin Staatsopera at this period, stars as Lyonel in this German film titled *Martha oder Letzte Rose* (Martha or The Last Rose). Carla Spletter is Lady Harriet, Fritz Kampers is Plumkett, Grethe Weiser is Nancy and Georg Alexander is Tristan. Harald Röbbeling and Arthur Pohl scripted, Herbert Korner was the cinematographer and Karl Anton directed. Black and white. In German. 106 minutes.

1936 Roger Bourdin film
Paris Opéra-Comique baritone Roger Bourdin stars as Lionel in this French version of the above production titled *Martha or les Dernières Roses*. Sim Viva is Lady Harriet, Arthur Devere is Plumkett, Fernande Saala is Nancy and Huguette Duflos is Queen Anne. Jacques Bousquet wrote the French screenplay, Herbert Korner was cinematographer and Karl Anton again directed. Black and white. In French. 99 minutes.

1970 Lucy Peacock film
American soprano Lucy Peacock stars as Lady Harriet with Elisabeth Steiner as her maid Nancy in this German film. Gustav Kogel, who scripted it, added a mime sequence during the overture. Klaus Hirte sings Lord Tristan. German conductor Horst Stein, known for his Wagner, conducts the Norddeutschen Rundfunks Orchestra and Chorus. Arno Assmann directed for ZDF. Color. In German. 112 minutes. Lyric video.

1986 Stuttgart State Opera
Krisztina Laki stars as Lady Harriet in this Stuttgart Staatsoper production by Loriot. Rüdiger Wohlers sings Lyonel, Waltraud Meier is Nancy, Helmut Berger-Tuna is Plumkett and Jörn W. Wilsing is Tristan. Loriot also designed the sets and costumes and Wolf Dieter Hauschild conducted the Stuttgart State Theater Orchestra.

Color. In German. 140 minutes. Lyric/Opera Dubs video.

Early/related films

1900 Edison opera film
This Edison film of four opera singers acting and singing their roles in the second act of *Martha* seems to be the first film of an actual opera. The director, probably Edwin S. Porter, filmed the performers on a set in Thomas Edison's New York studio. It was released in March 1900 as *Opera of Martha* with a promotion suggesting local church singers be engaged to sing the parts behind the scenes. Alternatively "the quartette can be engaged to travel with the exhibition." About 15 minutes.

1902 Lubin opera film
German-born Sigmund Lubin's Philadelphia-based Lubin Company also made a film of the very popular *Martha*. It was released in 1902, two years after the Edison film, and was meant to be screened with live music. About 10 minutes.

1908 Pathé sound film
This is a German film made by the Pathé company of a scene and aria from the opera. It was screened with the music played on a synchronized phonograph. In German. About 4 minutes.

1913 Michael Curtiz film
Casablanca director Michael Curtiz, one of Hungary's top directors in the silent era, made a full-length version of *Martha* in Budapest in 1913. It stars Matton Ratkai, Sari Fedak and Mihaly Varkonyi and was screened with live music. About 40 minutes.

1919 Delog film
The German Delog studio had an unusual solution to the silence of screen opera; they provided live musicians with their screen version of *Martha*. The company sent the film on tour with soloists, chorus and orchestra. It saved money on sets and was an attractive novelty. About 70 minutes.

1922 Dorothy Fane film
Dorothy Fane stars as Lady Henrietta in this British highlights version of the opera made by George Wynn for the *Tense Moments from Opera* series. Leslie Austin portrays Lionel and James

Knight is Plunkett. It was screened with live music. Gaumont. About 12 minutes .

1923 Walt Disney film
Walt Disney made an animated film called *Martha* in 1923 for his Song-o-Reel musical series. Black and white. About 6 minutes.

1927 Grizelda Hervey film
Grizelda Hervey stars as Lady Henrietta in this British highlights version of the opera made by H. B. Parkinson for the British *Cameo Opera* series. Gerald Rawlinson portrays Lionel and Albergon Hicks is Plunkett. Singers stood beside the screen and sang the arias played by the theater orchestra. Song Film. About 20 minutes.

1929 Frances Alda Vitaphone film
Metropolitan Opera soprano Frances Alda sings "The Last Rose of Summer" from *Martha* in this Vitaphone sound short released in August 1927. Black and white. About 8 minutes. Bel Canto Society video.

1929 Giovanni Martinelli film
Metropolitan opera tenor Giovanni Martinelli sings the famous aria "M'appari" from *Martha* in Italian in this Vitaphone sound film. He also performs a duet from Act II with soprano Livia Marracci. Black and white. About 10 minutes.

1937 When You're in Love
Beniamino Gigli is heard singing "M'appari" on a phonograph record in this Hollywood film about an opera star with Grace Moore. Robert Riskin directed. Columbia. Black and white. 104 minutes.

1939 Three Smart Girls Grow Up
Deanna Durbin sings "The Last Rose of Summer" arrangement from *Martha* in this film about three sisters and their romantic attachments. Henry Koster directed for Universal. Black and white. 87 minutes.

1943 The Phantom of the Opera
Nelson Eddy and chorus sing the Drinking Song from *Martha* in French at the Paris Opéra as the curtain raises on this famous version of the Leroux novel. The Phantom is watching in the wings. Arthur Lubin directed. Color. 92 minutes.

1946 The Whale Who Wanted to Sing at the Met
Nelson Eddy sings a stirring Italian version of the "Mag Der Himmel" ensemble at the end of this animated film about an operatic whale. In the finale he is shown in heaven singing "in a hundred glorious voices," all lent to him by Eddy. Hamilton Luske directed this Disney cartoon as part of the feature *Make Mine Music*. Color. 12 minutes.

1979 Breaking Away
"Ach so fromm" is widely known as the Italian aria "M'appari" because of the influence of Caruso. In this film about the ersatz Italian behavior of an Indiana boy who tries to be like his cycling heroes, it is used ironically. It is the "Italian" aria he sings while cycling. Peter Yates directed and Steve Tesich won an Oscar for his screenplay. Color. 100 minutes.

1982 The Grey Fox
An outdoor phonograph playing Caruso's recording of "M'appari" keys the chief romantic scene in this film. Richard Farnsworth portrays an aging train robber in the 1910s who is attracted through the aria to the woman of his life. Philip Borsos directed this fine Canadian film. Color. 92 minutes.

MARTINELLI, GIOVANNI
Italian tenor (1885-1969)

Giovanni Martinelli sang and starred in seventeen films, most of them operatic sound shorts made for Vitaphone from 1927 to 1931. He was Vitaphone's most admired and most prolific artist and was featured in fifteen films in four years, nearly a quarter of those made. Martinelli was born in 1885 in Montagnana and made his debut in Milan in 1910. In 1911 he sang Dick Johnson in *La Fanciulla del West* and his performance led to international fame. He sang at Covent Garden in 1912 and the Metropolitan in 1913 and the Met became the focal point of the rest of his career. He sang there until 1945 in over 900 performances. He made many records and continued to work into his 80s. See also METROPOLITAN OPERA (1966).

1927-31 Vitaphone Opera Films
Martinelli starred in fifteen opera films made for Vitaphone from 1927 to 1931, all filmed at Oscar Hammerstein's old Manhattan Opera House. The

film featuring Martinelli singing "Vesti la giubba" from *Pagliacci* was featured in the first Vitaphone evening on August 6, 1926 preceding the screening of *Don Juan*. It was greatly admired and led to many more. The other featured operas are *Aida, Carmen, Faust, Martha, Il Trovatore* and *La Juive*. Some of the films feature Russian, Mexican and Italian folk songs as well as art songs. Most of the Martinelli films are accessible. *Pagliacci* is on laser disc with the feature *Don Juan*, scenes from *Aida, La Juive* and *Il Trovatore* are on a Bel Canto Society video and the rest are in film archives. See also (all 1927-1930) AIDA, CARMEN, FAUST, LA JUIVE, MARTHA, PAGLIACCI, IL TROVATORE.

1967 Martinelli and Harewood
Martinelli is interviewed by Lord Harewood for BBC Television in this film telecast on Nov. 5, 1967. Martinelli is seen singing an aria from *La Juive*. Kenneth Gordon made the film as part of the International Music series. Black and white. 70 minutes. Print in National Film Archive, London.

1967 Seattle Opera
Martinelli's last stage performance at the age of 82 is shown in this film shot at the dress rehearsal of *Turandot* at the Seattle Opera in 1967. Martinelli was featured in the non-singing role of the Emperor. Color. 3 minutes. Print in National Film Archive, London.

MARTINI, NINO
Italian tenor (1905-1976)

Nino Martini was born in Verona, site of the famous open-air opera arena. He made his debut at La Scala in 1926 in *Rigoletto*. Jesse Lasky invited him to America in 1930 to appear in *Paramount on Parade*, after which he sang the Duke in *Rigoletto* with the Philadelphia Opera in 1932 and the Metropolitan Opera in 1933. He returned to Hollywood in the mid-1930s during the opera film boom and starred in three more films for Lasky. He continued to sing with the Met until 1946 and made a film in England in 1948.

1930 Paramount on Parade
Martini made his film debut in Technicolor in this musical revue where he was featured in the "Song of the Gondolier." He sings the Italian song "Torna a Sorrento" in a Venice canal. Paramount. Black and white and color. 100 minutes.

1935 Here's to Romance
Martini returned to Hollywood as an opera star. He appears in this film as a student of diva Ernestine Schumann-Heink, playing herself, who thinks he can become the greatest singer in the world. Through her help he is sent to study opera in Paris with financial assistance by Genevieve Tobin. Love problems make his Paris debut a disaster but he finally triumphs in *Tosca* at the Metropolitan. He also sings arias from *Manon, Cavalleria Rusticana* and *Pagliacci*. Alfred E. Green directed for Twentieth Century-Fox. Black and white. 83 minutes.

1936 The Gay Desperado
Martini is the singing hero of this musical western set in Mexico with Ida Lupino as the girl he gets in the end and Leo Carrillo as the bad bandit. It begins in a cinema where Martini quells a riot with his soothing singing and then gets pressganged by Carrillo. Many of the songs are in Spanish, there's a bit of *Aida* and the hit tune is "The World Is Mine." Rouben Mamoulian directed. Black and white. 85 minutes.

1937 Music For Madame
This entertaining film revolves around newly-arrived Italian immigrant Martini singing the "Vesta la giubba" aria from *Pagliacci*. He is hired to sing it in clown costume at a Hollywood wedding but discovers he has been used as a diversion for a robbery. If he sings again a famous conductor will recognize his voice and he will go to jail. Instead the conductor thinks he is so good that he hires him to sing at the Hollywood Bowl where he is a hit and wins Joan Fontaine. John Blystone directed. Black and white. 77 minutes. Lyric video.

1948 One Night With You
Martini portrays an Italian opera/movie star stranded in a village with Patricia Roc. They end up in jail but it all works out in the end. Martini sings both operatic arias and pop songs. This is a remake of the 1943 Italian film *Fuga a Due Voce* which featured tenor Gino Bechi. Terence Young directed. Black and white. 92 minutes.

MARTIN'S LIE
1964 TV opera by Menotti

Menotti's fourth TV commission was from CBS Television for this "church opera" about tolerance in a 16th century European orphanage. The orphan Martin lies and eventually dies to protect a man with different religious beliefs who could be his father. Menotti staged and narrated the opera at Bristol Cathedral. Michael Wennink sings the role of Martin, Donald McIntyre is the Stranger, William McAlpine is Father Cornelius, Noreen Berry is Naninga, Otakar Kraus is the Sheriff, , Keith Collins is Christopher and Roger Nicholas is Timothy. Anthony Powell designed the sets and costumes and Lawrence Leonard conducted the English Chamber Orchestra and St. Mary Redcliffe Secondary School Chorus. Kirk Browning directed the video on June 3, 1964 which was telecast by CBS on May 30, 1965. Black and white. In English. 52 minutes. Video at MTR. See also GIAN CARLO MENOTTI.

MARTINU, BOHUSLAV
Czech composer (1890-1959)

Bohuslav Martinu, one of the most important Czech composers, is well represented on CD but less so on video. He spent much of his life outside his homeland so he wrote operas in English, French and Italian as well as Czech. Martinu was in Paris from 1923 to 1940, in the U.S. from 1940 to 1953 and then mostly in France and Italy. He composed three screen operas. *Les Trois Souhaits* is a "film opera" and uses film in a major way to tell its story. *The Marriage* and *What Men Live By* were written for and premiered on American television. *Ariane* and *The Greek Passion* have been taped for television. See also ARIANE, THE GREEK PASSION, THE MARRIAGE, LES TROIS SOUHAITS.

1953 What Men Live By
Martinu's television opera *What Men Live By* (Czech title *Cím lide ziji*) is based on a short story by Tolstoy. Martinu wrote the English libretto and music in 1951-1952 and the opera premiered on American television in New York in May 1953. Black and white. In English. 55 minutes.

MARTON, EVA
Hungarian soprano (1943-)

Eva Marton has one of the most powerful soprano voices in opera today; she is noted for her performances in Wagner and Strauss though she is also formidable in Italian opera. Born Eva Heinrich in Budapest, she made her debut there in 1968, forged her early career in Frankfurt and made her Metropolitan Opera debut in 1976. She has sung in most major opera houses and can be seen on video in many of her best-known roles. See ANDREA CHÉNIER (1985), ELEKTRA (1989), DIE FRAU OHNE SCHATTEN (1992), DIVAS (1993), LA GIOCONDA (1986), GLYNDEBOURNE (1994), LOHENGRIN (1986), METROPOLITAN OPERA (1983, 1986), TANNHÄUSER (1982), TOSCA (1984, 1986), IL TROVATORE (1988), TURANDOT (1983, 1988, 1993), VERONA (1988).

1988 Eva Marton in Concert
This is a video record of a concert given by Eva Marton. She sings arias by Verdi, Puccini, Boito, Cilea, Ponchielli and Catalani. Color. 60 minutes. Pioneer Artists laserdisc.

MARUXA
1914 opera by Vives

Maruxa is Spanish composer Amadeo Vives's most successful opera, rivaling his zarzuelas in popularity. It is set in Galicia in northwest Spain and some of the characters sing in the local Gallegan language. The shepherdess Maruxa loves the shepherd Pablo but estate owner Rosa wants him for herself although she is already engaged to Antonio. After misunderstandings, storms, disguises, and folk dancing, the couples sort themselves out with help from Rufo. The libretto is by Luis Pascual Frutos. See also AMADEO VIVES.

1923 Henry Vorins film
French filmmaker Henry Vorins shot this silent Spanish film of the opera on location in Galicia with his wife Paulette Landais starring as Maruxa. It was presented in cinemas with the opera music played live by an orchestra. The cast includes Florian Rey, Asuncion Delgado, Elvira Lopez and Jose Mora. Luis R. Alonso was the cinematographer. Black and white. In Spanish. 80 minutes.

1968 Juan de Orduña film
Dolores Perez sings the role of Maruxa in this film directed by Juan de Orduña for the Spanish Television *Teatro Lirico Español* series. The other principal roles are sung by Luis Sagi-Vela as Pablo, Josefina Cubeiro as Rosa, Julio Julian and Chano Gonzalo. Non-singing actors are seen on screen. Manuel Tamayo wrote the script and Federico Moreno Torroba conducted the Spanish Lyric Orchestra and Madrid Chorus. TVE. Color. In Spanish. 110 minutes.

1979 Gran Teatro del Liceo, Barcelona

Carmen Hernandez stars as Maruxa in this stage production by Diego Monio at the Gran Teatro del Liceo in Barcelona. Sergio De Sales is Pablo, Antonio Borras is Rufo, Maria Uriz is Rosa and Emilo Belabal is Antonio, Gerardo Perez Busquier conducted the Gran Teatro del Liceo Symphonic Orchestra. Color. In Spanish. 116 minutes. Opera Dubs video.

MARY STUART
1835 opera by Donizetti

Donizetti's opera *Maria Stuarda* was written to be sung in Italian but it exists on video only in English. History it is not. The libretto by Giuseppe Bartari is based on a play by Schiller (also on video) which tells of a (fictional) meeting between Mary Queen of Scots and Queen Elizabeth. This is arranged by Leicester who is loved by Elizabeth though he actually loves Mary. Mary responds furiously to accusations about her loyalty and ends up on the scaffold. Janet Baker has been notable in the role on stage and her performance is on video. There are a number of films telling the story in a narrative form. See also GAETANO DONIZETTI.

1982 English National Opera

Janet Baker is in superb form as Mary Stuart in this splendid English National Opera English-language production. It was her last for the English stage, produced at her request at the ENO by John Copley. She is well partnered by Rosalind Plowright as Queen Elizabeth, David Rendal as Leicester, John Tomlinson as Talbot and Alan Opie as Cecil. The sets are by Desmond Heeley with Charles Mackerras conducting the ENO Orchestra and Chorus. Tom Hammond made the English translation and Peter Butler directed the video. Color. In English. 138 minutes. EMI/HBO video.

Early/related films

1908 Jeanne Delvair film

Jeanne Delvair stars as Mary Stuart in this French Pathé film made in color and titled *Marie Stuart*. It was directed by Albert Capellani and released in the U.S. and may have been based on the opera libretto. Color. 14 minutes.

1922 Mary, Queen of Scots

Cathleen Nesbit portrays Mary Stuart in this English film written by Eliot Stannard and directed by Edwin Greenwood for a series called *The Romance of British History*. About 10 minutes.

1927 Maria Stuart

A German version of the story based on the Schiller play and starring Fritz Kortner. It was directed by Friedrich Feher who wrote it with Leopold Jessner and Anton Kuh. About 70 minutes.

1936 Mary of Scotland

Katharine Hepburn stars as Mary Stuart with Florence Eldridge as Elizabeth in this American film based on the play by Maxwell Anderson. John Ford directed for RKO. Black and white. 123 minutes.

1971 Mary, Queen of Scots

Vanessa Redgrave portrays Mary Stuart with Glenda Jackson as Queen Elizabeth in this British film written by John Hale. Charles Jarrott directed. Color. 128 minutes.

1985 Mary Stuart

This is a German television production of the Schiller play on which the opera is based. Heinz Schirk wrote and directed the TV adaptation for Bavarian Television. In German or English. Color. 111 minutes. Inter Nationes video.

MASCAGNI, PIETRO
Italian composer (1863-1945)

Mascagni became famous overnight in 1890 with his one-act opera *Cavalleria Rusticana* (Rustic Chivalry). It marked the beginning of *verismo* opera and was the highpoint of Mascagni's career. He never again created an opera with such wide recognition and today is known almost wholly for this one opera. However, Mascagni wrote many others, some available on CD, including the influential *Iris* which was filmed in the silent era. He also composed a pioneer film score for the 1915 Italian movie *Rapsodia Satanica*, a popular operetta called *Sì* and music for a film starring tenor Giacomo Lauri-Volpi. See also CAVALLERIA RUSTICANA, GIACOMO LAURI-VOLPI (1933), IRIS, SÍ.

1915 Rapsodia Satanica

The libretto for this avant-garde film was sold as if it were for an opera and in some ways *Rapsodia Satanica* can be considered a "film opera." Mascagni wrote an original score for it in collaboration with scriptwriter Maria Martini and director Nino Oxilia. They described it as a "poema cinema-musical." Lyda Borelli, a major Italian cinema diva of the period, was the star opposite André Habay. Giorgio Ricci was the cinematographer. Black and white. In Italian. About 65 minutes.

1916 Amica

Amica is a 1905 opera by Mascagni that marked a return to his *verismo* style with a French libretto by Paul de Choudens. The composer conducted performances in Italy and its success led to a 1916 Italian film by Enrico Guazzoni made with Mascagni's cooperation. The film, a close reproduction of the opera, was screened with the opera music. It stars Leda Gys, Amleto Novelli, Augusto Mastipietri and Augusto Poggioli. Cines. Black and white. In Italian. About 60 minutes.

1952 Mascagni

Pierre Cressoy portrays Mascagni in this Italian biography of the composer. The film shows him studying at the Milan Conservatory, on tour with the Novarra operetta company orchestra and having a huge success with his first opera. Mario Del Monaco appears as the tenor Roberto Stagno who created the role of Turiddu in *Cavalleria Rusticana* in Rome in 1890 and Carla Del Poggio plays Mascagni's wife Lina. Giacomo Gentilomo directed for Lux. Alternative title: *Melodie Immortale*. Color. In Italian. 90 minutes. Opera Dubs/Lyric videos.

1994 La Scala, A Documentary of Performances

This film about the history of Teatro alla Scala includes two minutes of scenes of Mascagni conducting the 1935 premiere of his opera *Nerone*. It consists of newsreel footage shot in January 1935 and features Aureliano Pertile as Nerone and Margherita Carosio as Egloge. Black and white. With English narration. 63 minutes. VIEW video and on laser.

MASCOTTE, LA
1880 opéra comique by Audran

Edmond Audran, a popular French composer in the late 19th century, is best known for his 1880 opéra-comique *La Mascotte*. The mascot of the title is the heroine Bettina who becomes the good luck charm of the king. The opera is a tale about love, matchmaking and turkeys in 17th century Italy. Its arias remain popular in France to this day. See also EDMOND AUDRAN.

1935 Germaine Roger film

Germaine Roger stars as the King's mascot Bettina in this adaptation of the opera. Lucien Baroux portrays Laurent XVIII, Armand Dranem is Rocco, Thérèse Dorny is Dame Turlurette and René Lestelly is the Prince. Michel Lévine arranged the music, René Pujol wrote the screenplay and Léon Mathot directed. Black and white. In French. 100 minutes.

MASSARY, FRITZI
Austrian soprano (1882-1969)

Fritzi Massary, a popular Viennese singer of the early years of the century, is believed to be the first operetta star to sing in a film. At the end of 1896 German pioneer Max Skladanowsky made the first operetta film. It featured Massary at the beginning of her career with her comic partner Josef Gianpetro. They appeared in a scene from an operetta like *Der Vogelhander* or *Der Bettelstudent*. The film was supposedly shown with sound from a synchronized record. Massary and Pietro were also featured in duet in a 1903 Messter sound film. Massary, who created many notable operetta roles on stage, died in Beverly Hills in 1969. See MADAME POMPADOUR, DIE ROSE VON STAMBOUL, MAX SKLANDANOWSKY, A WOMAN WHO KNOWS WHAT SHE WANTS.

1903 Oskar Messter sound film

Fritzi Massary and her partner Josef Gianpetro were featured in a duet on an early sound film by German pioneer Oskar Messter. A print survives. 3 minutes.

MASSIMINI, SANDRO
Italian tenor/director

Italian tenor and operetta master Sandro Massimini organized a popular Italian TV series on the history of operetta called *Operette, Che Passione!* After telling the history of a classic operetta, he features musical numbers from it. Highlights from these shows have been released on Ricordi videos in Italy with three operettas on each tape. They feature some rare operettas unseen and unheard elsewhere. Massimini has also directed and starred in operettas on stage, notably *Die Csárdásfürstin, The Merry Widow* and *La Danza delle Libellule*, all of which are on video. See (all dated 1992) DIE BAJADERE, DIE CSÁRDÁSFÜRSTIN, LA DANZA DELLE LIBELLULE, LA DUCHESSA DEL BAL TABARIN, EVA, DIE FLEDERMAUS, GRÄFIN MARIZA, DER GRAF VON LUXEMBURG, DAS LAND DES LÄCHELNS, THE MERRY WIDOW, THE MIKADO, PAGANINI, GIUSEPPE PIETRI (L'ACQUA CHETA), LA REGINETTA DELLE ROSE), ROSE-MARIE, DIE ROSE VON STAMBOUL, SÌ, THE WHITE HORSE INN.

MASSENET, JULES
French composer (1841-1912)

Jules Massenet was one of the most successful French opera composers of the 19th century. His reputation is not as high as it once was but *Manon* and *Werther* remain in the opera house repertory and there appears to be a revival going on. Over a dozen of his operas are on now CD and *Cendrillon, Chérubin, Don Quichotte, Herodiade* and *Thaïs* have recently been staged. This is a big change from the 1950s when his operas were dismissed as dinner table music. Massenet's earlier popularity is reflected in the many silent films of his operas. He began creating operas in 1865 and continued until 1912 with *Don Quichotte* premiering when he was seventy. His relationships with singers Sibyl Sanderson and Lucy Arbell are the stuff of opera legend and Sanderson is said to be one of the models for the opera-singing mistress in *Citizen Kane*. See CENDRILLON, DON QUICHOTTE, MANON, WERTHER, THAÏS.

MASTERSON, VALERIE
English soprano (1937-)

Valerie Masterson, who made her debut at Salzburg in 1963, has a delightful range of roles from Gilbert & Sullivan to Mozart and Verdi. She was the principal soprano with the D'Oyly Carte company from 1966-1970 and can be seen on video in many of these roles. The combination of a fine voice and a winning stage personality can be observed in grander operas videos with a wide range of companies from the ENO and Glyndebourne to Geneva and Philadelphia. SEE THE ABDUCTION FROM THE SERAGLIO (1980), FAUST (1985), GIULIO CESARE (1984), H.M.S. PINAFORE (1974), THE MIKADO (1967, 1974), MIREILLE (1981), PAGLIACCI (1974), THE PIRATES OF PENZANCE (1974), THE TALES OF HOFFMANN (1974), LA TRAVIATA (1973), XERXES (1988).

MASTROCINQUE, CAMILLO
Italian film director (1901 -)

Camillo Mastrocinque, who began his directing career in 1937 with a film about La Scala, directed a number of films of operas and opera films during his long career including a biography of Donizetti. He also made films featuring opera singers Gino Bechi, Maria Caniglia and Mario Del Monaco. See THE BARBER OF SEVILLE (1955), GINO BECHI (1948), MARIA CANIGLIA (1947), MARIO DEL MONACO (1948), GAETANO DONIZETTI (1946), DON PASQUALE (1940 film), FEDORA (1942), IL MATRIMONIO SEGRETO (1943), PAGLIACCI (1941 film), TEATRO ALLA SCALA (1943).

MATRIMONIO SEGRETO, IL
1792 opera by Cimarosa

Domenico Cimarosa composed around sixty operas but is remembered for only one, the delightful *Il Matrimonio Segreto* (The Secret Marriage). It has always been considered as one of the most enjoyable comic operas and was performed numerous times during Cimarosa's lifetime. It has also enshrined itself in opera legend for having the longest encore. Emperor Leopold II enjoyed it so much at its premiere that he insisted the entire opera be repeated. And it was, all three hours. The story concerns a father's attempt to marry off a daughter to a lord but the lord prefers a second daughter who is already secretly married. See also DOMENICO CIMAROSA.

1943 Camillo Mastrocinque film
Italian director Camillo Mastrocinque, who made many narrative film adaptations of operas including *Pagliacci* and *Fedora*, shot this film in Spain in 1943. It was never released in Italy and

was probably not completed. Laura Solari, Miguel Ligero, Franco Coop and Nerio Barnardi are the stars. Appia-Safa production. Black and white. In Spanish.

1986 Schwetzingen Festival
Michael Hampe directed this charming Cologne Opera production at the Schwetzingen Festival. Barbara Daniels is Elisetta, Georgina Resick is Carolina, Carlos Feller is their father Geronimo, David Kübler is Carolina's secret husband Paolino, Claudio Nicolai is Count Robinson and Marta Szirmay is Aunt Fidalma. Hilary Griffiths conducts Sweden's Drottningholm Court Theater Orchestra with the authentic spirit its period instruments deserve. Jan Schlubach designed the sets and Claus Viller directed the video. Color. In Italian with subtitles. 140 minutes. Home Vision video and laserdisc.

MATZENAUER, MARGARET
Romanian contralto (1881-1963)

Contralto Margaret Matzenauer was born in Romania but her parents were German and she studied in Graz and Berlin before making her debut in Strasbourg in 1901. She came to the Metropolitan Opera in 1911 to sing Amneris in *Aida* under the direction of Arturo Toscanini and continued to sing there for nineteen years in a wide array of roles. She also performed soprano roles, was highly praised for her acting and was noted for having a photographic memory, able to memorize a new role in a day. She made many recordings but appeared in only one film where she was apparently meant to embody the public stereotype of an opera diva.

1936 Mr. Deeds Goes to Town
Matzenauer portrays opera diva Madame Pomponi in this Frank Capra film. Gary Cooper, a small-town tuba player, inherits $30 million dollars from an uncle and becomes chairman of a New York opera company. Matzenauer is the hostess of a fancy reception intended to introduce Deeds to society. She doesn't sing but she looks formidable. The film was based on Clarence Budington Kelland's short story *Opera Hat*. Columbia. Black and white. 118 minutes.

MAUREL, VICTOR
French baritone (1848-1923)

Victor Maurel, the French baritone who created the roles of Iago, Falstaff and Canio, was one of the first opera singers to be seen and heard in the movies. He was filmed in costume singing an aria from *Falstaff* in one film and from *Don Giovanni* in another. The pioneering sound films were shown at the Paris Exhibition in 1900. Maurel sang at La Scala, the Met and Covent Garden as well as the Paris Opéra, and was noted for his acting ability. See DON GIOVANNI (1900), FALSTAFF (1900).

MAY NIGHT
1889 opera by Rimsky-Korsakov

Nikolai Rimsky-Korsakov's comic opera *May Night* (*Maiskaya noch'*) is based on a story by Nikolai Gogol about the rivalry between a father and his son for a woman. The father, who is the village mayor, pretends to disapprove of his son Levko's love for Hanna because he wants her himself. The son leads a group of villagers who mock his father. With the help of some water sprites, he wins his father's consent. See also NIKOLAI RIMSKY-KORSAKOV.

1953 Alexander Rou film
Alexander Rou directed this Ukrainian film version of the opera story released in the U.S. in 1953 in a process called Magicolor. N. Losenko stars as Levko, T. Konukhova is Hannah, A. Khivlym is the father and G. Milliar is the village clerk. Critics thought Losenko sang well. The adaptation is by K. Idayev. Gorky Film Studios. Color. In Russian with English subtitles. 60 minutes.

MAYTIME
1917 operetta by Romberg

Sigmund Romberg's first successful operetta is based on Walter Kollo's love-through-three-generations German operetta *Wie einst im Mai*. Romberg wrote a new score while librettist Rida Johnson Young transmuted Bernauer and Schanzer's story into a New York tale. The story, however, is still a multi-generation romance with love finally conquering after sixty years. The Romberg song "Will You Remember" (aka "Sweetheart") became popular a second time through the MacDonald/Eddy film of the operetta. See also SIGMUND ROMBERG, WIE EINST IM MAI.

1923 Clara Bow/Harrison Ford film
Clara Bow was at the beginning of her film career when she appeared in this silent version of the Romberg operetta. She plays Alice, the girl the hero Harrison Ford marries on the rebound. Ethel Shannon is the other lead, Olga Printzlau wrote the script, Karl Struss photographed it and Louis Gasnier directed. It was shown in cinemas with the Romberg music. Black and white. About 80 minutes.

1927 John Charles Thomas/Vivienne Segal film
The first sound film based on an operetta was this Vitaphone short made in 1927. It's title tells it all: *John Charles Thomas, Outstanding American Baritone, and Vivienne Segal, Broadway Musical Comedy Star, Singing: Will You Remember, The Sweetheart Song from Maytime.* Black and white. 8 minutes.

1937 Jeanette MacDonald/Nelson Eddy film
This is the best Jeanette MacDonald/Nelson Eddy film though not much of the original music or plot is left except the hit song "Will You Remember." MacDonald plays an opera singer in Paris who falls in love with Eddy though she has promised to marry jealous voice teacher John Barrymore. MacDonald and Eddy finally end up as singing partners in an imaginary but enjoyable French opera with a Russian setting called *Czaritza* (composed by Herbert Stothart and based on Tchaikovsky's *Fifth Symphony*). MacDonald also sings the "Page Aria" from *Les Huguenots* and other arias in an opera montage while Eddy sings a delightful song about prima donnas titled "Viva l'opera"(lyrics by Bob Wright and Chet Forrest, music by Stothart). Noel Langley wrote the script and Robert Z. Leonard directed. Black and white. 132 minutes. MGM-UA video and laser.

MEDIUM, THE
1946 opera by Menotti

Gian Carlo Menotti's chamber opera *The Medium* is one of his most popular works with five screen adaptations including a film made by the composer. It premiered at Columbia University in New York in 1946 with Claramae Turner in the title role as the spiritualist Madame Flora/Baba. Marie Powers took over the role when the opera went to Broadway where it ran for 212

performances. The story is a Grand Guignol thriller about a fake medium who feels a ghostly hand on her throat in the middle of a séance. She blames her mute assistant Toby and banishes him despite protests from her daughter Monica. When he returns secretly, she thinks he is a ghost and shoots him. See also GIAN CARLO MENOTTI.

1948 Mary Davenport telecast
Mary Davenport, who alternated with Marie Powers on Broadway in *The Medium*, stars as Madame Flora in this TV production by Roger Englander. Leo Coleman is Toby with Lois Hunt as Monica, Edith Evans, Theodora Brandon and Emil Markow. The two-piano accompaniment is by Bertha Melnic and Alison Nelson. Paul Nickell directed the live telecast on Oct. 3, 1948, from NBC's Philadelphia station WTZ. Black and white. 60 minutes.

1948 Marie Powers telecast
Marie Powers, who starred in the role on Broadway, portrays Madame Flora in this TV production of the opera by Tony Miner. Lois Hunt plays Monica and Leo Coleman is again Toby with support from Beverly Dame, Catherine Mastice and Joe Bell. Alfredo Antonini conducted the orchestra. Paul Nickell directed the live telecast from New York on Nov. 15, 1948, for the CBS Studio One series. Black and white. 60 minutes. Video at MTR.

1951 Gian Carlo Menotti film
Menotti directed this adaptation of his opera, the only film ever made of an opera by its composer and one of the great opera films. He added twenty minutes of music and opened it up with street scenes. Marie Powers is superb as Madame Flora known as Baba, fourteen-year-old Anna Maria Alberghetti is outstanding as Monica and Leo Coleman is excellent as the mute Toby. Belva Kibler is Mrs. Nolan, Beverly Dame is Mrs. Gobineau and Donald Morgan is Mr. Gobineau. The film was shot in Rome with George Wakhevitch as art director and Enzo Serafin as the fine cinematographer. Thomas Schippers conducted the RAI Symphony Orchestra of Rome. Black and white. In English. 84 minutes. VAI video.

1959 Claramae Turner video
Claramae Turner, who created the role of Madame Flora, stars in this Omnibus production staged by

Menotti for NBC TV. Lee Ventura sings the role of Monica, José Perez is the mute Toby, Belva Kibler is Mrs. Nolan, Beverly Dame is Mrs. Gobineau and Donald Morgan is Mr. Gobineau. Henry May designed the sets while Werner Torkanowsky conducted the Symphony of the Air Orchestra. William A. Graham directed the telecast. Black and white. In English. 60 minutes. Video at MTR.

1975 Stratford Ensemble
Maureen Forrester stars as Madame Flora in this Stratford Ensemble production telecast from Canada in 1975. Raffi Armenian conducts the orchestra. Color. 80 minutes. Video at New York Public Library.

MEETING VENUS
1991 opera film by Szabó

One of the most intelligent films about opera, opera people and opera problems. Hungarian director István Szabó tells the funny/sad story of a multi-national European live satellite TV production of *Tannhäuser* in Paris. Glenn Close plays the Swedish diva soprano (Kiri Te Kanawa coached and provided her singing voice) while Niels Arestrup is the Hungarian conductor with major problems. The set looks like a post-modern nightmare, the dancers' union is on strike, the chorus is not cooperative, the singers are at each other's throats and the diva is an iceberg. When a love affair somehow develops between soprano and conductor, everyone finds out at once. When it seems the opera will never be staged, there is a surprise triumphant ending. The film is fascinating in its depiction of the inside world of opera production and the egos that need to be massaged. *Meeting Venus* was filmed in Budapest in the State Opera House and in Paris and produced by David Puttnam. Color. In English. 117 minutes. On video. See also ISTVÁN SZABÓ.

MEFISTOFELE
1868 opera by Boito

Master librettist Arrigo Boito's version of the Faust legend, based on Goethe's play, is a very different opera from Gounod's which focuses on Marguerite. Here Mefistofele is the focus and is seen betting with God that he can win Faust's soul. The ideas of Goethe are central to the opera with the battle between good and evil always present. The story of Faust and Margherita is still important

but there is also a remarkable scene at a Witches' Sabbath in which Helen of Troy appears. Mefistofele is one of the great roles for a bass. See also ARRIGO BOITO.

1989 San Francisco Opera
Samuel Ramey is devilishly compelling as Mefistofele in this famous San Francisco Opera production by Robert Carsen. He dominates from his first appearance when he climbs on stage from the orchestra pit. Gabriela Benackova is excellent as Margherita and Helen of Troy and Dennis O'Neill is grand as Faust. They have able support from Judith Christin as Marta, Emily Manhart as Pantalis, Daniel Harper as Wagner and Douglas Wunsch as Nereo. Carson and designer Michael Levine keep the stage a visual delight with bare breasts on both sexes in the bacchanalia, sensitive imagery and continuous surprises. Maurizio Arena conducts the San Francisco Opera Orchestra. Brian Large directed the video. Color. In Italian with English subtitles. 160 minutes. Home Vision video/Pioneer laserdisc.

1989 Genoa Opera
Paata Burchuladze is Mephistopheles in this extravagant Ken Russell production of the Boito opera for Genoa Opera. Those who enjoy Russell's style and playful ideas will love his updating of the story and costumes but non-admirers won't like it much. Ottavio Garaventa is a good Faust and Adriana Morelli a pleasant Margherita. Paul Dufficeny designed the costumes and sets while Richard Caceres did the choreography. Edoardo Muller conducted the Genoa Opera Orchestra and Chorus. Color. In Italian without subtitles. 137 minutes. In Italian. Pickwick (Germany) video.

Related film

1946 The Whale Who Wanted to Sing at the Met
Willie, the opera-singing whale with the voice of Nelson Eddy, imagines he is discovered and fantasizes a performance of *Mefistofele* at the Met. He breathes so much fire as the dominating Devil that firefighters standby to extinguish the flames. Hamilton Luske directed this Disney cartoon as part of the feature *Make Mine Music*. Color. 12 minutes.

MEHTA, ZUBIN
Indian-born conductor (1936-)

Zubin Mehta, who made his debut in 1964, has become one of the most popular contemporary conductors. He was the conductor chosen for some of the most popular opera television shows including both of the *Three Tenors* concerts and the live telecast of *Tosca* from Rome. See CARMEN (1991), CARNEGIE HALL (1991), FIDELIO (1979), GIAN CARLO MENOTTI (1966), MOZART REQUIEM (1994), LEONTYNE PRICE (1982), BEVERLY SILLS (1981), TANNHÄUSER (1994), THE THREE TENORS, TOSCA (1992).

1967 Zubin Mehta - A Man and His Music
This is a *Bell Telephone Hour* profile of the conductor at the age of thirty when he was with the Los Angeles Philharmonic Orchestra. The film shows him performing at the Hollywood Bowl and discussing his love of music and his philosophy. Black and white. 60 minutes. Video at MTR.

MEISTERSINGER VON NÜRNBERG, DIE
1868 opera by Wagner

Die Meistersinger Von Nürnberg (The Mastersingers of Nuremberg), Wagner's only naturalistic opera, was inspired by the life of Hans Sachs, a sixteenth century cobbler-poet and prominent member of the Mastersingers' Guild. It's set in 16th century Nuremberg where knight Walther wants to marry Eva. Her father Pogner has decided to give her hand to the winner of a singing contest so Walther is forced to learn the complex rules of the guild. He does so with the help of Sachs and, in the face of strong opposition from the town clerk Beckmesser, wins the contest and the woman. See also RICHARD WAGNER.

1969 Giorgio Tozzi film
Giorgio Tozzi stars as Sachs with Richard Cassilly as Walther and Arlene Saunders as Eva in this German film based on a Hamburg State Opera production. Toni Blankenheim is Beckmesser, Ernest Wiemann is David, Gerhard Unger is Pogner and Ursula Boese is Magdalene. Leopold Ludwig conducted the Hamburg State Opera Chorus and Philharmonic Orchestra. Rolf Liebermann produced and Leopold Lindtberg directed the film released theatrically in the U.S. Color. In German. 251 minutes.

1984 Bayreuth Festival
Bernd Weikl portrays Sachs, Siegfried Jerusalem is Walther and Mari Anne Haggander is Eva in this Bayreuth Festival production designed and staged by Wolfgang Wagner. Herman Prey is Beckmesser, Graham Clark is David, Manfred Schenk is Pogner, Jef Vermeersch is Kothner and Marga Schiml is Magdalene. Reinhard Heinrich designed the costumes and Horst Stein conducted the Bayreuth Festival Orchestra and Chorus. Brian Large directed the video. Color. In German with English subtitles. 269 minutes. Philips video and laser.

1988 Australian Opera
Donald McIntyre as Sachs and John Pringle as Beckmesser are the real stars of this excellent Australian Opera stage production by Michael Hampe. Paul Frey is seen as Walter, Helena Döse is Eva, Christopher Dig is David, Donald Shanks is Pogner, Robert Allman is Kothner and Rosemary Gunn is Magdalene. John Gunther designed the sets, Reinhard Heinrich designed the costumes and Sir Charles Mackerras conducted the Elizabethan Philharmonic Orchestra and Australian Opera Chorus. Peter Butler and Virginia Lumsden directed the video taped at a performance on Oct. 14, 1988. Color. In German with English subtitles. 277 minutes. Home Vision video.

1989 Bonn Opera
This highlights version of a Bonn Opera production of *Die Meistersinger* was arranged and directed for video by Werner Lütje. It includes what he considers the most memorable musical and dramatic passages of the opera. Color. In English. 53 minutes. Inter Nationes video.

Early/related films

1908 Pathé sound film
A German film of a scene and aria from the opera was made in 1908 by Pathé. It was screened with the music played on a synchronized phonograph.

1927 Ludwig Berger film
Ludwig Berger, a master of the musical film, directed this German silent film of the opera. Rudolf Rittner stars as Sachs with Maria Solveg as Eva, Gustav Frölich as Walther and Max Güstorff as Pogner with support from Julius Falkenstein, Viet Harlan and Elsa Wagner. Axel Graatkjaer and Karl Puth shot the film scripted by Berger, Rittner

and Robert Liebmann. Pheobus Film. Black and white. In German. About 82 minutes.

1987 Hope and Glory

Director John Boorman uses the "Dance of the Apprentices" from the opera in an ironic way in *Hope and Glory*. In Blitz-torn World War II London, a blimp is put up to protect the area from German planes. It floats into the sky accompanied by Wagner's music as the people of the neighborhood watch. Later it comes loose from its moorings, bounces around the houses to everyone's amusement and is shot out of the sky by the Home Guard. Color. 118 minutes. Nelson video.

MELBA, NELLIE
Australian soprano (1861-1931)

Nellie Melba inspired opera composers, film writers and chefs (peach melba and melba toast) but is still most famous for her voice. On record it has a silvery quality unmatched by any other singer. It was Melba who created the modern concept of the opera prima donna. She was born in Melbourne as Helen Porter Mitchell, studied with Mathilde Marchesi in Paris and made her debut in Belgium in 1887 as Gilda. The following year she sang in Paris and London and then reigned as the queen of Covent Garden until her retirement in 1926. She sang at the Met in New York from 1893 to 1910 and also at Oscar Hammerstein's Manhattan Opera House. In the later part of her career she concentrated on the role of Mimi in *La Bohème*. Melba made no films but there are many films about her.

1934 Evensong

Evensong is a British film based on a *roman á clef* novel by Beverly Nichols, Melba's private secretary and ghost writer of her autobiography. It stars Evelyn Laye as Irela, an Irish singer who elopes with musician Emlyn Williams, becomes an opera diva with the help of impresario Fritz Kortner, has an affair with archduke Carl Esmond and dies when a younger singer replaces her. Opera diva Conchita Supervia portrays Baba, the singer who challenges Irela's supremacy. The film includes excerpts from *La Bohème* and *La Traviata*. Supervia sings Musetta with Laye as Mimi. Victor Saville directed. Gaumont-British. Black and white. 83 minutes. Lyric video.

1953 Melba

Patrice Munsel portrays Nellie Melba in this opulent British film biography written by Harry Kurnitz. It tells the story of Melba's career beginning with a performance for Queen Victoria and flashing backwards and forwards. Covent Garden is central to the story. Martita Hunt portrays voice teacher Mathilde Marchesi, Robert Morley is opera impresario Oscar Hammerstein. and Sybil Thorndike is Queen Victoria. Munsel sings a wide array of arias from operas associated with Melba including *Rigoletto, Lucia di Lammermoor, Tosca, The Barber of Seville, The Daughter of the Regiment, Lohengrin, La Traviata, Romeo and Juliet* and naturally *La Bohème*. Australian Lewis Milestone directed. Color. 113 minutes.

1980 A Toast to Melba

Robyn Nevin portrays Melba with Roslyn Dunbar singing her arias in this Australian teleplay by Jack Hibbert telecast in August 1980. It traces the story of her career from tomboy in Australia to prima donna in Europe. Augustus Harris sings the role of Caruso and Michael Aitkens is Melba's husband Charles Armstrong. Other actors have multiple roles like Henri Szeps (who portrays Thomas Beecham as well as Buffalo Bill and the Mayor of Brisbane), Donald McDonald, Jane Harders, Anna Volska and Tim Eliot. Roger Kirk designed the sets and costumes and Alan Burke produced and directed. Color. 70 minutes.

1988 Melba

Actress Linda Cropper portrays Melba with soprano Yvonne Kenny singing the arias in this Australian TV film covering 45 years of the singer's life. She is shown leaving her unsympathetic husband, studying in Paris with Mathilde Marchesi, triumphing in Brussels, Paris and London, having a passionate affair with a pretender to the French throne and feuding with Tetrazzini and other singers. Joan Greenwood is a delight as voice teacher Mathilde Marchesi. William Motzing arranged the music, Roger McDonald wrote the novel on which the mini-series was based and Rodney Fisher directed. It was telecast on PBS in the U.S. in 1990. Color. In English. 480 minutes.

MELCHIOR, LAURITZ
Danish-born U.S. tenor (1890-1973)

Many consider Lauritz Melchior the greatest heldentenor of the century. He made his debut at the Royal Opera in Copenhagen in 1912 in *Pagliacci* and his Wagner career began in 1918. In 1924 he sang Parsifal at Bayreuth and in 1926 he began his Metropolitan Opera career with *Tannhäuser*. He sang there until 1950 when he had disagreements with Herman Bing and left the Met after 513 performances. He continued to perform until 1960 when he celebrated his 70th birthday singing Siegmund on the radio. Melchior starred in a number of films and showed he had an impressive personality as well as a glorious voice. There are no films of him in operas but he can be seen in performance in a *Voice of Firestone* video and in his movies.

1945 Thrill of a Romance
Melchior made his movie debut as Danish singer Nils Knunsen opposite Esther Williams in this mountain lodge musical. She portrays a swimmer who falls in love with returning serviceman Van Johnson. Melchior sings the aria "Vesti la giubba," the song "Please Don't Say No" and Schubert's "Serenade" and seems to enjoy himself. Richard Thorpe directed. Color. 105 minutes. MGM video.

1946 Two Sisters from Boston
Melchior portrays Metropolitan Opera tenor Olaf Ostrom in this turn-of-the-century New York musical. Kathryn Grayson pretend to be an opera singer and sneaks on stage to join him in an imaginary opera based on Mendelssohn. He later tries out an aria from *Die Meistersinger* for an early recording session and teams up again with Grayson at the end of the film for an imaginary opera called *Marie Antoinette* based on Liszt. The studio built a 500-foot-wide reproduction of the Old Met interior for the film directed by Henry Koster Black and white. 112 minutes. MGM video.

1947 This Time For Keeps
Melchior is opera star Richard Harald whose son Johnnie Johnston prefers modern music and swimming star Esther Williams. Melchior sings "M'appari" from *Martha*, "La donna è mobile" from *Rigoletto*, an aria from *Otello* and Cole Porter's song "You'd Be So Easy To Love." Jimmy Durante and Xaviar Cugat add to the musical mixture.

Richard Thorpe directed. Color. 105 minutes. MGM video.

1948 Luxury Liner
Melchior portrays opera tenor Olaf Eriksen in one of those delightful MGM shipboard musicals. Jane Powell is the stowaway daughter of liner captain George Brent. Melchior and Powell join in a duet from *Aida* and Melchior sings an aria from *Die Walküre*. Xaviar Cugat and his orchestra are also on board making music. Richard Whorf directed. Color. 98 minutes. MGM video.

1950-1951 Lauritz Melchior in Opera & Song
Melchior is shown in performance on *Voice of Firestone* television programs in 1950 and 1951. He sings "Wintersturme" from *Die Walküre*, "Prieslied" from *Die Meistersinger* and the Helmsman's Song from *The Flying Dutchman* plus songs by Richard Strauss, Tchaikovsky and Rodgers and Hammerstein. Howard Barlow conducts. Black and white. 45 minutes. VAI video.

1950-52 Lauritz Melchior in Opera & Song 2
The second of two videos featuring Melchior in performance on *Voice of Firestone* television programs in 1950, 1951 and 1952. He sings "In fernam Land" from *Lohengrin*, the Entrance of the Guests from *Tannhäuser*, "Vesti la giubba" from *Pagliacci*, the Prize Song from *Die Meistersinger* and "Serenade" from *The Student Prince*. Howard Barlow is the conductor. Black and white. 48 minutes. VAI video.

1953 The Stars Are Singing
Lauritz Melchior's last film is his best. He plays a former Metropolitan Opera star who befriends 15-year-old Anna Maria Alberghetti. She's an illegal immigrant and an aspiring opera singer. Melchior sings three times: once at the Met in a flashback performing "Vesta la giubba" in *Pagliacci* costume, once as Alberghetti makes him remember his singing career and once in duet with Alberghetti. Rosemary Clooney is the main star. Norman Taurog directed. Color. 99 minutes. Paramount video.

1990 Melchior Centennial Tribute
Melchior would have been 100 in 1990. Danish television devised this tribute program with excerpts and interviews. Melchior associates appearing include bass Aage Haugland, tenor Klaus König, Erich Leinsdorf, Eva Johannson and

Esther Williams. Color. In Danish, English and German. 101 minutes. Opera Dubs video.

MÉLIÈS, GEORGES
French film opera pioneer (1861-1938)

Georges Méliès was the first notable fiction filmmaker, a former magician who applied the tricks of his trade to the cinema and made films which still astonish. He was also the first important opera film producer and his early adaptations of the Faust operas of Gounod and Berlioz are a delight. Méliès played Mephistopheles in these 1903/1904 productions and the image of him in the role has become one of the icons of cinema. Méliès began making films in 1896 and two of his early films were views of the Place de L'Opéra. In 1898 he made two films based on the Faust story, a magic transformation film titled *Faust et Marguerite* and a second called *Damnation de Faust,* plus a film based on another opera-inspiring legend, *Guillaume Tell.* In 1899 the Paris public became interested in the Cinderella story because of the publicity around the premiere of Massenet's *Cendrillon.* Méliès made his own *Cendrillon,* an epic twenty-scene movie of the story. In 1903 he made a famous film about a music lover called *Le Mélomane* and the first of his two Faust opera adaptations. *Faust aux Enfers ou La Damnation de Faust* was composed of fifteen scenes and was based on the Berlioz opera *La Damnation de Faust.* In 1904 he made another epic Faust film in twenty scenes based on the Gounod opera *Faust* which he titled *Damnation du Docteur Faust.* The same year he made his final important opera film, a "reproduction" of Rossini's opera *The Barber of Seville* titled *Le Barbier de Séville.* Most of Méliès' films have survived and can still be viewed with pleasure today. See also THE BARBER OF SEVILLE (1904), CENDRILLON (1899), LA DAMNATION DE FAUST (1904), FAUST (1903).

MELTON, JAMES
American tenor (1904-1961)

James Melton is as well known today for his films as for his opera career, though he was a member of the Metropolitan Opera from 1942 to 1947. The Georgia tenor studied opera at Vanderbilt and began his singing career on radio and in concert in 1927. His film career started in 1933 with a cowboy song short and took off in 1935 with *Stars Over Broadway* which featured him singing opera at the Met. He began preparing for an opera career at this time and made his debut as Pinkerton in *Madama Butterfly* in Cincinnati in 1938. He then sang with the San Carlo and Chicago Opera companies. His career at the Met started in 1942 and he sang a variety of roles there over the next six years. Like many others he left with the arrival of Rudolph Bing. Melton's last film was the 1945 *Ziegfeld Follies* in which he appeared in a scene from *La Traviata.* In his later years he toured with *The Student Prince.*

1933 The Last Dogie
Melton's first film was a short in which he sang cowboy songs and performed rope tricks for his bunk mates. Black and white. 10 minutes.

1935 Stars Over Broadway
Melton's first film features him as hotel porter with such a good voice that manager Pat O'Brien decides to make him into an opera star. After long training he auditions at the Met with "Celeste Aida" and wins acclaim. O'Brien, however, is impatient to earn money and diverts him into crooning in clubs and radio. In the end Melton returns to opera and makes his debut in *Aida* at the Met. He also sings "M'appari" from *Martha* and some popular songs. His singing co-star is Jane Froman in her first film. William Keighley directed. Warner Bros. Black and white. 89 minutes.

1936 Sing Me a Love Song
Melton portrays the heir to a department store and sings Dubin and Warren songs in this musical. He works in the store incognito to learn about its problems and is soon involved with Patricia Ellis who works in the music department. His songs include "The Little House That Love Built" and "Shortnin' Bread." Warner Bros. Ray Enright directed. Black and white. 79 minutes.

1937 Melody for Two
Al Dubin and Harry Warren gave Melton some memorable songs to sing in this musical including "September in the Rain." He plays a bandleader who has problems with girlfriend Patricia Ellis. She ends up competing with him in the bandleading business but it all works out after they both start to play swing. Louis King directed. Warner Bros. Black and white. 60 minutes.

1946 Ziegfeld Follies

Melton actually filmed his sequence of this lavish Vincente Minnelli musical in 1944. He appears in a colorful scene from *La Traviata* with soprano Marion Bell and a group of elaborately costumed dancers. Melton and Bell duet on "Libiamo." The film is a Heavenly dream by Florenz Ziegfeld (William Powell) about putting on a new Follies. Color. 110 minutes. MGM-UA video.

MENOTTI, GIAN CARLO
Italian-American composer (1911-)

Gian Carlo Menotti was the best known American opera composer of the postwar period, partially because his operas were presented outside traditional venues. They were heard on radio, staged on Broadway, composed for television, sung in cathedrals and written for children. He was one of the first composers to write an opera for radio, the 1939 *The Old Man and the Thief*, and the first to write an opera for television, the 1951 *Amahl and the Night Visitors*. His success paved the way for the development of radio and TV opera. He was also the first (and still the only) composer to film his own opera, the 1951 *The Medium*. His theatrical skills led to a contract from MGM to write film scripts, one of which became the opera *The Consul*. Menotti was brought up in Milan but studied at the Curtis Institute in Philadelphia and most of his professional career was in the U.S. He had a close personal relationship with composer Samuel Barber (he wrote the librettos for two of Barber's operas) and with conductor Thomas Schippers (who became music director of his Festival of Two Worlds in Spoleto). Ten of Menotti's operas have been filmed or telecast. Though his operas are not currently in fashion, *Amahl and the Night Visitors*, *The Medium* and *The Telephone* are on commercial videos. See also AMAHL AND THE NIGHT VISITORS, THE CONSUL, GOYA, LABYRINTH, MARIA GOLOVIN, MARTIN'S LIE, THE MEDIUM, THE OLD MAID AND THE THIEF, THE SAINT OF BLEEKER STREET, SPOLETO, THE TELEPHONE.

1976 Landscapes & Remembrances

Menotti's cantata for soloists, chorus and orchestra is a nine-part autobiographical set of musical impressions from his arrival in New York as a teenager to his discovery of South Carolina. It was filmed when it premiered at the Performing Arts Center in Milwaukee. The performers are soloists Judith Blegen, Ani Yervanian, Vahan Khanzadian and Gary Kendall with the Milwaukee Symphony Orchestra and Bel Canto Chorus conducted by James A. Keeley. It was shot on May 14, 1976, and telecast on Nov. 14. Color. 60 minutes. Video at Library of Congress.

1979 Gian Carlo Menotti

The composer is shown at a rehearsal of his children's opera *Help, Help the Globolinks* and discusses his ideas about writing operas for children. The program is hosted by University of Michigan music professor John McCollum. Color. 30 minutes. On video.

1986 Gian Carlo Menotti: Musical Magician

Tom Bywaters' documentary film was made to eulogize the composer on his 75th birthday. It includes scenes shot at the Festivals of Two Worlds in Spoleto and Charleston and at his estate in Scotland. There are extracts from nine operas and interviews with colleagues like Luciano Pavarotti, John Butler, Colleen Dewhurst and Alwain Nikolais. The film was telecast in the Great Performances series on Nov. 21 1986. Color. 90 minutes.

MERCADANTE, SAVERIO
Italian composer (1795-1870)

Saverio Mercadante was the most important composer in Italy in the period immediately preceding Verdi and composed over fifty well-received operas. His fame was eclipsed by Verdi but a number of his works were revived for the centenary of his death in 1970. His most famous operas are *Il Giuramento* from 1837 and *Il Bravo* from 1839, both set in Venice, and the 1846 *Orazi e Curiazi*. *Il Bravo* is on CD and video.

1990 Il Bravo

The original source of this 1839 opera is James Fenimore Cooper's novel *The Bravo* as adapted by librettists Gaetano Rossi and Marco Marcello. The setting is 16th century Venice and the "bravo" of the title is an assassin hired by a woman to kidnap her own daughter. After this is done, the bravo reveals that he is the girl's father. It all gets very complicated. The opera was staged in the Palazzo Ducale in Martina Franca in 1990 with Dino di Dominico as the Bravo, Adelisa Tabiado as his wife Teodora and Stefano Antonucci as Foscari. The only video is a live non-professional recording. Color. In Italian. 165 minutes. Opera Dubs video.

MERRILL, ROBERT
American baritone (1917-)

Robert Merrill was the leading baritone at the Metropolitan Opera from 1945 to 1975. The Brooklyn-born singer made his debut as Germont and then sang in virtually all the available Italian and French baritone roles. He also sang Germont at La Fenice in 1961 and Covent Garden in 1967. He was much admired for his voice but acting was never his strong point. Merrill's film career was short and unfortunate. Rudolph Bing fired him for going off to make a Hollywood film instead of being available for a Met tour. It was Merrill's only feature and not a success. However, he made many recordings and appeared on television shows like *The Voice of Firestone*. He remains one of the best known American singers even today. See CARMEN (1950, 1959), DON CARLO (1950), METROPOLITAN OPERA (1953), ANNA MOFFO (1963), OTELLO (1963), RIGOLETTO (1963), LA TRAVIATA (1956).

1944 Toscanini: Hymn of the Nations
Merrill was noted for his emotional singing of the National Anthem and was captured singing it most splendidly at the end of this patriotic Oscar-nominated wartime documentary. He also does a fine job of singing Verdi's "Hymn of the Nations" with the Westminster Choir. The film was shot in December 1943 at the NBC studio with Arturo Toscanini leading the NBC Symphony Orchestra. The film made for the Office of War Information by avant-garde filmmaker Alexander Hammid. Black and white. 28 minutes. RCA Victor video and laser/ Video Yesteryear video.

1952 Aaron Slick from Punkin Crick
Robert Merrill portrays a city slicker who attempts to fleece widow Dinah Shore down on the farm in this old fashioned musical. *Variety* noted that Merrill had a good voice and screen presence but was not given a good role. His best song was the old church tune "Still Water" sung in duet. The new songs are by Ray Evans and Jay Livingstone. Claude Binyon directed. English title: *Marshmallow Moon*. Paramount. Color. 95 minutes.

1955-1959 Robert Merrill in Opera & Song
Merrill as he appeared on the *Voice of Firestone* TV series in six telecasts made from 1955 to 1959. He sings arias from *Carmen* ("Toreador Song"), *The Barber of Seville* ("Largo al factotum"), *Pagliacci* ("Prologue"), *Hamlet* (Drinking Song), *The Land of Smiles* ("Yours is My Heart Alone"), *The Red Mill* ("Every Day is Ladies" Day") and *Il Trovatore* ("Il Balen") plus songs. Howard Barlow conducted. Black and white. 52 minutes. VAI video.

1955-63 Robert Merrill in Opera & Song 2
The second of two videos featuring Merrill performing in *Voice of Firestone* telecasts from 1955 to 1963. He is seen in costume singing arias from *Faust*, *Hérodiade* and *La Traviata* plus songs by Romberg, Kern, Youmans and Rodgers and Hammerstein. Black and white. 55 minutes. VAI video.

MERRITT, CHRIS
American tenor (1952 -)

Oklahoma native Chris Merritt made his debut in Salzburg in 1978 after an apprenticeship in Santa Fe. He became a specialist in Rossini operas in Europe and his expressive voice led to invitations to sing in many of the composer's lesser-known operas in festivals and opera houses. A number of these Rossinii productions were televised and are available on video. See LA BOHÈME (1990 FILM), LA DONNA DEL LAGO (1992), ERMIONE (1987), OTELLO BY ROSSINI (1988), I PURITANI (1986), GIOACHINO ROSSINI (1992), I VESPRI SICILIANI (1990), WILLIAM TELL (1991).

MERRY WIDOW, THE
1905 operetta by Lehár

A *Merry Widow* craze swept the world after the premiere of *Der Lustige Witwe* in Vienna in 1905; it was widely staged and filmed and soon influenced both fashion and dance. Composer Franz Lehár conducted the first English-language performance in London in 1907 and it came to New York the same year. Within three months an American *Merry Widow* film was made and the operetta has been popular with filmmakers ever since. The German libretto by Victor Léon and Leo Stein is based on a French play by Henri Meilhac. Wealthy widow Hanna, the richest person in her small country, meets womanizing Prince Danilo in Paris and an old romance is rekindled. Although Ambassador Zeta asks Danilo to marry her to keep her fortune in the country, Danilo doesn't want to be seen as a fortune-hunter. The Ambassador's wife Valencienne is involved in a romantic subplot. The Merry Widow Waltz has become an audience favorite. For some reason the character

Hanna has become Sonia in most American films. See also FRANZ LEHÁR.

1934 Ernest Lubitsch film
Jeanette MacDonald stars as Sonia with Maurice Chevalier as Danilo in this stylish MGM film, one of the finest of all film operettas and most cleverly directed by Ernest Lubitsch. Edward Everett Horton bumbles his way through the role of the ambassador and Una Merkel is Queen Dolores. Sam Raphaelson and Ernest Vaja wrote the screenplay, Herbert Stothart arranged and conducted the music and masterful Lorenz Hart wrote the English lyrics. Black and white. In English. 99 minutes. MGM-UA video and laser.

1934 La Veuve Joyeuse
A French version of the operetta was made by MGM at the same time keeping MacDonald (renamed Missia) and Chevalier as the stars but with a different supporting cast. Fifi d'Orsay is Marcelle, Marcel Vallee is Ambassador Popoff and Danièle Parola is Queen Dolores. Ernest Lubitsch again directed. Black and white. In French. 105 minutes.

1952 Lana Turner film
Lana Turner stars as the Widow in this second MGM adaptation but it's Fernando Lamas as Danilo who sings most of the songs, including even "Vilja." This is a plush rewrite of the story with Turner portraying an American whose rich husband has just died. She is persuaded to visit his bankrupt native land where Danilo is ordered to marry her. It goes badly and she flees to Paris where they finally sort it out with the help of the famous waltz. The supporting cast is terrific with Una Merkel back again. Curtis Bernhardt directed. Color. In English. 105 minutes. MGM-UA video.

1954 Patrice Munsel video
Patrice Munsel sings the role of the Widow Sonia opposite Theodor Uppman as Prince Danilo in this CBS television production for Omnibus. Jerome Kilty is Baron Popoff, Martyn Green is Nisch and James Hawthorne is Georges. Cyril Ritchard staged the operetta and Eugene Ormandy conducted the Philadelphia Orchestra. It was telecast on Dec. 26, 1954. Black and white. In English. 90 minutes. On video.

1955 Anne Jeffreys telecast
Anne Jeffreys stars as Widow Sonia with Brian Sullivan as Danilo in this NBC Color Special produced and directed by Max Liebman. The other stars include Edward Everett Horton as Baron Zelta, Helena Bliss as Valencienne, Jack Russell as Lt. Nicholas and John Conte as Georges. Charles Sandford conducted. It was telecast on April 9, 1955. Black and white. 90 minutes. In English.

1962 Karin Hübner film
Karin Hübner, who has sung Polly Peachum and Eliza Doolittle on stage, stars as the Widow Hanna in this modernized film of the operetta. Peter Alexander is Count Danilo (and allowed to sing "Vilja"), Genevieve Cluny is Valencienne, Dario Moreno is Camille and Maurice Teynac is the Baron. The film was shot in Austria in French and German versions by Werner Jacobs. Color. In German. 91 minutes. Editions Montparnasse (France) video.

1963 Placido Domingo film
Placido Domingo stars in this Spanish-language film of the operetta made for Mexican television in 1963 as part of a series sponsored by Max Factor. His co-stars are his wife Marta Ornelas, Ernestina Garfias and Franco Inglesias. Black and white. In Spanish. 85 minutes.

1977 Beverly Sills video
Diva Beverly Sills stars as Widow Anna Glawari in this San Diego Opera production designed and produced by Tito Capobianca. Alan Titus is her Danilo, Andrew Foldi is Baron Zeta, Glenys Fowles is Valencienne and Henry Price is Camille. Kirk Browning directed the video telecast on PBS Nov. 27, 1977. Color. 120 minutes.

1988 Joan Sutherland video
Joan Sutherland stars as Widow Hanna in this Australian Opera English-language production by Lotfi Mansouri. Ronald Stevens portrays Danilo, Ann-Marie MacDonald is Valencienne and Anson Austin is Camille. Christopher Hassell wrote the English translation, Kristian Fredrickson designed the sets and costumes and Richard Bonynge conducted the Elizabethan Philharmonic Orchestra and Australian Opera Chorus and Ballet. Virginia Lumsden directed the video from a Feb. 23, 1988, performance. Color. In English. 151 minutes. Home Vision video

1992 Sandro Massimini video

Italian singer/director Sandro Massimini produced this Italian stage version of the operetta titled *La Vedova Allegra*. He stars as Danilo with Sonia Dorigo as Anna Glavari, Elio Crovetto as Mirko, Tamara Trojani as Valencienne and Vincenzo De Angelis as Camillo. Don Lurio arranged the choreography, Antonio Mastromattei designed the sets and Roberto Negri conducted the orchestra. Color. In Italian. 115 minutes. Ricordi (Italy) video.

1993 Mörbisch Festival

Elisabeth Kales sings the role of the widow in this production by Michael Murger for the Mörbischer Seefestspiele. She gets strong support from Peter Edelmann, Martina Dorak and Gideon Singer. Konstantin Schenk conducts the Bratislav Philharmonic Orchestra. Kurt Pongratz directed the HDTV video. Color. In German. 132 minutes. Taurus (German) video.

1996 New York City Opera

Jane Thorngren sings the role of Hanna with Michael Hayes as Danilo in this full-scale New York City Opera production by Robert Johanson telecast on March 27, 1996. George S. Irving is Baron Mirko, Patricia Johnson is Valencienne, Carlo Scibelli is Camille and Robert Creighton is Njegus. Michael Anania designed the sets, Gregg Barnes designed the costumes and Sharon Halley did the choreography. The English translation is by Johanson with lyrics by Albert Evans. Alexander Sander conducted the orchestra. The telecast included a three-part documentary titled "What's Behind *The Merry Widow*?" Color. In English. 180 minutes.

Early/related films

1907 Nordisk film

The first screen version of *The Merry Widow* was made in Sweden in 1907 by the Nordisk Company and was quite lengthy for its time. It features highlights from the operetta and was screened in theaters with live Lehár music. About 14 minutes.

1908 Kalem film

An enterprising film of scenes of the operetta was premiered by the Kalem Studio on Jan. 25, 1908, only three months after the New York stage premiere on Oct. 21, 1907. It was meant to be screened with live music and was intended to

show the rest of the U.S. what was happening on stage in New York. Three vocal numbers were pictured including Sonya singing "Vilja" and the famous waltz. The cast was not the stage cast but included C. Manthey, C. Davis, N. Morena and M. Katzer. About 15 minutes.

1908 The Merry Widow Waltz Craze

This is an American comedy film from the Edison studio about a man called Lightfoot who cannot stop dancing whenever he hears the Merry Widow Waltz. Edwin S. Porter directed the film released on April 29, 1908. About 10 minutes.

1908 The "Merry Widow" Hats

This is a Lubin comedy about the Merry Widow Hat craze in which two young women cause trouble everywhere they go with their strange headgear. They even get thrown out of a moving picture palace. Released May 14, 1908. About 9 minutes.

1908 The Merry Widow Hat

A Vitagraph company comedy film about the fashionable Merry Widow hat inspired by the operetta. A rival to the Lubin film released Oct. 24, 1908. About 9 minutes.

1908 La Valse de la Veuve Joyeuse

This Pathé Frères adaptation of the operetta's hit song was made in France and released in the U.S. on Nov. 28, 1908 as *Merry Widow Waltz*. It was screened with live music. About 6 minutes.

1908 The Merry Widow at a Supper Party

This Biograph Company comedy film, loosely based on the operetta, was shown with live music. Arthur Marvin directed. About 7 minutes.

1909 Brazilian Merry Widow

The Brazilian film industry produced humorous adaptations of operettas in the silent era. Singers stood behind the screen and sang the airs. One of the most successful was a "very merry" version of *The Merry Widow*. About 10 minutes.

1910 The Merry Widow Takes Another Partner

A humorous Vitagraph film based loosely on the operetta and shown with live music. About 14 minutes.

1912 Alma Rubens film
Alma Rubens stars as the Widow in this American silent film version of the operetta made for the Reliance-Majestic company. Wallace Reid portrays Prince Danilo. About 15 minutes.

1913 Alice Guy Blaché film
Pioneer woman director Alice Guy Blaché directed an early screen version of *The Merry Widow* for her Solax company. It was released on June 21, 1913. Marian Swayne stars as the widow. About 15 minutes.

1918 Michael Curtiz film
A Hungarian version of the operetta titled *A Víg Özvegy* was made by Michael Curtiz in his early years in Budapest. It stars Ica Lenkeffy, Frigyes Tarnay and Emil Fenivessy. About 70 minutes.

1925 Erich von Stroheim film
Mae Murray and John Gilbert star in this famous silent version of the operetta directed by Erich von Stroheim. Prince Danilo (Gilbert) is ordered to woo rich American widow Sally (Murray) whom he had earlier jilted. Their romance is rekindled when the movie theater pianist plays the *Merry Widow* Waltz on cue. Black and white. About 113 minutes. On video.

1943 Shadow of a Doubt
Alfred Hitchcock, with the help of composer Dmitri Tiomkin, uses the *Merry Widow* Waltz in a sinister way in this suspense thriller. It's the theme music of Teresa Wright's murderous uncle (Joseph Cotten) who is known as the Merry Widow Murderer. The music gradually become more disturbing as it is used in three crucial transitions. Black and white. 108 minutes.

1983 The Merry Widow ballet
A ballet adaptation of the operetta choreographed by Ruth Page and produced for television by Dick Carter. It tells the operetta story but is danced rather than sung to Lehár's music. Patricia McBride dances the role of the Widow with Peter Martin as Danilo and Rebecca Wright as Baroness de Popoff. The music is performed by the Chicago Symphony Orchestra. This adaptation premiered at Chicago's Lyric Opera in November 1955 and was telecast by Chicago's WTTW-TV on Sept. 21, 1983. Color. 60 minutes. On video.

1988 The Merry Widow ballet
This second ballet adaptation of *The Merry Widow* was written and choreographed by Ronald Hyde and Robert Helpmann. The dancers are Karen Kain as the Widow, John Meehan, Yoko Ichino, Raymond Smith, Charles Kirby and Jacques Gorrissen. Desmond Heeley designed the sets and costumes and Norman Campbell directed this Canadian video. CBC. Color. 120 minutes. On video.

MERRY WIVES OF WINDSOR, THE
1849 opera by Nicolai

Die Lustigen Weiber von Windsor, Otto Nicolai's charming Shakespearean opera with a libretto by Salomon Mosenthal, has almost the same story as Verdi's *Falstaff*. Falstaff sends love letters to two married women and they get revenge in a variety of ways. Some of the characters have been given German names, i.e., Mrs Ford is Frau Fluth and Mrs. Page is Frau Reich, but there is little difference in plot. The opera is mainly popular in Germanic countries but an American singer made an English-language film of it and the Chicago Opera Theater has telecast an English version. The German narrative film *Falstaff in Vienna* pretends to explain how Nicolai came to write it. See also OTTO NICOLAI.

1950 Georg Wildhagen film
Georg Wildhagen wrote and directed this realistic but entertaining film of the opera. Hans Krämer sings the role of Falstaff acted by Paul Esser, Martha Modl sings Frau Reich acted by Camilla Spira, Rita Streich sings Frau Fluth acted by Sonja Ziemann, Sonja Schoener sings Anna Reich acted by Ina Halley and Helmut Kregs sings Herr Fluth acted by Claus Holm. The film was released in the U.S. DEFA. Black and white. In German. 96 minutes.

1965 Norman Foster film
American bass Norman Foster stars as Falstaff in this lively English-language film of the opera which he himself adapted for the screen with a "reluctant" nod to Shakespeare. Canadian soprano Colette Boky sings Mistress Ford and has a steamy bathtub scene that cause comment when the film was released, Mildred Miller is a most enjoyable Mistress Page, Lucia Popp is excellent as Anne Page, Igor Gorin is good as the jealous Mr. Ford

and Ernst Schutz is Fenton. Milan Horvath conducts the Zagreb Symphony Orchestra. Foster produced and George Tressler directed this Yugoslav/Austrian co-production. Color. In English. 97 minutes. BHE video.

1968 Franco Enriquez film
Franco Enriquez directed a West German television film of the Nicolai opera in Munich. The music was performed by the Bavarian Television Orchestra and Chorus. Color. In German. 143 minutes.

1978 Chicago Opera Theater
A Chicago Opera Theater workshop production of the opera in English was videotaped and shown at the 1978 TV opera Colloquium sponsored by the National Opera Institute.

Early/related films

1915 German sound film
A German sound film was presented in 1915 showing a scene from the opera. The accompanying aria was played on a synchronized phonograph. In German. Black and white. About 4 minutes.

1935 Leo Slezak film
Der Lustigen Weiber is a German musical version of the story set in England about 1600 but it does not seem to be the opera as the music is credited to Ernest Fischer and Franz Grothe. Leo Slezak stars as Falstaff with Magda Schneider, Ida Wüst and Maria Krahn as the wives. Carl Hoffmann directed for Cine Allianz. Black and white. In German. 84 minutes.

1945 The Seventh Veil
This British melodrama about the romantic life of a concert pianist features a number of excerpts of classical music including the Overture from The Merry Wives of Windsor. Ann Todd and James Mason star under the direction of Compton Bennett. Black and white. In English.

1962 Musikalisches Rendezvous
This is an anthology film made up of excerpts from DEFA opera movies made in East Berlin and includes a 20-minute scene from the 1950 film of The Merry Wives of Windsor. There are also extracts from Zar and Zimmermann, The Marriage of Figaro

and The Beggar Student. Color. In German. 83 minutes.

MESSAGER, ANDRÉ
French composer (1853-1929)

André Messager was one of the last great French operetta composers and Fortunio and Véronique are still popular in France. He had also great success in the 1890s with La Basoche and Les P'tites Michu. His English 'romantic opera' Monsieur Beaucaire was produced in London and New York in 1919 and Maggie Teyte made one of its arias famous. Messager also wrote French operas including the 1893 Madame Chrysanthème, a predecessor of Madama Butterfly. Véronique has been filmed and was recently staged at the Salle Favart in Paris. There are also films of Messager's lesser-known operettas Passionnément, Deburau and Coups de Roulis. See also VÉRONIQUE.

1931 Coups de Roulis
Messager's 1928 operetta Coups de Roulis was filmed in France in 1931 with Max Dearly as the star. It's a musical love story set on a warship with echoes of H.M.S. Pinafore. Albert Willemetz' libretto centers around a government minister's daughter (loved by a ship captain and a humble sailor) and a government minister who gets involved with an actress. The cast includes Edith Manet, Lucienne Herval, Pierre Magnier and Roger Bourdin. Jean de la Cour directed the film. Black and white. In French. 115 minutes.

1932 Passionnément
Messager's 1926 operetta Passionnément centers around an American millionaire visiting Paris whose personality alters dramatically when he drinks. Not surprisingly his wife falls in love with a Frenchman. In this 1932 French film, René Koval plays the millionaire, Ketty Stevenson is the wife and Fernand Gravet is the French lover. Maurice Hennequin and Albert Willemetz wrote the libretto and Louis Mercant and René Guissart directed the film. Black and white. In French. 80 minutes.

1950 Deburau
Deburau is a 1926 operetta composed for Sacha Guitry who wrote the libretto. Guitry turned it into a film in 1950. It tells the story of a Paris mime in the 1840s who falls in love with Marie Duplessis. As she is the model for Violetta of La Traviata, she

naturally prefers Armand Duval. Guitry, who also directed, plays Deburau with Lana Marconi as Marie Duplessis. Black and white. In French. 93 minutes.

MESSIAH
1742 oratorio by Handel

Messiah is George Frideric Handel's best liked musical work and the most popular oratorio by any composer. It was composed in 1741 to an English libretto by Charles Jennens with the words taken from the *Bible*. It premiered in Dublin on April 13, 1742, at the Music Hall in Fishamble Street and has been in the repertory ever since, especially at Christmas. Its Hallelujah Chorus has become the best known single choral work. *Messiah* is featured on many videos and its music is often used in films. See also GEORGE F. HANDEL.

1982 Cardiff Polyphonic Choir
Roger Norrington conducts the London Baroque Players and the Cardiff Polyphonic Choir in this outstanding video of the oratorio. The soloists are Norma Burrowes, Willard White, Helen Watts and Robert Tear. Color. 140 minutes. Kultur video.

1983 Westminster Abbey, London
Christopher Hogwood conducts the Academy of Ancient Music and Choir of Westminster Cathedral at Westminster Abbey. The soloists are Judith Nelson, Emma Kirkby, Carolyn Watkinson, Paul Elliott and David Thomas. Roy Tipping directed the video. Color. 145 minutes. HBO video.

1984 St. Michaelis Church, Hamburg
Peter Schrieier conducts the North German Radio Symphony Orchestra and Choir in this performance taped at St. Michaelis Church in Hamburg, Germany. Gunther Bock directed the video. Color. 154 minutes. Inter Nationes video.

1987 Atlanta Symphony
Robert Shaw leads the Atlanta Symphony Orchestra and Chamber Chorus in this performance taped in Atlanta. The soloists are Sylvia McNair, Marietta Simpson, Jon Humphrey and William Stone. Phillip Byrd directed the video. Color. 141 minutes. VAI video.

1992 Point Theatre, Dublin
Neville Marriner conducts the St.-Martin-in-the-Fields Academy Orchestra and Chorus in this 250th anniversary performance at the Point Theatre in Dublin, the city where the oratorio was first performed. The soloists are Sylvia McNair, Anne Sofie von Otter, Michael Chance, Jerry Hadley and Robert Lloyd. Color. 147 minutes. Philips video. (Highlights version available in the *Great Moments* series as Volume 3.)

MESSTER, OSKAR
German film producer (1866-1943)

Oskar Messter was a major producer of early opera films as well as one of the important innovators in the early days of German cinema. He perfected his Kinematography system in 1895/1896 and began experimenting with sound as early as 1903. He succeeded in making films of opera arias that could be synchronized with phonograph records. They lasted about three or four minutes and Messter opened a cinema in Berlin to present them. Many notable opera and operetta stars sang for his Biophon-Tonbilder company and many movie actors began their careers in his films, most notably Henny Porten. In 1912 he made the first film biography of Richard Wagner. About 1500 sound films were made in Germany in this period, many of them by Messter, and a number survive. See FAUST (1907), FRA DIAVOLO (1908), LOHENGRIN (1907), LUCIA DI LAMMERMOOR (1907), FRITIZI MASSARY (1903), OTELLO (1907), HENNY PORTEN, SALOME (1906), LA TRAVIATA (1908), RICHARD WAGNER (1912).

MÉSZAROS, MÁRTA
Hungarian film director (1931-)

Márta Mészaros is one of the leading directors of the modern Hungarian cinema with a strong background in documentary, She is especially noted for her films about the situation of women including *Adoption* and *Nine Months*. Aside from the use of opera music in her films, she has made a fine documentary about *Don Pasquale* featuring American soprano Barbara Hendricks. See DON PASQUALE (1991).

METROPOLITAN OPERA
New York opera house (1883-)

The Metropolitan Opera in New York has been America's best-known opera house for over a hundred years and remains one of the best in the world. It is also of great importance in the history of opera on the screen. The first American telecast of an opera was *Pagliacci* by the Metropolitan Opera in 1940 and the first live telecast from any theater was *Otello* from the Met in 1948. The second was the Met's *Der Rosenkavalier* in 1949 and the third *Don Carlo* in 1950. There are more videos of operas at the Met than any other opera house as nearly every opera telecast is accessible. Most can be purchased while others can be viewed at the Museum of Television and Radio which held a major retrospective in 1986. Many fiction films with opera subjects feature scenes at or around the Met including *Moonstruck, A Night at the Opera, Metropolitan* and *The Stars are Singing.* MGM actually built a 500-foot-wide reproduction of the Old Met interior for the 1946 film *Two Sisters From Boston*. Most of the standard repertory operas are available as Met videos. For details see individual operas. See also ANTONY AND CLEOPATRA (1966), MARIA CALLAS (1956), JAMES LEVINE.

1940 Metropolitan Opera Gala Concert
This was the first American television broadcast of opera. The Met organized the telecast from an NBC stage in Radio City on March 10, 1940, in a program called *Metropolitan Opera Gala Concert*. In the first part singers in evening dress are featured in music from *Carmen* (Bruna Castagna and Lucia Albanese), *La Gioconda* (Frederick Jagel), *The Barber of Seville* (Leonard Warren) and *Rigoletto* (all four performing the Quartet). In the second half an highlights performance of *Pagliacci* is presented in costume with sets. Richard Bonelli sings the Prologue, Hilda Burke is Nedda, Armand Tokatyan is Canio and George Cehanovsky is Silvio. There were about 1000 television sets in the U.S. at this time and the audience for the show was estimated at 2000 people. Black and white. In English, French and Italian. 60 minutes.

1953 Metropolitan Opera Jamboree
Blanche Thebom, Richard Tucker, Leontyne Price and George London are the singers at this Met fund-raising celebration. Thebom sings "Amour viens aider" from *Samson et Dalila* and Tucker "Addio alla madre" from *Cavalleria Rusticana*. Deems Taylor, Milton Cross and Howard Dietz

also took part. Henry Souvaine produced and William Marshall and Marshall Diskin directed. The ABC telecast was made from the Ritz Theater in New York on April 6, 1953. Black and white. 60 minutes. Video at MTR.

1953 Toast to the Met
Ed Sullivan devoted his entire CBS show to the Met on Nov. 8, 1953, telecasting from the opera house stage. Among the stars shown in rehearsal and singing are Risë Stevens, Richard Tucker, Hilda Gueden, Robert Merrill, Cesare Siepi and Robert Peters. The studio audience actually wore black tie. Black and white. 60 minutes. Video at MTR.

1957 The Ed Sullivan Show
Renata Tebaldi and Richard Tucker are the guest stars from the Metropolitan on the *Ed Sullivan Show* on March 10, 1957. They sing one aria during the CBS television program. Black and white. 60 minutes. Video at MTR.

1966 The Met Yesterday and Tomorrow
A telecast tribute to the past history of the old Metropolitan Opera House which had just been razed when this program was show. The program ends with a discussion of the new opera house scheduled to open in September. Met stars of the past, including Caruso, Melba, Farrar and Chaliapin are featured in this NET program telecast on April 17, 1966. The guests include Richard Tucker, architect Wallace Harrison and Met president Anthony Bliss. Black and white. 90 minutes. Video at MTR.

1966 Open Mind
Lily Pons, Bidú Sayão, Lotte Lehmann, Giovanni Martinelli and Richard Crooks talk about the Golden Age of the Metropolitan Opera shortly after the razing of the old theater. This NBC program was telecast on April 17, 1966. Black and white. Video at the MTR.

1970 Opera with Henry Butler
Henry Butler, the stage director of the Metropolitan Opera when this film was made, talks about opera as a combination of music and theater. Included are as demonstration are scenes from *La Traviata* (the party scene with Anna Moffo) and *Pagliacci*. Color. 26 minutes.

1972 Salute to Sir Rudolf Bing

Forty-three Metropolitan Opera stars perform in a gala concert to honor Rudolf Bing retiring after 22 years as general manager. The singers include Luciano Pavarotti, Joan Sutherland, Placido Domingo, Montserrat Caballé, Roberta Peters, Birgitt Nilsson, Franco Corelli and Sherrill Milnes. The gala was produced by Charles Andrews, directed by Sydney Smith and telecast on April 30 on CBS. 60 minutes. Video at MTR.

1975 Danny Kaye's at the Metropolitan

Danny Kaye looks behind the scenes at scenery, lighting and special effects at the Metropolitan Opera in this CBS telecast in the Texaco Presents series. Seen on the show are Beverly Sills, Robert Merrill, Rosalind Elias, Enrico Di Giuseppe, James Morris and Judith Blegen. Robert Sheerer directed with Sylvia Fine as executive producer. The program aired on April 27, 1972. 60 minutes. Video at MTR.

1983 Centennial Gala

The Met celebrated its l00th birthday on Oct. 22, 1983 with an eight-hour gala telecast around the world with one hundred singers, seven conductors, the Met Orchestra, Chorus and Ballet and a live audience of 7,500. The participants include: Sopranos Kathleen Battle, Judith Blegen, Grace Bumbry, Montserrat Caballé, Ileana Cotrubas, Loretta Di Franco, Mirella Freni, Catherine Malfitano, Eva Marton, Leona Mitchell, Edda Moser, Birgit Nilsson, Roberta Peters, Leontyne Price, Katia Ricciarelli, Elisabeth Söderström, Joan Sutherland, Kiri Te Kanawa and Anna Tomowa-Sintow. Mezzo-sopranos Gail Dubinbaum, Marilyn Horne, Diane Kesling and Frederica von Stade. Tenors José Carreras, Giuliano Giannella, Placido Domingo, Nicolai Gedda, Alfredo Kraus, William Lewis, James McCracken, Robert Nagy, Luciano Pavarotti, Dano Raffanti and David Rendall. Baritones Renato Bruson, John Darrenkamp and Brian Schexnayder. Basses Ara Berberian, Sesto Bruscantini, Nicolai Ghiaurov, Ruggero Raimondi and Julien Robbins. Conductors Leonard Bernstein, Richard Bonynge, Thomas Fulton, James Levine, John Pritchard, David Stivender and Jeffrey Tate. Kirk Browning directed the telecast and video. Color. With English subtitles. 231 minutes. Paramount video/Pioneer laser.

1986 Live From the Met Highlights, Vol. I

A compilation video of excerpts from operas presented at the Met: *The Bartered Bride* (1978/overture conducted by James Levine), *Un Ballo in Maschera* (1980 with Judith Blegen and Luciano Pavarotti), *Don Carlo* (1983 with Mirella Freni and Placido Domingo), *La Bohème* (1982 with Teresa Stratas and José Carreras), *Tannhäuser* (1982 with Eva Marton) and *Lucia di Lammermoor* (1982 with Joan Sutherland). Color. 70 minutes. Paramount video.

1991 25th Anniversary Gala

A glittering gala with top stars celebrating the 25th anniversary of the Met's move to Lincoln Center. Luciano Pavarotti and Cheryl Studer are seen in Act III of *Rigoletto*, Placido Domingo and Mirella Freni appear in Act III of *Otello*, Domingo and Pavarotti sing together in a scene from *La Bohème* and a host of stars make guest appearances in Act II of *Die Fledermaus* including June Anderson, Kathleen Battle, Thomas Hampson and Frederica von Stade. James Levine conducts the Metropolitan Opera Orchestra. Color. With English subtitles. 115 minutes. On video.

1994 Meet the Met

This is a laserdsic compilation of favorite opera scenes from Met productions of *The Magic Flute, Il Trovatore, Otello, Un Ballo in Maschera, Aida, Ariadne auf Naxos, The Barber of Seville, Turandot, Die Fledermaus* and *Götterdämmerung*. Color. 101 minutes. In German and Italian with English titles. DG laser.

MEYERBEER, GIACOMO

French composer (1791-1864)

Giacomo Meyerbeer, born Jacob Meyer Beer, was the Cecil B. De Mille of grand opera. Although a Berlin-born German, he became the grand master of the French opera with librettist Eugène Scribe. Together they devised operas more spectacular and grandiose than anything seen on the stage before or since. His first success was the 1824 *Il Crociato in Egitto* but it was his 1931 collaboration with Scribe on *Robert le Diable* that began his triumphal grand opera career at the Paris Opéra. It scandalized Paris with dancing nuns. Meyerbeer afterwards collaborated with Scribe on the equally successful large-scale grand operas *Les Huguenots, Le Prophète* and *L'Africaine*. Although not currently in vogue, his operas remain on the stage. See L'AFRICAINE, LES HUGUENOTS.

MICHELENA, BEATRIZ
Americansilent film actress (1890-1942)

Beatriz Michelena, a star of the early American silent cinema, was also admired as an opera singer. She was the daughter of Spanish opera tenor Ferdinand Michelena and sister of Broadway musical comedy singer Vera Michelena. Beatriz was the top star of the California Motion Picture Corporation and was featured in an early screen adaptation of Ambroise Thomas's opera *Mignon*. When the film was first screened privately in December 1914, she sang Mignon's arias to accompany it. She was said to have been offered $5000 to sing at the Tivoli Opera House when the film opened in 1915 but preferred a movie career. Her other films include *Salomy Jane* and *Mrs Wiggs of the Cabbage Patch*, both 1914. See also MIGNON (1915).

MIDSUMMER MARRIAGE, THE
1955 opera by Tippett

Michael Tippett's first opera aroused a great deal of controversy when it premiered, mainly because of its libretto. It was too grand, too obscure, too mythological. It takes place in a clearing on a hilltop where the mysterious Mark is being rebuffed by the idealistic Jenifer whom he was to wed. Meanwhile the tycoon King Fisher is seeking them to stop the marriage. At the end the wedding finally takes place. See also MICHAEL TIPPETT.

1984 Thames Television
Philip Langridge is Mark, Lucy Shelton is Jenifer and Patricia O'Neill is Bella in this production of the opera adapted for Thames Television in London. David Atherton conducts the orchestra. Color. In English with Japanese subtitles. 120 minutes. On Japanese laserdisc.

MIDSUMMER NIGHT'S DREAM, A
1960 opera by Britten

Shakespeare's play is the basis of this opera but it has been somewhat altered by composer Benjamin Britten and co-librettist Peter Pears to emphasize the supernatural aspect. King Oberon gets his revenge on Queen Titania by giving her a love potion that causes her to fall for the rustic fool Bottom. He has been bewitched and now wears an ass's head. See also BENJAMIN BRITTEN.

1981 Glyndebourne Festival
Peter Hall staged this magical Glyndebourne Festival production of Britten's opera with atmospheric sets by John Bury. James Bowman portrays Oberon, Ileana Cotrubas is Titania, Ryland Davies is Lysander, Dale Duesing is Demetrius, Felicity Lott is Helena, Cynthia Buchan is Hermia, Curt Appelgren is Bottom, Robert Bryson is Quince, Andrew Gallacher is Snug, Donald Bell is Starveling, Patrick Power is Flute and Damien Nash is Puck. Bernard Haitink conducted the London Philharmonic Orchestra and David Heather directed the video. TVS. Color. In English. 156 minutes. Home Vision/ Kultur videos.

Related films

SHAKESPEARE FILMS
The best films of the Shakespeare play for comparison purposes are those made by Max Reinhardt in 1935 and Peter Hall in 1968. Reinhardt's lavish American version for MGM stars James Cagney, Mickey Rooney, Dick Powell and Olivia de Havilland. Hall's English film features members of the Royal Shakespeare Company including Diana Rigg, Helen Mirren, Ian Holm, David Warner and Judi Dench.

MIGENES, JULIA
American soprano (1945-)

Julie Migenes called herself Migenes-Johnson when she starred in Francesco Rosi's great 1984 opera film *Carmen* and won world renown. Her opera career began in her native New York as a three-year-old in a Metropolitan Opera production of *Madama Butterfly*. She made her adult debut in 1965 as Annina in the New York City Opera production of *The Saint of Bleeker Street* and then began to sing regularly with the Vienna Volksoper. She returned to the Met in 1979 and has been acclaimed there and in Europe for her performances in Berg's *Lulu* and in Weill operas. See CARMEN (1984), PLACIDO DOMINGO (1990), EINE NACHT IN VENEDIG (1974), LULU (1980), RISE AND FALL OF THE CITY OF MAHAGONNY (1976), SHERRILL MILNES (1985), THE THREEPENNY OPERA (1990).

MIGHTY CASEY, THE
1953 opera by Schuman

William Schuman's one-act opera concerns the mighty batter who struck out so unbelievably in a famous 1887 baseball game in the town of Mudville. Ernest L. Thayer's much-quoted poem "Casey at the Bat" provides the basis of the story used in the libretto by Jeremy Gury. There are no major singing roles and Casey himself is mimed. The opera premiered in Hartford on May 4, 1953, and is on CD. See also WILLIAM SCHUMAN.

1955 CBS Omnibus video
Schuman's short opera was presented live on the CBS Television *Omnibus* series on March 6, 1955. The large cast includes Danny Scholl, Elise Rhodes, Rufus Smith and Nathaniel Frey. Black and white. 60 minutes. Video at MTR.

MIGNON
1866 opera by Thomas

Ambroise Thomas's *Mignon* was very popular in the early part of the century so there are many silent films even though it is currently out of fashion. The opera is based on Goethe's 1796 novel *Wilhelm Meister's Apprenticeship* as adapted by Jules Barbier and Michel Carré. Mignon is a singer with a group of traveling gypsies who is rescued by Wilhelm. Lothario is a count disguised as a wandering minstrel who is looking for his long lost daughter. Not surprisingly she turns out to be Mignon. See also AMBROISE THOMAS.

1973 Joan Sutherland film
Joan Sutherland is in fine voice in this *Who's Afraid of Opera* highlights version of the opera. Sutherland portrays Philine with Huguette Turangeau as Mignon, Ian Caley as Wilhelm, Pieter Van Der Stolk as Lothario, Brian Ralph as Laertes and Gordon Wilcock as Jarno. Sutherland explains the plot in English to three puppets but she and the others sing in French. Herbert Wise directed, George Djurkovic designed the sets and Richard Bonynge conducted the London Symphony Orchestra. Color. 30 minutes. Kultur video.

1982 Trudeliese Schmidt film
Trudeliese Schmidt sings the role of Mignon in this West German television film made for ZDF with the Salzburg Marionette Theater. Like the Joan Sutherland highlights version, it mixes puppets with live actors. Color. In German. 59 minutes. German Language Video Center video.

1982 Mexico City Opera
Estrella Ramirez stars as Mignon in this Opera Nacional production by Carlos Diaz Dupond at the Teatro de Bellas Artes in Mexico City. Librado Alexander is Wilhelm, Angelica Dorantes is Philine, Rogelio Vargas is Lothario and Adrian Diaz de Leon is Frederick. The sets were designed by INBA. Enrique Padron De Hueda conducted the Teatro de Bellas Artes Orchestra and Chorus and Manuel Yrizar directed the telecast. The video is an off-air copy of a Mexican telecast. Color. In French with Spanish subtitles. 120 minutes. Lyric video.

Early/related films

1906 Chronographe film
A scene and aria from the opera was released with sound on disc in 1906 using the Gaumont Chronographe system. About 3 minutes.

1909 Lubin film
This American adaptation of the opera may also have been a singing version as the company that year was marketing a sound film system called the Lubin Synchronizer. About 9 minutes.

1911 Mary Runge film
Mary Runge sings the aria "Je suis Titania" from *Mignon* in this Oskar Messter sound film. It was made for his Berlin Biophon cinema using a sound-on-disc synchronization system. About 4 minutes.

1912 Marion Swayne film
Pioneer woman director Alice Guy Blaché directed an early screen version of *Mignon* for her Solax company. It stars Marion Swayne as Mignon, Blanche Cornwall as Philine, Darwin Karr as Wilhelm Meister and Billy Quirk as Frederick. They are all members of the Solax studio repertory company.

1915 Beatriz Michelena film
Soprano Beatriz Michelena gave a much praised performance as Mignon in this film of the opera shot in the San Francisco area. Michelena sang her arias live with the film at the premiere. House Peters is her Wilhelm, Andrew Robson is Lothario,

Will Pike is Frederick and Clara Beyers is Filina. Charles Kenyon adapted the opera for the screen and William Nigh directed for the California and World Film companies. Black and white. About 75 minutes (five reels).

1919 Tina Xeo film
Tina Xeo stars as Mignon in this Italian film of the Thomas opera and won wide acclaim for it. Franco Piersanti portrays Wilhelm and Renée de Saint-Léger and Dillo Lombardi lend support. Mario Gargiulo directed for the Flegrea Film company of Rome. About 70 minutes.

1943 The Life and Death of Colonel Blimp
Directors Michael Powell and Eric Pressburger use Mignon's aria "Je suis Titania" to help create a period ambiance in this fine film. Roger Livesey portrays a British Army officer in a Berlin cafe in 1902 on leave from the Boer War and accompanied by feminist Deborah Kerr. He is there to provoke a fight about allegations of British atrocities and he begins by asking the band to play the French aria. Color. 163 minutes.

1950 The Toast of New Orleans
The Thomas opera is seen on stage in this MGM musical. Kathryn Grayson sings an aria from *Mignon* in a production at the French Opera House in turn of the century New Orleans. Grayson portrays the opera house's prima donna who reluctantly instructs Mario Lanza about opera. Norman Taurog directed. Color. 97 minutes. MGM-UA video.

1975 The Wrong Movement
Wim Wenders German film *Falsche Bewegung* (The Wrong Movement) is a loose adaptation of the Goethe source novel *Wilhelm Meisters Lehrjahre*. It stars Rudiger Vogler as Wilhelm. Color. In German. 103 minutes. On video.

MIKADO, THE
1885 comic opera by Gilbert & Sullivan

The Mikado or The Town of Titipu is the most popular of the Gilbert and Sullivan operettas and this is reflected in a large number of films, videos and telecasts. It was first filmed in 1902 and a grandiose Technicolor version was made in 1939. While the setting is ostensibly Japan, the satire is entirely about English behavior. Nanki-Poo, the son of the Mikado, has come to the town of Titipu disguised as a minstrel to escape from marrying the old maid Katisha. He falls in love with Yum-Yum, the ward of Ko-Ko, the Lord High Executioner, who is planning to marry her with the help of Pooh-Bah, who holds most of the official positions. Many of the songs are classics including "A wandering minstrel" and "The flowers that bloom in the spring." See also GILBERT AND SULLIVAN.

1939 Victor Schertzinger film
Victor Schertzinger was brought to London to direct this lavish Technicolor film intended to be the British answer to *The Wizard of Oz*. It stars many of the best-known stars of the D'Oyly Carte Opera Company and is still enjoyable though certainly no match for *The Wizard*. Martyn Green is Ko-Ko, Jean Colin is Yum-Yum, John Barclay is the Mikado, Sydney Granville is Pooh-Bah and Constance Wills is Yum-Yum. American singer Kenny Baker was imported to play Nanki-Poo. Bernard Knowles and William Skall were the cinematographers and Geoffrey Toye conducted the London Symphony Orchestra. Color. In English. 91 minutes. Home Vision video.

1949 California Light Opera
The first American television production of the operetta was presented in 1949 by the California Light Opera company over KLAC in an abridged version with a cast of ten singers. They include Arthur Bradley, Phyllis Walker, Robert Kiber, John Hamilton and Mary Patrick. Luther Nuby directed the telecast on Jan. 25, 1949. The critics were not impressed. Black and white. In English. 50 minutes.

1959 Norman Campbell telecast
Eric House portrays Ko-Ko in this Canadian TV production by Norman Campbell. Alan Crofoot is Pooh-Bah, Roma Butler is Yum-Yum, Robert Reid is Nanki-Poo, Eric Treadwell is the Mikado and Irene Byatt is Katisha. Robert Lawson designed the sets, Suzanne Mess designed the costumes and Gladys Forrester staged the musical numbers. Godfrey Ridout conducted the CBC Orchestra. The critics liked it. Black and white. In English. 120 minutes.

1959 Ernie Ford video
Tennessee Ernie Ford featured a hillbilly version of *The Mikado* on his NBC TV series *The Ford Show* on

April 16, 1959. Ford portrays Ko-Ko and acts as narrator with support from Karen Wessler, Ken Remo, Ted Wills, Deltra Kamsler, Donna Cooke and Joanne Burgan. Writers Danny Arnold and Howard Leeds did the adaptation. Black and white. 30 minutes. Video at UCLA Film and Television Archive.

1960 Groucho Marx/Helen Traubel video
Groucho Marx and Helen Traubel star as Ko-Ko and Katisha in this amazing Bell Telephone Hour version of the operetta directed by Norman Campbell. Stanley Holloway plays Pooh-Bah, Robert Rounseville is Nanki-Poo, Barbara Meisteras is Yum-Yum and Dennis King is the Mikado. It was produced by Martyn Green and telecast on NBC on April 14, 1960. Color. In English. 60 minutes. Video at MTR.

1963 The Cool Mikado
Frankie Howerd stars as Ko-Ko with Stubby Kaye as Judge Mikado in this modernized film version of the operetta set in postwar Japan. Kevin Scott is Hank Mikado, Jill Mai Meredith is Yum-Yum, Lionel Blair is Nanki and Jacquelin Jones is Katie Shaw. Michael Winner directed this version written with Maurice Browning and Lew Schwartz and produced by Harold Baim. Color. In English. 81 minutes.

1967 D'Oyly Carte Company film
John Reed stars as Ko-Ko in this D'Oyly Carte Company film of the operetta based on Anthony Besch's classic 1966 stage production. Donald Adams is the Mikado, Valerie Masterson is Yum-Yum, Philip Potter is Nanki-Poo, Kenneth Sandford is Pooh-Bah and Christine Palmer is Katisha. Isidore Godfrey conducted the Birmingham City Symphony Orchestra and Stuart Burge directed the film shot at Golders Green Hippodrome in 1967 by Gerry Fisher. It was distributed in the U.S. by Warner Bros. Color. In English. 122 minutes. VAI video.

1974 World of Gilbert & Sullivan film
John Cartier stars as Ko-Ko in this English highlights version produced by John Seabourne for the *World of Gilbert and Sullivan* series. Donald Adams portrays the Mikado, Valerie Masterson is Yum-Yum, Lawrence Richard is Pooh-Bah, Thomas Round is Nanki-Poo and Helen Landis is Katisha. The music is played by the Gilbert and Sullivan Festival Orchestra and Chorus. Trevor

Evans directed the film. Color. In English. 50 minutes.

1982 George Walker film
American actor William Conrad portrays the Mikado in this British film produced by Judith De Paul for George Walker. Clive Revill is Ko-Ko, Kate Flowers is Yum-Yum, Stafford Dean is Pooh-Bah, John Steward is Nanki-Poo and Anne Collins is Katisha. The operetta was staged by Michael Geliot, designed by Allan Cameron and filmed by Rodney Greenberg. Alexander Faris conducts the London Symphony Orchestra and the Ambrosian Opera Chorus. Color. In English. 113 minutes. Pioneer laser/ Braveworld (England) video.

1982 Stratford Festival
Brian MacDonald staged this lively production for the Stratford Festival in Canada with updated references. Eric Donkin is Ko-Ko, Gideon Saks is the Mikado, Marie Baron is Yum-Yum, Henry Ingram is Nanki-Poo, Richard McMillan is Pooh-Bah and Christina James is Katisha. Susan Benson and Douglas A. McLean designed the sets and costumes and Berthold Carrière conducted the Stratford Festival Orchestra and Chorus. Norman Campbell directed the live video. CBC. Color. In English. 150 minutes. Home Vision/Connoisseur video/Japanese laser.

1987 English National Opera
Producer Jonathan Miller felt *The Mikado* was more English than Japanese so he moved its locale to 1920s England for this English National Opera production. It's set in a black-and-white art deco seaside resort with tap-dancing bellhops, white pianos and silver potted palms. It was filmed before a live audience at the London Coliseum using an array of period film techniques. Eric Idle is Ko-Ko, Richard Van Allen is Pooh-Bah, Richard Angas is the Mikado, Bonaventura Bottone is Nanki-Poo, Susan Bullock is Peep-Bo, Lesley Garrett is Yum-Yum and Felicity Palmer is Katisha. Anthony van Laast choreographed and Peter Robinson conducted the ENO Orchestra. John Michael Phillips directed the video. Thames TV. Color. In English. 130 minutes. HBO video.

1992 Christopher Renshaw video
The British critics were not very kind to this production of the operetta by Christopher Renshaw. Color. In English. Virgin Classics (England) video.

1992 Sandro Massimini video

Highlights from *Il Mikado* are sung in Italian by operetta master Sandro Massimini and his associates on the TV series *Operette, Che Passione!* Massimini gives a history of the operetta before he joins in the singing of "Tit willow" and "A more human Mikado." Color. In Italian. About 15 minutes. Ricordi (Italy) video.

1993 D'Oyly Carte Company

This is a production by the new D'Oyly Carte Company as originally staged by Andrew Wickes and restaged by Virginia Mason for filming at the Buxton Opera House. It features Jill Pert as Katisha with Julian Jensen, Lesley Echo Ross, Gary Montaine, Fenton Gray, Terence Sharpe and Deryck Hamon. Color. In English. 120 minutes. Polygram (England) video.

Early/related films

1902 Lubin film

The first film based on a Gilbert and Sullivan operetta featured a scene from *The Mikado*. It was filmed in the U.S. by the Lubin company and released in January 1902. About 3 minutes.

1904 Walterdaw sound film

The first sound film based on a Gilbert and Sullivan operetta. It utilized a British synchronized sound system devised by the Walterdaw company. A scene from *The Mikado* was screened with a record of the song pictured. About 3 minutes.

1907 Cinematophone Singing Pictures

This was an epic movie for its time with virtually all the hit songs from the operetta on twelve reels of film with sound provided by the Cinematophone system. Each individual film carried the title of a song from "A Wandering Minstrel" to "Three Little Maids" to "The Flowers that Bloom in the Spring." The song "Tit Willow" is identified as being sung by George Thorne portraying Ko-Ko. The films were directed by John Morland and made for the Walterdaw company. About 36 minutes.

1909 Vivaphone sound duet

A Hepworth Vivaphone sound film was made picturing a duet from *The Mikado*. This was a synchronized sound-on-disc system. About 4 minutes.

1918 Sidney Franklin film

This seems to be the first complete version of *The Mikado* on film. Retitled *Fan Fan* and with many of the characters renamed, it was produced by the Fox Film Corporation and directed by Sidney Franklin, later famous for movies like *The Barretts of Wimpole Street*. The film stars Virgina Lee Corbin as Fan Fan (ie, Yum Yum), Francis Carpenter as Hani Pan (Nanki-Poo), Carmen De Rue as Lady Shoot (Natisha), Violet Radcliffe as the High Executioner and Joe Singleton as the Mikado. The operetta libretto was rather freely adapted by Bernard McConville but the film was screened with music from the operetta. Black and white. About 70 minutes.

1926 D'Oyly Carte film

Scenes from a 1926 D'Oyly Carte production of *The Mikado* were filmed for a Gaumont Mirror movie house special program. It also shows Charles Ricketts working in the studio. About 10 minutes.

1937 The Girl Said No

This American film contains portions of *The Mikado* performed in a traditional manner by members of the New York Gilbert and Sullivan Opera Company. William Danforth, who sings the role of the Mikado, was said to have performed it for 25 years on stage. The other Savoyards are Frank Moulan, Vivian Hart and Vera Ross. The plot of the film revolves around staging *The Mikado* in New York. Grand National Films. Black and white. In English. 63 minutes. Video Yesteryear.

1978 Foul Play

The Mikado is central to the plot of this Hollywood thriller as the Pope is to be assassinated at a stage performance in San Francisco. Goldie Hawn and Chevy Chase race to the theater to foil the plot with Hitchcock-style cross-cutting to Dudley Moore who is conducting the operetta. Julius Rudel, however, is the real conductor of the music that is heard while *The Mikado* scenes are performed by members of the New York City Opera. Enrico di Giuseppe plays Nanki-Poo, Glenys Fowles is Yum-Yum, Kathleen Hegierski is Peep-Bo, Sandra Walker is Pitti-Sing, Jane Shaulis is Katisha, Thomas Jamerson is Pish-Tush and Richard McKee is Pooh-Bah. Colin Higgins directed the film for Paramount. Color. In English. 116 minutes.

1982 Gentlemen of Titipu
This is an abridged animated version of *The Mikado*. Color. In English. 27 minutes. Paragon video.

MIKI, MINORU
Japanese composer (1930-)

Minoru Miki is a Japanese composer who writes operas in Japanese in the European style using a Western orchestra. He incorporates Japanese themes, stories and musical ideas into the format. Miki began in 1963 with the chamber opera *Mendori Teischu* (The Henpecked Husband) which was staged in Japan and Europe. Equally successful was his full-scale 1975 *Shunkin-Sho* (The Story of Shunkin) about a boy who blinds himself for the sake of love. His only opera on video is called *Jojuri.*

1988 Jojuri
Miki's 1985 opera *Jojuri*, composed to a libretto by Colin Graham based on a play by Monzaemon Chikamatsu, was commissioned by the Opera Theater of St. Louis. It includes Japanese instruments in a Western style orchestra. After its premiere in St. Louis, it was reprised in 1988 and taped live in HDTV at the Nissei Theater in Tokyo. This Opera Theater of St. Louis production by Colin Graham features Faith Esham, Andrew Wentzel, John Brandstetter and Carrol Freeman. Joseph Rescigno conducts the Opera Theater of St. Louis Orchestra. Color. In English with Japanese subtitles. 160 minutes. On video and Japanese laserdisc.

MILLER, JONATHAN
English director (1936-)

Jonathan Miller has directed theater, television, opera and film and has brought a lively intelligence to each. He first became known with the *Beyond the Fringe* theater group and then began directing Chekhov and Shakespeare. He began to direct opera on stage in 1970 and developed a relationship with the English National Opera and Kent Opera companies. His most famous opera productions for the ENO, a 1950s New York gangster version of *Rigoletto* and a 1920s English version of *The Mikado*, are available on video. See THE BEGGAR'S OPERA (1983), LA FANCIULLA DEL WEST (1991), THE MARRIAGE OF FIGARO (1992), THE MIKADO (1987), RIGOLETTO (1982).

MILLION, LE
1931 opera film by Clair

René Clair's delightful opéra-bouffe film was quite probably the model for the Marx Brothers *A Night at the Opera*. The plot revolves around the chase after a winning lottery ticket which ends up in an opera house. Everyone descends on the Opéra-Lyrique stage where the imaginary opera *Les Bohèmiens* is being presented. The stout tenor Sopranelli is wearing a jacket with the ticket in the pocket and he and the soprano ironically sing about being alone in the forest. Actually there is a whole crowd watching and making furious attempts to get the lottery ticket. Complete chaos finally ensues and the opera ends in total anarchy. René Lefèvre and Annabella play the romantic leads. The music is by Georges van Pary (who also wrote stage operettas) with Philippe Parès and Armand Bernard. Black and white. In French. 91 minutes. Video Yesteryear/ Bel Canto Society videos. See also *Les Bohèmiens* under IMAGINARY OPERAS IN FILMS (1931).

MILLO, APRILE
American soprano (1958-)

Aprile Millo studied in San Diego and began her career starring in *Aida* in Salt Lake City in 1980. In 1982 she sang at La Scala in *Ernani* and in 1984 came to the Metropolitan as Amelia in *Simon Boccanegra*. She was soon a Met favorite in a wide variety of roles and can be seen on that stage on video as Aida and as Amelia in *Un Ballo in Maschera*. See AIDA (1989), UN BALLO IN MASCHERA (1991), DIVAS (1987), VERONA (1988).

MILLÖCKER, KARL
Austrian composer (1842-1899)

Karl Millöcker was a contemporary of Strauss and Suppé in Vienna's musical golden age and one of the major exponents of the Viennese operetta of the period though his name is not well known today outside the German-speaking world. His most famous operetta, the 1882 *Der Bettelstudent*, continues to be staged in Germany and is widely available on video. A revision of his *Gräfin Dubarry* (1879) was a hit on Broadway in the 1930s with Grace Moore as its star and *Gasparone* (1884) still has its admirers. See DER BETTELSTUDENT, DIE DUBARRY, GASPARONE, OPERETTE.

1945 Operettaklange

Operetta Tones is a German film about Millöcker centering on his struggles while composing his 1890 operetta *Der Arme Jonathan*. It stars Paul Hörbiger as the composer with support from Hans Holt and Margot Jahnen. Theo Lingen directed the film, originally titled *Glück Muss Man Haben*, which was unfinished when the war ended. When it was eventually completed, it was released with a different title. Black and white. In German. 78 minutes.

MILNES, SHERRILL
American baritone (1935-)

Illinois native Sherrill Milnes studied with Rosa Ponselle and made his opera debut in 1960 as Masetto. He then sang in Baltimore, Milan and with the New York City Opera. His principal career was with the Metropolitan Opera where he made his debut in 1965 and sang for over 25 years. His repertory includes most of the Verdi and Puccini baritone roles and he created the role of Adam Brant in Levy's *Mourning Becomes Electra*. He is featured in a number of films and videos of operas and recitals. See AIDA (1989), ERNANI (1983), OTELLO (1979) LUCIANO PAVAROTTI (1992), SIMON BOCCANEGRA (1984), TOSCA (1976), IL TROVATORE (1988).

1976 Sherrill Milnes: Homage to Verdi
Milnes goes on a pilgrimage to Verdi's birthplace and sings Verdi arias as he tells of the composer's life. He begins with "Di Provenza il mar" as he visits Villa Verdi at Sant'Agata and pays homage to Verdi's piano. He sings arias from *La Traviata, La Forza del Destino, I Vespri Siciliani, Attila, Rigoletto, Nabucco* and *Macbeth*. In addition he is seen rehearsing and performing *Rigoletto*. Gerald Krell produced and directed the film. Color. In English. 56 minutes. Kultur video.

1986 Sherrill Milnes at Juilliard
Milnes is shown giving an opera master class at the Juilliard Institute in 1986. He is featured giving advice and instructions to six advanced voice students who perform arias for him. Color. 75 minutes. Home Vision video.

1985 Sherrill Milnes All-Star Gala
Sherrill Milnes stars in this concert taped in Berlin. Milnes begins on a make-shift stage with the *Pagliacci* Prologue and ends with Iago's Credo. In between he duets with Julia Migenes on "Close as Pages in a Book" from *Up in Central Park*, with Mirella Freni on "Pura siccome un angelo" from *La Traviata* and with Placido Domingo on "Dio che nell'alma infondere" from *Don Carlo*. Milnes conducts the orchestra while Peter Schreier sings "Un aura amorosa." Georg Mielke directed. Color. 56 minutes. VAI video.

MIREILLE
1864 opera by Gounod

Charles Gounod's opera *Mireille* is set in Provence in the early 19th century. Mireille is in love with Vincent but her father is opposed and there is a dangerous rival in the form of the bullfighter Ourrias. The opera is based on a Provençal poem by Frédéric Mistral called *Mireio* with a libretto by Michel Carré. It was much discussed in its day for its agrarian setting and emphasis on class differences. See also CHARLES GOUNOD.

1981 Geneva Opera
Valerie Masterson stars as Mireille in this 1981 Geneva Opera production with a cast that also includes Luis Lima, Jane Berbie and Jules Bastin. Sylvain Cambreling conducts the orchestra. The video is an off-air tape of a telecast. Color. In French. 150 minutes. Lyric/Opera Dubs videos.

Early/related films

1906 Louis Feuillade film
This early French film of the story was made by pioneers Louis Feuillade and Alice Guy-Blaché. About 10 minutes.

1922 Ernest Servaës film
This French silent film of the story was based primarily on the poem by Mistral. It featured Joe Hamman as Ourrias, was directed by Ernest Servaës and was screened with music from the opera. About 75 minutes.

1933 Mireille Lurie film
Mireille Lurie stars as Mireille in this narrative version of the Gounod opera. The screenplay is based on the libretto and the score is based on the opera music. Jean Brunil plays Vincent, Joe Hamman is Ourrias, Marcel Boudouresque is Ramon, Mme. Clariot is Jeanne-Marie and Blanchet Le Sauvage is Ambroise. René Gaveau and Ernest

Servaës directed the film for the Société Chantereine d'Etudes Cinématographiques. Black and white. In French. 75 minutes.

MITRIDATE
1770 opera by Mozart

Mitridate, Re Di Ponto (Mithridates, King of Pontus) is an *opera seria* written by Mozart when he was fourteen and wanted desperately to please both singers and audience. It may not be a great opera but it has some great music. *Mitridate* tells the story of a king who has left his Black Sea country to fight the Romans. In his absence his sons Sifare and Farnace court his woman Aspasia. He returns having lost his war with the Romans but bringing Ismene as a bride for Farnace. He becomes suspicious of what has been happening in his absence and threatens to kill them all. The libretto by Vittorio Cigna-Santi is based on a Racine play. See also WOLFGANG A. MOZART.

1983 Opéra de Lyon
Rockwell Blake stars as Mitridate in this famous Lyons Opera production at Aix-en-Provence filmed in Cinemascope by Jean-Claude Fall. Yvonne Kenny sings the role of Aspasia, Ashley Putnam is Sifare, Brenda Boozer is Farnace, Patricia Rozario is Ismene, Christina Papis is Marzio and Catherine Dubosc is Arbate. Theodor Guschibauer conducts the Lyons Opera Orchestra. Color. In Italian. Polygram (France) video/ Japanese laser.

1986 Jean-Pierre Ponnelle film
Jean-Pierre Ponnelle filmed this inventive version of the *opera seria* at Palladio's Teatro Olimpico in Vicenza in March 1986 and it is quite marvelous. Gösta Winberg is Mitridate, Yvonne Kenny plays Aspasia, Ann Murray is Sifare, Anne Gjevang is Farnace, Joan Rodgers is Ismene, Peter Strakais Marzio and Massimiliano Roncato is Abbate. Xaver Schwarzenberger was the cinematographer and Nikolaus Harnoncourt conducted the Vienna Concentus Musicus. Color. In Italian with English subtitles. 124 minutes. London video.

1991 Royal Opera
Graham Vick's production of the opera for Covent Garden was praised by critics and won the Olivier Award for the outstanding opera achievement of the year. Vick and designer Paul Brown set the opera in a formal fantasy land full of pomp and ritual akin to Japanese Kabuki. Bruce Ford is Mitridate, Luba Orgonasova is Aspasia, Ann Murray is Sifare, Jochen Kowalski is Farnace, Lillian Watson is Ismene, Jacquelyn Fugell is Arbarte and Justin Lavender is Marzio. Paul Daniel conducted the Royal Opera Orchestra and Derek Bailey directed the video. Color. In Italian with English subtitles. 177 minutes. Home Vision video/ Pioneer Artists laser.

MLADA
1890 opera-ballet by Rimsky-Korsakov

Mlada is Nikolai Rimsky-Korsakov's gigantic answer to Wagner, a spectacular opera-ballet that demands expensive production values, amazing stage effects and uncommon casting and instruments. The heroine Mlada is a non-singing role for a dancer and is already dead when the opera begins. *Mlada* started as a collaborative project by four of the Famous Five composers but was then abandoned. Rimsky-Korsakov revised Viktor Krylov's libretto many years later refashioning Slavonic legend as Wagner had refashioned Germanic myths. The story, which takes places in pre-Christian times, concerns Prince Yaromir whose fiancée Mlada has been murdered by rival prince Mstiovsy. His evil daughter Voislava wants Yaromir for herself. Good and evil fight it out with titanic orchestration and lavish stage effects. Even the ghost of Cleopatra enters the fray. Good wins out, more or less. See also NIKOLAI RIMSKY-KORSAKOV.

1992 Bolshoi Opera
Dancer Nina Ananiashvili stars as Princess Mlada in this massive and inventive Bolshoi Opera production by the 83-year-old Boris Pokvrovsky. Oleg Kulko is Prince Yaromir, Maria Gavrilova is Princess Voislava, Gleb Nikolsky is Prince Mstivoy, Galina Borisova is Morena, Kirill Nikitin is the Soul of Yaromir and Yulia Malkhassiants is the Witch. Valery Levental designed the sets and Andrei Petrov was choreographer. Alexander Lazarev conducted the Bolshoi Symphony Orchestra and Chorus and Barrie Gavin directed the video. Color. In Russian. 139 minutes. Teldec video/laser.

MLLE. MODISTE

1905 comic opera by Herbert

Victor Herbert's *Mlle. Modiste*, one of his most popular operettas, helped make its star Fritzi Scheff famous, primarily because of its hit song "Kiss Me Again." Herbert had earlier persuaded her to give up her career at the Metropolitan Opera to star in his operettas. Henry Blossom's libretto tells the story of Fifi, an employee in a Parisian hat shop who becomes famous as the prima donna Madame Bellini. *Mlle. Modiste,* which had four hit songs, is still occasionally revived. There are three film versions including one with Fritzi Scheff herself. See also VICTOR HERBERT.

1926 Mademoiselle Modiste

Corinne Griffith stars as Mlle. Fifi in this silent feature film of the operetta which was screened in cinemas with Herbert's music. The cast includes Norman Kerry as Etienne, Willard Louis and Dorothy Cummings. Robert Leonard directed. Black and white. 70 minutes.

1930 Kiss Me Again/The Toast of the Legion

Bernice Claire stars as Mlle. Fifi in this enjoyable sound version of the operetta which includes all the main songs of the original. Walter Pidgeon sings the role of Paul de St. Cyr, Edward Everett Horton is Rene and Claude Gillingwater is the Count. William A. Seiter directed it and Lee Garmes photographed it in early Technicolor. The film is known as both *Kiss Me Again* and *The Toast of the Legion.* Color. 76 minutes.

1951 NBC Musical Comedy Time

Fritzi Scheff was 71 when she returned after 46 years to the operetta that made her famous in a television production on NBC's *Musical Comedy Time.* Scheff portrays Fifi's mother and sings "Kiss Me Again" one last time. Marguerite Piazza plays Mlle. Fifi with support from Frank McHugh and Brian Sullivan. Bernard Schubert produced, William Corrigan directed and Harry Sosnick was musical director. The operetta was telecast on Feb. 5, 1951. Black and white. 60 minutes.

MODL, MARTHA

German mezzo and soprano (1912-)

Martha Modl began her career as a mezzo-soprano making her debut as Hansel in *Hansel and Gretel* in 1942 and afterwards singing at Dusseldorf. In 1949 she joined the Hamburg State Opera as a dramatic soprano and in 1951 began to sing Wagner roles at Bayreuth. She sang in Carmen at Covent Garden in 1950 and came to the Metropolitan Opera in the late 1950s. In her later years she returned to mezzo roles and continued to sing onstage into her mid-70s. See ARABELLA (1977), THE MERRY WIVES OF WINDSOR (1950), POUSSIÈRES D'AMOUR, DER ZIGEUNERBARON (1975).

1984 Doppelgast in Aachen

Modl, aged 72, talks about her opera career and is shown in scenes from Reimann's *Mélusine* and Euripides' *The Trojans.* Peter Fuhrmann directed the video for WDR television in Germany. Color. In German. 30 minutes.

MOFFO, ANNA

American soprano (1934-)

Anna Moffo was born in Pennsylvania but made her start in opera in Italy. After studying in Rome, she made her debut in Spoleto in 1955. Her American debut came the following year in Chicago as Mimi and she joined the Metropolitan Opera in 1959 singing Violetta in *La Traviata.* It was this role that won her international acclaim for her coloratura versatility. Moffo achieved major recognition in Italy through her performance as Butterfly on television. She had her own Italian TV show, *The Anna Moffo Show,* in the 1960s. Her video of *La Traviata* is considered by one critic as the best recording of the opera in any form. Moffo starred in five opera films and appeared in fourteen non-operatic features. See LA BELLE HÉLÈNE (1975), DIE CSÁRDÁSFÜRSTIN (1971), LUCIA DI LAMMERMOOR (1971), LA SERVA PADRONA (1958), LA TRAVIATA (1966).

1958-1963 Anna Moffo in Opera and Song

Anna Moffo is seen in three appearances on *The Voice of Firestone* television series. On Sept. 22, 1958, she sings Musetta's Waltz and "Un bel di" with the orchestra conducted by Howard Barlow. On Jan. 3, 1963 she performs the Jewel Song from *Faust* with the orchestra conducted by Glenn Osser and is joined by Richard Merrill for Rodgers and Hammerstein duets. Her last appearance was on March 10, 1963 when she sang "Ballatella" from *Pagliacci* and two songs with the orchestra led by Arthur Fiedler. Black and white. 30 minutes. VAI video.

1964 The Anna Moffo Show

Anna Moffo hosted this RAI television show from Rome under the direction of her husband Mario Lanfranchi. She demonstrated charm and personality as well as a fine voice. The show usually included opera excerpts, especially from *La Traviata* and *Lucia di Lammermoor*. Black and white. In Italian . Each about 55 minutes.

1965 Menage all'Italiana

Moffo is featured as the wife of Ugo Tognazzi in this Italian comedy about a man who marries a singer but can't stop chasing other women. Moffo sings some popular songs and Franco Indovina directed. Color. In Italian. 95 minutes.

1969 Il Divorzio

Moffo stars opposite Vittorio Gassmann in *The Divorce*, an Italian film about a man who leaves his wife to chase younger women and finds himself replaced by a younger man when he returns home. Romolo Girolami directed for Fair Film. Color. In Italian. 100 minutes.

1970 Weekend Murders

Moffo stars opposite Eveline Stewart and Lance Percival in *Concerto per Pistolo Solista*, an Italian murder mystery directed by Michele Lupo. The plot revolves around an English family's quarrels. Released in the U.S. as *Weekend Murders*. Color. In Italian. 98 minutes.

1970 The Adventurers

Moffo play Dania Leonard in this Harold Robbins' potboiler and sings the *La Traviata* aria "Sempre libera." The film was based on his novel about a South American republic with a revolutionary history. Lewis Gilbert directed for Avco Embassy. Color. 171 minutes.

1970 La Ragazza di Nome Giulio

Moffo stars opposite Silvia Dionisio and Gianni Macchia in the Italian film *The Girl Named Giulio*. Tonino Valeri directed. Color. In Italian. 88 minutes.

MOJICA, JOSÉ
Mexican tenor (1896-1974)

José Mojica, the tenor who became a priest, was Mexico's greatest opera star before Placido Domingo and still has many admirers of his films and records. He came from a poor family but was still able to begin an opera career in Mexico City in 1916. He joined the Chicago Opera in 1923 and sang there until 1930 opposite stars like Mary Garden and Amelita Galli-Curci. In 1930 he began to star in Hollywood movies for Fox. He had major promotion as a new Latin lover at the time of his first film *One Mad Kiss* made in both English and Spanish versions. The studio was not happy with it, however and Mojica's other films for them were made strictly for the Spanish-speaking market. Mojica was featured in ten films for Fox between 1930 and 1934, all with musical and operatic elements. When Fox stopped producing Spanish-language films, he continued his career in Mexico and Argentina for another fifteen films. He returned to the opera stage in 1940 but gave it up when his mother died. He entered the priesthood in 1947 and became a missionary, sometimes singing when he had to raise funds. He published his autobiography *Yo Pecador* (I Sinner) in 1956 and it was made into a popular Mexican film. Mojica's American films are listed below as well as the Mexican and Argentine films available on video. One film was based on a Spanish opera. See DON GIL DE ALCALÁ.

1930 One Mad Kiss

Mojica's first Hollywood film was a musical made in both English and Spanish. He stars as a Spanish outlaw hero in Spain who fights corrupt official Antonio Moreno and finds love with dancehall girl Mona Maris. Mojica wrote the title song. Marcel Silver and James Tinling directed. Fox. Black and white. In English or Spanish. 70 minutes.

1931 Hay que Casar al Principe

Mojica's second film was a remake of a 1927 Fox film called *Paid To Love*. It's a love story with Mojica as a Ruritanian prince in Paris and Conchita Montenegro as the woman he loves. He sings popular songs for which he wrote the Spanish lyrics. Lewis Seiler directed. Fox. Black and white. In Spanish. 73 minutes.

1931 La Ley del Harem

Mojica plays an Arabian prince in *The Law of the Harem* opposite Carmen Larrabeita in this Fox remake of a 1928 film called Fazil. It features popular songs and was directed by Lewis Seiler. Fox. Black and white. In Spanish. 77 minutes.

1931 Their Mad Moment

Mojica had the Warner Baxter role in this Spanish-language version of the Fox romantic comedy *Their Mad Moment*. He also wrote the Spanish song lyrics. Andres De Segurola plays Lord Harry. Chandler Sprague directed. Black and white. In Spanish. 77 minutes.

1932 El Caballero de la Noche

Mojica plays English highwayman Dick Turpin opposite Mona Maris in this musical remake of the 1925 Fox film *Dick Turpin*. Andres De Segurola has a supporting role. James Tinling directed. Fox. Black and white. In Spanish. 83 minutes.

1933 La Melodia Prohibida

Mojica portrays a South Sea islander in *The Forbidden Song*, a musical co-starring Conchita Montenegro. Frank Strayer directed. Fox. Black and white. In Spanish. 82 minutes.

1933 El Rey de los Gitanos

The King of the Gypsies features Mojica as a gypsy monarch who has an affair with a princess he meets in disguise. The songs are gypsy-ish in style. Frank Strayer directed. Fox. Black and white. In Spanish. 82 minutes.

1934 Un Capitan de Cosacos

In *A Cossack Captain* Mojica portrays a 1910 Russian sea captain who falls in love with a woman he meets on a train. Andres De Segurola plays a general and John Reinhardt directed. Fox. Black and white. In Spanish. 81 minutes.

1934 La Cruz y la Espada

The Cross and the Sword is said to have influenced Mojica's thinking about the priesthood and religion. He portrays Brother Francisco in a story about an 18th century missionary in California. Frank Strayer directed. Fox. Black and white. In Spanish. 82 minutes.

1934 Las Fronteras del Amor

Mojica portrays an opera singer in *Frontiers of Love* and sings the Rigoletto aria "La donna è mobile." Most of the film takes place on a ranch and involves romance rather than opera. Frank Strayer directed. Fox. Black and white. In Spanish. 82 minutes.

1942 Melodias de las Americas

Melodies of the Americas is an Argentine film musical starring Mojica. Color. In Spanish. 82 minutes. Opera Dubs video.

1943 Sequire tus Pasos

Follow Your Steps is a Mexican film musical featuring Mojica. Black and white. 87 minutes. Opera Dubs video.

1952 El Portico de la Gloria

The Gate of Glory is a Mexican film musical featuring Mojica. Black and white. In Spanish. 91 minutes. Opera Dubs video.

1965 Yo Pecador - The Story of Jose Mojica

I, the Sinner is a Mexican film about the life of the singer based on his best-selling autobiography. Much of the film is a flashback showing his film and opera career in the U.S. There are excerpts from *Rigoletto*, *Il Trovatore*, *Madama Butterfly*, *La Bohème*, *La Favorita*, *Lucia di Lammermoor*, *L'Elisir d'Amore* and *Faust*. Pedro Geraldo portrays Mojica on screen but the singing voice is genuinely Mojica's. Alfonso Corona Blake directed. In Spanish. 90 minutes. Video Latino video.

MOLL, KURT
German bass (1938-)

Kurt Moll has become well known singing the bass roles in the Wagner operas but he is also impressive in Mozart as Osmin and Sarastro. He made his debut in 1961 in Aachen and stayed there until 1963. In 1970 he joined the Hamburg Staatsoper and soon was invited to sing at opera houses from Paris to Bayreuth. He made his debut at Covent Garden in 1977 and at the Metropolitan in 1978. Moll also sings Verdi and was well received as Don Quixote. Many of his great Wagner and Mozart performances are on video. See ABDUCTION FROM THE SERAGLIO, THE (1986), THE CREATION (1986), DON GIOVANNI (1990), THE MAGIC FLUTE (1983/1991), PARSIFAL (1993), DAS RHEINGOLD (1989), DER ROSENKAVALIER (1982/1984/1994), SIEGFRIED (1989), DIE WALKÜRE (1989/ 1990), WOZZECK (1972).

MONICELLI, MARIO
Italian film director (1915-)

Italian director Mario Monicelli, in addition to directing an excellent film biography of Rossini, also created a delightful operatic comedy with a clever use of Italian opera language. He is best known in the U.S. for his 1956 comedy *Big Deal on Madonna Street* (I Soliti Ignoti) and for his 1963 union film *The Organizer* (I Compagni). Monicelli has been nominated for two Oscars for his screenplays. See also GIOACHINO ROSSINI (1991).

1965 Casanova '70
This film includes Monicelli's delightful send-up of the oddities and pretensions of Italian operatic language. A Swedish woman visits Italy and arouses great merriment whenever she talks; she has learned the language from listening to Italian operas and always talks in the flowery operatic style. Marcello Mastroianni stars as a modern Casanova who is only interested in women if there is danger involved. Verna Lisi is the woman he loves. Color. In Italian. 113 minutes.

MONIUSZKO, STANISLAW
Polish composer (1819-1872)

Stanislaw Moniuszko is the major 19th century Polish opera composer and his 1848 opera *Halka* has become the Polish national opera. He studied in Berlin and began writing operettas in 1839, the best known being *The Lottery. Halka* was presented as a two-act opera in 1848 and revised to four acts for its major production in Warsaw in 1858. It made him an instant national celebrity and he had great success with his following operas, *The Raftsman* and *The Countess.* Most of his work is nationalist and patriotic and his 1865 opera *The Haunted Manor* was taken off stage because of its supposed ultra-patriotism. Moniuszko's operas and songs remain popular in Poland but are little known outside that country. Both *Halka* and The Haunted Manor have been filmed in Poland and are on CD. See HALKA, THE HAUNTED MANOR.

MONK, MEREDITH
American composer (1943-)

Meredith Monk is a multi-faceted multi-media artist-performer whose sometimes wordless "operas" may not be traditional but are certainly theatrical. *Juice,* her 1969 "theatre cantata," is scored for 85 voices, 85 jews harps and two violins. Her 1973 "opera" *Education of the Girlchild,* is for six women's voices, electric organ and piano. Her three-hour three-act opera *Atlas,* commissioned and staged by the Houston Grand Opera in 1991, is for chamber orchestra and voices. It tells of explorer Alexandra David-Neel whose journeys are spiritual as well as geographic. Monk even describes her film *Book of Days* as operatic.

1983 4 American Composers: Meredith Monk
British filmmaker Peter Greenaway shot this documentary portrait of Meredith Monk around theater performances she gave in London. She talks about her ideas, concerns, films, music and operas and there are excerpts from the opera *Education of a Girlchild* and the films *Quarry* and *Ellis Island.* Monk is seen in performance with her vocal group on *Dolmen Music* and *Turtle Dreams.* Channel Four/Transatlantic Films. Color. 60 minutes. Mystic Fire video.

1989 Book of Days
Monk's first film is a musical meditation on time and history and the connections of past and present. It is centered on a young Jewish woman in a medieval village who has visions of life today and tries to describe them to her grandfather. She dies in a plague but her drawings of airplanes and guns are found in our time. Black and white and color. In English. 77 minutes.

MONROE, MARILYN
American film actress (1926-1962)

Marilyn Monroe is the greatest myth figure of the modern cinema and has inspired at least two operas that have been staged. She has been transmuted from a real person into a myth that combines glamour with vulnerability. Excellent as she was in her best movies, like *Some Like It Hot* and *Gentleman Prefer Blondes,* it is Monroe's persona as an innocent with sexuality that has made her mythic. She projects the image of someone who needs to be protected and her relationships with Joe DiMaggio, Arthur Miller and the Kennedys helped bolster the legend. Monroe has inspired countless poems, books and paintings as well as operas.

MARILYN (1980)
Italian Lorenzo Ferrero composed his Fellini-esque opera about Monroe to a libretto by himself and

Floriana Bossi. It is subtitled "Scenes from the Fifties, after documents from American life" and presents portraits of the 1950s as well as Monroe's life. Ferrero looks at the Korean War, Joseph McCarthy and the persecution of Wilhelm Reich in the first half of the era and alternative culture heroes like Timothy Leary, Allen Ginsberg and the Beat writers in the second. Monroe's life disintegrates and she is shown rocking a doll to sleep after taking a drug overdose. The opera premiered at the Rome Opera Feb. 23, 1980.

MARILYN (1993)

American Ezra Laderman composed his documentary-like opera about Monroe to a libretto by playwright Norman Rosten. It consists of scenes from her life seen as flashbacks, memories and dreams but refrains from using real people as characters. It premiered at the New York City Opera in October 1993 with Kathryn Gamberoni portraying Monroe, Michael Rees Davis in the role of the Senator, Ron Baker as the Psychiatrist, Philip Cokorinos as husband Rick, Susanne Marsee as Rose, Michele McBride as Vinnie and John Lankston and Jonathan Green as Moguls. Jerome Sirlin designed and staged the opera while V. Jane Suttell created the costumes. Hal France conducted the New York City Opera Orchestra.

MONSIEUR CHOUFLEURI RESTERA CHEZ LUI LE...

1861 opérette bouffe by Offenbach

Mr. Cauliflower Will Be At Home On... is a delightful one-act operetta by Jacques Offenbach and librettist Conte de Morny. It's the story of a man attempting to break into Paris society through a musical soirée. When the singers don't appear, he and his daughter and her boyfriend impersonate them. The highlight of the operetta is a mock Italian trio called "Italia la bella." See also JACQUES OFFENBACH.

1951 NBC Opera Theatre

Virginia Haskins, Paul Franke and George Irving star in this English-language adaptation of the operetta titled *RSVP*. It was produced for NBC Opera Theatre by Samuel Chotzinoff as if the operetta were being imagined by Offenbach with Larry Weber portraying the composer. Dino Yannoulos wrote the adaptation and Peter Herman Adler conducted the Symphony of the Air Orchestra. Kirk Browning directed the telecast. Black and white. In English. 50 minutes. Video at MTR.

MONTALDO, GIULIANO

Italian film and opera director (1924-)

Giuliano Montaldo, one of the more important modern Italian film directors best known abroad for his 1953 *Chronicle of Poor Lovers*, has also directed a number of operas on stage. Two of his major Verona Arena productions are on video. See ATTILA (1985), TURANDOT (1983).

MONTARSOLO, PAOLO

Italian bass (1925-)

Paolo Montarsolo is a stylish basso buffo specialist who has been seen on stage in over 185 roles and can be experienced in many of them on film and video. He was born in Portici, studied at La Scala school and made his debut in Bologna in 1950. In 1957 he appeared at Glyndebourne in *L'Italiana in Algeri* and 1959 he starred in *Gianni Schicchi* at La Scala. He sang in Dallas in 1957 but did not reach the Metropolitan until 1975 when he starred in *Don Pasquale*. Among his popular roles are Basilio, Bartolo, Magnifico, Mustafa, Don Pasquale and Umberto in *La Serva Padrona*. See THE BARBER OF SEVILLE (1972), LA CENERENTOLA (1981), L' ELISIR D'AMORE (1959), THE MARRIAGE OF FIGARO (1976), LA SERVA PADRONA (1958).

MONTEMEZZI, ITALO

Italian composer (1875-1952)

Italo Montemezzi is remembered today for one opera, the 1913 *L'Amore dei Tre Re* (The Love of Three Kings), which was a smash hit at La Scala, the Met and Covent Garden in the early years of the century. It remained popular in the U.S. for many years but is currently out of fashion. Montemezzi's other major opera is the 1918 *La Nave* based on a famous play by D'Annunzio. See AMORE DEI TRE RE, L'.

MONTEVERDI, CLAUDIO

Italian composer (1567-1643)

Claudio Monteverdi is the earliest opera composer whose work is still in the repertory. He wrote his first great opera only a few years after the art form had been created, *Orfeo* in 1607, and nearly 400 years later that opera is still being staged. Monteverdi was born in Cremona, began his career in Mantua and spent most of his later years in Venice where he helped make opera spectacular and grandiose. Although he wrote some eighteen operas, only three survive. All are in the modern repertory and available on video. Monteverdi's operas received notable Zurich stage productions in the 1970s from director Jean-Pierre Ponnelle and conductor Nicholas Harnoncourt. The productions were later filmed and are on video. See L'INCORONAZIONE DI POPPEA, ORFEO; IL RITORNO D'ULISSE IN PATRIA.

1989 The Music of Man Vol. 3
Monteverdi and the growth of opera are central to *New Voices for Man*, Vol. 3 in the Canadian *The Music of Man* series. The video includes staged scenes from *Orfeo* and a brief history of the composer. Yehudi Menuhin is the narrator. Color. 60 minutes. Home Vision video.

1989 Vespro della Beata Vergine
Monteverdi's life as a composer is described by John Elliot Gardiner in Venice at the beginning of this video; afterward he leads a performance of the *Vespers of the Blessed Virgin* in St. Mark's Basilica. The soloists are sopranos Ann Monoyios and Marinella Pennicchi, countertenor Michael Chance, tenors Mark Tucker, Nigel Robson and Sandro Naglio and basses Bryn Terfel and Alastair Miles. They are supported by the Monteverdi Choir, the London Oratory Junior Choir, His Majesties Sagbutts & Cornetts and the English Baroque Soloists. Color. In English and Latin. 111 minutes. Archiv video.

1993 Banquet of the Senses
This is a program of Monteverdi madrigals performed like mini-operas at the palace of the Duke of Mantua where they were composed. They are sung and acted by Anthony Rooley's Consort of Musike with sopranos Emma Kirby and Evelyn Tubb, tenors Andrew King and Joseph Cornwell, alto Mary Nichols and bass Simon Grant. There is artistic and historical commentary by Rooley, who also directed the video, and the singing is counterpointed by scenes of the palace. Color. In Italian. 60 minutes. Musica Oscura/Columns Classics video.

MOORE, DOUGLAS
American composer (1893-1969)

Douglas Moore wrote twelve operas, mostly on American subjects, and was one of the chief architects of the modern American opera. He had his biggest success with the 1956 Colorado silver mining romance *The Ballad of Baby Doe*, which for a time was considered the great American opera. His other popular operas include *The Devil and Daniel Webster* (1938) and *Carrie Nation* (1966) about the anti-saloon campaigner. He won the Pulitzer Prize for *Giants in the Earth* (1949), which tells of a pioneer family in South Dakota. He also wrote music for films. *The Ballad of Baby Doe* and *Gallantry* have been telecast and *Ballad* and *Carrie Nation* have been recorded but surprisingly there are no commercial videos of any of Moore's operas. See THE BALLAD OF BABY DOE, GALLANTRY.

MOORE, GRACE
American soprano (1901-1947)

Glamorous Tennessee-born American opera diva Grace Moore became a major movie star at Columbia in the 1930s and her success created a new audience for opera as well as a rush of singers to Hollywood. None of the others quite repeated her success but the trend did ensure that opera singers of the period can usually be seen on film. Moore began her singing career very successfully in musical comedy and operetta in New York and then went to France to study opera. She made her Metropolitan Opera debut in 1928 as Mimi in *La Bohème* (it was a major social event after her Broadway success) and she was again successful, continuing to sing at the Met until 1944. Her first Hollywood films made for MGM, a Jenny Lind biography and the operetta *New Moon*, were not a success but after she starred on the New York stage in 1932 in a production of Millocker's operetta *Du Barry*, she was given a second chance by Columbia. *One Night of Love* was a critical and box-office hit, surprising even the studio and winning an Oscar nomination for the singer. Moore continued to make Hollywood films through the 1930s and then went to France to make a film of her favorite opera, *Louise*. She also took on Dorothy Kirsten as her protégé and published a 1944 autobiography called *You're Only Human Once*. She died in a plane crash in Denmark in 1947 while on a concert tour. Hollywood honored her with a film biography in 1953 titled *So This Is Love*. See also JENNY LIND (1930), LOUISE (1939), THE NEW MOON (1930).

1934 One Night of Love

Moore's best film. In the first ten minutes there are delightful operatic sequences like a balcony "Sempre libera" with Moore singing over a Milan courtyard full of competing musicians and a *Lucia di Lammermoor* Sextet devised to divert a landlady from collecting rent. Moore was liked by movie audiences for her personality as well as her voice. She looks wonderful, acts splendidly and sings superbly as an aspiring opera singer with a demanding teacher (Tullio Carminati). He turns her into a diva while falling in love with her and she ends up at the Met in *Madama Butterfly*. Moore also has a fine scene on stage singing *Carmen*. Spanish bass Andres De Segurola plays her first teacher and Luis Alberni is Carminati's pianist. The film won two Academy Awards and Moore was nominated for Best Actress but lost to Claudette Colbert. Pietro Cimini conducted the opera music and Victor Schertzinger directed the film. Columbia. Black and white. 80 minutes. Columbia video and laserdisc.

1935 Love Me Forever

Love Me Forever was also a hit for Moore. She portrays a poor but talented soprano who gets to sing in *La Bohème* at the Met opposite Michael Bartlett through the help of music-loving gangster Leo Carrillo. The film features a mockup of the old Met and an impersonation of Met general manager Giulio Gatti-Casazza by Thurston Hall. The *Rigoletto* quartet is expanded to include 40 voices, Hollywood-style, and Luis Alberni is in fine frenzied form. Victor Schertzinger wrote and directed. British title: *On Wings of Song*. Columbia. Black and white. 90 minutes.

1936 The King Steps Out

Josef von Sternberg directed Grace Moore in this musical based on Fritz Kreisler's 1932 Vienna operetta *Sissy*. She portrays Elizabeth (Cissy), the daughter of the Duke of Bavaria. Moore is in terrific frothy Viennese operetta voice and is allowed to sing quite a lot including the operetta's famous song "Stars in My Eyes." Franchot Tone plays the Emperor Franz Josef whom she marries in the end. This was a precursor of the famous Sissi films of the 1950s starring Romy Schneider. Columbia. Black and white. 85 minutes.

1937 When You're in Love

Moore portrays an Austrian opera star who pays Cary Grant to become her husband so she can sing in the United States. Naturally they fall in love by the end of the movie. Moore sings "Vissi d'arte" from *Tosca*, "Un bel di" from *Madama Butterfly* and the Waltz Song from Gounod's *Roméo et Juliette* as well as a delightful "Minnie the Moocher" in homage to Cab Calloway. The film was written and directed by the great screenwriter Robert Riskin. British title: *For You Alone*. Columbia. Black and white. 104 minutes.

1937 I'll Take Romance

Moore's last American film before she left to make *Louise* in Europe with Abel Gance. She portrays an opera diva romanced by Melvyn Douglas in a plot involving whether she will sing in Argentina or Paris. Moore sings arias from *La Traviata, Martha, Manon* and *Madama Butterfly*. Wilhelm Von Wymetal Jr. staged the opera sequences and Isaac Van Grove conducted the opera orchestra. Oscar Hammerstein II wrote the title tune and Edward H. Griffith directed the film. Black and white. 85 minutes.

1953 So This is Love

Kathryn Grayson portrays Grace Moore in this glossy film biography directed by Gordon Douglas. It finishes on stage at the Metropolitan Opera with Moore as Mimi in *La Bohème* and Grayson singing "Mi chiamano Mimi." Most of the film concerns Moore's early struggles to succeed, her success as a Broadway musical star and her departure to Paris to study opera. She returns in glory two years later for her 1928 Met debut. Also known as *The Grace Moore Story*. Warner Bros. Color. 101 minutes.

MORENO TORROBA, FEDERICO
Spanish composer (1891-1982)

Federico Moreno Torroba composed many operas but is mostly remembered for his zarzuelas, especially the 1932 *Luisa Fernanda*. The Madrid-born musician was also an important newspaper critic and a much-admired conductor. At the age of 80 he conducted thirteen classic zarzuelas for a major Spanish television film series called Teatro Lirico Español. At the age of 89 he wrote his last opera, *El Poeta*, on a commission from Placido Domingo who starred in the 1980 world premiere. See LUISA FERNANDA, EL POETA.

MORITZ, REINER
German opera video producer (1941-)

Reiner Moritz is relatively unknown to the opera public but is one of the key people in the filming and distribution of opera on video. He is the founder of RM Arts and it is often up to him to decide whether there will be a telecast and video of a production. Moritz, who is based in Munich, has been working in television for 35 years. A large number of the videos listed in this book were created through RM Arts.

MORRIS, JAMES
American bass-baritone (1947-)

James Morris studied with Rosa Ponselle in his native Baltimore where he made his debut in 1967 in *The Tales of Hoffmann*. He joined the Metropolitan Opera in 1970 starting with the King in *Aida* and later singing Don Giovanni and other lead roles. He found major international success in Wagner singing Wotan in the Ring cycle in Europe and America. His imposing voice and presence have made him particularly suitable in this role. See also LA BOHÈME (1982), LUISA MILLER (1979), DON GIOVANNI (1979), MACBETH (1972/1987), METROPOLITAN OPERA (1975/1991), DAS RHEINGOLD (1990), DER RING DES NIBELUNGEN (1990), SIEGFRIED (1990), THE TALES OF HOFFMANN (1988), DIE WALKÜRE (1990).

MOSES UND ARON
1930-1957 opera by Schoenberg

Moses and Aaron, a deeply religious opera, is the most often staged of Arnold Schoenberg's operas, though it has never been popular with the public. It was originally composed in 1930 but Schoenberg went on revising it until his death and never finished it. A concert version premiered in Hamburg in 1954. As Moses and Aaron lead the Israelites out of Egypt to the Promised Land, there is despair by the people as they wait for the Ten Commandments. They erect and worship the Golden Calf. Moses is a speaking part, Aaron is a tenor and the voice of God is six singers. See also ARNOLD SCHOENBERG.

1975 Jean-Marie Straub film
German filmmakers Jean-Marie Straub and Danièle Huillet created this austere film of the opera starring Gunter Reich as Moses and Louis Devos as Aaron. This is one of the most demanding opera films and has never been popular though it was widely shown at film festivals. Straub-Huillet adapted the opera to the screen emphasizing the philosophical rather than the dramatic content of the opera. They shot it on location in an ancient Roman amphitheater in the south of Italy. Everything in the film is said to be authentic, even the blood. Michael Gielen conducted the orchestra. Color. In German with English subtitles. 105 minutes. Opera Dubs video.

MOZART, WOLFGANG A.
Austrian composer (1756-1791)

Wolfgang Amadeus Mozart is arguably the greatest opera composer and unquestionably the most favored by filmmakers. There are numerous screen versions of his operas and nearly as many biographies. The most impressive videos as a group are the Drottningholm Court Theater productions in which Arnold Östman and his colleagues restore period charm to Mozart. Two of the truly great operas films are Ingmar Bergman's *The Magic Flute* and Joseph Losey's *Don Giovanni*; Mozart's music is also used in countless non-operatic films. The biographical films, which began as early as 1909, are romanticized but usually interesting for their music. See THE ABDUCTION FROM THE SERAGLIO, LA CLEMENZA DI TITO, COSÌ FAN TUTTE, DON GIOVANNI, LA FINTA GIARDINIERA, IDOMENEO, THE IMPRESARIO, THE MAGIC FLUTE, THE MARRIAGE OF FIGARO, MITRIDATE, MOZART AND SALIERI, MOZART REQUIEM, IL RE PASTORE, ZAIDE.

1909 Mozart's Last Requiem
French director Louis Feuillade's *La Mort de Mozart*, released in the U.S. with the above title, is the first film biography of the composer. Mozart feels compelled to write a Requiem Mass as he thinks death is near but his doctor orders him to rest. While listening to a student play violin, he has visions of scenes from *The Marriage of Figaro*, *Don Giovanni* and *The Magic Flute*. He cannot resist working on his *Requiem* and when it is finished a group of friends visit him. They sing the *Requiem* and he dies. The film was made by Gaumont, distributed in the U.S. by George Kleine and screened with live Mozart music. French title. Black and white. About 15 minutes. Prints survive.

1921 Mozarts Leben, Lieben und Leiden

Mozart's Life, Love and Suffering is a feature-length Austrian film biography starring Josef Zetenius as Mozart and Dora Kaiser as Konstanze. The cast includes Lili Fröhlich, Alice Grobois, Käte Schindler, Paul Gerhardt and Mizzi Trentin. It was directed by Otto Kreisler and Karl Toma and premiered at the Mozart Week celebrations in Salzburg in 1921. Black and white. In German. About 75 minutes.

1936 Whom the Gods Love

Stephen Haggard portrays Mozart in this British film biography written by Margaret Kennedy. Director Basil Dean's wife Victoria Hopper plays Mozart's wife Constance Weber, Liane Haid is Mozart's first love Aloysia Weber, Hubert Harben is Leopold Mozart, Jean Cadell is Mozart's mother and George Curzon is Lorenzo Da Ponte. The film consists of sketches about Mozart's life including Constance's rejection of a prince and the recognition of Mozart's genius just before his death. There are extracts from *The Marriage of Figaro* and *The Magic Flute*. Sir Thomas Beecham conducts the London Symphony Orchestra. The film was reissued in 1949 with the title *Mozart*. ATP. Black and white. In English. 82 minutes.

1939 Eine Kleine Nachtmusik

A Little Night Music is a German film based on a charming short novel by Eduard Mörike called *Mozart on the Road to Prague*. It describes an imaginary stopover the composer made in 1787 while on his way to Prague for the premiere of *Don Giovanni*. Hannes Stelzer stars as Mozart with a cast including Christl Mardayn, Heili Finkenzeller, Gustav Waldau and Kurt Meisel. The score consists of Mozart music arranged by Alois Melichar. Leopold Hainisch directed the film. Black and white. In German. 92 minutes.

1940 Melodie Eterne

Eternal Melodies is an Italian film biography starring Gino Cervi as Mozart and directed by opera film specialist Carmine Gallone. Luisella Beghi is Constanza, Conchita Montenegro is Aloysia, Maria Jocobini is mother Anna Maria Mozart, Jone Salina is sister Nannina Mozart and Luigi Pavese is father Leopoldo Mozart. The plot is devoted to Mozart's relationship with the Weber sisters as the film follows him from early years to great success. The voice singing Mozart arias on the soundtrack belongs to Margherita Carosio. Ernest Marischka wrote the screenplay and Achise Brizze was the cinematographer. Black and white. In Italian. 99 minutes.

1942 Wen die Götter lieben

Whom the Gods Love is an Austrian film biography starring Hans Holt as Mozart. It tells the story of the composer's life from the time he leaves Salzburg and focuses on his relationships with his wife and her sister. The cast includes Winnie Markus as Konstanze, René Deltgen as Beethoven, Paul Hörbiger, Irene von Meyerdorff and Walter Janssen. There are several opera scenes including one with Edna Berger as the Queen of the Night. There is also a non-historical visit by the young Beethoven to the dying Mozart. Karl Hartl directed from a screenplay by Richard Billinger and Eduard von Borsody. The music is played by the Vienna Philharmonic Orchestra. Black and white. 112 minutes. In German. On video.

1948 The Mozart Story

This American adaptation of the 1942 Austrian film *Wen die Götter lieben* is virtually a different film with an added framing structure featuring Salieri and Haydn. It is also a prototype for *Amadeus* as it begins with Salieri describing the events of the composer's life after his death. Envy has caused Salieri to oppose Mozart but now he wants to preserve his music and reputation. Karl Hartl directed the original film adapted for America by Frank Wisbar. Hans Holt stars as Mozart with Wilton Graff as Salieri, William Vedder as Haydn and Winnie Markus as Konstanze. The music is by the Vienna Philharmonic. Black and white. In English. 93 minutes. Opera Dubs/Video Yesteryear video.

1954 Unsterblicher Mozart

The Austrian film *Unsterblicher Mozart* (Immortal Mozart) features highlight version of three Mozart operas performed on stage by the Mozart Ensemble of the Vienna State Opera. They are *The Abduction from the Seraglio, Don Giovanni* and *The Marriage of Figaro*. Details under the operas. Color. In German. 95 minutes. Taurus (Germany) video.

1955 The Life and Loves of Mozart

Reich mir die Hand, mein Leben is an Austrian film starring Oskar Werner as Mozart. It was written and directed by Karl Hartl who made the 1942 Mozart film *Wen die Götter lieben*. Mozart is shown at the end of his life composing *The Magic Flute* and having a love affair with Nannina Gottlieb who created the role of Pamina. Johanna Mata portrays Gottlieb, Gertrud Kueckelman is Konstanze, Nadja Tiller is Aloysia, Erich Kuna is Schikaneder and Albin Skoda is Salieri. Hilde Gueden, Erika Köth, Gottlob Frick, Erich Kunz, Else Liebesberg and Anton Dermota are heard on the soundtrack with Hans Swarowsky conducting the Vienna Philharmonic Orchestra. Oskar Schnirch was the cinematographer. Black and white. In German. 100 minutes.

1967 The Life of Mozart
Das Leben Mozarts is an exemplary non-fiction German film about Mozart by Hans Conrad Fischer. It is a finely researched and comprehensive survey of the composer's life and music using original letters, documents, paintings and buildings. There are no enactments but there are photographs of places and cities associated with the composer all over Europe. Portraits of the period alternate with performances of Mozart's music by leading singers, orchestras and conductors including Fritz Wunderlich, Erika Koth, Maria Stader, Fiorenza Cossotto, Walter Berry and Lotte Schadle. Black and white. In German. 140 minutes. Hanssler (Germany) video.

1973 The Great Composers: W.A. Mozart
The Great Composers series consists of six documentary videos designed as introductions with selections from the composer's music. Featured on the Mozart video are Nina Milkina, the London Mozart Players and the Salzburg Puppet theater. Color. In English. 25 minutes. IFB video.

1974 Mozart: A Childhood Chronicle
Mozart: Autzeichnungen einer Jugend is an impressive German film biography by Klaus Kirschner. It depicts the composer from the age of seven to twenty using his family's letters as its off-screen narrative. Young Mozart is filmed traveling around Europe by coach and visiting various scenes of his early life. Pavlos Bekiaris portrays Mozart at seven, Diego Crovetti plays him at twelve and Santiago Ziesmer is the composer at twenty. Marianne Lowitz is his mother, Karl-Maria Schley is his father and Ingeborg Schroeder and Nina Palmers play his sister Nannerl aged eleven and seventeen. The soundtrack voices belong to Helen Donath, Eugene Ratti and Graziella Sciutti and Mozart's music is played on authentic instruments. Pitt Koch was cinematographer. Black

and white. In German with English subtitles. 224 mins. Kino video and laser.

1975 Mozart in Love
Experimental American filmmaker Mark Rappaport's Mozart biography does not resemble the standard biopic but it is still intriguing, funny and sometimes inspired. The composer's intense interest in the Weber sisters Aloysia and Konstanze is a focus of the film with the actors in costume standing in front of backdrop projections and miming their roles. Arias from Mozart operas provide the basis of the soundtrack. Color. 80 minutes.

1984 The Three of Us
Noi Tre is a charming Italian film by Pupi Avati about the fourteen-year-old Mozart and the summer he spent in Bologna in 1770. He was brought there by his father to prepare for an examination at the Philharmonic Institute and stayed at the country estate of a count. He becomes friends with the count's son and a girl neighbor and enjoys non-genius life so much that he tries to flunk the exam. Christopher Davidson portrays Mozart, Lino Capolicchio is Leopoldo, Dario Parsini is the young friend and Barbara Rebeschini is the girl. Color. In Italian. 90 minutes.

1984 Amadeus
The most famous film biography of the composer and a deserved multiple Academy Award winner. Czech-born American director Milos Forman knows his Mozart and did an excellent job of recreating the period and the attitudes of the protagonists. Tom Hulce portrays Mozart, Murray Abraham is Salieri, Elizabeth Berridge is Constanze, Simon Callow is Schikaneder, Roy Dotrice is Leopold Mozart and Jeffrey Jones is the Emperor. The opera scenes, staged by Twyla Tharpe, were filmed in Prague's Tyl Theater where *Don Giovanni* premiered. Major scenes are devoted to *The Marriage of Figaro* with Samuel Ramey as Figaro, *Don Giovanni* and *The Magic Flute*. Peter Shaffer wrote the screenplay based on his own play. Color. In English. 160 minutes. HBO video/ Pioneer laser (laserdisc includes a documentary about the film called *The Last Laugh* and a production book).

1985 Forget Mozart
Vergesst Mozart is a German film structured like a murder mystery and set on December 5, 1791, the

day of Mozart's death. When his friends gather around his deathbed, the chief of the secret police locks them in and begins to ask questions. Everyone seems to have had a motive to kill the composer and Mozart's connection with the Free Masons is particularly suspicious. There is also the idea that he committed slow suicide. Max Tidof portrays Mozart with Armin Mueller-Stahl as police chief Pergen, Catarina Raacke as Konstanze, Uwe Ochsenknecht as Schikaneder and Winfried Glatzeder as Salieri. The film features staged scenes from *The Marriage of Figaro* with Juraj Hrubant as Figaro and *The Magic Flute* with Ondrej Malachovsky as Sarastro. It was directed by Slavo Luther and written by Zdenek Mahler, Werner Uschkurat and Jirina Koenig. Color. In German with English subtitles. 93 minutes. Water Bearer Films video.

1987 Mozart
This short film about Mozart and his music, written and directed by Nicholas Vazsonyi, was made for the Klassix 13 series. It features Anthony Quayle and Balint Vazsony visiting Salzburg and Vienna and talking about the places the composer lived. There are staged enactments of scenes from his life and a good deal of Mozart music. The film was made for Canadian and Hungarian TV. Color. In English. 55 minutes. MPI video.

1991 Mozart on Tour series
The *Mozart on Tour* series of seven laser discs consists of thirteen documentary films about Mozart's travels in Europe and the music he composed on those trips plus fourteen piano concertos. They are presented by André Previn and were filmed in the European cities visited by the composer. Volume 1 is titled *London: The First Journey*, Volume 2 is *Mantua: Initial Steps* and Volume 3 is *Milan and Bologna: Learning by Traveling*, etc. The documentary films are from twenty to thirty minutes in length and are based on the letters and diaries of the Mozarts. Color. In English. Each laser disc is about 75 minutes.

1991 Following Mozart
A German film set in Mozart's era about a group of orphan musicians living near Dresden. They have entered a major competition and want to perform Mozart's famous piano rondo KV 382, "the one with the trill in it." It has not been published so the cleverest of the children, Trina (Maria Ferrens), follows Mozart around Germany trying to obtain a copy. Karl Heinz Lotz directed the film. Color. In German. 87 minutes.

1991 Mozart Gala
A three-hour celebration of Mozart's operas at the Verona Arena taped in August 1991 and released on three videos. Vol. One (63 minutes) features arias from *Don Giovanni* and *La Clemenza di Tito*, Vol. Two (72 minutes) has *Così Fan Tutte*, *Idomeneo* and *The Marriage of Figaro* and Vol. Three (63 minutes) features *The Abduction from the Seraglio* and *The Magic Flute*. The singers are sopranos Kathleen Cassello, Katia Ricciarelli, Anna Maria Blasi, Evelyn Holzschuh, Donna Ellen and Sona Ghzarin; mezzos Susan Quittmayer, Jutta Geister and Ann Murray; tenors Jerry Hadley, Franz Supper and Francisco Araiza; baritones Lucio Gallo, James Morris and Andrea Piccinni and bassos Evgeny Nesterenko and Hannes Jokel. The chorus came from the Linz Landestheater and the orchestra from the Vienna Mozart Academy. The conductors are Theodor Guschlbauer, Johannes Wildner and Ernst Dunschirm. Color. In Italian. 198 minutes. On video.

1992 Mozart: The Opera Experience
An instructive compilation of scenes from Mozart operas with commentary and introductions by Richard Baker. The excerpts, all from videos of performances at the Glyndebourne Festival, are from *Abduction from the Seraglio*, *Così Fan Tutte*, *Don Giovanni*, *Idomeneo*, *The Magic Flute* and *The Marriage of Figaro*. Performers include Kiri Te Kanawa, Benjamin Luxon and Leo Goeke. Mark Gasser portrays Mozart. Bob Carruthers and Graham Holloway produced. Color. 90 minutes. Options/Cromwell video.

1994 Mozart
A biographical documentary about the composer made for the *Biography* series on the Arts & Entertainment cable network. Performers includes Zubin Mehta and Isaac Stern. Color. 50 minutes. A& E video.

MOZART AND SALIERI
1898 opera by Rimsky-Korsakov

Pushkin's verse tragedy *Motsart i Salyeri* tells of Salieri's supposed murder of Mozart and provides the libretto for Nikolai Rimsky-Korsakov's chamber opera. It is based on the same folk legend as *Amadeus*. Salieri envies Mozart's divine genius and poisons him at a dinner at a inn after Mozart tells him about his *Requiem*. The opera is a brilliant homage to Mozart with quotations from his operas embedded in the score. The baritone role of Salieri was created by Chaliapin, the tenor role of Mozart by Vasily Skafter and the pianist by Sergei Rachmaninoff. See also NIKOLAI RIMSKY-KORSAKOV.

1962 Vladimir Gorikker film
The great Russian actor Innokenti Smoktunovsky stars as Mozart in this Soviet film of the opera made in Latvia. It was directed by opera film specialist Vladimir Gorikker assisted by his fine cinematographer Vadim Mass. Pyotry Glebov portrays Salieri and A. Milbret has the role of the blind musician. The film was distributed in the U.S. as *Requiem for Mozart*. Riga Film. Black and white. In Russian. 47 minutes. Corinth video.

Related film

1914 Symphony of Love and Death
Alexander Geirot portrays Mozart with A. Michurin as Salieri in *Simfoniya Lyubvi I Smerti*, an early Russian silent film based on the play by Pushkin that also inspired the opera. Victor Tourjansky, who later made many films in France and Germany, directed. Black and white. About 50 minutes.

MOZART REQUIEM
1891 Mass by Mozart

There are four videos of Mozart's *Requiem in D Minor*, a work featured in *Amadeus* and most of the biographical films about the composer. It was his last composition, K.626, and Mozart was convinced that he was composing it as his own requiem. While not an opera, it merits a separate entry because of its constant use in Mozart films and the many videos of it featuring major opera singers. See also WOLFGANG A. MOZART.

1988 Abbey Church, Bavaria
Marie McLaughlin, Maria Ewing, Jerry Hadley and Cornelius Hauptmann are the featured singers in this performance filmed in the Abbey Church, Diessen am Ammersee in Upper Bavaria. Leonard Bernstein conducts the Bavarian Radio Symphony Orchestra and Chorus. This beautifully sung and filmed production was directed for video by

Humphrey Burton Color. In Latin. 65 minutes. DG video.

1991 St. Stephen's Cathedral, Vienna
Cecilia Bartoli, Arleen Auger, Vinson Cole and René Pape are the featured singers in this performance in Vienna's St. Stephen's Cathedral. Mozart's funeral rites were held in this church and the video is of a Requiem Mass celebrated by Cardinal Groer on the 200th anniversary of his death. Georg Solti leads the Vienna Philharmonic Orchestra and Vienna State Opera Chorus. The Mass is preceded by a film telling the story of the Requiem. Humphrey Burton directed the video with Michael Weinmann. Color. In Latin. 93 minutes. London video and laser.

1991 Palace of Catalan Music, Barcelona
Barbara Bonney, Anne-Sofie Von Otter, Anthony Rolfe Johnson and Alastair Miles are featured in this performance of the *Requiem* plus the *Mass* in C Minor in the ornate Palau de la Musica Catalana in Barcelona. It was taped on Dec. 5, 1991, on the 200th anniversary of Mozart's death. John Eliot Gardiner conducts the Monteverdi Choir and the English Baroque Soloists. Jonathan Fuller directed the video. Color. In Latin. 106 minutes. Philips video and laser

1994 Requiem from Sarajevo
José Carreras, Ruggero Raimondi, Ildiko Komlosi and Cecilia Gasdia are the star soloists in this moving, dramatic performance of the Requiem in Sarajevo on the site of the city's devastated historic library. The film is intercut with scenes of the siege of the city. Zubin Mehta conducts the Sarajevo Cathedral Choir and the Sarajevo Philharmonic Orchestra. The film was produced by Mario Dradi and Francesco Stochino Weiss. Color. In Latin. 60 minutes. A & E video.

MUETTE DE PORTICI, LA
1828 opera by Auber

The Mute Girl of Portici is probably the only opera in which the title character can't talk let alone sing. Fenella, the mute girl of the title, mimes her role and leaps dramatically into Mount Vesuvius at the climax of the opera. The principal singer is her brother, a Neapolitan fisherman and revolutionary called Masaniello. He leads the revolt against the Spanish but is killed by his own men at the end. Daniel Auber's *La Muette de Portici* is considered the first grand opera and was celebrated for its revolutionary fervor in the 19th century. It has a complex French libretto by Germain Delavigne and Eugène Scribe. The early popularity of the story is attested by the number of films it inspired but there are currently no commercial videos of the opera. A non-professional version is available from Lyric and Opera Dubs. See also DANIEL AUBER.

1910 Ambrosio film
An early Italian silent version of the opera story was made in Turin by Ambrosio Films with the title *La Muta di Portici*. About 10 minutes

1916 Anna Pavlova film
Dancer Anna Pavlova starred as Fenella, the mute heroine of the opera, in this famous Universal feature called *The Dumb Girl of Portici*. Rupert Julien was featured as Masaniello. The musical accompaniment for the film, based on Auber's melodies, was arranged by Adolph Schmidt. Pioneer woman filmmaker Lois Wilson wrote and directed the film in collaboration with Phillips Smalley. Black and white. In English. About 80 minutes.

1924 Cecyl Tryan film
Cecyl Tryan stars as the mute Fenella with Livio Pavanelli as her brother Masaniello in this Italian film based on the libretto of the opera. Telemaco Ruggeri wrote and directed this *La Muta di Portici* made for AG Film in Rome. Black and white. In Italian. About 70 minutes.

1940 Luisa Ferida film
Mario Bonnard directed this Italian film of the story titled *La Fanciulla di Portici* (The Portici Girl) without the Auber music and apparently without the heroine being mute. Luisa Ferida stars as the Portici "girl" with Carlo Ninchi as Masaniello. Black and white. In Italian. 88 minutes.

1953 Flora Mariel film
Flora Mariel stars as the mute Lucia in this version of *La Muta di Portici*. The reason she is mute here is because she was tortured after refusing to reveal the hiding place of her brother Masaniello, portrayed by Paolo Carlini. Giorgio Ansoldi directed the film. Black and white. In Italian. 85 minutes.

MUSEUM OF TELEVISION AND RADIO

The Museum of Television and Radio (MTR), which has viewing facilities in New York and Los Angles, has over 70,000 videos for viewing including a large number of television programs devoted to opera. It has mounted full-scale tributes to the Metropolitan Opera and Leonard Bernstein, for example, and has comprehensive holdings on both. It also has extensive archives of historically important TV opera series like the *CBS Television Opera Theater*, *NBC Opera Theatre*, *Voice of Firestone*, *Bell Telephone Hour*, *Cameo Operas*, etc. It offers immediate viewing access to its tapes to anyone for a relatively small fee.

MUNSEL, PATRICE
American soprano (1923-)

Patrice Munsel has been as acclaimed for her light opera roles as for her coloratura performances. She was born in Spokane, Washington, and made her debut at the Metropolitan in 1943 at the age of eighteen in *Mignon*, the youngest singer ever signed by the Met. She sang a range of operas from *Lucia di Lammermoor* and *The Barber of Seville* to *Die Fledermaus* and *La Périchole*. Munsel retired from the Met in 1957 but sang with the Dallas Civic Opera in 1963 in *L'Incoronazione di Poppea*. She also hosted a 1950s TV variety show called the *Patrice Munsel Show* in which she sang opera arias and popular songs. Munsel starred in a film portraying Australian soprano Nellie Melba and sang on several *Voice of Firestone* shows available on video. See NELLIE MELBA (1953).

1951-1962 Patrice Munsel in Opera & Song
Highlights from the soprano's appearances on *The Voice of Firestone* television series in 1951 and 1962. Munsel sings arias from *Die Fledermaus*, *La Bohème*, *Louise*, *The Daughter of the Regiment* and *Madama Butterfly* and popular songs like "Home Sweet Home," "In the Still of the Night" and "I've Got You Under My Skin." Black and white. 55 minutes. VAI video.

MURDER AT THE OPERA
Mystery fiction on the screen

There are a great number of murders and assassinations in operas so it is no surprise to find that there have been a number of murder mystery movies with an operatic background. In *Fatal Lady*, opera diva Mary Ellis is accused of murders at two different opera houses. In *Charlie Chan at the Opera*, Boris Karloff is suspected of murdering another singer on-stage. In *Moonlight Murder*, a tenor is mysteriously murdered during a Hollywood Bowl performance of *Il Trovatore*. In the Beniamino Gigli film *Solo Per Te*, a baritone is murdered backstage during a performance of *Un Ballo in Maschera*. In *Find the Witness*, a temperamental female opera star is the murder victim. In Geraldine Farrar's film *The Turn of the Wheel*, she has to discover who really murdered the hero's wife. Opera singers Helen Traubel and Anna Moffo have both been featured in murder mystery movies and Traubel even wrote one titled *The Metropolitan Opera Murders* (it was actually ghostwritten by Harold Q. Masur). And finally the most famous of all opera murder mysteries, *The Phantom of the Opera* movies. The Phantom does in a goodly number of folks in a truly operatic manner. See CHARLIE CHAN AT THE OPERA, MARY ELLIS (1936), GERALDINE FARRAR (1918), BENIAMINO GIGLI (1937), HOLLYWOOD BOWL (1936), ANNA MOFFO (1970), THE PHANTOM OF THE OPERA, HELEN TRAUBEL (1967).

MUSIC IN THE AIR
1932 operetta by Kern

Jerome Kern's operetta *Music in the Air* is in the same pattern as his earlier *The Cat and the Fiddle* with a plot based around preparations for staging an operetta. Oscar Hammerstein II wrote the lyrics and book as he had for *Show Boat*. Bavarian villagers Sieglinde and Karl go to Munich and become involved with operetta writer Bruno and his diva Frieda. When Frieda walks out on the premiere of his new operetta, Sieglinde gets her chance to become a star. She flops. See also JEROME KERN.

1934 Gloria Swanson film
Gloria Swanson stars as the temperamental operetta diva quarreling with lyricist lover John Boles in this film version of the Kern operetta. Swanson takes up with Bavarian schoolteacher Douglas s Montgomery to make him jealous so Boles flirts with the teacher's sweetheart June Lang. One of Kern's finest scores including "I've told every little star." Billy Wilder and Howard Young wrote the script and Joe May directed. Black and white. 85 minutes.

MUSIC PERFORMANCE RESEARCH CENTER, LONDON

The Music Performance Research Center (MPRC) is a London audio-video library of live public music performances with a selection of opera videotapes. Its holdings, many quite rare, go back half a century and there is unique footage like Kirsten Flagstad and Maggie Teyte singing in *Dido and Aeneas* at the opening of the Mermaid Theatre in 1951. The donated BBC Television programs include a 1962 profile of Boris Christoff in which he sings arias from *Boris Godunov*. The MPRC is located at the Barbican Music Library in London.

MUSIC WITH ROOTS IN THE AETHER
1976 television opera by Ashley

American composer Robert Ashley created this unusual opera for television in seven two-hour episodes and premiered it at the Paris Festival D'Automne in 1976. It is devoted to contemporary musicians working in non-notational styles. Each episode includes an interview and a performance against a landscape backdrop with an ensemble led by the composer. Ashley is the focus of one video with an interview and performances of his operas *What She Thinks* and *Title Withdrawn* featuring Paul DeMarinis, Mimi Johnson, Robert Sheff and Ashley. The other six episodes center around Philip Glass (a scene from *Einstein on the Beach*), David Behrman, Alvin Lucier, Gordon Mumma, Pauline Oliveros and Terry Riley. The seven episodes were edited into one-hour television programs in 1985. Color. In English. 14 hours. Lovely Music video. See also ROBERT ASHLEY.

MUSSORGSKY, MODEST
Russian composer (1839-1881)

Modest Mussorgsky (or Musorgsky) created what many consider the greatest Russian opera, *Boris Godunov*, as well as the popular *Khovanshchina*. He began composing operas in 1856 but left most of his efforts unfinished. *Boris* was completed but did not become popular until it was (controversially) refashioned and smoothed out by Rimsky-Korsakov who also completed *Khovanshchina* after the composer's death. Mussorgsky's "Night on Bald Mountain," used to such dramatic effect in

Disney's *Fantasia*, was used by the composer in the opera project *Mlada* and the opera *The Fair at Sorochintsi*, both uncompleted. There are a number of films and videos of *Boris Godunov* and *Khovanshchina* and reasonable Soviet film biography of the composer. See BORIS GODUNOV, KHOVANSHCHINA.

1950 Mussorgsky

Alexander Borisov stars as Mussorgsky in the 1950 Soviet film biography Mussorgsky, a Cannes Film Festival prizewinner directed by Grigory Roshal and co-written with A. Abramova. Nikolai Cherkassov plays Mussorgsky's collaborator Stassov. Prominent in the film are the other members of the Russian musical "Five" with A. Popov as Rimsky-Korsakov, Y. Leonidov as Borodin, V. Friendlich as Cui and V. Balashov as Balakirev. The story focuses on the composer's problems getting recognition, especially for *Boris Godunov*, and includes staged sequences of the opera. The film was released in the U.S. Color. In Russian. 116 minutes.

MUTI, RICCARDO
Italian conductor (1941-)

Riccardo Muti is the chief conductor at La Scala and is featured on many of the videos of operas at the Milan theater. Muti has said that music should not be classified as "entertainment" but as a religious experience. Among his achievements is a famous revival of Pergolesi's *Lo Frate 'Nnamorato*, which is on video. See also ATTILA (1991), COSÌ FAN TUTTE (1989), DON CARLO (1992), DON GIOVANNI (1989), LA DONNA DEL LAGO (1992), ERNANI (1982), LO FRATE 'NNAMORATO (1992), BARBARA HENDRICKS (1990), CHRISTA LUDWIG (1992), NABUCCO (1986), LA TRAVIATA (1992), I VESPRI SICILIANI (1990), WILLIAM TELL (1991).

MY HEART'S IN THE HIGHLANDS
1970 TV opera by Beeson

American composer Jack Beeson adapted William Saroyan's wistful 1939 play for this opera which premiered on NET Opera Theatre on March 17, 1970. It tells the story of a poet and his unusual but fascinating family. Alan Crofoot portrays the poet Ben, Gerald Harrington III is the boy Johnny, Spiro Malas is the grocer Mr. Kosak, Lili Chookasian is Grandmother, Jack Beeson is the husband and Ken

Smith is Jasper, the runway from an old folks home. Peter Herman Adler produced and conducted the NBC Orchestrawhile Kirk Browning directed for television. Color. In English. 90 minutes. Video at MTR. See also JACK BEESON.

MYSHKIN
1973 TV opera by Eaton

John Eaton's television opera *Myshkin*, libretto by Patrick Creagh, is based on Dostoevsky's novel *The Idiot*. Prince Myshkin is the holy idiot of the title, a Christ-like figure subject to epileptic fits. The action is seen from Myshkin's point of view but as he is the camera he is never seen. The music reflects his swings between rationality and unreality and multiple time frames. The opera, composed in 1971, was presented on television by the Indiana University Opera Theater. Linda Anderson is Natasha, William Hartwell is Rogozhin, James Bert Neely is Dr. Schneider and William Oberholtzer is Yepanchin. Ross Allen and Herbert Selter produced and directed. The opera was telecast on PBS on April 23, 1973. Color. In English. 60 minutes. Video at MTR. See also JOHN EATON.

N

NABUCCO
1842 opera by Verdi

Nabucco was Verdi's first great success. The Hebrew chorus "Va, pensiero" in Act III became an anthem for Italian patriots and was sung at Verdi's funeral procession. The opera was seen as a metaphor about Italy under the control of Austria. Nabucco is the Babylonian king who orders the destruction of Jerusalem and takes the Hebrews prisoner, beginning the Babylonian captivity. The Hebrews are led by High Priest Zaccaria. Nabucco's daughters Fenena and Abigaille love the Israelite Ismaele and he loves Fenena. The libretto is by Temistocle Solera. See also GIUSEPPE VERDI.

1981 Verona Arena
Renato Bruson is a superb Nabucco in this massive production in the Verona Arena, matched by Ghena Dimitrova in a magnificent performance as his daughter Abigaille. Dimitur Petkov is the priest Zaccaria, Ottavio Garaventa is Ismaele and Bruna Baglioni is Fenena. The production was staged by Renzo Giacchieri with effective sets but rather odd costumes by Luciano Minguzzi. Maurizio Arena conducted the Verona Arena Orchestra and Chorus and Brian Large directed the video. Color. In Italian with English subtitles. 132 minutes. HBO video/Pioneer Artists laser.

1986 Teatro alla Scala
Renato Bruson and Ghena Dimitrova are again magnificent as Nabucco and Abigaille in this excellent La Scala production by Robert De Simone. Paata Burchuladze is terrific as Zaccaria, Raquel Pierott is Fenena and Bruno Becaria is Ismaele. Mauro Carosi designed the sets and Odette Nicoletti the costumes while Riccardo Muti conducted the Teatro alla Scala Orchestra and Chorus. Brian Large directed the video. Color. In Italian with English subtitles. 140 minutes Home Vision video/Japanese laser.

Related films

VERDI FILM BIOGRAPHIES
Scenes from the first performance of *Nabucco* are often featured in the film and video biographies of the composer with fairly authentic reproductions of the original staging. The most impressive is in the nine-hour 1982 epic *The Life of Verdi*. Also notable are the 1953 *Verdi King of Melody* with Tito Gobbi as Nabucco and the 1938 *Giuseppe Verdi*. For full details see GIUSEPPE VERDI.

1979 Inferno
Dario Argento's hypnotic supernatual horror film concerns three evil "mother" demons in New York and and Europe. Its soundtrack features "Va' pensiero" as performed by the Gaetano Riccitelli chorus led by Fernando Previtali. Color. In Italian. 110 minutes.

NACHT IN VENEDIG, EINE
1883 operetta by Strauss

One Night in Venice is one of Johann Strauss Jr.'s most popular operettas. It's set in 18th century Venice with the Duke of Urbino pursuing Barbara, an old senator's wife, who is more interested in a young sailor. The barber Caramello organizes a trap for her but his own girlfriend is mistakenly handed over to the Duke. There's also a masked ball with pastry cook Ciboletta and her boyfriend Pappacoda and lots of fine music. *A Night in Venice* was first presented in New York in 1884 and has been revived in modern times in both the U.S. and England but is most popular in Germany and Hungary. The libretto by F. Zell and Richard Genee is based on the play *Le Chateau Trompette*. See also JOHANN STRAUSS II.

1933 Robert Wiene film
Hungarian interest in the Strauss operetta led to the first film version being shot at the Hunnia Studios in Budapest as *Egy éj Velencében*. Director Robert Wiene and producer Emil Kovacs made a German version at the same time called *Eine Nacht in Venedig*. The stars are Tino Pattiere, Tina Eilers. Ludwig Stoessel and Oskar Sima. Black and white. In Hungarian or German. 80 minutes.

1942 Paul Verhoeven film
Paul Verhoeven, the actor-director father of new German cinema director Michael Verhoeven,

filmed this Tobis version of the Strauss operetta at the height of World War II. It stars Heidemarie Hatheyear, Lizzi Waldmuller, Hans Nielsen, Harald Paulsen and Erich Ponto.. Black and white. In German. 89 minutes.

1953 Georg Wildhagen film

Georg Wildhagen directed this Austrian film version of the operetta scripted by Rudolf Österreicher. It stars Herman Thimig as Pappacoda, Jeanette Schultze as Annina, Hans Olden as the Duke, Peter Pasetti as Caramello and Lotte Lang as Ciboletta. Nico Dostal conducted the orchestra. Black and white. In German. 90 minutes.

1973 Julia Migenes film

American mezzo-soprano Julia Migenes stars in this lavish German film of the operetta opposite Anton de Ridder, Trudeliese Schmidt, Sylvia Geszty and Erich Kunz. Burt Grund conducts the Munich Radio-Television Orchestra and Bavarian Radio Choir. Czech composer/ director Václav Kaslík shot the film in 35mm for German television. Unitel. Color. In German. 96 minutes.

1975 Frank de Quell film

Frank de Quell directed this German TV film of the operetta starring Wolfgang Brendel, Jeanette Scovotti, Carlo Bini and Elizabeth Steiner. Ernst Marzendorfer conducted the orchestra. Color. In German. 95 minutes. On Japanese laser.

NAMARA, MARGUERITE

American soprano (1888-1974)

Marguerite Namara, née Banks in Los Angeles, made her debut in Genoa in 1908 as Marguerite in *Faust*. She joined the Boston Opera Company and then went to Broadway to appear in Lehár and Gilbert & Sullivan operettas. In 1915 she starred opposite John Charles Thomas in Lehár's *Alone at Last*. She was with the Chicago Opera Company from 1919 to 1921 singing with Caruso and other major singers. In her first film in 1920 she played opposite Rudolph Valentino. Next was a 1931 British production of *Carmen* titled *Gypsy Blood* which she filmed following a European tour in the Bizet opera. Afterwards she appeared in supporting roles. Namara was married to British playwright Guy Bolton. See also CARMEN (1931).

1920 Stolen Moments

Namara stars opposite Rudolph Valentino in this melodramatic story about a woman infatuated with a South American novelist. After a heated argument over an incriminating letter, she thinks she may have killed him. American Cinema Corp. Black and white. About 70 minutes.

1934 Thirty Day Princess

Namara is lady-in-waiting to Sylvia Sidney who plays a double role as a princess and as an actress who substitutes for her on a tour. The other stars are Gary Grant and Edward Arnold. Marion Goring directed for Paramount. Black and white. 75 minutes.

1935 Peter Ibbetson

Namara appears as Madame Ginghi opposite Gary Cooper and Ann Harding in this romantic fantasy based on a novel by George du Maurier. Luis Buñuel called it "one of the world's ten best films" but few critics agree. Henry Hathaway directed for Paramount. Black and white. 85 minutes.

NANON

1877 operetta by Genée

Richard Genée, one of the great operetta librettists whose many masterworks include *Der Fledermaus*, also composed music. His major success as a composer was the operetta *Nanon, die Wirtin vom Goldenen Lamm*. It's set in France in the time of Louis XIV and the heroine Nanon is an innkeeper who falls in love with a marquis in disguise. When he gets in trouble she pleads to the king for his life and ends up as his marquise. See also RICHARD GENÉE.

1938 Erna Sack film

German opera coloratura Erna Sack stars as Nanon in this German film and was praised for being both a charming actress and a splendid singer. She falls in love with nobleman-in-disguise Johannes Heesters in her country inn and her problems begin. Otto Gebuehr portrays playwright Molière whose influence with the King helps resolve the romance. Herbert Maisch directed the film which was released in the U.S. UFA. Black and white. In German. 81 minutes.

NAPOLI MILIONARIA

1977 screen opera by Rota

Nino Rota's *Napoli Milionaria* is an usual type of screen opera for it is virtually an operatic homage to the composer's cinema career. It is based around music he wrote for the movies with a libretto by Eduardo De Filippo derived from the 1950 film *Napoli Milionaria*. The opera includes restructured music that Rota composed for that film plus music from Federico Fellini's *La Dolce Vita, Nights of Cabiria* and the *Toby Dammit* project, Luchino Visconti's *Rocco and His Brothers*, Sergei Bondarchuk's *Waterloo* and Eduardo De Filippo's *Filumena Marturano*. The opera premiered at Spoleto in 1977 but was criticized by the opera critics for its supposedly over-cinematic melodies. It was Rota's last opera. See also NINO ROTA.

NATIONAL FILM AND TELEVISION ARCHIVE

The National Film and Television Archive (NFTA) at the British Film Institute in London, one of the largest film and television archives in the world, has a notable collection of opera films and videos. Many of its copies of important films are unique and helped make the NFTA an invaluable resource center for opera film researchers.

NAUGHTY MARIETTA

1910 operetta by Herbert

Victor Herbert's most popular operetta was commissioned by impresario Oscar Hammerstein for his Manhattan Opera House and his prima donna Emma Trentina. Rida Johnson Young's libretto tells the story of Countess Marietta who flees to New Orleans on a ship with a group of husband-seeking French women. She ends up falling in love with ship captain Dick Warrington who wins her through his knowledge of a mysterious melody that has haunted her. We know it sung as "Ah! Sweet Mystery of Life." See also VICTOR HERBERT.

1935 Jeanette MacDonald/Nelson Eddy film

Nelson Eddy and Jeanette MacDonald were teamed for the first time in this entertaining MGM version of the operetta and its success led to their partnership on seven more films. The plot is somewhat changed with MacDonald transmuted into a French princess falling in love with American rescuer Eddy but the essentials are the same. Five of the stage songs were retained in the film with new lyrics by Gus Kahn for "Tramp, Tramp, Tramp" and "'Neath the Southern Moon". The cast includes Frank Morgan, Elsa Lanchester and Douglass Dumbrille. W.S. Van Dyke directed from a script by John Lee Mahin, Frances Goodrich and Albert Hackett. Black and white. 106 minutes. MGM video and laserdisc.

1955 Patrice Munsel/Alfred Drake video

Patrice Munsel and Alfred Drake star as Marietta and Captain Dick in this beautifully made and splendidly sung color television production by Max Liebman for NBC television. The cast includes John Conte as Governor Le Grange, Gale Sherwood as his light of love Yvonee, Donn Driver as Louis D'Arc, Robert Gallagher as the ship captain and Bambi Linn & Rod Alexander as the dancers. Charles Sanford conducts the NBC Orchestra. The excellent TV adaptation was written by playwright Neil Simon in collaboration with Fred Saidy, Will Glickman and William Friedberg. Color. 80 minutes. VAI video in black and white.

Related film

1974 Young Frankenstein

Mel Brooks provides an amusing variation on the haunting meaning of "Ah! Sweet Mystery of Life" in his horror movie spoof *Young Frankenstein*. Madeline Kahn sings it with ecstatic happiness in the arms of the Frankenstein monster (Peter Boyle). Color. 105 minutes.

NBC OPERA THEATRE

Television opera series (1949-1964)

NBC Opera Theatre presented the most important opera telecasts in the early years of American television. They were created by producer Samuel Chotzinoff, music director Peter Herman Adler and TV director Kirk Browning who together produced this unique English-language series of telecast operas. The operas began on Feb. 2, 1949, with the last act of *La Bohème* followed by abridged versions of *The Barber of Seville, The Bartered Bride* and *The Old Maid and the Thief*. The series premiered officially on Jan. 14, 1950, with Weill's *Down in the Valley*, and became famous in

1951 with the world premiere of the first television opera, *Amahl and the Night Visitors*. Famous productions include the American premiere of Britten's *Billy Budd*, Bernstein's *Trouble in Tahiti* and a mammoth production of Prokofiev's *War and Peace*. Among the operas Chotzinoff commissioned for the series were Martinu's *The Marriage*, Foss's *Griffelkin*, Dello Joio's *The Trial of Rouen*, Hollingworth's *La Grande Bretèche*, Menotti's *Maria Golovin* and Kastle's *Deseret*. The series ended with the death of Chotzinoff in 1964. Most of its productions can be seen at the Museum of Television and Radio (MTR). See PETER HERMAN ADLER, KIRK BROWNING, SAMUEL CHOTZINOFF.

NEDBAL, OSCAR
Czechoslovak composer (1874-1930)

Oscar Nedbal is the Czechoslovakian equivalent of Franz Lehár, a composer of popular operettas with Czech and Slovak folk rhythms that found success on the Vienna stage. He composed the operettas *Die Keusche Barbara* (1911), *Polenblut* (1913) and *Die Schöne Saskia* (1917), the comic opera *Sedlák Jakub* (1922) and many ballets. *Polenblut* was the most successful of his operettas, was filmed in Germany in 1934 and has remained in the repertory. Nedbal, who was also a noted conductor, settled in Bratislava in the latter part of his life and became a major figure in Slovak music. He was the director of the Bratislava Opera at the Slovak National Theater and music director of Bratislava Radio. See POLENBLUT.

NERONE
1924 opera by Boito

Arrigo Boito's opera *Nerone* was unfinished at his death in 1918, 56 years after he began it. Its libretto, however, had already been published and hailed as a masterwork and the posthumous premiere of the opera conducted by Toscanini at La Scala in 1924 was reasonably successful. The opera is a large-scale portrait of Rome in the time of the Emperor Nero and contrasts good Christians with decadent pagans. The only complete CD is from Hungary and the only video is from Croatia. See also ARRIGO BOITO.

1989 Split Summer Festival
A production of the opera in an appropriate ambiance, the courtyard of the Roman Emperor

Diocletian's palace. It was mounted as part of the Split Summer Festival in Croatia with a primarily Yugoslavian cast. The featured singers are Franjo Petrusanec, David McShane, Cigoj and Iveljic. The Split Summer Festival Orchestra is conducted by V. Barez. The video is an off-air copy of a telecast. Color. In Italian. 160 minutes. Lyric/ Opera Dubs video.

NESSLER, VIKTOR
Alsace composer (1841-1891)

Viktor Nessler is not a recognizable name to most opera lovers anymore because his Gothic fairy tale operas are no longer in vogue. At the turn of the century, however, he was highly popular for the operas *Der Rattenfänger von Hameln* and *Der Trompeter of Säkkingen*. Both were widely performed and provided the basis for German films in the early silent era.

1908 Der Trompeter of Säkkingen
The Trumpeter of Sakkingen, Nessler's 1884 opera based on a romance by J. V. von Scheffel, was so popular it was staged in Germany over 500 times following its Leipzig premiere. It also traveled to London and New York. Its popularity made it a natural choice for an early German sound opera film. Henny Porten, Germany's first film star, is featured as the heroine of a 1908 Messter film depicting a scene from the opera. Porten's father Franz, a former opera singer, directed the film shot in a Berlin studio using Oskar Messter's synchronization process. About 5 minutes.

1916 Der Rattenfänger von Hameln
The Flute Player of Hamelin, Nessler's 1879 variation on the Pied Piper legend, is based on a poetic romance by Julius Woolf. A German film of the opera libretto was made for the Union company in 1916 and screened with Nessler's music. It was directed and scripted by Paul Wegener who stars as the flute player. The cast includes Lyda Salmonova and Wilhelm Diegelmann. About 60 minutes.

NESTERENKO, YEVGENY
Russian bass (1938-)

Yevgeny Nesterenko has become the Russian bass of our time with a voice powerful enough to dominate even the Verona Arena when he sings the role of Attila. He was born in Moscow, studied in Leningrad and made his debut there in 1962. He joined the Bolshoi in 1971 and became one the company's best known performers. He has sung in most of the great opera houses including La Scala, Vienna, Covent Garden and the Metropolitan. Nesterenko performs many roles but is most admired and impressive in Russian operas. See ALEKO (1989), ATTILA (1985), BORIS GODUNOV (1978 /1987), KHOVANSHCHINA (1979), A LIFE FOR THE TSAR (1992), WOLFGANG A. MOZART (1991), PRINCE IGOR (1969).

NET OPERA
Educational television series (1957-1977)

NET, the National Educational Television collective network, first began to present opera programs in 1957. WGBH in Boston teamed with Boston University and the New England Conservatory of Music to present some opera rarities. They started with Mozart's *La Finta Giardiniera* and followed that in 1960 with Ravel's *L'Heure Español*. In 1961 they presented Purcell's *Dido and Aeneas* and in 1965 Nono's *Intolleranza*. In 1964 NET started a series called *This Is Opera* with the Metropolitan Guild and screened Bartók's *Bluebeard's Castle*. In 1967 the network televised Beeson's *Lizzie Borden*. NET also telecast eleven operas from European television companies. In 1969 the NET Opera Company was created by Peter Herman Adler and Kirk Browning from the old NBC Opera Theatre company. This ambitious series began in October 1969 with Janácek's *From the House of the Dead* and continued with the world premiere of Beeson's *My Heart's in the Highlands*. After a series of operas produced by BBC and CBC, NET continued its own productions with *The Abduction from the Seraglio* and *Queen of Spades*. In 1972 it successfully premiered Pasatieri's TV opera *The Trial of Mary Lincoln* but its next commissioned opera, Henze's *Rachel La Cubana*, ran so far over budget it ended all original productions. From that time on, NET acted only as a presentation forum for operas produced by others, mostly foreign TV companies. See PETER HERMAN ADLER, KIRK BROWNING.

NEWAY, PATRICIA
American soprano (1919 -)

Brooklyn-born Patrica Neway was gifted was an intense dramatic soprano voice and created leading roles in two operas by Gian Carlo Menotti. Neway made her debut in *Così Fan Tutte* in 1946, joined the New York City Opera in 1948 and created the role of Magda in *The Consul* in 1950. In 1952 she began to sing with the Opéra-Comique in Paris and in 1958 she created the role of the Mother in *Maria Golovin* at the Brussels World Fair. She also starred in a number of television operas and sang the role on Nettie in a TV production of *Carousel*. See THE ACCUSED, CAROUSEL (1967), THE CONSUL, LES DIALOGUES DES CARMÉLITES (1957), GOLDEN CHILD (1960), MACBETH (1953), MARIA GOLOVIN (1959).

NEW MOON, THE
1927 operetta by Romberg

Sigmund Romberg's tuneful operetta is set in 18th century New Orleans. A fugitive French nobleman, in the city to recruit freedom fighters, falls in love with a haughty woman. He is taken prisoner and sent back to France on the ship New Moon but the ship is captured by his men disguised as pirates. They establish a free colony on an island. The songs include "Softly as in a Morning Sunrise," "Stouthearted Men" and "Lover Come Back to Me." The lyrics and libretto are by Oscar Hammerstein II, Laurence Schwab and Frank Mandel. See also SIGMUND ROMBERG.

1930 Grace Moore/Lawrence Tibbett film
Metropolitan Opera stars Grace Moore and Lawrence Tibbett are featured in this rewritten MGM adaptation with the setting transposed to Russia. The couple meet on the Caspian Sea on the ship New Moon. Moore plays a Slavic princess who is fought over by Russian officer Tibbett and his commander Adolphe Menjou. Tibbett sings "Stouthearted Men," Moore sings "Softly as in a Morning Sunrise" and "One Kiss " and they duet on "Wanting You" and "Lover Come Back to Me." The film uses part of Romberg's score but also adds songs by Herbert Stothart. Jack Conway directed. Black and white. 85 minutes.

1940 MacDonald/Eddy film
Jeanette MacDonald and Nelson Eddy's film is much closer to the original stage operetta. It is set again in Louisiana with Eddy as the fugitive French freedom loving aristocrat and MacDonald as the haughty woman he falls in love with. Most of the famous songs are featured including "One Kiss," "Softly as in a Morning Sunrise," "Lover

Come Back to Me" and "Stout-Hearted Men." William Daniels was cinematographer and Robert Z. Leonard directed. Black and white. 105 minutes. On video.

1989 New York City Opera at Wolf Trap

This New York City Opera production of the Romberg operetta by Robert Johnson is the complete original version. It was staged at Wolf Trap where it was hosted by Beverly Sills. David Horn produced it for television and it was telecast on April 7, 1989. Color. 150 minutes.

NEW YEAR
1989 opera by Tippett

Michael Tippett's *New Year* is almost but not quite a TV opera. It was inspired by television shows and BBC-TV was a partner in commissioning it but it was not shown on television until after it had stage productions in Houston and Glyndebourne. It's a futuristic science-fiction space-time fantasy in which a spaceship from Nowhere Tomorrow controlled by computer wizard Merlin lands in the world of Somewhere Today. Pelegrin, the ship's pilot, has been attracted by the anguished face of child psychologist Jo Ann whose brother Donny is partially the cause of her grief. Pelegrin eventually finds Jo Ann in a crowd awaiting the New Year. See also MICHAEL TIPPETT.

1991 BBC-TV film

Helen Field stars as Jo Ann, Krister St. Hill is her foster brother Donny, James Maddalena is Merlin, Richetta Manager is Regan and Mike Henry is the presenter and narrator in this BBC Television film of the opera. Bruce Macadie and Jonathan Hills designed the sets and Anna Buruma created the costumes. Stephany Marks produced and Bill T. Jones and Dennis Marks directed. It was telecast on Sept. 21, 1991. Color. In English. 90 minutes.

NEW YORK CITY OPERA
New York opera company (1944-)

The New York City Opera was started as a low income alternative to the Met and has often outshone its richer rival in quality and adventurousness. Its star soprano Beverly Sills became a major American diva without singing at the Met. The NYCO become noted for its willingness to present new American operas and

has premiered many of the best. In 1971 it began to televise some of its productions including *The Ballad of Baby Doe, Street Scene* and *The Saint of Bleeker Street*. The company performed *The Mikado* for the film *Foul Play*. See ANNA BOLENA (1985), THE BALLAD OF BABY DOE (1976), THE BARBER OF SEVILLE (1976), CANDIDE (1986), CARMEN (1984), CAVALLERIA RUSTICANA (1992), THE CUNNING LITTLE VIXEN (1983), THE GOLDEN COCKEREL (1971), LIZZIE BORDEN (1967), MADAMA BUTTERFLY (1982), MANON (1977), THE MARRIAGE OF FIGARO (1991), MARILYN MONROE (1993), THE MIKADO (1978 film), PAGLIACCI (1992), LA RONDINE (1985), THE SAINT OF BLEEKER STREET (1978), BEVERLY SILLS, LA TRAVIATA (1995).

NEW YORK PUBLIC LIBRARY FOR THE PERFORMING ARTS

The New York Public Library for the Performing Arts at Lincoln Center (NYPL) has a division for music which contains the Rodgers & Hammerstein Archives of Recorded Sound. In this archive there is a large collection of opera videos, some of which appear to be unavailable elsewhere. It also includes all of the radio broadcasts of the Metropolitan Opera and the Bell Telephone Hour from the 1930s to the present day.

NICOLAI, OTTO
German composer (1810-1849)

Otto Nicolai is known primarily for his comic opera *Die Lustigen Weiber von Windsor* (The Merry Wives of Windsor) which preceded Verdi's version of the Shakespeare comedy by half a century. Nicolai's earlier operas were in Italian but he brought all his ideas together for this last opera in German. It was refused by the Vienna Hofoper, where Nicolai was music director, so he quit his post and moved to Berlin where the opera premiered. It has become a fixture of the German stage and is still a delight with a much-loved overture. There are a number of German films of the opera and a quite pleasant one in English. There is also a highly fictional film about Nicolai composing the opera. See THE MERRY WIVES OF WINDSOR.

1940 Falstaff In Wien

Falstaff in Vienna is a German film about Nicolai and the composition of *The Merry Wives Of Windsor* in Vienna. It pretends that events similar to the play happened in Nicolai's circle of friends and inspired him to write the opera. Scenes from the opera are also shown on stage. Hans Nielsen stars as Nicolai with support from Gusti Wolf, Paul Hörbinger and Lizzi Holtzschuh. The Berlin Staatsoper and Deutsches Operhaus singers include Erna Berger and Carla Spletter and the music is played by the Berlin Staatsoper Orchestra. Bruno Mondi was the cinematographer and Leopold Hainisch directed. Black and white. In German. 89 minutes. Lyric video.

NIGHT AT THE OPERA, A
1935 American opera film

The funniest of all opera films with the Marx Brothers invading the operatic world with devastating results. Groucho plays a tacky promoter in Milan trying to talk Margaret Dumont into investing money in Sig Rumann's New York Opera Company. Soprano Rosa Castaldi (Kitty Carlisle) and tenor Rodolfo Lassparri (Walter King) are seen on stage in a *Pagliacci* and hired to sing in New York. Chico sells tenor Allan Jones to Groucho in a delightful contract scene with a Sanity Clause and they all end up as stowaways on the boat to New York. After a series of ship scenes, including the famous crowded stateroom routine, they reach New York where Groucho is fired. The Marxes decide to sabotage the opening night of *Il Trovatore*. They change the orchestra music, sell peanuts, disrupt the Anvil Chorus, knock down sets, swing across the stage and get chased back and forth. When Lassparri is kidnapped, Jones takes over singing the role of Manrico and becomes a star. Carlisle plays Leonora, Olga Dane is Azucena, Luther Hoobner is Ruiz and Rodolfo Hoyos is Count di Luna who also sings. Other singers include Alexander Giglio for *Pagliacci* and Tandy McKenzie for *Il Trovatore*. Herbert Stothart arranged the music, George S. Kaufman and Morrie Ryskind wrote the script (which has been published) and Sam Wood directed for MGM. Black and white. 92 minutes. MGM-UA video.

NIGHTINGALE, THE
1914 opera by Stravinsky

The Nightingale was created by Igor Stravinsky in Russian as *Solovyei* with a libretto by the composer and Stepan Mitussov. It later premiered in Paris as *Le Rossignol*. The opera tells how the sweet song of the nightingale conquers even Death and saves the Emperor's life. It's based on the Hans Christian Anderson fairy tale *The Emperor's Nightingale*. See also IGOR STRAVINSKY.

1971 NET Opera
NET Opera presented the opera as part of a 1971 television program called *Stravinsky Remembered*. Reri Grist sings the role of the Nightingale, Lili Chookasian is Death, Emile Renan is the Emperor, Ellen Faul is the Cook and Sidney Johnson is the Fisherman. Peter Herman Adler, who also produced, conducts the CBC Symphony Orchestra. The program includes an interview with Stravinsky. Kirk Browning directed the telecast. Color. In English. 90 minutes. Video at MTR.

NILSSON, BIRGIT
Swedish soprano (1918-)

Birgit Nilsson, the finest Wagnerian soprano of her time, made her debut at the Royal Opera in Stockholm in 1946 as Agathe in *Der Freischütz* and sang there in a wide variety of roles. Her stardom, however, began in 1954 when she sang Brünnhilde in Stockholm and Munich and began a long Wagnerian association with Bayreuth. She made her debut at Covent Garden in the 1957 *Ring* and was at the Met in 1959 as Isolde. In addition to Wagner, she is admired for her recordings of Turandot and Elektra. Nilsson retired in 1984. See also BELL TELEPHONE HOUR (1967), ELEKTRA (1980), METROPOLITAN OPERA (1972/1983), DER RING DES NIBELUNGEN (1965 film), RUDOLF SCHOCK (1983), TOSCA (1983 film), TRISTAN UND ISOLDE (1967/1973), TURANDOT (1967).

1950s Bell Telephone Hour
Birgit Nilsson was at the peak of her vocal prowess in the 1950s when she appeared on a series of *Bell Telephone Hour* television shows. On the highlights video she is seen singing arias from the operas *Turandot* (In questa reggia), *Tannhäuser* (Elisabeth's Prayer), *Tosca* (Vissi d'arte), *La Forza del Destino* (Pace, mio Dio), *Macbeth* (Vieni! t'affretta) and *Götterdämmerung* (Brunhilde's Immolation). She also sings music from Handel's *Messiah*, Fauré's *Requiem* and Rossini's *Stabat Mater*. Donald Voorhees conducts the Bell Telephone Hour Orchestra. Color. 45 minutes. Kultur video.

1964 Swedish Opera Concert

Nilsson performs a program of arias from operas at a concert in Stockholm. They include *La Traviata, Aida, Oberon,* and *Tristan und Isolde*. She is accompanied by Swedish Radio Orchestra conducted by Stig Westerberg. Lars Egler directed the video for Swedish television on Sept. 26, 1964. 58 minutes.

1968 Swedish Verdi Concert

Nilsson performs a program of arias from Verdi operas at a concert in Stockholm. They are *Macbeth, Un Ballo in Maschera* and *La Forza del Destino*. She is accompanied by the Swedish Radio Symphonic Orchestra conducted by Sergiu Celibidache. Lars Egler directed the video for Swedish television on Sept. 5, 1968. 56 minutes.

1979 Skyline

Nilsson appeared on the PBS arts program *Skyline* in 1979. The program is primarily an interview about her career, with Beverly Sills asking the questions. Color. 30 minutes. Video at NYPL.

NIXON IN CHINA
1987 opera by Adams

Nixon in China was created by John Adams in collaboration with librettist Alice Goodman and director Peter Sellars on a commission from Houston Grand Opera. It is one of the most popular modern American operas and focuses on President Nixon's visit to China in 1972 and his meeting with Chairman Mao. The principal characters are Nixon, Mao, Pat Nixon, Madame Mao, Henry Kissinger and Chou En-Lai. The music is minimalist but accessible and a non-vocal work derived from it, "The Chairman Dances," has become popular in its own right. The complete opera is on CD but not yet on commercial video. See also JOHN ADAMS.

1988 Houston Grand Opera

The Houston production of the opera staged by Peter Sellars was taped in October/November 1987 and telecast on April 15, 1988 six months after its premiere. James Maddalena portrays Richard Nixon, Carol Ann Page is Pat Nixon, Sanford Sylvan is Chou en-Lai, John Duykers is Mao, Trudy Ellen Craney is Madame Mao and Thomas Hammons is Kissinger. John De Main conducts the Houston Grand Opera Orchestra. The opera was introduced by Walter Cronkite

who talks about the events on which it is based and Adams is interviewed during the interval. Brian Large directed the imaginative video. Color. In English. 180 minutes. Video at MTR.

NOAH AND THE FLOOD
See THE FLOOD

NORHOLM, IB
Danish composer (1931-)

Ib Norholm is a leading exponent of the "new simplicity" movement in Denmark music and one of its leading opera composers. His first major opera, *Invitation to the Scaffold*, was composed for Danish Television. His other major operas have also been televised in Denmark including the popular *The Young Park* (Den Unge Park/1970) and *The Garden Wall* (Havemuren/1976) which was also staged in England.

1967 Invitation to the Scaffold

Invitation til Skafottet is a 90-minute opera based on a story by Vladimir Nabokov with a libretto by P. Borum. It was composed for Danish Television and telecast on Oct. 10, 1967.

NORMA
1831 opera by Bellini

One of the great *bel canto* operas, *Norma* has been restored to the operatic repertory thanks to Maria Callas and Joan Sutherland. Vincenzo Bellini's opera is set in Gaul under the Roman occupation in First Century BC and tells the tragic story of the love affair of Druid priestess Norma and Roman proconsul Pollione. She has broken her vow of chastity for him but he now loves temple virgin Aldagisa. *Norma* contains one of the great soprano arias, "Casta Diva," Norma's prayer for peace. The libretto by Felice Romani is based on a play by Alexandre Soumet. See also VICENZO BELLINI.

1974 Montserrat Caballé at Orange Festival

Montserrat Caballé stars as Norma in this film of an outdoor production by Sandro Sequi at the ancient Roman amphitheater in Orange, France. Jon Vickers portrays Pollione, Josephine Veasey is Adalgisa, Agostino Ferrin is Orovese and Gino Sinimberghi is Flavio. Giuseppe Patanè conducts the Orchestra and Chorus of the Teatro Regio of Turin. Jean-Pierre Lazar is the cinematographer and Pierre Jourdan directed the film. Color. In Italian with Japanese subtitles. 161 minutes. Bel Canto Society/Lyric videos/Japanese laserdisc.

1978 Australian Opera
Joan Sutherland stars as Norma in this Australian Opera production by Sandro Sequi at the Sydney Opera House. This was one of her best roles and she is in excellent form. The cast includes Margarita Elkins as Adalgisa, Clifford Grant as Pollione and Ronald Stevens as Oroveso. Richard Bonynge conducts the Elizabethan Sydney Orchestra and Australian Opera Chorus. The opera was taped by the Australian Broadcasting Company. Color. In Italian. 153 minutes. Home Vision video.

Early/related films

1911 Film d'Arte Italian
Rina Adozzino Alessio stars as Norma in this silent Italian adaptation of the opera which was screened with live music. It stars Bianca Lorenzoni as Adalgisa and Alfredo Robert as Pollione. Gerolamo Lo Savio directed for Film d'Arte Italiana. Black and white. About 14 minutes.

1978 Blood Feud
Lina Wertmuller's bizarre love triangle film features the aria "Casta Diva" on the soundtrack every time lawyer Marcello Mastroianni gets together with widow Sophia Loren. The Italian title of the film is *Fatto de Sangue tra Due Uomini a Causa di una Vedova*. Color. In Italian. 112 minutes.

1980 Atlantic City
"Casta Diva" is memorably performed by Elizabeth Harwood and the London Philharmonic in the sensual opening scene of this fine movie. Burt Lancaster watches unobserved from his window as Susan Sarandon take a lemon bath. The aria sets the scene for their relationship in the film. Louis Malle directed this Venice Film Festival Grand Prize winner. Paramount. Color. 104 minutes. Paramount video.

1982 Casta Diva
Eric De Kuyper's experimental Dutch film uses the *Norma* aria and other opera music in unusual ways. Color. 110 minutes.

1990 Perfectly Normal
Norma is performed in drag at the hilarious climax of this odd Canadian film by Yves Simoneau. It takes place in a restaurant with operatic entertainment called La Traviata. Michael Riley plays Norma opposite Robbie Coltrane's Pollione. Color. 105 minutes.

1992 Lorenzo's Oil
Maria Callas is heard singing "Casta Diva" accompanied by the La Scala Orchestra and Chorus in George Miller's film about a couple fighting to save their child from a crippling illness. The La Scala Orchestra led by Tullio Serafin also plays the Introduction to Act II. Color. 135 minutes.

1995 The Bridges of Madison County
Maria Callas is heard on the radio singing "Casta Diva" in a prophetic moment for the Italian-born housewife Meryl Streep at the beginning of this romantic film directed by Clint Eastwood. The recording was made with the La Scala Orchestra conducted by Tullio Serafin. Color. 135 minutes.

NORMAN, JESSYE
American soprano (1945-)

Jessye Norman was born in Georgia, studied in American universities and then went to Europe. She made her debut in 1969 with the Deutsche Oper in Berlin as Elisabeth in *Tannhäuser*. In 1972 she sang Aida at La Scala and Cassandra at Covent Garden. She made her U.S. debut in Philadelphia singing Stravinsky's Jocasta and Purcell's Dido. She gave her first performance at the Metropolitan Opera in 1983 as Cassandra. Norman has a rare ability to make her voice as dramatic as it is beautiful. Her stage presence is impressive and she has been featured in several fine opera videos, including one with sister diva Kathleen Battle. See ARIADNE AUF NAXOS (1988), KATHLEEN BATTLE (1990), BLUEBEARD'S CASTLE (1989), CARMEN (1988 FILM), LES DIALOGUES DES CARMÉLITES (1987), HERBERT VON KARAJAN (1987), OEDIPUS REX (1972), LES TROYENS (1983), VERDI REQUIEM (1982).

1987 Songs by Handel, Schubert & Others
Jessye Norman sings Handel, Schubert, Schumann, Brahms and Strauss in a recital in June 1987 at the Schubertiade at the Hohenens Festival in Feld Kirch in Austria. Geoffrey Parson

accompanies her on piano and M. Kach directed the video. Color. 59 minutes. Phillips video.

1988 Jessye Norman's Christmastide
Norman sings Christmas carols at Ely Cathedral with the American Boychoir, Vocal Arts Chorus, Ely Cathedral Choristers and Bournemouth Symphony conducted by Robert DeCormier. Derek Jacobi introduces the concert, Timothy Woolford produced and John Michael Phillips directed the telecast and video on Nov. 30, 1988. Color. In English. 51 minutes. Phillips video.

1991 Symphony for the Spire
Norman sings at an outdoor concert at Salisbury Cathedral to raise funds to restore the cathedral's spire. The other performers are Placido Domingo, Ofra Harnoy, Charlton Heston and Kenneth Branagh. Richard Armstrong conducts the English Chamber Orchestra and Mike Mansfield directed the video. Color. 65 minutes. New Line video.

1991 Jessye Norman at Notre Dame
Norman gives a recital of spirituals, sacred music and Christmas carols at Notre Dame Cathedral in December 1991. She is accompanied by the Notre Dame Choir and the Radio France National Orchestra conducted by Lawrence Foster. The concert was televised in the U.S. Color. 55 minutes. Phillips video.

1991 Jessye Norman, Singer
A documentary film tracing Norman's life from her early years in Georgia through her training and international career. She offers insights into her cultural roots and how they effected her evolution as a singer. She also describes how she has developed her repertory and is working to expand her vocal capabilities. The film shows her in performance from London to Harlem. Malachite Production. Color. 74 minutes. Filmmakers Library video.

NORTON, FREDERIC
English composer (1975-1940)

Composer Frederic Norton and writer Oscar Asche created one of the great operetta successes of the London stage, *Chu Chin Chow*. It was actually a kind of cross between pantomime and operetta with a romantic story about a slave girl and a robber derived from Ali Baba and the Forty Thieves. It was a giant hit and ran for 2,238 performances, the longest run before *The Mousetrap*. It was silly escapism but it had pleasant tunes, including the popular "Robbers Chorus."

CHU CHIN CHOW
Chu Chin Chow was filmed twice but was never a big hit as a film. The first silent version was made by Herbert Wilcox in 1923 with Betty Blythe as the slave girl Zohrat and Herbert Langley as Hassan. Anna May Wong starred as the slave girl in Walter Forde's 1934 film of the operetta with George Robey as Ali Baba and Fritz Kortner as Hassan.

NOVELLO, IVOR
English composer (1893-1915)

Ivor Novello kept the old-fashioned romantic operetta alive in England when his contemporaries abandoned it for jazz rhythms and popular musical comedy. It may have been retrograde but it made him very popular as operettas like *Glamorous Night* (1935), *The Dancing Years* (1939) and *King's Rhapsody* (1949) were huge hits. Novello was also a notable performer on stage and film. His better known movies include *The White Rose* (1923), *The Rat* (1925) and *The Lodger* (1926 and 1932) and an adaptation of Balfe's opera *The Bohemian Girl*. See also MARY ELLIS, THE BOHEMIAN GIRL (1922).

1937 Glamorous Night
Metropolitan Opera soprano Mary Ellis stars as Gypsy prima donna Melitza in this film of Novella's operatic operetta. Novello was in the stage production opposite Ellis but he's not in the film. The main actors are Barry McKay, Otto Kruger and Victor Jory. Ellis is loved by a king and eventually leads her gypsies to save him from a wicked prime minister. Olive Gilbert of the Carl Rosa Opera Company appears in the film's opera sequence. Brian Desmond Hurst directed. Black and white. 81 minutes.

1950 The Dancing Years
Novello's charming operetta is set in Vienna in 1910 where a composer loves an opera star who marries a prince. The film stars Dennis Price, Giselle Preville, opera diva Olive Gilbert and Patricia Denton. Harold French directed. Color. 97 minutes.

1955 King's Rhapsody

Anna Neagle and Errol Flynn star in this English film of Novello's operetta about a Ruritanian king whose mistress tricks him into returning to his throne. Also in the cast are Patrice Wymore, Martita Hunt and Finlay Currie. Herbert Wilcox directed. Color. 93 minutes.

1975 The Music of Ivor Novello

This is a Canadian television tribute to Novello featuring performances of his songs by various singers. They include Mary Costa, Anna Shuttleworth, Judith Forst and Robert Jeffrey with Richard Bonynge accompanying on piano. Color. In English. 60 minutes. Opera Dubs video.

NOVOTNÁ, JARMILA
Czechoslovakian soprano (1907-1994)

Jarmila Novotná studied with the legendary Czech soprano Emmy Destinn and made her debut in Prague in 1925. In the 1930s she sang regularly in Vienna and Salzburg and created the title role of Lehár's *Giuditta* in 1934. She came to America in 1939 and was a stalwart at the Metropolitan Opera from 1940 to 1956, noted especially for performances as Violetta in *La Traviata*. Louis B. Mayer wanted her to make Hollywood musicals in the 1930s but she refused. She did make films in Czechoslovakia, Germany and Austria from 1925 on and appeared in a couple of Hollywood movies in the postwar period. Her most famous opera film is Max Ophuls' *The Bartered Bride* but she also starred in excellent German operetta films. See THE BARTERED BRIDE (1932), DER BETTELSTUDENT (1931), DIE FLEDERMAUS (1953), THE GREAT CARUSO, DER LETZTE WALZER (1936), FRASQUITA (1934), JOHANN STRAUSS (1955).

1930 Brand In Der Oper

Fire at the Opera or *Barcarolle* is an early opera film with Jarmila Novotná as one of the opera singers. It's set in an opera house where a rich man has arranged a production to star a chorus girl he loves. The theater burns down at the premiere. Carl Froelich directed the German version and Henry Roussell the French. Black and white. In German. 90 minutes.

1933 Die Nacht der Grossen Liebe

Novotná stars opposite Gustav Fröhlich in *The Night of Great Love*, a popular German musical with a score by Robert Stolz. The plot revolves around the competition between Novotná and her teenage daughter (Christiane Graufoff) for the love of a naval officer. Geza von Bolvary directed. Black and white. In German. 94 minutes.

1935 Der Kosak und die Nachtigall

Novotná portrays an opera singer in her last German-language film, *The Cossack and the Nightingale,* an espionage tale with music by Franz Lehár. Her co-stars include Ivan Petrovich, Rudolf Klein-Rogge and Fritz Imhoff. The movie was based on a novel by Georg C. Klaren and directed by Phil Jutzi. Black and white. In German. 85 minutes.

1937 Song of the Lark

Novotná sings in her native language in this Czech film about an opera singer who returns to her home village. A young man (Adolf Horalek) studying for the priesthood falls in love with her but she nobly decides to give him up to make his dying mother (Vera Ford) happy. Novotná sings arias from *Carmen* as well as Czech folk music. Svatopluk Inneman, who made the Czech *Bartered Bride*, directed. Black and white. In Czech. 85 minutes.

1948 The Search

Novotná is superb in a non-singing role portraying a desperate mother searching for her lost son around Europe after World War II. Montgomery Clift plays an American soldier in Germany who has been looking after the child. Audiences left the theaters in tears after seeing this three-handkerchief movie, It won four Oscar nominations for MGM. Master filmmaker Fred Zinnemann directed. Black and white. In English. 105 minutes. On video.

NOZZE DI FIGARO, LE
See THE MARRIAGE OF FIGARO

NUCCI, LEO
Italian baritone (1942-)

Leo Nucci began his career while still a student singing Figaro in *The Barber of Seville* at Spoleto in 1967 and it has remained one of his most popular roles. After a period in the La Scala chorus, his real professional career began at La Fenice in 1975 in *La Bohème* and at La Scala in 1976 as Figaro. He was at Covent Garden in 1978 and the Metropolitan in 1980 where he made his debut as Renato in *Un Ballo in Maschera*. He has been especially praised for his performances in Verdi operas. He has made a film of *The Barber of Seville* but most of his videos are of stage productions of Verdi operas. See UN BALLO IN MASCHERA (1991), THE BARBER OF SEVILLE (1988), FALSTAFF (1982), LA FORZA DEL DESTINO (1984), MACBETH (1987), VERONA (1988), I VESPRI SICILIANI (1986).

NYMAN, MICHAEL
English composer (1944-)

Michael Nyman, who has written five operas and was the first to use the word "minimalism" to describe music, has become widely known for his film music. He first attracted attention with his near-operatic scores for Peter Greenaway films including *The Draughtsman's Contract* and *The Cook, The Thief, His Wife and Her Lover*. He attracted an even wider audience with his music for Jane Campion's film *The Piano*. Nyman's operas are experimental in nature and include two written for television. The best known is *The Man Who Mistook his Wife for a Hat* (1986) which he helped make into a film after its stage premiere. See THE MAN WHO MISTOOK HIS WIFE FOR A HAT.

1984 The Kiss
Michael Nyman described *The Kiss*, his first opera, as a "video duet." It was created for England's Channel 4 television and premiered Oct. 13, 1984.

1991 Letters, Riddles And Writs
Nyman composed this excellent television opera to a libretto by director Jeremy Newson for the *Not Mozart* series. It's based on words by Leopold Mozart (sung by David Thomas) and son Wolfgang (sung by Ute Lemper) using their letters as source material. David Thomas is also seen on stage as Sarastro in *The Magic Flute*. The story is narrated by statues of Beethoven and Haydn with clever video effects by director Pat Gavin. Nyman appears in the opera as himself and is accused of pilfering Mozart's music. The opera was telecast on BBC on Nov. 10, 1991 and staged in London in June 1992. Color. 30 minutes. Connoisseur Academy (England) video.

O

OBERON

1826 opera by Weber

Oberon or the Elf King's Oath, Carl Maria von Weber's last opera, was written in English on a commission from Covent Garden to a libretto by James Robinson Planché. Elf King Oberon and Queen Titania have quarreled over whether man or woman is more inconstant and vow not to meet until they find a pair of faithful lovers. The test case is Huon who goes to Baghdad to marry the Caliph's daughter Reiza. With a little help from Oberon the pair are finally able to convince Titania they are faithful. See also CARL MARIA VON WEBER.

1968 Herbert Junkers film

Herbert Junkers directed this film of the opera for West German television in 1968. It stars René Kollo, Netta B. Ramati, Hans Putz, Ursula Schroeder-Feinen, and Heinz Bosi. Heinz Wallberg conducted the Bamberger Symphony Orchestra. Color. In German. 84 minutes.

1986 Frankfurt Opera

This German production of the opera is in the original English. Philip Langridge stars in a Frankfurt Opera telecast with Elizabeth Connell, Paul Frey and Benjamin Luxon. Seiji Ozawa conducts. Color. In English. 88 minutes. Lyric video.

OBRAZTSOVA, ELENA

Russian mezzo-soprano (1937-)

Russian mezzo Elena Obraztsova was born and brought up in Leningrad but later joined the Bolshoi in Moscow and made her debut there as Marina. She has performed around the world from La Scala and Covent Garden to the Metropolitan in both Russian and Western operas and is especially popular in *Carmen*, *A Midsummer Night's Dream* and *War and Peace*. The 1991 *Three Sopranos* concert video helped widen her reputation as did her film of *Cavalleria Rusticana* with Franco Zeffirelli. See

OCCASIONE FA IL LADRO, L'

1812 opera by Rossini

Opportunity Makes the Thief is a jaunty early Rossini opera that has been successfully revived on stage in recent years and is now available on video and CD. It's a switched-identity farce with libertine Don Parmenione pretending to be Count Alberto to win Marquise Berenice but she tricks him by switching identities with her maid Ernestina. In the end the right couples get together after a lot of joyful music and good Rossini fun. The libretto by Luigi Prividali is based on a play by Eugène Scribe. See also GIOACHINO ROSSINI.

1992 Schwetzingen Festival

A superbly staged and most appealing Schwetzingen Festival production of the comic opera by Michael Hampe. Natale de Carolis portrays the libertine Don Parmenione, while Monica Bacelli is his love-to-be Ernestina. Stuart Kale is Don Eusebio, Susan Patterson is Berenice and Robert Gambill is the Count. Gianluigi Gelmetti conducts the Stuttgart Radio Symphony Orchestra. Color. In Italian with English subtitles. 90 minutes. Teldec video and laser.

OEDIPUS REX

1927 opera by Stravinsky

Oedipus Rex is one of Stravinsky's most popular works and was originally composed in 1927 for Diaghilev's company Ballets Russes. Jean Cocteau wrote the libretto in Latin basing it on the Sophocles tragedy. Stravinsky wanted the opera in a dead language to give it a timeless quality and also wanted the characters masked. The story is the classic myth. Thebes is suffering from a plague because the murderer of Oedipus's father has not been punished. When Oedipus and his wife/mother Jocasta realize he is the guilty person, she hangs herself and he blinds himself. See also IGOR STRAVINSKY.

1973 Kollo/Troyanos at Harvard

René Kollo portrays Oedipus with Tatiana Troyanos as Jocasta and Tom Krause as Creon in this film of a notable stage production at Harvard University. Color. In Latin with English narration. 55 minutes. Kultur video.

1984 Carré Theater, Amsterdam

Neil Rosenshein stars as Oedipus with Felicity Palmer as Jocasta and Claudio Desderi as Creon in this stage production from the Carré Theater in Amsterdam. Color. In Latin with English narration. 58 minutes. Home Vision video and laser.

1992 Langridge/Norman in Matsumoto

This is a film of an inventive production staged in Japan by Julie Taymor and is stunning both visually and vocally. Philip Langridge portrays Oedipus, Jessye Norman is Jocasta, Bryan Terfel is Creon, Harry Peters is Tiresias, Kayoko Shiraishi is the Speaker, Min Tanaka is the Oedipus dancer, Robert Swenson is the Shepherd and Michio Tatara is the Messenger. Seiji Ozawa conducted the Saito Kinen Orchestra and the Tokyo Opera Singers. The video was produced by Peter Kelb and Pat Jaffe at the Saito Kinen Festival in Matsumoto with cinematography by Bobby Bukowski. Color. In Latin with English narration. 55 minutes. Philips video/on laser.

Related video

1961 Drama into Opera: Oedipus Rex

Leonard Bernstein examines Stravinsky's opera with the help of Metropolitan Opera singers and compares it to the Sophocles play as performed by Broadway actors. Inge Borkh sings Jocasta with David Lloyd as Oedipus in excerpts from the opera while Irene Worth plays Jocasta and Keith Mitchell is Oedipus in excerpts from the play. Bernstein comments on the differences between the two and conducts the New York Philharmonic on this CBS television program. David Greene directed the telecast on Feb. 16, 1951. Black and white. In English. 60 minutes. Video at MTR.

OFFENBACH, JACQUES
German/French composer (1819-1880)

Jacques Offenbach, who popularized the operetta, was born a German but is more identified with French light opera than any other composer. His tuneful operettas, from *Orpheus in the Underworld* to *La Périchole*, remain very popular in France while his opera, *The Tales of Hoffmann*, has become an international opera standard. Offenbach is not quite the father of the French operetta but it was his success that caused it to be recognized. His music has been used thematically in a great many films ranging from musicals like Jean Renoir's *French*

Cancan (1955) to Kenneth Branagh's romance *Peter's Friends* (1992). See BARBE-BLEUE, LA BELLE HÉLÈNE, LES BRIGANDS, LA GRANDE-DUCHESSE DE GÉROLSTEIN, MONSIEUR CHOUFLEURI RESTERA CHEZ LUI LE..., ORPHÉE AUX ENFERS, LA PÉRICHOLE, THE TALES OF HOFFMANN, LA VIE PARISIENNE.

1950 La Valse de Paris

A romantic French film about Offenbach's relationship with his favorite singer and sometime mistress Hortense Schneider. Pierre Fresnay stars as Offenbach but the focus of the film is on Yvonne Printemps as Hortense. She sings some of Offenbach's best music and there are 20 songs and many stage sequences. Both stars are splendid as is the re-creation of the period and the Dior costumes. *Valse* was written and directed by one of the leading theater directors of the period, Marcel Achard. Black and white. In French with English subtitles. 93 minutes. Bel Canto Society video.

1952 Le Plaisir

Max Ophüls' omnibus film of three Guy de Maupassant short stories uses as its music themes from several Offenbach operettas as arranged by Joe Hajos and Maurice Yvain. Jean Gabin heads the all-star cast. Black and white. In French. 97 minutes.

OF MEN AND MUSIC
1950 music film by Reis

This docudrama is a four-part homage to classical music with a twenty-minute segment devoted to Metropolitan Opera stars Jan Peerce and Nadine Conner. The story imagines them returning to a concert hall late at night where they put on a show in costume for the night watchman, a longtime fan. Peerce sings "O Paradiso" from *L'Africaine* and Leoncavallo's "Mattinata" and joins Conner for the farewell scene from *Lucia di Lammermoor*. Conner sings an aria from *Don Pasquale*. Victor Young conducts the unseen orchestra that accompanies them. The other three segments of the film feature pianist Artur Rubinstein, violinist Jascha Heifetz and conductor Dimitri Mitropoulos with the New York Philharmonic. The film was written by Harry Kurnitz and directed by Irving Reis. Twentieth Century Fox. Black and white. 95 minutes.

1977 Peerce, Anderson & Segovia

This 1977 compilation film includes the Jan Peerce-Nadine Conner segment from the film *Of Men and Music*. The other parts of the film feature Marion

Anderson and Andres Segovia. Black and white. 60 minutes. Kultur video.

OLD MAID AND THE THIEF, THE
1939 opera by Menotti

Gian Carlo Menotti's opera *The Old Maid and the Thief* was commissioned by Samuel Chotzinoff for NBC and was one of the first operas composed especially for radio. It was broadcast April 22, 1939, and later staged by the Philadelphia Opera company. In the opera Miss Todd and her servant Laetitia give shelter to the beggar Bob even after they discover he is an escaped thief. They also rob a liquor store when he wants some gin to drink. When Miss Todd threatens to turn him over to the police, he steals her car and elopes with her servant. See also GIAN CARLO MENOTTI.

1949 NBC Opera Theatre
Marie Powers stars as the Old Maid in this early NBC Opera Theatre production of *The Old Maid and the Thief*. Most of the cast came from the New York City Opera production of the opera staged by Roger Englander who produced the TV show. The television production was staged by Samuel Chotzinoff, who had originally commissioned it for radio, while Peter Herman Adler conducted the Symphony of the Air Orchestra. Kirk Browning directed the live telecast. Black and white. In English. 60 minutes.

OLIVERO, MAGDA
Italian soprano (1912-)

Magda Olivero, who made her debut in Turin in 1933, was a great favorite of the composer Francesco Cilea. She became identified with the title role of his opera *Adriana Lecouvreur* in the early 1950s after emerging from ten years of retirement. She then sang widely around the world for 30 more years, making her debut at the Met as Tosca in 1975 at the age of 60. She also continued to sing the role of Adriana Lecouvreur and even recorded it in 1993 at the age of 81. Small wonder that she has acquired a cult following in recent years. She can be seen in full form in a 1960 Tosca and in a documentary about that opera. See TOSCA (1960/1983 film).

1995 Magda Olivero: The Last Verismo Soprano
This is an amazing compilation video of highpoints from Olivero's career. She is first shown singing the role of Adriana Lecouvreur at

the age of 26 in 1938 opposite Beniamino Gigli. Then she is shown in 1993 at the age of 81 (that's 55 years later) singing the same role. There is also an appearance on a 1960 TV show with arias from *La Traviata* and *Iris*, an excerpt from a 1960 film of *Tosca* and an excerpt from *Manon Lescaut*. Color & black and white. 59 minutes. Bel Canto Society video.

OLOFSSON, THOMAS
Swedish TV director (1948-)

Thomas Olofsson produced and directed the videos of the outstanding Mozart productions at the Drottningholm Court Theater in Sweden which Arnold Östman conducted. He not only filmed them with discretion and taste, he sometimes added intriguing extras. *Così Fan Tutte*, for example, has a charming visual prelude: while the overture is playing, the cast is seen arriving by foot, bike and bus and then changing into costume and going on stage. See THE ABDUCTION FROM THE SERAGLIO (1991), AGRIPPINA (1985), LA CLEMENZA DI TITO (1987), COSÌ FAN TUTTE (1984), DON GIOVANNI (1987), LA FINTA GIARDINIERA (1988), IDOMENEO (1991), THE MAGIC FLUTE (1989), THE MARRIAGE OF FIGARO (1981).

OMNIBUS
American television series (1952-1959)

The culturally-oriented *Omnibus* series was involved with presenting opera and operetta from its beginning. Its first show on Nov. 9, 1952, included scenes from *The Mikado*. This was followed in the next program with scenes from *The Merry Widow* and then with the Menotti chamber opera *The Telephone*. In 1953 *Omnibus* teamed with the Metropolitan Opera to present a 65-minute version of *Die Fledermaus* in English involving over 300 people. Next was a 65-minute version of *La Bohème* adapted from the Met production by Joseph Mankiewicz. *Omnibus* also produced operas without involving the Met but productions were sporadic. They included Gershwin's *135th Street*, Respighi's Sleeping *Beauty in the Woods*, Schuman's *The Mighty Casey* and Moore's *The Ballad of Baby Doe*. The series was underwritten by the Ford Foundation and was seen originally on CBS and later on both ABC and CBS. Details are under the individual operas.

O'NEILL, DENNIS
Welsh tenor (1948-)

The Welsh tenor with the Irish name began his career with the Scottish Opera and joined the English Glyndebourne chorus in 1974. He was principal tenor with the South Australian Opera for two seasons and then sang with the Welsh National Opera and the Scottish Opera. He made his debut at Covent Garden in 1979 and was soon singing the leading tenor roles. His career has now widened to the U.S. and other European opera houses. See DIE FLEDERMAUS (1983), MACBETH (1987), MEFISTOFELE (1989), KIRI TE KANAWA (1994), ADELINA PATTI (1993), DER ROSENKAVALIER (1985).

ON THE TOWN
1944 musical by Bernstein

Leonard Bernstein's Broadway musical *On The Town* is not an opera but it is featured on a video starring opera singers in the principal roles. Betty Comden and Adolph Green wrote the fine lyrics and book, Jerome Robbins created the choreography and George Abbott staged it. *On the Town* is based on Bernstein's ballet *Fancy Free* and tells the story of three sailors in New York on 24-hour leave and the women they meet.

1949 Gene Kelly film
On the Town became a rather good MGM film musical in 1949 under the direction of Gene Kelly and Stanley Donen. It stars Kelly, Frank Sinatra and Jules Munshin as the sailors and Vera Allen, Ann Miller and Betty Garrett as their girlfriends. It was shot on location in New York. Color. 98 minutes. MGM-UA video.

1992 Barbican Hall concert
On the Town was filmed with opera singers in 1992 at a concert performance in London's Barbican Hall. The singers are Thomas Hampson, Samuel Ramey, Frederica von Stade, Marie McLaughlin, Kurt Ollman, Tyne Daley, Evelyn Lear and David Garrison. Adolph Green and Betty Comden narrated while Michael Tilson Thomas conducted the London Symphony Orchestra. Christopher Swann directed the video. Color. 107 minutes. DG video and laser.

OPERAS & OPERETTAS ABOUT THE MOVIES

There are a number of operas and operettas about movies and movie stars, some dating from the early days of silent cinema. Cinema-themed operettas were popular in Berlin, London, New York and Rome in the 1910s though none of them have been filmed or televised. The best-known movie-themed operas are recent American works dealing with the nearly mythical Hollywood stars Marilyn Monroe and Rudolph Valentino. The more generic cinema operettas and operas are described below. For individual star operas see THE DREAM OF VALENTINO, MARILYN MONROE.

1912 The Girl on the Film
Filmzauber (Film Magic) was the first operetta with cinema as its subject and was a big hit in Berlin in 1912. It came to London and New York in 1913 as *The Girl on the Film*. It centers around a film company making a movie about Napoleon in a small village. The girl of the title is a society lady on the run who pretends to be a boy to get a part in the film. *Filmzauber* was composed by Germany's Walter Kollo with help from Willy Bredschneider to a libretto by Rudolf Bernauer and Rudolph Schanzer. For England and America, James T. Tanner wrote the libretto, Adrian Ross wrote the lyrics and Albert Sirmay (Szirmai) composed new songs. The stars in both London and New York were George Grossmith, Emmy Wehlen and Madeleine Seymour.

1913 The Queen of the Movies
Die Kinokönigen (The Cinema Queen) was the second operetta about the movies. It opened in Berlin in March 1913 and reached London in 1914 as *The Cinema Star* and New York as *The Queen of the Movies*. The "queen" is a movie actress who pretends to be a princess to trick a stuffy businessman into acting in a film. German composer Jean Gilbert's Berlin operetta, composed to a libretto by Georg Okonkowski and Julius Freund, was first been staged in Hamburg as *Die Elfte Muse* (The Eleventh Muse). The English adaptation was by Glen MacDonough with lyrics by Edward Paulton. In London Jack Hulpert, Cicely Courtneidge and Dorothy Ward starred and in New York Alice Dovey, Frank Moulan and Valli Valli. Irving Berlin wrote new songs for the New York production.

1913 Der Kinotopponkel

Herman Höfert wrote the music for the German movie-oriented operetta *The Cinema Deal Uncle* to a libretto by Georg Schade. It premiered in Berlin on Dec. 17, 1913.

1914 La Signorina del Cinematografo

Carlo Lombardo created this Italian operetta about a movie queen when Italy was one of the film centers of the world. He based it on an 1896 Austrian operetta titled *Der Schmetterling* (The Butterfly) composed by Carlo Weinberger and written by A.M. Willner and Bernhard Buchbinder. As with his other adaptations, Lombardo completely revised the plot and libretto. It was a genuine hit in its new cinematic form and its libretto was even published in a popular edition.

1920 Der Filmstern

The Film Star is an Austrian operetta with a cinematic plot by Fritz Lehner and Willi Stick. It was first produced in Vienna on July 22, 1920.

1928 Les Trois Souhaits

Czech composer Bohuslav Martinu's *The Three Wishes*, is an opera with movies central to its story. The French libretto by Georges Ribemont-Dessaignes opens in a movie studio where a fairy-tale film titled *The Three Wishes* is being screened. A fairy grants the wishes of riches, youth and love to the couple Nina and Arthur. The wishes are seen being fulfilled in dream-like situations on a movie screen. Martinu's musical themes also contain strong references to 1920s pop music. *Troji prani* (its Czech title) was composed in 1928 but was not staged until 1971 in Brno.

1963 Il Pianista del Globe

The Globe Pianist is a fairly recent light opera dedicated to the music of the silent movie era and composed by Sergio Cafaro. The libretto was written by Mario Verdone, a leading Italian film historian and director with a particular interest in silent films and their music. *The Globe Pianist* revolves around a piano player who accompanies silent films in Italy in the early years of the century. Verdone (born 1917) also made a number of documentary films about the silent cinema.

OPERAS AS MOVIES

The "movie opera" is rare but a few operas have actually been created by composers on film. The most common movie opera is an imaginary opera whose highlights are created and staged as part of the plot of a film about opera singers. These are described under the entry IMAGINARY OPERAS IN FILMS. There are also films which are created for and used as an integral part of a stage opera.

1915 Rapsodia Satanica

Cavalleria Rusticana composer Pietro Mascagni wrote the score for this avant-garde film and its screenplay was sold as the "libretto dell'opera" so it would seem to qualify as a film opera. Mascagni created it in collaboration with writer Maria Martini and director Nino Oxilia and they called it a "poema cinema-musical." Lyda Borelli, a major Italian silent cinema diva, was the star and was featured opposite André Habay. Giorgio Ricci was the cinematographer. Mascagni's music was played live by the cinema orchestras in the theaters. Black and white. About 70 minutes. In Italian.

1922 Jenseits des Stromes

Jenseits des Stromes (The Other Side of the River), which was claimed to be the first opera written expressly for the movies, is the work of Berlin opera composer Ferdinand Hummel (1855-1928). He wrote seven operas for the stage, the most famous being the 1893 *Mara*, but they are now all forgotten. His film opera shares their fate. It was composed for singers and orchestra in the silent cinema era and provided its score literally on the screen. A strip of musical notation ran from left to right at the bottom of the image on screen as the picture progressed and this was meant to provide guidance to singers and orchestra in the theaters showing the film. Apparently not many did as the film made hardly a ripple in movie history.

1930 Zwei Kravaten

Zwei Kravaten (Two Ties) was described by *Variety* when it opened in America as an "attempt to create a film opera in the modern music sense of opera, something musically along the lines of Krenek's *Jonny Spielt Auf*, but strictly intended for filming." Metropolitan Opera bass-baritone Michael Bohnen does all the singing in this musical satire set in America. It revolves around a waiter (Bohnen) and his adventures after he exchanges his white tie for a gentleman criminal's black tie as part of an escape ruse. Olga Tschechowa plays the millionairess who sets him on his adventurous way. The music was composed by Micha Spoliansky with words and screenplay by Ladislaus Vajda based a on a novel by Georg Kaiser. Nikolaus Farkas was the cinematographer while Felix Basch and Richard Weichert co-directed. directed. It was distributed in the U.S. in 1932. Black and white. In German. 86 minutes.

1936 The Robber Symphony
This British film also claimed to be the first opera specially created for the screen. It was written, composed and directed by Austrian Friedrich Feher and has some similarities to *The Threepenny Opera*. It tells the story of a group of robber musicians and their search for a treasure hidden in a piano. There is no dialogue. Magda Sonja is the mother, Françoise Rosay is the fortuneteller, Hans Feher is Giannino, George Graves is the grandfather, Webster Booth is the singer and Oscar Ashe is the chief of police. Feher conducted the London Symphony Orchestra. Concordia Films. Black and white. 105 minutes.

1983 The Love Of Destiny
Petr Weigl, the Czech director known for his beautifully photographed opera films, wrote and directed this opera film pastiche. It uses arias from seven operas to tell the impressionistic story of a man's relationship with a mysterious woman. Peter Dvorsky stars as the man and sings arias from *Cavalleria Rusticana, Tosca, Un Ballo in Maschera, La Favorita, Manon, Madama Butterfly* and *Lucia di Lammermoor*. Emilia Aasaryova portrays the enigmatic woman. The film was photographed by Jiri Kadamka and the music is played by the Bratislava Symphony Orchestra. Bratislava Television. Color. In French and Italian. 60 minutes. Kultur video.

1969 La Cireuse Electrique
The Electric Waxer, described by director Jean Renoir as "a little opera," is the second of four episodes in his last film *Le Petit Théâtre par Jean Renoir*. It's the satirical story of a woman (Marguerite Cassan) who has a great love for her electric floor waxing machine and sings about it. Renoir wrote the words, Joseph Kosma wrote the music. Color. In French. 100 minutes. On video.

OPERAS BASED ON MOVIES

Operas based on movies or their screenplays has become a popular idea in recent years and appears to appeal to many modern composers. Philip Glass composed his operas *Orphée* and *La Belle et le Bête* to the screenplays of the Jean Cocteau films and *Belle* is actually sung while the movie is projected. Swiss composer Mathias Ruegg also wrote an opera based on *La Belle et le Bête*. Vaclav Kaslik created an opera based on the screenplay of Fellini's film *La Strada* and Polly Pen composed an opera based on Abraham Room's Soviet silent film *Bed and Sofa*. Harrison Birtwistle was inspired by *King Kong* to compose his opera *The Second Mrs. Kong*. William Balcon's *McTeague* is based on Erich Von Stroheim's film *Greed*. Dominick Argento, who composed the movie star opera *The Dream of Valentino*, plans to use the screenplay of Luchino Visconti's film *The Leopard* as a libretto. The earliest opera based on a movie scenario is the 1921 *La Forfaiture* by Claude Erlanger which is derived from the 1915 American film *The Cheat*. Malcolm Williamson's opera *Our Man in Havana* is based on the Graham Greene novel but the libretto is by screenwriter Sidney Gilliatt and was influenced by the 1959 film that preceded it. Conrad Susa's opera *The Dangerous Liaisons* is based on the French novel but was also influenced by the films that preceded it. See BED AND SOFA, LA BELLE ET LE BÊTE, THE DANGEROUS LIAISONS, LA FORFAITURE, MCTEAGUE, ORPHÉE, THE SECOND MRS. KONG, LA STRADA.

OPERA CAMEOS
American television series (1950-1955)

This television series *Opera Cameos* presented 30-minute highlight versions of famous Italian operas in Italian. They usually included three or four arias performed by well-known singers, sometimes from the Metropolitan, and including Mario del Monaco, Beverly Sills and Regina Resnick. The series was introduced by Giovanni Martinelli, produced by Carlo Vinti and written by Joseph Vinti. Giuseppe Bamboschek conducted the orchestra. *Opera Cameos* originated on the New York station WPIX-TV in 1950 and was later shown on the Dumont network. It was sponsored by Progress Quality Foods. Among the opera presented were CAVALLERIA RUSTICANA (1952), LA FORZA DEL DESTINO (1951), PAGLIACCI (1953), RIGOLETTO (1952), LA TRAVIATA (1953, 1954), IL TROVATORE (1953).

OPERA IMAGINAIRE
1993 animated opera anthology

This is a splendid compendium of twelve animated films of arias created by modern European animators. *Carmen* by Christophe Vallaux and

Pascal Roulin illustrates "Avec la garde montante" sung by Les Petits Chanteurs a Crois de Bois. *Cinderella* by Stephen Palmer features "Questa è un nodo avviluppato" sung by Giulietta Simionata, Paolo Montarsolo, Dora Carra, Giovanni Rionanni and Miti Truccato Pace. *Faust* by Hilary Audus has "Le veau d'or" sung by Nicolai Ghiaurov. *Lakmé* by Pascal Roulin depicts "Viens Malika" sung by Mady Mesplé and Danielle Millet. *Madama Butterfly* by Jonathan Hills illustrates "Un bel dì" sung by Felicia Weather. *The Magic Flute* by Raimund Krumme has "Du also bist mein Bräutigam?" sung by Lucia Popp. *The Marriage of Figaro* by Pascal Roulin portrays "Voi che sapete" sung by Susan Danco. *Pagliacci* by Ken Lidster depicts "Vesti la giubba" sung by Franco Corelli. *The Pearl Fishers* by Jimmy T. Murakami shows "Au fond du temple saint" sung by Nicolai Gedda and Ernest Blanc. *Rigoletto* by Monique Renault has "La donna è mobile" sung by Nicolai Gedda. *Tosca* by Jose Abel illustrates "E lucevan le stelle" sung by Carlo Bergonzi. *La Traviata* by Guionne Leroy depicts the "Gypsy Chorus" sung by the Santa Cecilia Academy Choir. Sue, Sarah and Tess Malinson produced the films for Pascavision. Commissioned by the Arts Council of Great Britain. Color. 52 minutes. Miramar video.

OPERALOGUE
1932 opera film series

The *Operalogue* short film series, made in 1932 for Educational Films by Howard Higgins and Lew Seller, condense opera stories to about twenty minutes and feature only the highlights of the story. The operas were usually given new titles so, for example, *Carmen* became *The Idol of Seville*, *Cavalleria Rusticana* was turned into *Vendetta* and *Martha* was promoted as *Milady's Escape*. See (all 1932) CARMEN, CAVALLERIA RUSTICANA, MARTHA.

OPERA NORTH
English opera company (1977-)

Opera North is a British opera company based in Leeds and founded in 1977 as the English National Opera North. It was renamed Opera North in 1981. The company has been very popular with operagoers in the north of England. See also BAA BAA BLACK SHEEP.

1992 Harry Enfield's Guide to Opera

Opera North is the operatic star of this six-part English TV series intended as a beginner's guide to opera. Paul Daniel of Opera North acts as Harry Enfield's guide and the illustrative opera scenes are performed by the Opera North company. Program One is about how a person becomes interested in opera, Two is concerned with opera plots, Three focuses on the opera voice, Four deals with Italian opera, Five features modern opera stars and Six concerns the Opera North company itself. There are interviews with Placido Domingo, José Carreras, Joan Sutherland and June Anderson and film showing Enrico Caruso, Maria Callas and Mario Lanza. The opera scenes staged by Opera North are *La Bohème, Carmen, Don Giovanni, Gianni Schicchi, Madama Butterfly, The Marriage of Figaro, Nabucco, The Pearl Fishers, Rigoletto, Tosca, La Traviata* and *Turandot*. The singers include Cheryl Barker, David Maxwell Anderson, Linda Kitchen, Claire Powell, Edmund Barham, Anne Dawson, Donald Maxwell, Robert Hayward, John Connell, Janice Cairns, Keith Latham, Joan Rodgers and Anthony Michaels-Moore. The opera extracts were staged by Jonathan Alver and the music is played by the English Northern Philharmonica conducted by Paul Daniel. The series was written by Paul Whitehouse, produced by Douglas Rae and directed by Robin Lough. The video is a condensed version of the TV series. Color. 70 minutes. PMI (England) video.

OPERA STARS IN CONCERT
1991 Madrid concert video

Ruggero Raimondi, Alfredo Kraus, Katia Ricciarelli, Paolo Coni and Lucia Valentini-Terrani are the stars of this colorful concert filmed at Madrid's Plaza de Toros Monumental in 1991 and released on two separate videos. On the first Raimondi sings the aria "Vieni la mia vendetta" from *Lucrezia Borgia*, duets with Coni on "Il rival salvar tu dei" from *I Puritani* and joins Kraus and Ricciarelli on the final trio from *Faust*. Ricciarelli sings Tosca's "Vissi d'arte" and joins Valentini-Terrani in a duet from *The Tales of Hoffmann*. Kraus sings "Lunge da lei" from *La Traviata* and Coni sings an aria from *Don Carlos*. In the second video Raimondi and Ricciarelli sing a duet from *Lucrezia Borgia* while Kraus sings "Una furtiva lagrima" and starts the quartet from *Rigoletto* on which he is joined by Valentini-Terrani, Coni and Ricciarelli. Ricciarelli sings "O mio babbino caro," Coni sings "Eri tu," Raimondi sings "La calunnia," Kraus sings Federico's lament from Cilea's *L'Arlesiana* and Valentina-Terrani closes with a *Carmen* aria. Gian Paolo Sanzogno conducts the Madrid Symphony Orchestra. Color. In Italian and French. Each video 60 minutes. Kultur video.

OPERA VS. JAZZ
1953 American TV series

Opera Vs. Jazz was a half-hour American television series on the ABC network that presented contrasting selections from opera and jazz. Jan Peerce and Alan Dale were regular performers, Nancy Kenyon was the moderator, Fred Heider produced the series and Charles Dubin directed. The series aired from May to September in 1953. There was also a segment in the film *Babes in Arms* titled *Opera Vs. Jazz.*

OPERAVOX
1995 animated operas

Operavox is six operas in animated form created through a collaboration by BBC, S4C and British and Moscow animation studios. The Welsh National Opera Orchestra plays the adapted scores for these films made with budgets of around $800,000. They were made with different animation techniques but are all in color and 27 minutes long. Christopher Grace was executive producer. The critics liked them all. See THE BARBER OF SEVILLE, CARMEN, THE MAGIC FLUTE, DAS RHEINGOLD, RIGOLETTO , TURANDOT.

OPERETTA

The operetta or "little opera," which originated in France, is usually light, tuneful and operatic with spoken dialogue and a happy ending. The musical comedy, which replaced it, does not necessarily have connections to opera as it also grew out of popular music, ragtime and jazz. Librettist Oscar Hammerstein, who wrote both, is the great link between the two genres. His musical masterpieces *Show Boat* and *Oklahoma* are clearly related to operetta though so different from *Der Fledermaus* as to be considered another species. For the purposes of this book modern American and British stage musicals are not considered operettas unless they were deliberately created in the old-fashioned Continental style. Modern French "opérettes" and Central European "Operette" are usually included even though they are also quite different from their 19th century predecessors. For the Spanish equivalent see ZARZUELA.

France
The light operas of Auber and Adam were transmuted into operettas in France in the 1850s when Offenbach defined the genre. Hervé, Lecoq and Messager created other operettas that are still in the French repertory. The form was revitalized in the 1920s by Christine and Hahn and exoticized by Lopez in the 1940s. Most of the films and videos of French operettas are, not surprisingly, French. Offenbach remains popular with opera companies but Lopez has the greatest number of videos. See ADOLPHE ADAM, DANIEL AUBER, EDMON AUDRAN, HENRI CHRISTINÉ, LOUIS GANNE, REYNALDO HAHN, FERDINAND HÉROLD, HERVÉ, CHARLES LECOCQ, FRANCIS LOPEZ, ANDRÉ MESSAGER, JACQUES OFFENBACH, YVONNE PRINTEMPS, VICTOR ROGER.

Central Europe
Suppé is said to have written the first Viennese operetta in 1860 but it was Strauss who made Vienna and the waltz synonymous with operetta. Zeller and Heuberger followed in the 1890s while Lehár, Kálmán and Straus gave the genre new impetus in the new century. The center of gravity shifted to Germany in the 1920s with a strong contribution from Hungarian composers. Nearly all the major German-language operettas have been filmed in Germany or Austria and most are on video. See PAUL ABRAHAM, RALPH BENATZSKY, LEO FALL, JEAN GILBERT, RICHARD HEUBERGER, GEORG JARNO, EMMERICH KÁLMÁN, WALTER KOLLO, FRANZ LEHÁR, PAUL LINCKE, KARL MILLÖCKER, OSCAR NEDBAL, FRED RAYMOND, FRANZ SCHUBERT, ROBERT STOLZ, OSCAR STRAUS, JOHANN STRAUSS, FRANZ VON SUPPÉ, CARL ZELLER, KARL MICHAEL ZIEHRER.

England
The English light operas of the early 19th century are no longer as visible as they once were but there is great charm in the works of Balfe, Benedict and Wallace and they have inspired several films. The comic opera composers Gilbert & Sullivan, however, remain popular and their operettas are nearly all available on video. Most of the English stage composers of the 20th century wrote what they liked to call "musical comedy" though Harold Fraser-Simon, Frederic Norton, Ivor Novello and Noel Coward occasionally created throwbacks to the old operetta style. See MICHAEL BALFE, JULIUS BENEDICT, NOËL COWARD, HAROLD FRASER-SIMSON, GILBERT AND SULLIVAN, FREDERIC NORTON, IVOR NOVELLO, VINCENT WALLACE.

America

The operetta was brought to the U.S. in its Viennese form by European-born composers who created superb additions to the genre. The earliest American operetta of note is De Koven's *Robin Hood* but it was Herbert who made the American operetta into a major force. He was followed by the equally tuneful Romberg and Friml. Gershwin composed one traditional operetta and Bernstein also paid homage to the genre. Although some critics consider the musicals of Kern, Gershwin and Rodgers to be operettas, it can be argued that they created a new American genre which is outside the boundaries of this book. Most of the films of their musicals are excluded unless they starred opera singers. The major period of filming traditional operettas in Hollywood was at the beginning of sound. See LEONARD BERNSTEIN, GEORGE GERSHWIN, JEROME KERN, REGINALD DE KOVEN, RUDOLF FRIML, VICTOR HERBERT, RICHARD RODGERS, SIGMUND ROMBERG, HARRY TIERNEY.

Italy

The light comic opera was created in Italy but the operetta as a separate form never really took root there. However, there are a few Italian operettas, mostly dating from the early 20th century, and some of them were written by major opera composers including Puccini (*La Rondine*), Mascagni (*Sì*) and Leoncavallo (*La Reginetta delle Rose*). See MARIO COSTA, RUGGERO LEONCAVALLO, CARLO LOMBARDO, PIETRO MASCAGNI, GIUSEPPE PIETRI, GIACOMO PUCCINI.

OPERETTE
1940 operetta film by Forst

This German film is essentially a love letter to the classic Viennese operetta. Leo Slezak stars as Franz von Suppé with Edmund Schellhammer as Johann Strauss Jr. and Kurt Jurgens as Karl Millöcker. The film is set in operetta's golden age in Imperial Vienna and includes operetta tunes from all three composers. Willi Forst, who wrote and directed the film, plays the main role. The film was not shown in the U.S. until 1949. Black and white. In German. 109 minutes. Lyric SRO video.

OPERNBALL, DER
1898 operetta by Heuberger

The Opera Ball is the most famous operetta by Austrian composer Richard Heuberger and continues to be revived in its native Vienna. The libretto by Victor Léon and Henrich von Waldberg is based on the play *Les Dominos Roses* by Alfred Hennequin and Alfred Delacour. The plot is similar to *Die Fledermaus* with the principal characters attending a masked ball in Paris wearing pink dominos. Its most famous tune is the waltz "Im chambre séparée" which has become a staple of operetta singers; Joan Sutherland included it on her influential album *The Golden Age of Operetta*. *The Opera Ball* was first staged in New York in 1912 with Marie Cahill as its star. See also RICHARD HEUBERGER.

1931 Liane Haid film
Liane Haid and Ivan Petrovich star in this Austrian film of the operetta directed by Max Neufeld. The cast also includes Betty Bird as Vicky the maid, Georg Alexander as Georg, Otto Wallburg as Von Arnolds and Irene Ambrus as Ilona. It was adapted for the screen by Neufeld, Jacques Bachrach and Ida Jenbach. It was released in the U.S. in 1931. Black and white. In German. 90 minutes.

1939 Marte Harell film
Marte Harell plays Elisabeth and Paul Hörbiger is her husband Georg in this lively German film of the operetta directed by Geza von Bolvary. The cast also includes Will, Dohm, Heli Finkenzeller, Hans Moser and Theo Lingen. Ernst Marischka wrote the adaptation while Willy Winterstein was the cinematographer. Black and white. In German. 93 minutes.

1956 Ernst Marischka film
Ernst Marischka, who wrote the 1939 version, directed this third film of the operetta. It stars Rudolf Vogel, Johannes Heesters, Sonja Ziemann, Fita Benkoff, Hertha Feilder and Theo Lingen. Brunbi Mondi was the cinematographer. Black and white. In German. 92 minutes.

1971 Helen Mané film
Helen Mané stars in this lavish German film of the operetta opposite Harald Serafin and Maria Tiboldi. Willy Mattes conducted the Kurt Graunke Symphony Orchestra and Eugen York directed the film in 35mm for German television. Unitel. Color. In German. 100 minutes.

OPHULS, MAX
German film director (1902-1957)

Max Ophuls was born in Germany but spent most of his life as a vagabond making films in different countries from Germany, Italy and France to America. His early German and French films are great, his middle-period American films are superb and his final French films are masterpieces; no one has ever used the camera as fluidly as Ophuls. There are many opera connections in his films and often their structure is operatic. The 1932 *Die Verkaufte Braut* is a German version of Smetana's Czech opera *The Bartered Bride* and one of the best films of the genre. *La Signora di Tutti* centers around an imaginary opera which helps bring about a love affair. *Letter from an Unknown Woman* reaches its climax at a performance of *The Magic Flute* at the Vienna Opera House. *Yoshiwara* has a *Madama Butterfly*-type plot but the opera at its center is *Fidelio*. *Le Plaisir* is influenced by and uses music by Offenbach. The plot of *Madame de...* revolves around earrings supposedly lost at the opera house and features musical themes from *Les Huguenots*. *Werther* is derived from the source novel of the Massenet opera of the same title. Oscar Straus, the creator of *The Merry Widow*, composed the famous theme for *La Ronde*. See THE BARTERED BRIDE (1932), FIDELIO (1937 film), LES HUGUENOTS (1951 film), IMAGINARY OPERAS IN FILMS (1934), THE MAGIC FLUTE (1948 film), JACQUES OFFENBACH (1952), OSCAR STRAUS (1950), WERTHER (1938 film).

1934 La Signora di Tutti
An imaginary opera is at the center of this film. Young Isa Miranda is taken to an opera by Memo Benassi and afterwards listens enthralled as he describes the plot in detail to his wife. Their illicit love is born during the telling. On the following night as the opera is heard on the radio by the wife, the girl and the man embrace in the garden. The wife is suspicious, sets out to look for them and dies when her wheelchair falls down the stairs. Miranda later imagines she hears this music even when it is not playing. The opera music was written by Daniel Amfitheatrof who began his professional career at La Scala. Black and white. In Italian. 89 minutes. Connoisseur video.

ORATORIO
Religious musical drama (1600-)

The oratorio and the opera are closely related and originated at almost the same time. An oratorio, in essence, is a religious opera for it has a story and vocal parts for soloists and ensembles even though it is presented without scenery, costumes or theatrical movement. Some modern oratorios, like Stravinsky's *Oedipus Rex*, are not even traditionally religious so it is not always easy to distinguish between the genres. Handel's Italian oratorios do not seem all that different from his Italian operas and have sometimes been staged like operas. A few operatic oratorios have entries in this book. See BELSHAZZAR, CARMINA BURANA, THE CREATION, JEANNE D'ARC AU BÛCHER, MESSIAH, OEDIPUS REX, WAR REQUIEM.

ORDUÑA, JUAN DE
Spanish film director (1907-1973)

Juan de Orduña y Fernández-Shaw began his film career as an actor starring in zarzuela films in the 1920s including *La Revoltosa*, *La Chavala* and *El Rey que Rabió*. He began to direct in 1943 and became one of the most commercially successful modern Spanish directors. His biggest hit was *El Último Cuplé* starring Sara Montiel. At the end of his career he returned to the zarzuela film and from 1967 to 1969 directed superb 35mm versions of classic zarzuelas for Spanish television. See EL BARBERILLO DE LAVAPIÉS, BOHEMIOS, JOSÉ SERRANO (La Canción del Olvidó), EL CASERIO, GIGANTES Y CABEZUDOS, LAS GOLONDRINAS, EL HUÉSPED DEL SEVILLANO, LUISA FERNANDA, MARUXA, LA REVOLTOSA, EL REY QUE RABIÓ, LOS SOBRINOS DEL CAPITÁN GRANT.

ORFEO
1607 opera by Monteverdi

Claudio Monteverdi's *Orfeo* is the earliest opera still regularly performed and the earliest on video. Monteverdi's version of the myth of Orpheus and Euridice, libretto by Alessandro Striggio, retells in elaborate form the legend of the musician who can charm Death but still lose the woman he loves. The opera has a number of singing roles in addition to Orpheus and Eurydice including Charon, Pluto, Apollo and Proserpina. See also CLAUDIO MONTEVERDI.

1971 Raymond Rouleau video

Raymond Rouleau created this Italian TV production of the opera staged as a Renaissance entertainment for a wealthy patron. Lajos Kozma sings the role of Orpheus while Nino Sanzogno conducts the RAI orchestra. The production was presented on NET Opera Theater in February 1971. Black and white. In Italian with English subtitles. 50 minutes. On video.

1978 Jean-Pierre Ponnelle film

Director Jean-Pierre Ponnelle and early music master Nikolaus Harnoncourt produced this outstanding film of the opera. It was filmed as an opera being performed for a period audience with singers, players and audience intermingling in a theatrically effective manner. The film grew out of a famous cycle of the Monteverdi operas at the Zurich Opera House, and the film cast is almost the same as that for the stage production. Philippe Huttenlocher is Orpheus, Dietlinde Turban is Eurydice, Roland Hermann is Apollo, Glenys Linos is the Messenger and Proserpina, Werner Gröschel is Pluto, Hans Franzen is Charon and Trudeliese Schmidt is Music and Hope. The film was written by Ponnelle, photographed by Wolfgang Treu, costumed by Pet Halmen and designed by Gerd Janka. Harnoncourt leads the Monteverdi Ensemble of the Zurich Opera House. Unitel Film. Color. In Italian with English subtitles. 102 minutes. London video/laser.

1985 Claude Goretta film

Swiss filmmaker Claude Goretta, known for *The Lacemaker*, premiered his film of the opera at the 1985 Venice Film Festival. A few critics objected to its stylized sets and lack of naturalism but most liked it for its sensitive direction, good acting and excellent singing. Gino Quilico stars as Orpheus, Audrey Michael is Eurydice, Carolyn Watkinson is the Messenger, Eric Tappy is Apollo, Colette Alliot-Lugas is Music, Danielle Borst is Proserpina, Frangiskos Voutsinos is Pluto and Filippo Da Garra is Charon. Michel Corboz conducts the Lyons Opera Orchestra and the Chapelle Royale vocal ensemble. Color. In Italian. 92 minutes.

ORFEO ED EURIDICE
1762 opera by Gluck

Christoph Gluck's version of the Orpheus and Eurydice myth was the first of his so-called simplified "reform" operas. Ranieri da Calzabigi wrote the original Italian libretto, and Pierre Louis Moline revised it in French as *Orphée et Eurydice*. The story is the traditional tale with Orpheus rescuing his dead wife from Hades by his music but losing her when he looks back. It has a smaller cast than the Monteverdi opera of the same myth and features only three singers. Orfeo is a contralto role while Euridice and Amore are both sopranos. See also CHRISTOPH WILLIBALD GLUCK.

1982 Glyndebourne Festival

This is an elegant neoclassic production with Dame Janet Baker at her best as Orfeo. She chose this work as her farewell to the opera stage with Sir Peter Hall directing a much-liked staging with sets designed by John Bury. Elizabeth Gale is excellent as Amore and Elisabeth Speiser is a charming Euridice. Hall breaks out of the stage in the final scene with a celebration that spills into the stalls and balconies. Raymond Leppard conducts the London Philharmonic Orchestra. Rodney Greenberg directed for video. Color. In Italian with English subtitles. 135 minutes. Home Vision video/Pioneer Artists laser.

1985 István Gaál film

István Gaál, one of Hungary's top filmmakers, premiered his version of the opera at the Venice Film Festival. He shot it in natural settings but still created a rather dream-like atmosphere. Baritone Lajos Miller sings the role of Orpheus acted by Sándor Téri, soprano Maddalena Bonifaccio is the voice of Eurydice acted by Eniko Eszenyi and soprano Veronika Kincses sings Amore acted by Ákos Sebestyén. Tamás Vásári conducts the Franz Liszt Chamber Orchestra and the Hungarian Radio and Television Choir. The sets are by Tamas Zanko and costumes by Judith Gombar. The cinematographers were Sandor Sara and Sandor Kurucz. The Hungarian title is *Orfeusz es Eurydike*. Color. In Italian. 95 minutes.

1987 Patricia Wise video

Patricia Wise stars as Euridice, Murray Dickie is Orfeo and Birgit Fandrey is Amor in this production created for East German and Austrian television. Max Pommer conducts the Leipzig Rundfunk Symphony Orchestra. Color. In German with Japanese subtitles. 82 minutes. On Japanese laser.

1989 Müllerschön/Werhahn film

This German film by Nikolai Müllerschön and Peter Werhahn features a highlights version of the opera. It uses key scenes from the Gluck opera to tell the story of the myth. The scenes were shot in a variety of settings including a Renaissance cloister, a quarry and a post-modern glass building. Color. In English or German. 55 minutes. Inter Nationes video.

1991 Royal Opera House

Director Harry Kupfer's modernized version was conceived for the Berlin Komische Opera but won the Olivier Award for Outstanding Achievement in Opera when it was staged at the Royal Opera House, Covent Garden. In this production, Orfeo wears a leather jacket and jeans, watches Eurydice die in a street accident, gets depressed, goes to a hospital/Hades and charms the beasts of the inner city. The complicated sets by Hans Schavernock are most impressive using projected imagery on revolving screens and mirrors to reflect performers, musicians and, eventually, the audience. German male alto Jochen Kowalski gives a virtuoso performance as Orfeo with British soprano Gillian Webster as Euridice and Jeremy Budd as Amore. Harmut Haenchen conducted the Royal Opera House Orchestra and Hans Hulscher directed the video. Color. In Italian with English subtitles. 80 minutes. RM Arts. Home Vision video/ Pioneer Artists laser.

Early/related films

1906 Danish film

When Gluck revised the opera for France he added a ballet in the second act. This early film shows that ballet as performed by the Royal Danish Ballet in 1906 for the silent camera. The soloists are Valborg Borchensenius, Ellen Price, Elisabeth Beck, Anna Agerhold. Black and white. About 10 minutes. Print in Danish film archive.

1949 Orphée

Jean Cocteau's superb film version of the Orpheus and Eurydice legend pays homage to Gluck by occasionally quoting music from the opera. Jean Marais portrays Orpheus and Maria Déa is Eurydice. Black and white. In French. 112 minutes.

1968 Hot Millions.

The "Dance of the Blessed Spirits" from the opera is played on the flute by Maggie Smith while Peter Ustinov listens seated at an antique keyboard. He is so impressed that romance blossoms. Eric Till directed. Color. 105 minutes.

1976 The Innocent

L'Innocente, Luchino Visconti's last film, has an ironic use of the aria "Che farò senza Euridice?" The story concerns an aristocrat who neglects his beautiful wife until she becomes interested in someone else at which he point he falls in love with her. Color. In Italian. 125 minutes

ORFF, CARL
German composer (1895-1982)

Carl Orff studied opera intensely as a young man and wrote many stage works though few are operas in the traditional sense. His influence on modern composers like the minimalists, however, is now becoming evident. His operas include *Antigonae* and *Oedipus der Tyran*, which are on CD, and the earlier and popular *Der Mond* and *Die Kluge*. Orff's best known stage work, and the most often recorded and videotaped, is his "staged cantata" *Carmina Burana*. It may not be an opera in the usual sense but it is one of the works that has helped alter modern ideas about what opera is. See CARMINA BURANA.

ORLANDO FURIOSO
1727 opera by Vivaldi

Antonio Vivaldi's Venetian opera, libretto by Grazio Braccioli, is based on an epic poem by Ludovico Ariosto. It centers around the crusader knight Orlando (Roland in English) who has fallen in love with a woman called Angelica. She, however, loves and marries someone else. This drives him mad. Meanwhile the sorceress Alcina has bewitched the knight Ruggiero. He is eventually saved by his fiancée Bradamante. See also ANTONIO VIVALDI.

1990 San Francisco Opera

This superb San Francisco Opera production of *Orlando Furioso* with Marilyn Horne is the only video of a Vivaldi opera. Horne is at her bel canto best portraying Orlando with Susan Patterson as the beloved Angelica, Kathleen Kuhlmann as the evil Alcina, counter tenor Jeffrey Gall as Ruggiero, Sandra Walker as Bradamante, William Matteuzzi as Angelica's lover Medoro and Kevin Langan as one of Alcina's victims. The production was designed and staged by Pier Luigi Pizzi. Randall Behr conducts the orchestra and chorus of the San Francisco Opera. Brian Large directed the video. Color. In Italian with English subtitles. 130 minutes. Home Vision video/Pioneer laserdisc.

ORMANDY, EUGENE
American conductor (1899-1985)

Eugene Ormandy began his operatic career conducting *Die Fledermaus* at the Metropolitan in 1950. It was such a hit that it was restaged as a television special in 1953 and won even wider acclaim. The following year he conducted the Philadelphia Orchestra for a CBS performance of *The Merry Widow* with Patrice Munsel. Both operettas are on video. See DIE FLEDERMAUS (1953), THE MERRY WIDOW (1954).

ORPHÉE
1993 screen opera by Glass

Philip Glass took his libretto for this opera directly from the screenplay of the 1949 French film *Orphée* written and directed by Jean Cocteau. The film is a surrealistic modern version of the Orpheus myth set in Paris. Death is a princess who falls in love with the poet Orpheus and helps him go to Hell to retrieve his lost love Eurydice. Francesca Zambello directed the first production of the Glass opera at the American Repertory Theater in Cambridge, Massachusetts with moveable sets by Robert Israel. Baritone Eugene Perry sang the role of Orpheus, Lynn Torgove was Eurydice and Wendy Hill was the Princess. Martin Goldray conducted the Philip Glass Ensemble. See also PHILIP GLASS.

ORPHÉE AUX ENFERS
1858 opéra-bouffe by Offenbach

Jacques Offenbach gave Paris and the world the can-can in his *Orpheus in the Underworld*, a delightful satire based around the legend of Orpheus and Eurydice and the Olympian gods. It is one of the best of the Offenbach operettas, a remarkable send-up of serious Gluck-style operas and still a tuneful delight. Orpheus and Eurydice are bored with each other and have other lovers. Public Opinion forces Orpheus to go to the afterworld for his wife though he is clearly not interested and Eurydice was happy to get away. Jupiter, Pluto and other gods then get involved and Jupiter even turns into a fly to seduce Eurydice. The operetta is usually produced in translation outside France. See also JACQUES OFFENBACH.

1962 Sadler Wells video
June Bronhill portrays Eurydice in this English Sadler's Wells production by Wendy Toye produced for Granada Television by Douglas Terry. Kevin Miller is Orpheus with Eric Shilling as Jupiter and Anna Pollak as Calliope. The cast also includes Heather Begg, Jon Weaving and Sophie Trant. Alexander Faris conducts the Sadler's Wells Orchestra and Chorus. The video was screened in the U.S. in the NET Playhouse series. Black and white. In English. 90 minutes.

1968 Joachim Hess film
Joachim Hess wrote and directed this *Orpheus in der Unterwelt*, a West German television film of the operetta sung in German. His co-adapter was Gunther Fleckenstein and Victor Reinshagen arranged the music. Color. In German. 106 minutes.

1974 Horst Bonnet film
Horst Bonnet wrote and directed this *Orpheus in der Unterwelt*, an East German film of the operetta sung in German. It stars Wolfgang Greese, Dorit Gabler and Rolf Habler. DEFA Production. Color. In German. 87 minutes.

1983 George Walker film
A charming English film of the operetta made by George Walker and presented as if being seen by Emperor Napoleon III and his Empress in a private theater in 1865. Dennis Quilley portrays Jupiter and Napoleon, Lillian Watson is Eurydice, Honor Blackman is the Empress, Alexander Oliver is Orpheus, Christopher Gable is Mercury, Emile Belcourt is Pluto, Elizabeth Gale is Cupid, Pauline Tinsley is Public Opinion, Felicity Palmer is Venus and Isobel Buchanan is Diana. Alexander Faris, who is made up to look like Offenbach, conducts the BBC Concert Orchestra and Ambrosian Opera Chorus. Christopher Renshaw staged the operetta, Judith De Paul produced and Derek Bailey directed the film for BBC TV. Color. In English. 90 minutes. Lyric video.

1990 Japanese HTDV video
Kanichi Suzuki stars as Orpheus opposite Yuko Shimada as Eurydice in this Japanese production sung in French. Mie Nakao portrays Public Opinion, Ruri Usami is Venus and Satsuki Adachi is Cupid. Shunsaku Tsutsumi conducts the

orchestra. The video was made by NHK and shot on HTDV. Color. In French. 94 minutes. On Japanese laserdisc.

Early films

1909 Nar jag var prins utav Arkadien
Oscar Bergstrom sings an Orphée aria in Swedish in this early Swedish sound film. Charles Magnusson directed using the pioneer Biophon sound system. Svenska Biografteatern. Black and white. About 4 minutes.

1910 Orfeus I Underjorden
A second early Swedish sound film with an aria from the operetta sung by Oscar Bergstrom. Charles Magnusson directed for Svenska Biografteatern. Black and white. About 4 minutes.

OSTEN, SUZANNE
Swedish film director

Susanne Osten, one of the top filmmakers in Sweden, had international success with her 1986 film *The Mozart Brothers* which dealt with the problems of staging *Don Giovanni*. The influence of the Marx Brothers and *A Night at the Opera* is evident but there is genuine empathy with Mozart. The film tells the story of a director who wants to stand the "old war-horse opera" on its head and create a vital new production. See DON GIOVANNI.

ÖSTMAN, ARNOLD
Swedish conductor (1939-)

Arnold Östman has made Mozart operas into a new and delightful experience through his authentic period performances at the Drottningholm Court Theater in Sweden, one of the last authentic chamber opera theaters in the world. The operas are presented with the orchestra in period costume playing period instruments. Östman became music director of the theater in 1979, and his recordings and videos of the operas have been highly acclaimed. He has now left Drottningholm but his videos and laserdiscs of these operas remain classics. He can also be seen on video conducting other early operas. See THE ABDUCTION FROM THE SERAGLIO (1991), AGRIPPINA (1985), LA CLEMENZA DI TITO (1987), COSÌ FAN TUTTE (1984), DON GIOVANNI (1987), LA DONNA DEL LAGO (1990), FALSTAFF BY SALIERI (1995), LA FINTA GIARDINIERA (1988), IDOMENEO (1991), THE MAGIC FLUTE (1989), THE MARRIAGE OF FIGARO (1981).

OTELLO
1887 opera by Verdi

Verdi had not written a new opera for 16 years when he was cajoled back into composing by poet-composer Arrigo Boito. Boito wrote one of the great opera librettos for Verdi and a few foolish critics even prefer his adaptation to the Shakespeare play. They are, of course, Italians. Boito made many changes but the basic story is not altered. Military leader Otello is married to beautiful Desdemona but is made jealous of her by Iago. Enraged he strangles her and kills himself. Iago's "Credo" is one of the great pieces of operatic dramatic writing and Desdemona's "Willow Song" is one of the most moving of all arias. See also GIUSEPPE VERDI.

1948 Metropolitan Opera telecast
Ramón Vinay stars as Otello, Leonard Warren sings the role of Iago and Licia Albanese is Desdemona in this historic telecast. This was the first complete opera ever televised live and it opened the 1948-1949 season at the Metropolitan Opera. Sponsor Texaco paid an extra $20,000 for the rehearsals of the telecast. Milton Cross introduced the acts and explained the action and Fritz Busch conducted the Metropolitan Opera orchestra. Burke Crotty produced and directed the telecast. Black and white. In Italian. 210 minutes.

1958 Mario Del Monaco film
Mario Del Monaco is a powerful and impressive Otello in this film made for Italian television. Rosanna Carteri is a sweet Desdemona and Renato Capecchi a mean Iago. They didn't want subtlety in these RAI productions aimed at the widest audience with pop song style close-ups. Gino Mattera is Cassio, Athos Cesarini is Roderigo and Luisella Ciaffi is Emilia. Mariano Mercuri designed the sets and Veniero Colasanti the costumes. Tullio Serafin conducted the RAI Orchestra and Chorus and Franco Enriquez directed the film. Black and white. In Italian. 136 minutes. Lyric video.

1959 Charles Holland film
African-American tenor Charles Holland stars as Otello in this production filmed by Rudolph Cartier for BBC Television. Ronald Lewis is Iago, Heidi Krall is Desdemona and the cast also includes John Ford, John Kentish, Forbes Robinson and Barbara

Hewitt. The opera was telecast on Oct. 1, 1959. Black and white. 123 minutes. Print at NFTA.

1961 Zurich Stadtheatre

American James McCracken, who became internationally famous as Otello, stars in this telecast production by Herbert Graf at the Zurich Stadtheatre. It was a huge success and helped make McCracken the top Otello of his time. Maria van Dongen sings Desdemona, Rudolf Knoll is Iago and American singers Mary Davenport and Robert Thomas are Emilia and Cassio. Black and white. In Italian. 150 minutes. On video.

1961 Del Monaco/Gobbi video

Mario Del Monaco sings Otello with Tito Gobbi as his Iago in this Japanese telecast of the opera. Gabriella Tucci takes the role of Desdemona and Franco Capuana conducts the Lirica Italiana Orchestra. Black and white. In Italian. 135 minutes. On Japanese laserdisc.

1962 Renata Tebaldi video

Renata Tebaldi stars as Desdemona with Hans Beirer as Otello in this fine Berlin Deutsche Opera production by Hans Peter Lehmann. William Dooley sings the role of Iago. Wilhelm Reinking designed the simple sets and Giuseppe Patané conducted the Deutsche Opera Orchestra. Korbinian Koeberle directed the video telecast in Tokyo on Sept. 1, 1962. Black and white. Soloists sing in Italian, chorus in German. 147 minutes. Legato Classics video/Japanese laserdisc.

1963 James McCracken video

James McCracken, now famous in the role, portrays Otello in this highlights version of the opera presented on the *Voice of Firestone* television show. Robert Merrill is Iago and Gabriella Tucci is Desdemona. The scenes are fully staged with sets and extras and the orchestra is conducted by Harry John Brown. It was telecast March 3, 1963. Black and white. In Italian with English introductions. About 22 minutes. VAI video *A Firestone Verdi Festival*.

1969 Walter Felsenstein film

Influential East Berlin stage director Walter Felsenstein produced this film of *Otello* in German with the Berlin Komischer Oper. Felsenstein seems to have been influenced in his cinematic style by Eisenstein and Pudovkin. Hanns Nocker portrays Otello, Christa Noack-Von Kamptz is Desdemona,

Vladimir Bauer is Iago, Hans-Otto Ragge is Cassio and Hanna Schmook is Emilia. Otto Merz and Hans-Jurgen Reinecke were the cinematographers, Alfred Tolle designed the sets and Kurt Masur conducted the Berlin Komischer Oper Orchestra. DEFA. Color. In German. 121 minutes. VIEW video.

1974 Herbert von Karajan film

Jon Vickers stars as Otello with Mirella Freni as Desdemona and Peter Glossop as Iago in this film produced by Herbert von Karajan. Cassio is played by Aldo Bottion, Roderigo is Michel Senechal and Stefania Malagu is Emilia. Karajan conducts the Berlin Philharmonic and the Deutsche Opera Chorus. Roger Benamou was the film director. Unitel. Color. In Italian with English subtitles. 145 minutes. DG video.

1978 Metropolitan Opera

Jon Vickers sings the role of Otello in this Metropolitan Opera production with Renata Scotto as Desdemona and Cornell MacNeil as Iago. Jean Kraft is Emilia, Raymond Gibbs is Cassio and Andrea Elis is Roderigo. The production was designed and originally produced by Franco Zeffirelli but this staging is by Fabrizio Melano with costumes designed by Peter J. Hall. Kirk Browning directed the Sept. 25. 1978 telecast. Color. In Italian with English subtitles. 140 minutes. Video at MTR.

1979 Metropolitan Opera

Placido Domingo sings the role of Otello in this Metropolitan Opera production with Gilda Cruz-Romo as Desdemona and Sherrill Milnes as Iago. Shirley Mills is Emilia and Giuliano Giannella is Cassio. The production was designed and originally produced by Franco Zeffirelli but this staging is by Fabrizio Melano. The telecast alos features a documentary film about Domingo's preparations for the role. Kirk Browning directed the telecast on Sept. 24, 1979. Color. In Italian with English subtitles. 140 minutes. Video at MTR.

1982 Verona Arena

Kiri Te Kanawa gives a wonderful performance as Desdemona in this large scale open-air Verona Arena production by Italian filmmaker Gianfranco de Bosio. Vladimir Atlantov sings the role of Otello and Piero Cappuccilli is Iago. The sets and costumes by Vittorio Rossi are awe-inspiring. Zoltan Pesko leads the Verona Orchestra and Chorus with vigor. Preben Montell directed the video. Color. In Italian with English subtitles. 145 minutes. HBO video.

1982 Opera Stories
A laserdisc highlights version of the above production narrated by Charlton Heston. The framing material was shot in Jerusalem in 1989 by Keith Cheetham. Color. In English and Italian with English subtitles. 52 minutes. Pioneer Artists laser.

1986 Franco Zeffirelli film
Franco Zeffirelli received criticism for this film by those who insist that operas be filmed exactly as they were written for the stage. Zeffirelli changes the opera considerably including having Otello kill Iago and cutting Desdemona's "Willow Song." All the same Zeffirelli has created a beautiful film, extraordinarily well photographed by Ennio Guarineri. The sets are impressive, the costumes were nominated for an Oscar, the opening storm is a powerhouse and the cast of singers is outstanding. Placido Domingo is one of the great Otellos, Katia Ricciarelli is fine as Desdemona, Justino Diaz is believable as Iago, Petra Malakova is Emilia and Cassio is sung by Ezio Di Cesare with Umberto Barberini acting the role. Lorin Maazel conducted the La Scala Orchestra and Chorus. 123 minutes. Color. In Italian with English subtitles. Kultur video.

1993 Covent Garden
Placido Domingo and Kiri Te Kanawa star as Otello and Desdemona in this superb Royal Opera production by Elijah Moshinsky. Sergei Leiferkus is Iago, Claire Powell is Emilia, Robin Leggate is Cassio and Ramon Remedio is Roderigo. Sir Georg Solti conducted the Royal Opera House Orchestra and Chorus and Brian Large directed the video. Color. 146 minutes. Home Vision video/ Pioneer laser.

1994 Verona Arena
Placido Domingo celebrated twenty five years of appearances at the Verona Arena with a special program of staged opera scenes that was televised in Italy. The program includes Act I of *Otello* with Domingo as Otello and Daniela Dessi as Desdemona. Nello Santi conducts the Verona Arena Orchestra. SACIS. Color. 90 minutes. On video.

1995 Metropolitan Opera
Placido Domingo once again stars as Otello but this time Renée Fleming as Desdemona won the got the most applause and best reviews. This fine Metropolitan Opera production by Elijah Moshinsky also features James Morris as a solid Iago, Richard Croft as Cassio, Charles Anthony as Rodrigo, Jane Bunnell as Emilia and Alexander Anisimov as Lodovico. Michael Yeargan designed the sets and Peter Hall the costumes. James Levine conducted the Met Orchestra and Chorus and Brian Large directed the video in October 1995. The opera was telecast on Feb. 1, 1996. Color. In Italian with English subtitles. 150 minutes.

Early/related Films

SHAKESPEARE FILMS
There are a great many films of the play *Othello* from the silent era onward. The best are the 1952 version directed by and starring Orson Welles and the 1965 version starring Laurence Olivier and directed by Stuart Burge. There is also an interesting Soviet ballet film based on the play and starring Vakhtang Chabukiani as a dancing Otello.

1907 The Death of Otello
Henny Porten stars as Desdemona with her father Franz as Otello and her sister Rosa as Emilia in this early German sound film. It uses Verdi's music synchronized on a record to accompany the final scenes of the opera. Franz directed the film in a Berlin studio using Oskar Messter's sound synchronization process. Black and white. In German. About 4 minutes.

1913 Bianco contro Negro
Ernesto Maria Pasquali made this Italian sound film of the Otello story in 1913 using Verdi's opera music. In *Bianco contro Negro* (White against Black), Alberto Capozzi portrays Otello with Mary Cleo Tarlarini as Desdemona. Pasquali Films. Black and white. In Italian. About 45 minutes.

1930 Frances Alda Vitaphone film
Metropolitan Opera soprano Frances Alda sings the "Ave Maria" aria from *Otello* in costume in this Vitaphone sound short. Black and white. About 8 minutes. Bel Canto Society video.

1930 Titta Ruffo Sings Iago's Credo
This early sound film made by the MGM studio features Italian baritone Tito Ruffo singing Iago's "Credo." It was filmed on a set with costume and

orchestra. Black and white. In Italian. About 8 minutes.

1979 Placido Domingo: Make-up for Otello
A PBS documentary about Placido Domingo's preparations for the 1979 Metropolitan Opera production of Otello. It was shown on Sept. 24, 1979, in connection with the telecast of the opera. Color. 55 minutes. Video at MTR.

OTELLO BY ROSSINI
1816 opera

Gioachino Rossini's opera version of Shakespeare's *Othello*, composed to a libretto by Francesco Beria di Salsa, was quite popular in the 19th century. It is less well known today as it has been replaced in the repertory by the Boito/Verdi masterpiece. Rossini's version does not follow the play as closely as Verdi. His opera is set in the Venetian first act of the Shakespeare play with Desdemona engaged to Rodrigo but in love with Otello. After being made jealous by Iago and fighting a duel, Otello is banished and returns secretly to kill Desdemona. Iago and Otello both commit suicide at the end of the opera. See also GIOACHINO ROSSINI.

1988 Pesaro Festival
June Anderson is Desdemona and Chris Merritt is Otello in this Pesaro Festival production by Pier Luigi Pizzi. Iago is Enzo di Cesare, Rodrigo is Rockwell Blake and Raquel Pierotti is Emilia in this excellent production designed by Pizzi. John Pritchard conducted the Turin RAI Symphony Orchestra and Ilio Catani directed the telecast. The video is an off-air tape of a RAI telecast. Color. In Italian. 184 minutes. Lyric video.

OTTER, ANNE-SOFIE VON
Swedish mezzo-soprano (1955-)

Anne-Sophie von Otter was born in Stockholm in 1955 and began her professional career in Basle in 1983 as Alcina in Haydn's *Orlando Paladino*. She sang there and at Aix-en-Provence for the next two years. She made her Covent Garden debut in 1985 as Cherubino and reached the Metropolitan in 1988 in the same role. Her career has now become truly international and she is noted for her trouser roles especially Cherubino, Sextus and the Composer. See DAMNATION DE FAUST, LA (1989), MESSIAH (1992), MOZART REQUIEM (1991), DER ROSENKAVALIER (1994).

OWEN WINGRAVE
1971 TV opera by Britten

Benjamin Britten's *Owen Wingrave* is one of the most important operas written for the screen. Britten was commissioned by BBC television to create it using TV techniques. Myfanwy Piper's libretto is based on a story by Henry James about a pacifist in 19th century England. When he refuses to go in the army, his military-oriented family shuns him and his fiancée accuses him of cowardice. The premiere performance, also available on CD, stars Benjamin Luxon as Owen Wingrave, Janet Baker as his bride-to-be Kate and John Shirley-Quirk as his tutor. Sylvia Fisher is Miss Windgrave, Heather Harper is Mrs Coyle, Jennifer Vyvyan is Mrs Julian and Peter Pears is the Narrator. Britten himself conducted the English Chamber Orchestra. John Culshaw produced and Colin Graham directed the telecast on May 16, 1971, on BBC in England and NET in America. Color. In English. 110 minutes. See also BENJAMIN BRITTEN.

OZAWA, SEIJI
American conductor (1935-)

Seiji Ozawa studied in Tokyo, won a number of international competitions and began to work with Herbert von Karajan and Leonard Bernstein. The first opera he conducted was *Così Fan Tutte* at Salzburg in 1969. One of his most notable was his *Eugene Onegin* at Covent Garden in 1974, repeated at the Vienna State Opera in 1988. He has also recorded several operas including both *Carmen* and *Oedipus Rex* with Jessye Norman. See CARMEN (1988 film), CARMINA BURANA (1989), OEDIPUS REX (1992).

1985 Ozawa
This is a film about the conductor by the noted documentary team of David and Albert Maysles, Susan Froemke and Diborah Dickson. Ozawa gives credit to Karajan and Bernstein for his rise to prominence in the world of conducting and to his Japanese teacher Professor Saitoh. The film shows him at work and home and discussing his ideas about conducting with colleagues. Also featured in the film are Jessye Norman, Edith Wiens, Rudolf Serkin, Yo-Yo Ma and the Boston Symphony Orchestra. Color. 60 minutes. CAMI video.

P

PAGANINI
1925 operetta by Lehár

Paganini, one of Franz Lehár's most melodious operettas, tells the story of the reputed greatest violin player of all time, Nicolo Paganini. The story revolves around his legendary love affair with Anna Luisa, the Duchess of Lucca. *Paganini* was not a success when it premiered in Vienna but was a triumph when Richard Tauber sang it in Berlin in 1926 with soprano Vera Schwarz. Tauber also presented it in London but not until 1937. The operetta's most popular song is Paganini's explanation of his success with women, "Girls Were Made to Love and Kiss." See also FRANZ LEHÁR.

1926 Eduard Von Winterstein film
Eduard Von Winterstein stars as Paganini in this silent German film version of the operetta. It was titled *Gern hab' ich die Frau'n geküsst* after the hit song "Girls were made to love and kiss." The film was directed by Bruno Rahn and screened with live music. Black and white. In German. About 70 minutes.

1934 Ivan Petrovich film
Ivan Petrovich stars as Paganini in this second German film of the operetta but this time with the music. Eliza Illiar is Anna Luisa in a cast that includes Theo Lingen, Rudolf Klein-Rogge and Veit Harlan. E. W. Emo directed. Black and white. In German. 85 minutes.

1972 Teresa Stratas film
Teresa Stratas stars as Anna Luisa in this well-produced German film of the operetta. Antonio Theba portrays Paganini in a strong cast that features Peter Kraus, Dagmar Koller and Johannes Heesters. Wolfgang Ebert conducted the Kurt Graunke Symphony Orchestra and Eugen York directed the film in 35mm and stereo for German television. Unitel. Color. In German. 108 minutes.

1992 Sandro Massimini video
Highlights from *Paganini* are sung by Italian operetta master Sandro Massimini and his associates on the Italian TV series *Operette, Che Passione!* Featured are "Se le donne vo baciar," "Bel ciela azzurro dell'Italia mia" and "Oh dolce malia." Color. In Italian. About 17 minutes. Ricordi (Italy) video.

PAGLIACCI
1892 opera by Leoncavallo

Pagliacci is not only one of the most popular operas of all time, it is also one of the most filmed and videotaped. Attempts have been made to film it since the beginning of cinema, often with primitive sound systems, and its music has been used with striking effect in many modern non-opera films. It was first staged in Milan in 1892 and made composer-librettist Ruggero Leoncavallo instantly famous. Unfortunately he was never to have another comparable success and it is his only opera in the standard repertory. A group of traveling players arrive in a Sicilian village and a drama of jealousy is played out like a Greek tragedy. Canio murders his wife Nedda and her lover Silvio during a *commedia dell'arte* performance after they are betrayed by Tonio. Canio's "Vesti la giubba" is probably the best known tenor aria. See also RUGGERO LEONCAVALLO.

1931 San Carlo Grand Opera film
This is the first sound film of a full opera and its credits claim it is the "world's first sound picture of a grand opera." It was filmed as a stage production on Long Island by Italian-Americans of the San Carlo Grand Opera Company. The music is performed by the San Carlo Symphony Orchestra led by Carlo Peroni. Producer Fortuno Gallo seems to have been the creative force behind the film with Joe W. Coffman as his director and Al Wilson as his cinematographer. Fernando Bertini portrays Canio, Alba Novella is Nedda, Mario Valle is Tonio, Giuseppe Interranti is Silvo and Francesco Curci is Beppe. The critics thought they sang well but that the film was crudely made. This historic film has survived and can still be viewed. Black and white. In Italian. 80 minutes.

1936 Richard Tauber film
Richard Tauber is the star of this surprisingly successful British film of the opera performed in English. He portrays Canio but also sings the

Prologue and the music written for Silvio and Beppe. In other words this a film for people who want to hear Tauber sing. Supporting him are Steffi Dune as Nedda, Diana Napier as Trina, Arthur Margetson as Tonio, Esmond Knight as Silvio and Jerry Verne as Beppe. Monckton Hoffe and Roger Burford made the adaptation with new English lyrics by poet John Drinkwater. Albert Coates conducted, Otto Kanturek was cinematographer and Karl Grune directed. Two scenes were shot in an early color process called Chemicolor. U.S. title: *A Clown Must Laugh.* 92 minutes. Black and white. In English. Lyric/Opera Dubs/Video Yesteryear videos.

1940 Metropolitan Opera

This was the first American television telecast of an opera and was performed by the Metropolitan Opera on an NBC stage in Radio City on March 10, 1940 as part of a Gala Concert. The opera is sung in a condensed version but with full sets and costumes. Richard Bonelli sings the Prologue, Hilda Burke is Nedda, Armand Tokatyan is Canio and George Cehanov is Silvio. Black and white. In Italian. 60 minutes.

1943 Laugh, Pagliacci

This German-Italian film is not quite the opera but contains most of it and purports to tell the story of how it originated. Beniamino Gigli stars as an opera singer who plays Canio on stage. The "real" Canio (Paolo Hörbiger) is a clown who killed his wife and her lover and has been let out of jail after 20 years. He seeks his daughter (Alida Valli) to ask forgiveness. Canio tells his story to composer Ruggero Leoncavallo (Carlo Romano) who then creates the opera. Gigli is the tenor who sings Canio on stage opposite Adriana Perris as Nedda, Leone Pacci as Tonio, Mario Boviello as Silvio and Adelio Zagonara as Beppe. The real Canio then disappears to the music of "Vesti la giubba." The great value of the film is Gigli in peak form. It opens with him singing the Prologue and includes snippets from other operas. The film was shot in Berlin with Leopold Hainisch directing *Lache Bajazzo* in German and Giuseppe Fatigati directing *Pagliacci* in Italian. In the German version, Monika Burg plays the Alida Valli role and Hans Hotter sings the Prologue. Black and white. In Italian or German. 84 minutes. Bel Canto Society/ Lyric video.

1948 Tito Gobbi film

Tito Gobbi stars as both Tonio and Silvio and also sings the Prologue in this undervalued Italian film released in the U.S. as *Love of a Clown*. Gina Lollobrigida is good as the on-screen Nedda sung by Onella Fineschi, Afro Poli plays Canio sung by Galliano Masini and Filippo Morucci is Beppe sung by Gino Sinimberghi. The film is well acted, directed and photographed with notable lighting effects. It begins with Leoncavallo talking to the audience and composing the opera on the piano. Gobbi is then seen on the stage of La Scala singing the Prologue. After that the opera begins in naturalistic settings. Giuseppe Morelli conducted the Rome Opera House Orchestra and Chorus and Mario Costa directed. Alternative title: *Amore Tragica.* Black and white. In Italian with English subtitles. 90 minutes. Lyric/ Bel Canto Society videos.

1951 NBC Opera Theatre

Elaine Malbin is Nedda with Joseph Mordino as Canio in this NBC Opera Theatre production by Samuel Chotzinoff. Paul Ukena is Tonio, Jack Russell is Silvio, Paul Franke is Beppe and Thomas L. Thomas sings the Prologue. Charles Polacheck directed and Peter Herman Adler conducted the orchestra. Townsend Brewster wrote the English translation and Kirk Browning directed the telecast. Black and white. In English. 60 minutes. Video at MTR.

1953 Mario Del Monaco Opera Cameo

Mario Del Monaco stars as Canio in this highlights version of the opera made for the Opera Cameos television series and shown in New York on the Dumont network. Nedda is sung by Mildred Ellar and Tonio by Paolo Silveri. The staging is by Fausto Bozza and the orchestra is conducted by Salvatore Dell'Isola. Louis Ames directed the film. Black and white. In Italian. 28 minutes. Lyric video.

1955 Jon Vickers video

Jon Vickers was 29 and at the beginning of his career when he starred in this Canadian television version of the opera. He portrays Canio, a role that was to be one of his greatest in later years. Eva Likova is Nedda, Robert Savoie is Tonio and Louis Quilico is Silvio. The music is performed by the Montreal Radio-Canada Orchestra. The opera was telecast on Nov. 3, 1955. CBC. Black and white. In Italian with English subtitles. 58 minutes. VAI video.

1961 Mario Del Monaco film
Mario Del Monaco stars as Canio in this Japanese television film of a Tokyo production sung on Oct. 25, 1961. He is at his Italian belting tenor best and the audience loves it. Gabriella Tucci as Nedda and Aldo Protti as Tonio lend their support. Giuseppe Morelli conducts the orchestra and chorus. Black and white. In Italian with English and Japanese subtitles. 75 minutes. VAI video/Japanese laserdisc.

1968 Teatro alla Scala
Jon Vickers stars as Canio with Raina Kabaivanska as Nedda and Peter Glossop as Tonio in this Teatro alla Scala production filmed in a studio by Herbert von Karajan with four cameras. Sergio Lorenzi portrays Beppe and Rolando Panerai is Silvio. The stage direction is by Paul Hager. Karajan conducts the La Scala Orchestra and Chorus. The film was shown theatrically in the U.S. Unitel. Color. In Italian. 79 minutes. London video and laser.

1974 Valerie Masterson film
Valerie Masterson sings Nedda with Kenneth Woollam as Canio and in this abridged version made in England for the *Focus on Opera* series. Malcolm Rivers is Tonio, David Young is Beppe and Michael Wakeham is Silvio. Peter Murray wrote the English translation, John J. Davies conducted the Classical Orchestra and Peter Seabourne directed the film. Chatsworth Film. Color. In English. 61 minutes.

1975 Covent Garden
Placido Domingo stars as Canio in this Royal Opera House, Covent Garden, production. It was telecast by the BBC in 1975 but not released on video until 1995. Color. In Italian. 70 minutes. Pioneer video and laser.

1978 Metropolitan Opera
Teresa Stratas is Nedda, Placido Domingo is Canio, Sherrill Milnes is Tonio and Allan Monk is Silvio in this Metropolitan Opera production. It was based on a production designed by Franco Zeffirelli but staged by Fabrizio Melano with James Levine conducting the Metropolitan Opera Orchestra and Chorus. Kirk Browning directed the telecast on April 5, 1978. Color. In Italian. 72 minutes. Video at MTR.

1982 Franco Zeffirelli film
Teresa Stratas portrays Nedda in Franco Zeffirelli's film of the opera with Placido Domingo as Canio, Juan Pons as Tonio, Florindo Andreolli as Peppe and Alberto Rinaldi as Silvio. Zeffirelli shifts the period of the story to the 1930s and gives it a Fellini-esque look with the help of set designer Gianni Quaranta and costume designer Anna Anni. The film was based on his La Scala production but was shot on a sound stage with a few scenes on location. Georges Pretre conducts the Teatro alla Scala Orchestra and Chorus. The film was telecast on PBS in 1984 with an introduction by Domingo from the Calabrian village of Montalto and won an Emmy. Color. In Italian with English subtitles. 72 minutes. Philips video/ laserdisc.

1992 New York City Opera
Sigmund Cowan is Tonio, Gwynne Geyer is Nedda and Antonio Barasorda is Canio in this New York City Opera production by Jonathan Eaton. He sets it in an Italian immigrant neighborhood in New York in the late 19th century. Paul Short designed the scenery and Eduardo V. Sicango the costumes. John Goberman produced for television with Kirk Browning directing the telecast on Sept. 20, 1992 in the Live from Lincoln Center series. Color. In Italian. 70 minutes. Video at MTR.

1994 Metropolitan Opera
Luciano Pavarotti is Canio in this Metropolitan Opera production by Fabrizio Melano. Teresa Stratas is Nedda, Juan Pons is Tonio, Dwayne Croft is Silvio and Kenn Chester is Beppe. Franco Zeffirelli designed the production, sets and costumes. James Levine conducted the Metropolitan Opera Orchestra and Chorus. Brian Large directed the video from a performance in September 1994 telecast on Dec. 18. Color. In Italian with English subtitles. 70 minutes.

Early/related films

1907 Luigi Maggi film
A early Italian film featuring scenes from the opera starring and directed by Luigi Maggi with Arthur Ambrosio. Mirra Principi is Nedda. Made for the Turin Ambrosio Company. About 5 minutes.

1907 Messter Prologue
This German sound film by Oskar Messter featured the Prologue as sung by Sigmund Lieban. It used the Biophon system of disc synchronization and may have been made as early as 1903. About 3 minutes.

1908 Deutsche Bioscop duet
This German sound film featured a duet sung by Nedda and Silvio. It was made by the Deutsche Bioscop company with synchronized sound on disc. About 4 minutes.

1909 Lubin film
An early sound film of scenes from the opera. It was made by the American Lubin company using the Lubin studio Synchronizer system. About 4 minutes.

1913 Vi-T-Ascope film
This film of *Pagliacci* is considered by the Guinness Book of Records as the first complete opera to be filmed in America. It was made in 1913 in three reels by the Vi-T-Ascope Co. using the Vi-T-Phone sound system. About 30 minutes.

1914 Webb's Electric Pictures
An abridged version of *Pagliacci* using a sound-on-film system devised by George Webb. It was shown in May 1914 at the Fulton Theater in New York with Elly Barnato as Nedda, W. Rossini as Tonio and Pilade Sinagra as Canio. About 30 minutes.

1914 Biophone Tonbilder films
Two early German sound films made by Oskar Messter's Biophon-Tonbilder company. On one the "Prologue" is sung by Emil Lieben, on the other Tonio's "Lament" is heard. Each about 4 minutes.

1914 Lache Bajazzo
Olaf Fons stars in this short German version of scenes from *Pagliacci* directed by Richard Oswald. About 15 minutes.

1915 Leoncavallo film
Composer Ruggero Leoncavallo was involved in this film helping to choose the actors and designing the production. Bianca Virginia Camagni stars as Nedda, Achille Vitti is Tonio, Paolo Colaci is Canio, Annnibale Nichi is Silvio and Umberto Zanuccoli is Peppe. Francesco Bertolini directed for the Mediolanum company. It was screened with live music. About 65 minutes.

1917 Enrico Caruso sound film
Enrico Caruso turned up in person at the Cohen & Harris Theater in New York on Jan. 14, 1917, for the premiere of this sound movie made by Webb's Singing Pictures. While actors appeared on screen in scenes from *Pagliacci*, Caruso's voice was heard singing the arias on loudspeakers from records. About 10 minutes.

1918 Enrico Guazzoni film
This Italian film called *I Pagliaccio* stars Amleto Novelli and Elena Sangro. It was directed by Enrico Guazzoni and based on the opera. About 70 minutes.

1923 Lillian Hall-Davis film
Lillian Hall-Davis stars as Nedda in this British feature film based on the opera. Adelqui Millar is Canio, Campbell Gullan is Tonio and Frank Dane is Silvio. George B. Samuelson produced and Adelqui Millar directed with Walter Summers. It was screened with live music. About 70 minutes.

1926 Giovanni Martinelli film
Metropolitan Opera tenor Giovanni Martinelli sings "Vesti la giubba" on stage in costume in this Vitaphone sound film accompanied by the Vitaphone Symphony Orchestra. It was presented before *Don Juan* in the first Vitaphone sound program Aug. 6, 1926, and was a huge hit. Black and white. 7 minutes. On video.

1927 John Charles Thomas film
Baritone John Charles Thomas sings the Prologue to *Pagliacci*, one of three Vitaphone short films based on music from the popular opera. He is accompanied by the Vitaphone Symphony Orchestra. Black and white. 8 minutes.

1927 John Barclay film
The full title of this Vitaphone short film is *John Barclay Offering Impersonations of Famous Characters Singing the Prologue from Pagliacci (and others)*. It features him performing the Prologue from *Pagliacci* followed by arias from *Faust*, *Boris Godunov* and *Carmen*. Black and white. 10 minutes.

1928 The Singing Fool
Al Jolson, heartbroken about the death of his little "Sonny Boy," emulates the protagonist of *Pagliacci* and puts on his blackface makeup to the music of "Vesti la giubbi." Audiences loved the overt sentimentality and the film became one of the biggest box-office successes of the decade. Lloyd Bacon directed. Black and white. 110 minutes.

1928 Richard Bonelli film
Richard Bonelli sings the Prologue in this operatic short made with the competing Fox Movietone sound-on-film system. The critics commented that his voice sounded splendid but rather loud. Black and white. 8 minutes.

1929 Electrocord film
A sound film of an aria from the opera was made as a part of the Electrocord Films series of opera arias and songs. Black and white. About 7 minutes.

1930 Call of the Flesh
Ramon Novarro's version of "Vesti la giubba" in this early Technicolor musical was generally liked by the critics. It's the story of a dancer turned opera singer. Charles Brabin directed. Color. 89 minutes.

1935 A Night at the Opera
Music from *Pagliacci* is played over the credits of this comic Marx Brothers homage to opera. It features a staged production of *Pagliacci* in Milan at the beginning of the film. Sam Wood directed. Black and white. 92 minutes.

1941 Ridi, Pagliaccio!
Despite the similarity of title this is not a film of the opera but it does use the opera music on its sound track. Camillo Mastrocinque directed this realistic story of a sad love affair. Black and white. 90 minutes.

1946 The Whale Who Wanted to Sing at the Met
Willie, the opera-singing whale with the voice of Nelson Eddy, fantasizes his performance in *Pagliacci* at the Met. He performs in clown costume and his tears flood the auditorium as he sings "Vesti la giubba." Hamilton Luske directed this Disney cartoon released as part of the feature *Make Mine Music*. Color. 12 minutes.

1987 The Untouchables
A scene from *Pagliacci* is used as a ironic counterpoint in this G-men vs. the Mafia movie directed by Brian De Palma. Al Capone (Robert De Niro) is shown at the opera shedding a tear for the clown on stage while Mario del Monaco sings "Vesti la giubba." Meanwhile, in crosscut scenes, we see incorruptible policeman Jim Malone (Sean Connery) being ambushed and killed by Capone's men. Color. 119 minutes.

1987 Bill Bryden film
Bill Bryden's segment of the British film *Aria* features John Hurt in *Pagliacci*. He enters an opera house, makes up as a clown, has a vision of a girl he once loved (Sophie Ward), mimes to Enrico Caruso singing "Vesti la giubba" and dies on stage. Bryden shot the scenes in Cremona. Color. 89 minutes.

PAGLIUGHI, LINA
Italian-American soprano (1907-1980)

Lina Pagliughi was born in New York but made her career in Italy where she was the leading light soprano after Toti dal Monte. She sang on stage from 1927 to 1957 and was a mainstay at La Scala and Rome though she also sang at Covent Garden as Gilda. She made many excellent recordings for RAI released on Cetra but had only a tiny movie career. She can be seen singing Gilda in Germany in 1931, is an impressive La Scala soprano in a 1943 film about the opera house and provides the voice of Gilda opposite Tito Gobbi in the 1947 film of *Rigoletto*. She was also the voice of Snow White in the Italian version of the Disney classsic *Snow White and the Seven Dwarfs*. See RIGOLETTO (1931/1947), TEATRO ALLA SCALA (1943).

1931 Lina Pagliughi sings "Caro Nome"
Lina Pagliughi portrays Gilda in *Rigoletto* and sings the aria "Caro Nome" on a small studio stage in Berlin in 1931. She is accompanied by Arturo Lucon and the Berlin Philharmonic Orchestra. Film of this scene from a 1931 German film is included in the video *Legends of Opera*. Black and white. About 5 minutes. Legato Classics video.

PAINTER, ELEANOR
American soprano (1886-1947)

Eleanor Painter made her debut in opera in Nuremberg in 1913 but was best known for performances in operettas. She created Victor Herbert's Princess in *Princess Pat* in 1915 and was the star of such shows as *The Lilac Domino, Gloriana, The Last Waltz* and *The Chiffon Girl*. She was married to opera singer Louis Graveure.

1929 Eleanor Painter, The Lyric Soprano
Eleanor Painter's only film is a sound short for Vitaphone titled *Eleanor Painter, The Lyric Soprano*. It features her singing the Habanera from *Carmen*, "Love is Best of All" from Herbert's *Princess Pat* (she had introduced it on stage) and the Irving

Berlin song "How About Me?" Black and white. About 10 minutes.

PAL, GEORGE
American producer (1908-1980)

Hungarian-born George Pal produced 42 Puppetoons films for Paramount using puppets animated by stop motion. Pal, who later became famous for his special effects science fiction movies, featured music by Johann Strauss in two of his puppet films. The first was the 1943 *Mr. Strauss Takes a Walk* with Strauss strolling around to his own tunes. The second, also in 1943, was *Bravo, Mr. Strauss* in which a statue of the composer comes to life when the Screwball Army (i.e., the Nazis) starts to destroy the Vienna Woods. He leads them into the Danube River like the Pied Piper by playing his violin.

PALACE, THE
1995 opera by Sallinen

Finnish composer Aulis Sallinen's opera *The Palace* premiered at the Savonlinna Festival in 1995. Irene Dische and Hans Magnus Enzenberger's libretto was inspired by Ryszard Kzpuscinski's book *The Emperor,* about the downfall of Haile Selassie of Ethiopia, and Mozart's *The Abduction from the Seraglio.* It's a satire about political power and its effect on those who have it. See also AULIS SALLINEN.

1995 Savonlinna Festival
Veijo Varpio portrays the King with Jaana Mantyne as the Queen in this production by Kalle Holmberg at the Savonlinna Festival in Finland. The cast includes Sauli Tilikainen, Jorma Silvasti, Tom Krause and Ritva-Liisa Korhonen. Okko Kamu conducts the Savonlinna Orchestra. Aarno Cronvall directed the telecast and video. RM Arts. Color. 130 minutes. On video.

PALERMO

The Palermo Opera house is featured in a number of narrative films. It provides the setting for the end of *The Godfather Part III* and a central scene in *Johnny Stecchino* when Roberto Benigni is mistaken for a mafia boss and empties the theater. At the end of *The Young Caruso* the tenor has his first public success in the Palermo Opera House.

PALIASHVILI, ZAKHARY
Georgian composer (1871-1933)

Zakhary Petrovich Paliashvili is considered the father of Georgian opera and the opera theater in Tbilisi is named after him. After helping to create awareness of Georgian folk music, he wrote three operas of which *Abesalom da Eteri* (Absalom and Etery) was the most influential. Based on an ancient Georgian legend and incorporating Georgian folk tunes, it was a huge success at its 1919 premiere. His second opera, almost as famous, is the highly patriotic 1923 *Daisi* (Twilight) which has been filmed.. See DAISI.

PALMER, FELICITY
English soprano/mezzo (1944-)

Felicity Palmer made her operatic debut as Dido with the Kent Opera in 1971. She then became a regular performer at the English National Opera singing Pamina, Donna Elvira and Katisha in the famous Jonathan Miller production of *The Mikado.* She has sung in Houston and Chicago and in recent years has taken on mezzo roles including Kabanicha in *Katya Kabanova.* She has a strong stage presence as is shown in her many videos. See ALBERT HERRING (1985), KATYA KABANOVA (1988), THE MIKADO (1987), OEDIPUS REX (1984), ORPHÉE AUX ENFERS (1983), THE QUEEN OF SPADES (1992).

PALMER, TONY
English film director (1935-)

Tony Palmer has been directing musical documentaries and films for television and the cinema since the 1960s and has devoted a good deal of time to opera. His biggest work by far is the epic nine-hour biographic film *Wagner* but he has also filmed operas including Britten's *Death in Venice.* His informative films on Berlioz, Britten, Callas and Stravinsky are of exceptional worth. See HECTOR BERLIOZ (1992), BENJAMIN BRITTEN (1976/ 1980), MARIA CALLAS (1987), DEATH IN VENICE (1981), GEORGE FRIDERIC HANDEL (1985), GIACOMO PUCCINI (1986), PETER SELLARS (1995), DIMITRI SHOSTAKOVICH (1987), IGOR STRAVINSKY (1982), RICHARD WAGNER (1983), WILLIAM WALTON (1987).

PARIS

Paris opera houses go back centuries but the main theaters today are the Paris Opéra (Palais Garnier,

1875), now the home of both ballet and opera; the $300 million Opéra Bastille (1990) which has four theaters and is the primary home of opera; the Opéra Comique (Salle Favert, 1898) which presents light opera; and the Chatelet Theater (taken over by the city in 1980 and renamed the Théâtre Musical de Paris), site of many fine Mozart productions. The first live telecast from the Paris Opéra was the Maria Callas gala evening on Dec. 19, 1958, which is on video. There are videos from all the theaters but not as many as there could be. The Paris Opéra archive has tapes of over 850 operas and ballets telecast since 1971. Most were televised only once and never released on video. There are now plans to make them available commercially. See THE ABDUCTION FROM THE SERAGLIO (1991), THE BARBER OF SEVILLE (1947), LES BORÉADES (1987), MARIA CALLAS (1958), COSÌ FAN TUTTE (1992), LA GRANDE-DUCHESSE DI GÉROLSTEIN (1981), THE MARRIAGE OF FIGARO (1993), MADO ROBIN, ROMÉO ET JULIETTE (1982), VÉRONIQUE (1979).

1983 Naissance d'un Opéra a la Bastille
The well-known French documentary filmmaker Francois Reichenbach made this short film, the first of a number of documentaries about the creation of the new Parisian opera house. Color. In French. 20 minutes.

1989 La Nuit d'Avant le Jour
This is a record of a concert in honor of the new Bastille Opera House. The featured singers are Placido Domingo, June Anderson, Teresa Berganza, Barbara Hendricks, Ruggero Raimondi, Alfredo Kraus, Martine Dupuy, Alain Fondary and Jean-Philippe Lafont. Georges Pretre leads the Orchestra. Color. In French. 90 minutes. Lyric video.

1990 L'Opéra Bastille
Jean-Francois Roudot made this French documentary film about the new opera house. Color. In French. 54 minutes.

1991 Histoires d'Opéra
The Opéra Bastille opened in March 1990 to controversy over prices, standards and staff. Robin Lough and Cathie Levy's documentary film shows the opera house during the preparations for two of its productions, Andrei Konchalovsky's staging of *The Queen of Spades* and Graham Vick's staging of Berio's *Un Re in Ascolto.* There is much comment about the pluses and minuses of the opera house and music director Myung-Whun Chung discusses

the criticism leveled at him. Color. With English narration. 59 minutes. On video.

PARSIFAL
1882 opera by Wagner

Richard Wagner's most religious and pretentious opera was meant to be performed only at Bayreuth. It is a variation on the Grail legend with Parsifal, the "holy fool" knight, sent to get the Holy Spear back from the evil sorcerer Klingsor. The Spear will cure the wounded King Amfortas but it is guarded by the irresistible enchantress Kundry and her euphemistically named "flower maidens." Hitler felt the opera was a close reflection of his philosophy. Thomas Edison made an "epic film" of it in 1904 during a copyright controversy and Hans-Jurgen Syberberg made a 1982 film that some critics consider "wacky." See also RICHARD WAGNER.

1981 Bayreuth Festival
Siegfried Jerusalem stars as Parsifal with Eva Randova as Kundry in this Bayreuth Festival production directed and designed by Wolfgang Wagner. Bernd Weikl is Amfortas, Matti Salminen is Titurel, Hans Sotin is Gurnemanz and Leif Roar is Klingsor. Reinhard Heinrich designed the costumes and Horst Stein conducted the Bayreuth Festival Orchestra and Chorus. Brian Large directed the video. Color. In German with English subtitles. 233 minutes. Philips video and laserdisc.

1982 Hans-Jurgen Syberberg film
Hans-Jurgen Syberberg's inventive but controversial film of the opera features three people as Parsifal: Reiner Goldberg sings the role while Michael Kutter and Karen Krick portray him/her on screen. Syberberg's favorite actress Edith Clever portrays Kundry with the role sung by Yvonne Minton. Robert Lloyd is Gurnemanz, Aage Haugland is Klingsor, Wolfgang Schöne sings the part of Amfortas acted by Armin Jordan and Hans Tschammer sings Titurel acted by Martin Sperr. Werner Achmann designed the sets (the background rocks are Wagner's death mask), Veronick Dorne and Hella Wolter created the costumes and Igor Luther was the cinematographer. Armin Jordan conducted the Monte Carlo Philharmonic Orchestra and the Prague Philharmonic Choir. Color. In German with English subtitles. 255 minutes. Kultur video.

1993 Metropolitan Opera

Siegfried Jerusalem stars as Parsifal with Waltraud Meier as Kundry in this Metropolitan Opera production by Otto Schenk. Kurt Moll is Gurnemanz, Franz Mazura is Klingsor, Bernd Weikl is Amfortas and Jan-Hendrick Rootering is Titurel. Phoebe Berkowitz was stage director, Gunther Schneider-Siemssen designed the sets and Rolf Langenfass designed the costumes. James Levine conducted the Metropolitan Orchestra and Chorus. Brian Large directed the video of a March 1992 performance telecast on April 7, 1993. Color. In German with English subtitles. 266 minutes. DG video and laser.

1993 Berlin State Opera

Paul Elming portrays Parsifal with Waltraud Meier as Kundry in this ultra modernist Berlin State Opera production by Harry Kupfer. In Kupfer's concept the story takes place in a kind of steel bank vault and the Flower Maidens are merely images on video screens. John Tomlinson is Gurnemanz, Falk Struckman is Amfortas and Gunter von Kannen is Klingsor. Daniel Barenboim conducted the Berlin State Opera Orchestra and Chorus. Hals Hulscher directed the video. Color. In German with English subtitles. 244 minutes. Teldec video and laser.

Early/related films

1904 Edison film

This is one of the important early opera films as it helped establish the right of authors to their work. When Wagner's opera opened in 1903 at the Metropolitan in New York despite hostility from Bayreuth, it attracted a lot of newspaper attention. The Edison studio decided to turn it into an epic film, a costly and ambitious production. Edwin S. Porter directed the movie in eight episodes with elaborate sets. Robert Whittier portrays Parsifal with Adelaide Fitz-Allen as Kundry. The film was to be screened with records of the Wagner music but the copyright lawsuit probably killed its release as it was not widely shown. The film survived in the paper print collection of the Library of Congress. Black and white. About 20 minutes. Prints at NFTA and LOC.

1912 Mario Caserini film

Mario Caserini directed this one-reel Italian film inspired by the opera. It was written by Arrigo Frusta for the Ambrosio company of Turin and stars Alberto Capozzi, Mary Cleo Tarlarini, Mario Caserini and Maria Gasperini Caserini. Black and white. About 15 minutes.

1952 Ludmilla Tcherina film

Dancer Ludmilla Tcherina stars as Kundry with Gustavo Rojo as Parsifal in this Spanish film inspired by the opera and directed by Daniel Mangrané and C. Serrano de Osma. The cast includes Carlo Tamberlani as Klingsor, Felix de Pomes and Alfonso Estela. Huguet production. Black and white. In Spanish. 95 minutes.

PASATIERI, THOMAS
American composer (1945-)

Thomas Pasatieri studied with Nadia Boulanger and at the Juilliard School. He composed two operas in 1964 but the first to be staged was his 1965 *The Women*. His most successful operas were based on Chekhov plays, *The Seagull* (1974) and *The Three Sisters* (1979). His only screen opera is *The Trial of Mary Lincoln*, a harrowing portrait of President Lincoln's widow on trial for her sanity. It was commissioned by the NET Opera Theater and telecast in 1972. Pasatieri's musical style has been compared to that of Menotti. See THE TRIAL OF MARY LINCOLN.

1977 The Operas of Thomas Pasatieri

This television program devoted to Pasatieri and his operas was presented in the adventurous CBS Camera Three series. It features the composer and four singers in conversation and performance. There is modest staging and costuming for scenes from three operas. Catherine Malfitano, Brent Ellis and Elaine Bonazzi perform the "Carriage Scene" from *Washington Square*, Joanna Simon sings the "Cradle Song" from *The Black Widow* and Ellis and Bonazzi duet with "Nina's Good-bye to Constantin" in *The Seagull*. Roger Englander produced and directed the telecast. Color. In English. 30 minutes. Video at MTR and from New York State Education Department.

PASINI, LAURA
Italian soprano (1894-1942)

Soprano Laura Pasini made her debut in Milan in 1921 and became a La Scala favorite from 1923 season on mostly in coloratura roles. She was particularly admired as the Queen of the Night in *The Magic Flute* and as the heroines of Rossini's *La Cenerentola* and *L'Italiana in Algeri*. She appeared in two Italian opera films. In the composer biography *Pergolesi* she sings the role of the wily servant Serpina in scenes from *La Serva Padrona*. In *The Opera Singer* she appears in the opera scenes. See also LA SERVA PADRONA (1932 film).

1932 La Cantante dell'Opera
The colorful Italian film *The Opera Singer* features soprano Pasini with her La Scala tenor colleague Alessio De Paolis in a number of opera scenes. The film revolves around a young opera singer in Venice and her involvement with a phony American. Nunzio Malasomma directed. Black and white. In Italian. 90 minutes.

PASTERNAK, JOE
American film producer (1901-1991)

Josef Pasternak was born in Hungary and began his career as a film producer in Budapest and Berlin. After he emigrated to the U.S., he became one of the major Hollywood producers at the Universal and MGM studios, usually of movies with opera content. His pictures featured such stars as Deanna Durbin, Mario Lanza, Kathryn Grayson, Anna Maria Alberghetti, Lauritz Melchior and Jane Powell. Pasternak, who was involved with over one hundred movies between 1929 and 1968, also produced films of the operettas *Spring Parade, The Merry Widow* and *The Student Prince.* He even built a reproduction of the old Met for *Two Sisters from Boston.* See ANNA MARIA ALBERGHETTI, DEANNA DURBIN, FRÜHJAHRSPARADE, KATHRYN GRAYSON, MARIO LANZA, LAURITZ MELCHIOR, THE MERRY WIDOW, JANE POWELL, THE STUDENT PRINCE.

PATIENCE
1881 comic opera by Gilbert & Sullivan

Patience or Bunthorne's Bride is a delightful spoof of Oscar Wilde, the aesthetes and the Pre-Raphaelite movement. It is one of W. S. Gilbert's cleverest librettos and its famous song about faking the esthetic game, "If you're anxious for to shine," is just as relevant today as when it was written. The story centers around the Oscar Wilde-type character Reginald Bunthorne and the twenty maidens who swoon over him to the annoyance of the Guards of the Dragoons who used to enjoy their favors. Reginald, however, loves the milkmaid Patience who knows nothing about estheticism; she is also loved by her childhood sweetheart Archibald Grosvenor. *Patience* was the first Gilbert and

Sullivan operetta performed at the Savoy Theater. See also GILBERT AND SULLIVAN.

1982 George Walker film
Derek Hammond-Stroud stars as Reginald Bunthorne with Sandra Dugdale as his Patience in this enjoyable film produced by Judith De Paul for George Walker. John Fryatt portrays Archibald Grosvenor, Donald Adams is Colonel Calverley, Terry Jenkins is the Duke of Dunstable, Roderick Kennedy is Major Murgatroyd, Anne Collins is Lady Jane and Shelagh Squires is Lady Saphir. Alexander Faris conducts the London Symphony Orchestra and the Ambrosian Opera Chorus. John Cox was the stage director and Dave Heather the film director. Color. In English. 117 minutes. Braveworld (England) video.

PATTI, ADELINA
Italian soprano (1843-1919)

Adelina Patti was born in Madrid but was brought up in New York City. She was a child prodigy able to sing "Casta diva" at the age of seven. Patti made her professional debut at sixteen in *Lucia di Lammermoor* at the New York Academy of Music and sang fourteen other roles the same year. She returned to Europe for her Covent Garden debut in 1861 as Amina in *La Sonnambula* and was the first Aida at Covent Garden. She continued singing around the globe until the turn of the century. Her records are still admired as she seems to have kept the purity of her voice to her final years. She is portrayed in many films.

1945 Pink String and Sealing Wax
English soprano Margaret Ritchie portrays Adelina Patti in this Ealing film set in Brighton in 1880. Ritchie sings the delightful "Hush, every breeze" which she later recorded with great success. The film is the story of a publican's wife and her plot to poison her husband. Robert Hamer directed. Black and white. 89 minutes.

1959 Gayarre
Spanish soprano Lina Huarte portrays Adelina Patti in this Spanish film about the 19th century tenor Julián Gayarre. Alfredo Kraus portrays Gayarre and Domingo Viladomat directed. Color. In Spanish. 90 minutes. Bel Canto/Lyric/ Opera Dubs videos.

1993 Adelina Patti, Queen of Song

American soprano June Anderson portrays Adelina Patti and sings arias associated with her in this English film by Chris Hunt. The focus is on a concert performance in her home theater in Wales but she is also pictured at Covent Garden and traveling with her jewel collection and her bodyguards. Dennis O'Neil appears as Patti's husband. Anderson is accompanied in her singing by the Welsh National Opera Orchestra conducted by Robin Stapleton. Color. 60 minutes. On video.

PAVAROTTI, LUCIANO
Italian tenor (1935-)

If one can measure popularity by videos, films, TV appearances and recordings, Luciano Pavarotti is one of the most popular opera singers of the century. The Modena tenor is certainly the most recognizable opera personality of our time. His World Cup success singing its theme "Nessun dorma" and the *Three Tenors* concert series confirmed that fame. There has not been a phenomenon like Pavarotti since Caruso, call it the opera singer as pop icon, and his clutched white handkerchief has become world famous. Like Caruso Pavarotti has remained firmly within the Italian repertoire. He made his debut in 1961 as Rodolfo in Reggio Emilia, went to Covent Garden in 1963 in the same role and then won fame touring with Joan Sutherland in Australia. He arrived at the Metropolitan in 1968 as Rodolfo and quickly became one of the Met's most popular performers. He can be seen on video in many operas, in a great number of recitals and concerts and even in a Hollywood film. See also AIDA (1986/1987 film), UN BALLO IN MASCHERA (1980/1991), LA BOHÈME (1977/1983/1986/1989), JOSÉ CARRERAS (1992), DON CARLO (1992), L'ELISIR D'AMORE (1981/1991), ERNANI (1983), DIE FLEDERMAUS (1990), LA GIOCONDA (1980/1980 film), MARILYN HORNE (1981), IDOMENEO (1982), I LOMBARDI ALLA PRIMA CROCIATA (1993), METROPOLITAN OPERA (1972/1983/1986/1991 PAGLIACCI (1994), RIGOLETTO (1981/1983), DER ROSENKAVALIER (1982), JOAN SUTHERLAND (1987), THE THREE TENORS, TOSCA (1978/1993), IL TROVATORE (1988), VERDI REQUIEM (1967/1991).

1979 Opera Master Class at Juilliard

There are number of films showing Pavarotti giving master classes and sharing his experience and knowledge with singers at the Juilliard School in New York. The most accessible is this video by Nathan Kroll which has commercial distribution.

Pavarotti sings "Per la gloria d'adorarvi" from Buononcini's Griselda and critiques six students as they sing. John Wustman is the accompanist. Color. 60 minutes. Kultur video.

1982 Yes, Giorgio

Pavarotti's sole attempt at Hollywood fame is an entertaining but plotless and old-fashioned story about a famous opera singer (Pavarotti) and his light-hearted affair with a doctor (Kathryn Harrold). It was a resounding commercial failure despite some pretty cinematography, rather good singing by Pavarotti including "Nessun Dorma" and deft direction by master filmmaker Franklin J. Schaffner. The film was apparently an attempt to make Pavarotti into a modern Mario Lanza but it was a misjudgement. Color. 110 minutes. On video.

1982 Pavarotti & Friends

This ABC-TV network special about Pavarotti was directed by Dwight Hemion and Gary Smith. It shows Pavarotti at home in Modena, talking with Jacqueline Bisset, meeting friends in Hollywood, singing in church and paying tribute to Caruso. Color. 60 minutes.

1982 Pavarotti In London

Pavarotti is in good form at this concert at the Royal Albert Hall in London on April 13, 1982. The program opens with Pavarotti singing "Recondita armonia" and includes music by Verdi, Donizetti, Cilea and de Curtis. Rodney Greenberg produced the video for the BBC. Color. 78 minutes. Columbia video.

1984 A Pavarotti Valentine

Pavarotti performs at the Teatro Petruzzelli in Bari on Feb. 14 1984. There are seven love songs by art song master Tosti and twelve other songs and arias by Gluck, Verdi, Donizetti, Puccini, Bononcini, Bizet and Caldara. Leone Magiera accompanies on piano. Color. 77 minutes. VAI video.

1984 Pavarotti

Pavarotti performs at the Riviera Hotel in Las Vegas. There are arias from *La Traviata, L'Elisir D'Amore, Un Ballo in Maschera, Werther, La Gioconda, La Bohème* and, of course, *Turandot* ("Nessun dorma"). Emerson Buckley conducts the Las Vegas Symphony Orchestra. Stan Harris directed the video produced by Jerry Harrison and Tibor Rudas. Color. 77 minutes. USA Home video.

1986 Luciano Pavarotti Gala Concert
Pavarotti gives a concert at Olympia Hall in Munich and sings arias from Verdi, Cilea, Giordano, Leoncavallo and Puccini. Emerson Buckley conducts the Munich Radio Orchestra and Karlheinz Hundorf directed the video for ZDF. Color. 60 minutes. Kultur video.

1987 Distant Harmony: Pavarotti in China
Pavarotti's visit to China in June 1986 was captured on film. He visits schools, dines in local restaurants, tries out some Chinese operatic gear and sings a good deal. He is seen and heard in rehearsal and performance of *Rigoletto*, *La Bohème*, *Turandot*, *Pagliacci* and *L'Arlesiana*. Dewitt Sage directed the film produced by John Goberman and Daniel Wigutow. Color. 85 minutes. Pacific Arts video.

1987 Pavarotti in Concert in China
A second video of Pavarotti's 1986 tour of China features him in performance at the Exhibition Hall in Beijing. He sings a selection of music from Verdi, Giordano and Puccini as well as "O Solo Mio." Emerson Buckley conducts the Genoa Municipal Opera Orchestra. Color. 96 minutes. Kultur video.

1988 Pavarotti and Levine in Recital
Pavarotti in recital at the Metropolitan Opera with conductor James Levine who accompanies him on piano. The program consists of twenty-one pieces including music by Mozart, Verdi, Rossini, Bellini, Massenet, Respighi, Flotow and Mascagni. Brian Large directed the video. Color. 71 minutes. London video and laser.

1988 Christmas with Luciano Pavarotti
Pavarotti performs Christmas classics at a recital in Montreal's Notre Dame Cathedral. He is joined by the Petits Chanteurs du Mont-Royal and The Disciples de Massenet. Franz-Paul Decker conducts the Montreal Symphony Orchestra. Color. 60 minutes. Video Treasures video.

1988 Mario Puzo's The Fortunate Pilgrim
Pavarotti's voice is featured on the soundtrack of this American TV film based on a Mario Puzo novel. Carlo Ponti produced it and Stuart Cooper directed. Color. 250 minutes. On video.

1990 Luciano Pavarotti: The Event
Subtitled *The World Cup Celebration Concert*, this concert features the tenor at Milan's Palatrussardi

Hall singing in honor of the 1990 World Cup players. Over 10,000 people attended and Pavarotti gives them six encores. The program includes Donizetti, Mozart, Verdi, Puccini, Massenet, Leoncavallo and Mascagni. Leone Magiera conducts the Bologna Chamber Orchestra and Pier Quinto Cariaggi produced the video. Color. 88 minutes. MCA Universal video.

1991 Pavarotti 30th Anniversary Concert
Pavarotti made his debut in 1961 in Reggio Emilia and returned 30 years later for an anniversary concert on April 29, 1991. The program includes selections from his debut opera *La Bohème* plus *Tosca*, *Don Giovanni*, *Lucia di Lammermoor*, *Il Trovatore*, *La Forza del Destino*, *La Favorita*, *L'Arlesiana* and *L'Elisir d'Amore*. Joining him are Raina Kabaivanska, June Anderson, Piero Cappuccilli, Shirley Verrett, Paolo Coni, Enzo Dara and Giuseppe Sabbatini. The Bologne Teatro Comunale Orchestra is led by Leone Magiera and Maurizio Benini. Color. 104 minutes. London video and laser.

1991 Pavarotti in Hyde Park
Pavarotti gives an impressive open air recital in Hyde Park, London, on July 30, 1991 with a massive crowd and good English rain. He sings a selection of arias from Verdi, Puccini, Mascagni, Wagner, Leoncavallo, Meyerbeer and Massenet. Leone Magiera leads the Philharmonia Orchestra and Chorus. Christopher Swann directed the filming. Color. 99 minutes. London video.
(Highlights version is available in *Great Moments* video series as Volume 12.)

1992 Pavarotti and Friends
This is a record of a concert in Pavarotti's hometown of Modena which was arranged for a local charity. The tenor's performing friends here include pop stars Sting, Suzanne Vega and the Neville Brothers among others. Color. 60 minutes. On video.

1992 Pavarotti & the Italian Tenor
Joshua Waletzky's documentary attempts to show how Italy nurtures its tenors. Pavarotti listens to records and talks about the four tenors who have most influenced him: Caruso, Gigli, Schipa and Di Stefano. The film shows him in his home town of Modena and includes early and recent performances, interviews with teachers and friends and a radio broadcast by his father. The film was

telecast in the *Great Performances* series Nov. 20, 1992. Color. 58 minutes. London video.

1992 Luciano Pavarotti
A video portrait of the great tenor made for the Italian opera singer series I Grandi della Lirica. Color. In Italian. 60 minutes. Center (Italy) video.

1991-1996 Pavarotti Plus
Pavarotti arranges a televised celebration with friends at Lincoln Center every year. Joining him in 1992 were Kallen Esperian, Raina Kabaivanska, Francesca Pedaci, Florence Quivar, Sherrill Milnes and Ferruccio Furlanetto. His guests in 1994 were Aprile Millo, Deborah Voigt, Elizabeth Holleque, Dolora Zajick, Stephen Mark Brown, Juan Pons and Roberto Scandiuzzi. Color. Each telecast program is about 60 minutes.

1993 Pavarotti In Paris
This is a most enjoyable record of an open-air recital by Pavarotti at the Champs de Mars in Paris before an audience of over 50,000 people. The program includes music by Puccini, Rossini, Verdi and Leoncavallo. Elliott Forest is the host. Color. 60 minutes.

1993 Pavarotti in Central Park
Pavarotti gives a splendid recital before an enthusiastic crowd in New York's Central Park in June 1993. The program includes selections from operas by Verdi, Puccini, Leoncavallo and Rossini. The concert was videotaped and shown on PBS on Aug. 10, 1993. Color. 60 minutes.

1993 Pavarotti: My Heart's Delight
Pavarotti is joined by soprano Nuccia Focile for a recital in his home town of Modena. They perform a wide array of opera arias and songs by Verdi, Puccini, etc. Maurizio Benini conducts the Royal Phiharmonic Orchestra. Color. In Italian. 60 minutes. On video.

1994 Pavarotti In Confidence
Peter Ustinov visits Pavarotti at his seaside villa in Pesaro and they discuss the tenor's life and career in a fairly forthright manner. Pavarotti also performs a range of arias by Verdi, Puccini and others with performance excerpts from *Rigoletto*, *Turandot, Madama Butterfly*, etc. Color. 50 minutes. Kultur video.

1994 Pavarotti Plus in London
This is a record of a charity concert given by Pavarotti and eight other singers for the Red Cross at the Royal Albert Hall in May 1994. The other singers, some of them winners of his annual singing competition,   include Dwayne Croft, Natalie Dessay, Elero D'Artenga and Dolora Zajick. Color. 80 minutes. Decca (England) video.

1995 Pavarotti: My World
This survey of Pavarotti's career was created for his 60th birthday and is basically a "greatest hits" compilation of scenes from concert videos with added comments and observations. Produced by Tibor Rudas and directed by David Horn, it includes memorable moments from concerts in Paris, Miami, London, Modena and Beijing as well as the Three Tenors events. The program was televised in December 1995. Color. 90 minutes. On video.

1995 Pavarotti: Children of Bosnia concert
This is a video of a concert given in Modena in September 1995 with the full title *Pavarotti & Friends: Together for the Children of Bosnia*. The friends who sing with Pavarotti include the Chieftains, Michael Bolton, Meat Loaf and Brian Eno. Color. 60 minutes. London video and laserdisc.

1996 Pavarotti in Miami Beach
Casually-dressed but in full form, the tenor performs at a Miami Beach seaside recital with soprano Cynthia Lawrence, a large back-up chorus and full orchestra. The crowd is enormous and enthusiastic and considering the venue, the microphones are probably necessary. The concert, which goes on until dusk, includes a wide range of arias from Puccini, Verdi, Mascagni and other Pavarotti favorites. The show, produced by Tibor Rudas, was telecast on PBS. Color. 60 minutes. On video.

1996 Pavarotti-Abbado Concert at Ferrara
Luciano Pavarotti is shown in performance in the Italian city of Ferrara with Claudio Abbado conducting the orchestra. Manuela Crivelli taped the concert for SACIS and Italian television. Color. In Italian. 90 minutes.

PEARS, PETER
English tenor (1910-1986)

Tenor Sir Peter Pears, who was Benjamin Britten's life partner and collaborator, created the leading roles in most of Britten's major operas from *Peter Grimes* to *Death in Venice*. He was also his co-librettist on *A Midsummer Night's Dream*. See BILLY BUDD (1966), BENJAMIN BRITTEN (1976/1980/1988), OWEN WINGRAVE (1971), A MIDSUMMER NIGHT'S DREAM, PETER GRIMES (1970), WAR REQUIEM (1988).

1975 Doria
Peter Pears was 65 when he was filmed at the Bergen Festival singing this poem by Ezra Pound. It was set to music at his request by composer Arne Nordheim. NRK.Color. 20 minutes.

PÊCHEURS DE PERLES, LES
1863 opera by Bizet

The Pearl Fishers is set in ancient Ceylon and tells the story of the friendship of tribal chief Zurga and fisherman Nadir and their rivalry over the priestess Leila. It was the second opera by Bizet to be staged and was written on commission to a libretto by Eugene and Michel Corman. Like *Carmen* it was originally an *opéra comique* with spoken dialogue later changed to recitative. A number of films have featured the famous tenor-baritone friendship duet "Au fond du temple saint" but the complete opera is badly represented on video. See also GEORGES BIZET.

1928 Gigli/De Luca duet
Tenor Beniamino Gigli and baritone Giuseppe De Luca perform the duet "Au fond du temple saint" in Italian on this early sound film made by the Vitaphone company. It is considered one of the all-time great performances of the duet and has also been released on CD. Black and white. In Italian. About 8 minutes.

1981 Gallipoli
Peter Weir's film about idealistic Australian soldiers in World War I features the friendship duet as an emotional highlight. On the night before an attack in which the commanding major knows he and many of his men are likely to be killed, he sits alone drinking champagne and listening to a recording of "Au fond du temple saint." The singers are Léopold Simoneau and René Bianco

with the Lamoureux Orchestra of Paris led by Jean Fournet. Color. 110 minutes. On video.

1991 Teatro Municipal, Santiago
The only video of the complete opera is of a production at the Teatro Municipal in Santiago, Chile, which features local singers. The video is a non-professional copy of a telecast. Color. In French. 119 minutes. Opera Dubs video.

1993 Opera Imaginaire
This English film includes a superb animated cartoon by Jimmy Murakami illustrating "Au fond du temple saint." The duet is sung by Nicolai Gedda and Ernest Blanc with the Paris Opéra-Comique Orchestra led by Paul Dervaux. See also OPERA IMAGINAIRE.

1994 Little Women
Friedrich (Gabriel Byrne) translates the French for Jo (Winona Ryder) as they watch the opera from free seats up among the scenery in this fine adaptation of the Louisa May Alcott novel. Barbara Hendricks (Leila) and John Aler (Nadir) sing the duet "Leïla! Leïla! Dieu puissant" from Act III accompanied by the Orchestra du Capitole du Toulouse under the baton of Michel Plasson. The actors seen on stage in the opera are Kate Robbins and David Adams. Color. 118 minutes. On video.

PEERCE, JAN
American tenor (1904-1984)

Jan Peerce began his opera career at the Metropolitan in 1941 and was one of the Met's top attractions for over 25 years. However, his singing career actually began at Radio City Music Hall where he appeared for nine years and became a popular radio singer. Only then did he begin to study opera. He made his Metropolitan debut as Alfredo in *La Traviata* and then stayed with the Met until 1968. He was the first American to sing at the Bolshoi Opera after the war and after leaving the Met became a Broadway musical star in 1971 portraying Tevye in *Fiddler on the Roof*. Peerce was featured in a number of films but never really had a Hollywood career though he became a regular on television. See also CARNEGIE HALL (1947), SOL HUROK (1956), OF MEN AND MUSIC, OPERA VS. JAZZ.

1943 Keep 'Em Rolling

Peerce sings a patriotic song by Richard Rodgers and Lorenz Hart in this wartime propaganda film. He encourages factory workers and buyers of Defense Bonds to keep them rolling. Black and white. In English. 8 minutes. Video Yesteryear video.

1946 Hymn of Nations

Jan Peerce is featured in this patriotic Office of War Information film with Arturo Toscanini conducting the NBC Symphony Orchestra. Peerce sings the tenor solo with the Westminster Choir on the "Hymn of Nations" following the overture to *La Forza del Destino*. The film was written by May Sarton and directed by Alexander Hammid. Black and white. 28 minutes. Video Yesteryear video

1947 Something in the Wind

Peerce teams up with Deanna Durbin to sing the "Misere" from *Il Trovatore* in this light comedy. She's a singing disc jockey, he's an opera singer and their voices match quite well. The plot is a romantic farrago that also features Donald O'Connor. Irving Pichel directed. U-I. Black and white. 89 minutes.

1950 Jan Peerce in Opera and Song

Peerce is seen as he appeared on the *Voice of Firestone* television series on Jan. 9, 1950. He sings songs and arias by Leoncavallo ("Vesti la giubba" from *Pagliacci*), Victor Herbert ("Thine Alone" from *Eileen*), Rossini ("La Danza") and Rodgers and Hammerstein ("Younger Than Springtime"). Howard Barlow conducts. Black and white. 25 minutes. VAI video.

1969 Goodbye, Columbus

Jan Peerce's son Larry directed his father in this 1969 Hollywood film based on Phillip Roth's portrait of a suburban Jewish family. The story is seen through the eyes of Richard Benjamin who falls in love with Ali MacGraw. Jan Peerce has a cameo role at the wedding. Color. 105 minutes.

1992 Jan Peerce: If I Were A Rich Man

A documentary about the tenor hosted and narrated by Isaac Stern with Peerce talking about his career and singing. The film clips are exceptionally interesting: Peerce is shown singing with Toscanini, being interviewed by Edward R. Murrow on *Person to Person*, on tour in the USSR in 1956, starring on Broadway in *Fiddler on The Roof* and in excerpts from *La Traviata*, *Rigoletto* and *Eugene Onegin*. Black and white and color. 59 minutes. Proscenium Entertainment video.

PELLÉAS ET MÉLISANDE
1902 opera by Debussy

Pelléas and Mélisande, one of the most popular operas of the twentieth century, is the only one Debussy finished. It's based on a play by Maurice Maeterlinck and tells a highly romantic story in a symbolist manner. Mélisande is a mysterious woman of unknown origin married to Golaud, grandson of King Arkel. Golaud becomes so jealous when his half-brother Pelléas and Mélisande fall in love that he kills Pelléas. Mélisande dies in childbirth. The opera is full of poetic symbols which are hard to explain from lost rings to deep wells to long flowing hair. It premiered in Paris with Mary Garden as Mélisande and she helped make it famous. Maeterlinck, however, quarreled viciously with Debussy about this as he wanted the part for his wife Georgette Leblanc. See also CLAUDE DEBUSSY.

1954 NBC Opera Theatre

Virginia Haskins stars as Mélisande with Davis Cunningham as Pelléas in this NBC Opera production by Samuel Chotzinoff. Carlton Gaud is Golaud with a supporting cast including Lee Cass and Mary Davenport. William Molyneux designed the sets and John Boxer the costumes while Jean Morel conducted the NBC Opera orchestra. Kirk Browning directed the telecast on April 10, 1954. Black and white. In English. 90 minutes. Video at MTR.

1987 Opéra de Lyon

José Van Dam portrays Goulaud with Colette Alliot-Lugoz as Mélisande and François Le Roux as Pelléas in this Opéra de Lyon production by Pierre Strosser. Roger Soyer is Arkel, Jocelyne Taillon is Geneviève and François Golfier is Yniold. Strosser sets the opera in an Edwardian living room and there is no well, ring or tower. John Eliot Gardiner conducts. The singing is wonderful but the production was disliked by most critics Color. In French with English subtitles. 137 minutes. Kultur video.

1992 Welsh National Opera

Alison Hagley stars as Mélisande with Neil Archer as Pélleas in this inventive and often magical Welsh National Opera production by Peter Stein. Donald

Maxwell is Golaud, Kenneth Cox is Arkel, Penelope Walker is Genevieve and Samuel Burkey is Yniold. Pierre Boulez conducts the Welsh National Opera Orchestra and Chorus. The opera was filmed in studio conditions in the New Theater, Cardiff, in March 1992 by its stage director Peter Stein. Color. In French with English subtitles. 158 minutes. DG video and laser.

Early films

1913 Constance Crawley film
Constance Crawley stars as Melisande with Arthur Maude as Pelleas in this early American feature film of the Maeterlinck play. It was directed by S. MacDonald and scripted by Harrison Del Ruth for the Bison division of Universal. About 45 minutes.

1916 Georgette Leblanc film
This historic French movie based on the source play stars Maeterlinck's wife Georgette Leblanc. She was finally able to portray Mélisande, even if it was in a movie a few years later, and Debussy's music was used as to accompany it at screenings. Gustave Labruyere directed for the Eclair company. Black and white. In French. About 70 minutes. Print in Romanian film archive.

PENDERECKI, KRZYSTOF
Polish composer (1933-)

Poland's Krzystof Penderecki has become one of the best known modern composers and his work is now performed around the world. One of his operas has a cinematic basis; the libretto of his 1978 *Paradise Lost* is based on a screenplay originally written for a film of Milton's epic poem. Penderecki's most famous opera, *The Devils of Loudun*, has been televised. See THE DEVILS OF LOUDUN.

PENELLA, MANUEL
Spanish composer (1880-1939)

Manuel Penella, one of the leading composers of Spanish stage music including operas and zarzuelas, is best known for a universally-known pasodoble. It was composed for his opera *El Gato Montés* and has become the theme music of the Spanish bullfight. Placido Domingo sang *El Gato Montés* in his early years in Mexico and has promoted it strongly in recent years including a telecast of the Los Angeles stage production, a complete recording and an excerpt in *Hommage a Sevilla*. Penella's other major opera is *Don Gil de Alcalá* which was made into a film starring Mexican tenor José Mojica. See DON GIL DE ALCALÁ, EL GATO MONTÉS.

PERFECT LIVES
1980 TV opera by Ashley

Robert Ashley's three-hour TV opera *Perfect Lives*, created for The Kitchen in New York, consists of seven 30-minute episodes: The Park, The Supermarket, The Bank, The Bar, The Living Room, The Church and The Backyard. It is set in a Midwestern town where the characters propose to "borrow" money from a bank for a day and return it the next. Ashley portrays the Narrator; "Blue" Gene Tyranny is Buddy, the World's Greatest Piano Player; Jill Kroesen is Isolde and David Van Tieghem is D, the Captain of the Football Team. The opera is full of imaginative techniques with orchestral tracks and video imagery created by John Sanborn. Ashley has said that television should feature re-viewable works of art that need to be seen again and again. Ashley wrote and created the opera, Peter Gordon produced the music and John Sanborn directed the video which is copyright 1983. Color. In English. 182 minutes. Lovely Music video. See also ROBERT ASHLEY.

1984 Music Word Fire: The Lessons
Music Word Fire and I Would Do It Again: The Lessons is a 1984 video of variations on the theme song from Episode Three of *Perfect Lives*. It contains four seven-minute portraits of the characters Isolde, NoZhay, Buddy and Donnie. Color. In English. 28 minutes. Lovely Music video.

PERFECTLY NORMAL
1990 opera film by Simoneau

Yves Simoneau's quirky Canadian film is about a man who loves opera so much that he opens an operatic restaurant which he calls La Traviata. *Norma* is performed in drag at the opening and there are also bits and pieces of *Il Trovatore, Tosca, La Traviata, Manon Lescaut* and *Salome*. Robbie Coltrane is the man with the opera dream and he also portrays Pollione in *Norma* while his friend Michael Riley dresses up as Norma. Eugene Lipinski and Paul Quarrington wrote the lovably eccentric screenplay. Color. In English. 105 minutes.

PERGOLESI, GIOVANNI

Italian composer (1710-1736)

Giovanni Pergolesi died young, barely 26, but in his few short years he helped change opera history. His intermezzo *La Serva Padrone* brought him posthumous fame when it came to be considered the model for *opera buffa* and brought about the famous "Guerre des Bouffons" in Paris in 1752. Pergolesi was born in Jesi, studied in Naples and had his first real success with his comic opera *Lo Frate 'Nnamorato*. His serious operas are now forgotten but his comic work remains popular. Many of them are available on CD and video and are still great fun. See LO FRATE 'NNAMORATO, LA SERVA PADRONA.

1932 Pergolesi

A romantic biography set in 1736, the year of the composer's death. It includes excerpts from *La Serva Padrona* sung by La Scala Opera House stars Laura Pasini and Vincenzo Bettoni. Pergolesi falls in love with a noble woman but her brother opposes the relationship and locks her up in his castle. The composer then becomes ill and dies in the monastery in Pozzuoli. Elio Steiner portrays Pergolesi and Dria Paola plays the woman he loves. Pergolesi's music was arranged by Vittorio Gui and conducted by Francesco Previtali. Gian Bistolfi wrote the film and Guido Brigone directed it. The French version is called *Les Amours de Pergolèse*. Black and white. In Italian. 80 minutes.

PÉRICHOLE, LA

1868 opéra-bouffe by Offenbach

Jacques Offenbach's operetta is romantic rather than satirical and tells the story of the 18th century Peruvian street singers La Périchole and Piquillo who are too poor to get married. When the love-stricken Viceroy offers La Périchole a position at court, she is obliged to marry for the sake of protocol. When a bogus marriage is arranged, she is married to Piquillo who is too drunk to know what is happening. The libretto by Henri Meilhac and Ludovic Halévy, based on a play by Prosper Mérimée, is loosely modeled on a real Peruvian actress who became the mistress of the Viceroy. Jean Renoir starred Anna Magnani in a film based on the story. See also JACQUES OFFENBACH.

1958 Metropolitan Opera on Omnibus

Theodore Uppman stars as the Viceroy with Laurel Hurley as La Périchole and Cyril Richard as Piquillo in this Metropolitan Opera production. It was created for the *Omnibus* television series by Richard Dunlap. Allessio de Paolis is the Prisoner and Osie Hawkin and Paul Franke are the VIPs. Jean Morel conducts the Metropolitan Opera Orchestra and Chorus. The operetta is sung in an English translation by Maurice Valency. Dunlap directed the NBC telecast of Acts I and II on Jan. 26, 1958. Black and white. In English. 90 minutes. Video at MTR and film at Library of Congress.

1972 Joan Sutherland video

Joan Sutherland stars in this highlights version in the series *Who's Afraid of Opera?* intended primarily for children. She tells the story of the opera to three puppets and takes the role of La Périchole with Pieter Van Der Stolk as Piquillo, Francis Egerton as the Viceroy, John Fryatt as Don Pedro, Gordon Wilcock as Panatellas and Alisa Gamely, Joy Mammen and Monica Sinclair as the Three Cousins. The dialogue is in English but the arias are sung in French. The music is played by the London Symphony Orchestra conducted by Richard Bonynge with sets designed by George Djurkovic. Piers Haggard directed. Color. In English and French. 30 minutes. Kultur video.

Related films

1952 The Golden Coach

Jean Renoir's classic film is based on the same Mérimée play as the opera. Anna Magnani stars as an actress with a touring *commedia dell'arte* troupe in 18th century Peru pursued by three lovers including the Viceroy. Renoir was inspired to make the film while listening to Vivaldi and so uses his music rather than Offenbach's on the soundtrack. The film was released in the U.S. in an English version. Color. In English. 101 minutes. On video.

1972 Ludwig

Luchino Visconti's elaborate biographical film about Bavarian King Ludwig II features mostly music by Wagner but also includes the overture to *La Périchole*. Helmut Berger stars as Ludwig. The music is played by the Hollywood Bowl Symphony Orchestra conducted by Carmen Dragon. Color. In Italian. 185 minutes.

PEROJO, BENITO
Spanish film director (1893-1974)

Benito Perojo, who began in the cinema in 1913 and continued for 60 years, was noted for his film musicals based on zarzuelas, operettas and operas. The most successful was his 1935 version of Breton's zarzuela *La Verbena de la Paloma* but he also produced films of Granados' *Goyescas*, Gilbert's *Die Keusche Susanne*, Vives' *Doña Francisquita*, *Carmen* and *The Barber of Seville*. See THE BARBER OF SEVILLE (1938 film), CARMEN (1959 film), DOÑA FRANCISQUITA (1952), GOYESCAS (1942), DIE KEUSCHE SUSANNE (1944), LA VERBENA DE LA PALOMA (1935/1963).

PETER GRIMES
1945 opera by Britten

Benjamin Britten's *Peter Grimes* was the first British opera to win international acclaim in the modern era. It is based on a narrative poem by George Crabbe called *The Borough*, and concerns a Suffolk fisherman whose apprentice is lost at sea. The village is full of suspicion and when a second boy dies, Grimes is driven to commit suicide. The libretto by George Slater changes Grimes from an evil man to a person victimized by his weaknesses and society. At the end it is unclear if he is to be blamed or pitied for what has happened. Peter Pears sang the role of Grimes at the premiere. See also BENJAMIN BRITTEN.

1970 The Maltings
Peter Pears stars as Peter Grimes in this production of the opera at The Maltings in Snape, Suffolk, with Britten leading the orchestra and the Ambrosian Opera Chorus. This was the first televised version of the opera, a collaboration between NET, BBC and CBC. The cast includes Heather Harper as Ellen Orford, Elizabeth Bainbridge, Owen Brannigan, Robert Tear and Bryan Drake. Brian Large directed the video. Color. In English. 148 minutes.

1981 Royal Opera House
Jon Vickers portrays Grimes in this fine production by Elijah Moshinsky taped at the Royal Opera House, Covent Garden. The cast includes Heather Harper as Ellen Orford, Norman Bailey as Captain Balstrode, Andrew Wilson as the boy, Elizabeth Bainbridge as Auntie, Marilyn Hill Smith and Anne Pashley as the nieces, John Dobson as Bob Boles and Patricia Payne as Mrs. Sedley. The set designers were Timothy O'Brien and Tazeena Firth. Colin

Davis leads the Royal Opera Orchestra and Chorus. John Vernon directed the video of a performance on June 31, 1981. Color. In English. 150 minutes. HBO video.

1994 English National Opera
Philip Langridge stars as Grimes in this English National Opera production by Tim Albery. Hildegard Bechtler designed the sets which create a rather abstract setting for the opera. Janice Cairns sings the role of Ellen, Alan Opie is Balstrode, Susan Gorton is Mrs Sedley, Ann Howard is Auntie, Edward Byles is the Rector, Alan Woodrow is Bob Doles and Robert Poulton is Ned Keene. David Atherton conducted the orchestra and Barry Gavin directed the video. Color. 146 minutes. London video.

PETERS, ROBERTA
American soprano (1930-)

Roberta Peters became an overnight star at the Metropolitan Opera as a last minute substitute for Nadine Conner, singing the role of Zerlina in *Don Giovanni*. She went on to even greater success with her brilliant performances in coloratura roles. Peters, who had no previous stage experience, was signed by the Met at nineteen to sing the Queen of the Night. She stayed with the company for 25 years and sang in 19 operas. She was especially noted for her Rosina, Lucia and Gilda and her voice ranked with those of Lily Pons and Amelita Galli-Curci. Peters can be seen on videos from her telecasts and in one Hollywood film. See SOL HUROK (1956), ROMÉO ET JULIETTE (1963), TONIGHT WE SING, TOSCA (1992 film).

1952-57 Roberta Peters in Opera and Song
This is a *Voice of Firestone* video featuring Peters in four appearances on the television program. On Aug. 4, 1952, she sings the Queen of the Night aria "Der Hölle Rache" plus other songs. On Nov. 15, 1954. she sings "Sempre libera," "I dreamt I dwelt in marble halls" and "Indian Love Call." On Sept. 20 1957, she is featured with the "Bell Song," "Stranger in Paradise" and "Song of India." Finally on Nov. 25, 1957, she sings "Ardon gl'incensi" from *Lucia di Lammermoor*. Black and white. 50 minutes. VAI video.

1952-59 Roberta Peters in Opera & Song 2
A second volume of highlights from appearances by Roberta Peters on the *Voice of Firestone* TV show.

She sings songs and arias from *Don Giovanni, The Tales of Hoffmann, Rigoletto* and *Naughty Marietta* plus "Greensleeves" and "One Night of Love." Black and white. 55 minutes. VAI video.

PHANTOM OF THE OPERA, THE
Film series based on Leroux novel

Gaston Leroux's 1911 novel *Le Fantôme de l'Opéra* has been popular with film makers since the 1925 Lon Chaney movie made it world famous. The story is a variation of the Faust legend and uses Gounod's *Faust* as a plot device. A mad composer who lives in the cellars of the Paris Opera House teaches a young soprano to sing and advances her career with acts of terror. She has effectively sold him her soul for the sake of her opera career. The films based on the book are of interest operatically both for their opera house settings and opera scenes. Gounod's *Faust* is central to most with the implication that the Phantom is playing Mephistopheles to his Faustian protégé Christine. The 1943 Nelson Eddy version, however, revolves around imaginary operas and in others the locale is shifted to London and Budapest. The novel has also spawned stage musicals and spin-off movies. Leroux (1868-1927) was a major French mystery writer and many of his stories have been made into French films but, surprisingly, not the *Phantom*.

1925 Lon Chaney film
Lon Chaney portrays the disfigured composer Erik who lives in the cellars of the Paris Opera House. He is the Phantom who loves understudy Christine Daaé (Mary Philbin) and makes her a star by forcing diva Carlotta (Virginia Pearson) to stop singing Marguerite in *Faust*. Edward Cecil portrays Faust, John Miljan is Valentin and Alexander Bevani is Mephistopheles. The film was re-issued with sound in 1929 with the Gounod arias. Elliot J. Clawson wrote the screenplay, Charles van Enger was the cinematographer and Rupert Julian directed. Universal. Two-color Technicolor & black and white. 79 minutes. On video and laserdisc.

1943 Nelson Eddy film
Nelson Eddy stars opposite soprano Susanna Foster in this operatic version of the Gaston Leroux tale. She plays the Paris Opera soprano Christine loved by Phantom Claude Rains, Eddy is the singer she loves and Jane Farrar is the diva she replaces. The film opens with Eddy and Foster on stage singing in Flotow's *Martha* in French. Composer Edward

Ward and librettist George Waggner created two imaginary operas which are elaborately staged in the movie. *L'Amour et la Gloire* is sung in French and based on themes by Chopin. *Le Prince Masque de la Caucasie* is a Russian opera based on Tchaikovsky's Fourth Symphony. William Wymetal staged the opera sequences, Samuel Hoffenstein and Eric Taylor wrote the screenplay, Hal Mohr was the cinematographer and Arthur Lubin directed the film. *Phantom* won Oscars for cinematography and art direction. Color. 92 minutes. MCA Universal video.

1955 Enrique Carreras film
The Argentine film titled *El Fantasma de la Operetta* is a spoof on *Phantom* and other similar horror films. It stars Amelita Vargas and Alfredo Barbieri and was directed by Enrique Carreras. Black and white. In Spanish. 70 minutes.

1960 Fernando Cortes film
This Mexican adaptation of the novel is titled *El Fantasma de la Operetta* and has a multitude of opera phantoms. It stars Tin-Tan and Ana Luisa Peluffo. Fernando Cortes directed. Color. In Spanish. 90 minutes.

1961 Renato Polselli film
This low-budget Italian variation on the story written and directed by Renato Polselli is titled *Il Mostro dell'Opera*. It stars Barbara Hawards, Marco Mariani Giuseppe Addobbati and Alberto Archetti. Color. In Italian 85 minutes.

1962 Terence Fisher film
The imaginary opera *Saint Joan* composed by the Phantom is the centerpiece of this Hammer film directed by horror master Terence Fisher. Lord Ambrose D'Arcy (Michael Gough) pretends he composed the opera and gets it staged. Herbert Lom portrays the Phantom with Heather Sears as the young singer Christine whom he teaches to sing his opera. The Phantom is depicted as a sympathetic character who dies to save Christine's life when a chandelier falls. The imaginary opera in the film was composed and conducted by Edwin Astley. Producer Anthony Hinds wrote the screenplay using the name John Elder and Arthur Grant was cinematographer. Color. 84 minutes.

1983 Maximilian Schell film
Maximilian Schell portrays the Phantom in this impressive TV film of the novel made and set in

Budapest with a British/Hungarian cast and crew. The Phantom has now become a Hungarian musician called Sandor Korvin. Jane Seymour plays a young soprano called Maria Gianelli whose stardom he orchestrates because she looks like his deceased opera singer wife. The central opera is again *Faust* with Pal Kovacs portraying Faust and Ferenc Begalyi as Mephistopheles. Michael York plays an opera producer who loves Christine and Diana Quick is the prima donna Brigida Bianchi. Sherman Yellen wrote the screenplay, Larry Pizer was the cinematographer and Robert Markowitz directed. Color. 100 minutes.

1987 Dario Argento film

Dario Argento's Italian film *Opera* is a variation on *The Phantom of the Opera* built around a production of Verdi's *Macbeth* in Parma. The plot is very close to *Phantom* with a mysterious figure prowling the secret corridors of the opera house, furthering the career of a young soprano and killing those involved with her. The scenes of the opera on stage at the Teatro Regio feature Cristina Marsillach as Lady Macbeth. The singers are Elisabetta Norberg Schulz, Paola Leolini, Andrea Piccini and Michele Pertusi with the Arturo Toscanini Symphony Orchestra of Emilia and Romagna. Maria Callas and Mirella Freni are heard singing arias from *Macbeth*, *Norma*, *La Traviata* and *Madama Butterfly*. The English title is *Terror at the Opera*. Color. In Italian. 90 minutes. South Gate video.

1987 Animated feature film

An American animated version of *The Phantom of the Opera* was reportedly made in 1987 credited to Aiden Grennell. No details are available. Color. In English. 60 minutes.

1989 Robert Englund film

Horror star Robert Englund portrays the Phantom in this handsome if rather gory film set in London at Covent Garden. The central opera is again *Faust* but there is also an aria from the Phantom's lost opera *Don Juan Triumphant* which is described in Leroux' novel. Jill Schoelen is the young soprano Christine who starts off in contemporary New York and ends up in 19th century London understudying and replacing diva Carlotta (Stephanie Lawrence) in *Faust*. Her stardom arrives after she sings the Jewel Song to a standing ovation. The *Faust* music is from a recording with Colin Davis conducting the Bavarian Radio Symphony Orchestra. Faust is Francisco Araiza and Mephistopheles is Yegeny

Nesterenko (on the recording Marguerite is sung by Kiri Te Kanawa). Misha Segal composed and conducted the music and Adras Miko directed the opera extracts. Duke Sandefur and Gerry O'Hara wrote the screenplay, Elemer Ragalyi was cinematographer and Dwight H. Little directed. Color. 90 minutes.

1990 Burt Lancaster film

Burt Lancaster is the Paris Opera House general manager and protective father of the Phantom (Charles Dance), actually his son, in this elaborate television variation of *The Phantom* devised by playwright Arthur Kopit. Things start to go wrong when villain Ian Richardson takes over the opera house so his wife Andrea Ferreol can be the diva. Teri Polo plays the young singer Christine who gets singing lessons from the Phantom with Michele LaGrange as her singing voice. Helia T'hezan sings for Ferreol and Gerard Carino sings for the Phantom. John Addison arranged the music and Tony Richardson directed. Color. 200 minutes.

PHI-PHI
1918 operetta by Christiné

Henri Christiné's tuneful French operetta *Phi-Phi*, libretto by Albert Willemetz and Francis Solar, is set in ancient Greece. It tells the story of the sculptor Phidias (known as Phi-Phi), the model/courtesan Aspasie, the sculptor's jealous wife Théodora and her paramour Prince Ardimedon. The operetta even tells how Venus de Milo lost her arms. See also HENRI CHRISTINÉ.

1927 Georges Pallu film

Phi-Phi was made into a French silent film in 1927 with Georges Gauthier starring as Phidias, Irène Wells as Aspasie, Rita Jolivet as Mrs. Phidias and Gaston Norès as Ardimedon. The film was presented in cinemas with live music from the operetta. Georges Pallu directed. Black and white. In French. About 80 minutes.

PICKWICK
1936 opera by Coates

This relatively obscure English opera by Albert Coates has a secure place in the history of music as it was the first televised opera. It was presented on BBC Television on Nov. 13, 1936, ten days before its world premiere at Covent Garden. Actually only 25 minutes of scenes from the opera were shown in a "special adaptation for television" made by Dallas Bower. The composer himself conducted the new BBC Television Orchestra with William Parsons singing the role of Mr. Pickwick and Dennis Noble as Sam Weller.

PIETRA DEL PARAGONE, LA
1812 opera by Rossini

Gioachino Rossini's comic opera *The Touchstone*, libretto by Luigi Romanelli, is a kind of houseparty where everyone plays mind games to see what people really feel about each other. The rich Count Asdrubale (bass), who is giving the party, pretends he is suddenly bankrupt. His beloved Clarice (contralto) tests his love for her by pretending to be her brother come to take her away. Poet Giocondo (tenor) is her great admirer. All ends more or less well. The CD of the opera features a young José Carreras as Giocondo. See also GIOACHINO ROSSINI.

1982 Bratislava Opera
Bass Alfredo Mariotti stars as the Count in this production at the Slovak National Theater in Bratislava. The cast includes Italian tenor Ugo Benelli as Giocondo with bass-baritone Claudio Desderi in support. Piero Bellugi conducts the Bratislava Opera Orchestra. Color. In Italian. 60 minutes. On Japanese video and laserdisc.

PIETRI, GIUSEPPE
Italian composer (1886-1946)

Giuseppe Pietri was the leading Italian operetta composer in the early part of the century and helped found an Italian operetta school. He began his career in 1910 with the opera *Calendimaggio* and then composed five other operas, most notably the 1934 *Maristella* featuring Gigli as its star. However, his real success came with operetta starting with the 1915 *Addio Giovinezza* based on a famous stage comedy that has been filmed four times. His other major success was the 1920 *L'Acqua Cheta*, also based on a stage play.

1992 L'Acqua Cheta
Pietri's 1920 operetta *L'Acqua Cheta* (Still Waters) tells the story of Ida, her sister Anita and their men friends and is based on a stage play by Augusto Novelli. Highlights of the operetta and its history are featured on the 1992 Italian TV series *Operette, Che Passione* hosted by Italian operetta master Sandro Massimini. Included on the video are the hit numbers "Oh com'è bello guidare i cavalli," "Canzone della Rificolona," "Su, le stelle sorridone chete" and "Serenata." Color. In Italian. About 19 minutes. Ricordi (Italy) video.

PINZA, EZIO
Italian/American bass (1892-1957)

Rome native Ezio Pinza was a major star at La Scala in Milan but it was the Metropolitan Opera in New York that made him internationally famous. He appeared there for 22 consecutive seasons beginning in 1926. He starred in 750 productions and was especially noted for his performances as Figaro and Don Giovanni. He left the Met at the age of 56 and became a major Broadway star appearing in *South Pacific* in 1949 and *Fanny* in 1954. He had a Hollywood career but was not given many good films. He also starred in two TV series in the early 1950s, the *Ezio Pinza Show* and the sitcom *Bonino* in which he portrayed a music-loving widower. Unfortunately he was never filmed in a complete opera. See BELL TELEPHONE HOUR (1947), CARNEGIE HALL (1947), TONIGHT WE SING.

1951 Mr. Imperium
Ezio Pinza is a prince who becomes a king in this colorful MGM musical romance. Lana Turner is the movie star he loves and leaves twice for the good of his country. Pinza and Turner both sing but not memorably. The film is stilted but has a certain charm, especially in the scene on a Hollywood set built to resemble their meeting place. Don Hartman directed. Color. 87 minutes.

1951 Strictly Dishonorable
Pinza portrays an opera star who dallies with Janet Leigh and then marries her to save her reputation. In the film he appears on stage in an opera written by Mario Castelnuovo-Tedesco and also sings the *Faust* aria "Le veau d'or" and two pop songs. The film was based on a Preston Sturges play, more daringly filmed in 1931, and scripted and directed by Melvin Frank and Norman Panama. MGM. Black and white. 86 minutes.

PIRATES OF PENZANCE, THE
1879 comic opera by Gilbert & Sullivan

The Pirates of Penzance or The Slave of Duty is one of the most popular Savoy operas and provided the music for a famous American song. The tune of "Hail, Hail, the Gang's All Here" was borrowed from the operetta where it is sung as "Come Friends, Who Plough the Sea." The story is wonderfully ridiculous. Frederic has been apprenticed to the pirates of Penzance by his nursemaid Ruth who misunderstood the word "pilot." The pirates are soft-hearted and especially partial to orphans. Frederic falls in love with Mabel, one of the daughters of Major General Stanley who happens to be an orphan. A band of policemen led by the Sergeant arrive to combat the pirates but all works out well. Mabel's song "Poor Wandering One" is virtually a coloratura aria. The popularity of the operetta is reflected in a large number of films and videos. See also GILBERT AND SULLIVAN.

1955 D'Oyly Carte Opera Company
Bridget D'Oyly Carte directed the D'Oyly Carte Opera Company for this television production of the operetta. The cast includes Joy Mornay, Joyce Wright and Neville Griffiths. Isadore Godfrey conducted the orchestra and Henry May designed the sets. Charles S. Dubin directed the telecast shown on CBS in the Omnibus series on Nov. 13, 1955. Black and white. In English. 35 minutes. Videos at MTR and Library of Congress.

1961 Stratford Festival
Norman Campbell directed this Canadian film based on a stage production of the operetta at the Stratford, Ontario, Festival in 1961. The singers include Andrew Downie, Eric House, Harry Mossfield, Irene Byratt, Howell Glynne and Marion Studholm. Louis Applebaum conducted the orchestra. CBC. Black and white. In English. 85 minutes.

1974 World of Gilbert & Sullivan film
Valerie Masterson stars as Mabel with Donald Adams as the Pirate King in this highlights version of the operetta produced by John Seabourne for the *World of Gilbert and Sullivan* series. Thomas Round is Frederic, Helen Landis is Ruth, John Cartier is the Major-General, Lawrence Richard is the Police Sergeant and Michael Wakeham is Samuel. The music is played by the Gilbert and Sullivan Festival Orchestra and the film was directed by Trevor Evans. Color. In English. 50 minutes.

1976 Sheila Graber animated film
English animator Sheila Graber made an animated cartoon version of one of the best known comic songs of the operetta and called it *I Am the Very Model of a Modern Major General*. Color. In English. 4 minutes.

1982 George Walker film
Peter Allen is the Pirate King in this film produced by Judith De Paul for George Walker. Keith Michell is the Major General, Janis Kelly is Mabel, Gillian Knight is Ruth, Alexander Oliver is Frederic and Paul Hudson is the Police Sergeant. Alexander Faris conducts the London Symphony Orchestra and the Ambrosian Opera Chorus. Michael Geliot was the stage director and Rodney Greenway the film director. Color. In English. 112 minutes. CBS Fox video/Pioneer laser.

1982 Linda Ronstadt film
Linda Ronstadt stars as Mabel with Kevin Kline as the Pirate King in this adaptation of Joseph Papp's stage production filmed by Wilford Leach. Angela Lansbury is Ruth, Rex Smith is Frederic, George Rose is the Major-General and Tony Azito is the Police Sergeant. Peter Howitt designed the sets and William Elliott conducted the orchestra. Universal Pictures. Color. In English. 112 minutes. MCA video and laser.

1985 Stratford Festival
Brian Macdonald's adaptation of the operetta was a major success on stage at the Stratford, Ontario, Festival in 1985 and was taped by Norman Campbell for presentation on CBC in Toronto. It stars Brent Carver as the Pirate King, Jeff Hyslop as Frederic, Caralyn Tomlin as Mabel, Ruth Galloway as Pat, Douglas Chamberlain as the Major General, Wendy Abbot as Blue Stocking and Stephen Beamis as the Police Chief. It was telecast on Dec. 29, 1985. Color. In English. 130 minutes.

PIROGOV, ALEXANDER
Russian bass (1899-1964)

Alexander Pirogov, one of the greatest Russian bass singers of the century and brother of the equally talented Grigory, made his debut in Moscow in 1922. He spent most of his career at the Bolshoi and was luckily captured on film by Soviet filmmaker Vera Stroyeva in two of his greatest roles. See BOLSHOI OPERA (1951) BORIS GODUNOV (1954), FAUST (1949 film), PRINCE IGOR (1951).

PLISHKA, PAUL
American bass (1941-)

Paul Plishka has been a mainstay of the Metropolitan Opera since 1967 and if he doesn't have the renown of a Pavarotti, he has the enduring admiration of all those who love opera. His career has been mostly centered around the Met though he has sung at La Scala, Berlin, Munich, Chicago and San Francisco. He is one of the most reliable of performers and often gets better notices than the stars. He is best known for his Verdi interpretations and is a notable Falstaff and a fine Leporello. His work is well represented on Met videos. See LA BOHÈME (1977), FALSTAFF (1992), LUCIA DI LAMMERMOOR (1982), LUISA MILLER (1988), RISE AND FALL OF THE CITY OF MAHAGONNY (1979), SIMON BOCCANEGRA (1984), LES TROYENS (1983), TURANDOT (1988), VERDI REQUIEM (1991).

POETA, EL
1980 opera by Morena Torroba

The Poet is an opera by Spanish zarzuela composer Federico Morena Torroba. He began his career in opera, built a reputation with zarzuelas and then returned to opera at the end of his life. Placido Domingo commissioned this opera and starred in it when it premiered. It's based on an episode in the life of the 19th century Spanish poet José Ignacio de Espronceda. See also FEDERICO MORENA TORROBA.

1980 Madrid Teatro La Zarzuela
Placido Domingo stars as the 19th century poet José Ignacio de Espronceda in this world premiere production at the Teatro La Zarzuela in Madrid. Garcia Navarro conducts the Teatro Orchestra. The video is a copy of a Spanish telecast. In Spanish. 137 minutes. Opera Dubs/Lyric video.

POLANSKI, ROMAN
Polish film director (1933-)

Roman Polanski became famous in 1962 with his first feature film, *Knife in the Water*. He became even better known after moving to the U.S. and making *Rosemary's Baby* and *Chinatown*. Polanski began to direct opera on stage in 1974 beginning with *Lulu* at the Festival of Two Worlds in Spoleto. He based his production of the Berg opera around the Pabst film of the story, *Pandora's Box*. Polanski has also staged *Rigoletto* in Munich and *The Tales of Hoffmann*

in Paris. In 1981 he returned to Poland to produce the Mozart play *Amadeus* on stage.

POLENBLUT
1913 operetta by Nebal

Oskar Nedbal's most popular operetta *Polenblut* (Polish Blood) is a kind of Polish counterpart to the patriotic Viennese operetta *Wiener Blut*. It's set in Russian-occupied Poland at the beginning of the century and is flavored with mazurkas and polonaises. Leo Stein's libretto tells the story of a high-spirited young woman who wins the affections of a high-living count after he spurns her for not being an aristocrat. It was presented in America in 1915 as *The Peasant Girl* with Emma Trentini in the starring role and new songs by Rudolf Friml. *Polenblut* has remained in the central European operetta repertory. See also OSKAR NEDBAL.

1934 Anny Ondra film
In 1934 *Polenblut* was made into a bi-lingual film in Prague with Anny Ondra portraying the clever daughter of rich Polish landowner Hans Moser. In the German version she wins the heart of aristocratic neighbor Ivan Petrovich. In the Czech version, titled *Polská Krev*, she wins Theodor Pistek. Karel Lamac directed. Black and white. In Czech or German. 87 minutes.

PONCHIELLI, AMILCARE
Italian composer (1834-1886)

Amilcare Ponchielli's first opera was based on the famous Italian novel *I Promessi Sposi* but he is remembered today for only one opera, *La Gioconda*. Even those who have never seen the opera know some of its music including the famous Dance of the Hours used in *Fantasia*. The masterful libretto is by the multi-talented Arrigo Boito. Ponchielli married soprano Teresina Brambilla whose descendants include Tullio Carminati, Grace Moore's co-star in the opera film *One Night of Love*. See LA GIOCONDA.

PONNELLE, JEAN-PIERRE
French director/designer (1932 -1988)

Jean-Pierre Ponnelle directed sixteen opera films and must be considered an important filmmaker even though he is not usually listed in film reference books. He is certainly one of the major auteurs of the opera film genre and could be compared to Franco Zeffirelli who also worked in film and theater. He has sometimes been called the "father of the opera film." His films are exciting visually as well as musically and have a style all their own. They were shot on 35mm and sometimes had theatrical release though they were normally made for television. Ponnelle was also an innovative stage director/designer and his theater productions were usually the basis of his films, most notably the Monteverdi cycle. His career began in Germany in 1952, he made his American debut designing sets for the San Francisco Opera in 1958 and he began to direct on stage in 1962. He died tragically from a fall into an orchestra pit while producing *Carmen* in Tel Aviv. Most of his films are available on video and his two Figaro operas are especially popular. See also THE ABDUCTION FROM THE SERAGLIO (1967), THE BARBER OF SEVILLE (1972), CARDILLAC (1986), CARMINA BURANA (1976), LA CENERENTOLA (1981), LA CLEMENZA DI TITO (1980), COSÌ FAN TUTTE (1988), FALSTAFF (1976), IDOMENEO (1982), L'INCORONAZIONE DI POPPEA (1978), L'ITALIANA IN ALGERI (1986), MADAMA BUTTERFLY (1974), THE MAGIC FLUTE (1982), MANON (1983), THE MARRIAGE OF FIGARO (1976), MITRIDATE (1981), ORFEO (1978), RIGOLETTO (1983), IL RITORNO D'ULISSE IN PATRIA (1979), TRISTAN UND ISOLDE (1983).

1986 Jean-Pierre Ponnelle or The Warpath
A documentary video portrait of Ponnelle by Brigitte Carreau which shows the director at work. Color. In German. 54 minutes.

PONS, LILY
French/American soprano (1904-1976)

Lily Pons, after Grace Moore, was the top female opera star in Hollywood in the 1930s and one of the finest coloratura sopranos in the world. She was born near Cannes, site of the world's best-known film festival, and made her debut in 1928 in Mulhouse in *Lakmé* with Reynaldo Hahn conducting. Despite her petite size (five foot high and barely 98 pounds), she made a sensational debut at the Metropolitan Opera on Jan. 1, 1931, starring in *Lucia di Lammermoor*. She continued to sing there for another 28 years. Pons made three reasonable films with good directors in Hollywood in the 1930s but then gave up on the movies. She was married to conductor André Kostelanetz from 1938 to 1958, the year she gave her farewell performance at the Met as Lucia. Her last stage performance was in Fort Worth where she opened the opera season as Lucia. See METROPOLITAN OPERA (1966).

1935 I Dream Too Much
Pons made her film debut opposite Henry Fonda in this enjoyable RKO picture directed by John Cromwell. Her delightful personality comes through well in her portrayal of a rising opera singer married to aspiring composer Fonda. His opera is not a success but becomes one when turned into a musical comedy. Pons sings her signature aria "Bell Song" from *Lakmé*, "Caro nome" from *Rigoletto* and songs by Jerome Kern and Dorothy Fields. She insisted that husband-to-be André Kostelanetz conduct the orchestra accompanying her arias. Black and white. 85 minutes. Turner video.

1936 That Girl From Paris
Pons' second RKO film featured her as a Parisian opera star who runs away from an arranged marriage. She ends up with Gene Raymond in the U.S. as an illegal immigrant involved in romantic mix-ups. Pons sings "Una voce poco fa" from *The Barber of Seville*, a Strauss waltz, a tarantella and songs by Arthur Schwartz and Edward Heyman. Lucille Ball plays a jealous friend. André Kostelanetz conducted the music and Leigh Jason directed. Black and white. 102 minutes. RKO video.

1937 Hitting a New High
Pons portrays a French jazz singer who wants to switch to opera in her last Hollywood film and is involved in a complicated ruse posing as a Bird Girl to deceive millionaire Edward Everett Horton. Her opera arias include the mad scene from *Lucia di Lammermoor* and "Je suis Titania" from *Mignon*. There are also songs by James McHugh and Harold Adamson. Pons left Hollywood complaining that there was comic business in this film even when she was singing. Raoul Walsh directed for RKO. Black and white. 80 minutes.

1973 Lily Pons
This is a documentary film portrait of Pons at the age of 70 in which she talks about her singing career and her life. The filmmakers follow along as she visits places associated with her career. The film was telecast on Feb. 21, 1973. Charos Productions. Color. 60 minutes. Video at Library of Congress.

PONSELLE, ROSA
American soprano (1897-1981)

Rosa Ponselle's life sounds like an unbelievable movie of a fairy tale. With no previous experience on an opera stage, this vaudeville singer made her debut at the Metropolitan Opera at the age of 21 opposite Enrico Caruso in *La Forza del Destino*. She was immediately acclaimed as a vocal miracle with a voice of pure gold and an actress with genuine ability. Ponselle was a Met favorite from her debut in 1918 until her too early retirement in 1937. Her records are still admired but she made no films.

1936 Carmen screen tests
Ponselle began to sing the mezzo role of Carmen in the last two years of her stage career and was tested for the role for a Hollywood movie. In the MGM screen tests, dated October 12, 1936, she talks about her love for *La Traviata* and her interest in seeing Greta Garbo in the film version of the story and about the difficulty of singing *Norma*. She is shown in costume singing the "Habanera" and the "Chanson bohemienne" and she looks and sounds splendid. She felt these tests of *Carmen* were the best recordings she ever made of the arias. The tests are included in the video *Legends of Opera*. Black and white. About 4 minutes. Legato Classics video.

1977 Metropolitan Opera
The Metropolitan Opera celebrated Ponselle's 80th birthday with a tribute to her during the interval of the telecast of the opera *Luisa Miller*. She was interviewed at her home in the Villa Pace for the program and her famous screen tests were also shown. Color & black and white. 10 minutes. On video.

POPP, LUCIA
Czech-born Austrian soprano (1939-1993)

Lucia Popp, who died tragically early at only 54 of a brain tumor, made her debut in 1963 in Bratislava as the Queen of the Night. She then moved to the Vienna Staatsoper, the opera house where she sang regularly for the rest of her life. She was a regular at the Salzburg Festival and came to the Met in 1967 as the Queen of the Night. Her specialties were Mozart and Strauss. Popp made a large number of recordings and can be seen in fine form on many videos. See THE BARTERED BRIDE (1980), THE CREATION (1986), FALSTAFF (1965), FIDELIO (1968/1978), HANSEL AND GRETEL (1984), THE MAGIC FLUTE (1983), DER ROSENKAVALIER (1979), ZAR UND ZIMMERMANN (1968).

1977 Four Last Songs
Popp sings the *Four Last Songs* of Richard Strauss with backing from the Chicago Symphony Orchestra led by Georg Solti. Humphrey Burton directed the video. Unitel. Color. 21 minutes.

1993 Opera Imaginaire
Popp is the featured singer on one of the films on this compendium of animated films of opera arias. Raimund Krumme animates her version of "Du also bist mein Brautigan?" from *The Magic Flute*. Color. 52 minutes. See OPERA IMAGINAIRE.

PORGY AND BESS
1935 opera by Gershwin

George Gershwin's *Porgy and Bess* is probably the major American opera and one of the few to be staged in the major opera houses of the world. It has taken a long time for it to get respect from the opera world because it was first staged on Broadway and was apparently considered too popular to be high art. There was also the question of whether a trio of white men could write an African-American opera. The question is now irrelevant as the opera has created its own universality. DuBose Heyward wrote the libretto based on his 1925 novel about people he observed in South Carolina, Ira Gershwin wrote most of the superb lyrics and George Gershwin composed music for their words that is likely to live as long as anything by Mozart or Verdi. The unforgettable arias of what Gershwin called a "folk opera" include "Summertime," "It Ain't Necessarily So" and "I Got Plenty Of Nothin'." The opera is set in an African-American ghetto in Charleston called Catfish Row. The crippled Porgy becomes involved with the beautiful Bess after her man Crown goes to jail but she eventually runs away with the gambler Sporting Life. See also GEORGE GERSHWIN.

1959 Otto Preminger film
Sidney Poitier stars as Porgy with Dorothy Dandridge as Bess and Sammy Davis Jr. as Sporting Life in this controversial Otto Preminger film of the opera. Pearl Bailey is Maria, Diahann Carroll is Clara, Brock Peters is Crown and writer Maya Angelou plays a dancer. Robert McFerrin is the singing voice of Porgy, Adele Addison sings Bess, Loulie Jean Norman sings Clara, Inez

Matthews sings Serena (acted by Ruth Attaway) and Bailey and Peters sing for themselves. The music arrangements by André Previn and Ken Darby won an Academy Award and the film was nominated for three other Oscars. This was the final and most expensive film of producer Samuel Goldwyn. Ira Gershwin said he liked it and *The New York Times* listed it as one of the Ten Best Films of the Year but it was not a commercial success. The film has been withdrawn from circulation by the Gershwin heirs but can be viewed at the Library of Congress. Color. In English. 138 minutes.

1989 Trevor Nunn film

Willard White stars as Porgy with Cynthia Haymon as Bess in this superb Trevor Nunn film shot in a London studio but based on his acclaimed Glyndebourne Festival/Covent Garden production. The cast is virtually the same as the stage production. Damon Evans sings the role of Sporting Life, Gregg Baker is Crown, Cynthia Clarey is Serena, Marietta Simpson is Maria and Paula Ingram is Clara (with the voice of Harolyn Blackwell). John Gunter designed the sets and Simon Rattle conducted the London Philharmonic Orchestra and Glyndebourne Festival Chorus. Color. 184 minutes. EMI Classics video and laser.

PORPORA, NICOLA
Italian composer (1686-1768)

Nicola Porpora was a notable rival to Handel during his heyday and produced five operas in London. He is said to have composed over fifty operas in the *opera seria* mode. He was also famous as a teacher with Haydn and the castrato Farinelli among his successful pupils. His operas emphasized vocal virtuosity and were popular with the castrati because of this. His work can be seen on stage in the film *Farinelli*. See FARINELLI.

PORTEN, HENNY
German film actress (1888-1960)

Henny Porten, Germany's first important film star, was the daughter of an opera singer and portrayed the heroine in early German opera sound films. Her first such "tonbilder" (sound-picture) was made in 1906. She usually worked with Oskar Messter who developed a synchronization process for his Biophon-Theater using phonograph records of opera arias. Porten's father, Franz, a former opera singer, directed and often acted in the films shot in

a Berlin studio. Henny also starred in the 1921 feature *Die Geier-Wally* based on the source story of Catalina's opera *La Wally*. It's not known exactly how many of these miniature opera films she made but it was probably about forty. Listed in this book are DER BETTELSTUDENT (1907), FAUST (1908), DON PASQUALE (1937 film), DER FREISCHÜTZ (1908), LOHENGRIN (1907), VIKTOR NESSLER (Der Trompeter von Sakkingen), OTELLO (1907), TANNHÄUSER (1908), IL TROVATORE (1908), LA WALLY (1921).

POSTILLON DE LONJUMEAU, LE
1844 opera by Adam

Adolphe Adam's French opera *The Coachman from Longjumeau* is the tuneful story of coachman Chapelou who abandons his bride Madeleine on their wedding night when he is taken off to sing at the Paris Opera. Ten years later they are reunited when he is famous and she is rich. This is Adam's most popular opera especially in German-speaking countries where tenors favor the role of Chapelou to show off their high D's. NB: "Longjumeau" is the English spelling of the French town while "Lonjumeau" is the spelling in French and German. See also ADOLPHE ADAM.

1936 Willy Eichberger film

Willy Eichberger stars as the coachman-turned-singer from Longjumeau in this German-language film shot in Vienna as *Der Postillon von Lonjumeau*. Rose Stradner portrays Madeleine, Alfred Neugebauer is King Louis XV, Leo Slezak is the Count de Latour and Thekla Ahrens is Mme. de Pompadour. It's good entertainment, if not quite the opera as written, and played as much for comedy as musical values. Carl Lamac directed. Shown in the U.S. as *King Smiles--Paris Laughs*. Black and white. In German. 91 minutes. Lyric Video.

1989 Grand Théâtre de Genève

This is a telecast of a Geneva Opera House stage production of the opera sung in French. It stars López-Yanez, Donna Brown, Maurice Sieyes and René Massis with Patrick Fournillier conducting the orchestra. The video is an taping of a telecast. Color. In French. 130 minutes. Lyric/ Opera Dubs video.

POTENZA DELLA MUSICA, LA
1549 musical interludes by various composers

The Power of Music is a collection of Italian musical interludes (intermedi) performed in Florence before the official birth of opera in 1599 and considered by some as virtually miniature operas. They were devised by Count Giovanni de' Bardi for a Medici wedding to be presented with Girolamo Bargagli's comedy *La Pellegrina*. Bardi was a central figure in the Camerata and the creation of opera with composers Jacobo Peri and Giulio Caccini who wrote some of the music for this event. The other composers were Luca Marenzio, Cristofano Malvezzi and Emile de' Cavaliere.

1989 Thames Television
The Power of Music was filmed by Thames Television in London as *Una Stravaganza dei Medici*. The singers are soprano Tessa Bonner, soprano Emma Kirkby, soprano Emily Van Evera and tenor Nigel Rogers. Andrew Parrott leads the Taverner Consort and Players. Color. In Italian. 71 minutes. EMI (England) video and laser/ Japanese laser.

POULENC, FRANCIS
French composer (1899-1963)

Francis Poulenc, one of the influential avant-garde group Les Six, came to opera late in his career and wrote only three operas. The first was the surrealistic 1947 *Les Mamelles de Terésias* based on a play by Apollinaire. It was followed by the powerful and strongly religious *Les Dialogues des Carmélites* in 1948. His last work was *La Voix Humaine* in 1958, a one-woman opera composed for Denise Duval. See LES DIALOGUES DES CARMÉLITES, LA VOIX HUMAINE.

POUSSIÈRES D'AMOUR
1996 opera film by Schroeter

German director Werner Schroeter's film *Poussières d'Amour*, known in English as both *Tears of Love* and *Love's Debris*, is a fascinating examination of opera singing and the emotions that the opera voice creates. Schroeter invited a number of major singers to the 13th Century Abbey of Roymaunt in France and worked with them on presenting a single aria. The arias were chosen from a wide range of operas from *Fidelio* to *Norma* to *Carmen*. The singers include Martha Mödl, Anita Cerquetti, Rita Gorr, Trudeliese Schmidt, Katherine and Kristine Ciesinski, Laurence Dale, Jenny Drivala, Gail Gilmore and Sergue Larin. They were accompanied on piano on their arias by Elizabeth Cooper. Film actresses also participated with Isabelle Huppert talking to Mödl and Carole Bouquet questioning Cerquetti. The film

is dedicated "to Maria Callas and all the others." France-Germany. In German, French, Italian, Russian and English. 120 minutes.

POWELL, JANE
American film soprano (1929-)

Jane Powell was MGM's answer to Deanna Durbin in the 1940s, a precocious teenage heroine with a high soprano voice who occasionally dabbled in opera or operetta. Her Hollywood career began in 1943 when she won a contest with an aria from *Carmen* and was signed to a movie contract. She sang classical music in her first film, the 1944 *Song of the Open Road*, and was taken up by Joe Pasternak who had been Durbin's producer. In 1948 she was featured with Jeanette MacDonald in *Three Daring Daughters*, a remake of Durbin's *Three Smart Girls*. Later that year she teamed with Metropolitan Opera tenor Lauritz Melchior in *Luxury Liner* and joined him in a duet from *Aida*. In 1951 she was paired with Fred Astaire in *Royal Wedding*. Her best film year was 1954. She starred opposite Howard Keel in the outstanding *Seven Brides for Seven Brothers*, sang an opera aria in *Athena* and was a guest star in the Sigmund Romberg biography *Deep in My Heart*. Her film career faded in the late 50s when the Hollywood musical died but she has continued to work on stage and in television. See LAURITZ MELCHIOR (1948).

1954 Athena
Powell plays Athena and sings the aria "Chacun le sait" from Donizetti's *The Daughter of the Regiment* in this minor musical about health fads. She was teamed with Vic Damone, Debbie Reynolds and Edmund Purdom. Richard Thorpe directed. Color. 96 minutes.

1954 Deep in My Heart
Powell is one of the guest stars in this lively film biography of operetta composer Sigmund Romberg directed by Stanley Donen. She and Vic Damone sing one of Romberg's most famous songs, "Will You Remember." José Ferrer portrays Romberg and Metropolitan Opera soprano Helen Traubel plays his restaurateur friend. Color. 132 minutes. MGM-UA video and laser.

POWELL, MICHAEL
English film director (1905-1990)

Michael Powell, one of the major British filmmakers, is best known for his ballet film *The Red Shoes* (1948) made with his usual collaborator Emeric Pressburger. They also produced two fine opera films, *The Tales of Hoffmann* and *O Rosalinda!*, a modern version of *Der Fledermaus*. In addition Powell directed a television film of Bartok's *Bluebeard's Castle*. Powell used opera on the soundtrack of some of his non-operatic films, most notably *Mignon* in *The Life and Death of Colonel Blimp*. See BLUEBEARD'S CASTLE (1964), DIE FLEDERMAUS (1955), MIGNON (1943 film), THE TALES OF HOFFMANN (1951).

POWERS, MARIE
American contralto (1910-1973)

Marie Powers, whose career was closely associated with operas by Gian Carlo Menotti, began her U.S. career touring with the San Carlo Opera company in the 1940s in *Aida* and *Un Ballo in Maschera*. In 1947 she sang Madame Flora, the medium, in the Broadway production of Menotti's *The Medium* in New York and then in 1948 in London. She starred in Menotti's *The Old Maid and the Thief* at the New York City Opera in 1948 and in 1950 created the role of the Mother in Menotti's *The Consul*. In the 1950s she sang at the Paris Opéra as Fricka and Mistress Quickly. She was a powerful singing actress as can be seen in her superb performance as Madame Flora in Menotti's great 1951 film of *The Medium*. See THE MEDIUM (1948/1951), THE OLD MAID AND THE THIEF (1949).

1950 Give Us Our Dream
Powers portrays Jessamine, an ex-opera star who still thinks she is performing at La Scala, in this Studio One play on CBS television. She is helped by neighbor Lily (Josephine Hall). Paul Nickell directed. Black and white. 60 minutes. Video at MTR.

PREMINGER, OTTO
Austrian/American director (1906-1986)

Otto Preminger began directing films in the 1930s and made his breakthrough in 1944 with *Laura*. He made three films with operatic content. His 1954 Bizet-derived *Carmen Jones* is undervalued but impressive, his 1959 film of Gershwin's *Porgy and Bess* remains controversial and out of circulation and his 1963 *The Cardinal* features Austrian soprano Wilma Lipp. See CARMEN (1954), WILMA LIPP, PORGY AND BESS (1959).

PREY, HERMANN
German baritone (1929-)

Herman Prey made his debut in Wiesbaden in 1952 and became internationally popular in the 1960s. He has a most engaging personality both as singer and actor as can be seen on his many videos. He is particular notable as Figaro in the Ponnelle film versions of *The Barber of Seville* and *The Marriage of Figaro*. See THE BARBER OF SEVILLE (1959/1972), COSÌ FAN TUTTE (1972), EUGENE ONEGIN (1968), DIE FLEDERMAUS (1983), HANSEL AND GRETEL (1981), THE MAGIC FLUTE (1975 film), THE MARRIAGE OF FIGARO (1976), MEISTERSINGER VON NÜRNBERG, DIE (1984), ZAR UND ZIMMERMANN (1976).

1985 Herman Prey Recital
Prey sings a selection of songs by Schumann with accompaniment by Leonard Hokanson. The video was made for German television. Unitel. Color. 66 minutes.

1986 Schubert's Schwanengesang
Herman Prey has made a number of recordings of Schubert's last songs. This studio recital is an excellent visual version with accompaniment by Leonard Hokanson. M. Kabelka directed the video. Color. In German. 70 minutes.

PRICE, LEONTYNE
American soprano (1927-)

Leontyne Price was the pre-eminent Verdi soprano in America for many years and can be seen and heard in fine form performing in Verdi operas on video. She was born in Mississippi, studied in Ohio and at the Juilliard and made her debut in 1952 on Broadway singing St. Cecilia in Barber's *Four Saints in Three Acts*. The next year she was Bess in the Gershwin opera at the Ziegfeld Theatre. She made her opera house debut in San Francisco in 1957 as Madame Lidoine in *Dialogue des Carmelites*. She was Aida at Covent Garden in 1958 and at La Scala in 1960 and reached the Metropolitan in 1961 as Leonora in *Il Trovatore*. She sang a wide series of roles at the Met, including Butterfly, Tosca and Pamina, and was Barber's Cleopatra in his *Anthony and Cleopatra* which opened the new Met. Price retired from the stage in 1985 after singing *Aida* at the Met. See AIDA (1958/ 1985), BELL TELEPHONE HOUR (1967), LES DIALOGUES DES CARMÉLITES (1957), DON GIOVANNI (1960), LA FORZA DEL DESTINO (1984), THE MAGIC FLUTE (1956), METROPOLITAN OPERA (1953/ 1966/1983), BEVERLY SILLS (1981), TOSCA (1955), GIUSEPPE VERDI (1956), VERDI REQUIEM (1967).

1982 Leontyne Price at Avery Fisher Hall

Leontyne Price performs at Avery Fisher Hall in this *Live from Lincoln Center* concert. Zubin Mehta conducts the New York Philharmonic Orchestra at the gala opening of the orchestra's 141st season. Price sings arias from operas by Mozart ("Come scoglio" from *Così Fan Tutte*), Verdi (Desdemona's "Willow Song" and "Ave Maria" from *Otello*) and Strauss (final scene from *Salome*). Price and Mehta have also recorded an album of arias from Verdi operas. The video, labeled *Zubin Mehta Leontyne Price*, was taped Sept. 15, 1982. Color. 152 minutes. Paramount video.

1983 Leontyne Price in Montreal

Price is shown in performance at a concert in Montreal with the Montreal Symphony Orchestra. The program includes arias by Mozart, Verdi, Gershwin and Puccini. Evelyne Robidas filmed the concert for Canadian TV. Color. 60 minutes.

1983 Leontyne Price Sings Noel

Price performs at a Christmas concert at Notre Dame Cathedral in Montreal and sings a range of carols from "Away in a Manger" to "O Come, Emanuel." She is accompanied by the Montreal Symphony Orchestra under the baton of Charles Dutoit. The concert was telecast by the Canadian Broadcasting Corporation from Montreal on Dec. 18, 1983, and released on video in 1987. Color. In English. 58 minutes. CBC video.

PRINCE IGOR

1890 opera by Borodin

This superb Russian opera by Alexander Borodin also provided the music for the pastiche operetta *Kismet*. *Prince Igor* (Kniaz Igor) was not finished when the composer died in 1887 but was completed by Rimsky-Korsakov and Glazounov. It revolves around the conflict between the Russians led by Prince Igor and the powerful Polovsti of Central Asia who invaded Russia in the 12th century. While Igor is a prisoner of the Polovsti, his son falls in love with the daughter of the enemy Khan. Borodin based his libretto on a 12th-century epic poem. The music of the Polovtsian Dances from the opera has become well-known. See also ALEXANDER BORODIN, KISMET.

1951 Vera Stroyeva film

Alexander Pirogov stars as Prince Igor in this condensed version of the opera filmed on stage at the Bolshoi for the film *Bolshoi Koncert*. Yevgeniya Smolenskaya portrays his wife and Maxim Mikhailov is Khan Konchak. Olga Lepeshinskaya is the main dancer in the Polovtsian Dances sequence. Vera Stroyeva directed this opera recital film which was released in the U.S. as *The Grand Concert*. Color. In Russian. 105 minutes.

1969 Roman Tikhomirov film

Roman Tikhomirov filmed this wide-screen spectacular on location on the steppes using actors whose singing is dubbed by Kirov Opera performers. Many of the arias are filmed as interior monologues while Mikhail Fokine's choreography helps make the Polovtsian Dances scene especially effective. Vladimir Kiniayev sings Prince Igor acted by Boris Khmelnitsky, Yevgeny Nesterenko sings Khan Konchak acted by Bimbolat Vatayev, Tamara Milashkina sings Princess Yaroslavna acted by Nelly Pshennaya and Virgilius Noreika sings Vladimir acted by Boris Takarev. Tikhomirov and Isaak Glikman wrote the adaptation and Gennady Provatorov conducted the Kirov Theater Orchestra and Chorus. Lenfilm. Color. In Russian with English subtitles. 105 minutes. Corinth video and laser.

1990 Royal Opera House

Sergei Leiferkus is outstanding as Prince Igor in this excellent Covent Garden production by Andrei Serban. Anna Tomowa-Sintow is Princess Yaroslavna, Alexei Steblianko is Vladimir, Paata Burchuladze is Khan Konchak, Nicola Ghiuselev is Galitsky, Elena Zaremba is Konchakovna, Francis Egerton is Eroshka, Eric Garrett is Skula and Robin Leggate is Ovlur. Liviu Ciulei designed the sets and Bernard Haitink conducted the Royal Opera Orchestra and Chorus. Humphrey Burton directed the video. Color. In Russian with English subtitles. 194 minutes. London video and laser.

Related film

1955 Fire Maidens from Outer Space

The Polovtsian Dances from *Prince Igor* provide seductive music for the lightly clad Fire Maidens of this cheap British science fiction movie. The Maidens' exotic dance to Borodin's music has helped make this really bad space opera into a cult classic. Cy Roth directed. Black and white. 80 minutes.

PRINCESS IDA
1884 comic opera by Gilbert and Sullivan

Princess Ida or Castle Adamant is a satire on the women's movement. Princess Ida, the daughter of King Gama, is head of a women's university at Castle Adamant to which men are denied access. As a child she was betrothed to Hilarion, son of King Hildebrand. He and his friends disguise themselves as women and become students. After some tomfoolery and war, Ida and Hilarion finally get together. The opera is written in blank verse and has never been among the most popular G & S operettas though it is quite entertaining. Film director Ken Russell staged a bizarre version of it at the English National Opera in 1994. See also GILBERT AND SULLIVAN.

1982 George Walker film

Frank Gorshin stars as King Gama with Neil Howlett as King Hildebrand in this enjoyable film produced by Judith De Paul for George Walker. Nan Christie portrays Princess Ida, Laurence Dale is Hilarion, Anne Collins is Lady Blanche, Bernard Dickerson is Cyril and Richard Jackson is Florian. Alexander Faris conducted the London Symphony Orchestra and the Ambrosian Opera Chorus. Terry Gilbert was the stage director and Dave Heather the film director. Color. In English. 117 minutes. Braveworld (England) video.

PRINTEMPS, YVONNE
French soprano (1894-1977)

Yvonne Printemps, the French soprano best known for her stage operettas and films, seems to be very popular with opera enthusiasts. *Opera* magazine devoted an article to her centennial in 1994 and the *New Grove* laments that she never sang the roles of Manon and Louise. Her wonderful voice and charm can be experienced on both record and video, most notably in the 1937 film of the Oscar Straus operetta *Les Trois Valses*. Yvonne (née Wigniole) was given the nickname "Printemps" (Springtime) as an ingenue. She rose to fame with Sacha Guitry (whom she married) and many composers wrote operettas especially for her. Her most famous stage appearances were in Reynaldo Hahn's *Mozart*, Noel Coward's *Conversation Piece* and Straus's *Mariette* and *Les Trois Valses*. Her second husband was Pierre Fresnay who usually appeared on stage and in films with her. Printemps can be seen as Offenbach's favorite singer Hortense Schneider in the 1949 film *La Valse de Paris*. See also ADRIANA LECOUVREUR (1938 film), JACQUES OFFENBACH (1949), LES TROIS VALSES (1938).

1934 La Dame aux Camélias

Yvonne Printemps' first film. She portrays the Parisian courtesan Marguerite Gautier whose life as described by Dumas provides the basis for Verdi's opera *La Traviata*. Printemps does not sing Verdi but music written for her by Reynaldo Hahn. Pierre Fresnay plays her lover Armand. Fernand Rivers directed under the supervision of Abel Gance. Black and white. In French. 118 minutes.

1939 Le Duel

Printemps was directed by husband Pierre Fresnay in this film about a widow wrongly persuaded to enter a convent rather than marry. Black and white. In French. 84 minutes.

1943 Je Suis avec Toi

Printemps portrays a wife who has doubts about the fidelity of her husband Pierre Fresnay. She pretends to be another woman and then seduces him. Henri Decoin directed. Black and white. In French. 95 minutes.

1947 Les Condamnés

Printemps plays a woman married to Pierre Fresnay who dies suspiciously after she falls in love with another man. Georges Lacambe directed. Black and white. In French. 100 minutes.

1951 Le Voyage en Amérique

Yvonne Printemps' last film includes a song written for her by Poulenc. She and Pierre Fresnay are a married couple in a French village who go to visit their daughter in America. Henri Lavorel directed. Black and white. In French. 91 minutes.

PROKOFIEV, SERGEI

Russian composer (1891-1953)

Sergei Prokofiev is as important musically for the cinema as for opera. He wrote some of the most powerful and influential film scores of all time for director Sergei Eisenstein. It has been argued that his music for *Ivan the Terrible* and *Alexander Nevsky* is operatic in effect and style and that these are effectively "opera films." His music for the film *Lieutenant Kije* is well known and he also composed music for the 1936 film *The Queen of Spades*. Prokofiev created a number of important stage operas that have been translated to the screen. The extraordinary *The Love of Three Oranges* had its world premiere in Chicago and the epic *War and Peace* had its American premiere on NBC television. His other major operas include *The Gambler* and *The Fiery Angel*. See SERGEI EISENSTEIN, THE FIERY ANGEL, IVAN THE TERRIBLE , THE LOVE OF THREE ORANGES, THE QUEEN OF SPADES (1936 film), WAR AND PEACE.

1961 Portrait of a Soviet Composer

Ken Russell's first television biography was a biography of Prokofiev. Even this early he was experimenting with editing film images to music, mostly newsreel footage in this case. There are stills and stock footage as well as live action footage but the BBC at this time would not allow Russell to use an actor to portray the composer. The film was telecast on June 18, 1961. Black and white. In English. 30 minutes.

PUCCINI, GIACOMO

Italian composer (1858-1924)

Filmmakers love to use Puccini's music and arias in movies, presumably because there are few more evocative and memorable melodies. Songwriters for the first half of the century, including those in Hollywood, made Puccini their role model. His major operas have been filmed and videotaped numerous times right back to the silent era. Puccini was born in Lucca into a musical family, studied under composer Amilcare Ponchielli and was a success with his first opera, *Le Villi*, staged at La Scala in 1884. His second, the 1889 *Edgar*, was a failure but the 1893 *Manon Lescaut* made him famous. *La Bohème* in 1896, *Tosca* in 1900 and *Madama Butterfly* in 1904 won Puccini international acclaim and remain among the most popular operas ever composed. *Butterfly* was badly received when it premiered but became a success after Puccini revised and restructured it. *La Fanciulla del West* premiered at the Met in 1910 but has never had the popularity of the big three. Puccini's 1917 light opera *La Rondine* is rarely staged today but the 1918 trilogy *Il Trittico* remains popular. Puccini's last opera *Turandot* was premiered after he died in 1924 and has now become an audience favorite. See LA BOHÈME, LA FANCIULLA DEL WEST, MADAMA BUTTERFLY, MANON LESCAUT, LA RONDINE, TOSCA, IL TRITTICO, TURANDOT, LE VILLI.

1952 Puccini

Gabriele Ferzetti portrays Puccini in Carmine Gallone's Italian film biography. Marta Toren is his wife Elvira, Carlo Duse is Boito, Oscar Andreani is Giacosa and René Clermont is Illica. The film includes many opera scenes and features opera singers Nelly Corradi in *Madama Butterfly*, Gino Sinimberghi in *La Bohème* and *Manon Lescaut* and the voices of Giulio Neri, Antonietta Stella, Rosanna Carteri, Dino Lo Patto, Dea Koronoff and Gino Penno. The US release title was *Two Hearts Have I*. Color. In Italian. 97 minutes. Bel Canto Society/ Opera Dubs videos.

1986 Puccini

Tony Palmer's British film biography stars Robert Stephens as Puccini and centers around a scandal that affected his career. His wife accused a maid of having an affair with the composer and the girl, though innocent, killed herself. Virginia McKenna is Elvira Puccini, Judith Howarth is the maid and Ronald Pickup is Giulio Ricordi. The film, written by Charles Wood, is intercut with rehearsal scenes of a Scottish Opera stage production of *Turandot* directed by Palmer. Color. In English. 113 minutes. Home Vision video.

1989 Opera Favorites By Puccini

This is a compilation video featuring scenes from five Puccini operas produced at the Royal Opera House in London and at the Verona Arena. The Verona operas are *Tosca* with Eva Marton, *Madama Butterfly* with Raina Kabaivanska and *Turandot* with Ghena Dimitrova. The Covent Garden operas are *La Bohème* with Ileana Cotrubas and *Manon Lescaut* with Kiri Te Kanawa. Also marketed as *Puccini Favorites*. Color. In Italian with English subtitles. 59 minutes. HBO video.

PUNCH AND JUDY
1968 opera by Birtwistle

Harrison Birtwistle's first opera *Punch and Judy* is not a children's opera but a stylized and ritualist drama for adults that uses the famous puppet show as its departure point. Stephen Pruslin's libretto takes Punch in search of Pretty Polly with the gallows and his nemeis choregos as constant companions. The music is said to be modeled on Bach's St. *Matthew Passion*. The opera premiered at the Aldeburgh Festival in 1968 and was revived by the London Sinfonietta in 1979. This concert performance was recorded and is on CD. See also HARRISON BIRTWISTLE.

1980 Keith Griffiths film
Birtwistle's riddles-and-rituals opera provides the basis for this powerful puppet film founded on the traditional Punch and Judy show. It was created for the Arts Council by Keith Griffiths in collaboration with Timothy and Stephen Quaij. Birtwistle's music is played by the London Sinfonietta. Color. 12 minutes.

1984 Opera Factory London
In 1982 the opera was revived and staged by David Freeman for Opera Factory London. This version was a major success and was televised in England in 1984. The telecast helped make the opera much better known. Color. In English. 103 minutes. Video at NFTA in London.

PUPPET OPERAS

There are number of videos which feature puppets and marionettes in operas. They are intended primarily for children but most are also interesting for adults. The best are the *Who's Afraid of Opera?* series with Joan Sutherland singing the principal roles and explaining eight operas. *The Maestro's Company* series features puppets in performance in four operas with the voices of noted opera singers. *Hansel and Gretel* was filmed with electronic puppets in 1954. Keith Griffiths has made a puppet film based on Birtwistle's opera *Punch and Judy*. Shari Lewis presents opera scenes with her hand puppets. See HANSEL AND GRETEL (1954).

1947 Largo al Factotum
Ferdinando Cerchio's Italian puppet film dramatizes Figaro's "Largo al factotum" aria from Rossini's *The Barber of Seville*. Black and white. 7 minutes.

1950 Magie di Figaro
Figaro's Magic is an Italian marionette film by Franco Cagnoli based on Rossini's *The Barber of Seville*. Color. 9 minutes.

1972-73 Who's Afraid of Opera?
Joan Sutherland stars in eight 30-minute highlight versions of operas intended for young audiences. They include operas she did not perform on stage like Offenbach's *La Périchole* and Thomas's *Mignon*. Sutherland tells the story of the opera to three puppets and performs the principal role on a small stage with supporting singers. The dialogue is in English but the arias are sung in their original language. The other operas are The *Barber of Seville, Daughter of the Regiment, Faust, Lucia di Lammermoor, Rigoletto* and *La Traviata*. The music is played by the London Symphony Orchestra conducted by Richard Bonynge with sets designed by George Djurkovic. The puppets were created by Larry Berthelson and the screenplays by Claire Merrill. The series was devised and produced by Nathan Kroll. Color. Each 30 minutes. Kultur Video. Details under each opera.

1984 Maestro's Company Puppets
The Australian Maestro's Company has taped highlights version of four operas with puppets borrowing the singing voices of major opera singers. The story involves two children who discover the puppets rehearsing their operas under an old theater. The dialogue is in English but the arias are sung in Italian. William Fitzwater directed and Jim George produced the videos for the series created by Marcia Hatfield. For details see THE BARBER OF SEVILLE, HANSEL UND GRETEL, RIGOLETTO, LA TRAVIATA.

1984 Kooky Classics: Shari Lewis
Children's TV star Shari Lewis features operas and classical music in this video in which she appears with her hand puppets Lamb Chop, Hush Puppy, Charley!Horse, et al. There is music from *The Marriage of Figaro* and *William Tell* and a *Carmen* with Lewis playing all the roles. Larry Granger conducts the orchestra. Color. In English. 55 minutes. MGM/UA video.

PURCELL, HENRY
English composer (1658-1695)

Henry Purcell wrote the first British opera *Dido and Aeneas* in 1689. Other stage works like *The Fairy Queen* and *King Arthur* are very like operas. Purcell has not been a popular composer with film makers though most of his operas are on record. There is a singular lack of commercial videos of his operas except for *Dido and Aeneas* and an off-air video of a 1989 Aix-en-Provence production of *The Fairy Queen*. See also DIDO AND AENEAS.

1995 England, My England
Michael Ball stars as Purcell in Tony Palmer's post-modern stylefilm about Purcell written by John Osborne and Charles Wood. Simon Callow portrays both King Charles II and an actor who is playing him and wants to find out more. Robert Stephens is Purcell's librettist John Dryden and there are opera scenes with John Eliot Gardiner conducting. Color. In English. 90 minutes. Warner Classics (England) video.

PURGATORY
1966 TV opera by Crosse

English composer Gordon Crosse created the one-act opera *Purgatory* for British television. It uses a libretto based on a poetic play by William Butler Yeats. The opera premiered in Cheltenham on July 7, 1966.

PURITANI, I
1835 opera by Bellini

The Puritans, Vincenzo Bellini's last opera, uses a libretto by Carlo Pepoli and is a tragic love story set in Plymouth during the English Civil War. Elvira is abandoned at the altar by Arturo whose duty forces him to leave her to save the Queen's life. Elvira feels betrayed and goes mad. The opera has one of the most famously difficult mad scenes and was revived in modern times for Maria Callas and Joan Sutherland. There are no commercial videos but there are some non-professional tapes. See also VINCENZO BELLINI.

1985 Australia Opera
Joan Sutherland sings the role of Elvira in an Australian Opera production at the Sydney Opera House with Anson Austin ass Arturo. Richard Bonynge conducts The Elizabethan Sydney Orchestra and Australian Opera Chorus. The video is a non-professional one shot from the audience. Color. In Italian. 155 minutes. Lyric video.

1986 Bari Opera
Katia Ricciarelli sings the role of Elvira and Chris Merritt is Arturo in this production of the Malibran version of the opera staged in Bari in southern Italy. Gabriele Ferro conducts the Bari Opera orchestra. Color. In Italian. 160 minutes. Lyric/ Opera Dubs video.

Related films

1987 The Dead
John Huston's adaptation of James Joyce's 1904 Dublin story features Elvira's aria "Son vergin vezzosa" at a party. It is sung in English as "Arrayed for the Bridal" by Cathleen Delany playing the elderly Aunt Julia. The aria is sung over a montage of mementos of her life. Color. 83 minutes.

1982 Fitzcarraldo
Fitzcarraldo, a film about a man obsessed by opera, ends with a whimsical production of *I Puritani* on a river boat with orchestra and singers. Isabel Jimenz de Cisneros sings Elvira and Liborio Simonella is Arturo with music by the Lima Repertory Symphony Orchestra. Color. 157 minutes. Warner video.

PUTNAM, ASHLEY
American soprano (1952 -)

Ashley Putnam began her career in 1976 singing Lucia in Norfolk and has continued to be a standout in bel canto operas. She is also known for her appearances in modern works including Moore's *The Mother of Us All* and Musgraves's Mary Queen, Queen of Scots. Putnam made her first appearance in Europe in 1978 singing Musetta at Glyndebourne and is featured in two videos there. She made her debut at the Met in 1991 as Marguerite in Faust. Her videos shown only part of her wide repertory. See ARABELLA (1984), LA CLEMENZA DI TITO (1991), DON GIOVANNI (1985 film), MITRIDATE (1983).

Q

QUEEN OF FRUIT

1993 TV opera by Scherrer

This British TV opera was written, composed and directed by Swiss-born Dominik Scherrer. He made it while still a student at the London College of Printing with help from the Channel 4 television company. It stars Lene Lovich as a woman whose fruitier husband Simon Packham is about to be crowned King of Fruit. He engages in a duel with her lover, taxidermist Martin Turner, in which the weapons are pieces of fruit and dead birds. The music is performed by the Béla Bartók Chamber Orchestra of Budapest. The opera was telecast on Channel 4 in June 1993. Color. In English. 20 minutes.

QUEEN OF SPADES, THE

1890 opera by Tchaikovsky

Peter Tchaikovsky's brother Modest wrote most of the libretto for this popular ghost story opera based on Pushkin's novella *The Queen of Spades* (Pikovaya Dama). Herman loves Lisa but he is a soldier without money while she is engaged to a prince. When he tries to force the Old Countess, her grandmother, to tell him her secret for winning at cards, he frightens her to death but she returns as a ghost and gives him the secret. He becomes obsessed with gambling, causes Lisa to drown herself and loses all his money when the Queen of Spades turns up instead of the expected Ace. There are many film and video versions of the original Pushkin story as well as the opera. See also PYOTR TCHAIKOVSKY.

1952 NBC Opera Theatre
David Poleri stars as Herman with Mararatia Zambrana as Lisa in this NBC Opera Theatre television production by Samuel Chotzinoff. The opera is sung in English in a revised format with the story told in flashbacks. Winifred Heidt portrays the Countess, Ralph Herbert is Tomsky and Guy Tano is the doctor-narrator. Charles

Polacheck was the stage director, Carl Kent designed the sets and Peter Herman Adler conducted the orchestra. Jean Karsavina made the English translation and Kirk Browning directed for television. Black and white. In English. 60 minutes. Video at MTR.

1960 Roman Tikhomirov film
Roman Tikhomirov's good but abridged Soviet film adaptation of the opera features singers from the Bolshoi Opera providing the voices for actors. Zurab Andzhaparidze sings the role of Herman acted by Oleg Strizhenov, Tamara Milashkina sings Lisa acted by Olga Krasina, Sofia Preobrazhenskaya sings the Countess acted by Yelena Polevitskaya and Vadim Nechipaylo sings Tomsky acted by Vadim Medvedev. Georgi and Sergei Vasilyev wrote the screenplay with Tikhomirov, Yevgeny Shapiro was cinematographer and Yevgeny Svetlanov conducted the Bolshoi Theater Orchestra and Choir. Color. In Russian with English subtitles. 105 minutes. Corinth video and laser.

1983 Bolshoi Opera
Vladimir Atlantov portrays Herman with Tamara Malashkina as Lisa in this opulent Bolshoi Opera stage production. Elena Obratsova sings the role of the Old Countess, Yuri Mazurok portrays Prince Yeletsky and Ludmilla Semtschkuk is Pauline. Yuri Simonov conducts the Bolshoi Opera Orchestra and Chorus. Color. In Russian with English subtitles. 174 minutes. Kultur video.

1992 Kirov Opera
Geǧam Grigorian stars as Herman with Maria Guleghina as Lisa in this Kirov Opera production by Yuri Temirkanov. Ludmilla Filatova portrays the Countess, Olga Borodina is Pauline, Sergei Leiferkus is Count Tomsky and Alexander Gergalov is Prince Yetetsky. Igor Ivanov designed the sets, Oleg Vinogradov was the choreographer and Valery Gergiev conducted the Kirov Opera, Chorus and Ballet. Brian Large directed the NHK HDTV video telecast in 1993. Color. In Russian. 210 minutes. Phillips Classics video and laser.

1992 Glyndebourne Festival
Russian tenor Yuri Marusin is Herman and Nancy Gustafson is Lisa in this Glyndebourne Festival Opera production by Graham Wick. Felicity Palmer sings the role of the Countess, Sergei Leiferkus is Tomsky, Dimitri Kharitonov is Yeletsky and Marie-Ange Todorovich is Pauline. Richard

Hudson designed the sets and Andrew Davis conducted the London Philharmonic Orchestra and Glyndebourne Chorus. Peter Maniuria directed the video. Color. In Russian. 168 minutes. Home Vision video.

Early/related films

1906 Alice Guy film
This French film by Alice Guy was made to be shown with a synchronized aria from the Tchaikovsky opera. It was made for the Gaumont Phonoscènes series. About 2 minutes.

1910 Petr Cardynin film
This Russian silent film was based on Pushkin and the libretto of the Tchaikovsky opera. It was directed by Petr Cardynin and stars P. Birjukov as Herman and A. Goncharova as Lisa. About 15 minutes.

1910 Deutsche Bioscop film
A German adaptation of the Pushkin story made by Deutsche Bioscop company. About 15 minutes.

1911 Cines film
This Italian silent film adaptation of the Pushkin story was made for the Cines studio and was screened with the opera music. About 12 minutes.

1913 Celio film
Leda Gys and Hesperia star in this Italian silent film adaptation of the Pushkin story made for the Celio studio. It was shown with the opera music. About 15 minutes.

1916 Yakov Protazanov film
Yakov Protazanov's famous Russian film was based on the Pushkin story but was shown in theaters accompanied by the music of the opera. Ivan Mozhukhin stars as Herman, Vera Orlova is Lisa, E. Shebujeva is the Old Countess, Tamara Duvan is the young Countess and P. Pavlov is her husband. The film has recently been restored. Black and white. Russian intertitles. About 63 minutes.

1922 Pal Fejos film
This Hungarian version of the Pushkin story was written and directed by Pal Fejos. Black and white. In Hungarian. About 70 minutes.

1925 Harry Fraser film
This is an American film of the Pushkin story starring Gordon Clifford and Charlotte Pierce. Harry Fraser directed. Black and white. In English. About 70 minutes.

1927 Alexander Rasumny film
A German film of the story starring Rudolf Forster and Jenny Jugo and directed by Alexander Rasumny. It was titled *Pique Dame, Das Geheimnis der Alten Grafin*. Black and white. In German. About 70 minutes.

1936 Mikhail Romm film
This unfinished Soviet film by Mikhail Romm is important musically because Sergei Prokofiev wrote a score for it in twenty-four scenes, twenty of which he orchestrated. When the film had to be abandoned in 1938 for political reasons, Prokofiev saved the lyrical theme he had composed for Lisa and used it as the slow movement of his Fifth Symphony.

1937 Fedor Ozep film
Pierre Blanchar stars as Herman in this noted French film by Fedor Ozep based on the Pushkin novel. Madeleine Ozeray portrays Lisa and Marguerite Moreno is the Old Countess. Black and white. In French. 100 minutes.

1949 Thorold Dickinson film
An outstanding British film version of the Pushkin novel starring Edith Evans as the Old Countess. Anton Walbrook portrays Herman and Yvonne Mitchell is Lisa. Thorold Dickinson directed. Black and white. In English. 95 minutes.

1966 Leonard Keigel film
Dita Parlo stars as the Old Countess in this French film version of the Pushkin novel with Michael Subor as Herman and Simone Bach as Lisa. Leonard Keigel directed. Color. In French. 92 minutes.

1972 Janusz Morgenstern film
Halina Mikolajska and Jan Englert star in this Polish TV film version of the novel directed by Janusz Morgenstern. The Polish title is *Dama Pikowa*. Color. In Polish. 90 minutes.

QUIET PLACE, A
1983 opera by Bernstein

Leonard Bernstein's opera *A Quiet Place*, libretto by Stephen Wadsworth, is a sequel to his 1952 *Trouble in Tahiti* and incorporates the earlier opera. The members of a dysfunctional American family meet for the first time in twenty years at the funeral of wife/mother Dinah who has been killed in a car accident. Her husband Sam, her son Junior, her daughter Dede and her son-in-law François remember events about her and each other. The next morning they meet in her garden, her "quiet place," and effect a reconciliation.

1986 Leonard Bernstein video
Leonard Bernstein conducts the ORF Symphony Orchestra in this Austrian television production of his opera. It was based on his production at the Vienna State Opera. The cast includes Chester Ludgin as old Sam, Edward Crafts as young Sam, Wendy White, Beverly Morgan and Jean Craft. Librettist Stephen Wadsworth directed. Color. In English. 163 minutes. On video.

QUILICO, GINO
Canadian baritone (1955-)

Gino Quilico, the son of baritone Louis Quilico, made his debut in 1978 on Canadian television as Mr. Gobineau in *The Medium*. He made his first appearance in Paris in 1980, sang at Covent Garden in 1983 and appeared at the Metropolitan in 1987. He can be seen on many videos but most notably as Figaro in *The Barber of Seville* opposite Cecilia Bartoli and in *The Ghost of Versailles* opposite Teresa Stratas. See THE BARBER OF SEVILLE (1988), LA BOHÈME (1988/1989), CARMEN (1991), LA CENERENTOLA (1989), DON PASQUALE (1991), THE GHOSTS OF VERSAILLES (1992), ORFEO (1985).

R

RACHEL LA CUBANA
1974 TV opera by Henze

Hans Werner Henze's TV opera is a Brecht/Weill-like twelve-tone memory piece, the reminiscences of a Cuban cabaret singer during the last days of the Battista regime. Lee Verona portrays young Rachel, Lili Darvas is the non-singing older Rachel and Alan Titus plays the three men in her life. Also in the cast are Robert Rounseville, Susanne Marsee, Ronald Young and Olympia Dukakis. The inventive sets and costumes were created by Rouben Ter-Arutunian. The opera was commissioned by Peter Herman Adler for NET Opera and telecast on March 4, 1974. The production costs were $505,000, four times its budget, and its huge overrun actually caused the demise of the whole opera series. Veteran director Kirk Browning quit because of problems on the production. Henze himself conducted the NET orchestra. The German title of the work is *La Cubana, oder Ein Leben für die Kunst.* Color. In English. 90 minutes. Video at MTR. See also HANS WERNER HENZE.

RACHMANINOFF, SERGEI
Russian composer (1873-1943)

Sergei Rachmaninoff (or Rakhmaninov) died in Beverly Hills; which seems appropriate; his music had a great influence on Hollywood film scores. His very first opera, *Aleko*, written when he was only nineteen, was produced at the Bolshoi. It became a popular success soon after when Chaliapin sang the title role in St. Petersburg. It is still in the Russian repertory and is his only opera on video. Rachmaninoff was also a noted conductor and premiered many Russian operas at the Bolshoi. See ALEKO.

RAIMONDI, RUGGERO
Italian bass-baritone (1941-)

Ruggero Raimondi is known to movie-goers as the star of two of the finest opera films. He is the irresistible Don in Joseph Losey's *Don Giovanni* and the full-of-himself bullfighter Escamillo in Franceso Rosi's *Carmen*. He also won praise for his Scarpia in the Live from Rome TV *Tosca* and his Boris in the Polish film of *Boris Godunov*. He has a strong screen presence as well as a fine resonant voice. Raimondi was born in Bologna and made his debut at Spoleto in 1964 as Colline in *La Bohème*. He began to sing soon after at La Scala and became internationally famous in 1969 as Don Giovanni at Glyndebourne. He came to the Metropolitan in 1970 in *Ernani*. Raimondi is also noted for his Don Quixote and Mephistopheles. See also BORIS GODUNOV (1989), CARMEN (1980/1984), CINOPERA, JOSÉ CARRERAS (1991), DON GIOVANNI (1978/1992), ERNANI (1983), GLYNDEBOURNE (1992), THE MARRIAGE OF FIGARO (1985/1992), MOZART REQUIEM (1994), METROPOLITAN OPERA (1983), OPERA STARS IN CONCERT, PARIS (1989), VERDI REQUIEM (1982), VERONA (1990), IL VIAGGIO A REIMS (1988), VIENNA (1993).

1991 Ruggero Raimondi
A French film portrait of the great bass showing him on stage at opera houses, talking about his singing and his career and interacting with directors and conductors. In his native Bologna he is shown in rehearsal for *Don Carlo* with conductor Myung Whun Ching. At the Rome Opera he sings the title role in Rossini's *Moses in Egypt* under the direction of Pier Luigi Pizzi. In Paris he sings Massenet's *Don Quichotte* with Piero Faggioni directing and Georges Prêtre conducting. He goes to Washington to sing the title role in *Boris Godunov* with Mstislav Rostropovitch conducting and is seen as Don Giovanni in Nancy in a production he himself directed. Color. 50 minutes. On video.

RAISA, ROSA
Polish-American soprano (1893-1963)

Rosa Raisa, one of the great dramatic sopranos of the century, created the role of Turandot in Puccini's last opera and was also the first Asteria in Boito's *Nerone*. She was born in Poland but began her career in Italy in 1913. She was a featured singer at La Scala and Covent Garden and a regular on the Chicago opera scene from 1916 to 1936. When she retired from the stage in 1937, she opened a singing school in Chicago with her husband, baritone Giacomo Rimini. Raisa left three short films showing her abilities as an actress and a singer.

1927/1928 Vitaphone opera films

"Mme Rosa Raisa" was featured on three Vitaphone sound films in 1927 and 1928. In the first, filmed in June 1927, she performs excerpts from Act IV of *Il Trovatore* with husband Giacomo Rimini who was also singing at the Chicago Opera. In the second, made in May 1928, she sings art songs by Tosti and Schindler. In the third, filmed in June 1928, she sings "Plaisir d'amour" and "La Paloma." Black and white. In Italian. Each about 8 minutes. Bel Canto Society video.

RAKE'S PROGRESS, THE

1951 opera by Stravinsky

Igor Stravinsky was inspired to write this unusual opera while visiting an exhibition of Hogarth drawings in Chicago that featured the 1735 cycle *A Rake's Progress*. The libretto by W. H. Auden and Chester Kallman keeps the 18th century English setting of the original and the character of the Rake but the story is mostly original. The strange Nick Shadow tells Tom Rakewell he has inherited a fortune and leads him down the road of vice and ruin, even to investing in a machine that makes bread out of stones. Nick turns out to be the Devil and takes Tom's sanity when he can't win his soul. Tom ends up in the Bedlam madhouse. See also IGOR STRAVINSKY.

1977 Glyndebourne Festival

Leo Goeke, Samuel Ramey and Felicity Lott star in this Glyndebourne Festival production famous for its colorful Hogarthian set designs by David Hockney. Goeke is the Rake Tom Rakewell, Ramey portrays Nick Shadow, Lott is Anne Trulove, Richard van Allen is her father and Rosalind Elias is Baba the Turk. Bernard Haitink leads the London Philharmonic Orchestra and the Glyndebourne Festival Chorus. The opera was staged by John Cox and directed for video by Dave Heather. Color. In English. 146 minutes. VAI video.

1982 Maggio Musicale Festival

English filmmaker Ken Russell staged this lively production for the Maggio Musicale Festival at the Teatro della Pergola in Florence with sets and costumes by another noted English filmmaker, Derek Jarman. Gösta Winbergh portrays Tom Rakewell, Cecilia Gasdia is Anne, Istvan Gatti is Nick Shadow, Carlo Del Bosco is Anne's father and Michael Aspinall is Mother Goose. Riccardo Chailly conducted the Maggio Musicale Fiorentino

Orchestra and Russell himself directed the video for Italy's RAI TV. Color. In English. 148 minutes. Opera Dubs video.

1992 Aix-en-Provence Festival

Samuel Ramey is Nick Shadow, Dawn Upshaw is Anne Trulove and Jerry Hadley is Tom Rakewell in this Aix-en-Provence Festival production of the opera by Alfredo Arias. The cast includes Victoria Vargara as Baba the Turk, John Macurdy and Steven Cole. Françoise Tournafond created the costumes and Robert Plate designed the sets. Kent Nagano conducted the Lyons Opera Orchestra and Aix-en-Provence Festival Choir. The opera was taped in High Definition TV. Color. In English. 150 minutes. On video.

1995 Inger Aby film

Swedish director Inger Aby shot this film version of the opera apparently inspired by Ingmar Bergman's 1961 stage production. Greg Fedderly stars as Tom Rakewell, Barbara Hendricks is Anne Trulove, Hakan Hagegard is Nick Shadow, Arild Hellegard is Sellem, Erk Saeden is Mr. Trulove, Gunilla Soderstrom is Mother Goose and countertenor Brian Asawa is Baba, the Turk. Gunnar Kallstrom was the cinematographer and Esa-Pekka Salonen conducted the Swedish Radio Symphony Orchestra. The film has been telecast in the U.S. Color. In English. 150 minutes.

RAMEY, SAMUEL

American bass (1942-)

Samuel Ramey made his debut with the New York City Opera in 1973 and then worked with the company for a number of years. He can be seen on a 1976 video with the NYCO singing Basilio opposite Beverly Sills in *The Barber of Seville*. He also sang Don Giovanni, Don Quichotte, Mephistopheles and *The Tales of Hoffmann* villains with the New York company. Ramey made his debut at Glyndebourne in 1977, at La Scala in 1981, at Covent Garden in 1982 and at the Metropolitan in 1984 in *Rinaldo*. Ramey is known for his performances in Verdi and Rossini operas but his range is quite wide. He is well represented on video including an outstanding performance in Boito's *Mefistofele* in San Francisco and a fine performance as Figaro in the Mozart biopic *Amadeus*. See ATTILA (1991), THE BARBER OF SEVILLE (1976), BLUEBEARD'S CASTLE (1989), CARMEN (1987), DON CARLO (1992), DON GIOVANNI (1987/1990), HERBERT VON KARAJAN (1987), I LOMBARDI ALLA

PRIMA CROCIATA (1993), MACBETH (1987), MANON (1977), THE MARRIAGE OF FIGARO (1984 film), MEFISTOFELE (1989), ON THE TOWN (1992), THE RAKE'S PROGRESS (1977/1992), GIOACHINO ROSSINI (1992), SEMIRAMIDE (1990), VERONA (1988), FREDERICA VON STADE (1990).

RAPSODIA SATANICA
1915 film opera by Mascagni

Italian composer Pietro Mascagni wrote an original score for this avant-garde film which is essentially a "film opera." The "libretto" of the film was even sold as if it were an opera libretto. Mascagni created *Rapsodia Satanica* in collaboration with scriptwriter Maria Martini and director Nino Oxilia and they described it as a "poema cinema-musical." Lyda Borelli, a major Italian cinema diva of the period, was the star appearing opposite André Habay. Giorgio Ricci was the cinematographer. Black and white. In Italian. About 70 minutes.

RATTLE, SIMON
English conductor (1955-)

Simon Rattle, who has worked in Berlin, Salzburg and Vienna as well as London, has become one of the most admired English conductors on the international circuit. He made his debut at Glyndebourne in 1977 and can now be heard leading orchestras around the world from London to Los Angeles. See L'ENFANT ET LES SORTILÈGES (1987), PORGY AND BESS (1989).

RAUTAVAARA, EINOJUHANI
Finnish composer (1938-)

Einojuhani Rautavaara is one of that group of new composers who have vitalized modern opera in Finland. His first opera, *Kaivos*, composed after his studies in America and Italy, is a 12-tone examination of liberty and state control. After an opera about Apollo, he began to create operas with Finnish backgrounds including two with ideas derived from the *Kalevala* and one about the first Bishop of Finland.

1963 Kaivos
Kaivos (The Mine) is a screen opera as it premiered on television although it was created for the stage. It was inspired by the Hungarian uprising against the Soviets in 1956 and tells the story of a miners' strike that is crushed by the Party. Because of its strong political comment in a period when Finland was nervous about its relationship with the USSR, it was rejected by the Finnish National Opera. It was premiered on Finnish Television on April 10, 1963. 120 minutes.

RAVEL, MAURICE
French composer (1875-1937)

Maurice Ravel is mostly known for his non-opera music but he did write two successful one-act operas. *L'Heure Espagnole* (1911) tells the amusing story of a clockmaker's wife who has to cope with three possible lovers when her husband goes away for a day. *L'Enfant et les Sortilèges* (1925) is the tale of an angry child sent to his room for misbehavior. See L'ENFANT ET LES SORTILÈGES, L'HEURE ESPAGNOLE..

1988 Ravel
Larry Weinstein's informative Canadian film about Ravel's life and music includes archival and home movie footage, interviews, photographs and letters as well as performances of his works. Among those performing are Victoria de los Angeles, Jean-Phillipe Collard, Augustin Dumay, Alicia de Larrocha, Charles Dutoit, the Montreal Symphony Orchestra and the Orford String Quartet. Len Gilday was the cinematographer. Color. In English. 105 minutes. On video.

RAYMOND, FRED
German composer (1900-1954)

Viennese-born Friedrich Vesely changed his name to Fred Raymond and became one of Germany's most popular operetta composers. His biggest success was *Maske in Blau* which premiered in 1937 at the Metropol Theater in Berlin and is still in that theater's repertory. It's a lavish revue-operetta, a love story involving theater people set in Latin American and the Italian Riviera. The libretto is by Heinz Hentschke.

MASKE IN BLAU
Raymond's still popular operetta has been filmed twice. The 1942 film was shot in Budapest and stars Clara Tabody, Wolf Albach-Retty and Hans Moser. Paul Martin directed. The second, made in Germany in 1953, stars Marika Rökk, Paul Hubschmid and Wilfried Seyfert. Georg Jacoby directed.

RED MILL, THE
1906 operetta by Herbert

Victor Herbert's tuneful operetta *The Red Mill,* book by Henry Blossom, was written as a vehicle for the comedians Fred Stone and David Montgomery. It remains one of the most popular Herbert operettas and had a successful Broadway revival in 1945. The plot revolves around two Americans in Holland, Kid Conner and Con Kidder, who work in the Red Mill Inn and help a woman marry the man she loves. Its most famous song is "In Old New York, in Old New York. See also VICTOR HERBERT.

1927 Marion Davies film
William Randolph Hurst bought the rights in *The Red Mill* for his mistress Marion Davies and produced this lavish silent film version for MGM through his Cosmopolitan company. Davies plays the Cinderella-like Tina, Owen Moore is the American Dennis who falls in love with her and Louise Fazenda portrays Gretchen. The film was directed by blacklisted comedian Fatty Arbuckle under the pseudonym William Goodrich from a screenplay by Frances Marion. Neither critics nor audiences were very fond of it. Black and white. About 70 minutes.

1958 Shirley Jones video
Shirley Jones and Donald O'Conner head an all-star cast in this lavish CBS Television color production directed by Delbert Mann as the Dupont Show of the Month. Writer Robert Alan Arthur updated the setting to the Brussels's World Fair. Featured were Mike Nichols, Elaine May, Elaine Stritch, Edward Andrews, Harpo Marx and Evelyn Rudie. Fred Coe was producer and Don Walker was musical director. This was one of the first major TV productions to be recorded on videotape. Color. 90 minutes. Video at MTR.

REGINETTA DELLE ROSE, LA
1912 operetta by Leoncavallo

Ruggero Leoncavallo is best known for his popular opera *Pagliacci* but he also tried his hand at lighter fare. His charming 1912 operetta *La Reginetta delle Rose* (The Little Queen of the Roses) was composed to a libretto by Gioacchino Forzano and was reasonably successful in Italy and France for a time. It was made into a silent film in 1914 but did not attract filmmakers in the sound era. See also RUGGERO LEONCAVALLO.

1992 Sandro Massimini video
Italian operetta master Sandro Massimini featured the Leoncavallo operetta on his TV series *Operette, Che Passione!* He talks about the history of the operetta and presents highlights from it in this video derived from the show. He talks about the history of the operetta and presents the ballet "Gavotta," the aria "Il valzer delle rose" sung by Sara Dilena and the duet "Tutte rose i tuoi capelli d'or" sung by Dilena and Max René Cosotti. Color. In Italian. About 17 minutes. Ricordi (Italy) video.

REICH, STEVE
American composer(1936 -)

Steve Reich, one of the leading composers of the American minimalist movement and a major influence on Philip Glass, has not written any traditional operas but he describes his 1993 *The Cave* as "documentary music video theater." It is, in effect, a complex screen opera, a collaboration with video artist Beryl Korot. It uses five video screens to tell an engrossing story about the underpinnings of the Middle East conflict with the focus on Hebron and the screens providing text as well as images and documentary material. See THE CAVE.

REINIGER, LOTTE
German animator (1899-1981)

Lotte Reiniger, who was born in Berlin but worked in Italy and England as well as Germany, was one of the great animation pioneers. She became famous for her silhouette films and in 1926 made the first animated feature, *The Adventures of Prince Achmed.* Many of her short films were based around music and operas. In 1930 she made *Ten Minutes of Mozart* in Germany. In 1933 she created a highly acclaimed silhouette version of *Carmen* in Italy. In 1935 she designed a *Papageno* that focused on the birdcatcher from *The Magic Flute.* In 1940, back in Italy, she made a version of Donizetti's *L'Elisir d'Amore* but was not able to complete it. Later in England she made films of *Hansel and Gretel* (1954), *La Belle Hélène* (1957) and *The Abduction from the Seraglio* (1958). See THE ABDUCTION FROM THE SERAGLIO (1958), LA BELLE HÉLÈNE (1957), CARMEN (1933), HANSEL AND GRETEL (1954), THE MAGIC FLUTE (1935).

RENOIR, JEAN
French film director (1894-1979)

Jean Renoir, one of the truly great filmmakers, worked on only one opera film but he also created a mini-opera on film and there are opera references in several of his movies. His opera film, *Tosca* (1941), was finished by another director when he had to abandon it because of the war. *La Grand Illusion* (1937) features an aria from *Faust* which is used as a signal by prisoners in a military camp. In *Madame Bovary* (1934) Renoir uses music from *Lucia di Lammermoor* in a key scene. *The Rules of the Game* (1939) contains music from *Die Fledermaus*. Renoir directed most of a Deanna Durbin film, *The Amazing Mrs. Holiday* (1943), in which she sings "Vissi d'arte" from *Tosca*. Kurt Weill wrote the music for Renoir's patriotic short film *Salute to France* (1944). His 1952 *The Golden Coach* is based on the same story as Offenbach's *La Périchole* and his 1955 *French CanCan* uses Offenbach's dance music. His last film, the 1969 *Le Petit Théâtre par Jean Renoir*, features what he called "a little opera." See FAUST, LUCIA DI LAMMERMOOR, LA PÉRICHOLE, TOSCA.

1969 La Cireuse Electrique
The Electric Waxer, described by Renoir as "a little opera," is the second of four episodes in his last film *Le Petit Théâtre par Jean Renoir*. It's the satirical story of a woman (Marguerite Cassan) who has a great love for her electric floor waxing machine and sings about it. Renoir wrote the words, Joseph Kosma wrote the music. Color. In French. Complete film is 100 minutes. On video.

RE PASTORE, IL
1775 opera by Mozart

Mozart composed *The Shepherd King*, a charming chamber opera or "serenata" when he was nineteen to a libretto by Metastasio. It has lovely music though not much plot. Alessandro (Alexander the Great) discovers that Aminta, the shepherd, is really the rightful heir to the throne of Sidon and insists he marry the former tyrant's daughter Tamiri. However, the couple are against this as Aminta loves Elisa and Tamiri loves Agenore. It finally gets sorted out.

1989 Salzburg Landestheater
John Cox staged this intriguing production in Salzburg like a series of concentric boxes. On the stage an 18th century audience in costume in a stately room watches the opera performed on a platform. Jerry Hadley sings the role of Alessandro, Angela Maria Blasi is Aminta, Silvia McNair is Elisa, Iris Vermillion is Tamiri and Claes H. Ahnsjo is Agenore. Elisabeth Dalton designed the sets and costumes and Neville Marriner conducted the Academy of St. Martin in the Fields orchestra. Brian Large directed the video. Color. In Italian with English subtitles. 116 minutes. Philips video.

RESNIK, REGINA
American mezzo-soprano (1922-)

New Yorker Regina Resnik made her debut as a soprano as Lady Macbeth with New York's New Opera Company in 1942 but later switched to mezzo roles. She sang with the Metropolitan Opera from 1944 to 1974 in a wide range of Italian and German operas. One of her most notable achievements was the creation of the role of the Baroness in Samuel Barber's *Vanessa*. She is a fine actress as well as a splendid singer but is not well represented on video. See CARMEN (1983 film), DIVAS (1991), ELEKTRA (1969).

RESPIGHI, OTTORINO
Italian composer (1879-1936)

Ottorino Respighi is not terribly well known as an opera composer for his fame mostly rests on tone poems like *The Fountains of Rome*. However, he wrote a number of operas including the relatively popular *La Bella Dormente nel Bosco* (Sleeping Beauty in the Woods). It has never entered the standard repertory but had considerable success around the world in a rather different way as it was written for Vittorio Podrecca's puppet theatre and is performed by puppets. The libretto by Gian Bistolfi follows the outlines of the Perrault fairy tale though Beauty's sleep lasts into the 20th century. See LA BELLA DORMENTE NEL BOSCO.

RETABLO DE MAESE PEDRO, EL
1923 opera by Falla

Manuel de Falla's one-act chamber opera *Master Peter's Puppet Show* is based on an episode in *Don Quixote* and was created for a princess for performance in her home. In it a puppet show is being performed by Master Peter and his boy assistant in the courtyard of a Spanish inn. They are continually interrupted by Don Quixote who is watching from the audience and seems to believe the story about the conflict between Crusaders and Moors is real. When the Moors chase the Christian lovers, he "rescues" them by wrecking the puppet show with his sword. Afterwards he explains that it was his duty as a knight errant. See also MANUEL DE FALLA.

1990 Opera Atelier

Justino Diaz portrays Don Quixote, Joan Cabero is Master Pedro and Xavier Cabero is the boy who narrates the puppet show in this splendid film of the opera by Larry Weinstein. The puppets really come alive in this production through fine crosscutting with live actors played by members of the Opera Atelier group. Charles Dutoit conducts the Montreal Symphony Orchestra. Color. In Spanish. 30 minutes. London video/ laser.

REVOLTOSA, LA
1897 zarzuela by Chapí

Ruperto Chapí's popular zarzuela *La Revoltosa* (The Mischievous Woman) centers around Mari Pepa, a flirtatious woman in a Madrid apartment block who dazzles the husbands of the other women living there. In revenge the wives send their husbands fake rendezvous notes and trap them in an embarrassing scene. This causes Felipe, the single man Mari Pepa has never been able to snare, to get jealous and allows the story to end in true romance. Carlos Fernández Shaw and J. Lopez Silva wrote the book. *La Revoltosa* has been filmed four times. See also RUPERTO CHAPÍ.

1925 Florián Rey film

Florián Rey directed the first film made of Chapí's popular zarzuela, a silent version that concentrates on the relationship between Mari Pepa and Felipe. Josefina Tapias stars as Mari-Pepa with Juan de Orduña as Felipe supported by José Moncayo and Ceferino Barrajon. Orduña later directed the same zarzuela for Spanish television. Black and white. In Spanish. About 85 minutes.

1949 José Diaz Morales film

Carmen Sevilla stars as Mari Pepa with Tony Leblanc as Felipe in this Spanish film directed by José Diaz Morales. The cast includes Maria Bru, Tomás Blanco and Mario Berriatua. Black and white. In Spanish. 91 minutes.

1963 José Diaz Morales film

Teresa Locke stars as Mari Pepa with German Cobos as Felipe in this Spanish film once again directed by José Diaz Morales. The cast includes Eulalia Soldevilla, Amalia Rodriguez, Matilde Munoz Sampedro and Julia Pachelo. Francisco Marin was cinematographer. Color. In Spanish. 94 minutes.

1968 Juan de Orduña film

Isabel Rivas sings the role of Mari-Pepa which is acted on screen by Elisa Ramirez while Luis Sagi-Vela sings Felipe acted by Jose Moreno in this film directed by Juan De Orduña. It was shot by Spanish Television in 35mm for its *Teatro Lirico Español* series. The other singers include Maria Carmen Ramirez and Luis Frutos. Manuel Tamayo wrote the script and Federico Larraya was the cinematographer. Federico Moreno Torroba conducts the Spanish Lyric Orchestra and Madrid Chorus. The soundtrack is on record. TVE. Color. In Spanish. 95 minutes. On video.

REY QUE RABIÓ, EL
1891 zarzuela by Chapí

Ruperto Chapí's charming zarzuela *El Rey que Rabió* (The King who was Rabid) is a comedy about a young king (a soprano role) who wanders around his country dressed like a shepherd to see what is actually going on. His general (a baritone role) accompanies him, also in disguise. The king falls in love with Rosa, an innkeeper's daughter, and they run off together. Her boyfriend Jeremías, who is somehow mistaken for the king, gets bitten by a rabid dog, hence the title. See also RUPERTO CHAPÍ.

1929 Amelia Munoz film

Amelia Munoz stars as the King in this silent version of the zarzuela written and directed by José Buchs. The cast includes Juan de Ordoña, José Montenegro and Pedro Barreto. Agustin Macasoli was the cinematographer. It was screened with music from the zarzuela. Black and white. In Spanish. About 90 minutes.

1939 Raquel Rodrigo film

Raquel Rodrigo stars as the King in the first sound version of the zarzuela again written and directed by José Buchs. The cast includes Luis Peña, Juan Bonate and Luis Heridia. Agustin Macasoli and Alfonso Nieva were cinematographers. Black and white. In Spanish. 93 minutes.

1968 Juan de Orduña film

Composer Federico Moreno Torroba conducts the Spanish Lyric Orchestra and Madrid Chorus in this 35mm film made for Spanish television. The principal roles are sung by Josefina Cubeiro as the King, Luis Sagi-Vela, Rosa Sarmiento, Manuel Gonzalez, Ramon Alonso and Jesus Aguirre with actors portraying the characters on screen. The film was directed by Juan De Orduña, written by Manuel Tamayo and produced by TVE for its *Teatro Lirico Español* series. The film soundtrack is on disc. Color. In Spanish. 96 minutes.

REY, FLORIÁN

Spanish film director (1894-1962)

Florian Rey began his film career in the early 1920s as an actor in zarzuelas like *La Verbena de la Paloma, Maruxa* and *La Chavala.* He turned director in 1925 with the zarzuela film *La Revoltosa* followed by *Gigantes y Cabezudos* and then won wide acclaim for his realistic *La Aldea Maldita* in 1929. He discovered and married Imperio Argentina, the top Spanish female star of the 1930s, and featured her in fifteen of his films. Their biggest success was *Morena Clara* in 1936. See CARMEN (1938 film), GIGANTES Y CABEZUDOS (1925), MARUXA (1923), LA REVOLTOSA (1925), LA VERBENA DE LA PALOMA (1921).

RHEINGOLD, DAS

1869 opera by Wagner

The Rhinegold is the first opera in Richard Wagner's epic *Der Ring des Nibelungen* tetralogy. Alberich, a member of the dwarf race of Nibelungs, steals the Rhinemaidens' magic gold and creates a Ring which can make its wearer master of the world. Wotan, chief of the gods, tricks it away from Alberich so the dwarf puts a terrible curse on it. Wotan is forced to give the ring to the giants Fafner and Fasolt as part of their payment for building Vahalla and freeing the goddess Freia. Fafner kills Fasolt and keeps the gold for himself. The curse has begun to take effect. See also RICHARD WAGNER.

1978 Herbert von Karajan film

The first film of *Das Rheingold* was made by conductor Herbert von Karajan in a Munich film studio in 1978 with a sound track recorded in 1974 at the Salzburg Festival. Thomas Stewart portrays Wotan, Brigitte Fassbaender is Fricka, Peter Schreier is Loge, Herman Esser is Froh, Zoltan Kelemen is Alberich, Jeannine Altmeyer is Freia, Leif Roar sings the role of Donner acted by Vladimir De Kanel, Louis Hendrikx is Fafner, Karl Ridderbusch sings the role of Fasolt acted by Gerd Nienstedt, Gerhard Stolze is Mime and Birgit Finnila is Erda. The Rhinemaidens are Eva Randova, Edda Moser and Liselotte Rebmann. Georges Wakhevitch designed the sets and costumes and Karajan conducted the Berlin Philharmonic Orchestra. Ernst Wild directed the film. Color. In German. 145 minutes. DG video.

1980 Bayreuth Festival

This is a record of Patrick Chéreau's controversial 1977 Bayreuth Festival Centenary production with Pierre Boulez conducting though it was not taped until three years after its premiere. Chéreau sets the story in the 19th century where the Rhinemaidens are whores cavorting around a hydro-electric dam and the gods wear aristocratic Victorian dress. Donald McIntyre is Wotan, Siegfried Jerusalem is Froh, Martin Egel is Donner, Hanna Schwarz is Fricka, Carmen Reppel is Freia, Hermann Becht is Alberich, Helmut Pampuch is Mime, Matti Salminen is Fasolt, Heinz Zednik is Loge, Fritz Hubner is Fafner and Ortrun Wenke is Erda. The Rhinemaidens are Norma Sharp, Ilse Gramatzki and Marga Schiml. Richard Peduzzi designed the sets and Jacques Schmidt the costumes. Brian Large directed the video. Color. In German with English subtitles. 150 minutes. Philips video and laserdisc.

1989 Bavarian State Opera

Robert Hale stars as Wotan in this modernized Bavarian State Opera production by Nikolas Lehnhoff with Wolfgang Sawallisch conducting. Marjana Lipovsek is Fricka, Nancy Gustafson is Freia, Ekkehard Wlaschiha is Alberich, Floria Cerny is Donner, Robert Tear has the role of Loge, Joseph Hopferweiser is Froh, Jan-Hendrick Rootering is Fasolt and Kurt Moll is Fafner. Erich Wonder designed the symbolic high-tech sets and Shokichi Amano directed the video. Color. In German with English subtitles. 152 minutes. EMI video/ Japanese laser.

1990 Metropolitan Opera

James Morris stars as Wotan in this traditional Metropolitan Opera production by Otto Schenk with James Levine conducting. Christa Ludwig is Fricka, Ekkehard Wlaschiha is Alberich, Siegfried Jerusalem is Fasolt, Matti Salminen is Loge, Alan Held is Donner, Mark Baker is Froh, Mari Anne Haggander is Freia, Heinz Zednik is Mime, Jan-

Hendrik Rootering is Fasolt, Matti Salminen is Fafner and Birgitta Svenden is Erda. The Rhinemaidens are Kaaren Erickson, Diane Kesling and Meredith Parson. Gunther Schneider-Siemssen designed the naturalistic sets and Rolf Langenfass designed the costumes. Brian Large directed the video telecast on PBS. Color. In German with English subtitles. 162 minutes. DG video and laserdisc

1991 Bayreuth Festival
John Tomlinson portrays Wotan in this modernized Bayreuth Festival production by Harry Kupfer with Daniel Barenboim conducting. Linda Finnie is Fricka, Bodo Brinkmann is Donner, Graham Clark is Loge, Kurt Schreibermayer is Froh, Eva Johannson is Freia, Helmut Pampuch is Mime, Günther von Kannen is Alberich, Philip Kang is Fafner, Matthias Hölle is Fasolt and Birgitta Svendén is Erda. The Rhinemaidens are Hilde Leidland, Annette Küttenbaum and Jane Turner. The minimalist sets are by Hans Schavernoch. Horant H. Hohlfeld directed the video. Color. In German with English subtitles. 153 minutes. Teldec video and laser.

Related films

1978 Rheingold
Director Niklaus Schilling sets this metaphorical German film on the Rheingold luxury train traveling along the Rhine River and uses as background Wagner's music and the Rhinegold legends. The symbolic plot is a murder mystery involving a diplomat, his wife and her lover. Color. In German. 91 minutes.

1979 Nosferatu the Vampyre
Director Werner Herzog uses the music of the Rheingold Prelude to emphasize the unworldly character of the story in the vampire film *Nosferatu Phantom der Nacht*. This modern version of the classic Murnau film stars Klaus Kinski as Nosferatu. Color. In German. 107 minutes.

1995 Operavox Animated Opera
The British animation studio Hibert Ralph created this animated version of *Rheingold* for the British Operavox series. The Welsh National Opera Orchestra plays a specially recorded score. David Seaman was music editor, John Cary produced and Graham Ralph directed. Color. 27 minutes.

RICCI, LUIGI and FEDERICO
19th century Italian composers

The Neapolitan brothers Luigi (1805-1859) and Federico (1809-1877) Ricci wrote many operas on their own but they are mostly remembered for their collaboration on the buffo comedy *Crispino e la Comare* (Crispino and the Fairy). After its premiere in Venice in 1850, it became one of the most popular comic operas of the 19th century. Luigi is also remembered for his scandalous *ménage a trois* with Fanny and Lidia Stolz, the twin sisters of the opera singer Teresa Stolz. He fell in love with both, lived with both, wrote an opera for both, had children by both and married one without giving up the other. See CRISPINO E LA COMARE.

RICCIARDO E ZORAIDE
1818 opera by Rossini

This lesser known opera by Gioachino Rossini has a libretto by Francesco Berio de Salsa who also wrote the book for Rossini's *Otello*. It tells a complicated story about the love affair between the Crusader knight Ricciardo and the Asian princess Zoraide. The music is splendid and there is a happy ending. See also GIOACHINO ROSSINI.

1990 Pesaro Festival
This Pesaro Festival production by Luca Ronconi was the first since the 19th century. June Anderson stars as Zoraide with William Matteuzzi as Ricciardo, Gloria Scalchi as Zomira and Bruce Ford as Agorante. Riccardo Chailly conducts the Bologna Teatro Communale Orchestra and Prague Philharmonic Chorus. The video is an off-air taping of an Italian telecast. Color. In Italian. 141 minutes. Lyric video.

RICCIARELLI, KATIA
Italian soprano (1946-)

Katia Ricciarelli was born in Rovigo, made her debut in Mantua in 1969 as Mimi and began to sing at La Scala in 1973. She made her first appearance in America in 1972 singing in Verdi's *I Due Foscari* in Chicago and then came to the Metropolitan in 1975 as Mimi. She has a wide repertory but is best known for her work in the Italian bel canto operas. Ricciarelli has an appealing screen presence that matches her warm voice as is evident in her performance as Desdemona in Franco Zefferelli's film of *Otello*. See UN BALLO IN MASCHERA (1980), I

CAPULETI ED I MONTECCHI (1991), CARMEN (1980), JOSÉ CARRERAS (1991), DIVAS (1991), PLACIDO DOMINGO (1984), FALSTAFF (1982), LUISA MILLER (1980), METROPOLITAN OPERA (1983), WOLFGANG A. MOZART (1991), OPERA STARS IN CONCERT, OTELLO (1986), I PURITANI (1986), TURANDOT (1983).

RIDERS TO THE SEA
1937 opera by Vaughan Williams

Ralph Vaughan Williams' one-act opera uses as libretto the exact text of John Millington's Synge's powerful 1904 Irish play *Riders to the Sea*. The story is set in the Aran Islands off the west coast of Ireland where Maurya has lost her husband and four of her sons to the sea. Her daughters Nora and Cathleen identify clothes taken from a drowned man as belonging to the missing son, their brother Michael. The last son Bartley leaves to take horses to Galway and drowns. Maurya sings mournfully that the sea can hurt her no more. See also RALPH VAUGHAN WILLIAMS.

1990 Louis Lentin video
Sarah Walker stars as Maurya, Yvonne Brennan is Cathleen, Kathleen Tynan is Nora and Hugh Mackey is Bartley in this excellent production for RTE Irish television. Martin Murphey appears in the prologue as J. M. Synge. Jay Clements designed the sets and Bryden Thomson conducted the Radio Telefis Eireann Concert Orchestra and Chamber Choir. Louis Lentin produced and directed both opera and video. Color. In English. 45 minutes. Opera Dubs video.

RIDIN' THE CHEROKEE TRAIL
1941 operatic cowboy film

This cheap Monogram B-western contains what is probably the most bizarre use of opera music in all cinema, transmuting arias from *Rigoletto* and *Carmen* into cowboy songs. Craven, the slick, sophisticated villain of the film, runs an outlaw empire in the Cherokee Strip at the turn of the century and is an opera enthusiast. He plays Caruso's version of "La donna é mobile" on a wind-up cylinder phonograph to demonstrate good music to hero Tex Ritter. Tex, however, claims that the aria is actually a cowboy song about Ol' Pete the Bandit. He strums Verdi's melody on his guitar and sings "Ol' Pete the Bandit-o/Held up the sheriff-o..." etc. He claims the "galoot Rigoletto" stole the tune from the cowboys. The astonished Craven then

plays the Toreador Song from *Carmen* on the piano and asks Tex what he thinks of it. Tex tells him that it actually another song about Pete the Bandit which he himself composed. He then sings an amazing cowboy-style song to the Bizet music beginning "Ol' Pete the Bandit/Robbed the country store/Smashed in the window/Tore down the door." Opera connoisseur Craven breaks out laughing and congratulates Tex on his inventiveness. All this happens in the middle of a perfectly ordinary cheapo cowboy movie about Texas Rangers trying to lure a bad guy over a border. Ritter, who sang on Broadway early in his career, presumably filmed the sequence tongue-in-cheek with the help of writer Edmund Kelso and director Spencer C. Bennett. Critics never took notice of this odd joke and B-western audiences simply laughed at the hokum. It has to be seen to be believed. Black and white. 62 minutes. Hollywood Nostalgia video.

RIGOLETTO
1851 opera by Verdi

This was the first of the major Verdi operas to become internationally popular. The libretto by Francesco Maria Piave is based on Victor Hugo's play *Le Roi s'Amuse* with the setting shifted to Mantua and the king transformed into a duke. Rigoletto, the hunchback jester, is cursed by a father whose daughter has been dishonored by the Duke. The curse is fulfilled when the Duke seduces Rigoletto's daughter Gilda. Rigoletto attempts to have the Duke killed by Sparafucile when he visits Maddalena in an inn. Besides the great Quartet, the opera contains such notable arias as "La donna è mobile" and "Caro nome." The opera and play have been popular with filmmakers since the early days of cinema and there is a wide choice of videos. Arias and music from the opera are often used in narrative films. See also GIUSEPPE VERDI.

1931-1981 Rigoletto Collection
This is a video anthology of excerpts from 50 years of *Rigoletto* on screen. The rarest excerpts are from a 1931 German film featuring four Italian singers: soprano Lina Pagliughi, baritone Carlo Galeffi, tenor Primo Montanari and mezzo Maria Castagna-Fullin. They each sing solo arias and join together for the Quartet accompanied by Arturo Lucon and the Berlin Philharmonic. The other films excerpted on the anthology are the 1947 *Rigoletto* with Tito Gobbi and Mario Filippeschi, the 1953 *Verdi King of Melody* with Tito Gobbi and Mario Del Monaco and

the 1981 Verona Arena *Rigoletto* with Garbis Boyagian, Alida Ferrarini and Vincenzo Bello. Black and white & color. In Italian. Japanese video and laserdisc.

1947 Tito Gobbi film

Tito Gobbi stars as Rigoletto in the first complete screen version of the opera. It was filmed at the Rome Opera House on stage without an audience by Anchise Brizzi. Gobbi is in marvelous form just starting his international career and critic Stephen Stroff considers this video the best recording of the opera in any form. The singers mime to their own voices except Gilda who is sung by the superb Lina Pagliughi and acted by Marcella Gavoni. Mario Filippeschi is the Duke, Giulio Neri is Sparafucile and Anna Maria Canali is Maddalena. Tullio Serafin is seen conducting the Rome Opera House orchestra as the film opens. Carmine Gallone directed for Excelsa Film. Black and white. In Italian. 98 minutes. Lyric video.

1952 Opera Cameo series

This highlights version of the opera stars La Scala's Irene Fratiza as Gilda with Robert Weede as Rigoletto and Salvatore Puma as the Duke. It was produced for the Opera Cameo series by Carlo Vinti and presented on television in New York in December 1952. Black and white. In Italian. 30 minutes. Video at MTR.

1954 Gobbi/Del Monaco film

This second Italian film of the opera is titled *Rigoletto, e la Sua Tragedia* and was made cinematically in contrast to the 1947 stage version. Tito Gobbi again sings the role of Rigoletto but the on-screen actor is Aldo Silvani while Mario Del Monaco sings the Duke with Gerard Landry on screen. Giuseppina Arnaldi sings Gilda acted by Janet Vidor, Cesare Polaco is Sparafucile and Franca Tamatini is Maddalena. Oliviero De Fabritiis conducts the Rome Opera Orchestra. Flavio Calzavara directed the film photographed by Adalberto Albertini. Color. In Italian. 90 minutes. VIEW/Video Yesteryear video.

1958 NBC Opera Theatre

Igor Gorin stars as Rigoletto with Oreste Kirkup as the Duke in this NBC Opera Theater production by Samuel Chotzinoff. Dorothy Coulter sings the role of Gilda, Joshua Hecht is Sparafucile and Gloria Lane is Maddalena. Jean Morel conducts the Symphony of the Air Orchestra and Peter Herman

Adler is music and artistic director. The opera is sung in English in a translation by Joseph Machlis. Kirk Browning directed the telecast on Feb. 16, 1958. Color. In English. 120 minutes. Lyric video.

1963 Voice of Firestone highlights

Richard Tucker is the Duke, Robert Merrill is Rigoletto and Anneliese Rothenberger is Gilda in this highlights version of *Rigoletto* presented on the *Voice of Firestone* television series on March 3, 1963. The scenes are fully staged with sets and extras and the orchestra is conducted by Emerson Buckley. Black and white. In Italian with English introductions. About 15 minutes. On VAI video *A Firestone Verdi Festival*.

1973 Who's Afraid of Opera? series

Joan Sutherland stars in this highlights version of the opera intended for children. She tells the story of the opera to three puppets and performs the role of Gilda with Pieter Van Der Stolk as Rigoletto, André Turp as the Duke, Huguette Turangeau as Maddalena and Nelson Taylor as Sparafucile. The dialogue is in English but the arias are sung in Italian. George Djurkovic designed the sets and Richard Bonynge conducted the London Symphony Orchestra. Herbert Wise directed. Color. In English and Italian. 30 minutes. Kultur video.

1974 Focus on Opera series

Malcolm Rivers stars as Rigoletto, John Brecknock is the Duke and Lillian Watson is Gilda in this abridged film version of the opera sung in English. Thomas Lawlor is Sparafucile and Antonia Butler is Maddalena. Peter Seabourne directed this British film shot at Knebworth House in Hertfordshire. The singers are accompanied by the Classical Orchestra led by John J. Davies. The English translation is by Peter Murray. Color. In English. 54 minutes.

1977 Metropolitan Opera

Placido Domingo is the Duke, Cornell MacNeill is Rigoletto and Ileana Cotrubas is Gilda in this Metropolitan Opera production by John Dexter. Isola Jones is Maddalena and Justino Diaz is Sparafucile. Tanya Moiseiwitsch designed the sets and James Levine conducted the Metropolitan Orchestra. Kirk Browning directed the video telecast on Nov. 7, 1977. Color. In Italian with English subtitles. 120 minutes. Video at MTR.

1981 Verona Arena

Garbis Boyagian portrays Rigoletto in this outsized production by Italian filmmaker Carlo Lizzani at the Arena di Verona. Vincenzo Bello plays the Duke, Alida Ferrarini is Gilda, Antonio Zerbini sings Sparafucile and Franca Mattiuci is Maddalena. Carlo Savi designed the mammoth sets for a fairly traditional production. Donato Renzetti conducts the Verona Arena Orchestra and Chorus and Brian Large directed the video. Color. In Italian. 115 minutes. Mastervision video/ Japanese laser.

1981 Metropolitan Opera

Luciano Pavarotti is the Duke, Louis Quilico is Rigoletto and Christiane Eda-Pierre is Gilda in this Metropolitan Opera production by John Dexter. Isola Jones is Maddalena and Ara Berberian is Sparafucile. Tanya Moiseiwitsch designed the sets, James Levine conducted the Metropolitan Opera Orchestra and Brian Large directed the video telecast on Dec. 15. 1981. Color. In Italian with English subtitles. 120 minutes. Video at MTR.

1982 Jonathan Miller at ENO

This is a famous English-language production by Jonathan Miller in which he moved the setting to New York's Little Italy in the 1950s and turned the Duke into a Mafia boss. John Rawnsley sings the role of Rigoletto, Arthur Davies is the Duke, Marie McLaughlin is Gilda, John Tomlinson is Sparafucile and Jean Rigby is Maddalena. The English translation is by James Fenton. Mark Elder conducts the English National Opera Orchestra and Chorus and John Michael Philips directed the video. Color. In English. 140 minutes. HBO video.

1983 Jean-Pierre Ponnelle Film

Luciano Pavarotti is the Duke, Ingvar Wixell is Rigoletto and Edita Gruberova is Gilda in this film by Jean-Pierre Ponnelle shot on location in the supposed sites of the opera in Mantua. Ferruccio Furlanetto is Sparafucile, Victoria Vergara is Maddalena and Kathleen Kuhlmann is Countess Ceprano. Pasqualino De Santis was the cinematographer and Riccardo Chailly conducts the Vienna Philharmonic Orchestra and Vienna State Opera Chorus. The film won an Emmy in 1985 when it was shown on U.S. television. Color. In Italian with English subtitles. 116 minutes. London video. (Highlights version available in the *Great Moments* video series as Volume 8).

1988 New York City Opera

Faith Esham stars as Gilda with Brent Ellis as Rigoletto and Mark S. Doss as the Duke in this televised New York City Opera production. The cast also includes Richard Leech as Sparafucile and Susanne Marsee as Maddalena. Elio Boncompagni conducts the New York City Opera Orchestra. Beverly Sills was host on the telecast on Sept. 21, 1988. Color. In Italian. 180 minutes.

Early/related films

1908 German sound films

Two German sound films from the Deutsche Bioscop company feature music from *Rigoletto*. The Quartet is presented on one and the aria "Ach wie so trügerisch" sung by Alberti Werner on the other. The films were screened with the music played on a synchronized phonograph. Each about 4 minutes. Prints in German film archive.

1908 Giovanni Vitrotti film

An early Italian film of scenes from the opera made for the Ambrosio studio. It was photographed and directed by the industrious Giovanni Vitrotti. Vitrotti made hundreds of films over a fifty year period from 1905 to 1954. About 10 minutes.

1909 D.W. Griffith film

A Fool's Revenge is a D. W. Griffith film made for the American Biograph company and based on the Verdi opera and the Hugo play. Owen Moore stars as the Duke, Charles Inslee is Rigoletto and Marion Leonard is Gilda. It was screened with Verdi's music. About l4 minutes.

1909 J. Stuart Blackton film

The Duke's Jester or A Fool's Revenge is an American film directed by J. Stuart Blackton for the Vitagraph company based on the Verdi opera and the Hugo play. It stars Maurice Costello and William Humphrey and was screened with Verdi's music. About l4 minutes.

1909 André Calmettes film

This French film by André Calmettes titled *Rigoletto* is based on the Verdi opera. It stars Paul Mounet and Rolla Norman and was made for the Film d'Art company in Paris. About l5 minutes.

1909 Le Roi s'Amuse
Alberto Capellani's Pathé film is based on the Hugo play but was released with the title *Rigoletto* in the U.S. and screened with Verdi's opera music. Paul Capellani stars as the hunchback, Marcelle Geniat is his daughter and Henri Sylvain is the King. In 20 scenes. About 13 minutes.

1910 Film d'Arte Italiana
This Italian film based on the opera was written and directed by Gerolamo Lo Slavio and stars Ferruccio Garavaglia and Vittoria Lepanto. It was made for the Film d'Arte Italiana company in Rome. About 12 minutes.

1917 Webb's Singing Pictures
Enrico Caruso turned up in person at the Cohen & Harris Theater in New York on January 14, 1917, for this attempt at sound cinema by George Webb and his Singing Pictures company. Caruso's voice was heard singing the aria "La donna è mobile" over loudspeakers in the auditorium while a costumed actor on screen mimed the words. A Caruso record provided the soundtrack. About 5 minutes.

1918 Liane Haid film
Hermann Benke portrays Rigoletto and Liane Haid is Gilda in this Austrian film based on the play and opera. Wilhelm Klitsch plays the libertine king. The film was known in Germany as both *Rigoletto* and *Der König amüsiert sich* and was screened with Verdi's music. Luise Kolm and Jacob Fleck directed. About 60 minutes.

1922 Clive Brook film
Clive Brook is the Duke, Gwyn Richmond is Gilda and A.B. Imeson is Rigoletto in this English film of scenes from the opera made for the *Tense Moments from Opera* series. It was directed by George Wynn and produced by H. B. Parkinson. About 12 minutes.

1926 British Phonofilm
The Guinness Book of Records considers this film of Act II of *Rigoletto* to be the first sound-on-film operatic production. It was made in England in 1926 and was produced with the De Forest Phonofilm sound process.

1926 Marion Talley film
Soprano "Marion Talley, Youthful Prima Donna of the New York Metropolitan Opera" sings Gilda's "Caro nome" from *Rigoletto* in this famous Vitaphone sound short. It premiered with the first sound feature *Don Juan* on August 26, 1926, but her performance was not much liked. Black and white. 7 minutes.

1927 Cameo Operas series
Herbert Langley is Rigoletto and Mme. Karina is Gilda in this English film of scenes from the opera directed by H. B. Parkinson for the *Cameo Opera* series. Off stage singers performed the arias when the film was screened. Black and white. 20 minutes.

1927 Beniamino Gigli Quartet
Beniamino Gigli sings the role of the Duke with Marion Talley as Gilda, Jeanne Gordon as Maddalena and Giuseppe De Luca as Rigoletto in this sound film of the *Rigoletto* Quartet made by the Vitaphone Company. It was shot in the Manhattan Opera House with music by the Vitaphone Symphony Orchestra. Black and white. In Italian. About 9 minutes. On video.

1927 Charles Hackett sings Rigoletto
Charles Hackett, the "leading tenor of the Chicago Civic Opera Co," performs "Questa o quella" and "La donna è mobile" in Italian in costume on this Vitaphone sound film. The arias were recorded in the old Manhattan Opera house with the Vitaphone Symphony Orchestra. Black and white. About 9 minutes. On video.

1935 I Dream Too Much
Lily Pons is a young opera singer who sings "Caro nome" during her music lesson with her uncle. Inspired by it she slips off to meet and fall in love with aspiring composer Henry Fonda. John Cromwell directed. Black and white. 95 minutes.

1935 Broadway Gondolier
Taxi driver Dick Powell sings "La donna è mobile" and is discovered by two music critics. When his radio career doesn't work out, he ends up in Venice as a singing gondolier. The film also includes an excerpt from the Quartet. Lloyd Bacon directed. Black and white. 98 minutes.

1941 The King's Jester
Il Re Si Diverte is an Italian narrative film of the story based on the Hugo play but using the Verdi opera music as its score. It stars Michel Simon as Rigoletto, Maria Mercader as Gilda and Rossano

Brazzi as King François I. The arias heard in the film are sung by Ferruccio Tagliavini and Toti dal Monte but only "La donna è mobile" is complete. Mario Bonnard directed. The film was shown in the U.S. as *The King's Jester*. Black and white. In Italian. 92 minutes.

1941 Ridin' the Cherokee Trail
This Tex Ritter B western contains what is surely the most bizarre version of "La Donna é mobile" in the cinema. See RIDIN' THE CHEROKEE TRAIL

1944 Leningrad Opera Company
This Soviet short film of excerpts from *Rigoletto* performed by the "Leningrad Opera Company" was distributed theatrically in the U.S. in 1944. Black and white. In Russian. About 10 minutes.

1952 The Importance of Being Earnest
Michael Redgrave as Ernest Worthing sings the Duke's aria "La donna è mobile" in his Albany bath as servants pour water over him. He sings it again on his way to meet the woman he loves and overhears Michael Denison as Algernon Moncrieff singing the same aria. Denison is told by his valet Walter Hudd that it is better to pretend not to have heard him. Anthony Asquith directed this fine adaptation of Oscar Wilde's play. Color. 95 minutes. On video.

1970 The Spider's Stratagem
Bernardo Bertolucci's superb film revolves around a plot to kill Mussolini during a performance of *Rigoletto* in the opera house in a provincial city. The son of the town's hero returns after many years to find out what really happened. His father, who betrayed the plan, had arranged his own operatic assassination to create a martyr hero and is killed in the opera house during the opera. *La Strategia del Ragno* stars Giulio Brogi and Alida Valli and is based on a Borges story. Color. In Italian. 110 minutes. On video.

1984 Maestro's Company Puppets
The Australian Maestro's Company presents scenes from the opera for children with puppets using the singing voices of opera singers. The story involves two children who discover puppets rehearsing operas under an old theater. The *Rigoletto* voices belong to Joan Sutherland, Cesare Siepi, Renato Cioni, Cornell MacNeil and Stefania Malagu. Nino Sanzogno conducts the Orchestra and Choir of the Santa Cecilia Academy. William Fitzwater directed

the video. Color. Dialogue in English, arias in Italian. 30 minutes. VAI video.

1987 Aria
Julien Temple's episode of the film *Aria* uses several arias from *Rigoletto* as ironic comment. A man and his wife sneak off separately for sexual dalliance at the same place, the Madonna Inn in San Luis Obispo. Buck Henry, Anita Morris, Beverly D'Angelo and Gary Kasper star. The singers are Alfredo Kraus, Robert Merrill and Anna Moffo. Sir Georg Solti conducts the RCA Italiana Orchestra. Color. In Italian. About 10 minutes.

1987 Wall Street
The tenor aria "Questa o quella" is heard on the soundtrack of Oliver Stone's film while ambitious young broker Charlie Sheen is having dinner with Daryl Hannah. Color. 124 minutes.

1992 Honeymoon in Vegas
The highly appropriate aria featured in Andrew Bergman's romantic fairytale is "La donna è mobile." The film features James Caan as a gambler who wins Nicolas Cage's fiancée Sarah Jessica Parker in a rigged poker game. Color. 95 minutes.

1995 Rigoletto
This is a musical fairy tale inspired by the opera though the music is not by Verdi and the story is not the same. The deformed Rigoletto character (Ribaldi) is played by Los Angles Civic Opera veteran Joseph Paur. He befriends singer Bonnie (Ivey Lloyd) in a beauty and the beast type story. Leo Paur directed. Color. 98 minutes.

1995 Operavox animated opera
The British animation studio Bare Boards created this model animation version of *Rigoletto* for the British Operavox series. The Welsh National Opera Orchestra plays a specially recorded score. Wyn Davies was the music editor. Color. 27 minutes.

RIMINI, GIACOMO
Italian baritone (1887-1952)

Giacomo Rimini sang with his wife Rosa Raisa in the world premiere of Puccini's *Turandot* in 1926; she was Turandot and he was Pong. Rimini was born in Italy in 1887, made his debut in 1910 singing Albert in *Werther* and in 1915 sang Falstaff for Arturo Toscanini in Milan. He sang regularly with his wife in Chicago and opened a singing school with her there in 1937. He left one film that shows his vocal and acting ability, in which he sings with his wife.

1927 Vitaphone II Trovatore
"Giacomo Rimini, Baritone, of the Chicago Opera Company" was featured with "Rosa Raisa, Soprano" in this Vitaphone film made in 1927 at the old Manhattan Opera House in New York. The film is devoted to excerpts from Act IV of Verdi's *Il Trovatore*. Black and white. About 8 minutes. Bel Canto Society video.

RIMSKY-KORSAKOV, NIKOLAI
Russian composer (1844-1908)

Nikolai Rimsky-Korsakov was one of the Russian Five who created the Russian nationalist style in the 19th century. He wrote fifteen operas beginning with *The Maid of Pskov (Ivan the Terrible)* in 1873. After concentrating on works for orchestra in the 1880s, seeing Wagner's *Ring* made him want to focus on creating operas. Most of them are based on Russian folklore and legend and contain delightful fantasy elements as well as unforgettable melodies. The popular "Flight of the Bumble Bee," for example, comes from his opera *The Legend of Tsar Saltan* and the famous television theme for *The FBI in Peace and War* series comes from *The Love of Three Oranges*. Rimsky-Korsakov was a superb arranger and was able to complete many of his colleagues' unfinished operas. See THE GOLDEN COCKEREL, IVAN THE TERRIBLE, MAY NIGHT, MLADA, THE LEGEND OF THE INVISIBLE CITY OF KITEZH, MOZART AND SALIERI, SADKO, THE TALE OF TSAR SALTAN, THE TSAR'S BRIDE.

1947 Song of Scheherazade
Jean-Pierre Aumont portrays Rimsky-Korsakov in this kitsch American film which is poor biography but enjoyable for its garish awfulness. It's set in 1865 when naval cadet Rimsky-Korsakov falls in love with dance hall girl Yvonne De Carlo and thus is inspired to write his greatest music. Walter Reisch directed with musical direction from Miklos Rozsa. Universal. Color. 107 minutes.

1952 Rimsky-Korsakov
Grigori Belov portrays the composer in this lavish if somewhat stolid Soviet film biography. Nikolai Cherkasov plays Stassov and basso Alexander Ognivtsev has the singing role of Chaliapin. There are some fascinating selections from the operas

Sadko, The Tale of Tsar Saltan, The Snow Maiden and *The Golden Cockerel*. They were staged for the film by the Kirov Opera with Boris Khaikin conducting the Kirov Opera Orchestra. The performances by Ognitsev and L. Grisasenko as the Snow Maiden are particularly fine. The film was written by Grigory Roshal and A. Abramova and directed by Roshal and Gennadi Kazansky. Color. In Russian. 113 minutes.

RINALDO
1711 opera by Handel

Handel's *Rinaldo* was the first opera he composed for London and the first Italian opera created for the English stage. It was a big success and began the rage for Handel operas in Italian. The story derives from Tasso's epic poem about the First Crusade, *Gerusalemme Liberata*, and revolves around the Crusader hero Rinaldo and his loves and adventures. The famous castrato Nicolini portrayed him at the London premiere. There is no film or video of the complete opera. See also GEORGE F. HANDEL.

1985 Honor, Profit and Pleasure
Anna Ambrose's British film biography of Handel features a performance of *Rinaldo*, beautifully reconstructed with a feeling for period and performance style. About five minutes of the opera are shown at the beginning of the film with authentic sets and special effects. James Bowman impersonates Nicolini singing Rinaldo's aria "Cara sposa" with support from Nicola Jenkin and Liz Anderson. Simon Callow portrays Handel and Alan Devlin plays Handel's friend James Quin, who narrates the film. Nicholas Kraemer was the musical director and Peter Luke was co-scripter. Color. 70 minutes. Films for the Humanities video.

RING DES NIBELUNGEN, DER
1876 opera tetralogy by Wagner

Richard Wagner's *The Nibelung's Ring* is the longest, most complex work in opera, an heroic fantasy of great power. The Nibelungs are mythological German dwarves and the ring is a magic ring of ultimate power. The four operas, *Das Rheingold, Die Walküre, Siegfried* and *Götterdämmerung*, were first staged as a group at Bayreuth in August 1876. Each opera is complete in itself but together they tell a multi-generational saga of greed, curses, love, incest, betrayal and heroism among the ancient

Norse gods and heroes. The story begins when the Nibelung Alberich steals magic gold from the Rhinemaidens and creates the Ring and a magic helmet called the Tarnhelm. It ends with the destruction of Valhalla and the retrieval of the gold by the Rhinemaidens. There are four complete versions of the *Ring* cycle on video and all are worthwhile but none is a clear-cut favorite. See also GÖTTERDÄMMERUNG, DAS RHEINGOLD, SIEGFRIED, RICHARD WAGNER, DIE WALKÜRE,.

1980 Bayreuth Festival
Director Brian Large and conductor Pierre Boulez created the first complete version of the tetralogy to be captured on film or video, a record of Patrick Chéreau's controversial Bayreuth Festival production that was televised worldwide. Chéreau sets the operas in the 19th century with the Rhinemaidens on a hydroelectric dam and the costumes ranging from medieval to Victorian. The casts include Donald McIntyre as Wotan, Peter Hofmann as Siegmund and Gwyneth Jones as Brünnhilde. The box set contains a film about the filming called *The Making of the Ring*. Philips video and laserdisc.

1989 Bavarian State Opera
Wolfgang Sawallisch was the conductor of the second complete tetralogy taped in Munich with the Bavarian State Opera. It is a somewhat science fiction-like production by Nikolas Lehnhoff. The casts include Robert Hale as Wotan, Hildegard Behrens as Brünnhilde and René Kollo as Siegfried. EMI video/ Japanese laser.

1990 Metropolitan Opera
James Levine was the conductor of the third complete tetralogy taped at the Metropolitan Opera. This is a solid, traditional production by Otto Schenk with naturalistic sets and costumes by Gunther Schneider-Siemssen. The casts include James Morris as Wotan, Hildegarde Behrens as Brünnhilde and Siegfried Jerusalem as Siegfried. The series was directed for video by Brian Large and telecast on PBS over four nights in June 1990. At 17 hours it was the longest opera telecast in U. S. television history. DG video and laser.

1991 Bayreuth Festival
Daniel Barenboim conducted the fourth complete tetralogy from the Bayreuth Festival, a modernist technological production by Harry Kupfer. Hans Schavernoch created the austere minimalist sets.

The casts include John Tomlinson as Wotan, Anne Evans as Brünnhilde and Poul Elming as Siegfried. The series was directed for video by Horant H. Hohlfeld. Teldec video and laser.

Early/related films

1910 I Nibelungi
This Italian film by the noted Milan-based Milano Film company was inspired by the Wagner epic and screened with the opera music. About 12 minutes.

1912 L'Epopea dei Nibelunghi
An Italian film of the Nibelungen legend directed by Mario Caserini for the Cines company of Rome. It was written by Arrigo Frusta and Alberto Capozzi and stars Capozzi, Franz Sala and Antonietta Calderari. Also known as *Siegfried*. About 13 minutes.

1924 Die Nibelungen
The most famous non-operatic version of the story was created by German director Fritz Lang and his scriptwriter wife Thea Von Harbou. It is based on a 13th century saga and differs considerably from the Wagner operas but features a truly great dragon. Paul Richter portrays Siegfried, Margarete Schön is Kriemhild, Hanna Ralph is Brünnhilde and Rudolph Klein-Rogge is Attila. The film was made in two parts, titled *Siegfried* and *Kriemhild's Revenge,* and released with music by Gottfried Huppertz. Black and white. In German. 249 minutes.

1927 The Ring
This is the shortest *Ring* on screen and is barely 22 minutes long. It was made for the English *Cameo Opera* series and based on the Wagner operas. H. H. Parkinson directed and John E Blakely produced. The film was silent but was screened with live orchestra and singers. Black and white. In English.

1957 La Leggenda dei Nibelunghi
This Italian film based on the Nibelungen legend, also known as *Sigfrido,* was directed by Giacomo Gentilomo. Sebastian Fischer portrays Sigfrido (i.e., Siegfried), Ilaria Occhini is Crimilde and Katharina Mayberg is Brunilde. The film borrows music from Wagner's *Siegfried* and *Götterdämmerung.* Color. In Italian. 95 minutes.

1957 What's Opera, Doc?

Chuck Jones' animated cartoon for Warner Brothers is a brilliant pastiche of the *Ring*. Elmer Fudd sings the role of Siegfried hunting down Bugs Bunny while singing to the Valkyries' music "Kill da wabbit, kill da wabbit." When Bugs disguises himself as Brünnhilde, they try a love duet together before Bugs loses his disguise and gets a lightning bolt thrown at him. The art is absolutely awe-inspiring. Color. 7 minutes.

1965 The Golden Ring

Humphrey Burton's *The Golden Ring: The Making of Solti's "Ring"* is a BBC film about the creation of the classic Decca recording by Georg Solti with the Vienna Philharmonic. It is mostly concerned with the recording of *Götterdämmerung* in 1964 and Burton brilliantly immerses the viewer in the task with record producer John Culshaw. The singers include Birgit Nilsson as Brünnhilde, Wolfgang Windgassen as Siegfried, Gottlob Frick as Hagen, Claire Watson as Gutrune and Dietrich Fischer-Dieskau as Gunther. The Solti *Ring* is available on CD. Black and white. In English. 87 minutes. London video and laserdisc.

1966 Die Nibelungen

A spectacular modern German narrative version of the story modeled on the 13th century saga and the Fritz Lang film. Uwe Beyer stars as Siegfried, Karin Dor is Brünnhilde, Maria Marlow is Kriemhild and Herbert Lom is Attila. It was released in the U.S. as *Whom The Gods Wish To Destroy*. Harald Reinl directed. Color. In German. 195 minutes.

1980 The Making of the Ring

Peter Wienberg's informative documentary about the filming of the 1980 Bayreuth *Ring* features Friedlind Wagner, Wolfgang Wagner, Patrice Chéreau, Pierre Boulez, Gwyneth Jones, Donald McIntyre and Brian Large. Written by John Ardoin and narrated by George Grizzard, it is included with the video of *Die Walküre*. Color. In English and German with English subtitles. About 59 minutes. Philips video and laserdisc.

1990 Scenes from the Ring at the Met

A compilation of scenes taken from the four videos of the Metropolitan Opera's 1990 Ring cycle. The tetralogy was produced by Otto Schenk and conducted by James Levine. Color. 90 minutes. DG video.

1992 Valhalla

A goofy but affectionate American film comedy built around the *Ring* cycle. The sons of an ailing opera buff stage a bargain basement lip-synched version of the four operas in his house using whomever and whatever they can get to help. The biker chick who plays Brünnhilde thinks of it as a musical version of *Conan the Barbarian* and the muscular surfer who portrays Siegfried really catches the musical waves. Jonathan D. Grift wrote and directed this Wagnerian homage. Color. 87 minutes

RIO RITA
1927 operetta by Tierney

Harry Tierney wrote this traditional-style operetta at the request of Broadway showman Florenz Ziegfeld and it was a spectacular hit on stage and screen. Joseph McCarthy wrote the lyrics and Guy Bolton & Fred Thompson wrote the book for this variation on the who-is-the-bandit? theme. A Texas Ranger, who is chasing a masked outlaw known as Kinkajou, falls in love with Rio Rita, who could be the bandit's sister. It has fairly typical operetta-type music including a stirring "Rangers' Song." See also HARRY TIERNEY.

1929 Bebe Daniels film

The 1929 color film version of *Rio Rita*, advertised as "The Radio Pictures Screen Operetta," was a major hit and helped create the operetta boom at the beginning of the sound era. Bebe Daniel stars as Rio Rita and John Boles portrays the Texas Ranger. Comedians Bert Wheeler and Robert Woolsey came from the stage production for their film debuts. Luther Reed directed for RKO. Black and white & color. 135 minutes.

1941 Kathryn Grayson film

The 1941 version of the operetta was updated as a vehicle for Bud Abbott and Lou Costello with Nazis is disguise on a Western ranch. Kathryn Grayson has the Rio Rita role opposite John Carroll. Black and white. 91 minutes.

RISE AND FALL OF THE CITY OF MAHAGONNY
1930 opera by Weill

Kurt Weill's German opera *Aufstieg und Fall der Stadt Mahagonny*, composed to a libretto by Bertolt

Brecht, is based on an earlier *songspiel* that was enlarged after the success of *The Threepenny Opera*. It is set in Mahagonny, an imaginary city of pleasures and criminals located in Alabama. Jenny Hill and Jim Mahoney have a love affair based on money and affection but in the end he is executed for the affair and for not paying his whiskey bill. The tone is cynical and satirical but more than just anti-capitalistic. The "Alabama Song," sung in English in the opera by Jenny and a group of whores, is one of Weill's best-known songs. See also KURT WEILL.

1965 BBC Television
Anne Pashley stars as Jenny with Emile Belcourt as Jim in this BBC Television production by Sydney Newman. The cast also features Monica Sinclair, Inia Te Waita and Trevor Anthony. Roger Andrew designed the sets and Lawrence Leonard conducted the English Chamber Orchestra. Philip Saville directed the telecast in March 1965. Black and white. In English. 90 minutes.

1976 Julia Migenes video
Julia Migenes stars as Jenny Hill in this fine German television production by Rudolf Küfner. Karl Walter Böhn is Jim Mahoney, Charlotte Berthold is Leokadja Begbick, Kurt Marschner is Fatty, Toni Blankenheim is Trinity Moses, Eberhard Katz is Jack O'Brien, Karl Heinz Lippe is Bill, Norbert Berger is Joe and Peter Schmitz is Toby. Christian Stalling conducts the Hessischer Rundfunk Orchestra and Bert Rhotert directed the video for Hessischer Rundfunk. Color. In German. 102 minutes. Opera Dubs video.

1979 Mahagonny songspiel
Peter Schweiger wrote and directed this fine Swiss Television adaptation of the original *Mahagonny* songspiel that provided the basis for the opera. Clementine Patrick sings Jessie, Brigitte Suschni is Bessie, Arley Reece is Charlie, Paul Späni is Billy, Allen Evans is Bobby and Hans Franzen is Jimmy. The music is played by a ten-piece band led by Armin Brunner. Color. In German. 32 minutes. Opera Dubs video.

1979 Metropolitan Opera
Teresa Stratas stars as Jenny in this Metropolitan Opera production by John Dexter sung in English. Richard Cassilly is Jimmy, Astrid Varnay is Begbick, Cornell MacNeil is Moses, Ragnar Ulfung is Fatty, Arturo Sergi is Jacob, Vern Shinall is Billy, Paul Plishka is Joe and Michael Bet is Toby. Jocelyn

Herbert designed the sets, Gil Wechsler created the lighting and James Levine conducted the Metropolitan Opera Orchestra and Chorus. David Drew and Michael Geliot made the translation and Brian Large directed the telecast on Nov. 27, 1979. Color. In English. 110 minutes. Video at MTR.

RITCHIE, MARGARET
English soprano (1903-1969)

Margaret Richie created roles in three important English operas: Vaughan Williams *The Poisoned Kiss*, Britten's *The Rape of Lucretia* (Lucia) and Britten's *Albert Herring* (Miss Wordsworth). Her most famous recording, however, is a wonderful version of James Hook's song "Hush, every breeze" which is included in the collection *The Record of Singing*. She originally sang it in a film in which she portrayed Adelina Patti.

1945 Pink String and Sealing Wax
Ritchie portrays Italian soprano Adelina Patti in this Ealing film set in Brighton in 1880. As Patti she sings James Hook's song "Hush, every breeze" which was so popular that she recorded it in 1948. The film is the story of a publican's wife who plots to poison her husband. Robert Hamer directed. Black and white. 89 minutes.

RITORNO D'ULISSE IN PATRIA, IL
1640 opera by Monteverdi

Claudio Monteverdi's Venetian opera *The Return of Ulysses to his Homeland* tells of the final adventure of the hero of the *Odyssey*. The weary traveler returns home after twenty years disguised as a beggar to see what has occurred in his absence. Penelope is still faithful but she is under siege from ardent suitors and his son Telemachus is loving but unable to take control. Ulysses eventually destroys the suitors in an extraordinary scene where his mighty bow becomes a test of strength. The libretto by Giacomo Badoara keeps fairly close to Homer. See also CLAUDIO MONTEVERDI.

1973 Glyndebourne Festival
Benjamin Luxon stars as a mighty Ulysses with Janet Baker as his faithful Penelope in this superb production by Peter Hall. Luxon and Baker are in marvelous form ably supported by Anne Howells as Minerva, Robert Lloyd as Neptune, Richard Lewis as the shepherd Emetes and Ian Caley as Telemachus. John Bury designed the sets. Raymond

Leppard conducted the London Philharmonic and Glyndebourne Festival Chorus. Dave Heather directed the video. Color. In Italian with English subtitles. 152 minutes. VAI video.

1980 Jean-Pierre Ponnelle film

Director Jean-Pierre Ponnelle joined with conductor Nikolaus Harnoncourt to produce this outstanding film. Like *Orfeo* and *L'Incoronazione di Poppea,* it grew out of a cycle of the operas they staged at the Zurich Opera House. Werner Hollweg is Ulysses, Trudeliese Schmidt is Penelope, Francisco Araiza is Telemaco, Simon Estes is Antinoo, Paul Esswood is Anfinomo, Philippe Huttenlocher is Eumete and Janet Perry is Melanto. Wolfgang Treu was the cinematographer with costumes by Pet Halmen and sets by Gerd Janka. Harnoncourt leads the Monteverdi Ensemble of the Zurich Opera House. Unitel. Color. In Italian with English subtitles. 154 minutes. On video.

1985 Salzburg Festival

Thomas Allen sings a powerful Ulysses opposite Kathleen Kuhlmann's strong Penelope in this Salzburg Festival production by Michael Hampe of an adaptation by Hans Werner Henze. Delores Ziegler is Minerva, Manfred Schenk is Neptune, James King is Jove, Alejandro Ramirez is Telemachus, Robert Tear is the shepherd Eumete and Curtis Rayam is Iro. Jeffrey Tate conducts the ORF Symphony Orchestra. Claus Viller directed the video. Color. In Italian with English subtitles. 187 minutes. Home Vision video/Pioneer Artists laser.

ROBERTO DEVEREUX

1837 opera by Donizetti

Robert Devereux is the Earl of Essex who was loved by Queen Elizabeth I but sentenced to death by her. Their stormy relationship was also the basis of a famous Hollywood film starring Bette Davis. Gaetano Donizetti's opera, composed to a libretto by Salvadore Cammarano, is based on a French play but like the film is more about the Queen than Essex. Elizabeth loves Devereux but he prefers Sarah, the Duchess of Nottingham, and the Duke is suspicious. When Devereux is accused of treason, Elizabeth sentences him to death out of spite and then cannot reprieve him in time. The opera is known in our time mostly through productions starring Monserrat Caballé and Beverly Sills. See also GAETANO DONIZETTI.

1975 Beverly Sills at Wolf Trap

Beverly Sills had one of her greatest successes in the role of Queen Elizabeth. She had sung the Donizetti opera for five years and perfected her characterization when this Wolf Trap production by Tito Capobianco was telecast in 1975. John Alexander portrays Devereux, Susanne Marsee is his beloved Duchess and Richard Fredricks is the jealous Duke. Julius Rudel conducts the Wolf Trap Orchestra. Kirk Browning directed the video. Color. In Italian with English subtitles. 145 minutes. VAI video.

1977 Monserrat Caballé at Aix

Monserrat Caballé is noted for her great performances as Queen Elizabeth in this opera. Here she sings opposite José Carreras as Devereux at the Aix-en-Provence festival in 1977. The cast includes Janet Coster and Franco Bordoni. Julius Rudel conducts the orchestra. In Italian. 140 minutes. Lyric video.

Related film

1939 The Private Lives of Elizabeth and Essex

This enjoyable and colorful film stars Bette Davis as Elizabeth and Errol Flynn as Devereux/Essex. It is based on the Maxwell Anderson play *Elizabeth the Queen* and makes an interesting comparison to the opera. Michael Curtiz directed. Color. 106 minutes. On video.

ROBIN, MADO

French soprano (1918-1960)

Coloratura Robin Mado is much admired in France but is still relatively little known in the U.S. She was noted for her vocal agility and extremely high range especially singing roles like Lucia, Lakmé and Stravinsky's Nightingale. She made her debut in Paris in 1945, first gained popular fame as Gilda and Rosina and was seen as Lucia and Gilda in San Francisco in 1954. She died tragically young of cancer but left some fil and television records of her performances.

1985 Mado Robin, Highest Voice in World

This is a French television documentary about the singer made by Ariane Adriani for Antennae 2. Robin is shown in performance on the Opéra Comique stage and on television singing a number of coloratura arias including her popular version of the "Bell Song" from *Lakme*. Arias associated with her career are also performed by young guest sopranos Christine Barbaux, Michele Langrande and Ghylaine Raphanel. Color. In French. 60 minutes. Lyric video.

1992 Mado Robin Live!
Robin's position as one of the most extraordinary coloratura sopranos of the century is evident in this fascinating video compilation. She is seen and heard in the *Lucia de Lammermoor* "Mad Scene" with a B-flat above high C, in *Hamlet* with an F-sharp and in *Mereille* with a G. The selections on the video, which also include *Lakmé*, *Rigoletto* and *The Barber of Seville*, come from French kinescopes of television appearances. Black and white. 24 minutes. Bel Canto video.

ROBESON, PAUL
American bass-baritone (1898-1976)

African-American Paul Robeson was not able to become a professional opera singer because of the racial bigotry of his time and it was a sad loss for American opera. Like his gifted female counterpart Marian Anderson, he had to settle for a concert career even though he had been George Gershwin's first choice for Porgy. He once commented that the only place he could sing opera was in the bathroom but he did record a number of opera arias. He was, however, able to forge an impressive concert career and to sing in some notable stage productions and films. He plays Joe in the fine 1936 version of *Show Boat* and his performance of the bass aria *Ol' Man River* is the highlight of the movie. His first film was the 1925 *Body and Soul* followed in 1933 by a version of Eugene O'Neill's *The Emperor Jones* in which he had starred on stage. His other important movies include *Sanders of the River* (1935), *Song of Freedom* (1936), *King Solomon's Mines* (1937) and *Proud Valley* (1940). See SHOW BOAT (1936).

ROBSON, CHRISTOPHER
English countertenor (1953-)

Christopher Robson made his debut in Birmingham in the opera *Sosarme* after studies with Paul Esswood. He sings both modern and baroque opera and has had success in both. He was Arsamene in *Xerxes* at the ENO and was very popular in the title role of Glass's *Akhnaten* in Houston. See AKHNATEN (1985), XERXES (1988).

RODGERS, RICHARD
American composer (1902 - 1979)

Richard Rodgers was for a time somewhat like the American equivalent of Verdi, the composer whose work represented the best of his country's musical theater. Although he did not compose operas or operettas, Rodgers helped forge a new genre of America musical beginning with *Pal Joey* and *Oklahoma*. He was a dominant force in American music for fifty years and his collaborations with Lorenz Hart and Oscar Hammerstein II are unparalleled. Although most of his work is outside the parameters of this book, some of his musicals have been staged with opera singers like Ezio Pinza and Risë Steven and those with opera singers in the screen versions are given entries. The New York Public Library for the Performing Arts at Lincoln Center maintains the Rodgers & Hammerstein Archives of Recorded Sound. See also CAROUSEL, OSCAR HAMMERSTEIN II, LORENZ HART, JEANETTE MACDONALD (1932/1942), SOUTH PACIFIC.

1948 Words and Music
Tom Drake portrays Rodgers with Mickey Rooney playing Hart in this musical biography. The film itself is not much but there are impressive musical numbers by Lena Horne, Judy Garland, Perry Como, Gene Kelly, Cyd Charisse and others. Norman Taurog directed for MGM. Color. 119 minutes.

RODRIGUE ET CHIMÈNE
1892 opera by Debussy

Claude Debussy did not finish this heroic opera so it was not staged in his lifetime but it was finally premiered in extract form at the Bibliothèque Nationale in 1987. It's a version of the story of the Spanish knight El Cid composed to a libretto by Catulle Mendès. Rodrigue, The Cid, is in love with Chimène, the daughter of Don Gomez who has insulted Rodrigue's father. Rodrigue sets out to win her love even though he knows he will have to avenge his father. See also CLAUDE DEBUSSY.

1993 Lyons Opera
This Opéra de Lyon production was the first staged performance of the Debussy opera in complete form and has also been released on CD. It was reassembled by Richard Langham Smith and orchestrated and completed by Edison Denisov. It stars British tenor Leo Dale as El Cid, Donna Brown

as his love Chimène, Jose Van Dam as his father Don Diègue and Jules Bastin as Don Gomez. American Kent Nagano conducts the Opéra de Lyon orchestra. RM Associates. Color. In French. 109 minutes. On video and laser.

ROEG, NICOLAS
English film director (1928-)

Nicolas Roeg began his cinema career as a cinematographer and switched to directing with the controversial 1970 film *Performance*. Even more successful were the films that followed, *Walkabout* and *Don't Look Now*. Roeg directed the excellent *Un Ballo in Maschera* episode of the 1987 English opera film *Aria* featuring his wife Theresa Russell. He also features opera on the soundtracks of other films including the *La Traviata* Brindisi in his 1973 Venice film *Don't Look Now*. See ARIA, UN BALLO IN MASCHERA (1987), LA TRAVIATA (1973).

ROGER, VICTOR
French composer (1853-1904)

Victor Roger created some thirty operettas in the latter part of the 19th century, more or less in the style of Offenbach and Lecocq, and they were staged in Paris with the major stars of the time. Most of them are forgotten today even in France except for *Joséphine Vendue par ses Soeurs* (1886), in which the Biblical Joseph is turned into a woman, and the *Les 28 Jours de Clairette* (1892) which has been filmed.

1933 Les Vingt-huit Jours de Clairette
The 28 days of Clairette are spent by newly-wed Clairette first in a Parisian department story and then with a troupe of soldiers as she tries to prevent her new husband from being won back by his former mistress. It was made into a French film in 1933 with Mireille as Clairette and Janine Guise as the former mistress. André Hugon directed. Black and white. In French. 98 minutes.

ROMBERG, SIGMUND
American composer (1887-1951)

Sigmund Romberg was born in Hungary and began his studies in Vienna with operetta master Richard Heuberger. He moved to New York in 1909 and his composing career was entirely American. Like his colleagues Victor Herbert and Rudolf Friml, he grafted the middle-European tradition of operetta onto the American theater. Romberg wrote over sixty theater shows and his songs are still surprisingly popular. In addition to the stage operettas that were filmed, he also created original film operettas with Oscar Hammerstein II and others. See THE DESERT SONG, DAS DREIMÄDERLHAUS (Blossom Time), LA FANCIULLA DEL WEST (The Girl of the Golden West), MAYTIME, THE NEW MOON, THE STUDENT PRINCE, UP IN CENTRAL PARK.

1930 Viennese Nights
Viennese Nights, with a book by Oscar Hammerstein II, is the best of several operettas that Romberg wrote directly for the screen. It is set in Vienna and New York and tells of a bittersweet romance that finally comes right for Vivienne Segal and Alexander Gray. The best-known song is "You Will Remember Vienna." Alan Crosland shot the film in two-color Technicolor for Warner Bros. 99 minutes.

1954 Deep in My Heart
José Ferrer portrays Romberg in this lively film biography directed by Stanley Donen. It traces Romberg's operetta career from early success to late problems. Metropolitan Opera soprano Helen Traubel plays the jolly woman who runs the restaurant where his career begins and she also sings some of his songs. Merle Oberon portrays Romberg's wife, Walter Pidgeon is J. J. Shubert and Paul Henried is Florenz Ziegfeld. Ferrer is superb, whether previewing a show by singing, dancing and acting all the parts or duetting with Traubel and Rosemary Clooney. The guest stars include Cyd Charisse, Gene and Fred Kelly, Jane Powell, Ann Miller, Howard Keel and Tony Martin. MGM. Color. 132 minutes. MGM-UA video and laser.

ROME

The main opera houses in Rome are the Teatro dell'Opera and the open-air Baths of Caracalla in the summertime. The Rome Opera House was built in 1880 as the Teatro Costanizi and was the Royal Opera House until the country became a republic after World War II. For a period it was a genuine rival of La Scala. Several operas were filmed there in the late 1940s, it has been featured in several films and there is a recent video of *Tosca*. There is no video of an opera at the 6,000-seat Baths of Caracalla but it is the site of the 1990 *Three Tenors* concert and a 1991 soprano concert, both on video. A Caracalla production is affectionately parodied in

Bertolucci's film *La Luna* and part of Ponnelle's film of *La Clemenza di Tito* was shot there. See THE BARBER OF SEVILLE (1946/ 1948), CARMEN (1948), LA CLEMENZA DI TITO (1980), DIVAS (1991), DON PASQUALE (1948), FRA DIAVOLO (1948), MARIO LANZA (1959), LUCIA DI LAMMERMOOR (1948), LA LUNA, THE MARRIAGE OF FIGARO (1948), RIGOLETTO (1947), THE THREE TENORS (1990), TOSCA (1946 film/ 1993), GIUSEPPE VERDI (1938), WILLIAM TELL (1948).

1942 Una Notte dopo l'Opera

One Night after the Opera is an Italian narrative film shot in and around what was then the Teatro Reale dell'Opera. It tells the story of a prima ballerina at the opera house and her love affair with a conductor. Beatrice Mancini and Mino Doro are the stars. Nicola Manzari and Nicola Fausto Neroni directed. Black and white. In Italian. 85 minutes.

ROMÉO ET JULIETTE
1867 opera by Gounod

Romeo and Juliet is Charles Gounod's French version of Shakespeare's tragic romance as adapted by librettists Jules Barbier and Michel Carré. It follows the play fairly closely and has been the most popular of the operatic adaptations of the story; Juliet's first act Waltz Song has been particularly admired. Most of the films of the story are based on the Shakespeare play but as early as 1900 a sound film featured the opera. Despite its early success Gounod's opera has not remained in the Anglo repertory though tenor Roberto Alagna attracted great attention in a recent London revival. See also CHARLES GOUNOD.

1963 Roberta Peters on Firestone

Roberta Peters is Juliet and Nicolai Gedda is Romeo in this highlights version of the opera shown on the *Voice of Firestone* television show on Feb. 10, 1963. The scenes are fully staged with sets and extras. William Walker portrays Mercutio and Wilfred Pelletier conducts the Firestone Orchestra. Black and white. In French with English introductions. 22 minutes. VAI video *Firestone French Opera Gala*.

1982 Paris Opéra

Barbara Hendricks made her Paris Opéra debut in 1982 as Gounod's Juliet singing opposite Neil Shicoff as Romeo. The video is an off-air copy of a telecast of the production. Color. In French. 120 minutes. Lyric video.

1994 Covent Garden

Roberto Alagna was hailed as a major new tenor after his success as Romeo in this outstanding production by Nicolas Joel at the Royal Opera, Covent Garden. Leontina Vaduva is also very impressive as Juliette. François Le Roux sings the role of Mercutio, Robert Lloyd is Friar Lawrence, Paul Charles Clarke is Tybalt, Peter Sidhom is Capulet and Anna Maria Panzarella is Stephano. Carlo Tommasi designed the sets and Charles Mackerras conducted the Royal Opera Orchestra and Chorus. Brian Large directed the video. Color. In French with English subtitles. 171 minutes. Home Vision video/Pioneer laser.

Early/related films

Films of the Shakespeare play

Most of the many films of the story are based on the Shakespeare play and go back to the earliest days of silent cinema. The most famous versions are George Cukor's 1936 MGM film' with Norma Shearer and Leslie Howard as the not-very-young lovers; Renato Castellani's 1954 version, with Laurence Harvey and Susan Shentall; and Franco Zeffirelli's 1968 film, starring the 15-year-old Olivia Hussey and 17-year-old Leonard Whiting.

1900 Emile Cossira sound film

Emile Cossira, a noted Romeo who sang the role at Covent Garden and the Paris Opéra, stars in what is considered the first sound opera film. It was presented on June 8, 1900 at the Phono-Cinéma-Théâtre at the Paris Exhibition with a connected synchronized phonographic cylinder. Cossira is seen and heard singing one air from *Roméo et Juliette*, probably "Ah! Léve-toi soleil." The film was made by Clément Maurice who created other early opera sound films. Also on the program were films of *Falstaff* and *Don Giovanni* with arias sung by Victor Maurel. They share first honors but are not advertised on the poster. Black and white. About 3 minutes.

1909 Luisa Tetrazzini film

Soprano Luisa Tetrazzini starred as Juliet in a sound film made in Germany in 1909 by Deutsche Vitascope. It was probably the first act scene featuring Juliet's Waltz Song. The film's German title is *Romeo und Julia*. Black and white. About 4 minutes.

1915 Francis X. Bushman Film

This famous Metro Studio *Romeo and Juliet* film is Shakespeare and not the opera but Gounod's music was used to accompany it in theaters. A special score for cinema orchestras was compiled based on the opera airs. Heroic Francis X. Bushman stars as Romeo with his wife Beverly Bayne as Juliet. They are not exactly young lovers but they were major stars at the time and the film was a big success. John W. Noble directed. Black and white. About 80 minutes.

1927 Vitaphone Tomb Scene

This Vitaphone sound film of the Tomb Scene in the final act features Charles Hackett and Rosa Low of the Chicago Opera. They sing from "C'est la! Salut! Tombeau" to the end of the opera accompanied by the Vitaphone Symphony Orchestra. Black and white. About 10 minutes.

1927 De Forest Phonofilm

Mary Cavanova and Otakar Mark star as Romeo and Juliet in this early British sound film made with the De Forest system. Black and white. About 7 minutes. Print without sound at NFTA, London.

1931 The Great Lover

Juliette's Waltz Song is sung at an opera dinner by Irene Dunne who portrays a rising young soprano. She is taken up by baritone Adolph Menjou who gives her a chance to sing at the Met. Ironically Dunne really did want to be an opera singer but was rejected by the Met. Harry Beaumont directed. Black and white. 79 minutes.

1936 Rose Marie

Jeanette MacDonald sings arias from *Roméo et Juliette* in this MGM film version of a Rudolph Friml operetta. She portrays an opera star and is on stage at the beginning of the film in the opera singing Juliette's "Waltz Song" and other snippets. W. S. Van Dyke directed. Black and white. 110 minutes. MGM-UA video and laser.

1938 That Certain Age

Deanna Durbin gets a crush on Melvyn Douglas and sings "Daydreams," an English version of "Ah! Je veux vivre" from *Roméo et Juliette*. Edward Ludwig directed. Universal. Black and white. 95 minutes.

1966 Fonteyn/Nureyev ballet film

Margot Fonteyn and Rudolf Nureyev star in Paul Czinner's film of the famous Royal Ballet production of Prokofiev's ballet based on the play. Color. 156 minutes.

RONDINE, LA
1917 opera by Puccini

The Swallow was Puccini's attempt to write an operetta-like light opera for Vienna but because of the war it had to premiere in neutral Monte Carlo. Light opera turned out to be rather more difficult than Puccini first envisioned and he revised the opera considerably for later productions. It has never been popular and has never even been staged at Covent Garden. Giuseppe Adami's libretto tells the story of Magda, the mistress of the banker Rambaldo, who has a bittersweet love affair with young Ruggero. See also GIACOMO PUCCINI.

1970 Teresa Stratas film

Teresa Stratas stars as Magda in this English-language television film of the opera produced by Norman Campbell in Toronto. The cast includes Cornelius Opthof as Rambaldo, Anastasios Vrenios, Barbara Shuttleworth and John Edward Walker with Brian Priestman conducting. The CBC film was telecast in the U.S. in May 1972. Color. In English. 90 minutes. Lyric video.

1985 New York City Opera

Elizabeth Knighton stars as Magda in this New York City Opera production by Lotfi Mansouri. Jon Garrison is Ruggero, Richard McKee is Rambaldo, Claudette Peterson is Lisette and David Eisler is Prunier. Alessandro Siciliani conducts the New York City Opera Orchestra. This is a *Live from Lincoln Center* production telecast on PBS on Oct. 30, 1985 with an introduction by Beverly Sills. Kirk Browning directed the video. Color. In Italian with English subtitles. 165 minutes.

1988 Puccini Festival, Torre del Lago

Elena Mauri-Nunziata stars as Magda in this production of the opera from the Puccini Festival in Torre del Lago. It was in this small village in Tuscany that Puccini composed most of his operas. The supporting cast includes Vincenzo Bello as Ruggero and Lucio Bizzi as Rambaldo. The orchestra is conducted by Pierluigi Urbini. The video is from an off-air telecast. Color. In Italian. 90 minutes. Opera Dubs video.

Related film

1985 A Room with a View

Kiri Te Kanawa sings the aria "Che il bel sogno di Doretta" from *La Rondine* on the soundtrack as confused young Helena Bonham Carter gets kissed by Julian Sands. The aria, not surprisingly, concerns a young girl awakening to love through a kiss. James Ivory directed this adaptation of an E. M. Forster novel set in the Florence of yesteryear. Color. 115 minutes.

ROSE-MARIE

1924 operetta by Friml & Stothart

Rose-Marie was a worldwide success for composers Rudolf Friml and Herbert Stothart. Its greatest attraction was a spectacular "Totem Tom Tom" number with a hundred dancers dressed as totem poles and its most famous tune is the "Indian Love Song." Otto Harbach and Oscar Hammerstein II wrote the libretto. Rose-Marie is the name of the Canadian heroine who is in love with the outlaw trapper Jim Kenyon. He is being pursued on a murder charge by Royal Canadian Mounted Policeman Sergeant Malone. The operetta has been filmed three times. See also RUDOLF FRIML, HERBERT STOTHART.

1928 Joan Crawford film

Joan Crawford stars in the first film adaptation of the operetta portraying Rose-Marie, a Canadian trading post woman who loves outlaw trapper James Murray. He is wanted for murder and is pursued by Mountie House Peters. The film was screened accompanied by the Friml/Stothart musical score but without singing. Lucien Hubbard wrote and directed the film for MGM. Black and white. 90 minutes.

1936 MacDonald/Eddy film

Jeanette MacDonald and Nelson Eddy are the stars of the second film of the operetta titled *Rome Marie* (without the hyphen) and with a much revised libretto by Frances Goodrich, Albert Hackett and Alice Duer Miller. Jeanette portrays an opera singer searching the Pacific northwest for fugitive brother James Stewart who is being sought by Canadian mountie Nelson Eddy. The film retains the stage show "Totem Tom-Tom" number and the "Indian Love Call" but drops the other Friml songs. It also adds scenes from *Tosca* and *Roméo et Juliette* for

MacDonald. William Daniel photographed the story on location at Lake Tahoe under the direction of W. S. Van Dyke. Herbert Stothart was the music director. MGM. Black and white. 110 minutes. MGM-UA video/laser.

1954 Keel/Blythe film

Howard Keel and Ann Blythe star in this third film of the operetta which is more faithful in plot to the original. It was shot in CinemaScope with a new screenplay by Ronald Millar. Keel is the Mountie Malone, Blythe is Rose-Marie and Fernando Lamas is the fugitive on the run. Bert Lahr sings "I'm the Mountie who Never Got his Man." Mervyn LeRoy directed. MGM Color. 115 minutes. MGM-UA video.

1992 Sandro Massimini video

Italian operetta master Sandro Massimini and his associates perform highlights from *Rose-Marie* on the Italian TV program *Operette, Che Passione!* The featured songs are "Oh Rose-Marie," "Indian Love Call" and "Pretty Things" plus an excerpt of the Totem dance from the Howard Keel film. The program with a history of the operetta given by Massimini has been issued on video. Color. In Italian. About 15 minutes. Ricordi (Italy) video.

ROSENKAVALIER, DER

1911 opera by Strauss

The Knight of the Rose, Richard Strauss's most popular opera, has an outstanding libretto by Hugo von Hofmannsthal. It's set in Vienna in the reign of the Empress Maria Thérèsa where the no-longer-young Marschallin has been having an affair with young Octavian (a soprano trouser role). He is sent as Rose Knight, an aristocratic marital emissary, to young Sophie whom the boorish Baron Ochs intends to wed. Octavian and Sophie fall in love at first sight, Ochs is humiliated and the Marschallin accepts the loss of her lover with grace. The Act III soprano trio is particularly famous and there are many fine waltz tunes. The opera has been popular with filmmakers and Strauss himself worked on a silent film version. See also RICHARD STRAUSS.

1949 Metropolitan Opera

Eleanor Steber is the Marschallin, Risë Stevens is Octavian and Erna Berger is Sophie in this pioneer telecast from the Metropolitan Opera on Nov. 21, 1949. It was the opening night of the 1949-1950 season and the television show was seen on ABC in six cities. Emanuel List portrays Baron Ochs and Fritz Reiner conducts the Metropolitan Opera Orchestra and Chorus. Burke Crotty directed for television with a staff of 41. The program includes comments from patrons and backstage interviews. Black and white. In German with English introductions and interviews. 240 minutes.

1953 NBC Opera Theatre
Wilma Spence stars as the Marschallin with Frances Bible as Octavian in this NBC Opera Theatre production by Samuel Chotzinoff. Virginia Haskins sings the role of Sophie, Ralph Herbert is Baron Ochs and Manfred Hecht plays Faninal. Peter Herman Adler conducted the Symphony of the Air Orchestra. The opera was presented in two sections on consecutive Saturdays in an English translation by John Gutman. Kirk Browning directed the live telecasts on April 25 and May 3. Black and white. In English. 150 minutes. Video at MTR.

1960 Salzburg Festival
Elisabeth Schwarzkopf stars as the Marschallin in Paul Czinner's classic film shot live at the Salzburg Festival in 1960 but not premiered in England until July 1962. Most critics feel Schwarzkopf's performance has never been surpassed. The film begins with cards that explain the action while Herbert von Karajan conducts the overture. Sena Jurinac is seen as Octavian with Anneliese Rothenberger as Sophie, Otto Edelmann as Baron Ochs and Erich Kunz as Faninal. Rudolf Hartmann directed the production, Teo Otto designed the sets and Erni Kniepert designed the costumes. Karajan leads the Mozarteum Orchestra, Vienna Philharmonic Orchestra and Vienna State Opera Chorus and C.D. Onions was the cinematographer. Color. In German with English subtitles. 192 minutes. Kultur video/Japanese laser.

1979 Bavarian State Opera
Gwyneth Jones is the Marshallin with Brigitte Fassbaender as Octavian and Lucia Popp as Sophie in this fine Bavarian State Opera production by Otto Schenk. Manfred Jungwirth portrays Baron Ochs, Francisco Araiza is the Italian Singer, David Thaw is Valzacchi and Benno Kusche is Faninal. Jurgen Rose designed the sets and costumes and Carlos Kleiber conducted the Bavarian Opera Orchestra and Chorus. Karlheinz Hundorf directed the video. Color. In German with English subtitles. 186 minutes. DG video and laser.

1982 Metropolitan Opera
Kiri Te Kanawa is the Marschallin, Tatiana Troyanos is Octavian, Judith Blegen is Sophie and Luciano Pavarotti is the Italian Singer in this Metropolitan Opera production by Nathaniel Merrill. Kurt Moll portrays Baron Ochs and Derek Hammond-Stroud is Faninal. Robert O'Herarn designed the sets and costumes and James Levine conducted the Metropolitan Opera Orchestra and Chorus. Kirk Browning directed the video telecast on Oct. 7, 1982. Color. In German with English subtitles. 200 minutes. Video at MTR.

1984 Salzburg Festival
Anna Tomowa-Sintow stars as the Marschallin with Agnes Baltsa as Octavian and Janet Perry as Sophie in this traditional Salzburg Festival production by Herbert von Karajan. Kurt Moll is outstanding as Baron Ochs, Gottfried Hornik is Faninal, Heinz Zednik is Valzacchi and Vinson Cole is the Italian Singer. Teo Otto designed the sets. Karajan conducted the Vienna Philharmonic Orchestra and Vienna State Opera Concert Chorus and directed the video. Color. In German. 196 minutes. Sony Classic video and laser.

1985 Royal Opera
Kiri Te Kanawa portrays the Marschallin in this outstanding Covent Garden stage production by British film director John Schlesinger. Anne Howells is nicely boyish as Octavian and Barbara Bonney is lovely as Sophie. Aage Haugland is Baron Ochs, Robert Tear is Valzacchi and Dennis O'Neill is the Italian Singer. The sets are by William Dudley and the costumes by Maria Bjoernson. Sir Georg Solti conducted the Royal Opera Orchestra and Chorus. Schlesinger uses his cinematic expertise to make the characterization as important as the singing and is ably supported by video director Brian Large who captures the nuances Schlesinger implies. Color. In German with English subtitles. 204 minutes. Home Vision video/Pioneer Artists laser.

1992 Berlin Philharmonic
Kathleen Battle is Sophie, Renee Fleming is the Marschallin and Frederica von Stade is Octavian in this concert performance of an excerpt from the opera. They sing the Trio and Act III finale as the conclusion of a New Year's concert by the Berlin Philharmonic conducted by Claudio Abbado. Andreas Schmidt sings the role of Faninal. The video is called *Richard Strauss Gala*. Color. In German. 77 minutes. Sony Classical video.

1994 Vienna State Opera

Felicity Lott is the Marschallin, Anne Sofie von Otter is Octavian and Barbara Bonney is Sophie in this outstanding Vienna State Opera production by Otto Schenk. Kurt Moll is Baron Ochs, Gottfried Hornik is Faninal, Heinz Zednik is Valzacchi and Keith Ikaia-Purdy is the Italian Singer. Carlos Kleiber conducts the Vienna Stage Opera Orchestra and Chorus. Horant H. Hohlfeld directed the video. Color. In German with English subtitles. 193 minutes. DG video and laser,

Early films

1910 Oskar Messter film

This early German sound film featuring an aria from the opera was made by the pioneering Oskar Messter for his cinema in Berlin. The film was shown with a synchronized phonograph record. Black and white. In German. About 3 minutes. Print survives in German archive.

1926 Richard Strauss film

Richard Strauss himself arranged the music, composed a new march and conducted the orchestra at the Vienna and London premieres of this famous Austrian film of his opera. Librettist Hugo von Hofmannsthal helped with the screenplay by adding a battle scene and a masked ball scene, replacing the inn scene and devising a new ending reconciling the Marshallin and the Field Marshall. The film was designed by Alfred Roller who worked on the original stage production. Huguette Duflos portrays the Marschallin, Jacques Catelain is Octavian, Elly Felisie Bergen is Sophie, Michael Bohnen is Baron Ochs, Paul Hartmann is the Field Marshall and Carl Forest is Faninal. Robert Wiene directed the film. A restored print was presented at Avery Fisher Hall in New York in 1993 with the music played by the American Symphony Orchestra led by Leon Botstein. Pan Film. Black and white. In German. About 110 minutes.

ROSE VON STAMBOUL, DIE

1916 operetta by Fall

Austrian soprano Fritzi Massary starred in the Berlin premiere of Leo Fall's operetta *The Rose of Stamboul* in 1916 and reprised her role as the Pasha's daughter in a film three years later. The daughter has been educated in Europe so she has modern ideas about the role of women in Turkey.

The operetta was written by Julius Brammer and Alfred Grünwald and was a major hit in German-speaking countries where it remains popular. It came to New York in 1922 with some new songs by Sigmund Romberg but did not catch on in the U.S. Tenor arias from the operetta have been recorded by Fritz Wunderlich and Rudolf Schock. See also Leo Fall.

1919 Fritzi Massary film

The first film of the operetta featured its great stage exponent Fritzi Massary reprising her role as Kondja Gül, the beautiful but rebellious daughter of the Pasha. Unfortunately, as the film was made in the silent era, Massary could not be heard singing her hit songs. The film was shown in theaters with the operetta music performed live. Black and white. About 70 minutes.

1953 Inge Egger film

The operetta was filmed for the second time in Germany in 1953 with Inge Egger starring as the rebel Turkish woman. The cast includes Albert Lieven, Paul Hörbiger and Laya Raki. Karl Lob was the cinematographer, Willy Schmidt-Gentner arranged the music and Karl Anton directed. Black and white. In German. 100 minutes

1992 Sandro Massimini video

Italian operetta master Sandro Massimini and his associates perform highlights from *La Rosa di Stambul* on the Italian TV program *Operette, Che Passione!* The featured songs are "Oh Rosa di Stambul," "Chiamami Pussy orsù" and "Lilly del Trianon." The program was released on video. Color. In Italian. About 17 minutes. Ricordi (Italy) video.

ROSHAL, GRIGORY

Russian film director (1899-?)

Director Grigory Roshal, who began working in the cinema in 1926, is best known for his Dostoevsky adaptation *St. Petersburg Nights.* It was made in 1934 in collaboration with his director wife Vera Stroyeva. Like her he turned to opera films in the 1950s and created a fine film version of Rachmaninoff's *Aleko* as well as biographies of Mussorgsky and Rimsky-Korsakov with opera sequences. See ALEKO (1954), MODEST MUSSORGSKY (1950), NIKOLAI RIMSKY-KORSAKOV (1953).

ROSI, FRANCESCO
Italian film director (1922-)

Director Francesco Rosi, who began his cinema career as assistant to opera-oriented Luchino Visconti, created one of the truly great opera films. Unlike other opera films his neo-realistic 1984 *Carmen* breathes the same air as a naturalistic movie. Rosi had a great understanding of the background having already made the superb bullfighting movie *The Moment of Truth*. As he was able to use Bizet's original spoken dialogue, his film of *Carmen* is probably as close as an opera movie can come to being totally cinematic. See CARMEN (1984).

ROSSELLINI, RENZO
Italian composer (1908-1982)

Film composer Renzo Rossellini saw Gian Carlo Menotti's opera *The Saint of Bleeker Street* in Italy in 1955 and because of it became interested in creating traditional romantic operas. Renzo was the brother of filmmaker Roberto Rossellini and wrote the scores for most of his great films. He wrote the screen opera *La Campane*, conducted the orchestra for a famous film of *Aida* with Sophia Loren and was artistic director of the Monte Carlo Opera in the 1970s. See AIDA (1953).

1959 La Campane
Renzo Rossellini wrote the libretto and composed the music for *The Bells*, a romantic opera commissioned by Italian television. It was telecast by the Italian TV network RAI from Milan on May 9, 1959.

ROSSELLINI, ROBERTO
Italian film director (1906-1977)

Roberto Rossellini, one of the most important filmmakers in the history of the cinema, was hugely influential on both Italian neorealism and the French *nouvelle vague*. His 1945 film *Rome Open City* launched neorealism and modern Italian cinema and his 1953 *Viaggio in Italia* became a role model for Jean-Luc Godard and his colleagues. Two of Rossellini's films have an overt operatic connection. He made a film of his stage production of Honneger's *Joan of Arc at the Stake* with Ingrid Bergman and he filmed *La Voix Humaine* with Anna Magnani. See JEANNE D'ARC AU BÛCHER (1954), LA VOIX HUMAINE (1947 film).

ROSS, HERBERT
American film director (1927-)

Herbert Ross began his film career in the opera genre when he was hired by Otto Preminger to choreograph *Carmen Jones*. Some of his most popular films were musicals including *Funny Girl* and *Funny Lady* with Barbra Streisand and *The Turning Point* with Shirley MacLaine but they are not operatic. Ross returned to opera in 1993 when he directed a stage production of *La Bohème* for the Los Angeles Music Center Opera.

ROSSINI, GIOACHINO
Italian composer (1792-1868)

Gioachino (or Gioacchino) Rossini has been a favorite of filmmakers since the earliest days of cinema, primarily because of *The Barber of Seville*. His popularity is reflected as early as 1898 when Italy's first filmmaker Leopoldo Fregoli made a movie impersonating Rossini conducting his music. There are two full film biographies and he often appears as a character in films about composers, e.g. the Bellini biopic *Casta Diva*. The two hundredth anniversary of Rossini's birth in 1992 was the stimulus for many new stage productions and subsequent videos of his rarer operas. He was born in Pesaro (which now has an opera festival held in his honor) and was a success almost at once. He composed all of his operas in an amazing 19-year burst of creativity from 1910 to 1929. He lived another 39 years after finishing *William Tell* but never wrote another opera. See THE BARBER OF SEVILLE, LA CAMBIALE DI MATRIMONIO, LA CENERENTOLA, LA DONNA DEL LAGO, ERMIONE, LA GAZZA LADRA, L'ITALIANA IN ALGERI, L'OCCASIONE FA IL LADRO, OTELLO BY ROSSINI, RICCIARDO E ZORAIDE, LA SCALA DI SETA, IL SIGNOR BRUSCHINO, TANCREDI, IL TURCO IN ITALIA, WILLIAM TELL.

1943 Rossini
Nino Besozzi stars as the composer in this Italian film which covers Rossini's life from 1815 to 1827. It features claques and controversies as well as his marriage to Isabella Colbran as it follows him from Naples to Rome to Paris where it ends as he begins *William Tell*. There is a good deal of opera in the film including excerpts from *The Barber of Seville*, *Otello* and *Moses*. The singers are Enzo De Muro Lomanto as Almaviva, Gianna Pederzina as Rosina, Mariano Stabile as Figaro, Tancredi Pasero as Don Basilio, Vito De Taranto as Don Bartolo, Pietro Pauli

as Otello and Gabriella Gatti as Desdemona. Vittorio Gui conducts the orchestra and Mario Bonnard directed the film. Black and white. In Italian. 112 minutes. Lyric/Bel Canto videos.

1988 Gioacchino Rossini

This is a straightforward but informative Italian documentary about the composer directed by Giuseppe Ferrara. Color. In Italian. 58 minutes. Mastervideo (Italy) video.

1991 Rossini! Rossini!

Mario Monicelli's Italian film biography, featuring Philippe Noiret as Rossini, was shot on location in sites associated with the composer. It begins with him an old man in a villa in Passy reminiscing about his rise to operatic fame. The women in his life are portrayed by Jacqueline Bissett and Sabine Azema. Monicelli wrote the screenplay with Suso Cecci Gori, Bruno Cagli (music consultant on the film) and Nicola Badalucco. Franco Di Giacomo was the cinematographer. Color. In Italian or French. 90 minutes

1992 Rossini Bicentennial Birthday Gala

Rossini's birthday is celebrated by singers who specialize in his operas at a Lincoln Center gala at Avery Fisher Hall. They include Marilyn Horne, Frederica von Stade, Rockwell Blake, Chris Merritt, Thomas Hampson, Samuel Ramey, Kathleen Kuhlmann and Deborah Voigt with Roger Norrington conducting the Orchestra of St. Luke's and Concert Chorale of New York. Aside from the usual *Barber* and *Cinderella*, there are selections from *Zelmira*, *Il Viaggio a Reims*, *Le Siege de Corinthe*, *Bianca e Falliero* and *William Tell*. Color. In English and Italian. 159 minutes. EMI video/laser.

ROTA, NINO
Italian composer (1911-1979)

Nino Rota is better known for his film music than for his operas but there is considerable overlap. His stage opera, *Napoli Milionaria* (1977), is based on a film and features music from such Rota movies as *La Dolce Vita*, *Nights of Cabiria*, *Waterloo* and *Rocco and His Brothers*. He also composed an imaginary opera for the film *The Glass* Mountain. Rota was born in Milan and was considered a child prodigy; he wrote his first opera at the age of fifteen. He began to compose for films in 1933, starting with *Treno Popolare*, and created memorable music for films by Fellini, Visconti, Zeffirelli, Wertmuller,

Bondarchuk and Coppola. His haunting music for *La Strada* has been turned into a La Scala ballet and his 1965 TV musical *Gian Burrasca* was a gigantic hit. His operas have also been produced in the U.S., most notably in Santa Fe. See NAPOLI MILIONARIA.

1950 The Glass Mountain

Nino Rota created an imaginary opera called *The Glass Mountain* (*La Montana di Cristallo*) for baritone Tito Gobbi for the English/Italian film *The Glass Mountain*. Michael Denison portrays an English composer who falls in love with Italian Valentina Cortese after his plane crashes in the Alps during World War II. Gobbi plays an opera singer partisan who joins with Elena Rizzieri to act in scenes from the opera that Denison composes in the film. Rota's music is played by the La Fenice Theater Orchestra of Venice led by Franco Ferrara. Henry Cass directed the film. Black and white. In English or Italian. 91 minutes. Lyric/ Opera Dubs videos.

ROTHENBERGER, ANNALIESE
German soprano (1924-)

Annaliese Rothenberger is probably best known for her performances in operetta but her opera background is formidable. She made her debut in 1943, sang with the Hamburg State Opera from 1946 to 1973 and has performed at Salzburg, Munich, Glyndebourne and the Met. She sings a range of heroines from Gilda, Susanna and Musetta to Sophie, Lulu and Adele and in 1967 created the title role in Sutermeister's *Madame Bovary*. She can been enjoyed on video as Sophie in Paul Czinner's *Der Rosenkavalier* film, as Adele in Michael Powell's version of *Die Fledermaus*, as Konstanze in a film of *Abduction from the Seraglio* and as Gilda in a Firestone *Rigoletto*. See THE ABDUCTION FROM THE SERAGLIO (1967), DIE FLEDERMAUS (1955), RIGOLETTO (1963), DER ROSENKAVALIER (1960).

1960 Marchenland Operette

Fairyland Operetta is a German television potpourri of scenes from operettas starring Rothenberger. They include Strauss's *Wienerblut*, Lehar's *Der Graf von Luxemburg*, Millocker's *Dubarry*, Nico Dostal's *Hungarian Wedding* and Fred Raymond's *Maske in Blau*. The other featured singers are Per Grunden, Rosl Schwaiger, Ferry Gruber and Luise Crame. Serner Schimidt-Boelcke conducts the Bavarian Radio Orchestra. Hermann Lanske directed the video telecast in March 1960. Black and white. In German. 90 minutes.

1970 Anneliese Rothenberger Gibt Sich die Ehre

Anneliese Rothenberg Honors Herself is a German TV program featuring arias associated with the soprano. It includes an excerpt from her ZDF film of *Madama Butterfly* as well as arias from *La Bohème, Gianni Schicchi, Pagliacci, Rusalka, Zigeunerliebe* and *Zwie Herzen im Dreiviertaltakt*. Color. In German. 60 minutes.

ROUNSEVILLE, ROBERT

American tenor (1914-1974)

New York Opera tenor Robert Rounseville is probably best known today for two films. He portrays Hoffmann in the Powell-Pressburger film version of *The Tales of Hoffmann* and he is Mr. Snow in the 1956 movie of *Carousel* opposite Claramae Turner. He also appeared regularly on NBC television opera productions in the 1950s. See CARMEN (1950, 1953), CAROUSEL (1956), LES DIALOGUES DES CARMÉLITES (1957), THE MIKADO (1960), RACHEL LA CUBANA, ELEANOR STEBER (1950-54), THE TALES OF HOFFMANN (1951).

ROYAL OPERA HOUSE

Covent Garden theater (1892-)

Opera has been performed at Covent Garden in London for the past 250 years though the buildings have changed over the years. The present 19th century edifice became the Royal Opera House in 1892 and has been one of the major centers of world opera for the past century. The first live opera telecast from Covent Garden was shown by the BBC in 1988 but union disagreements prevented continuing television presentations for some years. There are now regular telecasts and many videos of Covent Garden operas. See AIDA (1994), ANDREA CHÉNIER (1985), LA BOHÈME (1982), MARIA CALLAS (1962), CAVALLERIA RUSTICANA (1975), DON CARLO (1985), FALSTAFF (1982), LA FANCIULLA DEL WEST (1983), DIE FLEDERMAUS (1983), KIROV OPERA HOUSE (1992), LUISA MILLER (1980), MANON LESCAUT (1983), NELLIE MELBA (1953), ORFEO ED EURIDICE (1991), OTELLO (1993), PAGLIACCI (1975), ADELINA PATTI (1993), PETER GRIMES (1981), ROMÉO ET JULIETTE (1994), DER ROSENKAVALIER (1985), SALOME (1991), SAMSON ET DALILA (1981), SIMON BOCCANEGRA (1991), STIFFELIO (1993), THE TALES OF HOFFMANN (1981), KIRI TE KANAWA (1978), TOSCA (1964), LA TRAVIATA (1994).

1986 Fanfare for Elizabeth

The Royal Opera House organized an all-star gala concert in honor of Queen Elizabeth on April 21, 1986, The evening, which was televised, features fully-staged scenes from the following operas: *La Traviata* with Lucia Popp and Placido Domingo in the "Libiamo" scene; *Der Rosenkavalier* with Yvonne Kenny and Ann Murray in the Rose presentation scene; *The Bohemian Girl* with Jessye Norman singing "I dreamt I dwelt in marble halls;" *Tosca* with Domingo singing "E lucevan le stelle;" *Don Giovanni* with Popp and Thomas Allen singing "La ci darem la mano;" *Turandot* with Gwyneth Jones singing a duet with Giuseppe Giacomini; amd *Treemonisha* with Jessye Norman, Lisa Casteen and chorus singing "Marching onward." Edward Downes conducts the Royal Opera House Orchestra. Color. 90 minutes. Lyric video and at MPRC in London.

1995 The House

This is the ultimate opera house documentary, a six-part BBC Television film showing the inner workings of the Royal Opera House in all its glories, complications and problems. Director Michael Waldman's cameras filmed the meetings and work of the staff of "The House" from October 1993 to June 1994 and the edited six hours are considered the most candid film portrait ever of a major opera institution. When the series was first telecast in England it aroused mixed interpretations of what it reveals. There are a good few heroes and villains shown. Among the insiders seen at their best or worst in the film are general director Jeremy Isaacs, director Trevor Nunn and a marketing director with a mission. The series begins with American soprano Deynce Graves having problems with *Carmen*. Color. 360 minutes.

RUDDIGORE

1887 comic opera by Gilbert & Sullivan

Ruddigore or The Witch's Curse was not a success when it premiered but over the years has become one of the more popular Gilbert and Sullivan operettas. It's a burlesque Gothic melodrama with a witch's curse forcing the baronets of the Murgatroyd family to commit a crime every day. Ruthven flees the curse and lives as the simple farmer Robin while his brother Despard succeeds to the title and curse. Robin loves the maid Rose and asks his foster brother Richard to help in wooing her but Richard also falls in love. After many fine songs the curse is foiled and all is sorted out.

1967 Joy Batchelor animated film

Joy Batchelor produced and directed this British animated feature of the operetta for the Halas and Batchelor studio with designs by John Cooper. The plot follows the operetta closely even though it is abridged. The singers, all members of the D'Oyly Carte Opera Company, include John Reed, Ann Hood, David Palmer, Peggy Ann Jones, Donald Adams and Kenneth Sandford. James Walker conducts the Royal Philharmonic Orchestra. Color. In English. 55 minutes.

1974 World of Gilbert & Sullivan film

John Cartier stars as Ruthven in this highlights film produced by John Seabourne for the *World of Gilbert and Sullivan* series. Gillian Humphreys is Rose, Thomas Round is Richard, Helen Landis is Hannah, Lawrence Richard is Despard, Ann Hood is Margaret and Donald Adams is Roderick. The music is played by the Gilbert and Sullivan Festival Orchestra and Chorus and the film was directed by Trevor Evans. Color. In English. 50 minutes.

1982 Vincent Price film

Vincent Price is a delight as Sir Despard in this entertaining film produced by Judith De Paul for the George Walker Gilbert & Sullivan series. Keith Michell is Robin, Sandra Dugdale is Rose, Donald Adams is Roderick, Ann Howard is Margaret, John Treleaven is Richard, Paul Hudson is Adam and Johanna Peters is Hannah. Alexander Faris conducts the London Symphony Orchestra and the Ambrosian Opera Chorus. Christopher Renshaw was the stage director and Barrie Gavin the film director. Color. In English. 112 minutes. CBS Fox/Braveworld (England) video.

RUFFO, TITA
Italian baritone (1877- 1953)

Tita Ruffo was once hailed by conductor Tullio Serafin as one of the three singing miracles of the century (the others being Enrico Caruso and Rosa Ponselle). Ruffo made his debut in Rome in 1898 and sang at Covent Garden in 1903 where he had a famous dispute with Melba that made him world famous. He began to sing in Philadelphia in 1912 and was a regular there and in Chicago until 1926. He made his Metropolitan Opera debut in 1922 and then sang with the Met for eight seasons as Figaro, Don Carlo, Amonasro and Tonio. Ruffo is credited with changing the way baritones sang 19th century

opera. He can be seen in performance in three short films.

1929/1930 Metro Movietone Acts

Ruffo made three opera films for MGM in 1929 and 1930 singing in costume. On the first he performs Nelusko's invocation "Adamastor, re dell'onde profonde" from Meyerbeer's *L'Africaine*. On the second he presents Figaro's "Largo al Factotum" from *The Barber of Seville*. On the third he is featured singing Iago's "Credo" from *Otello*. The soundtracks of the Rossini and the Verdi films have also been issued on record. Black and white. Each about 8 minutes.

RUSALKA
1901 opera by Dvořák

Rusalka is Antonín Dvořák's best-known opera and has eclipsed Dargomizhsky's Russian opera about the same story. It is a retelling of the legend about a water spirit who falls in love with a prince and becomes human for his sake through the help of a witch. As she has to become mute to do this, she cannot explain her love and origin. Their relationship ends tragically with his death through a fatal kiss. The libretto by Jaroslav Kvapii is based on Friedrich Fouqué's play *Udine*. The opera's most famous aria is the soprano favorite "Song to the Moon." See also Antonín Dvořák.

1962 Václav Kaslík film

Czech director/conductor/composer Václav Kaslík created a film version of the Dvořák opera for Czechoslovakian television in 1962. It stars Jana Andrsova as Rusalka and Vladimir Raz as the Prince. Jan Stallich was the cinematographer. Color. In Czech. 120 minutes.

1978 Petr Weigl film

Czech filmmaker Petr Wiegl, who specializes in beautifully photographed film versions of classic operas, directed this stylish Czech film adaptation of the Dvořák opera. It stars Magda Vasaryova as Rusalka and Milan Knazko as the Prince. Color. In Czech. 100 minutes.

1986 English National Opera

Eilene Hannan stars as Rusalka with John Treleaven as the Prince in this English National Opera production by David Pountney. He turns the story into a fable about a young Victorian woman's journey into adulthood and makes her home into a playroom with dreamlike sets by Stefanos Lazaridis. Rodney Milnes created the updated English translation. Ann Howard portrays the witch Jezibaba, Rodney Macann is the Water Spirit, Fiona Kimm is the Kitchen Boy and Phyllis Cannan is the Foreign Princess. Mark Elder conducts the English National Opera Orchestra and Chorus and Derek Bailey directed the video. Color. In English. 160 minutes. Home Vision video.

Early/related films

1910 Vasilij Goncarov film
Vasilij Goncarov directed this Russian silent film of the Rusalka legend starring Aleksandra Goncarova as Rusalka and V. Stepanov as the Prince. Black and white. In Russian. About 12 minutes. Print in Russian archive.

1989 Driving Miss Daisy
It is spring in Atlanta in 1949 when Miss Daisy (Jessica Tandy) listens to "Song to the Moon" on the radio as sung by Gabriela Benackova with the Czech Philharmonic Orchestra. The water spirit tells of her need for love and Miss Daisy decides to be nice to her driver Hoke Colburn (Morgan Freeman). Australian director Bruce Beresford's fine film about the relationship between an African-American chauffeur and an elderly white woman won the Academy Award for Best Picture. Color. 99 minutes. Warner Brothers video.

1993 Dvorák in Prague
Mezzo-soprano Frederica von Stade sings the "Song to the Moon" in this tribute to Dvorák held at Smetana Hall in Prague. Seiji Osawa conducts the Boston Symphony Orchestra. Brian Large directed. Color. 90 minutes. Sony video.

RUSLAN AND LYUDMILA
1842 opera by Glinka

Mikhail Glinka's *Ruslan and Lyudmila* is famous historically as the first authentically Russian opera and was considered revolutionary in its time. It's based on a poem by Pushkin and is a magical romantic fairy tale about a princess (Lyudmila) and a warrior (Ruslan) who fall in love. Lyudmila is kidnapped by the dwarf Chernomor on the eve of their marriage. Ruslan sets out to rescue her and succeeds after many adventures including having to

battle sorcerers and witches. The music composed around the character of Chernomor is especially famous although it is a non-singing role.

1996 Kirov Opera
Soprano Anna Netrepko stars as Lyudmila with baritone Vladimir Ognovenko as Ruslan in this superb Kirov Opera production by Lotfi Mansouri. Galina Gorchakova portrays the enchanting Gorislava, Larissa Diadkova is the rival Ratmir, Mikhail Kit is King Svetozar, Yuri Marusin is the minstrel Bayan, Konstantin Plushinikova is the good wizard Finn and Gennady Bezzubenko is the comic villain Farlaf. The scenery and costumes are based on pre-Revolutionary designs by Alexander Golovin. Valery Gergiev conducts the Kirov Opera Orchestra. Hans Hulscher directed the video. Mosfilm. Color. In Russian with English subtitles. 145 minutes. On video.

Related films

1915 Wladyslaw Starewicz film
There are two Soviet feature films titled *Ruslan and Lyudmila* though both are based on the Pushkin poem rather than the opera. The first was this 1915 film written, photographed and directed by the great animation master Wladyslaw Starewicz. It stars Ivan Mozhukhin, S. Goslavskaya, A. Bibikov and E. Pukhalsky. Black and white. About 54 minutes.

1974 Alexandre Ptouchko film
This charming opulent epic-length film version of the Pushkin poem was directed by Alexandre Ptouchko, who also filmed two Rimsky-Korsakov operas. It stars Natala Petrova as Lyudmila and Valeri Kosinets as Ruslan with support from Vladimir Fiodorov, Maria Kapniste-Serko and Andrei Abrikossov. The special effects, sets and costumes are outstanding with notable cinematography by Igor Guelein and Valentine Zakharov. The original music is by Tikon Khrennikov. Color. In Russian. 225 minutes.

RUSSELL, ANNA
American soprano and satirist (1925-)

Anna Russell has been the diva of opera parody for nearly fifty years and is still a delight on record and video. She first became known from her recordings and then appeared on Broadway in 1953 in "Anna

Russell's Little Show." One of its highlights was a one-woman version of an old-fashioned operetta called "The Prince of Philadelphia." Russell has satirized everything from Wagner to modern opera and was featured as the witch in a Humperdinck opera. See HANSEL AND GRETEL (1954).

1984 Anna Russell: (First) Farewell Concert
Russell is in fine form in this concert for an appreciative audience at the Baltimore Museum of Art on Nov. 7, 1984. The program includes her devastating analysis of Wagner's *Ring* cycle in which she deconstructs the tale. "If you know of the chord of E-flat major, you know the prelude to *Rheingold*," she explains. She also creates her own Gilbert and Sullivan operetta, explains how to become a singer, talks about pink chiffon and remembers the wind instruments. Russell is accompanied by pianist Robert Rosenberger. Phillip Byrd directed the video. Color. 85 minutes. VAI video.

RUSSELL, KEN
English film director (1927-)

Ken Russell says that opera is the "last believable religion." This provocative but always stimulating filmmaker has directed biographies of opera composers for TV and cinema and produced stage operas which have been videotaped. He began his career in 1959 with the *Monitor* arts program on BBC and his first film of operatic interest was *Portrait of a Soviet Composer* (1961) about Prokofiev. It was followed in 1962 by *Lotte Lenya Sings Kurt Weill* and a famous *Elgar*. His other TV composer films include *Bartok, The Debussy Film, Song of Summer* (about Delius) and *The Dance of the Seven Veils: A Comic Strip in Seven Episodes on the Life of Richard Strauss*. His Tchaikovsky movie biography *The Music Lovers* aroused a good deal of controversy though his *Turandot* episode of *Aria* was liked for its visual extravagance and his *Salome's Last Dance* found admirers. Russell began directing opera on stage in 1982 in Florence with *The Rake's Progress* and the production is on video. He has since worked in opera houses in London, Genoa, Geneva, Spoleto, Lyons and Macerata. His Genoa stage version of Boito's *Mefistofele* is also on video. His ENO version of *Princess Ida* was much criticized. See Béla BARTÓK (1964), CLAUDE DEBUSSY (1965), FREDERICK DELIUS (1968), GUSTAV MAHLER (1974), MEFISTOFELE (1989), SERGEI PROKOFIEV (1961), THE RAKE'S PROGRESS (1982), SALOME (1998 film), RICHARD STRAUSS (1970), PYOTR TCHAIKOVSKY (1971),

RALPH VAUGHAN WILLIAMS (1984), TURANDOT (1987 film), KURT WEILL (1964).

1987 Ken Russell's ABC of British Music
Ken Russell celebrates his love of British composers with this idiosyncratic but rather enjoyable guide to the best and worst of British music. The video is organized on alphabetical principles with each letter standing for several composers or items, many of them operatic. Color. 78 minutes. On video.

RUSSELL, LILLIAN
American soprano (1861-1922)

Lillian Russell was known as the "Queen of Light Opera" in the 1890s. She remains a legend a century after her glory days for her charisma and colorful life as depicted in books and Hollywood films. Russell was born in Iowa as Helen Leonard, studied with Leopold Damrosch and became the Queen of Broadway with the help of Tony Pastor. She made her debut in *H.M.S. Pinafore* in 1879, starred in other Gilbert and Sullivan works and was a hit in the Offenbach operettas *The Brigands* and *The Grand Duchess*. Russell apparently had a wonderful voice, incredible charm and a great many feathered hats. She can be heard in recordings singing her signature tune "Come Down, My Evening Star." She starred in two early silent films and is the subject of a movie biography in which she is portrayed by Alice Faye. She is also portrrayed in four other films: In *Diamond Jim* (1935) she is played by Binnie Barnes, in *The Great Ziegfeld* (1936) by Ruth Gillette, in *Bowery to Broadway* (1944) by Louise Allbritton and in *My Wild Irish Rose* (1947) by Andrea King.

1906 Lillian Russell
Lillian Russell stars in this Biograph film directed by F. A. Dobson. It was made in October 1906 and released in November the same year. Black and white. About 2 minutes. A print survives.

1915 Wildfire
In this film Lillian Russell reprises her starring role in the 1906 Broadway play *Wildfire*. She plays Henrietta Barrington whose father's racing stable includes the star filly Wildfire. Russell's co-stars are Lionel Barrymore and Glen Moore. The play was written by George Hobart and George Broadhurst. Edward Middleton directed for World Film. Black and white. About 70 minutes.

1940 Lillian Russell

Alice Faye portrays Lillian Russell in this lavish Twentieth Century-Fox biopic. It begins in Iowa, shows her becoming a singing star with the help of Tony Pastor and shows her involvement with Gilbert and Sullivan. Faye sings a number of songs associated with Russell, including her signature tune "Come Down, My Evening Star." Leo Carillo plays Tony Pastor, Nigel Bruce is William S. Gilbert and Claude Allister is Arthur Sullivan. The men in her life are Henry Fonda, Don Ameche and Edward Arnold as Diamond Jim Brady. Irving Cummings directed. Black and white. 127 minutes.

RYSANEK, LEONIE

Austrian soprano (1926-)

Leonie Rysanek began her opera career in Innsbruck in 1949 and won fame as Sieglinde in Bayreuth in 1951. She became a Munich Opera regular, made her American debut in 1956 in San Francisco and came to the Metropolitan famously in 1959 as Lady Macbeth, replacing Maria Callas. She continues to have an active career in Vienna and New York and is on video as Elektra and Chrysothemis in *Elektra*, as Ortrud in *Lohengrin*, as Herodias in *Salome* and as Tosca in the documentary *I Live For Art*. See ELEKTRA (1980/1981), LOHENGRIN (1986), SALOME (1990), TOSCA (1983 film).

S

SACCHINI, ANTONIO
Italian composer (1730-1786)

Italian Antonio Sacchini was one of the major composers of *opera seria* in the late 18th century and lived most of his life in London and Paris. He was much admired in his time but his work is no longer in vogue. *Dardanus* and *Oedipe à Calone* are usually considered his finest operas.

1995 Jefferson in Paris
Sacchini's 1784 opera *Dardanus* was a big success while Thomas Jefferson was living in Paris and is justifiably featured in the 1995 film *Jefferson in Paris*. The opera revolves around the adventures of Dardanus, founder of the royal house of Troy. Director James Ivory includes a quite elaborate re-creation of the Paris staging with ballet and aria. Jean-Paul Fauchecourt sings the role of Dardanus, Sophie Daneman is Iphise and William Christie conducts Les Arts Florissants orchestra. The opera is the setting for the return of Jefferson (Nick Nolte) to Maria Cosway (Greta Scacci). Color. 139 minutes. On-video and laser.

SACK, ERNA
German soprano (1898-1972)

Berlin coloratura Erna Sack made her debut at the Berlin Staatsoper in 1928 and joined the Dresden Opera in 1933. She had a strong association with composer Richard Strauss, created Isotta in *Die Schweigsame Frau* for him and sang Zerbinetta under his direction at Covent Garden. She also toured America both in the 1930s and after the war. Sack made two German musical movies in the mid-1930s including a version of Richard Genée's operetta *Nanon*. Her looks, acting and voice charmed the film critics. See also NANON.

1936 Blumen aus Nizza
Flowers from Nice is a appealing musical set in the south of France. Sack portrays a gifted soprano who can sing above high C with no difficulty but can't get any recognition for it. In order to attract attention she hires a count (Karl Schönböck) to fake his suicide as a publicity stunt. She also performs several arias plus songs by D. V. Buday and Willy Schmidt-Gentner. Her co-stars are Friedl Czepa, Jane Tilden and Paul Kemp. Max Wallner wrote the screenplay and Augusto Genina directed. The film was released in the U.S. Gloria Film. Black and white. In German. 82 minutes.

SADKO
1898 opera by Rimsky-Korsakov

Nikolai Rimsky-Korsakov's *Sadko* is an adaptation of a Russian folk tale about a legendary merchant whose singing wins the heart of the Ocean King's daughter. It takes place in the realistic merchant world of Novgorod and in the fantasy land of an underwater kingdom. Sadko alone is able to exist in both realms and his travels and adventures are the story of the opera. The opera's best-known melody in the West is the "Song of India" which is sung to Sadko by an Indian merchant describing his homeland. Russian audiences, however, prefer the song by the Viking merchant. See also NICOLAI RIMSKY-KORSAKOV.

1927 Charles Hackett film
Chicago Opera tenor Charles Hackett sings the "Song of India" aria "Chanson Indoue" from *Sadko* in this early sound film made by the Vitaphone company. Black and white. 8 minutes.

1952 Alexander Ptushko film
Serge Stolyarov stars as Sadko in this dazzling, large-scale Soviet film adaptation. Director Alexander Ptushko thought big in his fantasy films and aimed for magnificence. K. Isayev's screenplay changes the plot somewhat with Sadko now sailing around the world looking for a magic bird but still ending up in the undersea kingdom. Anna Larionava portrays his wife Lyubava and the cast includes Olga Vikland, Sergei Kayukov, Nicolai Troyanofsky and Boris Surovtsev. Mosfilm. Color. In Russian. 88 minutes.

1975 Soviet marionette film
Vadim Kourtchevski directed an adaptation of the fantasy opera as a Soviet marionette film. Soyouz multfilm. Color. In Russian.

1994 Kirov Opera

Vladmir Galuzin stars as Sadko in this Kirov Opera stage production by Alexei Stepaniuk, the first full screen version of the complete opera. Valentina Tsidipova is the Ocean King's daughter, Marianna Tarasova is Lyubava, Larissa Diadkova is Nezhata and Alexander Gergalov, Bulat Minjelkiev and Gegam Grigoriam are the three merchants. Vitslav Opunke designed the sets and Valery Gergiev conducted the Kirov Opera Orchestra and Chorus. Brian Large directed the video on HDTV for NHK. Color. In Russian. 175 minutes. Phillips video and laser.

SAGI-VELA, LUIS
Spanish baritone (1914-)

Luis Sagi-Vela, one of the leading Spanish singers of zarzuela and light opera, is the son of bass-baritone Emilio Sagi-Barba and soprano Luisa Vela. He made his stage debut in 1932 and also had a notable film career. In the 1960s he starred in a series of zarzuelas produced for Spanish TV which were also issued as records. See EL BARBERILLO DE LAVAPIÉS (1968), EL CASERIO (1968), EL HUÉSPED DEL SEVILLANO (1939), LUISA FERNANDA (1968), MARUXA (1968), LA REVOLTOSA (1968), EL REY QUE RABIÓ (1968).

SAINT OF BLEEKER STREET, THE
1954 opera by Menotti

Gian Carlo Menotti's opera *The Saint of Bleeker Street* ran on Broadway for 92 performances and won the composer/librettist his second Pulitzer Prize. It is set in the Bleeker Street area in New York where the saintly but sickly Annina has been having visions and is being sought out to perform miracles. She wants to become a nun but her brother Michele objects strongly. When his mistress Desideria accuses him of loving his sister too much, he becomes so angry he kills her. Annina later meets her fugitive brother secretly in a subway station. See also GIAN CARLO MENOTTI.

1955 NBC Opera Theater

Virginia Copeland, one of the three sopranos who played the role on Broadway, stars as Annina in this excellent NBC Opera Theatre production by Samuel Chotzinoff. Richard Cassilly portrays her brother Michele, Leon Lishner is the priest Don Marco and Rosemary Kullmann is Desideria. Peter Herman Adler is the music and artistic director,

Trew Hocker designed the sets and Samuel Krachmalnick conducts the Symphony of the Air Orchestra. Kirk Browning directed the live telecast on May 15, 1955. Black and white. In English. 90 minutes. Video at MTR and 16mm print at NFTA.

1978 New York City Opera

Catherine Malfitano stars as Annina in this New York City Opera production by Francis Rizzo. Enrico di Giuseppe sings the role of her tormented brother Michele, Irwin Densen is the priest Don Marco, Sandra Walker is Desideria and Diane Soviero is Carmela. Beverly Sills interviews Menotti and Malfitano during the intermission. Cal Stewart Kellogg conducts the orchestra and Kirk Browning directed the *Live from Lincoln Center* series telecast on April 19, 1978. Color. In English. 100 minutes. Video at MTR.

SAINT-SAËNS, CAMILLE
French composer (1835-1921)

Camille Saint-Saëns composed twelve operas and the earliest original score for a film. His best known opera, the only one in the international repertory, is the Bible-based *Samson et Dalila*. His other notable opera is *Henry VIII* which deals with the English king's split with the Roman church. Film historians say that his score for the 1908 French movie *L'Assassinat du Duc de Guise* helped movies gain stature as an art form. See HENRY VIII, SAMSON ET DALILA.

1974 Effie Briest

All the music in R. W. Fassbinder's popular German film *Effie Briest* is based on themes taken from compositions by Saint-Saëns. Hanna Schygulla stars as the unhappy young heroine of this adaptation of the famous novel by Theodor Fontane. Color. In German. 141 minutes.

SALIERI, ANTONIO
Italian composer (1750-1825)

Antonio Salieri, Mozart's arch-rival in Vienna, has begun to return to fashion partially as a result of the film *Amadeus*. His operas are now available on CD and are being staged and televised and there are several books about him. Salieri's operas may not rival Mozart's but they still have quality. The most popular is *Tarare*, originally in French with a libretto by Beaumarchais, but better known in an Italian version by Lorenzo Da Ponte called *Axur*.

Also popular is Salieri's version of *The Merry Wives of Windsor* called *Falstaff*; it was one of the first operas based on Shakespeare. Of interest is *Prima la Musica e poi le Parole* which premiered with Mozart's *The Impresario*. There are no film biographies of Salieri but he is a major character in most Mozart films. In *Amadeus* he is portrayed by F. Murray Abraham who, rather ironically, won the Best Actor Oscar besting the Mozart actor Tom Hulce. There is also a Rimsky-Korsakov opera about their rivalry called *Mozart and Salieri*. See FALSTAFF BY SALIERI, WOLFGANG A. MOZART, MOZART AND SALIERI, TARARE.

1985 Mostly Mozart Meets Salieri

The musical abilities of Salieri and Mozart are compared and contrasted in this fascinating concert. Arias, overtures and concertos by each are performed by soprano Elly Ameling, pianist Horacio Gutierrez and the Mostly Mozart Festival Orchestra led by Gerard Schwarz. Patrick Watson is the narrator and host on the concert telecast July 10, 1985. Color. 120 minutes.

SALLINEN, AULIS

Finnish composer (1935-)

Finnish composer Aulis Sallinen has become one of the best known modern Finnish composers. His 1992 opera *Kullervo* premiered at the Los Angeles Music Center when the new Finnish National Opera House opening was delayed. Other operas of note include *The Horseman* (1975), *The Red Line* (1975) and *The King Goes Forth to France* (1984) which was staged at Covent Garden in 1987. Sallinen's operas are nationalist and enigmatic but quite accessible. See THE PALACE.

1992 Aulis Sallinen - Man, Music, Nature

Brad Oldenburg's documentary film about the composer includes extracts from his historically based operas *The Horseman* and *The Red Line* and excerpts from other compositions. Sallinen talks about himself and his ideas and there are critical comments from Arto Noras, Mstislav Rostropovitch, James de Priest and David Harrington. Amaya distribution. Color. With English narration. 56 minutes. On video.

SALOME

1905 opera by Strauss

The Salome craze caused by the Oscar Wilde play and the Richard Strauss opera is reflected in a large number of early films based on the story. The opera's popularity is probably due as much to its sexual connotations as to its intense drama and great music as there were many scandals about the Dance of the Seven Veils. Times have greatly changed, however, as both Maria Ewing and Catherine Malfitano went nude in their performances without controversy. Strauss wrote the libretto based on a German translation of the play that follows Wilde's original closely. The story is close to that in the Bible but the character of Salome is much more developed and the conflict here is between religious zeal and sexual obsession. Beautiful young Salome, is angered that holy man Jokanaan (John the Baptist) ignores her allure. She dances for King Herod who is lusting after her and then demands John's head as her reward. When she gets it and smothers it in kisses, Herod has her killed. See also RICHARD STRAUSS.

1954 NBC Opera Theatre

Elaine Malbin stars as Salome with dancer Carmen Guitterez taking her place for the Dance of the Seven Veils in this NBC Opera Theatre production by Samuel Chotzinoff. John Cassavetes, the filmmaker who was a top TV actor at this time, portrays Jokanaan with the singing by Norman Atkins. Sal Mineo is the Page sung by Carol Jones, Andrew McKinley is King Herod, Lorna Sidney is Herodias and Davis Cunninghan is Narraboth. William Molyneux designed the sets, Charles Polachek wrote the English translation and Peter Herman Adler conducted the Symphony of the Air Orchestra. Kirk Browning directed the live telecast on May 8, 1954. Black and white. In English. 90 minutes. Video at MTR.

1972 Werner Schroeter TV film

German new wave director Werner Schroeter, who has made a number of narrative films with opera content, directed a version of the Strauss opera for West German television in 1971. Color. In German. 110 minutes.

1974 Teresa Stratas film

Teresa Stratas stars as Salome in this studio film of a Vienna State Opera production by Götz Friedrich. Bernd Weikl portrays Jokanaan, Hans Beirer is King Herod, Astrid Varnay is Herodias, Wieslaw Oschman is Narraboth and Hanna Schwarz is the Page. Stratas never appeared on stage as Salome but is wonderfully effective in the soundstage setting. Gerd Staub designed the sets in Hollywood Biblical-style and Karl Böhm conducted the Vienna Philharmonic Orchestra. Color. In German with English subtitles. 112 minutes. DG video and laser.

1990 Deutsche Oper Berlin
Catherine Malfitano stars as Salome with Simon Estes as Jokanaan and Leonie Rysanek as Herodias in this Deutsche Oper Berlin production by filmmaker Petr Weigl. Horst Hiestermann sings the role of King Herod, Clemens Bieber is Narraboth and Camille Capasso is the Page. Malfitano is strong and intense as Salome and is defiantly nude at the end of her dance. Josef Svoboda designed the sets and Josef Jelinek the costumes. Giuseppe Sinopoli conducted the Deutsche Opera Berlin Orchestra and Chorus and Brian Large directed the video. Color. In German with English subtitles. 109 minutes. Teldec video.

1991 Royal Opera
Maria Ewing stars as Salome in this outstanding Royal Opera production at Covent Garden by Peter Hall and matches Malfitano by going nude at the end of her disturbing dance. Michael Devlin sings the role of Jokanaan, Kenneth Riegel is King Herod, Gillian Knight is Herodias, Robin Leggate is Narraboth and Fiona Kimm is the Page. John Burry designed the sets and lighting and Sir Edward Downes conducted the Royal Opera Orchestra. Hall. Derek Bailey directed the video. Color. In German with English subtitles. 108 minutes. Home Vision video/ Pioneer Artists laser.

Early/related Films

1906 Oskar Messter film
German film pioneer Oskar Messter shot this *Salome's Dance* based on the Wilde play. It features Adorée Villany Messter as Salome and concentrates on the dance and the reward of the head of John the Baptist. The film was made with synchronized sound. Black and white. 3 minutes.

1907 Billy Bitzer film
D. W. Griffith's great cameraman Billy Bitzer photographed this *Salome* in the New York studio of the American Mutoscope and Biograph Company. Black and white. About 7 minutes.

1908 Florence Lawrence film
Florence Lawrence stars as Salome with Maurice Costello as John the Baptist in this Vitagraph studio adaptation of the story. It's titled *Salome or the Dance of the Seven Veils* and the plot of the film is close to the plot of the opera. Black and white. About 10 minutes.

1908 Salome: The Dance of the Seven Veils
This is the Salome story as retold by Vitagraph's competitor the Lubin company. It uses a very similar title of *Salome: The Dance of the Seven Veils.* Black and white. About 10 minutes.

1908 Gaumont film
The French film companies were also willing to cash in on the Salome craze. This French *Salome* was made by Gaumont and released in the USA by Kleine. Black and white. About 9 minutes.

1909 Stacia Napierkowska film
Stacia Napierkowska stars as Salome with Paul Capellani as John the Baptist in this French *Salome* directed by Albert Capellani for Pathé. Black and white. About 10 minutes.

1908 The Saloon Dance
This is a satire on the Salome craze made by the Lubin studio. Two tramps find tickets for the opera and go to see *Salome*. They are so impressed that they get costumes so they can earn money imitating what they call the "Saloon" Dance. Black and white. About 10 minutes.

1908 Salome and the Devil to Pay
A satirical Lubin Studio comedy film about *Salome* and the people who go to see it on stage. A young man's family is shocked when he admits he has seen *Salome* but they all slip off later to see it themselves. Black and white. About 9 minutes.

1909 The Salome Craze
This is an American film about the public obsession with *Salome* made by the Phoenix Film Company. Black and white. About 8 minutes.

1909 The Salome Dance Music
This early British sound film pictures the "Dance of the Seven Veils" performed in synchronization with a phonograph record of the dance music. It was made by the Warwick Cinephone Films Company. Black and white. About 4 minutes.

1913 Suzanne de Laarboy film
French actress Suzanne de Laarboy stars as Salome in this nearly feature-length Italian version of the opera story. Salome does her famous dance on screen while the Strauss music is played live. The movie was made by the European Feature Film Company of Turin. Black and white. About 40 minutes.

1918 Theda Bara film
Theda Bara, the most famous of the silent vamps, stars as Salome in this Fox spectacular directed by J. Gordon Edwards. Albert Roscoe plays John the Baptist and G. Raymond Nye is King Herod. Critics were quick to noted the scantiness of Bara's costumes. The plot is about the same as that of the opera. Black and white. About 90 minutes.

1922 Nazimova film
Nazimova stars as Salome in this famous American film of the Wilde play directed by Charles Bryant. Nigel De Brulier portrays Jokaanan, Mitchell Lewis is King Herod and Rose Diane is Herodias. Natasha Rambova created the exotic sets and costumes based on designs by Aubrey Beardsley. Black and white. About 80 minutes.

1923 Diana Allen film
Diana Allen stars as Salome in this version of the story advertised as *Strauss' Salome*. The Strauss it refers to is not the German composer but the American producer/director Malcolm Strauss. Vincent Coleman portrays Herod with Christine Winthrop as Herodias. Black and white. About 75 minutes.

1945 Yvonne De Carlo film
Yvonne De Carlo became a star on the strength of her torrid dancing in the film *Salome, Where She Danced*, one of the all-time great bad movies. She plays a 19th century dancer-spy who comes to the American West and gets a town named after her. No music by Richard Strauss but some from Johann. Charles Lamont directed. Color. 90 minutes.

1953 Rita Hayworth film
Rita Hayworth is the star of this *Salome*, a really romantic Hollywood version of the story in which Salome wants to save John. Alan Badel is John the Baptist, Charles Laughton is King Herod and Judith Anderson is Herodias. The plot is similar and the Dance of the Seven Veils is prominent but the Strauss connection is slim. The music is by Daniel Amfitheatrof and George Duning. William Dieterle directed for Columbia Pictures. Color. In English. 102 minutes.

1953 The Man Between
Carol Reed's fine British thriller *The Man Between* features a key sequence when James Mason and Claire Bloom attend a production of the opera *Salome* at the East Berlin Staatsoper. Bulgarian soprano Ljuba Welitsch sings the role of Salome and is shown in her final scene as the couple slip away to try to escape to the West. Black and white. 101 minutes.

1972 Carmelo Bene film
Donyale Luna stars as Salome in this bizarre, experimental and generally over-the-top film of the Wilde play by Italian director Carmelo Bene. Color. In Italian. 77 minutes.

1986 Claude D'Anna film
French writer-director Claude D'Anna based his Salome film on the Strauss opera and the Wilde play and set it in vaguely modern times. Jo Champa portrays Salome, Fabrizio Bentivoglio is Jokanaan, Tomas Milian Is Herod and Pamela Salem is Herodias. Color. In English or French. 95 minutes.

1988 Ken Russell film
British director Ken Russell was denied use of the Strauss opera music for *Salome's Last Dance*. his excellent film adaptation of the Oscar Wilde play. He sets it in an 1892 brothel with Wilde himself watching. Imogen Millais-Scott plays Salome but Doug Howes performs the "Dance of the Seven Veils." Glenda Jackson is Herodias, Stratford John is Herod, Douglas Hodge is John the Baptist and Nicholas Grace is Wilde. Color. 89 minutes.

SALTIMBANQUES, LES
1899 opéra-comique by Ganne

French composer Louis Ganne's best-known stage work is *The Traveling Players*, a romantic operetta about a group of performers in a small traveling circus. It has pleasant tunes, colorful circus stage effects, and a clever libretto by Maurice Ordonneau that revolves around the poor heroine who is really an aristocrat plot. Malicorne and his wife run the circus with its strongman Grand Pingouin, beautiful tightrope walker Marion and sad clown Paillasse who loves little Suzanne the heroine. Her love for the soldier André causes a conflict and she runs away from the circus. There is a good French CD version with Mady Mesplé as Suzanne. See also Louis Ganne.

1930 Käthe von Nagy film
Käthe von Nagy stars as the heroine Suzanne in this film of the operetta made in three-languages in Germany in 1930. Nicolas Coline is Paillaise, Louis Ralph is Malicorne, Max Henson is André and Suzanne Gouts is Marion. Jaquelux and Robert Land directed for Nero Film and Albert Lauzin with a screenplay by Herbert Brown. Willy Goldberger was the cinematographer. The French title is *Les Saltimbanques*, the German is *Gaukler* and the Italian is *I Saltimbanchi*. Black and white. 88 minutes.

SALZBURG

Mozart's home town has a long history of opera performance going back to 1618 and two early Mozart operas premiered there. The Salzburg Festival itself dates only from 1922 when the Grosses Festspielhaus opened. One of the earliest major opera films of a stage production was made at Salzburg, Paul Czinner's pioneering 1954 *Don Giovanni*. It was followed in 1960 with his equally famous *Der Rosenkavalier*. Although it is impossible to go to an opera at the festival without booking very expensive tickets months in advance, it is fairly easy to visit the festival on video. There is a particularly wide range of choice as Herbert von Karajan, who ran the festival for many years, filmed nearly every opera he produced there. See THE ABDUCTION FROM THE SERAGLIO (1989), CAPRICCIO (1990), CARMEN (1966), JOSÉ CARRERAS (1985), LA CENERENTOLA (1989), DON CARLO (1986), DON GIOVANNI (1954/1987), FALSTAFF (1982), DIE FRAU OHNE SCHATTEN (1992), FROM THE HOUSE OF THE DEAD (1993), HERBERT VON KARAJAN (1987), IL RE PASTORE (1989), IL RITORNO D'ULISSE IN PATRIA (1985), DER ROSENKAVALIER (1960/1980), DIE SCHÖNE GALATHÉE (1967).

1931 Salzburg, City of Mozart
This early film about Salzburg has great historical interest as it shows opera scenes at the Festival as well as the Salzburg sights. Rosette Anday is seen in *Orpheus and Eurydice* with the legendary Bruno Walter conducting, and Richard Mayr is shown in *The Magic Flute* with Clemens Krauss conducting

the Vienna Philharmonic Orchestra. The film was made by Selenophon Talking Pictures. Black and white. 10 minutes. Print at National Film Archive, London.

1944 Musik in Salzburg
A romantic German film set in Salzburg during the period of the Festival. It stars Lil Dagover, Willy Birgel and Hans Nielsen. Herbert Maisch directed. Black and white. In German. 103 minutes.

1956 Salzburg Pilgrimage
This short film about the city and its opera festival was made by opera film pioneer Paul Czinner who shot *Don Giovanni* on stage there in 1954. Black and white. In English. 20 minutes.

SAMSON ET DALILA
1877 opera by Saint-Saëns

Camille Saint-Saëns' Biblical opera *Samson and Delilah* is best-known for its soprano aria "Mon coeur s'ouvre a ta voix " which is often featured in recitals and movies. Ferdinand Lemaire based the libretto on the story as it's told in *The Bible*. Strongman Hebrew warrior Samson leads a revolt against the Philistines but is seduced by beautiful Philistine spy Delilah who discovers the secret of his strength is in his hair. After it is cut off, he becomes weak and is taken prisoner. At the end God gives him the strength to pull down his captors' temple. See also CAMILLE SAINT-SAËNS.

1980 San Francisco Opera
Shirley Verrett sings Dalila and Placido Domingo is Samson in this San Francisco Opera production by John Goberman. Wolfgang Brendel is the High Priest of Dagon, Arnold Voketaitis is Abimelech and Kevin Langan is the Old Hebrew. Nicolas Joel was stage director, Douglas Schmidt designed the sets and Carrie Robbins created the costumes. Julius Rudel conducts the San Francisco Orchestra and Chorus and introduces the opera. Kirk Browning directed the video. Color. In French with English subtitles. 119 minutes. Home Vision video/ Pioneer laserdisc.

1981 Royal Opera
Shirley Verrett sings the role of Dalila with Jon Vickers as her Samson in this Royal Opera, Covent Garden, production by Elija Moshinsky. Jonathan Summer is the High Priest of Dagon, John

Tomlinson is Abimelech and Gwynne Howell is the Old Hebrew. Sidney Nolan designed the sets and costumes and Colin Davis conducted the Royal Opera House Orchestra and Chorus. John Vernon directed the video. Color. In French with English subtitles. 135 minutes. HBO video.

Early/related films

1902 Ferdinand Zecca film
Ferdinand Zecca's Pathé film *Samson et Dalila* features scenes from the story. It was inspired by the opera and screened with its music. It was released in the U.S. in 1904 by EdisonBlack and white. In French. About three minutes.

1907 Albert Capellani film
An Italian silent film by Albert Capellani was inspired by the opera and screened with its music. Black and white. In Italian. About 7 minutes. Print in British film archive.

1910 Gaumont film
This early French film, inspired by the opera and screened with its music, was made by Gaumont and distributed in the U.S. by Kleine. It was titled *Samson et Dalila* in France and *Samson's Betrayal* in the U.S. Black and white. About 8 minutes.

1922 Tense Moments from Opera series
Valia stars as Dalila with M. D. Waxman as Samson in this British highlights film of the opera. It was produced by H. B. Parkinson, written by Frank Miller and directed by Edwin J. Collins. It was screened with music from the opera. Black and white. In English. About 12 minutes.

1922 Samson and Delilah: Story of an Opera Singer
This is an Austrian film about an opera singer who is to sing the role of Dalila on stage. She seeks out a Jewish scholar to tell her the story of Samson and Delilah and then is able to relate the Biblical story to her own career. Maria Corda plays the prima donna under the direction of Alexander Korda. The cast includes Franz Herterich and Paul Lukas. Black and white. In German. About 70 minutes.

1927 Cameo Operas series
William Anderson portrays Samson in this film of scenes from the opera made by H. B. Parkinson for the British Cameo Opera series. The film was shown with singers off stage performing the arias. Black and white. 20 minutes.

1949 Cecil B. De Mille film
Cecil B. De Mille's epic sin-and-sandals film *Samson and Delilah* features Hedy Lamarr as Delilah and Victor Mature as Samson with music by Victor Young. The story is more or less the same as the opera but the film has more spectacular sets. Color. 128 minutes.

1955 Interrupted Melody
Polio-stricken Australian opera singer Marjorie Lawrence (Eleanor Parker) crawls across a room to knock over a phonograph playing her recording of "Mon coeur s'ouvre a ta voix." Husband Glenn Ford has set up the situation to force her to move unaided and so begin her recovery. The voice heard on the record actually belongs to Eileen Farrell. Curtis Bernhardt directed. Color. 106 minutes.

1957 The Lady from Philadelphia
Edward R. Murrow's film about Marian Anderson's goodwill tour of Southeast Asia for the State Department, shown on Murrow's CBS television program *See It Now*, features Anderson singing "Mon coeur s'ouvre a ta voix" with the Bombay Symphony Orchestra. The soundtrack is on LP. Black and white. 60 minutes. Video at MTR.

1984 Lee Phillips film
Lee Phillips directed this remake of De Mille's *Samson and Delilah* with Victor Mature now playing Samson's father. Antony Hamilton portrays Samson and Belinda Bauer is Delilah with a script by John Gay, music by Maurice Jarre and a starry supporting cast. Color. 100 minutes.

1987 Slamdance
Director Wayne Wang features the aria "Mon coeur s'ouvre a ta voix" (in an English translation as "My heart at thy voice") in a key scene about betrayal at the end of this psychological crime drama. The aria is sung by Billy Bizeau with musical backing by Richard Thompson, Alex Acuna, Jerry Scheff, Jim Keltner and Mitchell Froom. Color. 101 minutes.

1995 The Bridges of Madison County
Maria Callas is heard on the radio singing "Mon coeur s'ouvre a ta voix" in an appropriate moment for Italian-born housewife Meryl Streep. Clint Eastwood co-starred and directed this romantic

film. The Callas recording was made with the French National Radio Orchestra conducted by Georges Prêtre. Color. 135 minutes.

SAN FRANCISCO OPERA
Memorial Opera House (1932-)

The first opera was presented in San Francisco in 1851 and the city has been enthusiastic about opera ever since. The present building, the Memorial Opera House, dates from 1932. The company has been among the most adventurous in the U.S. and its premieres include such recent American operas as Susa's *The Dangerous Liaisons*. See L'AFRICAINE (1988), LA BOHÈME (1989), CAPRICCIO (1993), THE DANGEROUS LIAISONS (1994), LA GIOCONDA (1980), MEFISTOFELE (1989), ORLANDO FURIOSO (1990), SAMSON ET DALILA (1980), TURANDOT (1993).

1964 The Roving Boys at the Opera
Cartoonist Bill Bates and disc jockeys Don Sherwood and Carter B. Smith attend the opening night of the San Francisco Opera season in 1964 and poke fun at some of the things they see. Bates created a hundred sketches for this popular telecast on KGO-TV. Black and white. 30 minutes.

1991 In The Shadow Of The Stars
Subtitled *The Lives of Singers*, this is a fascinating Academy Award-winning documentary about the people who make up the chorus of the San Francisco Opera Company and swell the crowds on stage. The filmmakers allow them to explain the drive that makes them want to sing and the sacrifices they make to be in the chorus. As one chorus member explains, "all of us are stars." The yearning to take center stage is obvious and sometimes the dreams are fulfilled. There are scenes of rehearsals and from several productions including *L'Africaine*, *La Bohème*, *La Gioconda*, *Macbeth*, *Die Meistersinger*, *Parsifal* and *Il Trovatore* . Irving Saraf and Allie Light direct with real humanity. Color. 93 minutes. On video.

SATYAGRAHA
1980 opera by Glass

Philip Glass's opera gets its title from the Sanscrit words *sat* (truth) and *graha* (firmness), key ideas in Gandhi's passive resistance movement. The libretto by Constance De Jong working with Glass uses ideas taken from the *Bhagavad-Gita* to tell the story of Gandhi's years in South Africa. It was there that

he began to develop his revolutionary ideas as he fought to repeal the Black Act. The opera was premiered in Rotterdam by the Netherlands Opera. See also PHILIP GLASS.

1981 Stuttgart Opera
American Tenor Leo Goeke stars as Gandhi in this Stuttgart Opera production created by German designer/ director Achim Freyer. Freyer and his wife Ilona also designed the sets and costumes. Dennis Russell Davies conducted the Stuttgart State Opera Orchestra. NVC/RM Arts/DDF. Color. In Sanscrit and English. 170 minutes. Video at NFTA.

SAWALLISCH, WOLFGANG
German conductor (1923-)

Wolfgang Sawallisch was born in Munich and made his conducting debut in 1947; he has been closely associated with the Bavarian State Opera in Munich since 1971. Sawallisch is noted for his Wagner and Strauss (his complete *Ring* cycle is on video) but he can also be seen conducting Mozart and Hindemith opera. See BAYREUTH (1960), CARDILLAC (1986), DER FLIEGENDE HOLLÄNDER (1987, 1992), DIE GÖTTERDÄMMERUNG (1989), THE MAGIC FLUTE (1983), DAS RHEINGOLD (1989), SIEGFRIED (1989), DIE WALKÜRE (1989).

SAYÃO, BIDÚ
Brazilian soprano (1902-)

Bidú Sayão was born in Rio de Janeiro, studied in Nice with Jean De Reszke and returned to Rio in 1926 for her debut at the Teatro Municipal. By the early 1930s she was performing in major theaters in Paris and Italy. Her greatest success was in Massenet's *Manon* at the Metropolitan Opera in 1937 as it launched an American career that lasted until 1951. She was heard in a wide variety of roles but most especially in Mozart as Susanna and Zerlina. Sayão retired from the stage in 1958 but her silvery charm can be experienced on video. See also METROPOLITAN OPERA (1966).

1951 Bidú Sayão in Opera and Song
Highlights of appearances by the Brazilian soprano on the *Voice of Firestone* TV series in 1951 and 1952. She performs three arias: "Gavotte" from Massenet's *Manon*, "Un bel di" from Puccini's *Madama Butterfly* and "O mio babbino caro" from Puccini's *Gianni Schicchi*. She also sings songs by Arditi, Hahn, Sandoval, Padilla and Coward.

Howard Barlow leads the Firestone Orchestra. Black and white. 45 minutes. VAI video.

SCALA DI SETA, LA
1812 opera by Rossini

The Silk Ladder, a romantic farce with a famous overture and a libretto by Giuseppe Maria Foppa, is the second of three early one-act comedies Rossini premiered in Venice. Like the others it is concerned with young women being urged to marry against their will. In this case Giulia is already secretly married to Dorvil and he uses that silk ladder to climb up to her room. To remedy the situation she sets up her cousin Lucilla to marry her suitor Blansac so her guardian Dormant and his spy Germano have to accept the solution. See also GIOACHINO ROSSINI.

1989 Schwetzingen Festival
Michael Hampe staged this Cologne Opera production in a rococo theater in Schwetzingen as part of a Rossini opera cycle. The singers are Luciana Serra as the coloratura heroine Giulia, David Kuebler as Dorvil, Alexander Corbelli as Germano, Alberto Rinaldi as Blansac and Janice Hall as a servant. Gianluigi Gemetti conducts the Stuttgart Radio Symphony Orchestra with set designs by Carlo Tommasi and costumes by Carlo Diappi. Color. In Italian with English subtitles. 85 minutes. Teldec video and laser.

SCHAUSPIELDIREKTOR, DER
See THE IMPRESARIO

SCHEFF, FRITZI
Austrian soprano (1879-1954)

Fritzi Scheff created the role of Fifi in Victor Herbert's 1905 operetta *Mlle. Modiste* and is remembered for her memorable performance of its hit song "Kiss Me Again." She was known as the Little Devil of Grand Opera at the height of her Broadway fame. Scheff was born in Vienna and made her debut in 1897 in Frankfurt as Juliette in Gounod's opera. She moved to the U.S. in 1900 and sang Musetta in *La Bohème* in Los Angeles in 1900 and Marzelline in *Fidelio* at the Metropolitan the same year. After three years at the Met she switched to light opera. Her only film came in 1915 when she starred in a movie version of her Broadway stage success *Pretty Mrs. Smith*.

1915 Pretty Mrs. Smith
This is a straightforward film adaptation of Scheff's Broadway stage success written by Oliver Morosco and Elmer Harris. Scheff plays pretty Mrs. Drucilla Smith, a woman who marries three times and then finds that all three husbands are alive and she is a trigamist. All ends well. The film was produced by Morosco's company and directed by Hobart Bosworth for Paramount Pictures. Black and white. About 70 minutes.

SCHERTZINGER, VICTOR
American film director (1880-1941)

Victor Schertzinger, a composer and songwriter as well as a film director, wrote one of the first original film scores for the 1916 *Civilization*. He also made major contributions to the operatic film. His 1934 Grace Moore film *One Night of Love* virtually created the Hollywood opera film boom of the 1930s and was followed by another fine Moore picture *Love Me Forever* (1935). He wrote the songs for the Marian Talley opera film *Follow Your Heart* (1936) and his 1939 film of *The Mikado* was the first complete Gilbert and Sullivan operetta on screen. See THE MIKADO (1939), GRACE MOORE (1934/1935), MARION TALLEY (1936).

SCHIPA, TITO
Italian tenor (1888-1965)

Tito Schipa, one of the great tenors of the century, made his debut in 1910 in the provincial mosquito-ridden town of Vercelli. By 1915 he was singing at La Scala and in 1917 he created the role of Ruggero in Puccini's *La Rondine* in Monte Carlo. He sang in Chicago in the 1920s and at the Metropolitan in the 1930s but continued to perform at La Scala. He specialized in the lighter lyrical Italian roles but was also known for his performances in French operas like *Manon* and *Werther*. He began to star in Italian films in 1932 and had a big success with *Vivere* in 1936. See also MAD ABOUT OPERA.

1929/1930 Operatic Selections
Tito Schipa made two opera films for Paramount at the Astoria Studio in New York in 1929 and 1930, the studio's equivalent of the Warner Brothers Vitaphone opera shorts. In one of them he appears in costume singing the tenor aria from Flotow's *Martha* in its Italian translation as "M'appari," in the other he sings "Princesita." Black and white. About 8 minutes each.

1932 I Sing For You Alone

In Tito Schipa's first feature film he plays a tenor who has a great voice but crippling stage fright. He allows his voice to be used by a friend who becomes an opera star but eventually he wins recognition for himself. Mario Bonnard shot the film in three languages with different casts supporting Schipa. The English version, sometimes called *Three Lucky Fools*, features Roy Gilbert, Al Andrews, Claire Vaudry and Lester Charles. The Italian version, *Tre Uomini in Frak*, features Eduardo and Peppino De Filippo and the French version, *Trois Hommes in Habit*, features Alfred Pasqual, Jean Gobet and Charles Deschamps. Black and white. 70 minutes. Bel Canto Society videos in English or French.

1936 Vivere

Vivere, released in the U.S. as *To Live*, was Schipa's biggest film success. He plays a nightclub singer who becomes an opera star with the motto "Vivere", the title of his favorite song. His daughter Caterina Boratto marries a man he doesn't like but they become reconciled so he can sing the touching "Torna piccina mia" as well as arias by Cilea and Donizetti. Many years later Caterina Boratto would play the mystery woman in Fellini's *8 1/2* and Masina's mother in *Juliet of the Spirits*. Guido Brignone directed. Black and white. In Italian. 88 minutes.

1938 Chi é più Felice di Me!

Vivere was a hit so the producers reunited Schipa, Boratto and Brignone for a sequel called *Who is Happier than Me?* Schipa plays a Don Juanish middle-aged opera tenor who has an affair with a young woman. She bears his child while he is away but he marries her when he finds out and they live happily ever after. The film is three-handkerchief weepie with songs like "Bimbo mio" and arias from *Andrea Chénier*. Black and white. In Italian. 86 minutes.

1938 Terre de Feu

In *Land of Fire* Schipa is a jealous Italian tenor who kills a presumed rival. His innocent wife lies and says she was unfaithful so he will get a short prison sentence. When he is released, he discovers her innocence and begins his opera career again. Once of the highlights of the film is an aria from Massenet's *Werther*. The cast include Mireille Balin, Jean Servais and Marie Glory. Marcel L'Herbier directed in French but there is also an Italian version by Giorgio Ferroni titled *Terra di Fuoco*. Black and white. In French or Italian. 92 minutes.

1943 In Cerca di Felicità

In Search of Happiness stars Schipa as an opera singer who adopts a young woman who reminds him of his daughter. He disapproves of the young singer she loves. The cast includes Helen Luber, Alberto Rabagliati and Lucia D'Alberti. Giacomo Gentilomo directed. Black and white. In Italian. 82 minutes.

1946 The Life of Donizetti

Il Cavaliere del Sogno is an Italian film about composer Gaetano Donizetti. Schipa portrays the French tenor Gilbert Duprez who created the role of Edgardo in *Lucia di Lammermoor*. He also sings excerpts from *L'Elisir d'Amore* and *Don Pasquale*. Amedeo Nazzari portrays Donizetti and Camillo Mastrocinque directed. It was released in the U.S. as *The Life of Donizetti*. Black and white. In Italian. 89 minutes.

1950 Una Voce nel Tuo Cuore

The singing of Tito Schipa, Beniamino Gigli and Gino Bechi make the musical *A Voice in Your Heart* almost memorable. They play themselves as opera singers and their operatic sequences are the best thing in the film. Vittorio Gassman stars as a war correspondent who loves a nightclub performer who wants to be an opera singer. Alberto D'Aversa directed. Black and white. In Italian. 98 minutes.

1951 I Misteri di Venezia

Schipa's last film, *The Mysteries of Venice*, is a crime melodrama. He supports Virginia Belmont and Renato Valente in a complicated story about love, despair and smuggling. Ignazio Ferronetti directed. Black and white. In Italian. 85 minutes.

SCHIPPERS, THOMAS
American conductor (1930-1977)

Thomas Schippers made his conducting debut in 1948 with the Lemonade Opera Company in New York and began a long collaboration with Gian Carlo Menotti the following year when he took over as conductor of *The Consul*. He later became music director of Menotti's Festival of Two Worlds at Spoleto. Schippers started to conduct at the Metropolitan in 1955 and was the conductor chosen for the Met's reopening in 1966 with Barber's *Anthony and Cleopatra*. See AMAHL AND THE NIGHT

VISITORS (1951), ANTONY AND CLEOPATRA (1966 film), THE MEDIUM (1951), GIAN CARLO MENOTTI (1966).

SCHLESINGER, JOHN
English film director (1926-)

John Schlesinger, who directs stage opera as well as films, won an Academy Award for *Midnight Cowboy* and acclaim for such films as *Darling* and *Far From the Madding Crowd*. He sometimes uses opera extracts in his films, notably in *Sunday Bloody Sunday* (1971) which contains a brilliant scene with the *Così Fan Tutte* trio. He has directed opera documentaries for BBC television and he had a small role in Michael Powell's film of *Die Fledermaus*. Schlesinger began directing opera at Covent Garden in 1980 with *The Tales of Hoffmann* which was followed in 1984 by *Der Rosenkavalier*. Both are on video. In 1989 Schlesinger he won wide praise for a spectacular *Un Ballo in Maschera* at the Salzburg Festival. See BENJAMIN BRITTEN (1959), COSÌ FAN TUTTE (1971 film), DER ROSENKAVALIER (1984), THE TALES OF HOFFMANN (1980).

1959/1960 Opera TV films
John Schlesinger directed twenty-four films for the British BBC television series *Tonight* and *Monitor*. They included two opera-connected films made for *Monitor*, *Benjamin Britten* screened in 1959 and *The Italian Opera* screened in 1960.

SCHMID, DANIEL
Swiss film director (1941-)

Daniel Schmid, who began his cinema career in 1971, also directs operas on stage. His popular films include *Tonight or Never* and *Shadow of Angels*. In his 1974 film *La Paloma* he features Ingrid Caven and Peter Kern singing a duet from a German operetta in an Alpine landscape. In 1984 he made the documentary *Tosca's Kiss*, a study of a retirement home for opera singers. He began to produce operas on stage the same year starting with Offenbach's *Barbe-Bleue* in Geneva and continuing with Berg's *Lulu* in Geneva and Rossini's *William Tell* in Zurich. He also directed the video of his production of the Rossini opera. See CASA VERDI (1985), WILLIAM TELL (1988).

SCHMIDT, ANDREAS
German baritone (1960-)

Andreas Schmidt studied with Dietrich Fischer-Dieskau and has become one of the more sought-after baritones in the world in the past few years. He has a preference for Mozartian styles as can be seen in his videos including a *Magic Flute* at the Metropolitan and a *Marriage of Figaro* at Glyndebourne. See CAPRICCIO (1990), THE MAGIC FLUTE (1991), THE MARRIAGE OF FIGARO (1994), DER ROSENKAVALIER (1992).

SCHMIDT, JOSEF
Romanian tenor (1904-1942)

Joseph Schmidt, sometimes called the "German Caruso," never became an opera star because he was almost a dwarf and too short to be convincing on stage in tenor roles. Instead he became a German radio and record star singing opera arias to wide acclaim. After Hitler came to power, he was no longer allowed on Berlin radio because he was Jewish. Schmidt was born in Bucovina in Romania, studied in Vienna and appeared in concerts around the world including Carnegie Hall. He died in an internment camp in Switzerland. Schmidt starred in a number of German films and remains popular today because of his movies and recordings.

1931 Der Liebesexpress
Schmidt's first film, *The Love Express*, is a slight musical comedy in which he is only a featured singer, third billed after Georg Alexander and Dina Gralla. Robert Wiene directed. Black and white. In German. 84 minutes.

1932 Gehetzte Menschen
Schmidt is a featured performer in this crime drama set in the South of France and starring Maga Sonja and Hans Feher. Friedrich Feher directed. Black and white. In German. 92 minutes.

1933 My Song Goes Around the World
This semi-autobiographical film, made in English and German and set in Venice, tells how Schmidt becomes a singing star but loses his girl to a better-looking guy. He sings a wide range of opera and popular music. The English version has Charlotte Ander as Nina, John Loder as Rico, Jack Barty and Jimmy Godden with a screenplay by Clifford Grey and Frank Miller based on the German script by Ernest Neubach. Richard Oswald directed. The

German version, *Ein Lied geht um die Welt*, was banned by the Nazis in 1937. Black and white. 80 minutes. Lyric/ Opera Dubs videos.

1936 A Star Fell From Heaven
This bi-lingual British/Austrian musical was made in Vienna after Schmidt had to leave Germany. He portrays a singer who dubs the voice of a movie star and loses the woman he loves because of it. Paul Merzbach directed the English version with Anne Heinmeyer and Douglas Lincoln in support. Max Neufeld directed the German version as *Ein Stern Fellt von Himmel* with Egon V. Jordfan and Evi Panzer. Black and white. 70 minutes. Opera Dubs/SRO videos.

SCHMIDT, TRUDELIESE
German mezzo-soprano (1934-)

Trudeliese Schmidt made her debut in 1965 and joined the Dusseldorf Opera in 1967 where she specialized in trouser roles. She sang at Covent Garden as Cherubino in 1974, at Bayreuth in 1975 in the *Ring* and at Glyndebourne in 1976 as Dorabella. She is featured in all three of the wonderful Monteverdi opera films created by Jean-Pierre Ponnelle and in Werner Schroeter's film about opera singing, *Poussières d'Amour*. See ARIADNE AUF NAXOS (1978), L'INCORONAZIONE DI POPPEA (1979), MIGNON (1982), ORFEO (1978), POUSSIÈRES D'AMOUR, IL RITORNO D'ULISSE IN PATRIA (1980).

SCHOCK, RUDOLF
German tenor (1915-1986)

Rudolf Schock was acclaimed as the successor to Richard Tauber in post- World War II Germany and was said to be the most popular tenor in Europe in his time. He began his career in Duisburg at the age of 18, sang with the Hamburg Staatsoper from 1947 to 1956 in such roles as Lohengrin and Florestan and appeared as Rodolfo, Alfredo and Tamino at Covent Garden in 1949. His wider popularity came from operettas and movies. He starred in a number of films based on Lehár operettas, as Tauber had before him, and he portrayed Tauber in the film *The Richard Tauber Story*. See DAS DREIMÄDERLHAUS (1958), GIUDITTA (1972), GRÄFIN MARIZA (1958), EMMERICH KÁLMÁN (1958), SCHÖN IST DIE WELT (1958), RICHARD TAUBER (1953), DIE ZIRKUSPRINZESSIN (1973).

1955 Der Fröhliche Wanderer
Rudolf Schock stars as the director of a small town's children's choir in *The Happy Wanderer*, a pleasant rural musical. His co-stars are Elma Karlowa and Waltraud Haas. Hans Quest directed. Color. In German. 100 minutes.

1956 Die Stimme der Sehnsucht
Schock portrays an opera tenor with a marriage problem in the German film *The Voice of Yearning*. Everything is eventually sorted out by an orphan. Christine Kaufmann and Waltraud Haas are his co-stars. Thomas Engel directed. Color. In German. 89 minutes.

1983 Rudolf Schock Gala
This is a televised German gala in honor of the singer. The participants include Birgit Nilsson, René Kollo, Erika Koth, Renate Holm and Ludwig Baumann. Color. In German. 60 minutes. Lyric video.

SCHOENBERG, ARNOLD
Austrian/U.S. composer (1874-1951)

Arnold Schoenberg is probably the most influential composer of the century, for good or for bad, as his ideas were noted by all those who came after him. He virtually invented atonality and 12-tone serial music and his early compositions caused riots among listeners. Ironically the composer spent the last seventeen years of his life in Hollywood, a place not noted for its avant-garde taste. He was asked by MGM chief Irving Thalberg to compose the score for the 1937 *The Good Earth* and agreed to do it for $50,000 if the studio would agree not to change a single note. Thalburg refused and gave the task to another composerso Schoenberg's Hollywood career never happened. However, many notable film composers became his pupils, notably David Raksin and Leonard Rosenman. Schoenberg's operas are becoming more popular today with the Met daring to present *Ewartung* on television. However, *Moses und Aron* is the only Schoenberg opera currently available on commercial video. See ERWARTUNG, MOSES UND ARON.

1989 My War Years: Arnold Schoenberg
Niv Fichman directed this Canadian film about the most exciting period in Schoenberg's life, the years from 1906 to 1923 when he was transforming the language of music. The film combines home

movies, archival footage, new material and performances. There are comments from Anton Webern, Alban Berg, Alma Mahler and Wassily Kandinsky. Among those performing are Marianne Pousseur, Stefan Vladar, Arleen Auger, Pierre Boulez, Michael Tilson Thomas, the London Symphony Orchestra and the Schoenberg Quartet. Color. 83 minutes.

SCHÖN IST DIE WELT
1930 operetta by Lehár

Franz Lehár's German operetta *Schön ist die Welt* (The World is Beautiful) featured Berlin opera coloratura Gitta Alpar when it opened in 1930 at the Berlin Metropol. It was a revision of his 1914 mountain operetta *Endlich allein* featuring an aristocratic love affair on the Jungrau as a crown prince and a princess climb a mountain together. The sets were spectacular and the title song was a hit but the operetta never entered the repertory. The early version was staged in New York in 1915 as *Alone at Last* with Marguerite Namara and John Charles Thomas in the leading roles. See also FRANZ LEHÁR.

1954 Rudolf Schock film
Rudolf Schock, the postwar heir to Richard Tauber as the tenor star of Lehár operettas, plays opposite Renate Holm in this German film of Lehar's *Schön ist die Welt* with a completely new story line. He is now a famous singer and she is a beginner whom he - rejects. Schock and Holm also recorded highlights from the operetta. Geza von Bolvary directed. Color. In German. 87 minutes.

SCHÖNE GALATHÉE, DIE
1865 operetta by Suppé

The Beautiful Galathea is a one-act comic operetta by Franz von Suppé retelling the story of Pygmalion and the beautiful statue of Galathea that comes to life. According to L. Kohl von Kohlenegg's libretto, modeled after the style of Offenbach, she is not quite so charming once she becomes human. She starts flirting with Ganymede, demanding jewels and generally carrying on just like a human being. See also FRANZ VON SUPPÉ.

1967 Salzburg Festival
Paul Angerer conducts the orchestra for this 1967 production of *Die Schöne Galathée* at the Salzburg Festival. The singers are relatively unknowns and

the video is an off-air copy of a telecast. Black and white. In German. 80 minutes. Lyric video.

SCHORM, EVALD
Czech film director (1931-1988)

Czech director Evald Schorm was an opera singer before turning to cinema so it was natural for him to feature opera in his movies. *Five Girls to Deal With* (1967), for example, centers around some romantic girls attending Weber's *Der Freischütz* every night in a provincial opera house. His best known film is *Everyday Courage* (1964). After the Soviet invasion of Czechoslovakia in 1968, Schorm could no longer direct the films he wanted and instead turned to producing opera on stage. See DER FREISCHÜTZ (1967 film).

SCHREIER, PETER
German tenor/conductor (1935-)

Peter Schreier made his debut in 1961 in Dresden and was soon the leading tenor of the Berlin Staatsoper. He made his first appearance at the Metropolitan in 1967 as Tamino and became known all around the world for his performances in Mozart operas. His superb *Magic Flute* is on video. In 1971 he began a parallel career as a conductor and can be seen leading the orchestra on a video of Handel's *Giulio Cesare*. See BERLIN (1976), GIULIO CESARE (1970), THE MAGIC FLUTE (1982/1991), SHERRILL MILNES (1985), DAS RHEINGOLD (1978).

1972 Peter Schreier Recital
Schreier was filmed in recital in 1972 with Rudolf Bichbinder accompanying him on piano. The program consists of songs by Mozart, Beethoven, Schubert, Brahms, Schumann and Prokofiev. Hugo Kach directed the film in 35mm for television. Color. 64 minutes.

SCHROETER, WERNER
German film director (1945-)

Werner Schroeter is an extravagant German filmmaker who has been obsessed with opera since beginning his career in 1968 with amateur movies about Maria Callas. Opera music appears regularly on the soundtrack of his films and is often central to them. His early shorts include *Callas walking Lucia*, *Maria Callas Sings* and *Maria Callas Portrait*. *Eika Katappa* (1969) is a celebration of opera and was followed by an innovative *Salome* (1972) with music by Donizetti and Wagner as well as Strauss. His *Macbeth* (1972) crosses Shakespeare with Verdi. Schroeter celebrates the glories of the famous 19th century soprano in *The Death of Maria Malibran* (1971) and he features opera excerpts in *Willow Springs, The Black Angel* and *Goldflocken*. *Love's Debris* is all about opera and opera singers. He staged opera sequences for Werner Herzog's *Fitzcarraldo* including the Manhaus Opera production of *Ernani*. Schroeter began to direct opera on stage in 1979 beginning with *Lohengrin* at the Kassel Opera House. See also MARIA CALLAS (1968), ERNANI (1982 film), LOVE'S DESBRIS, MARIA MALIBRAN (1971), SALOME (1971).

1969 Eika Katappa
Schroeter's first feature is a celebration of opera in an extravagant, funny and sometimes hysterical manner with scenes from dozens of operas mixed in a frenzied manner. The film begins with a preview of coming attractions that includes a skinny Siegfried and a tough Brünnhilde and ends with a survey of opera highlights. Among the operas featured are *Rigoletto, Ernani, La Forza del Destino, Il Trovatore, Un Ballo in Maschera, Tosca, I Puritani, Hamlet, Fidelio* and *Carmen*. The actors include Magdalena Montezuma, Gisela Trowe, Carla Aulaulu, Rosy-Rosy and Rosa von Praunheim. Color. In German and Italian. 144 minutes.

1973 Willow Springs
This film, shot in Willow Springs in the American Mojave Desert, includes music from *Mignon, Die Fledermaus, Carmen, Samson et Dalila, Faust* and *Mephistofele*. Color. In English and German. 79 minutes.

1973 The Black Angel
This Werner Schroeter film includes music by Bizet, Giordano and Offenbach including *The Tales of Hoffmann*. Color. In German. 71 minutes.

1975 Goldflocken
The singers featured in this film include Emma Calvé and Conchita Supervia and the music comes from the operas of Bizet, Dvořák, Mozart, Rossini and Verdi. Color. In French and German. 163 minutes.

1986 Der Rosenkönig
Magdalena Montezuma, who starred in *Eika Katappa*, co-wrote and starred in this extravaganza

as her final testament when she was dying of cancer. It includes music from *Tosca, Aida, Il Trovatore, Casanova, Agnese di Hohenstaufen, Zaide, Louise* and *Otello*. The singing voices belong to Maria Callas, Beverly Sills, Franco Corelli, Elizabeth Schwartzkopf and Leontyne Price. The cast includes Karine Fallenstein, Mustafa Djadjam and Antonio Orlando. Color. In German, Portuguese, Italian, Spanish, French, English and Arabic. 110 minutes.

SCHUBERT, FRANZ
Austrian composer (1797-1828)

Franz Schubert wrote fourteen operas but none were successful, possibly because of weak librettos. The only one staged in his lifetime was the 1820 *Die Zwillingsbrüder*. However, his last and best opera, the 1823 *Fierrabras*, was revived with great success in Vienna in 1988. Ironically Schubert's music has been enormously popular on stage in another format. The 1916 Viennese pastiche operetta *Das Dreimäderlhaus*, which tells a fictional tale about the composer's love for a young woman, is totally derived from Schubert melodies. It has become one of the most popular operettas in the world with an English version starring Richard Tauber and an American version called *Blossom Time* arranged by Sigmund Romberg. Schubert's lovelife has also been a favorite film subject. See DAS DREIMÄDERLHAUS, FIERRABRAS.

1934 The Unfinished Symphony
A romantic film about Franz Schubert (Hans Jaray) and his love for Caroline Esterhazy (Marta Eggerth). As she's the daughter of the Count who hired him to give her music lessons and he doesn't approve of this love affair, Schubert gets sent back to Vienna. He doesn't return until her wedding to another. Eggerth sings Schubert's "Ave Maria." This is the English version of an Austrian film made in 1933 in German as *Schuberts Unvollendete Symphonie*. Willi Forst directed both. Black and white. In English. 90 minutes.

1939 Sérénade
Schubert (Bernard Lancret) has a bittersweet love affair with an English dancer (Lilian Harvey) in this highly romantic tale. It is told to Schubert's music as arranged by Paul Abraham. Jean Boyer directed. Black and white. In French. 90 minutes.

1941 The Melody Master

Hollywood's version of the composer's life stars Alan Curtis as Schubert with Ilona Massey and Binnie Barnes as the women in his life. Schubert finds the woman of his life on a sheep farm and takes her with him to Vienna. Her faith in his music plus encouragement from Beethoven (Albert Basserman) leads to success. Reinhold Schunzel directed. The film was originally titled *New Wine* and was shown in England as *The Great Awakening*. Black and white. In English. 89 minutes. Video Yesteryear video.

1948 La Belle Meunière

Tino Rossi portrays Schubert in this charming French film directed by Marcel Pagnol. It is based around the composer's famous song cycle *Die Schöne Müllerin* and imagines that he has a love affair with a miller's daughter (Jacqueline Pagnol) which inspires his music. Color. In French. 120 minutes.

1955 Schubert

Schubert is portrayed by Claude Laydu in this romantic Italian film biography of the composer. Gino Bechi is featured as baritone Johann Vogl, Schubert's friend and ideal interpreter. Lucia Bosé and Marina Vlady are the women in his life. Glauco Pellegrini directed. Also known as *Sinfonia d'Amore*. Color. In Italian or French. 100 minutes.

1988 Franz Peter Schubert

Subtitled *The Greatest Love & the Greatest Sorrow*, this documentary film by Christopher Nupen tells the story of Schubert's life and music. Andreas Schmidt sing the lieder and Wolfgang Sawallisch conducts the Bavarian Symphony Orchestra. Color. 60 minutes. Teldec video.

1989 Schubert: Klassix 13

Anthony Quayle and Balint Vaszonyi visit Schubert's "garage" where he composed many of his great works. This potted film biography uses actors to reconstruct scenes from Schubert's life in Vienna. There are scenes at authentic locations showing the night life and a gathering of 19th century students. Klassix 13 series. Color. 60 minutes. On video.

SCHUMAN, WILLIAM
American composer (1910-1992)

William Schuman won the first Pulitzer Prize in music in 1943 for his *A Free Song*. His first and his most famous opera is the one-act *The Mighty Casey* (1953) based on the famous baseball poem by Ernest L. Thayer. It was presented on television in 1955. His second opera was the 1989 *A Question of Taste* ; it's based on a Roald Dahl story about a man who bets his daughter in a winetasting contest. See THE MIGHTY CASEY.

SCHUMANN-HEINK, ERNESTINE
Austrian/U.S. contralto (1861-1936)

Ernestine Schumann-Heink, who took her last names from her first two husbands, sang professionally from the age of 17 to the age of 70. She made her debut in *Il Trovatore* in Dresden in 1878 and reached the Metropolitan in 1898. She was especially admired in Wagner operas and had a long association with Bayreuth. She also created the role of Clytemnestra in Strauss's *Elektra* but it was her many concert tours that made her into a singing legend. She gave her final performance at the Met in 1932 at the age of 70 singing Erda in *Siegfried*. She wanted to make movies and had many projects but was able to make only one Hollywood feature and three shorts. Deanna Durbin was to portray her as a girl in a film biography but Schumann-Heink died before it could be made.

1927 Vitaphone sound films

She was billed as "Mme. Ernestine Schumann-Heink, Contralto" when she made three sound shorts for Vitaphone in New York in 1927. In the first she sings "By the Waters of Minnetonka," Arditti's "Leggero Invisible" and Reimann's "Spinnerliedchen." The second includes "Danny Boy," "The Rosary" and "Stille Nacht, heilige Nacht." The third has Schubert's "Der Erlkönig" and the songs "Trees" and "Pirate Dreams" with piano accompaniment by Josefin H. Vollmer. Black and white. Each about 7 minutes. Bel Canto Society video.

1935 Here's to Romance

Schumann-Heink appears in this film as Nino Martini's singing teacher and sings Brahm's "Weigenleid (Cradle Song)," a great favorite of hers. The film revolves around Martini's relationship with a rich woman (Genevieve Tobin) who becomes his patron. Alfred E. Green directed for Twentieth Century-Fox. Black and white. 83 minutes.

SCHWARZKOPF, ELISABETH
German soprano (1915-)

Elisabeth Schwarzkopf, one of the great singers of the postwar period, began her career with the Berlin Städtische Oper in 1938 as a flowermaiden. She became a pupil of Maria Ivogün and Karl Böhm invited her to join the Vienna Staatsoper, where she gained her international reputation. Her status grew while she was at Covent Garden for five seasons from 1947 singing major roles in English. She was a featured performer at the Salzburg Festival from 1947 to 1964 and appeared there in one of the major opera films, Paul Czinner's influential 1960 *Der Rosenkavalier*. Her superb recordings of her major roles, made with her EMI record producer husband Walter Legge, ensure that her reputation will remain high. She retired from the stage in 1972 after a final *Rosenkavalier* in Brussels. Her relationship with the Nazi Party during World War II, however, became a subject of debate in 1996 when it was discussed in a biography by Alan Jefferson. She appeared in some films that were banned as propaganda after the war. See also BACH (1950), DIVAS (1995), DER ROSENKAVALIER (1960), TRILBY (1954).

1939 Drei Unteroffiziere
A young Elisabeth Schwarzkopf is seen in the role of Carmen in German opposite tenor Günther Treptow as José in a theater production of *Carmen* in *Three NCOs*. A soldier and his girlfriend attend the opera and music from *Carmen* becomes the *leitmotif* of their love story. As the story is about soldiers, the film was considered propagandistic and banned by the Allies after the war. Werner Hochbaum was actually a director of genuine discernment and the Nazis never let him work again after this film. Albert Hehn plays the soldier who goes to see Schwarzkopf and his girlfriend is portrayed by Ruth Hellberg. Black and white. In German. 92 minutes.

1943 Nacht ohne Abschied
Schwarzkopf appears as Violetta in a stage production of *La Traviata* opposite tenor Peter Anders of *Night Without Parting*. This was also considered a propaganda film and was banned by the Allies after World War II. Anna Damman and Karl Ludwig Diehl are the stars and Erich Waschneck directed. Black and white. In German. 77 minutes.

1944 Der Verteidiger hat das Wort
Schwarzkopf has a small role singing at a party in the crime thriller titled *The Defender has the Word*. It stars Heinrich George, and was directed by Werner Klingler. Schwartzkopf sings "Mona" in an elegant living room. Rudolf Fernau and Carla Rust are also in the film. Black and white. In German. 87 minutes.

1960 Elisabeth Schwarzkopf Recital
Schwartzkopf is filmed during a recital arranged for Canadian television accompanied by pianist George Reeves. The program includes works by Schubert, Schumann, Wolf and Martini. Radio-Canada. Black and white. 30 minutes.

1980 Master Class Elisabeth Schwarzkopf
Schwartzkopf is featured working with young singers as she leads a master class in New York City in this valuable video produced by Eve Ruggieri and directed by Ariane Adriani. Color. 60 minutes. Video at NYPL.

1988 Elisabeth Schwarzkopf: A Portrait
Schwartzkoph is interviewed about her life and career in this English documentary and is featured performing arias by Mozart and Strauss. Alan Benson directed the video for London Weekend Television. Color. 55 minutes.

1990 Schwarzkopf Master Classes
Schwarzkopf was taped by INA giving two master classes in 1990. In the first she works with student Tinuke Olafimihan on Mozart in a video directed by Ariane Adriani. 58 minutes. In the second she work with student Robert Brooks on Schubert. 66 minutes.

1995 Elisabeth Schwarzkopf: A Self-Portrait
Schwartzkopf narrates this documentary by Gérald Caillat about her life and career. It includes rare film material of her in performance in many of the roles associated with her including scenes from the films she made in Germany during the war. She also comments about developments in her career and her way of singing. The opera excerpts include *Carmen*, *La Traviata*, *The Marriage of Figaro*, *Don Giovanni* and *Der Rosenkavalier*. Black and white & color. 50 minutes. EMI Classics video.

SCHWARZWALDMÄDEL, DAS
1917 operetta by Jessel

Léon Jessel's lively country-style operetta *Das Schwarzwaldmädel* (The Black Forest Girl) premiered at the Komische Oper in Berlin in 1917 and has been popular ever since, no thanks to the Nazis who tortured and killed the Jewish composer. August Niedhart's libretto tells of a series of romantic entanglements in a town in the heart of the Black Forest. A number of young women in the operetta have to wear folksy peasant costumes before they can win their fellows. The central character of the operetta is the cathedral music master Blasius Römer, father of one of the young women. See also LÉON JESSEL.

1929 Viktor Janson film
Viktor Janson directed the first version of the Jessel operetta in 1929. The cast includes Käthe Haack, Fred Louis Lerch, Walter Janssen, Georg Alexander and Olga Limburg. Black and white. In German. About 80 minutes.

1933 Georg Zoch film
Hans Söhnker and Maria Beling star in this German film of the famous operetta, made just before Jessel and his work fell out of favor with the Nazis. The cast includes Walter Janssen, Kurt von Ruffin and Lotte Lorring. George Zoch directed. Black and white. In German. 89 minutes.

1950 Hans Deppe film
This adaptation of the operetta was the first color film made in postwar Germany. It stars Paul Hörbiger as music master Blasius Römer, Sonja Ziemann as Barbele, Lucie Englisch as Lorle, Gretl Schorg as Malwine and Rudolf Prack as Hans. Hans Deppe directed. Color. In German. 104 minutes.

SCHWETZINGEN FESTIVAL
German opera festival (1952-)

The 1752 rococo Schlosstheater in the small town of Schwetzingen is the only surviving German chamber opera theater of its kind. It has been the site of a spring opera festival since 1952 and is noted for its revivals of classical and baroque opera. This a charming place to visit on video and there are quite a number of videos available; the festival is sponsored by Süddeutscher Television. See AGRIPPINA (1985), THE BARBER OF SEVILLE (1988), LA CAMBIALE DI MATRIMONIO (1989), LE CINESI (1987), ECHO ET NARCISSE (1987), FALSTAFF BY SALIERI (1995), L'INCORONAZIONE DI POPPEA (1993), L'ITALIANA IN ALGERI (1987), IL MATRIMONIO SEGRETO (1986), L'OCCASIONE FA IL LADRO (1992), LA SCALA DI SETA (1989), IL SIGNOR BRUSCHINO (1989), TANCREDI (1992), TARARE (1993), THE TURN OF THE SCREW (1993).

SCORSESE, MARTIN
American film director (1942-)

Italian-American Martin Scorsese, one of the most impressive American directors to emerge in the 1970s and known for such films as *Raging Bull* and *Taxi Driver*, has used Italian opera and opera singers in many of his films. *Mean Streets* (1973) features Giuseppe de Stefano on the soundtrack. *Raging Bull* (1980) has excerpts from three of Pietro Mascagni's operas, *Cavalleria Rusticana*, *Guglielmo Ratcliff* and *Silvano*. *The Color of Money* (1985) features "Va pensiero" from *Nabucco*. *Life Lessons* (1989), Scorsese's episode in the *New York Stories*, features Mario Del Monaco singing "Nessun dorma" from *Turandot*. *Goodfellas* (1990) again feature Giuseppe de Stefano on the soundtrack. *Cape Fear* (1991) contains an aria from *Lucia di Lammermoor*. *The Age of Innocence* (1993) begins at a stage production of *Faust* in the 1870s and the plot unfolds as we watch Faust and Marguerite in Act III. Scorsese has also been an operatic actor. In the film *Pavlova* (1984) directed by Emil Lotianou, Scorsese portrays Metropolitan Opera general manager Giulio Gatti-Casazza. See also FAUST (1993 film), TURANDOT (1989 film).

SCOTTO, RENATA
Italian soprano (1934-)

Renata Scotto made her debut in 1952 at the age of 17 in Savona, sang in *La Wally* at La Scala in 1955 and reached London in 1957. She came to America in 1960 to sing Mimi in Chicago and made regular appearances at the Met from 1965 to 1987. Scotto sings a wide range of roles and is noted for the emotion she can convey. The *Washington Post* once called her the "greatest singing actress in the world." Scotto has been featured in many videos and was stage director of a 1995 *La Traviata*. See LA BOHÈME (1977,1982), DIVAS (1991/1991), DON CARLO (1980), FAUST (1973), FRANCESCA DA RIMINI (1984), GIANNI SCHICCHI (1981), LA GIOCONDA (1980), LUCIA DI LAMMERMOOR (1967), LUISA MILLER (1979), MANON LESCAUT (1980), OTELLO (1978), SUOR ANGELICA (1981), IL TABARRO (1981), LA TRAVIATA (1995).

1984 Renata Scotto, Prima Donna in Recital

Scotto is shown in recital at the NHK Auditorium in Tokyo on Sept. 2, 1984. She sings "Lascia ch'io pianga" from *Rinaldo*, "Tu che le vanitá" from *Don Carlos*, "Sole e amore" and "Nel villagio d'Edgar" from *Edgar*, "Senti , bambino" from *Zanetto*, "Vissi d'arte" from *Tosca* and "Tu? Tu? Piccolo Iddio!" from *Madama Butterfly*. There are also songs by Verdi, Rossini, Scarlatti, Respighi, Liszt and Mascagni. Thomas Fulton is the pianist. Color. 99 minutes. VAI video.

1991 Renata Scotto in Concert

Scotto is in fine form in this recital at the Franz Liszt Music Academy in Budapest, the site of the opera scenes in the film *Meeting Venus*. The centerpiece is *Les Nuits d'Été* by Berlioz but the recital also includes arias from *Giulio Cesare*, *La Clemenza di Tito*, *Manon*, *La Wally*, *Carmen*, *Gianni Schicchi* and *Adriana Lecouvreur*. Scotto is accompanied by the Budapest Symphony Orchestra led by Ervin Lukacs. Color. 86 minutes. VAI video.

1994 Christmas Concert from the Vatican

Renata Scotto is the operatic star of this Vatican Christmas concert arranged by RAI TV. Vladimiri Spivacov leads the St. Cecilia Academy Symphony Orchestra. Color. 90 minutes. On video.

SEABOURNE, PETER
English opera film director/producer

Peter Seabourne directed or produced fourteen films in 1974 ranging from highlights versions of *The Tales of Hoffman* and *La Traviata* featuring Valerie Masterson to Gilbert & Sullivan adaptations with singers like Donald Adams. They may not be on the highest level of operatic film but they are all enjoyable. A number of them are on video. See (all 1974) THE BARBER OF SEVILLE, THE GONDOLIERS, H.M.S. PINAFORE, IOLANTHE, THE MIKADO, PAGLIACCI, THE PIRATES OF PENZANCE, RIGOLETTO, RUDDIGORE, THE TALES OF HOFFMANN, LA TRAVIATA, TRIAL BY JURY, THE YEOMAN OF THE GUARD.

SECOND HURRICANE, THE
1937 opera by Copland

Aaron Copland's first opera was staged by Orson Welles who directed its world premiere before he went to Hollywood. It was intended as a "play opera" for high school students and the libretto by poet Edwin Denby tells of the adventures of six high school students. They have volunteered to help an aviator take supplies to an area hit by a hurricane and end up stranded on a hill. The story is about how Butch, Fat, Queenie and the others learn to cooperate. Leonard Bernstein brought the opera back to prominence in 1960 when he telecast and recorded it. See also AARON COPLAND.

1960 Leonard Bernstein video

Leonard Bernstein presents the opera at Carnegie Hall in concert form narrating the story and conducting the New York Philharmonic. The singers are students from the New York City High School of Performing Arts and the principals won high praise. The program was produced and directed by Roger Englander and telecast on April 24, 1960 in the CBS television series *Young People's Concerts*. Black and white. 60 minutes. Video at MTR.

SECOND MRS. KONG, THE
1994 screen opera by Birtwistle

Harrison Birtwistle's opera *The Second Mrs. Kong*, composed to a libretto by Russell Hoban, updates the story of King Kong mixing in computers, paintings and mythological beings like Orpheus and the Sphinx. Birtwistle and Hoban are great admirers of the RKO movie *King Kong* but have not tried to retell the film story. Their imaginative version uses Pearl from Vermeer's famous painting "Girl with a Pearl Earring" as the love object equivalent of Fay Wray. Kong and Pearl communicate via computer but eventually realize their love is not possible as they are creations of the artistic imagination who will never meet. The opera includes excerpts from the film *King Kong* as well as *Brief Encounter* and *Night Mail*. It premiered at the Glyndebourne Festival and was much liked by English critics. See also HARRISON BIRTWISTLE.

1995 Glyndebourne Festival

Philip Langridge stars as Kong in this dazzling Glyndebourne Festival production of the opera by Tom Cairns. Helen Field is Pearl, Michael Change is Orpheus, Nuala Willis is Madame Lena, Stephen Page is Anubis, Omar Ebrahim is Vermeer. Cairns also designed the impressive sets with Aletta Collins while Wolfgang Göbbel was the lighting designer. Elgar Howarth conducted the Glynebourne Orchestra. Color. In English. 118 minutes.

SEGUROLA, ANDRÉS DE
Spanish bass (1875-1953)

Andrés de Segurola was born in Valencia and made his debut in Barcelona in 1895. He was soon singing in Madrid, Lisbon, Milan and then in New York at the Metropolitan where he began in 1902. He created Jake in *La Fanciulla del West* opposite Enrico Caruso in 1910 and sang at the Met until 1913. His movie career began in 1927 when Gloria Swanson invited him to Hollywood to portray an opera impresario in *The Love of Sunya*. In 1928 he appeared in five films including *Glorious Betsy* with fellow Met singer Pasquale Amato. He had character roles in many Hollywood films including some in Spanish with tenor José Mojica. He also began to coach singers. His most prominent pupil was Deanna Durbin. He was given screen credit as vocal instructor on her films and wrote the introduction for her souvenir songbook of opera arias. Segurola appeared in many films but only those with some opera content are listed. See also JOSÉ MOJICA.

1927 The Love of Sunya
Segurola portrays opera impresario De Salvo who wants Gloria Swanson to become a singer. She opts instead to marry her first love. Albert Parker directed. Silent. Black and white. About 85 minutes.

1928 Glorious Betsy
Segurola sings a stirring "La Marseillaise" in this tale about Napoleon's younger brother falling in love with an American girl named Betsy. Fellow Met singer Pasquale Amato portrays Napoleon in this patriotic part-talkie. Dolores Costello, Conrad Nagel and Betty Blythe star and Alan Crosland directed. Black and white. 80 minutes.

1930 Song O' My Heart
Segurola portrays Guido, a former opera colleague of John McCormack, in this charming musical directed by Frank Borzage. Segurola reminds McCormack of their days together at La Scala when they meet in a New York impresario's office. Fox. Black and white. 91 minutes. VAI video.

1934 One Night of Love
Segurola is Grace Moore's voice teacher in Milan before she encounters Tullio Carminati and rises to stardom. There is a delightful scene in her apartment when he instigates a *Lucia di Lammermoor* sextet to divert Moore's landlady from collecting rent. He sings the bass role. Pietro Cimini conducted the music and Victor Schertzinger directed. Columbia Pictures. Black and white. 80 minutes. Columbia video/ laser.

1935 Public Opinion
Segurola portrays opera singer Enrico Martinelli in this film about an opera star (Lois Wilson) whose career causes her marriage to break up. Frank R. Strayer directed. Black and white. 70 minutes.

SELLARS, PETER
American opera director (1957-)

Peter Sellars has been the leading American exponent of modernized non-traditional opera staging since the early 1980s. He transposed *Pelléas et Mélisande* to modern Malibu, *The Marriage of Figaro* to the Trump Tower, *Così Fan Tutte* to Despina's Diner and *Giulio Cesare* to the Cairo Hilton. He has been admired by many and excoriated by others (his *Magic Flute* at Glyndebourne was the first ever booed there) but his productions have usually been innovative and thought provoking. His collaborations with composer John Adams on the operas *Nixon in China* and *The Death of Klinghoffer* have been greatly admired. Much of his work is available on video and there is a documentary about his filming of the Da Ponte/Mozart operas. See also COSÌ FAN TUTTE (1989), DON GIOVANNI (1990), GIULIO CESARE (1990), THE MARRIAGE OF FIGARO (1990), NIXON IN CHINA, THE SEVEN DEADLY SINS (1993).

1990 Destination: Mozart
Subtitled *A Night at the Opera with Peter Sellars*, this is a documentary about the modernized Mozart-Da Ponte opera films Sellars made in Vienna. It features interviews with Sellars and his cast members and their ideas regarding Mozart and the operas *Così Fan Tutte*, *Don Giovanni* and *The Marriage of Figaro*. Andrea Simon's video also includes performance extracts from the operas. Color. In English. 60 minutes. Kultur video.

1990 A Mind for Music with Peter Sellars
Bill Moyers talks to Sellars on his PBS series *A World of Ideas*. In the first part Sellars discusses his ideas about staging Mozart and Shakespeare and there are excerpts from his Mozart productions as well as *Nixon in China*. In the second part he talks about his ideas for working in Los Angeles.

Produced by Leslie Clark. Color. 56 minutes. PBS video.

1995 A Short Film about Loving
Tony Palmer's film profile of the director stresses that Sellars does not set out to be controversial but to make his productions relevant to modern society. Sellars is interviewed in Paris, Edinburgh and Salzburg and is seen in rehearsal and organizing the Los Angeles Festival. There are excerpts from films of his operas including *Così Fan Tutte, Don Giovanni* and *Giulio Cesare.* Color. 60 minutes.

SEMIRAMIDE
1823 opera by Rossini

Rossini's last Italian opera, based on Voltaire's play *Semiramis,* is set in ancient Babylonia. Queen Semiramide has murdered her husband with the help of her lover Assur but is now interested in giving her favors to the soldier Arsace. To her annoyance he prefers the princess Azema. When she finds out that he is actually her own son, she tries to protect him from Assur and is accidentally killed. See also GIOACHINO ROSSINI.

1980 Aix-en-Provence Festival
Montserrat Caballé stars as Semiramide opposite Marilyn Horne as Arsace and Samuel Ramey as Assur in this Aix-en-Provence Festival production. Jesús López-Cobos conducts the orchestra. Color. In Italian. 204 minutes. Lyric video and at New York Public Library.

1986 Australian Opera
Joan Sutherland stars as Semiramide opposite Marilyn Horne as Arsace in this Sydney Opera House production by John Copley. Richard Bonynge conducts the Elizabethan Sydney Orchestra. John Widdicombe directed the video for Australian television. Color. In Italian with English subtitles. 205 minutes. Sony video.

1990 Metropolitan Opera
June Anderson stars as Semiramide with Marilyn Horne as Arsace in this Metropolitan Opera production by John Copley. Samuel Ramey portrays Assur, Stanford Olsen is Idreno, John Cheek is Oroe, Young Ok Shin is Azema, Michael Forest is Mitrane and Jeffrey Wells is the Ghost of Nino. John Conklin designed the sets and Michael Stennet the costumes. James Conlon directed the Metropolitan

Opera Orchestra and Chorus. Brian Large directed the video at a performance on Dec. 22, 1990 telecast on Oct. 16, 1991. Color. In Italian. 220 minutes. Kultur video/Japanese laser.

Early/related films

1909 Albert Capellani film
This silent French film of the story titled *Semiramis* is based on the Voltaire source play and the opera. It was directed by Albert Capellani for Pathé in France and stars Stacia Napierkowska and Paul Capellani. Black and white. About 10 minutes. Print in National Film Archive, London.

1948 Unfaithfully Yours
Orchestra conductor Rex Harrison, convinced that his wife Linda Darnell is betraying him, imagines her murder while conducting the overture to *Semiramide.* Preston Sturges directed. Black and white. 105 minutes.

SENDAK, MAURICE
American designer/librettist (1928-)

American author/illustrator Maurice Sendak began writing children's books in 1956 but it was the 1963 *Where the Wild Things Are* that made him famous. It became the basis of a 1980 opera in collaboration with English composer Oliver Knussen. His subsequent book *Higglety Pigglety Pop!* was made into an opera by the same team in 1985. Sendak designed wondrous sets and costumes for his operas and for *The Love of Three Oranges, The Cunning Little Vixen* and two Ravel operas. See THE CUNNING LITTLE VIXEN (1983), L'ENFANT ET LES SORTILÈGES (1987), L'HEURE ESPAGNOLE (1987), HIGGLETY PIGGLETY POP!, THE LOVE OF THREE ORANGES (1982), WHERE THE WILD THINGS ARE.

1966 Maurice Sendak
An American film about the artist which takes the form of an informal visit to his studio apartment in New York. He talks about the music, art and ideas which have affected and influenced him. Produced and distributed by Weston Woods. Color. 14 minutes.

1987 Maurice Sendak: "Mon Cher Papa"
The "cher papa" of the title is Mozart whom Sendak adopted as his father and creative mentor after the death of his father in 1972. In this film he talks

about his ideas for set design for operas which he considers as illustration on a grand scale. The program was telecast on Aug. 31, 1987. Color. 60 minutes.

SERAFIN, TULLIO
Italian conductor (1878-1968)

Tullio Serafin was one of the most influential conductors of the modern era in both Italy and America. He was at the Metropolitan from 1924 to 1934 where he conducted the premieres of American operas and helped advance the career of Rosa Ponselle. Back in Europe he was associated with Maria Callas and Joan Sutherland and helped them to achieve greatness. He can be seen in three videos: *Aida* with Leyla Gencer, *Rigoletto* with Tito Gobbi and *Otello* with Mario del Monaco. See AIDA (1963), OTELLO (1958), RIGOLETTO (1947).

SERRANO, JOSÉ
Spanish composer (1873-1941)

José Serrano was one of the leading composers of zarzuela at the beginning of the century. He first became known in 1900 with *El Motete* after he worked with Manuel Fernandez Cabellero. Serrano wrote over fifty richly melodic zarzuelas. His major work is *La Dolorosa* but *La Alegría del Batallón, La Claveles* and *La Canción del Olvidó* are also popular. There are Spanish films of five of his zarzuelas, two of them directed by French master Jean Gremillon. See also LA ALEGRÍA DEL BATALLÓN.

1934 La Dolorosa
Serrano's 1930 *La Dolorosa*, written by Juan José Lorente, was inspired by the death of the composer's son and is virtually an opera. It was filmed in Valencia in 1934 by French director Jean Grémillon and critics rank it as one of the best films in the Spanish opera/zarzuela genre. Agustin Godoy, an important singer of the period, stars in the film with support from Rosita Diaz Gimeno, Mary Amparo Bosch and Pilar Carcia. Jacques Monterault was the cinematographer. Black and white. In Spanish. 100 minutes.

1935/1960 Los Claveles
Serrano's 1929 zarzuela *Los Claveles*, written by Luis Fernandez Sevilla and A.C. Carreño, has been filmed twice with zarzuela singers in the starring roles. The 1935 Valencia production features Maria Arias, Maria Amparo Bosch and Mario Gabarro and

was directed by Eusebio Fernandez Ardavin and Santiago Ontanon. The 1960 Barcelona production stars Lilian de Celis, Maruja Tamayo and Conchita Bautista and was directed by Miguel lluch.

1940 Los de Aragon
Serrano's 1927 zarzuela *Los de Aragon* (Those of Aragon) was filmed in Barcelona in 1940 with the title *Gloria del Moncayo*. It was adapted for the screen by Antonio Calderon and Martin Herzberg and directed by Juan Parellada. The principal actors are Eulalia Zazo, Polita Bedros, Manuel de Diego and Jorge Greiner and the cinematographer was Jose Gaspar. Black and white. In Spanish. 85 minutes.

1968 La Canción del Olvidó
The 1916 zarzuela *La Canción del Olvidó* (Song of Forgetfulness), written by Guillermo Fernandez-Shaw and Federico Romero, was made into a film in 1968. The leads are sung by Josefina Cubeiro, Dolores Preez, Vicente Sardinero and Francisco Saura with Federico Moreno Torroba conducting the Spanish Lyric Orchestra and actors portraying the characters on screen. It was directed by Juan De Orduña, written by Manuel Tamayo and produced by TVE for its *Teatro Lirico Español* series. The soundtrack is on record. Color. In Spanish. 91 minutes.

SERSE
See XERXES.

SERVA PADRONA, LA
1733 opera by Pergolesi

La Serva Padrona (The Maid Mistress), a seemingly throwaway comic intermezzo composed as the interlude in the middle of Giovanni Pergolesi's "serious" opera *Il Prigionier Superbo*, turned out to be one of the most influential operas of all time. It became the center of the "Guerre des Bouffons" in Paris in 1752, the model for *opera buffa* and the first opera televised in its entirety on Dec. 23, 1937, on BBC Television. *The Guinness Book of Records* also says that it was the first complete opera to be filmed with sound. *La Serva Padrona*, adapted by Gennarantonio Federico from a play, tells the story of the maid Serpina and how she tricks her master Umberto into marrying her by pretending to go off with another man. It is a chamber opera for two singers, a bass and a soprano. See also GIOVANNI PERGOLESI.

1932 Pergolesi
La Scala soprano Laura Pasini sings the role of the wily servant Serpina in scenes from *La Serva Padrona* in this Italian film biography of the composer. La Scala bass Vincenzo Bettoni is featured as her master Umberto whom she tricks into marriage. Francesco Previtali conducted the orchestra and Guido Brigone directed the film. Black and white. In Italian. 80 minutes.

1934 Bruna Dragoni Film
The *Guinness Book of Records* considers this Italian film the first complete opera on sound film though seems to have been preceded by the 1931 American film of *Pagliacci*. It is still a remarkable early effort and one of the first Italian sound films. Bruna Dragoni stars as the clever Serpina with Vincenzo Bettoni as her Uberto. Giorgio Mannini directed for Lirica Film. The film had a very limited release in Italy. Black and white. In Italian. 62 minutes.

1937 BBC Television First
This historic telecast on Dec. 23, 1937, by the fledgling BBC Television company was made from Alexander Palace in London. There weren't many receivers but Pergolesi's *La Serva Padrona* thus became the first opera ever televised in its entirety. The opera was probably chosen because of its small cast and short running time.

1958 Anna Moffo film
Anna Moffo stars as the wily maid Serpina in this fine Italian TV production of this historic opera. The great Paolo Montarsolo sings the role of her master Umberto. They are both in peak form singing and acting and the video is most enjoyable. Franco Ferrara conducts the Rome Philharmonic Orchestra. Black and white. In Italian. 60 minutes. VIEW video.

SEVEN DEADLY SINS, THE
1933 opera-ballet by Weill

Kurt Weill's *Die Sieben Todsünden*, composed to a text by Bertolt Brecht, is a "singing ballet" that tells the story of twin sisters named Anna I and II. Anna I, who tell us she is"practical," sings her role. Her sister Anna II, who is "beautiful," dances hers. As the sisters travel to seven cities to earn money to buy a house in Louisiana, they encounter the seven deadly sins and turn morality on its head. Each of the sins has its own musical sequence. Anna I was first sung by Lotte Lenya and Anna II was first danced by Tilly Losch. See also BERTOLT BRECHT, KURT WEILL.

1993 Lyons Opera
Peter Sellars' film version of the work stars Teresa Stratas as the singer Anna I and Norma Kimball as the dancer Anna II. It alternates between studio scenes and present day scenes of America. The family are played by Peter Rose as the "mother, Frank Kelley as first son, Herbert Perry as second son, and Howard Haskin. Kent Nagano conducts the Lyons Opera Orchestra. La Sept-Arte. Color. In German with English subtitles. 47 minutes. London video/Pioneer laser.

SHAKESPEARE AS OPERA

William Shakespeare's plays have been a major source of librettos for opera composers though only a few of the operas have remained in the repertory. The major adaptations, however, are mostly on film or video with the notable omission of Thomas's *Hamlet*. Many of the Shakespeare operas were also filmed in the silent era though it is not always possible to tell if the film is based on the opera libretto or the play. The outstanding authority is this area is Robert Hamilton Ball whose *Shakespeare on Silent Film* is invaluable. The best source of information about Shakespeare operas is *Shakespeare and Opera* by Gary Schmidgall. The entries on the Shakespeare operas in this guide also include a note on the major films of the plays. See ANTONY AND CLEOPATRA, I CAPULETI ED I MONTECCHI, FALSTAFF, MACBETH, THE MERRY WIVES OF WINDSOR, A MIDSUMMER NIGHT'S DREAM, OTELLO, OTELLO BY ROSSINI (1988), ROMÉO ET JULIETTE, THE TAMING OF THE SHREW.

SHOSTAKOVICH, DIMITRI
Russian composer (1906-1975)

Dimitri Shostakovich was famous at the age of 20 after the success of his first symphony and his first opera *The Nose*. He then had to tone down his experimental style because of the changing political climate. His second opera, *Lady Macbeth of the Mtensk District*, nearly destroyed his career. Stalin attended a performance, didn't like it and Shostakovich was attacked in Pravda. It was the beginning of the Terror. The opera was withdrawn and did not reappear until after Stalin's death in 1962 when the composer produced a revision titled *Katerina Ismailova*. In the intervening period he composed symphonic work and stayed away from the theater. There is no film yet of the original version but there is a good one of *Katerina Ismailova* starring Galina Vishnevskaya. See KATERINA ISMAILOVA.

1987 Testimony
Tony Palmer directed this epic film biography of the composer with Ben Kingsley giving a fine performance as Shostakovich. It's scripted by David Rudkin and based on a book by Solomon Vokov derived from memoirs. The film is as much about the composer's political problems with Stalin as his music. Nic Knowland was the cinematographer who shot most of the film in black and white and CinemaScope. Black and white & color. 157 minutes.

SHOW BOAT
1927 American musical by Kern

Jerome Kern's *Show Boat*, which virtually created the genre of the modern American musical, has now entered the opera house repertory. The New York City Opera was the first to stage it back in 1954 and the Houston Grand Opera mounted a most impressive production in 1983. A CD of the musical was recorded in 1988 starring opera singers Frederica von Stade, Teresa Stratas and Jerry Hadley in the main roles. *Show Boat*, based on a Edna Ferber novel and composed to a fine libretto by Oscar Hammerstein II, tells of the loves and woes of a group of people on a turn-of-the-century Mississippi river boat. Magnolia Hawks, the daughter of showboat owner Capt. Andy, falls in love with gambler Gaylord Ravenal after they sing "Make Believe." Singer Julie La Verne runs into race prejudice after she sings "Bill." Stevedore Joe sums up the problems of being black in Mississippi in the great bass aria "Ol' Man River". The musical has been filmed four times but not yet with opera singers. There is an excellent book about its history by Miles Kreuger.

1929 Laura La Plante/Joseph Schildkraut film
The first film of the musical stars Laura La Plante as Magnolia, Joseph Schildkraut as Ravenal, Alma Rubens as Julie and Stepin Fetchit as Joe. It was filmed soon after the success of the stage musical

with added songs and did not include much of Kern's music. An 18-minute prologue to the film features songs by members of the New York stage cast including Jules Bledsoe as Joe and Helen Morgan as Julie. Harry Pollard directed for Universal. Black and white. 85 minutes.

1936 Paul Robeson/James Whale film
The great bass Paul Robeson stars as Joe and sings "Ol' Man River" in this excellent second film version of the musical directed by James Whale. Irene Dunne is Magnolia, Allan Jones is Gaylord, Helen Morgan is Julie and Charles Winninger is Capt. Andy. Black and white. 113 minutes.

1946 Till the Clouds Roll By
This MGM film biography of Jerome Kern contains a highlights version of the musical. The singers include Kathryn Grayson as Magnolia, Tony Martin as Ravenal, Caleb Peterson as Joe and Lena Horne as Julie. Richard Whorf directed. Color. 137 minutes

1951 William Warfield/Kathryn Grayson film
Opera bass William Warfield, known for singing Porgy on stage, portrays Joe in this fine MGM film of the musical directed by George Sidney. Kathryn Grayson is Magnolia with Howard Keel as Ravenal, Ava Gardner as Julie (sung by Annette Warren) and Joe E. Brown as Capt. Andy. This is the film version that most people know and it is a pretty good one. Color. 107 minutes.

SÍ
1919 operetta by Mascagni

Pietro Mascagni is best known for his *verismo* opera *Cavalleria Rusticana* but he also tried his hand at lighter stage works including operettas like *Sí* composed to a libretto by the multi-talented entrepreneur Carlo Lombardo in collaboration with A. Franci. It tells the bittersweet story of a showgirl who can never say "no," only "sí," and the marital problems this leads to. The operetta opened at the Quirino Theatre in Rome in 1919 and was reasonably successful, helping Mascagi to regain favor with the Italian public that had been losing faith in him. See also PIETRO MASCAGNI.

1992 Sandro Massimini video
Highlights from Mascagni's operetta *Sí* (Yes) were featured by operetta master Sandro Massimini and his associates on the Italian TV series *Operette, Che*

Passione! In this video extract Massimini explains the history of the operetta and talks about its popularity. The featured songs from the operetta are the duet "Sì! Sì!" sung by Massimini with Sonia Dorigo, "Romanza del Sì" sung by Dorigo and "Bimbe la luce elettrica rimpiazza il sol" sung by Max René Costotti. Color. In Italian. About 18 minutes. Ricordi (Italy) video.

SIEGFRIED
1876 opera by Wagner

Siegfried is the third opera in Richard Wagner's epic *Der Ring des Nibelungen* tetrology. Siegfried, the son of Siegmund and Sieglinde, is reared by Alberich's brother Mime who wants him to regain the gold. Siegfried re-forges the heroic sword Nothung and uses it to kill the giant Fafner who has become a dragon. The Forest Bird then leads him to the Valkyries' Rock. Wotan, in his disguise as the Wanderer, tries to stop him but Siegfried breaks his spear and awakens Brünnhilde from her long sleep. See also DER RING DES NIBELUNGEN, RICHARD WAGNER.

1980 Bayreuth Festival
Manfred Jung stars as Siegfried in Patrick Chéreau's 1977 Bayreuth Festival Centenary production set in the 19th century with Pierre Boulez conducting. Donald McIntyre is Wotan, Heinz Zednik is Mime, Gwyneth Jones is Brünnhilde, Hermann Becht is Alberich, Fritz Hubner is Fafner, Ortrun Wenkel is Erda and Norma Sharp is the Forest Bird. Richard Peduzzi designed the sets and Jacques Schmidt the costumes. Brian Large directed the video. Color. In German with English subtitles. 225 minutes. Philips video and laserdisc.

1989 Bavarian State Opera
René Kollo portrays Siegfried in this modernist Bavarian State Opera production by Nikolas Lehnhoff with Wolfgang Sawallisch conducting. Robert Hale is Wotan, Hildegard Behrens is Brünnhilde, Helmut Pampuch is Mime, Eberhard Wlaschiha is Alberich, Kurt Moll is Fafner, Hanna Schwarz is Erda and Julie Kaufmann is the Forest Bird. Erich Wonder designed the symbolic high-tech sets and Shokichi Amano directed the video. Color. In German with English subtitles. 230 minutes. EMI video/Japanese laser.

1990 Metropolitan Opera
Siegfried Jerusalem is Siegfried in this fine traditional Metropolitan Opera production by Otto Schenk with James Levine conducting. James Morris is Wotan, Hildegarde Behrens portrays Brünnhilde, Heinz Zednik is Mime, Ekkehard Wlaschiha is Alberich, Matti Salminen is Fafner, Birgitta Svendén is Erda and Dawn Upshaw is the Forest Bird. Gunther Schneider-Siemssen designed the naturalistic sets and Rolf Langenfass the costumes. Brian Large directed the video and PBS telecast. Color. In German with English subtitles. 252 minutes. DG video and laserdisc.

1992 Bayreuth Festival
Siegfried Jerusalem is again Siegfried in this modernist Bayreuth Festival production by Harry Kupfer with Daniel Barenboim conducting. Helmut Pampuch is Mime, John Tomlinson is Wotan, Anne Evans is Brünnhilde, Gunter von Kannen is Alberich, Philip Kang is Fafner and Birgitta Svendén is Erda. The minimalist sets are by Hans Schavernoch and Horant H. Hohlfeld directed the video. Color. In German with English subtitles. 230 minutes. Teldec video and laser.

Early/related films

1905 Nothung scene
This German film features the scene in the opera when Siegfried forges his sword Nothung. It was screened with a synchronized phonograph record of the music. Black and white. About 2 minutes. Print in NFTA.

1912 Mario Caserini film
Mario Caserini directed this Italian film based on the opera for the Ambrosio film company of Turin. It stars Alberto Capozzi and Mary Cleo Tarlarini and was written by Arrigo Frusta Black and white. In Italian. About 14 minutes.

1930 L'Age d'Or
Spanish director Luis Buñuel was somewhat obsessed with Wagner's operas and used music from them in many films. He featured the "Forest Murmurs" from *Siegfried* in *L'Age d'Or*. Black and white. 60 minutes. On video.

SIEPI, CESARE

Italian bass (1923-)

Cesare Siepi is particularly admired for his performances in Mozart opera roles, and especially as Don Giovanni and Figaro. The Milan-born singer, who made his debut in 1941, began to sing at La Scala in 1946 and at Covent Garden in 1950. His place in opera film history was secured when he sang the role of the Don in the pioneer Salzburg Festival film of *Don Giovanni* in 1954. Siepi also starred in the Broadway musicals *Bravo, Giovanni* (1962) and *Carmelina* (1979). See also DON GIOVANNI (1954/1960), FAUST (1963 film/1965 film), METROPOLITAN OPERA (1953).

1963 RAI Concert
Siepi was filmed on stage for a RAI Italian television concert in 1963. Figaro's aria "Aprite un po' quegli occhi" from *The Marriage of Figaro* is included in the video *Legends of Opera*. Black and white. 4 minutes. Legato Classics video.

SIGNOR BRUSCHINO, IL

1813 opera by Rossini

This was the last of Gioachino Rossini's early romantic one-act farces. The libretto by Giuseppe Maria Foppa. based on a French play, centers around Sofia who is being married off by her guardian Guadenzio to the son of Signor Bruschino. Her lover Florville disguises himself as the young Bruschino and marries her instead. He is helped by Signor Bruschino who has complicated identity problems. See also GIOACHINO ROSSINI.

1988 Pesaro Festival
Mariella Devia stars as Sofia in this Pesaro Festival production by Roberto de Simone. Enzo Dara is Gaudenzio, Alberto Rinaldi is Bruschino, Eugenio Favano is his son and Dalmacio Gonzalez is Florville. The Turin RAI Symphonic Orchestra performs on stage in 18th century costume under the baton of Donato Renzetti. The sets and costumes are by Enrico Job. Claudio Codilupi and Luciana Ceci Mascola directed the video and telecast. Color. In Italian. 95 minutes. Lyric Video.

1989 Schwetzingen Festival
This is the third of the Cologne Opera productions of Rossini one-act operas staged in Schwetzingen by Michael Hampe. Amelia Fele plays Sofia, David Kuebler is her lover, Alexander Corbelli is Gaudenzio, Alberto Rinaldi is Signor Bruschino and Janice Hall is the servant. Carlo Tommasi designed the sets and Carlo Diappi did the costumes. Gianluigi Gemetti conducts the Stuttgart Radio Symphony Orchestra. Color. In Italian with English subtitles. 85 minutes. Teldec video and laser.

SILENT FILMS ABOUT OPERA

A great many films in the silent era from 1896 to 1927 featured opera and opera singers as a central plot theme. At the period the opera diva was considered the most glamorous of women and opera symbolized culture. The music from operas shown in the films was usually played live by orchestras and pianos. Films related to individual operas are listed under that opera. Some of the more generic opera films are described below. See also THE GREAT LOVER, THE PHANTOM OF THE OPERA, TRILBY.

1909 The Tenor Makes Conquests
The French film, *Le Ténor Fait des Conquêtes*, is a comedy made for Pathé. It stars Gabriel Moreau as an irresistible tenor looking for a woman admirer. About 7 minutes.

1914 Grand Opera in Rubeville
Richard Tucker (not the famous tenor) and Herbert Prior star in this Edison two-reel film written and directed by Ashley Miller for the Edison Studio. About 25 minutes.

1915 The Opera Singer's Romance
Gale Henry stars as a famous opera diva opposite William Franey in this Joker Studio romance directed by Allen Curtis. About 60 minutes.

1915 What Happened to Father
Frank Daniels stars as a father who writes a comic opera to make money and has to step in to sing the leading role. C. Jay Williams directed this comedy for Vitagraph. About 60 minutes.

1916 The Prima Donna's Husband
Kathryn Browne-Decker portrays an opera diva whose husband kills a man he believes is her lover. Julius Steger and Joseph Golden directed this melodrama for Triumph Film. About 60 minutes.

1916 The Yellow Passport
Silent film star Clara Kimball Young portrays a famous opera singer who is falsely accused of having once been a prostitute. Edwin August directed this melodrama for World Film. About 60 minutes.

1916 Two Seats at the Opera
William Garwood stars in this 1916 comedy made for the IMP company. The supporting cast includes Willam Welsh, Inez Marcel, Edwina Martin and William J. Dyer. About 12 minutes.

1917 The Master Passion
Mabel Trunnelle is obsessed with becoming an opera star in this Edison film. She abandons her husband and child to go to Paris to become famous. Richard Ridgely directed. About 65 minutes.

1917 The Snarl
Bessie Barriscale stars as twin sisters, one of whom is a great opera diva. After she is hurt in an accident she has to sing behind a curtain while her sister mimes her role on stage. Raymond West directed for Triangle. About 65 minutes.

1918 Das Leben einer Primadonna
Anetta Melton stars as an opera diva with problems in *The Live of a Prima Donna*, an Austrian film directed by Franz Köhler. About 50 minutes.

1919 Heartsease
Tom Moore portrays a composer who creates an opera called *Heartsease* and then dedicates it to Helene Chadwick. Harry Beaumont directed for Goldwyn Pictures. About 70 minutes.

1920 Greater Than Fame
Elaine Hammerstein stars in this Selznick Picture about an opera singer who finally becomes famous when composer Walter McGrail writes an opera for her. Alan Crosland directed. About 70 minutes.

1920 Out of the Storm
Margaret Hill portrays a nightclub singer who becomes an opera diva with help from an admirer. He turns out to be a criminal. William Parke directed for Goldwyn. About 70 minutes.

1920 Once to Every Woman
Dorothy Phillips become an opera singer with the help of an Italian admirer who eventually shoots her out of jealousy. Allen Houlbar directed for Universal. About 80 minutes.

1920 Greater Than Fame
Elaine Hammerstein becomes a star in a opera composed by her boyfriend Walter McGrail. Alan Crosland directed for Selznick. About 70 minutes.

1922 How Women Love
Betty Blythe becomes a famous opera singer and then tries to pay off her backer with stolen rubies. Kenneth Webb directed for B.B. Productions. About 75 minutes.

1926 The Torrent
Greta Garbo plays a famous opera diva who has an unhappy relationship with Spanish aristocrat Ricardo Cortez. Monta Bell directed this famous film for MGM. About 80 minutes.

SILENT FILMS OF OPERAS

Interest in opera was so intense in the early part of the century that silent films of operas became common. Most of the operas popular at the time were filmed and presented with live music when screened, with piano in small towns, orchestras in cities. There were also many films made to be shown with synchronized records. The Edison Studio made a notable film of *Martha* in 1900 and a version of *Parsifal* in 1904, a 22-minute epic shot at the time of the first New York stage production. Opera stars like Geraldine Farrar, Enrico Caruso and Mary Garden were often featured in silent operatic films and Farrar actually became a genuine movie star. The most important silent film of an opera is probably the 1926 version of Richard Strauss's *Der Rosenkavalier* for which composer and librettist wrote new scenes. It was recently restored and screened with live music. The most interesting film cinematically is probably King Vidor's version of *La Bohème* with Lillian Gish as Mimi.

SILJA, ANJA
German soprano (1935-)

Berliner Anja Silja became a major presence at Bayreuth during the 1960s when she was associated with Wieland Wagner who engaged her to sing the roles of Senta, Elsa, Eva, Elisabeth, Freia and Venus. Silja had made her debut in 1955 as Rosina at Brunswick and came to London in 1963 to sing *Fidelio* with the Frankfurt Opera at Sadler's Wells. Her American career began in Chicago as Senta and she reached the Metropolitan in 1971 in *Fidelio* and *Salome*. Silja has a magnetic stage personality as well as a fine voice as can be seen on her videos. See BAYREUTH (1960), JENUFA (1988), FIDELIO (1968).

SILLS, BEVERLY
American soprano (1929-)

Her nickname "Bubbles" is an indication of the personality of this extraordinary singer who became an American diva at the New York City Opera. Sills was born Belle Miriam Silverman in Brooklyn and made her debut in 1947 in the Lehár operetta *Frasquita* at the Philadelphia Civic Opera. She joined the NYCO in 1955, soon became its prima donna and gained wide recognition for her singing and her personality. She sang at La Scala, Vienna and Covent Garden in the 1960s and made a token Met appearance in 1975. She was general director of the NYCO from 1979 to 1989 and then headed the whole Lincoln Center arts complex. Her videos are almost as enjoyable for her sense of fun as for her exceptional voice. See THE BARBER OF SEVILLE (1976), THE DAUGHTER OF THE REGIMENT (1974), DON PASQUALE (1979), MANON (1977), THE MERRY WIDOW (1977), METROPOLITAN OPERA (1975), ROBERTO DEVEREUX (1975), LA TRAVIATA (1954/ 1976), IL TURCO IN ITALIA (1978).

1936 Uncle Sol Solves It
This, unfortunately, is Beverly Sills only film and it was made in New York when she was only seven years old. She had begun to appear on radio at the age of four on *Uncle Bob's Rainbow Hour* on station WOR and this led to this short film for Twentieth Century-Fox. Black and white. 10 minutes.

1974 Johnny Carson Show
Beverly Sills plays Jeanette MacDonald to Johnny Carson's Nelson Eddy on this *Johnny Carson Show*. He dressed up in a Mountie costume so they could sing the "Indian Love Song" together. Color. 60 minutes.

1976 Sills and Burnett at the Met
Beverly Sills and Carol Burnett sing and dance on the Metropolitan Opera stage beginning with the duet "Only an Octave Apart." Sills sings a number of arias and popular songs and joins Burnett in an opera spoof. Dave Powers directed. The video was telecast on Thanksgiving Day, Nov. 25, 1976. Color. 50 minutes. Video at MTR.

1976 Lifestyles with Beverly Sills
Beverly Sills made her debut as a talk show host with this program in October 1976. Her guests included Melba Moore, Phyllis Diller and Tammy Grimes. Color. 60 minutes.

1978 Beverly & Friends
Sills hosts this television show and seems to enjoy herself talking to the stars. She sang, danced and welcomed guests Burt Lancaster, Lily Tomlin and Joan Rivers. The program was telecast on Dec. 6, 1978. Color. 90 minutes.

1980 Beverly Sills Farewell
This is a kind of all-star farewell party for Beverly Sills held at the New York City Opera on Oct. 27, 1980. The setting is Act II of Die Fledermaus with Kitty Carlisle as the party-giver Prince Orlovsky. The guests include Placido Domingo, Sherrill Milnes, Leontyne Price, Renata Scotto, Zubin Mehta and Ethel Merman. Sills closes the party with a duet with Carol Burnett. Julius Rudel conducts the orchestra. The program was telecast Jan. 5, 1981 as a Lincoln Center special. Color. 60 minutes. Video at NYPL.

1985 Kennedy Center Honors
Beverly Sills is one of the honorees on this Kennedy Center Honors program in December 1985. Sherrill Milnes and Carol Burnett saluted her in a duet. The program was telecast on Dec. 27, 1985. Color. 120 minutes.

SIMIONATA, GIULIETTA
Italian mezzo-soprano (1910-)

Giulietta Simionata, who retired in 1966, was one of the most attractive voices and personalities to emerge from Italy after World War II. Her coloratura was vivacious and her acting charming. She began to sing at La Scala in 1939 and was invited to sing in London and New York in the 1950s. She made a few films, mostly just as a voice, but she can be seen on stage in person in *Casa Ricordi*. See also AIDA (1961/ 1963), THE BARBER OF SEVILLE (1955), CASA RICORDI, CAVALLERIA RUSTICANA

(1961/1963 film), OPERA IMAGINAIRE, IL TROVATORE (1964).

SIMON BOCCANEGRA
1857 opera by Verdi

The plot of this Verdi opera is as complicated as that of *Il Trovatore*, perhaps because it is based on a melodrama by the same overheated Spanish author, Antonio García Gutiérrez. *Simon Boccanegra* is set in 14th century Genoa. Simon, a plebian seaman, has become the Doge of Genoa. Many years before he loved the daughter of his patrician enemy Fiesco and had a daughter Maria who disappeared. She was brought up by Fiesco who thinks she is an orphan called Amelia. Plebian Paolo wants to marry her but she loves patrician Gabriele. Francesco Maria Piave's libretto was revised by Arrigo Boito in his first collaboration with Verdi. The opera is noted for its duets, especially between father and daughter. See also Giuseppe Verdi.

1978 Paris Opera
Giorgio Strehler's influential 1976 production of *Simon Boccanegra* for La Scala stessed the political and social aspects of the story. It later toured the world and was taped in Paris in 1978 by INA for French television. The production stars Piero Cappuccelli, Mirella Freni and Nicolai Ghiaurov with sets by Ezio Frigerio. Claudio Abbado conducted the Paris Opera Orchestra. Color. In Italian. 150 minutes. (There are also non-professional Lyric videos of the production in Paris in 1978 and at La Scala in 1979.)

1984 Metropolitan Opera
Sherrill Milnes stars as Simon Boccanegra with Anna Tomowa-Sintow as Amelia/Maria in this Metropolitan Opera production by Tito Capobianco. Paul Plishka is Jacopo Fiesco, Vasile Moldoveanu is Gabriele and Richard J. Clark is Paolo. James Levine conducts the Metropolitan Opera Orchestra and Chorus. Brian Large directed the video and telecast on Dec. 29, 1984. Color. In Italian with English subtitles. 153 minutes. Paramount video/Pioneer laser.

1991 Royal Opera House
Kiri Te Kanawa stars as Amelia with Alexandru Agache as Simon Boccanegra in this Royal Opera House, Covent Garden, production by Elijah Moskinsky. Roberto Scandiuzzi is Fiesco, Michael Sylvester is Gabriele and Alan Opie is Paolo. The sets are by Michael Yeargan and the costumes by Peter J. Hall. Sir George Solti leads the Royal Opera Orchestra and Chorus and Brian Large directed the video. Color. In Italian with English subtitles. 135 minutes. London video.

1995 Metropolitan Opera
Placido Domingo is Gabriele and Kiri Te Kanawa is Amelia in this Metropolitan Opera production by Giancarlo del Monaco. Vladimir Chernov is Simon Boccanegra, Robert Lloyd is Fiesco and Bruno Pola is Paolo. Michael Scott designed the costumes and sets and James Levine conducts the Metropolitan Opera Orchestra and Chorus. Brian Large directed the video at a January 1995 performance telecast on April 26. Color. In Italian with English subtitles. 152 minutes.

SINIMBERGHI, GINO
Italian tenor (1913-)

Gino Sinimberghi learned his craft in his native Rome but he spent the early years of his career from 1937 to 1944 singing with the Berlin Staaatsoper. After he returned to Italy, he was a fixture at the major opera houses until 1968. One of his finest moments was singing Ismaele opposite Maria Callas in *Nabucco* at San Carlo in 1949. He appeared in a number of Italian opera films during the 1940s and 1950s as both singer and actor. See LINA CAVALIERI (1955), L'ELISIR D'AMORE (1947), LA FAVORITA (1952), LA FORZA DEL DESTINO (1949), PAGLIACCI (1948), GIACOMO PUCCINI (1952), LA SONNAMBULA (1949), TOSCA (1946 FILM), IL TROVATORE (1949).

SKLADANOWSKY, MAX
German film pioneer (1863-1939)

Max Sklandanowsky occupies a position in German cinema similar to that of Edison in American and Lumière in France. He gave a public performance of moving pictures at the Berlin Wintergarten in a variety program on Feb. 1, 1985. At the end of 1896 he is believed to have shown the first operetta film which may also have been the first sound film. It featured Viennese operetta singer Fritzi Massary at the beginning of her career and her comic partner Josef Gianpietro. They appeared in a scene from an unknown operetta, probably *Der Vogelhander* or *Der Bettelstudent* in which Massary had appeared as a soubrette. The film was played with synchronized records. Massary made many recordings for Emile Berliner.

SLEZAK, LEO
Austrian-Czech tenor (1873-1946)

Leo Slezak was as popular with singers as with audiences and widely liked for his sense of humor. After he left the opera stage in 1932 he appeared in some 44 German films. Slezak was born in Moravia and made his debut as Lohengrin in 1896. He became forever associated with the opera when he missed his Lohengrin swan entrance and asked "What time is the next swan?" He was hugely popular in Vienna and also sang Wagnerian roles with the Metropolitan opera from 1909 to 1912. Listed below is a selection of his more musical films. See also CLO-CLO (1935), MARTA EGGERTH (1932/1935), GASPARONE (1937), MARIA JERITZA (1933), THE MERRY WIVES OF WINDSOR (1935 film), OPERETTE , LE POSTILLON DE LONJUMEAU (1936), DER VOGELHÄNDLER (1940).

1934 Rendezvous in Wien
 Slezak is an Austrian publisher with a charming daughter in this musical comedy directed by Viktor Janson. It tells the story of a romance between a poor composer and a tourist guide. Black and white. In German. 87 minutes.

1936 Das Frauenparadies
The Woman Parade is a Robert Stolz operetta set in the world of high fashion and starring Slezak opposite Hortense Raky and Ivan Petrovich. Operetta specialist Arthur Maria Rabenalt directed. Black and white. In German. 83 minutes.

1937 Liebe im Dreivierteltak
Slezak is one of several stars in *Love in Waltz Time,* a musical made in Czechoslovakia and Austria and featuring original music by Robert Stolz. Hubert Marischka directed. It was later released in the U.S. Black and white. In German. 94 minutes.

1938 Die 4 Gesellen
Ingrid Bergman is the star of this German film, her tenth as an emerging movie diva. Slezak and Sabine Peters lend support in a story set in upper-class Berlin. Carl Froelich directed from a play by Jochen Huth. Black and white. In German. 94 minutes.

1943 Baron Munchausen
Slezak is one of the many stars of this lavish color film fantasy about the tale-telling Baron Munchausen. It was made in the worst days of the war in Germany but still charms audiences today. Josef von Baky directed. Color. In German. 110 minutes. On video.

SLEZAK, WALTER
Austrian actor (1902-1983)

Walter Slezak was on stage at the Metropolitan Opera in 1957 in Johann Strauss's *The Gypsy Baron.* Although he was primarily a film and stage actor, he did sing at the Met and other opera houses. He was born in Vienna, the son of tenor Leo Slezak, and was discovered by Michael Curtiz who cast him in his 1922 *Sodom and Gomorrah.* He went on to play romantic leads on stage and film, made his Broadway debut in 1931 and started a Hollywood career in 1942 appearing in some thirty films. They include *Lifeboat* (1944), *The Pirate* (1948), *The Inspector General* (1949) and *Call Me Madame* (1953). In 1955 he won a Tony for singing on Broadway in *Fanny* and two years later he was singing at the Met.

SMETANA, BEDRICH
Czech composer (1824-1884)

Bedrich Smetana, the greatest Czech opera composer of the 19th century, is known abroad mostly for *The Bartered Bride* (1866). He actually composed seven other operas and they helped establish the pattern for nationalist opera in his country. The best known is the patriotic *Dalibor* which has striking similarities to *Fidelio. The Bartered Bride,* however, is certainly his greatest opera and for many years was the only Czech opera staged abroad. The other Smetana operas now on CD are *Libuse* and *The Two Widows.* See THE BARTERED BRIDE , DALIBOR.

1954 From My Life
Karel Hoger portrays Smetana in *Z Meho Zivota,* a Czech film adapted from Jiri Maranek's novel *The Song of the Heroic Life.* It shows Smetana's life in the context of the history of his period and includes a good deal of the music from his operas. Also in the cast are Zdenka Prochazkova, Ludmila Vendolova, Jaromir Spal and Bedrich Karen. Vaclav Krska, who also filmed Smetana's opera *Dalibor,* wrote the

screenplay and directed. Color. In Czech. 91 minutes.

SNOW MAIDEN, THE
1882 opera by Rimsky-Korsakov

The Snow Maiden (Snegurochka), described as a "spring fairy tale," is one of the most charming of Nikolai Rimsky-Korsakov's fifteen operas. He based the libretto on a Russian folk tale and a play by Alexander Ostrovsky. The Snow Maiden heroine is the daughter of Father Frost and Mother Spring. She is beautiful and sympathetic but her heart is made of ice and she will die if she falls in love because her heart will melt. She first falls in love with Lell, who rejects her, so she agrees to marry Mizgir. Her heart is warmed and melts. See also NIKOLAI RIMSKY-KORSAKOV.

1914 Wladyslaw Starewicz film
Wladyslaw Starewicz's silent Russian version of the story, based on the fable and a Gogol story, was screened in theaters with the Rimsky-Korsakov music. Black and white. In Russian. About 30 minutes.

1952 Ivan Ivanov-Vano film
Ivan Ivanov-Vano, one of the Soviet Union's finest animators, created an animated feature based on the opera. The story is the same with the cold and passionless Snow Maiden falling in love after her mother Spring gives her a magic gift. She is eventually melted by the Sun who hates Frost. The Rimsky-Korsakov opera music is performed by soloists and singers from the Bolshoi Opera and the Bolshoi Opera Orchestra. Soyuzmult-film Studio. Color. In Russian. 67 minutes.

Related film

1953 Mood Contrasts
Pioneer film artist Mary Ellen Bute created this abstract film as a visual interpretation of Rimsky-Korsakov opera music. The mood of the "The Dance of the Tumblers" from *The Snow Maiden* is contrasted to that of the "Hymn to the Sun" from *The Golden Cockerel*. Color. 7 minutes.

SOBRINOS DEL CAPITÁN GRANT, LOS
1877 zarzuela by Caballero

Spanish composer Manuel Fernández Caballero, best known for the zarzuela *Gigantes y Cabezudos*, also had a major success with his 1877 zarzuela *Los Sobrinos del Capitán Grant* (The Nephews of Captain Grant). It's based on a Jules Verne story with a libretto by Ramos Carrion. See also MANUEL FERNÁNDEZ CABALLERO.

1968 Juan De Orduña film
Caballero's zarzuela was made into a colorful Spanish television film by Juan De Orduña. Federico Moreno Torroba conducts the Spanish Lyric Orchestra with the principal roles sung by Josefina Cubeiro, Mari Carmen Ramirez, Vicente Sardinero and Andres Garcia Marti. Actors portray the characters on screen. Manuel Tamayo wrote the adaptation for the TVE *Teatro Lirico Español* series. The film soundtrack is also on record. Color. In Spanish. 92 minutes.

SOLDATEN, DIE
1965 screen opera by Zimmermann

Bernd Alois Zimmermann's controversial large-scale opera *The Soldiers* uses film as an integral part of the production with projections of scenes on three screens on the stage. Zimmermann wrote the anti-militaristic libretto based on a 1776 play by Jakob Lenz. It uses a very large orchestra and several kinds of music from jazz to electronic as well as ballet to tell a sad story of innocence seduced and abandoned. Young Marie is engaged to the draper Stolzius but is seduced and then humiliated by army officer Desportes. He later gives her to his servant who rapes her and she ends up as a whore and a beggar. See also BERND ZIMMERMANN.

1988 Stuttgart Staatstheater
Nancy Shade stars as the hapless Marie in this Stuttgart Staatstheater production by Harry Kupfer. William Cochran plays Desportes, Michael Ebbecke is Stolzius, Mark Munkittrick is Wesener, Milager Vargas is Charlotte and Grace Hoffmann is Marie's grandmother. Bernhard Kontarsky conducts the Stuttgart State Opera Orchestra and Chorus. Color. In German with English subtitles. 111 minutes. Home Vision video.

SOLDIER'S TALE, THE
1918 opera ballet by Stravinsky

Igor Stravinsky's *L'Histoire du Soldat* is sometimes classified as a ballet though it is also included in opera books like George Martin's *The Companion to Twentieth Century Opera*. The ambiguity is understandable as *The Soldier's Tale* is situated somewhere between opera and ballet with a narrated story told through and heightened by music and dance but without singing. Nowadays it is seen as a predecessor of post-modern operas. Swiss poet Charles F. Ramuz wrote the French libretto which is based on a Russian folk tale. A soldier on his way home from the war meets the devil and exchanges his violin for a magic book. He wins a princess but he eventually loses his soul. See also IGOR STRAVINSKY.

1963 Michael Birkett film
Robert Helpmann stars as the Devil with Brian Phelan as the Soldier and Svetlana Beriosova as the Princess in this British film written and directed by Michael Birkett. It was shot almost entirely on location in English villages, woodlands and mansions by Dennis Miller. The music is performed by the Melos Ensemble under the direction of Derek Hudson.. Color. In English. 52 minutes.

1984 R.O. Blechman animated film
New Yorker cartoonist R.O. Blechman's brilliant animated version *of The Soldier's Tale* is narrated in English. Swedish actor Max Von Sydow is the voice of the Devil, Yugoslav film director Dusan Makavejev is the Soldier, Galina Panova is the Princess and André Gregory is the narrator. The music is performed by the Los Angeles Chamber Orchestra conducted by Gerard Schwarz. Color. In English. 56 minutes. MGM/ UA video.

1983 Netherlands Dance Theater
This Nederlands Dans Theater TV production was designed by Czech choreographer Jiří Kylián The narration, in French, is on the soundtrack. Gabriele Cattano is the Storyteller, Aryeh Weiner is the Devil with the voice of Philip Clay, Nacho Dutao is the Soldier with the voice of Pierre-Marie Escourrou and Karin Heyninck is the Princess. The music is performed by the Nederlands Dans Theater Orchestra conducted by David Porcelijn. Torbjörn Ehrnvall directed the video. Color. 40 minutes. Phillips video and laser.

SOLTI, GEORG
Hungarian/English conductor (1912-)

Sir Georg Solti, who was music director of Covent Garden from 1960 to 1971, helped it to become one of the great opera houses of the world. He conducted his first opera in Budapest in 1938 but thought it prudent to move to Switzerland after the arrival of the German Army. In the postwar period he ran the Bavarian State Opera for six years and helped create its international reputation. He made his first visit to the Metropolitan Opera in 1960. Solti made the first complete recording of the Ring cycle and there is a film showing how it was done. See THE ABDUCTION FROM THE SERAGLIO (1967/1986), ARABELLA (1977), LUDWIG VAN BEETHOVEN (1994 film), BLUEBEARD'S CASTLE (1981), LA DAMNATION DE FAUST (1989), EUGENE ONEGIN (1988), FALSTAFF (1979), DIE FRAU OHNE SCHATTEN (1992), HANSEL AND GRETEL (1981), MOZART REQUIEM (1991), OTELLO (1993), DER RING DES NIBELUNGEN (1965 film), DER ROSENKAVALIER (1985), SIMON BOCCANEGRA (1991), RICHARD STRAUSS (1984), RICHARD WAGNER (1983).

1977 Solti Conducts Wagner
Solti leads the Chicago Symphony Orchestra in music from *The Flying Dutchman, Die Meistersinger, Tannhäuser* and *Tristan und Isolde*. The video was shown in the Great Performances series on March 1, 1977. Unitel. Color. 60 minutes. Video at LOC.

1978 Portrait of Solti
Portrait of Solti is an excellent documentary about the conductor's life and musical career. It includes scenes of German tanks rolling into his native Hungary at the beginning of World War II, the moment when he decided it was prudent to move elsewhere. Among those interviewed in the film are Hildegarde Behrens, Wolfgang Wagner and Isaac Stern. Valerie Pitts directed the 16mm film. Color and black and white. 73 minutes.

1990 The Maestro and The Diva
Solti was famous for his relationship to the music of Richard Strauss and proves to be the ideal conductor for Kiri Te Kanawa at this Strauss concert in Manchester. He leads the BBC Philharmonic Orchestra in selections that include the "Four Last Songs" and "Lieder." Humphrey Burton directed the video. Color. 118 minutes. On video.

1992 Sir Georg Solti

This is a London television salute to the conductor on his eightieth birthday made by the South Bank Show. It includes footage of his return to his native Hungary after a fifty year absence. Color. 60 minutes.

SONG OF THE FLAME

1925 "romantic opera" by Gershwin

Although this was advertised as a "romantic opera" when it opened on Broadway, it is actually George Gershwin's only Viennese-style operetta. It was a collaboration with composer Herbert Stothart and writers Otto Harbach and Oscar Hammerstein II, all three of whom knew the genre well. The plot is an operetta version of the Russian Revolution which appears to have been modelled on the story of Zorro. A Russian woman disguises herself as The Flame and sings to incite the downtrodden to rebel against the Czarist government. Handsome Prince Voloyda falls in love with her in this disguise and, after the Revolution turns sour, they find happiness in Paris. See also GEORGE GERSHWIN.

1930 Alice Gentle film

Metropolitan Opera mezzo soprano Alice Gentle is featured as Natasha, the Flame's rival, in this First National film version of the operetta. Bernice Claire stars as Aniuta the Flame with Alexander Gray as Prince Volodya and Noah Beery as Konstantin, the revolutionary who turns into the bad guy. Alan Crosland directed. Black and white. In English. 89 minutes. This is apparently a lost film.

1934 The Flame Song

Bernice Claire stars again as Aniuta the Flame in this abridged version of the operetta made for Vitaphone in 1934. J. Harold Murray takes the role of Prince Volodya. The film includes four of the operetta's songs. Black and white. 20 minutes.

SONNAMBULA, LA

1831 opera by Bellini

Sleepwalking seems an unlikely subject for an opera today but it was a common literary theme at the time Bellini composed *The Sleepwalker*. The libretto by Felice Romani is based on a Scribe play. It tells of a charming if somewhat innocent girl called Amina who sleepwalks into and spends the night in a man's room in an inn. It causes a scandal and she almost loses her fiancé Elvino because of it.

The music for Amina has a lot of vocal pyrotechnics and has been a favorite of agile sopranos like Maria Callas and Joan Sutherland. There are many silent films titled *The Somnambulist* but they do not seem to have been inspired by the opera. See also VICENZO BELLINI.

1949 Fiorella Ortis film

Fiorella Ortis sings the part of Amina most beautifully in this Italian film of the opera with Paola Bertini portraying her on screen. Cesare Berlacchi's film follows the action of the opera closely with an off-screen narrator explaining the action from time to time. Most of the actors do not sing but they look right for the roles and the singers from the Rome Opera House are excellent. Licinio Francardi sings the role of Elvino acted by Gino Sinimberghi with Alfredo Colella as Count Rodolpho. The other singers are Franca Tamatini, Rosetta Riscica and Maruizio Lolli. Graziano Mucci conducts the Rome Opera House Orchestra and Carlo Carlini was the cinematographer. Leeicum Films. Black and white. In Italian. 85 minutes. Lyric/ Opera Dubs videos.

1956 Anna Moffo telecast

American soprano Anna Moffo stars as Amina in this Italian RAI television production of the opera. She sings opposite Danilo Vega and Plinio Clabassi with Bruno Bartoletti conduction the orchestra. Black and white. In Itallian. 90 minutes. Lyric Legato Classics Archives video.

Related film

1942 La Sonnambula

This is not the opera but a film about Bellini's love affair with the sleepwalker who inspired the opera. Anyway that's what the film claims and the music is certainly by Bellini. It's set at Lake Como where the composer recovered from an illness in 1830, the year before the premiere of *La Sonnambula*. The story is based around the relationship between Bellini and Giuditta Turina, the most famous of his many lovers. Roberto Villa stars as Bellini, Germana Paolieri is Giuditta Turina and Anita Farra plays Giuditta Pasta, the singer who created Amina on stage. Piero Ballerini directed. Black and white. In Italian. 88 minutes.

SOUTH PACIFIC
1949 musical by Rodgers & Hammerstein

It's not an opera but Metropolitan Opera basses have sung the lead of this Richard Rodgers & Oscar Hammerstein II musical on stage and on film and it has been performed in concert by Kiri Te Kanawa and José Carreras. Ezio Pinza portrayed French planter Emile de Becque in the original Broadway production while Giorgio Tozzi sang the role in the film version and in the 1967 Lincoln Center stage production. The book of *South Pacific* was written by Hammerstein in collaboration with Joshua Logan and based on a story in James Michener's *Tales of the South Pacific*. It centers around two cross-cultural love affairs, an eventually happy one between de Becque and nurse Nellie Forbush and a tragic one between Lt. Joe Cable and the Polynesian woman Liat. See also OSCAR HAMMERSTEIN II, RICHARD RODGERS.

1958 Giorgio Tozzi film
Met basso Giorgio Tozzi does not appear on screen but is the singing voice of Rossano Brazzi who plays planter Emile de Beque in this film of the musical. Mitzi Gaynor is Nellie Forbush, John Kerr is Cable (with the singing voice of Bill Lee), France Nuyen is Liat, and Juanita Hall is Bloody Mary (with the singing voice of Muriel Smith). Cinematographer Leon Shamroy shot much of the film in Kauai and in the Fiji Islands. Joshua Logan, who produced the musical on Broadway, directed for Twentieth Century-Fox. Color. 151 minutes. On video.

1986 South Pacific: The London Sessions
Kiri Te Kanawa and José Carreras are the stars of this concert performance of *South Pacific* which is on video and CD. It has few admirers. Tenor Carreras sings the bass role of de Beque with the music transposed up while Te Kanawa sings Nellie Forbush with skill but not much character. Much better are Sarah Vaughan as Bloody Mary and Mandy Patinkin as Lt. Cable. Jonathan Tunich conducts the London Symphony Orchestra. Color. 60 minutes. On video.

SORCERER, THE
1877 comic opera by Gilbert & Sullivan

The Sorcerer or The Elixir of Love is one of the most entertaining of the Gilbert and Sullivan operettas and has some of their most delightful patter songs.

It tells the story of the sorcerer John Wellington Wells and a love potion that goes wrong. Alexis and Aline are betrothed, Dr. Daly loves Aline, Constance is attracted to Dr. Daly and Lady Sangazure has feelings about Sir Marmaduke. The elixir of love makes everyone fall for the wrong person but sorcerer Wells is able to sort it all out in the end. The song "My name is John Wellington Wells" is deservedly famous. See also GILBERT AND SULLIVAN.

1982 George Walker film
Clive Revill stars as John Wellington Wells in this first-class film produced by Judith De Paul for George Walker. Nan Christie is Aline, David Kernan is Dr. Daly, Donald Adams is Sir Marmaduke Pointdextre, Alexander Oliver is Alexis and Nuala Willis is Lady Sangazure. Alexander Faris conducts the London Symphony Orchestra and the Ambrosian Opera Chorus. Stephen Pimlott was the stage director and Dave Heather directed the film. Color. In English. 119 minutes. Pioneer laser/Braveworld (England) video.

SORCERESS, THE
1993 pastiche opera by Handel

The Sorceress originated as an idea by Kiri Te Kanawa and Christopher Hogwood who told the Canadian company Rhombus they wanted to make a video of Handel arias. Barbara Willis Sweet conceived the idea of a pastiche opera rather than a concert and stitched together pieces of six Handel operas to create the new work. As plot she inverted the story of Alcina so the enchantress falls in love with the mortal knight Ruggiero who is betrothed to Bradamante. The opera has only one singing role: Alcina is played by Te Kanawa while the other characters only dance or mime. She sings seven Handel arias including "Ombre pallide" from *Alcina*, "V'adoro pupille" from *Giulio Cesare* and "Bel piacere" from *Agrippina*. Andrew Kelley dances Ruggiero and Jeannette Zingg is Bradamante with support from the Scapino Ballet of Rotterdam and the Opera Atelier of Toronto. Zingg and Ed Wubbe devised the choreography and Christopher Hogwood conducts the Academy of Ancient Music. Color. In English and Italian. 51 minutes. Phillips video. See also GEORGE F. HANDEL.

SPOLETO

The Festival dei Due Mondi, which still continued, was created by Gian Carlo Menotti in the small town of Spoleto, Italy, in 1958 and expanded in 1977 to include a counterpart in Charleston, NC. It takes place annually in June and July and often revolves around new opera productions. Luchino Visconti staged important productions at the festival and its artistic directors have included Thomas Schippers and Romolo Valli.

1959 Ed Sullivan Show in Spoleto
Ed Sullivan hosted a program from the Festival of Two Worlds in July 1959. There are interviews with Menotti and others and scenes from productions. Eileen Farrell sings "Pace, pace, mio Dio" from *La Forza del Destino* and then joins Louis Armstrong on "On the Sunny Side of the Street". Bob Precht directed. Black and white. 60 minutes. Video at MTR.

1966 Festival of Two Worlds
This Bell Telephone Hour TV special was shot in Italy at the Festival of Two Worlds. Menotti explains his ideas about the festival and philosophizes about the arts. The musical excerpts include a scene from *Pelleas et Melisande*. The featured singers are Shirley Verrett, Judith Blegen and John Rearden. Thomas Schippers, Zubin Mehta and Sviatoslav Richter also make appearances. Robert Drew directed the film. Color. In English. 60 minutes.

1983 Festival! Spoleto, USA
A fascinating look at events held during Menotti's seventh annual festival in Charleston. There are scenes from his production of Samuel Barber's *Antony and Cleopatra*, chamber music selections, bits of jazz and views of sculpture and art. Kirk Browning directed the telecast on June 27. Color. 60 minutes.

SPONTINI, GASPARE
Italian composer (1774-1851)

Gaspare Spontini was an Italian composer who made his reputation in France through the patronage of the Empress Josephine. His grand opera *La Vestale* (1807) was his biggest success and was very popular during most of the 19th century. It was said to be a major influence on both Berlioz and Wagner. Many of Spontini's operas are on CD including *La Vestale* and OLYMPIE but they are not often found in the stage repertory. See AGNESE DI HOHENSTAUFEN.

STEBER, ELEANOR
American soprano (1916-1990)

Eleanor Steber was one of the pillars of the Metropolitan Opera when she sang there from 1940 to 1963. She began her career at the Met as Sophie in *Der Rosenkavalier*, was much admired in Mozart, starred in the U.S. premiere of several operas and created the title role in Samuel Barber's *Vanessa*. In later years she also sang in musical comedy. Steber was one of the most popular stars on the *Voice of Firestone* TV series and appeared 36 times; she is featured in six Firestone videos, including one with Leonard Warren. Steber is undervalued today but her status as one of the great American sopranos is evident on the small screen. See THE IMPRESARIO (1961), DER ROSENKAVALIER (1949), LEONARD WARREN (1949).

1950-54 Eleanor Steber in Opera & Oratorio
The first of the videos featuring Steber on the *Voice of Firestone* television series. She sings arias from *The Marriage of Figaro*, *Manon*, *La Bohème*, *Otello*, *Lohengrin*, *Pagliacci*, *La Traviata* and *Tosca* as well as music from Handel's *Messiah* and Rossini's *Stabat Mater*. Black and white. 65 minutes. VAI video.

1949-52 Eleanor Steber in Opera & Song
The second of the *Voice of Firestone* Steber videos features selections from *Louise*, *Naughty Marietta*, *The Marriage of Figaro* ("Dove sono" and "Porgi amor") and *La Forza del Destino* plus songs by Rodgers and Hammerstein, Victor Herbert, Kurt Weill and Cole Porter. Black and white. 50 minutes. VAI video.

1950-54 Eleanor Steber in Opera & Song 2
In the third selection of Steber appearances on the *Voice of Firestone* television series she sings arias from *Ernani*, *Madama Butterfly*, *Die Fledermaus*, *Porgy and Bess* and *The Chocolate Soldier*. There are also ensembles from *Rigoletto*, *Faust* and *Lucia de Lammermoor* with Risë Stevens, Jerome Hines, Thomas L. Thomas, Brian Sullivan and Robert Rounseville. Black and white. 50 minutes. VAI video.

1950-52 Eleanor Steber Sings Love Songs

The fourth *Voice of Firestone* selection of Steber appearances on the TV program features her performing popular love songs composed by Jerome Kern, Rodgers and Hammerstein, Cole Porter, Victor Herbert, Noel Coward and Oscar Straus. Black and white. 55 minutes. VAI video.

1950-57 Christmas with Eleanor Steber

This seasonal video features highlights from three of Steber's *Voice of Firestone* Christmas telecasts. Among the selections are *Silent Night, White Christmas, The First Noël, Deck The Halls, Joy to the World* and Mozart's *Alleluia*. The orchestras are conducted by Howard Barlow and Wilfrid Pelletier. Black and white. 30 minutes. VAI video.

STEVENS, RISË

American mezzo-soprano (1913-)

Risë Stevens sang *Carmen* 75 times at the Metropolitan Opera so it's not surprising that an aria from that opera turns up in most of her movies. In fact it was her *Carmen* aria in the movie *Going My Way* that identified her with the role before she actually sang it on an American stage. Stevens was born in New York City and studied at Juilliard and in Europe before making her debut in Prague in 1936. She became a Met singer in 1938 and appeared there regularly until 1960. She made her farewell to opera in 1961 in *Carmen*, sang in *The King and I* at Lincoln Center in 1964 and then joined the management side of the Met. Stevens made only a few movies but *Going My Way* was so popular that it made her a cultural icon. She was the most popular guest on the *Voice of Firestone* television series, performing on it 47 times. See also CARMEN (1952), CARNEGIE HALL (1947), THE CHOCOLATE SOLDIER (1941/1955), HANSEL AND GRETEL (1958), SOL HUROK (1956), METROPOLITAN OPERA (1953), DER ROSENKAVALIER (1949), ELEANOR STEBER (1950).

1944 Going My Way

Bing Crosby portrays a priest who needs to raise money for his church and goes to the Metropolitan Opera to ask for help from old friend Genevieve Linden (Risë Stevens). While there he watches from backstage as she sings the "Habanera." She then agrees to take Crosby's choir (played by the Robert Mitchell Boys' Choir) on tour and raise the needed funds. It was Stevens' husband's idea that she should sing an aria from *Carmen* in the film even though she had not yet appeared in it on the American stage. She also sings Schubert's "Ave Maria" and the title song in duet with Crosby. *Going My Way* won seven Oscars including Best Picture for Leo McCarey who wrote and directed it for Paramount. Black and white. In English. 126 minutes. Paramount video.

1951-54 Risë Stevens in Opera & Song

The first Stevens video from the *Voice of Firestone* television series is taken from programs telecast in 1951 and 1954. She sings three arias from *Carmen* plus songs by Schumann, Schubert, Irving Berlin, Jerome Kern and others. Black and white. 45 minutes. VAI video.

1951-62 Risë Stevens in Opera & Song 2

The second video from the *Voice of Firestone* television series features Stevens in performances telecast over eleven years from 1951 to 1962. She sings arias from *Samson et Dalila, The Marriage of Figaro* and *Carmen* and songs by Debussy, Rachmaninoff, Stolz, Herbert and Rodgers and Hammerstein. Black and white. 50 minutes. VAI video.

STIFFELIO

1850 opera by Verdi

Stiffelio is a tale about adultery in a religious community in 19th century Austria. Stiffelio is a devout minister whose wife Lina has been having an affair with a libertine nobleman named Raffaele. When her father Stankar discovers this, he challenges Raffaele to a duel. Stiffelio stops the duel but learns of his wife's unfaithfulness and has to confront her. Raffaele is killed by Stankar but in the church the minister and his congregation voice forgiveness of all. Francesco Maria Piave's libretto is based on a French play. See also GIUSEPPE VERDI.

1993 Royal Opera House

José Carreras stars as Stiffelio with Catherine Malfitano as his wife Lina in this fine Royal Opera, Covent Garden, production by Elija Moshinsky. The setting has been changed to a 19th century American frontier community. Gregory Yurisich is Stankar, Robin Leggate is Raffaele and Gwynne Howell is Jorg. Michael Yeargan based the sets on John Ford films and Peter J. Hall designed the costumes in a similar manner. Edward Downes conducts the Royal Opera House Orchestra and Chorus. Brian Large directed the video. Color. In

Italian with English subtitles. 123 minutes. Home Vision video/Pioneer laser.

1993 Metropolitan Opera

Placido Domingo is in fine voice as Stiffelio in this excellent Metropolitan Opera production by Giancarlo Del Monaco. Sharon Sweet is Lina, Vladimir Chernov is Stankar, Peter Ribert is Raffaele and Paul Pliska is Jorg. Michael Scott designed the Gothic sets and costumes and James Levine conducted the Metropolitan Opera Orchestra and Chorus. Brian Large directed the video on Nov. 1 telecast on PBS on Dec. 27. Color. In Italian with English subtitles. 130 minutes.

STILL, WILLIAM GRANT

American composer (1895-1978)

William Grant Still was the first African-American opera composer to win wide recognition and his *Troubled Island* was the first African-American opera to be staged by a major company. Still studied at Oberlin, worked for a while with Paul Whiteman and first became known for his 1930 *Afro-American Symphony*. He began to compose operas in collaboration with librettist Verna Arvey whom he married. Three of his operas were staged in his lifetime: *Troubled Island* was produced at the New York City Opera in 1949, *Highway No. 1 USA* in Florida in 1963 and *A Bayou Legend* in Mississippi in 1974. Opera South's production of *A Bayou Legend* was televised in 1981. *Minette Fontaine* was staged in Louisiana in 1985. See A BAYOU LEGEND.

STOCKHAUSEN, KARLHEINZ

German composer (1928-)

Karlheinz Stockhausen, the leading figure of the modern German avant-garde, did not begin to compose operas until 1977. He then began to create an ambitious cycle of seven operas with the collective title of *Licht* (light), each named after a day of the week. *Monday, Thursday* and *Saturday* have been completed and there is a video about *Monday.*

1988 Montag aus Light

Thomas Letocha and Henning Lohner's film is a documentary about the staging of Stockhausen's opera *Monday from Light* at La Scala in Milan in May 1988. It shows how the production was set up and how Stockhausen supervised the work of director Michael Bodanov. The video includes some scenes from the premiere. Color. In English or German. 28 minutes. Inter Nationes video.

STOLZ, ROBERT

Austrian composer (1880-1975)

Robert Stolz was the last purveyor of the traditional Viennese operetta style. He called himself "the last of the waltz kings" and composed in a style long out of fashion in most of the world. His popularity, however, remained high in German-speaking countries where he was a celebrity conductor. Stolz was music director of Vienna's Theater an der Wien in the golden age of operetta and he conducted the premieres of works by Lehár, Kálmán, Straus and Fall. He himself wrote over 65 stage operettas and several operetta films, one of which provided the basis for a Deanna Durbin film. He contributed to the Benatzky operetta *White Horse Inn*, worked in Hollywood from 1940 to 1946 and composed songs and scores for many films. He was the great nephew of Verdi's soprano friend Theresa Stolz. See FRÜHJAHRSPARADE, WHITE HORSE INN.

1930 Two Hearts in 3/4 Time

Zwei Herzen in Dreivierteltakt, a 1930 German film operetta, was Stolz's biggest success. It was a world hit, the U.S. included, and its title waltz was a huge hit. Geza von Bolvary directed the film which stars opera soprano Irene Eisinger (later very popular at Glyndebourne), Willi Forst, Gretl Theimer and Walter Janssen. Stolz turned the film into a stage operetta produced in Zurich in 1933 as *Der Verlorene Walzer* (The Lost Waltz). It was staged again in Vienna in 1948 but this time using the film title. Black and white. In German. 91 minutes.

1931 Die Lustigen Weiber von Wien

The stage operetta *The Merry Wives Of Vienna*, which premiered in Vienna in 1909, is based on a libretto by Joseph Braun written originally for Johann Strauss Jr. It takes place in Vienna in 1875 on New Year's Eve. In 1931 it was made into a German film starring opera singer Irene Eisinger and Willi Forst with Lee Parry and Paul Hörbiger. Geza von Bolvary directed. Black and white. In German. 106 minutes.

1967 Mein Leben, Meine Lieder Robert Stolz

My Life, My Songs: Robert Stolz is a TV tribute to the grand old man of Viennese operetta filmed as he approached his 85th birthday. It's a lavish full-scale portrait tracing his entire career with music, singers and dancers, clips from films and interviews with Stolz and his wife. His famous waltz "Two Hearts in Three-Quarter Time" is used as the theme music. Martin Jente produced and Alexis Neve directed. Color. In German. 105 minutes.

1990 Robert Stolz Gala
A Vienna television tribute to the music of Robert Stolz with top singers presenting his best known melodies. The performers include Marta Eggerth, Nicolai Gedda, Andrea Huber, Ulrike Steinsky, Michael Helteau and Frank Odjidja. Siegried Koehler conducts the orchestra. Color. In German. 60 minutes. Lyric video.

STONE GUEST, THE
1872 opera by Dargomizhsky

Alexander Dargomizhsky's opera *Kamenyi Gost* is a variation on the Don Giovanni story. Alexander Pushkin's 1830 poem, which was inspired by the first production of Mozart's *Don Giovanni* in St. Petersburg, is the libretto. Don Giovanni is banished for killing the Commander but returns under an assumed name with Leporello to see the actress Laura. He falls in love with Donna Anna, the Commander's widow whom he meets in the cemetery in front of the Commander's statue. The statue is invited to Anna's house where it seizes the Don and takes him to hell. *The Stone Guest* is Dargomizhsky's best-known opera though it is rarely staged in the West. See also ALEXANDER DARGOMIZHSKY.

1967 Vladimir Atlantov film
Russian tenor Vladimir Atlantov stars as Don Giovanni in *Kamenyi Gost*, a wide screen Soviet film of the opera directed by Vladimir Gorikker. The other actors are dubbed by opera singers. Donna Anna is sung by Tamara Milashkina and acted by Irina Pechernikova, Leporello is sung by Alexander Vedernikov and acted by Yevgeny Lebedev, Laura is sung by Tamara Sinyavskaya and acted by Larissa Trembovelskaya while Arthur Eisen sings the role of the Monk. Gorikker made the adaptation with Andrei Donatov and Leonid Kosmatov was cinematographer. Boris Khaikin conducts the orchestra. Color. In Russian. 83 minutes. Lyric/Opera Dubs videos.

STOTHART, HERBERT
American composer (1895-1949)

Herbert Stothart, who won an Oscar for *The Wizard of Oz*, often featured opera and operetta in his scores for MGM films and composed an imaginary opera called *Czarita* for the 1937 *Maytime*. He collaborated with Rudolf Friml on the stage operetta *Rose-Marie* and was the music director of the 1936 film (to which he added bits from *Tosca* and *Roméo et Juliette*). He also collaborated with George Gershwin on *Song of the Flame* and Emmerich Kálmán on *Golden Dawn*. He wrote songs for the Franz Lehár film *The Rogue Song* (1930) and adapted Lehár's music for Lubitsch's film of *The Merry Widow* (1934). He adapted music from *Il Trovatore* and *Pagliacci* for *A Night at the Opera* (1935) and included a stage production of *Eugene Onegin* in *Anna Karenina* (1935). He was music director on the opera-oriented *San Francisco* (1936) and worked on all the MacDonald and Eddy operetta films. Stothart's score for *Camille* (1937) is based entirely on themes from *La Traviata*. See also THE CHOCOLATE SOLDIER (1941), NELSON EDDY, EUGENE ONEGIN (1935 film), LA FANCIULLA DEL WEST (1938 film), THE FIREFLY (1937), GOLDEN DAWN, IMAGINARY OPERAS IN FILMS (1937), JEANETTE MACDONALD, MAYTIME (1937), THE MERRY WIDOW (1934), THE NEW MOON (1940), A NIGHT AT THE OPERA, ROSE-MARIE, SONG OF THE FLAME, SWEETHEARTS (1938), LA TRAVIATA (1937 film), ZIGEUNERLIEBE (1930).

STRADA, LA
1982 screen opera by Kaslík

Czech composer Václav Kaslík based his opera *La Strada* around the script of Federico Fellini's 1954 Academy Award-winning Italian film about a traveling circus. It features the film's strongman Zampano as a bass-baritone and the simple-minded Gelsomina as a soprano. The opera, with spoken dialogue like a singspiel, was staged in Prague in 1982. The film itself starred Anthony Quinn as the strongman with Giulietta Masina as Gelsomina. The screenplay, nominated for an Oscar, was written by Fellini in collaboration with Tullio Pinelli and Ennio Flaiano. The opera does not appear to have been filmed or televised. The film also provided the basis for an unsuccessful 1969 Broadway musical with a score by Lionel Bart. See also VÁCLAV KASLÍK.

STRATAS, TERESA
Canadian soprano (1938-)

Teresa Stratas, one of the finest singing actresses of our time, was born Anastasia Strataki in Canada of Greek parents. She made her debut in 1958 in Toronto with the Canadian Opera in the role of Mimi and sang at the Metropolitan Opera the following year in *Manon*. She was soon a regular at the Met and at major opera houses in Europe. Stratas created the role of Marie Antoinette in *The Ghosts of Versailles* in 1991 and celebrated 35 years on the Met stage when she opened the 1994-1995 season. Stratas began making films as early as 1970 including a number of operettas. Her amazing acting ability is notable in Zeffirelli's film of *La Traviata* and Friedrich's film of *Salome*. See AMAHL AND THE NIGHT VISITORS (1979), THE BARTERED BRIDE (1975/1978), LA BOHÈME (1982), COSÌ FAN TUTTE (1988), EUGENE ONEGIN (1968), THE GHOSTS OF VERSAILLES (1992), GIUDITTA (1972), METROPOLITAN OPERA (1986), PAGANINI (1973), PAGLIACCI (1978/ 1982/ 1994), RISE AND FALL OF THE CITY OF MAHAGONNY (1979), LA RONDINE (1970), SALOME (1974), THE SEVEN DEADLY SINS (1993), IL TABARRO (1994), LA TRAVIATA (1982), KURT WEILL (1994), DER ZAREWITSCH (1973).

1961 The Canadians
Teresa Stratas' first movie was this American-style Canadian Western. The plot is basically just pitting the Mounties against the Sioux. Robert Ryan and John Dehner are the stars and Burt Kennedy directed. Color. 85 minutes.

1983 Stratosphere: A Portrait of Teresa Stratas
Harry Rasky's excellent documentary surveys the life and career of the singer. In it she talks candidly about her early life in Toronto, her ties to her Crete heritage and her rise to success. The film includes archival footage of rehearsals with Franco Zeffirelli at the Metropolitan Opera and clips from performances of *Salome*, *Der Zarewitsch* and *La Bohème*. Stratas's quality both as singer and actress is amply demonstrated. CBC. Color. In English. 90 minutes. Kultur video.

STRAUS, OSCAR
Austrian composer (1870-1954)

Oscar Straus wrote cheerful, enjoyable operettas in the Viennese style that remain surprisingly popular. They have also attracted great interest from opera singers though they have not really entered the opera house repertory. Straus was born in Vienna and wrote his operettas in German but he had some of his biggest successes in translations. *Der Tapfer Soldat*, based on Shaw's play *Arms and the Man*, was a major hit in New York in its English-language version as *The Chocolate Soldier*. *Drei Wälzer* had its greatest success in Paris in its French incarnation as *Les Trois Valses*. *Hochzeit in Hollywood* was the first European operetta made into a sound film in Hollywood and was a hit as *Married in Hollywood*. *Ein Frau, di Weiss, Was sie Will* was popular on stage in London as *Mother of Pearl*. Straus, who settled in Hollywood for a time, also composed music for films and had a surprise hit at the age of 80 with his theme tune for the 1950 film *La Ronde*. See THE CHOCOLATE SOLDIER, HOCHZEIT IN HOLLYWOOD, DER LETZTE WALZER, RICHARD TAUBER (1936), LES TROIS VALSES, EIN WALZERTRAUM, A WOMAN WHO KNOWS WHAT SHE WANTS.

1950 La Ronde
Straus once again became popular all over the world with his memorable theme music for this superb Max Ophuls film. Based on an Arthur Schnitzler play, it's a cynical story about the way love (and sex) goes around in a circle. The all-star cast includes Anton Walbrook (who plays many roles and sings the theme tune), Isa Miranda and Simone Signoret. Straus wrote the music when he was 80. Black and white. In French. 97 minutes.

STRAUSS, JOHANN
Austrian composer (1825-1899)

Waltz King Johann Strauss Jr. is also the king of the Viennese operetta as *Die Fledermaus* is now welcome in most of the great opera houses of the world. There are few more enjoyable experiences than a really good *Fledermaus*, especially with the accepted practice of stars appearing as guests in the Act Two party scene. Equally admirable though not as well known is *The Gypsy Baron* which became a role model for operetta writers. Strauss wrote sixteen operettas and established the form of the Viennese operetta. There is also the popular *Wiener Blut*, which is a pastiche operetta of Strauss melodies. Strauss and his father, who together created the waltz as we know it, have been the subject of many films. The major ones are listed here though none are genuine biography. See DIE FLEDERMAUS, EINE NACHT IN VENEDIG, OPERETTE, LES TROIS VALSES, WIENER BLUT, DER ZIGEUNERBARON.

1925 Ein Walzer vom Strauss
A Waltz From Strauss is an Austrian film, the first major film biography of the Waltz King. Johann Strauss, the nephew of the composer, portrays his uncle in the film. He also conducted the orchestra which played Strauss melodies at the premieres in Vienna and London. Max Neufeld directed and Otto Kreisler supervised the film for Helios Film. Black and white. In German. About 70 minutes.

1929 Heut spielt der Strauss
Strauss, the Waltz King is a German film starring Imre Raday as Johann Strauss. The plot is based around the rivalry between father and son and the eventual triumph of young Strauss, the basic plot of most Strauss film biographies. The cast includes Alfred Abel as Strauss Sr., Hermine Sterler and Lillian Ellis. Robert Wiene wrote and Conrad Wiene directed the film. Black and white. In German. 84 minutes.

1930 Der Walzerkönig
The Waltz King is a German film biography starring Hans Stuwe as Johann Strauss II. The cast includes Claire Rommer, Ida Wust and Viktor Janson. Manfred Noa directed. Black and white. In German. 88 minutes.

1931 A Waltz From Strauss
Gustav Frölich portrays Johann Strauss in the German film *So Lang noch ein Walzer vom Strauss Erklingt* called simply *A Waltz from Strauss* in English. Hans Junkermann portrays the father who attempts to stop his son from following in his waltzing footsteps. Julia Serda is mother Strauss with Maria Paudler as his young sweetheart. Conrad Wiene directed. Black and white. In German. 88 minutes.

1932 Wiener Blut
This is not the operetta but the English title of a German film biography. It stars Metropolitan Opera bass-baritone Michael Bohnen as Strauss with a score based on waltzes like "Wiener Blut." The cast includes Gretl Theimer, Lee Parry and Paul Hörbiger. Conrad Wiene directed. The German title is *Johann Strauss, K. und K. Hofballmusikdirektor*. Black and white. In German. 99 minutes.

1934 Waltzes From Vienna
Esmond Knight stars as Strauss in this Alfred Hitchcock film of a 1931 London stage musical. It is based on the 1930 Vienna pastiche operetta *Walzer aus Wien* created by Erich Wolfgang Korngold before he went to Hollywood. It tells the traditional story of a Strauss father-son musical feud with young Strauss being helped to fame by Resi (Jessie Mathews) and Countess Baranskaja (Fay Compton). It was shown in the U.S. as *Strauss's Great Waltz*. Gaumont-British. Black and white. In English. 81 minutes.

1938 The Great Waltz
The London stage musical *Waltzes from Vienna* came to Broadway in 1934 in a revision by Moss Hart called *The Great Waltz*. MGM turned it into a film in 1938 with Fernand Gravet as Strauss, Polish soprano Miliza Korjus as Imperial Opera star Carla Donner and baritone George Houston as Imperial Opera star Fritz Schiller. Julien Duvivier directed this lavish production. Strauss loves Korjus but marries sweetheart Louise Rainer on the rebound. Korjus sings the waltz that get him a publisher and persuades him to write an operetta but faithful wife Rainer wins out in the end. The film won an Academy Award for its waltzing cinematography by Joseph Ruttenberg. Black and white. In English. 100 minutes. On video.

1938 Unsterbliche Melodien
The Austrian film *Unsterbliche Melodien* (Immortal Melodies) stars Alfred Jerger as Johann Strauss in a romantic film with plenty of waltzes and love interest. Lizzi Holschuh and Maria Paudler play the women who love him. The music is performed by the Vienna Philharmonic. Helen Moja wrote the screenplay and Heinz Paul directed. Black and white. In German. 90 minutes. 72 minutes.

1953 Johann Mouse
This delightful Tom and Jerry cartoon is about a musical mouse who lives in the house of Johann Strauss and is as fond of waltzes as the composer. It won the Best Cartoon Oscar for Hanna-Barbera. Color. 7 minutes.

1954 Eternal Waltz
Ewiger Walzer is an Austrian/German film, the romantic story of the loves and music of Strauss as portrayed by Bernhard Wicki. Much of it is concerned with his affair with singer Henriette Treffz played by Hilde Krahl. There are quite good re-creations of his operas on stage including his rarely seen first attempt, *Indigo*. Annemarie Düringer is Adele, Friedl Loor is Maria Geistinger, Gert Frobe is Gawrinoff and Jacques Offenbach is

Arnulf Schröder. Paul Verhoeven directed. Color. In German. 99 minutes. Toppic (Germany)/Video Yesteryear video.

1955 The Great Waltz
Patrice Munsel stars as Resi with Jarmila Novotna as Madame Baronska in this excellent television production by Max Liebman. Keith Andes is Strauss Henry Sharp is his father. and Bert Lahr is Bert Ebertede. Frederick Fox designed the sets and Charles Sanford was musical director. It was telecast on NBC on Nov. 5, 1955. Black and white. In English. 79 minutes. VAI video.

1961 Wien Tanzt
Vienna Waltzes is an Austrian film about the rise to fame of Johann Strauss the father with Anton Walbrook plaing the famous waltz composer. It includes the traditional rivalry and reconciliation with his son and music by both Strausses is used. Emile Edwin Reinert directed. Black and white. In German. 90 minutes.

1963 The Waltz King
Kerwin Mathews portrays Strauss with Brian Aherne as his father in this romantic Disney film directed by Steve Previn. Senta Berger is Strauss's love Jetty Treffz. It was shot in Germany and first shown in the US on television. Color. In English. 95 minutes.

1972 The Great Waltz
Horst Bucholz plays Strauss in this second MGM version of the story. Opera diva Mary Costa co-stars as opera singer Jetty Treffz, does most of the singing and encourages him to write operettas. The plots get revised but the music stays the same. Nigel Patrick portrays Strauss Sr. while Rossano Brazzi is a jealous Baron. Andrew Stone directed. Color. In English. 134 minutes. Opera Dubs video.

1972 The Strauss Family
A grand old style television mini-series from England devoted to the lives, ladies and conflicts of the Strauss dynasty. Eric Woofe is Johann Sr., Stuart Wilson is Johann Jr., Nicolas Simmonds is Josef Strauss, Derek Jacobi is Josef Lanner, Anne Stallybrass is Anna, Barbara Ferris is Emilie, Margaret Whiting is Hetti and Georgina Hale is Lili. David Reid produced, Anthony Skene wrote the screenplay and David Giles directed for ATV in Birmingham. The music is played by the London Symphony Orchestra conducted by Cyril Ornadel. Color. In English. 450 minutes.

1987 Johann Strauss - Der König ohne Krone
Johann Strauss: King without a Crown is an Austrian movie relating the life of Johann Jr. in flashback as imagined in a book written by Frédéric Morton. The film revolves around his music but focuses on love affairs with Olga in Moscow, Yvonne in Paris, Marie in Vienna and true love Adele. Oliver Tobias portrays Strauss with Zsa Zsa Gabor as his aunt Amalie. Franz Antel directed. It has been shown on American television. Color. In German. 124 minutes.

1996 Strauss: The King of Three-Quarter Time
Michael Riley stars as Strauss Jr. In this Canadian video biography aimed at young television viewers. Like the others in the *Composers Series* videos made by Devine Entertainment, it was shot in Central Europe and features a young person as a friend of the composer, in this case Derek Senft. The main musical theme of the bio is "Tales from the Vienna Woods." Color. In English. 50 minutes. Sony Classical video.

STRAUSS, RICHARD
German composer (1864-1949)

Richard Strauss is the most successful modern opera composer in terms of critical appreciation and audience acceptance. Of the fifteen operas he composed, ten have found a place in the international repertory. Strauss (who is not related to Johann) acquired fame and notoriety in 1905 through his scandal-creating operatic version of Oscar Wilde's infamous play *Salome* and there were a large number of early film versions to help spread the scandal. His collaboration with playwright Hugo von Hofmannsthal began in 1905 with *Electra* and resulted in some of the most popular and adventurous operas of the century including the classic *Der Rosenkavalier*. Strauss's work is well represented on video. See ARABELLA, ARIADNE AUF NAXOS, CAPRICCIO, ELEKTRA, DIE FRAU OHNE SCHATTEN, INTERMEZZO, DER ROSENKAVALIER, SALOME.

1970 The Dance of the Seven Veils
Ken Russell's controversial film, subtitled *A Comic Strip in Seven Episodes about Richard Strauss*, was made for the BBC television series *Omnibus*. It's based on a book by American George Marek that stresses the composer's relationship with the Nazis

and is a kind of satirical comic strip. Christopher Gable, Judith Paris and Vladek Sheybal are the principal actors with Imogen Claire seen as Salome. The film was telecast on Feb. 15, 1970, and caused such controversy that another program favorable to Strauss was presented as a balance. Strauss's son threatened to sue Russell over the "slanderous" portrayal of his father and the film was not shown again.

1984 Richard Strauss Remembered

This is a film portrait of the composer as seen through the eyes of his family and friends. Peter Adam, who wrote and directed it, filmed in the places where Strauss lived and performed and uses his letters and diaries as narration. There are extracts from operas, photographs, archival film and home movies. The interviewees include Sir John Gielgud, Frank Finlay, Sir George Solti and Herbert von Karajan. Blackford Carrington produced the film for BBC TV. Color. In English. 120 minutes.

STRAVINSKY, IGOR

Russian-born composer (1882-1971)

Igor Stravinsky composed unusual operas which broke the boundaries of what operas were expected to be and obviously influenced post-modern American opera composers like Robert Ashley. Many of his theater pieces are non-traditional halfway operas. *The Soldier's Tale*, for example, can be seen as an acted and narrated ballet-opera while *Oedipus Rex* is an oratorio-opera. All of them are full of ritual and magic and ideas derived from his revolutionary modern ballets. His internationalism is important because as he moved across borders he introduced Russian rhythms to western Europe and the USA. He composed specifically for the screen with the 1962 television opera *The Flood* and his music has been used to great effect in films from *Fantasia* to *La Belle Noiseuse*. See THE FLOOD, THE NIGHTINGALE, OEDIPUS REX, THE RAKE'S PROGRESS, THE SOLDIER'S TALE.

1958 Igor Stravinsky

This is an NBC film of an interview with the composer which was made available in the university *Wisdom Series*. Black and white. In English. 30 minutes.

1965 Stravinsky

This is an informal biography of the composer made by Roman Kroiter and Wolf Koenig for the National Film Board of Canada. Black and white. In English. 50 minutes.

1965 Stravinsky

This film profile of Stravinsky shows him conducting, visiting fellow artists and working on a project with choreographer George Balanchine. Charles Kuralt narrates the film. Black and white. 43 minutes. Carousel video.

1966 Stravinsky

This is a personal view of the composer as he reminiscences about the past and makes plans for the future. There are excerpts from new and old compositions. The film was made for a CBS News Special and telecast on May 3, 1966. Black and white. 60 minutes. Video at LOC.

1968 A Stravinsky Portrait

Richard Leacock directed, photographed and edited this film with help from Rolf Liebermann. It shows Stravinsky with wife and friends at his Beverly Hills home, conducting the West German Symphony Orchestra, discussing his work with colleagues and being interviewed. Appearing in the film are Pierre Boulez, George Balanchine and Christopher Isherwood. Black and white. 57 minutes. On video.

1982 "Once, at a border..." Aspects of Stravinsky

Tony Palmer's 100th anniversary film about Stravinsky's life and music was shown on television in three segments. Part One tells of the composer's life and career in Russia, Part Two is set in Western Europe and Part Three shows his life in America. The film includes documents, photographs, extracts from others films and musical performances plus appearances by Robert Craft, Marie Rambert, George Balanchine and Nadia Boulanger. The London Sinfonietta is the chief orchestra performing the music. LWT. Color and black & white. 166 minutes. Kultur video.

1982 America Celebrates Stravinsky

The 100th anniversary of the composer's birth is celebrated with a concert at the National Cathedral in Washington. Leonard Bernstein and Michael Tilson Thomas lead the National Symphony Orchestra in a program of non-operatic music. The video includes a documentary showing Stravinsky conducting. Humphrey Burton directed the telecast in 1982. Color. 90 minutes.

STREET SCENE
1947 American opera by Weill

Kurt Weill considered his "American opera" *Street Scene* to be his masterpiece. It's based on a Pulitzer Prize winning play by Elmer Rice and tells the story of 24 hours in the life of a group of people in a Manhattan tenement on a sweltering summer day. The loose plot revolves around Anna, who is killed by her jealous husband Frank, and their daughter Rose, who is loved by Sam. Rice wrote the libretto in collaboration with poet Langston Hughes. See also KURT WEILL.

1979 New York City Opera
Catherine Malfitano portrays Rose in this splendid New York City Opera production. Eileen Schauler is Anna, William Chapman is Frank, Harlan Foss is Harry and Alan Kays is Sam. John Mauceri conducts the New York City Opera Orchestra and Chorus. Beverly Sills interviews Lotte Lenya during the intermission. Kirk Browning directed the video which was telecast on Oct. 27, 1979, in the *Live from Lincoln Center* series. Color. In English. 180 minutes.

STREHLER, GIORGIO
Italian opera director (1921-)

Italian stage director Giorgio Strehler, famous for his influential theater productions with the Piccolo Teatro of Milan, was also a major opera producer at La Scala, Salzburg and Paris. After beginning in 1947 with *La Traviata*, he staged widely admired productions of *The Threepenny Opera*, *Simon Boccanegra*, *The Abduction from the Seraglio*, *Macbeth*, *Cavalleria Rusticana* and *The Magic Flute*. Although he did not make opera films, there are films and videos of many of his stage productions. See *The Abduction from the Seraglio* (1984), *Cavalleria Rusticana* (1968), *The Magic Flute* (1975 film), *The Marriage of Figaro* (1980), *Simon Boccanegra* (1978), *The Threepenny Opera* (1972).

1971 Giorgio Strehler Rehearses *Abduction from the Seraglio*
Strehler is shown at work in this documentary staging The *Abduction from the Seraglio*, a famous production that was originally created for the Salzburg Festival in 1965. It was hugely influential and featured radical *commedia dell'arte* ideas and memorable shadow-type silhouettes. Norbert

Beilharz directed the documentary for SDR television in Germany. Color. In German. 60 minutes.

STROYEVA, VERA
Russian opera film director (1903- ?)

Vera Stroyeva was a leading figure in the Soviet cinema from 1927, writing, directing and often working with her director husband Grigori Roshal. In the 1950s she turned to opera and dance films and made two of the more important movies in the genre as well as a concert film at the Bolshoi. See BOLSHOI OPERA (1951), BORIS GODUNOV (1954), KHOVANSHCHINA (1959).

STUDENT PRINCE, THE
1924 operetta by Romberg

Sigmund Romberg's operetta *The Student Prince in Heidelberg*, libretto by Dorothy Donnelly, is based on the 1902 German play *Alt Heidelberg* by Wilhelm Meyer-Forster. It tells the story of German Prince Karl-Franz, the heir to the throne, and his bittersweet romance with the innkeeper's daughter Kathie while at university in Heidelberg. In the end they know that it is his duty to marry Princess Margaret. The songs include "Deep in My Heart," "Serenade" and "The Drinking Song." See also SIGMUND ROMBERG.

1927 Ernst Lubitsch film
Ernst Lubitsch's silent version of the operetta, *The Student Prince in Old Heidelberg*, is outstanding even without the songs but as a visual rather than a vocal masterpiece. Ramon Novarro stars as Prince Karl Heinrich with Norma Shearer as the waitress Kathi who fascinates him. Lubitsch expanded the story to include the early years of the prince before he goes to university. Hans Kraly wrote the screenplay and John Mescall photographed it. The film was screened with a score by David Mendoza and William Axt and is on video with orchestral soundtrack. Black and white. 107 minutes. MGM/UA video.

1954 Mario Lanza film
Edmund Purdom stars as the Student Prince but he sings with Mario Lanza's voice in this musical version of the operetta. Lanza had already recorded the soundtrack when he left MGM so the studio hired Purdom to replace him on screen and dubbed in the songs. The voice alone was enough to make

the film a box-office hit. Ann Blyth is the barmaid he loves. Richard Thorpe directed. Color. 107 minutes. MGM/UA video.

Related films

1915 Wallace Reid

Wallace Reid stars as the student prince in *Old Heidelberg,* an American film based on the source play and made before the operetta. Dorothy Gish portrays Kathie with Erick Von Stroheim as Lutz. D. W. Griffith supervised and John Emerson directed and wrote the screenplay. Black and white. About 70 minutes.

1923 Paul Hartmann film

Paul Hartmann stars as the student prince in *Alt-Heidelberg,* a German film based on the source play directed by Hans Behrendt. Werner Krauss has a supporting role. Black and white. In German. About 70 minutes.

1959 Christian Wolff film

Christian Wolff stars as the prince in *Alt-Heidelberg,* a German film based on the play by Wilhelm Meyer-Förster. The cast includes Gert Grobe and Sabine Sinjen. Ernst Marischka directed. Color. In German. 105 minutes.

STUDER, CHERYL
American soprano (1955-)

Cheryl Studer was born in Michigan but prepared for her opera career in Vienna and made her debut in Munich in 1980. She has sung in most of the major opera houses in Europe and America in a wide range of roles from Verdi to Wagner and much of her work is available on video. She has won wide acclaim as one of the finest sopranos of her generation. See AIDA (1994), ATTILA (1991), MONTSERRAT CABALLÉ (1993), ELEKTRA (1989), DIE FRAU OHNE SCHATTEN (1992), LOHENGRIN (1990/1990), THE MARRIAGE OF FIGARO (1992), METROPOLITAN OPERA (1991), TANNHÄUSER (1990), I VESPRI SICILIANI (1990), WILLIAM TELL (1991).

STURRIDGE, CHARLES
English film director (1951-)

Charles Sturridge is best known internationally for his Evelyn Waugh adaptations, the television series *Brideshead Revisited* and the film *A Handful of Dust.*

He also directed the black-and-white *La Forza del Destino* episode of the collective film *Aria* and featured an excellent opera scene built around *Lucia Di Lammermoor* in his E. M. Forster film *Where Angels Fear to Tread* (1991). See LA FORZA DEL DESTINO (1987 film), LUCIA DI LAMMERMOOR (1991).

SULLIVAN, ARTHUR
See GILBERT AND SULLIVAN

SUMMER AND SMOKE
1971 opera by Hoiby

Composer Lee Hoiby and librettist Lanford Wilson's *Summer and Smoke* is based on a play by Tennessee Williams. It tells the story of the sexually repressed Southern minister's daughter Alma Winemiller who is unable to admit her love for doctor John Buchanan until it is too late. The title comes from the description of Alma as "suffocated in smoke from something on fire inside her." The opera, the first based on a Williams play, was commissioned and premiered by the St. Paul Opera company. See also LEE HOIBY.

1982 Chicago Opera Theater

Kirk Browning directed this national telecast of the opera based on a notable 1980 Chicago Opera Theatre production. Browning brought the Chicago Opera Theater into the studio to maintain the Williams atmosphere. The opera was telecast on PBS in June 1982. Color. In English. 90 minutes. Video at New York Public Library

SUOR ANGELICA
1918 one-act opera by Puccini

Sister Angelica is the second opera in Puccini's triple-bill *Il Trittico* which premiered at the Metropolitan Opera in 1918. The libretto by Gioacchino Forzano tells the story of Sister Angelica, a nun in 17th century Tuscany who was forced to give up her illegitimate child by her aristocratic family and enter a convent. Her aunt, a princess, comes to ask her to give up her inheritance and tell her the child is dead. Sister Angelica takes poison but the Madonna appears with the child to show her forgiveness. All the roles in the opera are women. See also GIACOMO PUCCINI.

1953 NBC Opera Theatre

Elaine Malbin stars as Sister Angelica with Winifred Heidt as her aunt in this NBC Opera Theatre production by Samuel Chotzinoff. It was sung in English and titled *Sister Angelica*. Townsend Brewster made the translation and Peter Herman Adler conducted the Symphony of the Air Orchestra. Kirk Browning directed the live telecast on March 7, 1953. Malbin also starred when the opera was repeated by NBC Opera Theatre in December 1954. Black and white. In English. 60 minutes. Video at MTR.

1981 Metropolitan Opera

Renata Scotto portrays the ill-fated Sister Angelica in this Metropolitan Opera production by Fabrizio Melano. Jocelyne Taillon is the Princess and Jean Kraft is the Abbess. David Reppa created the set designs and James Levine conducted the Metropolitan Orchestra. Kirk Browning directed the live performance which was telecast on Nov. 14 as part of *Il Trittico*. Color. 55 minutes. In Italian with English subtitles. Video at MTR.

1983 Teatro alla Scala

Rosalind Plowright stars as Sister Angelica with Dunja Vejzovich as the nasty Princess in this La Scala production by Silvano Bussoti. Gianandrea Gavazzeni conducted the La Scala Orchestra and Chorus. Brian Large directed the video of a live performance. Color. In Italian with English subtitles. 55 minutes. Home Vision video (with *Il Trittico*).

SUPERVIA, CONCHITA
Spanish mezzo-soprano (1895-1936)

Conchita Supervia was renowned for her vivacious personality but famous for singing Carmen and Rosina. She was born in Barcelona and began her stage career with a Spanish company in Argentina. She sang Octavian in *Der Rosenkavalier* in Rome in 1911, made her American debut in Chicago in 1915 and became a regular at La Scala In the 1920s. Her greatest fame came in the last decade of her life. She was living in London and singing at Covent Garden in 1934 when she appeared in her only film, *Melba*. She died tragically in childbirth in 1936 but was able to leave a notable recording legacy.

1934 Evensong

Evensong is a British film based on a novel by Beverly Nichols, Nellie Melba's private secretary.

Evelyn Laye stars as opera diva Irela while Supervia portrays Baba L'Etoile, a singer who challenges her stardom. Supervia performs the role of Musetta in *La Bohème* and is shown singing the famous aria "Quando me'n vo' soletta". Victor Saville directed. Gaumont-British. Black and white. 83 minutes. Lyric video.

SUPPÉ, FRANZ VON
Austrian composer (1819-1895)

Franz von Suppé is the father of the Viennese operetta and the predecessor of Strauss though he is now known primarily for his overtures. Admirers of the *Light Cavalry* and *Poet and Peasant* overtures are often surprised to learn they came from operettas staged in 1846 and 1866. Suppé, who began writing for the stage in 1841, was also an opera singer and conductor. His most popular operettas, and the best remembered, are *Die Schöne Galathee*, *Fatinitza* and *Boccaccio*. The diminished popularity of his operettas is reflected in a scarcity of videos. See BOCCACCIO, OPERETTE, DIE SCHÖNE GALATHÉE.

SUSA, CONRAD
American composer (1935-)

Conrad Susa has composed four operas and over a hundred scores for film, theater and television. His first opera *Transformations* (1973) is a setting of poems from the Anne Sexton book in which she retells fairy tales. It has been videotaped. *Black River* (1975) is based on Michael Lesy's powerful book *Wisconsin Death Trip*. More traditional is *The Love of Don Perlimpli* (1984) adapted from a play by Lorca and inspired by the music of Scarlatti. Susa's major achievement is *The Dangerous Liaisons* (1994), based on the epistolary novel by Pierre Choderlos de Laclos. It premiered at the San Francisco Opera where it was well received. See THE DANGEROUS LIAISONS.

1977 Transformations

Susa's 1973 opera, based on fairy tale poems by Anne Sexton, was given an experimental production by the Minnesota Opera in 1977 and then videotaped with reportedly inventive camera work. Robert Israel created the set designs. The video was shown at a TV Opera Colloquium in 1978 sponsored by the National Opera Institute. Color. 50 minutes.

SUSANNAH

1955 opera by Floyd

Carlisle Floyd's opera has claims to being the most performed and thus most popular American opera. There have been an estimated 200 productions since 1956, including four at the New York City Opera and a 1993 revival by the Chicago Lyric. Floyd's libretto is based on the Biblical story of Susanna and the Elders transposed to the mountains of Tennessee. After being condemned by the Church Elders who catch Susannah bathing, she is seduced by the preacher Blitch. When her brother Sam learns this, he shoots Blitch. The opera has square dance music, hymns and folk songs composed by Floyd. A CD version was recorded in France by the Lyons Opera with Cheryl Studer as Susannah and Samuel Ramey as Blitch but strangely there is as yet no professional video. See also CARLISLE FLOYD.

1979 Indiana Opera Theater

Jean Herzberg stars as Susannah in this performance by the Indiana Opera Theater taped live at the Musical Arts Center in Bloomington. William Parcher sings the role of Blitch, Jon Fay is Sam and Neil Jones is Little Bat. Brian Falkwill conducted the orchestra, Allan Ross directed the stage production and Mickey Klein directed the video for WTIV Television. Color. 90 minutes. Video at MTR.

1986 Chicago Opera Theater

The only readily available video of the opera is this low quality non-professional tape of a Chicago Opera Theater production shot from a balcony at a staged rehearsal. The singers are called Callahan, Bean and Stolze and the conductor is Larsen. It's interesting but hard to watch; the CD is much better. Black and white. 86 minutes. Opera Dubs video.

SUTERMEISTER, HEINRICH

Swiss composer (1910-)

Heinrich Sutermeister seems to have found the TV opera particularly suitable to his dramatic and musical concerns as he composed four operas for television. His best known stage opera is the 1940 Shakespeare adaptation *Romeo und Julia*. His TV operas, like his stage works, tend to have a literary basis.

1959 Seraphine

Sutermeister's television opera *Seraphine* is based on a story by Rabelais. It was telecast on Swiss Television on June 10, 1959 and staged the following year in Munich.

1962 Das Gespenst Von Canterville

Sutermeister's best known television opera, *The Canterville Ghost*, is based on a famous story by Oscar Wilde. It was telecast by ZDF on Sept. 6, 1962, and won the Salzburg Prize for best TV opera. The Wilde story was the basis of a Charles Laughton film in 1943, a Richard Kiley TV film in 1985 and a John Gielgud television movie in 1986.

1969 La Croisade des Enfants

The Children's Crusade was the composer's third television opera. It was commissioned by Swiss television and telecast in 1969.

1971 Das Flaschenteufel

Sutermeister's *The Bottle Imp* is a TV opera based on a famous short story by Robert Louis Stevenson with a libretto by R. K. Weibel. It was telecast by ZDF in 1971.

SUTHERLAND, JOAN

Australian soprano (1926-)

Dame Joan Sutherland has an extraordinarily beautiful voice which is well suited for *bel canto* roles but she is a delight in almost everything. She was born in Sydney and made her debut in 1947 as Purcell's Dido. She joined the Royal Opera House in London in 1952 and made her debut as the First Lady in *The Magic Flute*. She married conductor Richard Bonynge in 1954 and together they developed her *bel canto* repertoire culminating in her 1959 Covent Garden *Lucia di Lammermoor*. After Italian critics dubbed her "La Stupenda," she took her Lucia to Paris, La Scala and the Met and quickly became the reigning opera diva. She retired from the stage in 1990 but left a formidable legacy of recordings and videos. See ADRIANA LECOUVREUR (1984), ANNA BOLENA (1985), BELL TELEPHONE HOUR (1967/1968), THE DAUGHTER OF THE REGIMENT (1972/1986), LES DIALOGUES DES CARMÉLITES (1985), DON GIOVANNI (1978), FAUST (1973), DIE FLEDERMAUS (1982/1990), MARILYN HORNE (1981/1985), LES HUGUENOTS (1990), LAKMÉ (1976), LUCIA DI LAMMERMOOR (1973/1982/1986), LUCREZIA BORGIA (1977), THE MARRIAGE OF FIGARO (1972), THE MERRY WIDOW (1988), METROPOLITAN OPERA (1972/1983/

1986), MIGNON (1973), NORMA (1978), I PURITANI (1985), RIGOLETTO (1973), SEMIRAMIDE (1986), LA TRAVIATA (1973), IL TROVATORE (1983).

1963 Presenting Joan Sutherland
Sutherland is at her best on a *Voice of Firestone* TV show on April 21, 1963. She sings the arias "The Soldier Tir'd" from Arne's *Artaxerses*, "Bel raggio lusinghieri" from Rossini's *Semiramide*, "Donde lieta usci" from *La Bohème* and "O beau pays" from *Les Huguenots*. Richard Bonynge conducts the orchestra. Black and white. In English. 26 minutes. VAI video.

1963 Joan Sutherland Show
This Australian film is a showcase for the soprano. She performs arias from *Les Huguenots, La Traviata* and *Lucia di Lammermoor* and is joined on a duet by Margreta Elkins. Michael Denison introduces the music and Richard Bonynge conducts the London Symphony Orchestra. Peter Bernardos directed. Black and white. 60 minutes. Video at MTR and film at NFTA.

1963 Bell Telephone Hour
Sutherland appeared on this NBC television program on Feb. 11, 1963. She is seen singing "Casta Diva" from *Norma*. Sid Smith directs. Color. 60 minutes. Video at MTR.

1964 Joan Sutherland: La Prima Donna
Sutherland gives a concert for Canadian television with the Toronto Radio-Canada Orchestra conducted by Richard Bonynge. The program includes arias by Bellini, Rossini, Donizetti and Verdi. Franz Kraemer directed the video. Color. 60 minutes.

1965 An Hour with Joan Sutherland
Terry McEwen talks to Sutherland and her husband about her career in this homage. Sutherland sings arias by Handel, Paisello and Rossini plus Benedict's "The Gypsy and the Bird," joins in a duet from *Semiramide* with Marilyn Horne and a duet from *I Puritani* with John Alexander. Kirk Browning directed. Black and white. 60 minutes. Video at MTR.

1972/73 Who's Afraid of Opera? series
Sutherland stars in highlight versions of operas for young audiences, telling the story to puppets and performing the leading role. The operas are *The Barber of Seville, Daughter of the Regiment, Faust, Lucia*

di Lammermoor, Mignon, La Périchole, Rigoletto and *La Traviata*. George Djurkovic designed the sets and Richard Bonynge conducts the London Symphony Orchestra. Color. Each 30 minutes. Kultur Video.

1979 Joan Sutherland: A Life on the Move
Brian Adams spent a full year following Sutherland around the world for this documentary film about life. It traces her career from her early years in Sydney through her success in London to international stardom She is seen in rehearsal and performance at the Met and other opera houses. The film, made for Australian television, was first telecast in August 1979. Color. In English. 80 minutes.

1982 Joan Sutherland In Concert
This was the first recital Sutherland allowed to be televised live and it shows her in concert at the Perth Concert Hall in Australia on March 9, 1982. She performs arias from *La Traviata, Alcina, La Petite Bohèmienne, Semiramide* and *Les Huguenots* plus a selection of songs. Richard Bonynge accompanies her and Philip Booth directed the video. Color. 49 minutes. Kultur video.

1987 An Evening with Sutherland & Pavarotti
Sutherland and Luciano Pavarotti star in staged productions of scenes from three operas at this Metropolitan Opera gala. *La Traviata* (Act II) includes Leo Nucci as Germont and was staged by David Kneuss. The *Lucia di Lammermoor* scenes have Ariel Bybee as Alisa and Julien Robbins as Raimondo and were staged by David Kneuss. *Rigoletto* (Act III) features Leo Nucci as Rigoletto, Isola Jones as Maddalena and Ferruccio Furlanetto as Sparafucile and was staged by David Sell. Richard Bonynge conducts the Metropolitan Opera Orchestra. Kirk Browning directed the video on Jan. 11 telecast on March 4 as *The Sutherland/ Pavarotti Anniversary Gala*. Color. In Italian with English subtitles. 115 minutes. DG video/laser.

1991 La Stupenda
Subtitled *A Portrait of Dame Joan Sutherland*, this is the best biography of Sutherland, intelligently written and directed by Derek Bailey and narrated by Humphrey Burton. It traces Sutherland's career from its beginnings through to her rise to stardom at Covent Garden. There are many performance extracts including her fine *Lucia di Lammermoor*. Sutherland and husband Richard Bonynge talk about her singing and there are informative

interviews with Franco Zeffirelli and other associates. Color. 88 minutes. London video.

1993 The Essential Sutherland
This is an anthology of highlights from twelve Sutherland operas filmed at the Sydney Opera House by the Australian Broadcasting Corporation plus a scene with Marilyn Horne and Luciano Pavarotti in *Die Fledermaus* at Covent Garden. The operas are *Norma, Lucia di Lammermoor, Lucrezia Borgia, Daughter of the Regiment, Lakmé, Adriana Lecouvreur, Semiramide, La Traviata, Il Trovatore, The Merry Widow, Les Dialogues des Carmélites* and *Les Huguenots*. The excerpts are introduced by Sutherland and Richard Bonynge. Color. 116 minutes. On video.

1995 Dave and Dad On Our Selection
Sutherland portrays Mother Rudd with Leo McKern as her husband in this film based on Steele Rudd's stories of his family's hard life on their selection (farm) in Queensland. George Whaley wrote and directed Sutherland's first film as a non-singing actress and she received warm reviews as the tower of strength mother around whom the family revolves. Color. 105 minutes.

SWANN, CHRISTOPHER
English TV opera director

Christopher Swann has directed a large number of telecasts and videos of operas from Glyndebourne as well as films about Glyndebourne's history and its closing and reopening. He has also directed videos of concert stagings of Bernstein musicals in London with opera singers as well as notable operas at La Scala. See ATTILA (1991), GLYNDEBOURNE (1992/1994), HIGGLETY PIGGLETY POP! (1985), IDOMENEO (1983), ON THE TOWN (1992), LUCIANO PAVAROTTI (1991), I VESPRI SICILIANI (1990), WEST SIDE STORY (1985), WHERE THE WILD THINGS ARE (1985).

SWARTHOUT, GLADYS
American contralto (1900-1969)

Gladys Swarthout made her debut with the Chicago Civic Opera in 1924 in *Tosca*. She sang *La Gioconda* at the Metropolitan in 1929 and continued to appear there until 1945. Her most famous roles were Carmen and Mignon but she also sang in the premiere of Howard Hanson's neglected *Merry Mount*. In 1950 she starred in a CBS Televison production of *Carmen* and then, after a period on the concert circuit, she retired to Florence in 1954. Swarthout starred in five movies for Paramount in the 1930s during the cinematic opera boom. None of them used her talent properly and they were probably not helpful to her opera career. However, because of them she can still be seen performing today. She published her autobiography *Come Soon, Tomorrow* in 1945. See also CARMEN (1950).

1935 Rose of the Rancho
Swarthout's first film was a musical western with John Boles set in California in 1852. It's a *Mark of Zorro* variation with Swarthout as the masked mystery person who leads the ranchers against the villains. She sings to alert her followers to assemble and even dances on Boles' sombrero. Justice and true love triumph in the end. Marion Gering directed. Paramount. Black and white. 85 minutes.

1936 Give Us This Night
Swarthout stars opposite tenor Jan Kiepura in this operatic story. An off-key Italian tenor is pelted with eggs while singing *Il Trovatore* so fisherman Kiepura shows the audience how the aria should be sung. Later opera diva Swarthout refuses to sing with the ungifted Italian when proves himself once again inadequate at rehearsals of a new opera (written for the film by Eric Wolfgang Korngold). Kiepura is chosen to join her in the premiere of Korngold's *Romeo and Juliet*. They also have a chance to sing a duet from *Tosca*. Alexander Hall directed. Paramount. Black and white. 70 minutes.

1937 Champagne Waltz
Swarthout plays a Strauss named Elsa in this film set in Vienna. It concerns the rivalry between the Vienna Waltz Palace and the jazz club next door. Swarthout is romanced by jazzman Fred MacMurray and takes him to the waltz palace where they imagine its heyday when the "Blue Danube Waltz" was first played. Unfortunately the film doesn't have much fizz. Edward Sutherland directed. Paramount. Black and white. 87 minutes.

1938 Romance in the Dark
Swarthout is a naive Hungarian singer used by tenor John Boles to distract a rival away from another woman. She is finally allowed to sing at the Budapest opera house when she pretends to be an Egyptian princess but gets into difficulty. Boles rescues her by joining her on stage in the duet "La ci darem la mano" from *Don Giovanni*. Swarthout also sings the Berceuse from the Godard opera

Jocelyn, the Habanera from *Carmen* and the Song of India from *Sadko*. H.C. Potter directed. Paramount. Black and white. 80 minutes.

1939 Ambush
Swarthout's last film and her first dramatic non-singing role was a low-budget crime picture. Swarthout is the innocent sister of a man who joins a gang of bank robbers. She is taken hostage but rescued by truck driver Lloyd Nolan. Kurt Neumann directed. Paramount. Black and white. 60 minutes.

SWEETHEARTS
1913 operetta by Herbert

Victor Herbert's popular operetta *Sweethearts* has a Ruritanian-type plot about a young woman named Sylvia who works in a laundry in Belgium. She is really a princess, however, and so she finally wins a prince. The book is by Harry B. Smith and Fred de Grésac with lyrics by Robert B. Smith. The "Sweethearts Waltz" and "Pretty as a Picture" are the best-known songs. See also VICTOR HERBERT.

1938 MacDonald/Eddy film
Nelson Eddy and Jeanette MacDonald play a married couple who star in a long-running stage production of the operetta. The songs are retained but writers Dorothy Parker and Alan Campbell created an entirely new story. Producer Frank Morgan manipulates the couple into a marital spat and they split for a time. *Sweethearts* was MGM's first three-strip Technicolor film and the first in color for MacDonald and Eddy. W.S. Van Dyke directed and cinematographer Oliver Marsh won an Oscar for his colorful work. Color. In English. 114 minutes. MGM video and laser.

SYBERBERG, HANS JÜRGEN
German film director (1935-)

Hans Jürgen Syberberg, who earlier made films about Hitler and Karl May, directed one of the most controversial modern opera films, a highly symbolic but very beautiful *Parsifal*. He has also made films that feature Richard Wagner including the fictional *Ludwig, Requiem for a Virgin King* and the documentary *The Confessions of Winifred Wagner*. See LUDWIG II (1972), PARSIFAL (1982), RICHARD WAGNER (1975).

SYDNEY

Joan Sutherland and Australian Opera videos have made the beauty of the Sydney Opera house recognizable to the rest of the world, even to those who never heard of the controversy over its construction. It soars out over Sydney Harbor at the beginning of each video. There are also some fascinating documentaries about the opera house itself which opened in 1973. See ADRIANA LECOUVREUR (1984), LA BOHÈME (1993), THE DAUGHTER OF THE REGIMENT (1986), LES DIALOGUES DES CARMÉLITES (1986), DIE FLEDERMAUS (1982), LES HUGUENOTS (1990), LAKMÉ (1976), LUCIA DI LAMMERMOOR (1986), LUCREZIA BORGIA (1977), THE MAGIC FLUTE (1986), NORMA (1978), I PURITANI (1985), SEMIRAMIDE (1986), JOAN SUTHERLAND (1985/1993), TOSCA (1986), IL TROVATORE (1983).

1967 Sydney Opera House
A prize-winning short film about the construction of the Sydney Opera House which focuses on the design by Danish architect Jörn Utzon. John Fitzgerald directed it for the Commonwealth Film Unit. Color. 10 minutes.

1973 Opening of the Sydney Opera House
A newsreel film showing the official opening of the Sydney Opera House by Queen Elizabeth on Oct. 20 1973. Color. 8 minutes. Film at NFTA.

1973 The Fifth Facade
Danish architect Jörn Utzon provides the commentary for this film and notes that "one could not design a building for such an exposed position without paying attention to the roof - one must have a fifth facade." All the facades are shown during the construction and opening of the opera house. Also seen are rehearsals by the Sydney Symphony Orchestra and scenes from productions of *War and Peace* and *The Threepenny Opera*. Color. 28 minutes.

1984 As Frozen Music
This very lively documentary film tells the story of the Sydney Opera House and how it moved from being controversial to being a performing arts center. Featured in interviews are such opera folk as Joan Sutherland, Luciano Pavarotti and Janet Baker and there are extracts from a number of operas and plays. It was produced, directed and edited by John Davy Tristram and I. James Wilson for Juniper Film. Color. In English. 55 minutes. Brighton video.

SYLVA, MARGUERITA
Belgian/American soprano (1875-1957)

Marguerita Sylva, who sang the role of Carmen over 600 times on stages around the world, made an Italian film of it in 1916 to showcase her interpretation. She was compared to Calvé who sang the role over 1000 times. Sylva was born in Brussels with the plain name of Smith (her father was English) but when she became a protégé of William S. Gilbert at seventeen, he changed her name. He also helped her make her London debut in *Carmen* in 1892. She later sang in Paris, Berlin, Vienna and New York and all around the U.S. She starred in Victor's Herbert's operetta *The Fortune Teller* on Broadway in 1897 and in several films. Her last stage role was *Three Waltzes* on Broadway in 1937 and her last film was *The Gay Señorita* in 1945. Most of her recordings were destroyed in a 1914 fire which may explain why she is not as well remembered as others. See also CARMEN (1916).

1920 The Honey Bee
Sylva portrays a woman who falls in love with a married man and flees to Paris where she becomes involved with a boxer. Sylva's co-stars were Thomas Holding and Nigel Barrie. Rupert Julian directed and wrote the screenplay based on a novel by Samuel Merwin. American Film Company. Black and white. About 75 minutes.

1943 The Seventh Victim
Sylva has only a supporting role in this classic Val Lewton thriller directed by Mark Robson. Kim Hunter portrays a woman who meets up with a group of devil worshippers in New York. RKO. Black and white. 71 minutes.

1946 The Gay Señorita
Sylva has only a small role in this Columbia film starring Steve Cochran and Jinx Falkenburg. A builder falls in love and cancels a housing development that would have dispossessed the city's Mexicans. Arthur Dreifuss directed. Black and white. 70 minutes.

SZABÓ, ISTVÁN
Hungarian film director (1938-)

István Szabó, who won an Academy Award for his 1981 film *Mephisto*, began making films in Hungary in 1960 and gained international success with *Love Film* and *25 Fireman's Street*. His opera film *Meeting Venus* is one of the best screen portrayals of the problems of producing an opera. Szabó also directs opera on stage and *Meeting Venus* is said to be partially autobiographical. See MEETING VENUS.

SZIRMAI, ALBERT
Hungarian composer (1880-1967)

Albert Szirmai (or Sirmay) was one of a group of composers including Emmerich Kálmán and Viktor Jacobi who made Hungarian operettas famous in the early years of the century. He had a major success with his 1907 operetta *The Yellow Domino* and continued to compose in the genre until 1964. Szirmai was one of the collaborators on a notable 1913 London operetta about the movies called *The Girl on the Film*, adapted from the German *Filmzauber*. He moved to New York in 1926 and worked with Broadway composers as music editor at Chappell. His biggest hit was the 1916 operetta *Miska the Great* which has been filmed three times by the Hungarians.

MÁGNÁS MISKA
Miska the Great was a big success at its premiere in 1916 and was immediately turned into a film by Hungarian filmmaker Alexander Korda. A second version was made in 1942 with Pál Jávor and Klári Tolnay in the leading roles. The third version in 1948 was a huge hit and was said to be the most successful Hungarian film ever produced. It was directed by Márton Keleti from a screenplay by István Békeffy based on the libretto by Károly Bakonyi and Andor Gábor. The writers satirize the old ways of the aristocracy and hold the past up to ridicule. The cast included Kálmán Latabár (popular in a comedy role), Miklós Gábor, Árpád Latabár, Ági Mészáros and Marika Németh.

T

TABARRO, IL
1918 opera by Puccini

The Cloak is the first part of the Puccini trilogy *Il Trittico* which premiered at the Metropolitan Opera in 1918. It's a harsh, realistic story about a tragic love triangle. Seine River barge captain Michele finds out his wife Giorgetta is being unfaithful and kills her lover Luigi. He wraps the body in his cloak and gives it to his wife. The libretto by Giuseppe Adami is based on Didier Gold's play *La Houppelande*. See also GIACOMO PUCCINI.

1952 NBC Opera Theatre
Robert Weede stars as the jealous husband, Elaine Mabin is the unfaithful wife and Davis Cunningham is the luckless lover in this NBC Opera Theatre production by Samuel Chotzinoff. The opera is sung in an English translation by Townsend Brewster. Peter Herman Adler conducted the NBC orchestra and Kirk Browning directed the live telecast on Feb. 14, 1952. Black and white. In English. 50 minutes. Video at MTR.

1981 Metropolitan Opera
Renata Scotto sings the role of Giorgetta, Cornell MacNeil is Michele and Vasile Modoveanu is Luigi in this Metropolitan Opera production by Fabrizio Melano. David Reppa designed the sets, James Levine conducted the Metropolitan Orchestra and Kirk Browning directed the video and telecast on Nov. 14. 1981, as part of *Il Trittico*. Color. In Italian with English subtitles. 51 minutes. Video at MTR.

1983 Teatro alla Scala
Sylvia Sass stars as Giorgetta with Piero Cappuccilli as her jealous husband and Nicola Martinucci as her lover Luigi in this Teatro alla Scala production by Silvano Bussoti. Gianandrea Gavazzeni conducts the La Scala Orchestra and Chorus and Brian Large directed the video. Color. In Italian with English subtitles. 51 minutes. Home Vision video with complete *Il Trittico*.

1994 Metropolitan Opera
Placido Domingo stars as Luigi in this Metropolitan Opera production by Fabrizio Melano. Teresa Stratas is Giorgetta, Juan Pons is Michele, Florence Quivar is Frugola and Charles Anthony is Tinca. David Reppa designed the sets and costumes and James Levine conducted the Metropolitan Opera Orchestra and Chorus. Brian Large directed the video from a September 1994 performance telecast on Dec. 18. Color. In Italian with English subtitles. 52 minutes.

TADDEI, GIUSEPPE
Italian baritone (1916-)

Giuseppe Taddei made his debut in Rome in 1936 and sang regularly there until World War II. In the postwar period he sang in Vienna, London, Salzburg and La Scala and began to specialize in Mozart. He sang at Covent Garden and in America in the 1950s and has been particularly popular in comic roles like Verdi's Falstaff and Pergolesi's Music Master. See also ANDREA CHÉNIER (1955), FALSTAFF (1982), MAESTRO DI CAPELLA (1987), TOSCA (1983).

1956 Giuseppe Taddei in Tokyo
Taddei is see on stage in Tokyo in two of his favorite roles in the compilation video *Legends of Opera*. As Falstaff he sings "Quand'ero paggio" opposite Orietta Moscucci. As Figaro *in The Marriage of Figaro* he sings "Non piu andrai.". Black and white. In Italian. 8 minutes. Legato Classics video.

TAGLIAVINI, FERRUCCIO
Italian tenor (1913-1995)

Ferruccio Tagliavini, one of the great Italian postwar tenors, was a regular at the Metropolitan Opera from 1947 to 1954. He made his debut in Florence in 1938, sang widely in Italy during the war and had a strong international career from 1947 to 1965 when he retired from the stage. He had a small but memorable film career. He began singing though not acting in the 1941 *Tosca* and made his first screen appearance with Tito Gobbi in the 1946 *The Barber of Seville*. It opened in New York while he was having great success at the Met so it was promoted as a Tagliavini film. In addition to his films, he can be seen in fine form on videos of the Firestone television shows and a documentary about La Scala. See THE BARBER OF SEVILLE (1946),

L'ELISIR D'AMORE (1941 film/1959), TEATRO ALLA SCALA (1994), RIGOLETTO (1941 film), TOSCA (1941 film).

1941 The Lady Is Fickle
Voglio Vivere Così, Tagliavini's first film as an actor, is primarily an excuse for letting him sing and was released in the U.S. in 1948 as *The Lady Is Fickle*. He plays a schoolteacher who thinks he has been given an opera audition. It's a joke but he gets a job with the opera theater as a stage hand, steps in to replace the house tenor and becomes a star. Tagliavini's singing is splendid even if the film is a bit creaky. Mario Mattoli wrote and directed it. Black and white. In Italian. 83 minutes.

1942 La Donna è Mobile
Tagliavini sings arias from *La Bohème*, *La Sonnambula*, *Lohengrin* and *L'Elisir d'amore* in a story about another school teacher with a great voice. On a visit to Rome he loses his girl but is discovered as a singer. It was again directed by Mario Mattoli with a screenplay by Mario Monicelli and Steno. Black and white. In Italian. 78 minutes.

1944 Anything For a Song
Tagliavini portrays a man who would rather sing than eat despite his father's opposition in the Italian film *Ho Tanta Voglia di Cantare!* released in the U.S. in 1947 as *Anything For A Song*. The sound and photography are poor but this is not surprising as it was one of the few Italian films made in the chaos following Mussolini's downfall on July 25, 1943. Mario Monicelli directed. Black and white. In Italian. 80 minutes.

1949 One Night of Fame
Tagliavini plays himself in the Italian film *Al Diavolo la Celebrità*, shown in the U.S. as *One Night of Fame*. It's a clever comedy fantasy by Mario Monicelli and Steno about a man who gets a magic charm that allows him to become other people. One of the people he becomes is opera singer Ferruccio Tagliavini. Also featured is the voice of his wife Pia Tassinari. Black and white. In Italian. 91 minutes. Opera Dubs/ Lyric videos.

1950 I Cadetti di Guascogna
Ugo Tognazzi made his debut opposite Tagliavini and Walter Chiari in *The Cadets of Guascogna*, a "let's put on a show" type comedy. Tagliavini sings "Una furtiva lacrima" and "Santa Lucia" as a group of Army draftees hold a fund-raising show for stranded actors. Mario Mattoli directed. Excelsa Film. Black and white. In Italian. 90 minutes.

1950-54 Tagliavini in Opera & Song Vol. 1
Tagliavini is shown in performance on the *Voice of Firestone* television programs from 1950 to 1954. He sings arias from *Tosca*, *La Bohème*, *Martha*, *L'Elisir d'Amore* and *Rigoletto* and songs by Leoncavallo, Tchaikovsky, Schubert, di Capua, Tosti and de Curtis. Black and white. 50 minutes. VAI video.

1951 Anema e Core
Tagliavini plays a singer discovered by two crooks who become his manager but are baffled by his inability to sing in public. The title comes from a famous Neapolitan song. The cast includes Nino Manfredi, Dorian Gray and Mario Riva. Mario Mattoli directed. Excela Film. Color. In Italian. 86 minutes. Opera Dubs video.

1952-55 Tagliavini in Opera and Song Vol. 2
Tagliavini in performance on the *Voice of Firestone* television programs from 1952 to 1955. He sings arias and duets (with Margaret Broderson and Frances Wyatt) from *Carmen*, *Martha*, *Il Trovatore* and *La Traviata* plus songs by Rossini, di Capua and d'Esposito. Black and white. 30 minutes. VAI video.

1959 Vento di Primavera
Tagliavini portrays a famous Italian tenor in *Spring Wind*, a virtual remake of Gigli's first film *Forget Me Not*. He marries a German woman (Sabine Bethmann) on the rebound from a love affair and almost loses her when she meets up with her first love again. Giulio Del Torre directed the Italian version and Arthur Maria Rabenalt the German film titled *Vergiss Mein Nicht* (as was the Gigli film). Cineitalia-Trio Film. Color. 103 minutes.

1993 Ferruccio Tagliavini - L'Uomo, la Voce
Ferruccio Tagliavini - The Man, the Voice is an Italian video celebrating the glories of the great tenor. It was made in his native Reggio Emilia and published with a book devoted to his career and films. There are scenes at the Reggio Emilia theater where his career began, excerpts of performances from *Voice of Firestone* telecasts and commentary about his life and career. Umberto Bonafini produced the video. Color and black & white. In Italian. 60 minutes. Magis Books (Italy) video.

TAJO, ITALO
Italian bass (1915-1993)

Italo Tajo made his debut in 1935 in Turin and, amazingly, was still singing on stage in 1991. His early career was at the Rome Opera and La Scala and later he was a regular at Covent Garden, San Francisco and the Metropolitan. He made his Met debut in 1948 as Don Basilio in *The Barber of Seville* and was especially noted for his buffo roles. Tajo helped create the opera department at the University of Cincinnati and was active in teaching there. His longevity is evident in his screen career. He can be seen in films of operas made in Italy in the 1940s and videos of operas made in the U.S. in the 1980s. See THE BARBER OF SEVILLE (1946), LA BOHÈME (1977/1982/ 1989), CASA RICORDI, L'ELISIR D'AMORE (1947), FAUST (1949), LUCIA DI LAMMERMOOR (1948), TOSCA (1985).

TALE OF TSAR SALTAN, THE
1900 opera by Rimsky-Korsakov

The full name of Nikolai Rimsky-Korsakov's imaginative fantasy opera is *The Tale of Tsar Saltan, of his Son the Famous and Mighty Hero Prince Guidon Saltanovich, and of the Beautiful Swan Princess*. It tells the story of Tsar Saltan who marries Militrissa, the youngest of three sisters, and what happens to their son Prince Guidon after his exile to an island with the Swan Princess. The Princess changes the Prince into a bumble bee (the popular "Flight of the Bumble Bee" music) so he can spy on his family back home. Librettist Vladimir Bielsky took the story from Pushkin. The Russian title is *Skazka o Tsare Saltane*. See also NIKOLAI RIMSKY-KORSAKOV.

1966 Alexander Ptusko film
Soviet director Alexander Ptusko, who specialized in large-scale film fantasies, directed this Soviet adaptation of *The Tale of Tsar Saltan* for Mosfilm. He had earlier filmed Rimsky-Korsakov's opera *Sadko*. Color. In Russian. 92 minutes.

1978 Dresden State Opera
Harry Kupfer's Dresden State Opera production of *The Legend of Tsar Saltan* is in German not Russian but it is very imaginative and entertaining. Rolf Wollard portrays the Tsar, Lidija Rushizkaja is Militrissa, Stephan Spiewok is Prince Guidon, Ilse Ludwig is the Swan Princess, Barbara Hoene is Barbaricha and Elenore Elstermann and Barbara Gubisch are Militrissa's sisters. Peter Sykora designed the sets and costumes and Siegfried Kurz conducts the Dresden State Opera Orchestra and Chorus. Kupfer himself directed the video. Color. In German. 98 minutes. VIEW video.

TALES OF HOFFMANN, THE
1881 opera by Offenbach

Les Contes d'Hoffmann is Jacques Offenbach's only opera and is now probably more popular than his operettas. It has provided the basis for one of the great opera films and its Barcarolle is as famous as the Cancan from *Orpheus in the Underworld*. The opera revolves around the famous fantasy writer E. T. A. Hoffmann who describes three failed love affairs as he sits in a pub waiting for his new love. The first love turned out to be a mechanical doll, the second a young girl with an illness that killed her when she sings and the third a courtesan who could not be faithful. All are apparently aspects of his present love and the four women are often sung by the same soprano. Hoffmann's rival/enemy in each episode is also usually sung by the same baritone. The libretto by Jules Barbier is based on stories by the real Hoffmann, who lived from 1776 to 1822 and also wrote operas. See also JACQUES OFFENBACH.

1950 NBC Opera Theatre
David Cunningham stars as Hoffmann in this NBC Opera Theatre production by Samuel Chotzinoff in English. Dorothy Etherige dances the role of the doll Olympia sung by Barbara Gibson. Dorothy Warenskjold portrays the doomed singer Antonia, George Britten has the three villain roles and Johnny Silver plays the other parts. The Giulietta episode is omitted. Charles Polacheck directed the opera and Otis Riggs designed the sets. Peter Herman Adler conducted the Symphony of the Air Orchestra and Kirk Browning directed the telecast. Black and white. In English. 60 minutes.

1951 Michael Powell/Emeric Pressburger film
Michael Powell and Emeric Pressburger wrote and directed this great English film after the success of *The Red Shoes* and they used some of the same stars. Moira Shearer has a double role as ballet dancer Stella in the framing story and dancing doll Olympia in the first tale. Robert Rounseville gives a solid performance as Hoffmann with Ann Ayars as opera singer Antonia. Robert Helpmann appears in four villain roles sung by Bruce Dargavel, Frederick Ashton in two roles sung by Murray Dickie, Ludmilla Tcherina plays the courtesan Giulietta

sung by Margherita Grandi and Leonide Massine plays three roles sung by Grahame Clifford and Owen Brannigan. Pamela Brown appears as Hoffmann's sidekick Nicklaus with her singing by Monica Sinclair. Hein Heckroth designed the sets, Frederick Ashton was choreographer Christopher Challis was the cinematographer and Denis Arundell wrote the translation. Thomas Beecham appears in the film conducting the Royal Philharmonic Orchestra and Sadler's Wells Chorus. Technicolor. In English. 127 minutes. Home Vision video/Criterion Voyager laser with documentary material. (Note: The film is correctly titled on screen as *The Tales of Hoffmann* with two "n's." The hero's name is misspelled as "Hoffman" with one "n" in all standard film reference books including Maltin, Halliwell, Milne and Katz.)

1970 Walter Felsenstein film
Producer Walter Felsenstein wrote and directed *Hoffmanns Erzählungen*, a film of the opera based on his famous 1958 Komischer Oper production in East Berlin. Felsenstein seems to have been influenced in his cinematic style by Soviet filmmakers like Eisenstein. Hans Nocker sings the role of Hoffmann, Melitta Muszely portrays all four of the main female roles, Rudolf Asmus plays all four villain roles, Werner Enders plays four of the minor roles and Alfred Wroblewski is Crespel. The sets were created by Alfred Tolle while the cinematography was by Otto Merz and Hans-Jurgen Reinecke. Karl F. Voigtmann conducted the Komischer Oper Orchestra and George Miekle was co-director and writer. DEFA. Color. In German. 125 minutes. Lyric video/ Japanese video and laser.

1970 Rolf Liebermann film
Czech director/conductor Václav Kaslík made this German-language film version of the opera for West German television in 1970. It's based on a Hamburg State Opera production by Rolf Liebermann and stars Jon Piso as Hoffmann with Sylvia Geszty, Thomas Tipton and Herold Kraus in the other principal roles. Color. In German. 140 minutes.

1974 Valerie Masterson film
Valerie Masterson portrays Antonia with Kenneth Woollam as Hoffmann in this English highlights film of the opera made for the *Focus on Opera* series. Susan Miasey is Olympia and Janette Kearns is Giulietta while Malcolm Rivers sings the triple roles of Coppelius, Dappertutto and Doctor Miracle.

Peter Seabourne shot the film at Knebworth House, Hertfordshire, and John J. Davies conducted the Classical Orchestra. Color. In English. 52 minutes.

1981 Royal Opera
Placido Domingo is the unlucky-in-love Hoffmann in this Royal Opera, Covent Garden, production by filmmaker John Schlesinger. Luciana Serra is the doll Olympia, Agnes Baltsa is the courtesan Giulietta, Ileana Cotrubas is the frail Antonia and Deanne Bergsman is the disappointed Stella. Hoffmann's opposition includes Geraint Evans as Coppelius, Robert Lloyd as Lindorf, Robert Tear as Spalanzani, Siegmund Nimsgern as Dappertutto, Philip Gelling as Schlemil and Nicola Ghiuselev as Dr. Miracle. Claire Howell is Nicklaus, his companion and muse. The sets are by William Dudley and the matching costumes by Maria Bjornson. Georges Prêtre conducts the Royal Opera House Orchestra and Chorus and Brian Large directed the video. Color. In French with English subtitles. 149 minutes. HBO video/ Pioneer laser.

1988 Metropolitan Opera
Neil Shicoff stars as the poet Hoffmann in this Metropolitan Opera production by Otto Schenk. Tatiana Troyanos, Gwendolyn Bradley and Roberta Alexander portray the women he loves and loses and James Morris portrays the villains who cause him so much pain. Charles Dutoit conducts the Metropolitan Opera Orchestra and Chorus. Brian Large directed the video. Color. In French with English subtitles. 180 minutes. DG video/laser.

1993 Lyons Opera
This rather eccentric Opéra de Lyon production was devised by Louis Erlo who retitled it *...des Contes d'Hoffmann*. The setting is a madhouse with drab gray walls, Olympia is a catatonic inmate on a trolley, Giulietta is the matron and Stella wears evening dress but is bald. Daniel Galvez-Vallejo sings the role of Hoffmann, José Van Dam portrays the villains, Barbara Hendricks is Antonia, Natalie Dessay is Olympia, Isabelle Vernet is Giulietta, Gabriel Bacquier is Coppelius and Crespel and Brigitte Balleys both play Nicklaus. American Kent Nagano conducts the Lyons Opera Orchestra and Pierre Cavassilas directed the video. Color. In French with English subtitles. 158 minutes. Home Vision video/ Pioneer Artists laser.

Early/related films

1911 Kolm/Fleck film
The first film of the opera was a silent Austrian version made in Vienna in 1911 with Offenbach's music arranged by Erich Hiller to accompany the film live in cinemas. Luise Kolm, Anton Kolm, Jakob Fleck and Claudis Veltée wrote and directed. Black and white. In German. About 15 minutes.

1912 Barcarolle sound film
This early sound film of the Barcarolle was made by German sound film pioneer Oskar Messter for his Biophone Theater in Berlin with synchronized picture and record. It was copyrighted in the U.S. in 1915 but made earlier, probably in 1912. Black and white. In German. About 3 minutes.

1914 Richard Oswald film
Richard Oswald directed this German film of the opera with memorable set designs by Manfred Noa and fine cinematography by Ernst Krohn. It follows the opera closely with a prologue and three episodes with three women. Kurt Wolowsky plays young Hoffmann, Erich Kaiser-Titz is the old Hoffmann, Kathe Oswald is Stella, Ruth Oswald is Antonia, Alice Scheel-Hechy is Olympia, Thea Sandten is Giulietta and Werner Krauss is Desperdito. Black and white. In German. About 50 minutes.

1923 Max Neufeld film
Max Neufeld directed this Austrian film of the opera adapted for the screen by Josef Malina. It stars Dagny Servaes, Friedrich Feher, Eugen Neufel, Max Neufel, Karl Ehmann and Viktor Franz. Black and white. In German. 78 minutes.

1934 Barcarolle
Barcarolle is a narrative film set at Carnival time in Venice and based around the melodies of *The Tales of Hoffmann*. The German version stars Gustav Froelich as a young man willing to risk his life for a bet and Lida Baarova as the woman he bets on. In the French version Edwige Feuillère is the woman and Pierre Richard-Willm is the man. Gerhardt Lamprecht directed both versions. Black and white. In German or French. 83 minutes.

TALLEY, MARION
American soprano (1907-1983)

Marion Talley was a brilliant coloratura soprano whose too early rise to stardom probably ruined a promising career. She was only fifteen when excitement over her performance as Mignon in the Thomas opera led to a contract at the Metropolitan Opera. It was impossible for her to live up to hyped expectations so her debut at the Met in 1926 as Gilda in *Rigoletto* was inevitably a letdown. However, she continued to sing at the Met in various important roles until 1929 when, more or less burned out, she retired from opera. She later attempted comebacks but was never successful. The publicity around her Met debut was such that she was invited to star in three of the Vitaphone opera shorts, including two with tenor Beniamino Gigli. Republic Pictures signed her in 1936 in an attempt to cash in on her reputation and create prestige for the studio with a classy operatic film. It was not a success and her movie career ended.

1926/1927 Vitaphone opera films
She was billed as "Marion Talley, Youthful Prima Donna of the New York Metropolitan Opera" when she starred in three Vitaphone sound shorts, two made with tenor Beniamino Gigli. In the first, which premiered with the feature *Don Juan* in 1926, she sings Gilda's "Caro nome" from *Rigoletto*. In 1927 she made her two Gigli films. In one she sings Gilda in the Quartet from *Rigoletto* with Gigli, baritone Giuseppe De Luca and contralto Jeanne Gordon. In the other she is featured as Lucia with Gigli in the duet "Verranno a te sull'aura" from *Lucia di Lammermoor*. Black and white. About 8 minutes each.

1936 Follow Your Heart
Republic Pictures, the studio best known for Gene Autry cowboy films and thrill-a-minute serials, was a new studio in 1936 and needed a prestige picture to establish itself as something more than just a B-picture film factory. This was the time of the Grace Moore opera film boom in Hollywood so opera seemed the hot ticket but there weren't many unsigned big name singers around. Studio chief Herbert J. Yates and producer Nat Levine recalled the publicity around Talley's Met debut and thought they could garner prestige with a relatively high-budget opera film. And so the bizarre *Follow Your Heart* was born. Talley portrays a soprano with an eccentric Kentucky family. When Uncle Tony (Luis Alberni at his most frenzied) brings his down-

on-its luck opera company to the old homestead, she ends up as the star of an operetta composed by tenor Michael Bartlett. This is truly a down-home opera film for the folks, written tongue-in-cheek by top writers Nathaniel West, Lester Cole and Samuel Ornitz. Talley is introduced singing her first aria lying on a cellar floor poking a furnace. She sings the Page aria from *Les Huguenots* in a haymow accompanied by a phonograph. The *Lucia de Lammermoor* Sextet is turned into a comedy number with Bartlett singing to a baked ham while baritone Luis Alberni addresses a haddock. Despite all this Talley sings rather splendidly, especially the selection from Thomas's *Mignon*, the opera that had first made her famous years before. Aubrey Scotto directed the film. Black and white. 82 minutes. On video.

TAMING OF THE SHREW, THE
1953 opera by Giannini

American composer Vittorio Giannini's most popular opera is based on the Shakespeare play with a libretto by the composer and D. Fee. It first premiered in a concert version in Cincinnati in 1953 and was then performed by regional groups. It did not attract national attention until it qas given a large-scale production on NBC Opera Theatre in 1954. The story is more or less the same as the play and tells how clever wealth-seeking adventurer Petruchio tames tempestuous Katharina in medieval Italy. See also VITTORIO GIANNINI.

1954 NBC Opera Theatre
John Raitt stars as Petruchio and Susan Yager is Kate in this color television production by the adventurous NBC Opera Theatre. Sonia Stollin is Bianca, John Alexander is Lucentio, Donald Gramm is Hortensio and Leon Lishner is Baptista. It was produced by Samuel Chotzinoff, staged by Charles Polacheck, designed by William Molyneux and costumed by John Boxer. Artistic director Peter Herman Adler conducts the Symphony of the Air orchestra and Kirk Browning directed the telecast on March 13, 1954. The critics loved it. Color. In English. 90 minutes. Video at MTR.

Related film

SHAKESPEARE FILMS
The Shakespeare play has been filmed twice by famous acting couples. The static 1929 version stars Mary Pickford and Douglas Fairbanks as the battling pair and was directed by Sam Taylor. The rather more cinematic 1967 film stars Elizabeth Taylor and Richard Burton and was directed by Franco Zeffirelli.

1953 Kiss Me Kate
Cole Porter's 1948 stage musical version of *The Taming of The Shrew* was filmed in 1953, the same year Giannini's opera version was staged. Porter tells a double story paralleling the play with a back-stage plot and using lines from the play to begin songs like "I've Come to Wive it Wealthily in Padua" and "Were Thine that Special Face." Kathryn Grayson and Howard Keel star as the shrew and her tamer in this MGM film directed by George Sidney. Color. 109 minutes. On video.

TANCREDI
1813 opera by Rossini

Gioachino Rossini's biggest success before *The Barber of Seville* was this *opera seria* set in Syracuse in 1005. It's the legendary era of the heroic Christian knight Tancredi and the conflict between Christians and the Saracens. Tancredi loves Amenaide who refuses to marry Orbazzano who seeks revenge by false accusations. Tancredi fights as her champion and then defeats the Saracens. The libretto by Gaetano Rossi is based on Voltaire's *Tancréde* which was based on Tasso's *Gerusalemme Liberata*. See also GIOACHINO ROSSINI.

1981 Aix-en-Provence Festival
Marilyn Horne stars as Tancredi with Katia Ricciarelli as Amenaide in this Aix-en-Provence Festival production. Ralf Weikert conducts the Scottish Chamber Orchestra. Color. In Italian. 160 minutes. Lyric video and New York Public Library video.

1992 Schwetzingen Festival
Bernadette Manca di Nissi stars as Tancredi in this Schwetzingen Festival production by Pierluigi Pizzi who also designed sets and costumes. Maria Bayo is the heroine Amenaide, Ildebrando d'Arcangelo is Orbazzano, Raul Gimenez is Argirio and Katarzyna Bak is Isaura. Gianluigi Gelmetti conducts the Stuttgart Radio Symphony Orchestra. This is a so-called "interactive" video with Rossini's tragic and happy endings so you can choose which you want. Color. In Italian with English subtitles. 106 minutes. RCA video and laser.

TANNHÄUSER
1845 opera by Wagner

Tannhäuser und der Sängerkrieg auf Wartburg (Tannhäuser and the Wartburg Song Contest) is Richard Wagner's examination of redemption through love. The minstrel knight Tannhäuser, seduced by Venus, has been living a life of pure pleasure but decides to return home. There he attempts to win the hand of Elisabeth in a minstrel contest. He fails but he is redeemed by Elisabeth's self-sacrificing love. See also RICHARD WAGNER.

1978 Bayreuth Festival
Gwyneth Jones sings both Elisabeth and Venus opposite Spas Wenkoff's Tannhäuser in this Bayreuth Festival production by Götz Friedrich. Hans Sotin is the Landgrave, Bernd Weikl is Wolfram, Franz Manura is Biterolf and Klaus Brettschneider is the Young Shepherd. Jürgen Rose designed the costumes and sets and John Neumeier created the choreography and directed the Venusburg bacchanal scene. Colin Davis conducts the Bayreuth Festival Orchestra and Chorus and Thomas Oloffson directed the video. Color. In German with English subtitles. 190 minutes. Philips video and laser.

1982 Metropolitan Opera
Richard Cassilly sings Tannhäuser with Eva Marton as Elisabeth and Tatiana Troyanos as Venus in this attractive Metropolitan Opera production by Otto Schenk. Bernd Weikl is Wolfram, John Macurdy is the Landgrave, Richard J. Clark is Biterolf and Robert Nagy is Walter. Gunther Schneider-Siemssen designed the sumptuous sets, Patricia Zipprodt the costumes, Norbert Vesak the choreography and Gil Wechsler the lighting. James Levine conducts the Metropolitan Opera Orchestra and Chorus. Brian Large directed the video taped on Dec. 20, 1982, and telecast on March 23, 1983. Color. In German with English subtitles. 176 minutes. Paramount video/Pioneer laser.

1990 Bayreuth Festival
Richard Versalle sings Tannhäuser with Cheryl Studer as Elisabeth and Ruthild Engert-Ely as Venus in this Bayreuth Festival stage production by Wolfgang Wagner. Wolfgang Brendel portrays Wolfram and Hans Sotin sings the role of the Landgrave. Giuseppe Sinopoli conducts the Bayreuth Festival Orchestra and Chorus and Brian Large directed the video. Color. In German with English subtitles. 187 minutes. Philips video and laser.

1994 Munich Opera Festival
René Kollo stars as Tannhäuser with Nadine Secunde as Elisabeth in this innovative, modernized and quite controversial Munich Opera Festival production by David Alden. Waltraud Meier sings Venus, Jan-Hendrick Rootering is the Landgrave, Hans Gunter Nocker is Biterolf and Bernd Weikl is Wolfram. Buki Schiff created the costumes and Rini Toren designed the much-discussed sets which include the giant letters GERMANIA NOSTRA as a backdrop. Zubin Mehta conducts the Bavarian State Opera Orchestra and Chorus and Brian Large directed the video. Color. In German with English subtitles. 201 minutes. On video/Pioneer laserdisc.

Early/related films

1908 Henny Porten film
Henny Porten, Germany's first important film star, is featured as Elisabeth in this German Messter Biophone sound film using a record of an aria from the opera as its soundtrack. Porten's father Franz, a former opera singer, directed the film shot in a Berlin studio using Oskar Messter's synchronization process. Black and white. About 3 minutes.

1913 James Cruze film
James Cruze, later a noted director, stars as Tannhäuser with Marguerite Snow as Elisabeth in this American film of the opera made by the Thanhouser studio. Florence La Badie plays Venus and William Russell is Wolfram. Lucius J. Henderson directed. The film was screened with the music of the opera played by orchestra or piano. Black and white. About 35 minutes.

1938 Symphonic Films
Friedrich Feher conducted music from the opera for a one-reel film made for the Symphonic Films company. Black and white. 10 minutes.

1948 Unfaithfully Yours
Orchestra conductor Rex Harrison, convinced that his wife Linda Darnell is betraying him, imagines how to forgive her while conducting the "Pilgrim's Chorus" from *Tannhäuser*. Preston Sturges directed. Black and white. 105 minutes.

1974 Butley

Simon Gray's 1971 stage play *Butley* and the 1974 film based on it both open with the *Tannhäuser* overture. Teacher Alan Bates is attempting to listen to a record of it while mulling over his sex problems. Harold Pinter directed. Color. 127 minutes.

1982 The Night of the Shooting Stars

Paolo and Vittorio Taviani feature a star-themed aria from *Tannhäuser* in *La Notte di San Lorenzo*, their harsh but poetic film about the end of World War II in Tuscany. A retreating German soldier sings "O du mein holder Abendstern" and is watched by the villagers as he hurries ahead of the liberating American army. Color. In Italian with English subtitles. 107 minutes. MGM-UA video.

1991 Meeting Venus

István Szabó's bittersweet film centers around a TV production of *Tannhäuser* in Paris. Glenn Close plays the soprano (with the voice of Kiri Te Kanawa) and Niels Arestrup is the conductor. See MEETING VENUS.

TARARE

1787 opera by Salieri

Mozart's rival Antonio Salieri joined forces with Beaumarchais, the author of *The Marriage of Figaro*, for a revolutionary French opera in which a king is deposed. It premiered just two years before the French Revolution. King Atar is jealous of his general Tarare and his happiness with his wife Astasie so he kidnaps her for his harem. Atar is deposed by the eunuch Calpigi and his own soldiers and Tarare is made king. The opera was revised for Italy by Salieri and librettist Lorenzo da Ponte and became *Axur, Rè d'Ormus*. See also ANTONIO SALIERI.

1993 Schwetzingen Festival

Jean-Louis Martinoty directed this production of the rarely performed opera at the Schwetzingen Festival in 1993. The performers are Howard Crook, Jean Pierre Lafont, Anna Caleb and Eberhard Lorenz. Jean-Claude Malgoire conducts the German Handel Soloists. Claud Viler directed the film for television. EuroArts. Color. In French. 184 minutes. On video.

TARKOVSKY, ANDREI

Russian film & opera director (1932-1986)

Andrei Tarkovsky, considered by many critics to be among the finest film directors of all times, is known for such metaphysical achievements as *Andrei Roublev, Solaris, The Mirror* and *Stalker*. He moved into opera stage direction while in exile towards the end of his life. His masterful and hugely effective *Boris Godunov*, first staged at Covent Garden in 1983, was restaged and videotaped at the Kirov Opera in 1990. See BORISGODUNOV (1990).

TAUBER, RICHARD

Austrian tenor (1892-1948)

Richard Tauber was one of the leading tenors of the pre-war period in operas by Mozart and operettas by Lehár. Born in Linz, he made his debut in 1913 in *The Magic Flute* and sang with the Dresden Opera for many years. In the second part of his career he began to sing Lehár operettas and helped revive that composer's career. In 1931 he brought Lehár's *The Land of Smiles* to London and through it became a popular star in England. In 1933 when Hitler came to power, Tauber moved permanently to London where he continued to appear in both operas and operettas. Although never notable as an actor, he was able to develop a major film career in Germany and England through his singing. See also DAS LAND DES LÄCHELNS (1932), PAGLIACCI (1936).

1923 Achtung! Aufname!

This is a German promotional film made by Richard Tauber to help sell his recordings. It is silent but his records could be played with it. Black and white. 5 minutes. Print in NFTA in London.

1929 Ich Küsse Ihre Hand, Madame

Tauber performed (voice only) the title song of *I Kiss Your Hand, Madame*, the first German sound film, and made it an international hit. The stars of the film are Marlene Dietrich and Harry Liedtke who is seen singing on screen with Tauber's voice. Robert Land directed. Black and white. In German. 72 minutes.

1930 Never Trust a Woman

Tauber's first film as an actor was *Ich Glaub' Nie Mehr an eine Frau*, released in the U.S. as *Never Trust a Woman*. He portrays a wise old sailor who helps a young friend win music hall girl Maria Solveg.

Tauber mostly sings popular tunes by Paul Desseau. Max Reichmann directed. Black and white. In German. 96 minutes. Opera Dubs video.

1930 The End of the Rainbow

In Tauber's German film *Das Lockende Ziel* (shot simultaneously in English as *The End of the Rainbow)*, he plays a Bavarian singer who becomes an opera star in Berlin. The middle section of the film is devoted to a production of *Martha* at the Berlin Opera. The other actors include Sophie Pagay, Lucie English, and Oscar Sima. Tauber made the film for his own company with Max Reichmann directing. Black and white. In German or English. 92 minutes. Lyric video.

1931 Die Grosse Attraktion

In *The Great Attraction* Tauber sings some new songs by Franz Lehár including a tango called "Tauber-Lied." Other songs were provided by Bronislaw Kaper (who created a fox-trot called "Du warst mir ein Roman"), Paul Dessau and Franz Grothe. The cast includes Margiol Lion, Marianne Winkelstern and Teddy Bill. This was Tauber's last film for his own company, Max Reichmann directed. Black and white. In German. 85 minutes.

1932 Melodie der Liebe

In the German film *Melody of Love* Tauber plays an opera star who falls in love with a golddigger (Alice Treff). When he finds she is only interested in his money, he is heartbroken but pretty Lien Deyers consoles him. Tauber sings opera arias and popular songs. George Jacoby directed. Black and white. In German. 100 minutes.

1934 Blossom Time

Tauber portrays Franz Schubert in this excellent British musical about the life of the composer. It was derived from the 1916 pastiche operetta *Das Dreimaderlhaus* based on music by Schubert. In the film Tauber falls in love with a girl but loses her to a count even though he sings beautifully. The cast includes Jane Baxter, Athene Syeler and Carl Esmond. Paul L. Stein directed. U.S. title: *April Romance*. BIP. Black and white. In English. 91 minutes. Opera Dubs/Lyric video.

1935 Heart's Desire

Tauber plays a Viennese beer garden singer who goes to London and becomes an opera star but loses the woman he loves. The song "Vienna City of My Dreams" became a hit through this English film.

The cast includes Diana Napier, Kathleen Kelly, Leonora Corbett and Carl Harbord. Clifford Grey and Jack Davies wrote the screenplay and Paul L. Stein directed. BIP. Black and white. 82 minutes. Opera Dubs/Video Yesteryear videos.

1936 Land Without Music

In a bankrupt Ruritanian country, the ruling princess bans music so its overly musical people can concentrate on making money. Tauber and Jimmy Durante lead a revolution so people can get their music back and Tauber wins the hand of the princess played by his wife Diane Napier. Durante portrays an American newspaperman. Oscar Straus wrote the music for this British film directed by Walter Ford. U.S. title: *Forbidden Music*. Capitol Films. Black and white. 80 minutes.

1945 Waltz Time

Tauber has only a minor role in this English film set in Imperial Vienna. Empress Maria (Carol Raye) wants to marry one of her officers (Peter Graves) but he gets caught in a flirtation with Patrica Medina. Paul L. Stein directed. British National. Black and white. 100 minutes.

1946 Lisbon Story

Tauber's last feature is set in wartime Lisbon. Intelligence officer David Farrar uses his French actress fiancée Patricia Burke to foil Nazi Walter Rilla. Tauber has a small supporting role. Paul L. Stein directed. British National. Black and white. 103 minutes. Opera Dubs video.

1953 The Richard Tauber Story

Rudolf Schock portrays Tauber in *Du bist die Welt für mich*, an Austrian film biography released in the U.S. as *The Richard Tauber Story*. It pictures the singer rising from obscurity to fame with Tauber's recordings used as the singing voice. The plot revolves around the tenor's love for a ballerina who quits the stage because of a bad heart. Ernst Marischka wrote and directed it. Black and white. In German. 100 minutes. Opera Dubs video.

1958 Richard Tauber

American singer John Hendrik, a colleague of Tauber's, narrates this German SFB television film. It tells the story of Tauber's life, including his close collaboration with Lehar and the fact that he had to leave Germany in 1933 because he was Jewish. Excerpts from a 16mm film made by Tauber while he was touring the U.S. are featured as well as newsreel and other archival film. Black and white. In German. 30 minutes.

1971 This Was Richard Tauber

Charles Castle's film biography traces the history of the tenor's career over a thirty-year period. There are unique excerpts from films made by Tauber himself, films of scenes from stage shows, meetings with personalities and tributes to the singer. Castle's film was made with the help of Tauber's widow Diane Napier and is devoted primarily to his singing. The soundtrack was also released as a record. Color. In English. 90 minutes.

TAVIANI, VITTORIO/PAOLO
Italian film directors (1929/1931-)

The brothers Vittorio and Paolo Taviani have had wide success with such movies as *Padre Padrone* and *Allonsafan*. They say their childhood was dominated by live concerts and this helps explain why music is a major component of their films. *The Night of the Shooting Stars* and *Kaos* both feature music from operas. See THE MARRIAGE OF FIGARO (1984 film), TANNHÄUSER (1982 film).

TCHAIKOVSKY, PYOTR
Russian composer (1840-1893)

Peter Ilyich Tchaikovsky completed ten operas and devoted much of his time to composing them though he is probably better known for his piano and orchestral works. His first opera was *The Voyevoda* which premiered in 1868, the last was *Iolanta* in 1891. Tchaikovsky's personal life has been much gossiped about and has provided the basis for a number of not very enlightening films. Although he was homosexual, he jumped into a bad marriage that nearly drove him to suicide. It is worth noting that in his lifetime he was Russia's only full-time professional composer and that this was possible simply because he had a rich patroness. His most popular operas, *Eugene Onegin* and *The Queen of Spades*, are available in multiple film and video versions. See EUGENE ONEGIN, IOLANTA, THE MAID OF ORLEANS, THE QUEEN OF SPADES.

1948 Song of My Heart

Frank Sundstrom portrays Tchaikovsky in this American film about the composer written and directed by Benjamin Glazer. Its basic plot is that Tchaikovsky is tormented because he can't marry a princess. David Leonard plays Rimsky-Korsakov, Lewis Howard is Mussorgsky, Robert Barron is Borodin and William Ruhl is Cui. Jose Iturbi plays the piano music. The film was profoundly disliked by both critics and audiences and is now virtually forgotten. Allied Artists. Black and white. In English. 92 minutes.

1959 Tchaikovsky

This is a respectful Soviet documentary about the composer produced by the Central Documentary Film Studio of Moscow. It follows the life and career of the composer from childhood through his adult life and includes a number of musical excerpts. Pianists Sviatoslav Richter and Van Cliburn are among the featured performers. Color. In Russian. 50 minutes.

1964 The Peter Tchaikovsky Story

A Disney documentary film about the composer. It highlights his life with focus on successes, failures, loves and hates. Color. In English. 30 minutes.

1970 Tchaikovsky

Innokenti Smoktunovsky stars as Tchaikovsky in *Krasnaya Palatka*, a stolid 70mm Soviet biography of the composer directed by Igor Talankin. The composer is treated most reverently as his life and career is depicted from youth to old age. Dimitri Tiomkin arranged the music for the film including selections from *Eugene Onegin* and *The Queen of Spades*. The singers are Vladimir Atlantov, Irina Arkipova, Galina Oleinitchenko, Lev Vlasenko and Valentina Levko. The cinematography is by Margarita Pilikhina and the screenplay by Budimir Metalnikov, Yuri Naghibin and Talankin MGM-Mosfilm. Color. In Russian. 108 minutes.

1971 The Music Lovers

Director Ken Russell relishes the music but his vision of Tchaikovsky in this British film is more likely to dismay than enlighten. Richard Chamberlain plays Tchaikovsky with Glenda Jackson as his wife Nina. Like the curate's egg, the film is good in parts. Opera selections include the "Letter Song" from *Eugene Onegin* sung by April Cantelo and "Porgi Amor" from *The Marriage of Figaro*. Melvyn Bragg's screenplay is based on the book *Beloved Friend* by Catherine Drinker Bowen and Barbara von Meck. Douglas Slocombe was the cinematographer. Color. In English. 122 minutes.

1986 Tchaikovsky

Vladamir Ashkenazy portrays Tchaikovsky in two linked British films by writer/director Chrisopher Nupen. *Tchaikovsky's Women* tells the story of his life and career up to the time of his marriage and the opera *Eugene Onegin*. *Fate* is concerned with his life and musical ideas through *Manfred* and the Fifth and Sixth Symphonies. The music is played by the Swedish Radio Symphony Orchestra. Allegro Films. Color. In English 120 minutes. Teldec video.

1993 A Gala for Tchaikovsky

This is a record of a gala program at the Royal Opera House, Covent Garden, celebrating the 100th anniversary of the death of the composer. Placido Domingo sings Lensky's aria from *Eugene Onegin*, Dmitri Hvorostovsky sings arias from *Sadko* and The *Queen of Spades*, Anna Tomowa-Sintow sings Lisa's aria from *The Queen of Spades*, Paata Burchuladze sings arias from *Iolanta* and *Sadko* and Sergei Leiferkus sings an aria from *Aleko*. Kiri Te Kanawa sneaks in some Puccini and sings Musetta's aria from *La Bohème*. The evening includes ballet as well as opera with the music performed by the Royal Opera House Orchestra conducted by Bernard Haitink and Valeyr Gergiev. Color. 90 minutes. On video and Pioneer laser.

TEATRO ALLA SCALA
Milan opera house (1778-)

The Teatro alla Scala in Milan, Italy's most famous opera house, was built in 1778, partially destroyed in World War II and rebuilt and reopened in 1946. There are nearly as many videos of operas at La Scala as there are of operas at the Met. Most begin by showing La Scala from the square in front of the theater but Jean Pierre Ponnelle's film of *La Cenerentola* actually prowls around the theater lobby during the overture. The opera house is also featured in many Italian fiction films. See CLAUDIO ABBADO (1990), ADRIANA LECOUVREUR (1989), AIDA (1986), ANDREA CHÉNIER (1985), ATTILA (1991), LA CENERENTOLA (1981), COSÌ FAN TUTTE (1989), DON CARLO (1992), DON GIOVANNI (1989), LA DONNA DEL LAGO (1992), I DUE FOSCARI (1990), ERNANI (1982), LA FANCIULLA DEL WEST (1991), FEDORA (1993), LO FRATE 'NNAMORATO (1990), GIANNI SCHICCHI (1983), I LOMBARDI ALLA PRIMA CROCIATA (1984), LUCIA DI LAMMERMOOR (1992), MADAMA BUTTERFLY (1986), NABUCCO (1986), PAGLIACCI (1968), SUOR ANGELICA (1983), LA TRAVIATA (1992), IL TRITTICO (1983), IL TABARRO (1983), VERDI REQUIEM (1967), I VESPRI SICILIANI (1990), WILLIAM TELL (1991).

1937 Regina Della Scala

Queen of La Scala is an Italian feature film designed to glorify La Scala Opera House and much of it was shot on location inside the theater. *Regina della Scala*, in the film, is the name of an opera by a young composer which will be sung by his prima donna love. The director of La Scala tells the composer of the difficulties the architect Piermarini had when he designed the theater and the problems Verdi faced when audiences booed *Un Giorno di Regno*. The film includes excerpts from operas by Mascagni, Salieri, Pergolesi, Rossini, Donizetti, Puccini and Verdi. Mascagni himself appears in the film along with La Scala tenor Galliano Masini and a cross-section of Milan nobility. Guido Salvini and Camilo Mastrocinque wrote and directed the film. Black and white. In Italian. 88 minutes.

1943 La Primadonna

Two sopranos become deadly rivals at La Scala in the early 19th century in this Italian feature film. When a young singer substitutes for the theater's prima donna, she is such a success that the angry older woman decides to kill her. The prima donna is played by Anneliese Uhlig and sung by Maria Caniglia while the new singer is played by Maria Mercader and sung by Lina Pagliughi. The film is based on a novel by Filippo Sacchi. Ivo Perelli directed. Black and white. In Italian 88 minutes.

1994 La Scala, A Documentary of Performances

A fascinating film showing the history of Teatro alla Scala and those who have sung there. Much of it consists of opera scenes from the Italian movies *Follie per l'Opera*, *Giuseppe Verdi*, *Al Diavolo la Celebrita*, *Melodie Immortali* and *La Donna Piu Bella del Mondo*. There are scenes of Mascagni conducting the premiere of his *Nerone*, images of the devastated theater after World War II bombing wrecked it and a selection of rehearsals and opening nights. Mario Del Monaco, Tito Schipa, Tito Gobbi, Ferruccio Tagliavini and Arturo Toscanini are among those seen in performance with operas by Verdi, Puccini, Rossini and Bellini. Color & black and white. With English narration. 63 minutes. VIEW video and on laser.

1996 50th Anniversary Concert of Rebuilt La Scala

La Scala celebrated the 50th anniversary of its rebuilding in 1996 with a special concert conducted by Riccardo Muti. The event was filmed by the noted Italian filmmaker Liliana Cavani for SACIS and Italian television. Color. In Italian 100.

TEBALDI, RENATA
Italian soprano (1922-)

Renata Tebaldi was born in Pesaro, studied in Parma and made her debut in *Mefistofele* in 1944. She was one of those on stage at La Scala when it reopened in 1946 with Toscanini conducting and was a regular at the Milan theater until 1954. She first sang in England and the U.S in 1950, joined the Metropolitan Opera in 1955 and remained with the Met for twenty years. As her records and videos show, she had one of the most beautiful voices of her time and her reputation remains high. She was noted for her glorious Mimi which is heard on the soundtrack of the film *Moonstruck*. She also provided the singing voice for Sophia Loren in the famous Italian film of *Aida*. See AIDA (1953/1987 film), ANDREA CHÉNIER (1961), BELL TELEPHONE HOUR (1967), LA BOHÈME (1987 film), CASA RICORDI, LA FORZA DEL DESTINO (1958), LOHENGRIN (1947), METROPOLITAN OPERA (1957), OTELLO (1962), TOSCA (1983 film).

1958 Tebaldi Rehearses La Bohème
Tebaldi is shown rehearsing the aria "Sono andati" from *La Bohème* with a pianist in 1958. The film of the scene is included in the video *Legends of Opera*. Black and white. 2 minutes. Legato Classics video.

1959 Renata Tebaldi & Franco Corelli
Renata Tebaldi is seen in fine form in her performances on The *Voice of Firestone* TV series on Feb. 2; 1959. She sings three arias from Puccini operas: "Un bel dì" from *Madama Butterfly*, "Vissi d'arte" from *Tosca* and "Donde lieta usci" from *La Bohème*. Black and white. 35 minutes. VAI video.

1983 Tebaldi la Voce d'Angelo
Renata Tebaldi's musical career is the focus of this French TV documentary made for the Antenne 2 *Musiques au coeur* series. In addition to interviews, the program includes archival material of the young Tebaldi. She is seen in excerpts from *Otello, Aida, Andrea Chénier, Madama Butterfly, Adriana Lecouvreur, Tosca* and *Manon Lescaut*. Black and white. In French and Italian. 70 minutes.

TE KANAWA, KIRI
New Zealand soprano (1944-)

Dame Kiri Te Kanawa began her career in New Zealand but it was her singing Elena in *La Donna del Lago* at the Camden Festival in England in 1969 that began her rise to stardom. In 1971 she sang the Countess in *The Marriage of Figaro* at Covent Garden and international recognition began. She made her triumphant Metropolitan Opera debut in 1974 as Desdemona. Te Kanawa's voice, beauty and dignity have made her one of the most popular singers in the world today. Joseph Losey's *Don Giovanni* is probably her best film but the many videos of her stage performances are almost all splendid. See ANTHOLOGIES (1988/1992), CAPRICCIO (1993), CITIZEN KANE, DON GIOVANNI (1978), DIE FLEDERMAUS (1983/1986), DIVAS (1995), PLÁCIDO DOMINGO (1984), MANON LESCAUT (1983), THE MARRIAGE OF FIGARO (1973/1976), MEETING VENUS, METROPOLITAN OPERA (1983), OTELLO (1982/ 1993), DER ROSENKAVALIER (1982/1985), SIMON BOCCANEGRA (1991/ 1995), GEORG SOLTI (1990), THE SORCERESS, SOUTH PACIFIC (1986), TOSCA (1983 film), WEST SIDE STORY (1985), GIUSEPPE VERDI (1991).

1966 Don't Let It Get You
Kiri Te Kanawa was an unknown singer when she appeared in this New Zealand movie in which she has only eighth billing. *Variety* reviewed the film but Te Kanawa attracted little attention and wasn't even mentioned. The film, a tourist musical set in a New Zealand resort, centers around a drummer looking for a job. Most of the singing is by Maori singer Howard Morrison. John O'Shea directed. Pacific Films. Black and white. 80 minutes.

1978 Kiri Te Kanawa: Royal Gala Concert
This is a record of Te Kanawa's first recital at the Royal Opera House, Covent Garden. She looks stunning and sings beautifully accompanied by pianist Richard Amner. The program includes songs by Strauss, Schubert, Schumann, Wolf, Faure, Duparc, Walton and Dvořák. Richard Baker introduces the songs and David Heather directed the video on Dec. 3, 1978. Color. 60 minutes. Kultur video.

1985 Kiri Te Kanawa at Christmas
Te Kanawa celebrates Christmas with a concert at the Barbican Hall in London. She is joined by conductor Carl Davis and a hundred musicians and singers from the Philharmonia Orchestra and Tallis Chamber Choir. There are eleven Christmas songs including "Silent Night" and "White Christmas." Brian Kay is the TV presenter. Color. 50 minutes. View Video.

1989 Canteloube: Chants D'Auvergne
Te Kanawa sings Canteloube's famous Songs of the Auvergne in a concert with backing from the English Chamber Orchestra conducted by Jeffrey Tate. Peter Bartlett directed the video. Color. 52 minutes. London video.

1987 An Evening With Kiri Te Kanawa
Te Kanawa gives a concert at the Royal Albert Hall in London. In the first half she sings arias from *The Magic Flute, The Marriage of Figaro, Faust, Louise, Tosca* and *La Rondine*. In the second half she sings the role of Eliza Doolittle in a concert version of *My Fair Lady* with Jeremy Irons as Henry Higgins and Warren Mitchell as Eliza's father. John Mauceri leads the London Symphony Orchestra. Yvonne Littlewood directed the video. Color. 108 minutes. London video and on laser.
(Highlights version available in the *Great Moments* video series as Volume 9).

1989 Kiri in Concert
Te Kanawa is shown in concert at the Barbican in London on April 29, 1989, with Carl Davis leading the Royal Philharmonic Orchestra. Highlights include the Countess's arias from *The Marriage of Figaro*, "O mio babbino caro" from *Gianni Schicchi* and "Pace, pace, mio dio" from *La Forza del Destino*. She also sings arias and songs by Wolf-Ferrari, Charpentier, Puccini, Canteloube, Herbert, Gershwin and Rodgers and Hammerstein. Hefin Owen directed the video. Color. 100 minutes. EMI Classics video.

1990 Kiri Concert Special
Two 1990 concerts by Te Kanawa were filmed for her South Bank Show and later combined to create this video. In the first she sings at an open-air concert in Wellington in New Zealand. In the second she performs at the Royal Naval College chapel in Greenwich. Color. 60 minutes. Polygram (England) video.

1991 Kiri Sings Mozart
Te Kanawa sings at St. David's Hall with the Welsh National Opera Orchestra conducted by Sir Charles Mackerras. The concert includes arias from *Don Giovanni, The Magic Flute* and *La Clemenza di Tito*. Color. 90 minutes. On video.

1991 Together... Kiri & André on Broadway
This is a documentary film about the making of Te Kanawa's jazz album *Sidetracks*. André Previn plays piano and works with her as she picks the songs and learns how to swing them in a jazz manner with help from bassist Ray Brown and guitarist Mundell Lowe. The songs include "It Could Happen To You," "Honeysuckle Rose," "It Never Was You" and "Cute." Robin Lough directed the film. Color. 52 minutes. Phillips video.

1991 Kiri Te Kanawa
A superb South Bank Show profile of Te Kanawa in which she sings Mozart, Strauss, Handel, Gershwin and Maori songs. She is shown talking about her life, roles and future and preparing her role as the Countess in *Capriccio*. There is a touching scene of her in New Zealand singing "Now Is The Hour" as she remembers leaving years before to the same song. Nigel Wattis produced the film. Color. 60 minutes. On video.

1991 Nobel Jubilee Concert
Te Kanawa gives a concert in Stockholm to celebrate the Nobel Prize Jubilee. She is partnered by Georg Solti in a program that is mostly Mozart. Color. 86 minutes. Kultur video.

1994 Kiri: Her Greatest Hits Live
Te Kanawa celebrates her 50th birthday with a concert at the Royal Albert Hall, on March 13, 1994. She sings Korngold's aria from *Citizen Kane* that she helped revive, her famous "Porgi amor," "Art is Calling for Me" from Victor Herbert's *The Enchantress*, "Depuis le jour" and songs by Rodgers and Hammerstein and Andrew Lloyd Weber. Dennis O'Neill teams with her for duets from *La Bohème*, a Maori choir joins her for music from her native country and André Previn conducts her in a Strauss song and a Mozart aria. On the rest the London Symphony Orchestra is led by Stephen Barlow. Color. 90 minutes. London video and laser.

1994 Christmas with Kiri Te Kanawa
A record of a carol concert by Te Kanawa at Coventry Cathedral in December 1994. She is joined by bass Michael George, trumpeter Jouko Harjanne and the choirs of Coventry and Lichfield cathedrals. Robin Stapleton conducts the BBC Philharmonic Orchestra. Color. 60 minutes. Teldec (England) video.

TELEPHONE, THE

1947 opera by Menotti

Gian Carlo Menotti's one-act comic opera *The Telephone or L'Amour à Trois* was composed as a curtain raiser for *The Medium* on Broadway. It's a slight but enjoyable entertainment. Ben is trying to propose to Lucy but is always being interrupted by her talking on the telephone. He eventually solves the problem by leaving the house and phoning in his proposal. See also GIAN CARLO MENOTTI.

1948 NBC telecast
Barbara Cooper is the woman on the telephone with David Daniels the man trying to propose in this NBC TV studio production by Roger Englander. This was one of the first operas on network television. The singers, both students at the Curtis Institute of Music, are accompanied on piano by Maricarol Hanson. W.C. Smith designed the production directed by Paul Nickell. It was telecast on May 28, 1948, from NBC's Philadelphia station WPTZ. Black and white. 24 minutes.

1952 CBS Omnibus telecast
Edith Gordon stars as Lucy with Andrew Cainey as Ben in this CBS television production of *The Telephone* created for the *Omnibus* program. Emmanuel Balaban conducts the orchestra and Andrew McCullough directed the live telecast on Nov. 16, 1952. Black and white. In English. 25 minutes.

1992 BBC TV Scotland
Carole Farley gives a bravura performance as Lucy with Russell Smythe as her boyfriend Ben in this entertaining production of *The Telephone* for BBC TV in Scotland. Farley's husband José Serebrier conducts the Scottish Chamber Orchestra. Mike Newman produced and directed the opera. Color. In English. 23 minutes. PolyGram video/ London laserdisc.

TELEVISION OPERAS

Operas have been created for television for nearly half a century. The first was Gian-Carlo Menotti's *Amahl and the Night Visitors*, commissioned by NBC and telecast in 1951. It was so popular that it led to many further TV operas in the U.S. and Europe. The first BBC TV opera was Richard Arnell's *Love in Transit* telecast in 1955 followed by Arthur Benjamin's *Mañana* telecast on Feb. 1, 1956.

Television operas tend to be relatively short with small casts and strong stories. Listed below are some of the better known works. See the operas or composers for further details.

1951 - Menotti-*Amahl and the Night Visitors* (NBC)
1953 - Martinu - *The Marriage* (NBC)
1955 - Foss - *Griffelkin* (NBC)
1955 - Arnell - *Love in Transit* (BBC)
1956 - Benjamin - *Mañana* (BBC)
1957 - Hollingsworth - *La Grande Bretèche* (NBC)
1958 - Menotti - *Maria Golovin* (NBC)
1959 - Rossellini - *La Campane* (RAI)
1957 - Sutermeister - *Seraphine* (Swiss)
1959 - Badings - *Salto Mortale* (Dutch)
1960 - Bliss - *Tobias and the Angel* (BBC)
1961 - Prodromides - *Les Perses* (RTF)
1962 - Tate - *Dark Pilgrimage* (BBC)
1962 - Coleman - *Christmas Carol* (BBC)
1962 - Malipiero - *Battono alla Porta* (RAI)
1963 - Ton de Leeuw - *Alceste* (Holland)
1963 - Rautavaara - *Kaivos* (Finland)
1964 - Sutermeister-*The Canterville Ghost* (ZDF)
1966 - Krenek - *Der Zauberspiegel* (Bavaria)
1967 - Lidholm - *Holländarn* (Sweden)
1967 - Vlad - *La Fantarca* (RAI)
1967-Norholm-*Invitation to the Scaffold* (Denmark)
1971 - Britten - *Owen Wingrave* (BBC)
1976 -Hoddinott-*Murder the Magician* (C4)
1995 - Copeland - *Horse Opera* (C4)
1995 - Moore - *Camera* (Channel 4)

TEMPESTAD, LA

1882 zarzuela by Chapí

La Tempestad (The Storm) is one of Spanish composer Ruperto Chapí's most popular zarzuelas. Simon, an innkeeper in a Breton coastal village, has raised the orphan Angela whose father was murdered during a storm. She is in love with the fisherman Roberto (a soprano role) but Simon opposes their marriage. Simon accuses the rich Beltran of being the murderer but finally confesses that he is the guilty one. See also RUPERTO CHAPÍ.

1943 Javier Rivera film
Javier Rivera directed this Spanish film of the zarzuela for the Cepilsa company in Madrid. It stars Maria Luisa Gerona, Rufino Ingles, Julia Lajos and Manuel Arbo and was photographed by Manuel Beringola. Black and white. In Spanish. 91 minutes.

TENSE MOMENTS FROM OPERA
1922 English opera film series

This series of short opera films was produced by Harry B. Parkinson in 1922 for Master-British Exhibitors/Gaumont. It seems to have been an attempt to be cultural and popular at the same time. The operas were filmed in an abridged form with well-known stage players and had a format similar to the company's other series *Tense Moments from Great Plays* and *Tense Moments with Great Authors*. The directors included George Wynn, Challis Sanderson and Edwin J. Collins. The operas chosen for the series are a reflection of their popularity at the time. See (all 1922) CARMEN, DON GIOVANNI, FAUST, FRA DIAVOLO, THE LILY OF KILLARNEY, LUCIA DI LAMMERMOOR, MARITANA, MARTHA, RIGOLETTO, SAMSON ET DALILA, LA TRAVIATA, IL TROVATORE..

TEREZIN OPERAS

Two operas have been revived in recent years because of interest in Jewish composers Viktor Ullman and Hans Krása whose work was composed or staged in the World War II Terezin (Theresienstadt) concentration camp outside Prague. These operas have been filmed and have entries in this book. See BRUNDIBAR, DER KAISER VON ATLANTIS.

1994 The Music of Terezin
Simon Broughton's documentary film about the music and musicians of Terezin features excerpts from Ullman's and Krása's operas. Included are scenes of the original Terezin production of *Brundibar*, filmed by camp officials for a Nazi propaganda film, and staged scenes of *The Emperor of Atlantis*. Color. In English. 30 minutes.

TERFEL, BRYN
Welsh baritone (1965-)

Bryn Terfel, who made his debut in 1990 in *Così Fan Tutte* with the Welsh National Opera, has rapidly become one of the most acclaimed modern singers. He nearly rivaled Cecilia Bartoli in publicity when he made his first appearance at the Metropolitan Opera. He has been particularly admired for his Figaro in *The Marriage of Figaro* which he has sung widely and which is on video from Paris. See DIE FRAU OHNE SCHATTEN (1992), THE MARRIAGE OF FIGARO (1993), CLAUDIO MONTEVERDI (1985), OEDIPUS REX (1992).

1995 The Last Night of the Proms
Bryn Terfel is the featured singer in a performance of Walton's *Belshazzar's Feast* performed in the first half of this Proms concert in London. Andrew Davis conducts the BBC. Symphony Orchestra and Chorus. Color. 60 minutes. Teldec video.

TERRY, PAUL
Animated film producer (1887-1971)

Paul Terry and his Terrytoons were a staple in the Hollywood animated cartoon world from the 1910s to the 1950s. Among his famous cartoon characters are the Heckle and Jeckle crows and Mighty Mouse. Several of his cartoons had operatic content.

1935 Opera Night
A night at the opera cartoon-style in this Terrytoons Studio film directed by Paul Terry and Frank Moser. Black and white. 7 minutes.

1944 Carmen's Veranda
A veritable hodgepodge of opera music is used in this Terrytoon about the gallant knight Gandy Goose who rescues a fair damsel from a castle. There's a bit of Rossini, a little Gilbert and Sullivan and a touch of Bizet. Color. 7 minutes.

1952 Off to the Opera
A classic operatic cartoon about the argumentative magpies Heckle and Jeckle. It was made at the Terrytoons studio and directed by Connie Rasinski. Color. 7 minutes.

TETRAZZINI, LUISA
Italian soprano (1871-1940)

Luisa Tetrazzini was a major star in the first third of the century and one of the most dazzling singers ever to make records. She made her debut in 1890 and was acclaimed at the major opera houses for the beauty of her voice and for her technical agility. Tetrazzini made many recordings which are still admired today but unfortunately she does not seem to have been very interested in the cinema. Her popularity was so high that the 1909 Ziegfeld Follies featured a song called "I'm After Madame Tetrazzini's Job."

1909 Romeo und Julia
Tetrazzini stars as Juliet in a short scene from the Gounod opera *Roméo et Juliette*. This apparently lost

early sound film was made in Germany in 1909 by Deutsche Vitascope as one of the primitive synchronized sound films then popular. It's presumed that Tetrazzini sang the "Waltz Song" from the opera. Black and white. In German. About 5 minutes.

1932 Tetrazzini Listens to Caruso
Tetrazzini listens to a Caruso recording of "M'appari" from *Martha* and then joins him in song. Her voice may not be what it once was, she was 63 at the time, but the scene is a wonder. It is included in a number of videos but notably on *Legends of Opera*. Black and white. 2 minutes. Legato Classics video.

TEYTE, MAGGIE
English soprano (1988-1976)

Dame Maggie Teyte began her career singing Mozart with Jean de Reszke in Paris in 1906. She sang around the world from London to Chicago and was once partnered with Mary Garden whom she had succeeded in Paris as Mélisande. She can be seen on film with Kirsten Flagstad in scenes from a famous production of *Dido and Aeneas* in London. See DIDO AND AENEAS (1951).

THAÏS
1894 opera by Massenet

Thaïs is a fourth century prostitute rescued from evil ways by a monk who falls in love with her. They both die, of course, but not before they sing some fine music. Jules Massenet's opera is not well known today except for its contribution to the violin repertory. The "Meditation for Solo Violin," taken from Act Two, has acquired a life of its own and was used to memorable effect in a Hollywood film. The opera was written for American soprano Sibyl Sanderson, Massenet's mistress at the time and one of the prototypes for the opera singer/mistress in *Citizen Kane*. It's based on a scandalous Anatole France novel adapted by librettist Louis Gallet. *Thaïs* is currently out of vogue and there are no videos of major productions. See also JULES MASSENET.

1985 Bordeaux Ecole
Lysiane Leonard stars as Thaïs in this experimental French production of the opera by Jacques Bourgeois filmed by FR3 at the École de Bordeaux. Philippe Rouillon plays Athanael and Christian Papis is Nicias. Gerard Laurent directed the staging, Alain Gaucher designed the sets and costumes and Jacques Pernoo conducted the Bordeaux School Symphonic Orchestra. Patrice Bellot directed the video. Color. In French. 90 minutes. Lyric video.

Early/related films

1911 Louis Feuillade film
A French film based on the opera was directed by serial master Louis Feuillade for Gaumont. It was released in the US to a positive reception though *The New York Dramatic Mirror* did comment adversely on the operatic style of the acting. About 10 minutes.

1914 Constance Crawley film
Constance Crawley stars as Thaïs with Arthur Maude as her monk lover in this American film. It's based on the Anatole France novel rather than the opera or so its copyright-conscious producers claimed. Crawley and Maude also directed. About 20 minutes.

1916 Anton Giulio Bragaglia film
Anton Giulio Bragaglia, a major exponent of the Futurist art movement, used Futurist designs in this Italian film based on the opera. It was made for his Novissima Film company. About 60 minutes. A print survives.

1917 Mary Garden film
Opera diva Mary Garden portrays Thaïs in her debut film. She had starred in the opera at the Manhattan Opera House and it was hoped her reputation would make the film popular. It didn't though Garden herself was quite photogenic. The film was shot in operatic poses in a stilted stage acting style and audiences were not impressed. The support cast includes Hamilton Revelle, Crawford Kent and Lionel Adams. Frank H. Crane and Hugo Ballin directed at the Goldwyn Studios in Fort Lee, New Jersey. About 75 minutes.

1921 Stardust
Opera-singer-to-be Hope Hampton stars in this film based on a Fannie Hurst novel. It's the story of a young soprano from Iowa who goes to New York and becomes famous singing in *Thaïs*. The opera scene was accompanied by the Massenet music in theaters. About 80 minutes.

1939 Golden Boy
The "Meditation for Solo Violin" from Act II of *Thaïs* is played by musician-turned-boxer William Holden in this fine movie. He performs it on a violin given him by his father for his 21st birthday. Rouben Mamoulian directed. Black and white. 99 minutes

1993 L'Accompagnatrice
The Accompanist is a French film about a beautiful singer and her plain-jane accompanist in Paris in 1942. Soprano Irene (Elena Safonova, sung by Laurence Monteyrol) uses as her signature tune the Mirror Aria from *Thaïs* ("Dis-moi que je serai belle éternellement"). Pianist Sophie (Romane Bohringer, piano by Angeline Pondepeyre) is her accompanist. Claude Miller directed. Color. In French with English subtitles. 100 minutes.

THEBOM, BLANCHE
American mezzo-soprano (1918-)

Pennsylvania-born Blanche Thebom studied with opera divas Margaret Matzenauer and Edyth Walker and began her opera career with the Metropolitan on tour. She made her New York debut with the company in 1944 as Fricka in *Die Walküre* and stayed with the Met until 1967. She also sang at Covent Garden and Glyndebourne where she was noted for her Dorabella and Carmen. Thebom appeared briefly in opera sequences in two Hollywood films and a documentary but her best screen singing was on television; she was a frequent guest on the *Voice of Firestone* TV series and there is a fine video of highlights from her programs. See also BELL TELEPHONE HOUR (1947), THE GREAT CARUSO, SOL HUROK (1956), METROPOLITAN OPERA (1953).

1944 Irish Eyes Are Smiling
Blanche Thebom appears in an opera scene in this movie opposite Leonard Warren. The film is a tuneful biography of songwriter Ernest R. Ball starring Dick Haymes and June Haver. Gregory Ratoff directed. 20th Century-Fox. Color. 90 minutes.

1950-59 Blanche Thebom in Opera & Song
Thebom appeared on the *Voice of Firestone* television series 36 times when she was a major Metropolitan Opera star. This video shows highlights from three appearances with performances in operas and musicals. She is seen in arias from *Samson et Dalila*

and *Il Trovatore* and in songs from *My Fair Lady* and *A Connecticut Yankee*. Black and white. 28 minutes. VAI video.

THESPIS
1871 operetta by Gilbert & Sullivan

Thespis or The Gods Grown Old was the first collaboration between W. S. Gilbert and Arthur Sullivan and opened at the Gaiety theater on Dec. 26, 1871. It was modeled on Offenbach's *Orpheus in Hell* with mortals exchanging jobs with bored gods. It was successful but not a hit. The libretto has survived but most of the original music was lost or destroyed by Sullivan. See also GILBERT AND SULLIVAN.

1989 Gilbert & Sullivan Society video
Thespis, the "lost opera" was staged in 1989 in a reconstructed version created by the Connecticut Gilbert and Sullivan Society. This is said to be the only performance of *Thespis* staged this century! It was taped in performance for distribution by the society. Color. In English. 110 min. Gilbert & Sullivan Society video.

THOMAS, AMBROISE
French composer (1811-1896)

Ambroise Thomas was a very popular composer at the turn of the century when his operas *Hamlet* and *Mignon* were part of the standard repertory. Arias from these two operas are often found on phonograph records of this earlier era and both operas are available complete on CD. It is probable that his operas will come back into fashion but currently only *Mignon* is on video. See MIGNON.

THOMAS, JOHN CHARLES
American baritone (1891-1960)

John Charles Thomas was born in Pennsylvania and began his singing career in Broadway operettas and Gilbert and Sullivan. He starred opposite Marguerite Namara in Franz Lehár's operetta *Alone at Last* in 1915. In 1924 he made his opera debut as Amonasro in *Aida* at the Washington Opera. He made his first appearance in Europe in Brussels and went on to sing in Berlin, Vienna and Covent Garden. He came back to the U.S. in 1930, sang opera for a time in San Francisco and Chicago and then made his debut with the Metropolitan in 1934 as Germont in *La Traviata*. He sang at the Met until 1943 and in the 1940s also became an NBC radio singing star.

1923 Under the Red Robe
Thomas sang the Prologue to *Pagliacci* at the premiere of this epic in which he starred. It's an historical costume drama in which Thomas is ordered to catch a suspected traitor by Cardinal Richelieu. He does so but falls in love with the captive's sister, Alma Rubens. Alan Crosland directed for Goldwyn-Cosmopolitan. Black and white. About 100 minutes..

1927 Vitaphone sound films
"John Charles Thomas, Outstanding American Baritone," as he was billed, made three Vitaphone sound shorts in 1927. In the first he sings the Prologue to *Pagliacci* and in the second the popular songs "Danny Deever" and "In The Gloaming." The third Vitaphone film teams him with musical comedy soprano Vivienne Segal, a favorite of Rodgers and Hart, in Sigmund Romberg's "Will You Remember" from *Maytime*. Black and white. Each about 8 minutes.

1950-55 John Charles Thomas in Opera & Song
Highlights from early 1950s *Voice of Firestone* television programs on which Thomas performed. He sings arias from *Hamlet* and *Un Ballo in Maschera* plus songs by Rudolph Friml, Jerome Kern and Rodgers and Hammerstein. Black and white. 55 minutes. VAI video.

THOMSON, VIRGIL
American composer (1896-1989)

Virgil Thomson composed only three operas but the two with Gertrude Stein as librettist are among the most influential American operas. First was the amazing *Four Saints in Three Acts* (1934) with a fascinating non-narrative libretto, memorable poetry and an all-black cast. Second was *The Mother of Us All* (1947) based around Susan B. Anthony and women's suffrage. Thomson's last opera was *Lord Byron* (1972) with a libretto by Jack Larson. Thomson's operas are not on video but there are scenes from them on the documentary about Thomson and there was a WNET telecast of *Four Saints* in 1973 with Claudia Lindsey as Saint Teresa I. Thomson was also an influential composer for film and ballet and an important music critic.

1936-1964 Virgil Thomson's films
Virgil Thomson is one of the great film music composers though his output was small and mostly for documentaries. The best are probably Pare Lorentz's *The Plow That Broke The Plains* (1936) and *The River* (1937) and Robert Flaherty's *Louisiana Story* (1948). He also collaborated with Marc Blitzstein on the music for Joris Ivens' classic *Spanish Earth* (1937). Thomson's only fiction film was John Cromwell's *The Goddess* (1958) but he composed the music for Peter Brook's TV production of *King Lear* with Orson Welles. Thomson also wrote music for the documentaries *Tuesday in November* (1948), made for the U.S. Government, *Power Among Men* (1959), made for the United Nations, and *Voyage to America* (1964), made for the New York World's Fair.

1970 Gertrude Stein: When This You See Remember Me
This PBS documentary by Perry Miller Adato about poet/librettist Gertrude Stein includes commentary about and scenes from the Thomson/Stein opera *Four Saints in Three Acts*. Color. 60 minutes. Video at MTR.

1974 Day at Night: Virgil Thomson
James Day talks to Thomson about his life and work in this television show directed by Bob Hankal. Color. 29 minutes. Video at MTR.

1986 Virgil Thomson at 90
John Huszar's fine film tribute to the composer is primarily about his music but gives ample biographical background. Thomson sets the tone and guides the film along its way talking about his friendships with Picasso, Gertrude Stein and Alice B. Toklas and his film scores. There are amazing filmed scenes of the original 1934 "cellophane" production of *Four Saints in Three Acts* and bits of *The Mother of Us All* and *Lord Byron*. Librettist Jack Larson talks about working with Thomson on *Byron*, mezzo Betty Allen sings part of *Four Saints* and Stein's poem "Susie Asado" and there is an excerpt from the ballet *Filling Station*. The film was first telecast on Dec. 30, 1980, as *Virgil Thomson: Composer* and updated and shown as *Virgil Thomson at 90* on Nov. 30, 1986. Color. 60 minutes. FilmAmerica video.

THREEPENNY OPERA, THE
1928 opera by Weill

Die Dreigroschenoper is an adaptation of John Gay's *The Beggar's Opera* as rewritten by Bertolt Brecht with new music by Kurt Weill. Brecht kept the outline of the original but poured his ideas about society, corruption, love, crime and justice into the libretto while Weill composed a most tuneful popular opera. It tells the story of petty crook Macheath (Mack the Knife) and his love affair with Polly Peachum, daughter of the chief of beggars. When he commits the sin of marrying her, he sets in motion a series of events that leads him to the gallows. Weill's wife Lotte Lenya has portrayed Jenny on stage and screen. The opera was not popular in the U.S. until it was revived in New York in 1954 in a new translation by Marc Blitzstein. The song "Mack the Knife" became a hit parade favorite through the revival. See also BERTOLT BRECHT, KURT WEILL.

1931 G.W. Pabst film
Lotte Lenya stars as Jenny in this *Die Dreigroschenoper*, a famous German film of the opera directed by G.W. Pabst. Rudolf Forster is Macheath, Caroline Neher is Polly Peachum, Fritz Rasp is Peachum, Ernst Busch is the Street Singer, Valeska Gert is Mrs. Peachum and Reinhold Schunzel is Tiger Brown. Fritz Arno Wagner was cinematographer and Andrei Andreiev designed the sets. Theo Mackeben, who conducted the stage performances, worked with Weill to adapt the opera. Brecht and Weill sued Pabst because he altered script and music but critics still rank the film as one of the great achievements of German cinema. Nero Films. Black and white. In German with English subtitles. 113 minutes. Janus video/Voyager laser.

1931 L'Opéra de Quat'Sous
G. W. Pabst's French film version of the opera uses the same sets and lighting but has a different all-French cast. Albert Prejean is Macheath, Odette Florelle is Polly Peachum, Margo Lion is Jenny, Bill Bocketts is the Street Singer, Gaston Modot is Peachum, Lucy de Matha is Mrs. Peachum and Jacques Henley is Tiger Brown. This version looks like the German film but because it is sung in French it has quite a different tone. Black and white. In French. 100 minutes. René Chateau (France) video.

1963 Sammy Davis Jr. film
Sammy Davis Jr. is strong as the Street Singer in this *Die Dreigroschenoper*, a weak film of the opera shot in both English and German. Curt Jurgens is Macheath, Hildegarde Knef is Jenny and June Ritchie is Polly Peachum with Maria Korber doing some of her singing. Gert Frobe is Peachum, Hilde Hildebrand is Mrs. Peachum, Lino Ventura is Tiger Brown and Marlene Warrlich is Lucy Brown. Peter Sandloff arranged the music and Proger Fellous was the cinematographer. Wolfgang Staudte directed for Embassy. Color. In English or German. 124 minutes.

1971 Giorgio Strehler video
Giorgio Strehler created this short version of *Die Dreigroschenoper* for Italian television following his huge success with the opera on stage. He gave it fresh impact by setting the story in Little Italy in New York at the turn of the century and Brecht was full of praise for his ideas. Italo Dosca was the TV director. Color. In Italian. 45 minutes.

1990 Julia Migenes film
Julia Migenes stars as Jenny in *Mack the Knife*, a lavish but dull English-language film of the opera directed by Menahem Golan. The starry cast includes Raul Julia as Macheath, Roger Daltry as the Street Singer, Rachel Roberts as Polly Peachum, Richard Harris as Peachum, Julie Walters as Mrs Peachum and Bill Nighy as Tiger Brown. Dov Seltzer conducts the music. Despite all this talent, the film doesn't really work and the fault probably lies with the director. Cannon. Color. In English. 122 minutes. Columbia Tristar video/laser.

Related film

1979 City of Women
Federico Fellini's *La Città delle Donne*, a fantasy about the power of women starring Marcello Mastroianni, features "Mack the Knife" on the soundtrack. Color. In Italian. 139 minutes.

1994 Quiz Show
Robert Redford's film concerns a famous 1950s television scandal. Music from *The Threepenny Opera* is used to show the similarities between the sleazy behavior of the characters in the film and the crooks in the opera. Bobby Darin sings the Moritat as "Mack the Knife" over the opening credits while Lyle Lovett performs it again over the closing credits. Color. 130 minutes.

THREE TENORS, THE
Opera concert series

The Three Tenors concerts are among the most popular opera events ever organized. The televised shows, the records and the videos have all been runaway successes. The first concert sold some nine million copies on audio and video after more millions watched it on TV from Rome in 1990 on the night before the World Cup. It was equally successful in 1994 in Los Angeles with even more people watching. It may not be great opera but it is certainly great show business. José Carreras, Placido Domingo and Luciano Pavarotti are the stars but conductor Zubin Mehta, organizer Tibor Rudas and video director Brian Large deserve much credit.

1990 The Three Tenors in Rome
The most popular opera video and CD ever released is not called "The Three Tenors" on its box but is usually referred to by that name. The actual title is *Carreras Domingo Pavarotti in Concert*. The concert was taped on July 7, 1990, at the Baths of Caracalla in Rome on the night before the World Cup final. There are 16 numbers, mostly solos like Pavarotti's version of "Nessun dorma" which was used as the World Cup theme. The *Turandot* aria is sung again by the trio as an encore along with "O sole mio." Zubin Mehta conducts the Rome Opera and Florence Maggio Musicale Orchestras. Brian Large directed the video. Color. 86 minutes. London video and laser

1990 The Three Tenors Encore
Probably the first sequel in opera video history, *Three Tenors Encore* was released because of the continuing interest in the original concert video. It goes behind the scenes of the taping of the original event, shows how it was set up, includes interviews with the tenors, features more singing and describes this amazing evening from a different viewpoint. There are also some splendid scenes of the Baths of Caracalla. Derek Jacobi narrates Color. 57 minutes. New Line video.

1994 The 3 Tenors in Concert 1994
The success of the Rome concert almost guaranteed the success of this follow-up in Los Angeles on July 16, 1994, and certainly the hype was even greater. Despite efforts to make the concert as populist as possible, it is an enjoyable event both vocally and visually. Where else could you see Frank Sinatra acknowledging anyone else singing "My Way?" And some of the selections are hardly common fare with Carreras singing an aria from Massenet's *Le Cid*, Domingo from *Luisa Miller* and Pavarotti from *Werther*. Zubin Mehta conducts and seems to enjoy the evening as much as the tenors. William Cosel directed the video. Color. In English. 89 minutes. Teldec video and laser.

1994 The Making of the 3 Tenors
A backstage documentary about the Los Angeles Three Tenors concert was rushed out soon after the concert video was released, this time with commentary by Roger Moore. Sets for the show are shown being built in Hungary and flown to Los Angeles, Lalo Schifrin talks about the repertoire, the tenors are shown relaxing in Monte Carlo and the final dress rehearsal is captured on film. Tibor Rudas created and produced the film directed in Los Angles by David Dinkins Jr. Color. 62 minutes. Warnervision video.

TIBBETT, LAWRENCE
American baritone (1896-1960)

Lawrence Tibbett occupies a special place in the history of screen opera. He was the first opera singer to became a Hollywood movie star in the sound era and his films helped break down prejudices against opera. He was born in Bakersfield, grew up in Los Angeles and began his career as a member of a light opera company. He made his debut as Amonasro in *Aida* at the Hollywood Bowl in 1923 and began singing at the Met the same year. His performance as Ford in *Falstaff* in 1925 made him a major star and won acclaim for his acting. His film career began in 1930 with *The Rogue Song*, an adaptation of Franz Lehar's operetta *Zigeunerliebe*. His next film was an adaptation of Romberg's *New Moon* with Grace Moore but the combination and the film didn't sparkle. Two more films were not successful so he went back to opera and to radio. He returned to Hollywood in the mid-thirties for his last two films. His popularity as an opera singer continued into the 1950s and he was so well known that he was able to substitute for Frank Sinatra on the *Your Hit Parade* radio show. He left the Met in 1950 after disagreements with Rudolph Bing but remained an active singer until his death in 1960. See also THE NEW MOON (1930), ZIGEUNERLIEBE (1930).

1931 The Cuban Love Song

Tibbett plays a fun-loving Marine who goes to Cuba and gets entangled with a hot-tempered peanut vendor named Lupe Velez so he can sing the hit song "The Peanut Vendor." He got excellent reviews for his singing and acting and the film itself was liked. His other hit was "The Cuban Love Song." Tibbett's comic sidekicks are Ernest Torrence and Jimmy Durante. W.S. Van Dyke directed. MGM. Black and white. 80 minutes.

1931 The Prodigal

Tibbett is an aristocratic hobo with Roland Young and Cliff Edwards in this film in which he sings Straus's "Life Is a Dream," Youman's "Without a Song" and "Home Sweet Home." When he returns home, he falls in love with his brother's wife but does the right thing and goes back to being a hobo. Harry Pollard directed. The film is also known as *The Southerner*. MGM. Black and white. 76 minutes.

1935 Metropolitan

The film begins with Lawrence Tibbett singing Mephistopheles with socialite soprano Virginia Bruce as his Marguerite in the *Faust* trio. They are accompanied by a car radio on a country road. He is a spearbearer at the Metropolitan Opera where he has waited six years for a chance. When wealthy diva Alice Brady forms a rival opera company, she hires Tibbett as tenor and artistic director and elects herself prima donna, even if her voice is gone. Tibbett sings Figaro's "Largo al Factotum" as well as arias *from Carmen, Cavalleria Rusticana* and *Pagliacci*. Richard Boleslawski directed. Twentieth Century-Fox. Black and white. 75 minutes.

1936 Under Your Spell

Tibbett plays an opera star who becomes fed up with his manager's publicity stunts. Most of the story is about his romance with a Chicago socialite but he sings arias from *The Barber of Seville* and *Faust*. Tibbett was directed by Otto Preminger making his first American movie, and the story was adapted from José Mojica's Spanish-language Fox film *Las Fronteras del Amor*. MGM. Black and white. 63 minutes.

1991 Bugsy

Lawrence Tibbett is portrayed by actor Joe Baker in this Warren Beatty movie. Gangster Bugsy Siegel (Beatty) sees Tibbett's house in Beverly Hills, stops to say how much he admired him in *Rigoletto* the year before and then forces the singer to sell him the house. It is in a scene with Tibbett that Warren makes his famous diatribe against the appellation "Bugsy." Barry Levinson directed and James Toback wrote the screenplay. TriStar. Color. 135 minutes.

TIEFLAND

1903 opera by d'Albert

Eugen d'Albert's opera about sexual slavery, also known in English as *Marta of the Lowlands*, is based on the play *Terra Baixa* by the Catalan author Angel Guimera. Marta is the mistress of the landowner Sebastiano but he wants to marry someone else. He arranges for her to wed the shepherd Pedro who does not know of her past. The opera, still popular in Europe, was a favorite in Germany between the wars. It was one of the operas which helped launch the careers of both Kirsten Flagstad and Maria Callas. *Tiefland* was staged at the Met in 1908 but did not stay in the American repertory although there was a well received revival at the Washington Opera in 1995. The story has been filmed four times but not as the complete opera. See also EUGEN D'ALBERT.

1914 Bertha Kalich film

Opera singer Bertha Kalich stars as Marta in *Marta of the Lowlands*, an American silent film of the source play by Angel Guimera. It was screened with music from the opera. J. Searle Dawley directed for Famous Players. Black and white. In English. About 70 minutes.

1918 Marie Marchal film

Marie Marchal stars as Marta in this *Tiefland*, an Austrian silent film based on the source play. The cast also includes Wilhelm Klitsch and Tonton Edthofer. It was screened with music from the opera. Black and white. In German. About 45 minutes..

1922 Lil Dagover film

Lil Dagover stars as Marta in this *Tiefland*, a German film of the opera made with the composer's cooperation and performed with live music. Also featured in the film are the famous bass-baritone Michael Bohnen, director-to-be Wilhelm Dieterle, Ilka Gruning and Ida Perry. A. E. Licho produced and directed and Karl Freund was the cinematographer. Black and white. In German. About 75 minutes.

1954 Leni Riefenstahl film

Leni Riefenstahl stars as Marta and directed this famous *Tiefland*, her last film made over many years. The notorious cinematic genius, who made *Triumph of the Will* and the superb 1936 *Olympiad*, started this film in 1940 but didn't finish it until 1954. It's not the opera but a narrative film based on the libretto using the opera music as score. Also in the film are Academy Award winning actress Luise Rainer, Franz Eichberger and Maria Koppenhofer. Albert Benitz was the cinematographer. Black and white. In German. 95 minutes, On video.

TIERNEY, HARRY
American composer 1890-1965)

Harry Tierney was primarily a composer of music for Broadway shows and revues whose most enduring success is the splendid 1919 musical comedy *Irene*. However, at the request of Florenz Ziegfeld, he wrote a traditional operetta, the 1927 *Rio Rita*, which was a spectacular hit on stage and screen. It has some quite good tunes and has been filmed twice. See RIO RITA.

TIKHOMIROV, ROMAN
Russian film director (1915-1984)

Roman Tikhomirov, a Leningrad stage director turned filmmaker, transmuted three Russian operas into true films. He shot them on location in memorable landscapes with good actors whose singing voices were provided by first-class singers. Tikhomirov adapted the operas to the screen with many changes but with a real feeling for the essence of the operas. See EUGENE ONEGIN (1958), PRINCE IGOR (1969), THE QUEEN OF SPADES (1960).

TIPPETT, MICHAEL
English composer (1905-)

Sir Michael Tippett has never been really popular in America but he helped restore British opera to a position of prestige in postwar England and his work has had wide influence. He has always written his own librettos and they are famous for their literary and cultural allusions. His major postwar operas, created between 1946 and 1958, are *The Midsummer Marriage, King Priam, The Knot Garden, The Ice Break* and *New Year*. See KING PRIAM, THE MIDSUMMER MARRIAGE, NEW YEAR.

1975 Camera Three

This Camera Three program titled *A Composer For Our Time: Michael Tippett* is moderated by Andrew Porter. Tippett talks about his life and work and there are selections from his compositions. John Musill produced and directed the telecast on Feb. 23. Color. 30 minutes. Video at MTR.

1985 Sir Michael Tippett: A Musical Biography

This is a South Bank Show profile made for London Weekend TV and directed by Alan Benson. Tippett talks about his operas and there are scenes from *The Midsummer Marriage* performed by members of the Welsh National Opera with Richard Armstrong conducting. The singers are Raimund Herincx, Mary Davies, Mark Hamilton, Maureen Guy and Peter Massochi. Color. 85 minutes. Video at MTR.

TOBIAS AND THE ANGEL
1960 TV opera by Bliss

This television opera, one of two operas composed by Sir Arthur Bliss, was commissioned by BBC Television and telecast in May 1960. Christopher Hassall's libretto tells the Apocryphal story of Tobias who hires an angel called Azarias as his servant. The angel helps him conquer the devil who possesses the beautiful Sara, fight monsters and restore eyesight to his blind father Tobit. The superb television production by Rudolph Cartier stars John Ford as Tobias, Elaine Malbin as Sara and Ronald Lewis as the angel. Norman del Mar conducts the London Symphony Orchestra. Black and white. In English. 80 minutes. See also ARTHUR BLISS.

TONIGHT WE SING
1953 opera film by Leisen

Russian-born American impresario Sol Hurok, who helped popularize opera in America by bringing top singers on tour, is romanticized in this opera film. David Wayne portrays the entrepreneur in a cross between a biography and a classical music extravaganza. Anne Bancroft is his wife Emma, Ezio Pinza impersonates Russian bass Feodor Chaliapin and sings arias from *Faust* and *Boris Godunov*, Roberta Peters plays diva Elsa Valdine and sings Violetta's aria "Sempre libera," Jan Peerce is the voice of Gregory Lawrence and Tamara Toumanova portrays Anna Pavlova. Mitchell Leisen directed. Twentieth Century-Fox. Color. 109 minutes.

TORROBA MORENO, FEDERICO

See MORENO TORROBA, FEDERICO

TOSCA

1900 opera by Puccini

Tosca, one of the great opera melodramas, is set in Rome about 1800 in three famous buildings that still stand: the Church of Sant'Andrea della Valle, the Farnese Palace and the Castel Sant'Angelo. Opera singer Floria Tosca loves painter Mario Cavaradossi and is lusted after by police chief Baron Scarpia. When Cavaradossi is arrested for revolutionary activity, Tosca agrees to submit to Scarpia to save his life. After Scarpia arranges for a fake execution, she stabs him. The "fake" execution, however, is real and Cavaradossi is shot so Tosca leaps off the top of the castle. The libretto by Giuseppe Giacosa and Luigi Illica is based on Victorien Sardou's play *La Tosca*. The story has been very popular with filmmakers. Maria Callas, who is often associated with *Tosca*, can be seen in it on video. See also GIACOMO PUCCINI.

1955 Leontyne Price on NBC Opera Theatre
Leontyne Price stars as Tosca in this historic television production of the opera for NBC Opera Theatre. It was a breakthrough for Price in her first major opera role though some Southern TV stations refused to air the program. Josh Wheeler sings Scarpia with David Poleri as Cavaradossi. The opera is sung in an English translation by John Gutman. Samuel Chotzinoff produced, William Molyneux designed the sets and Peter Herman Adler conducted the Symphony of the Air Orchestra. Kirk Browning directed the live telecast. Black and white. In English. 120 minutes. Video at MTR.

1956 Carmine Gallone film
Opera film specialist Carmine Gallone shot this film on location in Rome at the sites specified in each act. Franco Corelli stars as Cavaradossi, Afro Poli is Scarpia and American soprano Franca Duval portrays Tosca with Maria Caniglia's voice used on the soundtrack. Gallone does a good job of capturing the feeling of the city with cinematographer Giuseppe Rotunno. Oliviero De Fabritis conducts the Rome Opera House Orchestra. Color. CinemaScope. In Italian. 111 minutes. Lyric/Bel Canto Society videos.

1956 Maria Callas on CBS
Maria Callas made her television debut with an 18-minute scene from *Tosca* on the Ed Sullivan Show on CBS on Nov. 25, 1956. The Act Two excerpt was staged by John Gutman with George London as Scarpia. Dimitri Mitropoulos conducts the Metropolitan Opera Orchestra. Black and white. 18 minutes. Video at MTR.

1958 Maria Callas in Paris
Maria Callas can be seen as Tosca in Act Two opposite Tito Gobbi as Scarpia in the video *Maria Callas Debuts at Paris*. With them are Louis Rialland, Albert Lance and Jean Paul Hurteau. The performance was taped at a concert given on Dec. 19, 1958, at the Théâtre National de l'Opéra in Paris. Georges Sebastian conducts the orchestra and Roger Benamou was stage director. Black and white. In Italian. About 40 minutes. EMI Classics video/Pioneer Artists laser.

1960 Magda Olivero film
Magda Olivera stars as Tosca in an Italian TV film of the opera opposite Alvinio Misciano as Cavaradossi and Giulio Fioravanti as Scarpia. Fulvio Vernizzi conducts the orchestra. Olivera made her debut at the Metropolitan Opera in the role in 1975 aged 60. Black and white. In Italian. 120 minutes. Lyric Legato Classics video.

1961 Renata Tebaldi in Stuttgart
Renata Tebaldi sings Tosca at the peak of her fame in this historic performance at the Stuttgart State Opera on June 3, 1961. This was probably the first international opera telecast and was transmitted to a consortium of European stations. George London is outstanding as Scarpia, Eugene Tobin is Cavaradossi, Heinz Kramer is the Sacristan and Gustav Grefe is Angelotti. Max Fritzsch designed the sets, Franco Patanè conducts the Stuttgart Staaatsoper Orchestra and Chorus, Werner Dobbertin was the stage director and Korbinian Koberte directed the telecast. Black and white. In Italian. 126 minutes. VAI video.

1964 Maria Callas at Covent Garden
The only visual record of Callas on stage in a performance of an opera is this Act II of *Tosca*. Franco Zeffirelli's production at the Royal Opera House, Covent Garden, was taped at a gala performance by Associated Television. Callas is in intense form as Tosca with Tito Gobbi as Scarpia and Renato Cioni as Cavaradossi. Tom Lingwood

designed the sets and Carlo Felice Cillaro conducted the Royal Opera House Orchestra and Chorus. This is the same act with the same Scarpia that was taped in concert in Paris in 1958. Bill Ward directed for live television on Feb. 9, 1964. Black and white. In Italian. 41 minutes. EMI Classics video.

1976 Gianfranco de Bosio Film
Italian film director Gianfranco de Bosio shot his *Tosca* on location in Rome with Raina Kabaivanska as Tosca, Placido Domingo as Cavaradossi and Sherrill Milnes as Scarpia. He filmed the first act at the Church of Sant' Andrea della Valle and the third act at the Castel Sant'Angelo but the Palazzo Farnese, site of the second act, could not be used. Domingo's ten-year-old son Placi is the Shepherd Boy. Giancarlo Pucci designed the sets and costumes while Bruno Bartoletti conducts the New Philharmonia Orchestra and Ambrosian Singers. Unitel. 116 minutes. Color. In Italian with English subtitles. London video.

1978 Metropolitan Opera
Shirley Verrett sings Tosca with Luciano Pavarotti as Cavaradossi and Cornell MacNeil as Scarpia in this Metropolitan Opera production by Tito Gobbi. Rudolf Heinrich designed the sets, James Conlon conducted the Metropolitan Orchestra and Chorus and Kirk Browning directed the video telecast on Dec. 19, 1978. Color. In Italian with English subtitles. 124 minutes. Video at MTR.

1983 Raina Kabaivanska with Taddei
Raina Kabaivanska sings the role of Tosca in Act II of the opera opposite Giuseppe Taddei as Scarpia in this Bulgarian television film. The film makes an interesting comparison to the video featuring Maria Callas and Tito Gobbi in the same act of the opera in 1964. Color. In Italian. 30 minutes. On video.

1984 Verona Arena
Eva Marton stars as Tosca with Giacomo Aragall as Cavaradossi and Ingvar Wixell as Scarpia in this excellent production by Silvano Bussotti in the open-air Arena in Verona. The singers are good but the sets tend to dominate. Fiorenzo Giorgi designed the sets and costumes and Daniel Oren conducted the Verona Arena Orchestra and Chorus. Video director Brian Large brings a real sense of intimacy to the viewer. Color. 126 minutes. In Italian with English subtitles. HBO Video.

1984 Opera Stories
This is a laser disc highlights version of the Verona Arena production with Eva Marton described above. It has an introduction and narration by Charlton Heston speaking from Rome. The framing material was shot in 1989 by Keith Cheetham. Color. In English and Italian with subtitles. 52 minutes. Pioneer Artists laser.

1985 Metropolitan Opera
Franco Zeffirelli's awe-inspiring Metropolitan Opera production stars Hildegard Behrens as Tosca, Placido Domingo as Cavaradossi and Cornell MacNeil as Scarpia. Italo Tajo portrays the Sacristan and James Courtney is Angelotti. Zeffirelli designed the sets and staged the opera in a grandiose manner with grand singing. Giuseppe Sinopoli conducts the Metropolitan Orchestra and Chorus and Kirk Browning directed this Live from the Met production that won him an Emmy. Color. In Italian with English subtitles. 127 minutes. Paramount video/Pioneer laser.

1986 Australian Opera
Eva Marton is an intense Tosca in this production by John Copley at the Sydney Opera House. John Shaw is Scarpia and Lamberto Furlan is Cavaradossi. Allan Lees designed the realistic sets and Michael Stennett the costumes while Alberto Erede conducted the Elizabethan Sydney Orchestra and Australian Opera Chorus. Peter Butler directed the video. Color. In Italian with English subtitles. 123 minutes. Kultur Video.

1991 Paris Opéra
Kiri Te Kanawa stars as Tosca in this production at the Paris Opéra. She is supported by Ernest Veronelli as Cavaradossi and Ingvar Wixell as Scarpia. Seiji Ozawa conducts the Paris Opéra Orchestra. Color. In Italian. 128 minutes. On video and Japanese laser.

1992 Tosca Live from Rome
This remarkable TV production was filmed at the sites of the three acts of the opera at the times specified in the libretto and was broadcast live in Europe in July 1992. Catherine Malfitano sings Tosca, Placido Domingo is Cavaradossi and Ruggero Raimondi is Scarpia. Giuseppe Patroni Griffi directed the show with Vittorio Stararo as his cinematographer. Zubin Mehta conducted the RAI Symphony Orchestra wearing headphones so he could hear the singers he watched on television

monitors. Act I was filmed at Sant'Andrea Church at noon, Act II at the Farnese Palace at sunset and Act III at the Castel Sant' Angelo at dawn the next day. TV/video director Brian Large does a fine job of keeping scenery and singers in balance. It's a terrific spectacle and a splendid concept by producer Andrea Andermann. Color. In Italian with English subtitles. 115 minutes Teldec video and laser.

1993 Rome Opera House

Luciano Pavarotti portrays Cavaradossi in this production at the Rome Opera House but the real star is Raina Kabaivanska, one of the great Toscas of our time. Ingmar Wixell is her Scarpia. Film director Mauro Bolognini staged the opera and filmed it for a live telecast while Daniel Oren conducted the Rome Opera Orchestra and Chorus. Sets, costumes and lighting are traditional but more than acceptable. Color. In Italian with English subtitles. 137 minutes. RCA video.

Early/related films

1908 The Queen's Love

This early Danish color film was titled *La Tosca* in Europe but released in the USA as *The Queen's Love*. It was supposedly based on the Sardou play rather than the opera. Viggo Larsen directed for Nordisk Films. Color. About 7 minutes.

1908 Sarah Bernhardt film

Victorien Sardou wrote the play *La Tosca* for Sarah Bernhardt and she was filmed in scenes from it by French director André Calmettes. It was presented in the USA by Universal in October 1912. Black and white. About 10 minutes.

1910 Cécile Sorel film

Cécile Sorel stars as Tosca in this French film based on the Sardou play screened with Puccini's music. It was directed by André Calmettes and Ferdinand Zecca. Alexandre Mosnier is Mario Cavaradossi with Charles Le Bargy as Scarpia. Film d'Art/Pathe. About 15 minutes.

1915 The Song of Hate

Betty Ansen stars as Floria Tosca in this American film based on the Sardou play. Arthur Hoops portrays Scarpia. This was a Fox film directed by J. Gordon Edwards. About 70 minutes.

1916 The Chalice of Sorrow

The story of *Tosca* was transposed to Mexico in revolutionary times for this American film. The names are different but the plot remains the same with Cleo Madison as an opera singer seeking to save her lover from a brutal governor. Rex Ingram wrote and directed this Bluebird Film. About 70 minutes.

1918 Pauline Frederick film

Pauline Frederick stars as Tosca in *La Tosca*, an American adaptation of the Sardou play directed by Edward José. Frank Losee plays Scarpia and Jules Raucourt is Cavaradossi. Famous Players-Lasky. About 70 minutes.

1918 Francesca Bertini film

Francesca Bertini, Italy's top star at this period, portrays Tosca in *La Tosca*, an Italian film based on the Sardou play. Gustavo Serena directed for Itala Film. About 70 minutes.

1919 Ebba Thomsen film

Ebba Thomsen stars as Tosca in this Danish film version of the story directed by Fritz Magnussen. About 80 minutes.

1934 My Heart Is Calling

The high point of this Jan Kiepura film is an open air performance of *Tosca*. It is staged by his traveling company on the steps of the Monte Carlo Opera House while the resident company performs the opera inside. The outsiders win and everyone exits the theater. Carmine Gallone directed. Black and white. 90 minutes.

1936 Rose Marie

Jeanette MacDonald, playing an opera diva, sings the finale from Act IV of *Tosca* with Allan Jones in this MGM film. W. S. Van Dyke directed. Black and white. 110 minutes. MGM-UA video and laser.

1941 The Story of Tosca

This famous Italian film uses music and arias from the opera and its screenplay is based on the opera and the play. Spain's Imperio Argentina stars as Tosca, Italy's Rossano Brazzi plays Cavaradossi and France's Michel Simon is Scarpia. The singing voices, however, belong to Ferrucio Tagliavini and Mafaldo Tavero. The production of the film, titled simply *Tosca* in Italy, was complicated by World War II. Jean Renoir was the original writer and director with Luchino Visconti as his assistant. Renoir had to leave when the war began so the film was finished by Carlo Koch. It was released in the U.S. in 1947 as a Tagliavini film because of his success at the Met. Black and white. In Italian. 105 mins. Italian video/Japanese laser.

1943 The Amazing Mrs Holliday
Deanna Durbin sings Tosca's aria "Vissi d'arte" during this film about a missionary and Chinese orphans. Jean Renoir directed most of the movie but Bruce Manning finished it. Universal. Black and white. 96 minutes.

1946 Before Him All Rome Trembled
Tito Gobbi is a superb Scarpia in scenes from a 1944 production of *Tosca* at the Rome Opera House in this film set during the German occupation. Anna Magnani plays an opera diva starring in *Tosca* whose "real life" parallels the opera plot. Her lover Gino Sinimberghi has rescued an English soldier and she is suspicious of his behavior. On stage Elisabetta Barbato is the voice of Tosca, Sinimberghi sings Cavaradossi and Gobbi is Scarpia. The Rome Opera House orchestra is led by Luigi Ricci. Carmine Gallone directed. The Italian title is *Davanti a lui Tremava Tutta Roma*, a line from the libretto describing Scarpia. Black and white. In Italian with English subtitles. 110 mins.

1973 Monica Vitti film
Monica Vitti stars as Tosca in *La Tosca*, an Italian film of the Sardou play with Puccini's music on the soundtrack. Her co-stars are Vittorio Gassmann, Luigi Proietti and Aldo Fabrizi. The film story follows the plot of the opera. Luigi Magni directed. Titanus. Color. In Italian. 100 minutes.

1973 Serpico
Al Pacino portrays Frank Serpico, an Italian-American cop who likes opera, in this police story. When he plays Cavaradossi's aria "E lucevan le stelle" on his phonograph and listens in his back yard, the woman next door asks if it is Björling. He says it is De Stefano but they become friends anyway. Sidney Lumet directed. Color. 130 minutes. On video.

1983 I Live for Art
A fine documentary about *Tosca* and the sopranos who have sung the role; it takes its title from Tosca's aria "Vissi d'arte." Among the many Toscas interviewed and heard singing are Licia Albanese, Grace Bumbry, Monserrat Caballé, Gina Cigna, Régine Crespin, Dorothy Kirsten, Zinka Milanov, Birgit Nilsson, Magda Olivero, Leonie Rysanek, Renata Tebaldi, Kiri Te Kanawa, Eva Turner, Galina Vishnevskaya and Lujba Welitsch. Maria Callas and Maria Jeritiza are also seen and discussed. The film, hosted by Robert Merrill, was written by Raymond Vanover, produced by Joseph Wishy and directed by Muriel Balash. Color. In English. 91 minutes. Kultur video.

1992 The Last Mile
Bernadette Peters portrays a young Met soprano in this teleplay written by Terence McNally. She is waiting nervously in her dressing room before her debut as Tosca. The story begins with the opening chords of *Tosca* and ends thirteen minutes later with Tosca's offstage cries of "Mario, Mario." The play was written for the 20th anniversary celebration of the Great Performances series and telecast on Oct. 9, 1992. Color. 13 minutes.

1993 Household Saints
Tosca's aria "Vissi d'arte" is sung on the soundtrack by Maria Caniglia in this offbeat story about the saintly lives of two Italian women in New York. Nancy Savoca directed the film based on a novel by Francine Prose. Color. 124 minutes.

1994 Heavenly Creatures
Peter Dvorsky is heard singing "E lucevan le stelle" in this fine New Zealand film set in the early 1950s. However, the tenor who dominates the film is Mario Lanza. Color. 95 minutes. On video.

TOSCAN DU PLANTIER, DANIEL
French film producer (1941-)

Daniel Toscan du Plantier, a French film producer who once headed the Gaumont film company in Paris, has specialized in producing opera films with major directors with no previous experience of opera. By so doing he has given the cinema some of the best opera films ever made. They include Joseph Losey's *Don Giovanni*, Francesco Rosi's *Carmen*, Luigi Comencini's *La Bohème* and Frederic Mitterand's *Madama Butterfly*. He can be seen talking about his work in the documentary *Cinopera*. See LA BOHÈME (1988), CARMEN (1984), CINOPERA, DON GIOVANNI (1978), MADAMA BUTTERFLY (1995).

TOSCANINI, ARTURO
Italian conductor (1867-1957)

Arturo Toscanini, one of the legends of modern music, began to conduct opera in 1886 at the age of nineteen. He was a major influence on La Scala, the Metropolitan, Bayreuth, Salzburg and the NBC. The Parma-born conductor was a valiant fighter for proper opera staging and presentation and a strong voice of protest in the fascist years of Italy and Germany. In his final years he was no longer simply a famous conductor but the person who symbolized classical music; he was *the* conductor. See AIDA (1949), CONDUCTORS (1995).

1944 Toscanini: Hymn of the Nations
Avant-garde filmmaker Alexander Hammid directed this Oscar-nominated documentary. It praises Toscanini's patriotism, talks about his career and shows him leading the NBC Symphony Orchestra in December 1943. He conducts the overture to Verdi's *La Forza del Destino* followed by the *Hymn of Nations* with Metropolitan tenor Jan Peerce and the Westminster Choir. May Sarton wrote the film made for the Office of War Information. Black and white. 28 minutes. RCA Victor video and laser/ Video Yesteryear video

1948-52 Toscanini: The Television Concerts
Eight concerts with Toscanini conducting the NBC Symphony Orchestra have been released on video and laser. They include one devoted to Wagner and a concert performance of *Aida*. The are all black and white kinescopes.

1988 Young Toscanini
Franco Zeffirelli's $14 million Italian film biography *Il Giovane Toscanini* stars C. Thomas Howell as the young Toscanini and Elizabeth Taylor as diva Nadina Bulichoff. It was not well received at its Venice Festival premiere and has been little seen since. It begins with Toscanini auditioning for La Scala in 1883 and is mainly concerned with the conductor's success in Brazil. High point of the film is Liz Taylor as Aida which has to be seen to be believed. Carlo Bergonzi is also in the film. William H. Stadiem wrote the screenplay. Color. In Italian. 120 minutes.

1985 Toscanini: the Maestro
Peter Rosen's outstanding film portrait of the conductor is hosted by James Levine and includes fascinating home movies as well as archival film and interviews. Remembering the great man are such colleagues as Herva Nelli, Jarmila Novotna, Robert Merrill, Bidyu Sayao and Licia Albanese. The members of the NBC Symphony Orchestra also recall his genius. Color. 74 minutes. RCA Victor video and laser.

TOTE STADT, DIE
1920 opera by Korngold

Eric Wolfgang Korngold's opera *The Dead City* is a symbolist dream tale set in Bruges at the end of the 19th century. The libretto by Korngold and his father Julius derives from Georges Rodenbuch's novel *Bruges-la-Morte*. Paul is obsessed by his love for his dead wife Marie. In his dreams a dancer named Marietta becomes confused with his wife and he imagines her seduction. Afterwards he feels disloyal and strangles her with a lock of Maria's hair. When he wakes from the dream, Paul decides to leave the city of death. See also ERIC WOLFGANG KORNGOLD.

1983 Berlin Deutsche Oper
James King sings the role of Paul and Karen Armstrong has the double role of Marie/Marietta in this video of a telecast of a Berlin Deutsche Oper production. Heinrich Hollreiser conducts the Berlin Deutsche Oper Orchestra. Color. In German. 120 minutes. Opera Dubs video/ Japanese laser.

1987 Bruce Beresford film
Australian director Bruce Beresford based his episode of the film *Aria* around the opera's famous aria known as Marietta's Song. A man (Peter Birch) and a woman (Elizabeth Hurley) share their love to the haunting "Gluck, das mir verblieb." The singers are Carol Neblett and René Kollo with the Munich Radio Orchestra conducted by Erich Leinsdorf. The film was shot in Belgium. Color. 89 minutes. Academy video and laser.

TOZZI, GIORGIO
American bass (1923-)

Giorgio Tozzi was born in Chicago where he studied with Rosa Raisa and Giacomo Rimini. He made his American debut on Broadway in 1948 in *The Rape of Lucretia*, his La Scala debut in *La Wally* in 1953 and his Met debut in 1955 in *La Gioconda*. His most popular roles include Don Giovanni, Boris Godunov and Phillip II. He created the role of the Doctor in Samuel Barber's *Vanessa* at the Met in

1958 and joined Joan Sutherland and Franco Corelli in the revival of *Les Huguenots* at La Scala in 1962. He also sang in musical comedy and had a minor Hollywood career. See also AMAHL AND THE NIGHT VISITORS (1978), DIE MEISTERSINGER VON NÜRNBERG (1969), SOUTH PACIFIC (1958).

1973 Shamus
Giorgio Tozzi got good notices for his performance as Il Dottore, a smooth gangster gourmet who dines with the police and gives away underworld secrets. Burt Reynolds stars in the film as a private detective. Buzz Kulik directed. Columbia. Color. 106 minutes.

1975 One of Our Own
Tozzi has a supporting role in this movie starring George Peppard as a hospital administrator who solves a hospital's problems. Richard C. Sarafian directed. Color. 100 minutes.

1979 Torn Between Two Lovers
Tozzi has a small role in this romantic TV movie. Lee Remick stars as a married woman having an affair with George Peppard. Delbert Mann directed. Color. 100 minutes.

TRAUBEL, HELEN
American soprano (1899-1972)

Helen Traubel, the foremost American Wagnerian of her time, had personality and grandeur as well as a remarkable voice. She was born in St. Louis and began her career in 1923 appearing in concerts. She did not make her debut in opera until 1937 when she sang in the premiere of Walter Damrosch's *The Man Without a Country* at the Metropolitan. In 1939 she sang the role of Sieglinde in *Die Walküre* and her Wagnerian career began. She was a major star at the Met until 1953 when she left after a disagreement with Rudolf Bing. She continued her career in television, concerts and nightclubs, starred on Broadway in the musical *Pipe Dream* and appeared in three films. See also THE MIKADO (1960), SIGMUND ROMBERG (1954).

1950 Helen Traubel in Opera and Song
Traubel made two appearances on the *Voice of Firestone* television show in 1950 singing songs and arias. The arias are both from *Die Walküre* ("Du bist der lenz" and "Ho-jo-to-ho") but the songs are wide ranging. They include "Deep River," "Vienna City

of My Dreams," "I Love Thee," "Loch Lochmond," "The World is Waiting for the Sunrise" and "Wish You Were Here." Black and white. 27 minutes. VAI video

1961 The Ladies' Man
Traubel stars opposite Jerry Lewis in this silly but fun comedy directed by Lewis. She's an ex-opera star called Welenmelon and runs a boarding house for career women. He's the girl-shy incompetent handyman who eventually becomes a ladies' man. Paramount. Color. 106 minutes. On video and laser.

1967 Gunn
Traubel is nightclub operator Mother in this film version of the Peter Gunn TV mystery series. Her waterfront club is being forced to pay protection money as Gunn (Craig Stevens) discovers when he begins to investigate a murder. Blake Edwards directed. Paramount. Color. 94 minutes.

TRAVIATA, LA
1853 opera by Verdi

The story of *La Traviata* has been very popular with filmmakers though many of the films are based on Alexandre Dumas' source novel and play *La Dame aux Camélias*. Dumas modeled his heroine on Alphonsine Plessis whose Paris grave has become a tourist site. In the Dumas play this glamorous lady of easy virtue is called Marguerite Gautier but in the opera Giuseppe Verdi and librettist Francesco Maria Piave call her Violetta. Despite this the stage, opera and screen stories are essentially the same. In the opera Violetta falls in love with Alfredo Germont and gives up her hedonistic life to live with him even though she knows she is dying. Alfredo's father persuades her to break up with his son for the good of his family and sister. The lovers are are reconciled at her deathbed but it is too late. Violetta/Marguerite has been portrayed on screen nearly as often as Carmen. See also GIUSEPPE VERDI.

1947 The Lost One
La Signora delle Camelie, Carmine Gallone's film of *La Traviata*, begins with Verdi and Dumas standing beside the grave of the Parisian courtesan who inspired the story and talking about her life and loves. The rest of the film is the opera. Nelli Corradi portrays Violetta with the role sung by Ornella Fineschi, Gino Mattera sings and acts Alfredo and Manfredi Polverosi plays Germont with the singing by Tito Gobbi. Giuseppe Morelli conducts the Rome

Opera Orchestra and Chorus. Black and white. In Italian. 84 minutes.

1950 CBS Opera Television Theatre

Lawrence Tibbett stars as Germont in this CBS Opera Television Theater production. Elaine Malbin sings the role of Violetta with Brooks McCormack as her Alfredo. The opera is sung in English in a translation by George Meade. Henry Souvaine was producer, Herbert Graf was stage director and Richard Rychtarik designed the sets. Faust Cleva conducts the CBS orchestra. Byron Paul directed the telecast. Black and white. In English. 95 minutes. Video at MTR.

1953 Lucia Evangelista film

Lucia Evangelista is Violetta in this highlights film made for the *Opera Cameos* series. Giulio Gari is Alfredo, Frank Valentini is Germont and Carlo Tomantelli is Dr. Grenville. The opera was staged by Anthony Stivanello and filmed by Carlo Vinti and Marion Rhodes. Giuseppe Bamboschek conducts the orchestra. The film was shown in the U.S. in a double bill with *Cavalleria Rusticana*. Color. In Italian. 53 minutes. Lyric/Video Yesteryear videos.

1954 Beverly Sills in Opera Cameos

Beverly Sills sings Violetta in this film of the third act of the opera produced for the *Opera Cameos* television series. John Druary is Alfredo and Frank Valentino is Germont. Tenor Giovanni Martinelli introduces the arias and Giuseppe Bamboschek conducts the orchestra. Carlo and Joseph Vinti wrote and directed the film. Black and white. 30 minutes. Video at MTR.

1957 NBC Opera Theatre

Metropolitan Opera baritone Igor Gorin sings Germont with Elaine Malbin as Violetta and John Alexander as Alfredo in this NBC Television Opera production by Samuel Chotzinoff. Peter Herman Adler was artistic director and Herbert Grossman conducts the Symphony of the Air Orchestra. The opera is sung in an English translation by Joseph Machlis. Kirk Browning directed the live telecast on April 21, 1957. Color. In English. 120 minutes. Lyric video.

1956 Richard Tucker on Voice of Firestone

Richard Tucker sings Germont in this highlights version of *La Traviata* performed on the *Voice of Firestone* television series on March 3, 1963. Elaine

Malbin is Violetta and Russell Hammar is Alfredo. The scenes are fully staged with sets and extras and the orchestra is conducted by Howard Buckley. Black and white. In Italian with English introductions. 14 minutes. On VAI video *A Firestone Verdi Festival*.

1966 Anna Moffo film

Anna Moffo stars as Violetta in this visually opulent and vocally splendid Italian film which one critic considers the best performance that exists in any form. Moffo is in peak form and ably partnered by the great Gino Bechi as Germont. He was 55 at the time but still in great voice. Franco Bonisoli is Alfredo and Afro Poli is Doctor Grenvil. Giuseppe Patanè conducts the Orchestra and Chorus of the Rome Opera House. Mario Lanfranchi directed the film. Color. In Italian with English plot summaries. 113 minutes. VAI video.

1973 Valerie Masterson film

Valerie Masterson is Violetta, Kenneth Woollam is Alfredo and Michael Wakeham is Germont in this English-language film made for the *Focus on Opera* series. It was filmed by Peter Seabourne at Knebworth House in Hertfordshire. John J. Davies conducts the Classical Orchestra. Color. In English. 57 minutes.

1973 Joan Sutherland video

Joan Sutherland stars in this highlights version made for the *Who's Afraid of Opera?* series. She tells the story to puppets and performs the role of Violetta with Ian Caley as Alfredo, Pieter Van Der Stolk as Germont, Alisa Gamley as Annina, Gordon Wilcock as Baron Douphol, John Gibbs as Dr. Grenvil and Monica Sinclair as Flora. The dialogue is in English, the singing is in Italian. George Djurkovic designed the sets and Richard Bonynge conducts the London Symphony Orchestra. Ted Kotcheff directed. Color. 30 minutes. Kultur video.

1973 Berlin State Opera

Mirella Freni stars as Violetta in this expansive three-nation telecast of a Berlin Staatsoper production. Franco Bonisolli sings Alfredo and Sesto Bruscantini is Germont. Lamberto Gardelli conducts the Berlin State Orchestra and Wolfgang Nagel directed the telecast for Austria, Italy and Germany. Color. In Italian. 90 minutes. On Japanese laserdisc.

1976 Beverly Sills at Wolf Trap

Beverly Sills is in peak form singing Violetta in this Wolf Trap production by Tito Capobianco. Henry Price is her beloved Alfredo while Richard Fredricks is Germont. Julius Rudel conducts the Wolf Trap Orchestra and Chorus and Kirk Browning directed the video. Color. In Italian with English subtitles. 145 minutes. VAI video.

1981 Metropolitan Opera

Ileana Cotrubas sings Violetta, Placido Domingo is Alfredo and Cornell MacNeil is Germont in this Metropolitan Opera production by Colin Graham. Ariel Bybee is Flora and Dana Talley is Gastone. Tanya Moiseiwitsch designed the sets and James Levine conducts the Metropolitan Opera Orchestra and Chorus. Brian Large directed the video taped on March 28 and telecast on Sept. 30, 1981. Color. In Italian with English subtitles. 140 minutes. Video at MTR.

1982 Franco Zeffirelli film

Teresa Stratas is an utterly believable and heart-breaking Violetta in this great opera film, Franco Zeffirelli's finest achievement in the genre. He uses a clever conceit to frame the story imagining the opera as a feverish memory by Violetta while she is dying. There are clever cinematic devices to retain interest and keep the narrative flowing including complex flashbacks and camera movements. The bravura rococo style is exactly in keeping with Violetta's memories and rightly romantic. Stratas is ably partnered by Placido Domingo as a powerful Alfredo and Cornell MacNeil as a convincing Germont. The film is beautifully photographed by Ennio Guarnieri, costumed by Piero Tosi and written and designed by Zeffirelli. James Levine conducts the Metropolitan Opera Orchestra and Chorus. Color. In Italian with English subtitles. 105 minutes. MCA video.

1987 Glyndebourne Festival

Marie McLaughlin is superb as Violetta in this Glyndebourne Festival production by Peter Hall. Walter MacNeil is Alfredo and Brent Ellis is Germont. John Gunter designed the sets and costumes while Bernard Haitink conducts the London Philharmonic Orchestra and Glyndebourne Festival Chorus. Hall also directed the video which was produced by Derek Bailey. Color. In Italian with English subtitles. 135 minutes. Home Vision video.

1992 Teatro alla Scala

Tiziana Fabbricini, who has been spoken of as a new Callas, portrays Violetta while Roberto Alagna, who some think may take over the mantle of Pavarotti, sings the role of Alfredo. Paolo Coni is fine as Germont. Italian film director Liliana Cavani staged the opera and shot it in HDTV giving it the gloss of 35mm film. Riccardo Muti conducts as if he is excited by this fine production with singers who can act. The sound and picture on the laser disc are especially notable. Color. In Italian with English subtitles. 148 minutes. Sony video and laser.

1992 La Fenice, Venice

Edita Gruberova is outstanding as Violetta with Neil Schicoff as Alfred and Giorgio Zancanaro as Germont in this excellent La Fenice production directed and designed by Pier Luigi Pizzi. It was recorded live in December 1992 in the Venice theater where Verdi premiered the opera in 1853. It may not have been a success that first night but it certainly looks splendid now. Carlo Rizzi conducts the Teatro La Fenice Orchestra and Chorus. Derek Bailey directed the video. Color. In Italian. 145 minutes. Teldec video and laser.

1994 Royal Opera

Romanian soprano Angela Gheorghiu was 29 when she was acclaimed for her performance as Violetta in this Royal Opera, Covent Garden, production by Richard Eyre. It was the first Traviata for both her and conductor Sir Georg Solti and the critics adored it. Frank Lopardo sings Alfredo with Leo Nucci as Germont. Bob Crowley designed the sets and Solti conducted the Royal Opera House Orchestra and Chorus. Peter Maniura and Humphrey Burton directed the video shown on BBC in December 1994. Color. In Italian with English subtitles. 135 minutes. London video and laserdisc.

1995 New York City Opera

Janice Woods sings the role of Violetta with Stephen Mark Brown as Alfredo in this New York City Opera production by Renata Scotto. Louis Otey is Germont, Carla Wood is Flora, Mark Delavan is the Baron and John Calvin West is Dr. Grenvil. Thierry Bosquet designed the costumes and sets and Yves Abel conducts the New York City Opera Orchestra. Sherrill Milnes hosted the backstage programs. Kirk Browning directed the video telecast on March 28, 1995 in the *Live from Lincoln Center* series. Color. In Italian with English subtitles. 175 minutes.

Early/related films

The role of Violetta-Marguerite was one of the most popular females roles in the cinema in the silent era. Though many of the films claimed to be based on the Dumas story rather than the opera, this was usually to avoid paying copyright and they were normally screened with music from the opera.

1907 Oda Alstrup film
Oda Alstrup stars as Marguerite in *Kamieladamen*, a Danish film of the Dumas/Verdi story released in the U.S. as *The Lady with the Camelias*. It was directed by Viggo Larsen for Nordisk Films. About 14 minutes.

1908 Oskar Messter sound film
This German film of an aria from the opera was screened with the music played on a synchronized phonograph. Many films of this kind were made by Oskar Messter in Berlin. About 4 minutes.

1909 Vittoria Lepanto film
Vittoria Lepanto stars as Marguerite in *La Signora delle Camelie*, an Italian film based on the Dumas novel but screened with music from the opera. Ugo Falena directed for Film d'Arte Italiana. About 14 minutes. A print survives.

1911 Sarah Bernhardt film
Stage immortal Sarah Bernhardt (ten aged 67) stars as Marguerite in *La Dame aux Camélias*, a French adaptation of the Dumas play. This was one of the most famous early silent films and was often screened with the Verdi music. André Calmettes and Henry Pouctal directed. About 12 minutes. Prints survive.

1912 Gertrude Shipman film
Gertrude Shipman stars as Marguerite in this American film version of the Dumas play. It was made for the Champion Film Company and directed by Herbert Brenon. About l5 minutes.

1915 Francesca Bertini film
Francesca Bertini, Italy's top film diva at this time, portrays Marguerite in *La Signore delle Camelie*, an Italian film based on the Dumas play. Gustavo Serena directed for Caesar Film. About 65 minutes.

1915 Hesperia film
Italian diva Hesperia stars as Marguerite in this *La Signore delle Camelie*, a rival 1915 Italian film of the Dumas play. Her husband Baldassarre Negroni directed for Tiber Film. Hesperia's real name was Olga Mabelli and Marguerite was her most famous role. About 70 minutes.

1915 Clara Kimball Young film
Clara Kimball Young stars as Marguerite in *Camille*, an American film based on the Dumas play. Albert Capellani directed for the World Film Corp. About 70 minutes.

1917 Theda Bara film
Theda Bara stars as Marguerite in *Camille*, an American film based on the Dumas play. J. Gordon Edwards directed for the Fox Film Corp. About 70 minutes.

1917 Erna Morena film
Erna Morena stars as Marguerite in *Die Kameliendame*, a German film of the Dumas play. Paul Leni, who later came to Hollywood, directed and also designed the sets and costumes. About 70 minutes.

1921 Alla Nazimova film
Alla Nazimova portrays Marguerite in *Camille* with newcomer Rudolph Valentino as her young lover in this American film of the Dumas play. Ray C. Smallwood directed for Metro. About 75 minutes.

1921 Pola Negri film
Pola Negri stars as Violetta in the German film *Arme Violetta* directed by Paul Ludwig Stein. About 80 minutes.

1922 Thelma Murray film
Thelma Murray stars as Violetta with Clive Brook as Alfredo in this British film of the Verdi opera made for the *Tense Moments from Operas* series. H. B. Parkinson produced and George Wynn directed. About 12 minutes.

1925 Tora Teje film
Swedish actress Tora Teje stars as Marguerite in *Damen med Kameliorna*, a Swedish film based on the Dumas play. Olof Molander directed. About 75 minutes.

1927 Norma Talmadge film
Norma Talmadge stars as Marguerite in *Camille*, an American film based on the Dumas play. Fred Niblo directed for First National. About 90 minutes.

1927 Peggy Carlisle film
Peggy Carlisle portrays Violetta, Anthony Ireland is Alfredo and Booth Conway is Baron Douphol in this English film of scenes from the opera. H. B. Parkinson directed for the Cameo Opera series. It was screened with singers on stage performing the arias. 18 minutes.

1934 Yvonne Printemps film
Yvonne Printemps stars as Marguerite in *La Dame aux Camélias*, a French film based on the Dumas novel. Abel Gance supervised and Fernand Rivers directed. In French. 118 minutes.

1936 Women of Glamour
Armanda Chirot is the soprano who sings Violetta's aria "Sempre libera" in this American feature film. Virginia Bruce portrays a modern gold digger. Gordon Wiles directed for Columbia Pictures. 72 minutes.

1936 Greta Carbo film
Herbert Stothart's score for George Cukor's *Camille* was created from themes from Verdi's *La Traviata*. Greta Garbo stars as Marguerite opposite Robert Taylor in this MGM film based on the Dumas novel and play. 108 minutes.

1937 100 Men and a Girl
Deanna Durbin sings Violetta's aria "Libiamo" in a story about the precocious daughter of a musician. Her co-star is conductor Leopold Stokowski. Henry Coster directed for Universal. Black and white. 83 minutes.

1938 The Goldwyn Follies
Metropolitan Opera soprano Helen Jepson sings Violetta opposite Met tenor Charles Kullmann's Alfredo on stage in *La Traviata* in this Goldwyn musical. They perform "Libiamo" and "Sempre libera." Jepson plays an opera singer who interests producer Adolphe Menjou. George Marshall directed. Black and white. 120 minutes.

1940 Amami, Alfredo!
This is an Italian "parallel film" of *La Traviata* made after the success of a similar film based on *Madama Butterfly*. Maria Cebotari stars as Maria Dalgeri, a famous singer who persuades La Scala to present an opera by Claudio Gora. Much Verdi music later, the illness that struck down the heroine of *La Traviata* threatens to destroy Cebotari. Luckily it's a poor diagnosis and she really isn't sick so there's a happy ending. Carmine Gallone directed. The German title is *Melodie der Liebe*. Black and white. In Italian. 86 minutes.

1943 Thousands Cheer
Kathyrn Grayson sings Violetta's aria "Sempre libera" in this all-star variety film in which she is the love interest of Army private Gene Kelly. George Sidney directed. Black and white. 126 minutes.

1945 The Lost Weekend
Writer/director Billy Wilder offers an ironic reason why alcoholics should avoid *La Traviata*. Ray Milland flees his seat at the Metropolitan Opera as the "Libiamo" drinking song reminds him of the bottle hidden in his coat in the cloakroom. He then has to sit out the opera waiting for Jane Wyman, the woman whose coat has been mixed with his. After all that the bottle gets broken but he wins the woman. Black and white. 101 minutes.

1952 Micheline Presle film
Micheline Presle stars as Marguerite in *La Dame aux Camélias*, a French film based on the Dumas novel. Raymond Bernard directed. Color. In French. 111 minutes.

1953 Maria Felix film
Maria Felix stars as Camelia in *Camelia, Passion Sauvage*, a Mexican film of the story based on the Dumas novel. Roberto Gavaldon directed. Black and white. In Spanish. 89 minutes.

1953 Barbara Laage film
Barbara Laage portrays the heroine in *Traviata 53*, a modernized Italian adaptation of the Verdi opera and Dumas novel. Vittorio Cottafavi directed. Black and white. In Italian. 92 minutes.

1962 Sarita Montiel film
Sarita Montiel stars as Marguerite aka Lola in *La Bella Lola*, a Spanish film version of the story directed by Alfonso Balcazar. Black and white. In Spanish. 88 minutes.

1965 Fists in the Pocket
Marco Bellochio's powerful Italian film *I Pugni in Tasca* uses Violetta's aria "Sempre libera" to emphasize the mental agony of Lou Castel, the

protagonist of the film. Black and white. In Italian. 113 minutes.

1966 Trans-Europ-Expres
Alain Robbe-Grillet's post-modernist film uses excerpts from *La Traviata* for most of its music. It was what the director said he wanted so Michael Fano arranged the Verdi opera music which was performed by the Prima Symphony Orchestra. Color. In French. 90 minutes.

1970 Camille 2000
Radley Metzer transfers the Dumas story to contemporary Rome with Danielle Gaubert as Margherita Gautier and Nino Castelnuovo as Armand Duval. It's also a bit more nude than usual. Color. In Italian. 104 minutes.

1973 Don't Look Now
Nicolas Roeg features the *La Traviata* Brindisi on the soundtrack of this erotic Daphne Du Maurier thriller set in Venice. Julie Christie and Donald Sutherland are the stars. Color. In English. 110 minutes.

1980 Isabelle Huppert film
Isabelle Huppert stars as Marguerite in *La Dama delle Camelie*, an Italian film based on the life of courtesan Alphonsine Plessis who inspired the Dumas novel. Mauro Bolognini directed. Color. In Italian. 92 minutes.

1984 Maestro's Company Puppets
The Australian Maestro's Company presents scenes from the opera with puppets. The story concerns two children who discover the puppets rehearsing operas under an old theater. The *La Traviata* voices belong to Pilar Lorengar in the role of Violetta, Giacomo Aragall as Alfredo and Dietrich Fischer-Diescau as Germont. Lorin Maazel conducts the Berlin Deutsche Oper Orchestra. William Fitzwater directed the video. Color. Dialogue in English, arias in Italian. 30 minutes. VAI video.

1984 Gretta Scacci film
Greta Scacci stars as Marguerite in *The Lady of the Camelias*, a British television film based on the Dumas novel and directed by Desmond Davis. Color. In English. 100 minutes.

1989 The Europeans
The Waltz from *La Traviata* is featured somewhat ironically at the ball in this splendid adaptation of the Henry James novel. James Ivory directed and Ismail Merchant produced. Color. 90 minutes.

1990 Pretty Woman
Verdi's pretty 19th century courtesan strikes a responsive chord in a pretty 20th century prostitute in this hit film. Hollywood streetwalker Julia Roberts is taken to San Francisco's War Memorial Opera House by millionaire Richard Gere who wants to observe her response to opera. Gere tells her that the first time one sees opera is very important because one falls in love with it at once or it never becomes a part of one's soul. Roberts naturally loves it. Karin Calabro sings the role of Violetta with Bruce Eckstut as Alfredo. Thomas Pastieri arranged and conducted the opera and Garry Marshall directed the film. Color. 117 minutes.

1994 The Adventures of Priscilla Queen of the Desert
A drag queen in an elaborate silvery costume on top of a pink bus on an empty highway in the Australian outback mimes to Violetta's aria "E strano!..forsa e lui." This is one of the odder opera scenes in modern cinema but perfectly justified in the context of a film about drag queens driving to the center of Australia. The actual singer is Joan Carden backed by the Sydney Symphony Orchestra. Stephan Elliot wrote and directed the film. Color. 103 minutes.

TREEMONISHA
1911 opera by Joplin

Scott Joplin's ragtime opera *Treemonisha* is the sleeping beauty of American music, forgotten for over fifty years after its 1915 premiere. The premiere was a sad affair, paid for by the composer himself and staged in Harlem with only a piano. The opera was judged a dismal failure and Joplin went crazy with disappointment, dying in an asylum. But *Treemonisha* won deserved acclaim when it was revived in 1972 and its wonderful climax "A Real Slow Drag" with its refrain of "Marching Onward" has become genuinely popular. Joplin was awarded a posthumous Pulitzer Prize for the opera in 1974. The story takes place on an abandoned Arkansas plantation in 1884. Treemonisha helps her people, who are former slaves, fight exploitative evil magicians who try to control them. She is kidnapped but rescued by Remus and all ends in forgiveness and fine music. See also SCOTT JOPLIN.

1982 Houston Grand Opera
Houston Grand Opera's colorful production of *Treemonisha* by Frank Corsaro in 1975 was a well-deserved success and is effectively captured on video. Carmen Balthrop stars as Treemonisha with Curtis Rayam as Remus, Obba Babatunde as Zodzetrick, Delores Ivory as Monisha, Dorceal Duckens as Ned, Kenn Hicks as Andy and Cora Johnson as Lucy. Gunther Schuller arranged and orchestrated the music, John DeMain conducts the Houston Grand Opera Orchestra, Franco Colabecchia designed the sets and costumes and Mabel Robinson created the choreography. Sid Smith directed the video. Color. In English. 86 minutes. Kultur video.

1986 Royal Opera House
Jessye Norman, Lisa Casteen and company sing the "A Real Slow Drag" ensemble "Marching Onward" in a staged scene at the Royal Opera House on April 21, 1986. It was one of the events in a telecast gala program arranged in honor of the Queen. Edward Downes conducts the Royal Opera House Orchestra. Color. 90 minutes. Lyric video and at MPRC.

TRIAL AT ROUEN, THE
1956 opera by Dello Joio

Norman Dello Joio's opera about the Maid of Orleans has had three incarnations. The first version was staged at Sarah Lawrence in 1950 as *The Trial of Joan*. Dello Joio then wrote a new libretto and score for NBC Opera Theatre and this opera was telecast in 1956 as *The Trial at Rouen*. When he revised it for the stage, it became *The Trial of St. Joan* and was produced by the New York City Opera in 1959 when it won the New York Music Critics Circle Award. The story focuses on Joan's trial at Rouen in 1431. In the first part the sympathetic Friar Julien urges Joan to submit to authority while Bishop Cauchon seems intent on destroying her. In the second part she is tried and condemned to death.

1956 NBC Opera Theatre
Elaine Malbin won high praise from the critics for her performance as Joan in this NBC Opera Theatre production by Samuel Chotzinoff. Her chief antagonist, Bishop Cauchon, is portrayed by Hugh

Thompson with Chester Watson as Friar Julien. The cast includes Paul Ukena, Loren Driscoll, Carole O'Hara and R. W. Barry. Trew Hocker designed the sets, Noel Polacheck designed the costumes and Peter Herman Adler conducted the Symphony of the Air Orchestra. Kirk Browning directed the telecast on April 8, 1956. Black and white. In English. 90 minutes.

TRIAL BY JURY
1875 comic opera by Gilbert & Sullivan

Trial by Jury, the first successful collaboration between William S. Gilbert and Arthur Sullivan, is the shortest of their operettas. It all takes place in a courtroom where a judge is called upon to decide a breach of promise action. Angelina is suing Edwin and arrives with her bridesmaids ready for a wedding. In the end the judge decides he will marry her himself. Gilbert's libretto is a satire on the English court system. See also GILBERT AND SULLIVAN.

1950 Patricia Morison Airflyte Theater
Patricia Morison stars as Angelina in this CBS television production by Marc Daniel created for the Nash Airflyte Theater. Ralph Riggs sings the role of the Judge and Donald Clark is the defendant Edwin. William Gaxton acted as host. It was telecast on Nov. 30, 1950. Black and white. In English. 30 minutes.

1953 Martyn Green Omnibus
Savoy opera specialist Martyn Green won high praise from the critics for his performance as the Judge in this CBS TV Omnibus production by William Spier. Arylne Frank portrays Angelina and Davis Cunningham is Edwin. Henry May designed the sets and Andrew McCullough directed the telecast on April 19, 1953. Black and white. In English. 25 minutes. Video at MTR & Library of Congress.

1974 Lawrence Richard film
Lawrence Richard stars as the Judge in this highlights version of the operetta produced by John Seabourne for the *World of Gilbert and Sullivan* film series. Gillian Humphreys is Angelina, Thomas Round is Edwin and Michael Wakeham is Angelina's counsel. The music is played by the Gilbert and Sullivan Festival Orchestra and Chorus and the film directed by Trevor Evans. Color. In English. 50 minutes.

1982 Frankie Howerd film

Frankie Howerd is sheer delight as the Judge in this lively film produced by Judith De Paul for George Walker. Kate Flowers is plaintiff Angelina, Ryland Davies is defendant Edwin, Anna Dawson is his new love Ann Other and Tom McDonnell is counsel for Angelina. Alexander Faris conducts the London Symphony Orchestra and the Ambrosian Opera Chorus. Wendy Toye was the stage director and Derek Bailey the film director. Color. In English. 40 minutes. Braveworld (England) video.

TRIAL OF MARY LINCOLN, THE
1972 TV opera by Pasatieri

President Lincoln's widow is put on trial for her sanity. Her son charges that her behavior is so peculiar that she should be committed to an asylum. American composer Thomas Pasatieri composed seven operas before creating this notable television opera with librettist Anne Howard Bailey. They tailored the opera specifically for TV with flashbacks, voice-overs and other screen techniques. It premiered on Feb. 26, 1972, on NET Opera Theater with mezzo-soprano Elaine Bonazzi. as Mary Lincoln. Critics particularly liked her Abraham Lincoln aria and her duet with her sister, soprano Carole Bogard. Baritone Wayne Turnage sings the role of her son. The cast also includes Chester Watson, Lizabeth Pritchett, Louise Parker, Julian Patrick and Alan Titus. William Ritman designed the sets and producer Peter Herman Adler conducted the Boston Symphony Orchestra. Kirk Browning directed the telecast which won an Emmy. Color. In English. 60 minutes. Video at MTR. See also THOMAS PASATIERI.

TRIALS OF GALILEO, THE
1967 TV opera by Laderman

American composer Ezra Laderman wrote the television opera *The Trials of Galileo* on commission from CBS. Joseph Darion's libretto concerns the problems of the 17th century astronomer who was forced to recant his heretical ideas by the Catholic Church. The trial is remembered in flashback by Galileo. The Cardinals Bellarmine and Barberini defend him at first but when Barberini becomes Pope Urban VIII, Galileo is tortured and imprisoned. His women friends also sing their feelings about him. The opera was telecast on May 14, 1967, in the CBS *Look Up and Live* series. It was put on the stage in a revised version in 1979 as *Galileo Galilei*. Color. In English. 75 minutes. See also EZRA LADERMAN.

TRILBY
Film series about opera singer

Trilby O'Farrell is the name of the tragic heroine of George du Maurier's 1894 novel *Trilby* about an artist's model who becomes a famous singer. She does this under the sinister hypnotic influence of Svengali, a Hungarian musician, who makes her into one of the great singers of Europe. She sings opera arias in controlled concerts but never appears in actual operas. When Svengali dies, Trilby loses her voice. The novel became a play in 1895 and has been enormously popular with filmmakers. The Trilby-Svengali myth is a powerful one and has been seen as an allegory about the harsh training of opera singers who are moulded into something strange and distant. Du Maurier is said to have modelled Trilby on the famous English contralto Clara Butt from the period when she was a music college student.

1896 Trilby Burlesque

The popularity of the play in London is reflected in its instant appearance in the movies in April 1896. This R. W. Paul English film simply shows the dancing girls at the Alhambra Theatre in London. About 1 minute.

1896 Trilby and Little Billee

The popularity in America of the play resulted in this Biograph film in September 1896. It shows the studio scene with Trilby and Little Billee. About 2 minutes.

1898 Ella Lola, á la Trilby

A short adaptation of the story featuring Svengali filmed by the Edison company. About 2 minutes.

1908 Oda Alstrup film

Danish actress Oda Alstrup portrays Trilby in this silent Danish film of the Du Maurier story. About 10 minutes.

1914 Viva Birkett film

English actress Viva Birkett plays Trilby with Sir Herbert Tree as her Svengali in this English silent film. Harold Shaw directed. Black and white. About 60 minutes.

1915 Clara Kimball Young film

Clara Kimball Young stars as Trilby with Wilton Lackaye as Svengali in this American film directed by Maurice Tourneur. Equitable Pictures. Black and white. About 70 minutes.

1922 Phyllis Neilson-Terry film

Phyllis Neilson-Terry portrays Trilby with Charles Garry as Svengali in this English film made for the *Tense Moments with Great Authors* series. H. B. Parkinson directed. Black and white. About 15 minutes.

1923 Andrée Lafayette film

Andrée Lafayette stars as Trilby with Arthur Edmund Carew as Svengali in this American film made for First National. James Young directed. Black and white. About 85 minutes.

1927 Anita Dorris film

Anita Dorris stars as Trilby with Paul Wagener as Svengali in this German film titled *Svengali*. Gennaro Righelli directed. Black and white. About 80 minutes.

1931 Marian Marsh film

This *Svengali* is the most famous film of the book with superb performances by Marian Marsh as Trilby and John Barrymore as Svengali. The sets by Anton Grot are a delight as is supporting actor Luis Alberni. Archie Mayo directed for Warner Bros. Black and white. 79 minutes.

1954 Elisabeth Schwarzkopf film

Trilby's beautiful singing voice is supplied by the great soprano Elisabeth Schwarzkopf in this English *Svengali*. Hildegarde Neff stars as Trilby with Donald Wolfit as Svengali. Noel Langley directed for MGM. Color. 82 minutes.

1983 Jodie Foster film

Operatic singing is left behind in this modernized *Svengali* set in the rock music world. Jodie Foster is the singer, Peter O'Toole is her Svengali and the cast includes Holly Hunter and Anthony Harvey. Color. 100 minutes.

TRISTAN UND ISOLDE

1865 opera by Wagner

The Celtic Tristan and Isolde legend originated in the mists of the time but Richard Wagner based his libretto on a 13th century German version written by Gottfried von Strassburg. Tristan is sent to Ireland by his King Mark of Cornwall to collect Mark's bride Isolde. Unfortunately they had met earlier and are secretly in love. When they attempt to take poison to avoid betrayal or suffering, Isolde's attendant Brangäne substitutes a love potion and passion overwhelms them. Mark discovers the betrayal and the lovers end up dying to the famous Liebestod. This is the best known melody in the opera and is often used as a musical comment in films. See also RICHARD WAGNER.

1967 Birgit Nilsson in Osaka

Birgit Nilsson stars as Isolde with Wolfgang Windgassen as her Tristan in this Osaka World Fair production originally designed and directed by Wieland Wagner for Bayreuth. Hans Hotter sings the role of King Mark, Hertha Töpper is Brangäne and Hans Andersson is Kursenal. Pierre Boulez conducts the Osaka Festival Chorus and Orchestra. The production was taped for Japanese television on April 10, 1967. Black and white. In German. 206 minutes. Legato Classics video.

1973 Birgit Nilsson in Orange

Birgit Nilsson plays Isolde opposite Jon Vickers as Tristan in this outdoor production by Nikolaus Lehnhoff at the Roman amphitheater in Orange. Walter Berry is Kursenal, Bengt Rundgren is King Mark and Ruth Hesse sings Brangäne. Karl Böhm conducts the ORTF Orchestra and the London New Philharmonic Chorus. Jean-Pierre Lazar was the cinematographer and Pierre Jourdan directed the film. Color. In German. 209 minutes. Lyric video/ Japanese video and laser.

1983 Bayreuth Festival

Johanna Meier portrays Isolde with René Kollo as Tristan in this Bayreuth Festival production designed, costumed and staged by Jean-Pierre Ponnelle. Matti Salminen is King Mark, Hanna Schwartz is Brangäne, Hermann Becht is Kurwenal and Robert Schunk is Melot. Daniel Barenboim conducts the Bayreuth Festival Orchestra and Chorus. Color. In German with English subtitles. 245 minutes. Philips video and laser.

1993 Deutsche Oper Berlin in Tokyo

Gwyneth Jones is Isolde and René Kollo is Tristan in this Deutsche Oper Berlin production by Götz Friedrich in Tokyo. The cast includes Robert Lloyd as King Mark, Gerd Feldhoff, Peter Edelmann,

Hanna Schwarz, Uwe Peper and Clemson Bieber. Jirí Kout conducts the Deutsche Opera Berlin Orchestra and Chorus. The opera was taped in HDTV. Color. In German. 243 minutes. On Japanese laserdisc.

Early/related films

1909 Tristan et Yseult
Stasia Napierkowska stars as Isolde with Paul Capellani as Tristan in this French Pathé film directed by Albert Capellani. Based on the opera and the legend, it was screened with the Wagner music. About 10 minutes.

1911 Tristano e Isotta
An Italian film version of the opera and legend shown in theaters with the Wagner music. It was made by the Film d'Arte Italiana studio. About 10 minutes.

1928 Un Chien Andalou
Spanish filmmaker Luis Buñuel was obsessed with *Tristan und Isolde* and featured music from it in three of his films. *Un Chien Andalou* is a silent film but it was usually screened accompanied by a gramophone record of the opera. When a sound version was made in 1960, the music of *Tristan und Isolde* was naturally used. Black and white. 17 minutes.

1930 L'Age d'Or
Luis Buñuel's masterpiece is as startling today as when it was made and again features music from *Tristan und Isolde*. An orchestra conducted by an aged bearded man is shown tuning up and playing the Liebestod. The orchestra's playing is crosscut with an erotic scene with a man and a woman in a garden. As they become passionate, the woman talks of murdering their children and blood appears on the man's face. The music stops after the conductor throws away his baton, goes to the couple and kisses the woman. Black and white. 60 minutes.

1943 Battle for Music
This is British film about the the problems and triumphs of the London Philharmonic Orchestra during World War II includes extracts from *Tristan und Isolde*. Among the conductors appearing in the film are Sir Adrian Boult, Warwich Braithwaite and Sir Malcolm Sargent. Donald Tayor directed for Strand Films. Black and white. In English. 87 minutes.

1946 Humoresque
Ambitious violinist John Garfield is performing the appropriate "Liebestod" music from *Tristan und Isolde* as the camera cuts to Joan Crawford walking melodramatically into the Atlantic Ocean to drown herself. The music was recorded for the film by master violinist Isaac Stern. Jean Negulesco directed. Black and white. 125 minutes.

1946 The Whale Who Wanted to Sing at the Met
Willie, the opera-singing whale with the voice of Nelson Eddy, fantasizes a performance in *Tristan* at the Met. He near blows his Isolde away with the wind he creates singing in duet with her. Hamilton Luske directed this Disney cartoon as part of the feature *Make Mine Music*. Color. 12 minutes.

1953 Wuthering Heights
Abismos de Pasión, Luis Buñuel's Mexican adaptation of *Wuthering Heights*, features themes from *Tristan und Isolde* as its entire musical soundtrack. Buñuel intended to feature the opera only in the climax of the film but ended up with fifty full minutes of Wagner. The music was arranged by Raul Lavista and played by the Philharmonic Society Orchestra. Black and white. In Spanish with English subtitles. 90 minutes.

1953 The Blue Gardenia
Fritz Lang uses the Liebestod music to indicate that a crime being reconstructed was committed in the name of love. Anne Baxter and Raymond Burr star in this fine *film noir* murder mystery. Black and white. 90 minutes.

1958 The Brain Eaters
Among the many pieces of classical music (mis)used in this cheap horror film are bits of *Tristan und Isolde*. A man called Tom Jonson claims he composed them but the piece he calls "Up the Hatch," for example, is really the Prelude to Act III of *Tristan*. Bruno Ve Sota directed. Black and white. 60 minutes.

1965 The Loved One
Tony Richardson's satirical film about a Hollywood cemetery includes a scene in which the loudspeakers play music appropriate for those

residing in that area. For the poets the music is from *Tristan und Isolde*. Black and white. 116 minutes.

1973 Tristan et Iseult

Writer/director Yvan Lagrange's French film is based on the legend but has an operatic musical background. Lagrange stars as Tristan with Claire Waution as his Isolde. This mannered but visually fascinating movie was shot in Iceland. Color. In French. 80 minutes.

1974 Mahler

The *Liebestod* as sung by Carol Mudie is heard on the soundtrack during a symbolic scene in Ken Russell's film about Mahler. His wife Alma buries the manuscript of her rejected song as the music plays. Robert Powell as Mahler recalls the events of his life during a trip with wife Georgina Hale. Color. In English. 115 minutes.

1975 Ron Hays Visualization

Ron Hays attempts to use video art to visualize music from the opera. He calls his piece *A Visualization of an Experience with Music - The Prelude and Liebestod from Tristan und Isold by Richard Wagner*. Color. 20 minutes. Video at Library of Congress.

1975 Black Moon

Louis Malle's futuristic fantasy uses the Prelude and Death of Isolde music to create a surrealistic atmosphere while men and women engage in deadly combat. Color. In French. 101 minutes.

1979 Tristan and Isolde

Richard Burton stars in this version of the legend made in Ireland by Tom Donovan with Kate Mulgrew as his Isolde. The cast includes Cyril Cusack, Nicholas Clay, Geraldine Fitzgerald and Niall Toibin. The film is also known as *Lovespell*. Color. 91 minutes,

1987 Franc Roddam film

English director Franc Roddam interprets the Liebestod aria in an episode of the opera film *Aria*. He places lovers Bridget Fonda and James Mathers in the night world of a Las Vegas hotel where they kill themselves after making love. The singer is Leontyne Price with the Philharmonia Orchestra conducted by Henry Lewis. Color. In German. About 10 minutes.

1990 Reversal of Fortune

Law professor Alan Dershowitz (Ron Silver) comes to interview suspected wife murderer Claus von Bulow (Jeremy Irons) and discovers him rather too appropriately enjoying the love and death Liebestod theme. Eva Marton is the singer backed by the London Philharmonic. Barbet Schroeder directed. Color. 120 minutes.

TRITTICO, IL
1918 one-act operas by Puccini

Il Trittico simply means *The Triptych* and is the collective name for a triple bill of one-act operas by Giacomo Puccini. They were premiered at the Metropolitan Opera in New York in 1918. For details on the individual operas, see GIANNI SCHICCHI, SUOR ANGELICA and IL TABARRO. See also GIACOMO PUCCINI.

1981 Metropolitan Opera

Renata Scotto stars in all three operas with casts that include Cornell MacNeil, Jean Kraft and Gabriel Bacquier. The operas were produced by Fabrizio Melano with set designs by David Reppa. James Levine conducted the Metropolitan Orchestra. Kirk Browning directed the telecast on Nov. 14, 1981. Color. In Italian with English subtitles. Video at MTR.

1983 Teatro alla Scala

Sylvano Bussoti's La Scala production features Sylvia Sass, Piero Cappuccilli and Nicola Martinucci in *Il Tabarro*, Rosalind Plowright and Dunja Vejzovich in *Suor Angelica* and Juan Pons and Cecilia Gasdia in *Gianni Schicchi*. Gianandrea Gavazzeni conducts the La Scala Orchestra and chorus and Brian Large directed the video. Color. In Italian with English subtitles. 150 minutes. Home Vision video.

TRIUMPH OF BEAUTY AND DECEIT, THE
1995 English TV opera by Barry

The Triumph of Beauty and Deceit is an English television opera based on Handel's oratorio *The Triumph of Time and Truth* and using the same characters. Composed by Gerald Barry to a libretto by Meredith Oakes, it is set in the Court of Pleasure and revolves around a struggle for the possession of Beauty. The singers are Richard Edgar Wilson as

Beauty, Nicholas Clapton as Pleasure, Stephen Richardson as Time, Denis Lakey as Truth and Adrian Clarke as Deceit. Diego Masson conducted the Composers Ensemble. Mary Jane Walsh produced the opera which was commissioned by Channel 4 and telecast on Feb. 19, 1995 with Donald Taylor Black directing. Color. In English. 51 minutes.

TROIS SOUHAITS, LES
1928 screen opera by Martinu

Czech composer Bohuslav Martinu's *The Three Wishes*, is a screen opera as movies are central to its plot and staging. It begins in a movie studio where a fairy-tale film titled *The Three Wishes* is being screened. A fairy grants the wishes of riches, youth and love to the couple Nina and Arthur. Their wishes are seen being fulfilled in the following acts in dream-like films. Georges Ribemont-Dessaignes wrote the French libretto. *Troji prani*, as it's called in Czech, was composed in 1928 but not staged until 1971 in Brno. It has been telecast and released on video iin France. See also BOHUSLAV MARTINU.

1991 Lyons Opera
Soprano Valerie Chevalier and bass-baritone Gilles Cachémaille star in this Opéra de Lyon production with support from Christian Papis, Valerie Millot, Jocelyne Taillon, Jules Bastin, Georges Gautier, Hélène Perrmouin, Beatrice Uria-Monzon and Riccardo Cassinelli. Kent Nagano conducts the Lyons Opera Chorus and Orchestra. In French. 101 minutes. France Telecom. Polygram (France) video.

TROIS VALSES, LES
1935 operetta by Straus

Drei Walzer (Three Waltzes), best known in French as *Les Trois Valses*, is an operetta by Oscar Straus composed with help from his great predecessors Johann Strauss Sr. and Jr. He created the music for this bitter-sweet story using tunes by Strauss Sr. for the first act set in 1865, Strauss Jr. for the second act set in 1900 and himself for the third act set in 1935. Paul Knepler and Armin Robinson's libretto takes place over three generations with the central character played by the same actress. She portrays a ballet dancer in the first act, her operetta star daughter in the second act and her film star granddaughter in the third act. In each the woman has to decide between career and love for a man (again the same actor) who is also a direct descendent. The operetta premiered in 1935 in Zurich in German but became famous in its 1937 French version as *Trois Valses* with Yvonne Printemps and Pierre Fresnay. It was filmed with the same cast. See also OSCAR STRAUS.

1938 Yvonne Printemps film
The French film of the operetta was splendidly directed by one of the masters of the waltz film, Ludwig Berger. Yvonne Printemps stars as Fanny, Yvette and Irene Grandpre in the three periods of the operetta. The times were slightly shifted (as on the Paris stage) to 1867, 1900 and 1937 to coincide with three world fairs. Printemps' husband Pierre Fresnay plays the man in all three time periods. The screenplay is by Leopold Marchant and Albert Willemetz who created the Paris stage adaptation. The cinematography is by Eugen Schüfftan, Paul Portier and Delattre. Black and white. In French. 104 minutes. Bel Canto Society/ Opera Dubs/ Editions Montparnasse (France) videos.

TROUBLE IN TAHITI
1952 opera by Bernstein

Dinah and Sam are stuck in a loveless marriage in a boring suburban home. Leonard Bernstein wrote music and libretto for this entertaining study in alienation. Particularly fine is a satirical aria by Dinah in which she describes the Hollywood South Seas sarong-and-volcano movie of the title. There are also fine pastiches of popular music sung by a Greek chorus-like jazz trio who comment on the action. The opera is incorporated in Bernstein's 1983 *A Quiet Place* as a flashback after the death of Dinah. See also LEONARD BERNSTEIN. A QUIET PLACE

1952 NBC Opera Theatre
Beverly Wolff is Dinah and David Atkinson is Sam in this excellent television production of the Bernstein opera. They are supported by the jazzy trio of Constance Brigham, Robert Kole and William Harder. Bernstein conducts the NBC Orchestra. Samuel Chotzinoff and Charles Polachek produced and Kirk Browning directed the Nov. 16, 1952 telecast. Some critics felt the opera worked better on television than it did on stage. Black and white. In English. 45 minutes. Video at MTR.

1973 London Weekend Television
This inventive British adaptation stars Nancy Williams as Dinah and Julian Patrick as Sam. The wonderful singing trio is Antonia Butler, Michael

Clark and Mark Brown. The singers perform in front of animated drawn sets with production design by Eileen Diss and graphic sequences by Pat Gavin. Leonard Bernstein leads the London Symphonic Wind Band. David Griffiths produced and Bill Hays directed the video for London Weekend Television. Color. In English. 45 minutes. Kultur Video.

TROVATORE, IL
1853 opera by Verdi

Giuseppe Verdi's *The Troubadour* has one of the most complicated plots in opera and also some of the best music, including the famous Anvil and Soldier Choruses and the great tenor aria "Di quella pira." Manrico is the troubadour of the title, a rebel leader in 15th century Spain, whose arch enemy Count di Luna leads the King's army. Both love Leonora but she prefers Manrico. Manrico's mother, the gypsy Azucena, is taken by Luna and Manrico is captured when he tries to rescue her. Leonora offers herself to Luna if he will free Manrico but takes poison after he agrees. When Luna finds he has been tricked, he executes Manrico anyway. Azucena then reveals that Manrico was not her son but Luna's lost brother. Salvatore Cammarano's libretto is based on an overheated Spanish play by Antonio Garcia Gutierrez. See also GIUSEPPE VERDI.

1949 Carmine Gallone film
Carmine Gallone directed this solid Italian film of the opera. Manrico is played by Gino Sinimberghi and sung by Antonio Salvarezza, Leonora is played by Vittorina Colonnello and sung by Franca Sacchi, mezzo Gianna Pederzini sings and acts Azucena and Enzo Mascherini is the Count di Luna. Gabriele Santini conducts the Rome Opera House Orchestra and Chorus. Black and white. In Italian. 105 minutes. Lyric/Bel Canto Society/ Mastervideo (Italy) videos.

1953 Opera Cameos film
A highlights version of the opera was telecast on the Dumont TV network in 1953. It was shown as part of the *Opera Cameos* series. Black and white. In Italian. 25 minutes.

1957 Mario Del Monaco film
Mario Del Monaco is in peak form as Manrico in this splendid production filmed for Italian TV. Critic Stephen Stroff rates it as the best recording as well as the best video of the opera. The strong cast includes Leyla Gencer as Leonora, Fedora Barbieri as Azucena and Ettore Bastianini as the Count di Luna. Fernando Previtali conducts the RAI Orchestra and Chorus. Claudio Fino directed the film. Black and white. In Italian. 124 minutes. Lyric Legato Classics/Bel Canto Society videos.

1964 Gwyneth Jones on BBC
Welsh soprano Gwyneth Jones stars as Leonora in this BBC highlights production of the opera. She is supported by Italian tenor Bruno Prevedi, Italian mezzo Giulietta Simionato and English baritone Peter Glossop Black and white. In Italian. 66 minutes. Print at NFTA in London.

1972 Montserrat Caballé at Orange
Montserrat Caballé stars as Leonora in this outdoor production by Charles Hamilton at the Roman amphitheater in Orange. Romanian tenor Ludovic Spiess sings Manrico, Irina Arkhipova is Azucena and Peter Glossop is the Count di Luna. Reynald Giovanetti conducts the Orchestra and Chorus. Pierre Jourdan directed the film of the opera live. Color. In German. 205 minutes. Lyric video/Japanese laserdisc.

1983 Australian Opera
Joan Sutherland stars as Leonora in this Sydney Opera House production by Elijah Moshinsky. Kenneth Collins sings Manrico, Lauris Elms is Azucena and Jonathan Summers is Count di Luna. Richard Bonynge conducts the Elizabethan Sydney Orchestra and Australian Opera Chorus. Brian Adams directed the video. Color. In Italian with English subtitles. 138 minutes. Sony video.

1984 Montreal Opera
Lynne Strow is Leonora, Vincenzo Bello is Manrico and Mariana Pounova is Azucena in this Montreal Opera production by Jean-Yves Landry. The cast includes Joseph Rouleau, Therese Sevigny and Richard Fredricks. Franz Paul Decker conducts the Montreal Opera Orchestra. The opera was telecast from Montreal on Jan. 1, 1984. Color. In Italian. 150 minutes. Lyric video.

1985 Verona Arena
Rosalind Plowright is Leonora, Franco Bonisolli is Manrico, Fiorenza Cossotto is Azucena and Giorgio Zancanaro is Count di Luna in this big Verona Arena production. It was staged by Italian playwright/filmmaker Giuseppe Patroni Griffi with sets designed by Mario Ceroli and costumes by

Gabriella Pescucci. Reynald Giovaninetti conducts the Verona Arena Orchestra and Chorus. Brian Large directed the video. Color. In Italian with English subtitles. 150 minutes. Home Vision video.

1985 Opera Stories
This is a laserdisc highlights version of the above Verona production with Charlton Heston setting the scene from Spain and describing the opera. The framing material was shot in 1989 by Keith Cheetham. Color. 52 minutes. Pioneer Artists laser.

1988 Metropolitan Opera
Luciano Pavarotti stars as Manrico with Eva Marton as Leonora in this fine Metropolitan Opera production by Fabrizio Melano. Sherrill Milnes sings the role of Count di Luna with Dolora Zajic as Azucena. Ezio Frigerio designed the sets and Franca Squarciapino the costumes. James Levine conducts the Metropolitan Opera Orchestra and Chorus and Brian Large directed the video. Color. In Italian with English subtitles. 139 minutes. DG video/laser.

Early/related films

1906 Chronophone sound films
Two early sound films of arias from *Il Trovatore* were made in England with the Chronophone system. Edith Albord and Frank Rowe are pictured singing the famous Miserere and "Home To Our Mountains." Arthur Gilbert directed. Each about 3 minutes.

1906 Gypsy Dance film
The Gypsy Dance from *Il Trovatore* is performed by the Royal Danish Ballet in this early Danish film. The soloist is Valborg Borchsenius. A print survives. About 4 minutes.

1908 Henny Porten film
Henny Porten, Germany's first major film star, is Leonora in this German sound film shot to a record of an *Il Trovatore* aria. Porten's father Franz, a former opera singer, directed in a Berlin studio using Oskar Messter's synchronization system. About 5 minutes.

1908 Deutsch Bioscop films
Two early German sound films were made by the German Deutsch Bioscop company of scenes from *Il Trovatore*. One shows the Trio, the other the Miserere. Both films survive in a German film archive. Each about 4 minutes.

1908 Pineschi sound film
This early Italian sound film made by the Pineschi company features scenes from the *Il Trovatore* synchronized with records of the music. About 10 minutes.

1909 Albert Capellani film
This French film of the story directed by Albert Capellani for Pathé stars Paul Capellani and Stacia Napierkowska. It includes scenes in color and was released in the U.S. in 1910 to favorable reviews. About l2 minutes.

1909 Lubin film
This early American film of the opera was made by the Lubin company for their Verdi series. About 10 minutes.

1909 Francesca Bertini film
Francesca Bertini stars as Leonora in this early Italian film based on the Verdi opera. It was directed by Ugo Falena for Film d'Arte Italiana in Rome. About 10 minutes.

1910 Animatophone film
This British sound film features arias from *Il Trovatore* synchronized with records. It was made by David Barnett for the Animatophone company. About 12 minutes.

1914 Centaur film
Agnes Mapes stars as Azucena in this feature-length American film based on the Verdi opera and the play. The cast includes Julia Hurley, Jean Thrall and Frank Holland. Charles Simone wrote and directed the film for the Nestor studio. About 60 minutes.

1922 Tense Moments from Opera series
Bertram Burleigh is Manrico, Lillian Douglas is Leonora, Cyril Dane is Count de Luna and Ada Grier is Azucena in this British silent film. It was made for the *Tense Moments from Opera* series and directed by Edwin J. Collins. About 10 minutes.

1927 Cameo Operas series
This is a British film of highlights from the opera made by A. E. Coleby for John E. Blakeley's *Song Films* series. The music accompanying the opera

scenes was played by the theater orchestra. About 18 minutes.

1927 Rosa Raisa/Giacomo Rimini film
Rosa Raisa and Giacomo Rimini, both then with the Chicago Opera, sing selections from Act IV of *Il Trovatore* in this Vitaphone sound film. About 8 minutes.

1930 Giovanni Martinelli film
Giovanni Martinelli performs selections from *Il Trovatore* in this Vitaphone sound film including "Ah, si ben mio" and "Di quella pira." He is assisted by soprano Livia Marraci and accompanied by the Vitaphone Symphony Orchestra. Black and white. About 9 minutes.

1935 A Night at the Opera
A production of *Il Trovatore* at the Met forms the background of the final scenes of this Marx Brothers comedy. Chico and Harpo mess up the music, Groucho sells peanuts, the sets fall down, the Anvil Chorus is guyed and Harpo swings across the stage. Everyone is chased around until the Manrico (Walter King) is kidnapped and Allan Jones is asked to sing in his place. Kitty Carlisle plays Leonora, Olga Dane is Azucena, Luther Hoobner is Ruiz and Rodolfo Hoyos is Count di Luna. Hoyos sings bits of *Il Trovatore* with Tandy McKenzie. Sam Wood directed. MGM. 90 minutes.

1936 Moonlight Murder
A tenor is killed at the Hollywood Bowl during a performance of *Il Trovatore* in this low-budget murder mystery. Leo Carrillo plays the tenor but the selections from the opera are actually sung by voice double Alfonso Pedroza. Edward R. Marin directed. Black and white. 80 minutes.

1944 The Anvil Chorus Girl
This Popeye cartoon features the famous Anvil Chorus as its musical focal point. The girl of the title creates the anvil music wherever she goes. I. Sparber directed for Paramount. Color. 7 minutes.

1947 Something in the Wind
Metropolitan opera tenor Jan Peerce and Deanna Durbin join voices in this film to sing the "Miserere" from *Il Trovatore* while they are in jail. Irving Pichel directed for Universal. Black and white. 89 minutes.

1954 Senso
Luchino Visconti's superb film opens with a production of *Il Trovatore* at La Fenice Theater in Venice in 1866 during the period of the Austrian occupation. When the tenor steps down stage and begins to sing "Di quella pira, " it is perceived as a patriotic statement by the Venetians and triggers leaflets and a riot. Color. In Italian. 115 minutes.

1993 Heart and Souls
Franco Corelli, Gabriella Tucci and Angelo Mercuriali are heard on the sound track of this Hollywood fantasy film performing "Ah! si ben mio...du quella pira." The music is performed by the Rome Opera House Orchestra led by Thomas Schippers. Robert Downey Jr. Stars, Ron Underwood directed. Color. 104 minutes.

TROYANOS, TATIANA
American mezzo-soprano (1938-1993)

Tatiana Troyanos, whose untimely death at the age of 54 robbed opera of a fine artist, was notable for her warmth and emotion as well as the range of her roles. She was born in a New York tenement, worked as a secretary while studying at Juilliard and endured two years as a chorus nun in *The Sound of Music* before breaking into opera. She made her debut in 1963 at the New York City Opera and then moved to Hamburg where she sang for ten years. Her breakthrough was her 1969 Covent Garden Octavian, a role she repeated in her debut at the Met in 1976. She created the main role in Pendercki's *The Devils of Loudun* in 1969 and the role of Isabella in Glass's *The Voyage* in 1992. She was much admired in trouser roles and can be seen on video in a number of these parts. See ARIADNE AUF NAXOS (1988), CAPRICCIO (1993), LA CLEMENZA DI TITO (1980), CAVALLERIA RUSTICANA (1978), THE DEVILS OF LOUDUN (1969), DON CARLO (1980), DIE FLEDERMAUS (1986), OEDIPUS REX (1973), DER ROSENKAVALIER (1982), THE TALES OF HOFFMANN (1988), TANNHÄUSER (1982), LES TROYENS (1983), WEST SIDE STORY (1985).

TROYENS, LES
1863 opera by Berlioz

The Trojans is Hector Berlioz' grand *opera maudit* and was never staged complete in his lifetime. Acts Three, Four and Five were presented at the premiere in 1863 but the complete five-act opera was not produced until 1890. The libretto is based on Virgil's *Aeniad*. The first half in Troy tells the story of Cassandra and the Trojan Horse while the second is set in Carthage after the fall of Troy and features Queen Dido. The problems Berlioz had with the opera are explored in Tony Palmer's film *I, Berlioz*. There are apparently only two complete recordings and one is the 1983 Met video. See also HECTOR BERLIOZ.

1983 Metropolitan Opera
Tatiana Troyanos stars as Dido, Queen of Carthage, with Jessye Norman as Cassandra and Placido Domingo as Aeneas in this major Metropolitan Opera production by Fabrizio Melano. Allan Monk sings Chorèbe, Paul Plishka is Narbal, Robert Nagy is Helenus, Claudia Catania is Ascagne, Barbara Conrad is Hecuba and John Macurdy is Priam. This is a grandiose production with sets and costumes by Peter Wexler. James Levine conducts the Metropolitan Orchestra and Chorus. Brian Large directed the video taped on Oct. 8, 1983, and telecast on March 24, 1984. Color. In French with English subtitles. 253 minutes. Paramount video/Pioneer laser.

1992 Zurich Opera House
Tony Palmer's film biography *I, Berlioz* contains sizable extracts from *Les Troyens* as staged by the Zurich Opera House. Ludmilla Schemtschuk sings Dido, Giorgio Lamberti is Aeneas, Agnes Habereder is Cassandra and Vesselina Kasarova is Anna. They perform with the Ensemble, Chorus and Orchestra of the Zurich Opera house conducted by Ralf Weikert. Palmer's film centers the difficulties Berlioz had composing the opera and having it staged. Color. In French with English subtitles. 90 min.

TSAR'S BRIDE, THE
1899 opera by Rimsky-Korsakov

The bride of Nikolai Rimsky-Korsakov's opera *Tsarskaya Nevesta* is a woman called Marfa who has been chosen to be the bride of Tsar Ivan the Terrible. She loves Lykov but is desired by Gryaznoy and this causes his jealous mistress Lyubasha to poison her. This leads to the execution of Lykov, who is blamed, and the murder of Lyubasha by Gryaznoy. Meanwhile poor dying Marfa goes mad. The story is gloomy but the music is splendid. See also NIKOLAI RIMSKY-KORSAKOV.

1965 Vladimir Gorikker film
Soviet opera film specialist Vladimir Gorikker produced this beautiful film of Rimsky-Korsakov's opera on location in Latvia. He seems to have been influenced by Eisenstein's film about the same Tsar but the effect is positive. The lovely Raissa Nedashkovskaya portrays Marfa with the fine singing voice of Galina Oleinichenko. Equally good are the villainous Lyubasha (acted by Natalya Rudnaya, sung by Larisa Avdeyeva), Gryaznoy (acted by Otar Koberidze and sung by Yevgeny Kibkalo) and Ivan the Terrible (acted by Pyotr Glebov). Vadim Mass was the superb cinematographer and Gorikker and Andrei Donativ wrote the adaptation. Yevgeni Svetlanov conducts the Bolshoi Theater Orchestra and Choir. Black and white. In Russian with English subtitles. 97 minutes. Kultur/Corinth video.

TUCKER, RICHARD
American tenor (1913-1975)

Richard Tucker made his debut in *La Traviata* in 1943 with the Salmaggi Opera in New York and reached the Met in 1945 in *La Gioconda*. In 1947 he sang in *La Gioconda* with Maria Callas at the Verona Arena when she made her Italian debut. Although he sang in most of the leading opera houses, the Metropolitan remained his center. He sang there for three decades in over 600 performances and was always an audience favorite. His screen opera debut was singing Ramades in a Toscanini telecast of *Aida* in 1949 which is on video. It's his only complete opera on video but he is featured on video in scenes from *Faust* and *Rigoletto* staged for the *Voice of Firestone* TV series and in a Metropolitan Opera telecast of *Carmen*. Tucker is remembered every year on television at an opera gala honoring the Richard Tucker Award winner. See AIDA (1949), CARMEN (1952), FAUST (1963), METROPOLITAN OPERA (1953/1953/1957/1966), RIGOLETTO (1963).

1949 Song of Surrender
This is was Richard Tucker's only Hollywood film and he is heard but not seen singing Schubert's "Ständchen." The film is set at the turn of the century and stars Wanda Hendrix as a young woman married to Claude Rains. Mitchell Leisen directed. Black and white. 93 minutes.

1957-63 Richard Tucker in Opera & Song
Richard Tucker is seen in performance on *Voice of Firestone* television programs from 1957 to 1963. He

sings arias from *Aida, Carmen, Pagliacci* and *Rigoletto* plus songs by Leoncavallo, Victor Herbert and Jerome Kern. Black and white. 40 minutes. VAI video.

1958 Lisa Della Casa in Opera & Song
Richard Tucker is featured with soprano Lisa Della Casa on this *Voice of Firestone* television show telecast on Sept. 22, 1958. He sings "E lucevan le stelle" from *Tosca* and joins the soprano on "O soave fanciulla" from *La Bohème*. Black and white. 30 minutes.

1970 Richard Tucker sings "Cielo e mar"
Tucker sings the aria "Cielo e mar" from *La Gioconda* on stage in a 1970 concert. The aria is included on the video *Legends of Opera*. Black and white. In Italian. 5 minutes. Legato Classics video.

1994 The Legacy of Richard Tucker
A compilation of arias and duets from the archives of the Richard Tucker Fountation. Included are arias from *Turandot, Pagliacci* and *Aida* and duets with *Renata Tebaldi* from *Manon Lescaut*. The video was produced by D'Alessio production. 30 minutes.

TURANDOT
1926 opera by Puccini

Turandot was Giacomo Puccini's last opera and some consider it his best. Its tenor aria "Nessun dorma," sung by Prince Calaf, has been a part of popular culture since Luciano Pavarotti's version was used as the theme song of the 1990 World Cup. The libretto by Renato Simoni and Giuseppe Adami is derived from a Chinese fairy tale by Carlo Gozzi. It tells of a cold-hearted princess named Turandot who beheads any man who attempts to win her but fails. Prince Calaf succeeds in thawing her out but not before the slave girl Liù has sacrificed herself to avoid betraying him. Puccini died before finishing the opera and it was completed by Franco Alfano from his notes. The aria "Nessun dorma," has been inserted effectively into a number of Hollywood movies. See also GIACOMO PUCCINI.

1958 Franco Corelli film
Franco Corelli stars as Prince Calaf with Lucille Udovick as his Turandot in this Italian television film. Corelli was in peak form when the film was made and gives a remarkable performance. Renata Mattioli is Liù and Plinio Clabassi plays Timur.

Fernando Previtali conducts the Milan RAI Orchestra and Chorus, Attilio Colonnello designed the sets and Mario Lanfranchi directed. Black and white. In Italian. 114 minutes. Lyric Legato Classics/ Bel Canto Society videos.

1969 Birgit Nilsson film
Birgit Nilsson sings Princess Turandot in this Italian TV film realistically directed by Margarita Wallman. Prince Calaf is sung by Gianfranco Cecchele, Gabriella Tucci is Liù and Boris Carmeli is Timur. The elaborate sets and costumes are by Eugenio Guglielminetti, Georges Prêtre conducts the RAI Orchestra and Chorus. Black and white. In Italian. 124 minutes. Lyric Legata Classics video.

1983 Verona Arena
Bulgarian soprano Ghena Dimitrova is a dominating Turandot and easily holds her own against the gigantic sets in this grand outdoor staging in the open-air Verona Arena. She is supported in this colorful production by Nicola Martinucci as Calaf, Cecila Gasdia as Liù and Ivo Vinco as Timur. The sets are by Luciano Rucceri, the costumes by Nana Cecchi and Italian filmmaker Giuliano Montaldo staged the production. Maurizio Arena conducts the Verona Arena Orchestra. Brian Large directed the video. Color. In Italian with English subtitles. 116 minutes. HBO video/Pioneer Artists laser.

1983 Vienna State Opera
A innovative Vienna production by Broadway's Hal Prince with a strong cast, intriguing direction and surprising sets. Eva Marton is the cold-hearted princess, José Carreras is the prince who thinks he can thaw her, Katia Ricciarelli is noble Liù and John Paul Bogart is Timur. Prince's dreamlike staging is supported by the designs of Tazeena Firth and Timothy O'Brien. Lorin Maazel conducts the Vienna State Opera Orchestra and Chorus and Vienna Boys Choir. Color. In Italian with English subtitles. 138 minutes. MGM/UA Home Video

1988 Metropolitan Opera
Franco Zeffirelli directed and designed the sets for this spectacular Metropolitan Opera production of *Turandot*. Eva Marton sings the role of Turandot, Placido Domingo is Calaf, Leona Mitchell is Liù and Paul Plishka is Timur. The opulent costumes and sets are almost as impressive as the singers but conductor James Levine keeps the music as relevant

as the scenery. Color. In Italian with English subtitles. 134 minutes. DG video.

1993 San Francisco Opera
This is one of those productions where you could go out happily whistling the sets. David Hockney's colorful designs dominate the San Francisco Opera stage with their brightness and zigzag angles and work well with the costumes and the singing. Eva Marton is the icy princess, Michael Sylvester is the warm-hearted Calaf, Lucia Mazzaria is an effective Liù and Kevin J. Langan is a strong Timur. The costumes are by Ian Falconer, Thomas J. Munn did the lighting and Peter McClintock was stage director. Donald Rummincles conducts the San Francisco Opera Orchestra and Brian Large directed the video. Color. In Italian with English subtitles. 124 minutes. Home Vision video/ Pioneer laser.

Early/related films

1934 Princess Turandot
This is a light musical version of the Turandot story written by Thea von Harbou, the leading German screenwriter of the time, and based on both the opera and the Gozzi play. Kathe von Nagy stars as Turandot with Willy Fritsch as Calaf in the German version and Pierre Blanchar as Calaf in the French. Gerhard Lamprecht directed the film in German as *Prinzessin Turandot* and in French as *Turandot, Princesse de Chine*. Black and white. 83 minutes.

1943 His Butler's Sister
Deanna Durbin sings the tenor aria "Nessun dorma" from *Turandot* at a butler's ball in this charming film about a girl and a composer. Frank Borzage directed. Universal. Black and white. 94 minutes.

1967 Martinelli at the Seattle Opera
Tenor Giovanni Martinelli's last stage performance at the age of 82 is shown in this film shot at the dress rehearsal of *Turandot* at the Seattle Opera in 1967. Martinelli was featured in the non-singing role of the Emperor. Color. 3 minutes. Print in National Film Archive, London.

1974 Gianini/Luzzati cartoon
The opera-oriented Italian animation team of Giulio Gianini and Emmanuele Luzzati created this *Turandot*, a splendid animated cartoon based the Puccini opera. Color. 8 minutes.

1984 The Killing Fields
"Nessun dorma" is sung by Franco Corelli in ironic counterpoint during a key scene of this film about the horrors of war in Cambodia. Sam Waterson wonders if his Cambodian assistant is still alive while Corelli sings on the stereo that his secret cannot be known. When Richard Nixon declaims about Cambodia on TV, Corelli sings that he will certainly conquer. Roland Joffe directed. Color. 141 minutes.

1987 Ken Russell film
Ken Russell's *Turandot* episode in the opera film *Aria* is a visually spectacular, surrealistic interpretation of "Nessun dorma." Linnzi Drew dreams she is being adorned with dazzling jewels but she is actually having visions on an operating table after a bad car accident. The singer is Jussi Björling with the Rome Opera House Orchestra conducted by Erich Leinsdorf. Color. In Italian. Color. About 10 minutes. See ARIA.

1987 The Witches of Eastwick
Luciano Pavarotti is heard singing "Nessun dorma" on the soundtrack at a particularly apt moment in this Jack Nicholson-as-the-Devil film directed by George Miller. Color. 118 minutes.

1989 New York Stories
Martin Scorsese's episode of the omnibus film *New York Stories* is *Life Lessons*, a story about a New York painter and his girlfriend. It features Mario Del Monaco singing "Nessun dorma." Color. 129 minutes.

1992 Over the Hill
Peter Dvorsky is heard singing "Nessun dorma" as characters in this romantic Australian comedy pass a sleepless night. Olympia Dukakis stars as a woman looking for herself in the Australian outback. George Miller directed. Color. 99 minute.

1995 Operavox Animated Opera
The Welsh animation studio Cartwn Cymru created this animated version of *Turandot* for the British Operavox series. The Welsh National Opera Orchestra plays a specially recorded score. Wyn Davies was music editor and Gary Hurst directed. Color. 27 minutes.

TURCO IN ITALIA, IL
1814 opera by Rossini

Gioachino Rossini's comic opera followed directly after the popular *L'Italiana in Algeri* with a kind of reverse emphasis of location and amorous intrigue. The setting here is Naples. The Turk of the title is Selim who is fancied by Zaide but attracted to Fiorilla who is married to Geronio but has Narciso as her lover. Meanwhile the poet Prosdocimo is looking for comic characters and finds a goodly number. See also GIOACHINO ROSSINI.

1978 New York City Opera
Beverly Sills stars as Fiorilla in this New York City Opera production sung in English and titled *The Turk in Italy*. Tito Capobianco staged the new translation by Andrew Porter. Donald Gramm portrays the Turk Selim, Susanne Marsee is Zaide, Alan Titus is Prosdocimo, James Billings is Geronio, Jonathan Green is Albazar and Henry Price is Narciso. Julius Rudel conducts the NYCO Orchestra and Chorus and Harold Prince acted as host. Kirk Browning directed the video and telecast on Oct. 4. 1980. Color. 180 minutes. Video at New York Public Library.

TURNAGE, MARK-ANTHONY
English composer (1960-)

Mark-Anthony Turnage studied with Oliver Knussen and John Lambert and then worked with Hans Werner Henze at Tanglewood. Henze commissioned Turnage's opera *Greek* for the Munich Biennale and it was later staged successfully in Edinburgh and London. Turnage composes in a modern idiom that includes influences from rock and jazz as well as Britten and Stravinsky. See GREEK.

TURNER, CLARAMAE
American contralto (1920-)

Claramae Turner began her career in the chorus of the San Francisco Opera and gradually moved into major roles. Gian-Carlo Menotti picked her to create the title role in *The Medium* at Columbia University in 1946 and she made her debut at the Metropolitan Opera the same year in *Faust*. She stayed with the Met for three years and then sang around the U.S. and Europe including the premiere of Copeland's *The Tender Land*. She has a major singing role as Nettie in the film version of Rodgers &

Hammerstein's *Carousel* and recreated her Madame Flora in *The Medium* for NBC television in 1959. See also CAROUSEL (1956), HANSEL AND GRETEL (1950), THE MEDIUM (1959).

TURNER, EVA
English soprano (1892-1990)

Eva Turner made her debut in 1916 as a page in *Tannhauser* with the Carl Rosa company and sang with that company for eight years. In 1924 she was Freia in *Das Rheingold* at La Scala and began her rise to stardom in the roles of Aida, Leonora and especially Turandot. She was associated with ice princess role for the rest of her life and many thought her its ideal singer. She was one of the major dramatic sopranos of the world in the 1930s and 1940s. She can be seen talking about and performing Aida and Tosca in the documentary films about the operas. See AIDA (1987 film), TOSCA (1983 film).

TURN OF THE SCREW, THE
1954 opera by Britten

Benjamin Britten's musical adaptation of Henry James' gothic ghost story about a supernatural war over two children was composed to a libretto by Myganwy Piper. A governess struggles to rescue two children in her care from the malign influence of the dead servants Peter Quint and Miss Jessel. She succeeds in wresting the girl Flora away with the help of the housekeeper Mrs. Grose but the boy Miles dies in the battle for his soul. See also BENJAMIN BRITTEN.

1959 Peter Morley telecast
Peter Morley directed this imaginative production of the opera for Associated-Rediffusion Television. It stars Jennifer Vyvyan, who originated the role of the Governess on stage, opposite Raymond Nilsson as Peter Quint. The others in the cast are Judith Pierce, Arda Mandikian, Tom Bevan and Janette Miller. Charles Mackerras conducted the English Opera Group Orchestra and John Piper designed the sets. Black and white. In English. 120 minutes.

1982 Petr Weigl film
Czech filmmaker Petr Weigl shot his film in a country estate in Czechoslovakia with actors miming to the voices of English singers. Weigl is good at this and though the film looks a bit

beautiful, it is very effective. Robert Tear sings Quint acted by Juraj Kukura, Helen Donath sings the Governess acted by Magdalena Vasaryova, Heather Harper sings Miss Jessel acted by Emilia Vasaryova, Lilian Watson sings Flora acted by Beata Blazickova, Michael Ginn sings Miles acted by Michael Gulyas, Ava June sings Mrs. Grose and Philip Langridge sings the Prologue. Sir Colin Davis conducts the Royal Opera House Orchestra. Unitel. Color. In English. 106 minutes. Philips video.

1990 Schwetzingen Festival
Helen Field sings the role of the Governess with Richard Greager as Quint in this production by Michael Hampe at the Schwetzingen Festival in Germany. The children are sung by treble Samuel Linay and soprano Machiko Obata. Stuart Bedford conducts the Stuttgart Radio Symphony Orchestra. Claud Viler directed the video. EuroArts. Color. In English. 114 minutes. On video and Japanese laser.

1994 Scottish Opera
David Leveaux's production for Scottish Opera, originally staged in Glasgow's Tramway, was taped and telecast by BBC Scotland. Philip Salmon sings the role of Peter Quint with Anne William-King in the role of the Governess. Mike Newman directed the video. Color. In English. 110 minutes.

U

UCLA FILM AND TELEVISION ARCHIVE

The UCLA Film and Television Archive in Los Angeles has one of the largest collections of film and television material in the United States. It has excellent research facilities and its holdings include not only opera films but many television programs with operatic content. Its comprehensive Hallmark collection is especially notable. It presents an annual preservation festival which often includes films of operatic interest.

UKRAINIAN OPERA

Ukrainian national opera began to take shape in the 19th century with Semyon Gulak-Artemovsky's comic opera *Cossacks beyond the Danube*. It developed while the country was still part of the Russian Empire and the Soviet Union. The composer Mykola Lysenko is credited with creating the model for Ukrainian grand opera with his *Taras Bulba* in 1891. There are several Ukrainian opera singers of note and even a film about the great Madama Butterfly Salomea Krusceniski. Ukrainian composer Oles Semenovich Chishko wrote an opera inspired by Eisenstein's famous Potemkin film. See BORIS GODUNOV (1953 film), IGOR GROIN, SERGEI EISENSTEIN, MAY NIGHT (1953), NINA KOSHETZ, SALOMEA KRUSCENISKI.

1944 Cossacks on the Danube
This is a Soviet compilation of excerpts from Gulak-Artemovsky's comic opera. The story concerns Ukrainians forced to take refuge in Turkey by Catherine the Great and the efforts of the refugees to return home at a later time. Artkino. In Russian. 30 minutes.

1953 Stars of the Ukraine
Stars of the Ukraine is a two-part Soviet film in MagiColor promoting the glories of Ukrainian composers and singers. Part One is a 52-minute version of the opera *May Night* based on a story by Ukrainian writer Nicolai Gogol. Part Two is the 74-minute *Ukrainian Concert Hall* featuring singers and dancers at the Shevchenko State Opera House. Ukrainian basso Boris Gmirya (or Borys Hmyrya in Ukrainian) is the star of the concert and his aria from *Boris Godunov* is a highlight. Mikhail Romensky, Lydia Rudenko and Dimitri Gnatok appear in scenes from Lyksenko's opera *Taras Bulba*. Ivan Patorchinsky and Maria Litvinenko perform in Gulak-Artemovsky's opera *Cossacks Beyond the Danube*. Boris Barnett directed the film which features the Dumka State Academy Choir and Shevchenko State Opera Orchestra, Chorus and Ballet. Color. In Russian and Ukrainian with English subtitles. 126 minutes.

ULLMANN, VIKTOR
Austro-Czech composer (1898-1944)

Jewish composer Viktor Ullmann, who died at Auschwitz, is remembered today primarily because of an opera he created in 1943 in the Terezin (Theresienstadt) concentration camp with librettist Peter Kien. They wrote *Der Kaiser von Atlantis* (The Emperor of Atlantis) on the back of SS deportation forms and were able to hold rehearsals of it but were sent to Auschwitz before they could stage it. The opera survived the war and premiered in Amsterdam in 1975. Ullmann composed earlier operas but none with the intensity of his last. See DER KAISER VON ATLANTIS.

UNDER THE ARBOR
1992 opera by Greenleaf

The modern American opera *Under the Arbor* tells the story of a romance between two teenage cousins in a town on the Chattahoochee River in Alabama in 1943. It was composed by Robert B. Greenleaf to a libretto by Marian Carcache. The music is traditional in style and somewhat akin to Copland's *The Tender Land*. It premiered in October 1992 at the Birmingham Civic Center Concert Hall in Birmingham, Alabama. Greenleaf teaches music at Auburn University.

1994 Opera Alabama
Sunny Joy Langton and Mark Calkins star as the young lovers Hallie and Robert in this production produced by Bob Cooley and directed by David Gately. Tichina Vaughn sings the role of Mattie, Claudia Cummings is Miss Nell, Carmen Balthrop

is Annie, Bruce Hall is Papa Brown, Vanessa Ayers is Duck and Ruby Hinds is Madame Queen. Charles Caldwell designed the sets and Paul Polivnick conducts the Alabama Symphony Orchestra. Bruce Kuerten directed the video and PBS telecast. Color. In English. 112 minutes. Kultur video.

UNDINE
1845 opera by Lortzing

Albert Lortzing's most popular opera, based on a story by Fouqué, is a fairy tale about the water nymph Undine. She falls in love with the knight Hugo and goes to his court to be with him. When he is unfaithful to her, she returns to the sea but they are reunited in the end. The same tale provided the basis for an opera by E.T.A. Hoffmann. The story was popular in the silent cinema era but there are no videos of the opera, only a CD. See also ALBERT LORTZING.

1912 Florence LaBadie film
Florence LaBadie stars as Undine in this American film of the story made for the Thanhauser studio. It follows the plot of the Lortzing opera quite closely. Theodore Marston directed. Black and white. About 30 minutes.

1916 Ida Schnall film
Ida Schnall, a champion swimmer, was chosen to star as Undine in this movie of the story because of her swimming ability as well as her beauty. It was filmed on location in the Santa Catalina area. Henry Otto directed for Bluebird. Black and white. About 65 minutes.

1919 Delog film
The German Delog company produced a film of the opera which required live singers and orchestra. The company sent the film (this was one of four they made) on tour with soloists, chorus and orchestra. Presumably it saved money on sets and was popular as a novelty in smaller cities. About 70 minutes.

UP IN CENTRAL PARK
1945 operetta by Romberg

Sigmund Romberg's vintage New York operetta *Up in Central Park* was a kind of comeback for the composer and his old-fashioned style of operetta.

Dorothy Fields' book and lyrics brought the Courier and Ives Manhattan of the 1870s back to life in a story about Boss Tweed and Tammany Hall graft. The song "Close as the Pages in a Book" was a hit. See also SIGMUND ROMBERG.

1948 Deanna Durbin film
Deanna Durbin plays Rosie Moore, the daughter of a Tweed crony, in this movie of the Romberg operetta. She falls in love with crusading New York Times reporter Dick Haymes and sings the best songs from the show as well as "Ave pace, mio dio" from *La Forza Del Destino*. Vincent Price portrays Boss Tweed. Karl Tunberg wrote the script and William Seiter directed. Universal-International. Black and white. 88 minutes.

UPPMAN, THEODOR
American baritone (1920-)

American Theodor Uppman created the role of Billy Budd in Benjamin Britten's opera at Covent Garden in 1951 and was also featured in premieres of operas by Floyd, Villa-Lobos and Pasatieri. He began his career in 1947 in his native California singing Pelléas with Maggie Teyte as Mélisande at San Francisco. He repeated the role at the Met and became internationally popular as his light baritone was much admired in its time. He was also a notable Papageno. See BILLY BUDD (1952), LA PÉRICHOLE (1958).

USANDIZAGA, JOSÉ MARIA
Basque composer (1887-1915)

José Maria Usandizaga was one of the best-known Basque composers and his zarzuela *Las Golondrinas* (The Swallows) remains popular in Spain. Usandizaga, who was born in San Sebastian, studied in Paris before returning to his Basque homeland to write an opera in the Basque language. *Mendi Mendiyan* (High in the Mountains) premiered in Bilbao in 1910 and was soon produced in other cities. *Las Golondrinas* won him national fame after its production in Madrid in 1914 but he died of TB in 1915 before completing any more operas. See LAS GOLONDRINAS.

V

VAGABOND KING, THE
1925 operetta by Friml

Rudolph Friml's last major stage operetta was based on Justin McCarthy's play *If I Were King*, a romantic tale about the French poet and rogue François Villon. The libretto by Brian Hooker and W. H. Post concentrates on his romance with his free-living companion Huguette and then with Lady Katherine. The stage production starred Dennis King, a fine singer and a trained Shakespearean actor. The score is one of Friml's best, and includes such memorable songs as "Only a Rose" and the "Huguette Waltz." See also RUDOLPH FRIML.

1930 Dennis King film
The first film of the Friml operetta stars Dennis King as François Villon in a repeat of the role he originated on stage. Jeanette MacDonald, at the beginning of her film career, plays his lady love Katherine. The film was made in early Technicolor and had excellent reviews but is considered a lost film. No prints are known to exist. Ludwig Berger directed for Paramount. Color. 120 minutes.

1956 Oreste Kirkop film
Maltese tenor Oreste Kirkop stars as François Villon with Kathryn Grayson as his Lady Katherine in this somewhat dull movie. Oreste was promoted by Paramount as a new Mario Lanza but this was his only movie. He sings well enough but his screen personality is not enough to carry a film. The cast also includes Rita Moreno, Walter Hampden and Cedric Hardwick. Robert Burks was the cinematographer for this VistaVision spectacular. Michael Curtis directed for Paramount Color. 88 minutes.

VAMPYR, DER
1828 opera by Marschner

Heinrich Marschner's opera is based on the famous story by Byron's doctor John Polidori that began the 19th century vampire craze. It premiered in Leipzig in 1828 and has remained popular, possibly because the vampire theme is still in vogue. The opera focuses on the vampire Lord Ruthven who has to sacrifice three brides in one day or be sent to Hell. He succeeds with the first two but is foiled when he attempts to marry Davenant's daughter Malvina. The libretto is by Wilhelm Wolhbrück. See also HEINRICH MARSCHNER.

1993 The Vampyr, A Soap Opera
This modernized BBC film version of the opera is set in present-day London. The vampire Riley has awakened after a 200-year sleep and become a successful businessman but now has to kill three women in three days or perish. The killings are quite nasty but then so are the seductions and there is a good deal of nudity. The singing, set designs, costumes, filming and acting are top notch. Omar Ebrahim portrays the Vampyr, Richard Van Allan is Davenant, Fiona O'Neill is Miranda, Willemijn Van Gent is Ginny, Philip Salmon is Alex, Colenton Freeman is George and Sally-Ann Shepherdson is Emma. Robert Stephens is the narrator, Jim Grant is the designer and David Parris conducts the BBC Philharmonic Orchestra and Britten Singers. Charles Hart wrote the new libretto and lyrics, Janet Street-Porter produced and Nigel Finch directed. The film won the Prix Italia for Music. Color. In English. 115 minutes. CBS Fox video.

VAN DAM, JOSÉ
Belgium bass-baritone (1940-)

José Van Dam, a superb actor, has been featured in three opera films including two versions of *Don Giovanni*. He was born in Brussels, made his debut in Liege in 1960 and sang minor roles in Paris for five years. His career took off in the late 1960s when he sang Figaro and Leporello with the Deutsche Oper in Berlin. He performed at Covent Garden in 1973 and at the Metropolitan in 1975 but the Théâtre de la Monnaie in Brussels is his main focus. He was Leporello in Joseph Losey's great film of *Don Giovanni* and he played the Don in the stage opera in the film *Babel Opera*. His performance as a singing teacher in *The Music Master* gained him international admiration. See LA DAMNATION DE FAUST (1989), DON GIOVANNI (1978/1985 FILM), PELLÉAS ET MÉLISANDE (1987), THE TALES OF HOFFMANN (1993).

1990 Music Lessons with José Van Dam

Van Dam, who intends to be a voice teacher when he retires and played the role of one in the film *The Music Master*, was filmed in this two-part music lesson in 1990. Part One, "The Construction of a Voice," shot in Liège, shows the training required to prepare a voice for a performance. The second part, "The Construction of a Role," was shot in Lyon and shows Van Dam giving advice to professional singers on the interpretations of their roles. Jean-François Jung directed. Color. 114 minutes. On video.

1988 The Music Teacher

José Van Dam is superb at acting as well as singing in *Le Maître de Musique*, a Belgian film that became popular around the world. He portrays an opera singer in 1900 who retires from the stage but decided to pass on his knowledge to two pupils, a beautiful young girl (Anne Roussel) and a wild young pickpocket (Philippe Volter). His training of their voices and personalities is the core of the film. At the climax they compete for and win a competition arranged by an old rival. Van Dam also sings in the film including an aria from *Rigoletto* and a charming Giovanni-Zerlina duet with the girl. The students, whose singing voices are dubbed by Dinah Bryant and Jérôme Pruett, are heard in duets from Verdi and Bellini and arias by Mozart and Mahler. Gérard Corbiau directed the film with loving care. Color. In French. 98 minutes.

VANESSA

1958 opera by Barber

Samuel Barber's *Vanessa* has been called the finest opera written by an American and has won wide acceptance and a Pulitzer Prize. It premiered at the Metropolitan Opera on Jan. 15, 1958, with Eleanor Steber, Rosalind Elias and Nicolai Gedda in the leading roles. Gian-Carlo Menotti wrote the libretto which tells of a love triangle on a northern estate where the fortyish Vanessa has been waiting twenty years for the return of her lover. Anatol, the man who finally comes, turns out to be her lover's son and is a fortune hunter attracted to Vanessa's niece Erika. See also SAMUEL BARBER.

1978 Spoleto Festival, USA

Johanna Meier sings Vanessa, Henry Price portrays Anatol and Katherine Ciesinski is Erika in this production by Gian Carlo Menotti filmed at the Spoleto Festival USA in Charleston. Alice Garrott is the Old Baroness, Irwin Densen is the Doctor and William Bender portrays Nicholas. Sidney Palmer and David Griffiths are the producers and Christopher Keene conducts the Spoleto Festival Orchestra. Kirk Browning directed the video and telecast for the South Carolina Educational Television Network. It was presented in the *Great Performances* series on Jan. 31, 1979. Color. In English. 119 minutes. Videos at New York Public Library and at Library of Congress.

VAUGHAN WILLIAMS, RALPH

English composer (1872-1958)

Ralph Vaughan Williams, one of the pioneers of modern English opera, wrote six very British operas during his long career, all based around British authors and folk song. The best known are *Hugh the Drover* (1924) and *The Pilgrim's Progress* (1951) but the most interesting is the 1937 *Riders to the Sea*. It's a word-for-word setting of John Millington's Synge's great Irish tragedy. Vaughan Williams also wrote music for several films including *49th Parallel*, *Story of a Flemish Farm*, *Coast Command* and *The Elizabeth of England*. See RIDERS TO THE SEA.

1984 Ralph Vaughan Williams

British music film specialist Ken Russell created this fine tribute to Vaughan Williams. It tells the story of the "quiet" composer through his music with stories and anecdotes from his widow Ursula and colleagues. It begins in Cornwall with the composer's *The Sea*, goes to a village green for the *Pastoral Symphony*, travels to the Antarctic for the *Seventh Symphony* and winds up on Salisbury Plain for the *Ninth Symphony*. Russell made the film for the South Bank Show and it was telecast on April 8, 1984. LWT. Color. 55 minutes. On film and video.

VENICE

La Fenice Theater in Venice, originally constructed in 1792, is one of the most beautiful large opera houses in the world. It was devastated by a fire recently but is being rebuilt in exactly the same way. La Fenice has been the site of numerous major opera premieres including both *Rigoletto* and *La Traviata*. It can be experienced on a number of opera videos and can be seen as it looked in the 19th century in the Verdi film biographies and in Visconti's film *Senso*. There are fine tours of the city and the canals in videos about Monteverdi and Wagner, good views in Visconti's film *Death in*

Venice and even a video of a soprano recital in St. Mark's Square. And, of course, many operas are set in Venice including Britten's *Death in Venice* and Ponchielli's *La Gioconda.* See CECILIA BARTOLI (1992), I CAPULETI ED I MONTECCHI (1991), DEATH IN VENICE, DIVAS (1991), GIUSEPPE VERDI, CLAUDIO MONTEVERDI (1989), LA TRAVIATA (1992).

VERBENA DE LA PALOMA, LA
1894 zarzuela by Breton

Tomás Breton's *La Verbena de la Paloma* (The Festival of the Dove) is one of the most popular Spanish zarzuelas. It is set in a working class area of Madrid in 1893 where the inhabitants are preparing for a street fair held on the annual saint's day of the Virgin of the Dove. Julian loves Susana but she doesn't seem to be interested. When the old chemist Don Hilarion takes her out to a dance hall, Julian's jealousy causes a fight and the police are called. The role of Don Hilarion is a favorite for comic tenors. The popularity of the zarzuela has led to three notable films and there is even an homage by Pedro Almodovar. See also TOMÁS BRETON.

1921 Jose Buchs film
Jose Buchs wrote and directed this film of the zarzuela that became so popular it helped launch the zarzuela as a cinematic genre. Although made in the silent era, it was not silent. The composer himself arranged his music to accompany the film and conducted the orchestra when it premiered. The film stars Elisa Ruiz Romero as Susana, Julia Lozano, Florian Rey and Jose Montenegro. Juan Sola was the cinematographer. Black and white. In Spanish. About 67 minutes.

1935 Benito Perojo film
Miguel Ligero stars as the comic Don Hilarion in this sound film of the zarzuela, still considered one of the best in the genre. It was adapted for the screen and directed by music film specialist Benito Perojo. Raquel Rodrigo sings Susanna, Roberto Rey is Julian, Charito Leonis is Casta, Dolores Cortes is Aunt Antonia and Selica Perez Carpios is Señora Rita. Fred Mendel was the cinematographer. This film was released in the U.S. Black and white. In Spanish. 69 minutes.

1963 Jose Luis Sáenz de Heredia film
Conchita Velasco stars as Susana in this lavish version of *Verbena* produced by Benito Perojo but written and directed by Jose Luis Sáenz de Heredia.

Miguel Ligero is once again featured as Don Hilarion, a role he often performed on stage, and he steals the acting honors. The cast includes Irán Eory, Vicente Parr and Mercedes Vecino. Color. In Spanish. 75 minutes.

1980 Pedro Almodovar film
There is a kind of inverted homage to *La Verbena* in Pedro Almodovar's film *Pepe, Luci, Bom y otros Chicas del Montón.* Pepi's punk rock group friends dress up like characters from *Verbena* and sing songs from the zarzuela as they go after a policeman who has raped Pepi. Color. In Spanish. 85 minutes.

VERDI, GIUSEPPE
Italian composer (1813-1901)

Composer Giuseppe Verdi has become synonymous with the Italian opera which he dominated for half a century and happily most of his operas are available on film and video. There are also many film biographies, some quite informative. He wrote his first opera in 1836 and his last in 1893. He became successful with *Nabucco* in 1842 and then world famous with *Rigoletto, Il Trovatore, La Traviata, Un Ballo in Maschera, La Forza del Destino* and *Aida.* When he died, he was an Italian national hero. He still is. See AIDA, ATTILA, UN BALLO IN MASCHERA, CASA RICORDI, CASA VERDI, DON CARLO, ERNANI, FALSTAFF, LA FORZA DEL DESTINO, GIOVANNA D'ARCO, I LOMBARDI ALLA PRIMA CROCIATA, MACBETH, SHERRILL MILNES (1976), NABUCCO, OTELLO, RIGOLETTO, SIMON BOCCANEGRA, STIFFELIO, LA TRAVIATA, IL TROVATORE, VERDI REQUIEM, I VESPRI SICILIANI.

1898 Fregoli as Verdi
Leopoldo Fregoli, the first Italian filmmaker, was a quick-change variety illusionist who transformed himself into famous people. With the help of his film *Maestri di Musica,* he impersonated Giuseppe Verdi conducting an opera. Fregoli stood by the screen and sang and talked in synchronization with the movie. Black and white. About 6 minutes.

1901 Giuseppe Verdi's Funeral in Milan
One of the first Italian non-fiction films, *Funerali di Giuseppe Verdi a Milano,* was made by pioneer filmmaker Italo Pacchioni. It was shot during Verdi's funeral and screened in Italy in March 1901. Black and white. About 3 minutes.

1913 Giuseppe Verdi nella Vita e nella Gloria

Paolo Rosmino stars as Verdi in *Giuseppe Verdi in Life and Glory*, an early Italian film biography. It was written and directed by Count Giuseppe de Luguoro-Presicce for Milano Film. Black and white. About 30 minutes.

1931 Verdi

This "sketch with music" about the composer was made by James J. FitzPatrick, the famous travelogue creator, and features an excerpt from *Aida*. Black and white. In English. 10 minutes.

1938 Giuseppe Verdi

Fosco Giachetti portrays Verdi in this epic Italian film directed by Carmine Gallone. Germana Paolieri is first wife Margherita Barezzi, Gaby Morlay is second wife Giuseppe Strepponi and Maria Cebotari is Teresina Stolz, the soprano who was Verdi's love interest in later life. Beniamino Gigli plays tenor Raffaele Mirate, who created the role of the Duke in *Rigoletto* and is seen practicing "La donna è mobile" with Verdi in a gondola before the premiere. Most of the people in Verdi's life and career appear in the film from family to Donizetti and Victor Hugo. The opera scenes were shot on stage at the Rome Royal Opera House and the film ends with the premiere of *Aida*. The singers include Tito Gobbi, Pia Tassinari, Gabriella Gatti and Apollo Granforte. Black and white. In Italian. 110 minutes. On video.

1948 Luoghi Verdiani

Italian filmmaker Luciano Emmer, who worked in non-fiction film from 1941 to 1950 before turning to features, was known for his fine studies of artists. His documentary *Luoghi Verdiani* (Verdi Places), also known as *Sulle Rome di Verdi*, is a splendid evocation of the composer through Roman locations used in his operas. Black and white. In Italian. 30 minutes.

1953 Verdi, King of Melody

Pierre Cressoy plays Verdi in this Italian film biography with an all-star cast. Mario Del Monaco is tenor Francesco Tamagno who created the role of Otello and Tito Gobbi is baritone Giorgio Ronconi who created the role of Nabucco. They are featured with singers Orietta Moscucci and Vito de Taranto in scenes from *Aida, Ernani, Falstaff, Nabucco, Otello, Rigoletto, La Traviata* and *Il Trovatore*. Gaby André portrays Giuseppina Strepponi, Emilio Cigoli is Donizetti and Loris Gizzi is Rossini. Raffaello

Matarazzo directed. The Italian title is *Giuseppe Verdi*. Color. In Italian. 117 minutes. VIEW video.

1956-1963 Firestone Verdi Festival

Highlights from Verdi operas were often featured on the *Voice of Firestone* television series. *La Traviata* (1956), *Aida* (1962), *Rigoletto* (1963) and *Otello* (1963) were performed in costume by leading opera singers of the period. Details are given under the individual operas. Black and White. In Italian with English introductions. 60 minutes. VAI video.

1976 Novecento

1900, Bernardo Bertolucci's epic operatic movie is virtually a tribute to Verdi. The protagonists of the film are born on the day in 1901 when the composer dies. The film surveys 20th century Italian history across families in Verdi's Emilia-Romagna region. There is Verdi music on the soundtrack and a hunchback clown named Rigoletto. Robert De Niro and Gérard Depardieu star. Color. In Italian. 320 minutes. On video.

1982 The Life of Verdi

Ronald Pickup stars as Verdi in this nine-hour docu-drama about the composer made by European television companies. This is a comprehensive biography from birth to death with documentary-like narration and reconstructed episodes of his life. It is narrated in English with Carla Fracci as Giuseppina Strepponi. Most of the film was shot at actual locations and there is a real feeling of place, notably in the re-creations of 19th century Milan and Venice. There are also many scenes from operas staged in period style. Mara Zampieri sings the roles introduced by Teresina Stolz but most of the excerpts are based on Fonit-Cetra recordings. Renato Castellani wrote and directed the film with Roman Vlad as musical director. The version shown on PBS and Bravo and now on video is in English. The Italian version is called *Verdi*. Color. 540 minutes. Kultur video.

1987 Little Dorritt

Christine Edzard's six-hour film of Charles Dickens' novel uses music from Verdi operas as its entire soundtrack. The music was arranged and conducted by Michael Sanvoisin with soloists Pat Halling, F. Gabarro and Jack Brynmer. Color. 357 minutes. Cannon video.

1989 Opera Favorites By Verdi

This is a compilation featuring scenes from six Verdi opera videos. Seen at Verona are *Aida* with Maria Chiara, *Nabucco* with Ghena Dimitrova, *I Lombardi* with José Carreras and *Otello* with Vladimir Atlantov. Seen at La Scala is *Ernani* with Mirella Freni. Seen at Covent Garden is *Falstaff* with Renato Bruson. Color. In Italian with English subtitles. 54 minutes. HBO video.

VERDI REQUIEM
1874 Mass by Verdi

Verdi's *Messa da Requiem*, written to honor the poet-patriot Alessandro Manzoni, is considered by some critics to be Verdi's best opera and is usually performed by opera singers. It has also been criticized by church officials for being too "theatrical." It premiered at Milan's San Marco Church on May 22, 1874, and was reprised three days later at La Scala Opera House where it received the applause not allowed in church. The videos of the *Requiem* all feature major opera singers.

1967 Teatro alla Scala

French filmmaker Henri-Georges Clouzot filmed this superb performance at La Scala without an audience. The featured singers are Leontyne Price, Luciano Pavarotti, Fiorenza Cossotto and Nicholai Ghiaurov with Herbert von Karajan conducting the La Scala Orchestra and Chorus. The singers are outstanding and the conducting first class but the most memorable aspect of this video is the direction of Clouzot. He demonstrates how a filmmaker of genius can make even a static Mass visually interesting and exciting. His choice of shots, cuts, camera movements and close-ups makes this a cinematic as well as a musical experience. Color. In Latin. 85 minutes. DG video and laser.

1982 Edinburgh Festival

Jessye Norman, José Carreras, Margaret Price and Ruggero Raimondi are the featured singers in this fine performance of the Mass filmed at the Usher Hall in Edinburgh. Claudio Abbado conducts the London Symphony Orchestra and the Edinburgh Festival Choir with real feeling. The performance is preceded by an introduction to the work by John Drummond. Color. In Latin. 112 minutes. HBO video and laser.

1982 Karajan at Salzburg

Anna Tomowa-Sintow, Agnes Baltsa, José Carreras and José Van Dam are the featured soloists in this film of the Verdi Requiem at the Salzburg Festival. Herbert von Karajan leads the Vienna State Opera Choir, Sofia National Opera Choir and the Vienna Philharmonic Orchestra. Color. Sony laserdisc. 111 minutes.

1991 Requiem in Moscow

Sharon Sweet, Luciano Pavarotti, Dolora Zajic and Paul Plishka are the featured singers at this performance of the Verdi *Requiem* in Moscow. Lorin Maazel leads the orchestra and chorus. Color. 96 minutes. Multigram (Italy) laserdisc.

VERNON, JOHN
British TV opera director

John Vernon directed a number of operas for television in England and Austria in the early 1980s and some of them are available on video including major productions from Glyndebourne, Covent Garden and Vienna. See ARABELLA (1984), ARIADNE AUF NAXOS (1978), LA CENERENTOLA (1983), LA FANCIULLA DEL WEST (1983), PETER GRIMES (1981), SAMSON ET DELILAH (1981).

VERONA
Italian open-air opera theater (1913-)

The Arena di Verona is the home of truly grand spectacle where even elephants on stage look natural and videos provide the best seats in the house. The Arena, an ancient Roman amphitheater seating 20,000 people with room for 3,000 on stage, began to present opera on a regular basis in 1913. It specializes in grand operas like *Aida* and *Nabucco* but also presents more intimate works like *Madama Butterfly*. It can be seen as it looked in the 1930s in the Giacomo Lauri-Volpi film *La Canzone del Sole* which features a production of *Les Huguenots*. It has also been the site of some grand gala recitals. See AIDA (1981), ATTILA (1985), PLACIDO DOMINGO (1994), GIACOMO LAURI-VOLPI (1933), MADAMA BUTTERFLY (1983), WOLFGANG A. MOZART (1991), NABUCCO (1981), OTELLO (1982), TOSCA (1984), IL TROVATORE (1985), TURANDOT (1983).

1988 La Grande Notte a Verona

Great Night at Verona is a spectacular concert celebrating the 75th anniversary of the Festival of the Verona Arena. It includes twenty-three singers with favorite arias from twenty operas. The singers are Leo Nucci (who opens the concert with "Largo al factotum"), Ghena Dimitrova, Peter Dvorsky, Sona Ghazarian, Giacomo Aragall, Ruggero Raimondi, Elena Obraztsova, Ferrucio Furlanetto, Natalie Troitskaya, Luca Canonici, Montserrat Caballé, Placido Domingo, Samuel Ramey, Aprile Millo, Vincenzo La Scola, Mara Zampieri, René Kollo ("In fernem land"), Silvano Carroli, Eva Marton, Juan Pons, Antonio Ordonez, Ileana Cotrubas and José Carreras. Carreras helped organize the concert as a benefit and closes the concert with "Granada." Jose Collado and Carlo Franci conduct the Madrid Symphony Orchestra. Karlheinz Hundorf directed the video. Color. 122 minutes. Kultur video.

1990 Gigli Memorial Tenor Concert
Carlo Bergonzi opens and closes *Concerto di Tenori*, a Gigli memorial concert with fourteen tenors at the Verona Arena. He begins the evening singing "Una furtiva lacrima" and closes it with "O paradiso" from *L'Africaine*. The other tenors are Piero Ballo, Franco Bonisilli, Alberto Cupido, Peter Dvorsky, Salvatore Fisichelli, Emil Ivanov, Mario Malagnini, Gianfranco Pastine, Vincenzo Scuderi, José Sempere, Anatoly Solovianenko, Giorgio Tieppo and Nunzio Todisco. Anton Guadagno conducts the Verona Arena Orchestra. Color. In Italian. 173 minutes. Multigram (Italy)/Lyric (USA) video.

1994 Verona Arena 25th Anniversary
Placido Domingo celebrated twenty five years of appearances at the Verona Arena with a special program of stage opera scenes that was televised in Italy. Joining him in Act I of *Otello*, Act III of *Aida* and Act III of *La Bohème* are Daniela Dessi, Leo Lucci and Cecilia Gasdia. Nello Santi conducts the Verona Arena Orchestra. SACIS. Color. 90 minutes. On video.

VÉRONIQUE
1898 opéra comique by Messager

André Messager's light opera, set in 1840 Paris, revolves around an amorous case of mistaken identity. Its most memorable tunes are duets known as the Donkey and Swing songs. Wealthy Hélène de Solanges pretends to be shopgirl Véronique to get revenge on playboy Viscount Florestan whom she had expected to marry. She is angry because she has discovered that he is having a dalliance with a married woman. He falls in love with Véronique

and wants to give up his noble bride-to-be, not realizing they are the same, even though it means he will be sent to debtors' prison. It works out in the end. The libretto is by Albert Vanloo and Georges Duval. See also ANDRÉ MESSAGER.

1949 Marina Hotine film
Messager's charming light opera was made into a pleasant French film in 1949. It stars Marina Hotine as Véronique/Hélène, Jean Desailly as Florestan, Giselle Pascal as Estelle, Mila Parély as Agathe, Jean Marchat as the Baron and Pierre Bertin as Coquenard. The libretto was adapted by Claude-André Puget and Jean Ferry and the music by Louis Beydts. Robert Vernay directed. Black and white. In French. 100 minutes.

1979 Paris Opéra Comique
Daniele Chlostowa portrays Véronique/Hélène with François Le Roux as her Florestan in this colorful production by Jean Laurent Cochet at the Salle Favart/Opéra Comique in Paris. Michel Roux is Coquenard, Annick Dutertre is Agathe and Odette Laure is Ermerance. François de la Mothe designed the sets and Rosine Delamare the costumes. Pierre Dervau conducts the Theâtre National de l'Opéra Orchestra and Chorus while Yvon Gerault directed the telecast. Color. In French. 110 minutes. Lyric video.

VERRETT, SHIRLEY
American mezzo/soprano (1931-)

New Orleans-born Shirley Verrett, whose most famous role is probably Carmen, prepared for her career in Los Angeles and Juilliard. She made her debut in Yellow Springs, Ohio, in 1957 as Lucretia in Britten's *The Rape of Lucretia* and came to the New York City Opera in 1958 as Irina in Weill's *Lost in the Stars*. Unusual roles continued in Europe where she made her debut in Hamburg in Nabokov's *Rasputin's End*. She first sang *Carmen* in 1962 in Spoleto and then repeated the role at the Bolshoi, La Scala, the NYCO, the Met and Covent Garden. Afterwards she began to widen her range at the Met with soprano roles like Norma, Tosca and Aida. Verrett has a memorable voice and a strong stage presence as can be seen in her videos. See L'AFRICAINE (1988), LA BOHÈME (1990 film), CAVALLERIA RUSTICANA (1990), ENRICO CARUSO (1994), PLACIDO DOMINGO (1989), MACBETH (1987), LUCIANO PAVAROTTI (1991), SAMSON ET DALILA (1980/ 1981), TOSCA (1978).

1985 Shirley Verrett

Subtitled *A Film Biography of the Black Diva*, Herbert Chappell's excellent documentary shows the singer's life over the course of a year with many performance extracts. She is seen as Carmen at La Scala, Tosca in Verona, Dalila at the Royal Opera House and Iphigenia at the Paris Opera singing with Placido Domingo, Ruggero Raimondi, Jon Vickers and Piero Faggioni. She also performs blues and spirituals, talks about her upbringing in the South and explains her experiences as a singer. NVC Arts. Color. 60 minutes. Kultur video.

1992 Songs of Freedom

Shirley Verrett is joined by guitarist John Williams and the Boston Pops Orchestra in a concert in tribute to the civil rights movement. There are also appearances by folk singer Odetta and the Boys Choir of Harlem. The program was telecast on PBS in February 1992. Color. 60 minutes.

VESPRI SICILIANI, I

1855 opera by Verdi

The Sicilian Vespers was a famous 1282 uprising in which revolutionaries massacred French overlords in Palermo. *Les Vêpres Siciliennes* was also Verdi's first French grand opera although it is usually sung in Italian as *I Vespri Siciliani*. Sicilian patriot Arrigo is the son of hated French governor Guido di Monforte but is involved with rebel Giovanni da Procida and Duchess Elena. He is accused of betrayal when he saves his father from assassination but then persuades Monforte to pardon the conspirators. He is allowed to marry Elena but the rebels use the wedding to launch the massacre. See also GIUSEPPE VERDI.

1986 Teatro Communale, Bologna

Veriano Luchetti sings Arrigo with Susan Dunn as Duchess Elena in this excellent though somewhat abridged Bologna production by Luca Ronconi. Leo Nucci is French governor Guido di Monforte and Bonaldo Gialotti is revolutionary leader Giovanni da Procida. Pasquale Grossi designed the sets and costumes. Riccardo Chailly conducts the Bologna Theater Orchestra and Chorus. Ronconi also directed the video. Color. In Italian with English subtitles. 155 minutes. Home Vision video.

1990 Teatro alla Scala

Chris Merritt is Arrigo and Cheryl Studer is Duchess Elena in this impressive La Scala production designed and staged by Pierluigi Pizzi. Ferruccio Furlanetto is Procida with Giorgio Zancanaro as Monforte. The production includes the third act Ballet of the Four Seasons danced by Carla Fracci and Wayne Eagling. Riccardo Muti leads the Teatro alla Scala Orchestra and Chorus. Christopher Swann directed the video. Color. In Italian with English subtitles. 210 minutes. Home Vision video/ Japanese video.

VETTER AUS DINGSDA, DER

1912 operetta by Künneke

A stranger is invited into a Dutch country house by a romantic young woman named Julia who believes he is the cousin she has been waiting to marry. He isn't. Edward Künneke's Berlin operetta *Der Vetter aus Dingsda* is his most successful stage work and is still in the German repertory. It has been staged in London as *The Cousin from Nowhere* and in New York as *Caroline*. The libretto is by Herman Haller and "Rideamus." See also EDWARD KÜNNEKE.

1934 Lien Deyers film

Lien Deyers stars as Julia in this film of the operetta made in Berlin by Georg Zoch. The cast includes Lizzi Holzschuh, Walter von Lennep and Rudolf Platte. Black and white. In German. 74 minutes.

1953 Vera Molnar film

Vera Molnar stars as Julia in this version of the operetta directed by Karl Anton. The cast includes Gerhard Riedmann, Joachim Brenneck, Ina Halley and Grethe Weiser. Central-Europa production. Black and white. In German. 95 minutes.

VIAGGIO A REIMS, IL

1825 opera by Rossini

The Voyage to Rheims never actually takes place in this delightful comic opera by Gioachino Rossini. A group of aristocrats stop at the Golden Lily Hotel on their way to the coronation of Charles X in Paris but a lack of horses keeps them from traveling on. They while away the time with stories and songs and, although there is not much plot, there are ten starring roles. The opera was virtually unstaged for a hundred years but was successfully revived in Pesaro in 1984. See also GIOACHINO ROSSINI.

1988 Vienna State Opera

Montserrat Caballé stars as Madama Cortese in this Vienna State Opera production by Luca Ronconi. Ruggero Raimondi is Don Profondo, Lella Cuberli is Contesssa di Folleville, Cecilia Gasdia is Corinna and Enzo Dara is Barone di Trombonok. Claudio Abbado conducted the Vienna State Opera Orchestra and Chorus and Brian Large directed the video. ORF/Unitel. Color. In Italian. 165 minutes.

Related films

1988 Backstage at *Il Viaggio a Reims*

A visit backstage at the Vienna State Opera during the premiere of the Luca Ronconi production. Claudio Abbado and Montserrat Caballé are among those interviewed. Michael Fischer-Ledinice directed the documentary. Color. In German. 30 minutes.

1994 Clear and Present Danger

Music from *Il Viaggio a Reims* in featured on the on the soundtrack of this thriller about skullduggery in the CIA. It's performed by the Plovdiv Philharmonic Orchestra. Phillip Noyce directed the movie. Color. 101 minutes.

VICK, GRAHAM

English director (1953-)

Graham Vick is considered one of the more radical and provocative stage directors working today. He began with the Scottish Opera in 1984, joined the Birmingham Touring Opera in 1987 and soon became famous throughout Europe and American for his innovative productions. Unfortunately his most controversial productions are not on video. See EUGENE ONEGIN (1994), MITRIDATE (1991), WAR AND PEACE (1991).

VICKERS, JON

Canadian tenor (1926-)

Jon Vickers made his stage debut in Toronto in 1954 and began almost at once to sing in televised operas which are now on video. He made his first appearance at Covent Garden in 1957 in *Un Ballo in Maschera* and then played Don Carlos in a famous production of the Verdi opera by Luchino Visconti. He sang in Dallas with Maria Callas in *Medea* and reached the Metropolitan Opera in 1960 as Canio in *Pagliacci*, one of his great roles. Vickers sang at the Met for the twenty-five years and was one of its most popular performers. See CARMEN (1966), FIDELIO (1977), OTELLO (1974/1978), PAGLIACCI (1955/1968), PETER GRIMES (1981), SAMSON ET DALILA (1981).

1954-56 Jon Vickers Sings Verdi and Puccini

This highlights video features excerpts from three operas starring Jon Vickers presented on Canadian television in the early 1950s before he went to London. The operas are *Manon Lescaut* shown on Dec. 30 1956, *Tosca* shown on May 25, 1955 and *Il Trovatore* presented on Jan. 5, 1956. The music is performed by the Radio Canada Orchestra in Montreal. CBC. Black and white. 80 minutes. VAI video.

1984 Jon Vickers in Concert

Vickers returned to Canada for this concert taped at the National Arts Center in Ottowa. He performs scenes in costume from several operas including *Otello*, *Peter Grimes* and Handel's *Samson*. Patrick Watson introduces the selections and puts them in context. Franz-Paul Decker conducts the orchestra and John Gemmill produced the show. Paddy Samson directed the video telecast by CBC on Dec. 6, 1984. Color. In English. 60 minutes.

VIDÉOTHÈQUES IN FRANCE

The vidéothèques in Paris and other cities in France are the Gallic equivalents of the Museum of Television and Radio in New York and Los Angeles. They allow visitors to view videos privately or on large screens and have strong opera components. The Vidéothèque International d'Art Lyrique et de Music in Aix-en-Provence has many opera videos that are not commercially available, most notably those from the Aix-en-Provence Festival and the Marseilles Opera. There also videos from Opéra de Lyon and other major opera houses of the world. Like the MTR it has individual viewing booths. Admission is free. The Vidéothèque de Paris also has a large collection of opera videos but its videos are shown on large screens, often with discussions. It often has weekends devoted to opera videos.

VIE PARISIENNE, LA

1866 opera-bouffe by Offenbach

Jacques Offenbach's operetta *Parisian Life*, set in Paris in 1867, is a lively satirical farce on Second

Empire morals by librettists Henri Meilhac and Ludovic Halévy. Raoul and Bobinet love Metello who spurns them. They set up an elaborate plot to make money out of tourists coming to Paris for the 1867 World Exhibition. A Swedish baron and his beautiful wife are tricked into believing that Raoul's house is a hotel so he can attempt to seduce the Swedish Baron's wife. The glovemaker Gabriele and a Brazilian millionaire add to the spicy fun. See also JACQUES OFFENBACH.

1935 Robert Siodmak films
Robert Siodmak made English and French films of an updated version of the operetta in 1935. They both star Max Dearly as the Brazilian millionaire and Conchita Montenegro as his granddaughter. Maurice Jaubert arranged the Offenbach music and Armand Thirard was cinematographer. The English version is titled *Parisienne Life*. Black and white. In English or French. 95 minutes.

1977 Christian-Jaque film
Costume film specialist Christian-Jaque directed this French film of the operetta which follows the original fairly closely. Bernard Alane portrays Gardefeu, Georges Aminel is the rich Brazilian, Evelyn Buyle is the glovemaker Gabrielle, Danvy Saval is Pauline, Jean-Pierre Darras is the Baron and Martine Sarcey is the Baroness Michel Carré was the cinematographer. Color. In French. 100 minutes.

1991 Opéra de Lyon
Alain Francon's stylized production with the Lyons Opera is lively if not exactly comic. Hélène Delavault is Metello, Jacques Verzier is Bobinet, Jean-François Sivadier is Gardefeu, Isabelle Mazin is Gabriele, Claire Wauthion is the Baroness and Jean-Yves Chateleais is the Baron. Carlo Tommasi designed the sets and Jean-Yves Ossonce conducts the Lyons Opera Orchestra. Pierre Cavassailas directed the video at the CDN Theatre. Color. In French with English subtitles. 159 minutes. Home Vision video/ Pioneer laser.

VIENNA

Vienna has two principal opera houses, the world famous Vienna State Opera (Staatsoper) and the delightful Volksoper, plus other beautiful venues which can be experienced on video. The Vienna City Hall is also used for concerts that include opera singers. See THE ABDUCTION FROM THE SERAGLIO (1954), ANDREA CHÉNIER (1979), ARABELLA (1977), ARIADNE AUF NAXOS (1978), THE BARTERED BRIDE (1980), CARMEN (1978), DON GIOVANNI (1954), ELEKTRA (1989), FIDELIO (1978), FIERRABRAS (1988), DIE FLEDERMAUS (1970), LA GIOCONDA (1986), THE IMPRESARIO (1989), KHOVANSHCHINA (1989), LOHENGRIN (1990), CHRISTA LUDWIG (1992/1994), MANON (1983), THE MARRIAGE OF FIGARO (1954/ 1992), MOZART REQUIEM (1991), A QUIET PLACE (1986), DER ROSENKAVALIER (1994), SALOME (1974), TURANDOT (1983), IL VIAGGIO A REIMS (1988), WOZZECK (1987).

1991 Vienna New Year's Day Celebration
Carlos Kleiber conducts the Vienna Philharmonic's 150th anniversary celebration with the focus on Viennese operetta. José Carreras sings Lehár's "Dein is mein ganzes Herz" with Placido Domingo conducting and there is film of Richard Tauber singing "Vienna City of My Dreams." Color. In German. 60 minutes.

1992 Christmas in Vienna
José Carreras and Placido Domingo are the stars of this Christmas concert telecast from the Vienna City Hall. Vjekoslav Sutej conducts the Vienna Symphony Orchestra. Christopher Swan directed the video. Color. 87 minutes. Sony Classical video.

1993 Christmas Time in Vienna
Ruggero Raimondi, Placido Domingo and Dionne Warwick are the stars of this Christmas concert telecast from the Vienna City Hall. Vjekoslav Sutej conducts the Vienna Symphony Orchestra and Mozart Boys Choir. RAI. Color. 77 minutes. On video.

1994 Christmas Concert in Vienna
Placido Domingo, Charles Aznavour and Sissel Kyrkjeboe are the stars of this Christmas concert telecast from the Vienna City Hall. Vjekoslav Sutej conducts the Vienna Symphony Orchestra. RAI TV. Color. 90 minutes. On video.

VIKTORIA UND IHR HUSSAR
1930 operetta by Abraham

Victoria and Her Hussar is the most popular operetta by the Hungarian composer Paul Abraham. It premiered in Budapest and then became a hit in Vienna, Berlin, Montreal and London. The plot resembles a travelogue as it moves around the world from Siberia, St. Petersburg and Hungary to Japan. It tells the story of a Hungarian countess who believes her beloved Hussar husband died in World War I. She re-marries and then finds her first husband alive. See also PAUL ABRAHAM.

1931 Michael Bohnen film
Metropolitan Opera bass-baritone Michael Bohnen stars in this 1931 German film of the operetta. The cast includes Friedel Schuster, Ivan Petrovitch and Willi Stettner. Richard Oswald directed. Black and white. In German. 96 minutes

1954 Eva Bartok film
Eva Bartok stars as the woman who finds that her cavalry captain husband from before the war is still much in evidence. Her co-stars include Frank Felder and Rudolf Forster. Rudolf Schündler directed. Black and white. In German. 95 minutes.

1994 Sandro Massimini video
Italian operetta specialist Sandro Massimini describes the history of the operetta known in Italian as *Vittoria e il suo Ussaro*. After he has outlined the highlights of its plot, he and his colleagues present excerpts on his Trieste television show *Operette, che Passione!* The TV series devoted to operetta, directed by Pierluigi Pagano is available on video. Color. In Italian. 52 minutes. Ricordi (Italy) video.

VILLAGE ROMEO AND JULIET, A
1907 opera by Delius

Frederick Delius's opera is in English but it's based on a story by Gottfried Keller set in Switzerland and was premiered in German in Berlin. A boy and girl grow up as the children of quarreling neighbor farmers. When they fall in love, they are encouraged by the mysterious Dark Fiddler to elope. They end up fleeing in a boat on the river that sinks as its floats downstream. See also FREDERICK DELIUS.

1989 Petr Weigl Film
Czech filmmaker Petr Weigl wrote and directed this adaptation of the opera shot on location in Czechoslovakia with most of the actors miming to the voices of the singers. Thomas Hampson sings and acts the role of the Dark Fiddler, Helen Field sings the young woman Vreli acted by Dana Moravkova, Arthur Davies sings the young man Sali acted by Michal Dlouhy, Barry Mora sings Manz acted by Leopold Haverl, Stafford Dean sings

Meri acted by Pavel Mikulik, Samuel Linday sings Sali as a child acted by Jan Kalous and Pamela Mildenhall sings Vreli as a child acted by Katerina Svobodova. Jaroslav Kucera was the cinematographer. Charles Mackerras conducts the ORF Symphony Orchestra and Arnold Schonberg Choir. Mediascope, Munich. Color. In English. 113 minutes. London video.

VILLER, CLAUS
TV opera director

Claus Viller has directed a number of important operas for television in Austria, France and Germany that are available on video. They include major productions from the Salzburg and Schwetzingen festivals and notably Cecilia Bartoli's breakthrough appearance in *The Barber of Seville*. See THE BARBER OF SEVILLE (1988), LA CENERENTOLA (1989), ITALIANA IN ALGERI, L' (1987), LUISA MILLER (1988), IL MATRIMONIO SEGRETO (1986), IL RITORNO D'ULISSE IN PATRIA (1985).

VILLI, LE
1884 opera by Puccini

Le Villi was Giacomo Puccini's first opera and was successful enough to encourage the young composer to make opera his career. The "villi" of the title are the ghosts of abandoned women who return to haunt untrue lovers and dance them to death. Anna is engaged to Roberto but he leaves to collect an inheritance and never returns. She dies of grief and her ghost is called back by her vengeful father. Roberto believes she is alive but she and the other *villi* force him to dance until he dies of exhaustion. The libretto by Ferdinado Fontana is based on the same story as the ballet *Giselle*. *Le Villi* did not become a part of the repertory and is rarely staged. See also GIACOMO PUCCINI.

1986 Tokyo television
The only available video of this rarely produced Puccini opera is a Japanese production that was telecast in Tokyo in 1986. A Ms. Yamagi plays Anna and a Mr. Atsuma is Roberto. The video is an off-air copy of the Japanese telecast. Color. In Italian. 75 minutes. Opera Dubs video.

VINAY, RAMÓN
Chilean tenor/baritone (1912-1996)

Ramón Vinay began his opera career in Mexico in 1931 as a baritone and shifted to tenor roles in 1943. He came to New York as Don José in *Carmen* and sang at the Metropolitan from 1946 to 1961. He was especially popular for his portrayal of *Otello* and inaugurated seasons with it at La Scala in 1947 and at the Met in 1948. He also recorded the role with Toscanini. Vinay began to sing Wagner roles at Bayreuth in the 1950s and then in 1962 resumed singing baritone parts. See OTELLO (1948).

VINGT-HUIT JOURS DE CLAIRETTE, LES
1892 operetta by Roger

Henry Roger composed some thirty operettas but *Clairette's 28 Days* is by far his most popular work and it has been filmed several times. The "28 days" of the title is the military service requirement of the time. Clairette spends them disguised as a soldier through a series of mix-ups. She is trying to prevent her husband Vivarel from being seduced by his former mistress, Bérénice, who doesn't know he is now married. An English version titled *Trooper Clairette* was staged in London in 1892 and an American one called *The Little Trooper* was produced in New York in 1894. See also HENRY ROGER.

1935 Mireille film
French actress Mireille stars as Clairette in this *Les Ving-Huit Jours de Clairette*, a French film of the operetta directed by André Hugon. Jean Guise is her sexy rival Bérénice and the cast includes Armand Bernard as Michonnet, Berval as Vivarel and Robert Hasti as the Captain. Black and white. In French. 98 minutes.

Early films

1902 De 28 Dagen van Clairette
One of the earliest sound films was *De 28 Dagen van Clairette*. It was screened in the Netherlands in September 1902 at Alber's Electro Talking Bioscope, fresh from France where the operetta was a recent success.

1927 I 28 Giorni de Claretta
Italian director Eugenio Perego wrote and directed *I 28 Giorni de Claretta*, a full-length silent version of the operetta. Diva Leda Gys stars as Clairette opposite Silvio Orsini. Pittaluga Film produced. Black and white. About 75 minutes.

VISCONTI, LUCHINO
Italian opera/film director (1906-1976)

Luchino Visconti occupies a unique position as a major figure in both opera and cinema. His influence on opera production was enormous, especially in restoring quality staging and through working with Maria Callas. He never made a film of an opera but he did feature opera scenes and music in many of his films. His filmmaking style has even been called "operatic realism." The operatic connection began at birth, he claimed, as he was born in Milan as the curtain went up at La Scala. His cinema career began with *Tosca* in 1940 assisting Jean Renoir. He directed his first film *Ossessione* in 1942 and followed it with the visually operatic *La Terra Trema*. His *Bellissima* (1951) uses music from Verdi's *L'Elisir d'Amore* in a most creative manner. *Senso* (1954) begins in Venice's La Fenice opera house with a striking production of *Il Trovatore*. *The Leopard* (1963) has many operatic elements in its account of an aristocratic Sicilian family faced with political changes. *The Damned* (1969) combines opera and politics in a Wagnerian account of the fall of a German industrial family. *Death in Venice* (1971) makes an interesting contrast to the Britten opera, especially through its use of Mahler's music. *Ludwig* (1973) returns to Wagner in a colorful rendition of the life of the Bavarian King. *L'Innocente* (1976) features an aria by Gluck. See L'ELISIR D'AMORE (1951 film), LUDWIG II (1973), MADAMA BUTTERFLY (1971), ORFEO ED EURIDICE (1976), TOSCA (1940 film), IL TROVATORE (1963 film).

VISHNEVSKAYA, GALINA
Russian soprano (1926-)

Galina Vishnevskaya's autobiography is a portrait of an era as well as a strong-minded singer. Vishnevskaya lived through the horrors of the siege of Leningrad and the madness of Stalin as well as the politics of the Bolshoi Opera. She joined the Bolshoi in 1952 and became famous for her portrayals of Tatiana in *Eugene Onegin* and Leonore in *Fidelio*. She created the role of Katherine in Shebalin's *The Taming of the Shrew* in 1957 and

Natasha in Prokofiev's *War and Peace*. She sang at the Met in 1961 as Aida and Butterfly and at Covent Garden in 1962 as Aida. She left the USSR in 1974 in political exile with her husband, Mstislav Rostropovich, and moved to the U.S. She stars in one Soviet opera film, is a featured singer in others and is one of the sopranos highlighted in a documentary about *Tosca*. Her return visit to the USSR with her husband is also on film. Her 1984 autobiography, *Galina: A Russian Story*, became the basis of Marcel Landowski's 1996 opera *Galina*. See BORIS GODUNOV (1989), EUGENE ONEGIN (1958), KATERINA ISMAILOVA (1960), TOSCA (1983 film), WAR REQUIEM (1988).

1990 Soldiers of Music

Galina Vishnevskaya and cellist husband Mstislav Rostropovich return to Moscow after sixteen years of exile. The film follows them as they meet friends, visit places where they lived or worked and remember the old days. Vishnevskay passes by the Bolshoi Opera but refuses to enter the building as the film shows photos of her Bolshoi roles and features her singing. The film also features a concert at which Vishnevskaya sings an aria from *Madama Butterfly* and a Tchaikovsky song. The filmmakers are Susan Froemke, Peter Gelb, Albert Maysles and Bob Eisenhardt. Color. In English. 89 minutes. Sony video.

VITAPHONE OPERA FILMS
Early sound opera films (1926-1930)

The Vitaphone Corporation, the sound-on-disc system that Warner Brothers used to launch the sound era in the cinema, made a first step towards what was described as " movie grand opera" when it signed a contract with the Metropolitan Opera Company in June 1926. The contract gave them the exclusive right to engage Met artists for its films. At the same time the company leased Oscar Hammerstein's old Manhattan Opera House for the filming of its productions. *The New York Times* predicted a great future for the system commenting that "If the plans of the corporation work as expected, Main Street will no longer have to journey to Broadway to hear grand opera. The 'movie grand opera' will be brought to Main Street." The first three opera films were shown on Aug. 6, 1926, preceding the John Barrymore *Don Juan* and featured Giovanni Martinelli, Marion Talley and Anna Case. The Vitaphone films were usually one reel and ran from four to ten minutes. William Sharman, who has written the definitive

study of these films, lists sixty-four films of opera content made from 1926 to 1930. Most of them have survived. For the individual films see the singer entries on FRANCES ALDA, PASQUALE AMATO, JOHN BARCLAY, ANNA CASE, GIUSEPPE DE LUCA, ADAM DIDUR, BENIAMINO GIGLI, CHARLES HACKETT, HOPE HAMPTON, MARY LEWIS, GIOVANNI MARTINELLI, ELEANOR PAINTER, ROSA RAISA, GIACOMO RIMINI, ERNESTINE SCHUMANN-HEINK, MARION TALLEY, JOHN CHARLES THOMAS.

VIVALDI, ANTONIO
Italian composer (1678-1741)

Antonio Vivaldi is best known for his violin music and concertos but he also made a notable contribution to opera in his native Venice. His first opera was produced in 1713 and he composed 44 more, 16 of which survive. Vivaldi worked in the *opera serie* style of the period with gods and mythology as his subject. His operas are not strong on drama but are a delight to listen to. While there are many videos of his Four Seasons concertos, there is presently only one of an opera, *Orlando Furioso*. However, there are other Vivaldi operas on CD. See ORLANDO FURIOSO.

VIVES, AMADEO
Spanish composer (1871-1932)

Amadeo Vives, one of Spain's major zarzuela composers, also wrote operas and operettas that are still being staged. He often wrote in the Catalan language though most his works premiered in Madrid. His best known opera is *Maruxa* (1914) which is set in Galicia and sung in the language of the region. Vives wrote over a hundred works for the stage but his biggest successes were his zarzuelas. The delightful *Bohemios* is a Spanish interpretation of Paris Bohemian life while *Doña Francisquita* is an updated version of a Lope de Vega play. They have been filmed many times. There is also a Spanish film of his lesser known Valencian zarzuela *Entre Barracas*. His operetta *La Generala*, a Ruritanian satire set in England, is still popular. See BOHEMIOS, DOÑA FRANCISQUITA, MARUXA.

VLAD, ROMAN
Romanian-born Italian composer (1919 -)

Roman Vlad was born in Romania but has lived most of his life in Italy. He is a notable editor as well as composer and was responsible for the prestigious *Enciclopedia dello Spettacolo*. His best-known stage operas are based on works by writers including Chekhov for *Il Gabbiano* (The Seagull) and Strindberg for *Il Sogno* (Dream Play). He has also composed operas for radio and television.

1967 La Fantarca

Vlad's Italian television opera *La Fantarca*, a satire about the Cold War, was composed to a libretto by G. Berto. It was telecast by RAI in 1967. Color. 60 minutes.

VOGELHÄNDLER, DER
1891 operetta by Zeller

Carl Zeller's charming and tuneful operetta *The Bird Seller* is a story about rustic folk mixing with the nobility in 18th century Rhineland and, naturally, features a princess in disguise. It has two famous songs that have helped make the roles of Adam, the bird seller, and Christel, the post mistress, quite popular with singers. Its song about roses in the Tyrol has almost become a folk tune. Moritz West and Ludwig Held based their libretto on a French play. See also CARL ZELLER.

1935 Lil Dagover film

Lil Dagover stars as the princess in bucolic disguise in this film of *Der Vogelhändler* made in Germany in 1935. Wolf-Albach Retty portrays Adam the bird seller while Maria Andergast plays singing postmistress Christel. Georg Alexander is Stanislaus, who pretends to be the prince, and Hans Zesch-Ballot is the real thing. E. W. Emo directed. Black and white. In German. 80 minutes.

1940 Marte Harell film

The second film of the operetta was called *Rosen in Tirol* after its most famous song. It stars Marte Harell, Johannes Heesters, Hans Moser, Leo Slezak and Theo Lingen. Geza von Bolvary directed. Black and white. In German. 97 minutes.

1953 Ilse Werner film

Ilse Werner stars in the third film of the operetta and the first in color. Gerhard Riedmann portrays Adam the bird seller and the cast includes Eva Probst and Ernie Mangold. The dancers are Sybill Verden and Gert Reinhold. Operetta film specialist Arthur Maria Rabenhalt directed. Berolina Film. Color. In German. 92 minutes.

1963 Conny Froboess film

Conny Froboess, Peter Weck and Maria Sebaldt are featured in the fourth film of the operetta, rather more lavish and also shot in color. It was directed by Geza von Cziffra. Color. In German. 87 minutes.

VOICE OF FIRESTONE
NBC television opera series (1949-1963)

The *Voice of Firestone* was an NBC television series featuring the top opera singers of the time in performance, most of them stars of the Metropolitan Opera. The program began as a 1928 radio show and in 1949 moved to television where it continued through 1963 as a weekly Monday night show. Kinescopes of these programs are a treasure trove of performances by top singers. Forty-one selections from the kinescopes, owned by the New England Conservatory of Music, have been issued on VAI video. Most focus on one singer but there are also compilations devoted to sopranos, tenors, Verdi and French opera. Risë Stevens was the most popular artist on the program (47 appearances) followed by Eleanor Thebom. The videos, all in black-and-white, begin and end with theme tunes written by Idabelle Firestone. The Firestone orchestra is usually conducted by Howard Barlow. For full details see entries on LICIA ALBANESE, JUSSI BJÖRLING, NADINE CONNER, FRANCO CORELLI, LISA DELLA CASA, IGOR GORIN, JEROME HINES, DOROTHY KIRSTEN, GEORGE LONDON, JAMES MCCRACKEN, JEANETTE MACDONALD, LAURITZ MELCHIOR, ROBERT MERRILL, ANNA MOFFO, PATRICE MUNSEL, JAN PEERCE, ROBERT PETERS, BIDU SAYÃO, ELEANOR STEBER, RISË STEVENS, JOAN SUTHERLAND, FERRUCCIO TAGLIAVINI, RENATA TEBALDI, BLANCHE THEBOM, JOHN CHARLES THOMAS, HELEN TRAUBEL, RICHARD TUCKER, GIUSEPPE VERDI, LEONARD WARREN.

1950-63 The Great Sopranos

This is a compilation of highlights from Firestone videos devoted to famous sopranos. Seen and heard on this tape are Albanese, MacDonald, Moffo, Munsel, Nilsson, Peters, Price, Sayao, Steber, Sutherland, Tebaldi and Traubel. Black and white. 58 minutes. VAI video.

1950-63 The Great Tenors

This is a compilation of highlights from Firestone programs that featured famous tenors. Seen and heard on this tape are Jussi Bjoerling, Franco Corelli, Nicolai Gedda, James McCracken, Lauritz Melchior, Jan Peerce, Ferruccio Tagliavini, Jess

Thomas and Richard Tucker. Black and white. 58 minutes. VAI video.

1959-63 French Opera Gala
This video features highlights from French operas presented on the *Voice of Firestone* television shows: *Carmen* with Robert Merrill, *Faust* with Richard Tucker and *Roméo et Juliette* with Roberta Peters. For details see entries under the opera. Black and white. In French with English introductions. 65 minutes. VAI video.

VOICES OF LIGHT
1994 film opera by Einhorn

American composer Richard Einhorn's opera/oratorio *Voices of Light* was created to be shown in synchronization with Carl Dreyer's 1928 silent film *La Passion de Jeanne d'Arc*. It is scored for orchestra, chorus and four soloists with the voice of Joan sung by two singers. The libretto is derived from writings by Joan and other medieval mystics. Dreyer's film, among the greatest and most powerful films ever made, stars Falconetti as Joan with a screenplay based on transcripts of her trial. The opera premiered in Northampton, MA, in 1994 and was presented with the film in the Hollywood Bowl in Los Angeles in 1995.

VOIX HUMAINE, LA
1959 opera by Poulenc

Jean Cocteau's 1928 play *The Human Voice* enjoyed success on stage, radio and film before it became an opera. Francis Poulenc used the play as the libretto for his opera and composed it as a vehicle for soprano Denise Duval. It's a one-woman one-act one-set tour-de-force. A woman takes an overdose of pills and then calls her lover on the phone. She knows he is with another woman but she cajoles, lies, begs and pleads for his love. See also FRANCIS POULENC.

1979 Karan Armstrong video
Karan Armstrong stars as the desperate woman on the phone in this adaptation by Barbara Karp who produced and directed it for television. Dino Anagnost conducted the orchestra. The opera was telecast on Nov. 28, 1979, in the PBS *Great Performance* series following the Cocteau play starring Liv Ullmann. Color. In English. 50 minutes.

1990 Gwyneth Jones film
Gwyneth Jones portrays the woman with the telephone in this French television production of the opera by Alain Francon. Yannis Kokkos designed the set and costume and Serge Baudo conducted the Ensemble Orchestra de Paris. Hugo Santiago directed the film. Amaya distribution. Color. In French. 57 minutes. On video.

1992 Carole Farley film
Carole Farley stars as the desperate woman in search of love in this BBC Scotland television production by Mike Newman. She sings and acts superbly and always retains our sympathy. Iain McDonald designed the set and David Beeton the costumes. José Serebrier conducts the Scottish Chamber Orchestra. Color. In French with English subtitles. 42 minutes. London video and laser.

Related films

1947 Roberto Rossellini film
Italian actress Anna Magnani stars as the woman on the phone in *La Voce Umana*, a film of the Cocteau play directed by Roberto Rossellini. Magnani won Italy's Best Actress award for her performance. It is one half of the feature film *Amore*. Black and white. In Italian. 50 minutes.

1979 Liv Ullman video
Swedish actress Liv Ullman stars as the distraught woman in this production in English by José Quintero. It was staged in Australia as part of a one-woman tour, taped by Quintero in 1978 and telecast in 1979 in the PBS *Great Performances* series with the Poulenc opera. Color. In English. 50 minutes.

VON STADE, FREDERICA
American mezzo-soprano (1945-)

Frederica Von Stade, one of the most admired singers of her generation, has created a number of roles in modern operas. Born in New Jersey, she studied in New York and made her debut at the Met in 1970 as Third Boy in *The Magic Flute*. She gained a reputation in Europe with 1973 Paris and Glyndebourne appearances as Cherubino in *The Marriage of Figaro*, a performance that is on video. She is much liked for her trouser roles including Octavian, Sestus and the Composer but is also a splendid Cinderella. Among the roles she has created are Merteuil in Susa's *The Dangerous Liaisons*, Tina in Argento's *The Aspern Papers*, Maria in Villa-Lobos's *Yerma* and Nina in Pasatieri's *The Seagull*. Her videos demonstrate her great charm on stage. See THE ASPERN PAPERS (1988), CARNEGIE HALL (1991), CENDRILLON (1979), LA CENERENTOLA (1981), THE DANGEROUS LIAISONS (1994), ANTONÍN DVORÁK (1993), SIMON ESTES (1990), HANSEL AND GRETEL (1982), IDOMENEO (1982), THE MARRIAGE OF FIGARO (1973/1985), METROPOLITAN OPERA (1983/1991), ON THE TOWN (1992), DER ROSENKAVALIER (1992), GIOACHINO ROSSINI (1992).

1987 Christmas with Flicka
Frederica's childhood nickname was Flicka. This video shows her celebrating Christmas in the Alpine village of St. Wolfgang with help from conductor Julius Rudel, Melba Moore, Rex Smith, some children and the townspeople. She sings eighteen seasonal airs from "O Tannebaum," "Deck the Halls," and "Rise Up Shepherd and Follow" to music by Handel and Mozart. Color. 58 minutes. VIEW video.

1990 Flicka and Friends
Von Stade is joined by bass Samuel Ramey and tenor Jerry Hadley in a program that runs from Rossini to Kern. They also perform works by Donizetti, Gounod, Massenet, Meyerbeer and Mozart. Henry Lewis conducts the Orchestra of St. Lukes and the New York Concert Singers. Telecast April 18, 1990. Color. 150 minutes.

W

WAGNER, RICHARD
German composer (1813-1883)

Richard Wagner is one of the most important and controversial figures in music history. He influenced almost everyone but it is sometimes difficult to separate his music from his ideas and the admiration he inspired in people like Hitler. Wagner wrote his own librettos and composed operas that admirers claim are the ultimate opera experience and detractors say are overblown. He began creating operas in 1832 and his musical genius quickly became evident with *Der Fliegende Holländer, Tannhäuser* and *Lohengrin*. As his ideas about unified music drama developed, he turned to pre-Christian Teutonic myth and wrote the longest and most complex work in opera, the *Ring Cycle*, which consists of four operas with a cotinuous narrative: *Das Rheingold, Die Walküre, Siegfried* and *Götterdämmerung*. Wagner thought so highly of them that he built an opera house in Bayreuth to stage them. His last opera *Parsifal* was meant to be presented nowhere else. Wagner's life has inspired numerous film biographies since the early days of cinema and he also figures prominently in films about his patron King Ludwig II. Among those who have impersonated him on screen are Richard Burton, Trevor Howard and Alan Badel. His music is often used for atmospheric effect in non-operatic films including such classics as *L'Age d'Or, Dracula* and *Apocalypse Now*. See also BAYREUTH, DER FLIEGENDE HOLLÄNDER, GÖTTERDÄMMERUNG, LOHENGRIN, LUDWIG II, DIE MEISTERSINGER VON NÜRNBERG, PARSIFAL, DAS RHEINGOLD, DER RING DES NIBELUNGEN, SIEGFRIED, TANNHÄUSER, TRISTAN UND ISOLDE , DIE WALKÜRE.

1913 The Life of Richard Wagner
Italian composer Giuseppe Becce stars as Wagner in this feature-length German film about the composer produced by Oskar Messter. Becce, who scored the Wagner music performed with the film, the first specially composed for a German film, became a top film music composer and wrote influential books about music for silent films. Director Carl Froelich continued to work in German cinema until 1951. The movie reached New York in November 1913. German title: *Richard Wagner*. Black and white. About 60 minutes.

1925 Wagner
This is a one-reel movie about Wagner's life and career made for the *British Music Master* series. It features a number of scenes from the operas which were screened with Wagner's music played by a small orchestra. Black and white. About 10 minutes.

1956 Magic Fire
Alan Badel stars as Wagner in this Hollywood-style biography based on a novel by Bertita Harding. It was filmed on location in Germany and describes his life from the age of twenty-one until his death. Yvonne De Carlo plays his first wife Minna, Rita Gam is Cosima, Carlos Thompson is Franz Liszt and Valentina Cortese is his patroness Mathilde. The opera scenes were staged in Munich by Rudolf Hartmann with the Bavarian State Opera and the orchestra conducted by Alois Melichar. Eric Wolfgang Korngold, who appears in the film as conductor Hans Richter, arranged and conducted the rest of the music ("to protect Wagner," he claimed) condensing the music of the *Ring* to three minutes. Ernest Haller was the cinematographer and Harding, E.A. Dupont and David Chantler wrote the screenplay. Wilhelm Dieterle directed. Color. 94 minutes.

1960 Song Without End
Lyndon March portrays Wagner in this very romantic Hollywood biography of the composer Franz Liszt. Dirk Bogarde plays Liszt. Charles Vidor and George Cukor directed the film. Color. 141 minutes

1982 Wagner and Venice
Orson Welles narrates this documentary film about Wagner's visits to Venice from 1858 to 1883. It uses as text the composer's own letters and poems. Wagner wrote much of *Tristan und Isolde* in Venice. The film includes a sequence built around Siegfried's Funeral March with the orchestra on a boat on the Grand Canal. Petr Ruttner wrote and directed the film. Color. 43 minutes. Italtoons video.

1975 The Confessions of Winifred Wagner

Hans-Jürgen Syberberg's film about Winifred Wagner, the 78-year-old English-born widow of Wagner's son Siegfried, is fascinating in its exploration of the Wagner-Hitler connection. Hitler attended over 100 performances at Bayreuth which he helped finance when Winifred administered it from 1931 to 1945. Hitler considered *Parsifal* a mirror of his own philosophy and made annual visits to Wagner's house Wanhfried. The German title of the film is *Winifred Wagner und die Geschichte des Hauses Wahnfried 1914-1975*. Color. In German. 105 minutes.

1975 Lisztomania

Paul Nicholas portrays Wagner in this extravagant Ken Russell biopic. Veronica Quilligan is seen as Cosima and Roger Daltry plays Liszt. Color. 105 minutes.

1983 Wagner

Richard Burton stars as Wagner in Tony Palmer's epic nine-hour film written by playwright Charles Wood. It was shot on location in two hundred sites in six countries including Ludwig's castles and Wagner's residences. Vanessa Redgrave portrays Cosima, Gemma Craven is Minna, László Gálffi is Ludwig II and the cast includes Laurence Olivier, John Gielgud, Ralph Richardson, Cyril Cusack, Franco Nero, Marthe Keller, Ronald Pickup, William Walton, Joan Plowright and Arthur Lowe. Vittorio Storaro was the cinematographer and Sir Georg Solti conducted the music. Color. 300 minutes as a film, 540 minutes as a video. Kultur video.

1984 Richard Wagner, the Man & His Music

This is a brief biography of Wagner combined with a mini-guide to the *Ring Cycle*. It explains Wagner's development as an opera composer, shows his relationship with family, friends and King Ludwig and discusses the influences of his stay in Venice. Color. 58 minutes. On video.

1987 Richard and Cosima

Peter Patzak's Austrian film about Wagner and his wife Cosima treats their love story as a romantic drama which becomes a tragic myth. Otto Sander stars as Wagner with Tatja Seibt as Cosima. Anton Peschke was the cinematographer and Reinhard Baumgart wrote the screenplay. The soundtrack music by Wagner and Liszt is played by the SWF Symphony Orchestra conducted by Pierre Boulez

and Erich Leinsdorf. Color. In German. 108 minutes.

1988 Wagner Concert in Leipzig

This is a record of a concert of overtures and vocal music from Wagner operas held at the new Leipzig Gewandhous and conducted by Kurt Masur. Theo Adam sings excerpts from *Die Meistersinger* and Karan Armstrong sings the "Liebestod" from *Tristan und Isolde*. Color. In German. 90 minutes. Kultur video.

WALKÜRE, DIE
1870 opera by Wagner

The Valkyrie is the second opera in Richard Wagner's epic *Der Ring des Nibelungen* tetralogy. Siegmund and Sieglinde, mortals who are the children of Wotan, do not know they are brother and sister. They fall in love and run away with the sword Nothung. Her husband Hunding and Siegmund fight and the Valkyrie Brünnhilde sides with her siblings against her father Wotan. Wotan kills Siegmund by shattering the sword and punishes Brünnhilde by putting her to sleep in a circle of fire. The "Ride of the Valkyries" music is often used in non-operatic films. See also RICHARD WAGNER.

1980 Bayreuth Festival

Gwyneth Jones portrays Brünnhilde in Patrick Chereau's 1977 Bayreuth Festival Centenary production set in the 19th century. Pierre Boulez conducts. Peter Hofman is Siegmund, Jeanine Altmeyer is Sieglinde, Donald McIntyre is Wotan, Matti Salminen is Hunding and Hanna Schwarz is Fricka. Richard Peduzzi designed the sets and Jacques Schmidt the costumes. Brian Large directed the video. Color. In German with English subtitles. 216 minutes. Philips video and laserdisc.

1989 Bavarian State Opera

Hildegard Behrens portrays Brünnhilde in this modernist Bavarian State Opera production by Nikolas Lehnhoff with Wolfgang Sawallisch conducting. Robert Schunk is Siegmund, Julia Varady is Sieglinde, Robert Hale is Wotan, Kurt Moll is Hunding and Marjana Lipovsek is Fricka. Erich Wonder designed the symbolic high-tech sets and Shokichi Amano directed the video. Color. In German with English subtitles. 235 minutes. EMI video/Japanese laser.

1989 Leonie Rysanek in Act I

Leonie Rysanek stars as Sieglinde in this video of a Madrid concert performance of Act I. She is ably supported by Siegfried Jerusalem and Philip Kang with Arpád Joó conducting the orchestra. Color. In German. 71 minutes. Lyric video.

1990 Metropolitan Opera

Hildegarde Behrens sings Brünnhilde in this traditional Metropolitan Opera production by Otto Schenk with James Levine conducting. Gary Lakes is Siegmund, Jessye Norman is Sieglinde, James Morris is Wotan, Kurt Moll is Hunding and Christa Ludwig is Fricka. Gunther Schneider-Siemssen designed the naturalistic sets and Rolf Langenfass the costumes. Brian Large directed the video telecast on PBS. Color. In German with English subtitles. 244 minutes. DG video and laserdisc.

1991 Bayreuth Festival

Anne Evans portrays Brünnhilde in this modernist Bayreuth Festival production by Harry Kupfer with Daniel Barenboim conducting. Poul Elming is Siegmund, Nadine Secunde is Sieglinde, John Tomlinson is Wotan, Matthias Hölle is Hunding and Linda Finnie is Fricka. Hans Schavernoch designed the minimalist sets and Horant H. Hohlfeld directed the video. Color. In German with English subtitles. 153 minutes. Teldec video and laser.

Related films

1915 The Birth of a Nation

Pioneer director D. W. Griffith compiled a potpourri of 19th century classics as the score for his epic movie masterpiece. One piece of music that was featured prominently was "The Ride of the Valkyries" from *Die Walküre*. Videos of performances that use the original score will include the Wagner music. Black and white. 159 minutes. On video.

1936 The Big Broadcast of 1938

Metropolitan Opera star Kirsten Flagstad is featured singing Brünnhilde's battle cry "Ho-jo-to-ho!" with the Metropolitan Opera Orchestra under the baton of Wilfred Pelletier. Flagstad's scene was shot at the Eastern Service Studios at Astoria, Long Island. However, the most famous musical number in the film is not Wagner but the Oscar-winning pop song "Thanks for the Memory" performed by Bob Hope and Shirley Ross. Mitchell Leisen directed for Paramount. Black and white. 100 minutes. On video.

1970 The Clowns

Italian director Federico Fellini features "The Ride of the Valkyries" music in this brilliant semi-documentary about the world of clowns. Color. In Italian 93 minutes.

1974 Mahler

One of the most bizarre uses of "The Ride of the Valkyries" music in all cinema occurs in Ken Russell's weird biography of composer Gustav Mahler. Russell wrote new English lyrics to the melody which are sung by Mahler (Robert Powell) and Cosima Wagner (Antonia Ellis) in a symbolic Vahalla scene. The scene is meant to show the composer converting from Judaism to Christianity. Cosmia begins by singing that he is "No longer a Jew boy, now you're a Goy." It's so strange it has to be seen to be believed. The film itself is structured as a flashback with Mahler recalling the events of his life. Color. In English. 115 minutes.

1977 That Obscure Object of Desire

The *Die Walküre* duet by the twins Siegmund and Sieglinde is featured in the final moments of *Cet Oscur Objet du Désir*, a satirical film by Luis Buñuel about sexual obsession. Fernando Rey is an old man obsessed with a young woman named Conchita, portrayed by both Carol Bouquet and Angela Molina. At the end of the film a loudspeaker in a Madrid shopping mall gives news about terrorist activity and then plays the duet. As Siegmund explains that at last he knows what has captured his heart, Rey watches a woman sewing threads of fate in a window. A few seconds later a bomb blows up the shopping mall. The duet is sung on the loudspeaker by James King and Leonie Rysanek with Karl Böhm conducting. Color. In French. 100 minutes. Embassy video.

1979 Apocalypse Now

Director Francis Ford Coppola made memorable and effective use of music from *Die Walküre* in his film *Apocalypse Now*. Air Cavalry Colonel Robert Duvall leads a noisy helicopter charge on the Vietcong by blasting them with "The Ride of the Valkyries" as well as guns and rockets. The music is played by the Vienna Philharmonic led by Georg Solti. Color. 150 minutes. Paramount video.

WALLACE, VINCENT
Irish composer (1812-1865)

Vincent Wallace was one of the major British opera composers of the 19th century, internationally famous for his 1845 *Maritana*. He was one of the big three of Irish composers (he was born in Waterford) with Balfe and Benedict and like them was a one-opera wonder. *Maritana* was such an enormous hit that it influenced other composers, including Bizet on *Carmen*. Wallace was never able to repeat this success though he wrote five more operas. *Maritana* has been filmed three times. See MARITANA.

WALLY, LA
1892 opera by Catalani

Italian composer Alfredo Catalani is remembered primarily for his wonderful opera *La Wally*. It's a kind of mountain Romeo and Juliet story with superb music. The Wally of the title is a young woman in a small Tyrolean village in the early 19th century who has an ill-fated love affair with the son of a family enemy. The libretto by Puccini collaborator Luigi Illica has resemblances to *La Bohème* and *Tosca* but is based on a story by Wilhelmine von Hillern called "Die Geyer-Wally." The wider cinema public became aware of the glories of Catalani's opera in 1981 when the French film *Diva* used its famous aria "Ebben...ne andro lontana" as a central plot point. See also ALFREDO CATALANI.

1932 Guido Brignone film
Guido Brignone's Italian film is based on Illica's libretto for *La Wally* and uses Catalani's music as its score but retains only a couple of arias from the opera. Germana Paolieri stars as the doomed mountain girl Wally opposite Carlo Ninchias as her stalwart love. The soprano heard in the film is Giannina Arangi Lombardi. Brignone's filming of the Alpine scenes was much admired at the time. Black and white. In Italian. 85 minutes.

1990 Bregenz Festival
Italian soprano Mara Zampieri stars as the heroine Wally in this modernized Bregenz Festival production by Tim Albery. Norman Bailey plays her father Stromminger, Michael Sylvester is her lover Hagenbach, David Malis is Gellner, Liliana Niehiteanu is Afra, Ildiko Raimondi sings the trouser role of Walter and Klos Kovacs is Infanterist. Pinchas Steinberg leads the Vienna Symphony Orchestra, Vienna Volksoper Choir, Sofia Kammerchor and the Bregenz Festival Choir. Hugo Kach directed the video. Color. In Italian. 121 minutes. Lyric video.

Related films

1921 Henny Porten film
Silent cinema star Henny Porten portrays Wally in *Die Geier-wally*, a German film written and directed by E. A. Dupont. It's based on the source novel by Wilhelmine von Hillern. Black and white. In German. About 75 minutes.

1940 Heidemarie Hatheyer film
Heidemarie Hatheyer stars as Wally in this *Die Geierwally*, a German sound film directed by Hans Steinhoff and based on the source novel. Black and white. In German. 97 minutes.

1956 Barbara Rutting film
Barbara Rutting stars as Wally in this *Die Geierwally*, a modern German film based on the source novel and directed by Franz Cap. Black and white. In German. 90 minutes

1988 Samy Orgen film
Samy Orgen stars as Wally in this *Geierwally*, still a musical but filmed as a comic parody of a mountain love affair. Walter Bockmayer directed. Color. In German. 93 minutes.

1981 Diva
This stylish French thriller uses the *La Wally* soprano aria "Ebben...ne andro lontana" as a central plot point. African-American diva Wilhelmina Wiggins Fernandez refuses to make records so a fanatic admirer tapes her in concert. The tape gets mixed up with one containing evidence of a crime ring. The film made the aria, composer and singer well known in cinephile circles. Jean-Jacques Beineix directed from a crime novel by Delacorta and was reportedly inspired to make the film after seeing Jessye Norman in a recital in Bordeaux. Color. In French with English subtitles. 117 minutes. MGM/UA Video.

1986 Dangerously Close
The aria "Ebben...ne andro lontana" is heard three times on the soundtrack of this films about fascist-style students who like to bully those who don't fit

in with their ideas. John Stockewell and J. Eddie Peck are the stars and Albert Pyun directed. Color. 95 minutes.

1987 Someone to Watch Over Me
Wilhelmina Wiggins Fernandez once again sings "Ebben...ne andro lontana" but this time only on the soundtrack. She is supported by the London Symphony Orchestra conducted by Vladimir Cosma. Ridley Scott directed this stylish thriller about cop Tom Berenger who is assigned to protect murder witness Lorraine Bracco. Color. 106 minutes.

1995 Crimson Tide
Miriam Gauci sings "Ebben...ne andro lontana" with the BRT Philharmonic Orchestra on the soundtrack of this hi-tech thriller set on a nuclear submarine. Denzel Washington and Gene Hackman are the stars, Tony Scott directed. Color. 116 minutes.

WALSKA, GANNE
Polish soprano (1891-1984)

Ganne Walska was probably the prototype for the cinema's greatest operatic failure, Susan Alexander in Orson Welles' *Citizen Kane*. She wasn't very talented but she was hugely ambitious and she had a rich New York husband and a powerful friend, Chicago newspaper magnate Harold McCormick. He hired Met diva Frances Alda to develop what there was of her voice and arranged for her to star in Leoncavallo's opera *Zaza* with the Chicago Opera Company of which he was a major funder. Like Alexander, Walska had a disastrous experience and fled the city before the opening night. Welles is to said to have kept copious notes on the Walska story. Walska's real name was Leszcynska and she made her singing debut as Sonia in *The Merry Widow* in Kiev. In New York she appeared in Herve's operetta *Mlle. Nitouche* in 1915. She acted in one film and wrote an autobiography called *Always Room at the Top*. After a recital at Carnegie Hall in 1929, *New York Times* critic Olin Downes commented that she had "leaped for glory before it was sensible or prudent to do so." During a performance of the opera *Fedora* in Havana, she went so far off key that the audience pelted her with vegetables. Walska went through six husbands, mostly rich, during her long life and finally ended up in Montecito, California, as a very wealthy gardener. Her legacy

was a horticultural folly called Lotusland which is filled with hundreds of exotic plans and can still be visited today. See also CITIZEN KANE.

1916 Child of Destiny
Walska gets only second billing in this Columbia/Metro film directed by William Nigh but she does get to be listed as "Madama Ganna Walska." She portrays Constance, an unfaithful woman who has been divorced and is now the rival of the heroine Irene Fenwich. She is quite remorseful at the end of the film and commits suicide. Black and white. In English. About 70 minutes.

WALTER, BRUNO
German conductor (1876-1962)

Bruno Walter made his conducting debut with Lortzing's *Der Waffenschmied* in 1894 in Cologne. He is known as a champion of Mahler but he also is associated with Hans Pfitzner whose operas he often premiered. After the Nazis took over in Germany, he moved to Austria, then France and finally America. After the war he decided to remain in the U.S. but he made visits to Salzburg, Edinburgh, Vienna and other opera houses. There is no film of him conducting a complete opera but he can be seen conducting in three films. See CARNEGIE HALL (1947), CONDUCTORS (1995), SALZBURG (1931).

WALTON, WILLIAM
British composer (1902-1983)

Sir William Walton had an intense love of Italian opera but composed only two operas himself, *Troilus and Cressida* in 1954 and *The Bear* in 1965. Unfortunately neither has yet been filmed. Walton's principal connection with the screen is as a composer for the cinema, most notably for Laurence Olivier's Shakespeare films. *Troilus and Cressida* was composed after Walton wrote the score for *Hamlet* and there are said to be many influences from the film, most noticeably in similarities between Ophelia's and Cressida's music.

1935-1972 British films
Walton began composing for the cinema in 1935 with the Elizabeth Bergner film *Escape Me Never* directed by her husband Paul Czinner. This was followed in 1936 with Czinner's Shakespeare

adaptation *As You Like It* with Bergner and Laurence Olivier. In 1938 he wrote the score for Czinner's *A Stolen Life* and in 1941 for Gabriel Pascal's *Major Barbara* and Charles Frend's *The Foreman Went to France*. In 1942 he created the music for Thorold Dickinson's *Next of Kin*, Alberto Cavalcanti's *Went the Day Well?* and (most notably) for Leslie Howard's *First of the Few* with its famous Spitfire "Prelude and Fugue." In 1944 he began his collaboration with Laurence Olivier on the Shakespeare epics *Henry V, Hamlet* and *Richard III*. This partnership has been compared in closeness and greatness to that between Eisenstein and Prokofiev. Walton's last two screen scores were for Guy Hamilton's *Battle of Britain* in 1969 and Olivier's *Three Sisters* in 1972.

1987 At the Haunted End of the Day...A Profile of Sir William Walton
Tony Palmer's film biography traces the life and career of the composer from his early years with fascinating commentary by Walton and his wife. There are twenty musical excerpts including Yvonne Kenny featured in *Troilus and Cressida*, Shakespeare film scores, other movies and the Coronation Ode "Crown Imperial." Among those appearing in the film are Julian Bream, Ralph Kirschbum, Yehudi Menuhin, Sacheverell Sitwell and Laurence Olivier. The film won the Prix Italia. Color. 100 minutes. Kultur video.

WALZERTRAUM, EIN
1907 operetta by Straus

The *Waltz Dream* contains one of the most popular waltzes that Oscar Straus ever wrote, the dreamy and memorable "Leise, ganze leise." The operetta itself was his first international hit and played in most of the world capitols. It has a bittersweet romance at its center. A princess marries a lieutenant of the Hussars. On their wedding night he slips off to see his old love, Franzi, a Viennese woman who leads a female orchestra. Eventually he finds that he has to give up his former love and accept that his new wife is the right one for him. See also OSCAR STRAUS.

1925 Ludwig Berger film
Ludwig Berger, the master of the waltz film, made this light romantic version of the Straus operetta towards the end of the silent era. Mady Christians takes the role of the princess who doesn't know what to expect from her new Hussar husband

Willy Fritsch. The cast includes Xenia Desni, Lydia Potechina, Hermann Picha and Julius Falkenstein. It was shown in the U.S. as *The Waltz Dream*. Black and white. In German. About 83 minutes.

1931 Ernst Lubitsch film
This delightful American version of *Ein Walzertraum* is called *The Smiling Lieutenant* and was directed with great style by Ernst Lubitsch. Maurice Chevalier stars as the Viennese Guards lieutenant who has to give up his mistress Franzi (Claudette Colbert) for a princess (Miriam Hopkins). The film received an Oscar nomination as Best Picture. Lubitsch had wanted to make the operetta as a silent film in 1925 but couldn't get the rights then. Black and white. In English. 88 minutes.

1960 Kurt Wilhelm film
Kurt Wilhelm directed this lavish German TV film of the operetta. Heidi Bruehl stars as Princess Helene with her singing voice provided by Luise Cramer and Hans von Borsody is Lt. Niki with his singing by Fritz Wunderlich. The cast includes Hans Timmerdings, Balduin Baas, Ernst Stankovsky, Waltraud Haas and Cissy Kramer. The music was provided by the Cologne Radio-Television Orchestra and Choir. It was telecast on May 23, 1960 by NWRV in Cologne. Black and white. In German. 135 minutes.

Early films

1907 First Austrian fiction film
This was the first ever Austrian fiction film. It shows a scene from the operetta at its premiere at the Carl Theater in Vienna on March 2, 1907. Black and white. About 4 minutes.

1908 Fritz Werner film
Fritz Werner sings the famous "Piccolo Duet" in this German Deutsche Bioscop sound film of a scene from the operetta. It was screened with the music played on a phonograph. Black and white. In German. About 5 minutes. Print in German film archive.

WAR AND PEACE
1946 opera by Prokofiev

Sergei Prokoviev shaped Tolstoy's sprawling novel *Voyna i Mir* into an opera libretto in collaboration with his companion Mira Mendelson. It doesn't encompass the whole novel but it does have big chunks of it with thirteen peace and war scenes and most of the important characters in the book. It is by far the most ambitious of Prokofiev's operas and possibly his greatest achievement. It was composed in 1941-1942 but the final version was not presented until 1959.

1957 NBC Opera Theatre
This grandiose television production by Samuel Chotzinoff on NBC Opera Theatre was the American premiere of the opera. It features a cast of 90 singers and a 63-piece orchestra in three studios at a cost of $160,000. Helen Scott plays Natasha, Morley Meredith portrays Prince Andrei, Linda McNaughton is Sonya, David Lloyd is Pierre, Beatrice Krebs is Mariya, Leon Lishner is Napoleon and Kenneth Smith is Kutuzov. Otis Riggs designed the sets, Peter Herman Adler conducted the orchestra and Joseph Machlis made the English translation. It was produced in the ten-scene version. Kirk Browning directed the telecast on Jan, 13, 1957. Color. In English. 150 minutes. Video at MTR.

1990 Seattle Opera
This spectacular Seattle Opera production by Francesca Zambello cost two million dollars with great input from designer John Conklin, costumer Bruno Schwengel and lighting director Neil Peter Jampolis. Sheri Greenawald sings Natasha, Vladimir Chernov is Andrei, Nicolai Ohotnikov is Kutusov, Peter Kazaras is Pierre, Alexander Morozov is Dolokhov and Julian Patrick is Napoleon. Mark Ermler of the Bolshoi Opera conducts the Seattle Opera Orchestra. It was taped on HDTV (High Definition TV) and has been presented in some theaters. Color. In Russian. 260 minutes. On video.

1993 Kirov Opera
Elena Prokina sings Natasha in this epic Kirov Opera production staged by England's Graham Vick. Alexander Gergalov is Prince Andrei, Nikolai Ohotnikov is Marshal Kutusov, Gegam Gregoriam is Pierre, Olga Borodina is Hélène, Yury Marusin is Anatol, Irina Bogacheva is Maria and Mikhail Kit is General Denisov. Timothy O'Brien designed the sets, Valentina Komolova created the costumes and Valery Gergiev conducted the Kirov Opera Orchestra and Chorus. Humphrey Burton directed for TV and video.

Color. In Russian with English subtitles. 270 minutes. Philips Classic video & laserdisc.

WARNER BROS. CARTOONS
Animated opera films

The animation geniuses at the Warner Brother studios were a match for their colleagues at Disney in creating great and stylish cartoon with opera music. Among the best were Chuck Jones, Tex Avery and Friz Freleng. For other WB cartoons see CHUCK JONES.

1941 Notes to You
An alley cat sets up a sheet music stand on a backyard fence and begins Figaro's Factotum aria from *The Barber of Seville* to the annoyance of Porky Pig who is trying to sleep. After the cat is eventually shot, ghost cats return singing the Sextet from *Lucia di Lammermoor*. Michael Maltese wrote the story, Carl Stalling conducted the music and Friz Freleng directed. Color. About 7 minutes.

1948 Back Alley Oproar
In this brilliant remake of *Notes to You* Sylvester is the cat and Elmer Fudd is the one trying to sleep as the feline tries out his Figaro aria. After much music the film ends in dynamite and a heavenly Sextet from *Lucia di Lammermoor*. Friz Freleng again directed. Color. 7 minutes.

1952 The Magical Maestro
Tex Avery's classic cartoon features the Great Poochini in a story about a man trying to sing an aria from *The Barber of Seville*. A magician transforms the opera singer in and out of outlandish costumes as he tries to keep singing. Color. 7 minutes.

WARREN, LEONARD
American baritone (1911-1960)

The great American baritone Leonard Warren virtually lived and died at the Metropolitan Opera, He began his career by winning a Met competition in 1938 and made his debut there in 1939 in a small role in *Simon Boccanegra*. In 1940 he sang with the Met in the first U.S. opera telecast and in 1948 sang Iago in *Otello* in the first live telecast of an opera from the stage. He sang at the Met for 21 years and died on stage singing Don Carlo in *La Forza del Destino*. He can be seen in performance in videos of

Met telecasts, in a Hollywood film and in *Voice of Firestone* TV shows. See also SOL HUROK (1956), METROPOLITAN OPERA (1940/1948), OTELLO (1948).

1944 Irish Eyes Are Smiling

Leonard Warren and Blanche Thebom portray turn-of-the-century Metropolitan Opera singers in this musical about songwriter Ernest R. Ball. Dick Haymes plays Ball and Gregory Ratoff directed. 20th Century-Fox. Color. 90 minutes.

1949-53 Leonard Warren in Opera and Song

A compilation of performances by the great baritone on the *Voice of Firestone* television shows. Warren sings the "Toreador Song" from *Carmen* in the telecast of Nov. 7, 1949. On June 2, 1952, he sings "Eri tu" from *Un Ballo in Maschera* plus other songs. On Aug. 24, 1953, he is featured in arias from *Faust*, *The Bartered Bride* and Friml's *The Three Musketeers*. Howard Barlow conducts. Black and white. 45 minutes. VAI video.

1949 Leonard Warren in Opera and Song 2

Warren is joined by Met soprano Eleanor Steber on this video of highlights from *Voice of Firestone* telecasts in 1949. On Nov. 7 he sings "On the Road to Mandalay." On Dec. 5 it is the "Largo al factotum" from *The Barber of Seville* and Huhn's "Invictus." Steber sings "Vissi d'arte" from *Tosca* and "My Hero" from *The Chocolate Soldier* and they join in duet on "Will You Remember" from *Maytime*. Black and white. 27 minutes. VAI video.

WAR REQUIEM
1988 oratorio by Britten

Benjamin Britten's pacifist oratorio *A War Requiem*, inspired by the poems of Wilfred Owen, was composed for the re-opening of Coventry Cathedral in 1962. The cathedral had been destroyed in an air raid during World War II. The oratorio mixes Owens' poems with traditional Latin texts. The premiere at Coventry featured German, Russian and English soloists.

1988 Derek Jarman film

War Requiem is not an opera but it nearly becomes one in this brilliant film by Derek Jarman. Jarman films it as a story remembered by old soldier Laurence Olivier and uses Owen's experiences in World War I as the narrative framework for Britten's 1963 London Symphony Orchestra recording. The soloists are Russia's Galina

Vishvevskaya, England's Peter Pears and Germany's Dietrich Fischer-Dieskau. The on-screen actors are Nathaniel Parker as Wilfred Owen, Tilda Swinton as the Nurse, and Patricia Hayes as the Mother. The film was shot at Darenth Park Hospital by Richard Greatrex and produced by Don Boyd. Color. In English. 93 minutes. Mystic Fire video.

1992 Barrie Gavin film

This performance of the oratorio was held to commemorate the restoration of the war-bombed Lübeck Marienkirche in August 1992. It was filmed by Barrie Gavin who uses a damaged bell from the church as a connecting symbol. The soloists are soprano Luba Organasova, tenor Anthony Rolfe Johnsson and baritone Boje Skovkus. John Eliot Gardiner conducts the Tölz Boys Choir, the Monteverdi Choir and the North German Radio Chorus and Symphony Orchestra. Color. 87 minutes. DG video and laser.

WEBB'S SINGING PICTURES
Early opera sound films

George Webb was a Baltimore entrepreneur who attempted to present opera on the screen with synchronized sound. His first program in May 1914, using a primitive sound-on-film system, included an abridged *Pagliacci*. Later presentations with sound-on-disc systems were called Webb's Singing Pictures. On Jan. 14, 1917, Enrico Caruso turned up in person at the Cohen & Harris Theater in New York for the premiere of a film in which he was the featured singer. The on-screen actors performed scenes from *Pagliacci* and *Rigoletto* while the voice of Caruso was heard on loudspeakers singing the arias. The second item was a full scene of *Carmen* starring Metropolitan Opera baritone Giuseppe Campanari as Escamillo. He was shown singing the "Toreador Song" with Marie Conesa as Carmen, Salvatore Giordano and Léon Rothier. Webb repeated this program at Westminster Cathedral Hall in London in 1921. Rothier, a Metropolitan Opera bass who was famous for his portrayal of Mephistopheles, reportedly made a film of *Faust* for Webb.

WEBER, CARL MARIA VON
German composer (1786-1826)

Carl Maria von Weber's *Der Freischütz* was the most popular German opera in the first half of the

19th century as it seemed to embody the ideas of Germanic romanticism. The mysterious Wolf Glen scene was particularly liked. Weber, who played a key role in the development of German Romantic opera, composed other successful operas like *Oberon, Abu Hassan* and *Euranthe* but *Der Freischütz* remains by far his most performed opera. All these operas are on CD but only *Der Freischütz* is currently on video. See DER FREISCHÜTZ, OBERON.

1934 Der Weg Carl Maria von Weber's

German baritone Willi Domgraf-Fassbänder of the Berlin Staatsoper stars in *Carl Maria von Weber's Way*, a romantic German film about the composer. It's a love story set in Dresden that uses Weber's music as score. The cast includes Eliza Illiard, Margo Kochlin, Ernst Rotmund and Else Botticher. Rudolf van der Noss directed. The film is also known as *Aufforderung sum Tanz*. Black and white. In German. 73 minutes.

WEIGL, PETR
Czechoslovak filmmaker (1938-)

Petr Weigl, who was born in Brno and brought up in Prague, learned his filmcraft at the FAMU film school. He began making films in 1964 and has directed over forty-five, including many based on operas or opera subjects. He has also directed an opera on stage and won Emmys for his TV work. Weigl's filmed operas are impressive though they tend to be overly beautiful as he usually shoots in lovely outdoor Czech locations with actors whose singing voices are dubbed. In addition to the operas listed below, he shot *Maria Stuart* in 1988 and *Lady Macbeth of the Mtsensk District* in 1991. His stage operas include *La Traviata* at the National Theatre in Prague and *Salome* at the Deutsche Oper in Berlin, which is on video. See EUGENE ONEGIN (1988), RUSALKA (1978), A VILLAGE ROMEO AND JULIET (1989), SALOME (1990), THE TURN OF THE SCREW (1982), WERTHER (1985).

1983 The Love Of Destiny

Weigl created this opera film pastiche which uses well-known arias to tell its impressionistic story. An opera singer remembers the woman he once loved who is now dead. It's a stylist tour-de-force that creates its own drama. Czech tenor Peter Dvorsky stars as the man while Emilia Aasaryova portrays the woman. Dvorsky sings arias from *Cavalleria Rusticana, Tosca, Una Ballo in Maschera, La Favorita, Manon, Madama Butterfly* and *Lucia di*

Lammermoor. The film was superbly photographed by Jiri Kadanka and the music is performed by the Bratislava Symphony Orchestra led by Ondrej Lenard. Bratislava Television/ WDR/FRG. Color. In French and Italian. 60 minutes. Kultur video.

WEIKL, BERND
Austrian baritone (1942-)

Austrian Bernd Weikl, who made his debut in 1968, has a repertory of over a hundred roles in Italian as well as German opera but is best known for his performances in Wagner and Strauss. His performance as Hans Sachs in *Die Meistersinger* is much admired for its acting as well as his voice quality. He can be seen on video in several Wagner and Strauss operas. See ARABELLA (1977), EUGENE ONEGIN (1988), LOHENGRIN (1982), MEISTERSINGER VON NÜRNBERG, DIE (1982), PARSIFAL (1981/1993), SALOME (1974), TANNHÄUSER (1978/1982).

WEILL, KURT
German/American composer (1900-1950)

Kurt Weill straddles the worlds of opera and musical as he created popular operas and serious musicals. The early Berlin part of his career used to be considered serious and the part in New York less so but in this post-modern age it is harder to compartmentalize his musical genius. He is a major stage composer however his music is described and his 1946 *Street Scene* is now recognized as one of the great American operas. Weill became famous in Berlin in the late 1920s collaborating with Bertolt Brecht on *Rise and Fall of the City of Mahagonny* and *The Threepenny Opera*. After he left Nazi Germany he was highly successful on Broadway with musicals like *Knickerbocker Holiday, Lady in the Dark* and *One Touch of Venus*. Weill died at the age of 50 before his full potential could be realized and before the New York revival of *The Threepenny Opera* in 1954 revitalized his reputation. See also BERTOLT BRECHT, MARC BLITZSTEIN, DOWN IN THE VALLEY, HAPPY END, DER LINDBERGHFLUG, RISE AND FALL OF THE CITY OF MAHAGONNY, THE SEVEN DEADLY SINS, STREET SCENE, THE THREEPENNY OPERA.

1944 Lady in the Dark

This film of Weill's 1941 stage musical with lyrics by Ira Gershwin and book by Moss Hart eliminates most of Weill's music. Ginger Roger stars as the woman who undergoes psychoanalysis. Mitchell

Leisen directed so it does have style. Color. 100 minutes.

1944 Knickerbocker Holiday
Only three Weill songs survive in this poor film version of his 1938 musical though one is the famous "September Song." Maxwell Anderson wrote the book for this political satire set in old Dutch New York. Nelson Eddy and Charles Coburn star and Harry Brown directed. Black and white. 85 minutes.

1945 Where Do We Go From Here?
Weill wrote a l2-minute mini-operetta about Christopher Columbus to a libretto by Ira Gershwin for this film musical. Fred MacMurray has a genie who allows him to travel backwards in time to observe American history. Gregory Ratoff directed. Color. 77 minutes.

1948 One Touch of Venus
Ava Gardner stars as the statue that comes to life in this poor version of Weill's 1943 stage musical with book and lyrics by S.J. Perelman and Ogden Nash. It contains one of Weill's finest songs, "Speak Low." William A. Seiter directed. Black and white. 81 minutes.

1954 Lady in the Dark
Ann Sothern stars as Liza opposite James Daly in Max Liebman's 1954 television production of Weill's 1941 stage musical. Color. 84 minutes. Video at MTR.

1964 Lotte Lenya Sings Kurt Weill
Ken Russell and Humphrey Burton directed this British film tribute to Weill for the *Monitor* television series. Weill's widow Lotte Lenya, the original stage Jenny, performs a selection of songs and arias from the musicals and operas. It was telecast on Sept. l0, 1962. Black and white. 60 minutes.

1964 The Broadway Years of Kurt Weill
An American television salute to Kurt Weill by Lotte Lenya. She sings a selection from *One Touch of Venus, Lady in the Dark, Knickerbocker Holiday, Street Scene* and what she describes as a smash flop, the forgotten 1945 musical *The Firebrand of Florence.* The program was produced by Jack Landau and telecast live on WCBS on Oct. 28, 1964. Black and white. 30 minutes. Video at MTR.

1974 Lost in the Stars
Weill's last musical, staged in 1949, was based on Alan Paton's novel *Cry, The Beloved Country* with a book by Maxwell Anderson. It tells a tragic tale about racial prejudice in South Africa. This American Film Theatre production stars Brock Peters and Melba Moore. Daniel Mann directed. Color. 114 minutes.

1992 Ute Lemper Sings Kurt Weill
German cabaret singer Ute Lemper sings airs from Weill operas and musicals at Les Bouffes du Nord in Paris. There are selections from *The Three Penny Opera, Mahagonny, Happy End, Marie Galante, Lady in the Dark, Lost in the Stars* and *One Touch of Venus.* Jeff Cohen accompanies her on piano. Tony Stavacre directed. Color. 60 minutes. London video.

1994 Kurt Weill in America
Barries Gavin directed this television documentary about Weill's American years. It was made for Germany's Hessischer Rundfunk. Color. 60 minutes.

1994 September Songs
Subtitled *The Music of Kurt Weill,* this Canadian film tribute to Weill's life and music is set in a kind of turn-of-the-century warehouse. The featured performers include Teresa Stratas, Stan Ridgeway, Betty Carter, Elvis Costello, Charlie Haden and Lou Reed. There is also archival film of Lotte Lenya and Weill. Horst Zeidler was the cinematographer and Larry Weinstein directed. Rhombus Media/ ZDF. Color. 85 minutes. On video.

1995 Lotte Lenya, an Invented Life
Lenya: ein Erfundenes Leben is a German documentary film about Weill's wife Lotte Lenya which is mostly concerned with her relationship with the composer and his music. It was produced by Hessian Television and directed by Barrie Gavin. Color. In German. 60 minutes. On video.

WEIR, JUDITH
Scottish composer (1954-)

Judith Weir is one of the most successful modern composers in the UK. She writes her own librettos and seems to have little trouble in getting her work produced. Her thirteen-minute *King Harald's Saga* (1979), described as a "grand opera in three acts for solo soprano," is popular on CD, possibly because the soprano sings the role of the whole Norwegian Army as well as eight other parts. Weir's first full-length opera was the 1987 *A Night at the Chinese Opera*. She has also written operas for television. Her opera *Blond Eckbert* was telecast in England in 1995. See BLOND ECKBERT.

1988 Missa Del Cid
Weir takes a cool look at violence in operatic form. The libretto combines a deadpan reading of the heroic actions of the famous medieval Spanish knight El Cid set against a mass for an ensemble of voices. It was televised in England in 1988. Color. 30 minutes.

1991 Scipio's Dream
This is Weir's revamping of Mozart's 1771 *Il Sogno di Scipione* for the Mozart centennial. It was created for and televised by BBC television. Color. 40 minutes.

WEIR, PETER
Australian film director (1944-)

Peter Weir, known for Australian films like *Picnic at Hanging Rock* and *Gallipoli* and American films like *Witness* and *Dead Poet's Society*, occasionally uses opera and opera singers on his film soundtracks. In *Gallipoli* there is a notable use of the duet "Au fond du temple saint" from Bizet's *Les Pecheurs de Perles*. In *The Year of Living Dangerously*, New Zealand soprano Kiri Te Kanawa sings "September" from the *Four Last Songs* by Richard Strauss.

WELITSCH, LJUBA
Bulgarian soprano (1913-1996)

Bulgarian soprano Ljuba Welitsch made her debut at the Sofia Opera in 1936 and began to sing in Graz, Hamburg and Munich. She joined the Vienna State Opera in 1946 and was especially popular as Tosca and Salome. After she appeared in productions of *Salome* at the Metropolitan and Covent Garden, she was hailed as one of the great voices of the world. When she retired from the stage, she continued to work in film and television in Europe, mostly in character and supporting roles. She is believed to have been featured in over 75 films and 45 television shows. A sampling is listed below. Welitsch talks about her opera career

in the *Tosca* film *I Live For Art*. See also GRÄFIN MARIZA (1973), TOSCA (1983 film).

1953 The Man Between
Ljuba Welitsch sings the role of Salome and is seen on stage in the final scene of the opera in this British spy film. James Mason and Claire Bloom attend a production of *Salome* at the East Berlin Staatsoper at the height of the Cold War and try to slip away to escape to the West. Carol Reed directed. Black and white. 101 minutes.

1960 Final Resolution
Ljuba Welitsch and Mario Del Monaco are the opera singers featured in *Schlussakkord*, a German/Italian film revolving around the premiere of an opera in Salzburg. There are the usual operatic problems of love, suspicion, jealousy and hate. The stars are Eleanora Rossi-Drago, Victor de Kowa and Christian Wolff. Wolfgang Liebeneiner directed. Black and white. In German. 102 minutes. Lyric/Opera Dubs videos.

1962 Arms and the Man
Ljuba Welitsch is the matronly rather operatic Katherina in this German adaptation of George Bernard Shaw's anti-war play. Liselotte Pulver stars as her daughter Raina who is charmed by the chocolate soldier Bluntschli, portrayed by O.W. Fischer. Kurt Kaznar plays Welitsch's husband. Franz Peter Wirth directed. Black and white. In German. 96 minutes.

1961 Adorable Julia
Welitsch plays Dolly de Fries in this French/Austrian adaptation of Somerset Maugham's novel *Theatre*. Lilli Palmer stars as a theatrical grande dame married to Charles Boyer who falls in love with young Jean Sorel. Alfred Weidemann directed. German title: *Julia, Du Bist Zauberhaft*. Color. In French or German. 97 minutes.

1989 Portrait of Ljuba Welitsch
Ljuba Welitsch was 75 and still very lively when this documentary portrait of her life and career was made for Bulgarian television. It focuses on her portrayals of Salome as she talks about the different productions in which she has starred. There is even a brief scene of her performing the Dance of the Seven Veils. Jordan Djoumaliev

directed the video. Color. In Bulgarian. 70 minutes. On video.

WELLES, ORSON
American film director (1915-1985)

Orson Welles once described himself as starting at the top in films and working his way down. Certainly there are many who consider *Citizen Kane*, which has a strong operatic element, the greatest film ever made. Welles also directed non-operatic versions of *Macbeth*, *Otello* and *Falstaff*. See CITIZEN KANE.

WERTHER
1892 opera by Massenet

Jules Massenet's operatic adaptation of Goethe's novel *Die Leiden des Jungen Werther* (The Sorrows of Young Werther) is currently his most popular and widely recorded opera. The story takes place in Frankfurt in 1772. Werther and Charlotte are in love but she is engaged to Albert. When Werther goes away for a time, Charlotte marries Albert. Werther returns, discovers what has happened and kills himself. The libretto is by Edouard Blaud, Paul Milliet and Georges Hartmann. See also DIE LEIDEN DES JUNGEN WERTHER, JULES MASSENET.

1985 Petr Weigl film
Peter Dvorsky portrays Werther in this stylish production by Czech film director Petr Weigl and is matched in brilliance by Brigitte Fassbaender as Charlotte. Weigl shot the opera outdoors somewhat modernized in ravishing locations which tend to make it look almost too beautiful. The other cast members are Czech actors dubbed by singers that include Hans Helm as Albert and Magdalena Vasary as Sophie. The music is performed by the Prague Radio Symphony Orchestra conducted by Libor Dvorsky. Color. In French. 108 minutes. European Video Distributors video/ Japanese laserdisc.

1991 Alfredo Kraus in Lisbon
Alfredo Kraus prepares for the title role of *Werther* at Lisbon's Teatro San Carlo in this documentary in the *My Favorite Opera* series. About 30 minutes of scenes from the stage production are presented in narrative order. Ileana Cotrubas sings the role of Charlotte, Elsa Saque is Sophie, J. Vaz de Carvalho is Albert and Jose de Freitas is Bailio. The opera was staged by Paolo Trevis with set designs by

Ferrucio Villagrossi. Gianpaolo Sanzogno conducts the Orchestra and Choir of the Teatro Nacional de Sao Carlos. German filmmaker Bernhard Sinkel directed. Color. In English and French. 60 minutes. Kultur video.

Early/related films

1910 André Brule film
The Massenet opera was the inspiration for the French silent film titled *Werther* made by the Film d'Art company and screened with Massenet's music. It stars André Brule as Werther, Phillipe Garnier and Mlle. Dulac. Black and white. About 10 minutes.

1938 Max Ophuls film
Max Ophuls directed this excellent French film version of the Goethe novel titled *Werther* or *Le Roman de Werther* and using music by Mozart, Grétry, Bach and Beethoven. Pierre-Richard Willm portrays Werther with Annie Vernay as Charlotte. Black and white. In France. 85 minutes.

1976 Egon Gunther film
Egon Gunther directed *Die Leiden des Jungen Werther*, a well-made East German version of the Goethe novel starring Hans-Jürgen Wolf as Werther. He uses music by Mozart and Siegfrid Matthus. Color. In German. 91 minutes.

1986 Pilar Miro film
Spanish filmmaker Pilar Miro's *Werther* is updated and reset in contemporary Spain with Eusebio Poncela starring as Werther. Miro uses music from Massenet's opera as the score for the film. It is sung by José Carreras and Federica von Stade with Colin Davis conducting the Royal Opera House Orchestra. Color. In Spanish. 110 minutes.

1992 Le Jeune Werther
Music from Massenet's opera is the basis for the soundtrack of this French film loosely derived from Goethe's novel. It's set in a contemporary French school where a group of 14-year-olds try to discover why a friend has committed suicide. The music was arranged by Philippe Sarde and Jacques Doillon directed the film. Color. In French. 94 minutes.

WEST SIDE STORY
1957 "American opera" by Bernstein

Leonard Bernstein's *West Side Story* has the structure of a Broadway musical but has been called an "American opera" because of its symphonic writing, vocal requirements and tragic libretto based on Shakespeare's *Romeo and Juliet*. It has certainly been sung by opera stars on video and it might someday enter the opera house repertory. The libretto by Arthur Laurents updates Shakespeare's story to New York City in the 1950s. The rival families are now youth gangs with the Italian Jets led by Riff and the Puerto Rican Sharks led by Bernardo. Tony, who is Riff's best friend, and Maria, who is Bernardo's sister, fall in love and the star-crossed tragedy begins. The superb lyrics are by Stephen Sondheim and the brilliant choreography was created by Jerome Robbins. See also LEONARD BERNSTEIN.

1961 Robert Wise film
This electrifying cinematic version of *West Side Story* was directed by Robert Wise and Jerome Robbins and adapted for the screen by Ernest Lehman. Natalie Wood portrays Maria with Marni Nixon doing her singing, Richard Beymer plays Tony with Jim Bryant doing his singing, Russ Tamblyn plays Riff and George Chakiris is Bernardo. Daniel Fapp was the cinematographer and Boris Leven the art director. The film won six Academy Awards including Best Picture, Director, Cinematographer and Art Director. Color. In English. 155 minutes. On video.

1985 The Making of West Side Story
Major opera singers make a recording of *West Side Story* with Leonard Bernstein and are captured on film in this splendid documentary. Kiri Te Kanawa sings the role of Maria, José Carreras is Tony, Tatiana Troyanos is Anita and Kurt Ollmann is Riff. Te Kanawa sings very well, Carreras has problems with his accent and Bernstein enjoys even the problems. This was the first time he conducted his opera. The film was photographed by John Else, produced by Humphrey Burton and directed by Christopher Swann. BBC/Unitel. Color. 89 minutes. On video.

WHALE WHO WANTED TO SING AT THE MET, THE
1946 animated opera film

Nelson Eddy is superb as the multiple voices of an operatic whale and the artwork of this animated classic is as grand as grand opera. Willie, who dreams of singing at the Metropolitan Opera, has three voices and can sing bass, baritone and tenor at the same time. When he arouses international attention by entertaining ships at sea, Met impresario Tetti-Tatti deduces he has swallowed an opera singer and sails to rescue him. Meanwhile the whale imagines he is about to be discovered and auditions with Figaro's "Largo al Factotum" aria from *The Barber of Seville* and the Sextet from *Lucia di Lammermoor*. He then fantasizes performances at the Metropolitan as a cavalier in *Lucia*, as a crying clown in *Pagliacci*, as Tristan singing the "Love Duet" to a diminutive Isolde in the Wagner opera and as a fire-breathing devil in *Mefistofele*. He is harpooned while performing Boito's ominous music and ends up in Heaven singing the great "May Heaven grant you pardon" ensemble from *Martha*. As the narrator points out he can now sing "in a hundred voices each more golden than the one before." He also sings in Italian which is apparently the preferred language of Heaven. Eddy is the narrator and all the other voices in the film which is based on a story by Irvin Graham adapted by Richmond Kelsey and T. Hee. Clyde Geronimi and Hamilton Luske directed the film which was originally released as part of the feature *Make Mine Music*. It is on video as *Willie The Operatic Whale*. Color. 12 minutes. Walt Disney video.

WHERE THE WILD THINGS ARE
1980 opera by Sendak and Knussen

American illustrator-author Maurice Sendak's popular and controversial children's book *Where the Wild Things Are* was turned into a fantasy opera by Sendak and English composer Oliver Knussen. It premiered in Brussels in 1980 but the definitive Glyndebourne version was not presented until 1984. The opera tells the story of Max, a rather naughty six-year-old boy who is sent to bed without supper. He imagines a journey to the land of the Wild Things where he becomes king and has a grand old time before having to flee back home. See also OLIVER KNUSSEN, MAURICE SENDAK.

1985 Glyndebourne Festival

Maurice Sendak is really the star of this Glyndebourne Festival production with imaginative characters, costumes and sets that appeal equally to children and adults. Karen Beardsley portrays Max with support from Mary King, Jenny Weston, Hugh Hetherington, Perry Davey and Jeremy Munro. Frank Corsaro staged and choreographed the production and composer Oliver Knussen conducted the London Sinfonietta. Christopher Swann directed the video. Color. In English. 40 minutes. Home Vision video/laser.

WHITE HORSE INN
1930 operetta by Benatzsky

Ralph Benatzsky's *Im Weissen Rössl*, a spectacular operetta-revue, was a big hit in the 1930s in Berlin, Vienna, Paris, London and New York. Its slight plot revolves around the woman who owns the famous White Horse Inn in St. Wolfgang near Salzburg and her relationship with her headwaiter. A good emperor resolves the problem. The story is mostly an excuse for extravagant sets and enjoyable songs. The basic score is by Benatzsky but some of the songs are by other composers like Robert Stolz and Robert Gilbert. The operetta has been filmed at least four times. See also RALPH BENATZSKY.

1935 Carl Lamac film

Christl Mardayn stars as the landlady of the beautiful hotel on Lake Wolfgang in the first film of the operetta. It was made by Czech director Carl Lamac as an Austrian/German co-production and shot in Vienna. The cast includes Herman Thimig, Theo Lingen and Annie Markart. Black and white. In German. 84 minutes.

1948 Benito Perojo film

Elisa Galve stars as the White Horse Inn manager in this lavish Argentine film version of the operetta. It was directed by Benito Perojo and was a huge hit in Buenos Aires. Juan Carlos Thorry plays a famous singer who visits the inn incognito to help boost its reputation. Black and white. In Spanish. 90 minutes.

1952 Eric Charell film

Eric Charell, the producer of the original stage show, created this spectacular Agfacolor film of the operetta. Johanna Matz stars as the hotel landlady Josepha, Walter Müller portrays her lovelorn headwaiter, Johannes Heesters is Dr. Seidler and Rudolf Forster plays the good-hearted Emperor Franz Joseph. The Austrian Tyrol scenery is as attractive as the songs. Willi Forst directed. Color. In German. 99 minutes.

1960 Werner Jacobs film

Werner Jacobs' film of the venerable operetta was actually shot on location at the White Horse Inn itself. It's certainly colorful and folksy even if it's updated. Karin Dor stars as the inn's landlady with strong support from Adrian Hoven, Günther Philipp, Estella Blain, Serner Finch and Erick Jelde. The film was made in German and French versions. The French film is titled *L'Auberge du Cheval Blanc*. Color. 95 minutes. Editions Montparnasse (France) video.

1992 Sandro Massimini video

Highlights from *Al Cavallino Bianco* are sung by Italian operetta master Sandro Massimini and his associates on the Italian TV series *Operette, Che Passione!* He also gives the history of the operetta over the years. The featured songs are "Sigismondi Al Cavallino è l'hotel più bel," "Meglio val sorridere" and "Occhione blu." Color. In Italian. About 16 minutes. Ricordi (Italy) video.

WIE EINST IM MAI
1913 operetta by Kollo

Walter Kollo's tuneful 1913 German operetta *Wie einst im Mai* (Once in May) provided the basis for Sigmund Romberg's hit *Maytime* though it is hardly known now outside Germany. The first of the love-through-three-generations operettas, it has a libretto by Rudolf Bernauer and Rudolf Schanzer with music by Kollo and Willy Bredschneider. The story continues from 1838 to 1913 as relationships evolve over the years. *Wie einst im Mai* was a big hit on stage in Berlin and continues to be presented there. It was filmed in 1926 and 1937 and a 1966 Berlin stage production starred opera tenor René Kollo, the composer's grandson. Meanwhile back in America Romberg composed a completely new score for his version and librettist Rida Johnson Young transmuted the story into a New York tale. *Maytime* was such a success that it has overshadowed the original except in Germany. See also WALTER KOLLO.

1926 Trude Hesterberg film

A German silent version of the Kollo operetta was produced in Berlin in 1926 starring Trude Hesterberg and Camilla Spira. It was shown in cinemas with music from the operetta played live. Willi Wolff directed. Black and white. About 80 minutes.

1937 Charlotte Ander film

Kollo's operetta was finally filmed with his music in Berlin in 1937 though it never achieved great popularity as a movie. The movie version stars Charlotte Ander, Paul Klinger, Otto Wernicke and Ilse Fürstenberg. The time period of the film was revised and set in 1900, 1913 and 1937. Richard Schneider-Edenkoben directed for Ariel Films. Black and white. In German. 91 minutes.

WIENER BLUT
1899 operetta by Strauss

Viennese Blood is not exactly an operetta by Johann Strauss Jr. even though he composed its music. It's really a *pasticcio*, a mosaic of pre-existing melodies. Strauss had wanted to rearrange some older compositions to fit a libretto written by Viktor Leon and Leo Stein but was too ill to work. He agreed to let Adolf Muller do the arrangements in his place but then died before it was completed. Like the 1931 film *Congress Dances* it is set at the Congress of Vienna in 1815 where everybody apparently had a very good time. Count Zedlau is trying to hide his relationship with his mistress Franzi from his wife Gabriele, who has unexpectedly turned up, but he is also creating a new friendship with the dress fitter Pepi. Most of the action revolves around various confusions with these women. All is sorted out at the end and their various misbehaviors are blamed on the powers of the ardent "Viennese blood." See also JOHANN STRAUSS.

1942 Willy Forst film

Willy Forst directed this wartime Austrian film of the operetta with Willy Fritsch as the Count and Maria Holst as his Countess. Doris Kreysler is the Count's very good friend, comedian Hans Moser is his portly valet and Theo Lingen is Jean. The adaptation was made by Forst working with Ernest Marischka and Axel Eggebrecht. It was not released in the U.S. until 1951. Black and white. In German. 104 minutes.

1971 René Kollo film

René Kollo stars as Count Zedlou in this lush Austrian film of the Strauss operetta. Ingeborg Hallstein sings the role of his wife Gabriele while Dagmar Koller portrays Franzi. Anton Paulik conducts the Kurt Graunke Symphony Orchestra, Schonbrunner Schrammeln and Munich Kammerchor. Hugo Wiener designed the sets with Herman Lanske and Lanske directed the film in 35mm and stereo for television. Unitel. Color. In German. 97 minutes. Taurus (Germany) video.

WILDER, ALEC
American composer (1907-1980)

Composer Alex Wilder began as a song writer and arranger and wrote one of the definitive studies of American popular song. He turned to opera in 1946 and composed thirteen stage works which have been performed. His years in popular song encouraged him to make them melodious. He also wrote one screen opera.

1953 Miss Chicken Little

This "musical fable" with libretto by W. Engwick was commissioned by CBS and premiered on the *Omnibus* series on Dec. 27, 1953. Black and white. In England. 30 minutes.

WILDHAGEN, GEORG
German film director

German filmmaker Georg Wildhagen directed three opera films of note. His version of *The Marriage of Figaro* in German was one of the first German opera films of importance in the postwar period. See THE MARRIAGE OF FIGARO (1949), THE MERRY WIVES OF WINDSOR(1950), EINE NACHT IN VENEDIG (1953).

WILLIAM TELL
1829 opera by Rossini

Guillaume Tell/Guglielmo Tell has the most famous overture in opera, so much so that an intellectual was once defined as a person who could listen to it and not think of *The Lone Ranger*. Gioachino Rossini's last opera was composed in Paris in French to a libretto by Etienne De Jouy and Hippolyte-Louis-Florent based on a play by Schiller. However, the versions on video are all in Italian and only the French speak of a *Guillaume Tell* Overture. The opera tells the legendary story of the rebel patriot archer who was forced to shoot an apple off his son's head. The main characters are William Tell, his conspirator friend Walter Furst, Arnold who loves Austrian princess Mathilde, Tell's son Melethal and the tyrant Gesler. The story has been filmed many times beginning as early as 1901. Most of the early films are based on the legend or the Schiller play though a 1925 Swiss film was actually based on the opera. The overture has been popular with animated cartoonist was with *The Lone Ranger*. See also GIOACHINO ROSSINI.

1948 Tito Gobbi film
Tito Gobbi sings the role of William Tell in this highlights version of the opera sung in Italian. It was made for George Richfield's *First Opera Film Festival* series. Gabriella Gatti sings the role of Mathilde acted by Pina Malgarini and José Soler sings the role of Arnaldo. The opera was filmed on stage at the Rome Opera House with singers from La Scala and Rome and the orchestra conducted by Angelo Questa. The story is told in English voice-over by Olin Downes. Black and white. 25 minutes. Lyric/Bel Canto videos.

1988 Zurich Opera
Swiss film director Daniel Schmid, who made the documentary *Tosca's Kiss*, produced and designed this Zurich Opera House production sung in Italian. Maria Chiara stars as Matilde, Antonio Salvadori is William Tell and Salvatore Fisichella is Arnoldo. Also in the cast are Margaret Chalker as Jemmy, Nadine Asher as Edwige and Alfred Muff as Gessler. Nello Santi conducts the Zurich Opera Orchestra and Choir. Schmid also directed the video. Color. In Italian. 172 minutes. Lyric video.

1991 Teatro alla Scala
Giorgio Zancanaro stars as Guglielmo Tell, Cheryl Studer is Matilde and Chris Merritt is Arnoldo in this Teatro alla Scala production sung in Italian. Luca Ronconi staged the theater production and directed the video. The sets were designed by Gianni Quaranta and the La Scala orchestra was conducted by Riccardo Muti. Color. In Italian with English subtitles. 142 minutes. Home Vision video/Japanese laser.

1991 Nello Santi film
Conductor Nello Santi is the focal point of this documentary film about the opera made for the *My Favorite Opera* series. Tomas Simerda's film mixes scenes from the opera with interviews with the conductor and views of the Swiss countryside where the opera takes place. Maria Chiara sings Matilde, Lee Roisum is William Tell and Salvatore Fisichella is Arnold. Santi conducts the Svizzera Italiana Orchestra. Color. 60 minutes. Kultur video.

Early/related films

THE LONE RANGER
The *Willian Tell* Overture was first used as the theme music for *The Lone Ranger* radio show which started in 1933. When the series moved on to television in 1949 with Clayton Moore as its star, the Rossini theme music became even better known. There have been many movies about the character but probably the most "authentic" is the 1956 *The Lone Ranger* directly derived from the TV series. Moore stars as the Lone Ranger and Stuart Heisler directed. Color. 86 minutes.

1925 Emil Harder film
Emil Harder directed this Swiss silent film based on the opera libretto. It was shown in the USA accompanied by live music from the opera. Felix Orell portrays William Tell, George Roberts is Albrecht and Robert Kleiner is Gesler. The cast also includes Heinrich Gretler, Elizabeth Jaun and Helene Kassewitcz. Black and white. In Italian. About 75 minutes.

1927 Henry Hadly Conducts the Overture
Henry Hadly, who wrote operas and operettas as well as having a major career as a conductor, starred in one of the early Vitaphone sound films. In it he is seen conducting the New York Philharmonic Orchestra in a performance of the William Tell Overture. Black and white. About 8 minutes.

1935 The Band Concert
Mickey Mouse conducts an animated band in the park in his first color film. First the audience cheers selections from *Zampa*, then the band plays the *William Tell* Overture until interrupted by Donald Duck. Wilfred Jackson directed. Color. 7 minutes.

1940 Popeye the Sailor Meets William Tell
The king of spinach meets the king of the bow and arrow to Rossini's music in this lively animated

cartoon. Dave Fleischer directed and Max Fleischer produced for Paramount. Color. 7 minutes.

1947 Overture to William Tell
Walter Lantz made this animated cartoon for his *Musical Miniatures* series and based it around the overture to the Rossini opera. It features the cartoon character Wally Walrus and was directed by Dick Lundy. Color. 7 minutes.

1948 Guglielmo Tell
This Italian narrative version of the story is based on the Schiller play but uses Rossini's music as its background score. Gino Cervi stars as Guglielmo Tell with Allegra Sander as Mathilde, Monique Orban as Berta and Paul Muller as Gessler. Fernando Previtali directed. Black and white. In Italian. 91 minutes.

1971 A Clockwork Orange
The *William Tell* Overture is featured on the soundtrack of this Stanley Kubrick film, a dystopian vision of England in the not-too-distant future as imagined by Anthony Burgess. Color. 136 minutes.

1993 Ludwig 1881
Helburt Berger stars in this German film about an attempt by King Ludwig II of Bavaria in 1881 to present Schiller's *William Tell* in its original setting at Lake Lucerne. Fosco and Donatello Dubini directed. Color. In German. 90 minutes.

WILLIE STARK
1981 opera by Floyd

Carlisle Floyd has specialized in operas with American settings like *Susannah* and *Of Mice and Men* but none is more American than *Willie Stark*. It's based on the life of Louisiana Governor Huey Long who is fictionally portrayed as Willie Stark in Robert Penn Warren's Pulitzer Prize-winning novel *All The King's Men*. Floyd himself wrote the libretto based on the book. Like the Hollywood film based on the novel, it portrays the rise and fall of one of the most corrupt and charismatic populist politicians in American history. The music has strong influences from jazz and folk song but maintains an operatic framework with arias and ensembles.

1981 Houston Grand Opera
Baritone Timothy Nolen stars as Willie Stark in this outstanding Houston Grand Opera production by Hal Prince. Alan Kay is the idealistic lawyer Jack, Jan Curtiz is the streetwise floozy Sadie, Julia Conwell is Ann, David Busby is Duffy, Robert Moulson is Sugar Boy and Don Garret is the Judge. Eugene Lee designed the sets. Director Brian Large taped the opera without an audience so he could place his cameras in the auditorium and on stage. The critics said it was magnificent screen opera. Color. In English. 120 minutes. Video at MTR.

RELATED FILM

1949 All the King's Men
Broderick Crawford stars as Willie Stark in this superb Academy Award-winning film of the Robert Penn Warren novel written and directed by Robert Rossen. It makes an enriching counterpoint to Floyd's musical adaptation of the story. Black and white. 109 minutes. On video.

1995 Kingfish: A Story of Huey P. Long
Thomas Schlamme directed this film telling the undisguised story of the Kingfish, Huey P. Long. He is portrayed by John Goodman. Paul Monoash wrote the screenplay for Turner Pictures for television. Color. 110 minutes.

WINDGASSEN, WOLFGANG
German tenor (1914-)

Wolfgang Windgassen, who made his debut in 1941, became one of the great Wagner tenors and was a regular at Bayreuth for twenty years from 1951 to 1970. He sang at the Metropolitan in 1957 in the role of Siegmund. Windgassen can be seen in two opera videos. In one he appears as Tristan, one of his great roles, opposite Renata Tebaldi. In the other he portrays Prince Orlofsky in the Strauss operetta. He also appears in the documentary film about the making of the first complete recording of the *Ring*. See DIE FLEDERMAUS (1971), DER RING DES NIBELUNGEN (1965 FILM), TRISTAN UND ISOLDE (1967).

WINDHEIM, MAREK
Polish/American tenor (1895-1960)

Tenor Marek Windheim came to America from Poland in 1926 after beginning his career in Vienna in 1914. He joined the Metropolitan Opera in 1928 and stayed with the company until 1936. Windheim was only five feet tall but he sang a range of roles at the Met, including the Lamplighter in *Manon Lescaut*, Walther in *Tannhäuser* and the dwarf in *Siegfried*. He began to appear in films in 1937 and played character parts in dozen of films including *Ninotchka* with Greta Garbo and *Mrs. Miniver* with Greer Garson. He was also in films with Metropolitan Opera singers Lily Pons and Grace Moore. His films include *Hitting a New High* and *Something to Sing About* in 1937; *Bringing Up Baby* and *Say It in French* in 1938; *Ninotchka* and *On Your Toes* in 1939; *Play Girl* and *Escape* in 1940; *Too Many Blondes* and *Marry the Boss's Daughter* in 1941, *Madame Curie* and *Mission to Moscow* in 1943, *Mrs. Parkington* and *In Our Time* in 1944, *A Royal Scandal* in 1945 and *The Razor's Edge* and *Two Smart People* in 1946.

WLASCHIHA, EKKEHARD
German baritone (1938-)

Ekkehard Wlaschiha has become one of the most popular German Wagnerian singers and has been featured on a number of videos. He made his debut in East Germany in 1961 in *The Merry Wives of Windsor* and began to sing at Leipzig and Dresden. He made his first Bayreuth appearance in 1986 and has now sung around the world from the Met to Covent Garden. He sings mostly in German opera but in a wide variety of roles. In addition to the operas listed below he was featured as Don Pizarro in a Leningrad TV film of *Fidelio*. See also DER FREISCHÜTZ (1985), GÖTTERDÄMMERUNG (1989/1990), LOHENGRIN (1990), DAS RHEINGOLD (1989/1990).

WO DIE LERCHE SINGT
1918 operetta by Lehár

Where the Lark Sings is a folksy Hungarian operetta by Franz Lehár. It premiered in Budapest in January 1918 as *A Pacsirta* (The Lark) and after revisions by librettists A. M. Willner and Heinz Reichert came to Vienna in March as *Wo die Lerche Singt*. It was such a hit with the Viennese that it held the stage for another 415 performances and was brought to New York in 1920. It tells the story of the love between a country maiden and a city artist.

1918 Hubert Marischka film
The popularity of the Lehár operetta led to a film version the same year as the stage premiere. Hubert Marischka wrote, directed and starred in the film which was based on the Theater an der Wien production. Marischka portrays the painter Sandor, Ernst Tautenhayn is the old farmer, Luise Kartousch is his granddaughter Margit, Marietta Weber is Vilma and Gustav Siege is the Baron. Lehár's music was played when the operetta was screened. Black and white. In German. About 80 minutes.

1936 Marta Eggerth film
Hungarian singer Marta Eggerth stars as the Hungarian country maiden in this version of *Where the Lark Sings* filmed in the Hunnia Studio in Budapest. She appears opposite Hans Söhnker, Lucie Englisch and Fritz Imhoff. Karel Lamac directed and Geza von Cziffra arranged the Lehár music. Black and white. In Hungarian or German. 95 minutes.

WOLF TRAP PARK

Notable productions of operas were telecast from the Filene Center Auditorium in Wolf Trap Park in Virginia before there were regular opera telecasts from the Met. They were organized by WETA (Washington Education Telecommunication Association) and began in 1974 with Beverly Sills in *The Daughter of the Regiment*. Four operas starring Sills were telecast from Wolf Trap and three of them are now available on video in the series *In Performance at Wolf Trap*. See THE DAUGHTER OF THE REGIMENT (1974), THE NEW MOON (1989), ROBERTO DEVEREUX (1975), LA TRAVIATA (1976).

WOMAN WHO KNOWS WHAT SHE WANTS, A
1932 operetta by Straus

Oscar Straus's operetta *A Woman Who Knows What She Wants* (Eine Frau, Die Weiss, Was Sie Will) was written for aging operetta diva Fritzi Massary who starred in the Berlin premiere. She portrayed a middle-aged actress somewhat like herself who finds she is losing her lover to her daughter. The bittersweet libretto is by Alfred Grunwald. The operetta went to London in 1933 retitled *Mother of Pearl* by adapter A. P. Herbert. It starred Alice

Delysia and was a major hit. It has been filmed twice.

1934 Lil Dagover film
Lil Dagover stars as the woman of the world with a few too many years in this Czechoslovakian film of the operetta. Director Viktor Janson shot the film in Prague in Czech and German. The cast includes Anton Edthofer, Maria Beling, Hans Junkermann and Kurt Bespermann. Black and white. In Czech or German. 82 minutes.

1957 Lilli Palmer film
Lilli Palmer stars in a double role in this somewhat surrealistic version of the operetta. She portrays both the woman of the world who knows what she wants and her rather virtuous granddaughter. The film was intended to be an homage to Fritzi Massary. Also starring are Maria Sebaldt and Peter Schütte. Arthur Maria Rabenalt directed for Bavaria Film. Color. In German. 101 minutes.

WORST OPERA ON FILM

There are a number of films of operas that are not very good but the 1936 British film of *Faust* is considered by many critics to be the worst film ever of a complete opera. Gounod's opera is reduced to 63 minutes of English words, poor singing, indifferent acting and bad color. The narrative film with the worst use of opera music may be a B-western. Parodies of *Rigoletto* and *Carmen* are sung as cowboy songs by Tex Ritter in the *Ridin' the Cherokee Trail* and are awe-inspiring in their awfulness. However, the incredibly bizarre lyrics sung to the "Ride of the Valkyries" music in Ken Russell's *Mahler* are even more excruciating. Both have to be heard to be believed. See FAUST (1936), RIDIN' THE CHEROKEE TRAIL, GUSTAV MAHLER (1974).

WORST OPERETTA ON FILM

Two operetta films made in Hollywood at the beginning of the sound era are clear contenders. Rudolf Friml's 1930 film operetta *The Lottery Bride* stars Jeanette MacDonald as the prize in an Alaskan marriage lottery. She is won by the man she is trying to forget who gives his winning ticket to his brother. When Jeanette arrives and he sees what has happened, he leaps on a passing German Zeppelin to forget his sorrows It gets lost in the frozen Arctic and Jeanette has to rescue him. It's pretty bad but worse is Emmerich Kálmán's 1927 stage operetta *Golden Dawn* which was turned into a film in 1930. It stars Vivienne Segal and features Viennese music sung in blackface in Africa in a World War II German prison camp. The hit song is the overseer's ode to his whip. As critic Lucius Beebe pointed out in a *Herald-Tribune* review, "Reason totters at the thought that any one could have conceived in seriousness such a definitive catalogue of vulgarity, witlessness, and utterly pathetic and preposterous nonsense." See GOLDEN DAWN, THE LOTTERY BRIDE.

WOZZECK
1925 opera by Berg

Alban Berg's powerful opera is based on the play *Woyzeck* by George Büchner. Despite its 19th century source, the opera seems very modern in its concern with a person brutalized by society. Wozzeck is a soldier who senses mysterious forces he does not understand. His captain uses him as a barber, his doctor uses him as an experimental guinea pig and his woman Marie has begun a dalliance with the Drum Major. His visions increase and eventually he kills Marie. Berg was influenced by the cinema in his libretto and uses cinematic rather than theatrical time flow for the action.

1967 Rolf Liebermann film
Toni Blankenheim stars as Wozzeck with Sena Jurinac as Marie in this film based on a Hamburg Opera production by Rolf Liebermann. Richard Cassilly portrays the Drum Major, Peter Haage is Andres, Gerhard Unger is the Captain, Hans Sotin is the Doctor and Elisabeth Steiner is Margret. The cinematography is by Wolfgang Peter Hassenstein, the sets were designed by Herbert Kirchhoff and the original stage director was Günther Rennert. Bruno Maderna conducts the Hamburg Philharmonic Orchestra. Joachim Hess directed the film. Polytel. Color. In German. 103 minutes.

1987 Vienna State Opera
Franz Grundheber stars as Wozzeck with Hildegarde Behrens as Marie in this Vienna State Opera production by Adolf Dresen. Walter Raffeiner is the Drum Major, Philip Langridge is Andres, Heinz Zednik is the Captain, Aage Haugland is the Doctor and Anna Conda is Margret. Herbert Kapplmüller designed the sets and costumes and Claudio Abbado conducted the

Vienna State Opera orchestra and chorus. Brian Large directed the video. Color. In German with English subtitles. 96 minutes. Home Vision video.

Related films

1947 Georg C. Klaren film

Kurt Meisel stars as Wozzek with Helga Zülch as Marie in this strong East German film adaptation of the Büchner play directed by Georg C. Klaren. It does not use Berg's music. Black and white. In German. 101 minutes.

1979 Werner Herzog Film

Werner Herzog's powerful and claustrophobic film adaptation of the Büchner play is titled *Woyzeck* and stars Klaus Kinski as Wozzeck and Eva Mattes as Marie. It is a brilliant transposition of the original which deserves comparison with the opera though it does not use Berg's music. Josef Bierbichler portrays the Drum Major, Willy Semmelrogge is the Doctor, Paul Burien is Andres and Wolfgang Reichmann is the Captain. Color. In German. 81 minutes.

1994 Janos Szasz film

Hungarian filmmaker Janos Szasz wrote and directed this bleak but beautiful adaptation of the Büchner play set in a grimy Hungarian railway yard. Woyzeck has become a point man humiliated by his boss and rejected by his wife Maria who prefers a policeman. Eventually he goes over the edge. Black and white. In Hungarian. 94 minutes.

WUNDERLICH, FRITZ
Austrian tenor (1930-1966)

Fritz Wunderlich, who died young in an accident, was Germany's top lyric tenor during his short career and was equally adept at opera and operetta. He made his debut in Stuttgart in 1955 as Tamino in *The Magic Flute*, joined the Munich Opera in 1960 and sang with the Vienna State Opera from 1962. He was noted for the sweetness and melodiousness of his voice and was especially admired in Mozart. His records remain popular. See THE BARBER OF SEVILLE (1959), EUGENE ONEGIN (1965), WOLFGANG A. MOZART (1967), EIN WALZERTRAUM (1960).

1990 Fritz Wunderlich: Portrait of a Singer

This German television documentary about the singer and his career was written and directed by Manfred Deide. Color. In German. 30 minutes. Video at NYPL.

1994 Fritz Wunderlich Live

This is a compilation of excerpts of scenes from operas on film or video featuring Wunderlich. The operas include *The Barber of Seville, Eugene Onegin, Maestro di Musica, The Magic Flute* and *The Abduction from the Seraglio*. Most of the material is from kinescopes of early television broadcasts. Black and white. In German. 47 minutes. Bel Canto Society video.

X

XERXES
1738 opera by Handel

Fredric Handel's splendid comic opera is *Serse* in the original Italian but the only video is in English and titled *Xerxes*. It is famous for its delightful hymn to a plane tree, "Ombra mai fu," which through the vagaries of time has been transmuted into the rather somber piece of music known as Handel's *Largo*. The opera, set in ancient Persia, concerns King Xerxes' efforts to win Romilda who loves his brother Arsamene. Xerxes, who already has a wife, finally contents himself with Romilda's sister Atalanta. The text is based on an Italian libretto by Stampiglia called *Il Xerse*. Odd as it seems, the historical King Xerxes really did revere a plane tree. See also GEORGE F. HANDEL.

1988 English National Opera
This delightful production by Nicholas Hytner stars Ann Murray as Xerxes with Valerie Masterson as Romilda and Christopher Robson as Arsamenes. It was filmed on stage at the Coliseum in London and sung in Hytner's English translation. Jean Rigby is Amastris, Lesley Garrett is Atalanta, Christopher Booth-Jones is Elviro and Rodney Macann is Ariodates. The production won the Laurence Olivier Opera Award. David Fielding designed the set and Sir Charles Mackerras conducted the ENO Orchestra. John Michael Phillips directed the video. Color. In English. 185 minutes. Home Vision video.

Related film

1988 Dangerous Liaisons
Stephen Frears' film *Dangerous Liaisons* features the Largo ("Ombra mai fu") from *Xerses*. John Malkovich and Glenn Close are the stars of the film. Color. In English. 120 minutes.

Y

YEOMAN OF THE GUARD, THE
1888 comic opera by Gilbert & Sullivan

The Yeoman of the Guard or The Merryman and His Maid comes the closest of the Savoy operas to being a "serious" opera and was compared after its premiere to Wallace's *Maritana*. It's set in the Tower of London in the 16th century. Colonel Fairfax wants to marry before he is executed and Elsie agrees to become his bride for the day. Jester Jack Point, her frustrated sweetheart, is most unhappy about this. Phoebe and her father Sgt. Meryll are admirers of the colonel so she wangles the cell key from jailer Wilfred and helps Fairfax escape. He is later reprieved but doesn't give up Elsie. *Yeoman* has been filmed a number of times. See also GILBERT AND SULLIVAN.

1907 Cinematophone Singing Pictures
This is an early British sound film of the final scene of Act One. John Morland directed *Great Finale* for Cinematophone Singing Pictures. 3 minutes.

1957 Alfred Drake video
Alfred Drake stars as Jack Point in this Hallmark Hall of Fame television production. Barbara Cook is Elsie, Celeste Holm is Phoebe, Bill Hayes is Colonel Fairfax, Henry Calvin is Wilfred and Robert Wright is Sir Richard. Paul Barnes designed the sets and George Schaefer directed. Telecast on April 10, 1957. Color. In English. 90 minutes. Video at UCLA.

1970 Tommy Steele film
Tommy Steele stars as Jack Point in this British film based on an Anthony Besch production at the Tower of London. It was made by Stanley Doreman with costumes designed by Peter Rice. Laureen Livingstone is Elsie, Terry Jenkins is Colonel Fairfax, Dennis Wicks is Wilfred, Anne Collins is Dame Carruthers, Della Jones is Phoebe, Tom McDonnell is Sir Richard and Paul Hudson is Sergeant Meryll. David Lloyd-Jones conducted the New World Philharmonic Orchestra. Color. In English. 105 minutes. Magnetic video.

1974 John Cartier film
John Cartier stars as Jack Point in this British highlights version of the operetta produced by John Seabourne for the *World of Gilbert and Sullivan* series. Valerie Masterston is Elsie, Thomas Round is Colonel Fairfax, Helen Landis is Dame Carruthers, Michael Wakeham is Sir Richard and Donald Adams is Sergeant Meryll. The music is played by the Gilbert and Sullivan Festival Orchestra and Chorus and the film was directed by Trevor Evans. Color. In English. 50 minutes.

1982 Joel Grey film
Joel Grey stars as Jack Point in this excellent film produced by Judith De Paul for George Walker. Elizabeth Gale is Elsie Maynard, Alfred Marks portrays Wilfred, David Hillman is Colonel Fairfax, Claire Powell is Phoebe, Geoffrey Chard is Sergeant Meryll, Elizabeth Bainbridge is Dame Carruthers and Peter Savidge is Sir Richard. Alexander Faris conducts the London Symphony Orchestra and the Ambrosian Opera Chorus. Anthony Besch was stage director and Dave Heather directed the film. Color. In English. 119 minutes. Pioneer laser/Braveworld (England) video.

YVAIN, MAURICE
French composer (1891-1965)

Maurice Yvain, who wrote film music as well as operettas and musical comedies, is most famous in America for the song "Mon Homme" which he created for Mistinguett. It was presented in the *Ziegfeld Follies of 1922* as "My Man" and became Fanny Brice's theme song. Yvain's most popular stage works were three operettas in the "Bouche" series and *Pas Sur la Bouche* was filmed. Among Yvain's many original film scores were the 1936 Julien Duvivier classic *La Belle Équipe* and the 1939 Pierre Fresnay movie *Le Duel* with Yvonne Printemps.

1931 Pas Sur la Bouche
Yvain's 1925 operetta *Not on the Mouth* was staged in London in 1926 as *Just a Kiss*. Gilberte is now happily married but was once secretly wed to an American who refused to allow her to kiss him on the mouth. It was made into a film in 1931 starring Mireille Perry as Gilberte, Jacques Grétillat as her present husband Georges, Nicolas Rimsky as her former husband Eric and Jeanne Marney as Huguette. Rimskey and Nicolas Evreimof directed. Black and white. In French. 80 minutes.

Z

ZAIDE
1780 opera by Mozart

Mozart never finished this opera, which is a sort of dry run for *The Abduction from the Seraglio*, but it has been completed by others and staged many times. It tells the story of a prisoner of a 16th century Turkish Sultan, his love affair with the Sultan's favorite Zaide and their escape together. A full production was mounted at Tanglewood in 1955 with Sarah Caldwell conducting. The only version of the opera available on video is an off-air copy of a telecast made in Madrid by the Warsaw Chamber Opera company in 1989 with Polish singers. It is distributed by Lyric and Opera Dubs. See also Wolfgang A. Mozart.

ZAMPA
1831 opéra comique by Hérold

Ferdinand Hérold's *Zampa ou La Fiancée de Marbre* (Zampa or the Marble Fiancée) was once a highly popular opera and a repertory regular throughout the 19th century. It is now known mostly for its overture and from vintage recordings. Zampa, the protagonist of the opera, is a pirate who attempts to steal his brother's bride-to-be. Like Don Giovanni, he is destroyed by a statue, in this case a marble one of a woman he seduced and abandoned. The libretto is by Mélesville. There does not seem to be a complete version of the opera on film or video. See also FERDINAND HÉROLD.

1930 William Cameron Menzies film
William Cameron Menzies, the highly imaginative art director and designer of films like *Things to Come*, made a series of brilliant musical short films in the early days of sound. His abbreviated but imaginative visualization of *Zampa* was made in 35mm in 1930 in a tinted version and remained popular in 16mm rental catalogs until the coming of video. Tinted black and white. 10 minutes.

1935 The Band Concert
Mickey Mouse conducts an animated band in the park in his first color film. First the audience cheers after a performance of selections from *Zampa*, then the band plays the *William Tell* Overture until interrupted by Donald Duck. Wilfred Jackson directed. Color. 7 minutes.

ZANDONAI, RICCARDO
Italian composer (1883-1944)

Riccardo Zandonai was considered the rival and successor of Puccini by the Ricordi publishing firm after his success in 1908 with the Dickens adaptation *Il Grillo del Focolare* (The Cricket on the Hearth). Zandonai also found admirers for his Spanish-flavored gypsy opera *Conchita* and his *Giulietta e Romeo*, a version of the Shakespeare play. Today he is known primarily for his 1914 opera *Francesca Da Rimini*, the only one available on video or CD. It tells the tragic story of the lovers immortalized in Dante's *Divine Comedy*. He also created an imaginary opera called Penelope for the 1940 Beniamino Gigli film *Traummusik*. See FRANCESCA DA RIMINI, IMAGINARY OPERAS IN FILMS (1940).

ZAR UND ZIMMERMANN
1837 opera by Lortzing

Albert Lortzing's *Tsar and Carpenter* remains popular in the German-speaking world but has not been much seen in America since its New York premiere back in 1851. It's a tuneful comic opera based on a legend about Tsar Peter I of Russia known as Peter the Great. He was said to have worked in disguise in Holland in 1698 to learn practical shipbuilding trades he could not study at home. He befriends a carpenter named Peter, who is in love with the Mayor's daughter Marie. Young Peter is wrongly identified as the Tsar and feted by local ambassadors and assorted fools but all is sorted out in the end with the help of the real Tsar. The libretto is by the composer. See also ALBERT LORTZING.

1955 Willy Kleinau film
Willy Kleinau portrays the Tsar, Bert Fortell plays young Peter and Lore Frisch takes the role of Marie in this East German film adaptation of the Lortzing opera. It was shot in East Berlin and directed by Hans Muller from a screenplay by Arthur Kuhnert. DEFA production. Color. In German. 101 minutes.

1962 Musikalisches Rendezvous

This is an opera anthology of DEFA opera films made in East Berlin. It includes 20 minutes of highlights from the 1955 film of *Zar und Zimmermann*. There are also scenes from *The Merry Wives of Windsor*, *The Marriage of Figaro* and *The Beggar Student*. Color. In German. 83 minutes.

1969 Raymond Wolansky film

American baritone Raymond Wolansky portrays the Tsar in this German film by Rolf Liebermann based on a Hamburg State Opera stage production. Lucia Popp plays Marie, Peter Haage is young Peter, Hans Sotin is Van Bett and Ursula Boese is Mistress Brown. Herbert Kirchhoff designed the sets and Charles Mackerras conducted the Philharmonic Orchestra and Hamburg State Opera Chorus. Joachim Hess directed the movie which was shown theatrically in the U.S. Polyphon Film. Color. In German. 137 minutes.

1976 Herman Prey film

German baritone Herman Prey stars as Tsar Peter in this Bavarian ZDF television film of the opera directed and introduced by the noted Austrian filmmaker Axel Corti. Lucia Popp is Marie and Adalbert Kraus is young Peter with Karl Ridderbusch as Van Bett, Werner Krenn as Chateauneuf, Alexander Malta as General Lefort and Helmut Berger-Tuna as Lord Syndham. Bernd Müller and Jörg Neumann designed the sets, Leo Bei designed the costumes, Hannes Winker arranged the choreography and Xaver Schwarzenberger and Sepp Vavra were the cinematographers. Heinz Wallberg conducted the Munich Radio-TV Orchestra and Bavarian Choir. Color. In German. 102 minutes. Lyric video.

ZAREWITSCH, DER

1927 operetta by Lehár

The Little Tsar tells the bittersweet story of a young Russian Crown Prince who dislikes women. When he is tricked into falling in love with a dancer named Sonja, however, he abandons his royal life and goes off to live with her in Italy. After he inherits the throne, duty gets the better of him and he gives her up to return home. *Der Zarewitsch* helped restore Franz Lehár's reputation which had gone into a decline. After he was championed by Richard Tauber, Lehár moved his base from Vienna to Berlin where this operetta had its premiere in 1927 with Tauber as the Crown Prince. It was a hit and is still popular in Germany. Bela Jenbach and Heinz Reichert's libretto is based on a play by Gabriela Zapolska. See also FRANZ LEHÁR.

1929 Ivan Petrovich film

Ivan Petrovich stars as the Crown Prince in this silent German film which was usually screened with live music from the operetta. Mariette Millner is his Sonja and the supporting cast includes Paul Otto, Albert Steinrück and John Hamilton. Jacob and Louise Fleck directed. Black and white. In German. About 80 minutes.

1933 Martha Eggerth film

Martha Eggerth stars as Sonja in this second German film of the operetta. Hans Sohnker portrays the Crown Prince while the supporting cast includes Ery Bos, Paul Otto, Georg Alexander and Ida Wüst. Viktor Janson directed. Black and white. In German. 85 minutes.

1933 Marie Glory film

Son Altesse Impériale is the French version of the above production and stars Marie Glory in the Sonja role (renamed Monique) and George Rigaud as Crown Prince Boris. Also in the cast are Germaine Aussey, Felix Oudart, Maurice Escande and Gaston Jacquet. Jean Bernard-Derosne directed. Black and white. In French. 85 minutes.

1954 Luis Mariano film

French operetta idol Luis Mariano is featured in this film version with the operetta featured inside a framing story. Mariano portrays a tenor who plays the Prince in a stage production of the operetta with Sonja Ziemann as the ballerina Sonja who loves him. After an accident she dreams the operetta and all ends happily. The cast includes Hans Richter, Maria Sebaldt and Ivan Petrovich. Arthur Maria Rabenalt directed German and French versions. The film was released in France as *Le Tzarewitch* and in the U.S. as *Der Zarewitsch*. CCC production. Color. 95 minutes. René Chateau (France) video.

1973 Teresa Stratas film

Teresa Stratas stars as Sonja opposite Wieslaw Ochmann as the Crown Prince in this colorful German film. This is a youthful Stratas at her peak in voice and charm. The film was lavishly made and won warm praise from German critics. Harald Juhnke plays Ivan, Birke Bruck is Mascha, Paul Esser is the Grand Duke and Lukas Amman is the Prime Minister. Willy Mattes conducts the Kurt

611

Graunke Symphony Orchestra. Arthur Maria Rabenalt directed in 35mm for German television. Unitel/ZDF. Color. In German. 92 minutes. Taurus (Germany) video.

ZARZUELA
Spanish light opera (1657-)

A zarzuela is a Spanish light opera with spoken dialogue, the counterpart of the operetta of central Europe but usually based on Spanish dance rhythms rather than the waltzes and czardas of Austria and Hungary. Zarzuelas are normally set in Spain and reflect aspects of regional culture from the street life of Madrid to the country life of Galicia. Their importance in Spanish cultural life is indicated by the many films based on them. Spanish critic J. F. Aranda says the best classic films of zarzuelas are Benito Perojo's *La Verbena de La Paloma* (1935), Jean Grémillon's *La Dolorosa* (1934) and Florian Rey's *El Novio de Mamá* (1934). The best modern films are the thirteen directed by Juan De Orduña for Spanish television in the late 1960s with top singers and actors. Spanish opera singers usually include zarzuela arias in their recitals. Placido Domingo, who starred in Mexican zarzuela films early in his career, also produced the only zarzuela ever featured on American television, *El Gato Montes*. One of the best descriptions of the zarzuela genre can be found in James A. Michener's excellent *Iberia*. For details about individual zarzuelas see the entries on the composers EMILIO ARRIETA, FRANCISCO BARBIERI, TOMAS BRETÓN, MANUEL FERNÁNDEZ CABALLERO, RUPERTO CHAPÍ, ENRIQUE GRANADOS, JACINTO GUERRERO, JESUS GURIDI, VICENTE LLEÓ, MANUEL PENELLA, JOSÉ SERRANO, FEDERICO MORENO TORROBA, JOSÉ MARIA USANDIZAGA, AMADEO VIVES.

1991 Zarzuela Royal Gala Concert
Placido Domingo is the best-known singer in this zarzuela concert held in the National Music Auditorium in Madrid in the presence of the Spanish King. Some of Spain's top zarzuela singers, including Guadalupe Sanchez, Teresa Verdera and Paloma Perez Inigo, join Domingo in this homage to the national music. They perform arias by Chapi, Chueca, Gimenez, Guerrero, Serrano, Sorozabal, Torroba and Vives with support from the Ballet Español and the Madrid Symphonic Orchestra. Enriques Garcia Asensio directed the video. Color. 69 minutes. Kultur video.

ZAUBERFLÖTE, DIE
See MAGIC FLUTE, THE

ZAUBERSPIEGEL, DER
1966 screen opera by Krenek

Austrian/American composer Ernest Krenek (1900-1991), who is best known for his jazz-inspired 1927 opera *Jonny Spielt Auf*, created the screen opera *Der Zauberspiegel* (The Magic Mirror) for German television. As with most of his other operas, he wrote his own libretto for this screen work. Krenek emigrated to the U.S. when the Nazis seized Austria and spent the rest of his life in America. He incorporated a variety of styles in operas ranging from atonality to dance music.

ZEFFIRELLI, FRANCO
Italian film/opera director (1923-)

Franco Zeffirelli is equally well known in the worlds of film, theater and opera and has had success in all three as director and designer. He first became famous for his revolutionary Shakespeare stage productions but he also helped guide Maria Callas to some of her greatest opera performances. His best opera film is his 1982 *La Traviata* with Maria Stratas, based on a revolutionary stage production, but there are many admirers of his other opera films. Zeffirelli began as an assistant to Luchino Visconti, a director who was also at home in opera and cinema. The first opera film he directed was *La Bohème* in 1965 but it was only a mild success. He won wide acclaim in 1967 for his Shakespearean adaptation, *The Taming of the Shrew*, with Richard Burton and Elizabeth Taylor. It was followed by a youthful *Romeo and Juliet*, another Shakespearean film modelled on his famous stage production His theatrical productions, like his films, are usually lavish with sumptuous sets and costumes. They have been so much admired at the Metropolitan Opera that one sponsor gives money earmarked only for his productions. Zeffirelli can be seen at work as a stage director in videos about Maria Callas and Teresa Stratas. His name, by the way, derives from the famous trio in *Così Fan Tutte*. It was misspelled on the birth certificate. See also LA BOHÈME (1967/1982), MARIA CALLAS, CAVALLERIA RUSTICANA (1982), CINOPERA, OTELLO (1978/1979/1986), PAGLIACCI (1982), TERESA STRATAS, TOSCA (1985), LA TRAVIATA (1982), TURANDOT (1988).

1973 Franco Zeffirelli: A Florentine Artist

This British documentary by Reginald Mills focuses on Zeffirelli making the film Brother Sun, Sister Moon. It presents a clear portrayal of the director at work and emphasizes his care about choosing locations and costumes. Color. In English. 51 minutes.

ZELLER, CARL

Austrian composer (1842-1898)

Carl Zeller, who began writing operettas in 1880, had his first major success in 1891 with *Der Vogelhändler* (The Bird Seller). While the operetta is particularly popular in German-speaking countries, Richard Tauber starred in a London production in 1947. Some of its tunes have become world favorites, including the rose-drenched "Schenkt man sich Rosen in Tirol." Zeller's 1894 operetta *Der Obersteiger* (The Mine Foreman) is also still popular in Germany. See DER VOGELHÄNDLER.

ZIEHRER, KARL MICHAEL

Austrian composer (1843-1922)

Karl Michael Ziehrer is more famous for composing waltzes than operettas but he did create twenty-two of them. The best-known is the 1899 *Die Landstreicher* which has been filmed. Ziehrer was a competitor of Strauss in the composition of traditional Viennese waltzes and had a big success with the *Vienna Madeln Waltz*. He was also a popular band master and took his band to the Chicago World's Fair in 1893. See DIE LANDSTREICHER.

1945 Wiener Madeln

Vienna Maiden is an early Agfacolor film biography of Ziehrer directed by and starring Willi Forst. It concerns the composer's rivalry and competition with Johann Strauss for attention as a waltz composer and climaxes with the creation of the famous *Vienna Maiden Waltz*. The cast also includes Dora Komar and Hans Moser. The film was shot in Vienna and Prague studios in 1945 but not released until 1949. Color. In German. 101 minutes.

ZIGEUNERBARON, DER

1885 operetta by Strauss

The Gypsy Baron is considered the best Johann Strauss operetta after *Die Fledermaus* and it became a model for later operetta writers. The complicated story focuses on aristocrat Sandor Barinkay who returns from exile to claim his land. The pig farmer Zsupan wants him to marry his daughter Arsena but Sandor falls in love with the gypsy Saffi. The libretto by Ignatz Schnitzer is based on the Hungarian story *Sáffi* by Mór Jókai. The operetta has remained very popular in Germany and France and there are many films based on it. See also JOHANN STRAUSS.

1927 Rudolf Klein-Rogge film

German actor Rudolf Klein-Rogge stars as Sandor in this German silent film version of the Strauss operetta with Lya Mara as his Saffi. The film was usually screened accompanied by the music of the operetta. The cast includes Michael Bohnen, Emil Fenyos, Wilhelm Dieterle and Vivan Gibson. Friedrich Zelnik directed. Black and white. In German. About 85 minutes.

1935 Kart Hartl film

Adolf Wahlbruck stars as Sandor, the tuneful gypsy baron, in this lavish German film of the operetta. Hansi Knoteck portrays Saffi with Fritz Kampers seen as Zsupan, Gina Falckenberg as Arsena and Edwin Jürgensen as Homonay. Kart Hartl directed. Black and white. In German. 105 minutes.

1935 Henri Chomette film

Adolf Wahlbruck stars again as the gypsy baron in this French version of the above production. *Le Baron Tzigane* was directed by Henri Chomette with a cast that features Jacqueline Francell as Saffi, Daniele Parola as Arsena, Gabriel Gabrio as Zsupan and Henri Bosc as Homonay. Black and white. In French. 105 minutes.

1954 Arthur Maria Rabenalt film

The first modern color film of the operetta was made in German and French versions with different stars. The German version, distributed in the U.S., features Gerhard Reidmann as Sandor, Margit Saad as Saffi, Maria Sebaldt is Arsena and Oskar Sima is Zsupan. The French version stars Georges Guetary as Sandor but again with Margit Saad as Saffi. Director Arthur Maria Rabenalt emphasized the visual qualities of the production and shot most of it on location. The Belgrade State Opera Ballet performs the dances. Herzog film. Color. In German or French. 105 minutes.

1962 Kurt Wilhelm film

Carlos Thompson is the gypsy baron in this modernized version of the operetta directed by Kurt Wilhelm. Heidi Bruhl is Saffi and Willy Millowitsch is Zsupan. Heinz Oskar Wuttig wrote the new screenplay and Willi Sohm was the cinematographer. Germany-France. Color. In German. 103 minutes.

1975 Siegfried Jerusalem film

Wagnerian tenor Siegfried Jerusalem began his singing career in this excellent modern German film of the operetta. He stars as Sandor Barinkay opposite Ellen Shade as Saffi with Martha Modl as Mirabella, Janet Perry as Arsena, Ivan Rebroff as Zsupan, Willi Brokmeier as Ottokar and Wolfgang Brendel as Count Homonay. Kurt Eichhorn conducted the Stuttgart Radio Orchestra and Chorus and Arthur Maria Rabenalt directed this 35mm film for television. Unitel. Color. In German. 97 minutes. Taurus (Germany) video.

ZIGEUNERLIEBE

1910 operetta by Lehár

Gypsy Love is a tuneful operetta by Franz Lehár about Zorika, a young woman in a Romanian village who worries about whom she should marry. She is attracted to the gypsy violinist Jószi though she is engaged to Jonel so she steals away from her engagement party to think it over. When she falls asleep by the river, she dreams what would happen if she went off with the gypsy. After the dream she is happy to pledge her love to husband-to-be Jonel without reservation. The libretto is by A. M. Willner and Robert Bodanzky. See also FRANZ LEHÁR.

1930 Lawrence Tibbett film

Metropolitan Opera star Lawrence Tibbett's first Hollywood film was *The Rogue Song*, a Technicolor musical based on Lehár's operetta. The plot is utterly changed. Tibbett portrays a bandit who steals from the Cossacks oppressing his people and falls in love with Princess Vera (Catherine Dale Owen), sister of the Cossack leader. The best known Lehár song in the film is "The White Dove" with lyrics by Clifford Grey but most of the music was by Herbert Stothart. Lionel Barrymore directed. The film is lost but the soundtrack is available on record and a few minutes of color footage survive. MGM. Color. In English. 107 minutes.

1974 Janet Perry film

Janet Perry stars as the confused bride-to-be Zorika in this enjoyable German film. Jon Buzea plays the gypsy violinist *Jozsi* with Adolf Dallapozza as the dependable Jonel, Colette Lorand as Ilona, Heinz Friedrich as Dragotin, Kurt Grosskurth as Mihaly, Helmut Wallner as Kajetan and Marianne Becker as Jolan. Heinz Wallberg conducts the Munich Radio-Television Orchestra and Bavarian Radio Choir. Václav Kaslík directed the film on 35mm for television. Unitel. Color. In German. 87 minutes. Taurus (Germany) video.

ZIMMERMANN, BERND

German composer (1918-1970)

Bernd Alois Zimmermann's opera *Die Soldaten* (The Soldiers) has been called the most important German opera after *Lulu*. Zimmermann, who was brought up under the Nazis, emerged as an important figure in avant-garde German music in the 1960s and killed himself in 1970. His despair is reflected in his opera which has established itself in the world repertory including U.S. productions. It is complicated to produce as it requires a large cast, three projection screens for film scenes and multiple stage levels. It is one of the few modern German operas available on video. See DIE SOLDATEN.

ZIRKUSPRINZESSIN, DIE

1926 operetta by Kálmán

Emmerich Kálmán's operetta *The Circus Princess* had to compete with popular revues in Vienna so librettists Julius Brammer and Alfred Grünwald added an exotic circus element to the usual princess. The circus is Russian and so is the wealthy Princess Fedora who becomes involved with a circus performer called Mr. X. As Mr. X is a baron in disguise, all ends romantically. The New York production of the operetta in 1927 was held at the Winter Garden so the circus element could be emphasized. See also EMMERICH KÁLMÁN.

1929 Harry Liedtke film

Harry Liedtke, who often worked with Ernst Lubitsch, stars as the aristocratic circus performer in this German silent film by Victor Janson. The film was screened with the music of the operetta. The cast includes Vera Schmitterlöw, Adele Sandrock, Hans Junkermann, Fritz Kampers, Hilde Rosch and Ernst Verebes. Guido Seeber was the cinematographer. Black and white. In German. About 85 minutes.

1969 Rudolf Schock film

Rudolf Schock stars as the circus baron with a past who loves princess Ingeborg Hallstein in this lavish modern film of the operetta. Werner Schmidt-Boelcke conducts the Kurt Graunke Symphony Orchestra. Manfred R. Kohler directed the 35mm film for West German television. Unitel. Color. In German. 111 minutes.

ZURICH

The Zurich Operhaus, which began life in 1891 as the Stadttheater, is one of the major opera houses of Europe and has been innovative and influential in recent years. One of its major productions was the Monteverdi trio of operas by Jean-Pierre Ponnelle and Nikolaus Harnoncourt which was filmed. Swiss film directors like Daniel Schmid have also staged operas at the theater. See L' INCORONAZIONE DI POPPEA (1979), ORFEO (1978), OTELLO (1961), IL RITORNO D'ULISSE IN PATRIA (1980), WILLIAM TELL (1988), LES TROYENS (1992).

1986 OperaFest

This is a record of a Gala Concert at the Zurich Opera. It was held to celebrate the reopening of the theater on Dec. 1, 1984. The performers include Mirella Freni, José Carreras, Lucia Popp, Thomas Hampson, Gwyneth Jones, Alfredo Kraus, Nicolai Ghiaurov, Mara Zampieri and Sona Ghazarian. There are arias, duets and ensembles by Wagner, Mozart, Strauss, Donizetti, Offenbach, Verdi, Bizet, Rossini and Dvorák. Gianni Paggi directed the video. Color. 92 minutes. VAI video.

1993 Der Opernhaus Direktor

The Opera House Director is a Swiss documentary film about Alexander Pereira, director of the Zurich Opera House since 1991. Color. 29 minutes.

****

LATE ADDITIONS

The following videos were issued or seen too late for inclusion in the main section of the book. They will be integrated into the text in the next edition.

1996 The Art of Singing: Golden Voices of the Century

A superb British collection of opera singers on film and video. It begins with Caruso, has memorable Vitaphone films of Martinelli and de Luca, features Ponselle's *Carmen* screen test and Callas's Lisbon *Traviata* appearance and includes a range of others from Chaliapin and Tauber through Price, Tebaldi and Sutherland. There is informed commentary by Thomas Hampson, Kirk Browning, Magda Olivero and others The excerpts are of excellent quality and there are written notes by John Steane. The video is based on a BBC TV production directed by Donald Sturrock. Color and black & white. 116 minutes. Warner Music (England) video.

1996 Legends of Opera

An American collection of singers on films and video comparable to the above and including some of the same scenes with Caruso, Ponselle, Callas, Tetrazzini and Supervia. Also featured are Tebaldi, Siepi, Wunderlich, Christoff, Bergonzi, Milankov, Tucker, Gigli, Taddei and Del Monaco. Mostly black and white. 77 minutes. Legato Classics video.

1996 Classic Opera

A fine collection of television appearances by top opera singers, mostly in color with splendid sound. Featured in arias and duets are Leontyne Price, Roberta Peters, Robert Merrill, Beverly Sills, Anna Moffo, Richard Tucker, Maria Callas, Lily Pons, Joan Sutherland, Marilyn Horne, Renata Tebaldi, Franco Corelli, Eileen Farrell, Birgit Nilsson, Jan Peerce and Dorothy Kirstin. Sources and dates are not identified but most seem to have originated on the Ed Sullivan show. Color and black & white. 90 minutes. MIA (England) video.

1996 Theodora

Dawn Upshaw stars as Theodora in this Glyndebourne Festival Opera production of Handel's oratorio originally set in ancient Rome. Director Peter Sellars' has updated the story and placed it in modern America. David Daniels takes the role of Didymus, Frode Olsen is Valens, Richard Croft is Septimius and Lorraine Hunt is Irene. William Christie conducts the Orchestra of the Age of Enlightenment. Sellars also directed the video. Color. In English with English subtitles. 206 minutes. Warner Music (England) video.

OPERA ON CD-ROM

The newest format for opera on screen is the CD-ROM though it is still very much in its formative period. However, there are already at least five CD-ROMs featuring opera (including this book) and four of them feature opera performances on screen with sound. In addition most major libraries now have CD-ROM indexes of opera and music publications. Whether the CD-ROM format for opera will become widely popular is not yet clear but it is already proving useful and informative.

1996 The Viking Opera Guide on CD-ROM
This excellent reference book, first published in 1993 and now virtually a standard work, has also been issued as a CD-ROM. It includes 300 pictures of operas and composers and three hours of audio excerpts from operas. It also features Indexes, Timelines, Maps, audio Pronunciation guides, Glossary, Bibliography and full Search capabilities. *The Viking Opera Guide* was edited by Amanda Holden with Nicholas Kenyon and Stephen Walsh. Penguin Books.

1996 The Art of Singing
This extraordinary CD-ROM is both entertaining and informative. It centers around an imaginary Academy of Music through which you travel via mouse clicks. In the concert hall there is 56 minutes of music and texts and translations as well as information about the performers. You can visit Joan Sutherland's or John Tomlinson's dressing rooms and learn about their repertory, drop in on the canteen and hear operatic anecdotes and even play cards in the porter's lodge. It was written and directed by Wilf Judd and Felicity Hayes-McCoy and produced by Ben Whittam Smith. Notting Hill, London.

1997 Opera on Screen on CD-ROM
The first edition features only words but it has full search capability of every word that appears in the book. It can be accessed through the A-Z system as in the book, through an alphabetical Index of every film and video and by a full Word Search. The advantage of words only is that it is small enough to be copied onto virtually any hard disk for instant access. All entries can be printed. Future editions will probably feature still and moving images. Beachwood Press.

1997 Microsoft Encarta Encyclopedia
The Microsoft multi-media encyclopedia is strong on images and video and audio excerpts and includes a number of opera entries with sound and image. Aside from the general opera entry there are biographies of composers and opera singers with photographs and posters, audio excerpts from selected operas and arias performed by singers from Enrico Caruso to Marian Anderson. Microsoft Corporation.

1997 Placido Domingo on CD-ROM
Placido Domingo appears to be the first opera singer featured solo on an operatic CD-ROM. Though not yet issued at the time of going to press, it is to include original audio and video material as well as excerpts from previous performances, behind-the-scenes interview material and background information. It is being published by Calliope Media. EMI Classics.

SELECTIVE BIBLIOGRAPHY - OPERA ON SCREEN

There is currently no substantial bibliography of publications relating to opera on the screen. This selective and lightly annotated bibliography is only a preliminary effort but it may be helpful to those interested in obtaining further information about opera and opera music featured in films, television programs and videos. It does not include most of the reviews of individual films or operas or indeed every available general article but hopefully it includes the most useful and relevant.

The primary sources of information about opera in the movies are national film catalogs, film festival catalogs, reviews in publications like *Variety* and *The New York Times* and book and magazine articles on opera and film. The primary sources of information about opera on television and video are the videos and programs themselves when available, opera magazine reviews, *Variety* reviews, the Museum of Television and Radio database and opera on video/laser publications and catalogs. Most film books and biographies and some television books contain information about opera and operetta on the screen. Most opera reference books have an entry on opera on the screen, the most helpful being *The New Grove Dictionary of Opera* which has articles on film, filming, videotaping and television plus information about TV operas in composer biographies.

1. OPERA ON FILM

AFI National Film Theater. *Opera on Film* program booklet. Washington, DC, 1974

Ainsley, Rob & Neil Evans (editors). *Music at the Movies: 100 Greatest Classical Cuts. Classic CD* magazine special issue. September 1995.

Anderson, Gillian B. *Music for Silent Films 1894-1929, A Guide.* Library of Congress, Washington, 1988..

Anderson, James. "Opera films." *Harper Dictionary of Opera and Operetta.* HarperCollins, New York, 1989.

Andreevsky, Alexander von. "Was soll der Opernfilm." *Weser Zeitung*, Bremen, May 15, 1930.

Ardoin, John. "Operatic Shadows." *The Opera Quarterly*, Autumn 1988 (opera singers in the movies)

Atkins, Irene Kahn. *Source Music in Motion Pictures.* Associated University Presses, East Brunswick, 1983. (information about operas composed for movies)

Ball, Robert Hamilton. *Shakespeare on Silent Film.* George Allen and Unwin, London, 1968. (information about Shakespeare operas in the silent era)

Barcelona Filmoteca. *Òpera al Cinema.* 1981 program booklet with essays on individual opera films.

Barrios, Richard. *A Song in the Dark, The Birth of the Musical Film.* Oxford University Press, 1995.

Batchelor, Joy. "From *Aida* to *Zauberflöte*,". *Screen*, xxv/3 1984.

Bauer, L. "Twice Told Tales: Translating Opera into Film." *Theatre Arts*, xxxv/6, 1951.

Bebb, Richard. *Opera and the Cinema.* National Film Theatre program booklet. London, 1969

Berchtold, William E. "Grand Opera Goes Hollywood." *North American Review*, February 1935.

Beyle, Claude with Jean-Michel Brèque, Michèle Friche, Philipe Godefroid and Fernand Leclercq. "Trente Classiques du Film-Opéra," Duault, *Cinéma et* Opéra, op cit. (essays on 30 opera films)

BFI National Film Theatre. *London International Opera Festival* annual programs.

Biamonte, S. G. (editor). *Musica e Film.* Edizioni dell'Ateneo, Rome, 1959. (articles about opera and operetta on film with filmography of opera movies)

Bierstadt, E. H. "Opera in Moving Pictures." *Opera Magazine*, October 1915.

Boll, André. "L'Opéra Cinématographique." *Musica* No. 38. Paris , May 1957. (UNESCO congress on "L'Opéra à la radio, à la télévision et dans le film")

Bourre, Jean-Paul. *Opéra et Cinéma.* Editions Artefact, Paris, 1987. (history of the opera film)

Breque, Jean-Michel. "Le Film-opera: vers une forme cinématographique autonome." Duault, *Cinéma et Opéra*, op cit.

Brook, Peter. *The Shifting Point: Theatre, Film, Opera 1946-1987.* Harper & Row, New York, 1987.

Buchau, Stephanie von. "Jean-Pierre Ponnelle: The Sensual Stylist." *Opera News*, September 1977.

Burton, Jack. *The Blue Book of Hollywood Musicals.* Century House, New York, 1953. (songs in Hollywood films from 1927 to 1952 including those performed by opera singers)

Cadars, Pierre. "Confession partielle d'un amoureux ambivalent." Dualt, *Cinéma et Opéra*, op cit.

Cannes Film Festival. *Cinéma et Opéra.* May 1987 program for opera film series.

Castello, Giulio Cesare. "Canzoni, riviste, operette nella storia del cinema." Biamonte, *Musica e Film,* op. cit. (survey of film operettas and musicals)

Citron, Marcia J. "A Night at the Cinema: Zeffirelli's *Otello* and the Genre of Film Opera." *The Musical Quarterly,* Winter 1994.

Colpi, Henri. *Defense et Illustration de la Musique dans le Film.* Sociètè d'Èdition, Lyon, 1963. (chapters devoted to opera, operetta and composer biographies on the screen)

Comuzio, Ermanno. "Il Film-opera." *Colonna Sonora.* Formichiere, Rome, 1980. (essay on opera and film)

Comuzio, Ermanno. "Opéra et Cinéma: des origines aux années soixante." Dualt, *Cinéma et Opéra,* op cit.

Crowther, Bosley. "Opera on the Screen." *New York Times,* Nov. 14, 1954. (Film vs. television opera)

De Fries, Tjitte. "Sound-on-Disc Films 1900-1926." FIAF Journal, 1980. (Early sound opera films)

Deslandes, Jacques. "Le Phono-Cinéma-Théâtre." *Le Cinéma d'Aujord'hui,* August 1976

Duault, Alain & Claude Beylie (editors). *Cinéma et Opéra.* Double issue of *L'Avant-Scene Opéra* 98 and *L'Avant-Scene Cinéma* 360. Paris, 1987. (opera film articles and opera filmography)

Durgat, Raymond. "Eternal Triangle: Opera, Film, Realism." *Monthly Film Bulletin,* October 1990.

Evidon, Richard. "Film." Sadie, *New Grove Dictionary of Opera,* op cit. (history of opera on film)

Ewen, David "Opera Performances: Motion Pictures." *The New Encyclopedia of the Opera,* Hill and Wang, New York, 1971

Fawkes, Richard. "Star Turns." *Opera Now,* March 1994. (opera singers in the movies)

----------------------. "Opera for the Masses." *Opera Now,* April 1994. (article on opera movies)

Franklin, Peter. "Movies as Opera (Behind the Great Divide)" in Tambling, *A Night in at the Opera,* op cit.

Gallone, Carmine. "Il Valore della music nel film e l'evoluzione dello spettacolo lirico sullo schermo." Biamonte, *Musica e Film,* op cit. (opera film director on opera in the cinema)

Garel, A. and M. Salmon. "Cinéma et Opéra." *La Revue du Cinéma* No. 429, Paris, 1987.

Giulianio, Elisabeth. "Opéra et Cinéma, un Uníon Légitime." Dualt, *Cinéma et Opéra,* op cit.

Grief, Lyndal. *The Operas of Gian Carlo Menotti, 1937-1972: A Selective Bibliography.* Scarecrow Press, Metuchen, 1974. (includes lists of articles about Menotti's screen operas)

Grodman, Jeanette & Maria De Monte. "Opera of the Future: Hollywood's Opera Films." *Opera News,* April 18, 1955.

Hamilton, Mary. "Opera on Film." *A-Z of Opera.* Facts on File, Oxford, 1990

Heinsheimer, Hans W. "Film Opera - Screen vs. Stage." *Modern Music,* March-April 1931.

Helm, Everett. "International Conference on Opera in Radio, TV and Film." *Musical Times,* February 1957.

Huckvale, David. "The Composing Machine: Wagner and Popular Culture" in Tambling, *A Night in at the Opera,* op cit.

Huntley, John. "Screen Opera." *British Film Music.* Skelton Robinson, London, 1947.

Jahn, Melvin. "Sight and Sound: Laserdisc Wish List," *Opera News,* Dec. 23, 1995. (operas on laser)

Kalbus, Oskar. "Der Operettenfilm." *Vom Werden Deutscher Filmkunst.* Altona, Berlin, 1935.

--------------------"Opern auf der Leinwand." Ibid.

Kauffman, Stanley." The Abduction from the Theater: Mozart Opera on Film." *On Mozart,* edited by James M. Morris. Cambridge University, Cambridge 1994. (on three Mozart opera films)

Kiepura, Jan. "L'Opera Lirica sullo Schermo." *Cinema* (Rome) No. 23, 1937.

Kobal, John. *Gotta Sing, Gotta Dance.* Hamlyn, London, 1977. (chapter on opera singers in Hollywood)

Kracauer, Siegfried. "Opera on the Screen." *Film Culture,* March-April 1955.

Lacombe, Alain & Claude Rocle. *La Musique du Film* Editions van de Velde, Paris, 1979. (biofilmographies of composers including Copland, Walton, Weill, , etc.)

Large, Brian. "Filming, videotaping." Sadie, *New Grove Dictionary of Opera,* op cit. (video opera director on techniques of filming and videotaping opera)

Lee, M. Owen. "I Heard It at the Movies." *The Opera Quarterly,* Spring 1986 and Winter 1991-1992. (survey of opera scenes in non-operatic movies)

Lehár, Franz. "L'Operetta Cinematografica." *Cinema* (Rome) No. 23, 1937.

Leonard, William Torbert. *Theatre: Stage to Screen to Television.* Scarecrow Press, Metuchen, 1981. (operas and operettas that were staged, filmed and televised)

Lunghi, Fernando Ludovico. "Il Film-opera." Biamonte, *Musica e Film,* op cit. (history of opera on film)

Mackay, Harper. "Going Hollywood." *Opera News,* April 13, 1991. (opera singers in Hollywood)

----------------------. "Reel Sound." *Opera News,* Feb. 15, 1992. (opera composers in the movies)

618

Manvell, Roger with John Huntley. *The Technique of Film Music.* Revised by Richard Arnell & Peter Day. Focal Press, London, 1975. (sections on opera films)

Musical America. "Problem of Film Opera Unresolved." March 1956.

Muziektheater, Amsterdam. *Bulletin Opera*, May 1994. (issue devoted to opera on film programs)

Myers, Eric. "Hollywood Goes to the Opera." *Opera News*, Jan. 8, 1994.

Parish, James Robert & Michael R. Pitts. *Hollywood Songsters, A Biographical Dictionary.* Garland, NY, 1991. (entries on opera singers in Hollywood)

Parker, David L. "Golden Voices, Silver Screen: Opera Singers as Movie Stars." *The Quarterly Journal of the Library of Congress*, Summer-Fall 1980 (also include European opera films)

Pasternak, Joe. *Easy the Hard Way.* W. H. Allen, London, 1956. (life of opera/operetta film producer)

Perlmutter, Donna. "Camera Angles: Film directors are bringing a cinematic eye to the opera stage." *Opera News*, Feb. 18, 1995.

Philharmonic Hall, Lincoln Center. *Opera on Film.* Program booklet for July 15-27, 1970.

Rabenalt, Arthur Maria. *Der Operetten-Bildband Bühne Film Fernsehen.* Olms Press, Hildesheim, 1980. (history of German operettas on film and on television)

Rattner, David S. "Opera and Films." *Film Music*, Spring 1956.

Robertson, Patrick. "Opera Films." *Guinness Film Facts and Feats.* Guinness Books, Enfield, 1985. (descriptions of the first opera films)

Rockwell, John. "Why Does Opera Lure Filmmakers?" *New York Times*, May 8, 1983.

Rosson, Alex. "An Unequal Partner Raises Its Lovely Face." *New York Times*, March 12, 1995.

Sadie, Stanley (editor). *The New Grove Dictionary of Opera.* Macmillan Press, London, 1992.

Serceau, M. and H. Puiseaux. "Cinéma et Opéra." *La Revue du Cinéma* No. 430, Paris, 1987.

Stanbrook, Alan. "The Sight of Music. "*Sight and Sound*, lvi/2, 1987 (essay on opera films)

Stein, Louise. "Pocket Divas and Prima Donnas." London NFT Program. (opera divas in Hollywood)

Swed, Mark. "Lights...Aria...Action." *Los Angeles Times*, Feb. 13, 1994.

Tambling, Jeremy. *Opera, Ideology and Film.* Manchester, 1957.

-----------------*Night in at the Opera, A: Media representations of opera.* (editor). Arts Council of England/ John Libbey, London. 1994. (13 essays about screen opera plus bibliography)

-----------------"Introduction: Opera in the Distraction Culture." Ibid.

Toscan du Plantier, Daniel. "Le Cinéma est l'(ardente) obligation de l'opéra" in Duault, *Cinéma et Opéra.*

Trask, C. Hooper. "Berlin turns to the Film Operetta." *Variety*, Nov. 13, 1932.

Turconi, David, Catherine Schapira & Michel Pazdro. "Filmographie: Cinéma et Opéra: du film muet à la video" in Duault, *Cinéma et Opéra*, op cit. (opera filmography up to 1987)

Uselton, Roi A. "Opera Singers on the Screen." *Films in Review*, April, May, June-July 1967 (comprehensive three-part article on opera singers in Hollywood)

Umshau. "Film-Opera und Musik." Frankfurt, 1921.

Villien, Bruno. "Opéra et Cinéma: le Suspense Continu." Duault, *Cinéma et Opéra*, op cit.

Warrack, John and Ewan West. "Film opera." *The Concise Oxford Dictionary of Opera.* Oxford University Press, Oxford, 1992. (brief history of opera in the cinema)

Weir, Judith. "Memoirs of an Accidental Film Artist" in Tambling, *A Night in at the Opera*, op cit.

William Shaman. "The Operatic Vitaphone Shorts." *ARSC Journal*, Spring 1951.

Wlaschin, Ken. "Success Drives the Reluctant Actor Away." Rome *Daily American*, April 7, 1963.

Zeffirelli, Franco." Une Aventure exaltante mais risquée." Duault, *Cinéma et Opéra*, op cit.

Zinger, Pablo. "An Operatic Armada Sweeps Ashore." *New York Times*, August 11, 1996. (on zarzuelas)

2. OPERA ON TELEVISION AND VIDEO

Adler, Peter Herman. "Opera on Television: The Beginning of an Era." *Musical America*, February 1952.

Allen, Peter. "Broadcasting." *The Metropolitan Opera Encyclopedia.* David Hamilton (editor). Simon and Schuster, New York, 1987. (on Met telecasts and broadcasts)

Almquist, Sharon G. (editor). *Opera Mediagraphy: Video Recordings and Motion Pictures.* Greenwood, Westport, 1993. (lists credits of operas on film and video)

Annals of the Metropolitan Opera: Complete Chronicle of Performances and Artists. G. K. Hall, Boston, 1989.

Ardoin, John. "Opera and Television." *The Opera Quarterly*, Spring 1983.

------------------ *The Stages of Menotti.* Doubleday, Garden City, 1985. (chapters on TV operas)

Barnes, John. *Manual of Television Opera Production.* CBC, Toronto, 1975.

Barnes, Jennifer. "Television Opera: A Non History" in Tambling, *A Night in at the Opera*, op cit.

Bate, Philip. "Ballet, Opera and Music." *Television in the Making*, edited by Paul Rotha. Focal Press, London, 1956. (on producing opera at BBC Television)

Bernheimer, Martin. "TV Opera: The Great Debate." *Los Angeles Times*, Oct. 8, 1978.

Bertz-Dostal, H.. *Oper im Fernsehen*. Vienna, 1970

Blythe, Alan. *Opera on Video: The Essential Guide*. Kyle Cathie, London, 1995. (Selected reviews)

Brooks, Tim and Earle Marsh. *The Complete Directory to Prime Time Network TV Shows*. Ballantine Books, New York, 1963. (entries on operatic programs)

Brunel, Claude. "Opéra et Télévision." *Cinéma et Opéra*. Op cit.

Burke, Richard C.: *A History of Televised Opera in the United States*. 1963 Michigan U. Ph.D. thesis.

------------------------"The NBC Opera Theater." *Journal of Broadcasting*, Winter 1965-66.

Cartier, R. "Producing Television Opera." *Opera*, May 1957

Croissant, Charles R. *Opera Performances in Video Format: a Check list of Commercially Released Recordings*. Music Library Association, Canton, MA, 1991.

Crutchfield, Will. "Karajan Faces Stiff Competition: Karajan." *New York Times*, July 18, 1993.

Dwyer, Edward J. *American Video Opera, An Introduction and Guidebook to its Production*. 1963 Columbia University Ph.D. thesis.

Eaton, Quaintance: "Great Opera Houses: NBC-TV." *Opera News*, Feb. 8, 1964.

------------------------ "Television Audiences Sees First Video Opera." *Musical America*, Dec. 15, 1948.

Englander, Roger. *Opera, What's All the Screaming About?* Walker, New York, 1994.

Ewen, David. "Opera Performance: Television." *The New Encyclopedia of the Opera*, Hill and Wang, New York, 1971

Falkenburg, Claudia & Andrew Wolt. *A Really Big Show: A Visual History of the Ed Sullivan Show*. Viking Studio Books, New York 1992 (information on opera singers on show)

Fawkes, Richard. "Opera in View." *Opera Now*. (opera on screen review column)

Gelb, Arthur. "The Future of Video Opera." *New York Times*, Dec. 28, 1952.

Graf, Herbert. *Opera for the People*. University of Minnesota Press, Minneapolis 1951. (chapter on TV opera in the 1940s by NBC TV producer)

Grimes, William. "Some Real Oldies Hit the Video Charts." *New York Times*, Aug. 18, 1992. (opera videos)

Gutman, John. "The Case for Opera on Television." *Theatre Arts*, December 1953.

Halliwell, Leslie. *Halliwell's Teleguide*. Granada, London, 1979. (operatic programs)

Hornak, Richard. "Taster's Choice." *Opera News* (column of opera on video reviews)

Internationales Musikzentrum. *Opera in Radio, TV and Film*. 1956 catalog, Salzburg.

Jahn, Melvin. *Tower Records Guide to the Classics on Video*. Tower Classics, Berkeley, November 1995. (opera and classical music videos and lasers on sale through Tower)

Johnson, Lawrence B. "When the Best Seat in the House Happens to Be at Home." *New York Times*, July 28, 1996. (on the joys of music and opera on the laserdisc)

Johnson, Trevor. "Diva delights." *Sight and Sound*, November 1993. (reviews of operas on video)

Kirstein, Lincoln. "Television Opera in the USA." *Opera*, April 1952.

Kraft, Rebecca. *The Arts on Television 1976-1990*. NEA, Washington, 1991. (operatic programs)

Kretschmer, Joan Thomson. "Face the Music." *Opera News*, June 1990. (on television opera)

Kuney, Jack. "Calling the Shots at the Metropolitan Opera." *Television Quarterly*, Number 4, 1984. (interview with Kirk Browning)

Laser Video File. New Visions, Westwood, NJ (semi-annual catalog with opera section)

Lee, M. O. "Video: Live by Laser from the Met." *Opera Quarterly* 4, 1986.

Levine, Robert. *Guide to Opera and Dance on Videocassette*. Consumers Union, Mount Vernon, 1989. (selective reviews of operas available on video)

Lipman, Samuel. "On the Air." *Commentary*, April 1980. (survey of TV opera of the period)

Marchetti, Giuseppe, Luciano Pinelli & Gabriele Rifilato. *VHS Film Guida*. Nuovi Eri, Rome, 1995. (catalog of videos available in Italy with opera section)

Marill, Alvin H. *Movies Made for Television: 1964-1986*. Baseline, New York, 1987.

McKee, David. "Video Trek: Lost In Space." *Opera News*, June 1995. (on the opera video industry)

McNeil, Alex. *Total Television*. Penguin Books, New York, 1984. (entries on operatic programs)

Museum of Broadcasting: *Leonard Bernstein, The Television Work*. 1985 catalog, New York.

--------------------------------*Metropolitan Opera: The Radio and Television Legacy*. 1986 catalog.

O'Connor, John J.. "Putting Life into *Live from the Met.*" *New York Times,* March 20, 1980. (Brian Large)

Phillips, Harvey E. "The Basics." *Opera News,* August 1991. (On collecting opera videos)

Ponnelle, Jean-Pierre. "Opera on the Small Screen." Essay in video of ZDF's 1988 *Marriage of Figaro.*

Pratt, Douglas. *The Laser Video Disc Companion.* Baseline Books, New York, 1995. (Includes reviews of operas available on laserdisc)

Price, Walter: "Before MTV, There Was Opera." *Los Angeles Times,* Nov. 1, 1992. (on *Voice of Firestone*)

----------------- "Voice of Firestone." *Opera News,* Dec. 8 1990. (*Voice of Firestone* telecasts and videos)

Reed, Robert M. & Maxine K. *The Encyclopedia of Television, Cable and Video.* Van Nostrand Reinhold, New York, 1992.(operatic information)

Riley, Brooks. "Camera Angles." *Opera News,* June 1990. (Differing styles of TV opera directors Kirk Browning, Brian Large and Peter Sellars)

Rockwell, John. "The Impact of TV on Opera." *New York Times,* Jan. 25, 1981.

Rohan, Michael Scott (editor). *The Classical Video Guide.* Victor Gollancz, London, 1994. (Selective reviews of opera videos available in England)

Rose, Brian G.: *Television and the Performing Arts.* Greenwood Press, Westport, 1986. (Includes comprehensive history of opera on American television with bibliography)

------------------ *Televising the Performing Arts: Interviews with Merrill Brockway, Kirk Browning, and Roger Englunder.* Greenwood Press, Westport, 1992

Rothstein,. Edward. "The Sight of Music." *The New Republic,* Sept. 2, 1991. (about opera on video)

SACIS International. *Straight to the Heart.* 1995 Italian TV catalogue with opera programs.

Salter, Lionel: "The Birth of TV Opera." *Opera.* March 1977. (BBC TV opera history 1936-1939)

----------------- "The Infancy of TV Opera." *Opera.* April 1977. (continuation of above article)

----------------- "Opera on Television." *Opera,* April 1957.

----------------- "Television." Sadie, *New Grove Dictionary of Opera,* op cit. (history of opera on television)

Schwartz, Lloyd. "Opera on Television." *The Atlantic,* January 1983.

Sykes, Margaret. *The Classical Catalog.* Gramophone, Harrow, 1995 (includes opera videos in England)

Tambling, Jeremy. "Revisions And Re-vampings: Wagner, Marschner and Mozart on Television and Video" in Tambling, *A Night in at the Opera,* op cit.

Taubman, Howard. "Televised Opera." *New York Times,* April 24, 1949.

UCLA Film and Television Archive. *Hallmark of Fame: The First Forty Years.* 1991 catalog, Los Angeles,.

Unitel. *Unitel Television Catalog,* 1986. Sections on TV "Operas " and "Operettas."

Verna, Tony. *Live TV, An Inside Look at Directing and Producing.* Focal Press, Boston, 1987. (With articles on TV opera by director Kirk Browning and producer John Goberman)

Warrack, John and Ewan West. "Television Opera." *The Concise Oxford Dictionary of Opera.* Oxford University Press, Oxford, 1992.

Wells, William H. "Opera Video." *Opera Monthly.* (column of opera video reviews)

Wexler, J. "Opera Taken Out of Mothballs, Given Exciting Vitality by NBC." *Billboard,* Oct. 13, 1951.

White, Jonathan. "Opera, Politics and Television: bel canto by Satellite" in Tambling, *A Night in at the Opera.*

Willey, George A. "Opera on Television." *The Music Review,* May 1959. (survey of TV opera)

3. INDIVIDUAL OPERAS & FILMS

Amadeus - *Amadeus.* Peter Shaffer. Signet, New York, 1984. (Film edition with photos)

- *The Mozart Firmament.* Charles Kiselyak. 1996 (Booklet on film in laser edition)

Amahl and the Night Visitors - *New York Times* critic Olin Downes makes TV opera history:

---- "Menotti Opera, the First for TV, Has Its Premiere." Dec. 25, 1951. (front page)

-----"Menotti's *Amahl* is a Historic Step in the Development of a New Medium." Dec. 30, 1951.

Bayou Legend, A - "A Bayou Legend." *Opera News,* June 1981. (William Grant Still opera telecast)

Beggar's Opera, The - "Beggar's Opera: A British Musical Film Version of Gay's Work." A.H. Weiler. *New York Times,* Aug. 30, 1953

Bed and Sofa - "New Life Off Broadway for Soviet Film of the 20s." Vincent Canby. *New York Times,* Feb. 2, 1996.

Belle et la Bête, La - "Glass Meets Cocteau: Beauty or Beast." Article by Chris Pasel & Kenneth Turan. *Los Angeles Times,* Nov. 11, 1995.

Billy Budd - "Billy Budd Scores in TV Bow." Olin Downes. *New York Times,* Oct. 20 ,1952.

Bohème, La - *"La Bohème*: Fidelité et Originalité." Luigi Comencini. *Cinéma et Opéra.* Op cit.

Boris Godunov - "A Propros de *Boris Godunov*," Andrzej Wajda. *Cinéma et Opéra*. Op cit.
Carmen:
- "The Carmen Connection." Glenn Loney. *Opera News*, Sept. 1983. (Peter Brook's *Carmen*)
- "Carmen Jones: un film d'Otto Preminger." Olivier Eyquem. *Avant-Scene du Cinéma*, July-Sept. 1978.
- "Fatal Charms." Peter Conrad. *Opera News*, 1986. (Carmen in the movies)
- "Gypsy." Leslie Rubinstein. *Opera News*, October 1984. (Francesco Rosi film)
Dalibor - "Prague." *Opera*, April 1957 (About film of the Smetana opera)
Don Giovanni:
---"Don Juan." David S. Rattner. *Film Music*, Jan-Feb. 1956. (Austrian film of opera)
 ---"Liebermann, Losey and the Libertine: *Don Giovanni* on film." Roland Gelatt. *Opera News*, Nov. 1979.
Dream of Valentino, The - Washington Opera program 1994:
----"Creating the Dream." Charles Nolte .
----"The Memory, The Movie Star, The Myth." Ken Wlaschin.
Elektra - "*Elektra* on the Screen." *Moving Picture World*, April 23, 1910. (Vitagraph film of opera)
Eugene Onegin - "Eugene Onegin." R. A. Tuggle. *Opera News*, Dec. 12, 1959. (Soviet film of opera)
Fitzcarraldo - *Fitzcarraldo, The Original Story*. Werner Herzog. Fjord Press, San Francisco, 1982.
Jean d'Arc au Bucher - "Give It a Hearing: Public Should be Allowed to see Film Version of Claudel-
        Honneger work." Howard Taubman. *New York Times*, May 22, 1955.
Lucia di Lammermoor - "The Maddening Popularity Swings of Lucia dì Lammermoor." Stephanie von
        Buchau. Los Angeles Opera Program 1994. (*Lucia* scene in *When Angels Fear to Tread*)
Macbeth - "Macbeth, la terrible parenthese." Director Claude d'Anna on his film. *Opéra et Cinéma*. Op cit.
Marriage, The - "Martinu Opera Scores in TV bow." Olin Downes. *New York Times*, Feb. 8, 1953.
Marilyn - "New Milieu for Monroe: Some Like It Operatic." Edward Rothstein. *New York Times*, Oct. 8,
        1993.
McTeague - "Tarnishing the Gilded Age: Altman Directs *McTeague*." Carrie Rickey. *Opera News*, 1994
Meeting Venus - "Close Encounters." Glenn Close. *Opera News*, November 1991. (film *Meeting Venus*)
Medium, The - "Film Version of *The Medium* directed by Menotti in Rome." Robert Sabin. *Musical America*,
April 15, 1951.
My Heart's in the Highlands - "Saroyan Story Charms as Opera." Raymond Ericson. *New York Times*,
        March 18, 1970.
Night at the Opera, A. - "The Singing Salami: Unsystematic Reflections on the Marx Brothers' *A Night at the
        Opera*." Lawrence Kramer in Tambling, *A Night in at the Opera*, op cit.
Nixon in China - "TV Adds New Dimension to *Nixon in China*." Alan Rich. *Los Angeles Herald Examiner*,
        April 10 1988.
Orphée - "Mood Painting." Mark Swed. *Opera News*, May 1993. (Philip Glass opera)
Perfect Lives - *Perfect Lives, an Opera*. Robert Ashley. Burning Books, San Francisco, 1991.
Porgy and Bess
    - *The Life and Times of Porgy and Bess*. Hollis Alpert. Knopf, New York, 1990. (Goldwyn film)
    - "It Takes a Long Pull..." Richard Fawkes. *Opera Now*, Dec. 1993. (Trevor Nunn film)
    - "Porgy in Hollywood." Harper Mackay. *Opera News*, Jan. 20, 1990. (Goldwyn film)
Ring of the Nibelungen
    - "Live from Valhalla." Fred Plotkin. *Opera News*, June 1990. (Met videotaping of Wagner *Ring* cycle)
    - "Ringing Response, A." Margaret Betley. *Opera News*, Jan 5, 1991. (Met *Ring* on television)
    - *Ring Resounding*. John Culshaw. Viking, New York, 1967. (Includes film *The Golden Ring*)
Rosa, A Horse Drama - "A Horse's Tale." Andrew Clements. *The Guardian*. Nov. 5, 1994.
Tales of Hoffmann, The - *The Tales of Hoffmann: A Study of a Film*. Monk Gibbon. London, Saturn, 1951.
Threepenny Opera, The - "De la pièce et du film..." Lotte Eisner on Pabst. *Cahiers du Cinéma*, June 1954.
Three Tenors series - "The Three Tenors Juggernaut." Ralph Blumenthal. *New York Times*, March 24, 1996.
Trovatore, Il
    - "*Trovatore* Begins Lyric Reform." *The Moving Picture World*, March 4, 1911.
    - "Film Music." Lawrence Morton. *Hollywood Quarterly*, Summer 1950. (Problems of filming in Italy)
Turandot - "Opera and Post-modern Cultural Politics: *Turandot* in Beijing." Ping-Hui Liao in Tambling, *A
        Night in at the Opera*, op cit.
War Requiem - *War Requiem, the Film*. Derek Jarman. Faber and Faber, London, 1989.
Willie Stark - "Hot Southern Politics Hits High-C on TV." Cynthia Lilley. *Los Angeles Reader*, Oct. 16, 1981.

4. INDIVIDUAL SINGERS & DIRECTORS

Alberghetti - "She Keeps Her Music Life in Tune." Jack Hawn. *Los Angeles Times*, May 1, 1985

Anderson - *Marian Anderson*. Anne Tedards. Chelsea House, New York, 1988.

Bertolucci - "The National Dimension? Verdi and Bernardo Bertolucci" in Tambling, *Night in at the Opera*.

Callas - "TV Honors a Grand Diva in a Grand Way." Tim Page. *New York Times*, Dec. 11, 1983

Caruso - "Two Opera Stars in Silent Films," *New York Times*, Dec. 2, 1918. (Caruso and Farrar)

Cebotari - "Maria Cebotari." John Steane. *Opera News*, March 1994

Chaliapin - *Chaliapin, an autobiography*. Nina Froud & James Hanley (editors). Macdonald, London, 1968

Domingo - *My First Forty Years*. Placido Domingo. New York, 1983.

Durbin - *The Child Stars*. Norman J. Zierold. Chapter on Durbin. Coward-McCann, New York, 1965.

Eggerth - "Queen of the Screen." Brendan Carroll on Marta Eggerth. *Opera Now*, October 1995

Ellis - "I Sang with Caruso." Michael Scott on Mary Ellis. *Opera News*, June 1988.

Farrar - *Always First Class: The Career of Geraldine Farrar*. E. Nash. Washington, 1982.

Hendricks - Mimi with a Method," Barbara Hendricks and *La Bohème* film. *Opera News*, August 1988.

Jepson - "Another View," F. Paul Driscoll. Helen Jepson in *The Goldwyn Follies*. *Opera News*, Feb. 18,1995.

Jeritza -"Maria Jeritza." Gustl Breuer. *Opera News*, September 1982.

Kiepura - "Magnetic Pole." Career of Jan Kiepura. *Opera Now*, 1984

Lanza - *Mario Lanza*. Derek Mannering. Robert Hale, London, 1993.

Lewis - "An American Tragedy." Michael B. Dougan on Mary Lewis. *Opera News*, July 1984.

McCormack - "John McCormack a Hit in Movietone." Mordaunt Hall. *New York Times*, March 12, 1930.

MacDonald & Eddy - *The Films of Jeanette MacDonald and Nelson Eddy*. Philip Castanza. Citadel Press, Secaucus, 1978.

Mariano - *Luis Mariano, Le Prince de Lumiere*. Daniel Ringold, Philippe Guiboust et al. TFI, Paris, 1995

McCracken - Wlaschin, Ken. "The Yanks are Coming to top the Bill." Rome *Daily American*, Jan. 6. 1963.

Melba -"Peach of a Diva, PBS miniseries salutes Nellie Melba." Jamie James, *Opera News*, Jan. 7, 1989

Melchior - "Lauritz Melchior" in *Hollywood Songsters*. Op cit.

Mojica - "Watch this Hombre." Photoplay, January 1930. (About José Mojica in Hollywood)

Moore - *You're Only Human Once*. Grace Moore. Doubleday, Doran. Garden City, 1944.

Novello - *Ivor*. Sandy Wilson. Information on his films. London, Joseph, 1975.

Novotná - "Jarmila Novotná 1907-1994." Walter Price. *Opera News*, April 2, 1994.

Pavarotti - "Pavarotti Goes Hollywood." Leslie Rubinstein on *Yes, Giorgio*. *Opera News*, September 1982.

Pons - "Lily Pons" in *Hollywood Songsters*. Op cit.

Ponselle - "The Ponselle Legacy." George Jellinek on Rosa Ponselle. *Opera News*, March 12 1977.

Printemps - "Yvonne Printemps - 100 Years of Springtime." Patrick O'Connor. *Opera*, July 1994.

Schroeter - Excess and Yearning: Operatic in Werner Schroeter's Cinema." Tambling, *Night in at the Opera*.

Schwarzkopf - *Elisabeth Schwarzkopf*. Alan Jefferson. Northeastern University Press, 1996.

Stevens - "Risë." Martin Mayer on career of Risë Stevens.. *Opera News*, Dec. 24, 1988.

Tagliavini - *Ferruccio Tagliavini, L'Uomo, la Voce*. Umberto Bonafini.Magis Books, Reggio Emilia, 1993.

Tauber - Tamino and Beyond." Michael Scott on Richard Tauber's career. *Opera News*, August 1991.

Tibbett -"Lawrence Tibbett" in *Hollywood Songsters*. Op cit.

Turner - "Call Me Madame." Brian Kelly on Claramae Turner. *Opera News*, Dec. 24, 1994.

Visconti - *Screen of Time, A: A Study of Luchino Visconti*. Monica Stirling. Secker & Warburg, London, 1979.

Van Dam - "Long Distance Master." Marylis Sevilla-Gonza on José Van Dam. *Opera News*, Jan 22, 1994.

Vishnevskaya - *Galina, A Russian Story*. Galina Vishnevskaya. Harcourt Brace Jovanovich, NY, 1984.

Zeffirelli - *Zeffirelli, The Autobiography of Franco Zeffirelli*. Weidenfeld and Nicolson, London, 1986.

5. PERIODICALS WITH SCREEN OPERA REVIEWS

Atlantic, The
Avant-Scene Cinéma, L'
Avant-Scene Opéra, L'
BBC Music Magazine
Billboard
Classic Images
Classical Pulse

Film Facts
Film Music
Gramophone
Hollywood Reporter, The
Journal of Broadcasting
Monthly Film Bulletin
Motion Picture Exhibitor
Motion Picture Herald Production Digest
Musica
Musical America
Nation, The
Newsweek
New Yorker, The
New York Times, The: Directory of the Film. Arno Press, New York. 1971
--------------------------*Film Reviews:* 1913 to 1980 (ten volumes). Arno Press.
Opera
Opera, L'
Opera International
Opera Monthly
Opera News
Opera Now
Opera Quarterly.
Operétte
Saturday Review
Television Quarterly
Theatre Arts
Time
Variety Film Reviews:
___1907 - 1986. (nineteen volumes). Garland Press, New York.
___1987 - 1992. (six volumes). R. W. Bower, New Providence.
---- 1993 - 1996.
Variety Television Reviews, 1905-1986. (eleven volumes). Garland, New York, 1988.

6. FILM CATALOGS

American films

American Film-Index 1908-1915. Amahl Lauritzen & Gunnar Lundquist. Film-Index, Stockholm, 1976
American Film Industry: A Historical Dictionary, The. Anthony Slide. Greenwood Press, Westport 1986
American Film Institute Catalog of Motion Pictures, The:
 - *Film Beginnings, 1893 - 1910.* (two volumes). Elias Savada (compiler), Scarecrow Press, Metuchen, 1995.
 - *Feature Films 1911-1920.* (two volumes). Patricia King Hanson (editor), UC Press, Berkeley, 1988.
 - *Feature Films 1921 -1930.* (two volumes). Kenneth W. Munden (editor), R. W. Bowker, New York, 1971.
 - *Feature Films 1931-1940.* (three volumes). Patricia King Hanson (editor), UC Press, Berkeley, 1993.
 - *Feature Films 1961- 1970.* (in two volumes). Richard P. Krafsur (editor), R. W. Bowker, New York, 1976.
Biograph Bulletins 1896-1908. Kemp R. Niven. Locare, Los Angeles, 1971.
Feature Films, 1940-1949, A United States Filmography. Alan G Fetrow. McFarland, Jefferson, 1994.
First Twenty Years, The: A Segment of Film History. Kemp R. Niven. Locare, Los Angeles, 1968.
Great Movie Shorts, The. Leonard Maltin. Bonanza Books, New York, 1972.

Animated films

Animated Film, The. Ralph Stephenson. Tantivy Press, London, 1973.
British Animated Films 1895-1985, A Filmography. Denis Gifford, McFarland, Jefferson 1987.
Fifty Greatest Cartoons. Edited by Jerry Beck. Turner Publishing, Atlanta, 1994.
Full Length Animated Features Films. Bruno Edera. Focas Press. London, 1977.
Looney Tunes and Merrie Melodies. Jerry Beck & Will Friedwald. Henry Holt, New York, 1989.

Argentina
Medio Signo de Cine: Argentina Sono Film. Claudio España. Editorial Abril, Buenos Aires, 1984.

Austria
Austrian Films. Annual catalogs. Austrian Film Commission, Vienna, 1987-1996
Österreicheschen Spielfilm der Stummfilmzeit (1907-1930). Walter Fritz. Austrian Film Archive, Vienna, 1967.
Österreicheschen Spielfilm der Tonfilmzeit (1929-1944). Walter Fritz. Austrian Film Archive, Vienna, 1968.

British films
British Film Catalogue: 1895-1985, The. Dennis Gifford. Facts on File, Oxford 1986.
British Film Catalogues. British Council, London. 1985 to 1996.
British Sound Films: The Studio Years 1928-1959. David Quinlan. B. T. Batsford, London 1984
History of the British Film, The:
    1896-1906. Rachel Low & Roger Manvell. Allen & Unwin, London, 1948.
    1906-1914. Rachel Low. Allen & Unwin, London, 1949
    1914-1918. Rachel Low. Allen & Unwin, London, 1948
    1918-1939. Rachel Low. Allen & Unwin, London, 1971.
Who's Who in British Cinema. Dennis Gifford. B. T. Batsford, London, 1978

Czechoslovakia
All the Bright Young Men and Women, History of the Czech Cinema. Josef Skvorecky. Take One, Toronto, 1971.
Outline of Czechoslovakian Cinema. Langdon Dewey. Informatics. London, 1971.

Denmark
Danske Titler og Biografier: Filmens Hvem-Hvad-Hvor. Bjorn Rasmussen. Politikens, Copenhagen 1968
Danish Films. Annual catalogs. Danish Film Institute. 1983 - 1996.

Finland
Finnish Cinema. Peter Cowie. VAPK Publishing, Helsinki 1990,
Finnish Films. Annual catalogs. Finnish Film Foundation. Helsinki, 1984-1996.

French films
Catalogue des Film Français de Long Métrage, Films de Fiction. Chirat, Raymond (editor).
    _____*1919 -1929.* Cinémathèque de Toulouse, 1984.
    _____*1929 -1939.* Cinémathèque Royale de Belgique, 1975.
    _____*1940 -1950.* Cinémathèque Municipale de Luxembourg, 1981.
Catalogue Pathé 1896 à 1914, Henri Bousquet. Edition Henri Bousquet, Paris, 1993.
Cinéma Français, Les Années 50. Jean-Charles Sabria (editor). Centre Pompidou, Paris, 1987
Cinema Francese 1930-1993. Mario Guidorizzi. Casa Editrice Mazziana, Verona, 1993.
Filmographie des Long Metrages Sonores du Cinéma Français. Vincent Pinel. Cinémathèque, Paris, 1985.
French Films. Annual catalogs. Unifrance Film, Paris, 1980-1996

Germany
Deutscher Spielfilm Almanach 1929-1950. Alfred Bauer. Filmladen Christoph Winterberg, München, 1976.
Films from the Federal Republic of Germany 1993-1994. Inter Nationes. Bonn, 1994
Films of Federal Republic of Germany. Catalogs. Export-Union des Deutschen Films. Munich 1985-1996
Germany (Screen Series), an Illustrated Guide and Index. Felix Bucher. Zwemmer, London, 1970.
Reclams Deutsches Filmlexikon. Herbert Holba, Gunter Knorr/Peter Spegel. Philipp Reclam, Stuttgart, 1984.
West German Cinema Since 1945: Reference Handbook. Richard & Marie Helt. Scarecrow, Metuchen, 1987.

Holland
Dutch Cinema, An Illustrated History. Peter Cowie. Tantivy Press, London, 1979.
Dutch Film. Annual catalogs. Holland Film Promotion, The Hague, 1988-1996.

Hungary
Pictorial Guide to Hungarian Cinema 1901-1984. Istvan Nemeskurty & Tibor Szanto. Revai, Budapest, 1985
Word and Image: History of the Hungarian Cinema. Istvan Nemeskurty. Corvina Press, Budapest, 1968

International - film dictionaries & encyclopedias
Dictionnaire du Cinéma. Two volumes. Jean Tulard. Robert Laffont, Paris, 1984/1985.
Directors and Their Films, 1895-1990. Brooks Bushnell. McFarland, Jefferson, 1993.
Encyclopedia of the Musical Film. Stanley Green. Oxford University Press, New York, 1981.
Faber Companion to Foreign Films, The. Ronald Bergan & Robyn Karney. Faber & Faber, London, 1992.
Film Encyclopedia, The. Ephraim Katz. HarperCollins, New York, 1994.
Film History. "Chronology of Cinema 1889-1896, A." Deac Rossell. Volume 7, No. 2, Summer 1995.
Halliwell's Filmgoer's and Video Viewer's Companion. John Walker (editor). HarperCollins, London, 1993
Halliwell's Film Guide. John Walker (editor). HarperCollins, London, 1991.
Hollywood Musical, The. John Russell Taylor and Arthur Jackson. McGraw-Hill, New York, 1971.
International Film Guides 1965-1996. Edited by Cowie Peter. Tantivy Press and Hamlyn Press, London
Leonard Maltin's Movie and Video Guide. Leonard Maltin (editor). Signet, New York, 1996
Musical, O. (Two volumes). Edited by Joao Benard da Costa & Manuel S. Fonseca. Lisbon, 1985.
National Film Archive Catalogue: Silent Fiction Films 1895-1930. British Film Institute, London 1960.
National Film Archive Catalogue: Silent Non-Fiction Films 1895-1934. British Film Institute, London 1966.
National Film Theatre Program Booklets. British Film Institute, London, 1952-1996
New York Times Encyclopedia of Film 1896-1979, The. Gene Brown (editor). Times Books, New York 1984.
Treasures from the Film Archives: Short Silent Fiction Films. Ronald S. Magliozzi. Scarecrow, Metuchen, 1988
Twenty Years of Silents, 1908-1928. John T. Weaver (compiler). Scarecrow , Metuchen, 1971.
Time Out Film Guide, The. Tom Milne. Penguin Books, London, 1989.
Variety International Film Guides. Peter Cowie (editor). Tantivy Press, later Hamlyn Press. 1965-1996.
Variety Obituaries 1905-1990. 13 volumes. Garland, New York, 1988.
World's Great Movie Stars and Their Films, The. Ken Wlaschin. Salamander Press, London, 1979

International - major film festival catalogs
AFI Fest, Los Angeles
Berlin Film Festival
Cannes Film Festival
Chicago Film Festival
Edinburgh Film Festival
Filmex, Los Angeles
Locarno Film Festival
London Film Festival
Montreal Film Festival
San Francisco Film Fetival
San Sebastian Film Festival
Sydney Film Festival
Toronto Film Festival
Venice Film Festival catalogs

Italian films
Cinema Muto Italiano, Il. 1919-1931. Four volumes. Vittorio Martinelli. Bianco e Nero, Rome.
Davanti allo Schermo, Cinema Italiano 1931-43. Mario Gromo. La Stampa, Turin, 1993
Dizionario del Cinema Italiano:
_____*I Film, Vol. 1, 1930 al 1944.* Roberto Chiti & Enrico Lancia. Gremese Editore, Roma, 1993.
_____*I Film, Vol. 2, 1945 al 1959.* Roberto Chiti & Roberto Poppi. Gremese Editore, Roma, 1991.
_____*I Film, Vol. 3, 1960 al 1969.* Roberto Poppi & Mario Pecorari. Gremese Editore, Roma, 1992
_____*I Film, Vol. 4 A-L, 1970 al 1979.* Roberto Poppi & Mario Pecorari. Gremese Editore, Roma, 1996
_____*I Registi, 1930 ai Giorni Nostri.* Roberto Poppi. Gremese Editore, Roma, 1993
Italian Film: A Who's Who. John Stewart. McFarland, Jefferson, 1994

Ma l'Amore No: Cinema Italiano di Regime (1930-1943). Francesco Savio, Sonzogno, Milan, 1975

Mexico
Mexican Cinema, Reflections of a Society 1896-1980. Carl J. Mora. University of California, Berkeley, 1982.

Norway
Norwegian Films. Annual catalogs. Norwegian Film Institute, 1975 - present.

Poland
Contemporary Polish Film. Stansilaw Kuszewski. Interpress Publishers, Warsaw, 1978.
Poland (World Cinema 1:). Frank Bren. Flicks Books, Trowbridge, 1990

Romania
Contributii la Istoria Cinematografiei in Romania 1896 -1948. Ion Cantacuzino. Academiei, Bucharest, 1971.

Sweden
Authors of Swedish Feature Films and Swedish TV Theatre. Sven G. Winquist (editor). SFI, Stockholm, 1969.
Svensk Filmografi 1920-1969. Four volumes. Swedish Film Institute, Stockholm 1977.
Swedish Films. Annual catalogs. Swedish Film Institute, 1983-1996.
Swedish Silent Pictures 1896-1931 and Their Directors. Edited by Sven G. Winquist. SFI, Stockholm 1967
Swedish Sound Pictures 1929-69 and Their Directors. Edited by Sven G. Winquist. SFI, Stockholm 1969.

Spain
Cine EspaÒol 1896-1983. Edited by August M. Torres, Ministerio de Cultura, Madrid, 1984
Cine EspaÒol. Annual film catalogues. Ministerio de Cultura. 1980-1996.
Diccionario del Cine EspaÒol 1896-1966. Fernando Vizcaino Casas. Editora Nacional, Madrid, 1968.

Switzerland
Swiss Films. Annual catalogs. Swiss Film Center, Zurich, 1988-1996.

USSR
Eastern Europe (Screen Series). Nina Hibbin. Zwemmer, London, 1969
Kino, A History of the Russian and Soviet Film. Jay Leyda. Allen & Unwin, London, 1960.
Soviet Film Catalogs. Sovexport Film, Moscow, undated.
Vingt Ans de Cinema Sovietique. Luda and Jean Schnitzer. Editions C.I.B., Paris, 1963
Who's Who in the Soviet Cinema. Galina Domatovskaya & Irina Shilova. Progress, Moscow, 1978.

7. OPERA & OPERETTA DICTIONARIES & ENCYCLOPEDIAS

Opera
Adam, Nicky. *Who's Who in British Opera*. Scolar Press, Aldershot, 1993.
Ewen, David. *Lighter Classics in Music*. Arco Publishing, New York, 1961
-------*The New Encyclopedia of the Opera*. Hill and Wang, New York, 1971.
Glasser, Alfred (editor). *The Lyric Opera Companion*. Andrews and McMeel, Kansas City, 1991
Henken, John E. *Francisco Asenjo Barbieri and ... Spanish National Music*. 1987 UCLA Ph.D. thesis.
Ho, Allan & Feofanov, Dmitry. *Biographical Dictionary of Soviet Composers*. Greenwood, Westport, 1989.
Holden, Amanda (editor). *The Viking Opera Guide*. Viking, London, 1993
Jacobs, Arthur. *The Penguin Dictionary of Musical Performers*. Penguin Books, London, 1991.
Johnson, H. Earle. *Operas on American Subjects*. Coleman-Ross, New York, 1964.
Kornick, Rebecca Hodell. *Recent American Opera, A Production Guide*. Columbia University, NY, 1991.
LaRue, C. Steven (editor). *International Dictionary of Opera*. St. James Press, Detroit, 1993.
Lebrecht, Norman. *Companion to 20th Century Music*. Simon & Schuster, New York, 1992.
Machlisi, Joseph. *American Composers of Our Time*. Thomas Y. Crowell, New York, 1963.
Martin, George. *The Opera Companion to Twentieth Century Opera*. Dodd Mead, New York, 1979.

Pokrovsky, Boris & Grigorovich, Yuri. *The Bolshoi*. William Morrow, New York, 1979
Rich, Maria F. (editor). *Who's Who in Opera*. Arno Press, New York, 1976.
Rockwell, John. *All American Music*. Alfred Knopf, New York, 1983.
Sadie, Stanley (editor). *The New Grove Dictionary of Opera*. Macmillan Press, London, 1992.
Schmidgall, Gary. *Shakespeare and Opera*. Oxford University Press, New York, 1990
Seeger, Horst. *Opernlexikon*. Florian Noetzel Verlag, Berlin, 1978.
Slonimsky, Nicolas. *Lectionary of Music*. Doubleday, *New York, 1989*
-------------*The Concise Baker's Biographical Dictionary of Musicians*. Schirmer Books, NY, 1988.
Stockdale, F. M & Dreyer, M. R. *The International Opera Guide*. Trafalgar Square , North Pomfret, 1990.
Warrack, John & West, Ewan. *Concise Oxford Dictionary of Opera*. Oxford University Press, Oxford, 1992.
Griffiths, Paul. *Encyclopedia of 20th Century Music*. Thames and Hudson, London, 1986.
Zentner, Wilhelm. *Reclams Opernführer*. Philipp Reclam Jun. Stuttgart, 1988

Operetta

Bloom, Ken. *American Song: Musical Theater Companion 1900-1984*. Facts on File. New York 1985.
Bordman, Gerald. *American Operetta: From H.M.S. Pinafore to Sweeney Todd*. Oxford, New York, 1981
Bradley, Edwin M. *The First Hollywood Musicals, A Critical Filmography of 171 Features 1927 through 1932*.
　　　　McFarland, Jefferson, 1996
Bruyr, José. *L'Opérette,*. Press Universitaires de France, Paris, 1962.
Ewen,David. *The Book of European Light Opera*. Holt, Rinehart & Winston, New York, 1962.
Gammond, Peter. *The Oxford Companion to Popular Music*. Oxford University Press, New York, 1991.
------------ & Clayton, Peter. *A Guide to Popular Music*. Phonexis House, London, 1960.
Gänzl, Kurt. *The Blackwell Guide to the Musical Theater on Record*. Blackwell, Oxford, 1990.
------- *The Encyclopedia of The Musical Theatre*. Blackwell Publishers, London, 1994.
------- *Gänzl's Book of the Musical Theatre*. Schirmer Books, New York, 1989.
Green, Stanley. *Encyclopedia of the Musical*. Cassell, London, 1977
Hischak, Thomas S. *The American Musical Theatre Song Encyclopedia*. Greenwood, Westport, 1995
Hughes, Gervase. *Composers of Operetta*. St. Martin's Press, New York, 1962
McSpadden, J. Walker. *Operas and Musical Comedies*. Thomas Crowell, New York, 1946.
Parker, Derek and Julia. *The Story and the Song: English Musical Plays, 1916-78*. Chappell, London, 1979.
Traubner, Richard. *Operetta, A Theatrical History*. Doubleday, Garden City, 1983.
Wurz, Anton. *Reclams Operetten-führer*. Philipp Reclam Jun. Stuttgart, 1988

****